Constitutional Law and Politics

VOLUME ONE

Eighth Edition

OTHER BOOKS BY DAVID M. O'BRIEN

Storm Center:
The Supreme Court in American Politics
9th ed.

Congress Shall Make No Law:
The First Amendment, Unprotected Expression, and
the U.S. Supreme Court

Animal Sacrifice and Religious Freedom:
Church of Lukumi Bababu Aye v. City of Hialeah

Privacy, Law, and Public Policy

The Public's Right to Know:
The Supreme Court and the First Amendment

What Process Is Due?:
Courts and Science-Policy Disputes

Judicial Roulette

The Politics of Technology Assessment:
Institutions, Processes and Policy Disputes
(co-editor)

Views from the Bench:
The Judiciary and Constitutional Politics
(co-editor)

Abortion and American Politics
(co-author)

The Politics of American Government
3rd ed.
(co-author)

Supreme Court Watch

To Dream of Dreams:
Religious Freedom and Constitutional Politics in Postwar Japan
(co-author)

Judges on Judging
3rd ed.
(editor)

The Lanahan Readings on Civil Rights and Civil Liberties
3rd ed.
(editor)

Judicial Independence in the Age of Democracy:
Critical Perspectives from Around the World
(co-editor)

Government by the People
22nd ed.
(co-author)

Courts and Judicial Policymaking
(co-author)

CONSTITUTIONAL LAW AND POLITICS

VOLUME ONE

Struggles for Power and Governmental Accountability

EIGHTH EDITION

DAVID M. O'BRIEN

UNIVERSITY OF VIRGINIA

W · W · NORTON & COMPANY · NEW YORK

For Claudine, Benjamin, Sara, and Talia

W. W. Norton & Company has been independent since its founding in 1923, when William Warder Norton and Mary D. Herter Norton first published lectures delivered at the People's Institute, the adult education division of New York City's Cooper Union. The firm soon expanded its program beyond the Institute, publishing books by celebrated academics from America and abroad. By midcentury, the two major pillars of Norton's publishing program—trade books and college texts—were firmly established. In the 1950s, the Norton family transferred control of the company to its employees, and today—with a staff of four hundred and a comparable number of trade, college, and professional titles published each year—W. W. Norton & Company stands as the largest and oldest publishing house owned wholly by its employees.

Composition by Matrix Publishing Services
Manufacturing by Courier Westford
Book design by Martin Lubin Graphic Design
Production Manager: Jane Searle
Project editor: Justin Hoffman
Drawn art by John McAusland.

Library of Congress Cataloging-in-Publication Data

O'Brien, David M.
    Constitutional law and politics / David M. O'Brien.— 8th ed.
        p. cm.
    Includes bibliographical references and index.
    ISBN 978-0-393-93549-3 (pbk. : v. 1)
    ISBN 978-0-393-93550-9 (pbk. : v. 2)
    1. Constitutional law—United States—Cases. 2. Constitutional history—United States—Cases. 3. Political questions and judicial power—United States—Cases. 4. Civil rights—United States—Cases.
    I. Title.
    KF4541.O27 2011
    342.73—dc22
                                                            2010046851

ISBN: 978-0-393-93549-3 (pbk.)

W. W. Norton & Company, Inc., 500 Fifth Avenue, New York, N.Y. 10110
www.wwnorton.com

W. W. Norton & Company Ltd., Castle House, 75/76 Wells Street, London W1T 3QT

1 2 3 4 5 6 7 8 9 0

CONTENTS

CHAPTER 4 ■ *The President as Chief Executive in Domestic Affairs* 346

CHAPTER 8 ■ *Representative Government, Voting Rights, and Electoral Politics* 833

CHAPTER 9 ■ *Economic Rights and American Capitalism*   1006

ILLUSTRATIONS

PREFACE

Because there is no dearth of casebooks, perhaps an explanation is needed of how this one differs from others. What distinguishes this casebook is its treatment and incorporation of material on constitutional history and American politics. Few casebooks pay adequate attention to the forces of history and politics on the course of constitutional law. Yet constitutional law, history, and politics are intimately intertwined.

The Constitution and Bill of Rights, of course, are political documents. Rooted in historic struggles and based on political compromises, their provisions and guarantees continue to invite competing interpretations and political contests over, for example, the separation of powers between Congress and the president, federalism, and civil rights and liberties. Because the Constitution says nothing about *who* should interpret it or about *how* it should be interpreted, constitutional law is animated by the politics of interpretation and the interpretation of politics. Neither do we have a single accepted theory of constitutional interpretation, nor do the justices write on a clean slate. Instead, we face constitutional choices and competing judicial and political philosophies, as well as new social, economic, and technological changes.

The Supreme Court's decisions do not occur in a political vacuum, standing apart from history and the political struggles within the Court and the country. Virtually every major political controversy raises questions of constitutional law, no less than do technological changes and social movements and economic forces. The development and direction of constitutional law also shift (more or less quickly) with the Court's changing composition. Members of the Court, just as other citizens, differ in their readings of the Constitution. Moreover, major confrontations in constitutional law and politics, such as those over the powers of the national government, school desegregation, abortion and the right of privacy, involve continuing struggles that run from one generation to another. In the course of those struggles, constitutional law evolves with changes in the Court and the country. The Constitution and the Bill of Rights bind the Court, other political institutions, and the people in an ongoing dialogue over the exercise of and limitations on governmental power.

By providing the historical context and explaining the political contests among the justices and between the Court and the country, this casebook aims to make constitutional law more accessible for students. History and politics are also important for students' analyzing of particular decisions and their relation to developments and changes in constitutional law and politics. They are crucial as well for students trying critically to evaluate competing interpretations and to appreciate the political consequences of alternative interpretations. And they are essential if students are to engage in the dialogue of constitutional law, confront constitutional choices, and come to terms with their and others' views of the Constitution and the Bill of Rights.

The casebook remains different in several ways. First, it comes in two very comprehensive, anthology-like volumes. Volume I, *Struggles for Power and Governmental Accountability*, deals with separation of powers, federalism, and the democratic process. Volume II, *Civil Rights and Civil Liberties*, is devoted to the enduring struggles to limit governmental power and guarantee civil rights and liberties. As a two-volume set, it not only includes more Court decisions than other casebooks but also permits more introductory background material. Instructors, therefore, have greater flexibility when assigning cases, and students will find useful the additional cases and guides to other cases and resources.

Second, two chapters dealing with the politics of constitutional interpretation and Supreme Court decision making contain material not usually found in casebooks. Chapter 1 goes beyond dealing with the establishment of the power of judicial review, and political criticisms of the Court's exercise of that power, to examining rival theories of constitutional interpretation. Students are introduced to differing judicial and political philosophies and referred to cases and opinions found in subsequent chapters that illustrate these different positions on constitutional interpretation. Chapter 2 combines an introduction to jurisdictional matters, such as standing, with a discussion of how the Court operates as an institution and in relation to other political institutions, which may help promote compliance with and implementation of its rulings, or thwart and even reverse them. In short, Chapter 1 prepares students for critically evaluating competing interpretations of constitutional provisions in subsequent chapters. And Chapter 2 prepares them for understanding the political struggles that take place within the Court as well as between the Court and other political institutions over its decisions. While the volumes together are designed for a two-semester course, both of these chapters, as well as The Constitution of the United States, are included in each volume for the convenience of teachers and students who might be involved in only one of the two-semester constitutional law course sequence. In addition, both volumes include in the Appendix discussions of how and why to brief cases, and there is a glossary of legal definitions.

As already noted, each chapter and subsection contains a lengthy introductory essay. These essays focus on particular provisions of the Constitution and the Bill of Rights, why they took the form they did, and what controversies surrounded them during the Founding period and later. Most begin with the debates at the Constitutional Convention of 1787 and those between the Federalists and Anti-Federalists during the ratification period, and then review subsequent cases and controversies. Besides providing a historical and political context for the cases in each chapter, the essays highlight the continuity and changes in the debates over constitutional law and politics that run from the Founding period to those rulings of the Roberts Court.

Something should also be said about the case excerpts. Most are preceded by "headnotes," short explanations of the facts and why the case was appealed to the Court. But, unlike the brief (and usually dry) headnotes typically found in casebooks, these reveal something about the personal and political struggles of those who appeal to the Court. Throughout, there is an attempt to help students understand the judicial and political process and appreciate how questions of constitutional law are embedded in everyday life. For this reason, students will also find excerpts from oral arguments before the Court and other materials bearing on the political struggles that they represent. Along with excerpts of the opinion announcing the decision of the Court, students will frequently encounter excerpts from separate concurring and dissenting opinions. These are included to help students appreciate the choices that the Court and they must make when interpreting the Constitution and the Bill of Rights. Related to this is a good suggestion made by a number of adopters of the first edition: the headnotes record the actual Court vote.

In addition, each volume contains four types of boxes, which include materials that further place constitutional interpretation and law in historical and political perspective. One set of boxes, CONSTITUTIONAL HISTORY, presents important background material, such as excerpts from John Locke on the connection between property and liberty and explanatory notes on the "Watergate crisis" and civil liberties in wartime. Another set, THE DEVELOPMENT OF LAW, shows changes and patterns in constitutional law and refers students to other cases on topics of special interest. The third, INSIDE THE COURT, illustrates the internal dynamics of the Court when engaged in the process of constitutional interpretation and deciding cases. Finally, IN COMPARATIVE PERSPECTIVE boxes illustrate how courts around the world have dealt with similar constitutional controversies. These boxes are indicated by □ in the contents. Also included at the end of each volume are brief biographies of the current sitting justices.

This eighth edition updates the introductions, the cases, and the four types of boxes, as well as incorporates the highlights of the Court's terms through the 2009–2010 term. Along with adding a number of new boxes on CONSTITUTIONAL HISTORY, THE DEVELOPMENT OF LAW, and IN COMPARATIVE PERSPECTIVE, this edition includes a number of other new features. RESEARCHING LEGAL MATERIALS provides a guide for students to access and to search for legal materials and law-related sources on the Internet. THE HOW, WHY, AND WHAT TO BRIEFING AND CITING COURT CASES discusses the how, why, and what to briefing and citing court decisions and opinions. In response to requests from adopters of past editions, the chapter titled "Economic Rights and American Capitalism" is included in both volumes; it appears as Chapter 9 in Volume One and remains Chapter 3 in Volume Two. Besides maintaining the SUPREME COURT WEB WATCH (at www.wwnorton .com/scww/), with links to pertinent information on the Supreme Court and the Constitution, in order to keep this edition up to date, I will continue to write, and Norton to publish each September, an annual supplement that we call SUPREME COURT WATCH.

What follows will, it is hoped, enrich students' understanding of constitutional law, politics, and history, as well as open them to the possibilities in interpreting the Constitution and the Bill of Rights. But the Constitution is where students should begin their study, and it is assuredly where they will return again and again.

D. M. O.

ACKNOWLEDGMENTS

I am indebted to my students and colleagues for the favorable reception that they gave earlier editions, but I still owe a larger debt to Claudine, my wife, for giving me the freedom to work as I do and to enjoy life's pleasures with Benjamin, Sara, and Talia. I continue to be grateful for the inspiration and support of my teacher, C. Herman Pritchett, University of California, Santa Barbara, and my colleagues at the University of Virginia, Henry J. Abraham and David Klein. Ira Carmen, University of Illinois; Phillip Cooper, University of Vermont; Jerome Hanus, The American University; and Gerald Rosenberg, University of Chicago, read and made very helpful suggestions on the first edition for which I am grateful. Also, I thank Thomas Baker, Florida International University; Sue Davis, University of Delaware; Susan Fino, Wayne State University; Christine Harrington, New York University; and H. N. Hirsch, University of California, San Diego, for offering comments that helped shape the casebook early on in its development.

I very much appreciate the support and suggestions made by countless undergraduate and graduate students. In particular, several current and former graduate students deserve special recognition: Christopher Banks, Stephen Bragaw, Steve Brown, John Blakeman, Richard Drew, Scott Gerber, Jeffrey Hockett, Robert Hume, Nathan Jones, Edward Kelly, Charles Kromkowski, William Mandel, Rick Mayes, Stacy Nyikos, Gavin Reddick, James Staab, Jon Talotta, Stephen Tauber, and James Todd. Numerous colleagues around the country offered support and very helpful suggestions for changes and corrections that have improved this edition. Among many other colleagues, I am grateful to the following: John Q. Adams, Maria Antonini, Gordon Baker, Jack Barlow, John Brigham, Joseph Callahan, David Carrithers, Richard Claude, George F. Cole, Ronald Collins, Sheila Collins, Akiba Covitz, John Domino, Louis Fisher, Jack Fruchtman, Jr., Hal Goldman, Leslie Goldstein, Susan Grogan, Robert Hardgrave, Jr., Harry N. Hirsch, Milton Heumann, Elizabeth Hull, Sidney Heyman, Michael Horan, Carolyn Johnson, Robert M. Johnstone, Nancy Kassop, Paul Kens, Byron Lander, Susan Lawrence, James Lennertz, Robert Katzmann, J. Morgan Kousser, Thomas Lewis, Kevin McGuire, Pricilla Macadeo, David T. Mason, Eddie L. Meaders, Lucas Morel, Bruce Murphy, Jill Norgren, Karen O'Connor, Jack W. Peltason, Marie Provine, Stephen Ross, John Scheb, Guy Scoffoni, David Skover, Rogers Smith, Neil Snortland, Donald Songer, Gene Straughan, Harold Sullivan, John Taylor, James Todd, and Mary Volcansek.

In preparing the last edition I benefited from the comments of several reviewers and remain indebted to John C. Blakeman, J. M. Bordelon, Steven Brown, Michelle D. Dearorff, Milton Heumann, Paul Kens, S. A. Dwyer-Shick, Cary Federman, Jack Fruchtman, Jr., David R. Manwaring, Wendy L. Martinek, W. McKercher, David Pogue, Alisa Rosenthal, Daniel E. Smith, Mark Caleb Smith, Steve Tauber, and Paul Weber.

This edition incurs even more debt. I am grateful to a number of reviewers, including: John Evans, Judy Failer, Martha Good, Laura Hatcher, Robert Howard, Susan Johnson, Paul Kens, Drew Noble Lanier, Quan Li, John Robey, Richard Sobel, Stephen Tauber, Jerold Waltman, Teena Wilheim, and John Winkle.

Finally, the generous support of the American Philosophical Society and the Earhart Foundation contributed to this project as well. Donald Fusting, a patient and wise editor, worked with me on the first two editions, as did Steve Dunn on the third, Sarah Caldwell on the fourth, Ann Marcy on the fifth edition, Aaron Javsicas on the sixth, Brian Baker and Matthew Arnold on the seventh, and Aaron Javiscas on this edition. Work on these volumes, I should also acknowledge, was indirectly but significantly helped by the U.S. Fulbright Commission. The first edition was largely completed during 1987–1988 while I was a Fulbright Lecturer in Constitutional Studies at Oxford University. The third edition was completed while I was a Fulbright Research Fellow in Japan. And the fourth edition was completed while I held the Fulbright Chair in History and Political Science at the University of Bologna. The seventh edition was worked on while I was a Visiting Professor at the Institut d'Etudes Politique, Universite Lyon-2, Lyon, France. I am thus deeply indebted to the Fulbright Commission and a number of scholars who made my stays so productive. In particular, I am grateful to Byron Shafer, Yasuo Ohkoshi, Vincent Michelot, and Tiziano Bonazzi. I am grateful as well for permission to reproduce materials here granted by the following individuals and organizations: Justices William J. Brennan, Jr., and Antonin Scalia; the curator of the Supreme Court of the United States; the Library of Congress; Justice Hans Linde of the Oregon State Supreme Court; the Supreme Court Historical Society; the National Portrait Gallery/Smithsonian Institution; *The New York Times*; the Roosevelt Library; Sygma/*New York Times Magazine*; Paula Oka-moto; and Wide World Photos.

Constitutional Law and Politics

VOLUME ONE

Eighth Edition

THE UNITED STATES CONSTITUTION AND AMENDMENTS

We the people of the United States, in Order to form a more perfect Union, establish Justice, insure domestic Tranquility, provide for the common defence, promote the general Welfare, and secure the Blessings of Liberty to ourselves and our Posterity, do ordain and establish this Constitution for the United States of America.

ARTICLE I

SECTION 1. All legislative Powers herein granted shall be vested in a Congress of the United States, which shall consist of a Senate and House of Representatives.

SECTION 2. The House of Representatives shall be composed of Members chosen every second Year by the People of the several States, and the Electors in each State shall have the Qualifications requisite for Electors of the most numerous Branch of the State Legislature.

No Person shall be a Representative who shall not have attained to the Age of twenty five Years, and been seven Years a Citizen of the United States, and who shall not, when elected, be an Inhabitant of that State in which he shall be chosen.

[Representatives and [direct Taxes] shall be apportioned among the several States [which may be included within this Union,] according to their respective Numbers, which shall be determined by adding to the whole Number of free Persons, including those bound to Service for a

Term of Years, and excluding Indians not taxed, three fifths of all other Persons. *(This clause was changed by section 2 of the Fourteenth Amendment.)*] The actual Enumeration shall be made within three Years after the first Meeting of the Congress of the United States, and within every subsequent Term of ten Years, in such Manner as they shall by Law direct. The Number of Representatives shall not exceed one for every thirty Thousand, but each State shall have at Least one Representative; and until such enumeration shall be made, the State of New Hampshire shall be entitled to chuse three, Massachusetts eight, Rhode-Island and Providence Plantations one, Connecticut five, New-York six, New Jersey four, Pennsylvania eight, Delaware one, Maryland six, Virginia ten, North Carolina five, South Carolina five, and Georgia three.

When vacancies happen in the Representation from any State, the Executive Authority thereof shall issue Writs of Election to fill such Vacancies.

The House of Representatives shall chuse their Speaker and other Officers; and shall have the sole Power of Impeachment.

SECTION 3. The Senate of the United States shall be composed of two Senators from each State, [chosen by the Legislature thereof, *(This provision was changed by section 1 of the Seventeenth Amendment.)*] for six Years; and each Senator shall have one Vote.

Immediately after they shall be assembled in Consequence of the first Election, they shall be divided as equally as may be into three Classes. The Seats of the Senators of the first Class shall be vacated at the Expiration of the second Year, of the second Class at the Expiration of the fourth Year, and of the third Class at the Expiration of the sixth Year, so that one third may be chosen every second Year; [and if Vacancies happen by Resignation, or otherwise, during the Recess of the Legislature of any State, the Executive thereof may make temporary Appointments until the next Meeting of the Legislature, which shall then fill such Vacancies. *(This clause was changed by section 2 of the Seventeenth Amendment.)*]

No Person shall be a Senator who shall not have attained to the Age of thirty Years, and been nine Years a Citizen of the United States, and who shall not, when elected, be an Inhabitant of that State for which he shall be chosen.

The Vice President of the United States shall be President of the Senate, but shall have no Vote, unless they be equally divided.

The Senate shall chuse their other Officers, and also a President pro tempore, in the Absence of the Vice President, or when he shall exercise the Office of President of the United States.

The Senate shall have the sole Power to try all Impeachments. When sitting for that Purpose, they shall be on Oath or Affirmation. When the President of the United States is tried, the Chief Justice shall preside: And no Person shall be convicted without the Concurrence of two thirds of the Members present.

Judgment in Cases of Impeachment shall not extend further than to removal from Office, and disqualification to hold and enjoy any Office of honor, Trust or Profit under the United States: but the Party convicted shall nevertheless be liable and subject to Indictment, Trial, Judgment and Punishment, according to Law.

SECTION 4. The Times, Places and Manner of holding Elections for Senators and Representatives, shall be prescribed in each State by the Legislature thereof; but the Congress may at any time by Law make or alter such Regulations, except as to the Places of chusing Senators.

The Congress shall assemble at least once in every Year, and such Meeting shall be [on the first Monday in December, (*This provision was changed by section 2 of the Twentieth Amendment.*)] unless they shall by Law appoint a different Day.

SECTION 5. Each House shall be the Judge of the Elections, Returns and Qualifications of its own Members, and a Majority of each shall constitute a Quorum to do Business; but a smaller Number may adjourn from day to day, and may be authorized to compel the Attendance of absent Members, in such Manner, and under such Penalties as each House may provide.

Each House may determine the Rules of its Proceedings, punish its Members for disorderly Behaviour, and, with the Concurrence of two thirds, expel a Member.

Each House shall keep a Journal of its Proceedings, and from time to time publish the same, excepting such Parts as may in their Judgment require Secrecy; and the Yeas and Nays of the Members of either House on any question shall, at the Desire of one fifth of those Present, be entered on the Journal.

Neither House, during the Session of Congress, shall, without the Consent of the other, adjourn for more than three days, nor to any other Place than that in which the two Houses shall be sitting.

SECTION 6. The Senators and Representatives shall receive a Compensation for their Services, to be ascertained by Law, and paid out of the Treasury of the United States. They shall in all Cases, except Treason, Felony and Breach of the Peace, be privileged from Arrest during their Attendance at the Session of their respective Houses, and in going to and returning from the same; and for any Speech or Debate in either House, they shall not be questioned in any other Place.

No Senator or Representative shall, during the Time for which he was elected, be appointed to any civil Office under the Authority of the United States, which shall have been created, or the Emoluments whereof shall have been encreased during such time; and no Person holding any Office under the United States, shall be a Member of either House during his Continuance in Office.

Section 7. All Bills for raising Revenue shall originate in the House of Representatives; but the Senate may propose or concur with Amendments as on other Bills.

Every Bill which shall have passed the House of Representatives and the Senate, shall, before it become a Law, be presented to the President of the United States; If he approve he shall sign it, but if not he shall return it, with his Objections to that House in which it shall have originated, who shall enter the Objections at large on their Journal, and proceed to reconsider it. If after such Reconsideration two thirds of that House shall agree to pass the Bill, it shall be sent, together with the Objections, to the other House, by which it shall likewise be reconsidered, and if approved by two thirds of that House, it shall become a Law. But in all such Cases the Votes of both Houses shall be determined by yeas and Nays, and the Names of the Persons voting for and against the Bill shall be entered on the Journal of each House respectively. If any bill shall not be returned by the President within ten Days (Sundays excepted) after it shall have been presented to him, the Same shall be a Law, in like Manner as if he had signed it, unless the Congress by their Adjournment prevent its Return, in which Case it shall not be a Law.

Every Order, Resolution, or Vote to which the Concurrence of the Senate and House of Representatives may be necessary (except on a question of Adjournment) shall be presented to the President of the United States; and before the Same shall take Effect, shall be approved by him, or being disapproved by him, shall be repassed by two thirds of the Senate and House of Representatives, according to the Rules and Limitations prescribed in the Case of a Bill.

Section 8. The Congress shall have Power To lay and collect Taxes, Duties, Imposts and Excises, to pay the Debts and provide for the common Defence and general Welfare of the United States; but all Duties, Imposts and Excises shall be uniform throughout the United States;

To borrow Money on the credit of the United States;

To regulate Commerce with Foreign Nations, and among the several States, and with the Indian tribes;

To establish an uniform Rule of Naturalization, and uniform Laws on the subject of Bankruptcies throughout the United States;

To coin Money, regulate the Value thereof, and of foreign Coin, and fix the Standard of Weights and Measures;

To provide for the Punishment of counterfeiting the Securities and current Coin of the United States;

To establish Post Offices and post Roads;

To promote the Progress of Science and useful Arts, by securing for limited Times to Authors and Inventors the exclusive Right to their respective Writings and Discoveries;

To constitute Tribunals inferior to the supreme Court;

To define and punish Piracies and Felonies committed on the high Seas, and Offences against the Law of Nations;

To declare War, grant Letters of Marque and Reprisal, and make Rules concerning Captures on Land and Water;

To raise and support Armies, but no Appropriation of Money to that Use shall be for a longer Term than two Years;

To provide and maintain a Navy;

To make Rules for the Government and Regulation of the land and naval Forces;

To provide for calling forth the Militia to execute the Laws of the Union, suppress Insurrections and repel Invasions;

To provide for organizing, arming, and disciplining, the Militia, and for governing such Part of them as may be employed in the Service of the United States, reserving to the States respectively, the Appointment of the Officers, and the Authority of training the Militia according to the discipline prescribed by Congress;

To exercise exclusive Legislation in all Cases whatsoever, over such District (not exceeding ten Miles square) as may, by Cession of particular States, and the Acceptance of Congress, become the Seat of the Government of the United States, and to exercise like Authority over all Places purchased by the Consent of the Legislature of the State in which the Same shall be, for the Erection of Forts, Magazines, Arsenals, dock-Yards, and other needful Buildings;—And

To make all Laws which shall be necessary and proper for carrying into Execution the foregoing Powers, and all other Powers vested by this Constitution in the Government of the United States, or in any Department or Officer thereof.

SECTION 9. The Migration or Importation of such Persons as any of the States now existing shall think proper to admit, shall not be prohibited by the Congress prior to the Year one thousand eight hundred and eight, but a Tax or duty may be imposed on such Importation, not exceeding ten dollars for each Person.

The Privilege of the Writ of Habeas Corpus shall not be suspended, unless when in Cases of Rebellion or Invasion the public Safety may require it.

No Bill of Attainder or ex post facto Law shall be passed.

No Capitation, or other direct, Tax shall be laid, unless in Proportion to the Census or Enumeration herein before directed to be taken.

No Tax or Duty shall be laid on Articles exported from any State.

No Preference shall be given by any Regulation of Commerce or Revenue to the Ports of one State over those of another: nor shall Vessels bound to, or from, one State, be obliged to enter, clear, or pay Duties in another.

No Money shall be drawn from the Treasury, but in Consequence of Appropriations made by Law; and a regular Statement and Account of the Receipts and Expenditures of all public Money shall be published from time to time.

No Title of Nobility shall be granted by the United States: And no Person holding any Office of Profit or Trust under them, shall, without the Consent of the Congress, accept of any present, Emolument, Office, or Title, of any kind whatever, from any King, Prince, or foreign State.

SECTION 10. No State shall enter into any Treaty, Alliance, or Confederation; grant Letters of Marque and Reprisal; coin Money; emit Bills of Credit; make any Thing but gold and silver Coin a Tender in Payment of Debts; pass any Bill of Attainder, ex post facto Law, or Law impairing the Obligation of Contracts, or grant any Title of Nobility.

No State shall, without the Consent of the Congress, lay any Imposts or Duties on Imports or Exports, except what may be absolutely necessary for executing it's inspection Laws: and the net Produce of all Duties and Imposts, laid by any State on Imports or Exports, shall be for the Use of the Treasury of the United States; and all such Laws shall be subject to the Revision and Controul of the Congress.

No State shall, without the Consent of Congress, lay any Duty of Tonnage, keep Troops, or Ships of War in time of Peace, enter into any Agreement or Compact with another State, or with a foreign Power, or engage in War, unless actually invaded, or in such imminent Danger as will not admit of delay.

ARTICLE II

SECTION 1. The executive Power shall be vested in a President of the United States of America. He shall hold his Office during the Term of four Years, and, together with the Vice President, chosen for the same Term, be elected, as follows

Each State shall appoint, in such Manner as the Legislature thereof may direct, a Number of Electors, equal to the whole Number of Senators and Representatives to which the State may be entitled in the Congress: but no Senator or Representative, or Person holding an Office of Trust or Profit under the United States, shall be appointed an Elector.

[The Electors shall meet in their respective States, and vote by Ballot for two Persons, of whom one at least shall not be an inhabitant of the same State with themselves. And they shall make a List of all the Persons voted for, and of the Number of Votes for each; which List they shall sign and certify, and transmit sealed to the Seat of the Government of the United States, directed to the President of the Senate. The President of the Senate shall, in the Presence of the Senate and House of Representatives, open all the Certificates, and the Votes shall then be counted. The Person having the greatest Number of Votes shall be the President, if such Number be a Majority of the whole Number of Electors appointed; and if there be more than one who have such Majority, and have an equal Number of Votes, then the House of Representatives shall immediately chuse by Ballot one of them for President; and if no Person have a Majority, then from the five highest on the List the said House shall in like Manner chuse the President. But in chusing the President, the Votes shall be taken by States, the Representation from each State having one Vote; A quorum for this purpose shall consist of a Member or Members from two thirds of the States, and a Majority of all the States shall be necessary to a Choice. In every Case, after the Choice of the President, the Person having the greatest Number of Votes of the Electors shall be the Vice President. But if there should remain two or more who have equal Votes, the Senate shall chuse from them by Ballot the Vice President. *(This clause was superseded by the Twelfth Amendment.)*]

The Congress may determine the Time of chusing the Electors, and the Day on which they shall give their Votes; which Day shall be the same throughout the United States.

No Person except a natural born Citizen, or a Citizen of the United States, at the time of the Adoption of this Constitution, shall be eligible to the Office of President; neither shall any Person be eligible to that Office who shall not have attained to the Age of thirty five

Years, and been fourteen Years a Resident within the United States.

[In Case of the Removal of the President from Office, or of his Death, Resignation, or Inability to discharge the Powers and Duties of the said Office, the Same shall devolve on the Vice President, and the Congress may by Law provide for the Case of Removal, Death, Resignation or Inability, both of the President and Vice President, declaring what Officer shall then act as President, and such Officer shall act accordingly, until the Disability be removed, or a President shall be elected. (*This clause was modified by the Twenty-Fifth Amendment.*)]

The President shall, at stated Times, receive for his Services, a Compensation, which shall neither be increased nor diminished during the Period for which he shall have been elected, and he shall not receive within that Period any other Emolument from the United States, or any of them.

Before he enter on the Execution of his Office, he shall take the following Oath or Affirmation:—"I do solemnly swear (or affirm) that I will faithfully execute the Office of President of the United States, and will to the best of my Ability, preserve, protect and defend the Constitution of the United States."

SECTION 2. The President shall be Commander in Chief of the Army and Navy of the United States, and of the Militia of the several States, when called into the actual Service of the United States; he may require the Opinion, in writing, of the principal Officer in each of the executive Departments, upon any Subject relating to the Duties of their respective Offices, and he shall have Power to grant Reprieves and Pardons for Offences against the United States, except in Cases of Impeachment.

He shall have Power, by and with the Advice and Consent of the Senate, to make Treaties, provided two thirds of the Senators present concur; and he shall nominate, and by and with the Advice and Consent of the Senate, shall appoint Ambassadors, other public Ministers and Consuls, Judges of the supreme Court, and all other Officers of the United States, whose Appointments are not herein otherwise provided for, and which shall be established by Law: but the Congress may by Law vest the Appointment of such inferior Officers, as they think proper, in the President alone, in the Courts of Law, or in the Heads of Departments.

The President shall have Power to fill up all Vacancies that may happen during the Recess of the Senate, by granting Commissions which shall expire at the End of their next Session.

SECTION 3. He shall from time to time give to the Congress Information of the State of the Union, and recommend to their Consideration such Measures as he shall judge necessary and expedient; he may, on extraordinary Occasions, convene both Houses, or either of them, and in Case of Disagreement between them, with Respect to the Time of Adjournment, he may adjourn them to such Time as he shall think proper; he shall receive Ambassadors and other public Ministers; he shall take Care that the Laws be faithfully executed, and shall Commission all the Officers of the United States.

SECTION 4. The President, Vice President and all civil Officers of the United States, shall be removed from Office on Impeachment for, and Conviction of, Treason, Bribery, or other high Crimes and Misdemeanors.

ARTICLE III

SECTION 1. The judicial Power of the United States, shall be vested in one supreme Court, and in such inferior Courts as the Congress may from time to time ordain and establish. The Judges, both of the supreme and inferior Courts, shall hold their Offices during good Behaviour, and shall, at stated Times receive for their Services, a Compensation, which shall not be diminished during their Continuance in Office.

SECTION 2. The judicial Power shall extend to all Cases, in Law and Equity, arising under this Constitution, the Laws of the United States, and Treaties made, or which shall be made, under their Authority;—to all Cases affecting Ambassadors, other public Ministers and Consuls;—to all Cases of admiralty and maritime Jurisdiction;—to Controversies to which the United States shall be a Party;—to Controversies between two or more States;—between a State and Citizens of another State;—between Citizens of different States,—between Citizens of the same State claiming Lands under Grants of different States, and between a State, or the Citizens thereof, and foreign States, Citizens or Subjects.

In all Cases affecting Ambassadors, other public Ministers and Consuls, and those in which a State shall be Party, the supreme Court shall have original Jurisdiction. In all the other Cases before mentioned, the supreme Court shall have appellate Jurisdiction, both as to Law and Fact, with such Exceptions, and under such Regulations as the Congress shall make.

The Trial of all Crimes, except in Cases of Impeachment, shall be by Jury; and such Trial shall be held in the State where the said Crimes shall have been committed; but when not committed within any State, the Trial shall be at such Place or Places as the Congress may by Law have directed.

SECTION 3. Treason against the United States, shall consist only in levying War against them, or in adhering to their Enemies, giving them Aid and Comfort. No Person shall be convicted of Treason unless on the Testimony of two Witnesses to the same overt Act, or on Confession in open Court.

The Congress shall have Power to declare the Punishment of Treason, but no Attainder of Treason shall work Corruption of Blood, or Forfeiture except during the Life of the Person attainted.

ARTICLE IV

SECTION 1. Full Faith and Credit shall be given in each State to the public Acts, Records, and judicial Proceedings of every other State; And the Congress may by general Laws prescribe the Manner in which such Acts, Records and Proceedings shall be proved, and the Effect thereof.

SECTION 2. The Citizens of each State shall be entitled to all Privileges and Immunities of Citizens in the several States.

A Person charged in any State with Treason, Felony, or other Crime, who shall flee from Justice, and be found in another State, shall on Demand of the executive Authority of the State from which he fled, be delivered up, to be removed to the State having Jurisdiction of the Crime.

[No Person held to Service or Labour in one State, under the Laws thereof, escaping into another, shall, in Consequence of any Law or Regulation therein, be discharged from such Service or Labour, but shall be delivered up on Claim of the Party to whom such Service or Labour may be due. (*This clause was superseded by the Thirteenth Amendment.*)]

SECTION 3. New States may be admitted by the Congress into this Union; but no new State shall be formed or erected within the Jurisdiction of any other State; nor any State be formed by the Junction of two or more States, or Parts of States, without the Consent of the Legislatures of the States concerned as well as of the Congress.

The Congress shall have Power to dispose of and make all needful Rules and Regulations respecting the Territory or other Property belonging to the United States; and nothing in this Constitution shall be so construed as to Prejudice any Claims of the United States, or of any particular State.

SECTION 4. The United States shall guarantee to every State in this Union a Republican Form of Government, and shall protect each of them against Invasion; and on Application of the Legislature, or of the Executive (when the Legislature cannot be convened) against domestic Violence.

ARTICLE V

The Congress, whenever two thirds of both Houses shall deem it necessary, shall propose Amendments to this Constitution, or, on the Application of the Legislatures of two thirds of the several States, shall call a Convention for proposing Amendments, which, in either Case, shall be valid to all Intents and Purposes, as Part of this Constitution, when ratified by the legislatures of three fourths of the several States, or by Conventions in three fourths thereof, as the one or the other Mode of Ratification may be proposed by the Congress; Provided that no Amendment which may be made prior to the Year One thousand eight hundred and eight shall in any Manner affect the first and fourth Clauses in the Ninth Section of the first Article; and that no State, without its Consent, shall be deprived of its equal Suffrage in the Senate.

ARTICLE VI

All Debts contracted and Engagements entered into, before the Adoption of this Constitution, shall be as valid against the United States under this Constitution, as under the Confederation.

This Constitution, and the Laws of the United States which shall be made in Pursuance thereof; and all Treaties made, or which shall be made, under the Authority of the United States, shall be the supreme Law of the Land; and the Judges in every State shall be bound thereby, any Thing in the Constitution or Laws of any State to the Contrary notwithstanding.

The Senators and Representatives before mentioned, and the Members of the several State Legislatures, and all executive and judicial Officers, both of the United States and of the several States, shall be bound by Oath or Affirmation, to support this Constitution; but no religious Test shall ever be required as a Qualification to any Office or public Trust under the United States.

ARTICLE VII

The Ratification of the Conventions of nine States, shall be sufficient for the Establishment of this Constitution between the States so ratifying the Same.

DONE in Convention by the Unanimous Consent of the States present the Seventeenth Day of September in the Year of our Lord one thousand seven hundred and Eighty seven and of the Independence of the United States of America the Twelfth.

IN WITNESS whereof We have hereunto subscribed our Names.

AMENDMENT I

[*The first ten amendments (the Bill of Rights) were ratified December 15, 1791.*]

Congress shall make no law respecting an establishment of religion, or prohibiting the free exercise thereof; or abridging the freedom of speech, or of the press, or the right of the people peaceably to assemble, and to petition the Government for a redress of grievances.

AMENDMENT II

A well regulated Militia, being necessary to the security of a free State, the right of the people to keep and bear Arms, shall not be infringed.

AMENDMENT III

No Soldier shall, in time of peace be quartered in any house, without the consent of the Owner, nor in time of war, but in a manner to be prescribed by law.

AMENDMENT IV

The right of the people to be secure in their persons, houses, papers, and effects, against unreasonable searches and seizures, shall not be violated, and no Warrants shall issue, but upon probable cause, supported by Oath or affirmation, and particularly describing the place to be searched, and the persons or things to be seized.

AMENDMENT V

No person shall be held to answer for a capital, or otherwise infamous crime, unless on a presentment or indictment of a Grand Jury, except in cases arising in the land or naval forces, or in the Militia, when in actual service in time of War or public danger; nor shall any person be subject for the same offence to be twice put in jeopardy of life or limb, nor shall be compelled in any criminal case to be a witness against himself, nor be deprived of life, liberty, or property, without due process of law; nor shall private property be taken for public use, without just compensation.

AMENDMENT VI

In all criminal prosecutions, the accused shall enjoy the right to a speedy and public trial, by an impartial jury of the State and district wherein the crime shall have been committed; which district shall have been previously ascertained by law, and to be informed of the nature and cause of the accusation; to be confronted with the witnesses against him; to have compulsory process for obtaining Witnesses in his favor, and to have the assistance of counsel for his defence.

AMENDMENT VII

In Suits at common law, where the value in controversy shall exceed twenty dollars, the right of trial by jury shall be preserved, and no fact tried by a jury, shall be otherwise re-examined in any Court of the United States, than according to the rules of the common law.

AMENDMENT VIII

Excessive bail shall not be required, nor excessive fines imposed, nor cruel and unusual punishments inflicted.

AMENDMENT IX

The enumeration in the Constitution, of certain rights, shall not be construed to deny or disparage others retained by the people.

AMENDMENT X

The powers not delegated to the United States by the Constitution, nor prohibited by it to the States, are reserved to the States respectively, or to the people.

AMENDMENT XI

[Ratified February 7, 1795.]

The Judicial power of the United States shall not be construed to extend to any suit in law or equity, commenced or prosecuted against one of the United States by Citizens of another State, or by Citizens or Subjects of any Foreign State.

AMENDMENT XII

[Ratified June 15, 1804.]

The Electors shall meet in their respective states, and vote by ballot for President and Vice-President, one of whom, at least, shall not be an inhabitant of the same state with themselves; they shall name in their ballots the person voted for as President, and in distinct ballots the person voted for as Vice-President, and they shall make distinct lists of all persons voted for as President, and of all persons voted for as Vice-President, and of the number of votes for each, which lists they shall sign and certify, and transmit sealed to the seat of the government of the United States, directed to the President of the Senate;—The President of the Senate shall, in the presence of the Senate and House of Representatives, open all the certificates and the votes shall then be counted;—The person having the greatest number of votes for President, shall be the President, if such number be a majority of the whole number of Electors appointed; and if no person have such majority, then from the persons having the highest numbers not exceeding three on the list of those voted for as President, the House of Representatives shall choose immediately, by ballot, the President. But in choosing the President, the votes shall be taken by states, the representation from each state having one vote; a quorum for this purpose shall consist of a member or members from two-thirds of the states, and a majority of all the states shall be necessary to a choice. [And if the House of Representatives shall not choose a President whenever the right of choice shall devolve upon them, before the fourth day of March next following, then the Vice-President shall act as President, as in the case of the death or other constitutional disability of the President—(*This clause was superseded by section 3 of the Twentieth Amendment.)*]. The person having the greatest number of votes as Vice-President, shall be the Vice-President, if such number be a majority of the whole number of Electors appointed, and if no person have a majority, then from the two highest numbers on the list, the Senate shall choose the Vice-President; a quorum for the purpose shall consist of two-thirds of the whole number of Senators, and a majority of the whole number shall be necessary to a choice. But no person constitutionally ineligible to the office of President shall be eligible to that of Vice-President of the United States.

AMENDMENT XIII

[*Ratified December 6, 1865.*]

SECTION 1. Neither slavery nor involuntary servitude, except as a punishment for crime whereof the party shall have been duly convicted, shall exist within the United States, or any place subject to their jurisdiction.

SECTION 2. Congress shall have power to enforce this article by appropriate legislation.

AMENDMENT XIV

[*Ratified July 9, 1868.*]

SECTION 1. All persons born or naturalized in the United States, and subject to the jurisdiction thereof, are citizens of the United States and of the State wherein they reside. No State shall make or enforce any law which shall abridge the privileges or immunities of citizens of the United States; nor shall any State deprive any person of life, liberty, or property, without due process of law; nor deny to any person within its jurisdiction the equal protection of the laws.

SECTION 2. Representatives shall be apportioned among the several States according to their respective numbers, counting the whole number of persons in each State, excluding Indians not taxed. But when the right to vote at any election for the choice of electors for President and Vice President of the United States, Representatives in Congress, the Executive and Judicial officers of a State, or the members of the Legislature thereof, is denied to any of the male inhabitants of such State, being twenty-one years of age, and citizens of the United States, or in any way abridged, except for participation in rebellion, or other crime, the basis of representation therein shall be reduced in the proportion which the number of such male citizens shall bear to the whole number of male citizens twenty-one years of age in such State.

Section 3. No person shall be a Senator or Representative in Congress, or elector of President and Vice President, or hold any office, civil or military, under the United States, or under any State, who, having previously taken an oath, as a member of Congress, or as an officer of the United States, or as a member of any State legislature, or as an executive or judicial officer of any State, to support the Constitution of the United States, shall have engaged in insurrection or rebellion against the same, or given aid or comfort to the enemies thereof. But Congress may by a vote of two-thirds of each House, remove such disability.

Section 4. The validity of the public debt of the United States, authorized by law, including debts incurred for payment of pensions and bounties for services in suppressing insurrection or rebellion, shall not be questioned. But neither the United States nor any State shall assume or pay any debt or obligation incurred in aid of insurrection or rebellion against the United States, or any claim for the loss of emancipation of any slave; but all such debts, obligations and claims shall be held illegal and void.

Section 5. The Congress shall have power to enforce, by appropriate legislation, the provisions of this article.

AMENDMENT XV

[Ratified February 3, 1870.]

Section 1. The right of citizens of the United States to vote shall not be denied or abridged by the United States or by any State on account of race, color, or previous condition of servitude.

Section 2. The Congress shall have power to enforce this article by appropriate legislation.

AMENDMENT XVI

[Ratified February 3, 1913.]

The Congress shall have power to lay and collect taxes on incomes, from whatever source derived, without apportionment among the several States, and without regard to any census or enumeration.

AMENDMENT XVII

[Ratified April 8, 1913.]

The Senate of the United States shall be composed of two Senators from each State, elected by the people thereof, for six years; and each Senator shall have one vote. The electors in each State shall have the qualifications requisite for electors of the most numerous branch of the State legislatures.

When vacancies happen in the representation of any State in the Senate, the executive authority of such State shall issue writs of election to fill such vacancies: *Provided*, That the legislature of any State may empower the executive thereof to make temporary appointments until the people fill the vacancies by election as the legislature may direct.

This amendment shall not be so construed as to affect the election or term of any Senator chosen before it becomes valid as part of the Constitution.

AMENDMENT XVIII

[Ratified January 16, 1919.]

SECTION 1. After one year from the ratification of this article the manufacture, sale, or transportation of intoxicating liquors within, the importation thereof into, or the exportation thereof from the United States and all territory subject to the jurisdiction thereof for beverage purposes is hereby prohibited.

SECTION 2. The Congress and the several States shall have concurrent power to enforce this article by appropriate legislation.

SECTION 3. This article shall be inoperative unless it shall have been ratified as an amendment to the Constitution by the legislatures of the several States, as provided in the Constitution, within seven years from the date of the submission hereof to the States by the Congress.

AMENDMENT XIX

[Ratified August 18, 1920.]

The right of citizens of the United States to vote shall not be denied or abridged by the United States or by any State on account of sex.

Congress shall have power to enforce this article by appropriate legislation.

AMENDMENT XX

[Ratified January 23, 1933.]

SECTION 1. The terms of the President and Vice President shall end at noon on the 20th day of January, and the terms of Senators and Representatives at noon on the 3d day of January, of the years in which such terms would have ended if this article had not been ratified; and the terms of their successors shall then begin.

SECTION 2. The Congress shall assemble at least once in every year, and such meeting shall begin at noon on the 3d day of January, unless they shall by law appoint a different day.

SECTION 3. If, at the time fixed for the beginning of the term of the President, the President elect shall have died, the Vice President elect shall become President. If a President shall not have been chosen before the time fixed for the beginning of his term, or if the President elect shall have failed to qualify, then the Vice President elect shall act as President until a President shall have qualified; and the Congress may by law provide for the case wherein neither a President elect nor a Vice President elect shall have qualified, declaring who shall then act as President, or the manner in which one who is to act shall be selected, and such person shall act accordingly until a President or Vice President shall have qualified.

SECTION 4. The Congress may by law provide for the case of the death of any of the persons from whom the House of Representatives may choose a President whenever the right of choice shall have devolved upon them, and for the case of the death of any of the persons from whom the Senate may choose a Vice President whenever the right of choice shall have devolved upon them.

SECTION 5. Sections 1 and 2 shall take effect on the 15th day of October following the ratification of this article.

SECTION 6. This article shall be inoperative unless it shall have been ratified as an amendment to the Constitution by the legislatures of three-fourths of the several States within seven years from the date of its submission.

AMENDMENT XXI

[Ratified December 5, 1933.]

SECTION 1. The eighteenth article of amendment to the Constitution of the United States is hereby repealed.

SECTION 2. The transportation or importation into any State, Territory, or possession of the United States for delivery or use therein of intoxicating liquors, in violation of the laws thereof, is hereby prohibited.

SECTION 3. This article shall be inoperative unless it shall have been ratified as an amendment to the Constitution by conventions in the several States, as provided in the Constitution, within seven years from the date of the submission hereof to the States by the Congress.

AMENDMENT XXII

[Ratified February 27, 1951.]

SECTION 1. No person shall be elected to the office of the President more than twice, and no person who has held the office of President, or acted as President, for more than two years of a term to which some other person was elected President shall be elected to the office of the President more than once. But this Article shall not apply to any person holding the office of President when this Article was proposed by the Congress, and shall not prevent any person who may be holding the office of President, or acting as President, during the term within which this Article becomes operative from holding the office of President or acting as President during the remainder of such term.

SECTION 2. This article shall be inoperative unless it shall have been ratified as an amendment to the Constitution by the legislatures of three-fourths of the several States within seven years from the date of its submission to the States by the Congress.

AMENDMENT XXIII

[Ratified March 29, 1961.]

SECTION 1. The District constituting the seat of Government of the United States shall appoint in such manner as the Congress may direct:

A number of electors of President and Vice President equal to the whole number of Senators and Representatives in Congress to which the District would be entitled if it were a State, but in no event more than the least populous State; they shall be in addition to those appointed by the States, but they shall be considered, for the purposes of the election of President and Vice President, to be electors appointed by a State; and they shall meet in the District and perform such duties as provided by the twelfth article of amendment.

SECTION 2. The Congress shall have power to enforce this article by appropriate legislation.

AMENDMENT XXIV

[Ratified January 23, 1964.]

SECTION 1. The right of citizens of the United States to vote in any primary or other election for President or Vice President, for electors for President or Vice President, or for Senator or Representatives in Congress, shall not be denied or abridged by the United States or any State by reason of failure to pay any poll tax or other tax.

SECTION 2. The Congress shall have power to enforce this article by appropriate legislation.

AMENDMENT XXV

[Ratified February 10, 1967.]

SECTION 1. In case of the removal of the President from office or of his death or resignation, the Vice President shall become President.

SECTION 2. Whenever there is a vacancy in the office of the Vice President, the President shall nominate a Vice President who shall take office upon confirmation by a majority vote of both Houses of Congress.

SECTION 3. Whenever the President transmits to the President pro tempore of the Senate and the Speaker of the House of Representatives his written declaration that he is unable to discharge the powers and duties of his office, and until he transmits to them a written declaration to the contrary, such powers and duties shall be discharged by the Vice President as Acting President.

SECTION 4. Whenever the Vice President and a majority of either the principal officers of the executive departments or of such other body as Congress may by law provide, transmit to the President pro tempore of the Senate and the Speaker of the House of Representatives their written declaration that the President is unable to discharge the powers and duties of his office, the Vice President shall immediately assume the powers and duties of the office as Acting President.

Thereafter, when the President transmits to the President pro tempore of the Senate and the Speaker of the House of Representatives his written declaration that no inability exists, he shall resume the powers and duties of his office unless the Vice President and a majority of either the principal officers of the executive department or of such other body as Congress may by law provide, transmit within four days to the President pro tempore of the Senate and the Speaker of the House of Representatives their written declaration that the President is unable to discharge the powers and duties of his office. Thereupon Congress shall decide the issue, assembling within forty-eight hours for that purpose if not in session. If the Congress, within twenty-one days after receipt of the latter written declaration, or, if Congress is not in session, within twenty-one days after Congress is required to assemble, determines by two-thirds vote of both Houses that the President is unable to discharge the powers and duties of his office, the Vice President shall continue to discharge the same as Acting President; otherwise, the President shall resume the powers and duties of his office.

AMENDMENT XXVI

[Ratified July 1, 1971.]

SECTION 1. The right of citizens of the United States, who are eighteen years of age or older, to vote shall not be denied or abridged by the United States or by any State on account of age.

SECTION 2. The Congress shall have power to enforce this article by appropriate legislation.

AMENDMENT XXVII

[Ratified May 7, 1992.]

No law varying the compensation for the services of Senators and Representatives shall take effect until an election of Representatives shall have intervened.

I

THE SUPREME COURT, JUDICIAL REVIEW, AND CONSTITUTIONAL POLITICS

Judicial review is one of the greatest and most controversial contributions of the Constitution to the law and politics of government. Article III of the Constitution simply provides that "[t]he judicial Power of the United States, shall be vested in one supreme Court, and in such inferior Courts as the Congress may from time to time ordain and establish." Remarkably, that power is not further defined in the Constitution. But in the course of constitutional politics, *judicial review* has come to be the power of the Supreme Court and the federal judiciary to consider and overturn any congressional and state legislation or other official governmental action deemed inconsistent with the Constitution, Bill of Rights, or federal law.

Like other provisions of the Constitution, the three brief sections in Article III register compromises forged during the Constitutional Convention; the Constitution, as the renowned historian and editor of *The Records of the Federal Convention of 1787*, Max Farrand, observed, is "a bundle of compromises."[1] The first section of Article III makes clear that the Supreme Court is the only federal court constitutionally required. The convention left it for the First Congress to establish a system of lower federal courts, which it did with the Judiciary Act of 1789. Both the convention and the First Congress rejected proposals that would have left the administration of justice entirely in the hands of state courts (with appeals to the Supreme Court). Also rejected was

James Madison's proposal to join justices and executive branch officials in a "council of revision" with a veto power over congressional and state legislation. Agreement on the importance of guaranteeing judicial independence resulted in the first section of Article III also providing that federal judges "hold their Offices during good Behaviour," subject only to impeachment, and forbidding the diminution of their salaries. That guarantee reflects colonial opposition to royalist judges under the English Crown. One of the grievances listed in the Declaration of Independence as a justification for the Revolutionary War was that King George III had "made Judges dependent on his Will alone."[2] The two remaining sections of Article III specify the kinds of cases and controversies that the federal judiciary may hear (that is, jurisdiction) (see Ch. 2) and empower Congress to punish individuals for treason.

The Framers, it is fair to say, failed to think through the power of judicial review and its ramifications for constitutional politics. "[T]he framers anticipated some sort of judicial review," noted political scientist Edward S. Corwin, but he added that "it is equally without question that the ideas generally current in 1787 were far from presaging the present role of the Court."[3] In a letter to Corwin, Max Farrand also concluded that "[t]he framers of the Constitution did not realize it themselves [how markedly different their conceptions of judicial review were]: they were struggling to express an idea and their experience was as yet insufficient."[4]

The Constitutional Convention left the power of the judiciary (and much else set forth in the Constitution) to be worked out in practice. As John Mercer, a delegate to the Constitutional Convention from Maryland, observed, "It is a great mistake to suppose that the paper we are to propose will govern the United States. It is the men whom it will bring into the government and interest in maintaining it that is to govern them. The paper will only mark out the mode and the form."[5] The Constitution, of course, is not self-interpreting and crucial principles—such as judicial review, separation of powers, and federalism—are presupposed rather than spelled out. Moreover, in creating separate institutions that share specific and delegated powers, the Constitution amounts to a prescription for political struggle and an invitation for an ongoing debate about enduring constitutional principles.

Almost immediately following the convention in 1787, controversy erupted over the powers granted the national government and in particular to the federal judiciary. Those opposed to the states' ratification of the Constitution, the Anti-Federalists, warned that "[t]here are no well defined limits of the Judiciary Powers, they seem to be left as a boundless ocean."[6] Fears that "the powers of the judiciary may be extended to any degree short of Almighty" were echoed by Thomas

Tredwell, among others, during New York's convention.[7] Robert Yates, one of the most articulate Anti-Federalists writing under the name of Brutus, attacked both the independence and the power of federal judges:

> There is no authority that can remove them, and they cannot be controuled [sic] by the laws of the legislature. In short, they are independent of the people, of the legislature, and of every power under heaven. Men placed in this situation will generally soon feel themselves independent of heaven itself. . . .
>
> And in their decisions they will not confine themselves to any fixed or established rules, but will determine, according to what appears to them, the reason and spirit of the constitution. The opinions of the supreme court, whatever they may be, will have the force of law; because there is no power provided in the constitution, that can correct their errors, or controul their adjudiciations. From this court there is no appeal.[8]

"This power in the judicial," charged Brutus, "will enable them to mould the government, into almost any shape they please."

Defenders of the Constitution countered that "the powers given the Supreme Court are not only safe, but constitute a wise and valuable part of the system."[9] In North Carolina's convention, Governor Johnston observed that "[i]t is obvious to every one that there ought to be one Supreme Court for national purposes."[10] During the fight for New York's ratification, Alexander Hamilton provided the classic defense of the judiciary as "the least dangerous branch." Responding to Brutus in *The Federalist*, No. 78, Hamilton argued,

> Whoever attentively considers the different departments of power must perceive, that in a government in which they are separated from each other, the judiciary, from the nature of its functions, will always be the least dangerous to the political rights of the constitution; because it will be least in a capacity to annoy or injure them. The executive not only dispenses the honors, but holds the sword of the community. The legislature not only commands the purse, but prescribes the rules by which the duties and rights of every citizen are to be regulated. The judiciary on the contrary has no influence over either the sword or the purse, no direction either of the strength or of the wealth of the society, and can take no active resolution whatever. It may truly be said to have neither Force nor Will, but merely judgment; and must ultimately depend upon the aid of the executive arm even for the efficacy of its judgments.
>
> If it be said that the legislative body are themselves the constitutional judges of their own powers, and that the construction they put upon them is conclusive upon other departments, it may be answered, that this cannot be the natural presumption, where it is not

to be collected from any particular provisions in the constitution. It is not otherwise to be supposed that the constitution could intend to enable the representatives of the people to substitute their *will* to that of their constituents. It is far more rational to suppose that the courts were designed to be an intermediate body between the people and the legislature, in order, among other things, to keep the latter within the limits assigned to their authority. The interpretation of the laws is the proper and peculiar province of the courts. A constitution is in fact, and must be, regarded by the judges as a fundamental law. It therefore belongs to them as to ascertain its meaning as well as the meaning of any particular act proceeding from the legislative body. If there should happen to be an irreconcilable variance between the two, that which has the superior obligation and validity ought of course to be preferred; or in other words, the constitution ought to be preferred to the statute, the intention of the people to the intention of their agents.

Nor does this conclusion by any means suppose a superiority of the judicial to the legislative power. It only supposes that the power of the people is superior to both; and that where the will of the legislature declared in its statutes, stands in opposition to that of the people declared in the constitution, the judges ought to be governed by the latter, rather than the former. . . .

If then the courts of justice are to be considered as the bulwarks of a limited constitution against legislative encroachments, this consideration will afford a strong argument for the permanent tenure of judicial offices, since nothing will contribute so much as this to that independent spirit in the judges, which must be essential to the faithful performance of so arduous a duty.

The Federalists' interpretation of Article III was advanced by others in the effort to win ratification. In Pennsylvania's convention, James Wilson, who was one of the first justices appointed by President George Washington, argued that

under this Constitution, the legislature may be restrained, and kept within its prescribed bounds, by the interposition of the judicial department. . . . [T]he power of the Constitution [is] paramount to the power of the legislature acting under that Constitution; for it is possible that the legislature, when acting in that capacity, may transgress the bounds assigned to it, and an act may pass, in the usual *mode*, notwithstanding that transgression; but when it comes to be discussed before *the judges*,—when they consider its principles, and find it to be incompatible with the superior power of the Constitution,—it is their duty to pronounce it *void*.[11]

In Connecticut, Oliver Ellsworth, another who was later appointed to the Court, declared, "If the general legislature should at any time overleap their limits, the judicial department is a constitutional check."[12]

Even among the Federalists, however, there were differing views of the judiciary's power. Alexander Hamilton and James Madison agreed that the Court would exercise some checking power over the states. The Court, in Madison's words, was "the surest expositor of . . . the [constitutional] boundaries . . . between the Union and its members."[13] But they were in less agreement on whether the Court had the power to check coequal branches, the Congress and the president. In *The Federalist*, Madison called the judiciary an "auxiliary precaution" against the possible domination of one branch of government over another. Later, during a debate in the First Congress in 1789, he observed that "in the ordinary course of Government, . . . the exposition of the laws and Constitution devolves upon the Judiciary." Still, Madison doubted that the Court's interpretation of the Constitution was superior to that given by Congress. "Nothing has been offered to invalidate the [view]," he argued, "that the meaning of the Constitution may as well be ascertained by the legislative as by the judicial authority."[14] The Court stood as a forum of last resort, Madison explained, but "this resort must necessarily be deemed the last in relation to the authorities of the other departments of the government; not in relation to the rights of the parties to the constitutional compact, from which the judicial, as well as the other departments, hold their delegated trusts."[15]

From the initial debate in the Constitutional Convention in 1787 to those between the Federalists and the Anti-Federalists over state ratification of the Constitution and into the First Congress, the power of judicial review and the meaning of other key provisions and principles of the Constitution have remained a continuing source of controversy in constitutional politics. And the Supreme Court has remained, as Justice Oliver Wendell Holmes observed, a "storm centre" of political controversy.

A | *Establishing and Contesting the Power of Judicial Review*

In its first decade, the Supreme Court had little business, frequent turnover in personnel, no chambers or staff, no fixed customs, and no institutional identity. When the Court initially convened on February 1, 1790, only Chief Justice John Jay and two other justices arrived at the Exchange Building in New York City. They adjourned until the next day when Justice John Blair arrived; the two other justices never arrived. With little to do other than admit attorneys to practice

■ HOW TO LOCATE DECISIONS
OF THE SUPREME COURT

[The decisions of the Supreme Court are published in the *United States Reports* by the U.S. Government Printing Office. Each decision is referred to by the names of the appellant, the person bringing the suit, and the appellee, the respondent: hence, *McCulloch v. Maryland*. After the name of the case is the volume number in which it appears in the *United States Reports* and the page number on which the Court's opinion begins, followed by the year of the decision. *McCulloch v. Maryland*, 17 U.S. 316 (1819), thus may be found in volume 17 of the *United States Reports* beginning on page 316.

Prior to the publication of the *United States Reports* in 1875, the Court's opinions used to be cited according to the name of the reporter of the Court, who published the Court's opinions at his own expense. Decisions thus would originally be cited as follows:

1789–1800	Dallas	(1–4 Dall., 1–4 U.S.)
1801–1815	Cranch	(1–9 Cr., 5–13 U.S.)
1816–1827	Wheaton	(1–12 Wheat, 14–25 U.S.)
1828–1842	Peters	(1–16 Pet., 26–41 U.S.)
1843–1860	Howard	(1–24 How., 42–65 U.S.)
1861–1862	Black	(1–2 Bl., 66–67 U.S.)
1863–1874	Wallace	(1–23 Wall., 68–90 U.S.)
1875–		(91– , U.S.)

The full citation for *McCulloch v. Maryland* is 4 Wheat. (17 U.S.) 316 (1819). But with volume 91 in 1875, the reporters' names were dropped, and decisions were then cited only by the volume number and the designation "U.S."

In addition, two companies print editions of the Court's decisions. There is the *Lawyers' Edition*, published by the Lawyer's Cooperative, and *The Supreme Court Reporter*, published by West Publishing Company. The *Lawyers' Edition* is cited as L.Ed. (e.g., 91 L.Ed. 575), and *The Supreme Court Reporter* is cited as S.Ct. (e.g., 104 S.Ct. 3005). See also Researching Legal Materials at the end of the book.

before its bar, the Court concluded its first sessions in less than two weeks.

When the capital moved from New York City to Philadelphia in the winter of 1790, the Court met in Independence Hall and in the

Old City Hall, until the capital again moved to Washington, DC, in 1800. Most of the first justices' time was spent riding circuit. That is, each would travel throughout a particular area, or circuit, in the country. Under the Judiciary Act of 1789, they were required twice a year to hold court, in the company of local district judges, in a circuit to hear appeals from the federal district courts. Hence, the justices resided primarily in their circuits, rather than in Washington, and felt a greater allegiance to their circuits than to the Court.

The Court's uncertain status was reflected in the first justices' exercise of their power of judicial review. Although in its initial years the Court had few important cases, *Chisholm v. Georgia*, 2 Dall. (2 U.S.) 419 (1793) precipitated the country's first constitutional crisis. In that case, Justice James Wilson, who had been a delegate to the Constitutional Convention and Pennsylvania's ratifying convention, ruled that citizens of one state could sue another state in federal courts. That provoked an angry dissent from Justice James Iredell, a southerner who had attended North Carolina's ratifying convention and a strong proponent of "states' rights." His dissent invited the adoption by Congress of the Eleventh Amendment in 1795, overturning *Chisholm* and guaranteeing state immunity from lawsuits brought by citizens of other states (see Vol. 1, Ch. 7 for further discussion). The outcry over *Chisholm* convinced Chief Justice John Jay that the Court would remain "the least dangerous branch." He resigned in 1795 to become New York's governor and later declined reappointment as chief justice.

The Court, though, in *Ware v. Hylton*, 3 Dall. (3 U.S.) 199 (1796), upheld the provisions of a federal treaty, the 1783 peace treaty with England, over state law. And *Hylton v. United States*, 3 Dall. (3 U.S.) 171 (1796), affirmed, over objections raised by the states, Congress's power to levy a carriage tax (and thus implicitly asserted the Court's power to nullify acts of Congress).

Still, two years later, *Calder v. Bull*, 3 Dall. (3 U.S.) 386 (1798), illustrates how uncertain and divided the justices were about exercising their power of judicial review. There the Court declined to assert its power when ruling that conflicts between state laws and state constitutions are matters for state, not federal, courts to resolve. But Justice Iredell maintained that a state law might run against principles of "natural justice" and the Court still have no power to strike it down. By contrast, Justice Samuel Chase contended that the Court had the power to overturn laws that violate fundamental principles, explaining,

> I cannot subscribe to the omnipotence of a State legislature, or that it is absolute and without controul; although its authority should not be expressly restrained by the Constitution, or fundamental

laws of the State. The people of the United States erected their Constitution . . . to establish justice, to promote the general welfare, to secure the blessings of liberty;and to protect their persons and property from violence. . . . There are acts which the Federal, or State, Legislature cannot do. . . . It is against all reason and justice to entrust a Legislature with SUCH [despotic] powers; and therefore, it cannot be presumed that they have done it. The genius, the nature, and the spirit of our State Governments, amount to a prohibition of such [unlimited] acts of legislation; and the general principles of law and reason forbid them.

Justice Chase was not alone in claiming that the judiciary had the power of judicial review. As an ardent Federalist, James Kent (1763–1847) staunchly defended the power of judicial review in his Introductory Law Lecture at Columbia University in 1794 (excerpted below). Like Alexander Hamilton, James Wilson, and other Federalists, Kent justified judicial review in terms of fundamental principles of constitutional government. But, unlike Hamilton's arguments in *The Federalist*, No. 78, Kent stressed the uniquely American basis for the doctrine of judicial review.

The uncertainty and controversy over the power of judicial review was, nevertheless, further underscored in 1798 with the passage of the Virginia and Kentucky Resolutions (excerpted below), in response to Congress's enactment of the Alien and Sedition Acts. Drafted by James Madison and Thomas Jefferson, the Virginia and Kentucky Resolutions not only contended that Congress had violated the First Amendment but claimed that state legislatures had the power to judge the constitutionality of federal laws. Jefferson went so far as to assert that states could nullify federal laws that they deemed unconstitutional. The "sovereign and independent" states, in his words, "have the unquestionable right to judge . . . and, that a nullification [by] those sovereignties, of all unauthorized acts done under the color of that instrument is the rightful remedy."

Jefferson remained opposed to the power of judicial review and the view that the Supreme Court's interpretation of the Constitution was binding on the other branches of government. In a 1819 letter to Spencer Roane, a Virginia state judge, Jefferson explained his departmental theory of constitutional interpretation:

My construction of the Constitution is . . . that each department is truly independent of the others, and has an equal right to decide for itself what is the meaning of the Constitution in the cases submitted to its action most especially where it is to act ultimately and without appeal. . . . Each of the three departments has equally the right to decide for itself what is its duty under the Constitution, without any regard to what the others may have decided for themselves under a similar question.[16]

Although less strident than Jefferson, Madison thought that the "true and safe construction" of the Constitution would emerge with the "uniform sanction of successive legislative bodies; through a period of years and under the varied ascendency of parties."[17]

Chief Justice John Marshall provided the classic justification for the power of judicial review in the landmark ruling in *Marbury v. Madison* (1803) (excerpted below; see also "The How, Why, and What to Briefing and Citing Court Cases" at the end of the book). Notice that Marshall's arguments draw on both general principles and the text of the Constitution and are not unassailable. In an otherwise unimportant state case, *Eakin v. Raub* 12 Sargeant & Rawle 330 (Pa., 1825), for example, Pennsylvania Supreme Court Justice John Gibson expressly refuted Marshall's arguments. It does not inexorably follow from Marshall's claim that the Constitution created a limited government that *only* the judiciary should enforce those limitations. No more persuasive is the argument that judges have the power to authoritatively interpret the Constitution based on their taking an oath to uphold the document, because all federal and state officers take an oath to support the Constitution. Like Madison and Jefferson, Justice Gibson rejected *Marbury's* implication that the judiciary has a monopoly (or supremacy) over interpreting the Constitution or, as Chief Justice Charles Evans Hughes later put it, "We are under a Constitution but the Constitution is what the judges say it is."[18] In providing a rationale for judicial self-restraint, Gibson embraces a departmental theory of constitutional interpretation—namely, that each branch has the authority to interpret the Constitution.

Chief Justice Marshall's arguments based on the text of the Constitution fare better. In specifying that the "judicial Power shall extend to" cases and controversies "arising under this Constitution," Article III implies that constitutional questions may be decided by the judiciary. And, as Marshall points out, the Supremacy Clause of Article VI makes it clear that the Constitution is "the supreme Law of the Land." Judicial review is thus a logical implication of the Constitution, for as Justice Joseph Story observed,

> The laws and treaties, and even the constitution, of the United States, would become a dead letter without it. Indeed, in a complicated government, like ours, where there is an assemblage of republics, combined under a common head, the necessity of some controlling judicial power, to ascertain and enforce the powers of the Union is, if possible, still more striking. The laws of the whole would otherwise be in continual danger of being contravened by the laws of the parts. The national government would be reduced to a servile dependence upon the states; and the same scenes would be again acted over in solemn mockery,

which began in the neglect, and ended in the ruin, of the con-federation.[19]

Still and undeniably, the power of judicial review is not expressly provided for in the Constitution and its exercise remains a continuing source of controversy.

The immediate political controversy over the exercise of judicial review in *Marbury* in striking down a section of the Judiciary Act of 1789 was defused by Chief Justice Marshall's conclusion that the Court had no power to order the delivery of Marbury's commission. Though outraged by Marshall's assertion of judicial review, Madison and Jefferson had not been compelled by the Court to do anything. Jefferson continued to maintain that each branch of government could interpret the Constitution and to deny that the Court's interpretations were binding on the president's exercise of executive powers. In a letter to Mrs. John Adams in 1804, explaining his decision to pardon those tried and convicted under the Sedition Act of 1798, Jefferson wrote,

> The Judges, believing the law constitutional, had a right to pass a sentence of fine and imprisonment; because that power was placed in their hands by the Constitution. But the Executive, believing the law to be unconstitutional, was bound to remit the execution of it; because that power has been confided to him by the Constitution. The instrument meant that its co-ordinate branches should be checks on each other. But the opinion which gives to the Judges the right to decide what Laws are constitutional, and what not, not only for themselves in their own sphere of action, but for the Leg-islative and Executive also in their spheres, would make the Judici-ary a despotic branch.[20]

Jefferson was not the last president to contest the authority of the Court. An irate President Andrew Jackson, on hearing of the decision in *Worcester v. Georgia*, 31 U.S. 515 (1832), holding that states could not pass laws affecting federally recognized Indian nations, reportedly declared, "John Marshall has made his decision, now let him enforce it."[21] Jackson elaborated his view in his Veto Message of 1832, explaining his vetoing of legislation rechartering the national bank (see Ch. 6). Besides con-tending that *McCulloch v. Maryland*, 17 U.S. 316 (1819) (see Ch. 6) was not binding on his actions, Jackson reiterated the position that

> [t]he Congress, the Executive, and the Court must each for itself be guided by its own opinion of the Constitution. Each public officer who takes an oath to support the Constitution swears that he will support it as he understands it, and not as it is understood by oth-ers. . . . The opinion of the judges has no more authority over Congress than the opinion of Congress has over the judges, and on that point the President is independent of both.[22]

Jackson's Veto Message drew an impassioned response from Senator Daniel Webster, who thundered in the halls of Congress that

> [t]he President is as much bound by the law as any private citizen. . . . He may refuse to obey the law, and so may a private citizen; but both do it at their own peril, and neither of them can settle the question of its validity. The President may say a law is unconstitutional, but he is not the judge. . . . If it were otherwise, there would be no government of laws; but we should all live under the government, the rule, the caprices of individuals. . . .
>
> [President Jackson's] message . . . converts a constitutional limitation of power into mere matters of opinion, and then strikes the judicial department, as an efficient department, out of our system. . . .
>
> [The message] denies first principles. It contradicts truths heretofore received as indisputable. It denies to the judiciary the interpretation of law.

Controversy over judicial review continues, but it bears emphasizing that Jefferson, Jackson, and subsequent presidents concede that the Court's rulings are binding for the actual cases decided and handed down. Technically, a decision of the Court is final only for the parties involved in the case. Yet, because the justices in their opinions give general principles for deciding a case and because they generally adhere to precedents (or tend to do so until the composition of the bench markedly changes), the Court's rulings are usually considered controlling for other similar cases and the larger political controversy they represent. But in major confrontations in constitutional politics—like those over the creation of a national bank, slavery, school desegregation, and abortion—the Court alone cannot lay those controversies to rest.

What presidents, Congress, the states, and others occasionally deny is *judicial supremacy* or the finality of the Court's interpretation of broad constitutional principles for resolving major political controversies. In his famous debates with Stephen Douglas, for instance, Abraham Lincoln denounced the Court's ruling in *Dred Scott v. Sandford*, 60 U.S. 393 (1857) (see Vol. 2, Ch. 12), that blacks were not citizens of the United States. While Lincoln doubted that "we, as a mob, will decide [Dred Scott] to be free," he exclaimed that

> we nevertheless do oppose that decision as a political rule which shall be binding on the voter, to vote for nobody who thinks it wrong, which shall be binding on the members of Congress or the President to favor no measure that does not actually concur with the principles of that decision. . . . We propose so resisting it as to have it reversed if we can, and a new judicial rule established upon this subject.[23]

Later, in his first Inaugural Address in 1861, Lincoln elaborated,

> I do not forget the position assumed by some, that constitutional questions are to be decided by the Supreme Court; nor do I deny that such decisions must be binding in any case, upon the parties to a suit, as to the object of that suit, while they are also entitled to a very high respect and consideration, in all parallel cases, by all other departments of government. And while it is obviously possible that such a decision may be erroneous in any given case, still the evil effect following it, being limited to that particular case, with the chance that it may be over-ruled, and never become a precedent for other cases, can better be borne than could the evils of a different practice. At the same time the candid citizen must confess that if the policy of the government, upon vital questions, affecting the whole people, is to be irrevocably fixed by the decisions of the Supreme Court, the instant they are made, in ordinary litigation between parties, in personal actions, the people will have ceased, to be their own rulers, having to that extent, practically resigned their government, into the hands of that eminent tribunal. Nor is there, in this view, any assault upon the court, or the judges. It is a duty, from which they may not shrink, to decide cases properly brought before them; and it is no fault of theirs, if others seek to turn their decisions to political purposes.

In major confrontations with the Court, other presidents have taken similar positions to that of President Lincoln. During the constitutional crisis of 1937, resulting from the Court's invalidation of much of the early New Deal progressive economic legislation, President Franklin D. Roosevelt proposed that Congress expand the size of the Court from nine to fifteen justices, and thereby enable him to secure a majority sympathetic to his programs and policies. And in a "Fireside Chat" in March 1937 (see excerpt below), FDR followed in the footsteps of Jefferson, Jackson, and Lincoln in attacking the Court for becoming a "super-legislature."

Judicial supremacy over interpreting the Constitution remains controversial. In *Marbury*, however, Chief Justice Marshall did not lay claim to judicial supremacy, only that the Court, no less than the president and Congress, has the authority and duty to interpret the Constitution.[24] By contrast, in this century justices have often asserted the supremacy of their decisions. In *United States v. Butler*, 297 U.S. 1 (1936), Justice (and later Chief Justice) Harlan Stone claimed that "[w]hile unconstitutional exercise of power by the executive and legislative branches of government is subject to judicial restraint, the only check upon our own exercise of power is our own sense of self-restraint." In the wake of massive resistance to the Court's watershed ruling on school desegregation, in *Brown v. Board of Education*, 347 U.S. 483 (1954) (see Vol. 2, Ch. 12), all nine justices took the unusual step of signing the opinion announcing *Cooper v. Aaron*, 358 U.S. 1 (1958) (see Vol. 2, Ch. 12), which ordered the desegregation of schools in Little Rock, Arkansas. And they interpreted *Marbury* to have

> declared the basic principle that the federal judiciary is supreme in the exposition of the law of the Constitution. . . . It follows that the interpretation of the Fourteenth Amendment enunciated by this Court in the *Brown* case is the supreme law of the land, and Article VI of the Constitution makes it have binding effect on the States. . . . Every state legislator and executive and judicial officer is solemnly committed by oath taken pursuant to Article VI, 3 "to support this Constitution."

The Court likewise proclaimed itself the "ultimate interpreter of the Constitution" in *Baker v. Carr*, 369 U.S. 186 (1962) (excerpted in Ch. 2), when holding that courts could decide disputes over the malapportionment of state legislatures. And again citing *Marbury* in *Powell v. McCormack*, 395 U.S. 486 (1969) (see Vol. 1, Ch. 5), involving a controversy over the House of Representatives' exclusion of a duly elected representative, the Court declared that "it is the responsibility of this Court to act as the ultimate interpreter of the Constitution." The Rehnquist Court underscored its authority, in *City of Boerne v. Flores*, 521 U.S. 507 (1997) (excerpted in Ch. 6 of Vols. 1 and 2), when reasserting that Congress's power under the Fourteenth Amendment is only remedial, not definitive, and thus only the Court, and not Congress, has the power to define constitutional rights. (See also *Boumediene v. Bush* (2008) (excerpted in Chapter 3), striking down Congress' stripping federal courts' jurisdiction over *habeas* petitions filed by enemy combatants held in Guantanamo Bay).

Despite the Court's occasional claims of judicial supremacy, the president, Congress, and the states may in various ways undercut and thwart compliance with, if not ultimately overturn, the Court's rulings (see Vol. 1, Ch. 2). By deciding only immediate cases, the Court infuses constitutional meaning into the larger surrounding political controversies by bringing them within the language, structure, and spirit of the Constitution. The Court may thus raise a controversial issue, as it did with school desegregation in *Brown* and with the right to abortion in *Roe*, to the national political agenda. But by itself the Court cannot lay those controversies to rest because its power, in Chief Justice Edward White's words, rests "solely upon the approval of a free people."[25] In areas of major and continuing political controversy, constitutional law is a kind of dialogue between the Court and the country over the meaning of the Constitution, and judicial review may be in historical perspective more provisional than final.

■ CONSTITUTIONAL HISTORY

Decisions of the Supreme Court Overruled and Acts of Congress Held Unconstitutional, and State Laws and Municipal Ordinances Overturned, 1789–2010★

Year	Supreme Court Decision Overruled	Acts of Congress Overturned	State Laws Overturned	Ordinances Overturned
1789–1800, Pre-Marshall				
1801–1835, Marshall Court	3	1	18	
1836–1864, Taney Court	4	1	21	
1865–1873, Chase Court	4	10	33	
1874–1888, Waite Court	13	9	7	
1889–1910, Fuller Court	4	14	73	15
1910–1921, White Court	5	12	107	18
1921–1930, Taft Court	6	12	131	12
1930–1940, Hughes Court	21	14	78	5
1941–1946, Stone Court	15	2	25	7
1947–1952, Vinson Court	13	1	38	7
1953–1969, Warren Court	45	25	150	16
1969–1986, Burger Court	52	34	192	15
1986–2005, Rehnquist Court	39	38	97	21
2005– , Roberts Court	9	7	11	2

★Note that in *Immigration and Naturalization Service v. Chadha* (1983), the Burger Court struck down a provision for a "one-house" legislative veto in the Immigration and Naturalization Act but effectively declared all one- and two-house legislative vetoes unconstitutional. While 212 statutes containing provisions for legislative vetoes were implicated by the Court's decision, *Chadha* is here counted as a single declaration of the unconstitutionality of congressional legislation. Note also that the Court's ruling in *Texas v. Johnson* (1989), striking down a Texas law making it a crime to desecrate the American flag, invalidated laws in forty-eight states and a federal statute. It is counted here, however, only once. This table includes cases through the 2009–2010 term.

Even more than Chief Justice Marshall's arguments in *Marbury*, the establishment of judicial review turned on public acceptance and the forces of history. That is not to gainsay Marshall's contributions. He had a keen understanding of the malleable nature of the young republic and the important role that the first generation would play in establishing the power of the national government. Marshall's long tenure (1801–1835) and that of others who served with him may have contributed as well. After *Marbury*, moreover, the Court did not again strike down another act of Congress or challenge a coequal branch of government until the 1857 ill-fated ruling in *Dred Scott*, which left the Court at a low ebb for two decades. Instead, the Marshall Court buttressed its own power by defending the interests of the national government against the states and striking down state laws.

Finally, social forces have shaped the Court's role in the kinds of cases and controversies brought to it for review. As already noted, the Court had little important business during its first decade. Over 40 percent of its business consisted in admiralty and prize cases (disputes over captured property at sea). About 50 percent raised issues of common law, and the remaining 10 percent dealt with matters like equity, including one probate case. By the late nineteenth century, the Court's business gradually changed in response to developments in American society. The number of admiralty cases, for instance, had by 1882 dwindled to less than 4 percent of the total. Almost 40 percent of the Court's decisions still dealt with either disputes of common law or questions of jurisdiction and procedure in federal courts. More than 43 percent of the Court's business, however, involved interpreting congressional statutes. Less than 4 percent of the cases raised issues of constitutional interpretation. The decline in admiralty and common-law litigation and the increase in statutory interpretation reflected the impact of the Industrial Revolution and the growing governmental regulation of social and economic relations. In the twentieth century, the trend continued. About 47 percent of the cases decided annually by the Court involve matters of constitutional law. Another 38 percent deal with the interpretation of congressional legislation. The remaining 15 percent involve issues of practice and procedure, administrative law, taxation, patents, and claims.

The Court is no longer "the least dangerous branch" or primarily concerned with correcting the errors of lower courts. In response to growing and changing litigation, the Court more frequently overturns prior rulings, congressional legislation, and state and local laws. The Court takes only "hard cases," involving major issues of legal policy and "not primarily to preserve the rights of the litigants," in the words of Chief Justice William Howard Taft: "The Supreme Court's function is for the purpose of expounding and stabilizing principles of law for the benefit of the people of the country, passing upon constitutional questions and other important questions of law for the public benefit."[26]

The Court and the country have changed with constitutional politics. From 1789 to the Civil War, the major controversies confronting the Court involved disputes between the national government and the states, and the Court employed its power to preserve the Union (see Chs. 6 and 7). Between 1865 and 1937, during the Reconstruction and the Industrial Revolution, the dominant political controversy revolved around balancing regulatory interests and those of businesses, and the Court defended the interests of American capitalism and private enterprise (see Vol. 2, Ch. 3). Only after 1937 did the Court begin to assume the role of "a guardian for civil liberties and civil rights" in defending the rights of minorities (see Vol. 2, Chs. 4–12). The Court's role has changed with constitutional politics, as the late Harvard Law School professor Paul Freund nicely expressed by analogy, "As Hamlet is to one generation a play of revenge, to another a conflict between will and conscience, and to another a study in mother-fixation, so the Constitution has been to one generation a means of cementing the Union, to another a protectorate of burgeoning property, and to another a safeguard of basic human rights and equality before the law."[27]

NOTES

1. See Max Farrand, *The Framing of the Constitution* (New Haven, CT: Yale University Press, 1913); Max Farrand, ed., *The Records of the Federal Convention of 1787*, 4 vols. (New Haven, CT: Yale University Press, 1911); and John P. Roche, "The Founding Fathers: A Reform Caucus in Action," 55 *American Political Science Review* 799 (1961).

2. The Supreme Court has enforced the tenure and salary provisions in *Ex parte Milligan*, 4 Wall. 2 (1867) (see Ch. 3), holding that civilians cannot be tried before military tribunals; in *O'Donoghue v. United States*, 289 U.S. 516 (1933), holding that judicial salaries cannot be reduced, even during the Great Depression; and *Northern Pipeline Construction Co. v. Marathon Pipe Line Co.*, 458 U.S. 50 (1982), striking down a statute expanding the power of bankruptcy judges.

3. Edward S. Corwin, "The Constitution as Instrument and as Symbol," 30 *American Political Science Review* 1078 (1936).

4. Letter from Max Farrand to Edward Corwin, Jan. 3, 1939, in Edward Samuel Corwin Papers, Box 3, Princeton University Library, Princeton, NJ.

5. Quoted in James Madison, *Notes of Debates in the Federal Convention of 1787* (Athens: Ohio University Press, 1966), 455–456.

6. A Columbia Patriot, in *The Complete Anti-Federalist*, Vol. 4, ed. Herbert J. Storing (Chicago: University of Chicago Press, 1981), 276.

7. Thomas Tredwell, in *The Debates in the Several State Conventions on the Adoption of the Federal Constitution*, Vol. 4, ed., Jonathan Elliot (New York: Burt Franklin, 1974), 401.

8. Brutus, in *The Complete Anti-Federalist*, Vol. 2, ed. Storing, 438–439, 420, 422.

9. James Wilson, in *The Debates*, Vol. 2, ed. Elliot, 494.

10. Governor Johnston, in *The Debates*, Vol. 4, ed. Elliot, 142.

11. James Wilson, in *The Debates*, Vol. 2, ed. Elliot, 445–446.

12. Oliver Ellsworth, in *The Debates*, Vol. 2, ed. Elliot, 196.

13. Letter from James Madison to an unidentified person, Aug. 1834, reprinted in *Letters and Other Writings of James Madison*, Vol. 4 (Philadelphia, 1865), 350.

14. James Madison, in *Annals of Congress*, Vol. 1 (Washington, DC: Gales & Seaton, 1789), 500, 546–547.

15. James Madison, "Report on the Virginia Resolutions," in *The Debates*, Vol. 5, ed. Elliot, 549.

16. Thomas Jefferson, *The Works of Thomas Jefferson*, Vol. 12, ed. Paul Ford (New York: G. P. Putnam's Sons, 1904–1905), 137–138.

17. Quoted in Robert J. Morgan, *James Madison on the Constitution and the Bill of Rights* (Westport, CT: Greenwood Press, 1988), 196. For more on Jefferson's and Madison's views, see the discussion of the controversy over Congress's creating a national bank and *McCulloch v. Maryland*, 17 U.S. 316 (1819) (excerpted in Ch. 6).

18. Charles Evans Hughes, *Address and Papers of Charles Evans Hughes* (New York: Columbia University Press, 1908), 139.

19. Joseph Story, *Commentaries on the Constitution*, (Durham, NC: Carolina Academic Press, 1987), reprint of 1833 ed.

20. Thomas Jefferson, Letter to John Adams, Sept. 11, 1804, as quoted in Charles Warren, *The Supreme Court in United States History*, Vol. 1 (Boston: Little, Brown, 1922), 265.

21. Quoted in Edward Corwin, *The Doctrine of Judicial Review* (Princeton, NJ: Princeton University Press, 1914), 22.

22. President's Veto Message (July 10, 1832), *A Compilation of the Messages and Papers of the Presidents*, Vol. 2, ed. J. Richardson (New York: Bureau of National Literature, 1917), 582.

23. Abraham Lincoln, *The Collected Works of Abraham Lincoln*, Vol. 2, Roy Basler, ed. (New Brunswick, NJ: Rutgers University Press, 1953), 401.

24. See David M. O'Brien, "Judicial Review and Constitutional Politics: Theory and Practice," 48 *University of Chicago Law Review* 1070 (1981).

25. Quoted in David M. O'Brien, *Storm Center: The Supreme Court in American Politics*, 9th ed. (New York: W. W. Norton, 2011).

26. William H. Taft, *Hearings before the House Committee on the Judiciary*, 67th Cong., 2d sess., 1922, 2.

27. Paul Freund, "My Philosophy of Law," 39 *Connecticut Bar Journal* 220 (1965).

Selected Bibliography

Corwin, Edward S. *The Doctrine of Judicial Review*. Princeton, NJ: Princeton University Press, 1914.

Ellis, Joseph. *Founding Brothers: The Revolutionary Generation*, New York: Knopf, 2000.

Fisher, Louis. *Constitutional Dialogues.* Princeton, NJ: Princeton University Press, 1988.

Hall, Kermit. *The Oxford Companion to the Supreme Court*, 2d ed. New York: Oxford University Press, 2007.

Lasser, William. *The Limits of Judicial Power.* Chapel Hill: University of North Carolina Press, 1988.

Nelson, William. *Marbury v. Madison: The Origins and Legacy of Judicial Review.* Lawrence: University of Kansas Press, 2000.

Warren, Charles. *The Supreme Court in United States History*, 3 vols. Boston: Little, Brown, 1922.

Whittington, Keith. *Political Foundations of Judicial Supremacy.* Princeton: Princeton University Press, 2007.

James Kent's Introductory Law School Lecture in 1794

James Kent (1763–1847) began a long legal career as a professor at Columbia University Law School in 1794. He later became a master of chancery and in 1804 the chief justice of New York's supreme court. His Columbia Law Lectures were later expanded into *Commentaries on the American Law* (1826–1830), which Justice Joseph Story called "our first judicial classic." Excerpted here is part of his "Introductory Lecture," which did not remain intact in his *Commentaries* but which uniquely justified judicial review in terms of established principles of republican government in America.

JAMES KENT: The British Constitution and Code of Laws, to the knowledge of which our Lawyers are so early and deeply introduced by the prevailing course of their professional inquiries, abounds, it is true, with invaluable Principles of Equity, of Policy, and of Social Order; Principles which cannot be too generally known, studied and received. It must however be observed at the same time, that many of the fundamental doctrines of their Government, and Axioms of their Jurisprudence, are utterly subversive of an Equality of Rights, and totally incompatible with the liberal spirit of our American Establishments. The Student of our Laws should be carefully taught to distinguish between the Principles of the one Government, and the Genius which presides in the other. He ought to have a correct acquaintance with genuine Republican Maxims, and be thereby induced to cultivate a superior regard for our own, and I trust more perfect systems of Liberty and Justice. . . .

The doctrine I have suggested, is peculiar to the United States. In the European World, no idea has ever been entertained (or at least until lately) of placing constitutional limits to the exercise of the Legislative Power. In England, where the Constitution has separated and designated the Departments of Government with precision and notoriety, the Parliament is still considered as transcendently absolute; and altho some Judges have had the freedom to observe, that a Statute made against natural equity was void, yet it is generally laid down as a necessary principle in their Law, that no Act of Parliament can be questioned or disputed. But in this country we have found it expedient to establish certain rights, to be deemed paramount to the power of the ordinary Legislature, and this precaution is considered in general as essential to perfect security, and to guard against the occasional violence and momentary triumphs of party. Without some express provisions of this kind clearly settled in the original compact, and constantly protected by the firmness and moderation of the Judicial department, the equal rights of a minor faction, would perhaps very often be disregarded in the animated competitions for power, and fall a sacrifice to the passions of a fierce and vindictive majority.

No question can be made with us, but that the Acts of the Legislative body, contrary to the true intent and meaning of the Constitution, ought to be absolutely null and void. The only inquiry which can arise on the subject is, whether the Legislature is not of itself the competent Judge of its own constitutional limits, and its acts of course to be presumed always conformable to the commission under which it proceeds; or whether the business of determining in this instance, is not rather the fit and exclusive province of the Courts of Justice. It is easy to see, that if the Legislature was left the ultimate Judge of the nature and extent of the barriers which have been placed against the abuses of its discretion, the efficacy of the check would be totally lost. The Legislature would be inclined to narrow or explain away the Constitution, from the force of the same propensities or considerations of temporary expediency, which would lead it to overturn private rights. Its will would be the supreme law, as much with, as without these constitutional safeguards. Nor is it probable, that the force of public opinion, the only restraint that could in that case exist, would be felt, or if felt, would be greatly regarded. If public opinion was in every case to be presumed correct and competent to be trusted, it is evident, there would have been no need of original and fundamental limitations. But sad experience has sufficiently taught mankind, that opinion is not an infallible standard of safety. When powerful rivalries prevail in the Community, and Parties become highly disciplined and hostile, every measure of the major part of the Legislature is sure to receive the sanction of that Party among their Constituents to which they belong. Every Step of the minor Party, it is equally certain will be approved by their immediate adherents, as well as indiscriminately misrepresented or condemned by the prevailing voice. The Courts of Justice which are organized with peculiar advantages to exempt them from the baneful influence of Faction, and to secure at the same time, a steady, firm and impartial interpretation of the Law, are therefore the most proper power in the Government to keep the Legislature within the limits of its duty, and to maintain the Authority of the Constitution. . . .

This power in the Judicial, of determining the constitutionality of Laws, is necessary to preserve the equilibrium of the government, and prevent usurpations of one part upon another; and of all the parts of government, the Legislative body is by far the most impetuous and powerful. A mere designation on paper, of the limits of the several departments, is altogether insufficient, and for this reason in limited Constitutions, the executive is armed with a negative, either qualified or complete upon the making of Laws. But the Judicial Power is the weakest of all, and as it is equally necessary to be preserved entire, it ought not in sound theory to be left naked without any constitutional means of defence. This is one reason why the Judges in this State are associated with the Governor, to form the Council of Revision, and this association renders some of these observations less applicable to our own particular Constitution, than to any other. The right of expounding the Constitution as well as Laws, will however be found in general to be the most fit, if not only effectual weapon, by which the Courts of Justice are enabled to repel assaults, and to guard against encroachments on their Chartered Authorities.

Nor can any danger be apprehended, lest this principle should exalt the Judicial above the Legislature. They are co-ordinate powers, and equally bound by the instrument under which they act, and if the former should at any time be prevailed upon to substitute arbitrary will, to the exercise of a rational Judgment, as it is possible it may do even in the ordinary course of judicial proceeding, it is not left like the latter, to the mere controul of public opinion. The Judges may be brought before the tribunal of the Legislature, and tried, condemned, and removed from office.

I consider then the Courts of Justice, as the proper and intended Guardians of our limited Constitutions, against the factions and encroachments of the Legislative Body. . . .

The Virginia and Kentucky Resolutions of 1798

In the spring of 1798, President John Adams and his Federalist-dominated Congress enacted the Alien and Sedition Acts, regulating immigration and making criticism of the government a crime of seditious libel. The laws aimed at silencing partisan criticism of the Adams administration's pro-British policies by Jeffersonian-Republicans. Although Jeffersonian-Republicans were prosecuted under the laws, often receiving stiff penalties, no court ruled on the constitutionality of the laws or whether they violated the First Amendment's guarantee for freedom of speech and press. The Kentucky legislature adopted a resolution secretly written by Thomas Jefferson, and Virginia adopted a similar resolution drafted by James Madison. Prosecutions for seditious libel ended in 1801, when the laws expired and Jefferson became president. Over 160 years later, the Supreme Court in a landmark ruling on libel, in the *New York Times Company v. Sullivan*, 376 U.S. 254 (1964) (see Vol. 2, Ch. 5), declared the Sedition Act and seditious libel unconstitutional and inconsistent with the First Amendment.

VIRGINIA RESOLUTIONS, DECEMBER 21, 1798

1. *Resolved*, That the General Assembly of Virginia doth unequivocally express a firm resolution to maintain and defend the Constitution of the United States, and the Constitution of this State, against every aggression, either foreign or domestic, and that it will support the government of the United States in all measures warranted by the former. . . .

3. That this Assembly doth explicitly and peremptorily declare that it views the powers of the Federal Government as resulting from the compact to which the States are parties, as limited by the plain sense and intention of the instrument constituting that compact; as no further valid than they are authorized by the grants enumerated in that compact; and that in case of a deliberate, palpable, and dangerous exercise of other powers not granted by the said compact, the States, who are the parties thereto, have the right, and are in duty bound, to interpose for arresting the progress of the evil, and for maintaining within their respective limits, the authorities, rights, and liberties appertaining to them.

4. That the General Assembly doth also express its deep regret that a spirit has in sundry instances been manifested by the Federal Government, to enlarge its powers by forced constructions of the constitutional charter which defines them; and that indications have appeared of a design to expound certain general phrases (which, having been copied from the very limited grant of powers in the former articles of confederation, were the less liable to be misconstrued), so as to destroy the meaning and effect of the particular enumeration, which necessarily explains and limits the general

phrases, and so as to consolidate the States by degrees into one sovereignty, the obvious tendency and inevitable result of which would be to transform the present republican system of the United States into an absolute, or at best, a mixed monarchy.

5. That the General Assembly doth particularly protest against the palpable and alarming infractions of the Constitution, in the two late cases of the "alien and sedition acts," passed at the last session of Congress, the first of which exercises a power nowhere delegated to the Federal Government; and which by uniting legislative and judicial powers to those of executive, subverts the general principles of free government, as well as the particular organization and positive provisions of the federal Constitution; and the other of which acts exercises in like manner a power not delegated by the Constitution, but on the contrary expressly and positively forbidden by one of the amendments thereto; a power which more than any other ought to produce universal alarm, because it is levelled against that right of freely examining public characters and measures, and of free communication among the people thereon, which has ever been justly deemed the only effectual guardian of every other right.

6. That this State having by its convention which ratified the federal Constitution, expressly declared, "that among other essential rights, the liberty of conscience and of the press cannot be cancelled, abridged, restrained, or modified by any authority of the United States," and from its extreme anxiety to guard these rights from every possible attack of sophistry or ambition, having with other States recommended an amendment for that purpose, which amendment was in due time annexed to the Constitution, it would mark a reproachful inconsistency and criminal degeneracy, if an indifference were now shown to the most palpable violation of one of the rights thus declared and secured, and to the establishment of a precedent which may be fatal to the other.

KENTUCKY RESOLUTIONS, NOVEMBER 10, 1798

1. *Resolved*, That the several states composing the United States of America, are not united on the principle of unlimited submission to their general government; but that by compact, under the style and title of a Constitution for the United States, and of amendments thereto, they constituted a general government for special purposes, delegated to that government certain definite powers, reserving, each state to itself, the residuary mass of right to their own self-government; and that whensoever the general government assumes undelegated powers, its acts are unauthoritative, void, and of no force: That to this compact each state acceded as a state, and is an integral party, its co-states forming as to itself, the other party: That the government created by this compact was not made the exclusive or final *judge* of the extent of the powers delegated to itself; since that would have made its discretion, and not the Constitution, the measure of its powers; but that, as in all other cases of compact among parties having no common judge, each party has an equal right to judge for itself, as well of infractions, as of the mode and measure of redress.

2. *Resolved*, That the Constitution of the United States having delegated to Congress a power to punish treason, counterfeiting the securities and current coin of the United States, piracies and felonies committed on the high

seas, and offences against the laws of nations, and no other crimes whatever, ... all other [of] their acts which assume to create, define, or punish crimes other than those enumerated in the Constitution, are altogether void, and of no force, and that the power to create, define, and punish such other crimes is reserved, and of right appertains, solely and exclusively, to the respective states, each within its own territory.

3. *Resolved,* That it is true as a general principle, and is also expressly declared by one of the amendments to the Constitution, that "the powers not delegated to the United States by the Constitution, nor prohibited by it to the states, are reserved to the states respectively, or to the people"; and that no power over the freedom of religion, freedom of speech, or freedom of the press, being delegated to the United States by the Constitution, nor prohibited by it to the states, all lawful powers respecting the same did of right remain, and were reserved to the states, or to the people; that thus was manifested their determination to retain to themselves the right of judging how far the licentiousness of speech and of the press may be abridged without lessening their useful freedom, and how far those abuses which cannot be separated from their use, should be tolerated rather than the use be destroyed; and thus also they guarded against all abridgment by the United States of the freedom of religious opinions and exercises, and retained to themselves the right of protecting the same, as this state by a law passed on the general demand of its citizens, had already protected them from all human restraint or interference: and that in addition to this general principle and express declaration, another and more special provision has been made by one of the amendments to the Constitution, which expressly declares, that "Congress shall make no law respecting an establishment of religion, or prohibiting the free exercise thereof, or abridging the freedom of speech, or of the press," thereby guarding in the same sentence, and under the same words, the freedom of religion, of speech, and of the press, insomuch, that whatever violates either, throws down the sanctuary which covers the others, and that libels, falsehoods, and defamations, equally with heresy and false religion, are withheld from the cognizance of federal tribunals: that therefore the act of the Congress of the United States, passed on the 14th day of July, 1798, entitled, "an act in addition to the act for the punishment of certain crimes against the United States," which does abridge the freedom of the press, is not law, but is altogether void and of no effect. . . .

Marbury v. Madison

1 Cr. (5 U.S.) 137 (1803)

This case grew out of one of the great early struggles over the course of constitutional politics. Shortly after the ratification of the Constitution, two rival political parties emerged with widely different views of the Constitution and governmental power. The Federalists supported a strong national government, including the power of the federal courts to interpret the Constitution. Their opponents, the Anti-Federalists and later the Jeffersonian-Republicans (who after the 1832 election became known as Democrats), remained distrustful of the national government and continued to favor the states and state courts. The struggle between the Federalists and the Jeffersonian-Republicans finally came to a head with the election of 1800. The Jeffersonians defeated the Federalists, who had held office since the creation of the republic and feared what the Jeffersonian-Republicans might do once in office.

Before leaving office, President John Adams and his Federalist-dominated Congress vindictively created a number of new judgeships and appointed all Federalists in the hope that they would counter the Jeffersonians once in office. But with time running out before the inauguration of Thomas Jefferson as president in 1801, not all of the commissions for the new judgeships were delivered. John Marshall, whom Adams had just appointed as chief justice, continued to work as secretary of state, delivering the commissions. But he failed to deliver seventeen commissions before Adams's term expired and left them for his successor as secretary of state, James Madison, to deliver. The Federalists' attempt to pack the courts infuriated the Jeffersonian-Republicans. And President Jefferson instructed Madison not to deliver the rest of the commissions.

William Marbury was one whose commission went undelivered. He decided to sue to force Madison to give him his commission. Specifically, he sought a *writ of mandamus*, which is simply a court order directing a government official (Madison) to perform a certain act (hand over the commission). Marbury argued that Section 13 of the Judiciary Act of 1789 had authorized the Supreme Court to issue such writs. He saw this as a way of getting back his commission and for the Marshall Court to take a stand against the Jeffersonians.

Marbury v. Madison was a politically explosive case for the Court and the country over the still-untested power of judicial review. The Court faced a major dilemma. On the one hand, if the Marshall Court ordered Marbury's commission, it was likely that Jefferson would refuse to comply. The Court would then be powerless, perhaps permanently. On the other hand, if the Court refused to issue the writ, it would appear weak and that would confirm the Jeffersonian argument that the courts had no power to intrude on the executive branch. Chief Justice Marshall's opinion, handed down on February 24, 1803, however, shrewdly asserted the power of judicial review and for the first time overturned part of an act of Congress but gave Jefferson no opportunity to retaliate and thus helped to defuse the political controversy surrounding the case. While Jeffersonians fervently disagreed with

Marshall's ruling, there was little for them to do because Marshall had not ordered the delivery of Marbury's commission.

The Court's decision was unanimous.

☐ *Chief Justice MARSHALL delivers the opinion of the Court.*

At the last term on the affidavits then read and filed with the clerk, a rule was granted in this case, requiring the secretary of state to show cause why a *mandamus* should not issue, directing him to deliver to William Marbury his commission as a justice of the peace for the county of Washington, in the District of Columbia.

No cause has been shown, and the present motion is for a *mandamus*. The peculiar delicacy of this case, the novelty of some of its circumstances, and the real difficulty attending the points which occur in it, require a complete exposition of the principles on which the opinion to be given by the court is founded.

These principles have been, on the side of the applicant very ably argued at the bar. In rendering the opinion of the court, there will be some departure in form, though not in substance, from the points stated in that argument.

In the order in which the court has viewed this subject, the following questions have been considered and decided.

1st. Has the applicant a right to the commission he demands?

2d. If he has a right, and that right has been violated, do the laws of his country afford him a remedy?

3d. If they do afford him a remedy, is it a *mandamus* issuing from this court?

The first object of inquiry is,

1st. Has the applicant a right to the commission he demands?

His right originates in an act of congress passed in February, 1801, concerning the District of Columbia.

After dividing the district into two counties, the 11th section of this law enacts, "that there shall be appointed in and for each of the said counties, such number of discreet persons to be justices of the peace as the president of the United States shall, from time to time, think expedient, to continue in office for five years."

It appears, from the affidavits, that in compliance with this law, a commission for William Marbury, as a justice of the peace for the county of Washington, was signed by John Adams, then President of the United States; after which the seal of the United States was affixed to it; but the commission has never reached the person for whom it was made out.

In order to determine whether he is entitled to this commission, it becomes necessary to inquire whether he has been appointed to the office. For if he has been appointed, the law continues him in office for five years, and he is entitled to the possession of those evidences of office, which, being completed, became his property.

The 2d section of the 2d article of the constitution declares, that "the president shall nominate, and, by and with the advice and consent of the senate, shall appoint, ambassadors, other public ministers and consuls, and all other officers of the United States, whose appointments are not otherwise provided for."

The 3d section declares, that "he shall commission all the officers of the United States."

An act of congress directs the secretary of state to keep the seal of the United States, "to make out and record, and affix the said seal to all civil commissions to officers of the United States, to be appointed by the president, by and with the consent of the senate, or by the president alone; provided, that the said seal shall not be affixed to any commission before the same shall have been signed by the President of the United States."

These are the clauses of the constitution and laws of the United States, which affect this part of the case. They seem to contemplate three distinct operations:

1st. The nomination. This is the sole act of the president, and is completely voluntary.

2d. The appointment. This is also the act of the president, and is also a voluntary act, though it can only be performed by and with the advice and consent of the senate.

3d. The commission. To grant a commission to a person appointed, might, perhaps, be deemed a duty enjoined by the constitution. "He shall," says that instrument, "commission all the officers of the United States." . . .

The last act to be done by the president is the signature of the commission. He has then acted on the advice and consent of the senate to his own nomination. The time for deliberation has then passed. He has decided. His judgment, on the advice and consent of the senate concurring with his nomination, has been made, and the officer is appointed. . . .

It is . . . decidedly the opinion of the court, that when a commission has been signed by the president, the appointment is made; and that the commission is complete when the seal of the United States has been affixed to it by the secretary of state.

Where an officer is removable at the will of the executive, the circumstance which completes his appointment is of no concern; because the act is at any time revocable; and the commission may be arrested, if still in the office. But when the officer is not removable at the will of the executive, the appointment is not revocable, and cannot be annulled. It has conferred legal rights which cannot be resumed. . . .

Mr. Marbury, then, since his commission was signed by the president, and sealed by the secretary of state, was appointed; and as the law creating the office, gave the officer a right to hold for five years, independent of the executive, the appointment was not revocable, but vested in the officer legal rights, which are protected by the laws of his country.

To withhold his commission, therefore, is an act deemed by the court not warranted by law, but violative of a vested legal right.

This brings us to the second inquiry; which is,

2d. If he has a right, and that right has been violated, do the laws of this country afford him a remedy?

The very essence of civil liberty certainly consists in the right of every individual to claim the protection of the laws, whenever he receives an injury. One of the first duties of government is to afford that protection. In

Great Britain the king himself is sued in the respectful form of a petition, and he never fails to comply with the judgment of his court. . . .

By the constitution of the United States, the president is invested with certain important political powers, in the exercise of which he is to use his own discretion, and is accountable only to his country in his political character and to his own conscience. To aid him in the performance of these duties, he is authorized to appoint certain officers, who act by his authority, and in conformity with his orders.

In such cases, their acts are his acts; and whatever opinion may be entertained of the manner in which executive discretion may be used, still there exists, and can exist, no power to control that discretion. The subjects are political. They respect the nation, not individual rights, and being intrusted to the executive, the decision of the executive is conclusive. . . .

But when the legislature proceeds to impose on that officer other duties; when he is directed peremptorily to perform certain acts; when the rights of individuals are dependent on the performance of those acts; he is so far the officer of the law; is amenable to the laws for his conduct; and cannot at his discretion sport away the vested rights of others.

The conclusion from this reasoning is, that where the heads of departments are the political or confidential agents of the executive, merely to execute the will of the president, or rather to act in cases in which the executive possesses a constitutional or legal discretion, nothing can be more perfectly clear than that their acts are only politically examinable. But where a specific duty is assigned by law, and individual rights depend upon the performance of that duty, it seems equally clear that the individual who considers himself injured, has a right to resort to the laws of his country for a remedy. . . .

It is, then, the opinion of the Court,

1st. That by signing the commission of Mr. Marbury, the President of the United States appointed him a justice of peace for the county of Washington, in the District of Columbia; and that the seal of the United States, affixed thereto by the secretary of state, is conclusive testimony of the verity of the signature, and of the completion of the appointment; and that the appointment conferred on him a legal right to the office for the space of five years.

2d. That, having this legal title to the office, he has a consequent right to the commission; a refusal to deliver which is a plain violation of that right, for which the laws of his country afford him a remedy.

It remains to be inquired whether,

3d. He is entitled to the remedy for which he applies. This depends on,

1st. The nature of the writ applied for; and,

2d. The power of this court.

1st. The nature of the writ. . . .

[T]o render the *mandamus* a proper remedy, the officer to whom it is to be directed, must be one to whom, on legal principles, such writ may be directed; and the person applying for it must be without any other specific and legal remedy.

1st. With respect to the officer to whom it would be directed. The intimate political relation subsisting between the President of the United States and the heads of departments, necessarily renders any legal investigation of the acts of one of those high officers peculiarly irksome, as well as delicate; and excites some hesitation with respect to the propriety of entering into such investigation. Impressions are often received without much reflection or examination, and it is not wonderful that in such a case as this the assertion, by an individual, of his legal claims in a court of justice, to which claims it is the duty of that court to attend, should at first view be considered by some, as an attempt to intrude into the cabinet, and to intermeddle with the prerogatives of the executive.

It is scarcely necessary for the court to disclaim all pretensions to such jurisdiction. An extravagance, so absurd and excessive, could not have been entertained for a moment. The province of the court is, solely, to decide on the rights of individuals, not to inquire how the executive, or executive officers, perform duties in which they have a discretion. Questions in their nature political, or which are, by the constitution and laws, submitted to the executive, can never be made in this court.

But, if this be not such a question; if, so far from being an intrusion into the secrets of the cabinet, it respects a paper which, according to law, is upon record, and to a copy of which the law gives a right. . . .

If one of the heads of departments commits any illegal act, under colour of his office, by which an individual sustains an injury, it cannot be pretended that his office alone exempts him from being sued in the ordinary mode of proceeding, and being compelled to obey the judgment of the law. How, then, can his office exempt him from this particular mode of deciding on the legality of his conduct if the case be such a case as would, were any other individual the party complained of, authorize the process?

It is not by the office of the person to whom the writ is directed, but the nature of the thing to be done, that the propriety or impropriety of issuing a *mandamus* is to be determined. . . .

This, then, is a plain case for a *mandamus*, either to deliver the commission, or a copy of it from the record; and it only remains to be inquired,

Whether it can issue from this court.

The act to establish the judicial courts of the United States authorizes the Supreme Court "to issue writs of *mandamus* in cases warranted by the principles and usages of law, to any courts appointed, or persons holding office, under the authority of the United States."★

The secretary of state, being a person holding an office under the authority of the United States, is precisely within the letter of the description, and if this court is not authorized to issue a writ of mandamus to such an officer, it must be because the law is unconstitutional, and therefore absolutely incapable of conferring the authority, and assigning the duties which its words purport to confer and assign.

The constitution vests the whole judicial power of the United States in one supreme court, and such inferior courts as congress shall, from time to

---

★ Note that Chief Justice Marshall selectively quotes from Section 13 of the Judiciary Act of 1789, which he construes ostensibly to confer authority on the Court to hear Marbury's case under the Court's original jurisdiction and, in turn, declares unconstitutional. The relevant part of Section 13 reads:

> The Supreme Court shall also have appellate jurisdiction from the circuit courts and courts of the several states, in the cases herein after specifically provided for; and shall have power to issue writs of prohibition to the district courts, when proceeding as courts of admiralty and maritime jurisdiction, and writs of *mandamus*, in cases warranted by the principles and usages of law, to any courts appointed, or persons holding office, under the authority of the United States.

time, ordain and establish. This power is expressly extended to all cases aris-ing under the laws of the United States; and, consequently, in some form, may be exercised over the present case; because the right claimed is given by a law of the United States.

In the distribution of this power it is declared that "the supreme court shall have original jurisdiction in all cases affecting ambassadors, other public ministers and consuls, and those in which a state shall be a party. In all other cases, the supreme court shall have appellate jurisdiction."

It has been insisted, at the bar, that as the original grant of jurisdiction, to the supreme and inferior courts, is general, and the clause, assigning orig-inal jurisdiction to the supreme court, contains no negative or restrictive words, the power remains to the legislature, to assign original jurisdiction to that court in other cases than those specified in the article which has been recited; provided those cases belong to the judicial power of the United States.

If it had been intended to leave it in the discretion of the legislature to apportion to the judicial power between the supreme and inferior courts ac-cording to the will of that body, it would certainly have been useless to have proceeded further than to have defined the judicial power, and the tribunals in which it should be vested. The subsequent part of the section is mere sur-plusage, is entirely without meaning, if such is to be the construction. If congress remains at liberty to give this court appellate jurisdiction, where the constitution has declared their jurisdiction shall be original; and original jurisdiction where the constitution has declared it shall be appellate; the distribution of jurisdiction, made in the constitution, is form without sub-stance.

Affirmative words are often, in their operation, negative of other objects than those affirmed; and in this case, a negative or exclusive sense must be given to them, or they have no operation at all.

It cannot be presumed that any clause in the constitution is intended to be without effect; and, therefore, such a construction is inadmissible, unless the words require it.

If the solicitude of the convention, respecting our peace with foreign powers, induced a provision that the supreme court should take original jurisdiction in cases which might be supposed to affect them; yet the clause would have proceeded no further than to provide for such cases, if no fur-ther restriction on the powers of congress had been intended. That they should have appellate jurisdiction in all other cases, with such exceptions as congress might make, is no restriction; unless the words be deemed exclusive of original jurisdiction.

When an instrument organizing fundamentally a judicial system, divides it into one supreme, and so many inferior courts as the legislature may or-dain and establish; then enumerates its powers, and proceeds so far to dis-tribute them, as to define the jurisdiction of the supreme court by declaring the cases in which it shall take original jurisdiction, and that in others it shall take appellate jurisdiction; the plain import of the words seems to be, that in one class of cases its jurisdiction is original, and not appellate; in the other it is appellate, and not original. If any other construction would render the clause inoperative, that is an additional reason for rejecting such other con-struction, and for adhering to their obvious meaning.

To enable this court, then, to issue a *mandamus*, it must be shown to be an exercise of appellate jurisdiction, or to be necessary to enable them to exercise appellate jurisdiction.

It has been stated at the bar that the appellate jurisdiction may be exercised in a variety of forms, and that if it be the will of the legislature that a *mandamus* should be used for that purpose, that will must be obeyed. This is true, yet the jurisdiction must be appellate, not original.

It is the essential criterion of appellate jurisdiction, that it revises and corrects the proceedings in a cause already instituted, and does not create that cause. Although, therefore, a mandamus may be directed to courts, yet to issue such a writ to an officer for the delivery of a paper, is in effect the same as to sustain an original action for that paper, and, therefore, seems not to belong to appellate, but to original jurisdiction. Neither is it necessary in such a case as this, to enable the court to exercise its appellate jurisdiction.

The authority, therefore, given to the supreme court, by the act establishing the judicial courts of the United States, to issue writs of *mandamus* to public officers, appears not to be warranted by the constitution; and it becomes necessary to inquire whether a jurisdiction so conferred can be exercised.

The question, whether an act, repugnant to the constitution, can become the law of the land, is a question deeply interesting to the United States; but, happily, not of an intricacy proportioned to its interest. It seems only necessary to recognize certain principles, supposed to have been long and well established, to decide it.

That the people have an original right to establish, for their future government, such principles, as, in their opinion, shall most conduce to their own happiness is the basis on which the whole American fabric has been erected. The exercise of this original right is a very great exertion; nor can it, nor ought it, to be frequently repeated. The principles, therefore, so established, are deemed fundamental. And as the authority from which they proceed is supreme, and can seldom act, they are designed to be permanent.

This original and supreme will organizes the government, and assigns to different departments their respective powers. It may either stop here, or establish certain limits not to be transcended by those departments.

The government of the United States is of the latter description. The powers of the legislature are defined and limited; and that those limits may not be mistaken, or forgotten, the constitution is written. To what purpose are powers limited, and to what purpose is that limitation committed to writing, if these limits may, at any time, be passed by those intended to be restrained? The distinction between a government with limited and unlimited powers is abolished, if those limits do not confine the persons on whom they are imposed, and if acts prohibited and acts allowed, are of equal obligation. It is a proposition too plain to be contested, that the constitution controls any legislative act repugnant to it; or, that the legislature may alter the constitution by an ordinary act.

Between these alternatives there is no middle ground. The constitution is either a superior paramount law, unchangeable by ordinary means, or it is on a level with ordinary legislative acts, and, like other acts, is alterable when the legislature shall please to alter it.

If the former part of the alternative be true, then a legislative act contrary to the constitution is not law: if the latter part be true, then written constitutions are absurd attempts, on the part of the people, to limit a power in its own nature illimitable.

Certainly all those who have framed written constitutions contemplate them as forming the fundamental and paramount law of the nation, and, consequently, the theory of every such government must be, that an act of the legislature, repugnant to the constitution, is void.

This theory is essentially attached to a written constitution, and, is consequently, to be considered, by this court, as one of the fundamental principles of our society. It is not therefore to be lost sight of in the further consideration of this subject.

If an act of the legislature, repugnant to the constitution, is void, does it, notwithstanding its invalidity, bind the courts, and oblige them to give it effect? Or, in other words, though it be not law, does it constitute a rule as operative as if it was a law? This would be to overthrow in fact what was established in theory; and would seem, at first view, an absurdity too gross to be insisted on. It shall, however, receive a more attentive consideration.

It is emphatically the province and duty of the judicial department to say what the law is. Those who apply the rule to particular cases, must of necessity expound and interpret that rule. If two laws conflict with each other, the courts must decide on the operation of each.

So if a law be in opposition to the constitution; if both the law and the constitution apply to a particular case, so that the court must either decide that case conformably to the law, disregarding the constitution; or conformably to the constitution, disregarding the law; the court must determine which of these conflicting rules governs the case. This is of the very essence of judicial duty.

If, then, the courts are to regard the constitution, and the constitution is superior to any ordinary act of the legislature, the constitution, and not such ordinary act, must govern the case to which they both apply.

Those, then, who controvert the principle that the constitution is to be considered, in court, as a paramount law, are reduced to the necessity of maintaining that courts must close their eyes on the constitution, and see only the law.

This doctrine would subvert the very foundation of all written constitutions. It would declare that an act which, according to the principles and theory of our government, is entirely void, is yet, in practice, completely obligatory. It would declare that if the legislature shall do what is expressly forbidden, such act, notwithstanding the express prohibition, is in reality effectual. It would be given to the legislature a practical and real omnipotence, with the same breath which professes to restrict their powers within narrow limits. It is prescribing limits, and declaring that those limits may be passed at pleasure.

That it thus reduces to nothing what we have deemed the greatest improvement on political institutions, a written constitution, would of itself be sufficient, in America, where written constitutions have been viewed with so much reverence, for rejecting the construction. But the peculiar expressions of the constitution of the United States furnish additional arguments in favour of its rejection.

The judicial power of the United States is extended to all cases arising under the constitution.

Could it be the intention of those who gave this power, to say that in using it the constitution should not be looked into? That a case arising under the constitution should be decided without examining the instrument under which it arises?

This is too extravagant to be maintained.

In some cases, then, the constitution must be looked into by the judges. And if they can open it at all, what part of it are they forbidden to read or to obey?

There are many other parts of the constitution which serve to illustrate this subject.

It is declared that "no tax or duty shall be laid on articles exported from any state." Suppose a duty on the export of cotton, of tobacco, or of flour; and a suit instituted to recover it. Ought judgment to be rendered in such a case? Ought the judges to close their eyes on the constitution, and only see the law?

The constitution declares "that no bill of attainder or *ex post facto* law shall be passed."

If, however, such a bill should be passed, and a person should be prosecuted under it; must the court condemn to death those victims whom the constitution endeavors to preserve?

"No person," says the constitution, "shall be convicted of treason unless on the testimony of two witnesses to the same overt act, or on confession in open court."

Here the language of the constitution is addressed especially to the courts. It prescribes, directly for them, a rule of evidence not to be departed from. If the legislature should change that rule, and declare one witness, or a confession out of court, sufficient for conviction, must the constitutional principle yield to the legislative act?

From these, and many other selections which might be made, it is apparent, that the framers of the constitution contemplated that instrument as a rule for the government of courts, as well as of the legislature.

Why otherwise does it direct the judges to take an oath to support it? This oath certainly applies in an especial manner, to their conduct in their official character. How immoral to impose it on them, if they were to be used as the instruments, and the knowing instruments, for violating what they swear to support!

The oath of office, too, imposed by the legislature, is completely demonstrative of the legislative opinion on this subject. It is in these words: "I do solemnly swear that I will administer justice without respect to persons, and do equal right to the poor and to the rich; and that I will faithfully and impartially discharge all the duties incumbent on me as ———, according to the best of my abilities and understanding agreeably to the constitution and laws of the United States."

Why does a judge swear to discharge his duties agreeably to the constitution of the United States, if that constitution forms no rule for his government? if it is closed upon him, and cannot be inspected by him?

If such be the real state of things, this is worse than solemn mockery. To prescribe, or to take this oath, becomes equally a crime.

It is also not entirely unworthy of observation, that in declaring what shall be the *supreme law* of the land, *the constitution* itself is first mentioned;

and not the laws of the United States generally, but those only which shall be made in *pursuance* of the constitution, have that rank.

Thus, the particular phraseology of the constitution of the United States confirms and strengthens the principle, supposed to be essential to all written constitutions, that a law repugnant to the constitution is void; and that *courts*, as well as other departments, are bound by that instrument.

The rule must be discharged.

President Jackson's Veto Message of 1832

President Andrew Jackson distrusted banks and, as a westerner, opposed the policies of the Bank of the United States which limited credit for land speculation. When Congress rechartered the Bank in 1832, Jackson vetoed the bill with this message,* drafted by Secretary of the Treasury (and later appointed as chief justice) Roger B. Taney. The controversy over the establishment of the national bank and its importance in shaping constitutional politics is dealt with further in Volume 1, Chapter 6.

☐ *To the Senate:*

The bill "to modify and continue" the act entitled "An act to incorporate the subscribers to the Bank of the United States" was presented to me on the 4th July instant. Having considered it with that solemn regard to the principles of the Constitution which the day was calculated to inspire, and come to the conclusion that it ought not to become a law, I herewith return it to the Senate, in which it originated, with my objections.

It is maintained by the advocates of the bank that its constitutionality in all its features ought to be considered as settled by precedent and by the decision of the Supreme Court. To this conclusion I can not assent. Mere precedent is a dangerous source of authority, and should not be regarded as deciding questions of constitutional power except where the acquiescence of the people and the States can be considered as well settled. So far from this being the case on this subject, an argument against the bank might be based on precedent. One Congress, in 1791, decided in favor of a bank; another in 1811, decided against it. One Congress, in 1815, decided against a bank, another, in 1816, decided in its favor. Prior to the present Congress, therefore, the precedents drawn from that source were equal. If we resort to the States, the expressions of legislative, judicial, and executive opinions against the bank have been probably to those in its favor as 4 to 1. There is nothing in precedent, therefore, which, if its authority were admitted, ought to weigh in favor of the act before me.

---

* From James D. Richardson, ed., *A Compilation of the Messages and Papers of the Presidents* (Washington, DC: Bureau of National Literature and Art, 1908), Vol. 2, 581–582.

If the opinion of the Supreme Court covered the whole ground of this act, it ought not to control the coordinate authorities of this Government. The Congress, the Executive, and the Court must each for itself be guided by its own opinion of the Constitution. Each public officer who takes an oath to support the Constitution swears that he will support it as he understands it, and not as it is understood by others. It is as much the duty of the House of Representatives, of the Senate, and of the President to decide upon the constitutionality of any bill or resolution which may be presented to them for passage or approval as it is of the supreme judges when it may be brought before them for judicial decision. The opinion of the judges has no more authority over Congress than the opinion of Congress has over the judges, and on that point the President is independent of both. The authority of the Supreme Court must not, therefore, be permitted to control the Congress or the Executive when acting in their legislative capacities, but to have only such influence as the force of their reasoning may deserve.

But in the case relied upon the Supreme Court have not decided that all the features of this corporation are compatible with the Constitution. It is true that the court have said that the law incorporating the bank is a constitutional exercise of power by Congress; but taking into view the whole opinion of the court and the reasoning by which they have come to that conclusion, I understand them to have decided that inasmuch as a bank is an appropriate means for carrying into effect the enumerated powers of the General Government, therefore the law incorporating it is in accordance with that provision of the Constitution which declares that Congress shall have power "to make all laws which shall be necessary and proper for carrying those powers into execution." Having satisfied themselves that the word "*necessary*" in the Constitution means "*needful,*" "*requisite,*" "*essential,*" "*conducive to,*" and that "a bank" is a convenient, a useful, and essential instrument in the prosecution of the Government's "fiscal operations," they conclude that to "use one must be within the discretion of Congress" and that "the act to incorporate the Bank of the United States is a law made in pursuance of the Constitution"; "but," say they, *"where the law is not prohibited and is really calculated to effect any of the objects intrusted to the Government, to undertake here to inquire into the degree of its necessity would be to pass the line which circumscribes the judicial department and to tread on legislative ground."*

The principle here affirmed is that the "degree of its necessity," involving all the details of a banking institution, is a question exclusively for legislative consideration. A bank is constitutional, but it is the province of the Legislature to determine whether this or that particular power, privilege, or exemption is "necessary and proper" to enable the bank to discharge its duties to the Government, and from their decision there is no appeal to the courts of justice. Under the decision of the Supreme Court, therefore, it is the exclusive province of Congress and the President to decide whether the particular features of this act are *necessary* and *proper* in order to enable the bank to perform conveniently and efficiently the public duties assigned to it as a fiscal agent, and therefore constitutional, or *unnecessary* and *improper*, and therefore unconstitutional. . . .

The bank is professedly established as an agent of the executive branch of the Government, and its constitutionality is maintained on that ground. Neither upon the propriety of present action nor upon the provisions of this act was the Executive consulted. It has had no opportunity to say that it neither needs nor wants an agent clothed with such powers and favored by such exemptions. There is nothing in its legitimate functions which makes it necessary or proper. Whatever interest or influence, whether public or private, has given birth to this act, it can not be found either in the wishes or necessities of the executive department, by which present action is deemed premature, and the powers conferred upon its agent not only unnecessary, but dangerous to the Government and country. . . .

Experience should teach us wisdom. Most of the difficulties our Government now encounters and most of the dangers which impend over our Union have sprung from an abandonment of the legitimate objects of Government by our national legislation, and the adoption of such principles as are embodied in this act. Many of our rich men have not been content with equal protection and equal benefits, but have besought us to make them richer by act of Congress. By attempting to gratify their desires we have in the results of our legislation arrayed section against section, interest against interest, and man against man, in a fearful commotion which threatens to shake the foundations of our Union. It is time to pause in our career to review our principles, and if possible revive that devoted patriotism and spirit of compromise which distinguished the sages of the Revolution and the fathers of our Union. If we can not at once, in justice to interests vested under improvident legislation, make our Government what it ought to be, we can at least take a stand against all new grants of monopolies and exclusive privileges, against any prostitution of our Government to the advancement of the few at the expense of the many, and in favor of compromise and gradual reform in our code of laws and system of political economy.

I have now done my duty to my country. If sustained by my fellow-citizens, I shall be grateful and happy; if not, I shall find in the motives which impel me ample grounds for contentment and peace.

President Roosevelt's Radio Broadcast, March 9, 1937

During President Franklin D. Roosevelt's first term (1933–1937), the Supreme Court by a vote of five to four invalidated much of his New Deal program and plan for the country's economic recovery from the Great Depression. After his landslide reelection in November 1936, FDR proposed in February 1937 that Congress expand the size of the Court from nine to fifteen justices and thereby give him the chance to secure a majority sympathetic to his policies. On March 9, 1937, the Democratic president made the following radio address in an effort to marshal public support for his "Court-packing plan." But that same month, while the Senate Judiciary Committee was considering his proposal, Justice Owen Roberts, who had previously cast the crucial vote for overturning progressive economic legislation, switched sides and voted to uphold New Deal legislation. The Court's proverbial "switch-in-time-that-saved-nine" then contributed to the Democrat-dominated Senate's defeat of FDR's proposal. The constitutional crisis that loomed over the Court and the country in 1937 is discussed further in Volume 1, Chapter 6, and in Volume 2, Chapter 3.

Tonight, sitting at my desk in the White House, I make my first radio report to the people in my second term of office.★

I am reminded of that evening in March, four years ago, when I made my first radio report to you. We were then in the midst of the great banking crisis.

Soon after, with the authority of the Congress, we asked the Nation to turn over all of its privately held gold, dollar for dollar, to the Government of the United States.

Today's recovery proves how right that policy was.

But when, almost two years later, it came before the Supreme Court its constitutionality was upheld only by a five-to-four vote. The change of one vote would have thrown all the affairs of this great Nation back into hopeless chaos. In effect, four Justices ruled that the right under a private contract to exact a pound of flesh was more sacred than the main objectives of the Constitution to establish an enduring Nation.

In 1933 you and I knew that we must never let our economic system get completely out of joint again—that we could not afford to take the risk of another great depression.

We also became convinced that the only way to avoid a repetition of those dark days was to have a government with power to prevent and to cure the abuses and the inequalities which had thrown that system out of joint.

We then began a program of remedying those abuses and inequalities—to give balance and stability to our economic system—to make it bomb-proof against the causes of 1929.

Today we are only part-way through that program—and recovery is speeding up to a point where the dangers of 1929 are again becoming possible, not this week or month perhaps, but within a year or two.

National laws are needed to complete that program. Individual or local or state effort alone cannot protect us in 1937 any better than ten years ago. . . .

The American people have learned from the depression. For in the last three national elections an overwhelming majority of them voted a mandate that the Congress and the President begin the task of providing that protection—not after long years of debate, but now.

The Courts, however, have cast doubts on the ability of the elected Congress to protect us against catastrophe by meeting squarely our modern social and economic conditions.

We are at a crisis in our ability to proceed with that protection. It is a quiet crisis. There are no lines of depositors outside closed banks. But to the far-sighted it is far-reaching in its possibilities of injury to America.

★ From 1937 *Public Papers and Addresses of Franklin D. Roosevelt* (1941), 122.

I want to talk with you very simply about the need for present action in this crisis—the need to meet the unanswered challenge of one-third of a Nation ill-nourished, ill-clad, ill-housed.

Last Thursday I described the American form of Government as a three horse team provided by the Constitution to the American people so that their field might be plowed. The three horses are, of course, the three branches of government—the Congress, the Executive and the Courts. Two of the horses are pulling in unison today; the third is not. Those who have intimated that the President of the United States is trying to drive that team, overlook the simple fact that the President, as Chief Executive, is himself one of the three horses.

It is the American people themselves who are in the driver's seat.

It is the American people themselves who want the furrow plowed.

It is the American people themselves who expect the third horse to pull in unison with the other two.

I hope that you have re-read the Constitution of the United States. Like the Bible, it ought to be read again and again.

It is an easy document to understand when you remember that it was called into being because the Articles of Confederation under which the original thirteen States tried to operate after the Revolution showed the need of a National Government with power enough to handle national problems. In its Preamble, the Constitution states that it was intended to form a more perfect Union and promote the general welfare; and the powers given to the Congress to carry out those purposes can be best described by saying that they were all the powers needed to meet each and every problem which then had a national character and which could not be met by merely local action.

But the framers went further. Having in mind that in succeeding generations many other problems then undreamed of would become national problems, they gave to the Congress the ample broad powers "to levy taxes . . . and provide for the common defense and general welfare of the United States."

That, my friends, is what I honestly believe to have been the clear and underlying purpose of the patriots who wrote a Federal Constitution to create a National Government with national power, intended as they said, "to form a more perfect union . . . for ourselves and our posterity." . . .

But since the rise of the modern movement for social and economic progress through legislation, the Court has more and more often and more and more boldly asserted a power to veto laws passed by the Congress and State Legislatures in complete disregard of this original limitation.

In the last four years the sound rule of giving statutes the benefit of all reasonable doubt has been cast aside. The Court has been acting not as a judicial body, but as a policy-making body.

When the Congress has sought to stabilize national agriculture, to improve the conditions of labor, to safeguard business against unfair competition, to protect our national resources, and in many other ways, to serve our clearly national needs, the majority of the Court has been assuming the power to pass on the wisdom of these Acts of the Congress—and to approve or disapprove the public policy written into these laws.

That is not only my accusation. It is the accusation of most distinguished Justices of the present Supreme Court. I have not the time to quote to you all the language used by dissenting Justices in many of these cases. But in the case holding the Railroad Retirement Act unconstitutional, for instance, Chief Justice Hughes said in a dissenting opinion that the majority opinion was "a departure from sound principles," and placed "an unwarranted limitation upon the commerce clause." And three other Justices agreed with him.

In the case holding the A.A.A. unconstitutional, Justice Stone said of the majority opinion that it was a "tortured construction of the Constitution." And two other Justices agreed with him.

In the case holding the New York Minimum Wage Law unconstitutional, Justice Stone said that the majority were actually reading into the Constitution their own "personal economic predilections," and that if the legislative power is not left free to choose the methods of solving the problems of poverty, subsistence and health of large numbers in the community, then "government is to be rendered impotent." And two other Justices agreed with him.

In the face of these dissenting opinions, there is no basis for the claim made by some members of the Court that something in the Constitution has compelled them regretfully to thwart the will of the people.

In the face of such dissenting opinions, it is perfectly clear, that as Chief Justice Hughes has said: "We are under a Constitution but the Constitution is what the Judges say it is."

The Court in addition to the proper use of its judicial functions has improperly set itself up as a third House of the Congress—a super-legislature, as one of the Justices has called it—reading into the Constitution words and implications which are not there, and which were never intended to be there.

We have, therefore, reached the point as a Nation where we must take action to save the Constitution from the Court and the Court from itself. We must find a way to take an appeal from the Supreme Court to the Constitution itself. We want a Supreme Court which will do justice under the Constitution—not over it. In our Courts we want a government of laws and not of men.

I want—as all Americans want—an independent judiciary as proposed by the framers of the Constitution. That means a Supreme Court that will enforce the Constitution as written—that will refuse to amend the Constitution by the arbitrary exercise of judicial power—amendment by judicial say-so. It does not mean a judiciary so independent that it can deny the existence of facts universally recognized.

How then could we proceed to perform the mandate given us? It was said in last year's Democratic platform "If these problems cannot be effectively solved within the Constitution, we shall seek such clarifying amendment as will assure the power to enact those laws, adequately to regulate commerce, protect public health and safety, and safeguard economic security." In other words, we said we would seek an amendment only if every other possible means by legislation were to fail.

When I commenced to review the situation with the problem squarely before me, I came by a process of elimination to the conclusion that short of amendments the only method which was clearly constitutional, and would at the same time carry out other much needed reforms, was to infuse new blood into all our Courts. We must have men worthy and equipped to carry out impartial justice. But, at the same time, we must have Judges who will bring to the Courts a present-day sense of the Constitution—Judges who will retain in the Courts the judicial functions of a court, and reject the legislative powers which the Courts have today assumed. . . .

What is my proposal? It is simply this: whenever a Judge or Justice of any Federal Court has reached the age of seventy and does not avail himself of the opportunity to retire on a pension, a new member shall be appointed by the President then in office, with the approval, as required by the Constitution, of the Senate of the United States.

That plan has two chief purposes. By bringing into the Judicial system a steady and continuing stream of new and younger blood, I hope, first, to make the administration of all Federal justice speedier and, therefore, less costly; secondly, to bring to the decision of social and economic problems younger men who have had personal experience and contact with modern facts and circumstances under which average men have to live and work. This plan will save our national Constitution from hardening of the judicial arteries.

The number of Judges to be appointed would depend wholly on the decision of present Judges now over seventy, or those who would subsequently reach the age of seventy.

If, for instance, any one of the six Justices of the Supreme Court now over the age of seventy should retire as provided under the plan, no additional place would be created. Consequently, although there never can be more than fifteen, there may be only fourteen, or thirteen, or twelve. And there may be only nine.

There is nothing novel or radical about this idea. It seeks to maintain the Federal bench in full vigor. It has been discussed and approved by many persons of high authority ever since a similar proposal passed the House of Representatives in 1869.

Why was the age fixed at seventy? Because the laws of many States, the practice of the Civil Service, the regulations of the Army and Navy, and the rules of many of our Universities and of almost every great private business enterprise, commonly fix the retirement age at seventy years or less.

The statute would apply to all the Courts in the Federal system. There is general approval so far as the lower Federal courts are concerned. The plan has met opposition only so far as the Supreme Court of the United States itself is concerned. If such a plan is good for the lower courts it certainly ought to be equally good for the highest Court from which there is no appeal.

Those opposing this plan have sought to arouse prejudice and fear by crying that I am seeking to "pack" the Supreme Court and that a baneful precedent will be established.

What do they mean by the words "packing the Court"?

Let me answer this question with a bluntness that will end all *honest* misunderstanding of my purposes.

If by that phrase "packing the Court" it is charged that I wish to place on the bench spineless puppets who would disregard the law and would decide specific cases as I wished them to be decided, I make this answer—that no President fit for his office would appoint, and no Senate of honorable men fit for their office would confirm, that kind of appointees to the Supreme Court.

But if by that phrase the charge is made that I would appoint and the Senate would confirm Justices worthy to sit beside present members of the

Court who understand those modern conditions—that I will appoint Justices who will not undertake to override the judgment of the Congress on legislative policy—that I will appoint Justices who will act as Justices and not as legislators—if the appointment of such Justices can be called "packing the Courts," then I say that I and with me the vast majority of the American people favor doing just that thing—now.

Is it a dangerous precedent for the Congress to change the number of the Justices? The Congress has always had, and will have, that power. The number of Justices has been changed several times before—in the Administrations of John Adams and Thomas Jefferson,—both signers of the Declaration of Independence—Andrew Jackson, Abraham Lincoln and Ulysses S. Grant.

I suggest only the addition of Justices to the bench in accordance with a clearly defined principle relating to a clearly defined age limit. Fundamentally, if in the future, America cannot trust the Congress it elects to refrain from abuse of our Constitutional usages, democracy will have failed far beyond the importance to it of any kind of precedent concerning the Judiciary. . . .

It is the clear intention of our public policy to provide for a constant flow of new and younger blood into the Judiciary. Normally every President appoints a large number of District and Circuit Judges and a few members of the Supreme Court. Until my first term practically every President of the United States had appointed at least one member of the Supreme Court. President Taft appointed five members and named a Chief Justice—President Wilson three—President Harding four including a Chief Justice—President Coolidge one—President Hoover three including a Chief Justice.

Such a succession of appointments should have provided a Court well-balanced as to age. But chance and the disinclination of individuals to leave the Supreme bench have now given us a Court in which five Justices will be over seventy-five years of age before next June and one over seventy. Thus a sound public policy has been defeated.

I now propose that we establish by law an assurance against any such ill-balanced Court in the future. I propose that hereafter, when a Judge reaches the age of seventy, a new and younger Judge shall be added to the Court automatically. In this way I propose to enforce a sound public policy by law instead of leaving the composition of our Federal Courts, including the highest, to be determined by chance or the personal decision of individuals.

If such a law as I propose is regarded as establishing a new precedent—is it not a most desirable precedent?

Like all lawyers, like all Americans, I regret the necessity of this controversy. But the welfare of the United States, and indeed of the Constitution itself, is what we all must think about first. Our difficulty with the Court today rises not from the Court as an institution but from human beings within it. But we cannot yield our constitutional destiny to the personal judgment of a few men who, being fearful of the future, would deny us the necessary means of dealing with the present.

This plan of mine is no attack on the Court; it seeks to restore the Court to its rightful and historic place in our system of Constitutional Government and to have it resume its high task of building anew on the Constitution "a system of living law."

B | *The Politics of Constitutional Interpretation*

Constitutional interpretation and law, Justice Felix Frankfurter observed, "is not at all a science, but applied politics."[1] The Constitution, of course, is a political document and as a written document is not self-interpreting; its interpretation is political. *How* the Constitution should be interpreted is thus as controversial as the ongoing debate over *who* should interpret it.

For much of the nineteenth century, theories of constitutional interpretation were generally not debated.[2] The Court's interpretation of the Constitution, of course, remained politically controversial. Yet, the great debates between Jeffersonian-Republicans and Federalists centered on disagreements over fundamental principles of constitutional politics (the power and structure of government and guarantees for civil rights and liberties), rather than competing interpretative theories. Their struggle was over rival political philosophies and interpretations of the political system created by the Constitution. That struggle continues except that contemporary debates, within the Court and the legal community, tend to be more complex and linked to rival theories of constitutional interpretation that aim to justify or criticize the Court's exercise of judicial review.

In 1833, for example, Justice Joseph Story in his influential *Commentaries on the Constitution of the United States* saw no need to offer a theory of constitutional interpretation, explaining that,

> [t]he reader must not expect to find in these pages any novel views and novel constructions of the Constitution. I have not the ambition to be the author of any new plan of interpreting the theory of the Constitution, or of enlarging or narrowing its powers by ingenious subtleties and learned doubts. . . . Upon subjects of government, it has always appeared to me, that metaphysical refinements are out of place. A constitution of government is addressed to the common sense of the people, and never was designed for trials of logical skill or visionary speculation.[3]

Story assumed that "[t]he first and fundamental rule in the interpretation of all instruments is, to construe them according to the sense of the terms and the intention of the parties."[4] This "plain meaning rule" was set forth by Chief Justice John Marshall in *Sturges v. Crowninshield,* 17 U.S. 122 (1819):

■ IN COMPARATIVE PERSPECTIVE

Written and Unwritten Constitutions: Britain's and Israel's Constitutions

What is a constitution? Does a constitution have to be written? Most of the world's 185 countries have written constitutions. Yet several do not, including Bosnia-Herzogovenia; Libya; New Zealand; Oman; Qatar; Saudi Arabia; Britain; and, at least until 1995, Israel. Furthermore, British legal scholars have long contended that Britain has a "historic constitution." By contrast, the Supreme Court of Israel declared its Basic Laws to constitute a constitution in 1995.

The British constitution, according to some legal scholars, is best understood not as an "unwritten" constitution but as a "historic constitution," a written and unwritten product of historical development, not of deliberate design; it is a romantic, pre-Enlightenment constitution. Parts of the British constitution are found in historic documents, such as the Magna Carta, the Act of Settlement, and the Parliament Acts. Still, as Vernon Bogdanor emphasizes:

> [T]here is a sense in which the British Constitution can be summed up in eight words: What the Queen in Parliament enacts is law. The essence of the British Constitution is thus better expressed in the statement that it is a historic constitution whose dominating characteristic is the sovereignty of Parliament, than in the statement that Britain has an unwritten constitution.

Because parliamentary sovereignty is at the heart of the British constitution, Bogdanor and others deem it "pointless to rationalise it in an enacted constitution which could forbid nothing, nor could it provide a list of basic freedoms which governments would be unable to infringe."[1]

In October 2000, however, Britain became subject to the European Convention on Human Rights, as a result of the going into effect of the Human Rights Act of 1998 which incorporates those guarantees into British law. British courts now have jurisdiction over human rights claims, though they still have no power to declare laws unconstitutional. If they find conflicts with legislation, they may issue declarations of incompatibility and the Parliament must decide whether to amend the legislation accordingly. Nonetheless, British judges are expected to increasingly look to rulings of the European Court of Human

Rights and to those of high courts in other member states of the European Union.

When Israel was proclaimed a state in 1948, it was expected to eventually enact a written constitution. But, due to initial opposition, the Knesset (parliament) in 1950 agreed, as a compromise, to the Harari Resolution, to build a constitution chapter by chapter through the enactment of Basic Laws. Accordingly, the Knesset enacted Basic Laws on The Knesset (1958); Israel Lands (1960); The President of the State (1964); The Government (1968); The State Economy (1975); Israel Defense Forces (1976); Jerusalem, The Capital of Israel (1980); The Judiciary (1984); and The State Comptroller (1988). These Basic Laws largely codified existing practices. But in 1992 the Knesset enacted two more, dealing for the first time with human rights: the Basic Laws on Freedom of Occupation and on Human Dignity and Liberty. Notably, Section 5 of the Basic Law on Freedom of Occupation also stipulated that it could not be changed "except by a Basic Law enacted by a majority of the Knesset members."

Until the 1990s, the prevailing view in Israel was that the Knesset's sovereignty was virtually unlimited and that the Supreme Court would exercise only limited judicial review, invalidating legislation only when in conflict with specific provisions of a Basic Law. But, in *United Mizrachi Bank plc v. Migdal Cooperative Village* (1995),[2] the Supreme Court reversed a lower court's ruling and proclaimed Israel's Basic Laws a constitution. A district court had struck down, as a violation of the 1992 Basic Law on Human Dignity and Liberty, a Knesset law aimed at providing agricultural relief. It was the first time an Israeli court had asserted "American-style" substantive judicial review of legislation. On appeal, though reversing that court's decision, all but one of the nine justices agreed that the Knesset had the "constituent authority" to frame a constitution, binding on its own powers, and that it had done so when enacting the 1992 Basic Laws on human rights. Furthermore, the Supreme Court held that Israel's constitution authorized the judiciary's exercise of "American-style" judicial review.

In *United Mizrachi Bank*, the Israeli Supreme Court embraced a theory that its President (or chief justice) Aharon Barak had championed following the enactment of the 1992 Basic Laws. According to Chief Justice Barak:[3]

> Under these new Basic Laws, several human rights—among them Dignity, Liberty, Mobility, Privacy, Property—acquired a constitutional force above regular statutes. . . . A regular Knesset (Parliamentary) statute can no longer infringe upon these rights,

(continues)

■ IN COMPARATIVE PERSPECTIVE
Written and Unwritten Constitutions:
Britain's and Israel's Constitutions (continued)

unless it fulfills the requirements of the Basic Laws (the "limitations clause"), namely, it befits the values of the State of Israel, it was passed for a worthy purpose and the harm caused to the constitutional Human Right is proportional to the purpose. Thus, we became a constitutional democracy. We joined the democratic, enlightened nations in which human rights are awarded a constitutional force above regular statutes. Similar to the United States, Canada, France, Germany, Italy, Japan, and other western countries, we now have a constitutional defense for Human Rights. We too have the central chapter in any written constitution, the subject-matter of which is Human Rights; we too have restrictions on the legislative power of the legislator; we too have judicial review of statutes which unlawfully infringe upon constitutionally protected human rights; we too have a written constitution, to which the Knesset in its capacity as legislator is subject and which it cannot alter. . . .

The Constitutional Revolution has led to a change in the judiciary's status. Great responsibilities have been imposed on it. It must fill the mould created by the "majestic generalities" in the new Basic Laws. The judiciary must be aware of the fundamental values of the people. It must balance them in accordance with the views of the "enlightened general public" in Israel. . . . Constitutional interpretation should not be formalistic or pedantic. It should be purposive. It should be done from a wide perspective and adopt a substantive approach. A constitution is a living organism. . . .

1. Vernon Bogdanor, "Britain: The Political Constitution," in Vernon Bogdanor, ed., *Constitutions and Democratic Politics* 53, 55 (Aldershot, England: Gower, 1988). See also Peter Leyland, *The Constitution of the United Kingdom* (Oxford: Hart Publishing, 2007).

2. A translation of and commentary on *United Mizrachi Bank plc v. Migdal Co-operative Village*, 48 (iv) P.D. 221 (1995), may be found in 31 *Israel Law Review* 754 (1997).

3. Aharon Barak, "The Constitutionalization of the Israeli Legal System as a Result of the Basic Laws and Its Effect on Procedural and Substantive Criminal Law," 31 *Israel Law Review* 3–23 (1997). See also Aharon Barak, *The Judge in a Democracy* (Princeton, NJ: Princeton University Press, 2006).

[A]lthough the spirit of an instrument, especially of a constitution, is to be respected not less than its letter, yet the spirit is to be collected chiefly from its words. . . . [I]f, in any case, the plain meaning of a provision, not contradicted by any other provision in the same instrument, is to be disregarded, because we believe the framers of that instrument could not intend what they say, it must be one in which the absurdity and injustice of applying the provision to the case, would be so monstrous that all mankind would, without hesitation, unite in rejecting the application.

While the plain meaning of the Constitution for Story and Marshall was derived from a commonsense, rather than a literal, reading of the Constitution, Jeffersonian-Republicans nevertheless charged them with distorting the plain meaning of the document to advance their nationalistic political vision.

One reason political struggles in the nineteenth century did not invite debates over competing theories of constitutional interpretation is that Federalists and Jeffersonian-Republicans largely professed acceptance of the English *declaratory theory of law*. This theory, or philosophy, of legal positivism holds that judges have no discretion, make no law, but simply discover and "declare" the law.[5] According to one of the most widely read English jurists, Sir William Blackstone, in his *Commentaries on the Laws of England* (1765–1768), judges were merely the "depositories of the laws; the living oracles" of law. Hamilton and Marshall considered themselves Blackstonians; judges, Hamilton wrote in *The Federalist*, No. 78, "may truly be said to have neither force nor will, but merely judgment."

By the late nineteenth century, the Blackstonian theory of law was under sharp attack. Oliver Wendell Holmes (1841–1935) was one of the first to debunk the idea that law is "a brooding omnipresence in the sky."[6] In his words, "The life of the law has not been logic; it has been experience. The felt necessities of the time, the prevalent moral and political theories, intuitions of public policy, avowed or unconscious, even the prejudices which judges share with their fellow-men, have had a good deal more to do than the syllogism in determining the rules by which men should be governed."[7] Holmes took it for granted that judges make law and pointed toward the empirical study of law: "The prophecies of what the courts will do in fact, and nothing more pretentious, are what I mean by the law."[8] Nor was Holmes alone in the revolt against legal formalism and the "mechanical jurisprudence" associated with the declaratory theory of judicial decision making.[9] Roscoe Pound (1870–1964), the founder of "sociological jurisprudence" and dean of Harvard Law School, encouraged the use of sociology and the study of law in relation to changing social forces. Unlike Holmes, though, Pound also encouraged judges to creatively mold law to the needs of society; judges should become "social engineers."[10]

One immediate consequence of this revolt against legal formalism was the innovation in legal argumentation that became known as "the

Brandeis brief," after its author, a progressive legal reformer and later justice, Louis D. Brandeis. In 1908, in support of Oregon's law limiting working hours for women, Brandeis filed a brief in *Muller v. Oregon*, 208 U.S. 412 (1908), which included only two pages of legal argumentation, followed by ninety-seven pages of statistics and other social science data documenting the health risks for women working long hours. Drawing on social science in legal argumentation was necessary, claimed Brandeis, if law was to keep "pace with the rapid development of our political, economic, and social ideals."[11]

By the 1920s and 1930s a diverse group of law professors, political scientists, economists, and sociologists emerged calling themselves "American legal realists."[12] They further questioned the determinacy of formal legal rules and the facts of cases for judicial decision making, thereby underscoring that judges interpret (and manipulate) both legal rules and the facts when deciding cases.[13] Karl Llewellyn, one of the most influential legal realists, brought these insights to bear on constitutional interpretation when calling for a "jurisprudence of a living Constitution":

> A "written constitution" is a system of unwritten practices in which the Document in question, by virtue of men's attitudes, has *a little influence. Where it makes no important difference which way the decision goes,* the Text—in the absence of countervailing practice—is an excellent traffic light. . . . The view advanced here *sounds* unorthodox. It sounds unorthodox only because it puts into words the *tacit* doing of the Court, and draws from that doing conclusions not to be avoided by a candid child. . . . Whatever the Court has *said,* it has repeatedly turned to established governmental practice in search of norms. What the Court has *said,* it has shaped the living Constitution to the needs of the day as it felt them. The whole expansion of the due process clause has been an enforcement of the majority's ideal of government-as-it-should-be, running free of the language of the Document.[14]

The Supreme Court was not immune from this change in legal thinking. On the bench sat Holmes (1902–1932), Brandeis (1916–1939), Benjamin Cardozo (1932–1938),[15] and Felix Frankfurter (1939–1962), among other legal progressives. Moreover, even judicial conservatives on the Court no longer denied that the process of interpreting the Constitution involves making law. As Chief Justice Harlan F. Stone, a political and judicial conservative, reflected in a letter to Edward Corwin, "I always thought the real villain in the play was Blackstone, who gave to both lawyers and judges artificial notions of the law which, when applied to constitutional interpretation made the Constitution a mechanical and inadequate instrument of government."[16] Justice Frankfurter, a former liberal professor at Harvard Law School who became an advocate of judicial self-restraint on the bench, elaborated his view in a letter to Justice Hugo Black:

> I think one of the evil features, a very evil one, about all this assumption that judges only find the law and don't make it, often becomes the evil of a lack of candor. By covering up the law-making function of judges, we miseducate the people and fail to bring out into the open the real responsibility of judges for what they do. . . .
>
> That phrase "judicial legislation" has become ever since a staple of a term of condemnation. I, too, am opposed to judicial legislation in its invidious sense; but I deem equally mischievous—because founded on an untruth and an impossible aim—the notion that judges merely announce the law which they find and do not themselves inevitably have a share in the law-making. Here, as elsewhere, the difficulty comes from arguing in terms of absolutes when the matter at hand is conditioned by circumstances, is contingent upon the everlasting problem of how far is too far and how much is too much. Judges as you well know, cannot escape the responsibility of filling in gaps which the finitude of even the most imaginative legislation renders inevitable. . . .
>
> So the problem is not whether judges make the law, but when and how and how much. Holmes put it in his highbrow way, that "they can do so only interstitially; they are confined from molar to molecular motions." I used to say to my students that legislatures make law wholesale, judges retail.[17]

Once constitutional interpretation was candidly conceded to be a lawmaking process, the Court and its commentators squarely faced what has been called the Madisonian dilemma and "the countermajoritarian difficulty" for judicial review. As former judge and unsuccessful 1987 Supreme Court nominee Robert Bork explains,

> The United States was founded as what we now call a Madisonian system, one which allows majorities to rule in wide areas of life simply because they are majorities, but which also holds that individuals have some freedoms that must be exempt from majority control. The dilemma is that neither the majority nor the minority can be trusted to define the proper spheres of democratic authority and individual liberty. The first would court tyranny by the majority; the second tyranny by the minority.[18]

When overturning legislation, the Court exercises a countermajoritarian power and substitutes its interpretation of the Constitution for that of elected representatives. Theories or rationalizations of the Court's interpretation of the Constitution thus appear necessary to justify the Court's countermajoritarian role in American politics, especially in the last sixty years as the Court increasingly overturned legislation in defense of civil rights and liberties.

In addition, in the aftermath of the American legal realist movement, legal scholarship became more pluralistic and interdisciplinary. Again quoting Judge Bork:

> The fact is that the law has little intellectual or structural resistance to outside influences, influences that should properly remain outside. The striking, and peculiar, fact . . . is that the law possesses very little theory about itself. . . . This theoretical emptiness at its center makes law, particularly constitutional law, unstable, a ship with a great deal of sail but a very shallow keel, vulnerable to the winds of intellectual or moral fashion, which it then validates as the commands of our most basic compact.[19]

Since World War II, legal scholars have turned not only toward moral and political philosophy as a guide for constitutional interpretation and the Court's exercise of judicial review, but they have also called for the development of a "political jurisprudence," combining normative theory with empirical studies;[20] proposed an economic approach to law, which would make rights turn on cost-risk-benefit analysis;[21] drawn on theories of literary criticism;[22] and advocated "legal pragmatism."[23] Still others in the feminist, Critical Race Theory, and the Critical Legal Studies movements attack theories of liberal legalism in an effort to deconstruct legal reasoning and law to show its drawbacks for minorities, women, and the poor.[24]

The rest of this section surveys and illustrates various theories of constitutional interpretation in terms of two broad approaches that have come to be known as *interpretivism* and *noninterpretivism*. Broadly speaking, interpretivists hold that constitutional interpretation should be limited solely to the text and historical context of particular provisions of the Constitution and Bill of Rights. By contrast, noninterpretivists maintain that constitutional interpretation frequently requires going beyond the text and historical context of specific provisions to articulate and apply broader principles of constitutional politics. Neither approach is inextricably linked to either a liberal or a conservative political philosophy; for example, a predominantly conservative Court in the late nineteenth century invented and wrote into constitutional law a "liberty of contract" to strike down progressive economic legislation (see Vol. 2, Ch. 3), while in the twentieth century a more liberal Court proclaimed and enforced a "right of privacy" to overturn legislation restricting the use of contraceptives and the availability of abortions (see Vol. 2, Ch. 11). Moreover, the distinction between interpretivists and noninterpretivists is one of degree, not a difference in kind.

NOTES

1. Felix Frankfurter, in *Law and Politics*, ed. E. Prichard, Jr., and Archibald Macleish (New York: Harcourt, Brace, 1939), 6.

2. See Robert H. Bork, "Styles in Constitutional Theory," 1984 *Supreme Court Historical Society Yearbook* 53 (1985).

3. Joseph Story, *Commentaries on the Constitution of the United States* (Durham, NC: Carolina Academic Press, 1987), vi, reprint of 1833 ed.

4. Ibid., 135.

5. See, generally, Lord Lloyd, *Lloyd's Introduction to Jurisprudence*, 5th ed. (London: Stevens & Sons, 1985); H. L. A. Hart, *Essays in Jurisprudence and Philosophy* (Oxford, UK: Clarendon Press, 1983), Chs. 1–5, 13; William Nelson, *Americanization of the Common Law* (Cambridge, MA: Harvard University Press, 1975); and Morton Horwitz, *The Transformation of American Law, 1780–1860* (Cambridge, MA: Harvard University Press, 1977).

6. *Southern Pacific Co. v. Jensen*, 244 U.S. 205 (1916).

7. Oliver W. Holmes, *The Common Law* (Boston: Little, Brown, 1881), 1.

8. Oliver W. Holmes, "The Path of Law," 10 *Harvard Law Review* 39 (1897).

9. See, generally, Morton White, *Social Thought in America: The Revolt against Formalism* (New York: Viking Press, 1949); and Benjamin Twiss, *Lawyers and the Constitution* (Princeton, NJ: Princeton University Press, 1942).

10. See Roscoe Pound, *An Introduction to the Philosophy of Law* (New Haven, CT: Yale University Press, 1922).

11. Louis Brandeis, "The Living Law," 10 *Illinois Law Review* 461 (1916).

12. See Wilfred Rumble, *American Legal Realism* (Ithaca, NY: Cornell University Press, 1968).

13. See Jerome Frank, *Law and the Modern Mind* (New York: Coward-McCann, 1930), and *Courts on Trial* (Princeton, NJ: Princeton University Press, 1949).

14. Karl Llewellyn, "The Constitution as an Institution," 34 *Columbia Law Review* 39–40 (1934).

15. See Benjamin Cardozo's highly acclaimed *The Nature of the Judicial Process* (New Haven, CT: Yale University Press, 1921).

16. Letter to E. Corwin, November 5, 1942, in Harlan F. Stone Papers, Box 10, Library of Congress, Washington, DC.

17. Letter to Justice Black, December 15, 1939, in Stone Papers, Box 13.

18. Bork, "Styles in Constitutional Theory," 53.

19. Robert H. Bork, "Tradition and Morality in Constitutional Law," in David M. O'Brien, ed., *Judges on Judging*, 3d ed. (Washington, DC: C.Q. Press, 2009).

20. See Martin Shapiro, "Political Jurisprudence," 52 *Kentucky Law Review* 294 (1964); Harry Stumpf, Martin Shapiro, David Danelski, Austin Sarat, and David O'Brien, "Whither Political Jurisprudence?: A Symposium," 36 *Western Political Quarterly* 533 (1983).

21. See, for example, Richard Posner, *Economic Analysis of Law*, 2d ed. (Boston: Little, Brown, 1977).

22. See William Bishin and Christopher Stone, *Law, Language and Ethics* (Mineola, NY: Foundation Press, 1972); James White, *The Legal Imagination* (Chicago: University of Chicago Press, 1973); James White, *When Words Lose Their Meaning* (Chicago:

University of Chicago Press, 1984); Richard Posner, *Law and Literature: A Misunderstood Relation* (Cambridge, MA: Harvard University Press, 1988); and James White, *Justice as Translation* (Chicago: University of Chicago Press, 1990).

23. See, e.g., Richard Posner, *The Problems of Jurisprudence* (Cambridge, MA: Harvard University Press, 1990); Richard Posner, *The Problematics of Moral and Legal Theory* (Cambridge, MA: Harvard University Press, 1999): Stephen Breyer, *Active Liberty: Interpreting Our Democratic Constitution* (New York: Knopf, 2005).

24. See David Kairys, ed., *The Politics of Law*, 3d ed. (New York: Pantheon, 1998); and Editors of the Harvard Law Review, *Essays on Critical Legal Studies* (Cambridge, MA: Harvard Law Review Association, 1986); Catharine MacKinnon, *Only Words* (Cambridge, MA: Harvard University Press, 1993); Richard Delgado et al., eds. *Critical Race Theory* (Philadelphia, PA: Temple University Press, 1999).

■ (1) THE TEXT AND HISTORICAL CONTEXT

The Supreme Court has been criticized by presidents from Thomas Jefferson to Ronald Reagan and George W. Bush for departing from a "strict" or "literal" interpretation of the Constitution. During the 1968 presidential election campaign, for instance, Republican nominee Richard Nixon attacked the "liberal jurisprudence" of the Warren Court (1953–1969) and promised to appoint only strict constructionists to the bench. *Strict constructionists* hold that constitutional interpretation should be confined to the "four corners" of the document, the literal language of the text of the Constitution.

Within the Court, Chief Justice Roger Taney expressed a strong version of strict constructionism in *Dred Scott v. Sandford*, 60 U.S. 393 (1857) (see Vol. 2, Ch. 12), when holding that blacks were not citizens of the United States within the meaning of "citizens" in Article III:

> No one, we presume, supposes that any change in public opinion or feeling, in relation to this unfortunate race [of blacks], in the civilized nations of Europe or in this country, should induce the court to give to the words of the Constitution a more liberal construction in their favor than they were intended to bear when the instrument was framed and adopted. . . .
>
> It [the Constitution] speaks not only in the same words, but with the same meaning and intent with which it spoke when it came from the hands of its framers, and was voted on and adopted by the people of the United States. Any other rule of construction would abrogate the judicial character of this Court and make it the mere reflex of the popular opinion or passion of the day.

This version of strict constructionism unrealistically (or disingenuously) denies the basic choices involved in constitutional interpretation. For example, much turns on whether the Court analyzes church–state controversies from the perspective of the First Amendment's free exercise clause or its establishment clause (see Vol. 2, Ch. 6). When applying the Fourth Amendment's guarantee against "unreasonable searches and seizures," the Warren Court chose to enforce strictly the requirements specified in that amendment's warrants and probable cause clauses. By contrast, the Burger Court (1969–1986), and the Rehnquist Court (1986–2005), tended to give less force to those requirements by relying instead on the justices' reading of what is "reasonable" under the amendment's reasonableness clause. Whether the Fourth Amendment is enforced primarily in terms of its reasonableness clause or its warrants and probable cause clauses represents a basic constitutional choice with important consequences for individual rights and law enforcement interests (see Vol. 2, Ch. 7).

Justice Hugo Black claimed to be an "absolutist," a "literalist." In his words:

> My view is, without deviation, without exception, without any if's, but's, or whereas, that freedom of speech means that government shall not do anything to people, or, in the words of the Magna Carta, move against people, either for the views they have or the views they express or the words they speak or write. Some people would have you believe that this is a very radical position, and maybe it is. But all I am doing is following what to me is the clear working of the First Amendment that "Congress shall make no law . . . abridging the freedom of speech or of the press."[1]

However, Justice Black acknowledged that the Constitution presents some interpretive problems and constitutional choices. In the controversy over the Court's application of the Bill of Rights to the states under the Fourteenth Amendment, for instance, Black became convinced that those guarantees were included in the amendment's privileges or immunities clause, whereas other justices contended that they were included in the Fourteenth Amendment's due process clause (see Vol. 2, Ch. 4).

Justice Black's absolutism was in response to the Court's *balancing* of First Amendment freedoms against governmental interests in national security in cases like *Dennis v. United States*, 341 U.S. 494 (1951) (see Vol. 2, Ch. 5), under the guise of the "clear and present danger" test. He opposed the Court's invention and use of such tests and metaphors. Still, much of constitutional law consists in metaphors created by the Court when explaining and applying constitutional provisions; consider the debates over executive privilege (see Vol. 1, Ch. 4), states' sovereignty (see Vol. 1, Ch. 7), the liberty of contract (see Vol. 2, Ch. 3), the high wall of separation between church and state (see Vol. 2, Ch. 6), or the controversy over whether the Constitution is color-blind (see Vol. 2, Ch. 12).

Interpretivism is usually only the beginning, not the end, of constitutional interpretation. The most frequently contested guarantees of the Constitution are neither unambiguous nor amenable to a literal or strict interpretation. What is the literal meaning of the reasonableness clause of the Fourth Amendment or of the due process and equal protection clauses of the Fourteenth Amendment? Nor do interpretivists, like Justice Black, deny First Amendment protection for posters and songs on the ground that they are not strictly speaking "speech"; although Black drew a line at extending protection to speech-plus-conduct and "symbolic speech" (see Vol. 2, Ch. 5).

Crucial provisions in the Constitution have what philosophers call an "open texture."[2] They are framed in general terms that are nonexhaustive of all future applications and have an essential incompleteness in dictating unforeseeable applications. The commerce clause in Article I, for example, gives Congress the power to regulate interstate commerce but fails to define *interstate commerce*. No one today, though, contends that interstate commerce should include only the methods of transportation available in 1787 or exclude modes of commerce, such as telecommunications and the Internet, that were unforeseen by the Constitutional Convention.

These are only some of the problems with strict constructionism, as federal court of appeals Judge Richard Posner notes in an essay titled, "What Am I? A Potted Plant? The Case against Strict Constructionism." Moreover, Posner underscores that nothing in the Constitution commands the Court to construe either "strictly" or "broadly" the document:

> Even the decision to read the Constitution narrowly, and thereby "restrain" judicial interpretation, is not a decision that can be read directly from the text. The Constitution does not say, "Read me broadly," "Read me narrowly." That decision must be made a matter of political theory, and will depend on such things as one's view of the springs of judicial legitimacy and of the relative competence of courts and legislatures in dealing with particular types of issues.[3]

Strict constructionism is incomplete as a theory of interpretation and inadequately deals with the fact that the Constitution was framed in generalities in order to express general principles. Because this is so, interpretivists often turn to the historical context of the Constitution. Consider, for example, the call for a *jurisprudence of original intention* by Ronald Reagan's attorney general, Edwin Meese III:

> As the "faithful guardians of the Constitution," the judges were expected to resist any political effort to depart from the literal provisions of the Constitution. The text of the document and the original intention of those who framed it would be the judicial standard in giving effect to the Constitution. . . . [But] it seems fair

to conclude that far too many of the court's opinions are, on the whole, more policy choices than articulations of constitutional principle. The voting blocs, the arguments, all reveal a greater allegiance to what the court thinks constitutes sound public policy than a deference to what the Constitution—its text and intention—demands.[4]

Meese was not the first to contend that the text and the Framers' intent should solely guide constitutional interpretation.[5] Nonetheless, he sparked considerable debate and provoked Justice William J. Brennan to respond in a speech, observing,

> In its most doctrinaire incarnation, this view demands that Justices discern exactly what the Framers thought about the question under consideration and simply follow that intention in resolving the case before them. It is a view that feigns self-effacing deference to the specific judgments of those who forged our original social compact. But in truth it is little more than arrogance cloaked as humility. It is arrogant to pretend that from our vantage we can gauge accurately the intent of the Framers on application of principle to specific, contemporary questions. All too often, sources of potential enlightenment such as records of the ratification debates provide sparse or ambiguous evidence of the original intention. Typically, all that can be gleaned is that the Framers themselves did not agree about the application or meaning of particular constitutional provisions, and hid their differences in cloaks of generality. Indeed, it is far from clear whose intention is relevant—that of the drafters, the congressional disputants, or the ratifiers in the states?—or even whether the idea of an original intention is a coherent way of thinking about a jointly drafted document drawing its authority from a general assent of the states. And apart from the problematic nature of the sources, our distance of two centuries cannot but work as a prism refracting all we perceive. . . .
>
> We current Justices read the Constitution in the only way that we can: as Twentieth Century Americans. We look to the history of the time of framing and to the intervening history of interpretation. But the ultimate question must be, what do the words of the text mean in our time. For the genius of the Constitution rests not in any static meaning it might have had in a world that is dead and gone, but in the adaptability of its great principles to cope with current problems and current needs. What the Constitution's fundamentals meant to the wisdom of other times cannot be their measure to the vision of our time. Similarly, what those fundamentals mean for us, our descendants will learn, cannot be the measure to the vision of their time.[6]

As Justice Brennan suggests, there are methodological difficulties with a "jurisprudence of original intention." For one thing, determining "intent" is a subjective enterprise; it proposes to discover what the

Framers had in mind when drafting and ratifying the Constitution. But as already noted, the Framers often disagreed and were forced to compromise on the language of the Constitution. At best, this approach considers the intentions of the drafters and ratifiers of the Constitution. And, who are "the Framers"? Should the views of only the thirty-nine signers of the document be considered, or should those of the other sixteen delegates who left before the Constitutional Convention concluded or refused to sign the document be considered as well? There are also compelling reasons for including the views of delegates to the thirteen state ratifying conventions, for as a result of those conventions the Bill of Rights was immediately added to the Constitution (see Vol. 2, Ch. 4).

Problems with discovering the intentions of the Framers also arise because the proceedings of the Constitutional Convention were conducted in secrecy and records of that convention and those in the states are far from complete and reliable. Moreover, it is debatable that the Framers intended their intentions to limit or guide constitutional interpretation.[7] Not until 1819 were speeches, resolutions, and votes of the delegates to the Constitutional Convention published. Almost another decade passed before Jonathan Elliot began publishing his collection of the debates in the state ratifying conventions. James Madison, who took notes of the debates at the Constitutional Convention and whose notes provide the only full record, refused to allow the publication of his notes until 1840, after his death. Madison insisted that the intent and literal reading of the text would be a "hard rule of construction." Instead, among the "obvious and just guides applicable to the Constn. of the U.S.," he listed

> 1. the evils & defects for curing which the Constitution was called for & introduced. 2. The comments prevailing at the times it was adopted. 3. The early, deliberate & continued practice under the Constitution as preferable to constructions adopted on the spur of occasions, and subject to the vicissitudes of party or personal considerations.[8]

In addition, it bears noting that in its first fifty years the Supreme Court infrequently cited works such as *The Federalist Papers* in its opinions. Between 1790 and 1839, *The Federalist Papers* were cited in only fifteen decisions; by comparison, since 1950 they were cited in more than 100 cases.[9]

Because of these difficulties, Chief Justice William Rehnquist, Justices Antonin Scalia and Clarence Thomas, among others associated with interpretivism and the "originalist" approach to constitutional interpretation, more modestly contend that the Court should remain faithful to the "original understanding" or "original meaning"[10] of the governing principles or political philosophy of the Framers. They do not claim to be uncovering the Framers' subjective intentions but rather limiting the interpretation of constitutional provisions to those principles that the Framers might be fairly said to have embraced when drafting and ratifying the Constitution. Judge Bork explains that

> [a] major problem with the idea of original intention is that the Framers articulated their principles in light of the world they knew, a world very different in important respects from that in which judges must decide cases today. . . . In order to protect the freedoms the Framers envisaged, the judge must discern a principle in the applications the Framers thought of and then apply that principle to circumstances they did not foresee.[11]

Nor do they claim that originalism eliminates the burden of making basic constitutional choices. Rather, they argue that this approach is superior to other noninterpretivist approaches because it ostensibly sharply limits the exercise of judicial review and thus proves more responsive to criticisms of the Court's countermajoritarian power. In Justice Scalia's words,

> The principal theoretical defect of nonoriginalism, in my view, is its incompatibility with the very principle that legitimizes judicial review of constitutionality. Nothing in the text of the Constitution confers upon the courts the power to inquire into, rather than passively assume, the constitutionality of federal statutes. . . . Quite to the contrary, the legislature would seem a much more appropriate expositor of social values, and *its* determination that a statute is compatible with the Constitution should, as in England, prevail.[12]

Justice Scalia concedes that originalism poses methodological problems in practice but nonetheless claims that it is "the lesser evil" in constitutional interpretation:

> [It] *is* true that it is often exceedingly difficult to plumb the original understanding of an ancient text. Properly done, the task requires the consideration of an enormous mass of material—in the case of the Constitution and its Amendments, for example, to mention only one element, the records of the ratifying debates in all the states. Even beyond that, it requires an evaluation of the reliability of that material—many of the reports of the ratifying debates, for example, are thought to be quite unreliable. And further still, it requires immersing oneself in the political and intellectual atmosphere of the time—somehow placing out of mind knowledge that we have which an earlier age did not, and putting on beliefs, attitudes, philosophies, prejudices and loyalties that are not those of

our day. It is, in short, a task sometimes better suited to the historian than the lawyer. . . .

I can be much more brief in describing what seems to me the second most serious objection to originalism. In its undiluted form, at least, it is medicine that seems too strong to swallow. Thus, almost every originalist would adulterate it with the doctrine of *stare decisis* [which holds that prior decisions should be respected]. . . . But *stare decisis* alone is not enough to prevent originalism from being what many would consider too bitter a pill. What if some state should enact a new law providing public lashing, or branding of the right hand, as punishment for certain criminal offenses? Even if it could be demonstrated unequivocally that these were not cruel and unusual measures [which are forbidden under the Eighth Amendment] in 1791, and even though no prior Supreme Court decision has specifically disapproved them, I doubt whether any federal judge—even among the many who consider themselves originalists—would sustain them against an Eighth Amendment challenge. It may well be . . . that this cannot legitimately be reconciled with originalist philosophy—that it represents the unrealistic view of the Constitution as a document intended to create a perfect society for all ages to come, whereas in fact it was a political compromise that did not pretend to create a perfect society even for its own age (as its toleration of slavery, which a majority of the founding generation recognized as an evil, well enough demonstrates). Even so, I am confident that public flogging and hand-branding would not be sustained by our courts, and any espousal of originalism as a practical theory of exegesis must somehow come to terms with that reality.[13]

Justice Scalia's discussion of public flogging and the Eighth Amendment is revealing not only in indicating that he is (in his words) "a faint-hearted originalist," because he would hold public flogging unconstitutional despite the fact that the Framers permitted that practice. The original understanding of constitutional guarantees, as Justice Anthony Kennedy observed during his 1987 Senate confirmation hearings, is a "necessary starting point," not an "adequate methodology" or "mechanical process" that "tells us how to decide a case."

What Scalia's discussion also points out is that crucial *concepts* in the Constitution give rise to competing *conceptions* and political philosophies.[14] Scalia would not limit the concept of cruel and unusual punishment in the Eighth Amendment to the Framers' conception of that punishment in 1791. Nor would Scalia go as far as Justice Brennan in interpreting the Eighth Amendment to bar capital punishment based on his "constitutional vision of human dignity" (see Vol. 2, Ch. 10). But, why not? What divides justices like Scalia and Thomas from Brennan, Souter, Ginsburg, and Breyer is their underlying judicial and political philosophies of the Constitution and the exercise of judicial review. So too, just as the Federalists and Anti-Federalists had competing political visions of the separation of powers and federalism, for example, even originalists such as Chief Justice Rehnquist and Justices Scalia and Thomas may have rival conceptions and interpretations of the separation of powers; see, for instance, *Morrison v. Olson*, 487 U.S. 654 (1988) (see Vol. 1, Ch. 4), and *McIntyre v. Ohio Elections Commission*, 514 U.S. 334 (1995) (excerpted in Vol. 1, Ch. 8).

An underlying problem for interpretivists and noninterpretivists is how broadly or narrowly they conceive and express the concept or principle of a constitutional provision. Consider, for example, the constitutional choices presented in interpreting and applying the Fourth Amendment and the equal protection clause of the Fourteenth Amendment.

The Fourth Amendment guarantees the people a right "to be secure in their persons, houses, papers, and effects against unreasonable searches and seizures." That guarantee was interpreted in *Olmstead v. United States*, 277 U.S. 438 (1928) (see Vol. 2, Ch. 7), not to cover wiretaps because a majority of the Court limited the amendment's application to Framers' conception of "unreasonable searches and seizures," giving the lowest level of generality to the amendment's principle, so as to bar only actual physical trespass by police and the seizure of tangible materials. By contrast, dissenting Justice Louis Brandeis argued for a broader conception of the amendment and a more general principle of privacy in the home that would have extended the guarantees of the amendment to cover electronic surveillance. Almost forty years later, in *Katz v. United States*, 389 U.S. 347 (1967) (see Vol. 2, Ch. 7), the Court finally embraced the broader principle of Fourth Amendment–protected privacy.

The Fourteenth Amendment guarantees "the equal protection of the laws." The principle of equality embodied there might be interpreted to bar only discrimination against blacks, because in the historical context of the post–Civil War period the Thirty-ninth Congress was indisputably primarily concerned with ensuring that states did not deny certain rights of newly freed blacks. However, the principle of equality has been given broader application and a higher level of generality so as to bar other kinds of racial discrimination against, for example, Hispanics and Asians. Even more broadly (as further discussed in Vol. 2, Ch. 12), the amendment has been construed to forbid forms of nonracial discrimination against women and homosexuals. But how and on what basis may this broader application of the equal protection clause be defended and the Court's exercise of judicial review in this way justified?

In sum and in Judge Bork's words, "The question is always the level of generality the judge chooses when he states the idea or object of the Framers."[15] Interpretivists, no less than noninterpretivists, cannot evade making basic constitutional choices in their conceptions and formulations of the underlying principles of constitutional provisions.

Notes

1. Hugo Black, *A Constitutional Faith* (New York: Knopf, 1968), 45.

2. See H. L. A. Hart, *The Concept of Law* (Oxford, UK: Clarendon Press, 1961), 124–132.

3. Richard Posner, "What Am I? A Potted Plant?" *The New Republic*, Sept. 28, 1987, 23.

4. Edwin Meese, "The Attorney General's View of the Supreme Court: Toward a Jurisprudence of Original Intention," in *Special Issue, Law and Public Affairs*, ed. Charles Wise and David O'Brien, 45 *Public Administration Review* 701 (1985).

5. See also Raoul Berger, *Government by Judiciary* (Cambridge, MA: Harvard University Press, 1977); and Walter Berns, *Taking the Constitution Seriously* (New York: Simon & Schuster, 1987).

6. William J. Brennan, Jr., "The Constitution of the United States: Contemporary Ratification," Georgetown University, Washington, DC (Oct. 12, 1985); reprinted in David M. O'Brien, ed., *Judges on Judging*, 3d ed. (Washington, DC: C.Q. Press, 2009).

7. See H. Jefferson Powell, "The Original Understanding of Original Intent," 98 *Harvard Law Review* 885 (1985); and James Hutson, "The Creation of the Constitution: The Integrity of the Documentary Record," 65 *Texas Law Review* 1 (1986).

8. Quoted in Robert Morgan, *James Madison on the Constitution and the Bill of Rights* (Westport, CT: Greenwood Press, 1988), 196–197.

9. See James Wilson, "The Most Sacred Text: The Supreme Court's Use of *The Federalist Papers*," 1985 *Brigham Young University Law Review* 65 (1985).

10. See Antonin Scalia, "Originalism: The Lesser Evil," 57 *Cincinnati Law Review* 849 (1989); reprinted in O'Brien, *Judges on Judging*.

11. Robert Bork, "Foreword" to Gary McDowell, *The Constitution and Contemporary Constitutional Theory* (Cumberland, VA: Center for Judicial Studies, 1985), x.

12. Scalia, "Originalism," 854.

13. Scalia, "Originalism," 856–857.

14. On the distinction between concepts and conceptions, see Ronald Dworkin, *Taking Rights Seriously* (Cambridge, MA: Harvard University Press, 1977), 135–137.

15. Bork, "Foreword," x.

Selected Bibliography

Amar, Akhill Reed. *America's Constitution: A Biography*. New York: Random House, 2005.

Amsterdam, Anthony, and Bruner, Jerome. *Minding the Law: How Courts Rely on Storytelling, and How Their Stories Change the Ways We Understand the Law—And Ourselves*. Cambridge, MA: Harvard University Press, 2000.

The Supreme Court, 2010. (*Steve Petteway, Collection of the Supreme Court of the United States.*)

Beeman, Richard. *Plain, Honest Men: The Making of the American Constitution.* New York: Random House, 2009.

Berger, Raoul. *Government by Judiciary: The Transformation of the Fourteenth Amendment.* Cambridge, MA: Harvard University Press, 1977.

Berns, Walter. *Taking the Constitution Seriously.* New York: Simon & Schuster, 1987.

Bickel, Alexander. *The Morality of Consent.* New Haven, CT: Yale University Press, 1975.

Black, Hugo. *A Constitutional Faith.* New York: Knopf, 1968.

Bork, Robert. *The Tempting of America.* New York: Free Press, 1989.

Brandwein, Pamela. *Reconstructing the Reconstruction: The Supreme Court and the Production of Historical Truth.* Durham, NC: Duke University Press, 1999.

Calabresi, Steven, ed. *Originalism: A Quarter-Century of Debate.* Washington, DC: Regnery, 2007.

Cogan, Neil, ed. *The Complete Bill of Rights: The Drafts, Debates, Sources, & Origins.* New York: Oxford University Press, 1997.

Crapanzano, Vincent. *Serving the Word: Literalism in America from the Pulpit to the Bench.* New York: New Press, 2000.

Gibson, Alan. *Interpreting the Founding.* Lawrence: University Press of Kansas, 2006.

Goldford, Dennis. *The American Constitution and the Debate over Originalism.* New York: Cambridge University Press, 2005.

Holton, Woody. *Unruly Americans and the Origins of the Constitution.* New York: Hill & Wang, 2007.

Jaffa, Harry V. *Original Intent and the Framers of the Constitution.* Washington, DC: Regnery Gateway, 1994.

Levy, Leonard. *Original Intent and the Framers' Constitution.* Chicago: Ivan Dee, 2000.

Lynch, Joseph. *Negotiating the Constitution: The Earliest Debates over Original Intent.* Ithaca, NY: Cornell University Press, 1999.

O'Neill, Jonathan. *Originalism in American Law and Politics.* Baltimore: Johns Hopkins University Press, 2005.

Rakove, Jack. *Original Meanings: Politics and Ideas in the Making of the Constitution.* New York: Knopf, 1996.

———, ed. *Interpreting the Constitution: The Debate over Original Intent.* Boston: Northeastern University Press, 1990.

Scalia, Antonin. *A Matter of Interpretation: Federal Courts and the Law.* Princeton, NJ: Princeton University Press, 1997.

Sunstein, Cass. *Radicals in Robes: Why Extreme Right-Wing Courts Are Wrong for America.* New York: Basic Books, 2005.

———. *A Constitution of Many Minds: Why the Founding Dowment Doesn't Mean What It Meant Before.* Princeton, NJ: Princeton University Press 2009.

Tamanaha, Brian. *On the Rule of Law: History, Politics, Theory.* New York: Cambridge University Press, 2004.

Thayer, Bradley. *Thayer's Legal Essays.* Boston: Boston Book Company, 1908.

Whittington, Keith. *Constitutional Interpretation: Textual Meaning, Original Intent, and Judicial Review.* Lawrence: University Press of Kansas, 1999.

■ (2) IN AND BEYOND THE TEXT

Noninterpretivism differs from interpretivism in the sources and kinds of argumentation marshaled in support of giving broader scope or higher levels of generality to constitutional principles. Whereas interpretivists confine analysis to the text and historical context of a provision, noninterpretivists tend to formulate more broadly the underlying principle of a constitutional provision. Noninterpretivists may turn to history and social science, for example, or appeal to natural law, natural rights, and moral or political philosophy, or call on process-oriented theories of judicial review and arguments about the structure of the Constitution.

Historical, economic, technological, and political changes are obviously relevant to constitutional interpretation. Yet, when and how should the Court use *history*? The Sixth Amendment, for instance, guarantees criminal defendants the right to a jury trial but does not define *jury*. When confronted with the question of whether juries must consist of twelve members, in *Thompson v. Utah*, 170 U.S. 343 (1882), the Court simply ruled that the Sixth Amendment incorporated the traditional common-law practice of twelve-member juries because that practice was firmly rooted in English history and familiar to the Framers of the Bill of Rights. The Court may also take *judicial notice* of historical events without the benefit of their being adjudicated, such as the fact that there was an economic depression in the 1930s. Chief Justice Morrison Waite drew heavily on history as a guide when upholding under the commerce clause the power of Congress, over that of the states, to regulate interstate telegraph lines, in *Pensacola Telegraph Co. v. Western Union Telegraph, Co.*, 96 U.S. 1 (1877):

> The powers thus granted are not confined to the instrumentalities of commerce . . . known or in use when the Constitution was adopted, but they keep pace with the progress of the country, and adapt themselves to the new developments of time and circumstance. They extend from the horse with its rider to the stagecoach, from the sailing-vessel to the steamboat . . . and from the railroad to the telegraph, as these new agencies are successively brought into use to meet the demands of increasing population and wealth. . . . As they were intrusted to the general government for the good of the nation, it is not only the right, but the duty, of Congress to see to it that intercourse among the States and the transmission of intelligence are not obstructed or unnecessarily encumbered by State legislation.

Justice Holmes took an even more expansive view of the use of history in the famous case dealing with the national government's treaty-making power in *Missouri v. Holland*, 252 U.S. 416 (1920) (see Ch. 3). Note his observation that "[t]he case before us must be considered in light of our whole experience and not merely in that of what was said a hundred years ago."

The Court's reliance on history is not unproblematic, however.[1] Justices are not trained as historians and they may confront problems in evaluating different schools of history and the works of revisionist historians. More fundamentally, Chief Justice William Rehnquist, among others, cautioned against turning to history because it encourages the notion that the "Constitution is a living document" and that the Court ought to keep the Constitution in "tune with the times." In Rehnquist's view, there are three serious flaws with the notion of a living Constitution:

> First, it misconceives the nature of the Constitution, which was designed to enable the popularly elected branches of government, not the judicial branch, to keep the country abreast of the times. Second, [it] ignores the Supreme Court's disastrous experiences when in the past it embraced contemporary, fashionable notions of what a living Constitution should contain. Third, however socially desirable the goals to be advanced, . . . advancing them through a

free-wheeling, non-elected judiciary is quite unacceptable in a democratic society.[2]

Social science may prove a no less controversial source of support for the Court's decisions. In the landmark school desegregation ruling in *Brown v. Board of Education*, 347 U.S. 483 (1954) (see Vol. 2, Ch. 12), for example, the Court cited in footnote 11 several social science studies in support of overturning the racial doctrine of "separate but equal facilities." Among those studies was Swedish economist and sociologist Gunnar Myrdal's book *An American Dilemma* (1944), the premier work on race relations in America. The Court's mention of *An American Dilemma* intensified the antagonism of powerful southerners, such as the South Carolina governor and former Supreme Court Justice James F. Byrnes and Mississippi Senator James O. Eastland. They and others attacked the Court for citing the work of "foreign sociologists," bad social science research, and, most of all, for drawing on social science in the first place, instead of simply sticking to the text and historical context of the Constitution.

The Court's use of social science materials may raise questions about judicial competence and the legitimacy of basing decisions on social science evidence.[3] Consider *Williams v. Florida*, 399 U.S. 78 (1970) (see Vol. 2, Ch. 9), upholding juries composed of fewer than twelve members, despite history and the ruling in *Thompson v. Utah* that the Sixth Amendment jury consisted "as it was at common law, of twelve persons, neither more nor less." *Williams* proved controversial because the Court held on the basis of psychological and sociological studies of small-group behavior that juries of fewer than twelve members were "functionally equivalent" to traditional twelve-member juries.

Natural law and *natural rights*, or what Edward Corwin termed, the "higher law" background of the Constitution, is an older tradition and source of constitutional interpretation.[4] The Framers took seriously natural law and natural rights in maintaining that individuals enjoy certain rights prior to the establishment of government and which may not be denied by government. Federalists, though, contended that the Constitution adequately safeguarded natural rights by creating a government of limited and specifically delegated powers. But the Anti-Federalists pushed for the addition of a bill of rights containing a statement of natural rights (see Vol. 2, Ch. 4).

Although the natural rights tradition runs throughout much of constitutional law, controversy has ensnarled appeals to natural law and rights ever since Justices Iredell and Chase debated, in *Calder v. Bull*, 3 Dall. 398 (1798), whether the Court has the power to strike down legislation based on principles of natural justice. Chief Justice John

Marshall faced the problem of enforcing his own acceptance of natural rights against the claims of Spanish and Portuguese slave traders in *The Antelope Case*, 23 U.S. 66 (1825). Slaves had been seized by pirates, who were later captured by an American naval ship, and the slave traders and owners sued to recover their "property." Of slavery and the slave trade, Chief Justice Marshall observed "[t]hat it is contrary to the law of nature will scarcely be denied. That every man has a natural right to the fruits of his own labor, is generally admitted, and [that] no other person can rightfully deprive him of those fruits, and appropriate them against his will, seems to be the necessary result of this admission." But Marshall concluded that

> [w]hatever might be the answer of a moralist to this question, a jurist must search for its legal solution, in those principles of action which are sanctioned by the usages, the national acts, and the general assent, of that portion of the world of which he considers himself as a part, and to whose law the appeal is made. If we resort to this standard as the test of international law, the question . . . is decided in favor of the legality of the [slave] trade.

Other members of the Court, though, have sided with Justice Chase's position in *Calder* that with respect to "certain vital principles . . . [a]n act of the Legislature (for I cannot call it a *law*) contrary to the *great first principles* of the social compact, cannot be considered a *rightful exercise* of legislative authority" and, therefore, must be overturned. Consider the debate over fundamental rights and the formulations and standards used by the Court when interpreting the Fourteenth Amendment's due process clause (see Vol. 2, Ch. 4). In *Hurtado v. California*, 110 U.S. 516 (1884) (see Vol. 2, Ch. 4), for example, Justice Stanley Matthews speaks of the "wellsprings of justice." In *Adamson v. California*, 332 U.S. 46 (1947) (see Vol. 2, Ch. 4), and *Rochin v. California*, 342 U.S. 165 (1952) (see Vol. 2, Ch. 4), Justice Frankfurter invokes "the shocks the conscience test" and "fundamental fairness standard" for determining what process is due under the due process clause.

The principal criticism of "natural law formulations" is levied in opinions by Justice Hugo Black, particularly in his dissent from the Court's recognition of a right of privacy in *Griswold v. Connecticut*, 381 U.S. 479 (1965) (see Vol. 2, Ch. 4), where he observes that

> [o]ne of the most effective ways of diluting or expanding a constitutionally guaranteed right is to substitute for the crucial word or words of a constitutional guarantee another word for the word or words, more or less flexible and more or less restricted in meaning. . . . Use of any such broad, unbounded judicial authority would make this Court's members a day-to-day constitutional convention.

This criticism of the Court for imposing its own substantive value choices applies as well to those arguing that the Court should draw on *moral* and *political philosophy.* Yet Professor Ronald Dworkin and other contemporary legal scholars call for "a fusion of constitutional law and moral theory" or political philosophy.[5] Contemporary legal scholarship is indeed marked by a proliferation of expressly normative theories that would rationalize and guide constitutional interpretation according to "abstract beliefs about morality and justice,"[6] the "voice of reason,"[7] "a moral patrimony" implicit in "our common heritage,"[8] "the circumstances and values of the present generation,"[9] "conventional morality,"[10] "public morality,"[11] "constitutional morality,"[12] "fundamental values,"[13] and the "essential principles of justice,"[14] or "the idea of progress."[15] But this movement toward more specialized and abstract theories of constitutional interpretation raises the ante for reaching consensus within the Supreme Court and the country.[16]

Interpretivists counter that the turn to moral and political philosophy only exacerbates the problems of constitutional interpretation and the countermajoritarian difficulty of judicial review. As former Stanford University Law School professor John Hart Ely cleverly put it, "The Constitution may follow the flag, but is it really supposed to keep up with the *New York Review of Books*?"[17] Judge Bork raises other concerns:

> The abstract, universalistic style of legal thought has a number of dangers. For one thing, it teaches disrespect for the actual institutions of the American polity. These institutions are designed to achieve compromise, to slow change, to dilute absolutisms. They embody wholesome inconsistencies. They are designed, in short, to do things that abstract generalizations about the just society tend to bring into contempt.[18]

Interpreting the Constitution, nevertheless, presupposes a judicial and political philosophy and poses inescapable questions of substantive value choices. As Justice Brennan explains,

> Faith in democracy is one thing, blind faith quite another. Those who drafted our Constitution understood the difference. One cannot read the text without admitting that it embodies substantive choices; it places certain values beyond the power of any legislature. . . .

> To remain faithful to the content of the Constitution, therefore, an approach to interpreting the text must account for the existence of these substantive value choices, and must accept the ambiguity inherent in the effort to apply them to modern circumstances. The Framers discerned fundamental principles through struggles against particular malefactions of the Crown; the struggle shapes the par-

■ CONSTITUTIONAL HISTORY

What Is the Constitution? Could a Constitutional Amendment Violate the Constitution?

What is the Constitution? Could a constitutional amendment violate the Constitution or fundamental principles of a constitution? These questions continue to be debated, especially in countries such as Germany and India that have constitutional provisions forbidding, or their high courts have interpreted their constitutions to forbid, amendments infringing on fundamental principles such as "human dignity." Other countries prohibit constitutional amendments changing official languages, national anthems, or the boundaries of subnational units; Turkey, for instance, forbids any amendment changing its constitutional provisions declaring the state a secular democracy and a republic.

The German Constitutional Court, for instance, struck down a provision of its Constitution in the *Southwest Case*, 1 BverfGE 14 (1951).[1] After World War II, the occupation forces divided two states, Baden and Wurttemberg, into three for the purposes of administration. When the new Constitution of the Federal Republic of Germany went into effect in 1949, these three territories became länder (states) with their own constitutions. Article 118 of Germany's Basic Law, however, provided that these three territories could be reorganized according to their own agreement or, if they failed to reach an agreement, by federal legislation and a referendum of the people. They were unable to reach an agreement and in 1951 the parliament passed two reorganization laws, creating a single länder to be called Baden-Wurttemberg. Baden immediately challenged the constitutionality of these laws on the ground that they diminished Baden's status as a länder and treated it unfairly and unequally by calling for a referendum of the people instead of just its own population. In holding unconstitutional Article 118, the German court observed:

> An individual constitutional provision cannot be considered as an isolated clause and interpreted alone. A constitution has an inner unity, and the meaning of any one part is linked to that of other provisions. Taken as a unit, a constitution reflects certain over-arching principles and fundamental decisions to which individual provisions are subordinate. Article 79, paragraph 3, makes it clear that the Basic Law agrees with the statement of the Bavarian Constitutional Court:

(continues)

■ CONSTITUTIONAL HISTORY
What Is the Constitution? Could a Constitutional Amendment Violate the Constitution? (continued)

That a constitutional provision itself may be null and void, is not conceptually impossible just because it is part of the constitution. There are constitutional principles that are so fundamental and to such an extent an expression of a law that precedes even the constitution that they also bind the framer of the constitution, and other constitutional provisions that do not rank so high may be null and void because they contravene these principles. . . .

From this rule of interpretation, it follows that any constitutional provision must be interpreted in such a way that it is compatible with those elementary principles and with the basic decisions of the framer of the constitution. This rule applies also to Article 118, sentence 2.

In the United States, some legal scholars also contend that the proposed constitutional amendment to forbid desecration of the American flag would violate the Constitution. Following the Supreme Court's ruling in *Texas v. Johnson* (excerpted in Vol. 2, Ch. 5), holding that flag-burning is protected speech under the First Amendment, Congress passed the Federal Flag Protection Act of 1989. That statute was then struck down in *United States v. Eichman* (1990). Following those rulings, an attempt in 1995 to override the Court's decisions by means of a constitutional amendment failed to pass the Senate by three votes. In 1997, the House of Representatives passed another proposed constitutional amendment and the Senate was closely divided on whether to send it to the states for ratification. Moreover, 49 state legislatures, far more than the 38 required to amend the Constitution, had indicated that they would ratify a constitutional amendment outlawing flag-burning. The Senate has reconsidered the matter several times but failed to muster the 67 votes needed for passage.

The constitutionality of constitutional amendments was raised previously in challenges to the validity of the Eighteenth and Nineteenth Amendments. The Eighteenth Amendment, ratified in 1919, prohibited the manufacturing, sales, and transportation of intoxicating liquors; it was later repealed by the Twenty-first Amendment in 1933. The Nineteenth Amendment, ratified in 1920, extended federal and state voting rights to women.

Shortly after the ratification of the Eighteenth Amendment, the Court consolidated seven lawsuits challenging the amendment's constitutionality in *The National Prohibition Cases, State of Rhode Island v. Palmer*, 253 U.S. 350 (1920). When arguing for Rhode Island, Herbert Rice contended that "the Amendment is an invasion of the sovereignty of the complaining State and her people . . ." Continuing, he argued:

> It is "This Constitution" that may be amended. "This Constitution" is not a code of transient laws but a framework of government and an embodiment of fundamental principles. By an amendment, the identity or purpose of the instrument is not to be changed; its defects may be cured, but "This Constitution" must remain. It would be the greatest absurdity to contend that there was a purpose to create a limited government and at the same time to confer upon that government a power to do away with its own limitations. . . .
>
> In the case of this so-called amendment, the representatives of the people of the United States have attempted, not to amend the Constitution of the United States, but to amend the constitution of every State in the Union. If the amending function is construed as extensive with absolute sovereignty, then the basis of our political system is no longer the right of the people of a State to make and alter their constitution, for their political institutions are at the mercy of others and may be changed against their will. . . .

Attorneys Elihu Root and William D. Guthrie also sought to persuade the Court of the amendment's unconstitutionality, arguing:

> If, as contended by the defendants, the power of amendment vested in Congress and three-fourths of the state legislatures be absolute and unrestricted, then there would be no limitation whatever upon their legislative authority. They could then by amendment establish a state religion, or oppress or discriminate against any denomination, or authorize the taking away of life, liberty and property, without due process of law, etc., etc. This would destroy the most essential limitation upon power under the American system of government, which is that the rights of the individual citizen shall be protected by withholding from the legislative function the power to do certain things inconsistent with individual liberty. This was the reason of the irresistible demand for the first ten amendments. . . .

By contrast, Solicitor General Alexander King countered, first, that whether the amendment was within the amending power of Article V and whether it in fact had been ratified "are questions committed by the Constitution to the political branch and not to the judicial branch of the Government." Second, "It has always been understood that there is no limitation upon the character of amendments which may be adopted, except such limitations as are imposed by Article V itself. . . . The fact that

(continues)

■ CONSTITUTIONAL HISTORY
What Is the Constitution? Could a Constitutional Amendment Violate the Constitution? (continued)

the Eighteenth Amendment confers upon Congress a power which had previously belonged exclusively to the States does not prevent that Amendment from being within the amending power conferred by Article V of the Constitution." Finally, he concluded: "No State by any provision of its laws or its constitutioncan make the ratification of an amendment to the Constitution of the United States by its legislature subject to a referendum vote of the people. The only method of ratification mentioned in the Constitution is through representatives assembled either in the legislature or a convention called for that purpose."

The arguments of the solicitor general prevailed and in a brief opinion for the Court Justice Van Devanter stated only "the conclusions of the Court," not its reasoning. Subsequently, the Nineteenth Amendment was challenged on the grounds that it was enacted without Maryland's consent and that state's constitution limited suffrage to men. Writing for the Court in *Leser v. Garnett*, 258 U.S. 130 (1922), Justice Brandeis dismissed that claim as well.[2]

Still, some scholars continue to maintain that amendments, such as the proposed one outlawing flag desecration, might run afoul of underlying constitutional principles. For further discussion, see Walter Murphy, "An Ordering of Constitutional Values," 53 *Southern California Law Review* 757 (1984); Sanford Levinson, ed., *Responding to Imperfection: The Theory and Practice of Constitutional Amendment* (Princeton, NJ: Princeton University Press, 1995); and the Constitutional History Boxes in Chapter 6.

1. The *Southwest Case* is translated and excerpted in Walter F. Murphy and Joseph Tanenhaus, eds., *Comparative Constitutional Law: Cases and Commentaries* (New York: St. Martin's Press, 1977). See also *Article 117 Case*, 3 BverfGE 225 (1953); *Privacy in Communications (Klass) Case*, 30 BverfGE 1 (1970); and Donald Kommers, ed., *The Constitutional Jurisprudence of the Federal Republic of Germany*, 2d ed. (Durham, NC: Duke University Press, 1997).

2. See also *Schneiderman v. United States*, 320 U.S. 118 (1943).

ticular contours of the articulated principles. But our acceptance of the fundamental principles has not and should not bind us to those precise, at times anachronistic, contours. Successive generations of Americans have continued to respect these fundamental choices and adopt them as their own guide to evaluating quite different historical practices. Each generation has the choice to overrule or add to the fundamental principles enunciated by the Framers; the Constitution can be amended or it can be ignored. Yet with respect to its fundamental principles, the text has suffered neither fate. . . .

The Constitution on its face is, in large measure, a structuring text, a blueprint for government. And when the text is not prescribing the form of the government it is limiting the powers of that government. The original document, before addition of any of the amendments, does not speak primarily of the rights of man, but of the abilities and disabilities of government. When one reflects upon the text's preoccupation with the scope of government as well as its shape, however, one comes to understand that what this text is about is the relationship of the individual and the state. The text marks the metes and bounds of official authority and individual autonomy. When one studies the boundary that the text marks out, one gets a sense of the vision of the individual embodied in the Constitution.

As augmented by the Bill of Rights and the Civil War Amendments, this text is a sparking vision of the supremacy of the human dignity of every individual. This vision is reflected in the very choice of democratic self-governance: the supreme value of a democracy is the presumed worth of each individual. . . . It is a vision that has guided us as a people throughout our history, although the precise rules by which we have protected fundamental human dignity have been transformed over time in response to both transformations of social conditions and evolution of our concepts of human dignity.[19]

Neither do alternative theories and modes of constitutional interpretation elude a dependence on political philosophy. Interpreting the Constitution frequently requires, as former Professor Charles L. Black, Jr., argued, "inference from the structure and relationships created by the constitution in all its parts or in some principal part."[20] Chief Justice Marshall's watershed opinion in *McCulloch v. Maryland*, 4 Wheat. (17 U.S.) 316 (1819) (see Vol. 1, Ch. 6), illustrates the role of *structural analysis* of the Constitution. There, Marshall upheld the constitutionality of the national bank as a necessary and proper exercise of Congress's powers based on inferences from the structure of federalism, instead of relying on the necessary and proper clause per se. Still, Jeffersonian-Republicans disagreed with the infusion of Marshall's nationalistic political philosophy into constitutional law. Moreover, differences rooted in rival political philosophies over the structure of federalism persist in the Court and the country (see Vol. 1, Ch. 6).

Nor do attempts to reconcile the exercise of the Court's power with majoritarian democracy in terms of what has become known as *process-oriented theory of judicial review* fare much better.[21] Justice Harlan Stone initially suggested that the Court's role ought to be limited to policing the political process and ensuring that it does not discriminate against "discrete and insular minorities," in footnote 4 of *United States*

■ THE DEVELOPMENT OF LAW

Comparative Constitutional Interpretation

Comparative constitutional interpretation increasingly commands greater attention. Scholars, along with members of the Supreme Court and other high courts around the world, are debating the uses and misuses of comparative constitutional law and interpretation.[1]

Several factors contribute to this development. For one, in the latter half of the twentieth century the European Court of Justice and constitutional courts in Western European countries have increasingly asserted their power and employed comparative constitutional analysis (see the In Comparative Perspective box in Vol. 1, Ch. 6). Following the collapse of the former Soviet Union, constitutional courts in Central and Eastern Europe also turned to comparative constitutional law analysis when construing their new constitutions. High courts in Canada, Germany, and Japan also frequently look to decisions of the U.S. Supreme Court when interpreting similar provisions in their post–World War II constitutions and bills of rights (see the In Comparative Perspective boxes in Vol. 2, Chs. 5 and 6). And the South African Constitution of 1996 and Bill of Rights specifically requires its judiciary to consider foreign and international law (see, for example, the In Comparative Perspective box in Vol. 2, Ch. 10). In addition, bar associations along with business and human rights organizations promote international exchanges, and comparative constitutional analysis became much easier with Internet access to court decisions from around the world.

Within the Supreme Court, however, the justices disagree about the use of comparative constitutional analysis. Unlike courts in Canada, Japan, South Africa, and elsewhere, the Supreme Court generally resists comparative constitutional law in justifying its decisions. Justice Scalia, in particular, is unapologetic, observing in *Printz v. United States*, 521 U.S. 898 (1997) that "comparative analysis [is] inappropriate to the task of interpreting a constitution, though it was of course relevant to the task of writing one." By contrast, Justice Breyer, the strongest supporter of comparative constitutional analysis, responded in his dissent that comparative law "may . . . cast an empirical light on the consequences of different legal solutions to a common legal problem." As a result, some foreign jurists have been highly critical of the U.S. Supreme Court for not paying more attention to comparative and international law, particularly with respect to human rights.[2]

Nonetheless, historically the Court has drawn on comparative law and experiences in several ways. First, such analysis has been employed to support the factual basis for the Court's rulings, highlighting relevant "constitutional facts." As a progressive attorney, before joining the Court, Louis D. Brandeis pioneered the idea in his famous "Brandeis brief." Filed in *Muller v. Oregon*, 208 U.S. 412 (1907), it cited in support of

Oregon's law restricting the number of hours that women could work, statutes and reports from Great Britain, France, Switzerland, Austria, Holland, Italy, and Germany. Brandeis did so to show the reasonableness of the legislation. In other words, the Court may take judicial notice of comparative law and experiences in its rulings. In striking down laws criminalizing homosexual sodomy in *Lawrence v. Texas* (2003) (excerpted in Vol. 2, Ch. 11), for instance, Justice Kennedy cites in support a decision of the European Court of Human Rights. In *Atkins v. Virginia* (2002) (excerpted in Vol. 2, Ch. 10), when holding that the execution of mentally retarded criminals violates the Eighth Amendment, Justice Stevens noted in a footnote that "within the world community, the imposition of the death penalty for crimes committed by mentally retarded offenders is overwhelmingly disapproved." But that reference invited a sharp rebuke from Chief Justice Rehnquist and Justice Scalia, who maintain that "the viewpoints of other countries simply are not relevant to interpreting constitutional standards."

Second, the Court sometimes uses comparative analysis in *dicta-dicta* that throws a comparative light on and ostensibly supports the interpretation given in the Court's opinion. Chief Justice Rehnquist, thus, in the doctor-assisted suicide ruling in *Washington v. Glucksberg*, 521 U.S. 702 (1997), cites comparative constitutional law in underscoring the importance of the issue, as have other justices in giving "kindred problems"[3] a comparative perspective. More frequently, such citations aim to buttress the Court's line drawing and announced principle based on our "traditions," especially historical and traditional links to English law and legal history; even Justice Scalia employs comparative constitutional analysis in this fashion.[4]

Third, closely related but more controversial are citations to developing international and comparative constitutional law as basis for a new interpretation of provisions of the Constitution and Bill of Rights. One of the most controversial illustrations, perhaps, is Justice Goldberg's 1963 opinion dissenting from the denial of *certiorari* in *Rudolph v. Alabama* (reproduced in the Inside the Court box in Vol. 2, Ch. 10), inviting challenges to the constitutionality of the death penalty.

1. For further discussion see, David M. O'Brien, "More Smoke than Fire: The Rehnquist Court's Use of Comparative Judicial Opinions and Law in the Construction of Constitutional Rights," 22 *Journal of Law & Politics* 83 (2006).

2. See, e.g., The Honourable Claire L'Heureux-Dube, Justice of the Supreme Court of Canada, "The Importance of Dialogue: Globalization and the International Impact of the Rehnquist Court," 34 *Tulsa Law Journal* 15 (1998).

3. *State Tax Commission of Utah v. Aldrich*, 316 U.S. 174 (1942) (Frankfurter, J., con. op.).

4. See, e.g., *Loving v. United States,* 517 U.S. 748 (1996). See also *Rogers v. Richmond,* 365 U.S. 534, 541 (1961) (on the roots of our adversary system); *McGowan v. State of Maryland,* 366 U.S. 101 (1961); *Thompson v. Oklahoma,* 487 U.S. 815, 868 (1988); and *McIntyre v. Ohio Elections Commission*, 514 U.S. 334 (1995) (Scalia, J., dis. op.).

v. Carolene Products Co., 304 U.S. 144 (1938) (see Vol. 2, Ch. 12). In a book titled *Democracy and Distrust*, Professor Ely further developed the theory that the Court's role should be limited to policing the democratic process and facilitating the representation of minorities in the electoral process: "[T]he general theory is one that bounds judicial review under the Constitution's open-ended provisions by insisting that it can appropriately concern itself only with questions of participation, and not with the substantive merits of the political choice under attack."[22] In this way, Ely aimed to justify the Court's supervision of the electoral process (see Vol. 1, Ch. 8) and reconcile judicial review with democratic theory. But Ely failed to provide a general theory in saying nothing about how the Court should handle cases involving disputes over presidential power and federalism, for example.[23] Moreover, the process-oriented theory of judicial review has been criticized for too sharply limiting the Court's role in protecting civil liberties and civil rights. As Justice Robert Jackson in *West Virginia State Board of Education v. Barnette*, 319 U.S. 624 (1943) (see Vol. 2, Ch. 5), observed, "The very purpose of a Bill of Rights was to withdraw certain subjects from the vicissitudes of political controversy, to place them beyond the reach of majorities and officials and to establish them as legal principles to be applied by the courts" (see also Vol. 2, Ch. 4).

Recently, some justices and scholars have advanced theories of *pragmatism* or *consequentialism*, avoiding "bright-line" rulings in favor of taking "one-case-at-a-time."[24] For example, see Justice Breyer's concurring opinion explaining his pivotal vote in *Van Orden v. Perry* and *McCreary v. American Civil Liberties Union* (2005) (both cases are excerpted in Vol. 2, Ch. 6). On the one hand, he agreed to join a majority upholding a 40-year-old six-foot granite monument engraved with the Ten Commandments on Texas public grounds, but on the other hand deemed a violation of the First Amendment (dis)Establishment Clause the more recent posting of the Ten Commandments in Kentucky courthouses, because of their different consequences and public reactions.

Ultimately, what divides the justices, and sometimes the Court and the country, has less to do with interpretivism and noninterpretivism than fundamentally rival political philosophies and views of the role of the Court in American politics. It is not just that constitutional interpretation draws on the text, structure, history, doctrines, practices, and moral and political philosophy that is important, but how these sources and modes of analysis are employed. Admittedly, as Justice Scalia has noted, there may be a "sense of dissatisfaction" with finding that we "do not yet have an agreed-upon theory" of constitutional interpretation. "But it should come as no surprise."[25] That conclusion has also led Judge Richard Posner of the Court of Appeals for the Seventh Circuit, a prolific author and advocate of pragmatism, to argue against the need for specialized constitutional theories to justify legal doctrines, and for more empirical research into the socioeconomic complexities underlying legal controversies.[26] To be sure, there is no denying that in constitutional politics there are no simple solutions but instead an invitation for reflection and enduring political struggles.

NOTES

1. See Willard Hurst, "The Role of History," in *Supreme Court and Supreme Law*, ed. Edmond Cahn (New York: Clarion Books, 1971); Charles Miller, *The Supreme Court and the Uses of History* (Cambridge, MA: Harvard University Press, 1969); and G. Edward White, "The Arrival of History in Constitutional Scholarship," 88 *Virginia Law Review* 485 (2002).

2. William Rehnquist, "The Notion of a Living Constitution," in David M. O'Brien, ed., *Judges on Judging*, 3d ed., (Washington, DC: C.Q. Press, 2009).

3. See Paul Rosen, *The Supreme Court and Social Science* (Urbana: University of Illinois Press, 1972); and David O'Brien, "The Seduction of the Judiciary: Social Science and the Courts," 64 *Judicature* 8 (1980).

4. See Edward S. Corwin, *The "Higher Law" Background of American Constitutional Law* (Ithaca, NY: Cornell University Press, 1955); Thomas Grey, "Do We Have an Unwritten Constitution," 27 *Stanford Law Review* 703 (1975); Robert Goldwin and William Schambra, eds., *How Does the Constitution Secure Rights?* (Washington, DC: American Enterprise Institute, 1985).

5. See Ronald Dworkin, *Taking Rights Seriously* (Cambridge, MA: Harvard University Press, 1977), 149; Ronald Dworkin, *A Matter of Principle* (Cambridge, MA: Harvard University Press, 1985); and Ronald Dworkin, *Law's Empire* (Cambridge, MA: Harvard University Press, 1986).

6. See G. Edward White, "Reflections on the Role of the Supreme Court: The Contemporary Debate and the Lessons of History," 63 *Judicature* 162 (1979); and Philip Bobbit, *Constitutional Fate* (New York: Oxford University Press, 1982).

7. Henry Hart, "Foreword: The Time Chart of the Justices," 73 *Harvard Law Review* 84 (1959).

8. Charles Black, "Old and New Ways in Judicial Review," address given at Bowdoin College, 1957.

9. Terrance Sandalow, "Constitutional Interpretation," 79 *Michigan Law Review* 1033 (1981).

10. Harry Wellington, "Common Law Rules and Constitutional Double Standards: Some Notes on Adjudication," 83 *Yale Law Journal* 221 (1973). See also Michael Perry, *The Constitution, the Courts, and Human Rights* (New Haven, CT: Yale University Press, 1982); and Michael Perry, *Morality, Politics & Law* (New York: Oxford University Press, 1988).

11. Owen Fiss, "Objectivity and Interpretation," 34 *Stanford Law Review* 739 (1982).

12. Dworkin, *Taking Rights Seriously*, 149.

13. Kenneth Karst, "The Freedom of Intimate Association," 89 *Yale Law Journal* 624

(1980); and Richard Richards, "Human Rights as the Unwritten Constitution: The Problem of Change and Stability in Constitutional Interpretation," 4 *University of Dayton Law Review* 295 (1979).

14. Michael Michelman, "In Pursuit of Constitutional Welfare Rights: One View of Rawls's Theory of Justice," 121 *University of Pennsylvania Law Review* 962 (1979).

15. Alexander Bickel, *The Supreme Court and the Idea of Progress* (New York: Harper & Row, 1970).

16. See David O'Brien, " 'The Imperial Judiciary:' Of Paper Tigers and Socio-Legal Indicators," 2 *Journal of Law & Politics* 1 (1985).

17. John Ely, *Democracy and Distrust* (Cambridge, MA: Harvard University Press, 1980), 58.

18. Robert Bork, "Tradition and Morality in Constitutional Law," in *Judges on Judging*, ed. O'Brien.

19. William Brennan, Jr., "The Constitution of the United States: Contemporary Ratification," speech given at Georgetown University, Oct. 12, 1985, reprinted in *Judges on Judging*, ed. O'Brien.

20. Charles Black, Jr., *Structure and Relationship in Constitutional Law* (Baton Rouge: Louisiana University Press, 1969).

21. See Laurence Tribe, "The Puzzling Persistence of Process-Based Constitutional Theories," 89 *Yale Law Journal* 1063 (1980); and Mark Tushnet, "Darkness on the Edge of Town: The Contributions of John Hart Ely," 89 *Yale Law Journal* 1037 (1980).

22. Ely, *Democracy and Distrust*, 181.

23. See David O'Brien, "Judicial Review and Constitutional Politics: Theory and Practice," 48 *University of Chicago Law Review* 1052 (1981).

24. See, e.g., Stephen Breyer, *Active Liberty* (New York: Knopf, 2005); Richard Posner, *Law, Pragmatism, and Democracy* (Cambridge, MA: Harvard University Press, 2003); and Cass Sunstein, *One Case at a Time: Judicial Minimalism on the Supreme Court* (Cambridge, MA: Harvard University Press, 1999).

25. Antonin Scalia, "Originalism: The Lesser Evil," 57 *Cincinnati Law Review* 850 (1989), 865, reprinted in *Judges on Judging*, ed. O'Brien.

26. Richard A. Posner, "Against Constitutional Theory," 73 *New York University Law* 1 (1998). See also R. Posner, *The Problematics of Moral and Legal Theory* (Cambridge, MA: Belknap Press, 1999).

SELECTED BIBLIOGRAPHY

Agresto, John. *The Supreme Court and Constitutional Democracy.* Ithaca, NY: Cornell University Press, 1984.

Barber, Sotirios, and Fleming, James, *Constitutional Interpretation: The Basic Questions.* New York: Oxford University Press, 2007.

Bickel, Alexander. *The Supreme Court and the Idea of Progress.* New York: Harper & Row, 1970.

———. *The Least Dangerous Branch.* New York: Bobbs-Merrill, 1961.

Black, Charles, Jr. *Decision According to Law.* New York: W. W. Norton & Company, 1981.

————. *Structure and Relationship in Constitutional Law.* Baton Rouge: Louisiana State University Press, 1969.

————. *A New Birth of Freedom: Human Rights, Named and Unnamed.* New York: Grosset/Putnam, 1997.

Bloom, Lackland H. *Methods of Interpretation: How the Supreme Court Reads the Constitution.* New York: Oxford University Press, 2009.

Bobbitt, Philip. *Constitutional Fate.* New York: Oxford University Press, 1982.

Bork, Robert. *Coercing Virtue: The Worldwide Rule of Judges.* Washington, DC: American Enterprise Institute, 2003.

Breyer, Stephen. *Active Liberty: Interpreting Our Democratic Constitution.* New York: Knopf, 2005.

Choper, Jesse. *Judicial Review and the National Political Process.* Chicago: University of Chicago Press, 1980.

Corwin, Edward. *The "Higher Law" Background of American Constitutional Law.* Ithaca, NY: Cornell University Press, 1955.

Delgado, Richard, and Stefancic, Jean. *Critical Race Theory: The Cutting Edge.* Philadelphia: Temple University Press, 1999.

Devins, Neal, and Fisher, Louis. *The Democratic Constitution.* New York: Oxford University Press, 2004.

Dworkin, Ronald. *Taking Rights Seriously.* Cambridge, MA: Harvard University Press, 1977.

————. *Law's Empire.* Cambridge, MA: Harvard University Press, 1986.

————. *Freedom's Law: The Moral Reading of the American Constitution.* Cambridge, MA: Harvard University Press, 1996.

————. *Justice in Robes,* Cambridge, MA: Belkap, 2006.

Ely, John. *Democracy and Distrust.* Cambridge, MA: Harvard University Press, 1980.

Erickson, Rosemary, and Simon, Rita. *The Use of Social Science Data in Supreme Court Decisions.* Urbana: University of Illinois Press, 1998.

Farber, Daniel, and Sherry, Suzanna. *Beyond All Reason: The Radical Assault on Truth in American Law.* New York: Oxford University Press, 1997.

————. *Desperately Seeking Certainty: The Misguided Quest for Constitutional Foundations.* Chicago: University of Chicago Press, 2003.

————. *Judgement Calls: Principle and Politics in Constitutional Law.* New York: Oxford University Press, 2008.

Fisher, Louis. *Constitutional Dialogues.* Princeton, NJ: Princeton University Press, 1988.

Fleming, James. *Securing Constitutional Democracy.* Chicago: University of Chicago Press, 2006.

George, Robert P. *In Defense of Natural Law.* New York: Oxford University Press, 1999.

Gerber, Scott. *To Secure These Rights: The Declaration of Independence and Constitutional Interpretation.* New York: New York University Press, 1995.

Goldstein, Leslie, ed. *Feminist Jurisprudence.* Lanham, MD: Rowman & Littlefield, 1992.

Hershovitz, Scott, ed. *Exploring Law's Empire: The Jurisprudence of Ronald Dworkin.* New York: Oxford University Press, 2007.

Hoffman, Daniel. *Our Elusive Constitution: Silences, Paradoxes, Priorities.* Albany: University of New York Press, 1996.

Kahn, Paul. *Legitimacy and History.* New Haven, CT: Yale University Press, 1992.

Kairys, David. *The Politics of Law.* 3d ed. New York: Pantheon Books, 1998.

Kersch, Ken I. *Constructing Civil Liberties: Discontinuities in the Development of American Constitutional Law.* New York: Cambridge University Press, 2004.

Levinson, Sanford. *Constitutional Faith.* Princeton, NJ: Princeton University Press, 1988.

Lipkin, Justin. *Constitutional Resolutions: Pragmatism and the Role of Judicial Review in American Constitutionalism.* Durham, NC: Duke University Press, 2000.

MacKinnon, Catharine, *Toward a Feminist Theory of the State.* Cambridge, MA: Harvard University Press, 1989.

———. *Feminism Unmodified.* Cambridge, MA: Harvard University Press, 1987.

Miller, Charles. *The Supreme Court and the Uses of History,* Cambridge, MA: Harvard University Press, 1969.

Murphy, Walter, *Constitutional Democracy: Creating and Maintaining a Just Political Order.* Baltimore, MD: Johns Hopkins University Press, 2007.

O'Brien, David M., ed. *Judges on Judging,* 3d ed. Washington, DC: C.Q. Press, 2009.

Peretti, Terri Jennings. *In Defense of a Political Court.* Princeton, NJ: Princeton University Press, 1999.

Posner, Richard. *The Problems of Jurisprudence.* Cambridge, MA: Harvard University Press, 1990.

———. *The Problematics of Moral and Legal Theory.* Cambridge, MA: Belknap Press, 1999.

———. *Law, Pragmatism, and Democracy.* Cambridge, MA: Harvard University, Press, 2003.

Powell, H. Jefferson. *Constitutional Conscience: The Moral Dimension of Judicial Decision.* Chicago: University of Chicago Press, 2008.

Redish, Martin. *The Constitution as Political Structure.* New York: Oxford University Press, 1995.

Ripstein, Arthur, ed. *Ronald Dworkin.* New York: Cambridge University Press, 2007.

Rosen, Paul. *The Supreme Court and Social Science.* Urbana: University of Illinois Press, 1972.

Seidman, Louis, and Tushnet, Mark. *Remnants of Belief: Contemporary Constitutional Issues.* New York: Oxford University Press, 1996.

Simmons, Nigel. *Law as a Moral Idea.* New York: Oxford University Press, 2007.

Smith, Rogers. *Liberalism and American Constitutional Law.* Cambridge, MA: Harvard University Press, 1985.

Strauss, David A. *The Living Constitution.* New York: Oxford University Press, 2010.

Sullivan, Michael. *Legal Pragmatism*. Bloomington: Indiana University Press, 2007.

Sunstein, Cass. *Radicals in Robes: Why Extreme Right-Wing Courts Are Wrong for America*. New York: Basic Books, 2005.

Tamanaha, Brian. *Law as a Means to an End: Threat to the Rule of Law*. New York: Cambridge University Press, 2006.

Tribe, Laurence. *Constitutional Choices*. Cambridge, MA: Harvard University Press, 1985.

———. *The Invisible Consitution*. New York: Oxford University Press, 2008.

Tribe, Laurence, and Dorf, Michael. *On Reading the Constitution*. Cambridge, MA: Harvard University Press, 1991.

Tushnet, Mark. *Red, White, and Blue: A Critical Analysis of Constitutional Law*. Cambridge, MA: Harvard University Press, 1988.

Vermeule, Adrian. *Judging under Uncertainty: An Institutional Theory of Legal Interpretation*. Cambridge, MA: Harvard University Press, 2006.

Weinrub, Lloyd. *Legal Reason: The Use of Analogy in Legal Argument*. New York: Cambridge University Press, 2005.

Wellington, Harry. *Interpreting the Constitution*. New Haven, CT: Yale University Press, 1990.

White, James. *Justice as Translation*. Chicago: University of Chicago Press, 1990.

———. *When Words Lose Their Meaning*. Chicago: University of Chicago Press, 1984.

2

LAW AND POLITICS IN THE SUPREME COURT: JURISDICTION AND DECISION-MAKING PROCESS

The Supreme Court is the only federal court in the United States to have complete power to decide what to decide, that is, which cases to hear. This power enables the Court to set its own agenda as well as to manage its docket. Like other courts, the Supreme Court, however, must await issues brought by lawsuits; it does not initiate its own. Also, like other social institutions, it is affected by social change. One hundred fifty years ago, the Court's docket did not include issues of personal privacy raised by electronic surveillance and computer data banks, for instance, or controversies over abortion and the patenting of organic life forms. As technology develops and society changes, courts respond. Law evolves more or less quickly in response to social change. Another change occurring over the past several decades has been a substantial increase in the number of cases, the caseload, sent to the Court. Unable to hear them all, the Court was given by Congress the power to pick which issues it will decide outside of those arising under Article III. The Court now functions like a roving commission in responding to social forces.

A | *Jurisdiction and Justiciable Controversies*

Jurisdiction is the authorized power of a court to hear a case and to exercise judicial review. The Court's jurisdiction derives from three sources: (1) Article III of the Constitution, which defines the Court's original jurisdiction; (2) congressional legislation, providing the basis for hearing appeals of lower courts' decisions, or appellate jurisdiction; and (3) the Court's own interpretation of 1 and 2 together with its own rules for accepting cases.

Article III of the Constitution provides that the judicial power extends to all federal questions, that is, "all Cases, in Law and Equity, arising under this Constitution, the Laws of the United States, and Treaties." The Court also has original jurisdiction over specific kinds of "cases or controversies": those affecting ambassadors and other public ministers and consuls; disputes to which the United States is a party; disputes between two or more states, disputes between a state and a citizen of another state, if a state waives its sovereign immunity under the Eleventh Amendment; and disputes between a state (or its citizens) and foreign countries. The Court today has only about ten cases each term (the first Monday in October through June) coming on original jurisdiction. Most involve states suing each other over land and water rights, and they tend to be rather complex and carried over for several terms before they are finally decided.

Congress establishes (and may change) the appellate jurisdiction of the federal judiciary, including the Supreme Court. Most cases used to come as direct appeals, requiring obligatory review. But as the caseload increased, Congress expanded the Court's discretionary jurisdiction by replacing appeals with petitions for *certiorari* (a petition asking a court to inspect the proceedings and decision of a lower court), which the Court may in its discretion grant or deny. Prior to the Judiciary Act of 1925, which broadened the Court's discretionary jurisdiction, appeals amounted to 80 percent of the docket and petitions for *certiorari*, less than 20 percent. Today, well over 99 percent of the docket comes on *certiorari*.

Although most cases now come as *certiorari* (*cert.*) petitions, Congress provides that appellate courts may submit a writ of certification to the Court, requesting the justices to clarify or "make more certain" a point of federal law. The Court receives only a handful of such cases each term. Congress also gave the Court the power to issue certain extraordinary writs, or orders. In a few cases, the Court may issue writs of *mandamus* and prohibition, ordering lower courts or public officials to either do something or refrain from some action. In addition, the Court has the power to grant writs of *habeas corpus* ("produce the body"), enabling it to review cases by prisoners who claim that their constitutional rights have been violated and they are unlawfully imprisoned.

Congress also established the practice of giving the poor, or the indigent, the right to file without the payment of fees. When filing an appeal or petition for *certiorari*, indigents may file an affidavit requesting that they be allowed to proceed *in forma pauperis* ("in the manner of a pauper,") without the usual filing fees and forms. The Court sets both the rules governing filing fees and the form that appeals, *cert.* petitions, and other documents must take. Except for indigents, the Court requires $300 for filing any case and another $100 if a case is granted oral argument. Indigents are exempt as well from the Court's rules specifying particular colors and lengths of paper for various kinds of filings. All *cert.* petitions, for instance, must have a white color, whereas opposing briefs are light orange. Any document filed by the federal government has a gray cover. No petition or appeal may exceed thirty pages, and for those few cases granted oral argument, briefs on the merits of cases are limited to fifty pages.

The Constitution and Congress thus stipulate the kinds of cases and controversies the Court may consider. Yet, as Charles Evans Hughes, who later became chief justice (1930–1941), candidly remarked, "We are under the Constitution, but the Constitution is what the Judges say it is."[1] The Court has developed its own doctrines for denying a large number of cases review and for setting its own agenda. Specifically, the Court considers whether it has jurisdiction over a "case or controversy," and then whether that dispute is justiciable, or capable of judicial resolution. Justices thus may, or may not, deny a case if it (1) lacks adverseness or (2) is brought by parties who lack "standing to sue," or poses issues that either (3) are not "ripe," (4) have become "moot," or (5) involve a "political question." What all this means is discussed below.

■ ADVERSENESS AND ADVISORY OPINIONS

The Court generally maintains that litigants, those involved in a lawsuit, must be real and adverse in seeking a decision that will resolve their dispute and not some hypothetical issue. The requirement of real and adverse parties means that the Court will not decide so-called friendly suits (when the parties do not have adverse interests in the out-

Avenues of Appeal:
The Two Main Routes to the Supreme Court

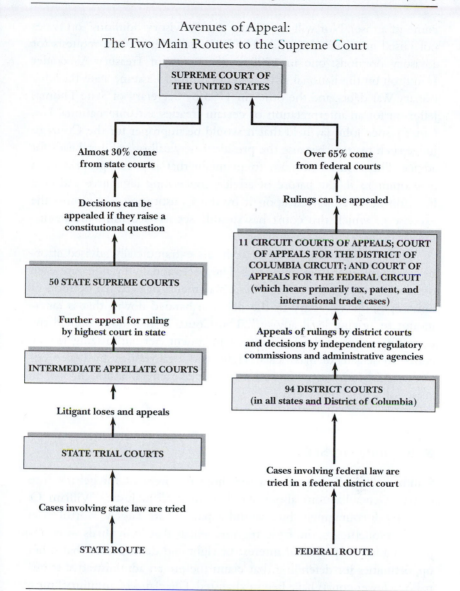

SUPREME COURT OF THE UNITED STATES

Almost 30% come from state courts

Over 65% come from federal courts

Decisions can be appealed if they raise a constitutional question

Rulings can be appealed

11 CIRCUIT COURTS OF APPEALS; COURT OF APPEALS FOR THE DISTRICT OF COLUMBIA CIRCUIT; AND COURT OF APPEALS FOR THE FEDERAL CIRCUIT (which hears primarily tax, patent, and international trade cases)

50 STATE SUPREME COURTS

Further appeal for ruling by highest court in state

Appeals of rulings by district courts and decisions by independent regulatory commissions and administrative agencies

INTERMEDIATE APPELLATE COURTS

94 DISTRICT COURTS (in all states and District of Columbia)

Litigant loses and appeals

STATE TRIAL COURTS

Cases involving state law are tried

Cases involving federal law are tried in a federal district court

STATE ROUTE

FEDERAL ROUTE

Note: In addition, some cases come directly to the Supreme Court from trial courts when they involve reapportionment or civil rights disputes. Appeals from the Court of Military Appeals also go directly to the Supreme Court. A few cases come on "original jurisdiction" and involve disputes between state governments.

come of a case). Nor will the Court give "advisory opinions" on issues not raised in an actual lawsuit. The Jay Court denied two requests for advisory opinions: one in 1790 by Secretary of Treasury Alexander Hamilton on the national government's power to assume state Revolutionary War debts, and the other in 1793 by Secretary of State Thomas Jefferson for an interpretation of certain treaties and international law. Chief Justice John Jay held that it would be improper for the Court to judge such matters, because the president may call on cabinet heads for advice. The Court continues to maintain that it is inappropriate "to give opinions in the nature of advice concerning legislative action, a function never conferred upon it by the Constitution and against the exercise of which this court has steadily set its face from the beginning."[2]

Historically, justices have nevertheless extrajudicially advised attorneys, congressmen, and presidents. They occasionally even accuse each other of including in opinions *dicta* (statements of personal opinion or philosophy not necessary to the decision handed down) that is tantamount to "giving legal advice."[3] The Court, furthermore, upheld the constitutionality of the Declaratory Judgment Act authorizing federal courts to declare, or make clear, rights and legal relationships even before a legislature has mandated a law to take effect, although only in "cases of actual controversy."[4]

■ STANDING TO SUE

Standing, like adverseness, is a threshold requirement for getting into court. "Generalizations about standing to sue," as Justice William O. Douglas discouragingly, but candidly, put it, "are largely worthless as such."[5] Nonetheless, the basic requirement is that individuals show injury to a legally protected interest or right and demonstrate that other opportunities for defending that claim (before an administrative tribunal or a lower court) have been exhausted. The claim of an injury "must be of a personal and not official nature" and of "some specialized interest of [the individual's] own to vindicate, apart from political concerns which belong to it."[6] The interest must be real as opposed to speculative or hypothetical.

The injuries and legal interests claimed traditionally turned on a showing of personal or proprietary damage. Typically, plaintiffs had suffered some "pocketbook" or monetary injury. But in the last fifty years, individuals have sought standing to represent nonmonetary injuries and "the public interest."

The law of standing is a combination of judge-made law and congressional legislation, as interpreted by the Court. During Earl Warren's tenure as chief justice (1953–1969) the Court substantially lowered the threshold for standing and permitted more litigation of public policy issues. *Frothingham v. Mellon*, 262 U.S. 447 (1923), was the leading case on taxpayer suits until it was overturned in *Flast v. Cohen* (1968) (see excerpt below). In *Frothingham*, the Taft Court had denied taxpayers standing to challenge the constitutionality of federal legislation. Mrs. Frothingham, a taxpayer, had attacked Congress's appropriation of federal funds to the states for a maternal and infant care program. She claimed that Congress exceeded its power and intruded on "the reserved rights of the states" under the Tenth Amendment of the Constitution. Writing for the Court, Justice George Sutherland avoided confronting the merits of her claim by denying standing. He did so on the grounds that an individual taxpayer's interest in the financing of federal programs is "comparatively minute and indeterminable," when viewed in light of all taxpayers. Frothingham's "injury" was neither direct nor immediate and the issue raised was basically "political, not judicial." As Sutherland put it,

> [T]he relation of a taxpayer of the United States to the Federal Government is very different [from that relationship with state and local governments]. His interest in the moneys of the Treasury—partly realized from taxation and partly from other sources—is shared with millions of others; is comparatively minute and indeterminable; and the effect upon future taxation, or any payment out of the funds, so remote, fluctuating and uncertain, that no basis is afforded for an appeal to the preventive powers of a court of equity.

To gain standing, according to Sutherland, a taxpayer "must be able to show not only that the statute is invalid but that he has sustained . . . some direct injury as the result of its enforcement, and not merely that he suffers in some indefinite way in common with people generally."

Frothingham's "direct injury" test was met in *Pierce v. Society of Sisters*, 268 U.S. 510 (1925). There, a religious school won a court order barring the enforcement of Oregon's 1922 constitutional amendment requiring children between the ages of eight and sixteen to attend public schools. The Court affirmed on the grounds that the law directly damages the business and property interests of the school and because it "unreasonably interferes with the liberty of parents and guardians to direct the upbringing and education of children under their control."

The federal government relied on *Frothingham* to provide an absolute barrier to subsequent federal taxpayer suits until the Warren Court made an exception to that doctrine in *Flast v. Cohen* (1968) (see excerpt below). In his opinion for the Court, Chief Justice Warren created a two-pronged standard for granting standing to federal taxpayers to challenge

Jurisdictional Map of the U.S. Courts of Appeal and
U.S. District Courts

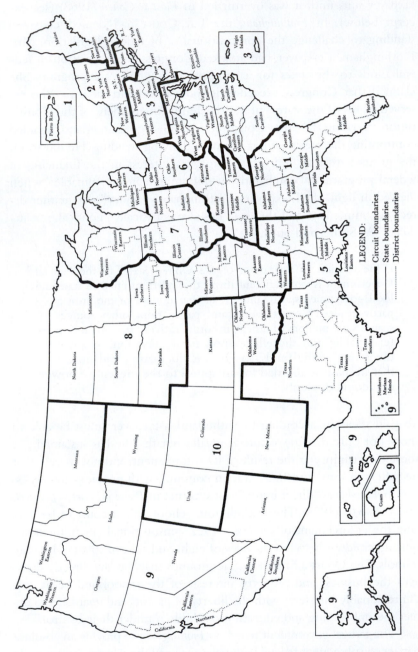

Note: The court of appeals for the federal circuit and the District of Columbia
circuit are located in the District of Columbia.
(*Administrative Office of the U.S. Courts, Washington, DC.*)

public expenditures for religious schools: taxpayers must show a logical relationship between their status as taxpayers and the challenged congressional statute as well as a connection between that status and the "precise nature of the constitutional infringement alleged."

The Burger Court (1969–1986) and the Rehnquist Court (1986–2005) tightened the requirements for standing in some cases, but relaxed them in others. In 1972, in two sharply divided decisions, the Burger Court denied standing to a group challenging military surveillance of lawful political protests in public places and to the Sierra Club when challenging the construction of a ski resort in Mineral King National Park. In both *Laird v. Tatum*, 408 U.S. 1 (1972), and *Sierra Club v. Morton*, 405 U.S. 727 (1972), a bare majority found that the groups failed to show a "personal stake in the outcome" of the litigation. The following year, however, standing was granted to a group of law students attacking a proposed surcharge on railroad freight. The students contended that the surcharge would discourage the recycling of bottles and cans, and thus contribute to environmental pollution. In *United States v. Students Challenging Regulatory Agency Procedure (SCRAP)*, 412 U.S. 669 (1973), the Burger Court granted standing, observing that "[a]esthetic and environmental well-being, like economic well-being, are important ingredients of the quality of life in our society, and the fact that particular environmental interests are shared by the many rather than the few does not make them less deserving of legal protection through the judicial process."

Plaintiffs, those bringing suit, must still claim a personal injury, but they could now act as surrogates for special interest groups. The personal injuries claimed thus embrace a public injury. Congress at the same time expanded the principle even more by providing that any individual "adversely affected or aggrieved" may challenge administrative decisions. Health, safety, and environmental legislation passed in the 1970s mandated such "citizen suits" and right to judicial review of regulatory action. Even when legislation does not provide for the citizen suits, individuals may claim personal injuries, or a "private cause of action," to gain access to the courts and to force agency compliance with the law.

The more conservative Burger and Rehnquist Courts restricted standing requirements in several ways. First, they refused to recognize new interests and injuries in granting standing. In *Linda R. S. v. Richard D.*, 410 U.S. 614 (1973), for instance, an unwed mother sought enforcement of child support under the Texas Penal Code because the local prosecutor refused to enforce the statute against fathers of illegitimate children. A majority of the Court ruled that she had no recognizable injury and no standing because she could not prove that payments stopped because that particular statute was unenforced.

■ The Development of Law

Other Important Rulings on Standing

CASE	VOTE	RULING
Schlesinger v. Reservists Committee to Stop the War, 418 U.S 208 (1974)	6:3	Held that members of an organization of present and past members of the military reserves opposed to the Vietnam War had no standing to file a class action suit against the secretary

of defense attacking the constitutionality of members of Congress holding commissions in the reserves and voting on appropriations for the war, as an alleged violation of Article I, Section 6, Clause 2, which declares that "no person holding any office under the United States, shall be a Member of either House during his continuance in office."

United States v. Richardson, 418 U.S. 166 (1974)	5:4	Denied taxpayer standing to bring suit against Congress's secret funding for the Central Intelligence Agency, as an alleged violation of Article I, Se-

tion 9, Clause 7, which provides that "no Money shall be drawn from the Treasury, but in Consequence of Appropriations made by Law; and a regular Statement of Account of the Receipts and Expenditures of all public money shall be published from time to time."

Warth v. Seldin, 422 U.S. 490 (1975)	5:4	Denied standing to various organizations in Rochester, New York, seeking to sue officials of the suburban town

of Penfield, claiming that the latter's zoning ordinance excluded low- and moderate-income persons from living in the town and violated their rights under the Bill of Rights. The Court held that the individuals and organizations failed to show that they had been "personally" injured.

Simon v. Eastern Kentucky Welfare Rights Organization, 426 U.S. 26 (1976)	9:0	Denied standing to indigents seeking to challenge federal tax regulations reducing the amount of free medical care hospitals must provide in order to receive certain tax benefits.

CASE	VOTE	RULING
City of Los Angeles v. Lyons, 461 U.S. 95 (1983)	5:4	Held that an arrestee had standing to sue the city for damages incurred as a result of police subjecting him to a "choke hold," but that he had no

standing to seek an injunction against the police practice of using choke holds, because he failed to show that he might ever be subjected to a choke hold again.

| *Allen v. Wright*, 468 U.S. 737 (1984) | 5:3 | Denied standing to parents of black children attending public schools in districts around the country tha were |

in the process of desegregation to sue various government officials and present their contention that the IRS failed to fulfill its obligation under the law to deny tax-exempt status to private schools engaged in racial discrimination.

| *Renne v. Geary*, 501 U.S. 312 (1991) | 7:2 | Held that a challenge to a section of California's constitution, which prohibits political parties from endorsing |

candidates in nonpartisan elections for judgeships and local government offices, was nonjusticiable because members of the San Francisco County Republican and Democratic Central committees did not have standing and failed to present a ripe case in challenging the state's restrictions as a violation of their First Amendment freedoms. Justices Blackmun and Marshall dissented.

| *Lujan v. Defenders of Wildlife*, 504 U.S. 555 (1992) | 7:2 | Writing for the Court, Justice Scalia denied standing to two environmentalists to bring a suit because they failed to show "imminent injury," or |

that they were inimmediate danger of suffering a concrete harm that supported their challenge to federal funding for projects in foreign countries, under the Endangered Species Act of 1973. Although Justice Stevens concurred, he would have granted standing, as would have dissenting Justices Blackmun and O'Connor.

(continues)

■ THE DEVELOPMENT OF LAW
Other Important Rulings on Standing (continued)

CASE	VOTE	RULING

Wyoming v. Oklahoma, 6:3 | Expanded standing for states to
502 U.S. 437 (1992) | sue one another, under the dorman
| commerce clause theory, on the
grounds that one state's regulations diminished the tax revenues of another. Dissenting Chief Justice Rehnquist and Justices Scalia and Thomas denounced the majority's expansive interpretation of standing under the commerce clause and warned that the ruling would invite a flood of litigation from the states.

Northeastern Florida 7:2 | Held that a building association had
Chapter of the Associated | standing to challenge an affirmative
General Contractors of | action set-aside program for contrac-
America v. City of Jack- | tors, even though during the course
sonville, Florida, 508 | of the litigation the city had repealed
U.S. 656 (1993) | its program and the building associa-
| tion did not pre-sent any evidence
that its members, in the absence of the program, would have received building contracts set aside for women and minorities. Justices Blackmun and O'Connor dissented.

Bennett v. Spear, 520 9:0 | Held that property owners, no less
U.S. 154 (1997) | than environmentalists, may assert
| standing to bring "citizen suits" under
the Endangered Species Act, and thereby challenge proposed environmental regulations. Writing for the Court, Justice Scalia ruled that the act's permitting "any person" to sue should be broadly interpreted because "the overall subject matter of this legislation is the environment . . . a matter in which it is common to think all persons have an interest." As a result, landowners have new legal standing to challenge environmental regulations.

Raines v. Byrd, 521 7:2 | Writing for the Court, Chief Justice
U.S. 811 (1997) | Rehnquist held that several members
| of Congress who challenged the con-
stitutionality of the Line Item Veto Act of 1996, delegating to the president the power of line-item vetoes, did not have standing to sue, because they did not assert any personal injury and "the institutional injury [to

Congress] they allege[d] is wholly abstract and widely dispersed." Dissenting Justices Stevens and Breyer would have granted standing and reached the merits presented.

CASE	VOTE	RULING

Friends of the Earth,   7:2   Upheld the right of Friends of the
Inc. v. Laidlaw Envi-   Earth, Inc., to sue Laidlaw Environ-
ronmental Services,   mental Services for failing to comply
528 U.S. 167 (2000)   with the Clean Water Act by impermissibly dumping mercury into a
South Carolina river on 489 occasions from 1987 to 1995. Writing for the Court, Justice Ginsburg held that the group had shown sufficient personal injury from their loss of enjoyment of the river to gain standing to sue without also having to prove "direct injury" to the river. The test for standing, in her words, is "not injury to the environment but injury to the plaintiff." Moreover, Justice Ginsburg ruled that the fact that fines won under such citizen suits go to the federal government, not to the individuals bringing the suits, does not diminish the personal injury at stake or deprive plaintiffs of standing. Justices Scalia and Thomas dissented.

Alexander v.   5:4   Writing for the Court, Justice Scalia
Sandoval, 532   held that individuals do not have
U.S. 275 (2001)   standing to sue in order to enforce
compliance with Title VI of the Civil
Rights Act, which bars state and local governments from spending federal funds in a discriminatory manner, unless they can show that the *intent* of the institution—a state, school district, hospital, etc.—was to discriminate. Previously, the Department of Justice and federal courts had held that, in most cases, individuals could sue upon showing that the *effect* of a particular practice or policy—hiring or admissions rules, for example—worked to disadvantage minorities and women. Thus, the threshold for standing for private individuals to enforce state and local government compliance with Title VI was raised and the filing of so-called disparate-impact lawsuits limited. Justices Stevens, Souter, Ginsburg, and Breyer dissented.

Palazzolo v. Rhode   5:4   Writing for the Court, Justice
Island, 533   Stevens held that Massachusetts
U.S. 606 (2001)   had standingto sue the EPA (EPA)
over its failure to regulate greenhouse
emissions. Justice Stevens reasoned that the state owned a great deal of the territory affected and had the sovereign prerogative to force reductions in the emissions, as well as that the EP Act granted a procedural

(continues)

■ The Development of Law
Other Important Rulings on Standing (continued)

right to challenge the EPA's rulemaking as arbitrary and capricious, since the state's risk was both "actual" and "imminent." Chief Justice Roberts and Justices Scalia, Thomas, and Alito dissented.

CASE	VOTE	RULING
Massachusetts v. *Environmental Protection* *Agency,* 549 U.S. 497 (2007)	6:3	Writing for the Court, Justice Kennedy held that once property owners take title to property that includes land-use restrictions, they have standing to challenge those

restrictions, even if the restrictions were imposed years earlier. In Justice Kennedy's words, the government may not be relieved "of its obligation to defend any action restricting land use, no matter how extreme or unreasonable." Although inviting more challenges to environmental regulations, on the merits the Court reaffirmed that to prevail such challenges must demonstrate that the owner was deprived of all economic value of the land. Justice Ginsburg, joined by Justices Souter and Breyer, dissented, contending that the case was not "ripe" for decision.

In *Paul v. Davis*, 424 U.S. 693 (1976), the Court's majority rejected a claim of injury to personal reputation by an individual who objected to the circulation of a flyer to local merchants that carried his photograph along with that of other alleged "active shoplifters." Rehnquist dismissed the claim out of hand. But Justice William Brennan in dissent responded that "[t]he Court by mere fiat and with no analysis wholly excludes personal interest in reputation from the ambit of 'life, liberty, of property' under the Fifth and Fourteenth Amendments, thus rendering due process concerns *never* applicable to the official stigmatization, however, arbitrary."

The Court went even further with its reinterpretation of the application of *Flast*'s test for taxpayer suits in *Valley Forge Christian College v. Americans United for Separation of Church and State, Inc.* (1982) (see excerpt below). And a bare majority of the Roberts Court (2005–) further limited taxpayers' standing to challenge federal policies under *Flast v. Cohen* in *Hein v. Freedom from Religion Foundation, Inc.* (2007) (excerpted below). Although declining to overrule *Flast*, writing for the majority Justice Alito limited *Flast* to permit taxpayer suits under the First Amendment (dis)establishment clause to challenges to congressional appropriations, but not to general expenditures for policies of the executive branch. Notably, concurring Justice Scalia, joined by Justice Thomas, would have overturned *Flast*. By contrast, Justice Souter, joined by Justices Stevens, Ginsburg, and Breyer, dissented and would have granted standing to challenge President George W. Bush's faith-based initiatives.

Almost two decades after the Court liberalized the law of standing so as to allow citizens' suits for environmental damages, a majority of the Rehnquist Court tightened standing requirements by raising new obstacles for citizens bringing environmental lawsuits. Writing for the majority in *Lujan v. Defenders of Wildlife*, 504 U.S. 555 (1992) (see excerpt below), Justice Scalia denied two environmentalists standing because they failed to show "imminent injury," or that they were in immediate danger of suffering a concrete harm that supported their filing a suit under the Endangered Species Act of 1973. Although Justice Stevens concurred, he would have granted standing, as would have the two dissenters, Justices Blackmun and O'Connor.

In another important ruling on standing, in *Northeastern Florida Chapter of the Associated General Contractors of America v. City of Jacksonville, Florida*, 508 U.S. 656 (1993) (see Vol. 2, Ch. 12), the Rehnquist Court made it easier for whites to gain standing to challenge affirmative action and minority set-aside programs. With Justices O'Connor and Blackmun dissenting, the Court held that a building association could challenge a city's set-aside program, even though during the course of the litigation the city had repealed its program. Writing for the majority, Justice Thomas held that in asserting standing to sue a building association did not have to show that any of its members, in the absence of the program, would have received building contracts set aside for women and minorities. While the ruling makes it easier to bring suits attacking set-aside and affirmative action programs, the decision more generally invites lawsuits against governments over the administration of benefit programs by individuals who need not show they were actually denied or would have obtained benefits.

In *Wyoming v. Oklahoma*, 502 U.S. 437 (1992), however, a majority of the Rehnquist Court expanded standing for states to challenge the constitutionality of other states' regulations under the commerce clause on the grounds those regulations diminished the state's tax revenues. In order to promote local jobs and to increase tax revenues, in 1986 Oklahoma enacted a law requiring its public utilities to purchase at least 10 percent of the coal they used from mines within the state. As a result, Oklahoma's public utilities purchased less Wyoming-mined coal, and Wyoming lost revenues from severance taxes on coal that would have otherwise been sold to Oklahoma's public utilities. Writing for the Court, Justice White struck down Oklahoma's statute as a violation of the Commerce Clause, which "prohibits economic protectionism—that is, regulatory measures designed to benefit in-state economic interests by burdening out-of-state competitors." In doing so, he held that states could invoke the Court's original jurisdiction, granted in Article III, and rejected Oklahoma's argument that Wyoming was neither engaged in interstate commerce nor had asserted an injury or interest covered by the commerce clause. "It is beyond peradventure," Justice White claimed, "that Wyoming has raised a claim of 'sufficient seriousness and dignity.' Oklahoma, acting in its sovereign capacity, passed the act, which directly affects Wyoming's ability to collect severance tax revenues, an action undertaken in its sovereign capacity." Having granted Wyoming standing to sue on the basis of its loss of revenue, Justice White struck down Oklahoma's law, observing that "when a state statute clearly discriminates against interstate commerce, it will be struck down, unless the discrimination is demonstrably justified by a valid factor unrelated to economic protectionism, see, e.g., *Maine v. Taylor*, 477 U.S. 131 (1986)" (Vol. 1, Ch. 7). By contrast, in a dissenting opinion joined by Chief Justice Rehnquist and Justice Thomas, Justice Scalia took strong exception to the majority's exercise of its original jurisdiction, granting of standing to Wyoming, and holding that a state's loss of revenue was within the "zone of interests" covered by the Commerce Clause. Wyoming, in his view, failed to assert a direct injury or an interest within the "zone-of-interests" embraced by the commerce clause; a state's interest in collecting taxes, as he put, was "only marginally related to the national market/free trade foundation of our jurisprudence" of applying the commerce clause in the absence of congressional legislation to strike state regulations deemed to burden interstate commerce.

Finally, the Court avoided the controversy over whether requiring school children to recite the Pledge of Allegiance violates the First Amendment by denying standing in *Elk Grove Unified School District v. Newdow* (2004) (excerpted below). Writing for the Court, Justice Stevens held that Michael A. Newdow, who challenged the policy on behalf of his daughter, even though he was not her legal custodian, lacked "prudential standing"—a Court-made rule. In other words, when legal claims are based on domestic relations law, a field largely left to states, "the prudent course is for the federal court to stay its hand rather than reach out to resolve a weighty question of federal constitutional law." But in concurring opinions, Chief Justice Rehnquist and Justices O'Connor and Thomas dismissed the ruling on "prudential standing" as "novel" and "like the proverbial excursion ticket—good for this day only." They would have granted standing and rejected Newdow's First Amendment claims. The controversy over the Pledge and the motto "In God We Trust" is nonetheless certain to continue and to return to the Court in another case.

■ RIPENESS AND MOOTNESS

With the doctrines of ripeness and mootness the Court wields a double-edged sword. Appellants, those appealing a lower court ruling, may discover that a case is dismissed because it was brought too early or because the issues are moot and the case was brought too late. Cases are usually rejected as not ripe if the injury claimed has not yet been realized, or if other avenues of appeal have not yet been exhausted. Petitioners raising a federal claim when appealing a state court ruling, for example, must exhaust all appeals in the state courts and the Court will not exercise jurisdiction until a "final judgment" has been rendered by the highest court in the state. The Court underscored its adherence to that rule when it dismissed *Johnson v. California*, 541 U.S. 428 (2004), because the petitioner failed to include (as required under the Court's rules) in an appendix to the petition for *certiorari* all opinions and final decisions in the case. Here, the state appellate court published only part of its decision (and, like other state and federal appellate courts in the last thirty years, withheld publication of part of its judgment, due to the mounting number of decisions annually handed down). Johnson included in the appendix only the published opinion and not the unpublished portion (which, like other unpublished opinions, was nonetheless available on Lexis). When the Court discovered from the unpublished opinion that the state appellate court's decision was not in all respects final, it dismissed the case. The Court thereby signaled petitioners to append any published and unpublished opinions of state high courts in order to establish that the decision appealed is indeed "final."

Alternatively, a case may be dismissed if pertinent facts or laws change so that there is no longer real adverseness or an actual case or controversy. The issue becomes moot because "there is no subject matter on which the judgment of the court can operate," and hence a ruling would not prove "conclusive" and final.[7] In practice both doctrines bend to the Court's will, because the requirement of ripeness permits the Court to avoid or delay deciding certain issues.

A finding of mootness likewise enables the Court to avoid, if not escape, deciding controversial political issues. *DeFunis v. Odegaard*, 416 U.S. 312 (1974), for example, involved a white student who was denied admission to the University of Washington Law School. The student claimed that the school's affirmative action program discriminated against him and allowed the entrance of minorities with lower LSAT test scores. After the trial judge ruled in his favor, he was admitted into law school but by the time his case reached the Supreme Court he was completing his final year and assured of graduation. Over four dissenters, the majority held that the case was moot. Yet, as the dissenters

■ THE DEVELOPMENT OF LAW

Class Action Suits

The Federal Rules of Civil Procedure provide for "class action" suits—suits filed by an individual for himself and for all others who have suffered the same injury. This rule enables individuals who have suffered small monetary damages to bring lawsuits that they might not otherwise have brought because of the prohibitively high cost of litigation. Specifically, Rule 23 provides that

> [o]ne or more members of a class may sue or be sued as representative parties on behalf of all only if (1) the class is so numerous that joinder of all members is impracticable, (2) there are questions of law or fact common to the class, (3) the claims or defenses of the representative parties are typical of the claims or defenses of the class, and (4) the representative parties will fairly and adequately protect the interests of the class....

> In any class action maintained under [this Rule], the court shall direct to the members of the class the best notice practicable under the circumstances, including individual notice to all members who can be identified.

The scope of this rule, however, was limited by *Eisen v. Carlisle & Jacquelin*, 417 U.S. 156 (1974), holding that when a representative of a class action

predicted, the issue would not go away. Within four years, the Burger Court reconsidered the issue of reverse discrimination in university affirmative action programs in *Regents of the University of California v. Bakke*, 438 U.S. 265 (1978) (see Vol. 2, Ch. 12).

The issue of mootness could have presented a problem when the Burger Court ruled on abortion in *Roe v. Wade*, 410 U.S. 113 (1973) (see Vol. 2, Ch. 11). There the Court struck down Texas's criminal statute prohibiting abortions, except when necessary to save a mother's life. When defending the law, the state's attorney general argued that the plaintiff was a single woman whose pregnancy had already resulted in birth by the time the case reached the Court, and hence her claim was moot. However, Justice Harry Blackmun, writing for the Court, rejected that view out of hand:

> [W]hen, as here, pregnancy is a significant fact in the litigation, the normal 266-day human gestation period is so short that the pregnancy will come to term before the usual appellate process is complete. If that termination makes a case moot, pregnancy litigation

suit refuses to pay the cost of giving actual notice to all reasonably identifiable class members, federal courts are required to dismiss the suit. Here, representatives had to notify 2,250,000 class members at a cost of $225,000.

In 2005, President George W. Bush signed into law the Class Action Fairness Act, which moved from state to federal courts large, interstate class-action lawsuits brought by consumers against businesses for fraud and faulty products. For over a decade business groups had lobbied for the legislation. They contended that businesses faced too many frivolous lawsuits and excessive punitive damage awards, and that lawyers filed such suits in states known to be favorable to consumers. Consumer advocates, trial lawyers, and the U.S. Judicial Conference opposed the law. They countered that the law would burden the federal judiciary; that federal courts were ill equipped to deal with such suits, which usually involve the application of state consumer protection laws; and that consumers would be discouraged from bringing such suits.

Under the law, class-action suits seeking $5 million or more remain in state courts only if the primary defendant and more than one-third of the plaintiffs are from the same state. If fewer than one-third of the plaintiffs are from the same state as the primary defendant, and more than $5 million is sought, the case goes to a federal court. In addition, the law also limits attorney fees when plaintiffs only receive discount coupons on products instead of financial settlements, by linking the fees to the coupon's redemption rate or the actual hours spent working on the case.

seldom will survive much beyond the trial stage, and appellate review will be effectively denied. Our law should not be that rigid. Pregnancy often comes more than once to the same woman, and in the general population, if man is to survive, it will always be with us. Pregnancy provides a classic justification for a conclusion of non-mootness. It truly could be "capable of repetition, yet evading review."

More recently, the Roberts Court dismissed as moot *Claiborne v. United States*, 551 U.S. 87 (2007), a case appealing an appellate court's reversal of a district court's sentencing of Mario Claiborne below the recommended mandatory federal sentencing guidelines, which the Court declared unconstitutional in *United States v. Booker*, 543 U.S. 220 (2005), in ruling that they are only advisory. Claiborne, a twenty-one-year-old convicted of selling cocaine, was sentenced to fifteen months in prison instead of the prescribed thirty-seven to forty-six months. But after serving his sentence, while his appeal was pending before the Court, he was shot to death. The Roberts Court thus dismissed his appeal and granted another case raising the issue of federal judges' discretion in sentencing, on which federal circuit courts are divided.

■ INSIDE THE COURT

Standing and the Connecticut Birth Control Cases

Between 1943 and 1965, the Court continually refused standing to individuals attacking the constitutionality of a late nineteenth-century Connecticut statute. The law prohibited virtually all single and married individuals from using contraceptives and physicians from giving advice about their use. In *Tileston v. Ullman*, 318 U.S. 44 (1943), a doctor sued charging that the statute prevented him from giving information to patients. But the Court ruled that he had no real interest or personal injury because he had not been arrested.

More than a decade later in *Poe v. Ullman*, 367 U.S. 497 (1961), a doctor, C. Lee Buxton, and a patient were likewise denied standing on the ground that the law had not been enforced for more than eighty years, even though the state had begun to close birth control clinics. This time the justices split five to four and only Chief Justice Warren and Justices Clark and Whittaker joined Justice Frankfurter's opinion for the Court (Justice Brennan concurred in the decision but not in the opinion). There, Frankfurter observed that

> [t]he Connecticut law prohibiting the use of contraceptives has been on the State's books since 1879. . . . During more than three-quarters of a century since its enactment, a prosecution for its violation seems never to have been initiated, save in [one] case. . . . Neither counsel nor our own researches have discovered any other attempt to enforce the prohibition of distribution or use of contraceptive devices by criminal process. The unreality of these law suits is illuminated by another circumstance. We were advised by counsel for appellants that contraceptives are commonly and notoriously sold in Connecticut drug stores. Yet no prosecutions are recorded. . . .
>
> The various doctrines of "standing," "ripeness," and "mootness," which this Court has evolved with particular, though not exclu-
>
> sive, reference to such cases are but several manifestations—each having its own "varied application"—of the primary conception that federal judicial power is to be exercised to strike down legislation, whether state or federal, only at the instance of one who is himself immediately harmed, or immediately threatened with harm, by the challenged action. . . .

By contrast, dissenting Justices Douglas, Harlan, and Stewart disagreed. Notably, Justice Harlan's dissent in *Poe v. Ullman* would have granted standing and reached the merits of the case in a lengthy and influential opinion, observing that

> I consider that this Connecticut legislation, as construed to apply to these appellants, violates the Fourteenth Amendment. I believe that a statute making it a criminal offense for married couples to use contraceptives is an intolerable and unjustifiable invasion of privacy in the conduct of the most intimate concerns of an individual's personal life. . . .

> [I]t is not the particular enumeration of rights in the first eight Amendments which spells out the reach of Fourteenth Amendment due process, but rather, as was suggested in another context long before the adoption of that Amendment, those concepts which are considered to embrace those rights "which are . . . fundamental; which belong . . . to the citizens of all free governments," *Corfield v. Coryell*, for "the purposes [of securing] which men enter into society," *Calder v. Bull*. Again and again this Court has resisted the notion that the Fourteenth Amendment is no more than a shorthand reference to what is explicitly set out elsewhere in the Bill of Rights. . . .

> Due process has not been reduced to any formula; its content cannot be determined by reference to any code. The best that can be said is that through the course of this Court's decisions it has represented the balance which our Nation, built upon postulates of respect for the liberty of the individual, has struck between that liberty and the demands of organized society. If the supplying of content to this Constitutional concept has of necessity been a rational process, it certainly has not been one where judges have felt free to roam where unguided speculation might take them. The balance of which I speak is the balance struck by this country, having regard to what history teaches are the traditions from which it developed as well as the traditions from which it broke. That tradition is a living thing. A decision of this Court which radically departs from it could not long survive, while a decision which builds on   what has survived is likely to be sound. No formula could serve as a substitute, in this area, for judgment and restraint. . .

> Precisely what is involved here is this: the State is asserting the right to enforce its moral judgment by intruding upon the most intimate details of the marital relation with the full power of the criminal law. Potentially, this could allow the deployment of all the inciden-tal machinery of the criminal law, arrests, searches and seizures; inevitably, it must mean at the very least the lodg-

(continues)

■ INSIDE THE COURT
Standing and the Connecticut Birth Control Cases (continued)

ing of criminal charges, a public trial, and testimony as to the *corpus delicti* [the body of crime]. . . . In sum, the statute allows the State to enquire into, prove and punish married people for the private use of their marital intimacy. . . .

I think the sweep of the Court's decisions, under both the Fourth and Fourteenth Amendments, amply shows that the Constitution protects the privacy of the home against all unreasonable intrusion of whatever character. . . .

Finally, after Dr. Buxton and Estelle Griswold, executive director of Planned Parenthood League of Connecticut, were tried and found guilty of prescribing contraceptives to a married couple, the Court in *Griswold v. Connecticut* (1965) (excerpted in Vol. 2, Ch. 4) struck down what Justice Potter Stewart called Connecticut's "uncommonly silly law." In his opinion for the Court, Justice Douglas explained why Buxton and Griswold were now granted standing:

The appellants were found guilty as accessories and fined $100 each, against the claim that the accessory statute as so applied violated the Fourteenth Amendment. . . . We think that appellants have standing to raise the constitutional rights of married people with whom they had a professional relationship. *Tileston v. Ullman*, is different, for there the plaintiff seeking to represent others asked for a declaratory judgment. In that situation, we thought that the requirements of standing should be strict, lest the standards of "case or controversy" in Article III of the Constitution become blurred. Here those doubts are removed by reason of a criminal conviction for serving married couples in violation of an aiding-and-abetting statute. Certainly the accessory should have standing to assert that the offense which he is charged with assisting is not, or cannot constitutionally be a crime.

Griswold was limited to the privacy and marital decisions of couples. Consequently, in *Eisenstadt v. Baird*, 405 U.S. 438 (1972), to gain standing to claim that single individuals also have a right to acquire and use contraceptives, a doctor arranged to be arrested after delivering a public lecture on contraceptives and handing out samples to single women in the audience. The Court accepted the case and ruled that single women also have the right to acquire and use contraceptives.

■ POLITICAL QUESTIONS

Even when the Court has jurisdiction over a properly framed suit, it may decline to rule because it decides that a case raises a "political question" that should be resolved by other political branches. Like other jurisdictional doctrines, the political question doctrine means what the justices say it means.

The doctrine has its origin in Chief Justice Marshall's observation in *Marbury v. Madison*, 5 U.S. 137 (1803) (see Ch. 1), that "[t]he province of the Court, is, solely, to decide on the rights of individuals. ... Questions in their nature political, or which are, by the constitution and laws, submitted to the executive can never be made in this Court." Yet as the French commentator Alexis de Tocqueville noted in the 1830s, "Scarcely any political question arises in the United States that is not resolved, sooner or later, into a judicial question."[8] Litigation that reaches the Court is political, and the justices for political reasons decide what and how to decide cases on their docket.

The Taney Court first developed the doctrine in *Luther v. Borden*, 7 How. [48 U.S.] 1 (1849). There, the Court held that whether Rhode Island had a "republican form of government," as guaranteed by Article IV of the Constitution, was a question for Congress, not the Court, to decide. Subsequent rulings elaborated other reasons for the doctrine besides deference to separation of powers. The Court may lack information and resources needed for a ruling. In some areas, as in foreign policy and international relations, the Court lacks both adequate standards for resolving disputes and the means to enforce its decisions.

For many decades the Court relied on the doctrine to avoid entering the "political thicket" of state representation and apportionment, that is, the ways by which a state is divided geographically as a basis for representation in state and federal elections. When declining to rule on the malapportionment of Illinois's congressional districts in *Colegrove v. Green*, 328 U.S. 549 (1946), Justice Felix Frankfurter explained,

> We are of the opinion that the petitioners ask of this Court what is beyond its competence to grant. This is one of those demands on judicial power which cannot be met by verbal fencing about "jurisdiction." It must be resolved by considerations on the basis of which this Court, from time to time, has refused to intervene in controversies. It has refused to do so because due regard for the effective working of our Government revealed this issue to be of a peculiarly political nature and therefore not meet for judicial determination.
>
> This is not an action to recover for damages because of the discriminatory exclusion of a plaintiff from rights enjoyed by other

citizens. The basis for the suit is not a private wrong, but a wrong suffered by Illinois as a polity. . . . In effect this is an appeal to the federal courts to reconstruct the electoral process of Illinois in order that it may be adequately represented in the councils of the Nation. Because the Illinois legislature has failed to revise its Congressional Representative districts in order to reflect great changes, during more than a generation, in the distribution of its population, we are asked to do this, for Illinois. . . .

Of course no court can affirmatively remap the Illinois districts so as to bring them more in conformity with the standards of fairness for a representative system. At best we could only declare the existing electoral system invalid. The result would be to leave Illinois undistricted and to bring into operation, if the Illinois legislature chose not to act, the choice of members for the House of Representatives on a statewide ticket. The last stage may be worse than the first. . . .

Nothing is clearer than that this controversy concerns matters that bring courts into immediate and active relations with party contests. From the determination of such issues this Court has traditionally held aloof. It is hostile to the democratic system to involve the judiciary in the politics of the people. And it is not less pernicious if such judicial intervention in an essentially political contest be dressed up in the abstract phrases of the law.

The one stark fact that emerges from the study of the history of Congressional apportionment is its enrollment in politics, in the sense of party contests and party interests. The Constitution enjoins upon Congress the duty of apportioning Representatives "among the several States . . . according to their respective Numbers. . . ." Article I, Sec. 2. Yet, Congress has at times been heedless of this command and not apportioned according to the requirements of the Census. It never occurred to anyone that this Court could issue mandamus to compel Congress to perform its mandatory duty to apportion.

Still, whites, blacks, and other minorities in urban and suburban areas were often denied equal representation in Congress and state legislatures until the Court reversed itself in *Baker v. Carr* (1962) (excerpted below).

In *Goldwater v. Carter* (1979) (excerpted below), the Court issued an order vacating (overturning) a lower court decision in a dispute between several congressmen, headed by conservative Senator Barry Goldwater, and Democratic President Jimmy Carter over the termination of a defense treaty with Taiwan. There, Justices Lewis F. Powell and William Rehnquist took quite different views of the application of the "political questions" doctrine in controversies between Congress and the president. *Goldwater v. Carter* also represents the Court's entertaining in the late twentieth century of *congressional standing*—members of the Senate and House of Representatives—challenging the constitutionality of congressional legislation and executive action; *see*, e.g. *Bowsher v.*

Synar, 478 U.S. 714 (1986) (excerpted in Vol. 1, Ch. 4). The Court, however, drew the line on congressional standing to challenge the constitutionality of newly enacted legislation in *Raines v. Byrd*, 521 U.S. 811 (1997), denying standing to challenge the Line Item Veto Act of 1996; subsequently the Court struck down that law in another suit brought by public and private parties in *Clinton v. City of New York*, 524 U.S. 417 (1998) (excerpted in Vol. 1, Ch. 4).

The Court also reconsidered the "political question" doctrine in *Nixon v. United States*, 506 U.S. 224 (1993) (see Vol. 1, Ch. 5). There, the Rehnquist Court held that a former federal judge's challenge to the Senate's expedited impeachment procedure was nonjusticiable. While also upholding the constitutionality of the Senate's procedure in his opinion for the Court, Chief Justice Rehnquist appeared to go out of his way to justify the application of the doctrine and ostensible exercise of judicial self-restraint.

The doctrine's logic is admittedly circular. "Political questions are matters not soluble by the judicial process; matters not soluble by the judicial process are political questions. As an early dictionary explained," political scientist John Roche says, "violins are small cellos, and cellos are large violins."[9] Still, Columbia Law School professor Louis Henkin points out, even when denying review because of a political question, "the court does not refuse judicial review; it exercises it. It is not dismissing the case or the issue as nonjusticiable; it adjudicates it. It is not refusing to pass on the power of the political branches; it passes upon it, only to affirm that they had the power which had been challenged and that nothing in the Constitution prohibited the particular exercise of it."[10]

Another illustrative controversy over the "political question" doctrine that continues to dog the Court involves the justiciability of political gerrymandering (redrawing voting district lines by the majority party in a legislature to benefit incumbents and to disadvantage candidates and voters in opposing parties). In *Davis v. Bandemer*, 478 U.S. 106 (1986), a plurality held that political gerrymandering controversies were justiciable, but failed to provide a standard for adjudicating such disputes. Almost twenty years later in *Vieth v. Juderlirer*, 541 U.S. 267 (2004) (excerpted in Ch. 8), a plurality would have overruled *Davis v. Bandemer* and held that such controversies are nonjusticiable. But Justice Kennedy, who cast the deciding vote, would not go along with that and maintained that a standard for adjudicating the matter might still evolve. The four dissenters—Justices Stevens, Souter, Ginsburg, and Breyer—countered that such disputes were justiciable and proposed their own standards, but they could not agree on a standard for determining when political gerrymanders are unconstitutional.

■ *STARE DECISIS* AND OTHER POLICIES

The justices occasionally rely on other self-denying policies to avoid reaching issues as well. They, for example, may invoke what has been called the doctrine of *strict necessity*, and thereupon formulate and decide only the narrowest possible issue.

Another doctrine, *stare decisis* ("let the prior decision stand"), is also not a mechanical formula. It is rather a judicial policy that promotes "the certainty, uniformity, and stability of the law." Even conservative Justice George Sutherland recognized that members of the Court "are not infallible, and when convinced that a prior decision was not originally based on, or that conditions have so changed as to render the decision no longer in accordance with, sound reason, [they] should not hesitate to say so."[11] "*Stare decisis* is usually the wise policy," Justice Louis Brandeis remarked, "because in most matters it is more important that the applicable rule of law be settled than that it be settled right."[12] On constitutional matters, however, Justice Douglas among others emphasizes, "*stare decisis*—that is, established law—was really no sure guideline because what did . . . the judges who sat there in 1875 know about, say, electronic surveillance? They didn't know anything about it."[13]

The Rehnquist Court's deference to *stare decisis* was a matter of controversy on and off the bench for several years. Indeed, Justice Scalia's sharp attack on a number of prior rulings prompted a response from retired Justice Lewis F. Powell, Jr., in his 1989 Leslie H. Arps Lecture, delivered to the Association of the Bar of the City of New York and entitled "*Stare Decisis* and Judicial Restraint." In Justice Powell's words:

> Those who would eliminate *stare decisis* in constitutional cases argue that the doctrine is simply one of convenience. . . . But elimination of constitutional *stare decisis* would represent explicit endorsement of the idea that the Constitution is nothing more than what five Justices say it is. This would undermine the rule of law. . . .
>
> It is evident that I consider *stare decisis* essential to the rule of law. . . . After two centuries of vast change, the original intent of the Founders is difficult to discern or is irrelevant. Indeed, there may be no evidence of intent. The Framers of the Constitution were wise enough to write broadly, using language that must be construed in light of changing conditions that could not be foreseen. Yet the doctrine of *stare decisis* has remained a constant thread in preserving continuity and stability.

But the debate over *stare decisis* continued and was especially sharp when by a six-to-three vote the Rehnquist Court overturned two of its own earlier decisions, in *Payne v. Tennessee*, 501 U.S. 808 (1991) (see Vol. 2, Ch. 10), striking down the use of "victim impact statements" in death penalty cases. Note, however, that subsequently Justices O'Connor, Kennedy, and Souter balked at applying *Payne's* analysis of *stare decisis* in *Planned Parenthood of Southeastern Pennsylvania v. Casey*, 505 U.S. 833 (1992) (see Vol. 2, Ch. 11). There, they gave the doctrine of *stare decisis* a new twist when justifying their refusal to overrule entirely the landmark abortion ruling in *Roe v. Wade* (1973) (see Vol. 2, Ch. 11) and drew sharp criticism from Chief Justice Rehnquist and Justices Scalia, Thomas, and White.

In sum, *stare decisis* and the precedential value of the Court's jurisdictional doctrines and policies, as Justice Jackson in half-jest quipped, "are accepted only at their current valuation and have a mortality rate as high as their authors."[14]

■ FORMAL RULES AND PRACTICES

Except for government attorneys and members of the practicing bar, few people pay any attention to the technical Rules of the Court. Yet, they are an exercise of political power and determine the nation's access to justice. The rules govern the admission and activities of attorneys in filing appeals, petitions, and motions and conducting oral arguments. They stipulate the fees, forms, and length of filings. Most important, they explain the Court's formal grounds for granting and disposing of cases.

To expedite the process of deciding what to decide, the Court periodically revises its rules. For example, even after the Judiciary Act of 1925 expanded the Court's discretionary jurisdiction, the justices still felt burdened by mandatory appeals. Accordingly, in 1928 the Court required the filing of a jurisdictional statement explaining the circumstances of an appeal, the questions presented, and why the Court should grant review. The requirement also allowed the justices to screen appeals just like petitions for *certiorari*.

One of the reasons for granting *certiorari* given in the Court's rules is whether "a federal court of appeals has rendered a decision in conflict with the decision of another federal court of appeals on the same matter." This rule is especially advantageous for the federal government. The Department of Justice has a relitigation policy. If it receives an adverse ruling from a circuit court of appeals, it will relitigate the issue in other circuits to obtain favorable decisions and generate a conflict among the circuits, which then may be brought to the Court. The rule for granting circuit conflicts, however important, does not control the justices' actual practice of granting *certiorari*. The government and individuals often allege circuit conflicts simply in an effort to get their cases accepted. But most circuit conflicts are "tolerable" and need not be immediately decided. The justices often feel that conflicts should percolate in the circuits before they take them. Sometimes, the justices may want to avoid or delay addressing an issue that has created a conflict among the circuits. Most crucial in granting *certiorari* is simply that at least four justices agree on the importance of the issue presented.

NOTES

1. Charles E. Hughes, *Addresses of Charles Evans Hughes* (New York: Putnam's, 1916), 185–186.

2. *Muskrat v. United States*, 219 U.S. 346 (1911).

3. See *Duke Power Co. v. Carolina Environmental Study Group*, 438 U.S. 59 (1978); and *Bellotti v. Baird*, 443 U.S. 622 (1979).

4. *Aetna Life Insurance Co. v. Haworth*, 300 U.S. 277 (1937).

5. *Data Processing Service v. Camp*, 397 U.S. 150, 151 (1970).

6. *Braxton County Court v. West Virginia*, 208 U.S. 192 (1908); and *Coleman v. Miller*, 307 U.S. 433 (1931) (Frankfurter, J., dissenting opinion).

7. *Ex parte Baez*, 177 U.S. 378 (1900).

8. Alexis de Tocqueville, *Democracy in America*, Vol. 1, ed. P. Bradley (New York: Vintage, 1945), 288.

9. John Roche, "Judicial Self-Restraint," 49 *American Political Science Review* 768 (1955).

10. Louis Henkin, "Is There a 'Political Question' Doctrine?" 85 *Yale Law Journal* 606 (1976).

11. Draft of an opinion, George Sutherland Papers, Manuscript Room, Library of Congress.

12. *Burnet v. Coronado Oil*, 285 U.S. 393 (1932) (Brandeis, J., dissenting opinion).

13. William O. Douglas, interview on *CBS Reports*, Sept. 6, 1972, CBS News, transcript p. 13.

14. Robert Jackson, "The Task of Maintaining Our Liberties: The Role of the Judiciary," 39 *American Bar Association Journal* 962 (1953).

SELECTED BIBLIOGRAPHY

Brenner, Saul, and Spaeth, Harold. *Stare Indecisis.* New York: Cambridge University Press, 1995.

Clayton, Cornell, and Gillman, Howard, eds. *Supreme Court Decision-Making.* Chicago: University of Chicago Press, 1999.

Gerhardt, Michael. *The Power of Precedent.* New York: Oxford University Press, 2008.

Hansford, Thomas, and Spriggs, James. *The Politics of Precedent on the U.S. Supreme Court.* Princeton, NJ: Princeton University Press, 2006.

Ivers, Gregg, and McGuire, Kevin T. eds. *Creating Constitutional Change.* Charlottesville: University of Virginia Press, 2004.

Kloppenberg, Lisa. *Playing It Safe: How the Supreme Court Sidesteps Hard Cases and Stunts the Development of Law.* New York: New York University Press, 2001.

Mourtada-Sabbah, Nada, and Cain, Bruce. *The Political Question Doctrine and the Supreme Court of the United States.* Lanham, MD: Rowman & Littlefield, 2007.

O'Brien, David. *Storm Center: The Supreme Court in American Politics.* New York: W. W. Norton & Company, 9th ed., 2011.

Posner, Richard. *The Federal Courts.* Cambridge, MA: Harvard University Press, 1996.

Rowland, C. K., and Carp, Robert. *Politics & Judgment in Federal District Courts.* Lawrence: University Press of Kansas, 1996.

Stern, Robert, Gressman, Eugene, Shapiro, Steven, and Geller, Kenneth. *Supreme Court Practice,* 7th ed. Washington, DC: Bureau of National Affairs, 1993.

Sterns, Maxwell L. *Constitutional Process: A Social Choice Analysis of Supreme Court Decisionmaking.* Ann Arbor: University of Michigan Press, 2000.

Urofsky, Melvin, ed. *100 Americans Making Constitutional History.* Washington, DC: C. Q. Press, 2004.

■ INSIDE THE COURT

The Supreme Court's Reversal of Precedent in Historical Perspective

The Supreme Court's reversal of prior rulings registers the politics of the changing composition of the high bench. Between 1791 and 1991, the Court reversed itself on average about once each term. In the nineteenth century, though, reversals were more infrequent, if only because there were fewer decisions to overturn. There were just 32 reversals in the nineteenth century, whereas the Court has reversed itself 179 times in the twentieth century, 166 since 1937.

The year 1937, of course, was a turning point for the Court and the country. An economically conservative Court had struck down much of the early New Deal program and, after his landslide reelection, Democratic President Franklin D. Roosevelt proposed that the number of justices be changed from nine to fifteen, thereby enabling him to pack the Court. In the spring of 1937, however, the Court abruptly reversed itself, upholding major pieces of New Deal legislation, and the Senate defeated FDR's "Court-packingplan." Conservative Justice Willis Van Devanter then retired and FDR had the first of eight opportunities during the next six years to fill vacancies on the Court, as well as the opportunity to elevate Justice Harlan F. Stone to the chief justiceship. Between 1937 and 1946, the Roosevelt Court overturned some thirty precedents.

(continues)

■ INSIDE THE COURT
The Supreme Court's Reversal of Precedent in Historical Perspective (continued)

When the Court's composition changes dramatically in a short period of time, or a pivotal justice leaves the bench, the Court tends to overturn prior rulings. The Warren Court (1953–1969) was even more activist than the Roosevelt Court in reversing forty-five precedents. Yet its record shows how crucial the timing of one or two changes on the bench may prove for the direction of the Court. From the landmark school desegregation ruling in *Brown v. Board of Education*, 347 U.S. 483 (1954) (see Vol. 2, Ch. 12), to the appointment of Justice Potter Stewart in 1959, the Warren Court reversed only six precedents. With Justice Stewart's arrival, six more precedents were overturned in the following four years. In 1962, the Court's composition changed again with Democratic President John F. Kennedy's appointments of Justices Byron White and Arthur Goldberg. Over the following three years fourteen prior rulings were discarded, and in the remaining four years of the Warren Court another twenty were reversed, as constitutional law was pushed in ever more liberal and egalitarian directions.

During Chief Justice Warren F. Burger's tenure (1969–1986), the Court gradually became more conservative, particularly in the area of criminal procedure. As its composition changed, the Burger Court also continued reconsidering precedents although typically liberal ones, reversing a total of fifty-two prior rulings. After Republican President Richard M. Nixon made the last two of his four appointments, Justices Harry Blackmun and William Rehnquist, ten decisions were reversed between 1972 and 1975. A critical conservative mass comparable to the liberal bloc on the Warren Court, however, failed to emerge. Then, liberal Justice William O. Douglas retired and his seat was filled by Republican President Gerald R. Ford's sole appointee, Justice John Paul Stevens. Between 1975 and 1981 the Burger Court then reversed no fewer than twenty-two decisions. Following the arrival of Republican President Ronald Reagan's first appointee, Justice Sandra Day O'Connor, another twelve precedents were overturned in the last five terms of the Burger Court.

The Rehnquist Court (1986–2005) reversed thirty-nine decisions. Notably, with each successive change in its composition the Rehnquist Court more actively reconsidered precedents laid down by its predecessors. In the year following Reagan's elevation of Justice Rehnquist to the chief justiceship and appointment of Justice Antonin Scalia, three precedents were reversed. After Reagan's fourth appointee, Justice Anthony Kennedy, joined the Court in 1988, another eight reversals came down in the 1987 to 1989 terms. Republican President George H. W. Bush's first appointee, Justice David H. Souter, then replaced the retired liberal Justice William J. Brennan. In the 1990 term, the Rehnquist Court overturned seven prior decisions. At the end of that term, Justice Thurgood Marshall announced his retirement and predicted, in *Payne v. Tennessee*, 501 U.S. 808 (1991) (excerpted in Ch. 10), that the Court would reverse many earlier liberal rulings. With Bush's second appointee, Justice Clarence Thomas, on the bench, the Court reversed, in whole or in part, five decisions during the 1991 term. But compare the treatment of the doctrine of *stare decisis* in the opinions in *Payne* with those in *Planned Parenthood of Southeastern Pennsylvania v. Casey*, 505 U.S. 833 (1992). A majority of the Roberts Court (2005—), however, has been less willing to overtly overturn prior decisions, but instead limited those decisions; see, for example, *Hein v. Freedom from Religion Foundation, Inc.* (2007) (in this chapter).

The following table places the Court's reversals of precedents in historical perspective.

COURT	NUMBER OF PRECEDENTS OVERTURNED
Marshall Court (1801–1836)	3
Taney Court (1836–1864)	4
Chase Court (1864–1873)	4
Waite Court (1874–1888)	13
Fuller Court (1888–1910)	4
White Court (1910–1921)	5
Taft Court (1921–1930)	6
Hughes Court (1930–1941)	21
Stone Court (1941–1946)	15
Vinson Court (1946–1953)	13
Warren Court (1953–1969)	45
Burger Court (1969–1986)	52
Rehnquist Court (1986–2005)	39
Roberts Court (2005–)	9
Total	233

This table updates data collected and analyzed by Christopher Banks. For a further discussion of the Supreme Court's reversal of precedents, see Christopher Banks, "The Supreme Court and Precedent: An Analysis of Natural Courts and Reversal Trends," 75 *Judicature* 262 (Feb./Mar. 1992). This table was updated through the 2009–2010 term by the author.

Flast v. Cohen

392 U.S. 83, 88 S.CT. 1942 (1968)

Florance Flast and several other taxpayers sought standing to challenge the constitutionality of the Elementary and Secondary Education Act of 1965. The act provided funding for instructional materials and purchase of textbooks for religious schools. Flast contended that the act violated the First Amendment's ban on the establishment of religion and guarantee for the free exercise of religion. In a federal district court in New York, she filed suit against Wilbur Cohen, the secretary of Health, Education, and Welfare, to enjoin the spending of funds authorized for religious schools. The district court denied standing and Flast appealed to the Supreme Court.

The Court's decision was eight to one, with the majority's opinion announced by Chief Justice Warren. There were concurrences by Justices Douglas, Stewart, and Fortas. Justice Harlan dissented.

■ *Chief Justice WARREN delivers the opinion of the Court.*

In *Frothingham v. Mellon* [262 U.S. 447] (1923), this Court ruled that a federal taxpayer is without standing to challenge the constitutionality of a federal statute. That ruling has stood for 45 years as an impenetrable barrier to suits against Acts of Congress brought by individuals who can assert only the interest of federal taxpayers. In this case, we must decide whether the *Frothingham* barrier should be lowered when a taxpayer attacks a federal statute on the ground that it violates the Establishment and Free Exercise Clauses of the First Amendment. . . .

This Court first faced squarely the question whether a litigant asserting only his status as a taxpayer has standing to maintain a suit in a federal court in *Frothingham v. Mellon, supra,* and that decision must be the starting point for analysis in this case. The taxpayer in *Frothingham* attacked as unconstitutional the Maternity Act of 1921, which established a federal program of grants to those States which would undertake programs to reduce maternal and infant mortality. . . . The Court noted that a federal taxpayer's "interest in the moneys of the Treasury . . . is comparatively minute and indeterminable" and that "the effect upon future taxation, of any payment out of the [Treasury's] funds, . . . [is] remote, fluctuating and uncertain." As a result, the Court ruled that the taxpayer had failed to allege the type of "direct injury" necessary to confer standing.

Although the barrier *Frothingham* erected against federal taxpayer suits has never been breached, the decision has been the source of some confusion and the object of considerable criticism. The confusion has developed as commentators have tried to determine whether *Frothingham* establishes a constitutional bar to taxpayer suits or whether the Court was simply im-posing a rule of self restraint which was not constitutionally compelled. The conflicting viewpoints are reflected in the arguments made to this Court by the parties in this case. The Government has pressed upon us the view that *Frothingham* announced a constitutional rule, compelled by the Article III limitations on federal court jurisdiction and grounded in considerations of the doctrine of separation of powers. Appellants, however, insist that *Frothingham* expressed no more than a policy of judicial self-restraint which can be disregarded when compelling reasons for assuming jurisdiction over a taxpayer's suit exist. The opinion delivered in *Frothingham* can be read to support either position. . . .

To the extent that *Frothingham* has been viewed as resting on policy considerations, it has been criticized as depending on assumptions not consistent with modern conditions. For example, some commentators have pointed out that a number of corporate taxpayers today have a federal tax liability running into hundreds of millions of dollars, and such taxpayers have a far greater monetary stake in the Federal Treasury than they do in any municipal treasury. To some degree, the fear expressed in *Frothingham* that allowing one taxpayer to sue would inundate the federal courts with countless similar suits has been mitigated by the ready availability of the devices of class actions and joinder under the Federal Rules of Civil Procedure, adopted subsequent to the decision in *Frothingham*. . . .

The jurisdiction of federal courts is defined and limited by Article III of the Constitution. In terms relevant to the question for decision in this case, the judicial power of federal courts is constitutionally restricted to "cases" and "controversies." As is so often the situation in constitutional adjudication, those two words have an iceberg quality, containing beneath their surface simplicity submerged complexities which go to the very heart of our constitutional form of government. Embodied in the words "cases" and "controversies" are two complementary but somewhat different limitations. In part those words limit the business of federal courts to questions presented in an adversary context and in a form historically viewed as capable of resolution through the judicial process. And in part those words define the role assigned to the judiciary in a tripartite allocation of power to assure that the federal courts will not intrude into areas committed to the other branches of government. Justiciability is the term of art employed to give expression to this dual limitation placed upon federal courts by the case-and-controversy doctrine.

Justiciability is itself a concept of uncertain meaning and scope. Its reach is illustrated by the various grounds upon which questions sought to be adjudicated in federal courts have been held not to be justiciable. Thus, no justiciable controversy is presented when the parties seek adjudication of only a political question, when the parties are asking for an advisory opinion, when the question sought to be adjudicated has been mooted by subsequent developments, and when there is no standing to maintain the action. Yet it remains true that "[j]usticiability is . . . not a legal concept with a fixed content or susceptible of scientific verification. Its utilization is the resultant of many subtle pressures," *Poe v. Ullman* [367 U.S. 497 (1961)].

Part of the difficulty in giving precise meaning and form to the concept of justiciability stems from the uncertain historical antecedents of the case-and-controversy doctrine. For example, Justice FRANKFURTER twice suggested that historical meaning could be imparted to the concepts of justiciability and case and controversy by reference to the practices of the courts of Westminster when the Constitution was adopted. . . .

However, the power of English judges to deliver advisory opinions was well established at the time the Constitution was drafted. And it is quite clear that "the oldest and most consistent thread in the federal law of justiciability is that the federal courts will not give advisory opinions." Thus, the implicit policies embodied in Article III, and not history alone, impose the rule against advisory opinions on federal courts. When the federal judicial power is invoked to pass upon the validity of actions by the Legislative and Executive Branches of the Government, the rule against advisory opinions implements the separation of powers prescribed by the Constitution and confines federal courts to the role assigned them by Article III. However, the rule against advisory opinions also recognizes that such suits often "are not pressed before the Court with that clear concreteness provided when a question emerges precisely framed and necessary for decision from a clash of adversary argument exploring every aspect of a multifaceted situation embracing conflicting and demanding interests." Consequently, the Article III prohibition against advisory opinions reflects the complementary constitutional considerations expressed by the justiciability doctrine: Federal judicial power is limited to those disputes which confine federal courts to a role consistent with a system of separated powers and which are traditionally thought to be capable of resolution through the judicial process.

Additional uncertainty exists in the doctrine of justiciability because that doctrine has become a blend of constitutional requirements and policy considerations. And a policy limitation is "not always clearly distinguished from the constitutional limitation." . . . The "many subtle pressures" which cause policy considerations to blend into the constitutional limitations of Article III make the justiciability doctrine one of uncertain and shifting contours.

It is in this context that the standing question presented by this case must be viewed and that the Government's argument on that question must be evaluated. As we understand it, the Government's position is that the constitutional scheme of separation of powers, and the deference owed by the federal judiciary to the other two branches of government within that scheme, present an absolute bar to taxpayer suits challenging the validity of federal spending programs. The Government views such suits as involving no more than the mere disagreement by the taxpayer "with the uses to which tax money is put." According to the Government, the resolution of such disagreements is committed to other branches of the Federal Government and not to the judiciary. Consequently, the Government contends that, under no circumstances, should standing be conferred on federal taxpayers to challenge a federal taxing or spending program. An analysis of the function served by standing limitations compels a rejection of the Government's position.

Standing is an aspect of justiciability and, as such, the problem of standing is surrounded by the same complexities and vagaries that inhere in justiciability. . . .

Despite the complexities and uncertainties, some meaningful form can be given to the jurisdictional limitations placed on federal court power by the concept of standing. The fundamental aspect of standing is that it focuses on the party seeking to get his complaint before a federal court and not on the issues he wishes to have adjudicated. The "gist of the question of standing" is whether the party seeking relief has "alleged such a personal stake in the outcome of the controversy as to assure that concrete adverseness which sharpens the presentation of issues upon which the court so largely depends for illumination of difficult constitutional questions," *Baker v. Carr*, [369 U.S. 186] (1962). In other words, when standing is placed in issue in a case, the question is whether the person whose standing is challenged is a proper party to request an adjudication of a particular issue and not whether the issue itself is justiciable. Thus, a party may have standing in a particular case, but the federal court may nevertheless decline to pass on the merits of the case because, for example, it presents a political question. A proper party is demanded so that federal courts will not be asked to decide "ill-defined controversies over constitutional issues," *United Public Workers of America v. Mitchell*, 330 U.S. 75 (1947), or a case which is of "a hypothetical or abstract character," . . . So stated, the standing requirement is closely related to, although more general than, the rule that federal courts will not entertain friendly suits. . . .

When the emphasis in the standing problem is placed on whether the person invoking a federal court's jurisdiction is a proper party to maintain the action, the weakness of the Government's argument in this case becomes apparent. The question whether a particular person is a proper party to maintain the action does not, by its own force, raise separation of powers problems related to improper judicial interference in areas committed to other branches of the Federal Government. Such problems arise, if at all, only from the substantive issues the individual seeks to have adjudicated. Thus, in terms of Article III limitations on federal court jurisdiction, the question of standing is related only to whether the dispute sought to be adjudicated will be presented in an adversary context and in a form historically viewed as capable of judicial resolution. It is for that reason that the emphasis in standing problems is on whether the party invoking federal court jurisdiction has "a personal stake in the outcome of the controversy," *Baker v. Carr*, and whether the dispute touches upon "the legal relations of parties having adverse legal interests." A taxpayer may or may not have the requisite personal stake in the outcome, depending upon the circumstances of the particular case. Therefore, we find no absolute bar in Article III to suits by federal taxpayers challenging allegedly unconstitutional federal taxing and spending programs. There remains, however, the problem of determining the circumstances under which a federal taxpayer will be deemed to have the personal stake and interest that impart the necessary concrete adverseness to such litigation so that standing can be conferred on the taxpayer *qua* taxpayer consistent with the constitutional limitations of Article III. . . .

Whether such individuals have standing to maintain that form of action turns on whether they can demonstrate the necessary stake as taxpayers in the outcome of the litigation to satisfy Article III requirements.

The nexus demanded of federal taxpayers has two aspects to it. First, the taxpayer must establish a logical link between that status and the type of legislative enactment attacked. Thus, a taxpayer will be a proper party to allege the unconstitutionality only of exercises of congressional power under the taxing and spending clause of Art. I, Sec. 8, of the Constitution. It will not be sufficient to allege an incidental expenditure of tax funds in the administration of an essentially regulatory statute. . . . Secondly, the taxpayer must establish a nexus between that status and the precise nature of the constitutional infringement alleged. Under this requirement, the taxpayer must show that the challenged enactment exceeds specific constitutional limitations imposed upon the exercise of the congressional taxing and spending power and not simply that the enactment is generally beyond the powers delegated to Congress by Art. I, Sec. 8. When both nexuses are established, the litigant will have shown a taxpayer's stake in the outcome of the controversy and will be a proper and appropriate party to invoke a federal court's jurisdiction.

The taxpayer-appellants in this case have satisfied both nexuses to support their claim of standing under the test we announce today. Their constitutional challenge is made to an exercise by Congress of its power under Art. I, Sec. 8, to spend for the general welfare, and the challenged program involves a substantial expenditure of federal tax funds. In addition, appellants have alleged that the challenged expenditures violate the Establishment and Free Exercise Clauses of the First Amendment. Our history vividly illustrates that one of the specific evils feared by those who drafted the Establishment Clause and fought for its adoption was that the taxing and spending power would be used to favor one religion over another or to support religion in general. James Madison, who is generally recognized as the leading architect of the religion clauses of the First Amendment, observed in his famous Memorial and Remonstrance Against Religious Assessments that "the same authority which can force a citizen to contribute three pence only of his property for the support of any one establishment, may force him to conform to any other establishment in all cases whatsoever." 2 *Writings of James Madison* 183, 186 (Hunt ed. 1901). The concern of Madison and his supporters was quite clearly that religious liberty ultimately would be the victim if government could employ its taxing and spending powers to aid one religion over another or to aid religion in general. The Establishment Clause was designed as a specific bulwark against such potential abuses of governmental power, and that clause of the First Amendment operates as a specific constitutional limitation upon the exercise by Congress of the taxing and spending power conferred by Art. I, Sec. 8.

The allegations of the taxpayer in *Frothingham v. Mellon, supra,* were quite different from those made in this case, and the result in *Frothingham* is consistent with the test of taxpayer standing announced today. The taxpayer in *Frothingham* attacked a federal spending program and she, therefore, established the first nexus required. However, she lacked standing because her constitutional attack was not based on an allegation that Congress, in enacting the Maternity Act of 1921, had breached a specific limitation upon its taxing and spending power. The taxpayer in *Frothingham* alleged essentially that Congress, by enacting the challenged statute, had exceeded the general powers delegated to it by Art. I, Sec. 8, and that Congress had thereby invaded the legislative province reserved to the States by the Tenth Amendment. To be sure, Mrs. Frothingham made the additional allegation that her tax liability would be increased as a result of the allegedly unconstitutional enactment, and she framed that allegation in terms of a deprivation of property without due process of law. However, the Due Process Clause of the Fifth Amendment does not protect taxpayers against increases in tax liability, and the taxpayer in *Frothingham* failed to make any additional claim that the harm she alleged resulted from a breach by Congress of the specific constitutional limitations imposed upon an exercise of the taxing and spending power. In essence, Mrs. Frothingham was attempting to assert the States' interest in their legislative prerogatives and not a federal taxpayer's interest in being free of taxing and spending in contravention of specific constitutional limitations imposed upon Congress' taxing and spending power.

We have noted that the Establishment Clause of the First Amendment does specifically limit the taxing and spending power conferred by Art. I, Sec. 8. Whether the Constitution contains other specific limitations can be determined only in the context of future cases. However, whenever such specific limitations are found, we believe a taxpayer will have a clear stake as a taxpayer in assuring that they are not breached by Congress. Consequently, we hold that a taxpayer will have standing consistent with Article III to invoke federal judicial power when he alleges that congressional action under the taxing and spending clause is in derogation of those constitutional provisions which operate to restrict the exercise of the taxing and spending power. The taxpayer's allegation in such cases would be that his tax money is being extracted and spent in violation of specific constitutional protections against such abuses of legislative power. Such an injury is appropriate for judicial redress, and the taxpayer has established the necessary nexus between his status and the nature of the allegedly unconstitutional action to support his claim of standing to secure judicial review. Under such circumstances, we feel confident that the questions will be framed with the necessary specificity, that the issues will be contested with the necessary adverseness and that the litigation will be pursued with the necessary vigor to assure that the constitutional challenge will be made in a form traditionally thought to be capable of judicial resolution. We lack that confidence in cases such as *Frothingham* where a taxpayer seeks to employ a federal court as a forum in which to air his generalized grievances about the conduct of government or the allocation of power in the Federal System.

☐ *Justice HARLAN, dissenting.*

The problems presented by this case are narrow and relatively abstract, but the principles by which they must be resolved involve nothing less than the proper functioning of the federal courts, and so run to the roots of our constitutional system. The nub of my view is that the end result of *Frothingham v. Mellon* was correct, even though, like others, I do not subscribe to all of its reasoning and premises. Although I therefore agree with certain of the conclusions reached today by the Court, I cannot accept the standing doctrine that it substitutes for *Frothingham*, for it seems to me that this new doctrine rests on premises that do not withstand analysis. Accordingly, I respectfully dissent. . . .

The lawsuits here and in *Frothingham* are fundamentally different. They present the question whether federal taxpayers *qua* taxpayers may, in suits in which they do not contest the validity of their previous or existing tax obligations, challenge the constitutionality of the uses for which Congress has authorized the expenditure of public funds. These differences in the purposes of the cases are reflected in differences in the litigants' interests. An action brought to contest the validity of tax liabilities assessed to the plaintiff is designed to vindicate interests that are personal and proprietary. The wrongs alleged and the relief sought by such a plaintiff are unmistakably private; only secondarily are his interests representative of those of the general population. I take it that the Court, although it does not pause to examine the question, believes that the interests of those who as taxpayers challenge the constitutionality of public expenditures may, at least in certain circumstances, be similar. Yet this assumption is surely mistaken. . . .

Presumably the Court recognizes at least certain . . . hazards, else it would not have troubled to impose limitations upon the situations in which, and purposes for which, such suits may be brought. Nonetheless, the limitations adopted by the Court are, as I have endeavored to indicate, wholly untenable. This is the more unfortunate because there is available a resolution of this problem that entirely satisfies the demands of the principle of separation of powers. This Court has previously held that individual litigants have standing to represent the public interest, despite their lack of economic or other personal interests, if Congress has appropriately authorized such suits. Any hazards to the proper allocation of authority among the three branches of the Government would be substantially diminished if public actions had been pertinently authorized by Congress and the President. I appreciate that this Court does not ordinarily await the mandate of other branches of the Government, but it seems to me that the extraordinary character of public actions, and of the mischievous, if not dangerous, consequences they involve for the proper functioning of our constitutional system, and in particular of the federal courts, makes such judicial forbearance the part of wisdom. It must be emphasized that the implications of these questions of judicial policy are of fundamental significance for the other branches of the Federal Government.

Such a rule could readily be applied to this case. Although various efforts have been made in Congress to authorize public actions to contest the validity of federal expenditures in aid of religiously affiliated schools and other institutions, no such authorization has yet been given.

This does not mean that we would, under such a rule, be enabled to avoid our constitutional responsibilities, or that we would confine to limbo the First Amendment or any other constitutional command. The question here is not, despite the Court's unarticulated premise, whether the religious clauses of the First Amendment are hereafter to be enforced by the federal courts; the issue is simply whether plaintiffs of an *additional* category, heretofore excluded from those courts, are to be permitted to maintain suits. The recent history of this Court is replete with illustrations, including even one announced today that questions involving the religious clauses will not, if federal taxpayers are prevented from contesting federal expenditures, be left "unacknowledged, unresolved, and undecided."

Accordingly, for the reasons contained in this opinion, I would affirm the judgment of the District Court.

Valley Forge Christian College v. Americans United for Separation of Church and State, Inc.

454 U.S. 464, 102 S.CT. 752 (1982)

Americans United for Separation of Church and State, an organization dedicated to the separation of religion from government, filed a suit in federal district court in Pennsylvania to stop the Department of Health,

Education, and Welfare (now the Department of Education) from conveying as "surplus property" a closed and former army hospital to Valley Forge Christian College. Under the Federal Property and Administrative Services Act of 1949, the department has authority to sell surplus government property for educational use to nonprofit, tax-exempt educational institutions. Congress has the power to "dispose of and make all needful Rules and Regulations respecting the . . . Property belonging to the United States," under Article IV, Section 3, Clause 2. But Americans United for Separation of Church and State contended that the department's conveyance here abridged its members' First Amendment rights to religious freedom and "deprived [them] of the fair and constitutional use of [their] tax dollars." The district court dismissed the suit but the Court of Appeals for the Third Circuit reversed. Thereupon, Valley Forge Christian College appealed to the Supreme Court.

The Court's decision was five to four, with the majority's opinion announced by Justice Rehnquist. Dissents were by Justices Stevens and Brennan, who was joined by Justices Blackmun and Marshall.

☐ *Justice REHNQUIST delivers the opinion of the Court.*

We need not mince words when we say that the concept of "Art. III standing" has not been defined with complete consistency in all of the various cases decided by this Court which have discussed it, nor when we say that this very fact is probably proof that the concept cannot be reduced to a one-sentence or one-paragraph definition. But of one thing we may be sure: Those who do not possess Art. III standing may not litigate as suitors in the courts of the United States. Article III, which is every bit as important in its circumscription of the judicial power of the United States as in its granting of that power, is not merely a troublesome hurdle to be overcome if possible so as to reach the "merits" of a lawsuit which a party desires to have adjudicated; it is a part of the basic charter promulgated by the Framers of the Constitution at Philadelphia in 1787, a charter which created a general government, provided for the interaction between that government and the governments of the several States, and was later amended so as to either enhance or limit its authority with respect to both States and individuals. . . .

[I]n *Flast v. Cohen*, [392 U.S. 83 (1968)], [t]he Court developed a two-part test to determine whether the plaintiffs had standing to sue. First, because a taxpayer alleges injury only by virtue of his liability for taxes, the Court held that "a taxpayer will be a proper party to allege the unconstitutionality only of exercises of congressional power under the taxing and spending clause of Art. I, Sec. 8, of the Constitution." Second, the Court required the taxpayer to "show that the challenged enactment exceeds specific constitutional limitations upon the exercise of the taxing and spending power and not simply that the enactment is generally beyond the powers delegated to Congress by Art. I, Sec. 8."

Unlike the plaintiffs in *Flast*, respondents fail the first prong of the test for taxpayer standing. Their claim is deficient in two respects. First, the source of their complaint is not a congressional action, but a decision by HEW to transfer a parcel of federal property. *Flast* limited taxpayer standing to challenges directed "only [at] exercises of congressional power." See *Schlesinger v. Reservists Committee to Stop the War*, [418 U.S. 208 (1974)] (denying standing because the taxpayer plaintiffs "did not challenge an enactment under Art. I, Sec. 8, but rather the action of the Executive Branch").

Second, and perhaps redundantly, the property transfer about which respondents complain was not an exercise of authority conferred by the Taxing and Spending Clause of Art. I, Sec. 8. The authorizing legislation, the Federal Property and Administrative Services Act of 1949, was an evident exercise of Congress' power under the Property Clause, Art. IV, Sec. 3, cl. 2. Respondents do not dispute this conclusion, and it is decisive of any claim of taxpayer standing under the *Flast* precedent.

☐ *Justice BRENNAN, with whom Justice MARSHALL and Justice BLACKMUN join, dissenting.*

The opinion of the Court is a stark example of this unfortunate trend of resolving cases at the "threshold" while obscuring the nature of the underlying rights and interests at stake. The Court waxes eloquent on the blend of prudential and constitutional considerations that combine to create our misguided "standing" jurisprudence. *But not one word is said about the Establishment Clause right that the plaintiff seeks to enforce.* And despite its pat recitation of our standing decisions, the opinion utterly fails, except by the sheerest form of *ipse dixit*, to explain why this case is unlike *Flast v. Cohen* (1968), and is controlled instead by *Frothingham v. Mellon* (1923). . . .

It is at once apparent that the test of standing formulated by the Court in *Flast* sought to reconcile the developing doctrine of taxpayer "standing" with the Court's historical understanding that the Establishment Clause was intended to prohibit the Federal Government from using tax funds for the advancement of religion, and thus the constitutional imperative of taxpayer standing in certain cases brought pursuant to the Establishment Clause. The two-pronged "nexus" test offered by the Court, despite its general language, is best understood as "a determinant of standing of plaintiffs alleging only injury as taxpayers who challenge alleged violations of the Establishment and Free Exercise Clauses of the First Amendment," and not as a general statement of standing principles. The test explains what forms of governmental action may be attacked by someone alleging *only* taxpayer status, and, without ruling out the possibility that history might reveal another similarly founded provision, explains why an Establishment Clause claim is treated differently from any other assertion that the Federal Government has exceeded the bounds of the law in allocating its largesse. . . .

The nexus test that the Court "announced," sought to maintain necessary continuity with prior cases, and set forth principles to guide future cases involving taxpayer standing. But *Flast* did not depart from the principle that no judgment about standing should be made without a fundamental understanding of the rights at issue. The two-part *Flast* test did not supply the rationale for the Court's decision, but rather is exposition: That rationale was supplied by an understanding of the nature of the restrictions on government power imposed by the Constitution and the intended beneficiaries of those restrictions.

It may be that Congress can tax for *almost* any reason, or for no reason at all. There is, so far as I have been able to discern, but one constitutionally imposed limit on that authority. Congress cannot use tax money to support a church, or to encourage religion. That is *"the* forbidden exaction." *Everson v. Board of Education* [330 U.S. 1 (1947)]. In absolute terms the history of the Establishment Clause of the First Amendment makes this clear. History also makes it clear that the federal taxpayer is a singularly "proper and appropriate party to invoke a federal court's jurisdiction" to challenge a federal bestowal of largesse as a violation of the Establishment Clause. Each, and indeed every, federal taxpayer suffers precisely the injury that the Establishment Clause guards against when the Federal Government directs that funds be taken from the pocketbooks of the citizenry and placed into the coffers of the ministry.

A taxpayer cannot be asked to raise his objection to such use of his funds at the time he pays his tax. Apart from the unlikely circumstance in which the Government announced in advance that a particular levy would be used for religious subsidies, taxpayers could hardly assert that they were being injured until the Government actually lent its support to a religious venture. Nor would it be reasonable to require him to address his claim to those officials charged with the collection of federal taxes. Those officials would be without the means to provide appropriate redress—there is no practical way to segregate the complaining taxpayer's money from that being devoted to the religious purpose. Surely, then, a taxpayer must have standing at the time that he learns of the Government's alleged Establishment Clause violation to seek equitable relief in order to halt the continuing and intolerable burden on his pocketbook, his conscience, and his constitutional rights.

Blind to history, the Court attempts to distinguish this case from *Flast* by wrenching snippets of language from our opinions, and by perfunctorily applying that language under color of the first prong of *Flast's* two-part nexus test. The tortuous distinctions thus produced are specious, at best: at worst, they are pernicious to our constitutional heritage.

First, the Court finds this case different from *Flast* because here the "source of [plaintiffs'] complaint is not a *congressional* action, but a decision by HEW to transfer a parcel of federal property." This attempt at distinction cannot withstand scrutiny. *Flast* involved a challenge to the actions of the Commissioner of Education, and other officials of HEW, in disbursing funds under the Elementary and Secondary Education Act of 1965 to "religious and sectarian" schools. Plaintiffs disclaimed "any intent[ion] to challenge . . . all programs under . . . the Act." Rather, they claimed that defendant-administrators' approval of such expenditures was not authorized by the Act, or alternatively, to the extent the expenditures were authorized, the Act was "unconstitutional and void." In the present case, respondents challenge HEW's grant of property pursuant to the Federal Property and Administrative Services Act of 1949, seeking to enjoin HEW "from making a grant of this and other property to the [defendant] so long as such a grant will violate the Establishment Clause." It may be that the Court is concerned with the adequacy of respondents' pleading; respondents have not, in so many words, asked for a declaration that the "Federal Property and Administrative Services Act is unconstitutional and void to the extent that it authorizes HEW's actions." I would not construe their complaint so narrowly.

More fundamentally, no clear division can be drawn in this context between actions of the Legislative Branch and those of the Executive Branch. To be sure, the First Amendment is phrased as a restriction on Congress' legislative authority; this is only natural since the Constitution assigns the authority to legislate and appropriate only to the Congress. But it is difficult to conceive of an expenditure for which the last governmental actor, either implementing directly the legislative will, or acting within the scope of legislatively delegated authority, is not an Executive Branch official. The First Amendment binds the Government as a whole, regardless of which branch is at work in a particular instance.

The Court's second purported distinction between this case and *Flast* is equally unavailing. The majority finds it "decisive" that the Federal Property and Administrative Services Act of 1949 "was an evident exercise of Congress' power under the Property Clause, Art. IV, Sec. 3, cl. 2," while the Government action in *Flast* was taken under Art. I, Sec. 8. The Court relies on *United States v. Richardson*, 418 U.S. [166] (1974), and *Schlesinger v. Reservists Committee to Stop the War*, 418 U.S. 208 (1974), to support the distinction between the two Clauses, noting that those cases involved alleged deviations from the requirements of Art. I, Sec. 9, cl. 7, and Art. I, Sec. 6, cl. 2, respectively. The standing defect in each case was *not*, however, the failure to allege a violation of the Spending Clause; rather, the taxpayers in those cases had not complained of the distribution of Government largesse, and thus failed to meet the essential requirement of taxpayer standing recognized in *Doremus* [*v. Board of Education*, 342 U.S. 429 (1952)]. . . .

Plainly hostile to the Framers' understanding of the Establishment Clause, and *Flast's* enforcement of that understanding, the Court vents that hostility under the guise of standing, "to slam the courthouse door against plaintiffs who [as the Framers intended] are entitled to full consideration of their [Establishment Clause] claims on the merits." *Barlow v. Collins*, 397 U.S. 159 (1970) (BRENNAN, J., concurring in result and dissenting). Therefore, I dissent.

Lujan v. Defenders of Wildlife

504 U.S. 555, 112 S.CT. 2130 (1992)

Under the Endangered Species Act (ESA) of 1973, federal agencies are required to consult with the Department of Interior (DOI) to make sure that their policies and actions will not jeopardize endangered or threatened species or their habitats. For more than a decade DOI interpreted that act to apply to federally funded projects at home and abroad. But in 1986 the Reagan administration reversed course, announcing that the law no longer applied to projects overseas. Immediately, Defenders of Wildlife, other environmental groups, and their members challenged that reinterpretation of the law.

To gain standing to file a lawsuit, members of Defenders of Wildlife—its president, Joyce Kelly, and another member, Amy Skilbred—filed affidavits alleging that they would suffer injuries due to the failure of the Agency for International Development (AID) and other agencies to consult with DOI about a federally funded irrigation project on the Mahaweli River in Sri Lanka and a redevelopment project on the Nile River in Egypt. Those projects, they claimed, threatened endangered elephants and leopards in Sri Lanka and the crocodile and other species in Egypt. And when asserting their standing to sue and personal injuries, Kelly and Skilbred testified that they were environmentalists and had traveled to each site, although neither indicated specifically when she would again visit those sites. A federal district court dismissed the suit for lacking standing, but the Court of Appeals for the Eighth Circuit reversed.

The George H. W. Bush administration appealed the appellate court's holding that Kelly and Skilbred had standing to sue under the ESA's provision conveying on citizens the right to sue the secretary of DOI for failure to consult with other federal agencies on projects potentially threatening to endangered species and their habitats, even though they failed to allege concrete injuries. Relying on *dicta* in several recent cases (see Justice Scalia's concurring opinion in *Gwaltney of Smithfield, Ltd. v. Chesapeake Bay Foundation*, 484 U.S. 49 [1987], and *Lujan v. National Wildlife Federation*, 497 U.S. 871 [1989]), the Bush administration asked the Court to sharply limit standing in such citizen suits.

The Court's decision was seven to two; the opinion was announced by Justice Scalia. Concurring opinions were delivered by Justice Kennedy, whom Justice Souter joined, and by Justice Stevens. Justice Blackmun dissented and was joined by Justice O'Connor.

☐ *Justice SCALIA delivers the opinion of the Court with respect to Parts I, II, III-A, and IV, and an opinion with respect to Part III-B in which Chief Justice REHNQUIST and Justices WHITE, KENNEDY, SOUTER, and THOMAS join.*

■ II

Over the years, our cases have established that the irreducible constitutional minimum of standing contains three elements: First, the plaintiff must have suffered an "injury in fact"—an invasion of a legally protected interest which is (a) concrete and particularized, *Warth v. Seldin*, 422 U.S. 490 (1975); *Sierra Club v. Morton*, 405 U.S. 727 (1972); and (b) "actual or imminent, not 'conjectural' or 'hypothetical.'" Second, there must be a causal connection between the injury and the conduct complained of—the injury has to be "fairly . . . traceable to the challenged action of the defendant, and not . . . the result [of] the independent action of some third party not before the court." *Simon v. Eastern Kentucky Welfare Rights Org.*, 426 U.S. 26 (1976). Third, it must be "likely," as opposed to merely "speculative," that the injury will be "redressed by a favorable decision."

When the suit is one challenging the legality of government action or inaction, the nature and extent of facts that must be averred (at the summary judgement stage) or proved (at the trial stage) in order to establish standing depends considerably upon whether the plaintiff is himself an object of the action (or foregone action) at issue. If he is, there is ordinarily little question that the action or inaction has caused him injury, and that a judgment preventing or requiring the action will redress it. When, however, as in this case, a plaintiff's asserted injury arises from the government's allegedly unlawful regulation (or lack of regulation) of someone else, much more is needed. In that circumstance, causation and redressability ordinarily hinge on the response of the regulated (or regulable) third party to the government action or inaction—and perhaps on the response of others as well. The existence of one or more of the essential elements of standing "depends on the unfettered choices made by independent actors not before the courts and whose exercise of broad and legitimate discretion the courts cannot presume either to control or to predict," *ASARCO Inc. v. Kadish*, 490 U.S. 605 (1989); and it becomes the burden of the plaintiff to adduce facts showing that those choices have been or will be made in such manner as to produce causation and permit redressability of injury. Thus, when the plaintiff is not himself the object of the government action or inaction he challenges, standing is not precluded, but it is ordinarily "substantially more difficult" to establish.

■ III

We think the Court of Appeals failed to apply the foregoing principles. . . . Respondents had not made the requisite demonstration of (at least) injury and redressability.

A. Respondents' claim to injury is that the lack of consultation with respect to certain funded activities abroad "increases the rate of extinction of endangered and threatened species." Of course, the desire to use or observe an animal species, even for purely aesthetic purposes, is undeniably a cognizable interest for purpose of standing. "But the 'injury in fact' test requires more than an injury to a cognizable interest. It requires that the party seeking review be himself among the injured." . . . [R]espondents had to submit affidavits or other evidence showing, through specific facts, not only that listed species were in fact being threatened by funded activities abroad, but also that one or more of respondents' members would thereby be "directly" affected apart from their " 'special interest' in the subject." . . .

We shall assume for the sake of argument that these affidavits contain facts showing that certain agency-funded projects threaten listed species—though that is questionable. They plainly contain no facts, however, showing how damage to the species will produce "imminent" injury to Mss. Kelly and Skilbred. That the women "had visited" the areas of the projects before the projects commenced proves nothing. . . .

Besides relying upon the Kelly and Skilbred affidavits, respondents propose a series of novel standing theories. The first, inelegantly styled "ecosystem nexus," proposes that any person who uses any part of a "contiguous ecosystem" adversely affected by a funded activity has standing even if the activity is located a great distance away. . . . [But to] say that the Act protects ecosystems is not to say that the Act creates (if it were possible) rights of action in persons who have not been injured in fact, that is, persons who use portions of an ecosystem not perceptibly affected by the unlawful action in question.

Respondents' other theories are called, alas, the "animal nexus" approach, whereby anyone who has an interest in studying or seeing the endangered animals anywhere on the globe has standing; and the "vocational nexus" approach, under which anyone with a professional interest in such animals can sue. Under these theories, anyone who goes to see Asian elephants in the Bronx Zoo, and anyone who is a keeper of Asian elephants in the Bronx Zoo, has standing to sue because the Director of AID did not consult with the Secretary regarding the AID-funded project in Sri Lanka. This is beyond all reason. . . .

B. The most obvious problem in the present case is redressability. Since the agencies funding the projects were not parties to the case, the District Court could accord relief only against the Secretary: He could be ordered to revise his regulation to require consulation for foreign projects. But this would not remedy respondents' alleged injury unless the funding agencies were bound by the Secretary's regulation, which is very much an open question. Whereas in other contexts the ESA is quite explicit as to the Secretary's controlling authority, with respect to consultation the initiative, and hence arguably the initial responsibility for determining statutory necessity, lies with the agencies. When the Secretary promulgated the regulation at issue here, he thought it was binding on the agencies. The Solicitor General, however, has repudiated that position here, and the agencies themselves apparently deny the Secretary's authority. . . .

A further impediment to redressability is the fact that the agencies generally supply only a fraction of the funding for a foreign project. AID, for example, has provided less than 10 percent of the funding for the Mahaweli Project. Respondents have produced nothing to indicate that the projects they have named will either be suspended, or do less harm to listed species, if that fraction is eliminated. . . .

We hold that respondents lack standing to bring this action.

☐ *Justice BLACKMUN, with whom Justice O'CONNOR joins, dissenting.*

I part company with the Court in this case in two respects. First, I believe that respondents have raised genuine issues of fact—sufficient to survive summary judgment—both as to injury and as to redressability. Second, I question the Court's breadth of language in rejecting standing for "procedural" injuries. I fear the Court seeks to impose fresh limitations on the constitutional authority of Congress to allow citizen-suits in the federal courts for injuries deemed "procedural" in nature. I dissent. . . .

To survive petitioner's motion for summary judgement on standing, respondents need not prove that they are actually or imminently harmed. They need show only a "genuine issue" of material fact as to standing. Federal Rules of Civil Procedure 56(c). This is not a heavy burden. A "genuine issue" exists so long as "the evidence is such that a reasonable jury could return a verdict for the nonmoving party respondents." *Anderson v. Liberty Lobby, Inc.*, 477 U.S. 242 (1986). "This Court's function is not itself to weigh the evidence and determine the truth of the matter but to determine whether there is a genuine issue for trial." . . .

I think a reasonable finder of fact could conclude from the information in the affidavits and deposition testimony that either Kelly or Skilbred will soon return to the project sites, thereby satisfying the "actual or imminent" injury standard. . . .

By requiring a "description of concrete plans" or "specification of when the same day [for a return visit] will be," the Court, in my view, demands what is likely an empty formality. No substantial barriers prevent Kelly or Skilbred from simply purchasing plane tickets to return to the Aswan and Mahaweli projects. . . .

In conclusion, I cannot join the Court on what amounts to a slash-and-burn expedition through the law of environmental standing. In my view, "the very essence of civil liberty certainly consists in the right of every individual to claim the protection of the laws, whenever he receives an injury." *Marbury v. Madison*, 1 Cranch 137 (1803).

Hein v. Freedom from Religion Foundation, Inc.

551 U.S. 587, 127 S.Ct. 2553 (2007)

In 2001, President George W. Bush issued an executive order creating the White House Office of Faith-Based and Community Initiatives, with the aim of ensuring "private and charitable community groups, including religious ones . . . have the fullest opportunity permitted by law to compete on a level playing field, so long as they achieve valid public purposes" and adhere to "the bedrock principles of pluralism, nondiscrimination, evenhandedness, and neutrality." The office was charged with the task of eliminating regulatory barriers that could impede such organizations' ability to compete equally for federal assistance. In separate executive orders, the president also created centers for Faith-Based and Community Initiatives within several federal agencies. They were given the job of ensuring that faith-based community groups would be eligible to compete for federal financial support, by holding conferences and giving assistance on grant applications. No congressional legislation specifically authorized the creation of the centers or appropriated funds for them. Instead, their activities were funded through general executive branch appropriations.

These faith-based initiatives were challenged by Freedom from Religion Foundation, Inc., a group of atheists and agnostics, who argued that these initiatives violated the First Amendment (dis)establishment clause by promoting religious community groups over secular ones. A federal district court dismissed the suit for lack of standing, concluding that under *Flast v. Cohen*, 392 U.S. 83 (1968), federal taxpayer standing is limited to challenges to the constitutionality of "'exercises of congressional power under the taxing and spending clause of Art. I, Sec. 8.'" Subsequently, a divided panel of the Court of Appeals for the Seventh Circuit reversed. That decision was appealed and the Supreme Court granted review.

The appellate court's decision was reversed by a five-to-four vote. Justice Alito delivered the opinion for the Court. Justices Scalia and Kennedy filed concurring opinions. Justice Souter issued a dissenting opinion, which was joined by Justices Stevens, Ginsburg, and Breyer.

☐ *Justice ALITO announced the judgment of the Court and delivered an opinion in which THE CHIEF JUSTICE and Justice KENNEDY join.*

This is a lawsuit in which it was claimed that conferences held as part of the President's Faith-Based and Community Initiatives program violated the Establishment Clause of the First Amendment because, among other things, President Bush and former Secretary of Education Paige gave speeches that used "religious imagery" and praised the efficacy of faith-based programs in delivering social services. The plaintiffs contend that they meet the standing requirements of Article III of the Constitution because they pay federal taxes.

It has long been established, however, that the payment of taxes is generally not enough to establish standing to challenge an action taken by the Federal Government. In light of the size of the federal budget, it is a complete fiction to argue that an unconstitutional federal expenditure causes an individual federal taxpayer any measurable economic harm. And if every federal taxpayer could sue to challenge any Government expenditure, the federal courts would cease to function as courts of law and would be cast in the role of general complaint bureaus.

In *Flast v. Cohen*, 392 U. S. 83 (1968), we recognized a narrow exception to the general rule against federal taxpayer standing. Under *Flast*, a plaintiff asserting an Establishment Clause claim has standing to challenge a law authorizing the use of federal funds in a way that allegedly violates the Establishment Clause. In the present case, Congress did not specifically authorize the use of federal funds to pay for the conferences or speeches that the plaintiffs challenged. Instead, the conferences and speeches were paid for out of general Executive Branch appropriations. The Court of Appeals, however, held that the plaintiffs have standing as taxpayers because the conferences were paid for with money appropriated by Congress.

The question that is presented here is whether this broad reading of *Flast* is correct. We hold that it is not. We therefore reverse the decision of the Court of Appeals. . . .

The only asserted basis for standing was that the individual respondents are federal taxpayers who are "opposed to the use of Congressional taxpayer appropriations to advance and promote religion." In their capacity as federal taxpayers, respondents sought to challenge Executive Branch expenditures for these conferences, which, they contended, violated the Establishment Clause. . . .

Article III of the Constitution limits the judicial power of the United States to the resolution of "Cases" and "Controversies," and " 'Article III standing . . . enforces the Constitution's case–or–controversy requirement.' "

The constitutionally mandated standing inquiry is especially important in a case like this one, in which taxpayers seek "to challenge laws of general application where their own injury is not distinct from that suffered in general by other taxpayers or citizens." This is because "[t]he judicial power of the United States defined by Art. III is not an unconditioned authority to determine the constitutionality of legislative or executive acts." *Valley Forge Christian College v. Americans United for Separation of Church and State, Inc.*, 454 U.S. 464 (1982). The federal courts are not empowered to seek out and strike down any governmental act that they deem to be repugnant to the Constitution. Rather, federal courts sit "solely, to decide on the rights of individuals," *Marbury v. Madison*, 1 Cranch 137 (1803), and must " 'refrai[n] from passing upon the constitutionality of an act . . . unless obliged to do so in the proper performance of our judicial function, when the question is raised by a party whose interests entitle him to raise it.' " *Valley Forge.* As we held over 80 years ago, in another case involving the question of taxpayer standing: "We have no power per se to review and annul acts of Congress on the ground that they are unconstitutional. The question may be considered only when the justification for some direct injury suffered or threatened, presenting a justiciable issue, is made to rest upon such an act. . . . The party who invokes the power must be able to show not only that the statute is invalid but that he has sustained or is immediately in danger of sustaining some direct injury as the result of its enforcement, and not merely that he suffers in some indefinite way in common with people generally." *Frothingham v. Mellon*, 262 U.S. 447 (1923). . . .

As a general matter, the interest of a federal taxpayer in seeing that Treasury funds are spent in accordance with the Constitution does not give rise to the kind of redressable "personal injury" required for Article III standing. Of course, a taxpayer has standing to challenge the collection of a specific tax assessment as unconstitutional; being forced to pay such a tax causes a real and immediate economic injury to the individual taxpayer. But that is not the interest on which respondents assert standing here. Rather, their claim is that, having paid lawfully collected taxes into the Federal Treasury at some point, they have a continuing, legally cognizable interest in ensuring that those funds are not used by the Government in a way that violates the Constitution.

We have consistently held that this type of *interest is too generalized and attenuated to support Article III standing.* In *Frothingham*, a federal taxpayer sought to challenge federal appropriations for mothers' and children's health, arguing that federal involvement in this area intruded on the rights reserved to the States under the Tenth Amendment and would "increase the burden of future taxation and thereby take [the plaintiff's] property without due process of law." We concluded that the plaintiff lacked the kind of particularized injury required for Article III standing: "[I]nterest in the moneys of the Treasury . . . is shared with millions of others; is comparatively minute and indeterminable; and the effect upon future taxation, of any payment out of the funds, so remote, fluctuating and uncertain, that no basis is afforded for an appeal to the preventive powers of a court of equity." . . .

Because the interests of the taxpayer are, in essence, the interests of the public-at-large, deciding a constitutional claim based solely on taxpayer standing "would be[,] not to decide a judicial controversy, but to assume a position of authority over the governmental acts of another and co-equal department, an authority which plainly we do not possess." . . .

In *Flast*, the Court carved out a narrow exception to the general consti-tutional prohibition against taxpayer standing. The taxpayer-plaintiff in that case challenged the distribution of federal funds to religious schools under the Elementary and Secondary Education Act of 1965, alleging that such aid violated the Establishment Clause. The Court set out a two-part test for de-termining whether a federal taxpayer has standing to challenge an allegedly unconstitutional expenditure: "First, the taxpayer must establish a logical link between that status and the type of legislative enactment attacked. Thus, a taxpayer will be a proper party to allege the unconstitutionality only of exer-cises of congressional power under the taxing and spending clause of Art. I, Sec. 8, of the Constitution. It will not be sufficient to allege an incidental ex-penditure of tax funds in the administration of an essentially regulatory statute. . . . Secondly, the taxpayer must establish a nexus between that status and the precise nature of the constitutional infringement alleged. Under this requirement, the taxpayer must show that the challenged enactment exceeds specific constitutional limitations imposed upon the exercise of the congres-sional taxing and spending power and not simply that the enactment is gen-erally beyond the powers delegated to Congress by Art. I, Sec. 8." . . .

Respondents argue that this case falls within the *Flast* exception, which they read to cover any "expenditure of government funds in violation of the Establishment Clause." But this broad reading fails to observe "the rigor with which the *Flast* exception to the *Frothingham* principle ought to be applied." *Valley Forge.*

The expenditures at issue in *Flast* were made pursuant to an express con-gressional mandate and a specific congressional appropriation. The plaintiff in that case challenged disbursements made under the Elementary and Secondary Education Act of 1965. That Act expressly appropriated the sum of $100 million for fiscal year 1966, and authorized the disbursement of those funds to local ed-ucational agencies for the education of low-income students. . . .

The expenditures challenged in *Flast*, then, were funded by a specific congressional appropriation and were disbursed to private schools (including religiously affiliated schools) pursuant to a direct and unambiguous congres-sional mandate. Indeed, the *Flast* taxpayer-plaintiff's constitutional claim was premised on the contention that if the Government's actions were " 'within the authority and intent of the Act, the Act is to that extent unconstitutional and void.' " . . .

Given that the alleged Establishment Clause violation in *Flast* was funded by a specific congressional appropriation and was undertaken pur-suant to an express congressional mandate, the Court concluded that the taxpayer-plaintiffs had established the requisite "logical link between [their taxpayer] status and the type of legislative enactment attacked." In the Court's words, "[t]heir constitutional challenge [was] made to an exercise by Congress of its power under Art. I, Sec. 8, to spend for the general welfare." But as this Court later noted, *Flast* "limited taxpayer standing to challenges directed 'only [at] exercises of congressional power' " under the Taxing and Spending Clause. *Valley Forge.*

The link between congressional action and constitutional violation that supported taxpayer standing in *Flast* is missing here. Respondents do not challenge any specific congressional action or appropriation; nor do they ask the Court to invalidate any congressional enactment or legislatively created program as unconstitutional. That is because the expenditures at issue here were not made pursuant to any Act of Congress. Rather, Congress provided general appropriations to the Executive Branch to fund its day-to-day activities. These appropriations did not expressly authorize, direct, or even mention the expenditures of which respondents complain. Those expenditures resulted from executive discretion, not congressional action. . . .

In short, this case falls outside "the narrow exception" that *Flast* "created to the general rule against taxpayer standing established in *Frothingham*." Because the expenditures that respondents challenge were not expressly authorized or mandated by any specific congressional enactment, respondents' lawsuit is not directed at an exercise of congressional power, and thus lacks the requisite "logical nexus" between taxpayer status "and the type of legislative enactment attacked.". . .

☐ *Justice SCALIA, with whom Justice THOMAS joins, concurring in the judgment.*

Today's opinion is, in one significant respect, entirely consistent with our previous cases addressing taxpayer standing to raise Establishment Clause challenges to government expenditures. Unfortunately, the consistency lies in the creation of utterly meaningless distinctions which separate the case at hand from the precedents that have come out differently, but which cannot possibly be (in any sane world) the reason it comes out differently. If this Court is to decide cases by rule of law rather than show of hands, we must surrender to logic and choose sides: Either *Flast v. Cohen* (1968), should be applied to (at a minimum) all challenges to the governmental expenditure of general tax revenues in a manner alleged to violate a constitutional provision specifically limiting the taxing and spending power, or *Flast* should be repudiated. For me, the choice is easy. *Flast* is wholly irreconcilable with the Article III restrictions on federal-court jurisdiction that this Court has repeatedly confirmed are embodied in the doctrine of standing. . . .

☐ *Justice SOUTER, with whom Justice STEVENS, Justice GINSBURG, and Justice BREYER join, dissenting.*

Flast v. Cohen (1968) held that plaintiffs with an Establishment Clause claim could "demonstrate the necessary stake as taxpayers in the outcome of the litigation to satisfy Article III requirements." Here, the controlling, plurality opinion declares that *Flast* does not apply, but a search of that opinion for a suggestion that these taxpayers have any less stake in the outcome than the taxpayers in *Flast* will come up empty: the plurality makes no such finding, nor could it. Instead, the controlling opinion closes the door on these taxpayers because the Executive Branch, and not the Legislative Branch, caused their injury. I see no basis for this distinction in either logic or precedent, and respectfully dissent. . . .

The plurality points to the separation of powers to explain its distinction between legislative and executive spending decisions, but there is no difference on that point of view between a Judicial Branch review of an executive decision and a judicial evaluation of a congressional one. We owe respect to each of the other branches, no more to the former than to the latter, and no one has suggested that the Establishment Clause lacks applicability to executive uses of money. It would surely violate the Establishment Clause for the Department of Health and Human Services to draw on a general appropriation to build a chapel for weekly church services (no less than if a statute required it), and for good reason: if the Executive could accomplish through the exercise of discretion exactly what Congress cannot do through legislation, Establishment Clause protection would melt away. . . .

Because the taxpayers in this case have alleged the type of injury this Court has seen as sufficient for standing, I would affirm.

Baker v. Carr

369 U.S. 186, 82 S.Ct. 691 (1962)

In 1901, the Tennessee legislature apportioned both houses and provided for subsequent reapportionment every ten years on the basis of the number of people in each of the state's counties as reported in the census. But for more than sixty years proposals to redistribute legislative seats failed to pass, while the state's population shifted from rural to urban areas. Charles Baker and several other citizens and urban residents sued various Tennessee officials. Baker claimed that as an urban resident he was being denied the equal protection of the law under the Fourteenth Amendment. He asked the court to order state officials to hold either an at-large election or an election in which legislators would be selected from constituencies in accordance with the 1960 federal census. The federal district court dismissed the suit, conceding that Baker's civil rights were being denied but holding that the court could offer no remedy. Baker made a further appeal to the Supreme Court.

When the Supreme Court granted review in *Baker v. Carr*, it faced two central issues: first, whether the malapportionment of a state legislature is a "political question" for which courts have no remedy and, second, the merits of Baker's claim that individuals have a right to equal votes and equal representation. With potentially broad political consequences, the case was divisive for the Court and was carried over and reargued for a term. Allies on judicial self-restraint, Justices Frankfurter and Harlan were committed to their view, expressed in *Colegrove v. Green*, 328 U.S. 549 (1946), that the "Court ought not to enter this political thicket." At conference, Justices Clark and Whittaker supported their view that the case presented a nonjusticiable political question. By contrast, Chief Justice Warren and Justices Black, Douglas, and Brennan thought that the issue was justiciable. They were also prepared to address the merits of the case. The pivotal justice, Potter Stewart, considered the issue justiciable, but he refused to address the merits of the case. He voted to reverse the lower court ruling only if the Court's decision was limited to holding that courts have jurisdiction to decide such disputes. He did not want the Court to take on the merits of re-apportionment in this case.

Assigned the task of drafting the opinion, Brennan had to hold on to Stewart's vote and dissuade Black and Douglas from writing opinions on the merits that would threaten the loss of the crucial fifth vote. After circulating his draft and incorporating suggested changes, he optimistically wrote Black, "Potter Stewart was satisfied with all of the changes. The Chief also is agreed. It, therefore, looks as though we have a court agreed upon this as circulated." It appeared that the decision would come down on the original five to four vote.

Clark, however, had been pondering the fact that in this case the population ratio for the urban and rural districts in Tennessee was more than nineteen to one. As he put it, "city slickers" had been "too long deprive[d] of a constitutional form of government." Clark concluded that citizens denied equal voting power had no political recourse; their only recourse was to the federal judiciary. Clark thus wrote an opinion abandoning Frankfurter and going beyond the majority to address the merits of the claim.

Brennan faced the dilemma of how to bring in Clark without losing Stewart, and thereby enlarge the consensus. Further negotiations were necessary but limited. Brennan wrote his brethren:

> The changes represent the maximum to which Potter will subscribe. We discussed much more elaborate changes which would have taken over a substantial part of Tom Clark's opinion. Potter felt that if they were made it would be necessary for him to dissent from that much of the revised opinion. I therefore decided it was best not to press for the changes but to hope that Tom will be willing to join the Court opinion but say he would go further as per his separate opinion.

Even though there were five votes for deciding the merits, the final opinion was limited to the jurisdictional question.★

The Court's decision was six to two, with Justice Whittaker not participating and with the majority's opinion delivered by Justice Brennan. There were concurrences by Justices Douglas, Clark, and Stewart. Justice Frankfurter dissented and was joined by Justice Harlan.

□ *Justice BRENNAN delivers the opinion of the Court.*

[W]e hold today only (a) that the court possessed jurisdiction of the subject matter: (b) that a justiciable cause of action is stated upon which

★ Sources of quotations are internal Court memos, located in the William J. Brennan, Jr., Papers, Library of Congress; and the Tom C. Clark Papers, University of Texas Law School.

appellants would be entitled to appropriate relief; and (c) because appellees raise the issue before this Court, that the appellants have standing to challenge the Tennessee apportionment statutes. Beyond noting that we have no cause at this stage to doubt the District Court will be able to fashion relief if violations of constitutional rights are found, it is improper now to consider what remedy would be most appropriate if appellants prevail at the trial.

JURISDICTION OF THE SUBJECT MATTER

The District Court was uncertain whether our cases withholding federal judicial relief rested upon a lack of federal jurisdiction or upon the inappropriateness of the subject matter for judicial consideration—what we have designated "nonjusticiability." The distinction between the two grounds is significant. In the instance of nonjusticiability, consideration of the cause is not wholly and immediately foreclosed: rather, the Court's inquiry necessarily proceeds to the point of deciding whether the duty asserted can be judicially identified and its breach judicially determined, and whether protection for the right asserted can be judicially molded. In the instance of lack of jurisdiction the cause either does not "arise under" the Federal Constitution, laws or treaties (or fall within one of the other enumerated categories of Art. III, Sec. 2), or is not a "case or controversy" within the meaning of that section; or the cause is not one described by any jurisdictional statute. Our conclusion that this cause presents no nonjusticiable "political question" settles the only possible doubt that it is a case or controversy. . . .

The appellees refer to *Colegrove v. Green*, 328 U.S. 549 [(1946)], as authority that the District Court lacked jurisdiction of the subject matter. Appellees misconceive the holding of that case. The holding was precisely contrary to their reading of it. Seven members of the Court participated in the decision. Unlike many other cases in this field which have assumed without discussion that there was jurisdiction, all three opinions filed in Colegrove discussed the question. Two of the opinions expressing the views of four of the Justices, a majority, flatly held that there was jurisdiction of that subject matter. Justice BLACK joined by Justice DOUGLAS and Justice MURPHY stated: "It is my judgment that the District Court had jurisdiction. . . ." Justice RUTLEDGE, writing separately, expressed agreement with this conclusion. . . . Indeed, it is even questionable that the opinion of Justice FRANKFURTER, joined by Justices REED and BURTON, doubted jurisdiction of the subject matter. . . .

JUSTICIABILITY

In holding that the subject matter of this suit was not justiciable, the District Court relied on *Colegrove v. Green*, *supra*, and subsequent *per curiam* cases. The court stated: "From a review of these decisions there can be no doubt that the federal rule . . . is that the federal courts . . . will not intervene in cases of this type to compel legislative reapportionment." We understand the District Court to have read the cited cases as compelling the conclusion that since the appellants sought to have a legislative apportionment held unconstitutional, their suit presented a "political question" and was therefore nonjusticiable. We hold that this challenge to an apportionment presents no nonjusticiable "political question." The cited cases do not hold the contrary.

Of course the mere fact that the suit seeks protection of a political right does not mean it presents a political question. Such an objection "is little more than a play upon words." Rather, it is argued that apportionment cases, whatever the actual wording of the complaint, can involve no federal constitutional right except one resting on the guaranty of a republican form of government, and that complaints based on that clause have been held to present political questions which are nonjusticiable.

We hold that the claim pleaded here neither rests upon nor implicates the Guaranty Clause and that its justiciability is therefore not foreclosed by our decisions of cases involving that clause. . . . To show why we reject the argument based on the Guaranty Clause, we must examine the authorities under it. But because there appears to be some uncertainty as to why those cases did present political questions, and specifically as to whether this apportionment case is like those cases, we deem it necessary first to consider the contours of the "political question" doctrine.

Our discussion, even at the price of extending this opinion, requires review of a number of political question cases, in order to expose the attributes of the doctrine—attributes which, in various settings, diverge, combine, appear, and disappear in seeming disorderliness. . . .

We have said that "In determining whether a question falls within [the political question] category, the appropriateness under our system of government of attributing finality to the action of the political departments and also the lack of satisfactory criteria for a judicial determination are dominant considerations." *Coleman v. Miller* [307 U.S. 433 (1939)]. The nonjusticiability of a political question is primarily a function of the separation of powers. Much confusion results from the capacity of the "political question" label to obscure the need for case-by-case inquiry. Deciding whether a matter has in any measure been committed by the Constitution to another branch of government, or whether the action of that branch exceeds whatever authority has been committed, is itself a delicate exercise in constitutional interpretation, and is a responsibility of this Court as ultimate interpreter of the Constitution. To demonstrate this requires no less than to analyze representative cases and to infer from them the analytical threads that make up the political question doctrine. We shall then show that none of those threads catches this case.

Foreign relations: There are sweeping statements to the effect that all questions touching foreign relations are political questions. Not only does resolution of such issues frequently turn on standards that defy judicial application, or involve the exercise of a discretion demonstrably committed to the executive or legislature; but many such questions uniquely demand single-voiced statement of the Government's views. Yet it is error to suppose that every case or controversy which touches foreign relations lies beyond judicial cognizance. Our cases in this field seem invariably to show a discriminating analysis of the particular question posed, in terms of the history of its management by the political branches, of its susceptibility to judicial handling in the light of its nature and posture in the specific case, and of the possible consequences of judicial action. . . .

Dates of duration of hostilities: Though it has been stated broadly that "the power which declared the necessity is the power to declare its cessation, and what the cessation requires," *Commercial Trust Co. v. Miller*, 262 U.S. 51 [1923], here too analysis reveals isolable reasons for the presence of political questions, underlying this Court's refusal to review the political departments' determination of when or whether a war has ended. Dominant is the need for finality in the political determination, for emergency's nature demands "A prompt and unhesitating obedience." *Martin v. Mott*, 12 Wheat. [256 U.S. 19 (1827)] [Calling up of militia.] . . . Further, clearly definable criteria for decision may be available. In such case the political question barrier falls away. . . .

Validity of enactments: In *Coleman v. Miller, supra*, this Court held that the questions of how long a proposed amendment to the Federal Constitution remained open to ratification, and what effect a prior rejection had on a subsequent ratification, were committed to congressional resolution and involved criteria of decision that necessarily escaped the judicial grasp. Similar considerations apply to the enacting process: "The respect due to coequal and independent departments," and the need for finality and certainty about the status of a statute contribute to judicial reluctance to inquire whether, as passed, it complied with all requisite formalities. *Field v. Clark*, 143 U.S. 649 [1892]. . . .

The status of Indian tribes: This Court's deference to the political departments in determining whether Indians are recognized as a tribe, while it reflects familiar attributes of political questions, also has a unique element in that "the relation of the Indians to the United States is marked by peculiar and cardinal distinctions which exist nowhere else. [The Indians are] domestic dependent nations. . . . Their relation to the United States resembles that of a ward to his guardian." *Cherokee Nation v. Georgia*, 5 Pet. 1 [1831]. Yet, here too, there is no blanket rule. . . .

It is apparent that several formulations which vary slightly according to the settings in which the questions arise may describe a political question, although each has one or more elements which identify it as essentially a function of the separation of powers. Prominent on the surface of any case held to involve a political question is found a textually demonstrable constitutional commitment of the issue to a coordinate political department; or a lack of judicially discoverable and manageable standards for resolving it; or the impossibility of deciding without an initial policy determination of a kind clearly for nonjudicial discretion; or the impossibility of a court's undertaking independent resolution without expressing lack of the respect due coordinate branches of government; or an unusual need for unquestioning adherence to a political decision already made; or the potentiality of embarrassment from multifarious pronouncements by various departments on one question.

Unless one of these formulations is inextricable from the case at bar, there should be no dismissal for nonjusticiability on the ground of a political question's presence. The doctrine of which we treat is one of "political questions," not one of "political cases." . . .

Republican form of government: Luther v. Borden, 7 How. 1 [1848], though in form simply an action for damages for trespass was, as Daniel Webster said in opening the argument for the defense, "an unusual case." The defendants, admitting an otherwise tortious breaking and entering, sought to justify their action on the ground that they were agents of the established lawful government of Rhode Island, which State was then under martial law to defend itself from active insurrection; that the plaintiff was engaged in that insurrection; and that they entered under orders to arrest the plaintiff. The case arose "out of the unfortunate political differences which agitated the people of Rhode Island in 1841 and 1842," and which had resulted in a situation wherein two groups laid competing claims to recognition as the lawful government. . . .

Chief Justice TANEY's opinion for the Court reasoned as follows: (1) If a court were to hold the defendants' acts unjustified because the charter government had no legal existence during the period in question, it would follow that all of that government's actions—laws enacted, taxes collected, salaries paid, accounts settled, sentences passed—were of no effect; and that "the officers who carried their decisions into operation [were] answerable as trespassers, if not in some cases as criminals." There was, of course, no room for application of any doctrine of *de facto* status to uphold prior acts of an officer not authorized *de jure*, for such would have defeated the plaintiff's very action. A decision for the plaintiff would inevitably have produced some significant measure of chaos, a consequence to be avoided if it could be done without abnegation of the judicial duty to uphold the Constitution.

(2) No state court had recognized as a judicial responsibility settlement of the issue of the locus of state governmental authority. Indeed, the courts of Rhode Island had in several cases held that "it rested with the political power to decide whether the charter government had been displaced or not," and that that department had acknowledged no change.

(3) Since "[t]he question relates, altogether, to the constitution and laws of [the] . . . State," the courts of the United States had to follow the state courts' decisions unless there was a federal constitutional ground for overturning them.

(4) No provision of the Constitution could be or had been invoked for this purpose except Art. IV, Sec. 4, the Guaranty Clause. Having already noted the absence of standards whereby the choice between governments could be made by a court acting independently, Chief Justice TANEY now found further textual and practical reasons for concluding that, if any department of the United States was empowered by the Guaranty Clause to resolve the issue, it was not the judiciary:

"Under this article of the Constitution it rests with Congress to decide what government is the established one in a State. For as the United States guarantee to each State a republican government, Congress must necessarily decide what government is established in the State before it can determine whether it is a republican or not. And when the senators and representatives of a State are admitted into the councils of the Union, the authority of the government under which they are appointed, as well as its republican character, is recognized by the proper constitutional authority. And its decision is binding on every other department of the government, and could not be questioned in a judicial tribunal. It is true that the contest in this case did not last long enough to bring the matter to this issue; and . . . Congress was not called upon to decide the controversy. Yet the right to decide is placed there, and not in the courts."

"So, too, as relates to the clause in the above-mentioned article of the Constitution, providing for cases of domestic violence. It rested with Congress, too, to determine upon the means proper to be adopted to fulfill this guarantee. . . . [B]y the act of February 28, 1795, [Congress] provided, that, 'in case of an insurrection in any State against the government thereof, it shall be lawful for the President of the United States, on application of the legislature of such State or of the executive (when the legislature cannot be convened) to call forth such number of the militia of any other State or States, as may be applied for, as he may judge sufficient to suppress such insurrection.'

"By this act, the power of deciding whether the exigency had arisen upon which the government of the United States is bound to interfere, is given to the President" [*Luther v. Borden*].

Clearly, several factors were thought by the Court in *Luther* to make the question there "political": the commitment to the other branches of the decision as to which is the lawful state government; the unambiguous action by the President, in recognizing the charter government as the lawful authority; the need for finality in the executive's decision; and the lack of criteria by which a court could determine which form of government was republican. . . .

But the only significance that *Luther* could have for our immediate purposes is in its holding that the Guaranty Clause is not a repository of judicially manageable standards which a court could utilize independently in order to identify a State's lawful government. The Court has since refused to resort to the Guaranty Clause—which alone had been invoked for the purpose—as the source of a constitutional standard for invalidating state action. . . .

We come, finally, to the ultimate inquiry whether our precedents as to what constitutes a nonjusticiable "political question" bring the case before us under the umbrella of that doctrine. A natural beginning is to note whether any of the common characteristics which we have been able to identify and label descriptively are present. We find none: The question here is the consistency of state action with the Federal Constitution. We have no question decided, or to be decided, by a political branch of government coequal with this Court. Nor do we risk embarrassment of our government abroad, or grave disturbance at home if we take issue with Tennessee as to the constitutionality of her action here challenged. Nor need the appellants, in order to succeed in this action, ask the Court to enter upon policy determinations for which judicially manageable standards are lacking. Judicial standards under the Equal Protection Clause are well developed and familiar, and it has been open to courts since the enactment of the Fourteenth Amendment to determine, if on the particular facts they must, that a discrimination reflects *no* policy, but simply arbitrary and capricious action.

This case does, in one sense, involve the allocation of political power within a State, and the appellants might conceivably have added a claim under the Guaranty Clause. Of course, as we have seen, any reliance on that clause would be futile. But because any reliance on the Guaranty Clause could not have succeeded it does not follow that appellants may not be heard on the equal protection claim which in fact they tender. . . .

We conclude that the complaint's allegations of a denial of equal protection present a justiciable constitutional cause of action upon which appellants are entitled to a trial and a decision. The right asserted is within the reach of judicial protection under the Fourteenth Amendment.

The judgment of the District Court is reversed and the cause is remanded for further proceedings consistent with this opinion.

Reversed and remanded.

☐ *Justice DOUGLAS, concurring.*

While I join the opinion of the Court and, like the Court, do not reach the merits, a word of explanation is necessary. I put to one side the problems of "political" questions involving the distribution of power between this Court, the Congress, and the Chief Executive. We have here a phase of the recurring problem of the relation of the federal courts to state agencies. More particularly, the question is the extent to which a State may weight one person's vote more heavily than it does another's.

So far as voting rights are concerned, there are large gaps in the Constitution. Yet the right to vote is inherent in the republican form of government envisaged by Article IV, Section 4 of the Constitution. . . .

Race, color, or previous condition of servitude is an impermissible standard by reason of the Fifteenth Amendment, and that alone is sufficient to explain *Gomillion v. Lightfoot*, 364 U.S. 339 [1960].

Sex is another impermissible standard by reason of the Nineteenth Amendment.

There is a third barrier to a State's freedom in prescribing qualifications of voters and that is the Equal Protection Clause of the Fourteenth Amendment, the provision invoked here. And so the question is, may a State weight the vote of one county or one district more heavily than it weights the vote in another?

The traditional test under the Equal Protection Clause has been whether a State has made "an invidious discrimination," as it does when it selects "a particular race or nationality for oppressive treatment." Universal equality is not the test; there is room for weighting. . . .

☐ *Justice CLARK, concurring.*

Although I find the Tennessee apportionment statute offends the Equal Protection Clause, I would not consider intervention by this Court into so delicate a field if there were any other relief available to the people of Tennessee. But the majority of the people of Tennessee have no "practical opportunities for exerting their political weight at the polls" to correct the existing "invidious discrimination." Tennessee has no initiative and referendum. I have searched diligently for other "practical opportunities" present under the law. I find none other than through the federal courts. The majority of the voters have been caught up in a legislative strait jacket. Tennessee has an "informed, civically militant electorate" and "an aroused popular conscience," but it does not sear "the conscience of the people's representatives." This is because the legislative policy has riveted the present seats in the Assembly to their respective constituencies, and by the votes of their incumbents a reapportionment of any kind is prevented. The people have been rebuffed at the hands of the Assembly; they have tried the constitutional convention route, but since the call must originate in the Assembly it, too, has been fruitless. They have tried Tennessee courts with the same result, and Governors have fought the tide only to flounder. It is said that there is recourse in Congress and perhaps that may be, but from a practical standpoint this is without substance. To date Congress has never undertaken such a task in any State. We therefore must conclude that the people of Tennessee are stymied and without judicial intervention will be saddled with the present discrimination in the affairs of their state government.

☐ *Justice FRANKFURTER, with whom Justice HARLAN joins, dissenting.*

The Court today reverses a uniform course of decision established by a dozen cases, including one by which the very claim now sustained was unanimously rejected only five years ago. The impressive body of rulings thus cast aside reflected the equally uniform course of our political history regarding the relationship between population and legislative representation—a wholly different matter from denial of the franchise to individuals because of race, color, religion or sex. Such a massive repudiation of the experience of our whole past in asserting destructively novel judicial power demands a detailed analysis of the role of this Court in our constitutional scheme. Disregard of inherent limits in the effective exercise of the Court's "judicial Power" not only presages the futility of judicial intervention in the essentially political conflict of forces by which the relation between population and representation has time out of mind been and now is determined. It may well impair the Court's position as the ultimate organ of "the supreme Law of the Land" in that vast range of legal problems, often strongly entangled in popular feeling, on which this Court must pronounce. The Court's authority—possessed of neither the purse nor the sword—ultimately rests on sustained public confidence in its moral sanction. Such feeling must be nourished by the Court's complete detachment, in fact and in appearance, from political entanglements and by abstention from injecting itself into the clash of political forces in political settlements.

A hypothetical claim resting on abstract assumptions is now for the first time made the basis for affording illusory relief for a particular evil even though it foreshadows deeper and more pervasive difficulties in consequence. The claim is hypothetical and the assumptions are abstract because the Court does not vouchsafe the lower courts—state and federal—guidelines for formulating specific, definite, wholly unprecedented remedies for the inevitable litigations that today's umbrageous disposition is bound to stimulate in connection with politically motivated reapportionments in so many States. In such a setting, to promulgate jurisdiction in the abstract is meaningless. It is as devoid of reality as "a brooding omnipresence in the sky," for it conveys no intimation what relief, if any, a District Court is capable of affording that would not invite legislatures to play ducks and drakes with the judiciary. For this Court to direct the District Court to enforce a claim to which the Court has over the years consistently found itself required to deny legal enforcement and at the same time found it necessary to withhold any guidance to the lower court how to enforce this turnabout, new legal claim, manifests an odd—indeed an esoteric—conception of judicial propriety. One of the Court's supporting opinions, as elucidated by commentary, unwittingly affords a disheartening preview of the mathematical quagmire (apart from divers judicially inappropriate and elusive determinants) into which this Court today catapults the lower courts of the country without so much as adumbrating the basis for a legal calculus as a means of extrication. Even assuming the indispensable intellectual disinterestedness on the part of judges in such matters, they do not have accepted legal standards or criteria or even reliable analogies to draw upon for making judicial judgments. To charge courts with the task of accommodating the incommensurable factors of policy that underlie these mathematical puzzles is to attribute, however flatteringly, omnicompetence to judges. . . .

We were soothingly told at the bar of this Court that we need not worry about the kind of remedy a court could effectively fashion once the abstract constitutional right to have courts pass on a statewide system of electoral districting is recognized as a matter of judicial rhetoric, because legislatures would heed the Court's admonition. This is not only a euphoric hope. It implies a sorry confession of judicial impotence in place of a frank acknowledgment that there is not under our Constitution a judicial remedy for every political mischief, for every undesirable exercise of legislative power. The Framers carefully and with deliberate forethought refused so to enthrone the judiciary. In this situation, as in others of like nature, appeal for relief does not belong here. Appeal must be to an informed, civically militant electorate. In a democratic society like ours, relief must come through an aroused popular conscience that sears the conscience of the people's representatives. In any event there is nothing judicially more unseemly nor more self-defeating than for this Court to make *in terrorem* pronouncements, to indulge in merely empty rhetoric, sounding a word of promise to the ear, sure to be disappointing to the hope. . . .

From its earliest opinions this Court has consistently recognized a class of controversies which do not lend themselves to judicial standards and judicial remedies. To classify the various instances as "political questions" is rather a form of stating this conclusion than revealing of analysis. Some of the cases so labelled have no relevance here. But from others emerge unifying considerations that are compelling.

1. The cases concerning war or foreign affairs, for example, are usually explained by the necessity of the country's speaking with one voice in such matters. While this concern alone undoubtedly accounts for many of the decisions, others do not fit the pattern. It would hardly embarrass the conduct of war were this Court to determine, in connection with private transactions between litigants, the date upon which war is to be deemed terminated. But the Court has refused to do so. A controlling factor in such cases is that, decision respecting these kinds of complex matters of policy being traditionally committed not to courts but to the political agencies of government for determination by criteria of political expediency, there exists no standard ascertainable by settled judicial experience or process by reference to which a political decision affecting the question at issue between the parties can be judged. . . .

2. The Court has been particularly unwilling to intervene in matters concerning the structure and organization of the political institutions of the States. The abstention from judicial entry into such areas has been greater even than that which marks the Court's ordinary approach to issues of state power challenged under broad federal guarantees. . . .

3. The cases involving Negro disfranchisement are no exception to the principle of avoiding federal judicial intervention into matters of state

government in the absence of an explicit and clear constitutional imperative. For here the controlling command of Supreme Law is plain and unequivocal. An end of discrimination against the Negro was the compelling motive of the Civil War Amendments. . . .

4. The Court has refused to exercise its jurisdiction to pass on "abstract questions of political power, of sovereignty, of government." *Massachusetts v. Mellon*, 262 U.S. 447 [1923]. The "political question" doctrine, in this aspect, reflects the policies underlying the requirement of "standing": that the litigant who would challenge official action must claim infringement of an interest particular and personal to himself, as distinguished from a cause of dissatisfaction with the general frame and functioning of government—a complaint that the political institutions are awry. . . . What renders cases of this kind non-justiciable is not necessarily the nature of the parties to them, for the Court has resolved other issues between similar parties; nor is it the nature of the legal question involved, for the same type of question has been adjudicated when presented in other forms of controversy. The crux of the matter is that courts are not fit instruments of decision where what is essentially at stake is the composition of those large contests of policy traditionally fought out in non-judicial forums, by which governments and the actions of governments are made and unmade. . . .

5. The influence of these converging considerations—the caution not to undertake decision where standards meet for judicial judgment are lacking, the reluctance to interfere with matters of state government in the absence of an unquestionable and effectively enforceable mandate, the unwillingness to make courts arbiters of the broad issues of political organization historically committed to other institutions and for whose adjustment the judicial process is ill-adapted—has been decisive of the settled line of cases, reaching back more than a century, which holds that Art. IV, Sec. 4, of the Constitution, guaranteeing to the States "a Republican Form of Government," is not enforceable through the courts. . . .

The present case involves all of the elements that have made the Guarantee Clause cases non-justiciable. It is, in effect, a Guarantee Clause claim masquerading under a different label. But it cannot make the case more fit for judicial action that appellants invoke the Fourteenth Amendment rather than Art. IV, Sec. 4, where, in fact, the gist of their complaint is the same—unless it can be found that the Fourteenth Amendment speaks with greater particularity to their situation. We have been admonished to avoid "the tyranny of labels." Art. IV, Sec. 4, is not committed by express constitutional terms to Congress. It is the nature of the controversies arising under it, nothing else, which has made it judicially unenforceable. Of course, if a controversy falls within judicial power, it depends "on how he [the plaintiff] casts his action," whether he brings himself within a jurisdictional statute. But where judicial competence is wanting, it cannot be created by invoking one clause of the Constitution rather than another. . . .

Appellants invoke the right to vote and to have their votes counted. But they are permitted to vote and their votes are counted. They go to the polls, they cast their ballots, they send their representatives to the state councils. Their complaint is simply that the representatives are not sufficiently numerous or powerful—in short, that Tennessee has adopted a basis of representation with which they are dissatisfied. . . . What is actually asked of the Court in this case is to choose among competing bases of representation—ultimately, really, among competing theories of political philosophy—in order to establish an appropriate frame of government for the State of Tennessee and thereby for all the States of the Union. . . .

To find such a political conception legally enforceable in the broad and unspecific guarantee of equal protection is to rewrite the Constitution. See *Luther v. Borden, supra.* Certainly, "equal protection" is no more secure a foundation for judicial judgment of the permissibility of varying forms of representative government than is "Republican Form." . . .

☐ *Justice HARLAN, with whom Justice FRANKFURTER joins, dissenting.*

I can find nothing in the Equal Protection Clause or elsewhere in the Federal Constitution which expressly or impliedly supports the view that state legislatures must be so structured as to reflect with approximate equality the voice of every voter. Not only is that proposition refuted by history, as shown by my Brother FRANKFURTER, but it strikes deep into the heart of our federal system. Its acceptance would require us to turn our backs on the regard which this Court has always shown for the judgment of state legislatures and courts on matters of basically local concern. . . .

Goldwater v. Carter

444 U.S. 996, 100 S.CT. 533 (1979)

In 1979, Senator Barry Goldwater and several other senators filed suit against President James ("Jimmy") Carter, challenging the constitutionality of Carter's termination of a defense treaty with Taiwan without the approval of the Senate. Underlying the case was the enduring support that the nation's conservative leadership extended toward Taiwan. A tiny island, Taiwan housed the Chinese nationalist government after it was forced out of the China mainland by the new communist government. Granting a petition for *certiorari* but without hearing oral arguments, the Court vacated a court of appeals ruling and remanded the case to a federal district court with directions to dismiss the complaint. In separate concurring opinions, Justice Powell rejected the application of the "political question" doctrine here, while Justice Rehnquist contended that it applies here and in other controversies over foreign policy. In his dissenting opinion, Justice Brennan rejected the idea that the question presented here is "political" and further discussed the scope of the judicial power.

The Court by a vote of six to three ordered the appellate court's judgment vacated and remanded the case to the district court. There were concurrences by Justices Powell and Rehnquist, who was joined by Chief Justice Burger and Justices Stewart and Stevens. Justice Marshall concurred without filing or joining an opinion. Justice Brennan filed a dissent. Justice Blackmun, joined by Justice White, filed a dissent from the Court's refusal to hear oral arguments in the case.

☐ *Justice POWELL, concurring.*

Although I agree with the result reached by the Court, I would dismiss the complaint as not ripe for judicial review.

This Court has recognized that an issue should not be decided if it is not ripe for judicial review. Prudential considerations persuade me that a dispute between Congress and the President is not ready for judicial review unless and until each branch has taken action asserting its constitutional authority. Differences between the President and the Congress are commonplace under our system. The differences should, and almost invariably do, turn on political rather than legal considerations. The Judicial Branch should not decide issues affecting the allocation of power between the President and Congress until the political branches reach a constitutional impasse. Otherwise, we would encourage small groups or even individual Members of Congress to seek judicial resolution of issues before the normal political process has the opportunity to resolve the conflict.

In this case, a few Members of Congress claim that the President's action in terminating the treaty with Taiwan has deprived them of their constitutional role with respect to a change in the supreme law of the land. Congress has taken no official action. In the present posture of this case, we do not know whether there ever will be an actual confrontation between the Legislative and Executive Branches. Although the Senate has considered a resolution declaring that Senate approval is necessary for the termination of any mutual defense treaty, no final vote has been taken on the resolution. Moreover, it is unclear whether the resolution would have retroactive effect. It cannot be said that either the Senate or the House has rejected the President's claim. If the Congress chooses not to confront the President, it is not our task to do so. I therefore concur in the dismissal of this case.

Justice REHNQUIST suggests, however, that the issue presented by this case is a nonjusticiable political question which can never be considered by this Court. I cannot agree. In my view, reliance upon the political-question doctrine is inconsistent with our precedents. As set forth in the seminal case of *Baker v. Carr*, [369 U.S. 186] (1962), the doctrine incorporates three inquiries: (i) Does the issue involve resolution of questions committed by the text of the Constitution to a coordinate branch of Government? (ii) Would resolution of the question demand that a court move beyond areas of judicial expertise? (iii) Do prudential considerations counsel against judicial intervention? In my opinion the answer to each of these inquiries would require us to decide this case if it were ready for review. . . .

In my view, the suggestion that this case presents a political question is incompatible with this Court's willingness on previous occasions to decide whether one branch of our Government has impinged upon the power of another. Under the criteria enunciated in *Baker v. Carr*, we have the responsibility to decide whether both the Executive and Legislative Branches have constitutional roles to play in termination of a treaty. If the Congress, by appropriate formal action, had challenged the President's authority to terminate the treaty with Taiwan, the resulting uncertainty could have serious consequences for our country. In that situation, it would be the duty of this Court to resolve the issue.

☐ *JUSTICE REHNQUIST, with whom THE CHIEF JUSTICE, Justice STEWART, and Justice STEVENS join, concurring.*

I am of the view that the basic question presented by the petitioners in this case is "political" and therefore nonjusticiable because it involves the authority of the President in the conduct of our country's foreign relations and the extent to which the Senate or the Congress is authorized to negate the action of the President. In *Coleman v. Miller*, 307 U.S. 433 (1939), a case in which members of the Kansas Legislature brought an action attacking a vote of the State Senate in favor of the ratification of the Child Labor Amendment, Chief Justice HUGHES wrote in what is referred to as the "Opinion of the Court":

> We think that . . . the question of the efficacy of ratifications by state legislatures, in the light of previous rejection or attempted withdrawal, should be regarded as a political question pertaining to the political departments, with the ultimate authority in the Congress in the exercise of its control over the promulgation of the adoption of the Amendment.
>
> The precise question as now raised is whether, when the legislature of the State, as we have found, has actually ratified the proposed amendment, the Court should restrain the state officers from certifying the ratification to the Secretary of State, because of an earlier rejection, and thus prevent the question from coming before the political departments. We find no basis in either Constitution or statute for such judicial action. Article V, speaking solely of ratification, contains no provision as to rejection.

Thus, Chief Justice HUGHES' opinion concluded that "Congress in controlling the promulgation of the adoption of a constitutional amendment has the final determination of the question whether by lapse of time its proposal of the amendment had lost its vitality prior to the required ratifications." . . .

I believe it follows *a fortiori* from *Coleman* that the controversy in the instant case is a nonjusticiable political dispute that should be left for resolution by the Executive and Legislative Branches of the Government. Here, while the Constitution is express as to the manner in which the Senate shall participate in the ratification of a treaty, it is silent as to that body's participation in the abrogation of a treaty. . . .

I think that the justifications for concluding that the question here is political in nature are even more compelling than in *Coleman* because it involves foreign relations—specifically a treaty commitment to use military force in the defense of a foreign government if attacked. In *United States v. Curtiss-Wright Corp.*, 299 U.S. 304 (1936), this Court said:

> Whether, if the Joint Resolution had related solely to internal affairs it would be open to the challenge that it constituted an un-

lawful delegation of legislative power to the Executive, we find it unnecessary to determine. The whole aim of the resolution is to affect a situation entirely external to the United States, and falling within the category of foreign affairs.

The present case differs in several important respects from *Youngstown Sheet & Tube Co. v. Sawyer*, 343 U.S. 579 (1952), cited by petitioners as authority both for reaching the merits of this dispute and for reversing the Court of Appeals. In *Youngstown*, private litigants brought a suit contesting the President's authority under his war powers to seize the Nation's steel industry, an action of profound and demonstrable domestic impact. Here, by contrast, we are asked to settle a dispute between coequal branches of our Government, each of which has resources available to protect and assert its interests, resources not available to private litigants outside the judicial forum. Moreover, as in *Curtiss-Wright*, the effect of this action, as far as we can tell, is "entirely external to the United States, and [falls] within the category of foreign affairs." Finally, as already noted, the situation presented here is closely akin to that presented in *Coleman*, where the Constitution spoke only to the procedure for ratification of an amendment, not to its rejection.

☐ *Justice BLACKMUN, with whom Justice WHITE joins, dissenting in part.*

In my view, the time factor and its importance are illusory; if the President does not have the power to terminate the treaty (a substantial issue that we should address only after briefing and oral argument), the notice of intention to terminate surely has no legal effect. It is also indefensible, without further study, to pass on the issue of justiciability or on the issues of standing or ripeness. While I therefore join in the grant of the petition for *certiorari*, I would set the case for oral argument and give it the plenary consideration it so obviously deserves.

☐ *Justice BRENNAN, dissenting.*

I respectfully dissent from the order directing the District Court to dismiss this case, and would affirm the judgment of the Court of Appeals insofar as it rests upon the President's well-established authority to recognize, and withdraw recognition from, foreign governments.

In stating that this case presents a non-justiciable "political question," Justice REHNQUIST, in my view, profoundly misapprehends the political-question principle as it applies to matters of foreign relations. Properly understood, the political-question doctrine restrains courts from reviewing an exercise of foreign policy judgment by the coordinate political branch to which authority to make that judgment has been "constitutional[ly] commit[ted]." *Baker v. Carr*. But the doctrine does not pertain when a court is faced with the *antecedent* question whether a particular branch has been constitutionally designated as the repository of political decisionmaking power. The issue of decisionmaking authority must be resolved as a matter of constitutional law, not political discretion; accordingly, it falls within the competence of the courts.

The constitutional question raised here is prudently answered in narrow terms. Abrogation of the defense treaty with Taiwan was a necessary incident to Executive recognition of the Peking Government, because the defense treaty was predicated upon the now-abandoned view that the Taiwan Government was the only legitimate political authority in China. Our cases firmly establish that the Constitution commits to the President alone the power to recognize, and withdraw recognition from, foreign regimes. That mandate being clear, our judicial inquiry into the treaty rupture can go no further.

Elk Grove Unified School District v. Newdow

542 U.S. 1, 124 S.Ct. 2301 (2004)

In 2000, Michael A. Newdow, an atheist, challenged the constitutionality of Elk Grove Unified School District's requirement that teachers lead their classes in reciting the Pledge of Allegiance. Because the Pledge contains the words "under God," he contended that the practice amounted to religious indoctrination and violates the First Amendment. At the time, his daughter was in kindergarten and Newdow was in a custody battle with her mother, Sandra Banning. Banning and Newdow were awarded shared "physical custody," but Banning had "exclusive legal custody." A federal district court dismissed Newdow's complaint, but the Court of Appeals for the Ninth Circuit reversed, holding Newdow had standing as a parent to sue and that the school district's policy violated the (Dis)establishment clause. Banning, then, filed a motion to have the case dismissed on the ground that she was the sole legal custodian and that she did not feel that it was in her daughter's interest to be a party to the suit. The Ninth Circuit, nonetheless, reaffirmed Newdow's standing to challenge allegedly unconstitutional governmental practices, and that under California law he retained the right to expose his child to his religious views, even though they contradicted her mother's Christian views. The school district appealed that decision to the Supreme Court, which granted review. Subsequently, Newdow filed a motion requesting Justice Scalia to recuse himself due to his off-the-bench comments criticizing the Ninth Circuit's ruling that the school district's policy violated the First Amendment.

The Ninth Circuit's decision was unanimously reversed, with Justice Scalia not participating. Justice Stevens delivered the opinion for the Court, holding that Newdow lacked "prudential standing" to raise the challenge on behalf of his daughter, and declined to reach the merits of the case. In three separate concurring opinions, Chief Justice Rehnquist and Justices O'Connor and Thomas indicate that Newdow had standing and they would, though each for different reasons, uphold the school district's policy over First Amendment objections.

☐ *Justice STEVENS delivered the opinion of the Court.*

As part of the nationwide interest in commemorating the 400th anniversary of Christopher Columbus' discovery of America, a widely circulated national magazine for youth proposed in 1892 that pupils recite the following affirmation: "I pledge allegiance to my Flag and the Republic for which it stands: one Nation indivisible, with Liberty and Justice for all." In the 1920's, the National Flag Conferences replaced the phrase "my Flag" with "the flag of the United States of America."

In 1942, in the midst of World War II, Congress adopted, and the President signed, a Joint Resolution codifying a detailed set of "rules and customs pertaining to the display and use of the flag of the United States of America." This resolution, which marked the first appearance of the Pledge of Allegiance in positive law, confirmed the importance of the flag as a symbol of our Nation's indivisibility and commitment to the concept of liberty.

Congress revisited the Pledge of Allegiance 12 years later when it amended the text to add the words "under God." The resulting text is the Pledge as we know it today: "I pledge allegiance to the Flag of the United States of America, and to the Republic for which it stands, one Nation under God, indivisible, with liberty and justice for all." . . .

We granted the School District's petition for a writ of *certiorari* to consider two questions: (1) whether Newdow has standing as a noncustodial parent to challenge the School District's policy, and (2) if so, whether the policy offends the First Amendment. . . .

The command to guard jealously and exercise rarely our power to make constitutional pronouncements requires strictest adherence when matters of great national significance are at stake. Even in cases concededly within our jurisdiction under Article III, we abide by "a series of rules under which [we have] avoided passing upon a large part of all the constitutional questions pressed upon [us] for decision." *Ashwander v. TVA*, 297 U.S. 288 (1936) (BRANDEIS, J., concurring).

Consistent with these principles, our standing jurisprudence contains two strands: Article III standing, which enforces the Constitution's case or controversy requirement; and prudential standing, which embodies "judicially self-imposed limits on the exercise of federal jurisdiction," *Allen [v. Wright*, 468 U.S. 737 (1984)]. . . . Although we have not exhaustively defined the prudential dimensions of the standing doctrine, we have explained that prudential standing encompasses "the general prohibition on a litigant's raising another person's legal rights, the rule barring adjudication of generalized grievances more appropriately addressed in the representative branches, and the requirement that a plaintiff's complaint fall within the zone of interests protected by the law invoked." *Allen.*

One of the principal areas in which this Court has customarily declined to intervene is the realm of domestic relations. Long ago we observed that "[t]he whole subject of the domestic relations of husband and wife, parent and child, belongs to the laws of the States and not to the laws of the United States." *In re Burrus*, 136 U.S. 586 (1890). [W]hile rare instances arise in which it is necessary to answer a substantial federal question that transcends or exists apart from the family law issue, in general it is appropriate for the federal courts to leave delicate issues of domestic relations to the state courts. . . .

Newdow's standing derives entirely from his relationship with his daughter, but . . . the interests of this parent and this child are not parallel and, indeed, are potentially in conflict.

Newdow's parental status is defined by California's domestic relations law. Our custom on questions of state law ordinarily is to defer to the interpretation of the Court of Appeals for the Circuit in which the State is located. In this case, the Court of Appeals, which possesses greater familiarity with California law, concluded that state law vests in Newdow a cognizable right to influence his daughter's religious upbringing. . . . Animated by a conception of "family privacy" that includes "not simply a policy of minimum state intervention but also a presumption of parental autonomy," the state cases create a zone of private authority within which each parent, whether custodial or noncustodial, remains free to impart to the child his or her religious perspective. . . .

In our view, it is improper for the federal courts to entertain a claim by a plaintiff whose standing to sue is founded on family law rights that are in dispute when prosecution of the lawsuit may have an adverse effect on the person who is the source of the plaintiff's claimed standing. When hard questions of domestic relations are sure to affect the outcome, the prudent course is for the federal court to stay its hand rather than reach out to resolve a weighty question of federal constitutional law. There is a vast difference between Newdow's right to communicate with his child—which both California law and the First Amendment recognize—and his claimed right to shield his daughter from influences to which she is exposed in school despite the terms of the custody order. We conclude that, having been deprived under California law of the right to sue as next friend, Newdow lacks prudential standing to bring this suit in federal court.

□ *Chief Justice REHNQUIST, with whom Justice O'CONNOR joins, and with whom Justice THOMAS joins as to Part I, concurring in the judgment.*

The Court today erects a novel prudential standing principle in order to avoid reaching the merits of the constitutional claim. I dissent from that ruling. On the merits, I conclude that the Elk Grove Unified School District policy that requires teachers to lead willing students in reciting the Pledge of Allegiance, which includes the words "under God," does not violate the Establishment Clause of the First Amendment.

[T]he Court does not dispute that respondent Newdow satisfies the requisites of Article III standing. But curiously the Court incorporates criticism of the Court of Appeals' Article III standing decision into its justification for its novel prudential standing principle. The Court concludes that respondent lacks prudential standing, under its new standing principle, to bring his suit in federal court.

We have, in the past, judicially self-imposed clear limits on the exercise of federal jurisdiction. In contrast, here is the Court's new prudential standing principle: "[I]t is improper for the federal courts to entertain a claim by a plaintiff whose standing to sue is founded on family law rights that are in dispute when prosecution of the lawsuit may have an adverse effect on the person who is the source of the plaintiff's claimed standing." . . .

First, the Court relies heavily on *Ankenbrandt v. Richards*, 504 U.S. 689 (1992), in which we discussed both the domestic relations exception and the abstention doctrine. . . . We . . . conclude[ed] that the domestic relations exception only applies when a party seeks to have a district court issue a "divorce, alimony, and child custody decree." We further held that abstention was inappropriate because "the status of the domestic relationship ha[d] been determined as a matter of state law, and in any event ha[d] no bearing on the underlying torts alleged."

The Court['s] conclusion does not follow from *Ankenbrandt*'s discussion of the domestic relations exception and abstention; even if it did, it would not be applicable in this case because, on the merits, this case presents a substantial federal question that transcends the family law. . . .

Although the Court may have succeeded in confining this novel principle almost narrowly enough to be, like the proverbial excursion ticket—good for this day only—our doctrine of prudential standing should be governed by general principles, rather than ad hoc improvisations. . . .

The phrase "under God" in the Pledge seems, as a historical matter, to sum up the attitude of the Nation's leaders, and to manifest itself in many of our public observances. Examples of patriotic invocations of God and official acknowledgments of religion's role in our Nation's history abound.

At George Washington's first inauguration on April 30, 1789, . . . "Washington put his right hand on the *Bible*, opened to Psalm 121:1: 'I raise my eyes toward the hills. Whence shall my help come.' The Chancellor proceeded with the oath: 'Do you solemnly swear that you will faithfully execute the office of President of the United States and will to the best of your ability preserve, protect and defend the Constitution of the United States?' The President responded, 'I solemnly swear,' and repeated the oath, adding, 'So help me God.' He then bent forward and kissed the Bible before him."

Later the same year, after encouragement from Congress, Washington issued his first Thanksgiving proclamation, which began: "Whereas it is the duty of all Nations to acknowledge the providence of Almighty God, to obey His will, to be grateful for his benefits, and humbly to implore his protection and favor—and whereas both Houses of Congress have by their joint Committee requested me 'to recommend to the People of the United States a day of public thanksgiving and prayer to be observed by acknowledging with grateful hearts the many signal favors of Almighty God especially by affording them an opportunity peaceably to establish a form of government for their safety and happiness.' "

Almost all succeeding Presidents have issued similar Thanksgiving proclamations. Later Presidents, at critical times in the Nation's history, have likewise invoked the name of God. . . .

The motto "In God We Trust" first appeared on the country's coins during the Civil War. [I]n 1956, Congress declared that the motto of the United States would be "In God We Trust."

Our Court Marshal's opening proclamation concludes with the words "God save the United States and this honorable Court." . . .

I do not believe that the phrase "under God" in the Pledge converts its recital into a "religious exercise" of the sort described in *Lee* [*v. Weisman*, 505 U.S. 577 (1992)]. Instead, it is a declaration of belief in allegiance and loyalty to the United States flag and the Republic that it represents. The phrase "under God" is in no sense a prayer, nor an endorsement of any religion. . . . Reciting the Pledge, or listening to others recite it, is a patriotic exercise, not a religious one; participants promise fidelity to our flag and our Nation, not to any particular God, faith, or church. . . .

When courts extend constitutional prohibitions beyond their previously recognized limit, they may restrict democratic choices made by public bodies. . . . The Constitution only requires that schoolchildren be entitled to abstain from the ceremony if they chose to do so. To give the parent of such a child a sort of "heckler's veto" over a patriotic ceremony willingly participated in by other students, simply because the Pledge of Allegiance contains the descriptive phrase "under God," is an unwarranted extension of the Establishment Clause, an extension which would have the unfortunate effect of prohibiting a commendable patriotic observance.

☐ *Justice O'CONNOR, concurring in the judgment.*

I join the concurrence of THE CHIEF JUSTICE in full. Like him, I would follow our policy of deferring to the Federal Courts of Appeals in matters that involve the interpretation of state law, and thereby conclude that the respondent does have standing to bring his constitutional claim before a federal court. Like THE CHIEF JUSTICE, I believe that petitioner school district's policy of having its teachers lead students in voluntary recitations of the Pledge of Allegiance does not offend the Establishment Clause. But while the history presented by THE CHIEF JUSTICE illuminates the constitutional problems this case presents, I write separately to explain the principles that guide my own analysis of the constitutionality of that policy. . . .

When a court confronts a challenge to government-sponsored speech or displays, I continue to believe that the endorsement test "captures the essential command of the Establishment Clause, namely, that government must not make a person's religious beliefs relevant to his or her standing in the political community by conveying a message 'that religion or a particular religious belief is favored or preferred.' " *County of Allegheny v. American Civil Liberties Union, Greater Pittsburgh Chapter*, 492 U.S. 573 (1989) (opinion of O'CONNOR, J.).

Endorsement, I have explained, "sends a message to nonadherents that they are outsiders, not full members of the political community, and an accompanying message to adherents that they are insiders, favored members of the political community." In order to decide whether endorsement has occurred, a reviewing court must keep in mind two crucial and related principles.

First, because the endorsement test seeks "to identify those situations in which government makes adherence to a religion relevant . . . to a person's standing in the political community," it assumes the viewpoint of a reasonable observer. Given the dizzying religious heterogeneity of our Nation, adopting a subjective approach would reduce the test to an absurdity. Nearly

any government action could be overturned as a violation of the Establishment Clause if a "heckler's veto" sufficed to show that its message was one of
endorsement.

The Court has permitted government, in some instances, to refer to or
commemorate religion in public life. . . . One such purpose is to commemorate the role of religion in our history. . . . For centuries, we have marked
important occasions or pronouncements with references to God and invocations of divine assistance. Such references can serve to solemnize an occasion
instead of to invoke divine provenance. . . .

This case requires us to determine whether the appearance of the phrase
"under God" in the Pledge of Allegiance constitutes an instance of such ceremonial deism. Although it is a close question, I conclude that it does, based
on my evaluation of the following four factors.

HISTORY AND UBIQUITY

The constitutional value of ceremonial deism turns on a shared understanding of its legitimate nonreligious purposes. That sort of understanding
can exist only when a given practice has been in place for a significant portion of the Nation's history, and when it is observed by enough persons that
it can fairly be called ubiquitous. By contrast, novel or uncommon references
to religion can more easily be perceived as government endorsements because the reasonable observer cannot be presumed to be fully familiar with
their origins. As a result, in examining whether a given practice constitutes
an instance of ceremonial deism, its "history and ubiquity" will be of great
importance. . . .

ABSENCE OF WORSHIP OR PRAYER

"[O]ne of the greatest dangers to the freedom of the individual to worship in his own way [lies] in the Government's placing its official stamp of
approval upon one particular kind of prayer or one particular form of religious services." *Engel v. Vitale*, 370 U.S. 421 (1962). Because of this principle,
only in the most extraordinary circumstances could actual worship or prayer
be defended as ceremonial deism. . . .

ABSENCE OF REFERENCE TO PARTICULAR RELIGION

"The clearest command of the Establishment Clause is that one religious denomination cannot be officially preferred over another." *Larson v.
Valente*, 456 U.S. 228 (1982). . . . As a result, no religious acknowledgment
could claim to be an instance of ceremonial deism if it explicitly favored one
particular religious belief system over another.

The Pledge complies with this requirement. It does not refer to a nation
"under Jesus" or "under Vishnu," but instead acknowledges religion in a general way: a simple reference to a generic "God." . . . The phrase "under God,"
conceived and added at a time when our national religious diversity was neither as robust nor as well recognized as it is now, represents a tolerable attempt to acknowledge religion and to invoke its solemnizing power without
favoring any individual religious sect or belief system.

MINIMAL RELIGIOUS CONTENT

A final factor that makes the Pledge an instance of ceremonial deism, in my view, is its highly circumscribed reference to God. [T]he brevity of a reference to religion or to God in a ceremonial exercise can be important for several reasons. First, it tends to confirm that the reference is being used to acknowledge religion or to solemnize an event rather than to endorse religion in any way. Second, it makes it easier for those participants who wish to "opt out" of language they find offensive to do so without having to reject the ceremony entirely. And third, it tends to limit the ability of government to express a preference for one religious sect over another. . . .

Michael Newdow's challenge to petitioner school district's policy is a well-intentioned one, but his distaste for the reference to "one Nation under God," however sincere, cannot be the yardstick of our Establishment Clause inquiry. Certain ceremonial references to God and religion in our Nation are the inevitable consequence of the religious history that gave birth to our founding principles of liberty. It would be ironic indeed if this Court were to wield our constitutional commitment to religious freedom so as to sever our ties to the traditions developed to honor it.

□ *Justice THOMAS, concurring in the judgment.*

Because I agree with THE CHIEF JUSTICE that respondent Newdow has standing, I would take this opportunity to begin the process of rethinking the Establishment Clause. I would acknowledge that the Establishment Clause is a federalism provision, which, for this reason, resists incorporation. Moreover, as I will explain, the Pledge policy is not implicated by any sensible incorporation of the Establishment Clause, which would probably cover little more than the Free Exercise Clause.

In *Lee* [*v. Weisman*], the Court held that invocations and benedictions could not, consistent with the Establishment Clause, be given at public secondary school graduations. . . . It brushed aside both the fact that the students were not required to attend the graduation, and the fact that they were not compelled, in any meaningful sense, to participate in the religious component of the graduation ceremony. The Court surmised that the prayer violated the Establishment Clause because a high school student could—in light of the "peer pressure" to attend graduation and "to stand as a group or, at least, maintain respectful silence during the invocation and benediction"— have "a reasonable perception that she is being forced by the State to pray in a manner her conscience will not allow."

Adherence to *Lee* would require us to strike down the Pledge policy, which, in most respects, poses more serious difficulties than the prayer at issue in *Lee*. A prayer at graduation is a one-time event, the graduating students are almost (if not already) adults, and their parents are usually present. By contrast, very young students, removed from the protection of their parents, are exposed to the Pledge each and every day. . . .

I conclude that, as a matter of our precedent, the Pledge policy is unconstitutional. I believe, however, that *Lee* was wrongly decided. *Lee* depended on a notion of "coercion" that . . . has no basis in law or reason. The kind of coercion implicated by the Religion Clauses is that accomplished "by force of law and threat of penalty." Peer pressure, unpleasant as it may be, is not coercion. But rejection of *Lee*-style "coercion" does not suffice to settle this case. Although children are not coerced to pledge their allegiance, they are legally coerced to attend school. Because what is at issue is a state action, the question becomes whether the Pledge policy implicates a religious liberty right protected by the Fourteenth Amendment.

I accept that the Free Exercise Clause, which clearly protects an individual right, applies against the States through the Fourteenth Amendment. But the Establishment Clause is another matter. The text and history of the Establishment Clause strongly suggest that it is a federalism provision intended to prevent Congress from interfering with state establishments. Thus, unlike the Free Exercise Clause, which does protect an individual right, it makes little sense to incorporate the Establishment Clause. In any case, I do not believe that the Pledge policy infringes any religious liberty right that would arise from incorporation of the Clause. Because the Pledge policy also does not infringe any free-exercise rights, I conclude that it is constitutional.

■ CONSTITUTIONAL HISTORY

Rules for Judicial Self-Restraint and Avoiding Constitutional Questions

Justice Louis D. Brandeis, concurring in *Ashwander v. Tennessee Valley Authority*, 297 U.S. 288 (1936), summarized some prudential rules for exercising judicial self-restraint and avoiding ruling on the constitutionality of congressional legislation:

> The Court developed, for its own governance in the cases confessedly within its jurisdiction, a series of rules under which it has avoided passing upon a large part of all the constitutional questions pressed upon it for decision. They are:
>
> 1. The Court will not pass upon the constitutionality of legislation in a friendly, non-adversary, proceeding, declining because to decide such questions "is legitimate only in the last resort, and as a necessity in the determination of real, earnest and vital controversy between individuals. . . .
>
> 2. The Court will not "anticipate a question of constitutional law in advance of the necessity of deciding it." *Liverpool, N.Y. & P. S. S. Co. v. Emigration Commissioners*, 113 U.S. 33 [(1885)]. . . .
>
> 3. The Court will not "formulate a rule of constitutional law broader than is required by the precise facts to which it is to be applied." *Liverpool*.

(continues)

■ CONSTITUTIONAL HISTORY
Rules for Judicial Self-Restraint and Avoiding Constitutional Questions (continued)

4. The Court will not pass upon a constitutional question although properly presented by the record, if there is also present some other ground upon which the case may be disposed of. . . . Appeals from the highest court of a state challenging its decision of a question under the Federal Constitution are frequently dismissed because the judgment can be sustained on an independent state ground.

5. The Court will not pass upon the validity of a statute upon complaint of one who fails to show that he is injured by its operation. Among the many applications of this rule, none is more striking than the denial of the right of challenge to one who lacks a personal or property right.

6. The Court will not pass upon the constitutionality of a statute at the instance of one who has availed himself of its benefits.

7. "When the validity of an act of the Congress is drawn in question, and even if a serious doubt of constitutionality is raised, it is a cardinal principle that this Court will first ascertain whether a construction of the statute is fairly possible by which the question maybe avoided." *Crowell v. Benson*, 285 U.S. 22 [(1932)].

B | *The Court's Docket and Screening Cases*

The justices' interpretation of their jurisdiction and rules governs access to the Court. But they also need flexible procedures for screening cases and deciding what to decide. This is because the Court's docket has grown phenomenally (see CONSTITUTIONAL HISTORY: Docket and Filings, 1800–2009, this chapter).

When any appeal or *cert.* petition arrives at the Court it immediately goes to the clerk's office. Staff look at whether it satisfies requirements as to form, length, and fees and if the filing is from an indigent whether there is an affidavit stating that the petitioner is too poor to pay fees. All unpaid cases are assigned a number in the order they arrive, and placed on what is called the Miscellaneous Docket. Paid cases are also assigned a number but placed on the Appellate Docket. The clerk then notifies the other party, or respondent, in each case that he or she must file a brief in response within thirty days. After receiving briefs from respondents, the clerk circulates to the justices' chambers a list of cases ready for consideration and a set of briefs for each case.

For much of the Court's history every justice was responsible for reviewing each case. The justices did not work by panels or delegate responsibility for screening cases to others. That is no longer true. In 1972 the "*cert.* pool" was established. Eight of the justices now share their collective law clerks' memos on all paid and unpaid cases. The memos explain the facts, issues raised, and lower court ruling as well as recommend whether the case should be granted or denied. Those justices not joining the pool—now only Alito—receive copies of unpaid cases along with other filings. Stevens also had his clerks screen all the cases and write memos only on those they thought were important enough for him to consider.

C | *The Rule of Four and Agenda Setting*

When Congress gave the Court discretionary jurisdiction in the Judiciary Act of 1925, by substituting petitions for *certiorari* for mandatory appeals, the justices developed the informal "rule of four" to decide which petitions they would grant. During conference, at least four justices must agree that a case warrants oral argument and consideration by the full Court.

The rule of four operates in a fraction of cases due to the increasing caseload, which is a result of a number of factors. Most important, institutional norms promote a shared conception of the role of the Court as a tribunal for resolving only issues of national importance. Justices agree that the overwhelming proportion of cases is "frivolous," and that there is a limited number of cases to which they may give full consideration.

The caseload and institutional norms push toward limiting the operation of the rule of four. But the rule remains useful, particularly if there is a bloc of justices who share the same ideological orientation. The rule of four thus enables a bloc of justices to work together in picking cases they want the Court to rule on.

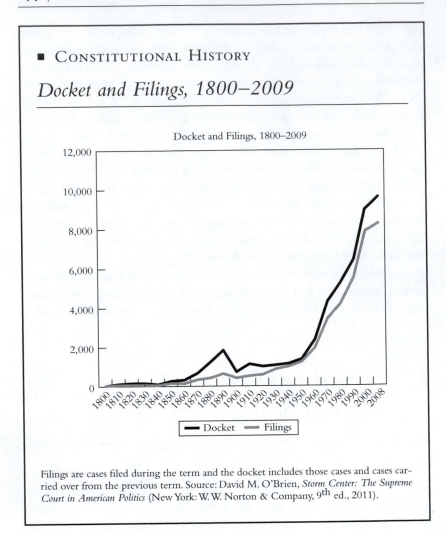

■ CONSTITUTIONAL HISTORY

Docket and Filings, 1800–2009

Docket and Filings, 1800–2009

Filings are cases filed during the term and the docket includes those cases and cases carried over from the previous term. Source: David M. O'Brien, *Storm Center: The Supreme Court in American Politics* (New York: W. W. Norton & Company, 9th ed., 2011).

Denial of *certiorari* is an important technique for managing the Court's caseload. But its meaning in particular cases may be far from clear. The Court has few fixed rules, and even the rule of four is not "an absolutely inflexible rule."[1] Although enabling the Court to manage its business, denials invite confusion and the suspicion, as Justice Jackson once observed, "that this Court no longer respects impersonal rules of law but is guided in these matters by personal impression which from time to time may be shared by a majority of the justices."[2]

The Court now decides less than 1 percent of the cases annually arriving on its docket.[3] That is far less than thirty years ago, when about 3 percent of a much smaller docket were granted and decided. Then, the docket was just reaching 5,000 cases and the justices decided between 150 and 180 cases a term. The docket now hovers around 9,000, yet the justices decide less than 80 cases a year. That is the same number decided by the Court in 1955 when the docket remained under 2,000. Even if the Court in the 1990s and 2000s had continued to grant as many cases as it did in the 1970s and 1980s, the percentage granted would have declined, of course, due to the continued growth in the caseload. Still, the diminished plenary docket is striking and probably reflects a combination of factors internal and external to the Court, which undoubtedly contributed to the inflation of the plenary docket during the Burger Court years (1969–1986) and to its contraction thereafter. Early in his chief justiceship, Burger expanded the size of the oral argument calendar in order to accommodate more cases, because of his concern about the Court's declining supervisory capacity. During Burger's chief justiceship, the discipline imposed by the rule of four was also weakened by the emergence of the practice of casting Join-3 votes and the increased circulation of dissents from denial of review, especially by Justice White who drew attention to cases raising conflicts among the lower courts that the Court was not resolving. A Join-3 vote is a vote to provide a fourth vote if others vote to grant review, but is otherwise considered as voting to deny. In the 1970s and 1980s, Join-3 votes arguably lowered the threshold for granting cases, thereby weakening the self-discipline imposed by the rule of four and contributing to the inflation of the plenary docket.

As the Court's composition changed from the 1990s through the first decade of the twenty-first century, so did the justices' voting practices when deciding what to decide: both Join-3 votes and dissents from denial became no longer commonplace and the justices became more tolerant of intercircuit conflicts. In addition, the Judicial Improvements and Access to Justice Act of 1988 eliminated virtually all remaining nondiscretionary appellate jurisdiction, thereby increasing the Court's "managerial capacity" for controlling the plenary docket by denying *cert.* to more cases. Finally, the institutionalization of the *cert.* pool over the past quarter of a century undoubtedly contributed to the shrinking plenary docket in several ways: more justices now rely, and rely to a greater degree than before, on their law clerks' *cert.* memos; there is, thus, less independent review of petitions by the justices themselves; and, as Stevens has suggested, the clerks tend to be "risk averse" when recommending that cases be granted.

■ IN COMPARATIVE PERSPECTIVE

The "European Model" of Constitutional Courts and Judicial Review

In most European states, the institution and power of "American-style" judicial review has been rejected. Instead, institutions called constitutional courts have been established in Austria (1945), Italy (1948), the Federal Republic of Germany (1949), France (1958), Portugal (1976), Spain (1978), and Belgium (1985), as well as in many of the post-communist countries in Eastern Europe (after 1989), including the Czech Republic, Hungary, Poland, Romania, Russia, and Slovakia.

In contrast to the United States federal judiciary, which has general jurisdiction over issues of constitutional and statutory law, European courts have historically been subordinate to legislatures and denied jurisdiction over constitutional matters. The constitutional courts created in post–World War II Europe thus were an innovation, although their powers of judicial review differed from the American model in several key respects. European constitutional courts are (1) formally detached from the judiciary, (2) given exclusive jurisdiction over constitutional questions, and (3) authorized to exercise review as well as to issue advisory opinions at the request of other governmental institutions.

Unlike the U.S. federal judiciary's jurisdiction over only actual cases or controversies, European constitutional courts may exercise abstract and concrete constitutional review of legislation. *Abstract constitutional review* of legislation is initiated by elected officials or national and regional governmental bodies with respect to legislation that has been recently adopted that either (1) has not yet been put into force (as in France) or (2) has not yet been enforced, or has been suspended, pending review by the constitutional court (as in Germany, Italy, and Spain). In short, before controversial legislation goes into effect the constitutional court must pass on its constitutionality, and thereafter the legislation may be revised. *Concrete constitutional review* arises from litigation in the courts when ordinary judges are uncertain about the constitutionality or the application of a statute or ordinance; in such cases the judges refer the constitutional question or complaint to the constitutional court for resolution.

The principal features of the European model of constitutional courts and judicial review in France, Germany, Italy, and Spain are summarized on the following page.

	FRANCE	GERMANY	ITALY	SPAIN
Court and Date of Creation	Constitutional Council (1958)	Federal Constitutional Court (1949)	Italian Constitutional Court (1956)	Spanish Constitutional Court (1978)
JURISDICTION				
Abstract review	Yes	Yes	Yes	Yes
Authority to initiate abstract review of legislation	President, Presidential Assembly, or Senate	Federal and länder (state) governments or one-third of the Bundestag	National government (against regional laws); regional governments (against national laws)	Prime minister, president of the Parliament, 50 deputies or senators, executives of autonomous regions, and ombudsmen
Laws referred	National	Federal and lander legislation	National and regional legislation	National and regional legislation
Laws must be referred	Within 15 days of adoption	Within 30 days of adoption	Within 30 days of adoption	Within 90 days of adoption
Concrete review	Yes (as of 2008)	Yes	Yes	Yes
Authority to initiate concrete review of legislation		Judiciary and individuals (after exhaustion of judicial remedies)	Judiciary	Judiciary, ombudsmen, and individuals (after exhaustion of judicial remedies)
COMPOSITION, RECRUITMENT, TENURE				
Number of judges	9	16	15	12
Recruitment	Named by the president (3) and assembly (6)	Elected by the Bundestag (8) and Bundesrat (8)	Named by the president (5), judiciary (5); elected by the Parliament (5)	Named by the federal government (2), judiciary (2); elected by the Congress (4) and Senate (4)

(continues)

■ In Comparative Perspective:
*The "European Model" of Constitutional Courts
and Judicial Review (continued)*

	FRANCE	GERMANY	ITALY	SPAIN
Length of term	9 years	12 years	9 years	9 years

For further reading, see Donald P. Kommers, *The Constitutional Jurisprudence of the Federal Republic of Germany* 2d ed., (Durham, NC: Duke University Press, 1997); Alex Stone, *The Birth of Judicial Politics in France* (New York: Oxford University Press, 1992); Mary Volcansek, *Constitutional Politics in Italy: The Constitutional Court* (New York: St. Martin's Press, 2000); Alec Stone Sweet, *Governing with Judges: Constitutional Politics in Europe* (New York: Oxford University Press, 2000); Carlo Guarnieri and Patrizia Pederzoli, *The Comparative Study of Courts and Democracy* (Oxford: Oxford University Press, 2002); and Georg Nolte, ed., *European and U.S. Constitutionalism (New York: Cambridge University Press, 2005).* See also Karen Alter, *The European Court's Political Power* (New York: Oxford University Press, 2009).

Notes

1. Potter Stewart, "Inside the Supreme Court," *The New York Times*, Oct. 1, 1979, p. 17A, col. 2.

2. *Brown v. Allen*, 344 U.S. 443, 535 (1953) (Jackson, J., concurring opinion).

3. This discussion draws on the author's analysis in "Join-3 Votes, the Rule of Four, the *Cert*. Pool, and the Supreme Court's Shrinking Plenary Docket," 13 *The Journal of Law & Politics* 779 (1997); and in "A Diminished Plenary Docket: A Legacy of the Rehnquist Court," 89 *Judicature* 134 (2005).

Selected Bibliography

Johnson, Timothy, and Goldman, Jerry, eds. *A Good Quarrel: America's Top Legal Reporters Share Stories from Inside the Supreme Court.* Ann Arbor: University of Michigan Press, 2008.

Pacelle, Richard L. *The Transformation of the Supreme Court's Agenda: From the New Deal to the Reagan Administration.* Boulder, CO: Westview Press, 1991.

Perry, H. W. *Deciding to Decide: Agenda Setting in the United States Supreme Court.* Cambridge, MA: Harvard University Press, 1991.

Provine, Doris Marie. *Case Selection in the United States Supreme Court.* Chicago: University of Chicago Press, 1980.

Scalia, Antonin, and Garner, Bryan. *Making Your Case: The Art of Persuading Judges.* St. Paul, MN: West, 2008.

Wrightsman, Lawrence. *Oral Arguments Before the Supreme Court.* New York: Oxford University Press, 2008.

D | *Summarily Decided Cases*

Even before the 1988 Act to Improve the Administration of Justice, which eliminated virtually all mandatory appeals, the distinction between mandatory and discretionary review of appeals and *cert.* petitions had largely disappeared in the Court's process of deciding what to decide. The Court annually received between 300 and 400 appeals, and the overwhelming majority were summarily decided (without hearing oral arguments and full consideration). They simply dismissed them for want of jurisdiction or failure to present a substantial federal question, or they ordered the lower court ruling affirmed or reversed.

Summarily decided cases enabled the Court to cut down on its workload. But they also engendered confusion among the lower courts. Summary decisions take the form of rather cryptic orders or *per curiam* (unsigned) opinions. Like denials of *cert.* petitions, they invite confusion over how the Court views the merits of a case and the lower court ruling. The problem is one of the Court's own making. The Court holds that summarily decided cases do not have the same precedential weight as plenary decisions, but they are nonetheless binding on lower courts "until such time as the Court informs [them] that [they] are not." *Hicks v. Arizona,* 422 U.S. 322 (1975).

E | *The Role of Oral Argument*

The Court grants a full hearing—that is, oral argument—to less than 80 of the approximately 9,000 cases on the docket each term. When cases are granted full consideration, attorneys for each side submit briefs setting forth their arguments and how they think the case should be decided. The clerk of the Court circulates the briefs to each chamber and sets a date for the attorneys to argue their views orally before the justices. After hearing oral arguments, the justices vote in private conference on how to decide the issues presented in a case.

Court..CA - 2..................   Voted on.....11./.8....../...., 19.90

Argued......./'./.>.q............., 19.90.   Assigned ...11./.13.c9....., 19.90.   No. 89-1391

Submitted............................, 19.....   Announced....5./.23..., 19.91.   Vide 89-1392

IRVING RUST, ETC., ET AL., Petitioners

VS.

LOUIS W. SULLIVAN, SECRETARY OF HEALTH AND HUMAN SERVICES

3/01/90 - Cert.

5/29/91 cert. granted

HOLD FOR	CERT.			JURISDICTIONAL STATEMENT				MERITS		MOTION			
	G	D	C&R	N	POST	DIS	AFF	REV	AFF	G	D		
Rehnquist, Ch. J. *assigned*									✓				
~~Brennan, J.~~									✓				
White, J.	✓								✓				
Marshall, J.	✓							✓					
Blackmun, J.								✓					
Stevens, J.								✓			*in part*		
O'Connor, J.								✓	✓				
Scalia, J.									✓				
Kennedy, J.								✓					

19020–2–88

Page from docket book.
(*Library of Congress, Justice Thurgood Marshall Papers.*)

For fourteen weeks each term, from the first Monday in October until the end of April, the Court hears arguments on Monday, Tuesday, and Wednesday about every two weeks. The importance of oral argument, Chief Justice Hughes observed, lies in the fact that often "the impression that a judge has at the close of a full oral argument accords with the conviction which controls his final vote."[1] The justices hold conference and take their initial, often decisive, vote on cases within a day or two after hearing arguments. Oral arguments come at a crucial time. They focus the minds of the justices and present the possibility for fresh perspectives on a case. It is the only opportunity for attorneys to communicate directly with the justices. Two basic factors appear to control the relative importance of oral argument. As Justice Wiley Rutledge observed, "One is brevity. The other is the preparation with which the judge comes to it."[2] When the Court revised its rules in 1980, the justices underscored that "*[t]he Court looks with disfavor on any oral argument that is read from a prepared text.*" Central to preparation and delivery is a bird's-eye view of the case, the issues and facts, and the reasoning behind legal developments. Crisp, concise, and conversational presentations are what the justices want. An attorney must never forget, in Chief Justice Rehnquist's words, that "[h]e is not, after all, presenting his case to some abstract, platonic embodiment of appellate judges as a class, but . . . nine flesh and blood men and women." Oral argument is definitely not a "brief with gestures."[3]

Notably, in 2000 the Supreme Court created its own web site (at www.supremecourt.gov) that makes available transcripts of oral arguments and the full text of its decisions and opinions, until they are officially published. In 2006, the Roberts Court began posting transcripts on its web site on the same day of hearing oral arguments. In addition, for the first time the transcripts indicated the name of the justice asking questions and responding to attorneys. The oral arguments in prior decisions may also be heard at the Oyez Project at www.oyez.org.

NOTES

1. Charles E. Hughes, *The Supreme Court of the United States* (New York: Columbia University Press, 1928), 61.

2. Wiley Rutledge, "The Appellate Brief," 28 *American Bar Association Journal* 251 (1942).

3. William Rehnquist, "Oral Advocacy: A Disappearing Art," Brainerd Currie Lecture, Mercer University School of Law, Oct. 20, 1983, msp. 4. See, generally, Timothy Johnson, *Oral Arguments and Decision Making on the U.S. Supreme Court* (Albany: SUNY Press, 2004).

F | *Conference Deliberations*

The justices meet alone in conference to decide which cases to accept and to discuss the merits of those few cases on which they hear oral arguments. Throughout the term during the weeks in which the Court hears oral arguments, conferences are held on Wednesday afternoons to take up the four cases argued on Monday, and then on Fridays to discuss new filings and the eight cases for which oral argument was heard on Tuesday and Wednesday. In May and June, when the Court does not hear oral arguments, conferences are held on Thursdays, from ten in the morning until four or four-thirty in the afternoon, with the justices breaking for a forty-five-minute lunch around twelve-thirty. A majority may vote to hold a special session during the summer months, when extraordinarily urgent cases arise.

Members of the Burger Court, in the tradition begun by Chief Justice Melville Fuller, shaking hands prior to going on the bench to hear oral arguments. (© *Yoichi Okamoto, Photo Researchers.*)

■ INSIDE THE COURT

On the Tentativeness of Votes and the Importance of Opinion Writing

In two controversial cases, involving claims by the press to a First Amendment right of access to visit and interview prisoners, Chief Justice Burger switched his vote after conference. During the conference discussion of *Pell v. Procunier* 417 U.S. 817 (1974) and *Saxbe v. Washington Post* 417 U.S. 843 (1974), the vote went five to four for recognizing that the press has a First Amendment right of access. But Burger later changed his mind and explained that the final outcome of the cases depended on how the opinions were written:

> This difficult case has few very clear cut and fixed positions but my further study over the weekend leads me to see my position as closer for those who would sustain the authority of the corrections administrators than those who would not! I would therefore reverse in 73–754, affirm in 73–918 and reverse in 73–1265.

> This is another one of those cases that will depend a good deal on "how it is written." The solution to the problem must be allowed time for experimentation and I fear an "absolute" constitutional holding adverse to administrators will tend to "freeze" progress.

The Court ultimately divided five to four but held that the press does not have a First Amendment right of access to interview inmates of prisons.

For other notable instances of vote switching that dramatically affected the outcome, see in Volume 1, Chapter 7, the box INSIDE THE COURT and the discussion of *Garcia v. San Antonio Metropolitan Transit Authority*, 469 U.S. 528 (1985) (excerpted there); and in Volume 2, Chapter 6, the box INSIDE THE COURT: Justice Kennedy Switches Positions and the Outcome in *Lee v. Weisman*; and Volume 2, Chapter 11, the box INSIDE THE COURT: Vote Switching in *Bowers v. Hardwick* and Justice Powell's April 8, 1986, Memorandum. These examples illustrate how important postconference deliberations and communications among the chambers have become for the Court's decision making.

Source: Library of Congress, Justice William J. Brennan, Jr., Papers, Manuscripts Room.

Summoned by a buzzer five minutes before the hour, the justices meet in the conference room, located directly behind the courtroom itself and next to the chief justice's chamber. The oak-paneled room is lined with *United States Reports* (containing the Court's decisions). Over the mantel of an exquisite fireplace at one end hangs a portrait of Chief Justice Marshall. Next to the fireplace stands a large rectangular table where the justices sit. The chief justice sits at the one end and the senior associate justice (Scalia) at the other. Along the right-hand side of the chief justice, next to the fireplace, sit Kennedy, Thomas, and Ginsburg; on the left-hand side, sit Breyer, Alito, Sotomayor, and Kagan, the most junior justice. The seating of the justices traditionally has been on the basis of seniority. But variations occur due to individual justices' preferences.

Two conference lists are circulated to each chamber by noon on Wednesday prior to the Friday conference. They structure conference discussion and enable the justices to get through their caseload. On the first list—Special List I, or the Discuss List—are jurisdictional statements, petitions for *certiorari*, and motions that are ready and worth discussing. The Discuss List typically includes between forty and fifty cases for each conference. Attached is a second list—Special List II, or what was called the Dead List—containing those cases considered unworthy of discussion. Any justice may request that a case be put on the Discuss List, and only after the chief's conference secretary has heard from all chambers do the lists become final. Over 90 percent of the cases on the conference lists are automatically denied without discussion, and most of those that do make the Discuss List are denied as well. The conference lists are an important technique for saving time and focusing attention on the few cases deemed worthy of consideration.

The significance of conference discussions has changed with the increasing caseload. Conference discussions do not play the role that they once did. When the docket was smaller in the nineteenth century, conferences were integral to the justices' collective deliberations. As the caseload grew, conferences became largely symbolic of past collective deliberations. They now serve only to discover consensus. There is no longer time to reach agreement and compromise on opinions for the Court. "In fact," Justice Antonin Scalia claims, "to call our discussion of a case a conference is really something of a misnomer. It's much more a statement of the views of each of the nine Justices."[1] More discussion, however, he admits would probably not contribute much or lead justices to change their minds when voting on cases. This is because the justices confront similar issues year after year and, as Chief Justice Rehnquist observed, "it would be surprising if [justices] voted differently than they had the previous time."[2]

The justices' votes are always tentative until the day the Court hands down its decision and opinion. Before, during, and after conference justices may use their votes in strategic ways to influence the disposition of a case.

NOTES

1. Antonin Scalia, comments at George Washington National Law Center, Feb. 16, 1988, quoted in "Ruling Fixed Opinions," *New York Times*, Feb. 22, 1988, p. 16A.

2. William H. Rehnquist, quoted in David M. O'Brien, *Storm Center: The Supreme Court in American Politics*, 9th ed. (New York: W. W. Norton & Company, 2011).

SELECTED BIBLIOGRAPHY

Dickson, Del. *The Supreme Court in Conference*. New York: Oxford University Press, 2001.

Hammond, Thomas; Bonneau, Chris; and Sheehan, Reginald. *Strategic Behavior and Policy Choice on the U.S. Supreme Court*. Stanford, CA: Stanford University Press, 2005.

Matltzman, Forrest; Spriggs, James F., II; and Wahlbeck, Paul. *Crafting Law on the Supreme Court: The Collegial Game*. Cambridge, MA: Cambridge University Press, 2000.

O'Brien, David M. *Storm Center: The Supreme Court in American Politics*, 9th ed. New York: W. W. Norton & Company, 2011.

Schwartz, Bernard. *Decision: How the Supreme Court Decides Cases*. New York: Oxford University Press, 1996.

G | *Postconference Writing and Circulation of Opinions*

Opinions justify or explain votes at conference. The opinion for the Court is the most important and most difficult to write because it represents a collective judgment. Because conference votes are tentative, the assignment, drafting, and circulation of opinions is crucial to the Court's rulings. At each stage justices compete for influence in determining the Court's final decision and opinion.

By tradition, when the chief justice is in the majority, he assigns the Court's opinion. If the chief justice did not vote with the majority, then the senior associate justice who was in the majority either writes the opinion or assigns it to another. Chief justices may keep cases for themselves. This is in the tradition of Chief Justice Marshall, but as modified by the workload and other justices' expectations of equitable opinion assignments. In unanimous decisions and landmark cases the chief justice often self-assigns the Court's opinion.

Parity in opinion assignment now generally prevails. But the practice of immediately assigning opinions after conference as Hughes did, or within a day or two as Stone did, was gradually abandoned by the end of Vinson's tenure as chief justice. Warren and Burger adopted the practice of assigning opinions after each two-week session of oral arguments and conferences. With more assignments to make at any given time, they thus acquired greater flexibility in distributing the workload. They also enhanced their own opportunities for influencing the final outcome of cases through their assignment of opinions.

Writing opinions is the most difficult and time-consuming task of the justices. Justices differ in their styles and approaches to opinion writing. They now more or less delegate responsibility to their clerks for assisting in the preparation of opinions. Chief Justice Rehnquist, for example, usually had one of his clerks do a first draft, without bothering about style, and gave him about ten days to prepare it. Before having the clerk begin work, Rehnquist went over the conference discussion with the clerk and explained how he thought an opinion could be written "supporting the result reached by the majority."

Only after a justice is satisfied with an initial draft does the opinion circulate to the other justices for their reactions. The practice of circulating draft opinions is pivotal in the Court's decision-making process because all votes are tentative until the final opinion is handed down.

Final published opinions for the Court are the residue of conflicts and compromises among the justices. But they also reflect changing institutional norms. In historical perspective, changes in judicial norms have affected trends in opinion writing, the value of judicial opinions, and the Court's contributions to public law.

"The business of the Court," Justice Stewart once observed, "is to give institutional opinions for its decisions." The opinion for the Court serves to communicate an institutional decision. For much of the Court's history, there were few concurring opinions (those in which a justice agrees with the Court's ruling but not the reasons given in its opinion) and dissenting opinions (those in which justices disagree with the Court's ruling and give an alternative interpretation). It was also rare for a justice to write a separate opinion in which he or she concurred and dissented from parts of the opinion for the Court. But in the last forty years there has been a dramatic increase in the total number of opinions issued each term, as depicted in CONSTITUTIONAL HISTORY: Opinion Writing, 1937–2009. However, during the last 20 years the Court has granted fewer cases plenary consideration and, hence, has annually handed down fewer opinions. In addition, from the 1990s through the first decade of the twenty-first century the justices also cut back somewhat on writing separate dissenting opinions, except

- CONSTITUTIONAL HISTORY

Opinion Writing, 1937–2009

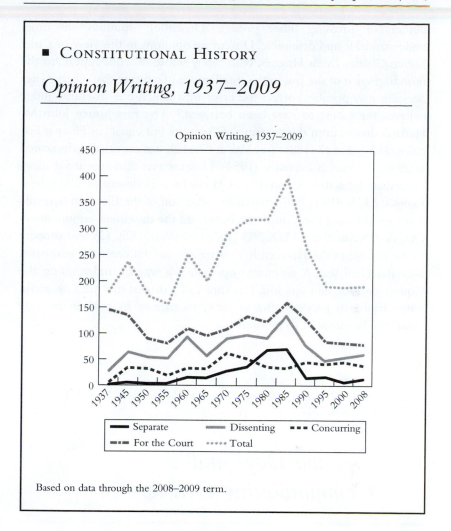

Opinion Writing, 1937–2009

Legend:
— Separate
— Dissenting
■■■ Concurring
■■■ For the Court
····· Total

Based on data through the 2008–2009 term.

in cases deemed especially important and divisive. The dissenters instead joined one another in a single dissenting opinion more frequently than was the prior practice.

The increase in the number of opinions reflects in part that the justices are now more interested in merely the tally of votes than arriving at an institutional decision and opinion. The number of cases decided by a bare majority has thus grown in the last few decades. In addition, sometimes a bare majority for deciding a case a certain way cannot agree on an opinion for the Court's decision and the author of the opinion announcing the Court's decision must write for only a plurality.

In contrast to the author of an opinion for the Court, a justice writing separate concurring or dissenting opinions does not carry the burden of amassing other justices. Dissenting opinions are more understandable and defensible. Dissenting opinions in the view of Chief Justice Charles Evans Hughes, who rarely wrote dissents, appeal "to the brooding spirit of the law, to the intelligence of a future day, when a later decision may possibly correct the error into which the dissenting judge believes the Court to have been betrayed."[1] The first Justice John M. Harlan's dissent from the doctrine of "separate but equal" in *Plessy v. Ferguson*, 163 U.S. 537 (1896) (see Vol. 2, Ch. 12), was eventually vindicated in *Brown v. Board of Education* (1954). Dissents may also appeal for more immediate legislative action: Justice James Iredell's dissent in *Chisholm v. Georgia*, 2 U.S. 419 (1793), invited the adoption of the Eleventh Amendment overturning the Court's decision; and the dissenters' arguments in *Dred Scott v. Sandford*, 60 U.S. 393 (1857) (see Vol. 2, Ch. 12), lent support to the passage of the Thirteenth, Fourteenth, and Fifteenth Amendments after the Civil War. A dissenting opinion is a way of undercutting the Court's decision and opinion. The threat of a dissent may thus be useful when trying to persuade the majority to narrow its holding or tone down the language of its opinion.

NOTE

1. Charles Evans Hughes, *The Supreme Court of the United States* (New York: Columbia University Press, 1928).

H | *Opinion Days and Communicating Decisions*

The justices announce their decisions in the courtroom, typically crowded with reporters, anxious attorneys, and curious spectators. When several decisions are to be handed down, the justices delivering the Court's opinions make their announcements in reverse order of seniority. Authors of concurring or dissenting opinions are free to give their views orally as well. By tradition there is no prior announcement as to when cases will be handed down. Most opinions are now announced in two to four minutes with justices merely stating the result in each case. In especially controversial cases, such as those concerning restrictions on abortion, justices may read portions of their opinions and, sometimes, dissents.

Justices appreciate that compliance with their decisions depends on public understanding of their opinions. And media coverage of the

Court has grown in the last thirty years. On "Opinion Days," journalists receive copies of the headnotes—prepared by the reporter of decisions—summarizing the main points of a decision. The Court has a public information office as well. The office serves primarily reporters (not members of the general public, whose inquiries are typically handled by the offices of the clerk, marshal, or curator) and provides space for a pressroom with sixteen assigned cubicles. The public information officer makes available all filings and briefs for cases on the docket, the Court's conference lists and final opinions, and speeches made by the justices. The Court also now makes its opinions and transcripts of oral arguments available on its web site at www.supremecourt.gov.

SELECTED BIBLIOGRAPHY

Johnson, Timothy, and Goldman, Jerry, eds. *A Good Quarrel: Reporters Share Stories from Inside the Supreme Court.* Ann Arbor: University of Michigan Press, 2009.

O'Brien, David M., ed. *Judges on Judging: Views from the Bench.* 3d ed. Washington, DC: C.Q. Press, 2009.

Slotnick, Elliot E., and Segal, Jennifer A. *Television News and the Supreme Court.* New York: Cambridge University Press, 1998.

I | *The Impact of Supreme Court Decisions: Compliance and Implementation*

"By itself," political scientist Robert Dahl observed, "the Court is almost powerless to affect the course of national policy."[1] This is because the Court's rulings are not self-executing. Enforcement and implementation require the cooperation and coordination of all three branches of government.

Brown v. Board of Education (1954) (see Vol. 2, Ch. 12), the public school desegregation case, dramatically altered the course of American life but also reflected the justices' awareness that their decisions are not self-executing. When striking down the "separate but equal" doctrine, which was practiced in segregated public school systems, the Warren Court waited a year after *Brown I* (1954) before issuing in *Brown II* its mandate for "all deliberate speed" in ending racial segregation in public education. The Court knew that there would be substantial public resistance to the social policy announced in *Brown I*. A rigid timetable for desegregation would have only intensified opposition. President Dwight Eisenhower refused to endorse the ruling for some time. Hence, implementation of *Brown* was deliberately slow and uneven. The Department of Justice had little role in ending school segregation before the passage of the Civil Rights Act of 1964 during Lyndon B. Johnson's presidency. For over three decades problems of implementing and achieving compliance with *Brown* persisted. Litigation by civil rights groups forced change, but it was piecemeal, costly, and modest. The judiciary alone could not achieve desegregation.

Public opinion serves to curb the Court when it threatens to go too far or too fast in its rulings. Life in the marble temple is not immune from shifts in public opinion.[2] But justices deny being directly influenced by public opinion. The Court's prestige rests on preserving the public's view that justices base their decisions on interpretations of the law, rather than on their personal policy preferences. Yet complete indifference to public opinion would be the height of judicial arrogance. In the highly controversial 1992 abortion ruling in *Planned Parenthood of Southeastern Pennsylvania v. Casey*, 505 U.S. 833 (1992) (see Vol. 2, Ch. 11), the justices engaged in an unusual debate over the influence of public opinion on the Court with the dissenters, Chief Justice Rehnquist and Justices Scalia, Thomas, and White, accusing the plurality (Justices O'Connor, Kennedy, and Souter) of bending to public opinion and following "not a principle of law . . . but the principle of Realpolitik."

Most of the Court's decisions do not attract widespread public attention. Most people find the Court remote and confusing or identify with its institutional symbols. The public perceives the Court as a temple of law rather than of politics—impartial and removed from the pressures of special partisan interests.[3] Issues such as school desegregation, school prayer, and abortion focus public attention and may mobilize public support or opposition for the Court. But those issues are also the most divisive within the country as well. Public opinion, therefore, tends to be diffuse and indirectly expressed by public officials and elected representatives.

Less concerned about public opinion than elected public officials, justices are sensitive to the attitudes of the Court's immediate constituents: the solicitor general, the attorney general and the Department of Justice, counsel for federal agencies, states' attorneys general, and the legal profession. Their responses to the Court's rulings help shape public understanding and determine the extent of compliance.

The solicitor general, attorney general, and agency counsel interpret the Court's decisions and advise the White House and agencies on compliance. Justices may find a favorable or unfavorable reception from the executive branch. The solicitor general decides which and what kinds of cases to take to the Court. In selecting cases he tries to offer the Court (or a majority) opportunities for pursuing their policy goals and those of the president.

The attorney general, cabinet heads, and agency counsel may likewise extend or thwart the Court's policies. They do so through their advisory opinions, litigation strategies, and development of agency policy and programs. The reactions of the fifty state attorneys general are no less important. Each has a pivotal role in advising governors, mayors, police chiefs, and others in his or her state. Their responses tend to reflect state and local reactions to the Court's rulings. Regional differences were evident in responses to the 1962 and 1963 school prayer decisions. In upholding separation of church and state, the Court struck down a state-composed prayer in *Engel v. Vitale*, 370 U.S. 421 (1962), and the reciting of the Lord's Prayer in public schools in *Abington School District v. Schempp*, 374 U.S. 203 (1963) (see Vol. 2, Ch. 6). Long-standing practices of school prayer in the East and South were not to be easily relinquished. Voluntary school prayer, silent meditation, and "the objective study of the Bible and of religion" were viewed as still permissible. Where school prayer received support in state constitutions or legislation, state and local officials denied the legitimacy of the Court's decrees and refused to obey.

The justices do consider anticipated reactions of the immediate audience of the Court's rulings. One example is that of Chief Justice Warren's opinion in *Miranda v. Arizona*, 384 U.S. 436 (1966) (see Vol. 2, Ch. 8), which held that police must read suspects their rights, granted them by the Fifth and Sixth Amendments, to remain silent and to consult and have the presence of an attorney during police questioning. A former attorney general in California, Chief Justice Warren knew full well that not all state attorneys general and police supported the Court's rulings on criminal procedure. He, therefore, strove to outline in *Miranda* a code for police procedures governing the interrogation of criminal suspects that police could not easily evade.

The Court's decisions have traditionally applied retroactively, permitting individuals to have retrials. In *Linkletter v. Walker* (1965) (see excerpt below), however, the Court refused to apply retroactively its controversial ruling in *Mapp v. Ohio*, 367 U.S. 643 (1961) (see Vol. 2, Ch. 7), which extended to the states the Fourth Amendment exclusionary rule, forbidding the use at trial of evidence obtained in violation of the requirements for a proper search and seizure. The Court subsequently developed what became known as its *ambulatory-retroactive doctrine*—the doctrine that a new ruling's retroactive application to prior decisions may depend on the ruling and its consequences, such as administrative costs; thus, not all new rulings apply retrospectively but only prospectively to new cases. "That doctrine," Justice Harlan explained, "was the product of the Court's disquietude with the impacts of its fast-moving pace in constitutional innovation in the criminal field." But he also objected that the doctrine merely rationalizes the Court's freedom "to act, in effect, like a legislature, making its new constitutional rules wholly or partially retroactive or only prospective as it deems wise."[4] In *Griffith v. Kentucky* (1987) (see excerpt below), Justice Blackmun further explains the Court's application of the doctrine of ambulatory retroactivity.

Subsequently, the Court established guidelines for when new decisions apply retroactively in *Teague v. Lane*, 489 U.S. 288 (1989). Under *Teague* an old ruling applies both on direct and collateral (an independent challenge to overturn a judgment) review, but a new rule, overturning a precedent, applies only to cases still on direct review and applies retroactively in collateral proceedings only if (1) it is substantive or (2) a watershed ruling bearing on "the fundamental fairness and accuracy of the criminal proceeding," like the Sixth Amendment right to counsel decision in *Gideon v. Wainwright*, 372 U.S. 335 (1963) (excerpted in Vol. 2, Ch. 9). In *Whorton v. Bockting* (2007) (excerpted below), the Roberts Court adhered to *Teague* in holding that the decision in *Crawford v. Washington*, 541 U.S. 36 (2004) (discussed in Vol. 2, Ch. 9), does not apply retroactively on collateral review. *Crawford* announced a new rule in ruling that "testimonial statements of witnesses absent from [a] trial" are admissible "only where the declarant is unavailable, and where the defendant has had a prior opportunity to cross-examine [the witness]," and overruling *Ohio v. Roberts*, 448 U.S. 56 (1980), as inconsistent with the Sixth Amendment's Confrontation Clause. In *Whorton*, writing for a unanimous Court Justice Alito held that although *Crawford* announced a new rule it was neither substantive nor a watershed ruling, like *Gideon*, and thus does not apply retroactively to cases on collateral review.

The Court directly and indirectly encourages interest groups and the government to litigate issues of public policy. The Court selects and decides "only those cases which present questions whose resolution will have immediate importance far beyond the particular facts and parties involved." Attorneys whose cases are accepted by the Court, Chief Justice Fred Vinson emphasized, "are, in a sense, prosecuting or defending class actions; that you represent your clients, but [more crucially] tremendously important principles, upon which are based the plans, hopes and aspirations of a great many people throughout the country."[5]

Interest groups from the entire political spectrum look to the Court to decide issues of public policy: from business organizations and corporations in the late nineteenth century to the Jehovah's Witnesses

The justices' private conference room. (*Franz Jantzen, Collection of the Supreme Court of the United States.*)

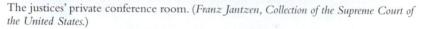

in the 1930s, to the ACLU and NAACP in the 1950s and 1960s, and to "liberal" women's rights groups and consumer and environmental protection groups—like the National Organization for Women (NOW), Common Cause, "Nader's Raiders," the Sierra Club, the Environmental Defense Fund, and the Natural Resources Defense Council—as well as to a growing number of conservative "public interest" law firms like the Pacific Legal Foundation, the Mountain States Legal Foundation, and the Washington Legal Foundation. "This is government by lawsuit," Justice Robert Jackson declared; "these constitutional lawsuits are the stuff of power politics in America."[6]

Interest group activities and public interest law firms offer a number of advantages for litigating policy disputes. They command greater financial resources than the average individual. A single suit may settle a large number of claims, and the issues are not as likely to be compromised or settled out of court. Interest group law firms typically specialize in particular kinds of lawsuits. They are, therefore, able to litigate more skillfully and over a longer period of time. There are also tactical opportunities. Litigants may be chosen to bring test cases, and those cases may be coordinated with other litigation and the activities of other organizations.

■ CONSTITUTIONAL HISTORY

The Southern Manifesto: A Declaration of Constitutional Principles

Following the Supreme Court's landmark school desegregation rulings in *Brown v. Board of Education* (1954 and 1955) (see Vol. 2, Ch. 12), 101 U.S. senators and representatives issued The Southern Manifesto, denouning the decision and the Court for running afoul of established constitutional principles. The excerpt reprinted here comes from 102 *Congressional Record* 4515 (1956).

The Founding Fathers gave us a Constitution of checks and balances because they realized the inescapable lesson of history that no man or group of men can be safely entrusted with unlimited power. They framed this Constitution with its provisions for change by amendment in order to secure the fundamentals of government against the dangers of temporary popular passion or the personal predilections of public officeholders.

We regard the decision of the Supreme Court in the school cases as a clear abuse of judicial power. It climaxes a trend in the federal judiciary undertaking to legislate, in derogation of the authority of Congress, and to encroach upon the reserved rights of the States and the people.

The original Constitution does not mention education. Neither does the 14th amendment nor any other amendment. The debates preceding the submission of the 14th amendment clearly show that there was no intent that it should affect the system of education maintained by the States.

The very Congress which proposed the amendment subsequently provided for segregated schools in the District of Columbia.

When the amendment was adopted in 1868, there were 37 States of the Union. Every one of the 26 States that had any substantial racial differences among its people, either approved the operation of segregated schools already in existence or subsequently established such schools by action of the same lawmaking body which considered the 14th amendment. . . .

This interpretation [the doctrine of "separate but equal"], restated time and again, became a part of the life of the people of many of the States and confirmed their habits, customs, traditions, and way of life. It is founded on elementary humanity and common sense, for parents should not be deprived by Government of the right to direct the lives and education of their own children.

Though there has been no constitutional amendment or act of Congress changing this established legal principle almost a century old, the Supreme Court of the United States, with no legal basis for such action, undertook to exercise their naked judicial power and substituted their personal political and social ideas for the established law of the land.

This unwarranted exercise of power by the Court, contrary to the Constitution, is creating chaos and confusion in the States principally affected. It is destroying the amicable relations between the white and Negro races that have been created through 90 years of patient effort by the good people of both races. It has planted hatred and suspicion where there has been heretofore friendship and understanding.

Without regard to the consent of the governed, outside agitators are threatening immediate and revolutionary changes in our public-school system. If done, this is certain to destroy the system of public education in some of the States.

With the gravest concern for the explosive and dangerous condition created by this decision and inflamed by outside meddlers:

We reaffirm our reliance on the Constitution as the fundamental law of the land.

We decry the Supreme Court's encroachments on rights reserved to the States and to the people, contrary to established law, and to the Constitution.

We commend the motives of those States which have declared the intention to resist forced integration by any lawful means.

We appeal to the States and people who are not directly affected by these decisions to consider the constitutional principles involved against the time when they too, on issues vital to them, may be the victims of judicial encroachment.

Even though we constitute a minority in the present Congress, we have full faith that a majority of the American people believe in the dual system of government which has enabled us to achieve our greatness and will in time demand that the reserved rights of the States and of the people be made secure against judicial usurpation.

We pledge ourselves to use all lawful means to bring about a reversal of this decision which is contrary to the Constitution and to prevent the use of force in its implementation.

In this trying period, as we all seek to right this wrong, we appeal to our people not to be provoked by the agitators and troublemakers invading our States and to scrupulously refrain from disorder and lawless acts.

The Court is an instrument of political power, but the justices remain dependent on the attitudes and actions of their immediate constitutents, elected officials, and the dynamics of pressure-group politics and public opinion. Implementation and compliance largely depend on lower courts, Congress, and the president.

Compliance with the Court's decisions by lower courts is invariably uneven. They may extend or limit decisions in anticipation of later rulings by the high Court. Following the watershed ruling on privacy in *Griswold v. Connecticut*, 381 U.S. 479 (1965) (see Vol. 2, Ch. 4), lower courts interpreted the newfound constitutional right of privacy to strike down a wide range of laws, from those limiting the length of male employees' and students' hair to ones forbidding certain sexual acts between consenting adults and the use of marijuana, to laws requiring psychological tests of applicants for government jobs, and to laws governing access to financial and medical records. The Court reversed or would not approve the extension of the right of privacy in many of these areas.

A simple model of compliance is not very useful: Decisions handed down by the Court are not necessarily or readily applied by lower courts. Ambiguity and plurality or five-to-four decisions invite lower courts to pursue their own policy goals. Crucial language in an opinion may be treated as *dicta*. Differences between the facts on which the Court ruled and the circumstances of a case at hand may be emphasized so as to distinguish or reach the opposite result of the Court's decision.

Lower federal courts may thus effectively delay implementation and compliance. Open defiance is infrequent but not unprecedented. *Jaffree v. Board of School Commissioners* (1983) (see excerpt below) is extreme but illustrative of lower court defiance. There, a federal district court judge in Alabama directly challenged the legitimacy of the Court in its public school prayer rulings. A majority of the Court rebuffed the lower court when it decided an appeal of the ruling and struck down the "moment of silence" law in *Wallace v. Jaffree*, 472 U.S. 38 (1985) (see Vol. 2, Ch. 6).

On the other hand, lower federal courts may anticipate the Court's future rulings, based on recent changes in its direction, in what has been termed "*anticipatory compliance.*" *Brzonkala v. Virginia Polytechnic Institute and State University*, 169 F.3d 820 (1999), for example, is based on the Court's rulings on federalism (see Vol. 1, Chs. 6 and 7) handed down after the passage of the Violence against Women Act of 1994, the Court of Appeals for the Fourth Circuit struck down provisions of that law. Subsequently, a bare majority of the Court affirmed that decision and extended its previous rulings in *United States v. Morrison* (2000) (excerpted in Vol. 1, Ch. 6).

In addition, as the Burger and Rehnquist Courts moved in more conservative directions in areas of civil rights and liberties, state supreme courts increasingly refused to follow the Court's construction of federal law and recognized new rights or extended protection on the basis of state constitutions to claims that the Supreme Court has declined to embrace (see Vol. 1, Ch. 7). State courts may do so if they base their decisions on their state constitutions and make a *"plain statement"* of *"adequate and independent state grounds"*; see *Michigan v. Long*, 463 U.S. 1036 (1983) (excerpted in Ch. 7). In *Bowers v. Hardwick*, 478 U.S. 186 (1986), for instance, a bare majority of the Court refused to extend the constitutional right of privacy in a challenge to Georgia's law punishing sodomy. But in *Commonwealth of Kentucky v. Wasson*, 842 S.W.2d 487 (1992) (see excerpt below), Kentucky's supreme court, as did other state courts, expressly declined to follow *Bowers* when striking down its state law against homosexual sodomy.

Major confrontations between Congress and the Court have occurred a number of times. With the election of Thomas Jefferson in 1800, Republicans gained control of Congress. Defeated President John Adams and the outgoing Federalists in Congress passed the Judiciary Act of 1801, creating new circuit court judgeships and stipulating that when the next vacancy on the Court occurred it should go unfilled. That attempt to maintain influence in the judiciary was quickly countered. In 1802, the Republican Congress repealed the Act of 1801, abolishing the judgeships and returning the number of justices to six. Congress also postponed the Court's next term to preclude it from immediately hearing a challenge, in *Stuart v. Laird*, 5 U.S. 299 (1803), to its repealing legislation. When the Court decided *Stuart*, it upheld Congress's power to repeal the Judiciary Act of 1801. The Jeffersonian-Republicans then impeached Justice Samuel Chase for expounding federalist doctrine. Although the Senate acquitted him, it would not confirm nominees for federal judgeships unless they were Republicans.

The Marshall Court approved the expansion of national governmental power, but in response Congress in the 1820s and 1830s threatened to remove the Court's jurisdiction over disputes involving states' rights. After the Civil War, Congress succeeded in repealing the Court's jurisdiction over certain denials of writs of *habeas corpus*—orders commanding that a prisoner be brought before a judge and cause shown for his imprisonment. In *Ex parte McCardle*, 74 U.S. 506 (1869), the Court upheld the repeal of its jurisdiction and thus avoided deciding a controversial case attacking the constitutionality of Reconstruction legislation. But most Court watchers and recent rulings indicate that the Court would likely strike down legislation stripping jurisdiction over areas involving fundamental rights; see, e.g., *Boumediene v. Bush*, 128 S. Ct. 2229 (2008) (excerpted in Vol. 1, Ch. 3).

At the turn of the century, Progressives in Congress unsuccessfully sought to pressure the Court—dominated at the time by advocates of laissez-faire social and economic policy. They proposed requiring a two-thirds vote by the justices when striking down federal statutes and permitting Congress to overrule the Court's decisions by a two-thirds majority. The confrontation escalated with the Court's invalidation of President Franklin D. Roosevelt's early New Deal program passed by Congress in the 1930s. FDR retaliated by attempting to pack the Court by increasing the number of justices. Even though it was upset by the Court's invalidation of the New Deal, Congress would not accept FDR's Court-packing plan. It did, though, pass legislation allowing justices to retire, after ten years of service at age seventy, with full rather than half salary. Congress thus made retirement more financially attractive and gave FDR opportunities to appoint justices who shared his political philosophy.

Congress may pressure the Court in a number of ways. The Senate may try to influence judicial appointments, and justices may be impeached. More often, institutional and jurisdictional changes are used as weapons against the Court. Congress has tried to pressure the Court when setting its terms and size and when authorizing appropriations for salaries, law clerks, secretaries, and office technology. Only once, in 1802 when repealing the Judiciary Act of 1801 and abolishing a session for a year, did Congress actually set the Court's term to delay and influence a particular decision.

The size of the Court is not preordained, and changes generally reflect attempts to control the Court. The Jeffersonian-Republicans' quick repeal of the act passed by the Federalists in 1801 reducing the number of justices was the first of several attempts to influence the Court. Presidents James Madison, James Monroe, and John Adams all claimed that the country's geographical expansion warranted enlarging the size of the Court. But Congress refused to do so until the last day of Andrew Jackson's term in 1837. During the Civil War, the number of justices increased to ten ostensibly due to the creation of a tenth circuit in the West. This gave Abraham Lincoln his fourth appointment and a chance to secure a pro-Union majority on the bench. Antagonism toward President Andrew Johnson's Reconstruction policies following the Civil War led to a reduction from ten justices to seven. After General Ulysses S. Grant was elected president, Congress again authorized nine justices—the number that has prevailed. In the nineteenth century at least, Congress rather successfully denied presidents additional appointments to preserve the Court's policies and increased the number of justices as a way to change the ideological composition of the Court.

Although Article III of the Constitution forbids reducing justices' salaries, Congress may withhold salary increases as punishment, especially in times of high inflation. More direct attacks are possible. Under Article III, Congress is authorized "to make exceptions" to the appellate jurisdiction of the Court. That authorization has been viewed as a way of denying the Court review of certain kinds of cases. Congress succeeded with the 1868 repeal of jurisdiction over writs of *habeas corpus*, which the Court upheld in *Ex parte McCardle*, 7 Wall. (74 U.S.) 506 (1869). More recently, in response to the rulings that "enemy combatants" held in Guantanamo Bay, Cuba, had a right to file a writ of *habeas corpus* and to trials by independent tribunals, in *Rasul v. Bush*, 542 U.S. 466 (2004) (excerpted in Vol. 1, Ch. 3) and *Hamdi v. Rumsfeld*, 542 U.S. 507 (2004), Congress enacted the Detainee Treatment Act (DTA) of 2005 which, among other things, withdrew jurisdiction over *habeas* writs filed by aliens detained outside of the United States. However, in *Hamdan v. Rumsfeld* (2006), without ruling on the constitutionality of that law, the Court held that enemy detainees whose *habeas* applications were pending at the time of the enactment of the DTA could invoke the judiciary's jurisdiction and ruled that they must be tried by civilian courts, courts martial, or military commissions as authorized by Congress. Subsequently, Congress passed and President George W. Bush signed into law the Military Commissions Act of 2006, which denies federal courts jurisdiction over *habeas* applications filed by "unlawful enemy combatants." Democrats opposed that court-stripping jurisdiction and Senator Arlen Spector (R–Pa), chair of the judiciary committee also deemed it unconstitutional but nonetheless voted for the bill. The Court struck down that jurisdiction-stripping legislation in *Boumediene v. Bush*, 128 S.Ct. 2229 (2008) (excerpted in Ch. 3).

Court-curbing legislation is not a very viable weapon. Rather than limiting judicial review, Congress has given the Court the power to set its own agenda and decide major issues of public law and policy—precisely the kinds of issues that Congress then seeks to deny the Court review. The Court has also suggested that it would not approve repeals of its jurisdiction that are merely attempts to dictate how particular kinds of cases should be decided.[7] Most proposals to curb the Court, of course, are simply that. During the McCarthy era, for instance, Republican Senator William Jenner spearheaded a drive to forbid review of cases challenging legislative committees investigating un–American activities. Another unsuccessful attempt was made in 1968 to amend the Omnibus Crime Control and Safe Streets Act so as to prevent the Court from reviewing state criminal cases raising *Miranda* issues.

Congress has had somewhat greater success in reversing the Court by constitutional amendment. Congress must pass a constitutional amendment that three-fourths of the states must then ratify. The process is cumbersome, and thousands of amendments to overrule the Court have failed. But four decisions have been overturned by constitutional amendment. *Chisholm v. Georgia*, 2 U.S. 419 (1793), holding that citizens of one state could sue another state in federal courts, was reversed by the Eleventh Amendment, guaranteeing sovereign immunity for states from suits by citizens of another state. The Thirteenth and Fourteenth Amendments, abolishing slavery and making blacks citizens of the United States, technically overturned the ruling in *Dred Scott v. Sandford* (1857) that blacks were not persons under the Constitution. With the ratification in 1913 of the Sixteenth Amendment, Congress reversed *Pollock v. Farmers' Loan and Trust Company*, 157 U.S. 429 (1895), which had invalidated a federal income tax. In 1970 an amendment to the Voting Rights Act of 1965 lowered the voting age to eighteen years for all elections. Although signing the act into law, President Richard Nixon had his attorney general challenge the validity of lowering the voting age by simple legislation, rather than by constitutional amendment. Within six months in *Oregon v. Mitchell*, 400 U.S. 112 (1970), a bare majority of the Court held that Congress exceeded its power by lowering the voting age for state and local elections. Less than a year later the Twenty-sixth Amendment was ratified extending the franchise to eighteen-year-olds in all elections.

More successful than Court curbing and amending the Constitution are congressional enactments and rewriting of legislation in response to the Court's rulings. Congressional reversals usually relate to both statutory and nonstatutory matters involving administrative policies.

Congress cannot overturn the Court's interpretations of the Constitution by mere legislation, as the Court underscored in *City of Boerne v. Flores*, 521 U.S. 507 (1997) (excerpted in Vol. 2, Ch. 6). But Congress can enhance or thwart compliance with the Court's rulings. After the Warren Court's landmark decision in *Gideon v. Wainwright*, 372 U.S. 335 (1963) (see Vol. 2, Ch. 9), that indigents have a right to counsel, Congress provided attorneys for indigents charged with federal offenses. By contrast, in the Crime Control and Safe Streets Act of 1968, Congress permitted federal courts to use evidence obtained from suspects who had not been read their *Miranda* rights, if their testimony appeared voluntary based on the "totality of the circumstances" surrounding their interrogation. Congress thus attempted to return to a pre-*Miranda* standard for federal agents' questioning of criminal suspects. Democratic and Republican administrations, however, declined to enforce that provision and instead complied with *Miranda* in federal prosecutions. Finally, in *Dickerson v. United States*, 530 U.S. 428 (2000) (excerpted in Vol. 2, Ch. 8), the Court rebuffed Congress's attempt to make an end run around *Miranda* and ruled that that decision applies to both federal and state police questioning of suspects.

Congress indubitably has the power to delay and undercut implementation of the Court's rulings. On major issues of public policy Congress is likely to prevail or, at least, temper the impact of the Court's rulings. But the Court forges public policy not only when invalidating federal legislation. No less importantly, the Court makes policy by overturning state and local laws and practices. The continuing controversies over decisions striking down state laws on school desegregation, school prayer, and abortion are a measure of the Court's influence on American life.

Charged with the responsibility of taking "care that the laws be faithfully executed," the president is the chief executive officer under the Constitution. As the only nationally elected public official, the president represents the views of the dominant national political coalition. A president's obligation to faithfully execute the laws, including decisions of the Court, thus may collide with his own perceived electoral mandate.

The Court has often been the focus of presidential campaigns and power struggles. But presidents rarely openly defy particular decisions by the Court. Presidential defiance is, perhaps, symbolized by the famous remark attributed to Andrew Jackson: "John Marshall has made his decision, now let him enforce it." Jackson's refusal to enforce the decision in *Worcester v. Georgia*, 31 U.S. 515 (1832), which denied state courts jurisdiction over crimes committed on Indian lands, in fact simply left enforcement problems up to the courts and legislatures. During the Civil War however, Lincoln ordered his military commanders to refuse to obey writs of *habeas corpus* issued by Chief Justice Taney.

In major confrontations, presidents generally yield to the Court. Richard Nixon complied with the ruling in *New York Times Co. v.*

United States, 403 U.S. 713 (1971) (see Vol. 1, Ch. 4), which struck down, as a prior restraint on freedom of the press, an injunction against the publication of the Pentagon Papers—a top secret report detailing the history of America's involvement in Vietnam. Then, during the Watergate scandal in 1974, Nixon submitted to the Court's decision in *United States v. Nixon*, 418 U.S. 683 (1974) (see Vol. 1, Ch. 4) ordering the release of White House tape recordings pertinent to the trial of his former attorney general John Mitchell and other presidential aides for conspiracy and obstruction of justice.

Although seldom directly defying the Court, in the short and long run presidents may undercut Supreme Court policymaking. By giving contradictory directives to federal agencies and assigning low priority for enforcement by the Department of Justice, presidents may limit the Court's decisions. Presidents may also make broad moral appeals in response to the Court's rulings, and those appeals may transcend their limited time in office. The Court put school desegregation and abortion on the national agenda. But President John F. Kennedy's appeal for civil rights captivated a generation and encouraged public acceptance of the Court's rulings. Similarly, President Ronald Reagan's opposition to abortion focused attention on "traditional family values" and served to legitimate resistance to the Court's decisions.

Presidential influence over the Court in the long run remains contingent on appointments to the Court. Vacancies occur on the average of one every twenty-two months. Four presidents—including Jimmy Carter—had no opportunity to appoint members of the Court. There is no guarantee how a justice will vote or whether that vote will prove sufficient in limiting or reversing past rulings with which a president disagrees. But through their appointments presidents may leave their mark on Supreme Court policymaking and possibly align the Court and the country or precipitate later confrontations.

For much of the Court's history, the work of the justices has not involved major issues of public policy. In most areas of public law and policy, the fact that the Court decides an issue is more important than what it decides. Relatively few of the major issues of public policy that arise in government reach the Court. When the Court does decide major questions of public policy, its rulings decide only the instant case and not the larger surrounding political controversies. Major confrontations in constitutional politics, like those over school desegregation and abortion, are determined as much by what is possible in a system of free government and pluralistic society as by what the Court says about the meaning of the Constitution. And on those controversial issues of public policy, constitutional law frames the political debate in the ongoing dialogue between the Court and the country. The Court's rulings and interpretation of the Constitution rest, in Chief Justice Edward White's words, "solely upon the approval of a free people."[8]

NOTES

1. Robert Dahl, "Decision-Making in a Democracy: The Supreme Court as a National Policy-Maker," 6 *Journal of Public Law* 293 (1957).

2. See Richard Funston, "The Supreme Court and Critical Elections," 69 *American Political Science Review* 795 (1975); Jonathan Casper, "The Supreme Court and National Policymaking," 70 *American Political Science Review* 5066 (1976); William Mishler and Reginald Sheehan, "The Supreme Court as a Countermajoritarian Institution?" 87 *American Political Science Review* 87 (1993); and Thomas Marshall, *Public Opinion and the Supreme Court* (New York: Longman, 1989).

3. See, for example, Walter Murphy, J. Tananhaus, and D. Kastner, *Public Evaluations of Constitutional Courts* (Beverly Hills, CA: Sage, 1973).

4. *Williams v. United States*, 401 U.S. 675 (1971).

5. Fred Vinson, speech given before the American Bar Association, Sept. 7, 1949, reprinted in 69 S.Ct. vi (1949).

6. Robert Jackson, *The Struggle for Judicial Supremacy* (New York: Knopf, 1951), 287.

7. *United States v. Klein*, 80 U.S. 128 (1872).

8. Edward White, "The Supreme Court of the United States," 7 *American Bar Association Journal* 341 (1921).

SELECTED BIBLIOGRAPHY

Baird, Vanessa. *Answering the Call of the Court: How Justices and Litigants Set the Supreme Court Agenda.* Charlottesville: University of Virginia Press, 2007.

Banks, Christopher, and O'Brien, David M. *Courts and Judicial Policymaking.* Upper Saddle River, NJ: Prentice-Hall, 2008.

Barnes, Jeb. *Overruled? Legislative Overrides, Pluralism, and Contemporary Court-Congress Relations.* Palo Alto, CA: Stanford University Press, 2004.

Canon, Bradley, and Johnson, Charles. *Judicial Policies: Implementation and Impact,* 2d ed. Washington, DC: CQ Press, 1999.

Cardozo, Benjamin. *The Nature of the Judicial Process.* New Haven, CT: Yale University Press, 1921.

Cooper, Phillip. *Hard Judicial Choices.* New York: Oxford University Press, 1988.

Dinan, John. *The American State Constitutional Tradition.* Lawrence: University Press of Kansas, 2006.

Epstein, Lee, and Kobylka, Joseph. *The Supreme Court & Legal Change.* Chapel Hill: University of North Carolina Press, 1992.

Fisher, Louis, and Devins, Neal. *Political Dynamics of Constitutional Law.* 3d. ed. St. Paul, MN: West, 2001.

Gates, John. *The Supreme Court and Partisan Realignment.* Boulder, CO: Westview, 1992.

Hall, Kermit, ed. *The Oxford Companion to the Supreme Court.* 2d ed. New York: Oxford University Press, 2005.

Kahn, Ronald, and Kersch, Ken I., eds. *The Supreme Court and American Political Development.* Lawrence: University Press of Kansas, 2006.

Marshall, Thomas. *Public Opinion and the Supreme Court.* Boston: Unwin Hyman, 1989.

McGuire, Kevin. *The Supreme Court Bar.* Charlottesville: University Press of Virginia, 1993.

Murphy, Walter. *Elements of Judicial Strategy.* Chicago: University of Chicago Press, 1964.

O'Brien, David M. *Storm Center: The Supreme Court in American Politics,* 9th ed. New York: W. W. Norton & Company, 2011.

Pacelle, Richard. *The Transformation of the Supreme Court's Agenda.* Boulder, CO: Westview, 1991.

Pickerill, J. Mitchell. *Constitutional Deliberations in Congress.* Durham: Duke University Press, 2004.

Rosen, Jeffrey. *The Most Democratic Branch: How the Courts Serve America.* New York: Oxford University Press, 2006.

Rosenberg, Gerald. *The Hollow Hope,* 2d ed. Chicago: University of Chicago Press, 2008.

Segal, Jeffrey, and Spaeth, Harold. *The Supreme Court and the Attitudinal Model.* 2d. ed. Cambridge, MA: Cambridge University Press, 2002.

Supreme Court Historical Society. *Journal of Supreme Court History.* Washington, DC: SCHS, 1976–present.

Urofsky, Melvin, ed. *The Public Debate Over Controversial Supreme Court Decisions.* Washington, DC: C.Q. Press, 2006.

Linkletter v. Walker

381 U.S. 618, 85 S.CT. 1731 (1965)

Victor Linkletter was tried and convicted in state court on evidence illegally obtained by police prior to *Mapp v. Ohio*, 367 U.S. 643 (1961) (see Vol. 2, Ch. 7), which barred states from using illegally obtained evidence at trial under the Fourth Amendment's exclusionary rule. Linkletter contended that *Mapp* should apply retroactively and he should be retried with the illegally obtained evidence excluded. A federal district court disagreed and after a court of appeals affirmed that ruling, Linkletter appealed to the Supreme Court.

The Court's decision was seven to two; with the majority's opinion announced by Justice Clark. The dissent was by Justice Black, who was joined by Justice Douglas.

☐ *Justice CLARK delivers the opinion of the Court.*

In *Mapp v. Ohio*, 367 U.S. 643 (1961), we held that the exclusion of evidence seized in violation of the search and seizure provisions of the Fourth Amendment was required of the States by the Due Process Clause of the Fourteenth Amendment. In so doing we overruled *Wolf v. People of State of Colorado*, 338 U.S. 25 (1949), to the extent that it failed to apply the exclusionary rule to the States. This case presents the question of whether this requirement operates retrospectively upon cases finally decided in the period prior to *Mapp*. The Court of Appeals for the Fifth Circuit held that it did not, and we granted *certiorari* in order to settle what has become a most troublesome question in the administration of justice. We agree with the Court of Appeals. . . .

At common law there was no authority for the proposition that judicial decisions made law only for the future. Blackstone stated the rule that the duty of the court was not to "pronounce a new law, but to maintain and expound the old one." 1 Blackstone, *Commentaries* 69 (15th ed. 1809). . . .

In the case of the overruled decision, *Wolf v. People of State of Colorado, supra*, here, it was thought to be only a failure at true discovery and was consequently never the law; while the overruling one, *Mapp*, was not "new law but an application of what is, and theretofore had been, the true law." . . .

On the other hand, [the late-nineteenth century legal philosopher John] Austin maintained that judges do in fact do something more than discover law; they make it interstitially by filling in with judicial interpretation the vague, indefinite, or generic statutory or common-law terms that alone are but the empty crevices of the law. Implicit in such an approach is the admission when a case is overruled that the earlier decision was wrongly decided. However, rather than being erased by the later overruling decision it is considered as an existing juridical fact until overruled, and intermediate cases finally decided under it are not to be disturbed.

The Blackstonian view ruled English jurisprudence and cast its shadow over our own. . . . However, some legal philosophers continued to insist that such a rule was out of tune with actuality largely because judicial repeal ofttime did "work hardship to those who [had] trusted to its existence." CARDOZO, Address to the N.Y. Bar Assn. (1932). . . .

It is true that heretofore, without discussion, we have applied new constitutional rules to cases finalized before the promulgation of the rule. Petitioner contends that our method of resolving those prior cases demonstrates that an absolute rule of retroaction prevails in the area of constitutional adjudication. However, we believe that the Constitution neither prohibits nor requires retrospective effect. As Justice CARDOZO said, "We think the Federal Constitution has no voice upon the subject." . . .

Once the premise is accepted that we are neither required to apply, nor prohibited from applying, a decision retrospectively, we must then weigh the merits and demerits in each case by looking to the prior history of the rule in question, its purpose and effect, and whether retrospective operation will further or retard its operation. We believe that this approach is particularly correct with reference to the Fourth Amendment's prohibitions as to un-reasonable searches and seizures. Rather than "disparaging" the Amendment we but apply the wisdom of Justice HOLMES that "[t]he life of the law has not been logic: it has been experience." Holmes, *The Common Law* 5 (Howe ed. 1963).

Since *Weeks v. United States*, 232 U.S. 383 (1914) this Court has adhered to the rule that evidence seized by federal officers in violation of the Fourth Amendment is not admissible at trial in a federal court. In 1949 in *Wolf v. People of State of Colorado, supra*, the Court decided that while the right to privacy—"the core of the Fourth Amendment"—was such a basic right as to be implicit in "the concept of ordered liberty" and thus enforceable against the States through the Fourteenth Amendment, "the ways of enforcing such a basic right raise questions of a different order. How such arbitrary conduct should be checked, what remedies against it should be afforded, the means by which the right should be made effective, are all questions that are not to be so dogmatically answered as to preclude the varying solutions which spring from an allowable range of judgment on issues not susceptible of quantitative solution."

Mapp was announced in 1961. The Court in considering "the current va-lidity of the factual grounds upon which *Wolf* was based" pointed out that prior to *Wolf* "almost two-thirds of the States were opposed to the use of the exclu-sionary rule, now, despite the *Wolf* case, more than half of those since passing upon it . . . have wholly or partly adopted or adhered to the *Weeks* rule." . . .

We believe that the existence of the *Wolf* doctrine prior to *Mapp* is "an operative fact and may have consequences which cannot justly be ignored. The past cannot always be erased by a new judicial declaration." The thou-sands of cases that were finally decided on *Wolf* cannot be obliterated. The "particular conduct, private and official," must be considered. Here "prior determinations deemed to have finality and acted upon accordingly" have "become vested." And finally, "public policy in the light of the nature both of the [*Wolf* doctrine] and of its previous application" must be given its proper weight. In short, we must look to the purpose of the *Mapp* rule; the reliance placed upon the *Wolf* doctrine; and the effect on the administration of justice of a retrospective application of *Mapp*.

It is clear that the *Wolf* Court, once it had found the Fourth Amend-ment's unreasonable Search and Seizure Clause applicable to the States through the Due Process Clause of the Fourteenth Amendment, turned its attention to whether the exclusionary rule was included within the com-mand of the Fourth Amendment. This was decided in the negative. It is clear that based upon the factual considerations heretofore discussed the *Wolf* Court then concluded that it was not necessary to the enforcement of the Fourth Amendment for the exclusionary rule to be extended to the States as a requirement of due process. *Mapp* had as its prime purpose the enforce-ment of the Fourth Amendment through the inclusion of the exclusionary rule within its rights. This, it was found, was the only effective deterrent to lawless police action. Indeed, all of the cases since *Wolf* requiring the exclu-sion of illegal evidence have been based on the necessity for an effective de-terrent to illegal police action. We cannot say that this purpose would be advanced by making the rule retrospective. The misconduct of the police prior to *Mapp* has already occurred and will not be corrected by releasing the prisoners involved. Nor would it add harmony to the delicate state-federal relationship of which we have spoken as part and parcel of the purpose of *Mapp*. Finally, the ruptured privacy of the victims' homes and effects cannot be restored. Reparation comes too late. . . .

Finally, there are interests in the administration of justice and the integrity of the judicial process to consider. To make the rule of *Mapp* retrospective would tax the administration of justice to the utmost. Hearings would have to be held on the excludability of evidence long since destroyed, misplaced or deteriorated. If it is excluded, the witnesses available at the time of the original trial will not be available or if located their memory will be dimmed. To thus legitimate such an extraordinary procedural weapon that has no bearing on guilt would seriously disrupt the administration of justice. . . .

All that we decide today is that though the error complained of might be fundamental it is not of the nature requiring us to overturn all final convictions based upon it. After full consideration of all the factors we are not able to say that the *Mapp* rule requires retrospective application.

Affirmed.

☐ *Justice BLACK, with whom Justice DOUGLAS joins, dissenting.*

The Court offers no defense based on any known principle of justice for discriminating among defendants who were similarly convicted by use of evidence unconstitutionally seized. It certainly cannot do so as between Linkletter and Miss Mapp. The crime with which she was charged took place more than a year before his, yet the decision today seems to rest on the fanciful concept that the Fourth Amendment protected her 1957 offense against conviction by use of unconstitutional evidence but denied its protection to Linkletter for his 1958 offense. In making this ruling the Court assumes for itself the virtue of acting in harmony with a comment of Justice HOLMES that "[t]he life of the law has not been logic: it has been experience." Justice HOLMES was not there talking about the Constitution; he was talking about the evolving judge-made law of England and of some of our States whose judges are allowed to follow in the common law tradition. It should be remembered in this connection that no member of this Court has ever more seriously criticized it than did Justice HOLMES for reading its own predilections into the "vague contours" of the Due Process Clause. But quite apart from that, there is no experience of the past that justifies a new Court-made rule to perpetrate a grossly invidious and unfair discrimination against Linkletter simply because he happened to be prosecuted in a State that was evidently well up with its criminal court docket. If this discrimination can be excused at all it is not because of experience but because of logic—sterile and formal at that—not, according to Justice HOLMES, the most dependable guide in law-making. . . .

As the Court concedes, this is the first instance on record where this Court, having jurisdiction, has ever refused to give a previously convicted defendant the benefit of a new and more expansive Bill of Rights interpretation. I am at a loss to understand why those who suffer from the use of evidence secured by a search and seizure in violation of the Fourth Amendment should be treated differently from those who have been denied other guarantees of the Bill of Rights. . . .

Griffith v. Kentucky

479 U.S. 314, 107 S.CT. 708 (1987)

Justice Blackmun's opinion for the Court discusses the issues presented here.

The Court's decision was six to three, with the majority's opinion announced by Justice Blackmun. Justice Powell concurred. There were dissents by Chief Justice Rehnquist and Justice White, who were joined by Justice O'Connor.

□ *Justice BLACKMUN delivers the opinion of the Court.*

Twenty-one years ago, this Court adopted a three-pronged analysis for claims of retroactivity of new constitutional rules of criminal procedure. See *Linkletter v. Walker*, 381 U.S. 618 (1965). In *Linkletter*, the Court held that *Mapp v. Ohio* [367 U.S. 643 (1961)], which extended the Fourth Amendment exclusionary rule to the States, would not be applied retroactively to a state conviction that had become final before *Mapp* was decided. The Court explained that "the Constitution neither prohibits nor requires retrospective effect" of a new constitutional rule, and that a determination of retroactivity must depend on "weigh[ing] the merits and demerits in each case." The Court's decision not to apply *Mapp* retroactively was based on "the purpose of the *Mapp* rule; the reliance placed upon the [previous] doctrine; and the effect on the administration of justice of a retrospective application of *Mapp*." . . .

Shortly after the decision in *Linkletter*, the Court held that the three-pronged analysis applied both to convictions that were final and to convictions pending on direct review. . . .

In *United States v. Johnson*, 457 U.S. 537 (1982), however, the Court shifted course. In that case, we reviewed at some length the history of the Court's decisions in the area of retroactivity and concluded, in the words of Justice HARLAN: " '[R]etroactivity' must be rethought." Specifically, we concluded that the retroactivity analysis for convictions that have become final must be different from the analysis for convictions that are not final at the time the new decision is issued. . . . The rationale for distinguishing between cases that have become final and those that have not, and for applying new rules retroactively to cases in the latter category, was explained at length by Justice HARLAN in *Desist v. United States*, 394 U.S. [244 (1969)] (dissenting opinion), and in *Mackey v. United States*, 401 U.S. 667 (1971) (opinion concurring in judgments). In *United States v. Johnson*, we embraced to a significant extent the comprehensive analysis presented by Justice HARLAN in those opinions.

In Justice HARLAN's view, and now in ours, failure to apply a newly declared constitutional rule to criminal cases pending on direct review violates basic norms of constitutional adjudication. First, it is a settled principle that this Court adjudicates only "cases" and "controversies." See U.S. Const.,

Art. III, Sec. 2. Unlike a legislature, we do not promulgate new rules of constitutional criminal procedure on a broad basis. Rather, the nature of judicial review requires that we adjudicate specific cases, and each case usually becomes the vehicle for announcement of a new rule. But after we have decided a new rule in the case selected, the integrity of judicial review requires that we apply that rule to all similar cases pending on direct review. . . .

As a practical matter, of course, we cannot hear each case pending on direct review and apply the new rule. But we fulfill our judicial responsibility by instructing the lower courts to apply the new rule retroactively to cases not yet final. . . .

Second, selective application of new rules violates the principle of treating similarly situated defendants the same. . . .

In *United States v. Johnson*, our acceptance of Justice HARLAN's views led to the holding that "subject to [certain exceptions], a decision of this Court construing the Fourth Amendment is to be applied retroactively to all convictions that were not yet final at the time the decision was rendered." The exceptions to which we referred related to three categories in which we concluded that existing precedent established threshold tests for the retroactivity analysis. In two of these categories, the new rule already was retroactively applied: (1) when a decision of this Court did nothing more than apply settled precedent to different factual situations, and (2) when the new ruling was that a trial court lacked authority to convict a criminal defendant in the first place. . . .

The third category—where a new rule is a "clear break" with past precedent—is the one at issue in these cases. . . .

Under this exception, a new constitutional rule was not applied retroactively, even to cases on direct review, if the new rule explicitly overruled a past precedent of this Court, or disapproved a practice this Court had arguably sanctioned in prior cases, or overturned a long-standing practice that lower courts had uniformly approved. . . .

For the same reasons that persuaded us in *United States v. Johnson* to adopt different conclusions as to convictions on direct review from those that already had become final, we conclude that an engrafted exception based solely upon the particular characteristics of the new rule adopted by the Court is inappropriate.

First, the principle that this Court does not disregard current law, when it adjudicates a case pending before it on direct review, applies regardless of the specific characteristics of the particular new rule announced. . . .

Second, the use of a "clear break" exception creates the same problem of not treating similarly situated defendants the same. . . .

We therefore hold that a new rule for the conduct of criminal prosecutions is to be applied retroactively to all cases, state or federal, pending on direct review or not yet final, with no exception for cases in which the new rule constitutes a "clear break" with the past. . . .

Whorton v. Bockting

549 U.S. 406, 127 S.Ct. 1173 (2007)

The facts and the issue of application of the retroactivity doctrine are discussed in Justice Alito's unanimous opinion for the Court, reversing the judgment of the Court of Appeals for the Ninth Circuit.

□ *Justice ALITO delivered the opinion of the Court.*

This case presents the question whether, under the rules set out in *Teague v. Lane,* 489 U.S. 288 (1989), our decision in *Crawford v. Washington,* 541 U.S. 36 (2004), is retroactive to cases already final on direct review. We hold that it is not.

Respondent Marvin Bockting lived in Las Vegas, Nevada, with his wife, Laura Bockting, their 3-year-old daughter Honesty, and Laura's 6-year-old daughter from a previous relationship, Autumn. One night, while respondent was at work, Autumn awoke from a dream crying, but she refused to tell her mother what was wrong, explaining: " '[D]addy said you would make him leave and that he would beat my butt if I told you.' " After her mother reassured her, Autumn said that respondent had frequently forced her to engage in numerous and varied sexual acts with him. . . .

[Subsequently, Bockting was charged and tried for sexual assault, but his step-daughter did not testify, rather her mother and a police detective recounted her out-of-court statements]. The jury found respondent guilty of three counts of sexual assault on a minor under the age of 14, and the trial court imposed two consecutive life sentences and another concurrent life sentence.

Respondent took an appeal to the Nevada Supreme Court, which handed down its final decision in 1993, more than a decade before *Crawford.* In analyzing respondent's contention that the admission of Autumn's out-of-court statements had violated his Confrontation Clause rights, the Nevada Supreme Court looked to *Ohio v. Roberts,* 448 U.S. 56 (1980), which was then the governing precedent of this Court. *Roberts* had held that the Confrontation Clause permitted the admission of a hearsay statement made by a declarant who was unavailable to testify if the statement bore sufficient indicia of reliability, either because the statement fell within a firmly rooted hearsay exception or because there were "particularized guarantees of trustworthiness" relating to the statement in question. . . .

Respondent then filed a petition for a writ of *habeas corpus* with the United States District Court for the District of Nevada, arguing that the Nevada Supreme Court's decision violated his Confrontation Clause rights. The District Court denied the petition [and Bockting] appealed to the United States Court of Appeals for the Ninth Circuit.

While this appeal was pending, we issued our opinion in *Crawford,* in which we overruled *Roberts* and held that "[t]estimonial statements of witnesses absent from trial" are admissible "only where the declarant is unavailable, and only where the defendant has had a prior opportunity to cross-examine [the witness]." We noted that the outcome in *Roberts*—as well as the outcome in all similar cases decided by this Court—was consistent with the rule announced in *Crawford*, but we concluded that the interpretation of the Confrontation Clause set out in *Roberts* was unsound in several respects. First, we observed that *Roberts* potentially excluded too much testimony because it imposed Confrontation Clause restrictions on nontestimonial hearsay not governed by that Clause. At the same time, we noted, the *Roberts* test was too "malleable" in permitting the admission of *ex parte* testimonial statements. . . .

In *Teague* and subsequent cases, we have laid out the framework to be used in determining whether a rule announced in one of our opinions should be applied retroactively to judgments in criminal cases that are already final on direct review. Under the *Teague* framework, an old rule applies both on direct and collateral review, but a new rule is generally applicable only to cases that are still on direct review. See *Griffith v. Kentucky*, 479 U.S. 314 (1987). A new rule applies retroactively in a collateral proceeding only if (1) the rule is substantive or (2) the rule is a " 'watershed rul[e] of criminal procedure' implicating the fundamental fairness and accuracy of the criminal proceeding."

In this case, it is undisputed that respondent's conviction became final on direct appeal well before *Crawford* was decided. We therefore turn to the question whether *Crawford* applied an old rule or announced a new one. A new rule is defined as "a rule that . . . was not 'dictated by precedent existing at the time the defendant's conviction became final.' "

Applying this definition, it is clear that *Crawford* announced a new rule. The *Crawford* rule was not "dictated" by prior precedent. Quite the opposite is true: The *Crawford* rule is flatly inconsistent with the prior governing precedent, *Roberts*, which *Crawford* overruled. . . .

Because *Crawford* announced a "new rule" and because it is clear and undisputed that the rule is procedural and not substantive, that rule cannot be applied in this collateral attack on respondent's conviction unless it is a " 'watershed rul[e] of criminal procedure' implicating the fundamental fairness and accuracy of the criminal proceeding." This exception is "extremely narrow," *Schriro v. Summerlin*, 542 U.S. 348 (2004). . . .

In order to qualify as watershed, a new rule must meet two requirements. First, the rule must be necessary to prevent "an 'impermissibly large risk' " of an inaccurate conviction. Second, the rule must "alter our understanding of the bedrock procedural elements essential to the fairness of a proceeding."

The *Crawford* rule does not satisfy the first requirement relating to an impermissibly large risk of an inaccurate conviction. To be sure, the *Crawford* rule reflects the Framers' preferred mechanism (cross-examination) for ensuring that inaccurate out-of-court testimonial statements are not used to convict an accused. But in order for a new rule to meet the accuracy requirement at issue here, "[i]t is . . . not enough . . . to say that [the] rule is aimed at improving the accuracy of trial," or that the rule "is directed toward the enhancement of reliability and accuracy in some sense." Instead, the question is whether the new rule remedied "an 'impermissibly large risk' " of an inaccurate conviction.

Guidance in answering this question is provided by *Gideon v. Wainwright*, 372 U.S. 335 (1963), to which we have repeatedly referred in discussing the meaning of the *Teague* exception at issue here. In *Gideon*, the only case that we have identified as qualifying under this exception, the Court held that counsel must be appointed for any indigent defendant charged with a felony. When a defendant who wishes to be represented by counsel is denied representation, *Gideon* held, the risk of an unreliable verdict is intolerably high. The new rule announced in *Gideon* eliminated this risk.

The *Crawford* rule is in no way comparable to the *Gideon* rule. The *Crawford* rule is much more limited in scope, and the relationship of that rule to the accuracy of the fact finding process is far less direct and profound. *Crawford* overruled *Roberts* because *Roberts* was inconsistent with the original understanding of the meaning of the Confrontation Clause, not because the Court reached the conclusion that the overall effect of the *Crawford* rule would be to improve the accuracy of fact finding in criminal trials. . . .

The *Crawford* rule also did not "alter our understanding of the bedrock procedural elements essential to the fairness of a proceeding." . . . We have frequently held that the *Teague* bar to retroactivity applies to new rules that are based on "bedrock" constitutional rights. Similarly, "[t]hat a new procedural rule is 'fundamental' in some abstract sense is not enough."

Instead, in order to meet this requirement, a new rule must itself constitute a previously unrecognized bedrock procedural element that is essential to the fairness of a proceeding. In applying this requirement, we again have looked to the example of *Gideon*, and "we have not hesitated to hold that less sweeping and fundamental rules" do not qualify.

In this case, it is apparent that the rule announced in *Crawford*, while certainly important, is not in the same category with *Gideon*. *Gideon* effected a profound and " 'sweeping' " change. The *Crawford* rule simply lacks the "primacy" and "centrality" of the *Gideon* rule, and does not qualify as a rule that "alter[ed] our understanding of the bedrock procedural elements essential to the fairness of a proceeding."

In sum, we hold that *Crawford* announced a "new rule" of criminal procedure and that this rule does not fall within the *Teague* exception for watershed rules. We therefore reverse the judgment of the Court of Appeals and remand the case for further proceedings consistent with this opinion.

Jaffree v. Board of School Commissioners of Mobile County

554 F.SUPP. 1104 (1983)

Ishmael Jaffree challenged the constitutionality of Alabama's law authorizing teachers to lead students in a moment of "silent meditation or voluntary prayer" as a violation of the First Amendment guarantees for religious freedom. Federal District Court Judge Brevard Hand rejected Jaffree's complaint in an opinion sharply critical of the Supreme Court's rulings on the First Amendment establishment clause. His ruling was subsequently appealed by Jaffree and overturned by a court of appeals. Governor George Wallace then appealed that ruling to the Supreme Court in *Wallace v. Jaffree*, 472 U.S. 38 (1985) (see Vol. 2, Ch. 6), which affirmed the appellant court's decision overturning Judge Hand's decision.

MEMORANDUM OPINION

☐ *Chief Judge BREVARD HAND.*

The United States Supreme Court has previously addressed itself in many cases to the practice of prayer and religious services in the public schools. As courts are wont to say, this court does not write upon a clean slate when it addresses the issue of school prayer.

Viewed historically, three decisions have lately provided general rules for school prayer. In *Engel v. Vitale*, 370 U.S. 421 [(1962)], *Abington v. Schempp*, 374 U.S. 203 (1963), and *Murray v. Curlett*, 374 U.S. 203 (1963) the Supreme Court established the basic considerations. As stated, the rule is that "[t]he First Amendment has erected a wall between church and state. That wall must be kept high and impregnable. We could not approve the slightest breach." *Everson v. Board of Education*, 330 U.S. 1 (1947).

The principles enunciated in *Engel v. Vitale, Abington v. Schempp*, and *Murray v. Curlett* have been distilled to this: "To pass muster under the Establishment Clause, the governmental activity must, first, reflect a clearly secular governmental purpose; second, have a primary effect that neither advances nor inhibits religion; and third, avoid excessive government entanglement with religion. *Committee for Public Education & Religious Liberty v. Nyquist*, 413 U.S. 756 (1973)." ...

In sum, under present rulings the use of officially-authorized prayers or Bible readings for motivational purposes constitutes a direct violation of the establishment clause. Through a series of decisions, the courts have held that the establishment clause was designed to avoid any official sponsorship or approval of religious beliefs. Even though a practice may not be coercive, active support of a particular belief raises the danger, under the rationale of the Court, that state-approved religious views may be eventually established. ...

In the face of this precedent the defendants argue that school prayers as they are employed are constitutional. The historical argument which they advance takes two tacks. First, the defendants urge that the first amendment to the U.S. Constitution was intended only to prohibit the *federal government* from establishing a *national* religion. Read in its proper historical context, the defendants contend that the first amendment has no application to the states. The intent of the drafters and adoptors of the first amendment was to prevent the establishment of a national church or religion, and to prevent any single religious sect or denomination from obtaining a preferred position under the auspices of the federal government. ...

Second, the defendants argue that whatever prohibitions were initially placed upon the federal government by the first amendment that those prohibitions were not incorporated against the states when the fourteenth amendment became law on July 19, 1868. The defendants have introduced the Court to a mass of historical documentation which all point to the intent of the Thirty-ninth Congress to narrowly restrict the scope of the fourteenth amendment. In particular, these historical documents, according to the defendants, clearly demonstrate that the first amendment was never intended to be incorporated through the fourteenth amendment to apply against the states. The Court [subsequently] examine[d] each historical argument in turn. . . .

[The Court concluded that] the establishment clause, as ratified in 1791, was intended only to prohibit the federal government from establishing a national religion. The function of the establishment clause was two-fold. First, it guaranteed to each individual that Congress would not impose a national religion. Second, the establishment clause guaranteed to each state that the states were free to define the meaning of religious establishment under their own constitutions and laws.

The historical record clearly establishes that when the fourteenth amendment was ratified in 1868 that its ratification did not incorporate the first amendment against the states. . . .

What is a court to do when faced with a direct challenge to settled precedent? In most types of cases "it is more important that the applicable rule of law be settled than that it be settled right." *Burnet v. Coronado Oil & Gas Co.*, 285 U.S. 393 (1932) (BRANDEIS, J., dissenting). This general rule holds even where the court is persuaded that it has made a serious error of interpretation in cases involving a statute. However, in cases involving the federal constitution, where correction through legislative action is practically impossible, a court should be willing to examine earlier precedent and to overrule it if the court is persuaded that the earlier precedent was wrongly decided. . . .

"[T]he ultimate touchstone of constitutionality is the Constitution itself and not what we have said about it." *Graves v. O'Keefe*, 306 U.S. 466 (1939) (FRANKFURTER, J., concurring). "By placing a premium on 'recent cases' rather than the language of the Constitution, the Court makes it dangerously simple for future Courts using the technique of interpretation to operate as a 'continuing Constitutional Convention.'" *Coleman v. Alabama*, 399 U.S. 1 (1970) (BURGER, C.J.). . . .

This Court's review of the relevant legislative history surrounding the adoption of both the first amendment and of the fourteenth amendment, together with the plain language of those amendments, leaves no doubt that those amendments were not intended to forbid religious prayers in the schools which the states and their political subdivisions mandate. . . .

If the appellate courts disagree with this Court in its examination of history and conclusion of constitutional interpretation thereof, then this Court will look again at the record in this case and reach conclusions which it is not now forced to reach.

Commonwealth of Kentucky v. Jeffrey Wasson

SUPREME COURT OF KENTUCKY, 842 S.W. 2D 487 (1992)

Jeffrey Wasson was arrested in a public parking lot and charged with soliciting an undercover police officer to engage in "deviate sexual intercourse." Under a Kentucky statute (KRS 510.100), "deviate sexual intercourse with another person of the same sex" is a criminal offense; the statute also provides that "consent of the other person shall not be a defense." At Wasson's trial, however, a district judge dismissed the charge and held that the statute violated provisions in the Kentucky Constitution that guarantee a "right of privacy" and the equal protection of the laws. A state appellate court affirmed and the Commonwealth of Kentucky appealed that ruling to its supreme court.

☐ *Opinion of the Court by Justice LEIBSON*

The Commonwealth maintains that the United States Supreme Court's decision in *Bowers v. Hardwick*, [478 U.S. 186 (1986)], is dispositive of the right to privacy issue; that the "Kentucky Constitution did not intend to confer any greater right to privacy than was afforded by the U.S. Constitution." Turning to the equal protection argument raised by a statute which criminalizes oral or anal intercourse between persons of the same sex, but not between persons of different sexes, which was not addressed in the *Bowers* case, the Commonwealth argues there is "a rational basis for making such a distinction." . . . The thrust of the argument advanced by the Commonwealth as a rational basis for criminalizing consensual intercourse between persons of the same sex, when the same acts between persons of the opposite sex are not punished, is that the level of moral indignation felt by the majority of society against the sexual preference of homosexuals justifies having their legislative representative criminalize these sexual activities. The Commonwealth believes that homosexual intercourse is immoral, and that what is beyond the pale of majoritarian morality is beyond the limits of constitutional protection.

The grounds stated by the District Court for striking down the statute as unconstitutional are: "KRS 510.100 clearly seeks to regulate the profoundly private conduct and in so doing impermissibly invades the privacy of the citizens of this state." . . . The Fayette Circuit Court "agreed with that conclusion," and further held the statute "unjustifiably discriminates, and thus is unconstitutional under Sections 2 and 3 of our Kentucky Constitution." These Sections are:

> Section 2. Absolute and arbitrary power over the lives, liberty and property of freemen exists nowhere in a republic, not even in the largest majority.
>
> Section 3. All men, when they form a social compact, are equal. . . .

These Sections [together with other provisions of the Kentucky Constitution] express the guarantee of equal treatment provided by the law in our Kentucky Constitution. The lower courts' judgments limit their finding of unconstitutionality to state constitutional grounds. *Bowers v. Hardwick* speaks neither to rights of privacy under the state constitution nor to equal protection rights under either federal or state constitutions. *Bowers* addressed the constitutionality of a Georgia statute prohibiting acts of consensual sodomy between persons of the same sex or the opposite sex. Because the Georgia statute embraced both heterosexual and homosexual conduct, the *Bowers* opinion did not involve the Equal Protection Clause of the Fourteenth Amendment.

For reasons that follow, we hold the guarantees of individual liberty provided in our 1891 Kentucky Constitution offer greater protection of the right of privacy than provided by the Federal constitution as interpreted by the United States Supreme Court, and that the statute in question is a violation of such rights; and, further, we hold that the statute in question violates rights of equal protection as guaranteed by our Kentucky Constitution.

I. RIGHTS OF PRIVACY

No language specifying "rights of privacy," as such, appears in either the federal or State Constitution. The Commonwealth recognizes such rights exist, but takes the position that, since they are implicit rather than explicit, our Court should march in lock step with the United States Supreme Court in declaring when such rights exist. Such is not the formulation of federalism. On the contrary, under our system of dual sovereignty, it is our responsibility to interpret and apply our state constitution independently. We are not bound by decisions of the United States Supreme Court when deciding whether a state statute impermissibly infringes upon individual rights guaranteed in the State Constitution so long as state constitutional protection does not fall below the federal floor, meaning the minimum guarantee of individual rights under the United States Constitution as interpreted by the United States Supreme Court. . . .

Kentucky cases recognized a legally protected right of privacy based on our own constitution and common law tradition long before the United States Supreme Court first took notice of whether there were any rights of privacy inherent in the Federal Bill of Rights. . . .

[Moreover,] the United States Supreme Court is extremely reticent in extending the reach of the Due Process Clauses in substantive matters [pertaining to privacy]. . . . *Bowers v. Hardwick* decides that rights protected by the Due Process Clauses in the Fifth and Fourteenth Amendments to the United States Constitution do not "extend a fundamental right to homosexuals to engage in acts of consensual sodomy."

Bowers decides nothing beyond this. But state constitutional jurisprudence in this area is not limited by the constraints inherent in federal due process analysis. Deviate sexual intercourse conducted in private by consenting adults is not beyond the protections of the guarantees of individual liberty in our Kentucky Constitution simply because "proscriptions against that conduct have ancient roots." Kentucky constitutional guarantees against government intrusion address substantive rights. . . . [T]he Kentucky Constitution of 1891 . . . amplifies [its guarantee of individual liberty] with a Bill of Rights in 26 sections, the first of which states:

Section 1. All men are, by nature, free and equal, and have certain inherent and inalienable rights, among which may be reckoned:

First: The right of enjoying and defending their lives and liberties. . . .

Third: The right of seeking and pursuing their safety and happiness. . . .

Section 2. Absolute and arbitrary power over the lives, liberty and property of freemen exists nowhere in a republic, not even in the largest majority. . . .

The leading case on this subject is *Commonwealth v. Campbell*, [133 Ky. 50 (1909)]. At issue was an ordinance that criminalized possession of intoxicating liquor, even for "private use." Our Court held that the Bill of Rights in the 1891 Constitution prohibited state action thus intruding upon the "inalienable rights possessed by the citizens" of Kentucky. Our Court interpreted the Kentucky Bill of Rights as defining a right of privacy, even though the constitution did not say so in that terminology. . . .

In the *Campbell* case our Court quoted at length from the "great work" *On Liberty* of the nineteenth-century English philosopher and economist, John Stuart Mill. . . . Mill's premise is that "physical force in the form of legal penalties," i.e., criminal sanctions, should not be used as a means to improve the citizen. The majority has no moral right to dictate how everyone else should live. Public indignation, while given due weight, should be subject to the overriding test of rational and critical analysis, drawing the line at harmful consequences to others. Modern legal philosophers who follow Mill temper this test with an enlightened paternalism, permitting the law to intervene to stop self-inflicted harm such as the result of drug taking, or failure to use seat belts or crash helmets, not to enforce majoritarian or conventional morality, but because the victim of such self-inflicted harm becomes a burden on society.

Based on the *Campbell* opinion, and on the Comments of the 1891 Convention Delegates, there is little doubt but that the views of John Stuart Mill, which were then held in high esteem, provided the philosophical underpinnings for the reworking and broadening of protection of individual rights that occurs throughout the 1891 constitution.

We have recognized protection of individual rights greater than the federal floor in a number of cases, most recently: *Ingram v. Commonwealth, Ky.*, 801 S.W.2d 321 (1900), involving protection against double jeopardy and *Dean v. Commonwealth, Ky.*, 777 S.W.2d 900 (1989), involving the right of confrontation. Perhaps the most dramatic recent example of protection of individual rights under the state constitution where the United States Supreme Court had refused to afford protection under the Federal Constitution is *Rose v. Council for Better Educ., Inc., Ky.*, 790 S.W.2d 186 (1989). In *Rose*, our Court recognized our Kentucky Constitution afforded individual school children from property poor districts a fundamental right to an adequate education such as provided in wealthier school districts, even though sixteen years earlier the United States Supreme Court held the Federal Constitution provided no such protection in *San Antonio Independent School District v. Rodriguez*, 411 U.S. 1 (1973). . . .

We view the United States Supreme Court decision in *Bowers v. Hardwick* as a misdirected application of the theory of original intent. To illustrate:

as a theory of majoritarian morality, miscegenation was an offense with ancient roots. It is highly unlikely that protecting the rights of persons of different races to copulate was one of the considerations behind the Fourteenth Amendment. Nevertheless, in *Loving v. Virginia*, 388 U.S. 1 (1967), the United States Supreme Court recognized that a contemporary, enlightened interpretation of the liberty interest involved in the sexual act made its punishment constitutionally impermissible.

According to *Bowers v. Hardwick*, "until 1961, all fifty States outlawed sodomy, and today, twenty-five States and District of Columbia continue to provide criminal penalties for sodomy performed in private and between consenting adults." In the space of three decades half the states decriminalized this conduct. . . . Two states [New York and Pennsylvania] by court decisions hold homosexual sodomy statutes of this nature unconstitutional for reasons similar to those stated here. . . . Thus our decision, rather than being the leading edge of change, is but a part of the moving stream. . . .

II. EQUAL PROTECTION

As stated earlier, in *Bowers v. Hardwick*, the Equal Protection Clause was not implicated because the Georgia statute criminalized both heterosexual and homosexual sodomy. Unlike the due Process Clause analysis provided in *Bowers v. Hardwick*, equal protection analysis does not turn on whether the law (KRS 510.100) transgresses "liberties that are 'deeply rooted in this Nation's history and tradition.' " *Bowers v. Hardwick*. . . .

Certainly, the practice of deviate sexual intercourse violates traditional morality. But so does the same act between heterosexuals, which activity is decriminalized. Going one step further, all sexual activity between consenting adults outside of marriage violates our traditional morality. The issue here is not whether sexual activity traditionally viewed as immoral can be punished by society, but whether it can be punished solely on the basis of sexual preference. . . .

We need not speculate as to whether male and/or female homosexuals will be allowed status as a protected class if and when the United States Supreme Court confronts this issue. They are a separate and identifiable class for Kentucky constitutional law analysis because no class of persons can be discriminated against under the Kentucky Constitution. All are entitled to equal treatment, unless there is a substantial governmental interest, a rational basis, for different treatment.

In the final analysis we can attribute no legislative purpose to this statute except to single out homosexuals for different treatment for indulging their sexual preference by engaging in the same activity heterosexuals are now at liberty to perform. By 1974 there had already been a sea change in societal values insofar as attaching criminal penalties to extramarital sex. The question is whether a society that no longer criminalizes adultery, fornication, or deviate sexual intercourse between heterosexuals has a rational basis to single out homosexual acts for different treatment. Is there a rational basis for declaring this one type of sexual immorality so destructive of family values as to merit criminal punishment whereas other acts of sexual immorality which were likewise forbidden by the same religious and traditional heritage of

Western civilization are now decriminalized? If there is a rational basis for different treatment it has yet to be demonstrated in this case.

The purpose of the present statute is not to protect the marital relation-ship against sexual activity outside of marriage, but only to punish one aspect of it while other activities similarly destructive of the marital relationship, if not more so, go unpunished. Sexual preference, and not the act committed, determines criminality, and is being punished. Simply because the majority, speaking through the General Assembly, finds one type of extramarital inter-course more offensive than another, does not provide a rational basis for criminalizing the sexual preference of homosexuals.

For the reasons stated, we affirm the decision of the Fayette Circuit Court, and the judgment on appeal from the Fayette District Court.

☐ *Justices LAMBERT, WINTERSHEIMBER, and REYNOLDS dissented.*

■ THE DEVELOPMENT OF LAW

Other Recent State Supreme Court Decisions Declining to Follow the U.S. Supreme Court's Rulings

State v. Bauder, 924 A.2d 38 (Vt. 2007)   Vermont's supreme court, like those in other states—New Jersey, New Mexico, Nevada, Pennsylvania, New York, Oregon, and Wyoming—declined to follow, based on its state constitution, the U.S. Supreme Court ruling in *New York v. Belton,* 453 U.S. 454 (1981), holding that upon a lawful custodial arrest of an occupant of a car, police may search the contents of any containers found within the passenger compartment, including consoles and receptacles. See also *State v. Eckel,* 185 N.J. 523 (2006); *Camacho v. State,* 119 Nev. 395 (2003); *Vasquez v. State,* 990 P.2d 476 (199); *State v. Arredondo,* 123 N.M. 628 (Ct. App., 2005); *Commonwealth v. White,* 543 Pa. 45 (1995); *People v. Blasich,* 73 N.Y. 673 (1989); and *State v. Fesler,* 68 Ore. App. 609 (1984).

Bush v. Holmes, 919 So.2d 392 (Fla. 2006)   The Supreme Court of Florida declined to follow the ruling in *Zelman v. Simmons-Harris,* 536 U.S. 639 (2002) (excerpted in Vol. 2, Ch. 6), upholding Ohio's voucher system over (dis)establishment clause objections. The court struck down Florida's voucher system based on provisions in its state constitution for an equal and uniform public educational system.

People v. Rodriguez, 112 P. 3d 693 78 (Colo. 2005)   The Supreme Court of Colorado declined to follow *Williams v. Florida,* 399 U.S. (1970) (excerpted in Vol. 2, Ch. 9), which held that the Sixth Amendment does not require juries of twelve in state criminal cases. Instead, based on the state constitution it held that twelve-person juries are required in felony, though not misdemeanor, criminal cases.

Indiana v. Gerschoffer, 763 N.E.2d 960 (Ind., 2002)   The Indiana Supreme Court held that a sobriety checkpoint for drivers violated the state constitution. See also *Brown v. State,* 653 N.E.2d 77 (Ind., 1995), holding that a warrantless search of defendant's car violated the state constitution.

Anchorage Police Department Employees Association v. Municipality of Anchorage, 24 P.3d 547 (Als., 2001)

Declining to follow *Vernonia School District No. 47J v. Acton,* 515 U.S. 646 (1995), the Alaska Supreme Court held that random drug testing of police and fire fighters violated the state constitution.

Shadler v. Florida, 761 So.2d 279 (Fla., 2000)

The Florida Supreme Court declined to follow *Arizona v. Evans,* 514 U.S. 1 (1995) (excerpted in Vol. 2, Ch. 7), in holding on state constitutional grounds that the "good-faith" exception to the exclusionary rule does not apply to arrests based on mistaken highway safety computerized records.

State v. Cline, 617 N.W.2d 277 (Iowa, 2000)

The Iowa Supreme Court declined to follow *Illinois v. Krull,* 480 U.S. 340 (1987), and *United States v. Leon,* 468 U.S. 897 (1984), in refusing to recognize a "good faith" exception to the exclusionary rule as a matter of state constitutional law. See also *Iowa v. Gillespie,* 619 N.W.2d 345 (Iowa, 2000)

Commonwealth v. Gonsalves, 711 N.E.2d 108 (Mass. 1999)

The Supreme Judicial Court of Massachusetts extended more rights than the U.S. Supreme Court, in *Pennsylvania v. Mimms,* 434 U.S. 106 (1977) and *Maryland v. Wilson,* 519 U.S. 408 (1977), based on its state constitution. The court held that the Massachusetts constitution requires a police officer, during the course of a routine traffic stop, to have a reasonable belief that the officer's safety is in danger before he can order the driver or passenger out of the vehicle.

Powell v. State of Georgia, 510 S.E.2d 18 (1998)

The Georgia Supreme Court struck down its state law criminalizing noncommercial, consensual sodomy and expressly rejected the ruling in *Bowers v. Hardwick,* 478 U.S. 186 (1986), which had upheld that state's law. Other state courts have struck their state laws criminalizing sodomy. See also *Kentucky v. Wasson,* 842 S.W.2d 487 (Ky. 1992) (excerpted in this chapter); *Michigan Organization for Human Rights v. Kelley,* No. 88-815820 CZ (Mich. Cir. Ct., July 9, 1990); and *State v. Cogshell,* 997 S.W.2d 534 (Mo. App. W.D., July 6, 1999).

(continues)

■ THE DEVELOPMENT OF LAW
Other Recent State Supreme Court Decisions Declining to
Follow the U.S. Supreme Court's Rulings (continued)

Commonwealth v. Labron,   The Pennsylvania Supreme Court re-
690 A.2D 228 (1997)   asserted, as a matter of state constitutional law, its earlier holding that the
automobile exception to search warrant requirements does not justify a
police search unless there exists probable cause for the search and a warrantless search is justified by the "exigencies of the circumstances,"
thereby declining to follow the ruling in *Pennsylvania v. Labron*, 518 U.S.
938 (1996).

American Academy of   By a vote of four to three, the Supreme
Pediatrics v. Lungren,   Court of California refused to follow
940 P.2d 797 (1997)   the U.S. Supreme Court's rulings upholding state restrictions on minors
seeking abortions by requiring them to obtain the permission of their
parents or a judge. Here, the court invalidated the parental consent and
judicial-bypass requirement for infringing on minors' right of privacy under the California Constitution.

Gryczan v. Montana,   Like the Supreme Court of Kentucky
942 P.2d 112 (1997)   in *Commonwealth of Kentucky v. Wasson*,
842 S.W. 2d (1992), the Montana
Supreme Court refused to follow the ruling in *Bowers v. Hardwick*, 478
U.S. 186 (1986) and based on its state constitution struck down its state
law criminalizing sodomy. Besides those two, other state supreme
courts have likewise invalidated their laws against sodomy. See, e.g.,
Tennessee v. Sundquist, 926 S.W.2d 250 (Tenn., 1996); *People v. Onofre*,
415 N.E.2d 936 (N.Y., 1980); and *Commonwealth v. Bonadio*, 415 A.2d
47 (Pa., 1980).

Smith v. Fair Employment   Among other state supreme courts re
and Housing Commission,   fusing to follow the U.S. Supreme
12 Cal. 4th 1143 (1996)   Court's ruling in *Employment Division,
Department of Human Resources of Ore-*
gon v. Smith, 494 U.S. 872 (1990) (excerpted in Vol. 2, Ch. 6), the California Supreme Court held that its state constitution "afford[s] the same
protection for religious exercise as the Federal Constitution [did] before
[the U.S. Supreme Court's decision in] *Employment Division v. Smith*."

State supreme courts in Alaska, Maine, Michigan, Minnesota, Ohio, New York, and Washington ruled likewise.

Sheff v. O'Neill,
238 Conn. 1 (1996)

Departing from the U.S. Supreme Court's holdings that only segregation brought about by intentional state action violates the Fourteenth Amendment, the Connecticut Supreme Court ruled that its state constitution explicitly bars unintentional racial segregation and guarantees a right to free and equal public education. In doing so, the state supreme Court found that *de facto* racial isolation and socioeconomic deprivation violated the right of equal opportunity to a free public education of students in Hartford, Connecticut. Whereas children from minority groups constitute 25 percent of the state's public school population, 92 percent of Hartford's public school students come from minority groups. "Because of the negative consequences of racial and ethnic isolation," the Court held unconstitutional a state law requiring that school districts coincide with municipal boundaries and ordered the state to integrate public schools across district lines.

*Commonwealth of
Pennsylvania v. Matos,*
672 A.2d 769 (1996)

Rejecting the reasoning and result in *California v. Hodari D.,* 499 U.S. 621 (1991) (see Vol. 2, Ch. 7), the Supreme Court of Pennsylvania held that under its state constitution, contraband discarded by a person fleeing a police officer was the fruit of an illegal search, because the officer possessed neither probable cause for an arrest nor a "reasonable suspicion" to stop the individual; and thus the contraband must be excluded as evidence against the accused. In the Court's words, "we reject *Hodari D.* as incompatible with the privacy rights guaranteed to the citizens of this Commonwealth under . . . the Pennsylvania Constitution." The Court noted as well that a number of other states had rejected the analysis in *Hodari D.*; those states include Connecticut, Hawaii, New Jersey, New York, and Oregon.

Florida v. White, 660
So. 2d 664 (1995)

Within months of the ruling in *Arizona v. Evans,* 514 U.S. 1 (see Vol. 2, Ch. 7), which extended the "good faith exception" to the Fourth Amendment's exclusionary rule to police officers' reliance on mistaken computerized records of an outstanding arrest warrant, the Supreme Court of Florida decided otherwise in holding that the "failure of the police to maintain up-to-date and accurate com-

(continues)

■ THE DEVELOPMENT OF LAW
Other Recent State Supreme Court Decisions Declining to
Follow the U.S. Supreme Court's Rulings (continued)

puter records results in an illegal arrest and search" and that "evidence obtained as a result of the illegal arrest is subject to the exclusionary rule" of
the state constitution.

Women of Minnesota v. Gomez,   In striking down its state's restrictions
542 N.W.2d 17 (1995)   on public funding for therapeutic
abortions, the Supreme Court of Min-
nesota observed that "in reaching our decision, we have interpreted the
Minnesota Constitution to afford broader protection than the United
States Constitution of a woman's fundamental right to reach a private decision on whether to obtain an abortion, and thus reject the United
States Supreme Court's opinion on this issue in *Harris v. McRae*, 448 U.S.
297 (1980)." Appellate courts in California, Connecticut, Massachusetts,
Michigan, and New Jersey have also struck down prohibitions on public
funding for abortions not necessary to save a pregnant woman's life on
the basis of their state constitutions.

Montana v. Bullock and   The Supreme Court of Montana ruled
Peterson, **901 P.2d 61 (1995)**   that under the state constitution individuals have "reasonable expectations
of privacy" and standing to challenge the legality of a police search of
property that they do not own, and thus declined to follow the U.S.
Supreme Court's rulings in *Rakas v. Illinois*, 439 U.S. 128 (1978). Other
state supreme courts have ruled likewise, including those in New Jersey,
in *State v. Alston*, 440 A.2d 1311 (1981); in Arizona, in *State v. White*, 574
P.2d 840 (1978); and New Hampshire, in *State v. Alosa*, 623 A.2d 218
(1993).

Torre Jenkins v. Chief Justice   The Massachusetts Supreme Court re-
of the District Court Department,   fused to follow the decision in *County*
416 Mass. 221 (1993)   *of Riverside v. McLaughlin*, 500 U.S. 44
(1991) (see Vol. 2, Ch. 7), that follow-
ing a warrantless arrest individuals may be incarcerated for up to forty-
eight hours before being given a hearing to determine the probable cause
for their arrest.

Sitz v. Michigan   The Supreme Court of Michigan re-
Department of State Police,   fused to abide by the U.S. Supreme
443 Mich. 744 (1993)   Court's holding, in *Michigan Depart-*

ment of State Police v. Sitz, 496 U.S. 444 (1990), that Michigan state police's use of sobriety checkpoints did not violate the Fourth Amendment. When that case was remanded back to the state appellate court, the state supreme court held that the state's policy of indiscriminate suspicionless stopping of automobiles violates the state constitution's prohibition against unreasonable searches and seizures. The Supreme Court of Washington also held that police checkpoints violate the privacy rights guaranteed by its state constitution, in *City of Seattle v. Mesiani,* 755 P.2d 775 (1988).

Derricott v. Maryland, 611 A.2d 592 (1992)

In *United States v. Sokolow,* 490 U.S. 1 (1989) (see Vol. 2, Ch. 7), the use of "drug courier profiles" by law enforcement officials was upheld over Fourth Amendment objections. But in *Derricott* the Court of Appeals of Maryland held that stopping and searching a car solely on the ground that the driver fit a "drug courier profile"—that is, was young, black, driving a sports car, and had a beeper—was not permissible under state constitutional law.

Gary v. Georgia, 422 S.E. 2d 426 (1992)

The Supreme Court of Georgia ruled that provisions of the state constitution precluded the adoption of a "good-faith" exception to the exclusionary rule and declined to follow the rulings in *United States v. Leon,* 468 U.S. 902 (1984), and *Massachusetts v. Sheppard,* 468 U.S. 981 (1984) (see Vol. 2, Ch. 7). Other state supreme courts that have refused to recognize a "good-faith exception" to the exclusionary rule as a matter of state constitutional law are in Connecticut, in *State v. Marsala,* 579 A.2d 58 (1990); Massachusetts, in *Commonwealth v. Upton,* 476 N.E.2d 548 (1985); Michigan, in *People v. Sundling,* 395 N.W.2d 308 (1986); New Jersey, in *State v. Novembrino,* 519 A.2d 820 (1987); New York, in *People v. Bigelow,* 488 N.E.2d 451 (1985); North Carolina, in *State v. Carter,* 370 S.E.2d 553 (1988); Pennsylvania, in *Commonwealth v. Edmunds,* 586 A.2d 887 (1991); Texas, in *Davis v. State,* 831 S.W.2d 426 (1992); and Vermont, in *State v. Oakes,* 598 A.2d 119 (1991).

New Jersey v. Hemple and Hemple, 576 A.2d 793 (1990)

Declining to follow *California v. Greenwood,* 486 U.S. 35 (1988), which held that under the Fourth Amendment individuals do not have "reasonable expectations of privacy" in the contents of garbage bags left for collection in public areas, the Supreme Court of New Jersey ruled otherwise, observing that, "When the United States Constitution affords our citizens less protection than does the New Jersey Constitution, we have not

(continues)

■ THE DEVELOPMENT OF LAW
Other Recent State Supreme Court Decisions Declining to
Follow the U.S. Supreme Court's Rulings (continued)

merely the authority to give full effect to the State protection, we have the duty to do so." The supreme courts of California and Hawaii have also ruled that their constitutions protect against warrantless searches of garbage in, respectively, *People of California v. Krivda*, 504 P.2d 457 (1973), and *State v. Tanaka*, 701 P.2d 1274 (1985).

In re T.W., 551 So.2d 1186 (1989)   In anticipation that the U.S. Supreme Court might overrule *Roe v. Wade*, 410 U.S. 113 (1973) (see Vol. 2, Ch. 11), or significantly cut back on its upholding a woman's right to secure an abortion, as occurred in *Planned Parenthood of Southeastern Pennsylvania v. Casey*, 505 U.S. 833 (1992) (see Vol. 2, Ch. 11), the Supreme Court of Florida interpreted a 1980 state constitutional amendment, providing that "Every natural person has the right to be let alone and free from government intrusion into his private life except as otherwise provided herein," to guarantee a woman the right to have an abortion and observed that its ruling "is beyond the reach" of the U.S. Supreme Court because the latter is "a bystander when it comes to interpreting state constitutions." Other state supreme courts have likewise ruled that their state constitutions protect a woman's right to abortion, including California, in *Committee to Defend Reproductive Rights v. Meyers*, 625 P.2d 779 (1981) (requiring state funding for abortions); Connecticut, in *Doe v. Maher*, 515 A.2d 134 (1986); Michigan, in *Doe v. Director of Michigan Department of Social Services*, 468 N.W. 2d 862 (1991); Massachusetts, in *Moe v. Secretary of Administration*, 417 N.E. 2d 387 (1981); Tennessee, in *Davis v. Davis*, 842 S.W. 588 (Tenn., 1992) (holding state constitution's right of privacy covered the choice not to procreate); and New Jersey, in *Right to Choose v. Byrne*, 450 A. 2d 925 (1982).

Edgewood Independent School District v. Kirby, 777 S.W.2d 391 (1989)   In a Fourteenth Amendment Equal Protection Clause challenge to disparities in Texas's system of public school financing, the U.S. Supreme Court held, in *San Antonio Independent School District v. Rodriguez*, 411 U.S. 1 (1973), that public education is not a "fundamental right" barring states from discriminatory public school financing. In *Edgewood Independent School District*, however, the Supreme Court of Texas ruled to the contrary, on the basis of its state constitution. Other state supreme courts have refused to follow *Rodriguez*; they include New Jersey [see *Robinson v. Cahill*, 303 A.2d 273 (N.J., 1973) to *Robinson VII*, 360 A.2d 400 (N.J., 1976)], California [*Serrano v. Priest*, 557 P.2d 929 (Cal., 1976)], Washington [*Seattle School District No. 1 v. State*, 585 P.2d 71 (Wash., 1978)], West Virginia [*Pauley v. Kelly*, 255 S.E.2d 859 (W. Va., 1979)], and Wyoming [*Washakie County School District No. 1 v. Herschler*, 606 P.2d 310 (Wyo., 1980)].

Witters v. State of Washington Commission for the Blind, 771 P.2d for 1119 (Wash., 1989)

On remand, the Supreme Court of Washington refused to follow the ruling in *Witters v. Washington Dept. of Services for the Blind*, 474 U.S. 481 (1981), holding that a state scholarship given to a handicapped person who attended a religious college did not violate the First Amendment's disestablishment clause. It found that such financial assistance violated its state constitution.

People v. P. J. Video, Inc., 68 N.Y. 2d 296 (1986)

In *New York v. P.J. Video, Inc.*, 475 U.S. 868 (1986), the U.S. Supreme Court reversed a ruling by the New York Court of Appeals, which had held that a state judge erred when issuing a search warrant for the seizure of allegedly obscene videos, which were subject to First Amendment protection and thus required a higher standard of probable cause than the usual "fair probability" that evidence of a crime would be found. When that case was remanded back to the state appellate court, the latter reaffirmed its earlier ruling on the basis of independent state grounds and refused to apply the "total of the circumstances/fair probability" test announced in *Illinois v. Gates*, 462 U.S. 213 (1983).

Montana v. Johnson, 719 P.2d 1248 (1986)

Departing from the ruling in *Fare v. Michael C.*, 442 U.S. 707 (1979), to the application and scope of the rights set forth in *Miranda v. Arizona*, 384 U.S. 436 (1966) (see Vol. 2, Ch. 8), to a juvenile who asked to see his probation officer, the Supreme Court of Montana held that the right to counsel is broader under its state constitutional law than under federal constitutional law, observing that "we refuse to 'march lock-step' with the United States Supreme Court where constitutional issues are concerned, even if the applicable State Constitution provisions are identical or nearly identical to those of the United States Constitution."

(continues)

■ THE DEVELOPMENT OF LAW
Other Recent State Supreme Court Decisions Declining to
Follow the U.S. Supreme Court's Rulings (continued)

Montana v. Solis,   Recognizing broader protection for
693 P.2d 518 (1984)   interests in privacy and against unreasonable searches and seizures, the
Supreme Court of Montana rejected the "assumption of risk" rule laid
down in *United States v. White*, 401 U.S. 745 (1971) (see Vol. 2, Ch. 7), with
respect to recording of conversations by undercover police, observing that
"[t]his Court is not bound by decisions of the United States Supreme
Court where independent grounds exist for reaching a contrary result,"
and noting that in *State v. Van Hyem*, 630 P.2d 202 (1981), it had ruled
"that independent state grounds existed for this Court to extend greater
privacy rights, and thereby greater protection against unreasonable search
and seizure, than would be afforded under the Federal Constitution."

South Dakota v. Neville,   In *South Dakota v. Neville*, 459 U.S.
346 N.W.2d 425 (1984)   553 (1983), the U.S. Supreme Court
held that the introduction as evidence
of the defendant's refusal to take a blood-alcohol test after being stopped
by police for failing to stop at a stop sign did not violate the Fifth
Amendment privilege against self-incrimination. On remand, however,
the Supreme Court of South Dakota ruled on the basis of its state constitution the defendant's refusal to submit to the test was inadmissible as evidence against him.

Washington v. Chrisman,
676 P.2d 419 (1984)

In *Washington v. Chrisman,* 455 U.S. 1 (1982), the U.S. Supreme Court reversed and remanded the decision of the Washington state supreme court that a campus police officer's warrantless entry and search of a dormitory room of two university students violated the Fourth Amendment, characterizing the decision as a "novel reading of the Fourth Amendment." On remand, the Supreme Court of Washington nonetheless found the officer's search to violate provisions of the state constitution.

People v. Long, **659
N.W. 2d 194 (1984)**

On remand, the Michigan state supreme court reasserted on independent state grounds its earlier ruling on the impermissibility of a police officer's search of a driver after its previous decision was reversed in *Michigan v. Long,* 463 U.S. 1032 (1983) (excerpted in Vol. 1, Ch. 7).

Right to Choose v. Byrne,
450 A.2d 925 (N.J., 1982)

After the ruling in *Harris v. McRae,* 448 U.S. 297 (1980) that a congressional prohibition on the use of Medicaid funds for abortions did not violate the Fourteenth Amendment's equal protection clause, the New Jersey Supreme Court held otherwise on the basis of its state constitution. State supreme courts in California, Connecticut, Massachusetts, Michigan, and Oregon have likewise upheld the right of indigent women to state-funded abortions.

3

Presidential Power, the Rule of Law, and Foreign Affairs

Article II of the Constitution establishes the basis for presidential power. It does so in both general and specific terms. "The executive Power shall be vested in a President" and "he shall take Care that the Laws be faithfully executed" are broad authorizations. In contrast with the lengthy enumeration of Congress's specific powers in Article I, those granted the president are few in number. The president is given, for example, power to veto legislation, power to pardon individuals of crimes, and power to act as commander in chief of the military. In addition, other powers—such as that of making treaties and appointing federal judges and other governmental officers—are shared with the Senate and their exercise subject to Senate approval.

A | Office and Powers: The Two Presidencies

The powers exercised by the contemporary presidency would have surprised those of the Founding generation. They expected, as James Madison put it in *Federalist*, No. 51, that "in republican government, the legislative authority necessarily predominates." Alexander Hamilton, however, prophetically championed the cause of a vigorous chief executive and maintained that the enumerated powers were not exhaustive of the powers of the president. In *Federalist,* No. 70, he set forth the principal arguments for a strong, independent president (see excerpt below).

The basis for broad presidential power was laid by the Constitutional Convention in 1787. Although many delegates distrusted executive power, there was agreement that the Articles of Confederation, which failed to provide for a separate executive, had proven disastrous. Accordingly, the executive power is lodged in a single individual, elected for a four-year term and eligible for reelection. Notably, election to the office is also based on the vote of the electoral college. That resulted as a compromise between congressional selection and direct popular election. And it reflects both a fear that Congress might overshadow the president as well as a distrust of direct democracy. Finally, certain powers—such as that of vetoing legislation—were granted to further ensure presidential independence from Congress.

"[T]he history of the presidency is a history of aggrandizement, but the story is a highly discontinuous one," observed Edward S. Corwin. "That is to say, what the presidency is at any particular moment depends in important measure on who is the President."[1] Undeniably, presidential character and understanding of the powers of the Oval Office are crucial. But presidential power has also grown enormously with the emergence of the United States as a world power and is due to the acquiescence of Congress, the courts, and the American people. Moreover, the power vested in the executive branch now resides in an institutionalized presidency, with more than two million employees, thousands of whom wield significant power.

The growth of the institutional presidency makes questions about the limitations imposed on the office of the president more pressing. For in keeping faith with the theory of our written Constitution, "[a]ll the officers of the Government, from the highest to the lowest, are creatures of the law and are bound to obey it."[2] However, in times of emergency and national crisis, presidents have asserted unauthorized power, even ignored constitutional constraints and suspended basic rights.

A central issue in constitutional politics thus involves whether the authority granted in Article II exhausts the powers of the president. To what extent does the president enjoy inherent power and extraordinary powers in times of emergency?

One classic theory is that the president, like the old English Crown, enjoys the sovereign's "prerogative" of asserting, when necessary, unauthorized power in pursuit of the public interest. Eighteenth-century English philosopher John Locke, in his *Two Treatises of Government*, described this prerogative as "the power to act according to discretion for the public good, *without the prescription of law and sometimes even against it*" (emphasis added). Periodically, throughout our history presidents have made similar claims. President Thomas Jefferson did so in 1803 when purchasing the Louisiana Territory, despite doubts about the authority to acquire new lands. At the outset of the Civil War, Abraham Lincoln took extraordinary measures—calling up state militias, spending unappropriated funds, and blockading Southern ports—without authorization. He later defended his actions as essential to preserving the Union:

> I [understood] my oath to preserve the constitution to the best of my ability, imposed upon me the duty of preserving, by every indispensable means, that government—that nation—of which that constitution was the organic law. Was it possible to lose the nation, and yet preserve the constitution? . . . I felt that measures, otherwise unconstitutional, might become lawful, by becoming indispensable to the preservation of the constitution, through the preservation of the nation.[3]

Franklin D. Roosevelt likewise claimed extensive powers during World War II. And as we will see later in this chapter, Harry S. Truman claimed the power to seize steel mills during the undeclared Korean War and, in 1971, Richard M. Nixon sought to suppress publication of the "Pentagon Papers," a history of the U.S. involvement in the Vietnam War.

During emergencies and national strife, Madison and Hamilton agreed that the national government enjoys extraordinary power. "It is in vain to oppose constitutional barriers to the impulse of self-preservation," Madison cautioned in *Federalist*, No. 41. Hamilton (in *Federalist*, No. 23) was even more emphatic about the powers that could be marshaled for national defense. They "ought to exist without limitation," he argued, "*because it is impossible to forsee or to define the extent and variety of the means which may be necessary to satisfy them. The circumstances that endanger the safety of nations are infinite, and for this reason no constitutional shackles can wisely be imposed on the power to which the care of it is committed*" (emphasis in original).

Still, how far presidents may go, without congressional authorization, when responding to perceived threats to national security remains a fundamental issue in constitutional politics. In *Ex parte Milligan* (1866) (excerpted below), the Court rejected Lincoln's suspension of the right of *habeas corpus* and order for trials of civilians by military commissions, with the poignant observation that "[t]he Constitution of the United States is a law for rulers and people, equally in war and in peace, and covers with the shield of its protection all classes of men, at all times,

Chief Justice William Howard Taft, the only president (1909–1913) also to serve on the Supreme Court (1921–1930). (*Library of Congress.*)

and under all circumstances." However, in *Korematsu v. United States* (1944) (excerpted below), the internment of Japanese-American citizens during World War II was upheld under legislation that made it a crime for persons of Japanese ancestry to be in "military zones" as designated by a commander under the secretary of war.

There are two rival theories of the nature and scope of the inherent presidential power; both are more restrictive than Locke's theory of the prerogative but also more generous than a rigid adherence to constitutional theory. Theodore Roosevelt took the position that inherent power extends to doing anything not expressly forbidden, so long as it serves the public interest and does not conflict with existing legislation. According to him,

> The executive power was limited only by specific restrictions and prohibitions appearing in the Constitution or imposed by the Congress under its Constitutional powers. . . . I declined to adopt the view that what was imperatively necessary for the Nation could not be done by the President unless he could find some specific authorization to do it. My belief was that it was not only his right but

his duty to do anything that the needs of the Nation demanded unless such action was forbidden by the Constitution or by the laws.[4]

By contrast, President (and later Chief Justice) William Howard Taft contended that inherent powers are limited and must be traceable to specific grants of power in the Constitution or legislation. In his words,

> The true view of the Executive function is, as I conceive it, that the President can exercise no power which cannot be fairly and reasonably traced to some specific grant of power or justly implied and included within such express grant as proper and necessary to its exercise. Such specific grant must be either in the Federal Constitution or in an act of Congress passed in pursuance thereof. There is no undefined residuum of power which he can exercise because it seems to him to be in the public interest.[5]

In addition, a distinction is usually drawn between the inherent powers of the president in domestic and in foreign affairs. As political scientist Aaron Wildavsky remarked, "The United States has one President, but it has two presidencies; one presidency is for domestic affairs, and the other is concerned with defense and foreign policy."[6] In the domestic area, claims to inherent presidential power are usually limited and sharply criticized, whereas Congress and the Court generally acknowledge presidential dominance in foreign affairs. The scope of presidential powers in this area, as Clinton Rossiter noted, has historically "been presidentially, not judicially, shaped; [the] exercise [of those powers] is for Congress and the people, not the Court, to oversee."[7]

This chapter examines the express and inherent powers of the president in foreign affairs. It does so in terms of basic interpretive choices that give rise to conflicts in constitutional politics. In addressing the president's powers as commander in chief and in foreign affairs, specific attention is given to the treaty-making and war-making powers. Chapter 4 examines the president's powers in domestic affairs.

Notes

1. E. Corwin, *The President*, 5th ed. (New York: New York University Press, 1984), 29–30.

2. *United States v. Lee*, 106 U.S. 196 (1882).

3. John Nicolay and John Hay, eds., *The Complete Works of Abraham Lincoln*, Vol. 10 (New York: Francis D. Tandy, 1894), 65–68.

4. T. Roosevelt, *Autobiography* (New York: Macmillan, 1931), 38.

5. W. Taft, *Our Chief Magistrate and His Powers* (New York: Columbia University, 1916), 139–140.

6. A. Wildavsky, "The Two Presidencies," 4 *Trans-Action* 230 (Dec. 1969).

7. C. Rossiter, *The Supreme Court and the Commander in Chief* (Ithaca, NY: Cornell University Press, 1976), 126.

SELECTED BIBLIOGRAPHY

Adler, David G., and George, Larry N., eds. *The Constitution and the Conduct of American Foreign Policy*. Lawrence: University Press of Kansas, 1996.

Bessette, Joseph, and Tulis, Jeffrey, eds. *The Constitutional Presidency*. Baltimore: The Johns Hopkins University Press, 2009.

Calabresi, Steven, and Yoo, Christopher. *The Unitary Executive: Presidential Power from Washington to Bush*. New Haven, CT: Yale University Press, 2008.

Casper, Gerhard. *Separating Power: Essays on the Founding Period*. Cambridge, MA: Harvard University Press, 1997.

Crovitz, L. Godron, and Rabkin, Jeremy, eds. *The Fettered Presidency*. Washington, DC: American Enterprise Institute, 1989.

Corwin, Edward. *The President: Office and Powers*, 5th rev. ed. New York: New York University Press, 1984.

Koh, Harold Hongju. *The National Security Constitution*. New Haven, CT: Yale University Press, 1990.

McGinty, Brian, *Lincoln and the Court*. Cambridge, MA: Harvard University Press, 2008.

Powell, H. Jefferson. *The President's Authority over Foreign Affairs*. Durham, NC: Carolina Academic Press, 2002.

Silverstein, Gordon. *Imbalance of Powers: Constitutional Interpretation and the Making of American Foreign Policy*. New York: Oxford University Press, 1996.

Taft, William Howard, with foreword by H. Jefferson Powell. *Our Chief Magistrate and His Powers*. Durham, NC: Carolina Academic Press, 2002.

■ CONSTITUTIONAL HISTORY

Alexander Hamilton, The Federalist, No. 70

Energy in the executive is a leading character in the definition of good government. It is essential to the protection of the community against foreign attacks; it is not less essential to the steady administration of the laws; to the protection of property against those irregular and high-handed combinations which sometimes interrupt the ordinary course of justice; to the security of liberty against the enterprises and assaults of ambition, of faction, and of anarchy. Every man the least conversant in Roman history knows how often that republic was obliged to take refuge in the absolute power of a single man, under the formidable title of dictator, as well as against the intrigues of ambitious individuals who aspired to the tyranny, and the seditions of whole classes of the community whose conduct threatened the existence of all government, as against the invasions of external enemies who menaced the conquest and destruction of Rome. . . .

The ingredients which constitute energy in the executive are unity; duration; an adequate provision for its support; and competent powers.

The ingredients which constitute safety in the republican sense are a due dependence on the people, and a due responsibility.

Those politicians and statesmen who have been the most celebrated for the soundness of their principles and for the justness of their views have declared in favor of a single executive and a numerous legislature. They have, with great propriety, considered energy as the most necessary

B | *As Commander in Chief and in Foreign Affairs*

The president's powers in foreign affairs flow from being commander in chief of the military and from specific powers (shared with the Senate) to make treaties and appoint ambassadors. Numerous other powers have developed in practice, from appointing diplomatic corps and negotiating with foreign governments, to using military forces to implement foreign policy independent of congressional authorization. Congressional legislation and treaties have also expanded presidential power. And presidents may defend controversial actions as necessary

qualification of the former, and have regarded this as most applicable to power in a single hand; while they have, with equal propriety, considered the latter as best adapted to deliberation and wisdom, and best calculated to conciliate the confidence of the people and to secure their privileges and interests.

That unity is conducive to energy will not be disputed. Decision, activity, secrecy, and dispatch will generally characterize the proceedings of one man in a much more eminent degree than the proceedings of any greater number; and in proportion as the number is increased, these qualities will be diminished. . . . In the legislature, promptitude of decision is oftener an evil than a benefit. The differences of opinion, and the jarring of parties in that department of the government, though they may sometimes obstruct salutary plans, yet often promote deliberation and circumspection, and serve to check excesses in the majority. When a resolution too is once taken, the opposition must be at an end. That resolution is a law, and resistance to it punishable. But no favorable circumstances palliate or atone for the disadvantages of dissention in the executive department. Here they are pure and unmixed. There is no point at which they cease to operate. They serve to embarrass and weaken the execution of the plan or measure to which they relate, from the first step to the final conclusion of it. They constantly counteract those qualities in the executive which are the most necessary ingredients in its composition—vigor and expedition, and this without any counterbalancing good. In the conduct of war, in which the energy of the executive is the bulwark of the national security, everything would be to be apprehended from its plurality.

under their obligation to "take Care that the Laws be faithfully executed." In addition, as Justice Frankfurter once noted, "Past practice does not, by itself, create power, but 'long-continued practice, known to and acquiesced in by Congress, would raise a presumption that the [action] has been [taken] in pursuance of its consent.'"

A principal justification—which has come to be known as the "sole organ theory"—for presidential independence in foreign affairs was offered by John Marshall in the House of Representatives in 1799. When defending President John Adams's extradition of a fugitive under the Jay Treaty, he proclaimed, "The President is the sole organ of the nation in its external relations, and its sole representative with foreign nations." Although Marshall contended that the president was the sole organ in communicating and negotiating with other countries, the theory has been expanded to include unilateral military action as well.

Such a broad view of inherent powers runs back to Alexander Hamilton, who warned in *Federalist*, No. 23, "The circumstances that endanger the safety of nations is infinite, and for this reason no constitutional shackles can wisely be imposed on the power to which the care of it is committed."

The Supreme Court in *United States v. Curtiss-Wright Export Corporation* (1936) (see excerpt below) wrote the sole organ theory into constitutional law. In upholding a delegation of power by Congress to the president that the Court would have invalidated had it been in the area of domestic—rather than foreign—affairs, Justice Sutherland agreed with Wildavsky that there are indeed two presidencies. And in the area of foreign affairs the president enjoys a large reservoir of inherent power. Notably, though, the opinion rests in part on a dubious reading of history: Sutherland maintains that sovereignty—including control over foreign affairs—passed directly from the English Crown to the national government, despite the fact that during the postindependence period the original thirteen states each acted on their own in foreign affairs and Article 2 of the Articles of Confederation recognized the sovereignty of the states (see Ch. 7).

Curtiss-Wright also exemplifies the Court's deference to the president in foreign affairs in recognition of the fact that Congress, not the judiciary, provides the most effective check. Congress is more effective because it has the power of authorization and appropriation of funds for the executive branch. Thus in *Goldwater v. Carter*, (1979) (see excerpt in Ch. 2), the Court refused to consider the merits of a suit filed by senators challenging President Jimmy Carter's termination, without congressional approval, of a Mutual Defense Treaty with Taiwan (an island off the coast of the People's Republic of China in which Chinese nationalists and non-Communists established a government-in-exile after the Chinese Communist revolution). Other cases also demonstrate the Court's recurrent deference. *Haig v. Agee*, 453 U.S. 280 (1981), for instance, held that "the President, acting through the Secretary of State, has authority to revoke a passport on the ground that the holder's activities in foreign countries are causing or are likely to cause serious damage to the national security or foreign policy of the United States." Subsequently, *Regan v. Wald*, 468 U.S. 222 (1984), upheld the Reagan administration's restrictions on travel to Cuba.

The Court's deference to, and recognition of, congressional acquiescence in the assertion of broad presidential powers in foreign affairs is further underscored by the ruling affirming President Carter's financial actions during the 1979 Iranian Hostage crisis, in *Dames & Moore v. Regan* (1981) (see excerpt below).

SELECTED BIBLIOGRAPHY

Adler, David, and George, Larry, eds. *The Constitution and the Conduct of American Foreign Policy*. Lawrence: University Press of Kansas, 1996.

Campbell, Colton, Rae, Nicol, and Stack, John, eds. *Congress and the Politics of Foreign Policy*. Upper Saddle River, NJ: Prentice-Hall, 2003.

Franck, Thomas. *Political Questions/Judicial Answers: Does the Rule of Law Apply to Foreign Affairs?* Princeton, NJ: Princeton University Press, 1992.

Howell, William G. *Power without Persuasion*. Princeton, NJ: Princeton University Press, 2003.

Irons, Peter. *Justice at War: The Story of the Japanese American Internment Cases*. New York: Oxford University Press, 1983.

————. *War Powers: How the Imperial Presidency Hijacked the Constitution*. New York: Metropolitan, 2005.

May, Christopher. *In the Name of War: Judicial Review and the War Powers since 1918*. Cambridge, MA: Harvard University Press, 1989.

Rossiter, Clinton. *The Supreme Court and the Commander in Chief*, rev. ed. Ithaca, NY: Cornell University Press 1976.

Wormuth, Francis, and Firmage, Edwin B. *To Chain the Dog of War: The War Power of Congress in History and Law*, 2d ed. Urbana: University of Illinois Press, 1989.

United States v. Curtiss-Wright Corporation
299 U.S. 304, 57 S.Ct. 216 (1936)

In 1934 Congress passed a joint resolution authorizing the president to prohibit the sale of munitions to two South American nations— Paraguay and Bolivia—who were embattled over the disputed land of Chaco, for as long as he believed that such an embargo would contribute to peace. President Roosevelt immediately issued a proclamation ordering an embargo on arms sales to the countries. Subsequently, the Curtiss-Wright Corporation was indicted for selling fifty machine guns to Bolivia. In the district court, the corporation contended that the president's actions were illegal because Congress had unconstitutionally delegated legislative powers to the executive. The district judge agreed and the government appealed directly to the Supreme Court, which reversed the lower court's ruling.

The Court's decision was seven to one; the opinion was announced by Justice Sutherland, with Justice Stone not participating. Justice McReynolds dissented.

☐ *Justice SUTHERLAND delivers the opinion of the Court.*

First. It is contended that by the Joint Resolution the going into effect and continued operation of the resolution was conditioned (a) upon the President's judgment as to its beneficial effect upon the reestablishment of peace between the countries engaged in armed conflict in the Chaco; (b) upon the making of a proclamation, which was left to his unfettered discretion, thus constituting an attempted substitution of the President's will for that of Congress; (c) upon the making of a proclamation putting an end to the operation of the resolution, which again was left to the President's unfettered discretion; and (d) further, that the extent of its operation in particular cases was subject to limitation and exception by the President, controlled by no standard. In each of these particulars, appellees urge that Congress abdicated its essential functions and delegated them to the Executive.

Whether, if the Joint Resolution had related solely to internal affairs, it would be open to the challenge that it constituted an unlawful delegation of legislative power to the Executive, we find it unnecessary to determine. The whole aim of the resolution is to affect a situation entirely external to the United States, and falling within the category of foreign affairs. The determination which we are called to make, therefore, is whether the Joint Resolution, as applied to that situation, is vulnerable to attack under the rule that forbids a delegation of the lawmaking power. In other words, assuming (but not deciding) that the challenged delegation, if it were confined to internal affairs, would be invalid, may it nevertheless be sustained on the ground that its exclusive aim is to afford a remedy for a hurtful condition within foreign territory?

It will contribute to the elucidation of the question if we first consider the differences between the powers of the federal government in respect of foreign or external affairs and those in respect of domestic or internal affairs. That there are differences between them, and that these differences are fundamental, may not be doubted.

The two classes of powers are different, both in respect of their origin and their nature. The broad statement that the federal government can exercise no powers except those specifically enumerated in the Constitution, and such implied powers as are necessary and proper to carry into effect the enumerated powers, is categorically true only in respect of our internal affairs. In that field, the primary purpose of the Constitution was to carve from the general mass of legislative powers *then possessed by the states* such portions as it was thought desirable to vest in the federal government, leaving those not included in the enumeration still in the states. That this doctrine applies only to powers which the states had is self-evident. And since the states severally never possessed international powers, such powers could not have been carved from the mass of state powers but obviously were transmitted to the United States from some other source. During the Colonial period, those powers were possessed exclusively by and were entirely under the control of the Crown. By the Declaration of Independence, "the Representatives of the United States of America" declared the United (not the several) Colonies to be free and independent states, and as such to have "full Power to levy War, conclude Peace, contract Alliances, establish Commerce and to do all other Acts and Things which Independent States may of right do."

As a result of the separation from Great Britain by the colonies, acting as a unit, the powers of external sovereignty passed from the Crown not to the colonies severally, but to the colonies in their collective and corporate capacity as the United States of America. Even before the Declaration, the colonies were a unit in foreign affairs, acting through a common agency—namely, the Continental Congress, composed of delegates from the thirteen colonies. That agency exercised the powers of war and peace, raised an army, created a navy, and finally adopted the Declaration of Independence. Rulers come and go; governments end and forms of government change; but sovereignty survives. A political society cannot endure without a supreme will somewhere. Sovereignty is never held in suspense. When, therefore, the external sovereignty of Great Britain in respect of the colonies ceased, it immediately passed to the Union. . . .

It results that the investment of the federal government with the powers of external sovereignty did not depend upon the affirmative grants of the Constitution. The powers to declare and wage war, to conclude peace, to make treaties, to maintain diplomatic relations with other sovereignties, if they had never been mentioned in the Constitution, would have vested in the federal government as necessary concomitants of nationality. . . .

Not only, as we have shown, is the federal power over external affairs in origin and essential character different from that over internal affairs, but participation in the exercise of the power is significantly limited. In this vast external realm, with its important, complicated, delicate and manifold problems, the President alone has the power to speak or listen as a representative of the nation. He *makes* treaties with the advice and consent of the Senate; but he alone negotiates. Into the field of negotiation the Senate cannot intrude; and Congress itself is powerless to invade it. As Marshall said in his great argument of March 7, 1800, in the House of Representatives, "The President is the sole organ of the nation in its external relations, and its sole representative with foreign nations." . . .

The marked difference between foreign affairs and domestic affairs in this respect is recognized by both houses of Congress in the very form of their requisitions for information from the executive departments. In the case of every department except the Department of State, the resolution *directs* the official to furnish the information. In the case of the State Department, dealing with foreign affairs, the President is *requested* to furnish the information "if not incompatible with the public interest." A statement that to furnish the information is not compatible with the public interest rarely, if ever, is questioned.

When the President is to be authorized by legislation to act in respect of a matter intended to affect a situation in foreign territory, the legislator properly bears in mind the important consideration that the form of the President's action—or, indeed, whether he shall act at all—may well depend, among other things, upon the nature of the confidential information which he has or may thereafter receive, or upon the effect which his action may have upon our foreign relations. This consideration, in connection with what we have already said on the subject discloses the unwisdom of requiring Congress in this field of governmental power to lay down narrowly definite standards by which the President is to be governed. . . . It is enough to summarize by saying that, both upon principle and in accordance with precedent, we conclude there is sufficient warrant for the broad discretion vested in the President to determine whether the enforcement of the statute will have a beneficial effect upon the re-establishment of peace in the affected countries; whether he shall make proclamation to bring the resolution into operation; whether and when the resolution shall cease to operate and to make proclamation accordingly; and to prescribe limitations and exceptions to which the enforcement of the resolution shall be subject. . . .

The judgment of the court below must be reversed and the case remanded for further proceedings in accordance with the foregoing opinion.

It is so ordered.

☐ *Justice McREYNOLDS does not agree. He is of opinion that the court below reached the right conclusion and its judgment ought to be affirmed.*

Dames & Moore v. Regan

453 U.S. 654, 101 S.Ct. 2972 (1981)

After the seizure of the U.S. embassy in Tehran, Iran, in November 1979 and the taking of diplomatic personnel as hostages, President Carter invoked the International Emergency Economic Powers Act (IEEPA) and ordered a freeze on Iranian assets within the United States. On January 20, 1981, the hostages were released by Iran on the basis of an agreement that the government would "terminate all legal proceedings in the United States courts involving claims of United States persons and institutions against Iran and its state enterprises, to nullify all attachments and judgments obtained therein, [and] to prohibit future litigation based on these claims." Various executive orders implementing the agreement issued by Carter were subsequently reaffirmed by the Reagan administration. Dames & Moore sought to regain over $3 million owed to it under a contract for services performed for the Iranian government. In the trial court, the company claimed that the executive orders went beyond the president's statutory and constitutional powers. After the district court held against Dames & Moore, the company appealed to the Supreme Court, which granted *certiorari* on an expedited basis and upheld the actions of the president.

The Court's decision was eight to one; the opinion was announced by Justice Rehnquist. Justice Stevens concurred. A separate opinion, in part dissenting and concurring, was delivered by Justice Powell.

□ *Justice REHNQUIST delivers the opinion of the Court.*

The questions presented by this case touch fundamentally upon the manner in which our Republic is to be governed. Throughout the nearly two centuries of our Nation's existence under the Constitution, this subject has generated considerable debate. We have had the benefit of commentators such as John Jay, Alexander Hamilton, and James Madison writing in *The Federalist Papers* at the Nation's very inception, the benefit of astute foreign observers of our system such as Alexis de Tocqueville and James Bryce writing during the first century of the Nation's existence, and the benefit of many other treatises as well as more than 400 volumes of reports of decisions of this Court. As these writings reveal it is doubtless both futile and perhaps dangerous to find any epigrammatical explanation of how this country has been governed. . . .

Our decision today will not dramatically alter this situation, for the Framers "did not make the judiciary the overseer of our government." We are confined to a resolution of the dispute presented to us. That dispute involves various Executive Orders and regulations by which the President nullified attachments and liens on Iranian assets in the United States, directed that these assets be transferred to Iran, and suspended claims against Iran that may be presented to an International Claims Tribunal. This action was taken in an effort to comply with an Executive Agreement between the United States and Iran. . . .

[T]he decisions of the Court in this area have been rare, episodic, and afford little precedential value for subsequent cases. The tensions present in any exercise of executive power under the tripartite system of Federal Government established by the Constitution have been rejected in opinions by Members of this Court more than once. . . . Justice JACKSON in his concurring opinion in *Youngstown* [*Sheet & Tube Co. v. Sawyer*, 343 U.S. 579 (1952)], which both parties agree brings together as much combination of analysis and common sense as there is in this area, focused not on the "plenary and exclusive power of the President" but rather responded to a claim of virtually unlimited powers for the Executive by noting:

> The example of such unlimited executive power that must have most impressed the forefathers was the prerogative exercised by George III, and the description of its evils in the Declaration of Independence leads me to doubt that they were creating their new Executive in his image. . . .

As we now turn to the factual and legal issues in this case, we freely confess that we are obviously deciding only one more episode in the never-ending tension between the President exercising the executive authority in a world that presents each day some new challenge with which he must deal and the Constitution under which we all live and which no one disputes embodies some sort of system of checks and balances.

■ I

On November 4, 1979, the American Embassy in Tehran was seized and our diplomatic personnel were captured and held hostage. In response to that crisis,

President Carter, acting pursuant to the International Emergency Economic Powers Act (hereinafter "IEEPA"), declared a national emergency on November 14, 1979, and blocked the removal or transfer of "all property and interests in property of the Government of Iran, its instrumentalities and controlled entities and the Central Bank of Iran which are or become subject to the jurisdiction of the United States." . . . On November 15, 1979, the Treasury Department's Office of Foreign Assets Control issued a regulation providing that "[u]nless licensed or authorized . . . any attachment, judgment, decree, lien, execution, garnishment, or other judicial process is null and void with respect to any property in which on or since [November 14, 1979] there existed an interest of Iran." . . .

On December 19, 1979, petitioner Dames & Moore filed suit in the United States District Court for the Central District of California against the Government of Iran, the Atomic Energy Organization of Iran, and a number of Iranian banks. In its complaint, petitioner alleged that its wholly owned subsidiary, Dames & Moore International, S. R. L., was a party to a written contract with the Atomic Energy Organization, and that the subsidiary's entire interest in the contract had been assigned to petitioner. . . . Petitioner contended . . . that it was owed $3,436,694.30 plus interest for services performed under the contract prior to the date of termination. The District Court issued orders of attachment directed against property of defendants, and the property of certain Iranian banks was then attached to secure any judgment that might be entered against them.

On January 20, 1981, the Americans held hostage were released by Iran pursuant to an Agreement entered into the day before. . . . The Agreement stated that "it is the purpose of [the United States and Iran] . . . to terminate all litigation as between the Government of each party and the nationals of the other, and to bring about the settlement and termination of all such claims through binding arbitration." In furtherance of this goal, the Agreement called for the establishment of an Iran-United States Claims Tribunal which would arbitrate any claims not settled within 6 months. Awards of the Claims Tribunal are to be "final and binding" and "enforceable . . . in the courts of any nation in accordance with its law." . . . Under the Agreement, the United States is obligated:

> to terminate all legal proceedings in United States courts involving claims of United States persons and institutions against Iran and its state enterprises, to nullify all attachments and judgments obtained therein, to prohibit all further litigation based on such claims, and to bring about the termination of such claims through binding arbitration. . . .

In addition, the United States must "act to bring about the transfer" by July 19, 1981, of all Iranian assets held in this country by American banks. One billion dollars of these assets will be deposited in a security account in the Bank of England, to the account of the Algerian Central Bank, and used to satisfy awards rendered against Iran by the Claims Tribunal. . . .

On January 19, 1981, President Carter issued a series of Executive Orders implementing the terms of the Agreement. . . .

On February 24, 1981, President Reagan issued an Executive Order in which he "ratified" the January 19th Executive Orders. Moreover, he "suspended" all "claims which may be presented to the . . . Tribunal" and provided that such claims "shall have no legal effect in any action now pending in any court of the United States."The suspension of any particular claim terminates if the Claims Tribunal determines that it has no jurisdiction over that claim; claims are discharged for all purposes when the Claims Tribunal either awards some recovery and that amount is paid, or determines that no recovery is due. . . .

The parties and the lower courts confronted with the instant questions have all agreed that much relevant analysis is contained in *Youngstown Sheet & Tube Co. v. Sawyer* (1952). Justice BLACK's opinion for the Court in that case, recognized that "[t]he President's power, if any, to issue the order must stem either from an act of Congress or from the Constitution itself." Justice JACKSON's concurring opinion elaborated in a general way the consequences of different types of interaction between the two democratic branches in assessing presidential authority to act in any given case. When the President acts pursuant to an express or implied authorization from Congress, he exercises not only his powers but also those delegated by Congress. In such a case the executive action "would be supported by the strongest of presumptions and the widest latitude of judicial interpretation, and the burden of persuasion would rest heavily upon any who might attack it." When the President acts in the absence of congressional authorization he may enter "a zone of twilight in which he and Congress may have concurrent authority, or in which its distribution is uncertain." In such a case the analysis becomes more complicated, and the validity of the President's action, at least so far as separation of powers principles are concerned, hinges on a consideration of all the circumstances which might shed light on the views of the Legislative Branch toward such action, including "congressional inertia, indifference or quiescence." Finally, when the President acts in contravention of the will of Congress, "his power is at its lowest ebb," and the Court can sustain his actions "only by disabling the Congress from acting upon the subject." . . .

Although we have in the past and do today find Justice JACKSON's classification of executive actions into three general categories analytically useful . . . Justice JACKSON himself recognized that his three categories represented "a somewhat over-simplified grouping," and it is doubtless the case that executive action in any particular instance falls, not neatly in one of three pigeon-holes, but rather at some point along a spectrum running from explicit congressional authorization to explicit congressional prohibition. This is particularly true as respects cases such as the one before us, involving responses to international crises the nature of which Congress can hardly have been expected to anticipate in any detail. . . .

The Government . . . has principally relied on Sec. 1702 of IEEPA as authorization for these actions. [It] provides in part:

> At the times and to the extent specified in section 1701 of this title, the President may, . . . nullify, void, prevent or prohibit, any acquisition, holding, withholding, use, transfer, withdrawal, transportation, importation or exportation of, or dealing in, or exercising any right, power or privilege with respect to, or transactions involving, any property in which any foreign country or a national thereof has any interest; by any person, or with respect to any property, subject to the jurisdiction of the United States.

The Government contends that the acts of "nullifying" the attachments and ordering the "transfer" of the frozen assets are specifically authorized by the plain language of the above statute. . . .

Petitioner contends that we should ignore the plain language of this statute because an examination of its legislative history as well as the history of Sec. 5(b) of the Trading With the Enemy Act (hereinafter "TWEA"), 50 U.S.C. App. Sec. 5(b), from which the pertinent language of Sec. 1702 is directly drawn, reveals that the statute was not intended to give the President such extensive power over the assets of a foreign state during times of national emergency. . . .

We do not agree and refuse to read out of Sec. 1702 all meaning to the words "transfer," "compel," or "nullify." Nothing in the legislative history of either Sec. 1702 or Sec. 5(b) of the TWEA requires such a result. To the contrary, we think both the legislative history and cases interpreting the TWEA fully sustain the broad authority of the Executive when acting under this congressional grant of power. . . .

Because the President's action in nullifying the attachments and ordering the transfer of the assets was taken pursuant to specific congressional authorization, it is "supported by the strongest of presumptions and the widest latitude of judicial interpretation, and the burden of persuasion would rest heavily upon any who might attack it." *Youngstown* (JACKSON, J., concurring). Under the circumstances of this case, we cannot say that petitioner has sustained that heavy burden. A contrary ruling would mean that the Federal Government as a whole lacked the power exercised by the President, and that we are not prepared to say.

Although we have concluded that the IEEPA constitutes specific congressional authorization to the President to nullify the attachments and order the transfer of Iranian assets, there remains the question of the President's authority to suspend claims pending in American courts. Such claims have, of course, an existence apart from the attachments which accompanied them. In terminating these claims through Executive Order No. 12294 the President purported to act under authority of both the IEEPA and 22 U.S.C. Sec. 1732, the so-called "Hostage Act." . . .

We conclude that although the IEEPA authorized the nullification of the attachments, it cannot be read to authorize the suspension of the claims. . . .

Concluding that neither the IEEPA nor the Hostage Act constitutes specific authorization of the President's action suspending claims, however, is not to say that these statutory provisions are entirely irrelevant to the question of the validity of the President's action. We think both statutes highly relevant in the looser sense of indicating congressional acceptance of a broad scope for executive action in circumstances such as those presented in this case. . . . [T]he IEEPA delegates broad authority to the President to act in times of national emergency with respect to property of a foreign country. The Hostage Act similarly indicates congressional willingness that the President have broad discretion when responding to the hostile acts of foreign sovereigns. . . .

Although we have declined to conclude that the IEEPA or the Hostage Act directly authorizes the President's suspension of claims for the reasons noted, we cannot ignore the general tenor of Congress' legislation in this area in trying to determine whether the President is acting alone or at least with the acceptance of Congress.... Congress cannot anticipate and legislate with regard to every possible action the President may find it necessary to take or every possible situation in which he might act. Such failure of Congress specifically to delegate authority does not, "especially ... in the areas of foreign policy and national security," imply "congressional disapproval" of action taken by the Executive. *Haig v. Agee*, [453 U.S. 280] (1981). On the contrary, the enactment of legislation closely related to the question of the President's authority in a particular case which evinces legislative intent to accord the President broad discretion may be considered to "invite" "measures on independent presidential responsibility." *Youngstown* (JACKSON, J., concurring). At least this is so where there is no contrary indication of legislative intent and when, as here, there is a history of congressional acquiescence in conduct of the sort engaged in by the President. It is to that history which we now turn.

Not infrequently in affairs between nations, outstanding claims by nationals of one country against the government of another country are "sources of friction" between the two sovereigns. To resolve these difficulties, nations have often entered into agreements settling the claims of their respective nationals....

Under such agreements, the President has agreed to renounce or extinguish claims of United States nationals against foreign governments in return for lump sum payments or the establishment of arbitration procedures....

Crucial to our decision today is the conclusion that Congress has implicitly approved the practice of claim settlement by executive agreement. This is best demonstrated by Congress' enactment of the International Claims Settlement Act of 1949....

In light of all of the foregoing—the inferences to be drawn from the character of the legislation Congress has enacted in the area, such as the IEEPA and the Hostage Act, and from the history of acquiescence in executive claims settlement—we conclude that the President was authorized to suspend pending claims pursuant to Executive Order No. 12294. As Justice FRANKFURTER pointed out in *Youngstown*, "a systematic, unbroken executive practice, long pursued to the knowledge of Congress and never before questioned ... may be treated as a gloss on 'Executive Power' vested in the President by Sec. 1 of Art. II." Past practice does not, by itself, create power, but "long-continued practice, known to and acquiesced in by Congress, would raise a presumption that the [action] has been [taken] in pursuance of its consent...."

Our conclusion is buttressed by the fact that the means chosen by the President to settle the claims of American nationals provided an alternate forum, the Claims Tribunal, which is capable of providing meaningful relief....

Just as importantly, Congress has not disapproved of the action taken here. Though Congress has held hearings on the Iranian Agreement itself, Congress has not enacted legislation, or even passed a resolution, indicating its displeasure with the Agreement. Quite the contrary, the relevant Senate Committee has stated that the establishment of the Tribunal is "of vital importance to the United States." We are thus clearly not confronted with a situation in which Congress has in some way resisted the exercise of presidential authority.

Finally, we re-emphasize the narrowness of our decision. We do not decide that the President possesses plenary power to settle claims, even as against foreign governmental entities. . . . But where, as here, the settlement of claims has been determined to be a necessary incident to the resolution of a major foreign policy dispute between our country and another, and where, as here, we can conclude that Congress acquiesced in the President's action, we are not prepared to say that the President lacks the power to settle such claims.

C | *The Treaty-Making Power and Executive Independence*

The president makes treaties "by and with the Advice and Consent of the Senate." Although President George Washington initially sought Senate consultation when negotiating an Indian treaty in 1789, presidents since him have tended to negotiate treaties independently and only later to obtain ratification by a two-thirds vote of the Senate. There are times, though, when senators become involved in negotiations, dealing with trade or especially controversial agreements like the Strategic Arms Limitations Treaty (SALT) II treaty in 1979. (See the CONSTITUTIONAL HISTORY box, The Treaty-Reinterpretation Controversy, in this section.) Presidential dominance nevertheless is now the norm.

Treaties are on a par with federal legislation and considered part of the supreme law of the land. Moreover, in *Missouri v. Holland* (1920) (see excerpt below), the Court ruled that a treaty on migratory birds gave Congress the authority to pass regulations forbidding the killing of such birds, which it would not have had in the absence of the treaty. Treaties thus may be a source of law and a basis of power that neither the president nor Congress had before their adoption. They often serve, for example, as the basis for presidents making *executive agreements* with foreign countries in order to implement treaty provisions.

Independent of treaties and congressional authorization, presidents increasingly enter into executive agreements with other countries. In *United States v. Belmont*, 301 U.S. 324 (1937), the Court upheld such agreements as valid international compacts and then ruled that they have the same legal effect as treaties in *United States v. Pink* (1942) (see excerpt below).

As a result of the rulings in *Belmont* and *Pink*, presidents have circumvented the treaty-making provision, and executive agreements now outnumber treaties (see the CONSTITUTIONAL HISTORY box, Alternatives to Treaties, in this section). Many of the most sensitive agreements were not even made known to Congress until it passed the Case Act in 1972, requiring notification within sixty days of "any international agreement." After Congress discovered that the Ford and Carter administrations had not fully complied and had made a number of secret "executive arrangements," the act was amended to require notification within twenty days of any "oral international agreement, which shall be reduced to writing." Notably, though, because of opposition in the Senate to the North American Free Trade Agreement (NAFTA) of 1993, which eliminated trade barriers in uniting Canada, the United States, and Mexico in a free-trade zone, the president was given "fast-track authority" and the NAFTA was approved by simple majorities of both houses of Congress, instead of ratified as a treaty by a two-thirds vote of the Senate.

In general, the Court defers to the president and tries to avoid deciding issues arising from the independence of the executive branch in the conduct of foreign affairs. Questions thus remain over the president's unilateral termination of treaties (see *Goldwater v. Carter* [1979]; excerpt in Vol. 1, Ch. 2), and reinterpretation of the language of treaties over Senate opposition. (See the box on CONSTITU-TIONAL HISTORY: The Treaty-Reinterpretation Controversy in this section).

However, the Court has, albeit infrequently and reluctantly, recognized constitutional limitations on the scope of treaties and executive agreements. In *Geofroy v. Riggs*, 133 U.S. 258 (1890), the Court rejected the contention that the treaty power "extends so far as to authorize what the Constitution forbids, or a change in the character of the government." But Justice Holmes's sweeping opinion in *Missouri v. Holland* (see excerpt below) raised anew questions about the scope of treaties and executive agreements. The Court finally qualified that ruling in *Reid v. Covert*, 354 U.S. 1 (1957), holding that executive agreements could not deprive individuals of the guarantees of the Bill of Rights. At issue in *Reid v. Covert* was the constitutionality of an executive agreement permitting dependents of American military residing in Great Britain to be tried for crimes committed there by military courts under the Uniform Code of Military Justice, which does not extend the same guarantees as those in the Bill of Rights to criminal trials. Notably, when invalidating the executive agreement the Court was bitterly divided and forced to overrule a five-to-four decision of one year earlier, in *Reid v. Covert*, 351 U.S. 487 (1956), that had reached the opposite conclusion.

Finally, during the presidencies of Ronald Reagan, George H. W. Bush, and George W. Bush, the executive branch staunchly asserted its power to reinterpret what it deemed ambiguous congressional statutes

■ CONSTITUTIONAL HISTORY

Alternatives to Treaties: The Rise of Executive Agreements and Arrangements

Since 1945, U.S. presidents have increasingly used executive agreements, which do not require Senate approval, as substitutes for traditional treaties.

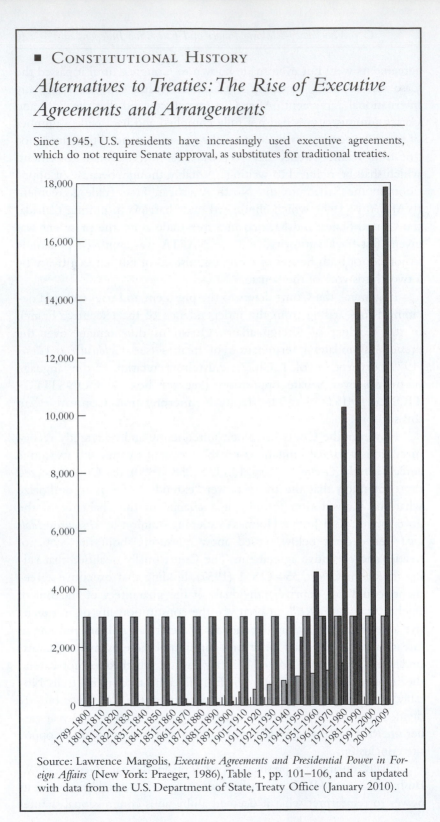

Source: Lawrence Margolis, *Executive Agreements and Presidential Power in Foreign Affairs* (New York: Praeger, 1986), Table 1, pp. 101–106, and as updated with data from the U.S. Department of State, Treaty Office (January 2010).

and treaties with foreign governments. In *Rust v. Sullivan*, 500 U.S. 173 (1991) (see Vol. 2, Ch. 5), the Court upheld the administration's reinterpretation of a congressional statute to forbid organizations receiving federal funding from providing counseling on abortion. The Court has not squarely confronted the related issue of the president's reinterpretation of a treaty that contravenes the understanding of the Senate when it consented to the treaty. However, in *United States v. Alvarez-Machain*, 504 U.S. 655 (1992) (see excerpt below), the Court upheld the George H. W. Bush administration's reinterpretation of an extradition treaty to permit it to order the kidnapping and bringing of a foreign national to the United States for trial. Subsequently, Mexico filed a formal protest with the government and requested a renegotiation of its treaty with the United States.

Finally, the Roberts Court rebuffed President George W. Bush's broad assertion of executive power with respect to the enforcement of interpretations of treaty provisions. In 2004, the International Court of Justice (ICJ) ruled against the denial of certain procedural rights under provisions of the Vienna Convention. Subsequently, President Bush issued a memorandum directing Texas state courts to comply with the ICJ's decision, but they balked and held that the president exceeded his constitutional authority over the conduct of foreign affairs and intruded on the independence of state court proceedings. On appeal in *Medellin v. Texas* (2008) (excerpted below), six members of the Court rejected the administration's interpretation of the Vienna Convention and position on presidential power. Writing for the majority, Chief Justice Roberts held that the convention was a non-self-executing treaty, requiring further congressional legislation to make the ICJ's ruling binding on domestic courts, in contrast to self-executing treaties that have immediate binding legal effect. In addition, he held that President Bush's order had no binding legal effect because it exceeded his authority under the treaty-making provision of the Constitution. Thus, neither the ICJ's decision nor President Bush's memorandum, in the absence of federal legislation, compelled state courts to alter their procedures for granting writs of *habeas corpus*. Justice Breyer issued a dissenting opinion, which Justices Souter and Ginsburg joined, countering that the Vienna Convention was a self-executing treaty and had binding legal effect.

Selected Bibliography

Aust, Anthony. *Modern Treaty Law and Practice*. Cambridge, UK: Cambridge University Press, 2000.

Campbell, Colton C.; Rae, Nicol; and Stack, John, eds. *Congress and the Politics of Foreign Policy.* Upper Saddle River, NJ: Prentice Hall, 2003.

Cohen, David, and Wells, John, eds. *American National Security and Civil Liberties in an Era of Terrorism.* New York: Palgrave, 2004.

Corwin, Edward S. *National Supremacy: Treaty Power vs. State Power.* New York: Henry Holt, 1913.

Fisher, Louis. *Constitutional Conflicts between Congress and the President.* 5th ed. Lawrence: University of Kansas Press, 2007.

Krutz, Glen, and Peake, Jeffrey. *Treaty Politics and the Rise of Executive Agreements.* Ann Arbor: University of Michigan Press, 2009.

Margolis, Lawrence. *Executive Agreements and Presidential Power in Foreign Affairs.* New York: Praeger, 1986.

Sutherland, George. *Constitutional Power and World Affairs.* New York: Columbia University Press, 1919.

Missouri v. Holland

252 U.S. 416, 40 S.Ct. 382 (1920)

Pursuant to a treaty between the United States and Great Britain in 1916 for the protection of birds migrating between Canada and the United States, legislation and regulations were adopted in 1918 to establish closed hunting seasons and to prevent the killing of certain migratory birds. The state of Missouri contended that the treaty and regulations violated the Tenth Amendment's provision that "powers not delegated to the United States by the Constitution . . . are reserved to the States." After unsuccessfully seeking in a federal district court a bill of equity to stop a U.S. game warden from enforcing the regulations, the state appealed to the Supreme Court, which then affirmed the lower court's ruling.

The Court's decision was seven to two, and the opinion was announced by Justice Holmes. The dissent, without opinions, was by Justices Van Devanter and Pitney.

☐ *Justice HOLMES delivers the opinion of the Court.*

This is a bill in equity brought by the State of Missouri to prevent a game warden of the United States from attempting to enforce the Migratory Bird Treaty Act of July 3, 1918, and the regulations made by the Secretary of Agriculture in pursuance of the same. The ground of the bill is that the statute is an unconstitutional interference with the rights reserved to the States by the Tenth Amendment. . . . It is unnecessary to go into any details, because, as we have said, the question raised is the general one whether the

■ THE DEVELOPMENT OF LAW

Senate Rejection of Proposed Treaties

Although the Senate has ratified over 1,500 treaties, it has rejected 21 proposed treaties.

DATE OF VOTE	COUNTRY	SUBJECT
March 9, 1825	Colombia	Suppression of African slave trade
June 11, 1836	Switzerland	Property rights
June 8, 1844	Texas	Annexation
June 15, 1844	Germany	Commercial reciprocity
May 31, 1860	Mexico	Transit and commercial rights
June 27, 1860	Spain	Cuban claims commission
April 13, 1869	Britain	Arbitration of claims
June 1, 1870	Hawaii	Commercial reciprocity
June 30, 1870	Dominican Republic	Annexation
January 29, 1885	Nicaragua	Interoceanic canal
April 20, 1886	Mexico	Mining claims
August 21, 1888	Britain	Fishing rights
February 1, 1889	Britain	Extradition
May 5, 1897	Britain	Arbitration
March 19, 1920	Multilateral	Treaty of Versailles
January 18, 1927	Turkey	Commercial rights
March 18, 1934	Canada	St. Lawrence Seaway
January 29, 1935	Multilateral	World Court
May 26, 1960	Multilateral	Law of the Sea Convention
March 8, 1983	Multilateral	Montreal Aviation Protocol
October 14, 1999	Multilateral	Comprehensive Test Ban

Source: U.S. Senate Library

treaty and statute are void as an interference with the rights reserved to the States.

To answer this question it is not enough to refer to the Tenth Amendment, reserving the powers not delegated to the United States, because by Article 2, Section 2, the power to make treaties is delegated expressly, and by Article 6 treaties made under the authority of the United States along with the Constitution and laws of the United States made in pursuance thereof, are declared the supreme law of the land. If the treaty is valid there can be no dispute about the validity of the statute under Article 1, Section 8, as a necessary and proper means to execute the powers of the Government. The language of the Constitution as to the supremacy of treaties being general, the question before us is narrowed to an inquiry into the ground upon which the present supposed exception is placed.

It is said that a treaty cannot be valid if it infringes the Constitution, that there are limits, therefore, to the treaty-making power, and that one such limit is that what an act of Congress could not do unaided, in derogation of the powers reserved to the States, a treaty cannot do. An earlier act of Congress that attempted by itself and not in pursuance of a treaty to regulate the killing of migratory birds within the States had been held bad in the District Court. *United States v. Shauver*, [214 F.Supp. 154 (1914)]; *United States v. McCullagh*, [221 F.Supp. 288(1915)]. Those decisions were supported by arguments that migratory birds were owned by the States in their sovereign capacity for the benefit of their people, and that under cases like *Geer v. Connecticut*, 161 U.S. 519 [(1896)], this control was one that Congress had no power to displace. The same argument is supposed to apply now with equal force.

Whether the two cases cited were decided rightly or not they cannot be accepted as a test of the treaty power. Acts of Congress are the supreme law of the land only when made in pursuance of the Constitution, while treaties are declared to be so when made under the authority of the United States. It is open to question whether the authority of the United States means more than the formal acts prescribed to make the convention. We do not mean to imply that there are no qualifications to the treaty-making power; but they must be ascertained in a different way. It is obvious that there may be matters of the sharpest exigency for the national well being that an act of Congress could not deal with but that a treaty followed by such an act could, and it is not lightly to be assumed that, in matters requiring national action, "a power which must belong to and somewhere reside in every civilized government" is not to be found, *Andrews v. Andrews*, 188 U.S. 14 [(1903)]. What was said in that case with regard to the powers of the States applies with equal force to the powers of the nation in cases where the States individually are incompetent to act. We are not yet discussing the particular case before us but only are considering the validity of the test proposed. With regard to that we may add that when we are dealing with words that also are a constituent act, like the Constitution of the United States, we must realize that they have called into life a being the development of which could not have been foreseen completely by the most gifted of its begetters. It was enough for them to realize or to hope that they had created an organism; it has taken a century and has cost their successors much sweat and blood to prove that they created a nation. The case before us must be considered in the light of our whole experience and not merely in that of what was said a hundred years ago. The treaty in question does not contravene any prohibitory words to be found in the Constitution. The only question is whether it is forbidden by some invisible radiation from the general terms of the Tenth Amendment. We must consider what this country has become in deciding what that amendment has reserved.

The State as we have intimated founds its claim of exclusive authority upon an assertion of title to migratory birds, an assertion that is embodied in statute. No doubt it is true that as between a State and its inhabitants the State may regulate the killing and sale of such birds, but it does not follow that its authority is exclusive of paramount powers. To put the claim of the State upon title is to lean upon a slender reed. Wild birds are not in the possession of anyone; and possession is the beginning of ownership. The whole foundation of the State's rights is the presence within their jurisdiction of birds that yesterday had not arrived, tomorrow may be in another State and in a week a thousand miles away. If we are to be accurate we cannot put the case of the State upon higher ground than that the treaty deals with creatures that for the moment are within the state borders, that it must be carried out by officers of the United States within the same territory, and that but for the treaty the State would be free to regulate this subject itself. . . .

Here a national interest of very nearly the first magnitude is involved. It can be protected only by national action in concert with that of another power. The subject matter is only transitorily within the State and has no permanent habitat therein. But for the treaty and the statute there soon might be no birds for any powers to deal with. We see nothing in the Constitution that compels the Government to sit by while a food supply is cut off and the protectors of our forests and our crops are destroyed. It is not sufficient to rely upon the States. The reliance is vain, and were it otherwise, the question is whether the United States is forbidden to act. We are of opinion that the treaty and statute must be upheld. . . . Decree affirmed.

☐ Justice VAN DEVANTER and Justice PITNEY dissent.

United States v. Pink
315 U.S. 203, 62 S.CT. 552 (1942)

Following diplomatic recognition of Soviet Russia in 1933 President Franklin Roosevelt negotiated the "Litvinov Assignment," under which it was stipulated that instead of each government prosecuting claims for recovery of assets against citizens of the other, the Soviet Union would give title to claims to assets in America to the U.S. government and vice versa. In *United States v. Belmont*, 301 U.S. 324 (1937), a New York banker, August Belmont, contended that funds deposited in his bank by the Petrograd Metal Works prior to the Russian Revolution in 1918 were subject to New York laws and thus could not be confiscated by the federal government. Justice Sutherland, relying on his earlier opinion in *United States v. Curtiss-Wright Export Corporation* (1936) (excerpted in this chapter, section B), however, upheld the agreement as a valid international compact that superseded the laws of New York. Subsequently, the federal government sought to recover the assets of the New York branch of the First Russian Insurance Company and sued Louis H. Pink, Superintendent of

Insurance for the state of New York. The state supreme court dismissed the government's complaint and a federal court of appeals affirmed, whereupon the government appealed to the Supreme Court.

The Court's decision was six to one, and the majority's opinion was announced by Justice Douglas, with Justices Reed and Jackson not participating. Justice Frankfurter delivered a separate opinion and Chief Justice Stone dissented.

☐ *Justice DOUGLAS delivers the opinion of the Court.*

This Court, speaking through Justice SUTHERLAND, held [in *United States v. Belmont* (1937)] that the conduct of foreign relations is committed by the Constitution to the political departments of the Federal Government; that the propriety of the exercise of that power is not open to judicial inquiry; and that recognition of a foreign sovereign conclusively binds the courts and "is retroactive and validates all actions and conduct of the government so recognized from the commencement of its existence." It further held that recognition of the Soviet Government, the establishment of diplomatic relations with it, and the Litvinov Assignment were "all parts of one transaction, resulting in an international compact between the two governments." After stating that "in respect of what was done here, the Executive had authority to speak as the sole organ" of the national government, it added, "The assignment and the agreements in connection therewith did not, as in the case of treaties, as that term is used in the treaty making clause of the Constitution (Art. 2, Sec. 2), require the advice and consent of the Senate." It held that the "external powers of the United States are to be exercised without regard to state laws or policies. The supremacy of a treaty in this respect has been recognized from the beginning." And it added that "all international compacts and agreements" are to be treated with similar dignity for the reason that "complete power over international affairs is in the national government and is not and cannot be subject to any curtailment or interference on the part of the several states." . . .

The holding in the *Belmont* case is therefore determinative of the present controversy unless the stake of the foreign creditors in this liquidation proceeding and the provision which New York has provided for their protection call for a different result. . . .

We recently stated in *Hines v. Davidowitz*, 312 U.S. 52 [1941], that the field which affects international relations is "the one aspect of our government that from the first has been most generally conceded imperatively to demand broad national authority"; and that any state power which may exist "is restricted to the narrowest of limits." There we were dealing with the question as to whether a state statute regulating aliens survived a similar federal statute. We held that it did not. Here we are dealing with an exclusive federal function. If state laws and policies did not yield before the exercise of the external powers of the United States, then our foreign policy might be thwarted. These are delicate matters. If state action could defeat or alter our foreign policy, serious consequences might ensue. The nation as a whole would be held to answer if a State created difficulties with a foreign power. . . .

The action of New York in this case amounts in substance to a rejection of a part of the policy underlying recognition by this nation of Soviet Russia. Such power is not accorded a State in our constitutional system. To permit it would be to sanction a dangerous invasion of Federal authority. For it would "imperil the amicable relations between governments and vex the peace of nations." *Oetjen v. Central Leather Co.* [246 U.S. 297 (1918)]. It would tend to disturb that equilibrium in our foreign relations which the political departments of our national government had diligently endeavored to establish.

We repeat that there are limitations on the sovereignty of the States. No State can rewrite our foreign policy to conform to its own domestic policies. Power over external affairs is not shared by the States; it is vested in the national government exclusively. It need not be so exercised as to conform to state laws or state policies whether they be expressed in constitutions, statutes, or judicial decrees. And the policies of the States become wholly irrelevant to judicial inquiry, when the United States, acting within its constitutional sphere, seeks enforcement of its foreign policy in the courts. . . .

We hold that the right to the funds or property in question became vested in the Soviet Government as the successor to the First Russian Insurance Co.; that this right has passed to the United States under the Litvinov Assignment; and that the United States is entitled to the property as against the corporation and the foreign creditors.

The judgment is reversed. . . .

It is so ordered.

■ CONSTITUTIONAL HISTORY

The Treaty-Reinterpretation Controversy*

In May 1988, by a vote of 93 to 5 the Senate approved a landmark treaty—the INF Treaty—banning, among other things, intermediate-range nuclear force (INF) missiles. The Senate's action made possible ratification of the treaty that June at a Moscow meeting of Republican President Ronald Reagan and Soviet leader Mikhail S. Gorbachev. The INF treaty was the first arms-control accord ratified since 1972, when the strategic arms limitation (SALT I) and the antiballistic missile (ABM) treaties were approved; in 1979 the Senate refused to consent, as required under the Constitution, to the SALT II treaty.

(continues)

*For further discussion, see "INF Missile Treaty Wins Senate Approval," 1988 *CQ Almanac* 379 (Washington, DC: Congressional Quarterly Press, 1989); U.S. Cong., Senate, Comm. on Foreign Relations, 100th Cong., 2nd Sess., *Hearings before the Committee on Foreign Relations, U.S. Senate, 100th Cong., 2d Sess., on the Treaty between the United States of America and the Union of Soviet Socialist Republics on the Elimination of their Intermediate-Range and Shorter-Range Missiles*, 5 vols. (Washington, DC: Government Printing Office, 1988); and U.S. Cong., Senate, Committee on Foreign Relations, 100 Cong., 2d Sess., *The INF Treaty* (Washington, DC: Government Printing Office, 1988).

■ CONSTITUTIONAL HISTORY
The Treaty-Reinterpretation Controversy (continued)

The INF treaty was politically controversial and brought to a head an underlying dispute over the power of the president to reinterpret the provisions and original understanding of a treaty after it has been approved by the Senate and ratified. The Constitution offers no guidance in resolving that dispute; and its silence on treaty reinterpretation, along with the power to terminate treaties (see *Goldwater v. Carter*, 444 U.S. 996 [1979]) pitted the Senate against the Reagan administration in a political struggle not only over the INF treaty but also over the respective roles of the Senate and the president in determining the meaning of treaties.

The treaty-reinterpretation controversy erupted in 1987, when the Reagan administration sought to reinterpret the 1972 ABM treaty so as to authorize the testing of so-called star wars antimissile laser-based technology—the Strategic Defense Initiative (SDI). Senate Democrats balked and led by Georgia's Democratic senator, Samuel Nunn, argued (a) that the ABM treaty barred the testing of SDI and (b) that the executive branch could not significantly modify or reinterpret provisions and the original understanding of a treaty without the approval of the Senate. In fact, in 1983 when Reagan unveiled his "star wars" program, the administration adhered to the prevailing interpretation of the ABM treaty: tests of SDI space-based laser missile systems would violate the treaty. But by 1985, a State Department legal adviser, Abraham Sofaer, advanced a broader interpretation of the treaty, which permitted SDI testing. What became known as the "Sofaer doctrine" had three prongs: (1) the ABM treaty—its design, genesis, text, and implementation—was fraught with ambiguities; (2) the president, not the Senate, was empowered to resolve those ambiguities; and (3) whatever the Senate was told in the process of consenting to a treaty—about, for example, negotiations behind and the mean-ing of key provisions of a treaty—is not itself binding on the president's subsequent interpretation of, and obligation to carry out, the treaty.

Whereas Republican senators tended to support the administration, Democratic members of the Senate Foreign Relations Committee claimed that the record of the ABM treaty was unambiguous in prohibiting SDI testing. Democratic senators also took strong exception to the Reagan administration's "*constitutional* assertion of a clearly delineated and unprecedented doctrine under which the president has wide latitude for treaty 'reinterpretations,' notwithstanding what the Senate may have been told in the course of granting consent to ratification."

A compromise was finally reached on the permissibility of the Reagan administration's reinterpretation of the ABM treaty. After lengthy hearings, the Senate ultimately agreed not to contest the "broad-versus-narrow" interpretation of the ABM treaty. Instead, the Senate resolved to allow its continuing disputes with the Reagan administration over SID testing to be worked out in the defense budget process and in future negotiations among the superpowers.

When consenting to the INF treaty, though, the Senate added an amendment, a reservation, to its resolution approving of the treaty's ratification. By a vote of seventy-two to twenty-seven the Senate agreed to add to its resolution consenting to the INF treaty the following:

> subject to the following principles, which derive, as a necessary implication, from the provisions of the Constitution (Article II, Section 2, Clause 2) for the making of treaties:
>
> (a) the United States shall interpret this Treaty in accordance with the understanding of the Treaty shared by the Executive and the Senate at the time of Senate consent to ratification;
>
> (b) such common understanding is:
>> (i) based on the text of the Treaty;
>> (ii) reflected in the authoritative representations provided by the Executive Branch to the Senate consent to ratification, inso-far as such representations are directed to the meaning and legal effect of the Treaty;
>
> (c) the United States shall not agree to or adopt an interpretation different from that common understanding except pursuant to Senate advice and consent to a subsequent treaty or protocol, or the enactment of a statute.

The Reagan administration in turn expressed concerns about the constitutionality of this treaty-interpretation amendment as a limitation on the president's treaty-making power and, more generally, presidential powers.

Notably, Congress enacted and President George W. Bush signed into law the Military Commissions Act of 2006, which authorized the president to reinterpret guarantees for detaining "unlawful enemy combatants" under the Geneva Conventions so long as the procedures are not "grave breaches" of the conventions and do not constitute "cruel, unusual, or inhumane treatment." (See also the Constitutional History box on presidential signing statements in Vol. 1, Ch. 4).

Goldwater v. Carter

444 U.S. 996, 100 S.Ct. 533, (1979) (reprise)

This case, arising from President Carter's termination of a defense treaty with Taiwan, is reprinted in Volume 1, Chapter 2.

United States v. Alvarez-Machain

504 U.S. 655, 112 S.Ct. 2188 (1992)

Humberto Alvarez-Machain, a citizen and resident of Mexico, was indicted for participating in the kidnapping and murder of a U.S. Drug Enforcement Administration (DEA) special agent. The DEA believed that Alvarez-Machain, a medical doctor, participated in the murder by prolonging the agent's life so that others could torture and interrogate him. In 1990, Alvarez-Machain was forcibly kidnapped from his medical office and flown by private plane to Texas, where he was arrested by DEA officials. Alvarez-Machain moved to dismiss the indictment on the grounds that his abduction constituted outrageous governmental conduct and that federal courts lacked jurisdiction to try him because he was abducted in violation of a treaty between the United States and Mexico. A federal district court ruled that it lacked jurisdiction to try Alvarez-Machain because his abduction violated the Extradition Treaty. The Court of Appeals for the Ninth Circuit affirmed that decision, relying on its own ruling in *United States v. Verdugo-Urquidez*, 939 F. 2d 1341 (CA 9 1991). In that case, the court of appeals held that the forcible abduction of a Mexican national with the authorization or participation of the United States violates the Extradition Treaty between the United States and Mexico. The Bush administration appealed that ruling to the Supreme Court of the United States, which granted review. Following the Rehnquist Court's ruling upholding the unusual bounty-hunting operation in apprehending Dr. Alvarez-Machain, the federal government's prosecution was dismissed by a federal district court judge for lack of evidence that he had participated in the torture and murder of a DEA agent. And Dr. Alvarez-Machain was permitted to return to Mexico.

The Court's decision was six to three; the opinion was announced by Chief Justice Rehnquist. Justice Stevens's dissent was joined by Justices Blackmun and O'Connor.

☐ *Chief Justice REHNQUIST delivers the opinion of the Court.*

The issue in this case is whether a criminal defendant, abducted to the United States from a nation with which it has an extradition treaty, thereby acquires a defense to the jurisdiction of this country's courts. We hold that he does not, and that he may be tried in federal district court for violations of the criminal law of the United States. . . .

Although we have never before addressed the precise issue raised in the present case, we have previously considered proceedings in claimed violation of an extradition treaty, and proceedings against a defendant brought before a court by means of a forcible abduction. We addressed the former issue in *United States v. Rauscher*, 119 U.S. 407 (1886); more precisely, the issue of whether the Webster-Ashburton Treaty of 1842, which governed extraditions between England and the United States, prohibited the prosecution of defendant Rauscher for a crime other than the crime for which he had been extradited. Whether this prohibition, known as the doctrine of specialty, was an intended part of the treaty had been disputed between the two nations for some time. Justice MILLER delivered the opinion of the Court. . . . [and] reached the following conclusion:

[A] person who has been brought within the jurisdiction of the court by virtue of proceedings under an extradition treaty, can only be tried for one of the offences described in that treaty, and for the offence with which he is charged in the proceedings for his extradition, until a reasonable time and opportunity have been given him, after his release or trial upon such charge, to return to the country from whose asylum he had been forcibly taken under those proceedings. . . .

In *Ker v. Illinois,* 119 U.S. 436 (1886), also written by Justice MILLER and decided the same day as *Rauscher*, we addressed the issue of a defendant brought before the court by way of a forcible abduction. Frederick Ker had been tried and convicted in an Illinois court for larceny; his presence before the court was procured by means of forcible abduction from Peru. A messenger was sent to Lima with the proper warrant to demand Ker by virtue of the extradition treaty between Peru and the United States. The messenger, however, disdained reliance on the treaty processes, and instead forcibly kidnapped Ker and brought him to the United States. We distinguished Ker's case from *Rauscher*, on the basis that Ker was not brought into the United States by virtue of the extradition treaty between the United States and Peru, and rejected Ker's argument that he had a right under the extradition treaty to be returned to this country only in accordance with its terms. We rejected Ker's due process argument more broadly, holding in line with "the highest authorities" that "such forcible abduction is no sufficient reason why the party should not answer when brought within the jurisdiction of the court which has the right to try him for such an offence, and presents no valid objection to his trial in such court." . . .

The only differences between *Ker* and the present case are that *Ker* was decided on the premise that there was no governmental involvement in the abduction, and Peru, from which Ker was abducted, did not object to his prosecution. Respondent finds these differences to be dispositive, as did the Court of appeals in *Verdugo*, contending that they show that respondent's prosecution, like the prosecution of Rauscher, violates the implied terms of a valid extradition treaty. The Government, on the other hand, argues that *Rauscher* stands as an "exception" to the rule in Ker only when an extradition treaty is invoked, and the terms of the treaty provided that its breach will limit the jurisdiction of a court. . . .

According to respondent, [provisions of the treaty embody a] bargain which the United States struck: if the United States wishes to prosecute a Mexican national, it may request that individual's extradition. . . .

We do not read the Treaty in such a fashion. [It] does not purport to specify the only way in which one country may gain custody of a national of the other country for the purposes of prosecution. In the absence of an extradition treaty, nations are under no obligation to surrender those in their country to foreign authorities for prosecution. Extradition treaties exist so as to impose mutual obligations to surrender individuals in certain defined sets of circumstances, following established procedures. The Treaty thus provides a mechanism which would not otherwise exist, requiring, under certain circumstances, the United States and Mexico to extradite individuals to the other country, and establishing the procedures to be followed when the Treaty is invoked. . . .

Thus, the language of the Treaty, in the context of its history, does not support the proposition that the Treaty prohibits abductions outside of its terms. . . .

The judgment of the Court of Appeals is therefore reversed, and the case is remanded for further proceedings consistent with this opinion.

☐ *Justice STEVENS, with whom Justices BLACKMUN and O'CONNOR join, dissenting.*

A critical flaw pervades the Court's entire opinion. It fails to differentiate between the conduct of private citizens, which does not violate any treaty obligation, and conduct expressly authorized by the Executive Branch of the Government, which unquestionably constitutes a flagrant violation of international law, and in my opinion, also constitutes a breach of our treaty obligations. Thus, at the outset of its opinion, the Court states the issue as "whether a criminal defendant, abducted to the United States from a nation with which it has an extradition treaty, thereby acquires a defense to the jurisdiction of this country's courts." That, of course, is the question decided in *Ker v. Illinois*, 119 U.S. 436 (1886); it is not, however, the question presented for decision today.

The importance of the distinction between a court's exercise of jurisdiction over either a person or property that has been wrongfully seized by a private citizen, or even by a state law enforcement agent, on the one hand, and the attempted exercise of jurisdiction predicated on a seizure by federal officers acting beyond the authority conferred by treaty, on the other hand, is explained by Justice BRANDEIS in his opinion for the Court in *Cook v. United States*, 288 U.S. 102 (1933). That case involved a construction of a prohibition era treaty with Great Britain that authorized American agents to board certain British vessels to ascertain whether they were engaged in importing alcoholic beverages. A British vessel was boarded 11½ miles off the coast of Massachusetts, found to be carrying unmanifested alcoholic beverages, and taken into port. The Collector of Customs assessed a penalty which he attempted to collect by means of libels against both the cargo and the seized vessel.

The Court held that the seizure was not authorized by the treaty because it occurred more than 10 miles off shore. The Government argued that the illegality of the seizure was immaterial because, as in *Ker*, the Court's jurisdiction was supported by possession even if the seizure was wrongful. Justice BRANDEIS acknowledged that the argument would succeed if the seizure had been made by a private party without authority to act for the Government, but that a different rule prevails when the Government itself lacks the power to seize. . . .

The same reasoning was employed by Justice MILLER to explain why the holding in *Rauscher* did not apply to the *Ker* case. The arresting officer in *Ker* did not pretend to be acting in any official capacity when he kidnapped Ker. . . . The exact opposite is true in this case, as it was in *Cook*. . . .

As the Court observes at the outset of its opinion, there is reason to believe that respondent participated in an especially brutal murder of an American law enforcement agent. That fact, if true, may explain the Executive's intense interest in punishing respondent in our courts. Such an explanation, however, provides no justification for disregarding the Rule of Law that this Court has a duty to uphold. That the Executive may wish to reinterpret the Treaty to allow for an action that the Treaty in no way authorizes should not influence this Court's interpretation. . . .

Medellin v. Texas

128 S.Ct. 1346 (2008)

Jose Medellin was convicted of murder and sentenced to death in Texas. He filed in state courts for a writ of *habeas corpus*, contending that he had a right as a foreign national to consult Mexican authorities, under the Vienna Convention on Consular Relations, and he had not been informed of that right at his trial. After his appeal was dismissed, Mexico filed a suit against the United States in the International Court of Justice (ICJ), which has jurisdiction over disputes arising from the convention and other treaties. Mexico contended that Medellin and fifty other Mexican nationals had been denied their procedural rights under the treaty. The ICJ, in the *Case Concerning Avena and Other Mexican Nationals* (*Mex. v. U.S.*), 2004 ICJ 12 (*Avena*), held that the nationals were entitled to reconsideration of their convictions and sentences in the United States.

Medellin appealed his conviction, relying on the ICJ's *Avena* ruling. But a federal appellate court dismissed his petition, holding that it was procedurally barred from *habeas* relief because he had not raised the claim during his original trial. He in turn appealed that decision and his death sentence to the Supreme Court. While the Court was considering his appeal, in February 2005 President George W. Bush issued a memorandum announcing that the

United States would comply with *Avena* "by having state courts give effect to the [ICJ] decision in accordance with general principles of comity filed by the 51 Mexican nationals addressed in that decision." Subsequently, the Court by a five-to-four vote dismissed Medellin's appeal in an unsigned decision to allow Texas courts to comply with the presidential memorandum. Medellin once again appealed to the Texas courts, contending that they should comply with the ICJ's ruling and Bush's memorandum. But in 2006 the Texas Court of Criminal Appeals dismissed his petition and held that the ICJ's ruling was not binding on state courts. The state appellate court also held that President Bush exceeded his constitutional authority over foreign affairs and intruded on the independent powers of state courts. Medellin, again, appealed to the Supreme Court, which granted review.

The state appellate court's decision was affirmed by a six-to-three vote. Chief Justice Roberts delivered the opinion for the Court. Justice Stevens filed a concurring opinion. Justice Breyer issued a dissenting opinion, which Justices Souter and Ginsburg joined.

☐ *Chief Justice ROBERTS delivered the opinion of the Court.*

The International Court of Justice (ICJ), located in the Hague, is a tribunal established pursuant to the United Nations Charter to adjudicate disputes between member states. In the *Case Concerning Avena and Other Mexican Nationals (Mex. v. U.S.)*, 2004 ICJ 12 (Judgment of Mar. 31) (*Avena*), that tribunal considered a claim brought by Mexico against the United States. The ICJ held that, based on violations of the Vienna Convention, 51 named Mexican nationals were entitled to review and reconsideration of their state-court convictions and sentences in the United States. This was so regardless of any forfeiture of the right to raise Vienna Convention claims because of a failure to comply with generally applicable state rules governing challenges to criminal convictions.

In *Sanchez-Llamas v. Oregon*, 548 U.S. 331 (2006)—issued after *Avena* but involving individuals who were not named in the *Avena* judgment—we held that, contrary to the ICJ's determination, the Vienna Convention did not preclude the application of state default rules. After the *Avena* decision, President George W. Bush determined, through a Memorandum to the Attorney General (Feb. 28, 2005), App. to Pet. for Cert. 187a (Memorandum or President's Memorandum), that the United States would "discharge its international obligations" under *Avena* "by having State courts give effect to the decision." . . .

In 1969, the United States, upon the advice and consent of the Senate, ratified the Vienna Convention on Consular Relations (Vienna Convention or Convention), the Optional Protocol Concerning the Compulsory Settlement of Disputes to the Vienna Convention (Optional Protocol or Protocol). . . . Article 36(1) provides that if a person detained by a foreign country "so requests, the competent authorities of the receiving State shall, without delay, inform the consular post of the sending State" of such detention, and "inform the [detainee] of his righ[t]" to request assistance from the consul of his own state. . . .

Under Article 94(1) of the U. N. Charter, "[e]ach Member of the United Nations undertakes to comply with the decision of the [ICJ] in any case to which it is a party." The ICJ's jurisdiction in any particular case, however, is dependent upon the consent of the parties. The ICJ Statute delineates two ways in which a nation may consent to ICJ jurisdiction: It may consent generally to jurisdiction on any question arising under a treaty or general international law, or it may consent specifically to jurisdiction over a particular category of cases or disputes pursuant to a separate treaty. The United States originally consented to the general jurisdiction of the ICJ when it filed a declaration recognizing compulsory jurisdiction under Article 36(2) in 1946. The United States withdrew from general ICJ jurisdiction in 1985. By ratifying the Optional Protocol to the Vienna Convention, the United States consented to the specific jurisdiction of the ICJ with respect to claims arising out of the Vienna Convention. On March 7, 2005, subsequent to the ICJ's judgment in *Avena*, the United States gave notice of withdrawal from the Optional Protocol to the Vienna Convention. . . .

Medellín first contends that the ICJ's judgment in *Avena* constitutes a "binding" obligation on the state and federal courts of the United States. He argues that "by virtue of the Supremacy Clause, the treaties requiring compliance with the *Avena* judgment are already the 'Law of the Land' by which all state and federal courts in this country are 'bound.'" Accordingly, Medellín argues, *Avena* is a binding federal rule of decision that preempts contrary state limitations on successive *habeas* petitions.

No one disputes that the *Avena* decision—a decision that flows from the treaties through which the United States submitted to ICJ jurisdiction with respect to Vienna Convention disputes—constitutes an international law obligation on the part of the United States. But not all international law obligations automatically constitute binding federal law enforceable in United States courts. The question we confront here is whether the *Avena* judgment has automatic domestic legal effect such that the judgment of its own force applies in state and federal courts.

This Court has long recognized the distinction between treaties that automatically have effect as domestic law, and those that—while they constitute international law commitments—do not by themselves function as binding federal law. The distinction was well explained by Chief Justice Marshall's opinion in *Foster v. Neilson*, 2 Pet. 253 (1829), overruled on other grounds, *United States v. Percheman*, 7 Pet. 51 (1833), which held that a treaty is "equivalent to an act of the legislature," and hence self-executing, when it "operates of itself without the aid of any legislative provision." When, in contrast, "[treaty] stipulations are not self-executing they can only be enforced pursuant to legislation to carry them into effect." *Whitney v. Robertson*, 124 U.S. 190 (1888). In sum, while treaties "may comprise international commitments . . . they are not domestic law unless Congress has either enacted implementing statutes or the treaty itself conveys an intention that it be 'self-executing' and is ratified on these terms." . . .

As a signatory to the Optional Protocol, the United States agreed to submit disputes arising out of the Vienna Convention to the ICJ. The Protocol provides: "Disputes arising out of the interpretation or application of the [Vienna] Convention shall lie within the compulsory jurisdiction of the International Court of Justice." Of course, submitting to jurisdiction and agreeing to be bound are two different things. A party could, for example, agree to compulsory nonbinding arbitration. Such an agreement would require the party to appear before the arbitral tribunal without obligating the party to treat the tribunal's decision as binding.

The most natural reading of the Optional Protocol is as a bare grant of jurisdiction. It provides only that "[d]isputes arising out of the interpretation or application of the [Vienna] Convention shall lie within the compulsory jurisdiction of the International Court of Justice" and "may accordingly be brought before the [ICJ] . . . by any party to the dispute being a Party to the present Protocol." The Protocol says nothing about the effect of an ICJ decision and does not itself commit signatories to comply with an ICJ judgment. The Protocol is similarly silent as to any enforcement mechanism.

The obligation on the part of signatory nations to comply with ICJ judgments derives not from the Optional Protocol, but rather from Article 94 of the United Nations Charter—the provision that specifically addresses the effect of ICJ decisions. Article 94(1) provides that "[e]ach Member of the United Nations undertakes to comply with the decision of the [ICJ] in any case to which it is a party." The Executive Branch contends that the phrase "undertakes to comply" is not "an acknowledgement that an ICJ decision will have immediate legal effect in the courts of U. N. members," but rather "a commitment on the part of U. N. Members to take future action through their political branches to comply with an ICJ decision."

We agree with this construction of Article 94. The Article is not a directive to domestic courts. It does not provide that the United States "shall" or "must" comply with an ICJ decision, nor indicate that the Senate that ratified the U. N. Charter intended to vest ICJ decisions with immediate legal effect in domestic courts. In other words, the U. N. Charter reads like "a compact between independent nations" that "depends for the enforcement of its provisions on the interest and the honor of the governments which are parties to it." *Head Money Cases* [112 U.S. 580 (1884)].

The remainder of Article 94 confirms that the U. N. Charter does not contemplate the automatic enforceability of ICJ decisions in domestic courts. Article 94(2)—the enforcement provision—provides the sole remedy for noncompliance: referral to the United Nations Security Council by an aggrieved state. . . .

If ICJ judgments were instead regarded as automatically enforceable domestic law, they would be immediately and directly binding on state and federal courts pursuant to the Supremacy Clause. Mexico or the ICJ would have no need to proceed to the Security Council to enforce the judgment in this case. Noncompliance with an ICJ judgment through exercise of the Security Council veto—always regarded as an option by the Executive and ratifying Senate during and after consideration of the U. N. Charter, Optional Protocol, and ICJ Statute—would no longer be a viable alternative. There would be nothing to veto. In light of the U. N. Charter's remedial scheme, there is no reason to believe that the President and Senate signed up for such a result.

In sum, Medellin's view that ICJ decisions are automatically enforceable as domestic law is fatally undermined by the enforcement structure established by Article 94. His construction would eliminate the option of noncompliance contemplated by Article 94(2), undermining the ability of the political branches to determine whether and how to comply with an ICJ judgment. Those sensitive foreign policy decisions would instead be transferred to state and federal courts charged with applying an ICJ judgment directly as domestic law. And those courts would not be empowered to decide whether to comply with the judgment—again, always regarded as an option by the political branches—any more than courts may consider whether to comply with any other species of domestic law. This result would be particularly anomalous in light of the principle that "[t]he conduct of the foreign relations of our Government is committed by the Constitution to the Executive and Legislative—'the political'—Departments." *Oetjen v. Central Leather Co.*, 246 U.S. 297 (1918).

The ICJ Statute, incorporated into the U. N. Charter, provides further evidence that the ICJ's judgment in *Avena* does not automatically constitute federal law judicially enforceable in United States courts. To begin with, the ICJ's "principal purpose" is said to be to "arbitrate particular disputes between national governments." Accordingly, the ICJ can hear disputes only between nations, not individuals. More important, Article 59 of the statute provides that "[t]he decision of the [ICJ] has no binding force except between the parties and in respect of that particular case." The dissent does not explain how Medellin, an individual, can be a party to the ICJ proceeding. . . .

Our Framers established a careful set of procedures that must be followed before federal law can be created under the Constitution—vesting that decision in the political branches, subject to checks and balances. U.S. Const., Art. I, Sec. 7. They also recognized that treaties could create federal law, but again through the political branches, with the President making the treaty and the Senate approving it. Art. II, Sec. 2. The dissent's understanding of the treaty route, depending on an ad hoc judgment of the judiciary without looking to the treaty language—the very language negotiated by the President and approved by the Senate—cannot readily be ascribed to those same Framers.

The dissent's approach risks the United States' involvement in international agreements. It is hard to believe that the United States would enter into treaties that are sometimes enforceable and sometimes not. Such a treaty would be the equivalent of writing a blank check to the judiciary. Senators could never be quite sure what the treaties on which they were voting meant. Only a judge could say for sure and only at some future date. This uncertainty could hobble the United States' efforts to negotiate and sign international agreements.

In this case, the dissent—for a grab bag of no less than seven reasons—would tell us that this particular ICJ judgment is federal law. That is no sort of guidance. Nor is it any answer to say that the federal courts will diligently police international agreements and enforce the decisions of international tribunals only when they should be enforced. The point of a non-self-executing treaty is that it "addresses itself to the political, not the judicial department; and the legislature must execute the contract before it can become a rule for the Court." . . .

Our holding does not call into question the ordinary enforcement of foreign judgments or international arbitral agreements. Indeed, we agree with Medellin that, as a general matter, "an agreement to abide by the result" of an international adjudication—or what he really means, an agreement to give the result of such adjudication domestic legal effect—can be a treaty obligation like any other, so long as the agreement is consistent with the Constitution. The point is that the particular treaty obligations on which Medellin relies do not of their own force create domestic law. . . .

In sum, while the ICJ's judgment in *Avena* creates an international law obligation on the part of the United States, it does not of its own force constitute binding federal law that preempts state restrictions on the filing of successive *habeas* petitions. Nothing in the text, background, negotiating and drafting history, or practice among signatory nations suggests that the President or Senate intended the improbable result of giving the judgments of an international tribunal a higher status than that enjoyed by "many of our most fundamental constitutional protections."

Medellin next argues that the ICJ's judgment in *Avena* is binding on state courts by virtue of the President's February 28, 2005 Memorandum. The United States contends that while the *Avena* judgment does not of its own force require domestic courts to set aside ordinary rules of procedural default, that judgment became the law of the land with precisely that effect pursuant to the President's Memorandum and his power "to establish binding rules of decision that preempt contrary state law." Accordingly, we must decide whether the President's declaration alters our conclusion that the *Avena* judgment is not a rule of domestic law binding in state and federal courts.

The United States maintains that the President's constitutional role "uniquely qualifies" him to resolve the sensitive foreign policy decisions that bear on compliance with an ICJ decision and "to do so expeditiously." In this case, the President seeks to vindicate United States interests in ensuring the reciprocal observance of the Vienna Convention, protecting relations with foreign governments, and demonstrating commitment to the role of international law. These interests are plainly compelling.

Such considerations, however, do not allow us to set aside first principles. The President's authority to act, as with the exercise of any governmental power, "must stem either from an act of Congress or from the Constitution itself." *Youngstown* [*Sheet & Tube v. Sawyer*, 343 U.S. 579 (1952)].

Justice Jackson's familiar tripartite scheme provides the accepted framework for evaluating executive action in this area. First, "[w]hen the President acts pursuant to an express or implied authorization of Congress, his authority is at its maximum, for it includes all that he possesses in his own right plus all that Congress can delegate." *Youngstown*. Second, "[w]hen the President acts in absence of either a congressional grant or denial of authority, he can only rely upon his own independent powers, but there is a zone of twilight in which he and Congress may have concurrent authority, or in which its distribution is uncertain." In this circumstance, Presidential authority can derive support from "congressional inertia, indifference or quiescence." Finally, "[w]hen the President takes measures incompatible with the expressed or implied will of Congress, his power is at its lowest ebb," and the Court can sustain his actions "only by disabling the Congress from acting upon the subject." ...

The President has an array of political and diplomatic means available to enforce international obligations, but unilaterally converting a non-self-executing treaty into a self-executing one is not among them. The responsibility for transforming an international obligation arising from a non-self-executing treaty into domestic law falls to Congress. ...

The requirement that Congress, rather than the President, implement a non-self-executing treaty derives from the text of the Constitution, which divides the treaty-making power between the President and the Senate. The Constitution vests the President with the authority to "make" a treaty. If the Executive determines that a treaty should have domestic effect of its own force, that determination may be implemented "in mak[ing]" the treaty, by ensuring that it contains language plainly providing for domestic enforceability. If the treaty is to be self-executing in this respect, the Senate must consent to the treaty by the requisite two-thirds vote consistent with all other constitutional restraints.

Once a treaty is ratified without provisions clearly according it domestic effect, however, whether the treaty will ever have such effect is governed by the fundamental constitutional principle that "'[t]he power to make the necessary laws is in Congress; the power to execute in the President.'" *Hamdan v. Rumsfeld*, 548 U.S. 557 (2006). As already noted, the terms of a non-self-executing treaty can become domestic law only in the same way as any other law—through passage of legislation by both Houses of Congress, combined with either the President's signature or a congressional override of a Presidential veto. Indeed, "the President's power to see that the laws are faithfully executed refutes the idea that he is to be a lawmaker." *Youngstown*.

A non-self-executing treaty, by definition, is one that was ratified with the understanding that it is not to have domestic effect of its own force. That understanding precludes the assertion that Congress has implicitly authorized the President—acting on his own—to achieve precisely the same result. We therefore conclude, given the absence of congressional legislation, that the non-self-executing treaties at issue here did not "express[ly] or implied[ly]" vest the President with the unilateral authority to make them self-executing. Accordingly, the President's Memorandum does not fall within the first category of the *Youngstown* framework. . . .

The United States nonetheless maintains that the President's Memorandum should be given effect as domestic law because "this case involves a valid Presidential action in the context of Congressional 'acquiescence.'" Under the *Youngstown* tripartite framework, congressional acquiescence is pertinent when the President's action falls within the second category—that is, when he "acts in absence of either a congressional grant or denial of authority." Here, however, as we have explained, the President's effort to accord domestic effect to the *Avena* judgment does not meet that prerequisite. . . .

We thus turn to the United States' claim that—independent of the United States' treaty obligations—the Memorandum is a valid exercise of the President's foreign affairs authority to resolve claims disputes with foreign nations. The United States relies on a series of cases in which this Court has upheld the authority of the President to settle foreign claims pursuant to an executive agreement. . . .

This argument is of a different nature than the one rejected above. Rather than relying on the United States' treaty obligations, the President relies on an independent source of authority in ordering Texas to put aside its procedural bar to successive *habeas* petitions. Nevertheless, we find that our claims-settlement cases [*United States v. Pink*, 315 U.S. 202 (1942); *United States v. Belmont*, 301 U.S. 324 (1937)] do not support the authority that the President asserts in this case. . . .

☐ *Justice BREYER, with whom Justice SOUTER and Justice GINSBURG join, dissenting.*

The Constitution's Supremacy Clause provides that "all Treaties . . . which shall be made . . . under the Authority of the United States, shall be the supreme Law of the Land; and the Judges in every State shall be bound thereby." The Clause means that the "courts" must regard "a treaty . . . as equivalent to an act of the legislature, whenever it operates of itself without the aid of any legislative provision." *Foster v. Neilson*, 2 Pet. 253 (1829).

In the *Avena* case the International Court of Justice (ICJ) (interpreting and applying the Vienna Convention on Consular Relations) issued a judgment that requires the United States to reexamine certain criminal proceedings in the cases of 51 Mexican nationals. The question here is whether the ICJ's *Avena* judgment is enforceable now as a matter of domestic law, i.e., whether it "operates of itself without the aid" of any further legislation. . . .

To understand the issue before us, the reader must keep in mind three separate ratified United States treaties and one ICJ judgment against the United States. The first treaty, the Vienna Convention, contains two relevant provisions. The first requires the United States and other signatory nations to inform arrested foreign nationals of their separate Convention-given right to contact their nation's consul. The second says that these rights (of an arrested person) "shall be exercised in conformity with the laws and regulations" of the arresting nation, provided that the "laws and regulations . . . enable full effect to be given to the purposes for which" those "rights . . . are intended."

The second treaty, the Optional Protocol, concerns the "compulsory settlement" of Vienna Convention disputes. It provides that for parties that elect to subscribe to the Protocol, "[d]isputes arising out of the interpretation or application of the [Vienna] Convention" shall be submitted to the "compulsory jurisdiction of the International Court of Justice." It authorizes any party that has consented to the ICJ's jurisdiction (by signing the Optional Protocol) to bring another such party before that Court.

The third treaty, the United Nations Charter, says that every signatory Nation "undertakes to comply with the decision of the International Court of Justice in any case to which it is a party." Article 94(1). In an annex to the Charter, the Statute of the International Court of Justice states that an ICJ judgment has "binding force . . . between the parties and in respect of that particular case." Article 59.

The critical question here is whether the Supremacy Clause requires Texas to follow, i.e., to enforce, this ICJ judgment. The Court says "no." And it reaches its negative answer by interpreting the labyrinth of treaty provisions as creating a legal obligation that binds the United States internationally, but which, for Supremacy Clause purposes, is not automatically enforceable as domestic law. In the majority's view, the Optional Protocol simply sends the dispute to the ICJ; the ICJ statute says that the ICJ will subsequently reach a judgment; and the U. N. Charter contains no more than a promise to "'undertak[e] to comply'" with that judgment. Such a promise, the majority says, does not as a domestic law matter (in Chief Justice Marshall's words) "operat[e] of itself without the aid of any legislative provision." *Foster.* Rather, here (and presumably in any other ICJ judgment rendered pursuant to any of the approximately 70 U.S. treaties in force that contain similar provisions for submitting treaty-based disputes to the ICJ for decisions that bind the parties) Congress must enact specific legislation before ICJ judgments entered pursuant to our consent to compulsory ICJ jurisdiction can become domestic law.

In my view, the President has correctly determined that Congress need not enact additional legislation. The majority places too much weight upon treaty language that says little about the matter. The words "undertak[e] to comply," for example, do not tell us whether an ICJ judgment rendered pursuant to the parties' consent to compulsory ICJ jurisdiction does, or does not, automatically become part of our domestic law. To answer that question we must look instead to our own domestic law, in particular, to the many treaty-related cases interpreting the Supremacy Clause. Those cases, including some written by Justices well aware of the Founders' original intent, lead to the conclusion that the ICJ judgment before us is enforceable as a matter of domestic law without further legislation. . . .

I would find the relevant treaty provisions self-executing as applied to the ICJ judgment before us (giving that judgment domestic legal effect) for the following reasons, taken together.

First, the language of the relevant treaties strongly supports direct judicial enforceability, at least of judgments of the kind at issue here. The Optional Protocol bears the title "Compulsory Settlement of Disputes," thereby emphasizing the mandatory and binding nature of the procedures it sets forth. The body of the Protocol says specifically that "any party" that has consented to the ICJ's "compulsory jurisdiction" may bring a "dispute" before the court against any other such party. And the Protocol contrasts proceedings of the compulsory kind with an alternative "conciliation procedure," the recommendations of which a party may decide "not" to "accep[t]." Article III. Thus, the Optional Protocol's basic objective is not just to provide a forum for settlement but to provide a forum for compulsory settlement. . . .

Second, the Optional Protocol here applies to a dispute about the meaning of a Vienna Convention provision that is itself self-executing and judicially enforceable. The Convention provision is about an individual's "rights," namely, his right upon being arrested to be informed of his separate right to contact his nation's consul. . . .

Third, logic suggests that a treaty provision providing for "final" and "binding" judgments that "settl[e]" treaty-based disputes is self-executing insofar as the judgment in question concerns the meaning of an underlying treaty provision that is itself self-executing. Imagine that two parties to a contract agree to binding arbitration about whether a contract provision's word "grain" includes rye. They would expect that, if the arbitrator decides that the word "grain" does include rye, the arbitrator will then simply read the relevant provision as if it said "grain including rye." They would also expect the arbitrator to issue a binding award that embodies whatever relief would be appropriate under that circumstance.

Why treat differently the parties' agreement to binding ICJ determination about, e.g., the proper interpretation of the Vienna Convention clauses containing the rights here at issue? Why not simply read the relevant Vienna Convention provisions as if (between the parties and in respect to the 51 individuals at issue) they contain words that encapsulate the ICJ's decision? Why would the ICJ judgment not bind in precisely the same way those words would bind if they appeared in the relevant Vienna Convention provisions—just as the ICJ says, for purposes of this case, that they do?

To put the same point differently: What sense would it make (1) to make a self-executing promise and (2) to promise to accept as final an ICJ judgment interpreting that self-executing promise, yet (3) to insist that the judgment itself is not self-executing (i.e., that Congress must enact specific legislation to enforce it)?

I am not aware of any satisfactory answer to these questions. . . .

Fourth, the majority's very different approach has seriously negative practical implications. The United States has entered into at least 70 treaties that contain provisions for ICJ dispute settlement similar to the Protocol before us. Many of these treaties contain provisions similar to those this Court has previously found self-executing—provisions that involve, for example, property rights, contract and commercial rights, trademarks, civil liability for personal injury, rights of foreign diplomats, taxation, domestic-court jurisdiction, and so forth. If the Optional Protocol here, taken together with the U. N. Charter and its annexed ICJ Statute, is insufficient to warrant enforcement of the ICJ judgment before us, it is difficult to see how one could reach a different conclusion in any of these other instances. And the consequence is to undermine longstanding efforts in those treaties to create an effective international system for interpreting and applying many, often commercial, self-executing treaty provisions. . . .

Fifth, other factors, related to the particular judgment here at issue, make that judgment well suited to direct judicial enforcement. The specific issue before the ICJ concerned "'review and reconsideration'" of the "possible prejudice" caused in each of the 51 affected cases by an arresting State's failure to provide the defendant with rights guaranteed by the Vienna Convention. This review will call for an understanding of how criminal procedure works, including whether, and how, a notification failure may work prejudice. As the ICJ itself recognized, "it is the judicial process that is suited to this task." Courts frequently work with criminal procedure and related prejudice. Legislatures do not. Judicial standards are readily available for working in this technical area. Legislative standards are not readily available. Judges typically determine such matters, deciding, for example, whether further hearings are necessary, after reviewing a record in an individual case. Congress does not normally legislate in respect to individual cases. Indeed, to repeat what I said above, what kind of special legislation does the majority believe Congress ought to consider?

Sixth, to find the United States' treaty obligations self-executing as applied to the ICJ judgment (and consequently to find that judgment enforceable) does not threaten constitutional conflict with other branches; it does not require us to engage in nonjudicial activity; and it does not require us to create a new cause of action. The only question before us concerns the application of the ICJ judgment as binding law applicable to the parties in a particular criminal proceeding that Texas law creates independently of the treaty. I repeat that the question before us does not involve the creation of a private right of action (and the majority's reliance on authority regarding such a circumstance is misplaced).

Seventh, neither the President nor Congress has expressed concern about direct judicial enforcement of the ICJ decision. To the contrary, the President favors enforcement of this judgment. . . .

For these seven reasons, I would find that the United States' treaty obligation to comply with the ICJ judgment in *Avena* is enforceable in court in this case without further congressional action beyond Senate ratification of the relevant treaties. . . .

In sum, a strong line of precedent, likely reflecting the views of the Founders, indicates that the treaty provisions before us and the judgment of the International Court of Justice address themselves to the Judicial Branch and consequently are self-executing. In reaching a contrary conclusion, the Court has failed to take proper account of that precedent and, as a result, the Nation may well break its word even though the President seeks to live up to that word and Congress has done nothing to suggest the contrary.

For the reasons set forth, I respectfully dissent.

D | *War-Making and Emergency Powers*

An enduring struggle between the president and Congress over the power to wage war took root at the Constitutional Convention. Delegates initially gave Congress the power "to make war" but finally settled on giving it the power "to declare war" in Article I, Section 8. This reflected a recognition that the president as commander in chief may need "to repel sudden attacks," but also that the nation must be safeguarded against unchecked presidential power to wage or initiate war. The war-making power is thus a shared power. The president oversees all military operations in peace and wartime, yet Congress has the power to "raise and support Armies" as well as to "provide for calling forth the Militia to execute the Laws of the Union, suppress Insurrections and repel Invasions."

Although Congress has the power to declare war, the president's power to order the military into conflict in foreign countries and to wage war has been firmly demonstrated. In fact, just five wars have been "declared" and only with the War of 1812 did Congress actively debate the merits of entering the conflict. As earlier noted, at the outset of the Civil War, Lincoln asserted expansive powers before seeking congressional approval. During World Wars I and II, Congress simply recognized a state of war when passing broad legislation delegating vast discretionary powers to the president. Moreover, every president from Theodore Roosevelt to George W. Bush has ordered troops into foreign conflicts without congressional assent and with little or no prior notification; indeed, presidents have ordered forces abroad over 130 times.

In historical perspective, restraints on the president's power to wage war remain almost entirely in the hands of Congress. The Court is especially reluctant to question the wisdom of a president's military decisions. It also recognizes the potential futility of declaring unconstitutional presidential actions during wartime and international emergencies. The Court tends to agree with the view expressed by Charles Evans Hughes, before becoming chief justice, that "[t]he power to wage war is the power to wage war successfully. . . . That is, there are constantly new applications of unchanged powers. . . . So, also, we have a *fighting* Constitution."[1]

A basic constitutional dilemma in enforcing constraints on presidential power to wage war nevertheless remains. Thomas Jefferson, the renowned "strict constructionist," posed the problem of, on the one hand, adhering to constitutional constraints and guarantees and, on the other hand, of taking unauthorized action deemed necessary to preserve the country. In the Kentucky Resolutions of 1798, he argued in opposition to the Alien and Sedition acts and partisan prosecution of critics of the Federalists that "[i]n questions of power then let no more be heard of confidence in man, but bind him down by the chains of the Constitution." Yet Jefferson later took a broad view of the government's power to respond to national emergencies, "A strict observance of the written laws is doubtless *one* of the high duties of a good citizen, but it is not *the highest*. The laws of necessity, of self-preservation, of saving our country when in danger, are of higher obligation."[2]

The dilemma of preserving the Constitution and the country was put well in 1967 by Chief Justice Earl Warren: " '[N]ational defense' cannot be deemed an end in itself. . . . Implicit in the term . . . is the notion of defending those values and ideas which set this Nation apart. . . . It would indeed be ironic if, in the name of national defense, we would sanction the subversion of one of those liberties . . . which makes the defense of the Nation worthwhile."[3]

Justices no less than others are often sharply divided over ignoring or enforcing and broadly or narrowly interpreting constraints on the president's war-making powers. The Court's rulings in controversies arising from Lincoln's actions at the start of the Civil War are illustrative. The full Court never ruled on Lincoln's orders suspending the writ of *habeas corpus*. But Chief Justice Taney in *Ex parte Merryman*, 17 Fed. Cases 144 (1861), declared them unconstitutional on the ground that Article I, Section 9, gives Congress, not the president, the power to suspend the writ "when in Cases of Rebellion or Invasion the public Safety may require it." Lincoln nonetheless disregarded Taney's opinion and continued to contend that the president shares with Congress the power to suspend the writ. The president's military orders for a blockade of Confederate ports was subsequently upheld by a bare majority in *The Prize Cases* (1863) (excerpted below). Four dissenters, though, point out that the Constitution grants only Congress the power to call up the militia to suppress insurrections. Three years later and notably after the end of the Civil War, however, a unanimous Court ruled in *Ex parte Milligan* (1866) (see excerpt below) that Lincoln's orders for the trial of civilians by military courts were unconstitutional.[4]

During World War II the Court again proved reluctant to enforce constitutional guarantees against claims of broad emergency powers. The forced evacuation of over 100,000 Japanese and Japanese-Americans from the West Coast was based on both congressional legislation and executive orders. The Court initially avoided ruling on the questions arising from the denial of civil liberties and property rights by the evacuation and internment program. *Hirabayashi v. United States*, 320 U.S. 91 (1943), upheld a curfew imposed on Japanese-Americans but avoided ruling on their evacuation. The next year, in *Korematsu v. United States* (1944) (see excerpt below), one of the most libertarian justices, Hugo Black, handed down an opinion finding the evacuation program constitutional. The three dissenters all disagreed on different grounds, but notably Justice Robert Jackson sharply criticized the sanctioning of "a military expedient that has no place in law under the Constitution." To partially deflect some of the criticism of *Korematsu*, on the same day as that ruling came down Justice Douglas announced the decision in *Ex parte Endo*, 323 U.S. 283 (1944). In that case the Court upheld the right of a loyal Japanese-American woman to a writ of *habeas corpus* releasing her from a relocation camp but again refused to address the constitutionality of the detention program. Despite the outcry over these rulings, Justices Black and Douglas never regretted their decisions, and the latter once explained, "The decisions were extreme and went to the verge of wartime power; and they have been severely criticized. It is, however, easy in retrospect to denounce what was done, as there actually was no invasion of our country. . . . But those making plans for defense of the nation had no such knowledge and were planning for the worst."[5] Over forty years later in 1988, President Reagan signed legislation providing reparations for those interned in relocation camps during World War II.

Controversies arising from the undeclared war in Vietnam were evaded by the Court as well, even though several of the justices maintained that it ought to consider cases challenging the constitutionality of the war.[6] Presidents from Eisenhower to Nixon justified their sending military advisers and troops to Vietnam on their power as commander in chief. In addition, Johnson and Nixon defended their escalation of the war and bombing of North Vietnam on a joint resolution passed by Congress in 1964 after alleged attacks by torpedo boat on two U.S. destroyers in the Gulf of Tonkin. The Gulf of Tonkin Resolution, as it was called, supported "the determination of the President, as commander in chief, to take all necessary measures to repel any armed attack against the forces of the United States and to prevent further aggression." Both the Johnson and Nixon administrations claimed that the resolution gave the president as much power as a declaration of war. But as military involvement increased and opposition to the war grew, Congress tried to curb the president with legislation—prohibiting the use of funds for combat forces in Cambodia and Laos and repealing the Gulf of Tonkin Resolution. These limitations proved unavailing because continued military presence in Vietnam could be justified as necessary to protect troops there until they could be safely withdrawn. One major result of the struggle between Congress and the president over the Vietnam War was the passage in 1973 of the War Powers Resolution, over Nixon's veto (see excerpt below).

More recently, the Court has also consistently declined to review cases challenging, for example, President George H. W. Bush's sending military forces into Saudi Arabia in 1990 after Iraq invaded Kuwait, and President Bill Clinton's decision to authorize military intervention in Yugoslavia in 1999. Lower federal courts have held that suits challenging the constitutionality of those actions filed by members of Congress either raised political questions or that members of Congress lacked standing to file the lawsuits.[7]

The Court, however, could not avoid ruling on challenges to the administration of President George W. Bush's claim that he had the power to indefinitely detain foreign nationals who had been seized after the September 11, 2001, terrorist attacks and held in Guantanamo Bay, Cuba, as well as U.S. citizens held as "enemy combatants." See also the CONSTITUTIONAL HISTORY box in this chapter, Citizens, Noncitizens, "Enemy Combatants," and Civil Rights in Wartime. In *Rasul v. Bush* (2004) (excerpted below) the Court rejected the administration's position that federal courts lacked jurisdiction over foreign nationals held in Cuba and affirmed the right of these individuals to seek judicial review of the basis for their detention. In *Hamdi v. Rumsfeld,* 542 U.S. 507 (2004), a bare majority held that the president was authorized to detain U.S. citizens as enemy combatants, but on a six-to-three vote held that citizens have a right to consult with an attorney and to contest the basis for their detention before an independent tribunal. For a bare majority Justice O'Connor ruled that the Authorization on the Use of Military Force Act (AUMF) of 2001, enacted after the 9/11 terrorist attacks, authorized the detaining of U.S. citizens, though not indefinitely, but that Hamdi was entitled to *habeas* relief. By a six-to-three vote, Justice O'Connor also ruled that due process entitled Hamdi to consult an attorney and to a hearing before a tribunal—whether civil or military was left open. In an opinion concurring and dissenting in part, Justice Souter, joined by Justice Ginsburg, agreed with the rejection of the Bush administration's position on the role of courts but concluded that the Non-Detention Act of 1971, which stipulates that Congress must enact legislation expressly authorizing the detention of individuals, was run afoul by the unauthorized detention of enemy combatants. Justice Souter disagreed with Justice O'Connor's position that the AUMF authorized such detentions. Justice Scalia, joined by Justice Stevens, also rejected the Bush administration's position and contended that the proper course would be to try citizen combatants for treason. In Justice Scalia's words:

> Where the Government accuses a citizen of waging war against it, our constitutional tradition has been to prosecute him in federal court for treason or some other crime. Where the exigencies of war prevent that, the Constitution's Suspension Clause, Art. 1, Sec. 9, cl. 2, allows Congress to relax the usual protections temporarily. Absent suspension [of *habeas* review], however, the Executive's assertion of military exigency has been thought sufficient to permit the detention without charge. No one contends that the congressional Authorization for Use of Military Force, on which the Government relies to justify its actions here, is an implementation of the Suspension Clause.

Only dissenting Justice Thomas embraced Bush's broad claims of presidential power, observing that:

> The Founders intended that the President have primary responsibility—along with the necessary power—to protect the national security and to conduct the Nation's foreign relations. They did so principally because the structural advantages of a unitary Executive are essential in these domains. "Energy in the executive is a leading character in the definition of good government. It is essential to the protection of the community against foreign attacks." The *Federalist* No. 70 (A. Hamilton). . . .

Subsequently, in a plea agreement *Hamdi* renounced his U.S. citizenship and was returned to Saudia Arabia.

In response to the ruling in *Hamdi* Congress enacted the Detainee Treatment Act (DTA) of 2005, which stripped federal courts of jurisdiction over *habeas* appeals from detainees. And Bush on his own authority established military tribunals to review the basis for detaining enemy combatants, but their procedures did not comply with those of the Uniform Code of Military Justice (UCMJ) or the Geneva Conventions.

When the DTA and Bush's orders establishing military tribunals were challenged in *Hamdan v. Rumsfeld*, 542 U.S. 507 (2006), the Court split six to three. Writing for the majority, Justice Stevens held that Hamdan—who was Osama Bin Ladin's driver and was captured in Afghanistan—had a statutory right to *habeas* relief, because his case was pending when the DTA was enacted. But again the Court avoided ruling on whether detainees had a constitutional right to a writ of *habeas corpus* and on the constitutionality of Congress's stripping federal courts of *habeas* jurisdiction. Justice Stevens, however, also rejected Bush's claim of inherent power to establish the military tribunals in holding that express congressional authorization was needed to try combatants and to try them in accord with the Geneva Conventions and that the tribunals failed to comply with the UCMJ and the procedures of a regularly constituted court. By contrast, Justices Scalia, Thomas, and Alito maintained that Bush had authority as commander in chief under Article 2 to create the tribunals, and the president was entitled to judicial deference.

Congress in turn responded to *Hamdan* by enacting the Military Commissions Act (MCA) of 2006. That law denied federal courts' jurisdiction over *habeas* appeals by detainees and authorized the president to establish military commissions and interrogation methods, as well as gave the president the authority to interpret procedural guarantees for detainees so long as they did not pose "grave breaches" of the Geneva Conventions or constitute "cruel, unusual or inhumane treatment." The MCA, though, also rejected the right to a speedy trial, required military defense attorneys, and specified that the commissions' decisions need not be unanimous.

When provisions of the MCA were initially challenged in *Boumediene v. Bush*, 549 U.S. 1328 (2007), the Roberts Court denied review but subsequently reversed course and granted review. A bare majority then held that even foreign nationals have a *constitutional* right to apply to federal courts for writs of *habeas corpus* and to judicial review of the basis for their detention. Writing for the Court, in *Boumediene v. Bush* (2008) (excerpted below), Justice Kennedy observed that "The laws and Constitution are designed to survive, and remain in force, in extraordinary times." Chief Justice Roberts and Justice Scalia each filed dissenting opinions, which were joined by Justices Thomas and Alito.

In a related case, *Munaf v. Green*, 128 S.Ct. 2229 (2008), an unanimous Court held that U.S. citizens held by U.S. forces in Iraq had the right to file *habeas* petitions, but that federal courts did not have the authority to bar their transfer to and trial by Iraqi authorities for charges of terrorism-related crimes. Chief Justice Roberts delivered the opinion of the Court, while Justice Souter filed a concurring opinion, joined by Justices Ginsburg and Breyer. In their view, the ruling would not foreclose U.S. courts from preventing the transfer of citizens into foreign custody when "the probability of torture is well documented, even if the Executive fails to acknowledge it."

NOTES

1. C. E. Hughes, "War Powers under the Constitution," 62 *American Bar Association Reports* 238 (1917).

2. T. Jefferson, Letter to J. B. Colvin, in *The Writings of Thomas Jefferson*, Vol. 12, ed. Andrew A. Lipscomb (Washington, DC: The Thomas Jefferson Memorial Association, 1903), 418.

3. *United States v. Robel*, 389 U.S. 258 (1967).

4. Military trials of captured saboteurs and enemies during World War II, however, were upheld in *Ex parte Quirin*, 317 U.S. 1 (1942), and *In re Yamashita*, 327 U.S. 1 (1946). But the Court has maintained that citizens and military dependents may not be tried by military courts either for capital offenses, in *Reid v. Covert*, 351 U.S. 487 (1957), or noncapital offenses, in *Kinsella v. United States ex rel. Singleton*, 361 U.S. 234 (1960), and *McElroy v. United States ex rel. Guagliardo*, 361 U.S. 281 (1960).

5. *DeFunis v. Odegaard*, 416 U.S. 312 (1973).

6. See *Mora v. McNammara*, 389 U.S. 934 (1967); *Massachusetts v. Laid*, 400 U.S. 886 (1970); and *Sarnoff v. Schultz*, 409 U.S. 929 (1972).

7. See *Lowry v. Reagan*, 676 F. Supp. 333 (D.C. Cir., 1987); *Dellums v. Bush*, 752 F. Supp. 1141 (D.C. Cir., 1990); and *Campbell v. Clinton*, 203 F. 3d 19 (9th Cir., 2000).

SELECTED BIBLIOGRAPHY

9/11 Commission. *The 9/11 Commission Report*. New York: W. W. Norton & Company, 2004.

Ackerman, Bruce. *Before the Next Attack: Preserving Civil Liberties in an Age of Terrorism*. New Haven, CT: Yale University Press, 2006.

Ball, Howard. *Bush, the Detainees and the Constitution*. Lawrence: University Press of Kansas, 2007.

Bobbitt, Philip, *Terror and Consent: The Wars for the Twenty-First Century*. New York: Knopf, 2008.

Burgess, Susan. *Contest for Constitutional Authority: The Abortion and War Powers Debates*. Lawrence: University Press of Kansas, 1992.

Cole, David. *Enemy Aliens*. New York: New Press, 2003.

————, and Dempsey, James. *Terrorism and the Constitution* 3d ed. New York: New Press, 2006.

Delgado, Richard. *Justice at War*. New York: New York University Press, 2003.

Ely, John Hart. *War and Responsibility: Constitutional Lessons of Vietnam and Its Aftermath*. Cambridge, MA: Harvard University Press, 1993.

Farber, Daniel. *Lincoln's Constitution*. Chicago: University of Chicago Press, 2003.

Fisher, Louis. *Presidential War Power*. 2d ed. Lawrence: University Press of Kansas, 2004.

————. *Congressional Abdication on War and Spending*. College Station: Texas A & M University Press, 2000.

————. *Nazi Saboteurs on Trial: A Military Tribunal and American Law*. 2d ed. Lawrence: University Press of Kansas, 2005.

————. *Military Tribunals and Presidential Power*. Lawrence: University Press of Kansas; 2005.

————. *In the Name of National Security: Unchecked Presidential Power and the Reynolds Case*. Lawrence: University Press of Kansas, 2006.

————. *The Constitution and 9/11*. Lawrence: University Press of Kansas, 2008.

Goldsmith, Jack. *The Terror Presidency: Law and Judgment Inside the Bush Administration*. New York: W. W. Norton & Company, 2007.

Heymann, Philip B. *Terrorism, Freedom, and Security: Winning without War.* Cambridge, MA: MIT Press, 2003.

Irons, Peter. *Justice at War.* New York: Oxford University Press, 1983.

Keynes, Edward. *Undeclared War: Twilight Zone of Constitutional Power.* University Park: Pennsylvania State University Press, 1982.

Kurnaz, Murat. *Five Years of My Life: An Innocent Man in Guantanamo.* New York: Palgrave, 2008.

Lehman, Charles. *Making War: The 200-Year-Old Battle between the President and Congress over How Americans Go to War.* New York: Scribner's Sons, 1992.

Levinson, Stanford, ed. *Torture: A Collection.* New York: Oxford University Press, 2004.

Mahler, Jonathan. *The Challenge: Hamdan v. Rumsfeld and the Fight over Presidential Power.* New York: Farrar, Straus and Giroux, 2008.

■ CONSTITUTIONAL HISTORY

Citizens, Noncitizens, "Enemy Combatants," and Civil Rights in Wartime

Shortly after the attacks on the World Trade Center and the Pentagon on September 11, 2001, President George W. Bush declared war against al Qaeda forces in Afghanistan and international terrorism. He issued an order authorizing the indefinite detention of captured terrorists and their trial by military tribunals, without appeal. Bush's order invited controversy because the detainees were not treated as prisoners of war according to international law. Under the Third Geneva Convention of 1949, prisoners of war are entitled to an independent and impartial trial, the assistance of counsel, and the right of appeal. Less than two months later, Bush signed into law the 342-page USA PATRIOT Act. Its provisions expand surveillance by law enforcement agencies, provide for greater cooperation among federal agencies, and create new crimes. Civil libertarians and other critics contend that the government overreacted, especially in detaining immigrants and holding U.S. citizens as "enemy combatants."

In historical perspective, threats to national security have tended to be exaggerated and civil liberties curbed. When on the verge of war with France, in 1798 Congress enacted the Alien and Sedition Acts, empowering the president to expel any alien deemed dangerous. The Sedition Act made it unlawful to "write, print, utter or publish . . . any false, scandalous and malicious writing . . . against" the government. It led to twenty-five arrests, fifteen indictments, and ten convictions. All of them were

Posner, Eric, and Vermeule, Adrian. *Terror in the Balance: Security, Liberty, and the Courts.* New York: Oxford University Press, 2007.

Pyle, Christopher. *Getting Away with Torture: Secret Government, War Crimes, and the Rule of Law.* Washington, DC: Potomac Books, 2009.

Rehnquist, William H. *All The Laws but One: Civil Liberties in Wartime.* New York: Knopf, 1998.

Sidhu, Dawinder and Gohil, Neha S. *Civil Rights in Wartime: The Post-9/11 Sikh Experience.* Surrey, UK: Ashgate, 2009.

Yoo, John. *The Powers of War and Peace: The Constitution and Foreign Affairs after 9/11.* Chicago: University of Chicago Press, 2006.

Wittes, Benjamin. *Law and the Long War: The Future of Justice in the Age of Terror.* New York: Penguin, 2008.

Jeffersonian-Republican opponents of the Federalists, who were then in power. The laws expired in 1801. The Supreme Court took the extraordinary step over 150 years later of declaring them unconstitutional, in *New York Times Company v. Sullivan*, 376 U.S. 254 (1964) (excerpted in Vol. 2, Ch. 5).

In 1798, Congress also enacted the Enemy Alien Act, still in effect, authorizing the president during a war to detain and expel citizens of a country with which we are at war. James Madison invoked it during the War of 1812; President Woodrow Wilson did so during World War I to arrest over 6,000 German nationals and hold about 2,300 in internment camps; and during World War II President Franklin D. Roosevelt invoked the law to classify almost one million foreigners as "enemy aliens."

World War I brought other restrictions, particularly for immigrants from East Europe and Russia. The Senate debated a bill that would have turned the country into a military zone and made it a crime to publish anything endangering national security, with trials by military tribunals and convictions punishable by death. But President Wilson persuaded Congress to enact the less extreme Espionage Act of 1917, making it a crime to interfere with war efforts. Still, as amended in 1918, the law criminalized any "disloyal, profane, scurrilous or abusive" language about the government. Approximately 2,000 individuals were prosecuted under the law. By the time appeals reached the Court, World War I was over, but the "Red Scare" remained and most of the convictions were upheld. In *Schenck v. United States*, 249 U.S. 47 (1919) (excerpted in Vol. 2, Ch. 5), Justice Oliver Wendell Holmes proposed his "clear and present danger" test for protecting speech, yet upheld the conviction, observing: "When a nation is at war many things that might be said in time of peace are such

(continues)

- ■ Constitutional History
*Citizens, Noncitizens, "Enemy Combatants," and
Civil Rights in Wartime (continued)*

a hindrance to its effort that their utterance will not be endured so long as men fight." When another appeal reached the Court, *Abrams v. United States*, 250 U.S. 616 (1919), Justices Holmes and Louis D. Brandeis dissented and explained: "The power undoubtedly is greater in time of war than in time of peace because war opens dangers that do not exist at other times. But as against dangers peculiar to war, as against others, the principle of the right of free speech is always the same." (See also *Gitlow v. People of the State of New York*, 268 U.S. 652 (1925), excerpted in Vol. 2, Ch. 5.)

During World War II and the Cold War, the Court again did not seriously question wartime hysteria or the prosecution of "subversives." Notably, the Court upheld the convictions of leaders of the Communist Party under the Smith Act of 1940, in *Dennis v. United States*, 341 U.S. 494 (1951) (excerpted in Vol. 2, Ch. 5). That law made it a crime "to organize any society . . . advocat[ing] . . . the overthrow or destruction of any government of the United States." Subsequently, Congress enacted the Internal Security Act of 1950 and the Communist Control Act of 1954, aimed at flushing out communists and others belonging to "subversive organizations."

The Cold War in the 1950s and 1960s also led to congressional "witch hunts." The House Un-American Activities Committee (HUAC), established in 1938 and not abolished until 1974, and the Senate Permanent Investigations Subcommittee, chaired by Wisconsin Senator Joseph R. McCarthy, subpoenaed hundreds of individuals to testify about alleged communist activities. In response to challenges to the investigations, the Court ruled that witnesses may refuse to answer vague and irrelevant questions; see *Watkins v. United States*, 354 U.S. 178 (1957); and *Barenblatt v. United States*, 360 U.S. 109 (1959) (both excerpted in Vol. 1, Ch. 5). But, the Court was initially reluctant to check Congress or the executive branch. However, *United States v. Robel*, 389 U.S. 258 (1967), struck down a section of the Internal Security Act, making it unlawful for a member of a communist-action organization to work in a defense facility, for sweeping "too indiscriminately" and "literally establish[ing] guilt by association."

Besides limiting freedom of speech, press, and association, the government also detained and incarcerated immigrants and citizens, along with suspending other guarantees of the Bill of Rights. In *Ex parte Milligan*, 71 U.S. 2 (1866) (excerpted in Ch. 3), the Court overruled President Abraham Lincoln's use of military courts to try civilians accused of disloyalty during the Civil War. Yet during World War II it upheld the internment of over 110,000 Japanese-Americans—70,000 of whom were U.S. citizens—as "enemy aliens" without evidence of their disloyalty, in *Korematsu v. United States*, 323 U.S. 214 (1944) (excerpted in Vol. 1, Ch. 3). On the same day *Korematsu* came down, though, the Court ruled, in *Ex parte Endo*, 323 U.S. 283 (1944), that, although the evacuation was permissible, the detention of loyal Japanese-Americans was unconstitutional.

During World War II the Court also approved the use of military tribunals to try eight German saboteurs, including one naturalized U.S. citizen, for sabotaging bridges and utility plants. In *Ex parte Quirin*, 317 U.S. 1 (1942), the Court ruled that the president has the "power . . . to carry into effect . . . all laws defining and punishing offenses against the law of nations, including those which pertain to the conduct of war." Chief Justice Stone added that there was no distinction between U.S. citizens and noncitizens deemed belligerents. As he put it: "citizenship in the United States of an enemy belligerent does not relieve him from the consequences of a belligerency which is unlawful."

At the end of World War II, the Court upheld the use of military commissions to try leaders of the Japanese Imperial Military in *In re Yamashita*, 327 U.S. 1 (1946). The Court also held, in *Johnson v. Eisentrager*, 339 U.S. 763 (1950), that federal courts have no jurisdiction over *habeas corpus* petitions filed by foreign nationals held overseas by U.S. military forces. In *Reid v. Covert*, 354 U.S. 1 (1957), though, the Court ruled that U.S. citizens who are dependents of military personnel stationed abroad may not be subject to courts-martial or denied rights guaranteed in the Bill of Rights. For that reason, John Walker Lindh, the young American captured fighting with the Taliban in Afghanistan, was accorded counsel and prosecuted in federal court.

In the aftermath of the 9/11 terrorist attacks, the boundaries between the rights of citizens and noncitizens were once again blurred. International and constitutional law has long recognized that during wartime the government has special powers over foreign nationals from a country at war. The Bush administration advanced the position that the war against international terrorism was different because it was against Al Qaeda and other terrorists, not a nation. Over 3,000 foreign nationals from the Middle East were detained and another 6,000 targeted for deportation. The administration rejected international criticism of its indefinite and incommunicado detention of about 650 foreign nationals as "enemy combatants" in Guantánamo Bay, Cuba. The administration initially distinguished between the rights of citizens and foreign nationals, but then blurred the line, drawing sharp criticism from commentators and some lower federal courts, for its treatment of U.S. citizens as "enemy combatants."

(continues)

■ CONSTITUTIONAL HISTORY
Citizens, Noncitizens, "Enemy Combatants," and
Civil Rights in Wartime (continued)

The line between the rights of citizens and foreign nationals has been breached in the past. The Constitution expressly distinguishes the rights of citizenship in certain respects: only citizens may run for elective federal office and their right to vote may not be denied discriminatorily. In addition, Article IV guarantees citizens "privileges and immunities" and they may involve diversity jurisdiction of the federal courts under the Eleventh Amendment. Yet all other rights are not so literally limited. The Fourth Amendment guarantee against "unreasonable searches and seizures," for instance, extends to all "people." The Fifth and Fourteenth Amendment guarantees of due process and equal protection extend to all "persons," including resident foreign nationals.

Accordingly, the Court has held that neither the First nor the Fifth Amendment "acknowledges any distinction between citizens and resident aliens," *Kwong Hai Chew v. Colding*, 344 U.S. 590 (1953). The Court re-affirmed that "the Due Process Clause applies to all 'persons' within the United States, including aliens, whether their presence here is lawful, un-lawful, temporary, or permanent," in *Zadvydas v. Davis*, 533 U.S. 678 (2001). It also has repeatedly held that equal protection is "universal in [its] application to all persons within the territorial jurisdiction, without regard to differences of . . . nationality," *Yick Wo v. Hopkins*, 118 U.S. 356 (1886); see also *Plyer v. Doe*, 457 U.S. 2002 (1982) (excerpted in Vol. 2, Ch. 12, rejecting the denial of public education to children of illegal aliens).

At the same time, citizens and noncitizens are not similarly situated. Al-though the Court has held that state laws discriminating against aliens may be presumptively invalid, in *Graham v. Richardson*, 403 U.S. 365 (1971), it has permitted states to bar foreign nationals from public employment as police officers, schoolteachers, and probation officers; see *Foley v. Connelie*, 435 U.S. 291 (1978); *Ambach v. Norwick*, 441 U.S. 68 (1979); and *Cabell v. Chavez-Salido*, 454 U.S. 432 (1982).

The status of citizens and noncitizens diverges most sharply with re-spect to detention, deportation, and immigration. Citizens may not be expelled from the country, whereas noncitizens may be expelled for even minor infractions. As the Court observed in *Mathews v. Diaz*, 426 U.S. 67 (1976): "In the exercise of its broad power over naturalization and immi-gration, Congress regularly makes rules that would be unacceptable if ap-plied to citizens." The Court has, thus, permitted the exclusion and expulsion of foreign nationals on the basis of their race and if they have committed certain crimes, in *Chae Chan Ping v. United States*, 130 U.S. 581 (1889) and *Yamataya v. Fisher*, 189 U.S. 861 (1903); it has also allowed their deportation because of political associations, in *Shaughnesy v. United States ex rel. Mezei*, 345 U.S. 206 (1953).

In *United States v. Salerno*, 481 U.S. 739 (1987), the Court nonetheless blurred the line between citizens and noncitizens when upholding the pretrial detention for two years, without bail, of a citizen as "regulatory, not penal," and hence not a violation of due process. In *dictum*, referring to times of "war or insurrection," Chief Justice Rehnquist added that "the government may detain individuals whom the government believes to be dangerous." However, in *Zadvydas v. Davis*, 533 U.S. 678 (2001), the Court ruled that legal immigrant felons are entitled to due process and may not be held indefinitely—longer than six months—under deportation orders when countries refuse to take them back. Subsequently, though, a bare majority in *Demore v. Kim*, 538 U.S. 510 (2003), upheld a federal statute mandating preventive detention during deportation proceedings of foreign nationals accused of certain crimes, based on statistics showing that a high percentage of "criminal aliens" commit more offenses after their release and fail to reappear at deportation hearings.

The detentions and deportations of immigrants of Middle East origins in the aftermath of 9/11 gave rise to a new series of litigation. The adoption by the Immigration and Naturalization Service (INS) of secret deportation hearings resulted in conflicting lower federal court rulings. The U.S. Court of Appeals for the Sixth Circuit held that the First Amendment guarantees a right of access for the press and the media to the proceedings, while the Third and District of Columbia Circuit courts ruled contrariwise. The Supreme Court denied review of the latter decisions (for further discussion of claims to a right of access see Vol. 2, Ch. 5).

The Court had inexorably to consider appeals of the treatment of "enemy combatants" and to clarify the rights of foreign nationals, as well as U.S. citizens. The Court reviewed cases involving foreign nationals captured in Afghanistan and Pakistan, in *Rasul v. Bush* (2004) (excerpted in this chapter). *Rasul* posed the question of whether federal courts have jurisdiction over challenges to the legality of holding foreign nationals detained in Guan-tánamo Bay. By a six-to-three vote the Court ruled that federal courts have jurisdiction over foreign nationals held in Guantánamo Bay, Cuba, and that these nationals have the right to seek independent review of their detention.

The Court also granted the appeal of a U.S. citizen declared an "enemy combatant," Yaser Esam Hamdi. Hamdi was born in Baton Rouge, Louisiana, then moved as a child to his parents' homeland in Saudi Arabia, where he was raised. He eventually went to Afghanistan, where he was captured fighting alongside the Taliban. He was initially taken to Guantánamo, but once his U.S. citizenship was discovered he was designated an "enemy combatant" and moved to a brig in Norfolk, Virginia. Hamdi

(continues)

■ CONSTITUTIONAL HISTORY
*Citizens, Noncitizens, "Enemy Combatants," and
Civil Rights in Wartime (continued)*

challenged his detention and denial of legal representation as a violation of the Fifth and the Fourteenth Amendments. Before the government could respond, a federal district court judge appointed a public defender and ordered the government to allow Hamdi to consult with an attorney. The Bush administration appealed and the Court of Appeals for the Fourth Circuit reversed. In December 2003, the Bush administration decided to allow Hamdi to consult with an attorney, though maintaining that it could hold him without further judicial hearings. The Court granted an appeal and held in *Hamdi v. Rumsfeld,* 542 U.S. 507 (2004) that Hamdi had the right to contest his detention before an independent tribunal. Writing for a bare majority, Justice O'Connor ruled that the Authorization on the Use of Military Force Act (AUMF) of 2001, enacted after the 9/11 terrorist attacks, authorized the detaining of U.S. citizens, though not indefinitely, but that Hamdi was entitled to *habeas* relief. By a six-to-three vote, Justice O'Connor also ruled that due process entitled Hamdi to the right to consult an attorney and to a hearing before a tribunal—whether civil or military was left open. In an opinion concurring and dissenting in part, Justice Souter, joined by Justice Ginsburg, agreed with the rejection of the Bush administration's position on the role of courts but concluded that the Non–Detention Act of 1971, which stipulates that Congress must enact legislation expressly authorizing the detention of individuals, was run afoul by the unauthorized detention of enemy combatants. Justice Souter disagreed with Justice O'Connor's position that the AUMF authorized such detentions. Justice Scalia, joined by Justice Stevens, also rejected the Bush administration's position in pointing out that Congress had not suspended access to courts for *habeas* relief. In their view, the proper course would be to try citizen combatants for treason. Only dissenting Justice Thomas embraced Bush's broad claims of presidential power. Subsequently, in a plea agreement Hamdi renounced his U.S. citizenship and was returned to Saudia Arabia.

In response to the ruling in *Hamdi* Congress enacted the Detainee Treatment Act (DTA) of 2005, which stripped federal courts of jurisdiction over *habeas* appeals from detainees. And Bush on his own authority established military tribunals to review the basis for detaining enemy combatants, but their procedures did not comply with those of the Uniform Code of Military Justice (UCMJ) or the Geneva Conventions.

When the DTA and Bush's orders establishing military tribunals were challenged in *Hamdan v. Rumsfeld*, 542 U.S. 507 (2006), the Court split six to three. Writing for the majority, Justice Stevens held that Hamdan—who was

Osama Bin Ladin's driver and was captured in Afghanistan—had a statutory right to *habeas* relief, because his case was pending when the DTA was enacted. But again the Court avoided ruling on whether there was a constitutional right to a writ of *habeas corpus* and on the constitutionality of Congress's stripping federal courts of *habeas* jurisdiction. Justice Stevens, however, furthermore rejected Bush's claim of inherent power to establish the military tribunals in holding that express congressional authorization was needed to try combatants and to try them in accord with the Geneva Conventions and that the tribunals failed to comply with the UCMJ and the procedures of a regularly constituted court. By contrast, Justices Scalia, Thomas, and Alito maintained that Bush had authority as commander in chief under Article 2 to create the tribunals, and the president was entitled to judicial deference.

Congress in turn responded to *Hamdan* by enacting the Military Commissions Act (MCA) of 2006. That law denied federal courts jurisdiction over *habeas* appeals by detainees, authorized the president to establish military commissions and interrogation methods, as well as gave the president the authority to interpret procedural guarantees for detainees so long as they did not pose "grave breaches" of the Geneva Conventions or constitute "cruel, unusual or inhumane treatment." The MCA, though, also rejected the right to a speedy trial, required military defense attorneys, and specified that the commissions' decisions need not be unanimous.

When provisions of the MCA were challenged in *Boumediene v. Bush*, 549 U.S. 1328 (2007), the Roberts Court initially denied review but subsequently reversed course and granted review. A bare majority then held that even foreign nationals have a *constitutional* right to apply to federal courts for writs of *habeas corpus* and to judicial review of the basis for their detention. Writing for the Court, in *Boumediene v. Bush* (2008) (excerpted in this chapter), Justice Kennedy observed that "The laws and Constitution are designed to survive, and remain in force, in extraordinary times." Chief Justice Roberts and Justice Scalia each filed dissenting opinions, which were joined by Justices Thomas and Alito.

Subsequently, during the 2008 presidential election Barack Obama vowed to close by January 2010 the prison in Guantanamo Bay, Cuba, in which over 650 "enemy combatants" had been held after the 9/11 terrorist attacks. A large number had been repatriated or sent to third-party countries by late 2009, when President Obama's administration announced that it would no longer claim the power to detain suspects as "enemy combatants" and also that meeting the January deadline would be impossible until later in 2010. Additionally, the administration announced that some of the detainees—including Khalid Sheikh Mohammed and four other co-conspirators involved in the 9/11 terrorist attacks—would be tried in civil courts, while others would be tried by military commissions; and most of the remaining detainees would be repatriated or transferred to federal prisons.

■ IN COMPARATIVE PERSPECTIVE

The House of Lords Rules against the Indefinite Detention of Terrorists

As a result of the continued conflicts in North Ireland, the United Kingdom enacted the Terrorism Act of 2000, which broadened the definition of terrorism, prohibited fund-raising for terrorist organizations, and expanded law enforcement powers to stop, search, arrest, and detain suspected terrorists. But after the international terrorist attacks on September 11, 2001, on the Twin Towers and the Pentagon, the Parliament enacted the Anti-Terrorism, Crime, and Security Act of 2001, which, among other things, derogated obligations under Article 5 of the European Convention on Human Rights that prohibit detention without trial.

The provisions of the Anti-Terrorism, Crime, and Security Act were subsequently challenged and the House of Lords in an eight-to-one decision, in *A(FC) and others (FC) v. Secretary of State for the Home Department*, [2004] UKHL 56, held that indefinite detention of suspected terrorists without charge or trial violates Articles 5 and 14 of the European Convention on Human Rights, issuing a "declaration of incompatibility" (since English courts have no power to invalidate legislation), and referring the matter back to Parliament. Lord Bingham issued the lead opinion and found that the flaw in the detention policy was the way it discriminated against foreign nations. In his words:

> The appellants share certain common characteristics which are central to their appeals. All are foreign (non-UK) nationals. None has been subject of any criminal charge. In none of their

The Prize Cases

2 BL. (67 U.S.) 935, 17 L.ED. 459 (1863)

After the outbreak of the Civil War in April 1861 but before convening a special session of Congress, President Abraham Lincoln declared the Southern states in rebellion and ordered a blockade of their ports. Congress subsequently passed legislation authorizing his actions, yet Lincoln

cases is a criminal trial in prospect. All challenge the lawfulness of their detention. More specifically, they all contend that such detention was inconsistent with obligations binding on the United Kingdom under the European Convention on Human Rights. . . .

The appellants were treated differently from both suspected international terrorists who were not UK nationals but could be removed and also from suspected international terrorists who were UK-nationals and could not be removed. There can be no doubt but that the difference in treatment was on grounds of nationality or immigration status (one of the proscribed grounds under Article 14).

Lord Walker, the lone dissenter, countered that:

The appropriate intensity of scrutiny of decisions in this crucial area—involving both national security and individual rights—presents a dilemma. . . . The court should show a high degree of respect for the Secretary of State's appreciation, based on secret intelligence sources, of the security risks; but at the same time the court should subject to a very close scrutiny the practical effect which derogating measures have on human rights, the importance of the rights affected, and the robustness of any safeguards intended to minimize the impact of the derogating measures on individual human rights.

In 2005, Parliament enacted a new anti-terrorism act that authorizes judges to impose a range of restrictions on terrorist suspects, short of imprisonment, including placing them under house arrest, imposing nighttime curfews, requiring electronic tagging, and barring their use of cell phones and computers. The law expired in 2006, some provisions were renewed and suspected terrorists may be held without charges for twenty-eight days.

maintained that his actions were justifiable given his inherent powers as commander in chief and legislation in 1795 and 1807 that had delegated certain war powers to the president. The owners of several ships, which had been seized and confiscated in the blockade, unsuccessfully challenged the legality of the blockade in federal district courts and then appealed to the Supreme Court. Justice Robert Grier's opinion for the Court affirming the actions of the president prompted dissenting Justice Samuel Nelson to issue a sharply worded reminder of the importance of the rule of law and constitutional constraints on the president.

The Court's decision was five to four, and the majority's opinion was announced by Justice Grier. Justice Nelson dissented, as did Chief Justice Taney and Justices Clifford and Catron.

☐ *Justice GRIER delivers the opinion of the Court.*

Had the President a right to institute a blockade of ports in possession of persons in armed rebellion against the government, on the principles of international law, as known and acknowledged among civilized States? . . .

That the President, as the Executive Chief of the Government and Commander-in-Chief of the Army and Navy, was the proper person to make such notification, has not been, and cannot be disputed.

The right of prize and capture has its origin in the "*jus belli,*" and is governed and adjudged under the laws of nations. To legitimate the capture of a neutral vessel or property on the high seas, a war must exist *de facto*, and the neutral must have a knowledge or notice of the intention of one of the parties belligerent to use this mode of coercion against a port, city or territory, in possession of the other.

Let us inquire whether, at the time this blockade was instituted, a state of war existed which would justify a resort to these means of subduing the hostile force.

War has been well defined to be, "That state in which a nation prosecutes its right by force." . . .

By the Constitution, Congress alone has the power to declare a national or foreign war. It cannot declare war against a State or any number of States, by virtue of any clause in the Constitution. The Constitution confers on the President the whole executive power. He is bound to take care that the laws be faithfully executed. He is Commander-in-Chief of the Army and Navy of the United States, and of the militia of the several States when called into the actual service of the United States. He has no power to initiate or declare a war either against a foreign nation or a domestic State. But by the Acts of Congress of Feb. 28th, 1795, ch. 36 (1 Stat. at L., 424), and 3d of March 1807, ch. 39 (1 Stat. at L., 443), he is authorized to call out the militia and use military and naval forces of the United States in case of invasion by foreign nations, and to suppress insurrection against the government of a State or of the United States.

If a war be made by invasion of a foreign Nation, the President is not only authorized but bound to resist force, by force. He does not initiate the war, but is bound to accept the challenge without waiting for any special legislative authority. And whether the hostile party be a foreign invader, or States organized as rebellion, it is none the less a war, although the declaration of it be *"unilateral."* . . .

Whether the President in fulfilling his duties, as Commander-in-Chief, in suppressing an insurrection, has met with such armed hostile resistance, and a civil war of such alarming proportions as will compel him to accord to them the character of belligerents, is a question to be decided by him, and this court must be governed by the decisions and acts of the Political Department of the government to which this power was intrusted. "He must determine what degree of force the crisis demands." The proclamation of blockade is, itself, official and conclusive evidence to the court that a state of war existed which demanded and authorized a recourse to such a measure, under the circumstances peculiar to the case.

☐ *Justice NELSON, joined by Chief Justice TANEY and Justices CATRON and CLIFFORD, dissenting.*

[W]e are asked: what would become of the peace and integrity of the Union, in case of an insurrection at home or invasion from abroad, if this power could not be exercised by the President in the recess of Congress, and until that body could be assembled?

The framers of the Constitution fully comprehended this question, and provided for the contingency. Indeed, it would have been surprising if they had not, as a rebellion had occurred in the State of Massachusetts while the Convention was in session, and which had become so general that it was quelled only by calling upon the military power of the State. The Constitution declares that Congress shall have power "to provide for calling forth the militia to execute the laws of the Union, suppress insurrections, and repel invasions." Another clause, "that the President shall be Commander-in-chief of the Army and Navy of the United States, and of the Militia of the several States when called into the actual service of the United States;" and, again: "He shall take care that the laws shall be faithfully executed." Congress passed laws on this subject in 1792 and 1795.

The last Act provided that whenever the United States shall be invaded or be in imminent danger of invasion from a foreign nation, it shall be lawful for the President to call forth such number of the militia most convenient to the place of danger, and in case of insurrection in any State against the government thereof, it shall be lawful for the President, on the application of the Legislature of such State, if in session, or if not, of the Executive of the State to call forth such number of militia of any other State or States, as he may judge sufficient to suppress such insurrection. . . .

It has also been argued that this power of the President from necessity should be construed as vesting him with the war power, or the Republic might greatly suffer or be in danger from the attacks of the hostile party before the assembling of Congress. But we have seen that the whole military and naval forces are in his hands under the municipal laws of the country. He can meet the adversary upon land and water with all the forces of the government. The truth is, this idea of the existence of any necessity for clothing the President with the war power, under the Act of 1795, is simply a monstrous exaggeration; for, besides having the command of the whole of the army and navy, Congress can be assembled within any thirty days, if the safety of the country requires that the war power shall be brought into operation. . . .

So the war carried on by the President against the insurrectionary districts in the Southern States, as in the case of the King of Great Britain in the American Revolution, was a personal war against those in rebellion, and with encouragement and support of loyal citizens with a view to their cooperation and aid in suppressing the insurgents, with this difference, as the war making power belonged to the King, he might have recognized or declared the war at the beginning to be a civil war which would draw after it all the rights of a belligerent, but in the case of the President no such power existed; the war, therefore, from necessity, was a personal war, until Congress assembled and acted upon this state of things.

Down to this period the only enemy recognized by the government was the persons engaged in the rebellion, all others were peaceful citizens, entitled to all the privileges of citizens under the Constitution. Certainly it cannot rightfully be said that the President has the power to convert a loyal citizen into a belligerent enemy or confiscate his property as enemy's property.

Congress assembled on the call for an extra session the 4th July, 1861, and among the first Acts passed was one in which the President was authorized by proclamation to interdict all trade and intercourse between all the inhabitants of States in insurrection and rest of the United States, subjecting vessel and cargo to capture and condemnation as prize, and also to direct the capture of any ship or vessel belonging in whole or in part to any inhabitant of a State whose inhabitants are declared by the proclamation to be in a state of insurrection, found at sea or in any part of the rest of the United States. Act of Congress of 13 July, 1861, Secs. 5, 6. The 4th section also authorized the President to close any port in a Collection District obstructed so that the revenue could not be collected and provided for the capture and condemnation of any vessel attempting to enter.

The President's Proclamation was issued on the 16th August following, and embraced Georgia, North and South Carolina, part of Virginia, Tennessee, Alabama, Louisiana, Texas, Arkansas, Mississippi and Florida.

This Act of Congress, we think, recognized a state of civil war between the government and the Confederate States. . . .

Upon the whole, after the most careful consideration of this case which the pressure of other duties has admitted, I am compelled to the conclusion that no civil war existed between this Government and the States in insurrection till recognized by the Act of Congress 13th July, 1861; that the President does not possess the power under the Constitution to declare war or recognize its existence within the meaning of the law of nations, which carries with it belligerent rights, and thus change the country and all its citizens from a state of peace to a state of war; that this power belongs exclusively to the Congress of the United States and, consequently, that the President had no power to set on foot a blockade under the law of nations, and the capture of the vessel and cargo in this case, and in all cases before us in which the capture occurred before the 13th July, 1861, for breach of blockade, or as enemies' property, are illegal and void, and that the decrees of condemnation should be reversed and the vessel and cargo restored.

Ex parte Milligan

4 WALL. (71 U.S.) 2, 18 L.ED. 281 (1866)

In 1862, President Abraham Lincoln ordered the suspension of the writ of *habeas corpus* and that all persons disloyal to the Union should be tried and punished by court-martial or military commissions. In 1863,

Congress passed legislation suspending the writ. A year later, Lambdin P. Milligan, a lawyer sympathizing with the Confederacy, was seized and tried by a military commission in Indiana. He appealed to the federal circuit court for a writ of *habeas corpus* and challenged the commission's jurisdiction, because Indiana was not a state in insurrection and had functioning civil courts. The circuit judges were sharply divided and decided to certify certain questions—pertaining to the issuance of a writ of *habeas corpus* and the jurisdiction of the military commission— to the Supreme Court for decision. The Court unanimously ruled against the president's actions on the grounds that Congress had not authorized the use of courts-martial in an opinion by Justice David Davis, an appointee of President Lincoln. But Chief Justice Salmon Chase, in a separate opinion joined by three other justices, took strong exception to Justice Davis's opinion, also holding that it is not within Congress's power to establish military commissions.

The Court's decision was five to four, and the majority's opinion was announced by Justice Davis. Chief Justice Chase concurred in part and dissented in part, and was joined by Justices Wayne, Swayne, and Miller.

☐ *Justice DAVIS delivers the opinion of the Court.*

The controlling question in the case is this: Upon *the facts* stated in Milligan's petition, and the exhibits filed, had the military commission mentioned in it *jurisdiction*, legally, to try and sentence him? Milligan, not a resident of one of the rebellious states, or a prisoner of war, but a citizen of Indiana for twenty years past, and never in the military or naval service, is, while at his home, arrested by the military power of the United States, imprisoned, and, on certain criminal charges preferred against him, tried, convicted, and sentenced to be hanged by a military commission, organized under the direction of the military commander of the military district of Indiana. Had this tribunal the *legal* power and authority to try and punish this man?

No graver question was ever considered by this court, nor one which more nearly concerns the rights of the whole people; for it is the birthright of every American citizen when charged with crime, to be tried and punished according to law. The power of punishment is alone through the means which the laws have provided for that purpose, and if they are ineffectual, there is an immunity from punishment, no matter how great an offender the individual may be, or how much his crimes may have shocked the sense of justice of the country, or endangered its safety. By the protection of the law human rights are secured; withdraw that protection, and they are at the mercy of wicked rulers, or the clamor of an excited people. If there was law to justify this military trial, it is not our province to interfere; if there was not, it is our duty to declare the nullity of the whole proceedings. The decision of this question does not depend on argument or judicial precedents, numerous and highly illustrative as they are. These precedents inform us of the extent of the struggle to preserve liberty and to relieve those in civil life from military trials. The founders of our government were familiar with the history of that struggle; and secured in a written constitution every right which the people had wrested from power during a contest of ages. By the Constitution and the laws authorized by it this question must be determined. The provisions of that instrument on the administration of criminal justice are too plain and direct, to leave room for misconstruction or doubt of their true meaning. Those applicable to this case are found in that clause of the original Constitution which says, "That the trial of all crimes, except in case of impeachment, shall be by jury"; and in the fourth, fifth, and sixth articles of the amendments. . . .

The Constitution of the United States is a law for rulers and people, equally in war and in peace, and covers with the shield of its protection all classes of men, at all times, and under all circumstances. No doctrine, involving more pernicious consequences, was ever invented by the wit of man than that any of its provisions can be suspended during any of the exigencies of government. Such a doctrine leads directly to anarchy or despotism, but the theory of necessity on which it is based is false; for the government, within the Constitution, has all the powers granted to it, which are necessary to preserve its existence, as has been happily proved by the results of the great effort to throw off its just authority. . . .

Have any of the rights guaranteed by the Constitution been violated in the case of Milligan? and if so, what are they?

Every trial involves the exercise of judicial power; and from what source did the military commission that tried him derive their authority? Certainly no part of the judicial power of the country was conferred on them; because the Constitution expressly vests it "in one supreme court and such inferior courts as the Congress may from time to time ordain and establish," and it is not pretended that the commission was a court ordained and established by Congress. They cannot justify on the mandate of the President; because he is controlled by law, and has his appropriate sphere of duty, which is to execute, not to make, the laws; and there is "no unwritten criminal code to which resort can be had as a source of jurisdiction."

But it is said that the jurisdiction is complete under the "laws and usages of war."

It can serve no useful purpose to inquire what those laws and usages are, whence they originated, where found, and on whom they operate; they can never be applied to citizens in states which have upheld the authority of the government, and where the courts are open and their process unobstructed. This court has judicial knowledge that in Indiana the Federal authority was always unopposed, and its courts always open to hear criminal accusations and redress grievances; and no usage of war could sanction a military trial there for any offence whatever of a citizen in civil life, in nowise connected with the military service. Congress could grant no such power; and to the honor of our national legislature be it said, it has never been provoked by the state of the country even to attempt its exercise. One of the plainest constitutional provisions was, therefore, infringed when Milligan was tried by a court not ordained and established by Congress, and not composed of judges appointed during good behavior.

Why was he not delivered to the Circuit Court of Indiana to be proceeded against according to law? No reason of necessity could be urged against it; because Congress had declared penalties against the offences charged, provided for their punishment, and directed that court to hear and determine them. And soon after this military tribunal was ended, the Circuit Court met, peacefully transacted its business, and adjourned. It needed no bayonets to protect it, and required no military aid to execute its judgments. It was held in a state, eminently distinguished for patriotism, by judges commissioned during the Rebellion, who were provided with juries, upright, intelligent, and selected by a marshal appointed by the President. The government had no right to conclude that Milligan, if guilty, would not receive in that court merited punishment; for its records disclose that it was constantly engaged in the trial of similar offences, and was never interrupted in its administration of criminal justice. If it was dangerous, in the distracted condition of affairs, to leave Milligan unrestrained of his liberty, because he "conspired against the government, afforded aid and comfort to rebels, and incited the people to insurrection," the law said arrest him, confine him closely, render him powerless to do further mischief; and then present his case to the grand jury of the district, with proofs of his guilt, and, if indicted, try him according to the course of the common law. If this had been done, the Constitution would have been vindicated, the law of 1863 enforced, and the securities for personal liberty preserved and defended.

Another guarantee of freedom was broken when Milligan was denied a trial by jury. The great minds of the country have differed on the correct interpretation to be given to various provisions of the Federal Constitution; and judicial decision has been often invoked to settle their true meaning; but until recently no one ever doubted that the right of trial by jury was fortified in the organic law against the power of attack. It is now assailed; but if ideas can be expressed in words, and language has any meaning, *this right*—one of the most valuable in a free country—is preserved to every one accused of crime who is not attached to the army, or navy, or militia in actual service. The sixth amendment affirms that "in all criminal prosecutions the accused shall enjoy the right to a speedy and public trial by an impartial jury," language broad enough to embrace all persons and cases; but the fifth, recognizing the necessity of an indictment, or presentment, before any one can be held to answer for high crimes, "*except* cases arising in the land or naval forces, or in the militia, when in actual service, in time of war or public danger"; and the framers of the Constitution, doubtless, meant to limit the right of trial by jury, in the sixth amendment, to those persons who were subject to indictment or presentment in the fifth. . . .

It is claimed that martial law covers with its broad mantle the proceedings of this military commission. The proposition is this: that in a time of war the commander of an armed force (if in his opinion the exigencies of the country demand it, and of which he is to judge), has the power, within the lines of his military district, to suspend all civil rights and their remedies, and subject citizens as well as soldiers to the rule of *his will*; and in the exercise of his lawful authority cannot be restrained, except by his superior officer or the President of the United States.

If this position is sound to the extent claimed, then when war exists, foreign or domestic, and the country is subdivided into military departments for mere convenience, the commander of one of them can, if he chooses, within his limits, on the plea of necessity, with the approval of the Executive, substitute military force for and to the exclusion of the laws, and punish all persons, as he thinks right and proper, without fixed or certain rules.

The statement of this proposition shows its importance; for, if true, republican government is a failure, and there is an end of liberty regulated by law. Martial law, established on such a basis, destroys every guarantee of the Constitution, and effectually renders the "military independent of and superior to the civil power"—the attempt to do which by the King of Great Britain was deemed by our fathers such an offence, that they assigned it to the world as one of the causes which impelled them to declare their independence. Civil liberty and this kind of martial law cannot endure together; the antagonism is irreconcilable; and, in the conflict, one or the other must perish.

This nation, as experience has proved, cannot always remain at peace, and has no right to expect that it will always have wise and humane rulers, sincerely attached to the principles of the Constitution. Wicked men, ambitious of power, with hatred of liberty and contempt of law, may fill the place once occupied by Washington and Lincoln; and if this right is conceded, and the calamities of war again befall us, the dangers to human liberty are frightful to contemplate. If our fathers had failed to provide for just such a contingency, they would have been false to the trust reposed in them. They knew—the history of the world told them—the nation they were founding, be its existence short or long, would be involved in war; how often or how long continued, human foresight could not tell; and that unlimited power, wherever lodged at such a time, was especially hazardous to freemen. For this, and other equally weighty reasons, they secured the inheritance they had fought to maintain, by incorporating in a written constitution the safeguards which *time* had proved were essential to its preservation. Not one of these safeguards can the President, or Congress, or the Judiciary disturb, except the one concerning the writ of *habeas corpus*.

It is essential to the safety of every government that, in a great crisis, like the one we have just passed through, there should be a power somewhere of suspending the writ of *habeas corpus*. In every war, there are men of previously good character, wicked enough to counsel their fellow-citizens to resist the measures deemed necessary by a good government to sustain its just authority and overthrow its enemies; and their influence may lead to dangerous combinations. In the emergency of the times, an immediate public investigation according to law may not be possible; and yet, the peril to the country may be too imminent to suffer such persons to go at large. Unquestionably, there is then an exigency which demands that the government, if it should see fit in the exercise of a proper discretion to make arrests, should not be required to produce the persons arrested in answer to a writ of *habeas corpus*. The Constitution goes no further. It does not say after a writ of *habeas corpus* is denied a citizen, that he shall be tried otherwise than by the course of the common law; if it had intended this result, it was easy by the use of direct words to have accomplished it. The illustrious men who framed that instrument were guarding the foundations of civil liberty against the abuses of unlimited power; they were full of wisdom, and the lessons of history informed them that a trial by an established court, assisted by an impartial jury, was the only sure way of protecting the citizen against oppression and wrong. Knowing this, they limited the suspension to one great right, and left the rest to remain forever inviolable. But, it is insisted that the safety of the country in time of war demands that this broad claim for martial law shall be sustained. If this were true, it could be well said that a country, preserved at the sacrifice of all the cardinal principles of liberty, is not worth the cost of preservation. Happily, it is not so.

It will be borne in mind that this is not a question of the power to proclaim martial law, when war exists in a community and the courts and civil authorities are overthrown. Nor is it a question what rule a military commander, at the head of his army, can impose on states in rebellion to cripple their resources and quell the insurrection. The jurisdiction claimed is much more extensive. The necessities of the service, during the late Rebellion, required that the loyal states should be placed within the limits of certain military districts and commanders appointed in them; and, it is urged, that this, in a military sense, constituted them the theatre of military operations; and, as in this case, Indiana had been and was again threatened with invasion by the enemy, the occasion was furnished to establish martial law. The conclusion does not follow from the premises. If armies were collected in Indiana, they were to be employed in another locality, where the laws were obstructed and the national authority disputed. On *her* soil there was no hostile foot; if once invaded, that invasion was at an end, and with it all pretext for martial law. Martial law cannot arise from a *threatened* invasion. The necessity must be actual and present; the invasion real, such as effectually closes the courts and deposes the civil administration.

It is difficult to see how the *safety* of the country required martial law in Indiana. If any of her citizens were plotting treason, the power of arrest could secure them, until the government was prepared for their trial, when the courts were open and ready to try them. It was as easy to protect witnesses before a civil as a military tribunal; and as there could be no wish to convict, except on sufficient legal evidence, surely an ordained and established court was better able to judge of this than a military tribunal composed of gentlemen not trained to the profession of the law.

It follows, from what has been said on this subject, that there are occasions when martial rule can be properly applied. If, in foreign invasion or civil war, the courts are actually closed, and it is impossible to administer criminal justice according to law, *then*, on the theatre of active military operations, where war really prevails, there is a necessity to furnish a substitute for the civil authority, thus overthrown, to preserve the safety of the army and society; and as no power is left but the military, it is allowed to govern by martial rule until the laws can have their free course. As necessity creates the rule, so it limits its duration; for, if this government is continued *after* the courts are reinstated, it is a gross usurpation of power. Martial rule can never exist where the courts are open, and in the proper and unobstructed exercise of their jurisdiction. It is also confined to the locality of actual war. Because, during the late Rebellion it could have been enforced in Virginia, where the national authority was overturned and the courts driven out, it does not follow that it should obtain in Indiana, where that authority was never disputed, and justice was always administered. And so in the case of a foreign invasion, martial rule may become a necessity in one state, when, in another, it would be "mere lawless violence." . . .

The two remaining questions in this case must be answered in the affirmative. The suspension of the privilege of the writ of *habeas corpus* does not suspend the writ itself. The writ issues as a matter of course; and on the return made to in the court decides whether the party applying is denied the right of proceeding any further with it.

If the military trial of Milligan was contrary to law, then he was entitled, on the facts stated in his petition, to be discharged from custody by the terms of the act of Congress of March 3d, 1863.

☐ *Chief Justice CHASE delivers the following opinion.*

[T]he opinion which has just been read . . . asserts not only that the Military Commission held in Indiana was not authorized by Congress, but that it was not in the power of Congress to authorize it; from which it may be thought to follow, that Congress had no power to indemnify the officers who composed the commission against liability in civil courts for acting as members of it.

We cannot agree to this. . . .

We think that Congress had power, though not exercised, to authorize the Military Commission which was held in Indiana.

Congress has the power not only to raise and support and govern armies, but to declare war. It has, therefore, the power to provide by law for carrying on war. This power necessarily extends to all legislation essential to the prosecution of war with vigor and success, except such as interferes with the command of the forces and conduct of campaigns. That power and duty belong to the President as Commander-in-Chief. Both these powers are derived from the Constitution, but neither is defined by that instrument. Their extent must be determined by their nature, and by the principles of our institutions. . . .

We think that the power of Congress, in such times and in such localities, to authorize trials for crimes against the security and safety of the national forces, may be derived from its constitutional authority to raise and support armies and to declare war, if not from its constitutional authority to provide for governing the national forces. . . .

Justice WAYNE, Justice SWAYNE and Justice MILLER concur with me in these views.

Korematsu v. United States

323 U.S. 214, 65 S.CT. 193 (1944)

Following the Japanese attack on Pearl Harbor in December 1941 and amid growing fears that the West Coast might be invaded, President Franklin D. Roosevelt issued in February 1942 an executive order authorizing the creation of "military zones" in which military commanders could impose curfews and exclude individuals to prevent espionage and sabotage. Congress a month later passed legislation approving these orders and providing criminal penalties for their violation. Tens of thousands of Japanese-Americans along the West Coast were subsequently subjected to curfews, evacuations, and internment in "relocation camps," which were set up farther inland. The constitutionality of these orders was immediately challenged. In *Hirabayashi v. United States*, 320 U.S. 81 (1943), the orders for curfews were upheld, but the Court avoided ruling on the evacuation program. The Court then squarely confronted a challenge to the latter when Toyosaburo Korematsu, a citizen of Japanese ancestry, refused to leave his home in California and was convicted in district court for violating the exclusion order. The Supreme Court granted his petition for *certiorari* after a court of appeals upheld his conviction.

The Court's decision was six to three, and the majority's opinion was announced by Justice Black. A concurring opinion was delivered by Justice Frankfurter. Justices Roberts, Murphy, and Jackson dissented.

☐ *Justice BLACK delivers the opinion of the Court.*

The 1942 Act was attacked in the *Hirabayashi* case [320 U.S. 81] as an unconstitutional delegation of power; it was contended that the curfew order and other orders on which it rested were beyond the war powers of the Congress, the military authorities and of the President, as Commander in Chief of the Army; and finally that to apply the curfew order against none but citizens of Japanese ancestry amounted to a constitutionally prohibited discrimination solely on account of race. To these questions, we gave the serious consideration which their importance justified. We upheld the curfew order as an exercise of the power of the government to take steps necessary to prevent espionage and sabotage in an area threatened by Japanese attack.

In the light of the principles we announced in the *Hirabayashi* case, we are unable to conclude that it was beyond the war power of Congress and the Executive to exclude those of Japanese ancestry from the West Coast war area at the time they did. True, exclusion from the area in which one's home is located is a far greater deprivation than constant confinement to the home from 8 P.M. to 6 A.M. Nothing short of apprehension by the proper military authorities of the gravest imminent danger to the public safety can constitutionally justify either. But exclusion from a threatened area, no less than curfew, has a definite and close relationship to the prevention of espionage and sabotage. The military authorities, charged with the primary responsibility of defending our shores, concluded that curfew provided inadequate protection and ordered exclusion. They did so, as pointed out in our *Hirabayashi* opinion, in accordance with Congressional authority to the military to say who should, and who should not, remain in the threatened areas.

In this case the petitioner challenges the assumptions upon which we rested our conclusions in the *Hirabayashi* case. He also urges that by May 1942, when Order No. 34 was promulgated, all danger of Japanese invasion of the West Coast had disappeared. After careful consideration of these contentions we are compelled to reject them.

Japanese–Americans in an internment camp during World War II.
(*AP/Wide World Photos, Inc.*)

Here, as in the *Hirabayashi* case, "we cannot reject as unfounded the judgment of the military authorities and of Congress that there were disloyal members of that population, whose number and strength could not be precisely and quickly ascertained. We cannot say that the war-making branches of the Government did not have ground for believing that in a critical hour such persons could not readily be isolated and separately dealt with, and constituted a menace to the national defense and safety, which demanded that prompt and adequate measures be taken to guard against it."

Like curfew, exclusion of those of Japanese origin was deemed necessary because of the presence of an unascertained number of disloyal members of the group, most of whom we have no doubt were loyal to this country. It was because we could not reject the finding of the military authorities that it was impossible to bring about an immediate segregation of the disloyal from the loyal that we sustained the validity of the curfew order as applying to the whole group. In the instant case, temporary exclusion of the entire group was rested by the military on the same ground. The judgment that exclusion of the whole group was for the same reason a military imperative answers the contention that the exclusion was in the nature of group punishment based on antagonism to those of Japanese origin. That there were members of the group who retained loyalties to Japan has been confirmed by investigations made subsequent to the exclusion. Approximately five thousand American citizens of Japanese ancestry refused to swear unqualified allegiance to the United States and to renounce allegiance to the Japanese Emperor, and several thousand evacuees requested repatriation to Japan.

We uphold the exclusion order as of the time it was made and when the petitioner violated it. . . . In doing so, we are not unmindful of the hardships imposed by it upon a large group of American citizens. . . . But hardships are part of war, and war is an aggregation of hardships. All citizens alike, both in and out of uniform, feel the impact of war in greater or lesser measure. Citizenship has its responsibilities as well as its privileges, and in time of war the burden is always heavier. Compulsory exclusion of large groups of citizens from their homes, except under circumstances of direst emergency and peril, is inconsistent with our basic governmental institutions. But when under conditions of modern warfare our shores are threatened by hostile forces, the power to protect must be commensurate with the threatened danger. . . .

Since the petitioner has not been convicted of failing to report or to remain in an assembly or relocation center, we cannot in this case determine the validity of those separate provisions of the order. It is sufficient here for us to pass upon the order which petitioner violated. To do more would be to go beyond the issues raised, and to decide momentous questions not contained within the framework of the pleadings or the evidence in this case. It will be time enough to decide the serious constitutional issues which petitioner seeks to raise when an assembly or relocation order is applied or is certain to be applied to him, and we have its terms before us.

Some of the members of the Court are of the view that evacuation and detention in an Assembly Center were inseparable. After May 3, 1942, the date of Exclusion Order No. 34, Korematsu was under compulsion to leave the area not as he would choose but via an Assembly Center. The Assembly Center was conceived as a part of the machinery for group evacuation. The power to exclude includes the power to do it by force if necessary. And any forcible measure must necessarily entail some degree of detention or restraint whatever method of removal is selected. But whichever view is taken, it results in holding that the order under which petitioner was convicted was valid.

It is said that we are dealing here with the case of imprisonment of a citizen in a concentration camp solely because of his ancestry, without evidence or inquiry concerning his loyalty and good disposition towards the United States. Our task would be simple, our duty clear, were this a case involving the imprisonment of a loyal citizen in a concentration camp because of racial prejudice. Regardless of the true nature of the assembly and relocation centers—and we deem it unjustifiable to call them concentration camps with all the ugly connotations that term implies—we are dealing specifically with nothing but an exclusion order. To cast this case into outlines of racial prejudice, without reference to the real military dangers which were presented, merely confuses the issue. Korematsu was not excluded from the Military Area because of hostility to him or his race. He was excluded because we are at war with the Japanese Empire, because the properly constituted military authorities feared an invasion of our West Coast and felt constrained to take proper security measures, because they decided that the military urgency of the situation demanded that all citizens of Japanese ancestry be segregated from the West Coast temporarily, and finally, because Congress, reposing its confidence in this time of war in our military leaders—as inevitably it must—determined that they should have the power to do just this. There was evidence of disloyalty on the part of some, the military authorities considered that the need for action was great, and time was short. We cannot—by availing ourselves of the calm perspective of hindsight—now say that at that time these actions were unjustified.

Affirmed.

□ *Justice FRANKFURTER, concurring.*

According to my reading of Civilian Exclusion Order No. 34, it was an offense for Korematsu to be found in Military Area No. 1, the territory wherein he was previously living, except within the bounds of the established Assembly Center of that area. Even though the various orders issued by General DeWitt be deemed a comprehensive code of instructions, their tenor is clear and not contradictory. They put upon Korematsu the obligation to leave Military Area No. 1, but only by the method prescribed in the instructions, i.e., by reporting to the Assembly Center. I am unable to see how the legal considerations that led to the decision in *Kiyoshi Hirabayashi v. United States* fail to sustain the military order which made the conduct now in controversy a crime. And so I join in the opinion of the Court, but should like to add a few words of my own.

The provisions of the Constitution which confer on the Congress and the President powers to enable this country to wage war are as much part of the Constitution as provisions looking to a nation at peace. And we have had recent occasion to quote approvingly the statement of former Chief Justice HUGHES that the war power of the Government is "the power to wage war successfully." *Hirabayashi v. United States*. Therefore, the validity of action under the war power must be judged wholly in the context of war. That action is not to be stigmatized as lawless because like action in times of peace would be lawless. To talk about a military order that expresses an allowable judgment of war needs by those entrusted with the duty of conducting war as "an unconstitutional order" is to suffuse a part of the Constitution with an atmosphere of unconstitutionality. The respective spheres of action of military authorities and of judges are of course very different. But within their sphere, military authorities are no more outside the bounds of obedience to the Constitution than are judges within theirs. "The war power of the United States, like its other powers . . . is subject to applicable constitutional limitations," *Hamilton v. Kentucky Distilleries Co.*, 251 U.S. 146 [(1919)]. To recognize that military orders are "reasonably expedient military precautions" in time of war and yet to deny them constitutional legitimacy makes of the the Constitution an instrument for dialectic subtleties not reasonably to be attributed to the hard-headed Framers, of whom a majority had had actual participation in war. If a military order such as that under review does not transcend the means appropriate for conducting war, such action by the military is as constitutional as would be any authorized action by the Interstate Commerce Commission within the limits of the constitutional power to regulate commerce. And being an exercise of the war power explicitly granted by the Constitution for safeguarding the national life by prosecuting war effectively, I find nothing in the Constitution which denies to Congress the power to enforce such a valid military order by making its violation an offense triable in the civil courts. . . . To find that the Constitution does not forbid the military measures now complained of does not carry with it approval of that which Congress and the Executive did. That is their business, not ours.

☐ *Justice ROBERTS, dissenting.*

I dissent, because I think the indisputable facts exhibit a clear violation of Constitutional rights.

This is not a case of keeping people off the streets at night as was *Kiyoshi Hirabayashi v. United States*, nor a case of temporary exclusion of a citizen from an area for his own safety or that of the community, nor a case of offering him an opportunity to go temporarily out of an area where his presence might cause danger to himself or to his fellows. On the contrary, it is the case of convicting a citizen as a punishment for not submitting to imprisonment in a concentration camp, based on his ancestry, and solely because of his ancestry, without evidence or inquiry concerning his loyalty and good disposition towards the United States. If this be a correct statement of the facts disclosed by this record, and facts of which we take judicial notice, I need hardly labor the conclusion that Constitutional rights have been violated.

☐ *Justice MURPHY, dissenting.*

This exclusion of "all persons of Japanese ancestry, both alien and non-alien," from the Pacific Coast area on a plea of military necessity in the absence of martial law ought not to be approved. Such exclusion goes over "the very brink of constitutional power" and falls into the ugly abyss of racism.

In dealing with matters relating to the prosecution and progress of a war, we must accord great respect and consideration to the judgments of the military authorities who are on the scene and who have full knowledge of the military facts. The scope of their discretion must, as a matter of necessity and common sense, be wide. And their judgments ought not to be overruled lightly by those whose training and duties ill-equip them to deal intelligently with matters so vital to the physical security of the nation. . . .

The judicial test of whether the Government, on a plea of military necessity, can validly deprive an individual of any of his constitutional rights is whether the deprivation is reasonably related to a public danger that is so "immediate, imminent, and impending" as not to admit of delay and not to permit the intervention of ordinary constitutional processes to alleviate the danger. Civilian Exclusion Order No. 34, banishing from a prescribed area of the Pacific Coast "all persons of Japanese ancestry, both alien and non-alien," clearly does not meet that test. Being an obvious racial discrimination, the order deprives all those within its scope of the equal protection of the laws as guaranteed by the Fifth Amendment. It further deprives these individuals of their constitutional rights to live and work where they will, to establish a home where they choose and to move about freely. In excommunicating them without benefit of hearings, this order also deprives them of all their constitutional rights to procedural due process. Yet no reasonable relation to an "immediate, imminent, and impending" public danger is evident to support this racial restriction which is one of the most sweeping and complete deprivations of constitutional rights in the history of this nation in the absence of martial law. . . .

No adequate reason is given for the failure to treat these Japanese Americans on an individual basis by holding investigations and hearings to separate the loyal from the disloyal, as was done in the case of persons of German and Italian ancestry. It is asserted merely that the loyalties of this group "were unknown and time was of the essence." Yet nearly four months elapsed after Pearl Harbor before the first exclusion order was issued; nearly eight months went by until the last order was issued; and the last of these "subversive" persons was not actually removed until almost eleven months had elapsed. Leisure and deliberation seem to have been more of the essence than speed. And the fact that conditions were not such as to warrant a declaration of martial law adds strength to the belief that the factors of time and military necessity were not as urgent as they have been represented to be. . . .

I dissent, therefore, from this legalization of racism. Racial discrimination in any form and in any degree has no justifiable part whatever in our democratic way of life. It is unattractive in any setting but it is utterly revolting among a free people who have embraced the principles set forth in the Constitution of the United States.

☐ *Justice JACKSON, dissenting.*

Korematsu was born on our soil, of parents born in Japan. The Constitution makes him a citizen of the United States by nativity and a citizen of California by residence. No claim is made that he is not loyal to this country. There is no suggestion that apart from the matter involved here he is not law-abiding and well disposed. Korematsu, however, has been convicted of an act not commonly a crime. It consists merely of being present in the state whereof he is a citizen, near the place where he was born, and where all his life he has lived.

Even more unusual is the series of military orders which made this conduct a crime. They forbid such a one to remain, and they also forbid him to leave. They were so drawn that the only way Korematsu could avoid violation was to give himself up to the military authority. This meant submission to custody, examination, and transportation out of the territory, to be followed by indeterminate confinement in detention camps.

A citizen's presence in the locality, however, was made a crime only if his parents were of Japanese birth. Had Korematsu been one of four—the others being, say, a German alien enemy, an Italian alien enemy, and a citizen of American-born ancestors, convicted of treason but out on parole—only Korematsu's presence would have violated the order. The difference between their innocence and his crime would result, not from anything he did, said, or thought, different than they, but only in that he was born of different racial stock.

Now, if any fundamental assumption underlies our system, it is that guilt is personal and not inheritable. Even if all of one's antecedents had been convicted of treason, the Constitution forbids its penalties to be visited upon him, for it provides that "no Attainder of Treason shall work Corruption of Blood, or Forfeiture except during the Life of the Person attained." Article 3, Sec. 3, cl. 2. But here is an attempt to make an otherwise innocent act a crime merely because this prisoner is the son of parents as to whom he had no choice, and belongs to a race from which there is no way to resign. If Congress in peace-time legislation should enact such a criminal law, I should suppose this Court would refuse to enforce it.

But the "law" which this prisoner is convicted of disregarding is not found in an act of Congress, but in a military order. Neither the Act of Congress nor the Executive Order of the President, nor both together, would afford a basis for this conviction. It rests on the orders of General DeWitt. And it is said that if the military commander had reasonable military grounds for promulgating the orders, they are constitutional and become law, and the Court is required to enforce them. There are several reasons why I cannot subscribe to this doctrine.

It would be impracticable and dangerous idealism to expect or insist that each specific military command in an area of probable operations will conform to conventional tests of constitutionality. When an area is so beset that it must be put under military control at all, the paramount consideration is that its measures be successful, rather than legal. The armed services must protect a society, not merely its Constitution. The very essence of the military job is to marshal physical force, to remove every obstacle to its effectiveness, to give it every strategic advantage. Defense measures will not, and often should not, be held within the limits that bind civil authority in peace. No court can require such a commander in such circumstances to act as a reasonable man; he may be unreasonably cautious and exacting. Perhaps he should be. But a commander in temporarily focusing the life of a community on defense is carrying out a military program; he is not making law in the sense the courts know the term. He issues orders, and they may have a certain authority as military commands, although they may be very bad as constitutional law.

But if we cannot confine military expedients by the Constitution, neither would I distort the Constitution to approve all that the military may deem expedient. That is what the Court appears to be doing, whether consciously or not. I cannot say, from any evidence before me, that the orders of General DeWitt were not reasonably expedient military precautions, nor could I say that they were. But even if they were permissible military procedures, I deny that it follows that they are constitutional. If, as the Court holds, it does follow, then we may as well say that any military order will be constitutional and have done with it.

The limitations under which courts always will labor in examining the necessity for a military order are illustrated by this case. How does the Court know that these orders have a reasonable basis in necessity? No evidence whatever on that subject has been taken by this or any other court. There is sharp controversy as to the credibility of the DeWitt report. So the Court, having no real evidence before it, has no choice but to accept General DeWitt's own unsworn, self-serving statement, untested by any cross-examination, that what he did was reasonable. And thus it will always be when courts try to look into the reasonableness of a military order.

In the very nature of things military decisions are not susceptible of intelligent judicial appraisal. They do not pretend to rest on evidence, but are made on information that often would not be admissible and on assumptions that could not be proved. Information in support of an order could not be disclosed to courts without danger that it would reach the enemy. Neither can courts act on communications made in confidence. Hence courts can never have any real alternative to accepting the mere declaration of the authority that issued the order that it was reasonably necessary from a military viewpoint.

Much is said of the danger to liberty from the Army program for deporting and detaining these citizens of Japanese extraction. But a judicial construction of the due process clause that will sustain this order is a far more subtle blow to liberty than the promulgation of the order itself. A military order, however unconstitutional, is not apt to last longer than the military emergency. Even during that period a succeeding commander may revoke it all. But once a judicial opinion rationalizes such an order to show that it conforms to the Constitution, or rather rationalizes the Constitution to show that the Constitution sanctions such an order, the Court for all time has validated the principle of racial discrimination in criminal procedure and of transplanting American citizens. The principle then lies about like a loaded weapon ready for the hand of any authority that can bring forward a plausible claim of an urgent need. Every repetition imbeds that principle more deeply in our law and thinking and expands it to new purposes. All who observe the work of courts are familiar with what Judge CARDOZO described as "the tendency of a principle to expand itself to the limit of its logic." A military commander may overstep the bounds of constitutionality, and it is an incident. But if we review and approve, that passing incident becomes the doctrine of the Constitution. There it has a generative power of its own, and all that it creates will be in its own image. Nothing better illustrates this danger than does the Court's opinion in this case.

It argues that we are bound to uphold the conviction of Korematsu because we upheld one in *Kiyoshi Hirabayashi v. United States*, when we sustained these orders in so far as they applied a curfew requirement to a citizen of Japanese ancestry. I think we should learn something from that experience.

In that case we were urged to consider only the curfew feature, that being all that technically was involved, because it was the only count necessary to sustain Hirabayashi's conviction and sentence. We yielded, and THE CHIEF JUSTICE guarded the opinion as carefully as language will do. He said: "Our investigation here does not go beyond the inquiry whether, in the light of all the relevant circumstances preceding and attending their promulgation, the challenged orders and statute *afforded a reasonable basis for the action taken in imposing the curfew.*" . . . "We decide only the issue as we have defined it—we decide only that the curfew order as applied, and at the time it was applied, was within the boundaries of the war power." And again: "It is unnecessary to consider whether or to what extent *such findings would support orders differing from the curfew order.*" [Italics supplied.] However, in spite of our limiting words we did validate a discrimination on the basis of ancestry for mild and temporary deprivation of liberty. Now the principle of racial discrimination is pushed from support of mild measures to very harsh ones, and from temporary deprivations to indeterminate ones. And the precedent which it is said requires us to do so is *Hirabayashi*. The Court is now saying that in *Hirabayashi* we did decide the very things we there said we were not deciding. Because we said that these citizens could be made to stay in their homes during the hours of dark, it is said we must require them to leave home entirely; and if that, we are told they may also be taken into custody for deportation; and if that, it is argued they may also be held for some undetermined time in detention camps. How far the principle of this case would be extended before plausible reasons would play out, I do not know.

I should hold that a civil court cannot be made to enforce an order which violates constitutional limitations even if it is a reasonable exercise of military authority. The courts can exercise only the judicial power, can apply only law, and must abide by the Constitution, or they cease to be civil courts and become instruments of military policy. . . .

My duties as a justice as I see them do not require me to make a military judgment as to whether General DeWitt's evacuation and detention program was a reasonable military necessity. I do not suggest that the courts should have attempted to interfere with the Army in carrying out its task. But I do not think they may be asked to execute a military expedient that has no place in law under the Constitution. I would reverse the judgment and discharge the prisoner.

Rasul v. Bush

542 U.S. 466, 124 S.CT. 2686 (2004)

On September 11, 2001, al Qaeda terrorists hijacked four airliners and used them as missiles to attack the World Trade Center in New York and the Pentagon in Virginia, killing approximately 3,000 people and destroying hundreds of millions of dollars of property. In response, Congress passed a joint resolution, Authorization for Use of Military Force (AUMF), authorizing the president to use "all necessary and appropriate force against those nations, organizations, or persons he determines planned, authorized, committed, or aided the terrorist attacks . . . or harbored such organizations or persons." Pursuant to that authorization, President George W. Bush sent forces into Afghanistan to fight al Qaeda and the Taliban regime that supported it.

Subsequently, two Australian citizens and twelve Kuwaiti citizens who were captured in Afghanistan and held at the U.S. naval base at Guantánamo Bay, Cuba, filed petitions for writ of *habeas corpus*, seeking access to counsel, release from custody, and review by an independent tribunal or federal court. The naval base is occupied by the United States pursuant to a 1903 Lease Agreement executed with Cuba in the aftermath of the Spanish–American War. Under the agreement, "the United States recognizes the continuance of the ultimate sovereignty of the Republic of Cuba over the [leased areas]," while "the Republic of Cuba consents that during the period of the occupation by the United States . . . the United States shall exercise complete jurisdiction and control over and within said areas." The federal district court for the District of Columbia dismissed their petitions on the ground that it lacked jurisdiction, since in *Johnson v.*

Eisentrager, 339 U.S. 763 (1950), the Court held that "aliens detained outside the sovereign territory of the United States [may not] invok[e] a petition for a writ of *habeas corpus.*" The Court of Appeals for the District of Columbia Circuit affirmed and an appeal was made to the Supreme Court, which granted review.

The appellate court's decision was reversed by a vote of six to three. Justice Stevens delivered the opinion of the Court. Justice Kennedy filed a concurring opinion. Justice Scalia filed a dissenting opinion, which Chief Justice Rehnquist and Justice Thomas joined.

□ *Justice STEVENS delivered the opinion of the Court.*

Congress has granted federal district courts, "within their respective jurisdictions," the authority to hear applications for *habeas corpus* by any person who claims to be held "in custody in violation of the Constitution or laws or treaties of the United States." [U.S. Code, Section 2241 (a).] The statute traces its ancestry to the first grant of federal court jurisdiction: Section 14 of the Judiciary Act of 1789 authorized federal courts to issue the writ of *habeas corpus* to prisoners "in custody, under or by colour of the authority of the United States, or committed for trial before some court of the same." In 1867, Congress extended the protections of the writ to "all cases where any person may be restrained of his or her liberty in violation of the constitution, or of any treaty or law of the United States."

Habeas corpus is, however, "a writ antecedent to statute, . . . throwing its root deep into the genius of our common law." The writ appeared in English law several centuries ago, became "an integral part of our common-law heritage" by the time the Colonies achieved independence, and received explicit recognition in the Constitution, which forbids suspension of "[t]he Privilege of the Writ of *Habeas Corpus* . . . unless when in Cases of Rebellion or Invasion the public Safety may require it," Art. I, Sec. 9, cl. 2. . . .

Consistent with the historic purpose of the writ, this Court has recognized the federal courts' power to review applications for *habeas* relief in a wide variety of cases involving Executive detention, in wartime as well as in times of peace. The Court has, for example, entertained the *habeas* petitions of an American citizen who plotted an attack on military installations during the Civil War, *Ex parte Milligan*, 4 Wall. 2 (1866), and of admitted enemy aliens convicted of war crimes during a declared war and held in the United States, *Ex parte Quirin*, 317 U.S. 1 (1942), and its insular possessions, *In re Yamashita*, 327 U.S. 1 (1946).

The question now before us is whether the *habeas* statute confers a right to judicial review of the legality of Executive detention of aliens in a territory over which the United States exercises plenary and exclusive jurisdiction, but not "ultimate sovereignty."

Respondents' primary submission is that the answer to the jurisdictional question is controlled by our decision in *Eisentrager*. In that case, we held that a Federal District Court lacked authority to issue a writ of *habeas corpus* to 21 German citizens who had been captured by U.S. forces in China, tried and convicted of war crimes by an American military commission headquartered in Nanking, and incarcerated in the Landsberg Prison in occupied Germany. The Court of Appeals in *Eisentrager* had found jurisdiction, reasoning that "any person who is deprived of his liberty by officials of the United States, acting under purported authority of that Government, and who can show that his confinement is in violation of a prohibition of the Constitution, has a right to the writ." In reversing that determination, this Court summarized the six critical facts in the case: "We are here confronted with a decision whose basic premise is that these prisoners are entitled, as a constitutional right, to sue in some court of the United States for a writ of *habeas corpus.* To support that assumption we must hold that a prisoner of our military authorities is constitutionally entitled to the writ, even though he (a) is an enemy alien; (b) has never been or resided in the United States; (c) was captured outside of our territory and there held in military custody as a prisoner of war; (d) was tried and convicted by a Military Commission sitting outside the United States; (e) for offenses against laws of war committed outside the United States; (f) and is at all times imprisoned outside the United States." On this set of facts, the Court concluded, "no right to the writ of *habeas corpus* appears."

Petitioners in these cases differ from the *Eisentrager* detainees in important respects: They are not nationals of countries at war with the United States, and they deny that they have engaged in or plotted acts of aggression against the United States; they have never been afforded access to any tribunal, much less charged with and convicted of wrongdoing; and for more than two years they have been imprisoned in territory over which the United States exercises exclusive jurisdiction and control.

Not only are petitioners differently situated from the *Eisentrager* detainees, but the Court in *Eisentrager* made quite clear that all six of the facts critical to its disposition were relevant only to the question of the prisoners' constitutional entitlement to *habeas corpus.* The Court had far less to say on the question of the petitioners' statutory entitlement to *habeas* review. Its only statement on the subject was a passing reference to the absence of statutory authorization: "Nothing in the text of the Constitution extends such a right, nor does anything in our statutes." . . .

Because subsequent decisions of this Court have filled the statutory gap that had occasioned *Eisentrager*'s resort to "fundamentals," persons detained outside the territorial jurisdiction of any federal district court no longer need rely on the Constitution as the source of their right to federal *habeas* review. In *Braden v. 30th Judicial Circuit Court of Ky.,* 410 U.S. 484 (1973), this Court held that the prisoner's presence within the territorial jurisdiction of the district court is not "an invariable prerequisite" to the exercise of district court jurisdiction under the federal *habeas* statute. Rather, because "the writ of *habeas corpus* does not act upon the prisoner who seeks relief, but upon the person who holds him in what is alleged to be unlawful custody," a district court acts "within [its] respective jurisdiction" within the meaning of Sec. 2241 as long as "the custodian can be reached by service of process." . . .

Because *Braden* overruled the statutory predicate to *Eisentrager*'s holding, *Eisentrager* plainly does not preclude the exercise of Sec. 2241 jurisdiction over petitioners' claims. . . .

Application of the *habeas* statute to persons detained at the base is consistent with the historical reach of the writ of *habeas corpus*. At common law, courts exercised *habeas* jurisdiction over the claims of aliens detained within sovereign territory of the realm, as well as the claims of persons detained in the so-called "exempt jurisdictions," where ordinary writs did not run, and all other dominions under the sovereign's control. As Lord Mansfield wrote in 1759, even if a territory was "no part of the realm," there was "no doubt" as to the court's power to issue writs of *habeas corpus* if the territory was "under the subjection of the Crown." *King v. Cowle*, 2 Burr. 834, 97 Eng. Rep. 587 (K. B.). Later cases confirmed that the reach of the writ depended not on formal notions of territorial sovereignty, but rather on the practical question of "the exact extent and nature of the jurisdiction or dominion exercised in fact by the Crown." *Ex parte Mwenya*, [1960] 1 Q. B. 241 (C. A.) (Lord Evershed, M. R.).

In the end, the answer to the question presented is clear. Petitioners contend that they are being held in federal custody in violation of the laws of the United States. No party questions the District Court's jurisdiction over petitioners' custodians. Section 2241, by its terms, requires nothing more. We therefore hold that Sec. 2241 confers on the District Court jurisdiction to hear petitioners' *habeas corpus* challenges to the legality of their detention at the Guantánamo Bay Naval Base. . . .

Whether and what further proceedings may become necessary after respondents make their response to the merits of petitioners' claims are matters that we need not address now. What is presently at stake is only whether the federal courts have jurisdiction to determine the legality of the Executive's potentially indefinite detention of individuals who claim to be wholly innocent of wrongdoing. Answering that question in the affirmative, we reverse the judgment of the Court of Appeals and remand for the District Court to consider in the first instance the merits of petitioners' claims. It is so ordered.

□ *Justice KENNEDY, concurring in the judgment.*

The Court is correct, in my view, to conclude that federal courts have jurisdiction to consider challenges to the legality of the detention of foreign nationals held at the Guantánamo Bay Naval Base in Cuba. While I reach the same conclusion, my analysis follows a different course. . . . In my view, the correct course is to follow the framework of *Eisentrager*.

Eisentrager considered the scope of the right to petition for a writ of *habeas corpus* against the backdrop of the constitutional command of the separation of powers. . . . The Court began by noting the "ascending scale of rights" that courts have recognized for individuals depending on their connection to the United States. Citizenship provides a longstanding basis for jurisdiction, the Court noted, and among aliens physical presence within the United States also "gave the Judiciary power to act." This contrasted with the "essential pattern for seasonable Executive constraint of enemy aliens." . . . Because the prisoners in *Eisentrager* were proven enemy aliens found and detained outside the United States, and because the existence of jurisdiction would have had a clear harmful effect on the Nation's military affairs, the matter was appropriately left to the Executive

Branch and there was no jurisdiction for the courts to hear the prisoner's claims.

The decision in *Eisentrager* indicates that there is a realm of political authority over military affairs where the judicial power may not enter. The existence of this realm acknowledges the power of the President as Commander in Chief, and the joint role of the President and the Congress in the conduct of military affairs. A faithful application of *Eisentrager*, then, requires an initial inquiry into the general circumstances of the detention to determine whether the Court has the authority to entertain the petition and to grant relief after considering all of the facts presented. A necessary corollary of *Eisentrager* is that there are circumstances in which the courts maintain the power and the responsibility to protect persons from unlawful detention even where military affairs are implicated.

The facts here are distinguishable from those in *Eisentrager* in two critical ways, leading to the conclusion that a federal court may entertain the petitions. First, Guantánamo Bay is in every practical respect a United States territory, and it is one far removed from any hostilities. . . .

The second critical set of facts is that the detainees at Guantánamo Bay are being held indefinitely, and without benefit of any legal proceeding to determine their status. In *Eisentrager*, the prisoners were tried and convicted by a military commission of violating the laws of war and were sentenced to prison terms. Having already been subject to procedures establishing their status, they could not justify "a limited opening of our courts" to show that they were "of friendly personal disposition" and not enemy aliens. Indefinite detention without trial or other proceeding presents altogether different considerations. . . .

In light of the status of Guantánamo Bay and the indefinite pretrial detention of the detainees, I would hold that federal-court jurisdiction is permitted in these cases. This approach would avoid creating automatic statutory authority to adjudicate the claims of persons located outside the United States, and remains true to the reasoning of *Eisentrager*. For these reasons, I concur in the judgment of the Court.

☐ *Justice SCALIA, with whom THE CHIEF JUSTICE and Justice THOMAS join, dissenting.*

The Court today holds that the *habeas* statute, [Section] 2241 extends to aliens detained by the United States military overseas, outside the sovereign borders of the United States and beyond the territorial jurisdictions of all its courts. This is not only a novel holding; it contradicts a half-century-old precedent on which the military undoubtedly relied, *Johnson v. Eisentrager*, 339 U.S. 763 (1950). The Court's contention that *Eisentrager* was somehow negated by *Braden v. 30th Judicial Circuit of Ky.*, 410 U.S. 484 (1973)—a decision that dealt with a different issue and did not so much as mention *Eisentrager*—is implausible in the extreme. This is an irresponsible overturning of settled law in a matter of extreme importance to our forces currently in the field. I would leave it to Congress to change Sec. 2241, and dissent from the Court's unprecedented holding. . . .

■ IN COMPARATIVE PERSPECTIVE

The Supreme Court of Canada's Rulings on the Rights of Detainees

The Supreme Court of Canada struck down a law authorizing the government to detain foreign-born terrorist suspects indefinitely in *R. v. Hape*, [2007] 2 S.C.R. 292, 2007 S.C.C. 26. Subsequently, in 2008 the court held that the U.S. "regime" for detaining and interrogating a teenage Canadian in Guantanamo Bay since 2002 amounted to "a clear violation of fundamental human rights protected by international law," in *Canada v. Khadr*, 2008 S.C.C 28. The U.S. Supreme Court also ordered Canadian officials to disclose the records of interrogation of Omar Ahmed Khadr for the defense lawyers' use in defending him against war crimes charges made by the U.S. military. Khadr was captured in Afghanistan when he was fifteen years old and subsequently held in Guantanamo Bay.

The decision's conclusion that the detention and questioning of Khadr was illegal rested on the rulings of the U.S. Supreme Court in *Ra-*

Boumediene v. Bush

128 S.CT. 2229 (2008)

In 2002 Lakhdar Boumediene and several other Algerian nationals were seized by Bosnian police when U.S. intelligence officers suspected them of plotting to attack an embassy. Boumediene and the others were classified as "enemy combatants" and held in Guantanamo Bay, Cuba. Boumediene filed a petition for *habeas corpus*. A federal district court granted the government's motion to have all claims dismissed on the ground that Boumediene was an alien detained overseas and, hence, had no right to a *habeas* petition. The U.S. Court of Appeals for the District of Columbia Circuit affirmed, but the U.S. Supreme Court reversed in *Rasul v. Bush*, 542 U.S. 466 (2004) (excerpted above), holding that noncitizen detainees in Guantanamo were entitled to *habeas* relief. In response, Congress passed the Detainee Treatment Act of 2005, which basically stripped the federal courts of jurisdiction over *habeas* petitions from those held in Guantanamo Bay. The detainees, however, argued that the act did not apply to their cases since they were pending before its passage and that they were denied due process. On appeal, the Supreme Court agreed in *Hamdan v. Rumsfeld*, 548 U.S. 557 (2006). Congress in turn

sul v. Bush, 542 U.S. 466 (2004), and *Hamdan v. Rumsfeld*, 548 U.S. 557 (2006). The Court did not mention the developments following *Hamdan* or Congress's passage of the Military Commissions Act of 2006. In the Court's words: "The process in place at the time Canadian officials interviewed Mr. Khadr and passed the fruits of the interviews on to U.S. officials has been found by the U.S. Supreme Court to violate U.S. domestic law and international human rights obligations to which Canada is a party." Because of this, the Canadian security agents who interrogated Khadr violated the Canadian Charter of Rights and Freedoms. Hence, the Court ordered the disclosure to defense counsel of all documents in Canadian government hands bearing on the war crimes charges that Khadr faces before a U.S. military commission. However, the Court ruled that the remedy under the Charter did not require that Khadr have access to completely unedited versions of the documents and interrogations. Unredacted copies of those materials, the Court noted, had already been turned over to a Canadian judge. And that judge should review the material and "decide which documents fall within the scope of the disclosure obligation." In doing so, the Court stressed that what was ultimately disclosed depended on a "balancing of national security and other considerations" under Canada's laws of evidence.

passed the Military Commissions Act (MCA) of 2006, which eliminated federal courts' jurisdiction over *habeas* petitions filed by Guantanamo Bay detainees who had been designated "enemy combatants" under the procedures established, following the Court's ruling in *Hamdi v. Rumsfeld*, 542 U.S. 507 (2004), for Combatant Status Review Tribunals (CSRTs) to review the military's designation of "enemy combatant" status. Boumediene and other Guantanamo Bay prisoners challenged their detention, but a federal district court agreed with the government and dismissed their petitions. But shortly thereafter another district court rejected the government's motion to dismiss the petitions of detainees, ruling that they were entitled to due process. A divided panel of the U.S. Court of Appeals for the District of Columbia Circuit, then, vacated the district court judgments and dismissed the cases for lack of jurisdiction. The majority concluded that the Military Commissions Act of 2006 stripped the federal courts of jurisdiction over *habeas* petitions filed by Guantanamo Bay detainees and rejected the claim that the MCA ran afoul of Article 1, Section 9 of the Constitution, which stipulates that "The Privilege of the Writ of *Habeas Corpus* shall not be suspended, unless when in Cases of Rebellion or Invasion the public Safety may require it." Boumediene appealed the appellate court's decision and the Supreme Court granted review.

The appellate court's decision was reversed by a bare majority. Justice Kennedy delivered the opinion for the Court. Justice Souter filed a concur-

"Enemy combatants" held in Guantanamo Bay, Cuba. (*Ron Sachs/CNP/ Corbis.*)

ring opinion, which Justices Ginsburg and Breyer joined. Chief Justice Roberts and Justice Scalia each filed dissenting opinions, which were joined by Justices Thomas and Alito. Subsequently, Boumediene was transferred to France.

☐ *Justice KENNEDY delivered the opinion of the Court.*

Petitioners present a question not resolved by our earlier cases relating to the detention of aliens at Guantanamo: whether they have the constitutional privilege of *habeas corpus*, a privilege not to be withdrawn except in conformance with the Suspension Clause, Art. I, Sec. 9, cl. 2. We hold these petitioners do have the *habeas corpus* privilege. Congress has enacted a statute, the Detainee Treatment Act of 2005 (DTA), that provides certain procedures for review of the detainees' status. We hold that those procedures are not an adequate and effective substitute for *habeas corpus*. Therefore Sec. 7 of the Military Commissions Act of 2006 (MCA) operates as an unconstitutional suspension of the writ. We do not address whether the President has authority to detain these petitioners nor do we hold that the writ must issue. These and other questions regarding the legality of the detention are to be resolved in the first instance by the District Court.

Under the Authorization for Use of Military Force (AUMF), the President is authorized "to use all necessary and appropriate force against those nations, organizations, or persons he determines planned, authorized, committed, or aided the terrorist attacks that occurred on September 11, 2001, or harbored such organizations or persons, in order to prevent any future acts of international terrorism against the United States by such nations, organizations or persons."

In *Hamdi v. Rumsfeld*, 542 U.S. 507 (2004), five Members of the Court recognized that detention of individuals who fought against the United States in Afghanistan "for the duration of the particular conflict in which they were captured, is so fundamental and accepted an incident to war as to be an exercise of the 'necessary and appropriate force' Congress has authorized the President to use." After *Hamdi*, the Deputy Secretary of Defense established Combatant Status Review Tribunals (CSRTs) to determine whether individuals detained at Guantanamo were "enemy combatants," as the Department defines that term. A later memorandum established procedures to implement the CSRTs. The Government maintains these procedures were designed to comply with the due process requirements identified by the plurality in *Hamdi*. . . .

The first actions commenced in February 2002. The District Court ordered the cases dismissed for lack of jurisdiction because the naval station is outside the sovereign territory of the United States. The Court of Appeals for the District of Columbia Circuit affirmed. We granted *certiorari* and reversed, holding that 28 U.S.C. Sec. 2241 extended statutory *habeas corpus* jurisdiction to Guantanamo. See *Rasul v. Bush*, 542 U. S. 466 (2004). The constitutional issue presented in the instant cases was not reached in *Rasul*.

As a threshold matter, we must decide whether MCA Sec. 7 denies the federal courts jurisdiction to hear *habeas corpus* actions pending at the time of its enactment. We hold the statute does deny that jurisdiction, so that, if the statute is valid, petitioners' cases must be dismissed. . . .

We acknowledge, moreover, the litigation history that prompted Congress to enact the MCA. In *Hamdan* [v. *Rumsfeld*, 548 U.S. 557 (2006)] the Court found it unnecessary to address the petitioner's Suspension Clause arguments but noted the relevance of the clear statement rule in deciding whether Congress intended to reach pending *habeas corpus* cases. This interpretive rule facilitates a dialogue between Congress and the Court. If the Court invokes a clear statement rule to advise that certain statutory interpretations are favored in order to avoid constitutional difficulties, Congress can make an informed legislative choice either to amend the statute or to retain its existing text. If Congress amends, its intent must be respected even if a difficult constitutional question is presented. The usual presumption is that Members of Congress, in accord with their oath of office, considered the constitutional issue and determined the amended statute to be a lawful one; and the Judiciary, in light of that determination, proceeds to its own independent judgment on the constitutional question when required to do so in a proper case.

If this ongoing dialogue between and among the branches of Government is to be respected, we cannot ignore that the MCA was a direct response to *Hamdan's* holding that the DTA's jurisdiction-stripping provision had no application to pending cases.

In deciding the constitutional questions now presented we must determine whether petitioners are barred from seeking the writ or invoking the protections of the Suspension Clause either because of their status, i.e., petitioners' designation by the Executive Branch as enemy combatants, or their physical location, i.e., their presence at Guantanamo Bay. The Government contends that noncitizens designated as enemy combatants and detained in territory located outside our Nation's borders have no constitutional rights and no privilege of *habeas corpus*. Petitioners contend they do have cognizable constitutional rights and that Congress, in seeking to eliminate recourse to *habeas corpus* as a means to assert those rights, acted in violation of the Suspension Clause.

We begin with a brief account of the history and origins of the writ. Our account proceeds from two propositions. First, protection for the privilege of *habeas corpus* was one of the few safeguards of liberty specified in a Constitution that, at the outset, had no Bill of Rights. In the system conceived by the Framers the writ had a centrality that must inform proper interpretation of the Suspension Clause. Second, to the extent there were settled precedents or legal commentaries in 1789 regarding the extraterritorial scope of the writ or its application to enemy aliens, those authorities can be instructive for the present cases.

The Framers viewed freedom from unlawful restraint as a fundamental precept of liberty, and they understood the writ of *habeas corpus* as a vital instrument to secure that freedom. Experience taught, however, that the common-law writ all too often had been insufficient to guard against the abuse of monarchial power. That history counseled the necessity for specific language in the Constitution to secure the writ and ensure its place in our legal system.

Magna Carta decreed that no man would be imprisoned contrary to the law of the land. The development was painstaking, even by the centuries-long measures of English constitutional history. The writ was known and used in some form at least as early as the reign of Edward I. Yet at the outset it was used to protect not the rights of citizens but those of the King and his courts. The early courts were considered agents of the Crown, designed to assist the King in the exercise of his power. Thus the writ, while it would become part of the foundation of liberty for the King's subjects, was in its earliest use a mechanism for securing compliance with the King's laws. . . .

Still, the writ proved to be an imperfect check. Even when the importance of the writ was well understood in England, *habeas* relief often was denied by the courts or suspended by Parliament. Denial or suspension occurred in times of political unrest, to the anguish of the imprisoned and the outrage of those in sympathy with them. . . .

This history was known to the Framers. It no doubt confirmed their view that pendular swings to and away from individual liberty were endemic to undivided, uncontrolled power. The Framers' inherent distrust of governmental power was the driving force behind the constitutional plan that allocated powers among three independent branches. This design serves not only to make Government accountable but also to secure individual liberty. . . .

That the Framers considered the writ a vital instrument for the protection of individual liberty is evident from the care taken to specify the limited grounds for its suspension: "The Privilege of the Writ of *Habeas Corpus* shall not be suspended, unless when in Cases of Rebellion or Invasion the public Safety may require it." Art. I, Sec. 9, cl. 2. The word "privilege" was used, perhaps, to avoid mentioning some rights to the exclusion of others. (Indeed, the only mention of the term "right" in the Constitution, as ratified, is in its clause giving Congress the power to protect the rights of authors and inventors. See Art. I, Sec. 8, cl. 8.)

Surviving accounts of the ratification debates provide additional evidence that the Framers deemed the writ to be an essential mechanism in the separation-of-powers scheme. . . .

Post–1789 *habeas* developments in England, though not bearing upon the Framers' intent, do verify their foresight. Those later events would underscore the need for structural barriers against arbitrary suspensions of the writ. Just as the writ had been vulnerable to executive and parliamentary encroachment on both sides of the Atlantic before the American Revolution, despite the *Habeas Corpus* Act of 1679, the writ was suspended with frequency in England during times of political unrest after 1789. Parliament suspended the writ for much of the period from 1792 to 1801, resulting in rampant arbitrary imprisonment. . . .

The broad historical narrative of the writ and its function is central to our analysis, but we seek guidance as well from founding-era authorities addressing the specific question before us: whether foreign nationals, apprehended and detained in distant countries during a time of serious threats to our Nation's security, may assert the privilege of the writ and seek its protection. The Court has been careful not to foreclose the possibility that the protections of the Suspension Clause have expanded along with post–1789 developments that define the present scope of the writ. . . .

We know that at common law a petitioner's status as an alien was not a categorical bar to *habeas corpus* relief. See, e.g., *Sommersett's Case*, 20 How. St. Tr. 1 (1772) (ordering an African slave freed upon finding the custodian's return insufficient) . . . .

We find the evidence as to the geographic scope of the writ at common law informative, but, again, not dispositive. Petitioners argue the site of their detention is analogous to two territories outside of England to which the writ did run: the so-called "exempt jurisdictions," like the Channel Islands; and (in former times) India. There are critical differences between these places and Guantanamo, however.

As the Court noted in *Rasul*, common-law courts granted *habeas corpus* relief to prisoners detained in the exempt jurisdictions. But these areas, while not in theory part of the realm of England, were nonetheless under the Crown's control. . . .

In the end a categorical or formal conception of sovereignty does not provide a comprehensive or altogether satisfactory explanation for the general understanding that prevailed when Lord Mansfield considered issuance of the writ outside England. In 1759 the writ did not run to Scotland but did run to Ireland, even though, at that point, Scotland and England had merged under the rule of a single sovereign, whereas the Crowns of Great Britain and Ireland remained separate (at least in theory). But there was at least one major difference between Scotland's and Ireland's relationship with England during this period that might explain why the writ ran to Ireland but not to Scotland. English law did not generally apply in Scotland (even after the Act of Union) but it did apply in Ireland. . . .

Drawing from its position that at common law the writ ran only to territories over which the Crown was sovereign, the Government says the Suspension Clause affords petitioners no rights because the United States does not claim sovereignty over the place of detention.

Guantanamo Bay is not formally part of the United States. And under the terms of the lease between the United States and Cuba, Cuba retains "ultimate sovereignty" over the territory while the United States exercises "complete jurisdiction and control." Under the terms of the 1934 Treaty, however, Cuba effectively has no rights as a sovereign until the parties agree to modification of the 1903 Lease Agreement or the United States abandons the base. . . .

Were we to hold that the present cases turn on the political question doctrine, we would be required first to accept the Government's premise that *de jure* sovereignty is the touchstone of *habeas corpus* jurisdiction. This premise, however, is unfounded. For the reasons indicated above, the history of common-law *habeas corpus* provides scant support for this proposition; and, for the reasons indicated below, that position would be inconsistent with our precedents and contrary to fundamental separation-of-powers principles.

The Court has discussed the issue of the Constitution's extraterritorial application on many occasions. These decisions undermine the Government's argument that, at least as applied to noncitizens, the Constitution necessarily stops where *de jure* sovereignty ends. . . .

Fundamental questions regarding the Constitution's geographic scope first arose at the dawn of the 20th century when the Nation acquired noncontiguous Territories: Puerto Rico, Guam, and the Philippines—ceded to the United States by Spain at the conclusion of the Spanish-American War—and Hawaii—annexed by the United States in 1898. At this point Congress chose to discontinue its previous practice of extending constitutional rights to the territories by statute.

In a series of opinions later known as the *Insular Cases*, the Court addressed whether the Constitution, by its own force, applies in any territory that is not a State. The Court held that the Constitution has independent force in these territories, a force not contingent upon acts of legislative grace. . . .

Practical considerations weighed heavily as well in *Johnson v. Eisentrager*, 339 U.S. 763 (1950), where the Court addressed whether *habeas corpus* jurisdiction extended to enemy aliens who had been convicted of violating the laws of war. The prisoners were detained at Landsberg Prison in Germany during the Allied Powers' postwar occupation. The Court stressed the difficulties of ordering the Government to produce the prisoners in a *habeas corpus* proceeding. It "would require allocation of shipping space, guarding personnel, billeting and rations" and would damage the prestige of military commanders at a sensitive time. In considering these factors the Court sought to balance the constraints of military occupation with constitutional necessities.

True, the Court in *Eisentrager* denied access to the writ, and it noted the prisoners "at no relevant time were within any territory over which the United States is sovereign, and [that] the scenes of their offense, their capture, their trial and their punishment were all beyond the territorial jurisdiction of any court of the United States." The Government seizes upon this language as proof positive that the *Eisentrager* Court adopted a formalistic, sovereignty-based test for determining the reach of the Suspension Clause. We reject this reading for three reasons.

First, we do not accept the idea that the above-quoted passage from *Eisentrager* is the only authoritative language in the opinion and that all the rest is *dicta*.

Second, because the United States lacked both *de jure* sovereignty and plenary control over Landsberg Prison, it is far from clear that the *Eisentrager*

Court used the term sovereignty only in the narrow technical sense and not to connote the degree of control the military asserted over the facility. . . .

Third, if the Government's reading of *Eisentrager* were correct, the opinion would have marked not only a change in, but a complete repudiation of, the *Insular Cases*' functional approach to questions of extraterritoriality. We cannot accept the Government's view. Nothing in *Eisentrager* says that *de jure* sovereignty is or has ever been the only relevant consideration in determining the geographic reach of the Constitution or of *habeas corpus*. Were that the case, there would be considerable tension between *Eisentrager*, on the one hand, and the *Insular Cases*, on the other. Our cases need not be read to conflict in this manner. A constricted reading of *Eisentrager* overlooks what we see as a common thread uniting the *Insular Cases* [and] *Eisentrager*; the idea that questions of extraterritoriality turn on objective factors and practical concerns, not formalism.

The Government's formal sovereignty-based test raises troubling separation-of-powers concerns as well. The political history of Guantanamo illustrates the deficiencies of this approach. The United States has maintained complete and uninterrupted control of the bay for over 100 years. At the close of the Spanish-American War, Spain ceded control over the entire island of Cuba to the United States and specifically "relinquishe[d] all claim[s] of sovereignty . . . and title." See Treaty of Paris, Dec. 10, 1898. From the date the treaty with Spain was signed until the Cuban Republic was established on May 20, 1902, the United States governed the territory "in trust" for the benefit of the Cuban people. And although it recognized, by entering into the 1903 Lease Agreement, that Cuba retained "ultimate sovereignty" over Guantanamo, the United States continued to maintain the same plenary control it had enjoyed since 1898. . . .

As we recognized in *Rasul*, the outlines of a framework for determining the reach of the Suspension Clause are suggested by the factors the Court relied upon in *Eisentrager*. In addition to the practical concerns discussed above, the *Eisentrager* Court found relevant that each petitioner: "(a) is an enemy alien; (b) has never been or resided in the United States; (c) was captured outside of our territory and there held in military custody as a prisoner of war; (d) was tried and convicted by a Military Commission sitting outside the United States;(e) for offenses against laws of war committed outside the United States; (f) and is at all times imprisoned outside the United States." Based on this language from *Eisentrager*, and the reasoning in our other extraterritoriality opinions, we conclude that at least three factors are relevant in determining the reach of the Suspension Clause: (1) the citizenship and status of the detainee and the adequacy of the process through which that status determination was made; (2) the nature of the sites where apprehension and then detention took place; and (3) the practical obstacles inherent in resolving the prisoner's entitlement to the writ.

Applying this framework, we note at the onset that the status of these detainees is a matter of dispute. The petitioners, like those in *Eisentrager*, are not American citizens. But the petitioners in *Eisentrager* did not contest, it seems, the Court's assertion that they were "enemy alien[s]." In the instant cases, by contrast, the detainees deny they are enemy combatants. They have been afforded some process in CSRT proceedings to determine their status;

but, unlike in *Eisentrager*, there has been no trial by military commission for violations of the laws of war. The difference is not trivial. The records from the *Eisentrager* trials suggest that, well before the petitioners brought their case to this Court, there had been a rigorous adversarial process to test the legality of their detention. The *Eisentrager* petitioners were charged by a bill of particulars that made detailed factual allegations against them. To rebut the accusations, they were entitled to representation by counsel, allowed to introduce evidence on their own behalf, and permitted to cross-examine the prosecution's witnesses.

In comparison the procedural protections afforded to the detainees in the CSRT hearings are far more limited, and, we conclude, fall well short of the procedures and adversarial mechanisms that would eliminate the need for *habeas corpus* review. Although the detainee is assigned a "Personal Representative" to assist him during CSRT proceedings, the Secretary of the Navy's memorandum makes clear that person is not the detainee's lawyer or even his "advocate." The Government's evidence is accorded a presumption of validity. The detainee is allowed to present "reasonably available" evidence, but his ability to rebut the Government's evidence against him is limited by the circumstances of his confinement and his lack of counsel at this stage. And although the detainee can seek review of his status determination in the Court of Appeals, that review process cannot cure all defects in the earlier proceedings.

As to the second factor relevant to this analysis, the detainees here are similarly situated to the *Eisentrager* petitioners in that the sites of their apprehension and detention are technically outside the sovereign territory of the United States. . . .

As to the third factor, we recognize, as the Court did in *Eisentrager*, that there are costs to holding the Suspension Clause applicable in a case of military detention abroad. *Habeas corpus* proceedings may require expenditure of funds by the Government and may divert the attention of military personnel from other pressing tasks. While we are sensitive to these concerns, we do not find them dispositive. Compliance with any judicial process requires some incremental expenditure of resources. Yet civilian courts and the Armed Forces have functioned alongside each other at various points in our history. . . .

We hold that Art. I, Sec. 9, cl. 2, of the Constitution has full effect at Guantanamo Bay. If the privilege of *habeas corpus* is to be denied to the detainees now before us, Congress must act in accordance with the requirements of the Suspension Clause. The MCA does not purport to be a formal suspension of the writ; and the Government, in its submissions to us, has not argued that it is. Petitioners, therefore, are entitled to the privilege of *habeas corpus* to challenge the legality of their detention.

In light of this holding the question becomes whether the statute stripping jurisdiction to issue the writ avoids the Suspension Clause mandate because Congress has provided adequate substitute procedures for *habeas corpus*. The Government submits there has been compliance with the Suspension Clause because the DTA review process in the Court of Appeals provides an adequate substitute. Congress has granted that court jurisdiction to consider "(i) whether the status determination of the [CSRT] . . . was consistent with the standards and procedures specified by the Secretary of Defense . . . and

(ii) to the extent the Constitution and laws of the United States are applicable, whether the use of such standards and procedures to make the determination is consistent with the Constitution and laws of the United States." . . .

Our case law does not contain extensive discussion of standards defining suspension of the writ or of circumstances under which suspension has occurred. This simply confirms the care Congress has taken throughout our Nation's history to preserve the writ and its function. Indeed, most of the major legislative enactments pertaining to *habeas corpus* have acted not to contract the writ's protection but to expand it or to hasten resolution of prisoners' claims.

We do not endeavor to offer a comprehensive summary of the requisites for an adequate substitute for *habeas corpus*. We do consider it uncontroversial, however, that the privilege of *habeas corpus* entitles the prisoner to a meaningful opportunity to demonstrate that he is being held pursuant to "the erroneous application or interpretation" of relevant law. And the *habeas* court must have the power to order the conditional release of an individual unlawfully detained—though release need not be the exclusive remedy and is not the appropriate one in every case in which the writ is granted. . . .

Where a person is detained by executive order, rather than, say, after being tried and convicted in a court, the need for collateral review is most pressing. A criminal conviction in the usual course occurs after a judicial hearing before a tribunal disinterested in the outcome and committed to procedures designed to ensure its own independence. These dynamics are not inherent in executive detention orders or executive review procedures. In this context the need for *habeas corpus* is more urgent. The intended duration of the detention and the reasons for it bear upon the precise scope of the inquiry. *Habeas corpus* proceedings need not resemble a criminal trial, even when the detention is by executive order. But the writ must be effective. The *habeas* court must have sufficient authority to conduct a meaningful review of both the cause for detention and the Executive's power to detain.

To determine the necessary scope of *habeas corpus* review, therefore, we must assess the CSRT process, the mechanism through which petitioners' designation as enemy combatants became final. Whether one characterizes the CSRT process as direct review of the Executive's battlefield determination that the detainee is an enemy combatant—as the parties have and as we do—or as the first step in the collateral review of a battlefield determination makes no difference in a proper analysis of whether the procedures Congress put in place are an adequate substitute for *habeas corpus*. What matters is the sum total of procedural protections afforded to the detainee at all stages, direct and collateral. Petitioners identify what they see as myriad deficiencies in the CSRTs. The most relevant for our purposes are the constraints upon the detainee's ability to rebut the factual basis for the Government's assertion that he is an enemy combatant. As already noted, at the CSRT stage the detainee has limited means to find or present evidence to challenge the Government's case against him. He does not have the assistance of counsel and may not be aware of the most critical allegations that the Government relied upon to order his detention. The detainee can confront witnesses that testify during the CSRT proceedings. But given that there are in effect no limits on the admission of hearsay evidence—the only requirement is that the tribunal deem the evidence "relevant and helpful"—the detainee's opportunity to question witnesses is likely to be more theoretical than real. . . .

Even if we were to assume that the CSRTs satisfy due process standards, it would not end our inquiry. *Habeas corpus* is a collateral process that exists, in Justice HOLMES' words, to "cu[t] through all forms and g[o] to the very tissue of the structure. It comes in from the outside, not in subordination to the proceedings, and although every form may have been preserved opens the inquiry whether they have been more than an empty shell." *Frank v. Mangum*, 237 U.S. 309 (1915). Even when the procedures authorizing detention are structurally sound, the Suspension Clause remains applicable and the writ relevant. . . .

Although we make no judgment as to whether the CSRTs, as currently constituted, satisfy due process standards, we agree with petitioners that, even when all the parties involved in this process act with diligence and in good faith, there is considerable risk of error in the tribunal's findings of fact. And given that the consequence of error may be detention of persons for the duration of hostilities that may last a generation or more, this is a risk too significant to ignore.

For the writ of *habeas corpus*, or its substitute, to function as an effective and proper remedy in this context, the court that conducts the *habeas* proceeding must have the means to correct errors that occurred during the CSRT proceedings. This includes some authority to assess the sufficiency of the Government's evidence against the detainee. It also must have the authority to admit and consider relevant exculpatory evidence that was not introduced during the earlier proceeding. Federal *habeas* petitioners long have had the means to supplement the record on review, even in the post conviction *habeas* setting. Here that opportunity is constitutionally required.

Consistent with the historic function and province of the writ, *habeas corpus* review may be more circumscribed if the underlying detention proceedings are more thorough than they were here. In two *habeas* cases involving enemy aliens tried for war crimes, *In re Yamashita*, 327 U.S. 1 (1946), and *Ex parte Quirin*, 317 U.S. 1 (1942), for example, this Court limited its review to determining whether the Executive had legal authority to try the petitioners by military commission. We need not revisit these cases, however. For on their own terms, the proceedings in *Yamashita* and *Quirin*, like those in *Eisentrager*, had an adversarial structure that is lacking here.

The extent of the showing required of the Government in these cases is a matter to be determined. We need not explore it further at this stage. We do hold that when the judicial power to issue *habeas corpus* properly is invoked the judicial officer must have adequate authority to make a determination in light of the relevant law and facts and to formulate and issue appropriate orders for relief, including, if necessary, an order directing the prisoner's release.

We now consider whether the DTA allows the Court of Appeals to conduct a proceeding meeting these standards. . . .

The DTA does not explicitly empower the Court of Appeals to order the applicant in a DTA review proceeding released should the court find that the standards and procedures used at his CSRT hearing were insufficient to justify detention. This is troubling. Yet, for present purposes, we can assume congressional silence permits a constitutionally required remedy. In that case it would be possible to hold that a remedy of release is impliedly provided for. . . .

The absence of a release remedy and specific language allowing AUMF challenges are not the only constitutional infirmities from which the statute potentially suffers, however. The more difficult question is whether the DTA permits the Court of Appeals to make requisite findings of fact. The DTA enables petitioners to request "review" of their CSRT determination in the Court of Appeals, but the "Scope of Review" provision confines the Court of Appeals' role to reviewing whether the CSRT followed the "standards and procedures" issued by the Department of Defense and assessing whether those "standards and procedures" are lawful. Among these standards is "the requirement that the conclusion of the Tribunal be supported by a preponderance of the evidence . . . allowing a rebuttable presumption in favor of the Government's evidence."

Assuming the DTA can be construed to allow the Court of Appeals to review or correct the CSRT's factual determinations, as opposed to merely certifying that the tribunal applied the correct standard of proof, we see no way to construe the statute to allow what is also constitutionally required in this context: an opportunity for the detainee to present relevant exculpatory evidence that was not made part of the record in the earlier proceedings.

On its face the statute allows the Court of Appeals to consider no evidence outside the CSRT record. In the parallel litigation, however, the Court of Appeals determined that the DTA allows it to order the production of all "'reasonably available information in the possession of the U.S. Government bearing on the issue of whether the detainee meets the criteria to be designated as an enemy combatant,'" regardless of whether this evidence was put before the CSRT. For present purposes, we can assume that the Court of Appeals was correct that the DTA allows introduction and consideration of relevant exculpatory evidence that was "reasonably available" to the Government at the time of the CSRT but not made part of the record. Even so, the DTA review proceeding falls short of being a constitutionally adequate substitute, for the detainee still would have no opportunity to present evidence discovered after the CSRT proceedings concluded.

Under the DTA the Court of Appeals has the power to review CSRT determinations by assessing the legality of standards and procedures. This implies the power to inquire into what happened at the CSRT hearing and, perhaps, to remedy certain deficiencies in that proceeding. But should the Court of Appeals determine that the CSRT followed appropriate and lawful standards and procedures, it will have reached the limits of its jurisdiction. There is no language in the DTA that can be construed to allow the Court of Appeals to admit and consider newly discovered evidence that could not have been made part of the CSRT record because it was unavailable to either the Government or the detainee when the CSRT made its findings. This evidence, however, may be critical to the detainee's argument that he is not an enemy combatant and there is no cause to detain him. . . .

By foreclosing consideration of evidence not presented or reasonably available to the detainee at the CSRT proceedings, the DTA disadvantages the detainee by limiting the scope of collateral review to a record that may not be accurate or complete. In other contexts, e.g., in post-trial *habeas* cases where the prisoner already has had a full and fair opportunity to develop the factual predicate of his claims, similar limitations on the scope of *habeas* review may be appropriate. In this context, however, where the underlying detention proceedings lack the necessary adversarial character, the detainee cannot be held responsible for all deficiencies in the record. . . .

We do not imply DTA review would be a constitutionally sufficient replacement for *habeas corpus* but for these limitations on the detainee's ability to present exculpatory evidence. For even if it were possible, as a textual matter, to read into the statute each of the necessary procedures we have identified, we could not overlook the cumulative effect of our doing so. To hold that the detainees at Guantanamo may, under the DTA, challenge the President's legal authority to detain them, contest the CSRT's findings of fact, supplement the record on review with exculpatory evidence, and request an order of release would come close to reinstating the *habeas corpus* process Congress sought to deny them. The language of the statute, read in light of Congress' reasons for enacting it, cannot bear this interpretation. Petitioners have met their burden of establishing that the DTA review process is, on its face, an inadequate substitute for *habeas corpus.* . . .

Although we hold that the DTA is not an adequate and effective substitute for *habeas corpus*, it does not follow that a *habeas corpus* court may disregard the dangers the detention in these cases was intended to prevent. [T]he Suspension Clause does not resist innovation in the field of *habeas corpus*. Certain accommodations can be made to reduce the burden *habeas corpus* proceedings will place on the military without impermissibly diluting the protections of the writ. . . .

In considering both the procedural and substantive standards used to impose detention to prevent acts of terrorism, proper deference must be accorded to the political branches. See *United States v. Curtiss-Wright Export Corp.*, 299 U.S. 304 (1936). Unlike the President and some designated Members of Congress, neither the Members of this Court nor most federal judges begin the day with briefings that may describe new and serious threats to our Nation and its people. The law must accord the Executive substantial authority to apprehend and detain those who pose a real danger to our security. . . .

We hold that petitioners may invoke the fundamental procedural protections of *habeas corpus*. The laws and Constitution are designed to survive, and remain in force, in extraordinary times. Liberty and security can be reconciled; and in our system they are reconciled within the framework of the law. The Framers decided that *habeas corpus*, a right of first importance, must be a part of that framework, a part of that law.

The determination by the Court of Appeals that the Suspension Clause and its protections are inapplicable to petitioners was in error. The judgment of the Court of Appeals is reversed. The cases are remanded to the Court of Appeals with instructions that it remand the cases to the District Court for proceedings consistent with this opinion. It is so ordered.

☐ *Justice SOUTER, with whom Justice GINSBURG and Justice BREYER join, concurring.*

Four years ago, this Court in *Rasul v. Bush*, 542 U.S. 466 (2004) held that statutory *habeas* jurisdiction extended to claims of foreign nationals imprisoned by the United States at Guantanamo Bay, "to determine the legality of the Executive's potentially indefinite detention" of them. Subsequent legislation eliminated the statutory *habeas* jurisdiction over these claims, so that now there must be constitutionally based jurisdiction or none at all. Justice SCALIA is thus correct that here, for the first time, this Court holds there is (he says "confers") constitutional *habeas* jurisdiction over aliens imprisoned by the military outside an area of *de jure* national sovereignty. But no one who reads the Court's opinion in *Rasul* could seriously doubt that the jurisdictional question must be answered the same way in purely constitutional cases, given the Court's reliance on the historical background of *habeas* generally in answering the statutory question.

Indeed, the Court in *Rasul* directly answered the very historical question that Justice SCALIA says is dispositive; it wrote that "[a]pplication of the *habeas* statute to persons detained at [Guantanamo] is consistent with the historical reach of the writ of *habeas corpus*," Justice SCALIA dismisses the statement as *dictum*, but if *dictum* it was, it was *dictum* well considered, and it stated the view of five Members of this Court on the historical scope of the writ. Of course, it takes more than a quotation from *Rasul*, however much on point, to resolve the constitutional issue before us here, which the majority opinion has explored afresh in the detail it deserves. But whether one agrees or disagrees with today's decision, it is no bolt out of the blue.

A second fact insufficiently appreciated by the dissents is the length of the disputed imprisonments, some of the prisoners represented here today having been locked up for six years. Hence the hollow ring when the dissenters suggest that the Court is somehow precipitating the judiciary into reviewing claims that the military (subject to appeal to the Court of Appeals for the District of Columbia Circuit) could handle within some reasonable period of time. . . .

It is in fact the very lapse of four years from the time *Rasul* put everyone on notice that *habeas* process was available to Guantanamo prisoners, and the lapse of six years since some of these prisoners were captured and incarcerated, that stand at odds with the repeated suggestions of the dissenters that these cases should be seen as a judicial victory in a contest for power between the Court and the political branches. The several answers to the charge of triumphalism might start with a basic fact of Anglo-American constitutional history: that the power, first of the Crown and now of the Executive Branch of the United States, is necessarily limited by *habeas corpus* jurisdiction to enquire into the legality of executive detention. And one could explain that in this Court's exercise of responsibility to preserve *habeas corpus* something much more significant is involved than pulling and hauling between the judicial and political branches. Instead, though, it is enough to repeat that some of these petitioners have spent six years behind bars. After six years of sustained executive detentions in Guantanamo, subject to *habeas* jurisdiction but without any actual *habeas* scrutiny, today's decision is no judicial victory, but an act of perseverance in trying to make *habeas* review, and the obligation of the courts to provide it, mean something of value both to prisoners and to the Nation.

□ *Justice SCALIA, with whom THE CHIEF JUSTICE, Justice THOMAS, and Justice ALITO join, dissenting.*

Today, for the first time in our Nation's history, the Court confers a constitutional right to *habeas corpus* on alien enemies detained abroad by our military forces in the course of an ongoing war. THE CHIEF JUSTICE's dissent, which I join, shows that the procedures prescribed by Congress in the Detainee Treatment Act provide the essential protections that *habeas corpus* guarantees; there has thus been no suspension of the writ, and no basis exists for judicial intervention beyond what the Act allows. My problem with today's opinion is more fundamental still: The writ of *habeas corpus* does not, and never has, run in favor of aliens abroad; the Suspension Clause thus has no application, and the Court's intervention in this military matter is entirely *ultra vires.* . . .

America is at war with radical Islamists. The enemy began by killing Americans and American allies abroad: 241 at the Marine barracks in Lebanon, 19 at the Khobar Towers in Dhahran, 224 at our embassies in Dares Salaam and Nairobi, and 17 on the USS *Cole* in Yemen. On September 11, 2001, the enemy brought the battle to American soil, killing 2,749 at the Twin Towers in New York City, 184 at the Pentagon in Washington, DC, and 40 in Pennsylvania. It has threatened further attacks against our homeland; one need only walk about buttressed and barricaded Washington, or board a plane anywhere in the country, to know that the threat is a serious one. Our Armed Forces are now in the field against the enemy, in Afghanistan and Iraq.

The game of bait-and-switch that today's opinion plays upon the Nation's Commander in Chief will make the war harder on us. It will almost certainly cause more Americans to be killed. That consequence would be tolerable if necessary to preserve a time-honored legal principle vital to our constitutional Republic. But it is this Court's blatant abandonment of such a principle that produces the decision today. . . .

In the long term, then, the Court's decision today accomplishes little, except perhaps to reduce the well-being of enemy combatants that the Court ostensibly seeks to protect. In the short term, however, the decision is devastating. At least 30 of those prisoners hitherto released from Guantanamo Bay have returned to the battlefield. But others have succeeded in carrying on their atrocities against innocent civilians. In one case, a detainee released from Guantanamo Bay masterminded the kidnapping of two Chinese dam workers, one of whom was later shot to death when used as a human shield against Pakistani commandoes.

These, mind you, were detainees whom the military had concluded were not enemy combatants. Their return to the kill illustrates the incredible difficulty of assessing who is and who is not an enemy combatant in a foreign theater of operations where the environment does not lend itself to rigorous evidence collection. Astoundingly, the Court today raises the bar, requiring military officials to appear before civilian courts and defend their decisions under procedural and evidentiary rules that go beyond what Congress has specified. . . .

And today it is not just the military that the Court elbows aside. A mere two Terms ago in *Hamdan v. Rumsfeld*, 548 U.S. 557 (2006), when the Court held (quite amazingly) that the Detainee Treatment Act of 2005 had not stripped *habeas* jurisdiction over Guantanamo petitioners' claims, four Members of today's five-Justice majority joined an opinion saying the following: "Nothing prevents the President from returning to Congress to seek the authority [for trial by military commission] he believes necessary." . . .

The Suspension Clause of the Constitution provides: "The Privilege of the Writ of *Habeas Corpus* shall not be suspended, unless when in Cases of Rebellion or Invasion the public Safety may require it." Art. I, Sec. 9, cl. 2. As a court of law operating under a written Constitution, our role is to determine whether there is a conflict between that Clause and the Military Commissions Act. A conflict arises only if the Suspension Clause preserves the privilege of the writ for aliens held by the United States military as enemy combatants at the base in Guantanamo Bay, located within the sovereign territory of Cuba.

We have frequently stated that we owe great deference to Congress's view that a law it has passed is constitutional. Indeed, we accord great deference even when the President acts alone in this area.

In light of those principles of deference, the Court's conclusion that "the common law [does not] yiel[d] a definite answer to the questions before us," leaves it no choice but to affirm the Court of Appeals. The writ as preserved in the Constitution could not possibly extend farther than the common law provided when that Clause was written. The Court admits that it cannot determine whether the writ historically extended to aliens held abroad, and it concedes (necessarily) that Guantanamo Bay lies outside the sovereign territory of the United States. Together, these two concessions establish that it is (in the Court's view) perfectly ambiguous whether the common-law writ would have provided a remedy for these petitioners. If that is so, the Court has no basis to strike down the Military Commissions Act, and must leave undisturbed the considered judgment of the coequal branches.

How, then, does the Court weave a clear constitutional prohibition out of pure interpretive equipoise? The Court resorts to "fundamental separation-of-powers principles" to interpret the Suspension Clause. According to the Court, because "the writ of *habeas corpus* is itself an indispensable mechanism for monitoring the separation of powers," the test of its extraterritorial reach "must not be subject to manipulation by those whose power it is designed to restrain."

That approach distorts the nature of the separation of powers and its role in the constitutional structure. The "fundamental separation-of-powers principles" that the Constitution embodies are to be derived not from some judicially imagined matrix, but from the sum total of the individual separation-of-powers provisions that the Constitution sets forth. Only by considering them one-by-one does the full shape of the Constitution's separation-of-powers principles emerge. It is nonsensical to interpret those provisions themselves in light of some general "separation-of-powers principles" dreamed up by the Court. Rather, they must be interpreted to mean what they were understood to mean when the people ratified them. And if the understood scope of the writ of *habeas corpus* was "designed to restrain" (as the Court says) the actions of the Executive, the understood limits upon that scope were (as the Court seems not to grasp) just as much "designed to restrain" the incursions of the Third Branch. "Manipulation" of the territorial reach of the writ by the Judiciary poses just as much a threat to the proper separation of powers as "manipulation" by the Executive. . . .

The Court purports to derive from our precedents a "functional" test for the extraterritorial reach of the writ, which shows that the Military Commissions Act unconstitutionally restricts the scope of *habeas*. That is remarkable because the most pertinent of those precedents, *Johnson v. Eisentrager*, conclusively establishes the opposite. There we were confronted with the claims of 21 Germans held at Landsberg Prison, an American military facility located in the American Zone of occupation in postwar Germany. They had been captured in China, and an American military commission sitting there had convicted them of war crimes—collaborating with the Japanese after Germany's surrender. Like the petitioners here, the Germans claimed that their detentions violated the Constitution and international law, and sought a writ of *habeas corpus*. Writing for the Court, Justice JACKSON held that American courts lacked *habeas* jurisdiction: "We are cited to [sic] no instance where a court, in this or any other country where the writ is known, has issued it on behalf of an alien enemy who, at no relevant time and in no stage of his captivity, has been within its territorial jurisdiction. Nothing in the text of the Constitution extends such a right, nor does anything in our statutes." Justice JACKSON then elaborated on the historical scope of the writ: "The alien, to whom the United States has been traditionally hospitable, has been accorded a generous and ascending scale of rights as he increases his identity with our society." "But, in extending constitutional protections beyond the citizenry, the Court has been at pains to point out that it was the alien's presence within its territorial jurisdiction that gave the Judiciary power to act." . . .

Eisentrager thus held—held beyond any doubt—that the Constitution does not ensure *habeas* for aliens held by the United States in areas over which our Government is not sovereign.

The Court would have us believe that *Eisentrager* rested on "[p]ractical considerations," such as the "difficulties of ordering the Government to produce the prisoners in a *habeas corpus* proceeding." Formal sovereignty, says the Court, is merely one consideration "that bears upon which constitutional guarantees apply" in a given location. This is a sheer rewriting of the case. *Eisentrager* mentioned practical concerns, to be sure—but not for the purpose of determining under what circumstances American courts could issue writs of *habeas corpus* for aliens abroad. It cited them to support its holding that the Constitution does not empower courts to issue writs of *habeas corpus* to aliens abroad in any circumstances. As Justice BLACK accurately said in dissent, "the Court's opinion inescapably denies courts power to afford the least bit of protection for any alien who is subject to our occupation government abroad, even if he is neither enemy nor belligerent and even after peace is officially declared." . . .

What drives today's decision is neither the meaning of the Suspension Clause, nor the principles of our precedents, but rather an inflated notion of judicial supremacy. . . . That cannot be, the Court says, because it is the duty of this Court to say what the law is. . . . Our power "to say what the law is" is circumscribed by the limits of our statutorily and constitutionally conferred jurisdiction. And that is precisely the question in these cases: whether the Constitution confers *habeas* jurisdiction on federal courts to decide petitioners' claims. It is both irrational and arrogant to say that the answer must be yes, because otherwise we would not be supreme.

But so long as there are some places to which *habeas* does not run—so long as the Court's new "functional" test will not be satisfied in every case—then there will be circumstances in which "it would be possible for the political branches to govern without legal constraint." Or, to put it more impartially, areas in which the legal determinations of the other branches will be (shudder!) supreme. In other words, judicial supremacy is not really assured by the constitutional rule that the Court creates. The gap between rationale and rule leads me to conclude that the Court's ultimate, unexpressed goal is to preserve the power to review the confinement of enemy prisoners held by the Executive anywhere in the world. The "functional" test usefully evades the precedential landmine of *Eisentrager* but is so inherently subjective that it clears a wide path for the Court to traverse in the years to come.

Putting aside the conclusive precedent of *Eisentrager*, it is clear that the original understanding of the Suspension Clause was that *habeas corpus* was not available to aliens abroad.

The Suspension Clause reads: "The Privilege of the Writ of *Habeas Corpus* shall not be suspended, unless when in Cases of Rebellion or Invasion the public Safety may require it." The proper course of constitutional interpretation is to give the text the meaning it was understood to have at the time of its adoption by the people. That course is especially demanded when (as here) the Constitution limits the power of Congress to infringe upon a pre-existing common-law right. The nature of the writ of *habeas corpus* that cannot be suspended must be defined by the common-law writ that was available at the time of the founding.

It is entirely clear that, at English common law, the writ of *habeas corpus* did not extend beyond the sovereign territory of the Crown. To be sure, the writ had an "extraordinary territorial ambit," because it was a so-called "prerogative writ," which, unlike other writs, could extend beyond the realm of England to other places where the Crown was sovereign.

But prerogative writs could not issue to foreign countries, even for British subjects; they were confined to the King's dominions—those areas over which the Crown was sovereign. Thus, the writ has never extended to Scotland, which, although united to England when James I succeeded to the English throne in 1603, was considered a foreign dominion under a different Crown—that of the King of Scotland.

The common-law writ was codified by the *Habeas Corpus* Act of 1679, which "stood alongside Magna Charta and the English Bill of Rights of 1689 as a towering common law lighthouse of liberty—a beacon by which framing lawyers in America consciously steered their course." The writ was established in the Colonies beginning in the 1690's and at least one colony adopted the 1679 Act almost verbatim. Section XI of the Act stated where the writ could run. It "may be directed and run into any county palatine, the cinque-ports, or other privileged places within the kingdom of England, dominion of Wales, or town of Berwick upon Tweed, and the islands of Jersey or Guernsey."

The Act did not extend the writ elsewhere, even though the existence of other places to which British prisoners could be sent was recognized by the Act. . . .

In sum, all available historical evidence points to the conclusion that the writ would not have been available at common law for aliens captured and held outside the sovereign territory of the Crown. . . .

Today the Court warps our Constitution in a way that goes beyond the narrow issue of the reach of the Suspension Clause, invoking judicially brainstormed separation-of-powers principles to establish a manipulable "functional" test for the extraterritorial reach of *habeas corpus* (and, no doubt, for the extraterritorial reach of other constitutional protections as well). It blatantly misdescribes important precedents, most conspicuously Justice JACKSON's opinion for the Court in *Johnson v. Eisentrager*. It breaks a chain of precedent as old as the common law that prohibits judicial inquiry into detentions of aliens abroad absent statutory authorization. And, most tragically, it sets our military commanders the impossible task of proving to a civilian court, under whatever standards this Court devises in the future, that evidence supports the confinement of each and every enemy prisoner.

The Nation will live to regret what the Court has done today. I dissent.

□ *Chief Justice ROBERTS, with whom Justice SCALIA, Justice THOMAS, and Justice ALITO join, dissenting.*

Today the Court strikes down as inadequate the most generous set of procedural protections ever afforded aliens detained by this country as enemy combatants. The political branches crafted these procedures amidst an ongoing military conflict, after much careful investigation and thorough debate. The Court rejects them today out of hand, without bothering to say what due process rights the detainees possess, without explaining how the statute fails to vindicate those rights, and before a single petitioner has even attempted to avail himself of the law's operation. And to what effect? The majority merely replaces a review system designed by the people's representatives with a set of shapeless procedures to be defined by federal courts at some future date. One cannot help but think, after surveying the modest practical results of the majority's ambitious opinion, that this decision is not really about the detainees at all, but about control of federal policy regarding enemy combatants. . . .

I believe the system the political branches constructed adequately protects any constitutional rights aliens captured abroad and detained as enemy combatants may enjoy. I therefore would dismiss these cases on that ground. With all respect for the contrary views of the majority, I must dissent. . . .

War Powers Resolution

87 STAT. 555 (1973)

In response to opposition to the continuation of the Vietnam War in 1973, Congress passed the War Powers Resolution. It imposed a number of limitations on presidential commitment of troops abroad without specific congressional authorization and requires the president to notify and consult with Congress before sending armed forces into actual or potential hostilities. The act remains controversial and its constitutionality a matter of dispute.*

There are those who defend Congress's power to limit the president's war-making powers. For example, S. Carter argues that

> [t]he "inherent" powers to which opponents of the War Powers Resolution make reference are really [powers] thought to be inherent because the President has historically exercised them. But they are powers the President has exercised in the absence of any congressional objection. . . . [Moreover,] historical acquiescence by Congress in the President's exercise of a particular power does not by itself prove that Congress lacks the authority to limit the exercise of that power when it gathers the wisdom and courage to do so.†

Contrariwise, others contend that the act is far too broad and a congressional intrusion on inherent presidential powers. Among them Eugene V. Rostow points out,

> The pattern against which the [War Powers Resolution] protests is old, familiar, and rooted in the nature of things. There is nothing constitutionally illegitimate or even dubious about "undeclared" wars. We and other nations fought them frequently in the eighteenth and nineteenth centuries, as well as in the twentieth. . . . [This act] would turn the clock back to the Articles of Confederation, and destroy the Presidency which it was one of the chief aims of the men of Annapolis and Philadelphia to create.‡

> *Resolved by the Senate and House of Representatives of the United States of America in Congress assembled, That:*

---

* See Robert Scigliano, "The War Powers Resolution and the War Powers," in *The Presidency in the Constitutional Order*, ed. Joseph M. Bessette and Jeffrey Tulis (Baton Rouge: Louisiana State University Press, 1981).

† S. Carter, "The Constitutionality of the War Powers Resolution," 70 *Virginia Law Review* 101 (1984).

‡ Eugene V. Rostow, "Great Cases Make Bad Law: The War Powers Act," 50 *Texas Law Review* 833 (1972).

Section 1. This joint resolution may be cited as the "War Powers Resolution."

Sec. 2. (a) It is the purpose of this joint resolution to fulfill the intent of the framers of the Constitution of the United States and insure that the collective judgment of both the Congress and the President will apply to the introduction of United States Armed Forces into hostilities, or into situations where imminent involvement in hostilities is clearly indicated by the circumstances, and to the continued use of such forces in hostilities or in such situations.

(b) Under article I, section 8, of the Constitution, it is specifically provided that the Congress shall have the power to make all laws necessary and proper for carrying into execution, not only its own powers but also all other powers vested by the Constitution in the Government of the United States, or in any department or officer thereof.

(c) The constitutional powers of the President as Commander-in-Chief to introduce United States Armed Forces into hostilities, or into situations where imminent involvement in hostilities is clearly indicated by the circumstances, are exercised only pursuant to (1) a declaration of war, (2) specific statutory authorization, or (3) a national emergency created by attack upon the United States, its territories or possessions, or its armed forces.

Sec. 3. The President in every possible instance shall consult with Congress before introducing United States Armed Forces into hostilities or into situations where imminent involvement in hostilities is clearly indicated by the circumstances, and after every such introduction shall consult regularly with the Congress until United States Armed Forces are no longer engaged in hostilities or have been removed from such situations.

Sec. 4. (a) In the absence of a declaration of war, in any case in which United States Armed Forces are introduced—

(1) into hostilities or into situations where imminent involvement in hostilities is clearly indicated by the circumstances;

(2) into the territory, airspace or waters of a foreign nation, while equipped for combat, except for deployments which relate solely to supply, replacement, repair, or training of such forces; or

(3) in numbers which substantially enlarge United States Armed Forces equipped for combat already located in a foreign nation; the President shall submit within 48 hours to the Speaker of the House of Representatives and to the President pro tempore of the Senate a report, in writing, setting forth—

(A) the circumstances necessitating the introduction of United States Armed Forces;

(B) the constitutional and legislative authority under which such introduction took place; and

(C) the estimated scope and duration of the hostilities or involvement. . . .

(b) The President shall provide such other information as the Congress may request in the fulfillment of its constitutional responsibilities with respect to committing the Nation to war and to the use of United States Armed Forces abroad.

(c) Whenever United States Armed Forces are introduced into hostilities or into any situation described in subsection (a) of this section, the President shall, so long as such armed forces continue to be engaged in such hostilities or situation, report to the Congress periodically on the status of such hostilities or situation as well as on the scope and duration of such hostilities or situation, but in no event shall he report to the Congress less often than once every six months.

Sec. 5. (a) Each report submitted pursuant to section 4(a)(1) shall be transmitted to the Speaker of the House of Representatives and to the President pro tempore of the Senate on the same calendar day. Each report so transmitted shall be referred to the Committee on Foreign Affairs of the House of Representatives and to the Committee on Foreign Relations of the Senate for appropriate action. If, when the report is transmitted, the Congress has adjourned sine die or has adjourned for any period in excess of three calendar days, the Speaker of the House of Representatives and the President pro tempore of the Senate, if they deem it advisable (or if petitioned by at least 30 percent of the membership of their respective Houses) shall jointly request the President to convene Congress in order that it may consider the report and take appropriate action pursuant to this section.

(b) Within sixty calendar days after a report is submitted or is required to be submitted pursuant to section 4(a)(1), whichever is earlier, the President shall terminate any use of United States Armed Forces with respect to which such report was submitted (or required to be submitted), unless the Congress (1) has declared war or has enacted a specific authorization for such use of United States Armed Forces, (2) has extended by law such sixty-day period, or (3) is physically unable to meet as a result of an armed attack upon the United States. Such sixty-day period shall be extended for not more than an additional thirty days if the President determines and certifies to the Congress in writing that unavoidable military necessity respecting the safety of United States Armed Forces requires the continued use of such armed forces in the course of bringing about a prompt removal of such forces.

(c) Notwithstanding subsection (b), at any time that United States Armed Forces are engaged in hostilities outside the territory of the United States, its possessions and territories without a declaration of war or specific statutory authorization, such forces shall be removed by the President if the Congress so directs by concurrent resolution.

Sec. 6. (a) Any joint resolution or bill introduced pursuant to section 5(b) at least thirty calendar days before the expiration of the sixty-day period specified in such section shall be referred to the Committee on Foreign Affairs of the House of Representatives or the Committee on Foreign Relations of the Senate, as the case may be, and such committee shall report one such joint resolution or bill, together with its recommendations, not later than twenty-four calendar days before the expiration of the sixty-day period specified in such section, unless such House shall otherwise determine by the yeas and nays.

(b) Any joint resolution or bill so reported shall become the pending business of the House in question (in the case of the Senate the time for debate shall be equally divided between the proponents and the opponents), and shall be voted on within three calendar days thereafter, unless such House shall otherwise determine by yeas and nays.

(c) Such a joint resolution or bill passed by one House shall be referred to the committee of the other House named in subsection (a) and shall be reported out not later than fourteen calendar days before the expiration of the sixty-day period specified in section 5(b). The joint resolution or bill so reported shall become the pending business of the House in question and shall be voted on within three calendar days after it has been reported, unless such House shall otherwise determine by yeas and nays.

(d) In the case of any disagreement between the two Houses of Congress with respect to a joint resolution or bill passed by both Houses, conferees shall be promptly appointed and the committee of conference shall make and file a report with respect to such resolution or bill not later than four calendar days before the expiration of the sixty-day period specified in section 5(b). In the event the conferees are unable to agree within 48 hours, they shall report back to their respective Houses in disagreement. Notwithstanding any rule in either House concerning the printing of conference reports in the Record or concerning any delay in the consideration of such reports, such report shall be acted on by both Houses not later than the expiration of such sixty-day period.

Sec. 7. (a) Any concurrent resolution introduced pursuant to section 5(c) shall be referred to the Committee on Foreign Affairs of the House of Representatives or the Committee on Foreign Relations of the Senate, as the case may be, and one such concurrent resolution shall be reported out by such committee together with its recommendations within fifteen calendar days, unless such House shall otherwise determine by the yeas and nays.

(b) Any concurrent resolution so reported shall become the pending business of the House in question (in the case of the Senate the time for debate shall be equally divided between the proponents and the opponents) and shall be voted on within three calendar days thereafter, unless such House shall otherwise determine by yeas and nays.

(c) Such a concurrent resolution passed by one House shall be referred to the committee of the other House named in subsection (a) and shall be reported out by such committee together with its recommendations within fifteen calendar days and shall thereupon become the pending business of such House and shall be voted upon within three calendar days, unless such House shall otherwise determine by yeas and nays.

(d) In the case of any disagreement between the two Houses of Congress with respect to a concurrent resolution passed by both Houses, conferees shall be promptly appointed and the committee of conference shall make and file a report with respect to such concurrent resolution within six calendar days after the legislation is referred to the committee of conference. Notwithstanding any rule in either House concerning the printing of conference reports in the Record or concerning any delay in the consideration of such reports, such report shall be acted on by both Houses not later than six calendar days after the conference report is filed. In the event the conferees are unable to agree within 48 hours, they shall report back to their respective Houses in disagreement.

Sec. 8. (a) Authority to introduce United States Armed Forces into hostilities or into situations wherein involvement in hostilities is clearly indicated by the circumstances shall not be inferred—

(1) from any provision of law (whether or not in effect before the date of the enactment of this joint resolution), including any provision contained in any appropriation Act, unless such provision specifically authorizes the introduction of United States Armed Forces into hostilities or into such situations and states that it is intended to constitute specific statutory authorization within the meaning of this joint resolution; or

(2) from any treaty heretofore or hereafter ratified unless such treaty is implemented by legislation specifically authorizing the introduction of United States Armed Forces into hostilities or into such situations and stating that it is intended to constitute specific statutory authorization within the meaning of this joint resolution.

(b) Nothing in this joint resolution shall be construed to require any further specific statutory authorization to permit members of United States Armed Forces to participate jointly with members of the armed forces of one or more foreign countries in the headquarters operations of high–level military commands which were established prior to the date of enactment of this joint resolution and pursuant to the United Nations Charter or any treaty ratified by the United States prior to such date.

(c) For purposes of this joint resolution, the term "introduction of United States Armed Forces" includes the assignment of members of such armed forces to command, coordinate, participate in the movement of, or accompany the regular or irregular military forces of any foreign country or government when such military forces are engaged, or there exists an imminent threat that such forces will become engaged, in hostilities.

(d) Nothing in this joint resolution—

(1) is intended to alter the constitutional authority of the Congress or of the President, or the provisions of existing treaties; or

(2) shall be construed as granting any authority to the President with respect to the introduction of United States Armed Forces into hostilities or into situations wherein involvement in hostilities is clearly indicated by the circumstances which authority he would not have had in the absence of this joint resolution.

Sec. 9. If any provision of this joint resolution or the application thereof to any person or circumstance is held invalid, the remainder of the joint resolution and the application of such provision to any other person or circumstance shall not be affected thereby.

Sec. 10. This joint resolution shall take effect on the date of its enactment.

[Passed over Presidential veto November 7, 1973.]

■ THE DEVELOPMENT OF LAW

The USA PATRIOT Act of 2001, Wiretaps, and the Foreign Intelligence Surveillance Court★

Enacted in response to the terrorist attacks of September 11, 2001, the USA PATRIOT Act authorizes sweeping changes in law enforcement, notably lowering the standards for searching and seizing individuals suspected of terrorism, for example, as well as expanding investigatory powers. Among the changes, the law authorizes

- Roving wiretaps—wiretaps on any telephone used by a person suspected of terrorism—and the use of key-logger devices, which register every stroke made on a computer, and Internet wiretaps.
- Police searches of private property without prior notification of the owners and without a search warrant.
- A lower standard for judicial approval of wiretaps for individuals suspected of terrorist activities.
- The attorney general to designate domestic groups as terrorist organizations and to block the entry into the country of foreigners aligned with them.
- The Central Intelligence Agency to investigate Americans suspected of having connections to terrorism.
- The Department of Treasury to monitor financial transactions—bank accounts, mutual funds, and brokerage deals—and to obtain medical and other electronic records on individuals.
- The detention and deportation of foreigners suspected of having connections to terrorist organizations.

One of the most controversial provisions of the USA PATRIOT Act removes restrictions on information sharing and foreign intelligence gathering. Section 203 requires the attorney general to disclose to the director of the Central Intelligence Agency (CIA) "foreign intelligence" obtained from a federal criminal investigation, including wiretaps and grand jury hearings. The CIA may also share information with domestic law enforcement agencies.

★The full title of the law is Uniting and Strengthening America by Providing Appropriate Tools Required to Intercept and Obstruct Terrorism (USA PATRIOT) Act of 2001. For the text and other information go to www.personalinfomediary.com/USAPATRIOTACT_Text.htm.

(continues)

■ The Development of Law
The USA PATRIOT Act of 2001, Wiretaps, and the
Foreign Intelligence Surveillance Court (continued)

Critics charged that the broad language of the act's disclosure requirements permits the Department of Justice (DoJ) to give the CIA all information related to a foreigner or to a citizen's contacts with a foreign government or organization, not merely pertaining to international terrorism. Moreover, the act did not establish any standards or safeguards for restricting the disclosure of "foreign intelligence information." Critics therefore contended that the intelligence community may collect information about individuals who have committed no crimes but who are involved in lawful protests of American foreign policies.

Furthermore, the USA PATRIOT Act changed the Foreign Intelligence Surveillance (FIS) Act of 1978, which created a special FIS court, staffed by sitting federal judges on special assignments, to approve wiretaps and to ensure that "the sole purpose" of domestic intelligence gathering was to obtain foreign intelligence information. That law was enacted because of abuses in domestic surveillance of anti-Vietnam war protesters and leaders of the civil rights movement in the 1960s and 1970s. Section 218 of the USA PATRIOT Act, however, changed the law so the DoJ need only show that the collection of foreign intelligence information has "a significant purpose," instead of being "the sole purpose" of an investigation.

Based on those provisions in 2002, Attorney General John Ashcroft issued new guidelines allowing federal prosecutors to consult with law enforcement agents conducting foreign intelligence surveillance. Those guidelines were in turn challenged as a violation of the Fourth Amendment and for permitting the use of special FIS wiretaps for investigating and prosecuting ordinary criminals, and not just spies and terrorists. In May 2002, the U.S. Foreign Intelligence Surveillance Court unanimously rejected the new guidelines and for the first time in the history of the court released a published opinion, *In re All Matters Submitted to the Foreign Intelligence Surveillance Court*, No. Multiple 02-429 F.Supp. 2d C (U.S. Foreign Intel. Surv. Ct., 17 May 2002). Emphasizing the special and intrusive nature of FIS Act surveillance, the seven judges on the court maintained that the "walls" prohibiting criminal prosecutors from conducting investigations of suspected foreign spies and terrorists should not be torn down and that the DoJ's new guidelines were not "reasonably designed."

However, the DoJ successfully appealed that decision to a special three-judge court of appeals, as authorized by the FIS Act and whose judges are assigned from other federal appellate courts by the chief justice of the Supreme Court. Subsequently, the FIS appellate court upheld the DoJ's new guidelines, in *In re: Sealed Case* (U.S. Foreign Intelligence Surveillance Court of Review No. 02-001 and 02-002), available at www.cadc.uscourts.gov/common/newsroom/02001.pdf. In doing so, the appellate court stressed that the USA PATRIOT Act aimed to eliminate "walls" between foreign intelligence and domestic law enforcement agencies, and explained: "Effective counterintelligence, as we have learned, requires the whole-hearted cooperation of all the government's personnel who can be brought to the task. A standard which punishes such cooperation could well be thought dangerous to national security." As a result, federal criminal prosecutors may use information against citizens obtained from wiretaps authorized by the FIS court, based on less than probable cause and on more searching surveillance than permitted under traditional wiretaps.

The principal provisions of the USA PATRIOT Act were renewed in 2006. Yet another controversy erupted over the revelation that President George W. Bush issued a secret executive order authorizing the National Security Agency (NSA) to conduct warrantless electronic surveillance of "communications where one . . . party to the communication is outside of the United States" and there is "a reasonable basis to conclude that one party" is a member of or supporting al Qaeda or other terrorists. The surveillance involves monitoring e-mails, through Google-like searches, and tracking cell phone calls and other Internet and satellite communications. Foreign intelligence surveillance was supposed to be governed by the Foreign Intelligence Surveillance Act (FISA), but the Bush administration defended the NSA's warrantless surveillance on three grounds. First, the president has the inherent power and power as commander in chief to do so during times of war. Prior presidents made similar claims. President Abraham Lincoln ordered the warrantless wiretapping of telegraph wires during the Civil War. Likewise, during World Wars I and II Presidents Woodrow Wilson and Franklin D. Roosevelt ordered the interception of international communications. Similar claims to presidential power were made by subsequent administrations, including those of Presidents Jimmy Carter and Bill Clinton.

Second, the joint resolution for the Authorization for the Use of Military Force (AUMF) of 2001 provides for the use of "all necessary and appropriate" force to combat terrorists, and thus justifies the president's action. Third, the AUMF justifies not complying with the provisions of the FISA, since it superseded FISA. In addition, *Smith v. Maryland*, 442

(continues)

■ THE DEVELOPMENT OF LAW
The USA PATRIOT Act of 2001, Wiretaps, and the
Foreign Intelligence Surveillance Court (continued)

U.S. 735 (1979), upheld the use of pen registers, which record the telephone numbers called from phones but not the conversations. Accordingly, by extension the NSA's collection of "meta-data"—the time and to and from of Internet and satellite communications—was permissible.

By contrast, some members of Congress and civil liberties groups countered that the president has no inherent power to authorize warrantless domestic security surveillance; that neither the AUMF nor the FISA permit such a program; and that *United States v. United States District Court*, 407 U.S. 297 (1972), the so-called *Keith* case, held that domestic intelligence surveillance requires prior judicial approval of a warrant in order to satisfy the Fourth Amendment's guarantee against unreasonable searches and seizures, though the decision left open the matter of warrantless foreign surveillance. After months of negotiations in 2006 Congress enacted legislation reasserting the authority of the FISA court, while permitting wiretapping without a warrant for up to forty-five days but requiring the attorney general to certify and explain why such warrantless surveillance is necessary to a subcommittee of the Senate Intelligence Committee.

Subsequently, in 2006 it was also revealed that the NSA had been monitoring the phone numbers dialed by millions of U.S. citizens in order to search for telephone calling patterns and possible links to terrorists, as well as that the Central Intelligence Agency and the Department of Treasury mines the transactions of 7,800 financial institutions worldwide. A Belgian cooperative routed daily about $6 trillion in international transactions. And its database is monitored to find customers' names, account numbers, and other information that establishes links to al Qaeda and other terrorist organization.

In 2006, a federal district court declared the NSA program unconstitutional. Then, in 2007 a FISA court judge held that the Bush administration overstepped its authority in monitoring telephone calls and e-mails that pass through U.S. networks between foreign nationals. In response, however, Congress enacted and President Bush signed into law the Protect America Act of 2007 that expanded the administration's authority to conduct warrantless wiretaps without FISA approval, including telephone calls and e-mails of U.S. citizens, so long as officials indicate that they are targeting someone overseas suspected of terrorism. The constitutionality of that law was immediately challenged by the Center for Constitutional Rights as a violation of the First and Fourth Amendments.

In 2008, Congress revised the Foreign Intelligence Surveillance Act, which was created to issue warrants for domestic spying cases related to espionage and terrorism. It did so because of controversies over the Bush administration's bypassing the court and conducting warrantless searches of electronic communications. The major provisions of the law, which will expire in 2012, provide that:

(1) Telecommunication companies that assisted the government in warrantless surveillance on the Internet after the September 11, 2001, terrorist attacks are shielded from lawsuits for invasion of privacy.

(2) Procedures for monitoring telephone calls and e-mails of foreigners must be approved by the Foreign Intelligence Surveillance Court, and the government's surveillance of U.S. citizens, including those abroad, require that court's approval of individual warrants.

(3) The government is prohibited from targeting a foreigner in order to secretly eavesdrop on U.S. citizen's telephone calls and e-mails without court approval.

(4) The government may conduct emergency eavesdropping without a court-approved warrant but must seek approval within one week.

For further reading see U.S. Department of Justice, "Legal Authorities Supporting the Activities of the National Security Agency Described by the President" (Washington, DC: Department of Justice, January 19, 2006), and compare Congressional Research Service, "Memorandum: Presidential Authority to Conduct Warrantless Electronic Surveillance to Gather Foreign Intelligence Information" (Washington, DC: Congressional Research, January 5, 2006).

The Supreme Court of Israel's Ruling against the Use of Torture

The disclosure of the abuse of prisoners by U.S. soldiers at the Abu Ghraib prison in Iraq, and the further revelations in 2006 that torture continued in some Iraqi jails, fueled the controversy over the application of international human rights standards to interrogations for military intelligence purposes during wartime. Torture and other cruel, inhuman, or degrading treatment and punishment violates the Third Geneva Convention of 1949, the Convention against Torture and Other Cruel, Inhuman or Degrading Treatment or Punishment, and the International Covenant on Civil and Political Rights, all of which the United States joined. In addition, a 1994 federal law makes the use of torture by U.S. officials abroad a criminal offense.

The Supreme Court of Israel, in the 1999 *Judgment Concerning the Interrogation Methods Implied* [sic] *by the General Security Services*, ruled against the use of certain techniques involving inhuman treatment and torture used when interrogating Palestinians suspected of terrorism.

President [Chief Justice Aharon] Barak:

> The General Security Service (hereinafter, the "GSS") investigates individuals suspected of committing crimes against Israel's security. . . . The interrogations are conducted on the basis of directives regulating interrogation methods. These directives equally authorize investigators to apply physical means against those undergoing interrogation (for instance, shaking the suspect and the *"Shabach"* position [the cuffing of the suspect, seating him on a low chair, covering his head with an opaque sack (head covering) and playing powerfully loud music in the area]. The basis for permitting such methods is that they are deemed immediately necessary for saving human lives. . . .
>
> The State of Israel has been engaged in an unceasing struggle for both its very existence and security, from the day of its founding. Terrorist organizations have established as their goal Israel's annihilation. Terrorist acts and the general disruption of order are their means of choice. In employing such methods, these groups do not distinguish between civilian and military targets. They carry out terrorist attacks in which scores are murdered in public areas, public transportation. . . .
>
> We asked the applicants' attorneys whether the "ticking time bomb" rationale was not sufficiently persuasive to justify the use of physical means, for instance, when a bomb is known

to have been placed in a public area and will undoubtedly explode causing immeasurable human tragedy if its location is not revealed at once. This question elicited a variety of responses from the various applicants before the Court. There are those convinced that physical means are not to be used under any circumstances; the prohibition on such methods to their mind is absolute, whatever the consequences may be. On the other hand, there are others who argue that even if it is perhaps acceptable to employ physical means in most exceptional "ticking time bomb" circumstances, these methods are in practice used even in absence of the "ticking time bomb" conditions. The very fact that, in most cases, the use of such means is illegal provides sufficient justification for banning their use altogether, even if doing so would inevitably absorb those rare cases in which physical coercion may have been justified. . . .

[A] reasonable investigation is necessarily one free of torture, free of cruel, inhuman treatment of the subject and free of any degrading handling whatsoever. There is a prohibition on the use of "brutal or inhuman means" in the course of an investigation. Human dignity also includes the dignity of the suspect being interrogated. This conclusion is in perfect accord with (various) International Law treaties—to which Israel is a signatory—which prohibit the use of torture, "cruel, inhuman treatment" and "degrading treatment." These prohibitions are "absolute." . . .

We shall now turn from the general to the particular. Plainly put, shaking is a prohibited investigation method. It harms the suspect's body. It violates his dignity. It is a violent method which does not form part of a legal investigation. It surpasses that which is necessary. . . .

It was argued before the Court that one of the investigation methods employed consists of the suspect crouching on the tips of his toes for five minute intervals. The State did not deny this practice. This is a prohibited investigation method. It does not serve any purpose inherent to an investigation. It is degrading and infringes upon an individual's human dignity.

The "*Shabach*" method is composed of a number of cumulative components: the cuffing of the suspect, seating him on a low chair, covering his head with an opaque sack (head covering) and playing powerfully loud music in the area. [W]e accept that the suspect's cuffing, for the purpose of preserving the investigators' safety, is an action included in the general power to investigate. Provided the suspect is cuffed for this purpose, it is within the investigator's authority to cuff him. . . . Notwithstanding, the cuffing associated with the "*Shabach*" position is

(continues)

■ IN COMPARATIVE PERSPECTIVE
The Supreme Court of Israel's Ruling against the
Use of Torture (continued)

unlike routine cuffing. The suspect is cuffed with his hands tied behind his back. One hand is placed inside the gap between the chair's seat and back support, while the other is tied behind him, against the chair's back support. This is a distorted and unnatural position. The investigators' safety does not require it. Therefore, there is no relevant justification for handcuffing the suspect's hands with particularly small handcuffs, if this is in fact the practice. The use of these methods is prohibited. . . .

This is the law with respect to the method involving seating the suspect in question in the "*Shabach*" position. We accept that seating a man is inherent to the investigation. This is not the case when the chair upon which he is seated is a very low one, tilted forward facing the ground, and when he is sitting in this position for long hours. This sort of seating is not encompassed by the general power to interrogate. . . . [Such] methods do not fall within the sphere of a "fair" interrogation. They are not reasonable. They impinge upon the suspect's dignity, his bodily integrity and his basic rights in an excessive manner (or beyond what is necessary). . . .

A similar—though not identical—combination of interrogation methods [was] discussed in the case of *Ireland v. United Kingdom* (1978) 2 EHRR 25. In that case, the Court probed five interrogation methods used by England for the purpose of investigating detainees suspected of terrorist activities in Northern Ireland. The methods were as follows: protracted standing against the wall on the tip of one's toes; covering of the suspect's head throughout the detention (except during the actual interrogation); exposing the suspect to powerfully loud noise for a prolonged period and deprivation of sleep, food and drink. The Court held that these methods did not constitute "torture." However, since they treated the suspect in an "inhuman and degrading" manner, they were nonetheless prohibited. . . .

This decision opens with a description of the difficult reality in which Israel finds herself security wise. We shall conclude this judgment by re-addressing that harsh reality. We are aware that this decision does not ease dealing with that reality. This is the destiny of democracy, as not all means are acceptable to it, and not all practices employed by its enemies are open before it. Although a democracy must often fight with one hand tied behind its back, it nonetheless has the upper hand. Preserving the Rule of Law and recognition of an individual's liberty constitutes an important component in its understanding of security. At the end of the day, they strengthen its spirit and its strength and allow it to overcome its difficulties. This having been said, there are those who argue that Israel's security problems are too numerous, thereby requiring the authorization to use physical means. If it will nonetheless be decided that it is appropriate for Israel, in light of its security difficulties to sanction physical means in interrogations (and the scope of these means which deviate from the ordinary investigation rules), this is an issue that must be decided by the legislative branch which represents the people. We do not take any stand on this matter at this time. It is there that various considerations must be weighed. The pointed debate must occur there. It is there that the required legislation may be passed, provided, of course, that a law infringing upon a suspect's liberty "befitting the values of the State of Israel," is enacted for a proper purpose, and to an extent no greater than is required. (Article 8 to the Basic Law: Human Dignity and Liberty). . . .

4

THE PRESIDENT AS CHIEF EXECUTIVE IN DOMESTIC AFFAIRS

The growth in the legislative powers of the president might appear paradoxical given the principle of separation of powers. Article I vests "[a]ll legislative powers" in Congress, while Article II provides that "[t]he executive Power shall be vested in a President." Yet the Constitution provides the president with certain legislative powers as well. He has the power to inform Congress about "the State of the Union," to convene both houses of Congress on extraordinary occasions, and to veto legislation. As chief executive, the president also has the power to appoint subordinate officers in the government and thereby influence the development and implementation of legislation.

The legislative and administrative role of the president has nonetheless grown enormously with the development of White House staff and the institutionalized presidency. The state of the union address, for instance, has become an occasion for presidents to announce their own broad legislative programs. Even more important, Congress has delegated vast legislative powers to the executive branch. As a result, administrative agencies, under the control and supervision of the president, are responsible for developing and implementing the overwhelming majority of all federal regulations. Besides these statutory grants of power to the executive branch, presidents may assert legislative powers through executive orders, presidential proclamations, and White House oversight of regulatory rule making. In addition, presidents may claim inherent or implied powers as chief executive and under their obligation to "take Care that the Laws be faithfully executed."

This chapter examines the president's powers as chief executive in regard to controversies over national security, the appointment and removal of federal officials, and the legislative role of the presidency in the administrative state. The chapter concludes by taking up issues involving presidential immunity and accountability, dealing particu-larly with claims to executive privilege and the impeachment of the president.

SELECTED BIBLIOGRAPHY

Barber, Sotirios. *The Constitution and the Delegation of Congressional Power*. Chicago: University of Chicago Press, 1975.

Cooper, Phillip. *By Order of the President: The Use and Abuse of Executive Direct Action*. Lawrence: University Press of Kansas, 2002.

Fisher, Louis. *Constitutional Conflicts between Congress and the President*. 5th ed. Lawrence: University Press of Kansas, 2007.

Marcus, Maeva. *Truman and the Steel Seizure Case*. New York: Columbia University Press, 1977.

A | *National Security and Inherent and Emergency Powers*

In times of emergency and in response to perceived threats to national security, presidents claim inherent or implied powers over domestic as well as foreign affairs. They do so as chief executive and as empowered to "take Care that the Laws be faithfully executed." But the Court has been more troubled by claims to inherent presidential powers in domestic, as opposed to foreign, affairs. As Chief Justice Hughes observed in *Home Building & Loan Association v. Blaisdell*, 290 U.S. 398 (1934) (see Vol. 2, Ch. 3),

> Emergency does not create power. Emergency does not increase granted power or remove or diminish the restrictions imposed upon power granted or reserved. The Constitution was adopted in a period of grave emergency. Its grants of power to the federal government and its limitations of the power of the States were determined in the light of emergency, and they are not altered by emergency. . . .
>
> While emergency does not create power, emergency may furnish the occasion for the exercise of power. . . . The constitutional question presented in the light of an emergency is whether the power possessed embraces the particular exercise of it in response to particular conditions.

The Court first confronted claims of inherent presidential powers in domestic affairs in *In re Neagle*, 135 U.S. 546 (1890). David Neagle, a U.S. marshal, had been assigned by the attorney general to protect Justice Stephen Field, after a disgruntled litigant threatened his life, while riding circuit in California. Neagle subsequently shot and killed the litigant and was charged with murder by state authorities. The federal government sought his release, contending that he was simply performing his duties as a marshal, even though there was no statutory authority for the president to assign bodyguards to federal judges. Over the dissent of Chief Justice Fuller and Justice Lamar, the Court ruled that the president's power to faithfully execute the laws was not "limited to the enforcement of acts of Congress." According to the majority it was unthinkable that the president should have "within the domain of [his] powers no means of protecting . . . judges."

In another late-nineteenth-century case, the Court underscored that the president's obligation to faithfully execute the laws conveyed certain inherent powers as well. In *In re Debs*, 158 U.S. 564 (1895), the Court unanimously upheld the contempt conviction of Eugene Debs, a prominent Socialist and labor leader, for violating an injunction against a labor union strike aimed at preventing the operation of certain railroads. Although there was no express authority for the government's injunction, Justice Brewer upheld the convictions and injunction on the grounds that "[t]he national government, given by the Constitution power to regulate interstate commerce, has by express statute assumed jurisdiction over such commerce when carried on railroads. It is charged, therefore, with the duty of keeping those highways of interstate free from obstruction."

By contrast, in the twentieth century the Court has on several occasions rejected broad claims of inherent presidential powers in domestic affairs. In the famous "Steel Seizure Case," *Youngstown Sheet & Tube v. Sawyer* (1952) (see excerpt below), the justices divided six to three in striking down President Harry Truman's order for the secretary of commerce to seize and operate the nation's steel mills so as to avert a nationwide strike that might have jeopardized an undeclared war in Korea. However, only Justices Black and Douglas took the position that the president has no such inherent powers. The four others in the majority took more pragmatic approaches, emphasizing that Congress contemplated but rejected passing legislation authorizing the president to seize steel mills in the event of labor strikes. While contending that in different circumstances such an exercise of power might be justified, these justices found the president's actions in this case too drastic. Chief Justice Fred Vinson, along with two other dissenters, nevertheless adhered to the view advanced by *Neagle* in maintaining that Truman was simply "faithfully execut[ing] the laws by acting in an emergency to maintain the status quo, thereby preventing collapse of the legislative programs until Congress could act."

During the Nixon presidency, the Court once again confronted claims to inherent presidential powers invoked to protect national security interests. In the "Pentagon Papers" case, *New York Times Co. v. United States* (1971) (see excerpt below), a bitterly divided Court agreed only on a brief *per curiam* opinion rejecting, as a prior restraint on freedom of the press, the administration's efforts to enjoin the publication of a history of America's involvement in Vietnam that was prepared by a California think tank, the Rand Corporation, for the Department of Defense and classified top secret. Although all nine justices issued separate opinions in the six-to-three decision, five justices—Black, Douglas, Stewart, White, and Marshall—indicated that the president has no power, without prior congressional authorization, to suppress the publication of classified documents in the interests of national security.

The following year in *United States v. United States District Court*, 407 U.S. 297 (1972), the Court dealt another blow to claims of inherent power by the Nixon presidency. The administration had wiretapped the offices of a number of domestic organizations to gather intelligence information in the interest of national security. The justices (eight to zero) ruled that such domestic security surveillance, conducted without congressional guidelines or judicially issued search warrants, ran afoul of the Fourth Amendment's guarantee against unreasonable searches and seizures. Subsequently, Congress passed the Foreign Intelligence Surveillance Act of 1978, requiring the government to obtain a warrant prior to undertaking electronic surveillance for the purpose of obtaining foreign intelligence information. But the USA PATRIOT Act of 2001 eliminated many of the safeguards earlier provided; see THE DEVELOPMENT OF LAW box in the preceding section.

Despite these rulings, the permissible scope of presidential power that may be invoked in the interest of national security remains a matter of considerable contention, especially when supported by congressional legislation but challenged as infringing on First Amendment freedoms. Although the Court has not squarely addressed this controversy, note that five justices in the "Pentagon Papers" case suggest that the president may enjoin the publication of documents in the interest of "national security" when expressly authorized to do so by Congress. Also, in *Snepp v. United States* 444 U.S. 507 (1980), the Court upheld over First Amendment objections, the requirements of the Central Intelligence Agency's (CIA) based in part on statutory authority, that employees and former employees submit any writing related to the agency for prepublication review to safeguard interests in foreign affairs and national security.

In *United States v. The Progressive, Inc.*, 467 F.Supp. 990 (1979), the government sought and obtained from a federal district court a temporary injunction against the publication of an article titled "The H–Bomb Secret: How We Got It, Why We're Telling It." It did so under the Atomic Energy Act, which authorizes the government to obtain a temporary or permanent injunction against the dissemination of any "restricted data" concerning the construction of atomic weapons. Judge Robert W. Warren found "no plausible reason why the public needs to know the technical details about hydrogen bomb construction to carry on an informed debate" about nuclear proliferation. And he distinguished this case from the *New York Times* case, observing,

> In the first place, the study involved in the *New York Times* case contained historical data relating to events that occurred some

■ THE DEVELOPMENT OF LAW

The State Secrets Privilege

The state secrets privilege is a common-law evidentiary rule, which traces back to English law and was recognized in *United States v. Reynolds*, 345 U.S. 1 (1953). The privilege is invoked by the executive branch to exclude evidence from discovery and other court proceedings that allegedly endanger national security and/or military secrets. When the privilege is invoked, plaintiffs often cannot continue civil lawsuits without the privileged information, and the cases are dismissed or dropped. (The Classified Information Procedures Act provides a similar rule for criminal cases.)

The basis for the state secrets privilege has been claimed, on the one hand, on the president's powers as commander in chief and as "the sole organ" in foreign affairs, as suggested in *United States v. Nixon*, 418 U.S. 683 (1974) (excerpted in this chapter); and, on the other hand, derived from the principle of separation of powers, as *Reynolds* held.

Since *Reynolds* the privilege has been increasingly claimed. After the September 11, 2001, terrorist attacks, President George W. Bush's administration invoked the privilege in a wide range of cases in order to not only withhold information, but also to have lawsuits dismissed. The privilege was claimed in cases challenging the detention of enemy combat-

three to twenty years previously. Secondly, the Supreme Court agreed with the lower court that no cogent reasons were advanced by the government as to why the article affected national security except that publication might cause some embarrassment to the United States. A final and most vital difference between these two cases is the fact that a specific statute is involved here. Section 2274 of The Atomic Energy Act prohibits anyone from communicating, transmitting or disclosing any restricted data to any person "with reason to believe such data will be utilized to injure the United States or to secure an advantage to any foreign nation."

But when a similar article appeared in another publication, the government abandoned its efforts to permanently enjoin *The Progressive* magazine's article. The Supreme Court thus did not rule on the government's actions and whether the Atomic Energy Act is overly broad or so vague as to infringe on First Amendment freedoms.

ants, for example, and the National Security Agency's secret wiretapping. In addition, Bush issued Executive Order 13233 to extend the privilege to allow former presidents and high government officials to bar the release of records from their tenures in office.

Critics counter that courts are too reluctant to scrutinize claims of state secrets, though in some recent cases lower courts have rejected claims to the privilege. Critics also charge that the privilege has been invoked simply to prevent embarrassing facts rather than legitimate state secrets, and that evidence that has been excluded from court cases has later been revealed to contain no state secrets. In *Reynolds*, widows of crew members of a crashed B-29 bomber sought accident reports but were denied on the ground of state secrets. The Court held that the executive branch could bar the release of the reports because it would impair national security. However, in 1996 the reports were declassified and in 2000 found to contain no secret material. They do, though, indicate the poor condition of the bomber, and prompted critics to charge that the government had abused the state secrets privilege.

For further discussion, see Louis Fisher, *The Reynolds Case*. Lawrence: University Press of Kansas, 2006; Carrie Newton Lyons, "The State Secrets Privilege: Expanding Scope Through Government Misuse," 11 *Lewis & Clark Law Review* (2007); Louis Fisher, "The State Secrets Privilege: Relying on Reynolds," 122 *Political Science Quarterly* 385 (2007); and William G. Weaver and Robert Pallitto, "State Secrets and Executive Power," 120 *Political Science Quarterly* 85 (2005).

■ INSIDE THE COURT

The Argument for Inherent and Emergency Presidential Powers in "the Steel Seizure Case"

During oral arguments before federal district court Judge David A. Pine, Assistant Attorney General Holmes Baldridge contended in the following exchange that the president enjoys inherent and unreviewable powers in times of national emergency.

THE COURT: Now, Mr. Attorney General . . . I wonder if you would give me such assistance as you can . . . as to your power or as to your client's power.

As I understand it you do not assert any statutory power.

MR. BALDRIDGE: That is correct.

THE COURT: And you do not assert any express constitutional power.

MR. BALDRIDGE: Well, your Honor, we base the President's power on Sections 1, 2 and 3 of Article II of the Constitution, and whatever inherent, implied or residual powers may flow therefrom. . . .

We say that when an emergency situation in this country arises that is of such importance to the entire welfare of the country that something has to be done about it and has to be done now, and there is no statutory provision for handling the matter, that it is the duty of the Executive to step in and protect the national security and the national interests. . . .

THE COURT: So you contend the Executive has unlimited power in time of an emergency?

MR. BALDRIDGE: He has the power to take such action as is necessary to meet the emergency.

THE COURT: If the emergency is great, it is unlimited, isn't it?

MR. BALDRIDGE: I suppose if you carry it to its logical conclusion, that is true. But I do want to point out that there are limitations on the Executive power. One is the ballot box and the other is impeachment. . . .

THE COURT: And that the Executive determines the emergencies and the Courts cannot even review whether it is an emergency.

MR. BALDRIDGE: That is correct.

SELECTED BIBLIOGRAPHY

Ackerman, Bruce, *The Failure of the Founding Fathers: Jefferson, Marshall and the Rise of Presidential Democracy.* Cambridge, MA: Belknap, 2005.

Ellsberg, Daniel, *Secrets: A Memoir of Vietnam and the Pentagon Papers.* New York: Viking, 2002.

Fisher, Louis. *In the Name of National Security: Unchecked Presidential Power and the Reynolds Case.* Lawrence: University Press of Kansas, 2006.

Gup, Ted, *Nation of Secrets: The Threat to Democracy and the American Way of Life.* New York: Doubleday, 2007.

O'Brien, David. *The Public's Right to Know: The Supreme Court and the First Amendment.* New York: Praeger, 1981.

Marcus, Maeva. *Truman and the Steel Seizure Case.* New York: Columbia University Press, 1977.

Pallitto, Robert, and Weaver, Kenneth. *Presidential Secrecy and the Law.* Baltimore: Johns Hopkins University Press, 2007.

Posner, Richard. *Not a Suicide Pact: The Constitution in a Time of National Emergency.* New York: Oxford University Press, 2006.

Prados, John, and Potter, Margaret P., eds. *Inside the Pentagon Papers.* Lawrence: University Press of Kansas, 2004.

Randall, James. *Constitutional Problems under Lincoln.* Urbana: University of Illinois Press, 1994.

Rudenstine, David. *The Day the Presses Stopped: A History of the Pentagon Papers Case.* Berkeley: University of California Press, 1996.

Stone, Geoffrey. *Top Secret: When Our Government Keeps Us in the Dark.* Lanham: Rowman and Littlefield, 2007.

Westin, Alan. *Anatomy of a Constitutional Law Case.* New York: Macmillan, 1958.

Youngstown Sheet & Tube Co. v. Sawyer

343 U.S. 579, 72 S.CT. 863 (1952)

A labor dispute that began in 1951 during the "police action" (undeclared war) in Korea eventually led the United Steel Workers to call a strike to shut down steel mills in April 1952. Instead of invoking provisions of the Taft-Hartley Act, which passed over a presidential veto and provided for a cooling-off period in labor-management disputes, hours before the strike President Harry S. Truman issued Executive Order 10340. It directed Secretary of Commerce Charles Sawyer to seize and operate the steel mills. The steel companies immediately sought an injunction in a federal district court to restrain Sawyer from seizing the mills. Judge David Pine ruled against the president, observing,

> There is no express grant of power in the Constitution authorizing the President to direct this seizure. There is no grant of power from which it reasonably can be implied. There is no enactment of Congress authorizing it. . . .
>
> The President therefore must derive this broad "residuum of power" or "inherent" power from the Constitution itself, more particularly Article II thereof, which contains that grant of Executive power. . . .
>
> [But, t]here is no undefined residuum of power which he can exercise because it seems to him to be in the public interest, and there is nothing in the *Neagle* case and its definition of a law of the United States, or in other precedents, warranting such an inference.

When the labor unions then called another strike, the government obtained from an appellate court a stay on Judge Pine's order pending direct appeal to the Supreme Court. The Court expedited the case, granting *certiorari* on May 3, hearing oral arguments on May 12, and handing down its decision within a month, on June 12, 1952. President Truman was angered by the six-to-three ruling that he had exceeded his powers, particularly because the majority included two of his own appointees, Justices Tom Clark and Harold Burton, and Clark, earlier as attorney general, had advised Truman that he had the power to deal with such emergencies. Chief Justice Fred Vinson and Justice Sherman Minton, two other appointees of Truman, dissented along with Justice Stanley Reed.

The Court's decision was six to three, and the majority's opinion was announced by Justice Black. There were concurrences by Justices Jackson, Burton, Clark, Douglas, and Frankfurter. Chief Justice Vinson dissented and was joined by Justices Reed and Minton.

☐ *Justice BLACK delivers the opinion of the Court.*

We are asked to decide whether the President was acting within his constitutional power when he issued an order directing the Secretary of Commerce to take possession of and operate most of the Nation's steel mills. The mill owners argue that the President's order amounts to lawmaking, a legislative function which the Constitution has expressly confided to the Congress and not to the President. The Government's position is that the order was made on findings of the President that his action was necessary to avert a national catastrophe which would inevitably result from a stoppage of steel production, and that in meeting this grave emergency the President was acting within the aggregate of his constitutional powers as the Nation's Chief Executive and the Commander in Chief of the Armed Forces of the United States. The issue emerges here from the following series of events:

In the latter part of 1951, a dispute arose between the steel companies and their employees over terms and conditions that should be included in

(*Library of Congress.*)

new collective bargaining agreements. Long-continued conferences failed to resolve the dispute. On December 18, 1951, the employees' representative, United Steelworkers of America, C. I. O., gave notice of an intention to strike when the existing bargaining agreements expired on December 31. The Federal Mediation and Conciliation Service then intervened in an effort to get labor and management to agree. This failing, the President on December 22, 1951, referred the dispute to the Federal Wage Stabilization Board to investigate and make recommendations for fair and equitable terms of settlement. This Board's report resulted in no settlement. On April 4, 1952, the Union gave notice of a nation-wide strike called to begin at 12:01 A.M. April 9. The indispensability of steel as a component of substantially all weapons and other war materials led the President to believe that the proposed work stoppage would immediately jeopardize our national defense and that governmental seizure of the steel mills was necessary in order to assure the continued availability of steel. Reciting these considerations for his action, the President, a few hours before the strike was to begin, issued Executive Order 10340. The order directed the Secretary of Commerce to take possession of most of the steel mills and keep them running. The Secretary immediately issued his own possessory orders, calling upon the presidents of the various seized companies to serve as operating managers for the United States. They were directed to carry on their activities in accordance with regulations and directions of the Secretary. The next morning the President sent a message to Congress reporting his action. Cong. Rec., April 9, 1952, p. 3962. Twelve days later he sent a second message. Cong. Rec., April 21, 1952, p. 4192. Congress has taken no action.

Obeying the Secretary's orders under protest, the companies brought proceedings against him in the District Court. Their complaints charged that the seizure was not authorized by an act of Congress or by any constitutional provisions. The District Court was asked to declare the orders of the President and the Secretary invalid and to issue preliminary and permanent injunctions restraining their enforcement. Opposing the motion for preliminary injunction, the United States asserted that a strike disrupting steel production for even a brief period would so endanger the well-being and safety of the Nation that the President had "inherent power" to do what he had done—power "supported by the Constitution, by historical precedent, and by court decisions." The Government also contended that in any event no preliminary injunction should be issued because the companies had made no showing that their available legal remedies were inadequate or that their injuries from seizure would be irreparable. Holding against the Government on all points, the District Court on April 30 issued a preliminary injunction restraining the Secretary from "continuing the seizure and possession of the plant . . . and from acting under the purported authority of Executive Order No. 10340." On the same day the Court of Appeals stayed the District Court's injunction. Deeming it best that the issues raised be promptly decided by this Court, we granted *certiorari* on May 3 and set the cause for argument on May 12. . . .

The President's power, if any, to issue the order must stem either from an act of Congress or from the Constitution itself. There is no statute that expressly authorizes the President to take possession of property as he did here. Nor is there any act of Congress to which our attention has been directed from which such a power can fairly be implied. Indeed, we do not understand the Government to rely on statutory authorization for this seizure. There are two statutes which do authorize the President to take both personal and real property under certain conditions. However, the Government admits that these conditions were not met and that the President's order was not rooted in either of the statutes. The Government refers to the seizure provisions of one of these statutes (Sec. 201 (b) of the Defense Production Act) as "much too cumbersome, involved, and time-consuming for the crisis which was at hand."

Moreover, the use of the seizure technique to solve labor disputes in order to prevent work stoppages was not only unauthorized by any congressional enactment; prior to this controversy, Congress had refused to adopt that method of settling labor disputes. When the Taft-Hartley Act was under consideration in 1947, Congress rejected an amendment which would have authorized such governmental seizures in cases of emergency. Apparently it was thought that the technique of seizure, like that of compulsory arbitration, would interfere with the process of collective bargaining. Consequently, the plan Congress adopted in that Act did not provide for seizure under any circumstances. Instead, the plan sought to bring about settlements by use of the customary devices of mediation, conciliation, investigation by boards of inquiry, and public reports. In some instances temporary injunctions were authorized to provide cooling-off periods. All this failing, unions were left free to strike after a secret vote by employees as to whether they wished to accept their employers' final settlement offer.

It is clear that if the President had authority to issue the order he did, it must be found in some provisions of the Constitution. And it is not claimed that express constitutional language grants this power to the President. The contention is that presidential power should be implied from the aggregate of his powers under the Constitution. Particular reliance is placed on provisions in Article II which say that "the executive Power shall be vested in a President . . ."; that "he shall take Care that the Laws be faithfully executed"; and that he "shall be Commander in Chief of the Army and Navy of the United States."

The order cannot properly be sustained as an exercise of the President's military power as Commander in Chief of the Armed Forces. The Government attempts to do so by citing a number of cases upholding broad powers in military commanders engaged in day-to-day fighting in a theater of war. Such cases need not concern us here. Even though "theater of war" [is] an expanding concept, we cannot with faithfulness to our constitutional system hold that the Commander in Chief of the Armed Forces has the ultimate power as such to take possession of private property in order to keep labor disputes from stopping production. This is a job for the Nation's lawmakers, not for its military authorities.

Nor can the seizure order be sustained because of the several constitutional provisions that grant executive power to the President. In the framework of our Constitution, the President's power to see that the laws are faithfully executed refutes the idea that he is to be a lawmaker. The Constitution limits his functions in the lawmaking process to the recommending of laws he thinks wise and the vetoing of laws he thinks bad. And the Constitution is neither silent nor equivocal about who shall make laws which the President is to execute. The first section of the first article says that "All legislative Powers herein granted shall be vested in a Congress of the United States. . . ." After granting many powers to the Congress, Article I goes on to provide that Congress may "make all Laws which shall be necessary and proper for carrying into Execution the foregoing Powers and all other Powers vested by this Constitution in the Government of the United States, or in any Department or Officer thereof."

The President's order does not direct that a congressional policy be executed in a manner prescribed by Congress—it directs that a presidential policy be executed in a manner prescribed by the President. The preamble of the order itself, like that of many statutes, sets out reasons why the President believes certain policies should be adopted, proclaims these policies as rules of conduct to be followed, and again, like a statute, authorizes a government official to promulgate additional rules and regulations consistent with the policy proclaimed and needed to carry that policy into execution. The power of Congress to adopt such public policies as those proclaimed by the order is beyond question. It can authorize the taking of private property for public use. It can make laws regulating the relationships between employers and employees, prescribing rules designed to settle labor disputes, and fixing wages and working conditions in certain fields of our economy. The Constitution did not subject this law-making power of Congress to presidential or military supervision or control.

It is said that other Presidents without congressional authority have taken possession of private business enterprises in order to settle labor disputes. But even if this be true, Congress has not thereby lost its exclusive constitutional authority to make laws necessary and proper to carry out the powers vested by the Constitution "in the Government of the United States, or in any Department or Officer thereof."

The Founders of this Nation entrusted the law making power to the Congress alone in both good and bad times. It would do no good to recall the historical events, the fears of power and the hopes for freedom that lay behind their choice. Such a review would but confirm our holding that this seizure order cannot stand.

The judgment of the District Court is affirmed.

Affirmed.

☐ *Justice JACKSON, concurring.*

That comprehensive and undefined presidential powers hold both practical advantages and grave dangers for the country will impress anyone who has served as legal adviser to a President in time of transition and public anxiety. While an interval of detached reflection may temper teachings of that experience, they probably are a more realistic influence on my views than the conventional materials of judicial decision which seem unduly to accentuate doctrine and legal fiction. But as we approach the question of presidential power, we half overcome mental hazards by recognizing them. The opinions of judges, no less than executives and publicists, often suffer the infirmity of confusing the issue of a power's validity with the cause it is invoked to promote, of confounding the permanent executive office with its temporary occupant. The tendency is strong to emphasize transient results upon policies—such as wages or stabilization—and lose sight of enduring consequences upon the balanced power structure of our Republic.

A judge, like an executive adviser, may be surprised at the poverty of really useful and unambiguous authority applicable to concrete problems of executive power as they actually present themselves. Just what our forefathers did envision, or would have envisioned had they foreseen modern conditions, must be divined from materials almost as enigmatic as the dreams Joseph was called upon to interpret for Pharaoh. A century and a half of partisan debate and scholarly speculation yields no net result but only supplies more or less apt quotations from respected sources on each side of any question. They largely cancel each other. And court decisions are indecisive because of the judicial practice of dealing with the largest questions in the most narrow way.

The actual art of governing under our Constitution does not and cannot conform to judicial definitions of the power of any of its branches based on isolated clauses or even single Articles torn from context. While the Constitution diffuses power the better to secure liberty, it also contemplates that practice will integrate the dispersed powers into a workable government. It enjoins upon its branches separateness but interdependence, autonomy but reciprocity. Presidential powers are not fixed but fluctuate, depending upon their disjunction or conjunction with those of Congress. We may well begin by a somewhat over-simplified grouping of practical situations in which a

President may doubt, or others may challenge, his powers, and by distinguishing roughly the legal consequences of this factor of relativity.

1. When the President acts pursuant to an express or implied authorization of Congress, his authority is at its maximum, for it includes all that he possesses in his own right plus all that Congress can delegate. In these circumstances, and in these only, may he be said (for what it may be worth), to personify the federal sovereignty. If his act is held unconstitutional under these circumstances, it usually means that the Federal Government as an undivided whole lacks power. A seizure executed by the President pursuant to an Act of Congress would be supported by the strongest of presumptions and the widest latitude of judicial interpretation, and the burden of persuasion would rest heavily upon any who might attack it.

2. When the President acts in absence of either a congressional grant or denial of authority, he can only rely upon his own independent powers, but there is a zone of twilight in which he and Congress may have concurrent authority, or in which its distribution is uncertain. Therefore, congressional inertia, indifference or quiescence may sometimes, at least as a practical matter, enable, if not invite, measures on independent presidential responsibility. In this area, any actual test of power is likely to depend on the imperatives of events and contemporary imponderables rather than on abstract theories of law.

3. When the President takes measures incompatible with the expressed or implied will of Congress, his power is at its lowest ebb, for then he can rely only upon his own constitutional powers minus any constitutional powers of Congress over the matter. Courts can sustain exclusive Presidential control in such a case only by disabling the Congress from acting upon the subject. Presidential claim to a power at once so conclusive and preclusive must be scrutinized with caution, for what is at stake is the equilibrium established by our constitutional system.

Into which of these classifications does this executive seizure of the steel industry fit? It is eliminated from the first by admission, for it is conceded that no congressional authorization exists for this seizure. That takes away also the support of the many precedents and declarations which were made in relation, and must be confined, to this category.

Can it then be defended under flexible tests available to the second category? It seems clearly eliminated from that class because Congress has not left seizure of private property an open field but has covered it by three statutory policies inconsistent with this seizure. In cases where the purpose is to supply needs of the Government itself, two courses are provided: one, seizure of a plant which fails to comply with obligatory orders placed by the Government, another, condemnation of facilities, including temporary use under the power of eminent domain. The third is applicable where it is the general economy of the country that is to be protected rather than exclusive governmental interests. None of these were invoked. In choosing a different and inconsistent way of his own, the President cannot claim that it is necessitated or invited by failure of Congress to legislate upon the occasions, grounds and methods for seizure of industrial properties.

This leaves the current seizure to be justified only by the severe tests under the third grouping, where it can be supported only by any remainder of executive power after subtraction of such powers as Congress may have over the subject. In short, we can sustain the President only by holding that seizure of such strike-bound industries is within his domain and beyond control by Congress. Thus, this Court's first review of such seizures occurs under circumstances which leave Presidential power most vulnerable to attack and in the least favorable of possible constitutional postures.

I did not suppose, and I am not persuaded, that history leaves it open to question, at least in the courts, that the executive branch, like the Federal Government as a whole, possesses only delegated powers. The purpose of the Constitution was not only to grant power, but to keep it from getting out of hand. However, because the President does not enjoy unmentioned powers does not mean that the mentioned ones should be narrowed by a niggardly construction. Some clauses could be made almost unworkable, as well as immutable, by refusal to indulge some latitude of interpretation for changing times. I have heretofore, and do now, give to the enumerated powers the scope and elasticity afforded by what seem to be reasonable practical implications instead of the rigidity dictated by a doctrinaire textualism. . . .

Loose and irresponsible use of adjectives colors all non-legal and much legal discussion of presidential powers. "Inherent" powers, "implied" powers, "incidental" powers, "plenary" powers, "war" powers and "emergency" powers are used, often interchangeably and without fixed or ascertainable meanings.

The vagueness and generality of the clauses that set forth presidential powers afford a plausible basis for pressures within and without an administration for presidential action beyond that supported by those whose responsibility it is to defend his actions in court. The claim of inherent and unrestricted presidential powers has long been a persuasive dialectical weapon in political controversy. While it is not surprising that counsel should grasp support from such unadjudicated claims of power, a judge cannot accept self-serving press statements of the attorney for one of the interested parties as authority in answering a constitutional question, even if the advocate was himself. But prudence has counseled that actual reliance on such nebulous claims stop short of provoking a judicial test.

The Solicitor General, acknowledging that Congress has never authorized the seizure here, says practice of prior Presidents has authorized it. He seeks color of legality from claimed executive precedents, chief of which is President Roosevelt's seizure on June 9, 1941, of the California plant of the North American Aviation Company. Its superficial similarities with the present case, upon analysis, yield to distinctions so decisive that it cannot be regarded as even a precedent, much less an authority for the present seizure.

The appeal, however, that we declare the existence of inherent powers *ex necessitate* to meet an emergency asks us to do what many think would be wise, although it is something the forefathers omitted. They knew what emergencies were, knew the pressures they engender for authoritative action, knew, too, how they afford a ready pretext for usurpation. We may also suspect that they suspected that emergency powers would tend to kindle emergencies. Aside from suspension of the privilege of the writ of *habeas corpus* in time of rebellion or invasion, when the public safety may require it, they made no express provision for exercise of extraordinary authority because of a crisis. I do not think we rightfully may so amend their work, and, if we could, I am not convinced it would be wise to do so, although many modern nations have forthrightly recognized that war and economic crises may upset the normal balance between liberty and authority. Their experience with emergency powers may not be irrelevant to the argument here that we should say that the Executive, of his own volition, can invest himself with undefined emergency powers. . . .

In view of the ease, expedition and safety with which Congress can grant and has granted large emergency powers, certainly ample to embrace this crisis, I am quite unimpressed with the argument that we should affirm possession of them without statute. Such power either has no beginning or it has no end. If it exists, it need submit to no legal restraint. I am not alarmed that it would plunge us straightway into dictatorship, but it is at least a step in that wrong direction.

As to whether there is imperative necessity for such powers, it is relevant to note the gap that exists between the President's paper powers and his real powers. The Constitution does not disclose the measure of the actual controls wielded by the modern presidential office. That instrument must be understood as an Eighteenth-Century sketch of a government hoped for, not as a blueprint of the Government that is. Vast accretions of federal power, eroded from that reserved by the States, have magnified the scope of presidential activity. Subtle shifts take place in the centers of real power that do not show on the face of the Constitution.

Executive power has the advantage of concentration in a single head in whose choice the whole Nation has a part, making him the focus of public hopes and expectations. In drama, magnitude and finality his decisions so far overshadow any others that almost alone he fills the public eye and ear. No other personality in public life can begin to compete with him in access to the public mind through modern methods of communications. By his prestige as head of state and his influence upon public opinion he exerts a leverage upon those who are supposed to check and balance his power which often cancels their effectiveness.

Moreover, rise of the party system has made a significant extra-constitutional supplement to real executive power. No appraisal of his necessities is realistic which overlooks that he heads a political system as well as a legal system. Party loyalties and interests, sometimes more binding than law, extend his effective control into branches of government other than his own and he often may win, as a political leader, what he cannot command under the Constitution. Indeed, Woodrow Wilson, commenting on the President as leader both of his party and of the Nation, observed, "If he rightly interpret the national thought and boldly insist upon it, he is irresistible. . . . His office is anything he has the sagacity and force to make it." I cannot be brought to believe that this country will suffer if the Court refuses further to aggrandize the presidential office, already so potent and so relatively immune from judicial review, at the expense of Congress.

But I have no illusion that any decision by this Court can keep power in the hands of Congress if it is not wise and timely in meeting its problems. A crisis that challenges the President equally, or perhaps primarily, challenges Congress. If not good law, there was worldly wisdom in the maxim attributed to Napoleon that "The tools belong to the man who can use them." We may say that power to legislate for emergencies belongs in the hands of Congress, but only Congress itself can prevent power from slipping through its fingers.

The essence of our free Government is "leave to live by no man's leave, underneath the law"—to be governed by those impersonal forces which we call law. Our Government is fashioned to fulfill this concept so far as humanly possible. The Executive, except for recommendation and veto, has no legislative power. The executive action here originates in the individual will of the President and represents an exercise of authority without law. No one, perhaps not even the President, knows the limits of the power he may seek to exert in this instance and the parties affected cannot learn the limit of their rights. We do not know today what powers over labor or property would be claimed to flow from Government possession if we should legalize it, what rights to compensation would be claimed or recognized, or on what contingency it would end. With all its defects, delays and inconveniences, men have discovered no technique for long preserving free government except that the Executive be under the law, and that the law be made by parliamentary deliberations.

Such institutions may be destined to pass away. But it is the duty of the Court to be last, not first, to give them up.

☐ *Justice CLARK, concurring.*

The limits of presidential power are obscure. However, Article II, no less than Article I, is part of "a constitution intended to endure for ages to come, and, consequently, to be adapted to the various crises of human affairs." Some of our Presidents, such as Lincoln, "felt that measures otherwise unconstitutional might become lawful by becoming indispensable to the preservation of the Constitution through the preservation of the nation." Others, such as Theodore Roosevelt, thought the President to be capable, as a "steward" of the people, of exerting all power save that which is specifically prohibited by the Constitution or the Congress. In my view—taught me not only by the decision of Chief Justice MARSHALL in *Little v. Barreme*, 2 Cranch 170 [(1804)], but also by a score of other pronouncements of distinguished members of this bench—the Constitution does grant to the President extensive authority in times of grave and imperative national emergency. In fact, to my thinking, such a grant may well be necessary to the very existence of the Constitution itself. As Lincoln aptly said, "[is] it possible to lose the nation and yet preserve the Constitution?" In describing this authority I care not whether one calls it "residual," "inherent," "moral," "implied," "aggregate," "emergency," or otherwise. I am of the conviction that those who have had the gratifying experience of being the President's lawyer have used one or more of these adjectives only with the utmost of sincerity and the highest of purpose.

I conclude that where Congress has laid down specific procedures to deal with the type of crisis confronting the President, he must follow those procedures in meeting the crisis; but that in the absence of such action by Congress, the President's independent power to act depends upon the gravity of the situation confronting the nation. I cannot sustain the seizure in question because . . . Congress had prescribed methods to be followed by the President in meeting the emergency at hand.

☐ *Justice DOUGLAS, concurring.*

There can be no doubt that the emergency which caused the President to seize these steel plants was one that bore heavily on the country. But the emergency did not create power; it merely marked an occasion when power should be exercised. And the fact that it was necessary that measures be taken to keep steel in production does not mean that the President, rather than the Congress, had the constitutional authority to act. The Congress as well as the President, is trustee of the national welfare. The President can act more quickly than the Congress. The President with the armed services at his disposal can move with force as well as with speed. All executive power—from the reign of ancient kings to the rule of modern dictators—has the outward appearance of efficiency.

Legislative power, by contrast, is slower to exercise. There must be delay while the ponderous machinery of committees, hearings, and debates is put into motion. That takes time; and while the Congress slowly moves into action, the emergency may take its toll in wages, consumer goods, war production, the standard of living of the people, and perhaps even lives. Legislative action may indeed often be cumbersome, time-consuming, and apparently inefficient. . . .

We therefore cannot decide this case by determining which branch of government can deal most expeditiously with the present crisis. The answer must depend on the allocation of powers under the Constitution. . . .

The legislative nature of the action taken by the President seems to me to be clear. When the United States takes over an industrial plant to settle a labor controversy, it is condemning property. The seizure of the plant is a taking in the constitutional sense. A permanent taking would amount to the nationalization of the industry. A temporary taking falls short of that goal. But though the seizure is only for a week or a month, the condemnation is complete and the United States must pay compensation for the temporary possession. . . .

The power of the Federal Government to condemn property is well established. *Kohl v. United States*, 91 U.S. 367 [(1876)]. It can condemn for any public purpose; and I have no doubt but that condemnation of a plant, factory, or industry in order to promote industrial peace would be constitutional. But there is a duty to pay for all property taken by the Government. The command of the Fifth Amendment is that no "private property be taken for public use, without just compensation." That constitutional requirement has an important bearing on the present case.

The President has no power to raise revenues. That power is in the Congress by Article I, Section 8 of the Constitution. The President might seize and the Congress by subsequent action might ratify the seizure. But until and unless Congress acted, no condemnation would be lawful. The branch of government that has the power to pay compensation for a seizure is the only one able to authorize a seizure or make lawful one that the President had effected. That seems to me to be the necessary result of the condemnation provision in the Fifth Amendment. It squares with the theory of checks and balances expounded by Justice BLACK in the opinion of the Court in which I join.

If we sanctioned the present exercise of power by the President, we would be expanding Article II of the Constitution and rewriting it to suit the political conveniences of the present emergency. . . .

We pay a price for our system of checks and balances, for the distribution of power among the three branches of government. It is a price that today may seem exorbitant to many. Today a kindly President uses the seizure power to effect a wage increase and to keep the steel furnaces in production. Yet tomorrow another President might use the same power to prevent a wage increase, to curb trade unionists, to regiment labor as oppressively as industry thinks it has been regimented by this seizure.

☐ *Justice FRANKFURTER, concurring.*

. . .

The pole-star for constitutional adjudications is John MARSHALL's greatest judicial utterance that "it is *a constitution* we are expounding." *McCulloch v. Maryland*, 4 Wheat. 316 [(1819)]. That requires both a spacious view in applying an instrument of government "made for an undefined and expanding future," *Hurtado v. People of State of California*, 110 U.S. 516 [(1884)], and as narrow a delimitation of the constitutional issues as the circumstances permit. Not the least characteristic of great statesmanship which the Framers manifested was the extent to which they did not attempt to bind the future. It is no less incumbent upon this Court to avoid putting fetters upon the future by needless pronouncements today.

MARSHALL's admonition that "it is *a constitution* we are expounding" is especially relevant when the Court is required to give legal sanctions to an underlying principle of the Constitution—that of separation of powers. . . .

The issue before us can be met, and therefore should be, without attempting to define the President's powers comprehensively. I shall not attempt to delineate what belongs to him by virtue of his office beyond the power even of Congress to contract; what authority belongs to him until Congress acts; what kind of problems may be dealt with either by the Congress or by the President or by both, what power must be exercised by the Congress and cannot be delegated to the President. It is as unprofitable to lump together in an undiscriminating hotch-potch past presidential actions claimed to be derived from occupancy of the office, as it is to conjure up hypothetical future cases. The judiciary may, as this case proves, have to intervene in determining where authority lies as between the democratic forces in our scheme of government. But in doing so we should be wary and humble. Such is the teaching of this Court's role in the history of the country.

It is in this mood and with this perspective that the issue before the Court must be approached. We must therefore put to one side consideration of what powers the President would have had if there had been no legislation whatever bearing on the authority asserted by the seizure, or if the seizure had been only for a short, explicitly temporary period, to be terminated automatically unless Congressional approval were given. These and other questions, like or unlike, are not now here. I would exceed my authority were I to say anything about them.

The question before the Court comes in this setting. Congress has frequently—at least 16 times since 1916—specifically provided for executive seizure of production, transportation, communications, or storage facilities. In every case it has qualified this grant of power with limitations and safeguards. This body of enactments—summarized in tabular form in Appendix I— demonstrates that Congress deemed seizure so drastic a power as to require that it be carefully circumscribed whenever the President was vested with this extraordinary authority. The power to seize has uniformly been given only for a limited period or for a defined emergency, or has been repealed after a short period. Its exercise has been restricted to particular circumstances such as "time of war or when war is imminent," the needs of "public safety" or of "national security or defense," or "urgent and impending need." The period of governmental operation has been limited, as, for instance, to "sixty days after the restoration of productive efficiency." Seizure statutes usually make executive action dependent on detailed conditions: for example, (a) failure or refusal of the owner of a plant to meet governmental supply needs or (b) failure of voluntary negotiations with the owner for the use of a plant necessary for great public ends. Congress often has specified the particular executive agency which should seize or operate the plants or whose judgment would appropriately test the need for seizure. Congress also has not left to implication that just compensation be paid; it has usually legislated in detail regarding enforcement of this litigation–breeding general requirement. . . .

In adopting the provisions which it did, by the Labor Management Relations Act of 1947, for dealing with a "national emergency" arising out of a breakdown in peaceful industrial relations, Congress was very familiar with Government seizure as a protective measure. On a balance of considerations Congress chose not to lodge this power in the President. It chose not to make available in advance a remedy to which both industry and labor were fiercely hostile. In deciding that authority to seize should be given to the President only after full consideration of the particular situation should show such legislation to be necessary, Congress presumably acted on experience with similar industrial conflicts in the past. It evidently assumed that industrial shutdowns in basic industries are not instances of spontaneous generation, and that danger warnings are sufficiently plain before the event to give ample opportunity to start the legislative process into action.

In any event, nothing can be plainer than that Congress made a conscious choice of policy in a field full of perplexity and peculiarly within legislative responsibility for choice. In formulating legislation for dealing with industrial conflicts, Congress could not more clearly and emphatically have withheld authority than it did in 1947. Perhaps as much so as is true of any piece of modern legislation, Congress acted with full consciousness of what it was doing and in the light of much recent history. Previous seizure legislation had subjected the powers granted to the President to restrictions of varying degrees of stringency. Instead of giving him even limited powers, Congress in 1947 deemed it wise to require the President, upon failure of attempts to reach a voluntary settlement, to report to Congress if he deemed the power of seizure a needed shot for his locker. The President could not ignore the specific limitations of prior seizure statutes. No more could he act in disregard of the limitation put upon seizure by the 1947 Act. . . .

By the Labor Management Relations Act of 1947, Congress said to the President, "You may not seize. Please report to us and ask for seizure power if you think it is needed in a specific situation." . . .

It is not a pleasant judicial duty to find that the President has exceeded his powers and still less so when his purposes were dictated by concern for the Nation's well-being, in the assured conviction that he acted to avert danger. But it would stultify one's faith in our people to entertain even a momentary fear that the patriotism and the wisdom of the President and the Congress, as well as the long view of the immediate parties in interest, will not find ready accommodation for differences on matters which, however close to their concern and however intrinsically important, are overshadowed by the awesome issues which confront the world.

☐ *Chief Justice VINSON, with whom Justice REED and Justice MINTON join, dissenting.*

Those who suggest that this is a case involving extraordinary powers should be mindful that these are extraordinary times. A world not yet recovered from the devastation of World War II has been forced to face the threat of another and more terrifying global conflict.

Accepting in full measure its responsibility in the world community, the United States was instrumental in securing adoption of the United Nations Charter, approved by the Senate by a vote of 89 to 2. The first purpose of the United Nations is to "maintain international peace and security, and to that end: to take effective collective measures for the prevention and removal of threats to the peace and for the suppression of acts of aggression or other breaches of the peace." . . . In 1950, when the United Nations called upon member nations "to render every assistance" to repel aggression in Korea, the United States furnished its vigorous support. For almost two full years, our armed forces have been fighting in Korea, suffering casualties of over 108,000 men. Hostilities have not abated. The "determination of the United Nations to continue its action in Korea to meet the aggression" has been reaffirmed. Congressional support of the action in Korea has been manifested by provisions for increased military manpower and equipment and for economic stabilization. . . .

One is not here called upon even to consider the possibility of executive seizure of a farm, a corner grocery store or even a single industrial plant. Such considerations arise only when one ignores the central fact of this case—that the Nation's entire basic steel production would have shut down completely if there had been no Government seizure. Even ignoring for the moment whatever confidential information the President may possess as "the Nation's organ for foreign affairs," the uncontroverted affidavits in this record amply support the finding that "a work stoppage would immediately jeopardize and imperil our national defense." . . .

In passing upon the grave constitutional question presented in this case, we must never forget, as Chief Justice MARSHALL admonished, that the Constitution is "intended to endure for ages to come, and consequently, to be adapted to the various *crises* of human affairs," and that "[i]ts means are adequate to its ends." Cases do arise presenting questions which could not have been foreseen by the Framers. In such cases, the Constitution has been treated as a living document adaptable to new situations. But we are not called upon today to expand the Constitution to meet a new situation. For, in this case, we need only look to history and time-honored principles of constitutional law—principles that have been applied consistently by all branches of the Government throughout our history. It is those who assert the invalidity of the Executive Order who seek to amend the Constitution in this case.

A review of executive action demonstrates that our Presidents have on many occasions exhibited the leadership contemplated by the Framers when they made the President Commander in Chief, and imposed upon him the trust to "take Care that the Laws be faithfully executed." With or without explicit statutory authorization, Presidents have at such times dealt with national emergencies by acting promptly and resolutely to enforce legislative programs, at least to save those programs until Congress could act. Congress and the courts have responded to such executive initiative with consistent approval. . . .

The President reported to Congress the morning after the seizure that he acted because a work stoppage in steel production would immediately imperil the safety of the Nation by preventing execution of the legislative programs for procurement of military equipment. And, while a shutdown could be averted by granting the price concessions requested by plaintiffs, granting such concessions would disrupt the price stabilization program also enacted by Congress. Rather than fail to execute either legislative program, the President acted to execute both. . . .

The absence of a specific statute authorizing seizure of the steel mills as a mode of executing the laws—both the military procurement program and the anti-inflation program—has not until today been thought to prevent the President from executing the laws. . . .

There is no statute prohibiting seizure as a method of enforcing legislative programs. Congress has in no wise indicated that its legislation is not to be executed by the taking of private property (subject of course to the payment of just compensation) if its legislation cannot otherwise be executed. Indeed, the Universal Military Training and Service Act authorizes the seizure of *any* plant that fails to fill a Government contract or the properties of *any* steel producer that fails to allocate steel as directed for defense production. And the Defense Production Act authorizes the President to requisition equipment and condemn real property needed without delay in the defense effort. Where Congress authorizes seizure in instances not necessarily crucial to the defense program, it can hardly be said to have disclosed an intention to prohibit seizures where essential to the execution of that legislative program.

Whatever the extent of Presidential power on more tranquil occasions, and whatever the right of the President to execute legislative programs as he sees fit without reporting the mode of execution to Congress, the single Presidential purpose disclosed on this record is to faithfully execute the laws by acting in an emergency to maintain the status quo, thereby preventing collapse of the legislative programs until Congress could act. The President's action served the same purposes as a judicial stay entered to maintain the status quo in order to preserve the jurisdiction of a court. In his Message to Congress immediately following the seizure, the President explained the necessity of his action in executing the military procurement and anti-inflation legislative programs and expressed his desire to cooperate with any legislative proposals approving, regulating or rejecting the seizure of the steel mills. Consequently, there is no evidence whatever of any Presidential purpose to defy Congress or act in any way inconsistent with the legislative will. . . .

The diversity of views expressed in the six opinions of the majority, the lack of reference to authoritative precedent, the repeated reliance upon prior dissenting opinions, the complete disregard of the uncontroverted facts showing the gravity of the emergency and the temporary nature of the taking all serve to demonstrate how far afield one must go to affirm the order of the District Court.

The broad executive power granted by Article II to an officer on duty 365 days a year cannot, it is said, be invoked to avert disaster. Instead, the President must confine himself to sending a message to Congress recommending action. Under this messenger-boy concept of the Office, the President cannot even act to preserve legislative programs from destruction so that Congress will have something left to act upon. There is no judicial finding that the executive action was unwarranted because there was in fact no basis for the President's finding of the existence of an emergency for, under this view, the gravity of the emergency and the immediacy of the threatened disaster are considered irrelevant as a matter of law. . . .

As the District Judge stated, this is no time for "timorous" judicial action. But neither is this a time for timorous executive action. Faced with the duty of executing the defense programs which Congress had enacted and the disastrous effects that any stoppage in steel production would have on those programs, the President acted to preserve those programs by seizing the steel mills. There is no question that the possession was other than temporary in character and subject to congressional direction—either approving, disapproving or regulating the manner in which the mills were to be administered and returned to the owners. The President immediately informed Congress of his action and clearly stated his intention to abide by the legislative will. No basis for claims of arbitrary action, unlimited powers or dictatorial usurpation of congressional power appears from the facts of this case. On the contrary, judicial, legislative and executive precedents throughout our history demonstrate that in this case the President acted in full conformity with his duties under the Constitution. Accordingly, we would reverse the order of the District Court.

New York Times Co. v. United States

403 U.S. 670, 91 S.Ct. 2140 (1971)

In 1971, amid growing opposition to the undeclared Vietnam War, the Nixon administration sought to enjoin the *New York Times* and the *Washington Post* from publishing a series of articles based on a forty-seven-volume study, *History of U.S. Decision Making Process on Viet Nam Policy.* The study was prepared in 1968 and was classified top secret—sensitive. The *New York Times* received duplicates of the study from Daniel Ellsberg, who had secretly copied them while working for a think tank and after his unsuccessful efforts to persuade leading politicians to publicize the study.

After several months of reviewing the documents, the *New York Times* commenced publication of selected items on June 13, 1971. Following the third installment the Department of Justice sought an injunction against publication of the balance of the series and obtained a temporary restraining order prohibiting further publication until June 19. On June 18 the *Washington Post* also printed two articles based on the study, and by five o'clock that day the government had filed a similar suit against its further publication of the material.

The next morning a district court denied the government's request for a preliminary injunction, but later in the day a circuit court judge extended the temporary restraining order until noon, June 21, to give a panel of the Court of Appeals for the District of Columbia Circuit the opportunity to consider the government's application. On June 22, the circuit court remanded the case to the district court to determine whether any of the other materials posed "such grave and immediate danger" to the security of the country as to warrant prior restraint and a continued stay on publication until June 25. The *New York Times* promptly appealed to the Supreme Court to vacate the stay on publication and to expedite consideration of the case. On June 25 the Court granted *certiorari* and heard arguments the next day. Remarkably, four days later the Court issued no fewer than ten opinions: one brief *per curiam* opinion, six concurring and three dissenting opinions.

The Court's decision was six to three, and the majority's opinion was announced *per curiam*. Justices Black, Douglas, Brennan, Stewart, White, and Marshall delivered concurring opinions. Chief Justice Burger and Justices Harlan and Blackmun dissented.

PER CURIAM

We granted *certiorari* in these cases in which the United States seeks to enjoin the *New York Times* and the *Washington Post* from publishing the contents of a classified study entitled "History of U.S. Decision-Making Process on Viet Nam Policy."

"Any system of prior restraints of expression comes to this Court bearing a heavy presumption against its constitutional validity." *Bantam Books, Inc. v. Sullivan*, 372 U.S. 58 (1963); see also *Near v. Minnesota ex rel. Olson*, 283 U.S. 697 (1931). The Government "thus carries a heavy burden of showing justification for the imposition of such a restraint." *Organization for a Better Austin v. Keefe*, 402 U.S. 415 (1971). The District Court for the Southern District of New York in the *New York Times* case, 328 F.Supp. 324, and the District Court for the District of Columbia Circuit, 446 F.2d 1327, in the *Washington Post* case held that the Government had not met that burden. We agree.

The judgment of the Court of Appeals for the District of Columbia is therefore affirmed. The order of the Court of Appeals for the Second Circuit is reversed and the case is remanded with directions to enter a judgment affirming the judgment of the District Court for the Southern District of New York. The stays entered June 25, 1971, by the Court are vacated.

☐ *Justice BLACK, with whom Justice DOUGLAS joins, concurring.*

I believe that every moment's continuance of the injunctions against these newspapers amounts to a flagrant, indefensible, and continuing violation of the First Amendment. . . . In my view it is unfortunate that some of my Brethren are apparently willing to hold that the publication of news may sometimes be enjoined. Such a holding would make a shambles of the First Amendment. . . .

In seeking injunctions against these newspapers and in its presentation to the Court, the Executive Branch seems to have forgotten the essential purpose and history of the First Amendment. When the Constitution was adopted, many people strongly opposed it because the document contained no Bill of Rights to safeguard certain basic freedoms. They especially feared that the new powers granted to a central government might be interpreted to permit the government to curtail freedom of religion, press, assembly, and speech. . . . Madison and the other Framers of the First Amendment, able men that they were, wrote in language they earnestly believed could never be misunderstood: "Congress shall make no law . . . abridging the freedom . . . of the press. . . ." Both the history and language of the First Amendment support the view that the press must be left free to publish news, whatever the source, without censorship, injunctions, or prior restraints. . . .

The Government's case here is based on premises entirely different from those that guided the Framers of the First Amendment. The Solicitor General has carefully and emphatically stated:

> Now, Justice [BLACK], your construction of . . . [the First Amendment] is well known, and I certainly respect it. You say that no law means no law, and that should be obvious. I can only say, Mr. Justice, that to me it is equally obvious that "no law" does not mean "no law," and I would seek to persuade the Court that that is true. . . . [T]here are other parts of the Constitution that grant powers and responsibilities to the Executive, and . . . the First Amendment was not intended to make it impossible for the Executive to function or to protect the security of the United States.

And the Government argues in its brief that in spite of the First Amendment, "[t]he authority of the Executive Department to protect the nation against publication of information whose disclosure would endanger the national security stems from two interrelated sources: the constitutional power of the President over the conduct of foreign affairs and his authority as Commander-in-Chief."

In other words, we are asked to hold that despite the First Amendment's emphatic command, the Executive Branch, the Congress, and the Judiciary can make laws enjoining publication of current news and abridging freedom of the press in the name of "national security." The Government does not even attempt to rely on any act of Congress. Instead it makes the bold and dangerously farreaching contention that the courts should take it upon themselves to "make" a law abridging freedom of the press in the name of equity, presidential power and national security. . . . To find that the President has "inherent power" to halt the publication of news by resort to the courts would wipe out the First Amendment and destroy the fundamental liberty and security of the very people the Government hopes to make "secure." No one can read the history of the adoption of the First Amendment without being convinced beyond any doubt that it was injunctions like those sought here that Madison and his collaborators intended to outlaw in this Nation for all time.

The word "security" is a broad, vague generality whose contours should not be invoked to abrogate the fundamental law embodied in the First Amendment. The guarding of military and diplomatic secrets at the expense of informed representative government provides no real security for our Republic. The Framers of the First Amendment, fully aware of both the need to defend a new nation and the abuses of the English and Colonial Governments, sought to give this new society strength and security by providing that freedom of speech, press, religion, and assembly should not be abridged.

☐ *Justice DOUGLAS, with whom Justice BLACK joins, concurring.*

The Government says that it has inherent powers to go into court and obtain an injunction to protect the national interest, which in this case is alleged to be national security.

Near v. Minnesota ex rel. Olson, 283 U.S. 697 [(1931)], repudiated that expansive doctrine in no uncertain terms. . . .

Secrecy in government is fundamentally anti-democratic, perpetuating bureaucratic errors. Open debate and discussion of public issues are vital to our national health. On public questions there should be "uninhibited, robust, and wide-open" debate.

☐ *Justice BRENNAN, concurring.*

I write separately in these cases only to emphasize what should be apparent that our judgments in the present cases may not be taken to indicate the propriety, in the future, of issuing temporary stays and restraining orders to block the publication of material sought to be suppressed by the Government. So far as I can determine, never before has the United States sought to enjoin a newspaper from publishing information in its possession. The relative novelty of the questions presented, the necessary haste with which decisions were reached, the magnitude of the interests asserted, and the fact that all the parties have concentrated their arguments upon the question whether permanent restraints were proper may have justified at least some of the restraints heretofore imposed in these cases. . . . But even if it be assumed that some of the interim restraints were proper in the two cases before us, that assumption has no bearing upon the propriety of similar judicial action in the future. . . . More important, the First Amendment stands as an absolute bar to the imposition of judicial restraints in circumstances of the kind presented by these cases.

☐ *Justice STEWART, with whom Justice WHITE joins, concurring.*

In the governmental structure created by our Constitution, the Executive is endowed with enormous power in the two related areas of national defense and international relations. This power, largely unchecked by the

Legislative and Judicial branches, has been pressed to the very hilt since the advent of the nuclear missile age. For better or for worse, the simple fact is that a President of the United States possesses vastly greater constitutional independence in these two vital areas of power than does, say, a prime minister of a country with a parliamentary form of government.

In the absence of the governmental checks and balances present in other areas of our national life, the only effective restraint upon executive policy and power in the areas of national defense and international affairs may lie in an enlightened citizenry—in an informed and critical public opinion which alone can here protect the values of democratic government. For this reason, it is perhaps here that a press that is alert, aware, and free most vitally serves the basic purpose of the First Amendment. For without an informed and free press there cannot be an enlightened people.

Yet it is elementary that the successful conduct of international diplomacy and the maintenance of an effective national defense require both confidentiality and secrecy. Other nations can hardly deal with this Nation in an atmosphere of mutual trust unless they can be assured that their confidences will be kept. And within our own executive departments, the development of considered and intelligent international policies would be impossible if those charged with their formulation could not communicate with each other freely, frankly, and in confidence. In the area of basic national defense the frequent need for absolute secrecy is, of course, self-evident.

I think there can be but one answer to this dilemma, if dilemma it be. The responsibility must be where the power is. If the Constitution gives the Executive a large degree of unshared power in the conduct of foreign affairs and the maintenance of our national defense, then under the Constitution the Executive must have the largely unshared duty to determine and preserve the degree of internal security necessary to exercise that power successfully. It is an awesome responsibility, requiring judgment and wisdom of a high order. I should suppose that moral, political, and practical considerations would dictate that a very first principle of that wisdom would be an insistence upon avoiding secrecy for its own sake. For when everything is classified, then nothing is classified, and the system becomes one to be disregarded by the cynical or the careless, and to be manipulated by those intent on self-protection or self-promotion. I should suppose, in short, that the hallmark of a truly effective internal security system would be the maximum possible disclosure, recognizing that secrecy can best be preserved only when credibility is truly maintained. But be that as it may, it is clear to me that it is the constitutional duty of the Executive—as a matter of sovereign prerogative and not as a matter of law as the courts know law—through the promulgation and enforcement of executive regulations, to protect the confidentiality necessary to carry out its responsibilities in the fields of international relations and national defense.

This is not to say that Congress and the courts have no role to play. Undoubtedly Congress has the power to enact specific and appropriate criminal laws to protect government property and preserve government secrets. . . . Moreover, if Congress should pass a specific law authorizing civil proceedings in this field, the courts would likewise have the duty to decide the constitutionality of such a law as well as its applicability to the facts proved.

But in the cases before us we are asked neither to construe specific regulations nor to apply specific laws. We are asked, instead, to perform a function that the Constitution gave to the Executive, not the Judiciary. We are asked, quite simply, to prevent the publication by two newspapers of material that the Executive Branch insists should not, in the national interest, be published. I am convinced that the Executive is correct with respect to some of the documents involved. But I cannot say that disclosure of any of them will surely result in direct, immediate, and irreparable damage to our Nation or its people. That being so, there can under the First Amendment be but one judicial resolution of the issues before us. I join the judgments of the Court.

□ *Justice WHITE, with whom Justice STEWART joins, concurring.*

I concur in today's judgments, but only because of the concededly extra-ordinary protection against prior restraints enjoyed by the press under our constitutional system. I do not say that in no circumstances would the First Amendment permit an injunction against publishing information about government plans or operations. Nor, after examining the materials the Government characterizes as the most sensitive and destructive, can I deny that revelation of these documents will do substantial damage to public interests. Indeed, I am confident that their disclosure will have that result. But I nevertheless agree that the United States has not satisfied the very heavy burden that it must meet to warrant an injunction against publication in these cases, at least in the absence of express and appropriately limited congressional authorization for prior restraints in circumstances such as these.

The Government's position is simply stated: The responsibility of the Executive for the conduct of the foreign affairs and for the security of the Nation is so basic that the President is entitled to an injunction against publication of a newspaper story whenever he can convince a court that the information to be revealed threatens "grave and irreparable" injury to the public interest; and the injunction should issue whether or not the material to be published is classified, whether or not publication would be lawful under relevant criminal statutes enacted by Congress, and regardless of the circumstances by which the newspaper came into possession of the information.

At least in the absence of legislation by Congress, based on its own investigations and findings, I am quite unable to agree that the inherent powers of the Executive and the courts reach so far as to authorize remedies having such sweeping potential for inhibiting publications by the press. Much of the difficulty inheres in the "grave and irreparable danger" standard suggested by the United States. If the United States were to have judgment under such a standard in these cases, our decision would be of little guidance to other courts in other cases, for the material at issue here would not be available from the Court's opinion or from public records, nor would it be published by the press. Indeed, even today where we hold that the United States has not met its burden, the material remains sealed in court records and it is properly not discussed in today's opinions. Moreover, because the material poses substantial dangers to national interests and because of the hazards of criminal sanctions, a responsible press may choose never to publish the more sensitive materials. To sustain the Government in these cases would start the courts down a long and hazardous road that I am not willing to travel, at least without congressional guidance and direction.

☐ *Justice MARSHALL, concurring.*

The problem here is whether in these particular cases the Executive Branch has authority to invoke the equity jurisdiction of the courts to protect what it believes to be the national interest. See *In re Debs*, 158 U.S. 564 (1895). The Government argues that in addition to the inherent power of any government to protect itself, the President's power to conduct foreign affairs and his position as Commander in Chief give him authority to impose censorship on the press to protect his ability to deal effectively with foreign nations and to conduct the military affairs of the country. Of course, it is beyond cavil that the President has broad powers by virtue of his primary responsibility for the conduct of our foreign affairs and his position as Commander in Chief. . . .

It would, however, be utterly inconsistent with the concept of separation of powers for this Court to use its power of contempt to prevent behavior that Congress has specifically declined to prohibit. There would be a similar damage to the basic concept of these co-equal branches of Government if when the Executive Branch has adequate authority granted by Congress to protect "national security" it can choose instead to invoke the contempt power of a court to enjoin the threatened conduct. The Constitution provides that Congress shall make laws, the President execute laws, and courts interpret laws. It did not provide for government by injunction in which the courts and the Executive Branch can "make law" without regard to the action of Congress. It may be more convenient for the Executive Branch if it need only convince a judge to prohibit conduct rather than ask the Congress to pass a law, and it may be more convenient to enforce a contempt order than to seek a criminal conviction in a jury trial. Moreover, it may be considered politically wise to get a court to share the responsibility for arresting those who the Executive Branch has probable cause to believe are violating the law. But convenience and political considerations of the moment do not justify a basic departure from the principles of our system of government.

☐ *Chief Justice BURGER, dissenting.*

I suggest . . . these cases have been conducted in unseemly haste. . . .

Here, moreover, the frenetic haste is due in large part to the manner in which the *Times* proceeded from the date it obtained the purloined documents. It seems reasonably clear now that the haste precluded reasonable and deliberate judicial treatment of these cases and was not warranted. . . .

The newspapers make a derivative claim under the First Amendment; they denominate this right as the public "right to know"; by implication, the *Times* asserts a sole trusteeship of that right by virtue of its journalistic "scoop." The right is asserted as an absolute. Of course, the First Amendment right itself is not an absolute, as Justice HOLMES so long ago pointed out in his aphorism concerning the right to shout "fire" in a crowded theater if there was no fire. There are other exceptions, some of which Chief Justice HUGHES mentioned by way of example in *Near v. Minnesota ex rel. Olson*. There are no doubt other exceptions no one has had occasion to describe or discuss. . . .

It is not disputed that the *Times* has had unauthorized possession of the documents for three to four months, during which it has had its expert analysts studying them, presumably digesting them and preparing the material for publication. During all of this time, the *Times*, presumably in its capacity as trustee of the public's "right to know," has held up publication for purposes it considered proper and thus public knowledge was delayed. No doubt this was for a good reason; the analysis of 7,000 pages of complex material drawn from a vastly greater volume of material would inevitably take time and the writing of good news stories takes time. But why should the United States Government, from whom this information was illegally acquired by someone, along with all the counsel, trial judges, and appellate judges be placed under needless pressure? After these months of deferral, the alleged "right to know" has somehow and suddenly become a right that must be vindicated instanter.

Would it have been unreasonable, since the newspaper could anticipate the Government's objections to release of secret material, to give the Government an opportunity to review the entire collection and determine whether agreement could be reached on publication? Stolen or not, if security was not in fact jeopardized, much of the material could no doubt have been declassified, since it spans a period ending in 1968. With such an approach—one that great newspapers have in the past practiced and stated editorially to be the duty of an honorable press—the newspapers and Government might well have narrowed the area of disagreement as to what was and was not publishable, leaving the remainder to be resolved in orderly litigation, if necessary. To me it is hardly believable that a newspaper long regarded as a great institution in American life would fail to perform one of the basic and simple duties of every citizen with respect to the discovery or possession of stolen property or secret government documents. That duty, I had thought—perhaps naively—was to report forthwith, to responsible public officers. This duty rests on taxi drivers, Justices, and the *New York Times*. The course followed by the *Times*, whether so calculated or not, removed any possibility of orderly litigation of the issues. If the action of the judges up to now has been correct, that result is sheer happenstance.

☐ *Justice HARLAN, with whom THE CHIEF JUSTICE and Justice BLACKMUN join, dissenting.*

With all respect, I consider that the Court has been almost irresponsibly feverish in dealing with these cases.

Both the Court of Appeals for the Second Circuit and the Court of Appeals for the District of Columbia Circuit rendered judgment on June 23. The *New York Times'* petition for *certiorari*, its motion for accelerated consideration thereof, and its application for interim relief were filed in this Court on June 24 at about 11 A.M. The application of the United States for interim relief in the *Post* case was also filed here on June 24 at about 7:15 P.M. This Court's order setting a hearing before us on June 26 at 11 A.M., a course which I joined only to avoid the possibility of even more peremptory action by the Court, was issued less than 24 hours before. The record in the *Post* case was filed with the Clerk shortly before 1 P.M. on June 25; the record in the *Times* case did not arrive until 7 or 8 o'clock that same night. The briefs of the parties were received less than two hours before argument on June 26.

This frenzied train of events took place in the name of the presumption against prior restraints created by the First Amendment. Due regard for the extraordinarily important and difficult questions involved in these litigations should have led the Court to shun such a precipitate timetable. In order to decide the merits of these cases properly, some or all of the following questions should have been faced:

1. Whether the Attorney General is authorized to bring these suits in the name of the United States. . . .

2. Whether the First Amendment permits the federal courts to enjoin publication of stories which would present a serious threat to national security. . . .

3. Whether the threat to publish highly secret documents is of itself a sufficient implication of national security to justify an injunction on the theory that regardless of the contents of the documents harm enough results simply from the demonstration of such a breach of secrecy.

4. Whether the unauthorized disclosure of any of these particular documents would seriously impair the national security.

5. What weight should be given to the opinion of high officers in the Executive Branch of the Government with respect to questions 3 and 4.

6. Whether the newspapers are entitled to retain and use the documents notwithstanding the seemingly uncontested facts that the documents, or the originals of which they are duplicates, were purloined from the Government's possession and that the newspapers received them with knowledge that they had been feloniously acquired. . . .

7. Whether the threatened harm to the national security or the Government's possessory interest in the documents justifies the issuance of an injunction against publication in light of—

a. The strong First Amendment policy against prior restraints on publication;

b. The doctrine against enjoining conduct in violation of criminal statutes; and

c. The extent to which the materials at issue have apparently already been otherwise disseminated.

These are difficult questions of fact, of law, and of judgment: the potential consequences of erroneous decision are enormous. The time which has been available to us, to the lower courts, and to the parties has been wholly inadequate for giving these cases the kind of consideration they deserve. It is a reflection on the stability of the judicial process that these great issues—as important as any that have arisen during my time on the Court—should have been decided under the pressures engendered by the torrent of publicity that has attended these litigations from their inception.

Forced as I am to reach the merits of these cases, I dissent from the opinion and judgments of the Court. . . .

It is plain to me that the scope of the judicial function in passing upon the activities of the Executive Branch of the Government in the field of foreign affairs is very narrowly restricted. This view is, I think, dictated by the concept of separation of powers upon which our constitutional system rests.

In a speech on the floor of the House of Representatives, Chief Justice John MARSHALL, then a member of that body, stated:

The President is the sole organ of the nation in its external relations, and its sole representative with foreign nations. 10 Annals of
Cong. 613.

From that time, shortly after the founding of the Nation, to this, there has
been no substantial challenge to this description of the scope of executive
power. . . . I agree that, in performance of its duty to protect the values of the
First Amendment against political pressures, the judiciary must review
the initial Executive determination to the point of satisfying itself that the
subject matter of the dispute does lie within the proper compass of the
President's foreign relations power. Constitutional considerations forbid "a
complete abandonment of judicial control." Moreover the judiciary may
properly insist that the determination that disclosure of the subject matter
would irreparably impair the national security be made by the head of the
Executive Department concerned—here the Secretary of State or the Secretary of Defense—after actual personal consideration by that officer. This safeguard is required in the analogous area of executive claims of privilege for
secrets of state. . . .

But in my judgment the judiciary may not properly go beyond these
two inquiries and redetermine for itself the probable impact of disclosure on
the national security.

☐ *Justice BLACKMUN, dissenting.*

The country would be none the worse off were the cases tried quickly,
to be sure, but in the customary and properly deliberative manner. The most
recent of the material, it is said, dates no later than 1968, already about three
years ago, and the *Times* itself took three months to formulate its plan of procedure and, thus, deprived its public for that period.

The First Amendment, after all, is only one part of an entire Constitution. Article II of the great document vests in the Executive Branch primary
power over the conduct of foreign affairs and places in that branch the responsibility for the Nation's safety. Each provision of the Constitution is important, and I cannot subscribe to a doctrine of unlimited absolutism for the
First Amendment at the cost of downgrading other provisions. First Amendment absolutism has never commanded a majority of this Court. . . .

What is needed here is a weighing, upon properly developed standards,
of the broad right of the press to print and of the very narrow right of the
Government to prevent.

■ THE DEVELOPMENT OF LAW

The National Security Agency's Warrantless Electronic Surveillance

In 2005, a controversy erupted over the revelation that after the September 11, 2001, terrorist attacks President George W. Bush issued a secret executive order authorizing the National Security Agency (NSA) to conduct warrantless electronic surveillance of "communications where one . . . party to the communication is outside of the United States" and there was "a reasonable basis to conclude that one party" has contacts with terrorists. The surveillance involved monitoring e-mails, through Google-like searches, and tracking Internet and satellite communications.

Foreign intelligence surveillance was supposed to be governed by the Foreign Intelligence Surveillance Act (FISA) of 1978 (see The Development of Law: The USA PATRIOT Act of 2001 box in Vol. 1, Ch. 3 and in Vol. 2, Ch. 7). Under that law, the government must seek a warrant from a special FISA court, though in emergencies warrantless searches may be conducted for three days prior to requesting a warrant. The law also makes it a crime for government officials to conduct "electronic surveillance under color of law except as authorized by statute." The USA PATRIOT Act amended the FISA to require a "significant purpose" for an investigation of foreign intelligence information; in 2006 the major provisions of the USA PATRIOT Act were extended and made permanent.

The Bush administration defended the NSA's warrantless surveillance on three grounds. First, the president has the inherent power and power as commander in chief to do so during times of war. Prior presidents made similar claims. President Abraham Lincoln ordered the warrantless wiretapping of telegraph wires during the Civil War. Likewise, during World Wars I and II Presidents Woodrow Wilson and Franklin D. Roosevelt ordered the interception of international communications. Similar claims to presidential power were made by subsequent administrations, including those of Presidents Jimmy Carter and Bill Clinton.

Second, the joint resolution for the Authorization for the Use of Military Force (AUMF) of 2001 provides for the use of "all necessary and appropriate" force to combat terrorists, and thus justifies the president's action. Third, the AUMF justifies not complying with the provisions of the FISA, since it superseded FISA. In addition, *Smith v. Maryland*, 442 U.S. 735 (1979), upheld the use of pen registers, which record the telephone numbers called from phones but not the conversations. Accordingly, by extension the NSA's collection of "meta-data"—the time and to and from of Internet and satellite communications—was permissible.

By contrast, some members of Congress and civil liberties groups countered that the President has no inherent power to authorize warrantless domestic security surveillance; that neither the AUMF nor the FISA permit such a program; and that *United States v. United States District Court*, 407 U.S. 297 (1972), the so-called *Keith* case, held that domestic intelligence surveillance requires prior judicial approval of a warrant in order to satisfy the Fourth Amendment's guarantee against unreasonable searches and seizures, though the decision left open the matter of warrantless foreign surveillance. After months of negotiations in 2006 Congress enacted legislation reasserting the authority of the FISA court, while permitting wiretapping without a warrant for up to 45 days but requiring the attorney general to certify and explain why such warrantless surveillance is necessary to a subcommittee of the Senate Intelligence Committee.

Subsequently, it was also revealed that the NSA had been monitoring the phone numbers dialed by millions of U.S. citizens in order to search for telephone calling patterns and possible links to terrorists, as well as that the Central Intelligence Agency and the Department of Treasury monitored the transactions of 7,800 financial institutions worldwide.

In response to criticisms and lawsuits filed by civil liberties groups challenging the constitutionality of the NSA's warrantless surveillance, President Bush agreed to legislation that would consolidate litigation and give jurisdiction to the FISA court. But he also exacted concessions permitting revisions of the program after the court's ruling and permitting in emergency situations warrantless surveillance for up to one week (instead of the previous seventy-two hours) before requesting a warrant. However, before that legislation was enacted a federal district court, in *American Civil Liberties Union v. National Security Agency* (2006), ruled that the president did not have the inherent power to conduct such surveillance without judicial review, and that the FISA controlled the government's electronic eavesdropping. Subsequently, in 2007 the Bush administration agreed to give the FISA court exclusive jurisdiction over the NSA's wiretapping program and to end its warrantless eavesdropping on citizens suspected of having ties to terrorists.

For further reading, see U.S. Department of Justice, "Legal Authorities Supporting the Activities of the National Security Agency Described by the President" (Washington, DC: Department of Justice, January 19, 2006), and compare Congressional Research Service, "Memorandum: Presidential Authority to Conduct Warrantless Electronic Surveillance to Gather Foreign Intelligence Information" (Washington, DC: Congressional Research, January 5, 2006).

B | *Appointment and Removal Powers*

With the power given in Article II, Section 2, the president shall "nominate, and by and with the advice and consent of the Senate, shall appoint ambassadors, other public ministers and consuls, judges of the supreme Court, and all other Officers of the United States, whose Appointments are not herein otherwise provided for, and which shall be established by Law." He also has the power to make "recess appointments" when the Senate is not in session, and those appointees may hold office through the next session even without Senate confirmation. However, Article II also provides that "Congress may by Law vest the Appointment of such *inferior Officers*, as they may think proper, in the President alone, in the Courts of Law, or in the Heads of Departments" (emphasis added). Thus while the president has the power to nominate and, with the consent of the Senate, appoint high government officials, Congress has the power to condition, and even deny the president, the appointment power over "inferior" government officials.

In theory, the nomination of government officials is the "sole act of the President," as Chief Justice Marshall observed in *Marbury v. Madison* (1803) (see excerpt in Ch. 1). Appointment of high-ranking officials—members of the cabinet and the Supreme Court—is generally a matter of personal presidential prerogative, although in extraordinary circumstances the Senate may deny confirmation for broad political reasons. The Constitutional Convention, however, envisioned some senatorial participation in the nomination and appointment process. And since the 1840s the tradition of "senatorial courtesy" has guaranteed a high degree of Senate participation in the nomination process, depending on the political strength or weakness of the president and whether the Senate is controlled by a loyal or opposition party. According to this tradition, the White House pays deference to a senator's preferences in filling vacancies in that senator's home state for offices, such as U.S. marshals, attorneys, and district judges. Moreover, the Civil Service Act of 1883 restricts the president's prerogative over appointments within the executive branch to those among the highest grades of the civil service.

By contrast with the appointment power, the Constitution is silent about the removal power. It expressly provides only that the president, federal judges, and all civil officials are subject to "[i]mpeachment for, and Conviction of, Treason, Bribery, or other high Crimes and Misdemeanors." As a result, there are competing views of the power to remove government officials for other than impeachable offenses. Presidents have long contended that they enjoy the sole power of removal. Yet, because appointees are subject to Senate confirmation, it is sometimes claimed that the Senate shares in the removal power. Furthermore, because Congress creates offices, arguably it may place conditions on appointees' tenure and removal.

The Constitutional Convention left the issue of the removal power to be debated in 1789 in connection with the creation of the departments of foreign affairs, war, and the treasury. In the House of Representatives, James Madison initially argued that the secretaries of these departments should be "removable by the President." The "executive power" is vested in the president, who is obligated to "faithfully execute the Laws," Madison reasoned, and the removal power would render the department heads more accountable to the president. But he subsequently drew a distinction among the secretaries of foreign affairs and war and the comptroller of the treasury. The latter was not "purely of an Executive nature," Madison pointed out, suggesting that "there may be strong reasons why an officer of this kind should not hold his office at the pleasure of the Executive branch of the Government." The House nevertheless passed a bill creating all three departments without specifying the president's power of removal. The Senate, however, distinguished among "executive departments" in giving the president the power to remove the secretaries of foreign affairs and war, while denying him that power over the head of the treasury. But when the House and Senate bills had to be reconciled, the Senate split evenly and Vice President Adams cast the deciding vote giving the removal power to the president over all three departments.

Despite presidential claims to the sole power of removal, Congress in the nineteenth century specified conditions for removing a number of government officials and even subjected the removal of some to "the advice and consent of the Senate." In the few cases dealing with the removal power that came before it, the Supreme Court indicated that presidential power could be limited when Congress clearly specified the conditions for removing certain inferior appointees from office. (See *Parsons v. United States*, 167 U.S. 324 (1897) (removal of a U.S. attorney); *Shurtleff v. United States*, 189 U.S. 311 (1903) (customs official); and *Wallace v. United States*, 257 U.S. 541 (1922) (dismissal of officer of Quartermaster Corps.)

An expansive view of the president's removal power was, nonetheless, embraced by Chief Justice William Howard Taft in *Myers v. United States* (1926) (see excerpt below) over the sharp dissents of Justices Brandeis, Holmes, and McReynolds. But less than a decade later *Humphrey's Executor v. United States* (1935) (see excerpt below) unanimously held that a member of the Federal Trade Commission (FTC) could not be removed simply for policy reasons. Writing for the Court, Justice Sutherland drew a distinction between "purely executive" officials—such as the postmaster in *Myers*—which the president may remove at his discretion, and those like an FTC commissioner who have "quasi-judicial and quasi-legislative" duties, who are removable only for reasons specified by Congress.

The distinction between purely executive and quasi-judicial and quasi-legislative officials, as Justice Sutherland concedes, is inexact and invites controversy. *Humphrey's Executor* also remained sharply criticized for limiting the powers of the president.

The Court reassessed the removal powers of Congress and the president in two other major rulings. In *Bowsher v. Synar* (1986) (see excerpt below), the Court relied on *Humphrey's Executor* in striking down a portion of the Balanced Budget and Emergency Deficit Control Act because it empowered the comptroller general, who may be removed by a joint resolution of Congress, to make across-the-board reductions in federal spending if yearly maximums set for federal deficits were not met. Then in *Morrison v. Olson* (1988) (see excerpt below) Chief Justice Rehnquist reconsidered and rejected *Humphrey's Executor*'s reasoning when upholding the appointment of independent counsel to investigate the misconduct of executive branch officials under the Ethics in Government Act. Compare the majority's view of the separation of powers with that of Justice Scalia in his dissenting opinion in *Morrison*. Justice Scalia again stood alone in dissenting from *Mistretta v. United States*, 488 U.S. 361 (1989). There, the Court upheld the Sentencing Reform Act of 1984, which created the U.S. Sentencing Commission and authorized it to promulgate binding guidelines for a range of determinate sentences for all categories of federal crime. In *Mistretta*, the majority held that Congress had not violated the principle of separation of powers by conferring on the president the power to appoint and to remove "for cause" members of the commission, including federal judges; nor did Congress run afoul of the nondelegation doctrine (discussed in the next section) by broadly delegating to the commission its power to make law.

In *Weiss v. United States*, 510 U.S. 163 (1994), the Court confronted a challenge under the appointments clause of Article II and the Fifth Amendment's due process clause to the way judges are appointed in military courts. Under the Uniform Code of Military Justice (UCMJ), a special and general court-martial trial is heard before a military judge and from three to five court-martial members, all of whom are temporarily assigned by the Judge Advocate General. Weiss, a Marine who was found guilty of larceny at a special court-martial, appealed on the grounds that the UCMJ's prescribed appointment method violated Article II and the due process clause. Writing for the majority, Chief Justice

Rehnquist rejected the contentions that the appointment as judges of commissioned military officers runs afoul of Article II. Furthermore, he did not find any merit to the claim that the position of a military judge is so similar to other positions specified in Article II as to require Senate confirmation, nor did he agree that military judges are akin to other high government officials, such as the chairman of the Joint Chiefs of Staff, subject to a second appointment proceeding under Article II.

Finally, while not overturning the Sarbanes-Oxley Act, passed in response to the accounting scandals of Enron and Worldcom, a bare majority of the Roberts Court relied on *Humphrey's Executor v. United States*, 295 U.S. 602 (1935), (excerpted below) to rule that the provision for removing members of the Public Company Accounting Oversight Board (PCAOB), which oversees firms that audit publically traded companies, violated the separation of powers by giving executive branch responsibility to members of the Securities and Exchange Commission (SEC). The SEC is beyond the president's control because its members cannot be removed except for "good cause" or "inefficiency, neglect of duty, or malfeasance in office." Writing for the majority in *Free Enterprise Fund v. Public Company Accounting Oversight Board*, 130 S.Ct. 3138 (2010), Chief Justice Roberts distinguished prior decisions limiting the president's power of removal of subordinates by focusing on the fact that members of the PCAOB could be removed for "good cause" by the SEC but the SEC's members could not be removed by the president. In the majority's view that provision violated Article II's vesting of the executive power in the president. Justices Stevens, Ginsburg, Breyer, and Sotomayor dissented.

Selected Bibliography

Abraham, Henry. *Justices, Presidents, and Senators: A History of the U.S. Supreme Court Appointments from Washington to Bush II.* Lanham, MD: Rowman & Littlefield, 2008.

Goldman, Sheldon. *Picking Federal Judges: Lower Court Selection from Roosevelt through Reagan.* New Haven, CT: Yale University Press, 1997.

Harriger, Katy. *The Special Prosecutor in American Politics.* 2d ed. Lawrence: University Press of Kansas, 2000.

Massaro, John. *Supremely Political: The Role of Ideology and Presidential Management in Unsuccessful Supreme Court Nominations.* Albany: State University of New York Press, 1990.

McKenzie, G. Galvin. *The Politics of Presidential Appointments.* New York: Free Press, 1981.

O'Brien, David. *Judicial Roulette: Report of the Twentieth Century Fund Task Force on Judicial Appointments.* New York: The Twentieth Century Fund, 1988.

Watson, George, and Stookey, John. *Shaping America: The Politics of Supreme Court Appointments.* New York: HarperCollins, 1995.

■ CONSTITUTIONAL HISTORY

Supreme Court Nominations Rejected, Postponed, or Withdrawn Due to Senate Opposition[a]

NOMINEE	YEAR NOMINATED	NOMINATED BY	ACTIONS[b]
William Paterson[c]	1793	Washington	Withdrawn (for technical reasons)
John Rutledge[d]	1795	Washington	Rejected
Alexander Wolcott	1811	Madison	Rejected
John J. Crittenden	1828	J. Q. Adams	Postponed, 1829
Roger B. Taney[e]	1835	Jackson	Postponed
John C. Spencer	1844	Tyler	Rejected
Reuben H. Walworth	1844	Tyler	Withdrawn
Edward King	1844	Tyler	Postponed
Edward King[f]	1844	Tyler	Withdrawn, 1845
John M. Read	1845	Tyler	No action
George W. Woodward	1845	Polk	Rejected, 1846
Edward A. Bradford	1852	Fillmore	No action
George E. Badger	1853	Fillmore	Postponed
William C. Micou	1853	Fillmore	No action
Jeremiah S. Black	1861	Buchanan	Rejected
Henry Stanbery	1866	Johnson	No action
Ebenezer R. Hoar	1869	Grant	Rejected, 1870
George H. Williams[d]	1873	Grant	Withdrawn, 1874
Caleb Cushin[d]	1874	Grant	Withdrawn
Stanley Mathews[c]	1881	Hayes	No action
William B. Hornblower	1893	Cleveland	Rejected, 1894
Wheeler H. Peckham	1894	Cleveland	Rejected
John J. Parker	1930	Hoover	Rejected
Abe Fortas[g]	1968	Johnson	Withdrawn
Homer Thornberry	1968	Johnson	No action
Clement F. Haynsworth, Jr.	1969	Nixon	Rejected
G. Harold Carswell	1970	Nixon	Rejected
Robert H. Bork	1987	Reagan	Rejected
Douglas H. Ginsburg	1987	Reagan	Withdrawn
Hariett Meyers	2005	G. W. Bush	Withdrawn

[a]Article II of the Constitution provides the president shall nominate Supreme Court justices and lower court judges "with the advice and consent of the Senate." These are the nominees to the Supreme Court that the Senate has rejected or forced to be withdrawn from consideration.
[b]A year is given if different from the year of nomination.
[c]Reappointed and confirmed.
[d]Nominated for chief justice.
[e]Taney was reappointed and confirmed as chief justice.
[f]Second appointment.
[g]Associate justice nominated for chief justice.

Myers v. United States

272 U.S. 52, 47 S.CT. 21 (1926)

A series of confrontations between the president and Congress over the removal power began with Andrew Jackson's "spoils system" and removal of more officials than all preceding presidents. Congress eventually passed the Tenure of Office Act in 1867, providing that every appointee confirmed by the Senate was entitled to hold office until a successor was appointed by the president with the advice and consent of the Senate. During the post–Civil War period Congress also passed legislation permitting the removal of officials only with senatorial approval. Among these laws was an 1876 statute requiring senatorial advice and consent for the removal of all first-, second-, and third-class postmasters. Presidential opposition to such restrictions persisted and Congress eventually repealed the Tenure of Office Act in 1887, but others including the 1876 statute governing the removal of postmasters remained in force.

In 1920, President Woodrow Wilson was battling with Congress over a section of the budget and accounting bill that provided that the comptroller general could be removed only by impeachment or a concurrent resolution of Congress. He contended that Congress could not in this way limit presidential power. Amid the struggle Wilson directed the postmaster general to remove, in violation of the 1876 law, Frank S. Myers, a postmaster in Portland, Oregon. Myers sued to recover his lost salary in the U.S. Court of Claims, which ruled against him. Louis Myers, the administrator of his estate, then appealed to the Supreme Court and challenged the constitutionality of the president's actions.

The Court's decision was six to three, and the majority's opinion was announced by Chief Justice Taft. Justices McReynolds, Brandeis, and Holmes dissented.

☐ *Chief Justice TAFT delivers the opinion of the Court.*

This case presents the question whether under the Constitution the President has the exclusive power of removing executive officers of the United States whom he has appointed by and with the advice and consent of the Senate. . . .

The debates in the Constitutional Convention indicated an intention to create a strong executive, and after a controversial discussion the executive power of the government was vested in one person and many of his important functions were specified so as to avoid the humiliating weakness of the Congress during the Revolution and under the Articles of Confederation.

Mr. Madison and his associates in the discussion in the House dwelt at length upon the necessity there was for construing article 2 to give the President the sole power of removal in his responsibility for the conduct of the executive branch, and enforced this by emphasizing his duty expressly declared in the third section of the article to "take care that the laws be faithfully executed." Madison, 1 *Annals of Congress*, 496, 497.

The vesting of the executive power in the President was essentially a grant of the power to execute the laws. But the President alone and unaided could not execute the laws. He must execute them by the assistance of subordinates. This view has since been repeatedly affirmed by this court. As he is charged specifically to take care that they be faithfully executed, the reasonable implication, even in the absence of express words, was that as part of his executive power he should select those who were to act for him under his direction in the execution of the laws. The further implication must be, in the absence of any express limitation respecting removals, that as his selection of administrative officers is essential to the execution of the laws by him, so must be his power of removing those for whom he cannot continue to be responsible. It was urged that the natural meaning of the term "executive power" granted the President included the appointment and removal of executive subordinates. If such appointments and removals were not an exercise of the executive power, what were they? They certainly were not the exercise of legislative or judicial power in government as usually understood. . . .

The power to prevent the removal of an officer who has served under the President is different from the authority to consent to or reject his appointment. When a nomination is made, it may be presumed that the Senate is, or may become, as well advised as to the fitness of the nominee as the President, but in the nature of things the defects in ability or intelligence or loyalty in the administration of the laws of one who has served as an officer under the President are facts as to which the President, or his trusted subordinates, must be better informed than the Senate, and the power to remove him may therefore be regarded as confined for very sound and practical reasons, to the governmental authority which has administrative control. The power of removal is incident to the power of appointment, not to the power of advising and consenting to appointment, and when the grant of the executive power is enforced by the express mandate to take care that the laws be faithfully executed, it emphasizes the necessity for including within the executive power as conferred the exclusive power of removal. . . .

The view of Mr. Madison and his associates was that not only did the grant of executive power to the President in the first section of article 2 carry with it the power of removal, but the express recognition of the power of appointment in the second section enforced this view on the well-approved principle of constitutional and statutory construction that the power of removal of executive officers was incident to the power of appointment. It was agreed by the opponents of the bill, with only one or two exceptions, that as a constitutional principle the power of appointment carried with it the power of removal. Roger Sherman, 1 *Annals of Congress*, 491. This principle as a rule of constitutional and statutory construction, then generally conceded, has been recognized ever since. . . . The reason for the principle is that those in charge of and responsible for administering functions of government, who select their executive subordinates, need in meeting their responsibility to have the power to remove those whom they appoint.

Under section 2 of article 2, however, the power of appointment by the executive is restricted in its exercise by the provision that the Senate, a part of the legislative branch of the government, may check the action of the executive by rejecting the officers he selects. Does this make the Senate part of the removing power? And this, after the whole discussion in the House is read attentively, is the real point which was considered and decided in the negative by the vote already given.

The history of the clause by which the Senate was given a check upon the President's power of appointment makes it clear that it was not prompted by any desire to limit removals. As already pointed out, the important purpose of those who brought about the restriction was to lodge in the Senate, where the small states had equal representation with the larger states, power to prevent the President from making too many appointments from the larger states. . . .

It is reasonable to suppose also that had it been intended to give to Congress power to regulate or control removals in the manner suggested, it would have been included among the specifically enumerated legislative powers in article 1, or in the specified limitations on the executive power in article 2. The difference between the grant of legislative power under article 1 to Congress which is limited to powers therein enumerated, and the more general grant of the executive power to the President under article 2 is significant. The fact that the executive power is given in general terms strengthened by specific terms where emphasis is appropriate, and limited by direct expressions where limitation is needed, and that no express limit is placed on the power of removal by the executive is a convincing indication that none was intended. . . .

It is argued that the denial of the legislative power to regulate removals in some way involves the denial of power to prescribe qualifications for office, or reasonable classification for promotion, and yet that has been often exercised. We see no conflict between the latter power and that of appointment and removal, provided of course that the qualifications do not so limit selection and so trench upon executive choice as to be in effect legislative designation. As Mr. Madison said in the First Congress:

> The powers relative to offices are partly legislative and partly executive. The Legislature creates the office, defines the powers, limits its duration, and annexes a compensation. This done, the legislative power ceases. They ought to have nothing to do with designating the man to fill the office. That I conceive to be of an executive nature. Although it be qualified in the Constitution, I would not extend or strain that qualification beyond the limits precisely fixed for it. We ought always to consider the Constitution with an eye to the principles upon which it was founded. In this point of view, we shall readily conclude that if the Legislature determines the powers, the honors, and emoluments of an office, we should be insecure if they were to designate the officer also. The nature of things restrains and confines the legislative and executive authorities in this respect; and hence it is that the Constitution stipulates for the independence of each branch of the government. 1 *Annals of Congress*, 581, 582.

Made responsible under the Constitution for the effective enforcement of the law, the President needs as an indispensable aid to meet it the disciplinary influence upon those who act under him of a reserve power of removal. But it is contended that executive officers appointed by the President with the consent of the Senate are bound by the statutory law, and are not his servants to do his will, and that his obligation to care for the faithful execution of the laws does not authorize him to treat them as such. The degree of guidance in the discharge of their duties that the President may exercise over executive officers varies with the character of their service as prescribed in the law under which they act. The highest and most important duties which his subordinates perform are those in which they act for him. In such cases they are exercising not their own but his discretion. This field is a very large one. It is sometimes described as political. . . .

The duties of the heads of departments and bureaus in which the discretion of the President is exercised and which we have described are the most important in the whole field of executive action of the government. There is nothing in the Constitution which permits a distinction between the removal of the head of a department or a bureau, when he discharges a political duty of the President or exercises his discretion, and the removal of executive officers engaged in the discharge of their other normal duties. The imperative reasons requiring an unrestricted power to remove the most important of his subordinates in their most important duties must therefore control the interpretation of the Constitution as to all appointed by him.

But this is not to say that there are not strong reasons why the President should have a like power to remove his appointees charged with other duties than those above described. The ordinary duties of officers prescribed by statute come under the general administrative control of the President by virtue of the general grant to him of the executive power, and he may properly supervise and guide their construction of the statutes under which they act in order to secure that unitary and uniform execution of the laws which article 2 of the Constitution evidently contemplated in vesting general executive power in the President alone. Laws are often passed with specific provision for the adoption of regulations by a department or bureau head to make the law workable and effective. The ability and judgment manifested by the official thus empowered, as well as his energy and stimulation of his subordinates, are subjects which the President must consider and supervise in his administrative control. Finding such officers to be negligent and inefficient, the President should have the power to remove them. Of course there may be duties so peculiarly and specifically committed to the discretion of a particular officer as to raise a question whether the President may overrule or revise the officer's interpretation of his statutory duty in a particular instance. Then there may be duties of a quasi judicial character imposed on executive officers and members of executive tribunals whose decisions after hearing affect interests of individuals, the discharge of which the President cannot in a particular case properly influence or control. But even in such a case he may consider the decision after its rendition as a reason for removing the officer, on the ground that the discretion regularly entrusted to that officer by statute has not been on the whole intelligently or wisely exercised. Otherwise he does not discharge his own constitutional duty of seeing that the laws be faithfully executed.

We have devoted much space to this discussion and decision of the question of the presidential power of removal in the First Congress, not because a congressional conclusion on a constitutional issue is conclusive, but first because of our agreement with the reasons upon which it was avowedly based, second because this was the decision of the First Congress on a question of primary importance in the organization of the government made within two years after the Constitutional Convention and within a much shorter time after its ratification, and third because that Congress numbered among its leaders those who had been members of the convention. It must necessarily constitute a precedent upon which many future laws supplying the machinery of the new government would be based and, if erroneous, would be likely to evoke dissent and departure in future Congresses. It would come at once before the executive branch of the government for compliance and might well be brought before the judicial branch for a test of its validity. As we shall see, it was soon accepted as a final decision of the question by all branches of the government.

It was, of course, to be expected that the decision would be received by lawyers and jurists with something of the same division of opinion as that manifested in Congress, and doubts were often expressed as to its correctness. But the acquiescence which was promptly accorded it after a few years was universally recognized. . . .

We come now to consider an argument, advanced and strongly pressed on behalf of the complainant, that this case concerns only the removal of a postmaster, that a postmaster is an inferior officer, and that such an office was not included within the legislative decision of 1789, which related only to superior officers to be appointed by the President by and with the advice and consent of the Senate. This, it is said, is the distinction which Chief Justice MARSHALL had in mind in *Marbury v. Madison* in the language already discussed in respect to the President's power of removal of a District of Columbia justice of the peace appointed and confirmed for a term of years. We find nothing in *Marbury v. Madison* to indicate any such distinction. It cannot be certainly affirmed whether the conclusion there stated was based on a dissent from the legislative decision of 1789, or on the fact that the office was created under the special power of Congress exclusively to legislate for the District of Columbia, or on the fact that the office was a judicial one, or on the circumstance that it was an inferior office. In view of the doubt as to what was really the basis of the remarks relied on and their obiter dictum character, they can certainly not be used to give weight to the argument that the 1789 decision only related to superior officers. . . .

Our conclusion on the merits, sustained by the arguments before stated, is that article 2 grants to the President the executive power of the government—i.e., the general administrative control of those executing the laws, including the power of appointment and removal of executive officers—a conclusion confirmed by his obligation to take care that the laws be faithfully executed; that article 2 excludes the exercise of legislative power by Congress to provide for appointments and removals, except only as granted therein to Congress in the matter of inferior offices; that Congress is only given power to provide for appointments and removals of inferior officers after it has vested, and on condition that it does vest, their appointment in other authority than the President with the Senate's consent; that the provisions of the second section of article 2, which blend action by the legislative branch, or by part of it, in the work of the executive, are limitations to be strictly construed, and not to be extended by implication; that the President's power of removal is further established as an incident to his specifically enumerated function of appointment by and with the advice of the Senate, but that such incident does not by implication extend to removals the Senate's power of checking appointments; and, finally, that to hold otherwise would make it impossible for the President, in case of political or other difference with the Senate or Congress, to take care that the laws be faithfully executed.

We come now to a period in the history of the government when both houses of Congress attempted to reverse this constitutional construction, and to subject the power of removing executive officers appointed by the President and confirmed by the Senate to the control of the Senate, indeed finally to the assumed power in Congress to place the removal of such officers anywhere in the government.

This reversal grew out of the serious political difference between the two houses of Congress and President Johnson. There was a two-thirds majority of the Republican party, in control of each house of Congress, which resented what it feared would be Mr. Johnson's obstructive course in the enforcement of the reconstruction measures in respect to the states whose people had lately been at war against the national government. This led the two houses to enact legislation to curtail the then acknowledged powers of the President.

[T]he chief legislation in support of the reconstruction policy of Congress was the Tenure of Office Act of March 2, 1867, providing that all officers appointed by and with the consent of the Senate should hold their offices until their successors should have in like manner been appointed and qualified; that certain heads of departments, including the Secretary of War, should hold their offices during the term of the President by whom appointed and one month thereafter, subject to removal by consent of the Senate. The Tenure of Office Act was vetoed, but it was passed over the veto. . . . [Objections to Congress's limiting the removal power of the President, from Grant to Coolidge, were then discussed by the Chief Justice.]

In spite of the foregoing presidential declarations, it is contended that, since the passage of the Tenure of Office Act, there has been general acquiescence by the executive in the power of Congress to forbid the President alone to remove executive officers, an acquiescence which has changed any formerly accepted constitutional construction to the contrary. Instances are cited of the signed approval by President Grant and other Presidents of legislation in derogation of such construction. We think these are all to be explained, not by acquiescence therein, but by reason of the otherwise valuable effect of the legislation approved. Such is doubtless the explanation of the executive approval of the act of 1876, which we are considering, for it was an appropriation act on which the section here in question was imposed as a rider. . . .

The fact seems to be that all departments of the government have constantly had in mind, since the passage of the Tenure of Office Act, that the question of power of removal by the President of officers appointed by him with the Senate's consent has not been settled adversely to the legislative action of 1789, but, in spite of congressional action, has remained open until the conflict should be subjected to judicial investigation and decision.

The action of this court cannot be said to constitute assent to a departure from the legislative decision of 1789, when the Parsons and Shurtleff Cases, one decided in 1897, and the other in 1903, are considered, for they certainly leave the question open. *Wallace v. United States*, 257 U. S. 541 [1922]. Those cases indicate no tendency to depart from the view of the First Congress. This court has since the Tenure of Office Act manifested an earnest desire to avoid a final settlement of the question until it should be inevitably presented, as it is here.

An argument *ab inconvenienti* has been made against our conclusion in favor of the executive power of removal by the President, without the consent of the Senate, that it will open the door to a reintroduction of the spoils system. The evil of the spoils system aimed at in the Civil Service Law and its amendments is in respect to inferior offices. It has never been attempted to extend that law beyond them. . . .

For the reasons given, we must therefore hold that the provision of the law of 1876 by which the unrestricted power of removal of first-class postmasters is denied to the President is in violation of the Constitution and invalid. This leads to an affirmance of the judgment of the Court of Claims.

☐ *Justice McREYNOLDS, dissenting.*

May the President oust at will all postmasters appointed with the Senate's consent for definite terms under an act which inhibits removal without consent of that body? May he approve a statute which creates an inferior office and prescribes restrictions on removal, appoint an incumbent, and then remove without regard to the restrictions? Has he power to appoint to an inferior office for a definite term under an act which prohibits removal except as therein specified, and then arbitrarily dismiss the incumbent and deprive him of the emoluments? I think there is no such power. Certainly it is not given by any plain words of the Constitution; and the argument advanced to establish it seems to me forced and unsubstantial.

A certain repugnance must attend the suggestion that the President may ignore any provision of an act of Congress under which he has proceeded. He should promote and not subvert orderly government. The serious evils which followed the practice of dismissing civil officers as caprice or interest dictated, long permitted under congressional enactments, are known to all. It brought the public service to a low estate and caused insistent demand for reform. "Indeed, it is utterly impossible not to feel, that, if this unlimited power of removal does exist, it may be made, in the hands of a bold and designing man, of high ambition and feeble principles, an instrument of the worst oppression and most vindictive vengeance." *Story on the Constitution.* . . .

Constitutional provisions should be interpreted with the expectation that Congress will discharge its duties no less faithfully than the executive will attend to his. The Legislature is charged with the duty of making laws for orderly administration obligatory upon all. It possesses supreme power over national affairs and may wreck as well as speed them. It holds the purse; every branch of the government functions under statutes which embody its will; it may impeach and expel all civil officers. The duty is upon it "to make all laws which shall be necessary and proper for carrying into execution" all powers of the federal government. We have no such thing as three totally distinct and independent departments; the others must look to the legislative for direction and support. "In republican government the legislative authority necessarily predominates." *The Federalist*, XLVI, XVII. Perhaps the chief duty of the President is to carry into effect the will of Congress through such instrumentalities as it has chosen to provide. . . .

I find no suggestion of the theory that "the executive power" of article 2, Sec. 1, includes all possible federal authority executive in nature unless definitely excluded by some constitutional provision, prior to the well-known House debate of 1789, when Mr. Madison seems to have given it support. A resolution looking to the establishment of an executive department—Department of Foreign Affairs (afterwards State)—provided for a secretary, "who shall be appointed by the President by and with the advice and consent of the Senate and to be removable by the President." Discussion arose upon a motion to strike out, "to be removable by the President." The distinction between superior and inferior officers was clearly recognized; also that the proposed officer was superior and must be appointed by the President with the Senate's consent. The bill prescribed no definite term—the incumbent would serve until death, resignation or removal. In the circumstances most of the speakers recognize the rule that where there is no constitutional or legislative restriction power to remove is incidental to that of appointment. Accordingly, they thought the President could remove the proposed officer; but many supposed he must do so with consent of the Senate. They maintained that the power to appoint is joint. . . .

In any rational search for answer to the questions arising upon this record, it is important not to forget—

That this is a government of limited powers, definitely enumerated and granted by a written Constitution.

That the Constitution must be interpreted by attributing to its words the meaning which they bore at the time of its adoption, and in view of commonly-accepted canons of construction, its history, early and long-continued practices under it, and relevant opinions of this court.

That the Constitution endows Congress with plenary powers "to establish post offices and post roads."

That, exercising this power during the years from 1789 to 1836, Congress provided for postmasters and vested the power to appoint and remove all of them at pleasure in the Postmaster General.

That the Constitution contains no words which specifically grant to the President power to remove duly appointed officers. And it is definitely settled that he cannot remove those whom he has not appointed—certainly they can be removed only as Congress may permit.

That postmasters are inferior officers within the meaning of Article 2, Sec. 2, of the Constitution.

That from its first session to the last one Congress has often asserted its right to restrict the President's power to remove inferior officers, although appointed by him with consent of the Senate.

That many Presidents have approved statutes limiting the power of the executive to remove, and that from the beginning such limitations have been respected in practice.

That this court, as early as 1803, in an opinion never overruled and rendered in a case where it was necessary to decide the question, positively declared that the President had no power to remove at will an inferior officer appointed with consent of the Senate to serve for a definite term fixed by an act of Congress.

That the power of Congress to restrict removals by the President was recognized by this court as late as 1903, in *Shurtleff v. United States* [189 U.S. 311 (1903)].

That the proceedings in the Constitutional Convention of 1787, the political history of the times, contemporaneous opinion, common canons of construction, the action of Congress from the beginning and opinions of this court, all oppose the theory that by vesting "the executive power" in the President the Constitution gave him an illimitable right to remove inferior officers.

That this court has emphatically disapproved the same theory concerning "the judicial power" vested in the courts by words substantially the same as those which vest "the executive power" in the President. "The executive power shall be vested in a President of the United States of America." "The judicial power of the United States, shall be vested in one Supreme Court, and in such inferior courts as the Congress may from time to time ordain and establish."

That to declare the President vested with indefinite and illimitable executive powers would extend the field of his possible action far beyond the limits observed by his predecessors, and would enlarge the powers of Congress to a degree incapable of fair appraisement.

Considering all these things, it is impossible for me to accept the view that the President may dismiss, as caprice may suggest, any inferior officer whom he has appointed with consent of the Senate, notwithstanding a positive inhibition by Congress. In the last analysis, that view has no substantial support, unless it be the polemic opinions expressed by Mr. Madison (and eight others) during the debate of 1789, when he was discussing questions relating to a "superior officer" to be appointed for an indefinite term. Notwithstanding his justly exalted reputation as one of the creators and early expounder of the Constitution, sentiments expressed under such circumstances ought not now to outweigh the conclusion which Congress affirmed by deliberate action while he was leader in the House and has consistently maintained down to the present year, the opinion of this court solemnly announced through the great CHIEF JUSTICE more than a century ago, and the canons of construction approved over and over again.

Judgment should go for the appellant.

□ *Justice BRANDEIS, dissenting.*

May the President, having acted under the statute in so far as it creates the office and authorizes the appointment, ignore, while the Senate is in session, the provision which prescribes the condition under which a removal may take place?

It is this narrow question, and this only, which we are required to decide. We need not consider what power the President, being Commander-in-Chief, has over officers in the Army and the Navy. We need not determine whether the President, acting alone, may remove high political officers. We need not even determine whether, acting alone, he may remove inferior civil officers when the Senate is not in session. . . .

Over removal from inferior civil offices, Congress has, from the foundation of our government, exercised continuously some measure of control by legislation. The instances of such laws are many. Some of the statutes were directory in character. Usually, they were mandatory. Some of them, comprehensive in scope, have endured for generations. During the first 40 years of our government, there was no occasion to curb removals. . . .

In the later period, which began after the spoils system had prevailed for a generation, the control of Congress over inferior offices was exerted to prevent removals. The removal clause here in question was first introduced by the Currency Act of February 25, 1863, which was approved by President Lincoln. That statute provided for the appointment of the Comptroller, and that he "shall hold his office for the term of five years unless sooner removed by the President, by and with the advice and consent of the Senate." In 1867 this provision was inserted in the Tenure of Office Act of March 2, 1867, which applied, in substance, to all presidential offices. It was passed over President Johnson's veto. . . .

The practice of Congress to control the exercise of the executive power of removal from inferior offices is evidenced by many statutes which restrict it in many ways besides the removal clause here in question. Each of these restrictive statutes became law with the approval of the President. Every President who has held office since 1861, except President Garfield, approved one or more of such statutes. Some of these statutes, prescribing a fixed term, provide that removal shall be made only for one of several specified causes. Some provide a fixed term, subject generally to removal for cause. Some provide for removal only after hearing. Some provide a fixed term, subject to removal for reasons to be communicated by the President to the Senate. Some impose the restriction in still other ways. . . .

The historical data submitted present a legislative practice, established by concurrent affirmative action of Congress and the President, to make consent of the Senate a condition of removal from statutory inferior, civil, executive offices to which the appointment is made for a fixed term by the President with such consent. They show that the practice has existed, without interruption, continuously for the last 58 years; that throughout this period, it has governed a great majority of all such offices; that the legislation applying the removal clause specifically to the office of postmaster was enacted more than half a century ago; and that recently the practice has, with the President's approval, been extended to several newly created offices. The data show further that the insertion of the removal clause in acts creating inferior civil offices with fixed tenures is part of the broader legislative practice, which has prevailed since the formation of our government, to restrict or regulate in many ways both removal from and nomination to such offices. A persistent legislative practice which involves a delimitation of the respective powers of Congress and the President, and which has been so established and maintained, should be deemed tantamount to judicial construction, in the absence of any decision by any court to the contrary. . . .

The persuasive effect of this legislative practice is strengthened by the fact that no instance has been found, even in the earlier period of our history, of concurrent affirmative action of Congress and the President which is inconsistent with the legislative practice of the last 58 years to impose the removal clause. Nor has any instance been found of action by Congress which involves recognition in any other way of the alleged uncontrollable executive power to remove an inferior civil officer. The action taken by Congress in 1789 after the great debate does not present such an instance. The vote then taken did not involve a decision that the President had uncontrollable power. It did not involve a decision of the question whether Congress could confer upon the Senate the right, and impose upon it the duty, to participate in removals. It involved merely the decision that the Senate does not, in the absence of legislative grant thereof, have the right to share in the removal of an officer appointed with its consent, and that the President has, in the absence of restrictive legislation, the constitutional power of removal without such consent. Moreover, as Chief Justice MARSHALL recognized, the debate and the decision related to a high political office, not to inferior ones.

It is true that several Presidents have asserted that the Constitution conferred a power of removal uncontrollable by Congress. But of the many statutes enacted since the foundation of our government which in express terms controlled the power of removal, either by the clause here in question or otherwise, only two were met with a veto: The Tenure of Office Act of 1867, which related to high political officers among others, and the Budget Act of 1921, which denied to the President any participation in the removal of the Comptroller and Assistant Comptroller. One was passed over the President's veto; the other was approved by the succeeding President. It is true also that several Presidents have and others at times insisted that for the exercise of their power they were not accountable to the Senate. But even these Presidents have at other times complied with requests that the ground of removal of inferior officers be stated. Many of the Presidents have furnished the desired information without questioning the right to request it. And neither the Senate nor the House has at any time receded from the claim that Congress has power both to control by legislation removal from inferior offices and to require the President to report to it the reasons for removals made there from. . . .

The separation of the powers of government did not make each branch completely autonomous. It left each in some measure, dependent upon the others, as it left to each power to exercise, in some respects, functions in their nature executive, legislative and judicial. Obviously the President cannot secure full execution of the laws, if Congress denies to him adequate means of doing so. Full execution may be defeated because Congress declines to create offices indispensable for that purpose; or because Congress, having created the office, declines to make the indispensable appropriation; or because Congress, having both created the office and made the appropriation, prevents, by restrictions which it imposes, the appointment of officials who in quality and character are indispensable to the efficient execution of the law. If, in any such way, adequate means are denied to the President, the fault will lie with Congress. The President performs his full constitutional duty, if, with the means and instruments provided by Congress and within the limitations prescribed by it; he uses his best endeavors to secure the faithful execution of the laws enacted.

The doctrine of the separation of powers was adopted by the convention of 1787 not to promote efficiency but to preclude the exercise of arbitrary power. The purpose was not to avoid friction, but, by means of the inevitable friction incident to the distribution of the governmental powers among three departments, to save the people from autocracy.

☐ *Justice HOLMES, dissenting.*

The arguments drawn from the executive power of the President, and from his duty to appoint officers of the United States (when Congress does not vest the appointment elsewhere), to take care that the laws be faithfully executed, and to commission all officers of the United States, seem to me spiders' webs inadequate to control the dominant facts.

We have to deal with an office that owes its existence to Congress and that Congress may abolish tomorrow. Its duration and the pay attached to it while it lasts depend on Congress alone. Congress alone confers on the President the power to appoint to it and at any time may transfer the power to other hands. With such power over its own creation, I have no more trouble in believing that Congress has power to prescribe a term of life for it free from any interference than I have in accepting the undoubted power of Congress to decree its end. I have equally little trouble in accepting its power to prolong the tenure of an incumbent until Congress or the Senate shall have assented to his removal. The duty of the President to see that the laws be executed is a duty that does not go beyond the laws or require him to achieve more than Congress sees fit to leave within his power.

Humphrey's Executor v. United States
295 U.S. 602, 55 S.Ct. 869 (1935)

William E. Humphrey was a conservative nominated by President Herbert Hoover and confirmed by the Senate as a commissioner of the Federal Trade Commission in 1931. According to the FTC Act, a commissioner could be removed by the president only for "inefficiency, neglect of duty, or malfeasance in office." However, in 1933 President Franklin D. Roosevelt asked Humphrey to resign, because the FTC had jurisdiction over many New Deal programs that Humphrey opposed. When he refused, the president dismissed him on policy grounds, rather than those specified in the FTC Act. Shortly thereafter Humphrey died, but the executor of his estate challenged the dismissal and sought to recover his salary in the court of claims and eventually in the Supreme Court. The justices unanimously agreed that Humphrey had been improperly removed from office and with Justice George Sutherland's opinion for the Court that limited the earlier ruling in *Myers v. United States* (1926) (see preceding excerpted case).

The Court's decision was unanimous, and the opinion was delivered by Justice Sutherland. Justice McReynolds concurred.

☐ *Justice SUTHERLAND delivers the opinion of the Court.*

The question first to be considered is whether, by the provisions of section 1 of the Federal Trade Commission Act, . . . the President's power is limited to removal for the specific causes enumerated therein. . . .

The commission is to be nonpartisan; and it must, from the very nature of its duties, act with entire impartiality. It is charged with the enforcement of no policy except the policy of the law. Its duties are neither political nor executive, but predominantly quasi judicial and quasi legislative. Like the Interstate Commerce Commission, its members are called upon to exercise the trained judgment of a body of experts "appointed by law and informed by experience." . . .

The legislative reports in both houses of Congress clearly reflect the view that a fixed term was necessary to the effective and fair administration of the law. . . .

The debates in both houses demonstrate that the prevailing view was that the Commission was not to be "subject to anybody in the government but . . . only to the people of the United States"; free from "political domination or control" or the "probability or possibility of such a thing"; to be "separate and apart from any existing department of the government—not subject to the orders of the President." . . .

Thus, the language of the act, the legislative reports, and the general purposes of the legislation as reflected by the debates, all combine to demonstrate the congressional intent to create a body of experts who shall gain experience by length of service; a body which shall be independent of executive authority; *except in its selection*, and free to exercise its judgment without the leave or hindrance of any other official or any department of the government. To the accomplishment of these purposes, it is clear that Congress was of the opinion that length and certainty of tenure would vitally contribute. And to hold that, nevertheless, the members of the commission continue in office at the mere will of the President, might be to thwart, in large measure, the very ends which Congress sought to realize by definitely fixing the term of office.

We conclude that the intent of the act is to limit the executive power of removal to the causes enumerated, the existence of none of which is claimed here; and we pass to the second question.

Second: To support its contention that the removal provision of section 1, as we have just construed it, is an unconstitutional interference with the executive power of the President, the government's chief reliance is *Myers v. United States*, 272 U.S. 52 [(1926)]. That case has been so recently decided, and the prevailing and dissenting opinions so fully review the general subject of the power of executive removal, that further discussion would add little of value to the wealth of material there collected. These opinions examine at length the historical, legislative, and judicial data bearing upon the question, beginning with what is called "the decision of 1789" in the first Congress and coming down almost to the day when the opinions were delivered. They occupy 243 pages of the volume in which they are printed. Nevertheless, the narrow point actually decided was only that the President had power to remove a postmaster of the first class, without the advice and consent of the Senate as required by act of Congress. In the course of the opinion of the court, expressions occur which tend to sustain the government's contention, but these are beyond the point involved and, therefore, do not come within the rule of *stare decisis*. In so far as they are out of harmony with the views here set forth, these expressions are disapproved. . . .

The office of a postmaster is so essentially unlike the office now involved that the decision in the *Myers* Case cannot be accepted as controlling our decision here. A postmaster is an executive officer restricted to the performance of executive functions. He is charged with no duty at all related to either the legislative or judicial power. The actual decision in the *Myers* Case finds support in the theory that such an officer is merely one of the units in the executive department and, hence, inherently subject to the exclusive and illimitable power of removal by the Chief Executive, whose subordinate and aide he is. Putting aside *dicta*, which may be followed if sufficiently persuasive but which are not controlling, the necessary reach of the decision goes far enough to include all purely executive officers. It goes no farther;—much less does it include an officer who occupies no place in the executive department and who exercises no part of the executive power vested by the Constitution in the President.

The Federal Trade Commission is an administrative body created by Congress to carry into effect legislative policies embodied in the statute in accordance with the legislative standard therein prescribed, and to perform other specified duties as a legislative or as a judicial aide. Such a body cannot in any proper sense be characterized as an arm or an eye of the executive. Its duties are performed without executive leave and, in the contemplation of the statute, must be free from executive control. In administering the provisions of the statute in respect of "unfair methods of competition," that is to say, in filling in and administering the details embodied by that general standard, the commission acts in part quasi legislatively and in part quasi judicially. In making investigations and reports thereon for the information of Congress under section 6, in aid of the legislative power, it acts as a legislative agency. Under section 7, which authorizes the commission to act as a master in chancery under rules prescribed by the court, it acts as an agency of the judiciary. To the extent that it exercises any executive function, as distinguished from executive power in the constitutional sense, it does so in the discharge and effectuation of its quasi legislative or quasi judicial powers, or as an agency of the legislative or judicial departments of the government.

If Congress is without authority to prescribe causes for removal of members of the trade commission and limit executive power of removal accordingly, that power at once becomes practically all-inclusive in respect of civil officers with the exception of the judiciary provided for by the Constitution. The Solicitor General, at the bar, apparently recognizing this to be true, with commendable candor, agreed that his view in respect of the removability of members of the Federal Trade Commission necessitated a like view in respect of the Interstate Commerce Commission and the Court of Claims. We are thus confronted with the serious question whether not only the members of these quasi legislative and quasi judicial bodies, but the judges of the legislative Court of Claims exercising judicial power . . . continue in office only at the pleasure of the President. . . .

We think it plain under the Constitution that illimitable power of removal is not possessed by the President in respect of officers of the character of those just named. The authority of Congress, in creating quasi legislative or quasi judicial agencies, to require them to act in discharge of their duties independently of executive control cannot well be doubted; and that authority includes, as an appropriate incident, power to fix the period during which they shall continue, and to forbid their removal except for cause in the meantime. For it is quite evident that one who holds his office only during the pleasure of another cannot be depended upon to maintain an attitude of independence against the latter's will.

The fundamental necessity of maintaining each of the three general departments of government entirely free from the control or coercive influence, direct or indirect, of either of the others, has often been stressed and is hardly open to serious question. So much is implied in the very fact of the separation of the powers of these departments by the Constitution; and in the rule which recognizes their essential coequality. The sound application of a principle that makes one master in his own house precludes him from imposing his control in the house of another who is master there.

The result of what we now have said is this: Whether the power of the President to remove an officer shall prevail over the authority of Congress to condition the power by fixing a definite term and precluding a removal except for cause will depend upon the character of the office; the *Myers* decision, affirming the power of the President alone to make the removal, is confined to purely executive officers; and as to officers of the kind here under consideration, we hold that no removal can be made during the prescribed term for which the officer is appointed, except for one or more of the causes named in the applicable statute.

To the extent that, between the decision in the *Myers* Case, which sustains the unrestrictable power of the President to remove purely executive officers, and our present decision that such power does not extend to an office such as that here involved, there shall remain a field of doubt, we leave such cases as may fall within it for future consideration and determination as they may arise.

☐ *Justice McREYNOLDS concurred in a separate opinion.*

Bowsher v. Synar

478 U.S. 714, 106 S.Ct. 3181 (1986)

Faced with mounting federal budget deficits, Congress in 1985 enacted the Balanced Budget and Emergency Deficit Control Act—known also as the Gramm-Rudman-Hollings Act. It set annual ceilings for deficits and, if these are exceeded, required across-the-board reductions in federal spending. To achieve the reductions, the act requires the Office of Management and Budget of the executive branch and the Congressional Budget Office to submit deficit estimates and possible budget reductions to the comptroller general, who makes his own recommendations for budget reduction to the president, who then must order the spending reductions. Opposition to the bill in Congress focused on whether the principle of separation of powers was violated by delegating the power to recommend budget reductions to the comptroller general, who is removable by a joint resolution of Congress. As a result, a "fallback" provision was included in the event that a federal court struck down the delegation to the comptroller general.

Immediately after President Reagan signed the bill into law, Congressman Michael Synar and eleven others opposed to the law filed suit in the Court of Appeals for the District of Columbia Circuit challenging the constitutionality of the Act. A three-judge panel held, in an opinion joined by then-Judge Antonin Scalia, that the empowerment of the comptroller general was unconstitutional. An appeal was promptly made to the Supreme Court which expedited consideration of the case.

The Court's decision was seven to two, and the majority's opinion was announced by Chief Justice Burger. Justice Stevens concurred and was joined by Justice Marshall. Dissents were by Justices White and Blackmun.

☐ *Chief Justice BURGER delivers the opinion of the Court.*

The question presented by these appeals is whether the assignment by Congress to the Comptroller General of the United States of certain functions under the Balanced Budget and Emergency Deficit Control Act of 1985 violates the doctrine of separation of powers.

On December 12, 1985, the President signed into law the Balanced Budget and Emergency Deficit Control Act of 1985, popularly known as the "Gramm-Rudman-Hollings Act." The purpose of the Act is to eliminate the federal budget deficit. To that end, the Act sets a "maximum deficit amount" for federal spending for each of fiscal years 1986 through 1991. The size of that maximum deficit amount progressively reduces to zero in fiscal year 1991. If in any fiscal year the federal budget deficit exceeds the maximum deficit amount by more than a specified sum, the Act requires across-the-board cuts in federal spending to reach the targeted deficit level, with half of the cuts made to defense programs and the other half made to nondefense programs. The Act exempts certain priority programs from these cuts. Sec. 255.

These "automatic" reductions are accomplished through a rather complicated procedure, spelled out in Sec. 251, the so-called "reporting provisions" of the Act. Each year, the Directors of the Office of Management and Budget (OMB) and the Congressional Budget Office (CBO) independently estimate the amount of the federal budget deficit for the upcoming fiscal year. If that deficit exceeds the maximum targeted deficit amount for that fiscal year by more than a specified amount, the Directors of OMB and CBO independently calculate, on a program-by-program basis, the budget reductions necessary to ensure that the deficit does not exceed the maximum deficit amount. The Act then requires the Directors to report jointly their deficit estimates and budget reduction calculations to the Comptroller General.

The Comptroller General, after reviewing the Directors' reports, then reports his conclusions to the President. Sec. 251 (b). The President in turn must issue a "sequestration" order mandating the spending reductions specified by the Comptroller General. Sec. 252. There follows a period during which Congress may by legislation reduce spending to obviate, in whole or in part, the need for the sequestration order. If such reductions are not enacted, the sequestration order becomes effective and the spending reductions included in that order are made. . . .

Within hours of the President's signing of the Act, Congressman Synar, who had voted against the Act, filed a complaint seeking declaratory relief that the Act was unconstitutional. Eleven other Members later joined Congressman Synar's suit. A virtually identical lawsuit was also filed by the National Treasury Employees Union. The Union alleged that its members had been injured as a result of the Act's automatic spending reduction provisions, which have suspended certain cost-of-living benefit increases to the Union's members.

A three-judge District Court, appointed pursuant to 2 U.S.C.A. Sec. 922(a)(5) (Supp. 1986), invalidated the reporting provisions. *Synar v. United States*, 626 F.Supp. 1374 (DC 1986) (SCALIA, JOHNSON, GASCH, JJ.). . . .

We noted recently that "[t]he Constitution sought to divide the delegated powers of the new Federal Government into three defined categories, Legislative, Executive, and Judicial," *INS v. Chadha*, 462 U.S. 919 (1983). The declared purpose of separating and dividing the powers of government, of course, was to "diffus[e] power the better to secure liberty." *Youngstown Sheet & Tube Co. v. Sawyer*, 343 U.S. 579 (JACKSON, J., concurring). Justice JACKSON's words echo the famous warning of Montesquieu, quoted by James Madison in *The Federalist* No. 47, that " 'there can be no liberty where the legislative and executive powers are united in the same person, or body of magistrates'. . . ." *The Federalist* No. 47.

Even a cursory examination of the Constitution reveals the influence of Montesquieu's thesis that checks and balances were the foundation of a structure of government that would protect liberty. The Framers provided a vigorous legislative branch and a separate and wholly independent executive branch, with each branch responsible ultimately to the people. The Framers also provided for a judicial branch equally independent with "[t]he judicial Power . . . extend[ing] to all Cases, in Law and Equity, arising under this Constitution, and the Laws of the United States." Art. III, Sec. 2.

Other, more subtle, examples of separated powers are evident as well. Unlike parliamentary systems such as that of Great Britain, no person who is an officer of the United States may serve as a Member of the Congress. Art. I, Sec. 6. Moreover, unlike parliamentary systems, the President, under Article II, is responsible not to the Congress but to the people, subject only to impeachment proceedings which are exercised by the two Houses as representatives of the people. Art. II, Sec. 4. And even in the impeachment of a President the presiding officer of the ultimate tribunal is not a member of the legislative branch, but the Chief Justice of the United States. Art. I, Sec. 3.

That this system of division and separation of powers produces conflicts, confusion, and discordance at times is inherent, but it was deliberately so structured to assure full, vigorous and open debate on the great issues affecting the people and to provide avenues for the operation of checks on the exercise of governmental power.

The Constitution does not contemplate an active role for Congress in the supervision of officers charged with the execution of the laws it enacts. The President appoints "Officers of the United States" with the "Advice and Consent of the Senate. . . ." Article II, Sec. 2. Once the appointment has been made and confirmed, however, the Constitution explicitly provides for removal of Officers of the United States by Congress only upon impeachment by the House of Representatives and conviction by the Senate. An impeachment by the House and trial by the Senate can rest only on "Treason, Bribery or other high Crimes and Misdemeanors." Article II, Sec. 4. A direct con-gressional role in the removal of officers charged with the execution of the laws beyond this limited one is inconsistent with separation of powers. . . .

This Court first directly addressed this issue in *Myers v. United States.* At issue in *Myers* was a statute providing that certain postmasters could be removed only "by and with the advice and consent of the Senate." The President removed one such postmaster without Senate approval, and a lawsuit ensued. Chief Justice TAFT, writing for the Court, declared the statute unconstitutional on the ground that for Congress to "draw to itself, or to either branch of it, the power to remove or the right to participate in the exercise of that power . . . would be . . . to infringe the constitutional principle of the separation of governmental powers." . . .

A decade later, in *Humphrey's Executor v. United States* (1935), relied upon heavily by appellants, a Federal Trade Commissioner who had been removed by the President sought back pay. *Humphrey's Executor* involved an issue not presented either in the *Myers* case or in this case—i.e., the power of Congress to limit the President's powers of removal of a Federal Trade Commissioner. . . . The relevant statute permitted removal "by the President," but only "for inefficiency, neglect of duty, or malfeasance in office." Justice SUTHERLAND, speaking for the Court, upheld the statute, holding that "illimitable power of removal is not possessed by the President [with respect to Federal Trade Commissioners]." The Court distinguished *Myers*, reaffirming its holding that congressional participation in the removal of executive officers is unconstitutional. The Court reached a similar result in *Weiner v. United States*, 357 U.S. 349 (1958), concluding that, under *Humphrey's Executor*, the President did not have unrestrained removal authority over a member of the War Crimes Commission.

In light of these precedents, we conclude that Congress cannot reserve for itself the power of removal of an officer charged with the execution of the laws except by impeachment. To permit the execution of the laws to be vested in an officer answerable only to Congress would, in practical terms, reserve in Congress control over the execution of the laws. As the District Court observed, "Once an officer is appointed, it is only the authority that can remove him, and not the authority that appointed him, that he must fear and, in the performance of his functions, obey." The structure of the Constitution does not permit Congress to execute the laws; it follows that Congress cannot grant to an officer under its control what it does not possess. . . .

The dangers of congressional usurpation of Executive Branch functions have long been recognized. "[T]he debates of the Constitutional Convention, and the *Federalist Papers*, are replete with expressions of fear that the Legislative Branch of the National Government will aggrandize itself at the expense of the other two branches." *Buckley v. Valeo*, 424 U.S. 1 (1976). Indeed, we also have observed only recently that "[t]he hydraulic pressure inherent within each of the separate Branches to exceed the outer limits of its power, even to accomplish desirable objectives, must be resisted." With these principles in mind, we turn to consideration of whether the Comptroller General is controlled by Congress. . . .

The critical factor lies in the provisions of the statute defining the Comptroller General's office relating to removability. Although the Comptroller General is nominated by the President from a list of three individuals recommended by the Speaker of the House of Representatives and the President pro tempore of the Senate and confirmed by the Senate, he is removable only at the initiative of Congress. He may be removed not only by impeachment but also by Joint Resolution of Congress "at any time" resting on any one of the following bases:

(i) permanent disability;
(ii) inefficiency;
(iii) neglect of duty;
(iv) malfeasance; or
(v) a felony or conduct involving moral turpitude.

This provision was included, as one Congressman explained in urging passage of the Act, because Congress "felt that [the Comptroller General] should be brought under the sole control of Congress, so that Congress at the moment when it found he was inefficient and was not carrying on the duties of his office as he should and as the Congress expected, could remove him without the long, tedious process of a trial by impeachment."

It is clear that Congress has consistently viewed the Comptroller General as an officer of the Legislative Branch. The Reorganization Acts of 1945 and 1949, for example, both stated that the Comptroller General and the GAO are "a part of the legislative branch of the Government." Similarly, in the Accounting and Auditing Act of 1950, Congress required the Comptroller General to conduct audits "as an agent of the Congress."

Against this background, we see no escape from the conclusion that, because Congress had retained removal authority over the Comptroller General, he may not be entrusted with executive powers. The remaining question is whether the Comptroller General has been assigned such powers in the Balanced Budget and Emergency Deficit Control Act of 1985. . . .

The primary responsibility of the Comptroller General under the instant Act is the preparation of a "report." This report must contain detailed estimates of projected federal revenues and expenditures. The report must also specify the reductions, if any, necessary to reduce the deficit to the tar-get for the appropriate fiscal year. The reductions must be set forth on a program-by-program basis. . . .

The executive nature of the Comptroller General's functions under the Act is revealed in Sec. 252(a)(3) which gives the Comptroller General the ultimate authority to determine the budget cuts to be made. Indeed, the Comptroller General commands the President himself to carry out, without the slightest variation (with exceptions not relevant to the constitutional issues presented), the directive of the Comptroller General as to the budget reductions:

> The [Presidential] order *must provide* for reductions in the manner specified in section 251(a)(3), *must incorporate* the provisions of the [Comptroller General's] report submitted under section 251(b), and *must be consistent with such report in all respects.* The President *may not modify or recalculate any of the estimates, determinations, specifications, bases, amounts, or percentages* set forth in the report submitted under section 251(b) in determining the reductions to be specified in the order with respect to programs, projects, and activities, or with respect to budget activities, within an account. . . . Sec. 252(a)(3) (emphasis added).

Congress of course initially determined the content of the Balanced Budget and Emergency Deficit Control Act; and undoubtedly the content of the Act determines the nature of the executive duty. However, as *Chadha* makes clear, once Congress makes its choice in enacting legislation, its participation ends. Congress can thereafter control the execution of its enactment only indirectly—by passing new legislation. *Chadha.* By placing the responsibility for execution of the Balanced Budget and Emergency Deficit Control Act in the hands of an officer who is subject to removal only by itself, Congress in effect has retained control over the execution of the Act and has intruded into the executive function. The Constitution does not permit such intrusion. . . .

No one can doubt that Congress and the President are confronted with fiscal and economic problems of unprecedented magnitude, but "the fact that a given law or procedure is efficient, convenient, and useful in facilitating functions of government, standing alone, will not save it if it is contrary to the Constitution. Convenience and efficiency are not the primary objectives—or the hallmarks—of democratic government. . . ." *Chadha.* . . .

We conclude the District Court correctly held that the powers vested in the Comptroller General under Sec. 251 violate the command of the Constitution that the Congress play no direct role in the execution of the laws. Accordingly, the judgment and order of the District Court are affirmed.

□ *Justice STEVENS, with whom Justice MARSHALL joins, concurring.*

When this Court is asked to invalidate a statutory provision that has been approved by both Houses of the Congress and signed by the President, particularly an Act of Congress that confronts a deeply vexing national problem, it should only do so for the most compelling constitutional reasons. I agree with the Court that the "Gramm-Rudman-Hollings" Act contains a constitutional infirmity so severe that the flawed provision may not stand. I disagree with the Court, however, on the reasons why the Constitution prohibits the Comptroller General from exercising the powers assigned to him by Sec. 251(b) and Sec. 251(c)(2) of the Act. It is not the dormant, carefully circumscribed congressional removal power that represents the primary constitutional evil. Nor do I agree with the conclusion of both the majority and the dissent that the analysis depends on a labeling of the functions assigned to the Comptroller General as "executive powers." Rather, I am convinced that the Comptroller General must be characterized as an agent of Congress because of his longstanding statutory responsibilities; that the powers assigned to him under the Gramm-Rudman-Hollings Act require him to make policy that will bind the Nation; and that, when Congress, or a component or an agent of Congress, seeks to make policy that will bind the Nation, it must follow the procedures mandated by Article I of the Constitution—through passage by both Houses and presentment to the President. In short, Congress may not exercise its fundamental power to formulate national policy by delegating that power to one of its two Houses, to a legislative committee, or to an individual agent of the Congress such as the Speaker of the House of Representatives, the Sergeant at Arms of the Senate, or the Director of the Congressional Budget Office. *INS v. Chadha* (1983). That principle, I believe, is applicable to the Comptroller General.

☐ *Justice WHITE, dissenting.*

The Court, acting in the name of separation of powers, takes upon itself to strike down the Gramm-Rudman-Hollings Act, one of the most novel and far-reaching legislative responses to a national crisis since the New Deal. The basis of the Court's action is a solitary provision of another statute that was passed over sixty years ago and has lain dormant since that time. I cannot concur in the Court's action. Like the Court, I will not purport to speak to the wisdom of the policies incorporated in the legislation the Court invalidates; that is a matter for the Congress and the Executive, *both* of, which expressed their assent to the statute barely half a year ago. I will, however, address the wisdom of the Court's willingness to interpose its distressingly formalistic view of separation of powers as a bar to the attainment of governmental objectives through the means chosen by the Congress and the President in the legislative process established by the Constitution. . . .

Before examining the merits of the Court's argument, I wish to emphasize what it is that the Court quite pointedly and correctly does *not* hold: namely, that "executive" powers of the sort granted the Comptroller by the Act may only be exercised by officers removable at will by the President. The Court's apparent unwillingness to accept this argument, which has been tendered in this Court by the Solicitor General, is fully consistent with the Court's longstanding recognition that it is within the power of Congress under the "Necessary and Proper" Clause, Art. I, Sec. 8, to vest authority that falls within the Court's definition of executive power in officers who are not subject to removal at will by the President and are therefore not under the President's direct control. See, *e.g., Humphrey's Executor v. United States* (1935); *Wiener v. United States* (1958). In an earlier day, in which simpler notions of the role of government in society prevailed, it was perhaps plausible to insist that all "executive" officers be subject to an unqualified presidential removal power, see *Myers v. United States* (1926); but with the advent and triumph of the administrative state and the accompanying multiplication of the tasks undertaken by the Federal Government, the Court has been virtually compelled to recognize that Congress may reasonably deem it "necessary and proper" to vest some among the broad new array of governmental functions in officers who are free from the partisanship that may be expected of agents wholly dependent upon the President. . . .

If, as the Court seems to agree, the assignment of "executive" powers under Gramm-Rudman to an officer not removable at will by the President would not in itself represent a violation of the constitutional scheme of separated powers, the question remains whether, as the Court concludes, the fact that the officer to whom Congress has delegated the authority to implement the Act is removable by a joint resolution of Congress should require invalidation of the Act. The Court's decision, as I have stated above, is based on a syllogism: the Act vests the Comptroller with "executive power"; such power may not be exercised by Congress or its agents; the Comptroller is an agent of Congress because he is removable by Congress; therefore the Act is invalid. I have no quarrel with the proposition that the powers exercised by the Comptroller under the Act may be characterized as "executive" in that they involve the interpretation and carrying out of the Act's mandate. I can also accept the general proposition that although Congress has considerable authority in designating the officers who are to execute legislation, the constitutional scheme of separated powers does prevent Congress from reserving an executive role for itself or for its "agents." *Buckley v. Valeo*, (WHITE, J., concurring in part and dissenting in part). I cannot accept, however, that the exercise of authority by an officer removable for cause by a joint resolution of Congress is analogous to the impermissible execution of the law by Congress itself, nor would I hold that the congressional role in the removal process renders the Comptroller an "agent" of the Congress, incapable of receiving "executive" power. . . .

The deficiencies in the Court's reasoning are apparent. First, the Court baldly mischaracterizes the removal provision when it suggests that it allows Congress to remove the Comptroller for "executing the laws in any fashion found to be unsatisfactory"; in fact, Congress may remove the Comptroller only for one or more of five specified reasons, which "although not so narrow as to deny Congress any leeway, circumscribe Congress' power to some extent by providing a basis for judicial review of congressional removal." *Ameron, Inc. v. United States Army Corps of Engineers*, 787 F.2d 875 (CA 3 1986) (BECKER, J., concurring in part). Second, and more to the point, the Court overlooks or deliberately ignores the decisive difference between the congressional removal provision and the legislative veto struck down in *Chadha*: under the Budget and Accounting Act, Congress may remove the Comptroller only through a joint resolution, which by definition must be passed by both Houses and signed by the President. See *United States v. California*, 332 U.S. 19 (1947). In other words, a removal of the Comptroller under the statute *satisfies the requirements of bicameralism and presentment laid down in Chadha.* The majority's citation of *Chadha* for the proposition that Congress may only control the acts of officers of the United States "by passing new legislation," in no sense casts doubt on the legitimacy of the removal provision, for that provision allows Congress to effect removal only through action that constitutes legislation as defined in *Chadha.* . . .

The statute does not permit anyone to remove the Comptroller at will; removal is permitted only for specified cause, with the existence of cause to be determined by Congress following a hearing. Any removal under the statute would presumably be subject to post-termination judicial review to ensure that a hearing had in fact been held and that the finding of cause for removal was not arbitrary. See *Ameron, Inc. v. United States Army Corps of Engineers* (BECKER, J., concurring in part). These procedural and substantive limitations on the removal power militate strongly against the characterization of the Comptroller as a mere agent of Congress by virtue of the removal authority. Indeed, similarly qualified grants of removal power are generally deemed to protect the officers to whom they apply and to establish their independence from the domination of the possessor of the removal power. See *Humphrey's Executor v. United States.* Removal authority limited in such a manner is more properly viewed as motivating adherence to a substantive standard established by law than as inducing subservience to the particular institution that enforces that standard. That the agent enforcing the standard is Congress may be of some significance to the Comptroller, but Congress' substantively limited removal power will undoubtedly be less of a spur to subservience than Congress' unquestionable and unqualified power to enact legislation reducing the Comptroller's salary, cutting the funds available to his department, reducing his personnel, limiting or expanding his duties, or even abolishing his position altogether.

More importantly, the substantial role played by the President in the process of removal through joint resolution reduces to utter insignificance the possibility that the threat of removal will induce subservience to the Congress. As I have pointed out above, a joint resolution must be presented to the President and is ineffective if it is vetoed by him, unless the veto is overridden by the constitutionally prescribed two-thirds majority of both Houses of Congress. The requirement of presidential approval obviates the possibility that the Comptroller will perceive himself as so completely at the mercy of Congress that he will function as its tool. If the Comptroller's conduct in office is not so unsatisfactory to the President as to convince the latter that removal is required under the statutory standard, Congress will have no independent power to coerce the Comptroller unless it can muster a two-thirds majority in both Houses—a feat of bipartisanship more difficult than that required to impeach and convict. The incremental *in terrorem* effect of the possibility of congressional removal in the face of a presidential veto is therefore exceedingly unlikely to have any discernible impact on the extent of congressional influence over the Comptroller.

The practical result of the removal provision is not to render the Comptroller unduly dependent upon or subservient to Congress, but to render him one of the most independent officers in the entire federal establishment. Those who have studied the office agree that the procedural and substantive limits on the power of Congress and the President to remove the Comptroller make dislodging him against his will practically impossible. As one scholar put it nearly fifty years ago, "Under the statute the Comptroller General, once confirmed, is safe so long as he avoids a public exhibition of personal immorality, dishonesty, or failing mentality." H. Mansfield, *The Comptroller General* 75–76 (1939). The passage of time has done little to cast doubt on this view: of the six Comptrollers who have served since 1921, none has been threatened with, much less subjected to, removal. Recent students of the office concur that "[b]arring resignation, death, physical or mental incapacity, or extremely bad behavior, the Comptroller General is assured his tenure if he wants it, and not a day more." F. Mosher, *The GAO* 242 (1979). The threat of "here-and-now subservience," is obviously remote indeed.

Realistic consideration of the nature of the Comptroller General's relation to Congress thus reveals that the threat to separation of powers conjured up by the majority is wholly chimerical. The power over removal retained by the Congress is not a power that is exercised outside the legislative process as established by the Constitution, nor does it appear likely that it is a power that adds significantly to the influence Congress may exert over executive officers through other, undoubtedly constitutional exercises of legislative power and through the constitutionally guaranteed impeachment power. Indeed, the removal power is so constrained by its own substantive limits and by the requirement of presidential approval "that, as a practical matter, Congress has not exercised, and probably will never exercise, such control over the Comptroller General that his non-legislative powers will threaten the goal of dispersion of power, and hence the goal of individual liberty, that separation of powers serves." *Ameron, Inc. v. United States Army Corps of Engineers* (BECKER, J., concurring in part).

The majority's contrary conclusion rests on the rigid dogma that, outside of the impeachment process, any "direct congressional role in the removal of officers charged with the execution of the laws . . . is inconsistent with separation of powers." Reliance on such an unyielding principle to strike down a statute posing no real danger of aggrandizement of congressional power is extremely misguided and insensitive to our constitutional role. . . .

I dissent.

Morrison v. Olson
487 U.S. 654, 108 S.Ct. 2597 (1988)

In the wake of the "Watergate crisis" (see "Unraveling the Watergate Affair" later in this chapter) Congress passed the Ethics in Government Act in 1978, which expired in 1999 due to bipartisan opposition and disgust over Kenneth Starr's over $40 million investigation of President and Mrs. Clinton's Whitewater land deal in Arkansas and the president's affair with White House intern Monica Lewinsky. The law provided for independent counsel to investigate presidential subordinates if warranted after a preliminary review by the attorney general. The attorney general must request the appointment of counsel from a "Special Division" of the U.S. Court of Appeals for the District of Columbia. Once appointed, counsel may be removed by the attorney general only for reasons specified in the act.

Independent counsels initially provoked controversy with the appointment of a special prosecutor assigned to investigate President Nixon's involvement in the Watergate cover-up. In 1973, Nixon ordered the dismissal of Archibald Cox, the Watergate special prosecutor. After the attorney general and his assistant resigned rather than remove Cox, Acting Attorney General Robert H. Bork discharged him. A lower federal court, in *Nader v. Bork*, 366 F.Supp. 104 (D.D.C., 1973), later held that the dismissal was illegal.

The constitutionality of independent counsel was controversial again in 1987, when four separate counsels were investigating the Iran-Contra affair and allegations of wrongdoing by Attorney General Edwin Meese III and other former presidential aides. This case, however, arose from independent counsel Alexia Morrison's 1986 investigation of allegations that former Assistant Attorney General Theodore Olson (who was later President George W. Bush's solicitor general) lied before a congressional subcommittee in 1983 concerning the withholding of Environmental Protection Agency documents from Congress. Olson challenged the constitutionality of Morrison's appointment in the U.S. Court of Appeals for the District of Columbia. A three-judge panel split two to one when finding the appointment of independent counsel to violate principles of separation of powers. Morrison then appealed to the Supreme Court, which expedited briefing and oral arguments in the spring of 1988. President Ronald Reagan's last appointee to the Court did not participate in the decision. With the exception of Justice Antonin Scalia, who issued a sharp dissenting opinion, the rest of the Court joined in Chief Justice William Rehnquist's opinion upholding the constitutionality of the appointment of special prosecutors. Three months after the Court's ruling, Morrison concluded her two-year investigation, deciding that there was not enough evidence to seek an indictment of Olson. The independent counsel law expired in 1999.

The Court's decision was seven to one, and the majority's opinion was announced by Chief Justice Rehnquist, with Justice Kennedy not participating. Justice Scalia dissented.

☐ *Chief Justice REHNQUIST delivers the opinion of the Court.*

This case presents us with a challenge to the independent counsel provisions of the Ethics in Government Act of 1978. We hold today that these provisions of the Act do not violate the Appointments Clause of the Constitution, Art. II, Sec. 2, cl. 2, or the limitations of Article III, nor do they impermissibly interfere with the President's authority under Article II in violation of the constitutional principle of separation of powers. . . .

The Appointments Clause of Article II reads as follows:

[The President] shall nominate, and by and with the Advice and Consent of the Senate, shall appoint Ambassadors, other public Ministers and Consuls, Judges of the Supreme Court, and all other Officers of the United States, whose Appointments are not herein otherwise provided for, and which shall be established by Law: but the Congress may by Law vest the Appointment of such inferior

Officers, as they think proper, in the President alone, in the Courts of Law, or in the Heads of Departments.

The parties do not dispute that "[t]he Constitution for purposes of appointment . . . divides all its officers into two classes." *United States v. Germaine*, 99 U.S. (9 Otto) 508 (1879). As we stated in *Buckley v. Valeo*, 424 U.S. 1 (1976), "[p]rincipal officers are selected by the President with the advice and consent of the Senate. Inferior officers Congress may allow to be appointed by the President alone, by the heads of departments, or by the Judiciary." The initial question is, accordingly, whether appellant is an "inferior" or a "principal" officer. If she is the latter, as the Court of Appeals concluded, then the Act is in violation of the Appointments Clause.

The line between "inferior" and "principal" officers is one that is far from clear, and the Framers provided little guidance into where it should be drawn. . . . We need not attempt here to decide exactly where the line falls between the two types of officers, because in our view appellant clearly falls on the "inferior officer" side of that line. Several factors lead to this conclusion.

First, appellant is subject to removal by a higher Executive Branch official. Although appellant may not be "subordinate" to the Attorney General (and the President) insofar as she possesses a degree of independent discretion to exercise the powers delegated to her under the Act, the fact that she can be removed by the Attorney General indicates that she is to some degree "inferior" in rank and authority. Second, appellant is empowered by the Act to perform only certain, limited duties. An independent counsel's role is restricted primarily to investigation and, if appropriate, prosecution for certain federal crimes. Admittedly, the Act delegates to appellant "full power and independent authority to exercise all investigative and prosecutorial functions and powers of the Department of Justice," but this grant of authority does not include any authority to formulate policy for the Government or the Executive Branch, nor does it give appellant any administrative duties outside of those necessary to operate her office. The Act specifically provides that in policy matters appellant is to comply to the extent possible with the policies of the Department. . . .

Third, appellant's office is limited in jurisdiction. Not only is the Act itself restricted in applicability to certain federal officials suspected of certain serious federal crimes, but an independent counsel can only act within the scope of the jurisdiction that has been granted by the Special Division pursuant to a request by the Attorney General. Finally, appellant's office is limited in tenure. . . . In our view, these factors relating to the "ideas of tenure, duration . . . and duties" of the independent counsel, *Germaine*, are sufficient to establish that appellant is an "inferior" officer in the constitutional sense. . . .

This does not, however, end our inquiry under the Appointments Clause. Appellees argue that even if appellant is an "inferior" officer, the Clause does not empower Congress to place the power to appoint such an officer outside the Executive Branch. They contend that the Clause does not contemplate congressional authorization of "interbranch appointments," in which an officer of one branch is appointed by officers of another branch. The relevant language of the Appointments Clause is worth repeating. It reads: ". . . but the Congress may by Law vest the Appointment of such inferior Officers, as they think proper, in the President alone, in the courts of Law, or in the Heads of Departments." On its face, the language of this "excepting clause," admits of no limitation on interbranch appointments. Indeed, the inclusion of "as they think proper" seems clearly to give Congress significant discretion to determine whether it is "proper" to vest the appointment of, for example, executive officials in the "courts of Law." . . .

We also note that the history of the clause provides no support for appellees' position. Throughout most of the process of drafting the Constitution, the Convention concentrated on the problem of who should have the authority to appoint judges. [T]here was little or no debate on the question of whether the Clause empowers Congress to provide for interbranch appointments, and there is nothing to suggest that the Framers intended to prevent Congress from having that power.

We do not mean to say that Congress' power to provide for interbranch appointments of "inferior officers" is unlimited. In addition to separation of powers concerns, which would arise if such provisions for appointment had the potential to impair the constitutional functions assigned to one of the branches, [*Ex parte*] *Siebold* [100 U.S. 371 (1880)] itself suggested that Congress' decision to vest the appointment power in the courts would be improper if there was some "incongruity" between the functions normally performed by the courts and the performance of their duty to appoint. . . . In this case, however, we do not think it impermissible for Congress to vest the power to appoint independent counsels in a specially created federal court. . . . Congress of course was concerned when it created the office of independent counsel with the conflicts of interest that could arise in situations when the Executive Branch is called upon to investigate its own high-ranking officers. If it were to remove the appointing authority from the Executive Branch, the most logical place to put it was in the Judicial Branch. In the light of the Act's provision making the judges of the Special Division ineligible to participate in any matters relating to an independent counsel they have appointed, we do not think that appointment of the independent counsels by the court runs afoul of the constitutional limitation on "incongruous" interbranch appointments.

Appellees next contend that the powers vested in the Special Division by the Act conflict with Article III of the Constitution.

Most importantly, the Act vests in the Special Division the power to choose who will serve as independent counsel and the power to define his or her jurisdiction.

Clearly, once it is accepted that the Appointments Clause gives Congress the power to vest the appointment of officials such as the independent counsel in the "courts of Law," there can be no Article III objection to the Special Division's exercise of that power, as the power itself derives from the Appointments Clause, a source of authority for judicial action that is independent of Article III. . . .

The Act also vests in the Special Division various powers and duties in relation to the independent counsel that, because they do not involve appointing the counsel or defining her jurisdiction, cannot be said to derive from the Division's Appointments Clause authority. These duties include granting extensions for the Attorney General's preliminary investigation; re-

ceiving the report of the Attorney General at the conclusion of his preliminary investigation . . . referring matters to the counsel upon request, receiving reports from the counsel regarding expenses incurred . . . receiving a
report from the Attorney General following the removal of an independent
counsel; granting attorney's fees upon request to individuals who were investigated but not indicted by an independent counsel; receiving a final report
from the counsel, Sec. 594(h)(1)(B); deciding whether to release the counsel's
final report to Congress or the public and determining whether any protective orders should be issued, Sec. 594(h)(2); and terminating an independent
counsel when his task is completed, Sec. 596(b)(2).

Leaving aside for the moment the Division's power to terminate an independent counsel, we do not think that Article III absolutely prevents Congress from vesting these other miscellaneous powers in the Special Division
pursuant to the Act. As we observed above, one purpose of the broad prohibition upon the courts' exercise of "executive or administrative duties of a
nonjudicial nature," *Buckley*, is to maintain the separation between the judiciary and the other branches of the Federal Government by ensuring that
judges do not encroach upon executive or legislative authority or undertake
tasks that are more properly accomplished by those branches. In this case, the
miscellaneous powers described above do not impermissibly trespass upon the
authority of the Executive Branch. Some of these allegedly "supervisory"
powers conferred on the court are passive: the Division merely "receives" reports from the counsel or the Attorney General, it is not entitled to act on
them or to specifically approve or disapprove of their contents. Other provisions of the Act do require the court to exercise some judgment and discretion, but the powers granted by these provisions are themselves essentially
ministerial. The Act simply does not give the Division the power to "supervise" the independent counsel in the exercise of her investigative or prosecutorial authority. And, the functions that the Special Division is empowered
to perform are not inherently "Executive"; indeed, they are directly analogous to functions that federal judges perform in other contexts, such as deciding whether to allow disclosure of matters occurring before a grand jury,
see Fed. Rule Crim.Proc. 6(e), deciding to extend a grand jury investigation,
Rule 6(g), or awarding attorney's fees. . . .

We are more doubtful about the Special Division's power to terminate
the office of the independent counsel pursuant to Sec. 596(b)(2). As appellees
suggest, the power to terminate, especially when exercised by the Division
on its own motion, is "administrative" to the extent that it requires the Special Division to monitor the progress of proceedings of the independent
counsel and come to a decision as to whether the counsel's job is "completed." It also is not a power that could be considered typically "judicial," as
it has few analogues among the court's more traditional powers. Nonetheless,
we do not, as did the Court of Appeals, view this provision as a significant
judicial encroachment upon executive power or upon the prosecutorial discretion of the independent counsel. . . .

Nor do we believe, as appellees contend, that the Special Division's exercise of the various powers specifically granted to it under the Act poses any
threat to the "impartial and independent federal adjudication of claims
within the judicial power of the United States." We reach this conclusion for
two reasons. First, the Act as it currently stands gives the Special Division it-

self no power to review any of the actions of the independent counsel or any of the actions of the Attorney General with regard to the counsel. Accordingly, there is no risk of partisan or biased adjudication of claims regarding the independent counsel by that court. Second, the Act prevents members of the Special Division from participating in "*any* judicial proceeding concerning a matter which involves such independent counsel while such independent counsel is serving in that office or which involves the exercise of such independent counsel's official duties, regardless of whether such independent counsel is still serving in that office." (emphasis added); see also Sec. 596(a)(3) (preventing members of the Special Division from participating in review of the Attorney General's decision to remove an independent counsel). We think both the special court and its judges are sufficiently isolated by these statutory provisions from the review of the activities of the independent counsel so as to avoid any taint of the independence of the judiciary such as would render the Act invalid under Article III. . . .

We now turn to consider whether the Act is invalid under the constitutional principle of separation of powers. Two related issues must be addressed: The first is whether the provision of the Act restricting the Attorney General's power to remove the independent counsel to only those instances in which he can show "good cause," taken by itself, impermissibly interferes with the President's exercise of his constitutionally appointed functions. The second is whether, taken as a whole, the Act violates the separation of powers by reducing the President's ability to control the prosecutorial powers wielded by the independent counsel.

Unlike both *Bowsher v. Synar*, [478 U.S. 714 (1986)] and *Myers*, this case does not involve an attempt by Congress itself to gain a role in the removal of executive officials other than its established powers of impeachment and conviction. The Act instead puts the removal power squarely in the hands of the Executive Branch; an independent counsel may be removed from office, "only by the personal action of the Attorney General, and only for good cause." There is no requirement of congressional approval of the Attorney General's removal decision, though the decision is subject to judicial review. In our view, the removal provisions of the Act make this case more analogous to *Humphrey's Executor v. United States*, 295 U.S. 602 (1935), and *Wiener v. United States*, 357 U.S. (1958), than to *Myers* or *Bowsher*. . . .

Appellees contend that *Humphrey's Executor* and *Wiener* are distinguishable from this case because they did not involve officials who performed a "core executive function." They argue that our decision in *Humphrey's Executor* rests on a distinction between "purely executive" officials and officials who exercise "quasi-legislative" and "quasi-judicial" powers. In their view, when a "purely executive" official is involved, the governing precedent is *Myers*, not *Humphrey's Executor*. And, under *Myers*, the President must have absolute discretion to discharge "purely" executive officials at will.

We undoubtedly did rely on the terms "quasi-legislative" and "quasi-judicial" to distinguish the officials involved in *Humphrey's Executor* and *Wiener* from those in *Myers*, but our present considered view is that the determination of whether the Constitution allows Congress to impose a "good cause"-type restriction on the President's power to remove an official cannot be made to turn on whether or not that official is classified as "purely executive." The analysis contained in our removal cases is designed not to define rigid categories of those officials who may or may not be removed at will by the President, but to ensure that Congress does not interfere with the President's exercise of the "executive power" and his constitutionally appointed duty to "take care that the laws be faithfully executed" under Article II. *Myers* was undoubtedly correct in its holding, and in its broader suggestion that there are some "purely executive" officials who must be removable by the President at will if he is to be able to accomplish his constitutional role. . . . But as the Court noted in *Wiener*,

> The assumption was short-lived that the *Myers* case recognized the President's inherent constitutional power to remove officials no matter what the relation of the executive to the discharge of their duties and no matter what restrictions Congress may have imposed regarding the nature of their tenure. . . .

At the other end of the spectrum from *Myers*, the characterization of the agencies in *Humphrey's Executor* and *Wiener* as "quasi-legislative" or "quasi-judicial" in large part reflected our judgment that it was not essential to the President's proper execution of his Article II powers that these agencies be headed up by individuals who were removable at will. We do not mean to suggest that an analysis of the functions served by the officials at issue is irrelevant. But the real question is whether the removal restrictions are of such a nature that they impeded the President's ability to perform his constitutional duty, and the functions of the officials in question must be analyzed in that light.

Considering for the moment the "good cause" removal provision in isolation from the other parts of the Act at issue in this case, we cannot say that the imposition of a "good cause" standard for removal by itself unduly trammels on executive authority. There is no real dispute that the functions performed by the independent counsel are "executive" in the sense that they are law enforcement functions that typically have been undertaken by officials within the Executive Branch. As we noted above, however, the independent counsel is an inferior officer under the Appointments Clause, with limited jurisdiction and tenure and lacking policymaking or significant administrative authority. Although the counsel exercises no small amount of discretion and judgment in deciding how to carry out her duties under the Act, we simply do not see how the President's need to control the exercise of that discretion is so central to the functioning of the Executive Branch as to require as a matter of constitutional law that the counsel be terminable at will by the President.

Nor do we think that the "good cause" removal provision at issue here impermissibly burdens the President's power to control or supervise the independent counsel, as an executive official, in the execution of her duties under the Act. This is not a case in which the power to remove an executive official has been completely stripped from the President, thus providing no means for the President to ensure the "faithful execution" of the laws. Rather, because the independent counsel may be terminated for "good cause," the Executive, through the Attorney General, retains ample authority to assure that the counsel is competently performing her statutory responsibilities in a manner that comports with the provisions of the Act. Although we need not decide in this case exactly what is encompassed within the term "good cause" under the Act, the legislative history of the removal provision also makes clear that the Attorney General may remove an independent counsel for "misconduct." Here, as with the provision of the Act conferring the appointment authority of the independent counsel on the special court, the congressional determination to limit the removal power of the Attorney General was essential, in the view of Congress, to establish the necessary independence of the office. We do not think that this limitation as it presently stands sufficiently deprives the President of control over the independent counsel to interfere impermissibly with his constitutional obligation to ensure the faithful execution of the laws.

The final question to be addressed is whether the Act, taken as a whole, violates the principle of separation of powers by unduly interfering with the role of the Executive Branch. . . .

We observe first that this case does not involve an attempt by Congress to increase its own powers at the expense of the Executive Branch. Unlike some of our previous cases, most recently *Bowsher v. Synar*, this case simply does not pose a "dange[r] of congressional usurpation of Executive Branch functions." Indeed, with the exception of the power of impeachment—which applies to all officers of the United States—Congress retained for itself no powers of control or supervision over an independent counsel. The Act does empower certain members of Congress to request the Attorney General to apply for the appointment of an independent counsel, but the Attorney General has no duty to comply with the request, although he must respond within a certain time limit. Sec. 529(g). Other than that, Congress' role under the Act is limited to receiving reports or other information and oversight of the independent counsel's activities, Sec. 595(a), functions that we have recognized generally as being incidental to the legislative function of Congress. . . .

Similarly, we do not think that the Act works any *judicial* usurpation of properly executive functions. As should be apparent from our discussion of the Appointments Clause above, the power to appoint inferior officers such as independent counsels is not in itself an "executive" function in the constitutional sense, at least when Congress has exercised its power to vest the appointment of an inferior office in the "courts of Law." . . .

Finally, we do not think that the Act "impermissibly undermine[s]" the powers of the Executive Branch or "disrupts the proper balance between the coordinate branches [by] prevent[ing] the Executive Branch from accomplishing its constitutionally assigned functions," *Nixon v. Administrator of General Services*, [433 U.S. 425 (1977)]. It is undeniable that the Act reduces the amount of control or supervision that the Attorney General and, through him, the President exercises over the investigation and prosecution of a certain class of alleged criminal activity. The Attorney General is not allowed to appoint the individual of his choice; he does not determine the counsel's jurisdiction; and his power to remove a counsel is limited. Nonetheless, the Act does give the Attorney General several means of supervising or controlling the prosecutorial powers that may be wielded by an independent counsel. Most importantly, the Attorney General retains the power to remove the counsel for "good cause," a power that we have already concluded provides the Executive with substantial ability to ensure that the laws are "faithfully executed" by an independent counsel. . . .

In sum, we conclude today that it does not violate the Appointments Clause for Congress to vest the appointment of independent counsels in the Special Division; that the powers exercised by the Special Division under the Act do not violate Article III; and that the Act does not violate the separation of powers principle by impermissibly interfering with the functions of the Executive Branch. The decision of the Court of Appeals is therefore

Reversed.

☐ *Justice SCALIA, dissenting.*

The principle of separation of powers is expressed in our Constitution in the first section of each of the first three Articles. Article I, Sec. 1 provides that "[a]ll legislative Powers herein granted shall be vested in a Congress of the United States, which shall consist of a Senate and House of Representatives." Article III, Sec. 1 provides that "[t]he judicial Power of the United States, shall be vested in one supreme Court, and in such inferior Courts as the Congress may from time to time ordain and establish." And the provision at issue here, Art. II, Sec. 1, cl. 1 provides that "[t]he executive Power shall be vested in a President of the United States of America."

But just as the mere words of a Bill of Rights are not self-effectuating, the framers recognized "[t]he insufficiency of a mere parchment delineation of the boundaries" to achieve the separation of powers. *Federalist* No. 73, (Hamilton). "[T]he great security," wrote Madison, "against a gradual concentration of the several powers in the same department consists in giving to those who administer each department the necessary constitutional means and personal motives to resist encroachments of the others. The provision for defense must in this, as in all other cases, be made commensurate to the danger of attack." *Federalist* No. 51. Madison continued:

> But it is not possible to give to each department an equal power of self-defense. In republican government, the legislative authority necessarily predominates. The remedy for this inconveniency is to divide the legislature into different branches; and to render them, by different modes of election and different principles of action, as little connected with each other as the nature of their common functions and their common dependence on the society will admit. . . . As the weight of the legislative authority requires that it should be thus divided, the weakness of the executive may require, on the other hand, that it should be fortified.

The major "fortification" provided, of course, was the veto power. But in addition to providing fortification, the founders conspicuously and very consciously declined to sap the executive's strength in the same way they had weakened the legislature: by dividing the executive power. . . .

That is what this suit is about. Power. The allocation of power among Congress, the President and the courts in such fashion as to preserve the equilibrium the Constitution sought to establish—so that "a gradual concentration of the several powers in the same department," *Federalist* No. 51 (J. Madison), can effectively be resisted. Frequently an issue of this sort will come before the Court clad, so to speak, in sheep's clothing: the potential of the asserted principle to effect important change in the equilibrium of power is not immediately evident, and must be discerned by a careful and perceptive analysis. But this wolf comes as a wolf. . . .

[B]y the application of this statute in the present case, Congress has effectively compelled a criminal investigation of a high-level appointee of the President in connection with his actions arising out of a bitter power dispute between the President and the Legislative Branch. Mr. Olson may or may not be guilty of a crime; we do not know. But we do know that the investigation of him has been commenced, not necessarily because the President or his authorized subordinates believe it is in the interest of the United States, in the sense that it warrants the diversion of resources from other efforts, and is worth the cost in money and in possible damage to other governmental interests; and not even, leaving aside those normally considered factors, because the President or his authorized subordinates necessarily believe that an investigation is likely to unearth a violation worth prosecuting; but only because the Attorney General cannot affirm, as Congress demands, that there are *no reasonable grounds to believe* that further investigation is warranted. The decisions regarding the scope of that further investigation, its duration, and, finally, whether or not prosecution should ensue, are likewise beyond the control of the President and his subordinates. . . .

The Court devotes most of its attention to such relatively technical details as the Appointments Clause and the removal power, addressing briefly and only at the end of its opinion the separation of powers. As my prologue suggests, I think that has it backwards. Our opinions are full of the recognition that it is the principle of separation of powers, and the inseparable corollary that each department's "defense must . . . be made commensurate to the danger of attack," *Federalist* No. 51 (J. Madison), which gives comprehensible content to the appointments clause, and determines the appropriate scope of the removal power. Thus, while I will subsequently discuss why our appointments and removal jurisprudence does not support today's holding, I begin with a consideration of the fountainhead of that jurisprudence, the separation and equilibration of powers. . . .

To repeat, Art. II, Sec. 1, cl. 1 of the Constitution provides: "The executive Power shall be vested in a President of the United States." As I described at the outset of this opinion, this does not mean *some of* the executive power, but *all of* the executive power. It seems to me, therefore, that the decision of the Court of Appeals invalidating the present statute must be upheld on fundamental separation-of-powers principles if the following two questions are answered affirmatively: (1) Is the conduct of a criminal prosecution (and of an investigation to decide whether to prosecute) the exercise of purely executive power? (2) Does the statute deprive the President of the United States of exclusive control over the exercise of that power? Surprising to say, the Court appears to concede an affirmative answer to both questions, but seeks to avoid the inevitable conclusion that since the statute vests some purely executive power in a person who is not the President of the United States it is void.

The Court concedes that "[t]here is no real dispute that the functions performed by the independent counsel are 'executive'," though it qualifies that concession by adding "in the sense that they are 'law enforcement' functions that typically have been undertaken by officials within the Executive Branch." The qualifier adds nothing but atmosphere. In what *other* sense can one identify "the executive Power" that is supposed to be vested in the President (unless it includes everything the Executive Branch is given to do) *except* by reference to what has always and everywhere—if conducted by Government at all—been conducted never by the legislature, never by the courts, and always by the executive. There is no possible doubt that the independent counsel's functions fit this description. She is vested with the "full power and independent authority to exercise all *investigative and prosecutorial* functions and powers of the Department of Justice [and] the Attorney General." Governmental investigation and prosecution of crimes is a quintessentially executive function. . . .

As for the second question, whether the statute before us deprives the President of exclusive control over that quintessentially executive activity: The Court does not, and could not possibly, assert that it does not. That is indeed the whole object of the statute. Instead, the Court points out that the President, through his Attorney General, has at least *some* control. That concession is alone enough to invalidate the statute, but I cannot refrain from pointing out that the Court greatly exaggerates the extent of that "some" presidential control. "Most importan[t]" among these controls, the Court asserts, is the Attorney General's "power to remove the counsel for 'good cause.' " This is somewhat like referring to shackles as an effective means of locomotion. As we recognized in *Humphrey's Executor v. United States* (1935)—indeed, what *Humphrey's Executor* was all about—limiting removal power to "good cause" is an impediment to, not an effective grant of, presidential control. We said that limitation was necessary with respect to members of the Federal Trade Commission, which we found to be "an agency of the legislative and judicial departments," and "wholly disconnected from the executive department" because "it is quite evident that one who holds his office only during the pleasure of another, cannot be depended upon to maintain an attitude of independence against the latter's will." What we in *Humphrey's Executor* found to be a means of eliminating presidential control, the Court today considers the "most importan[t]" means of assuring presidential control. Congress, of course, operated under no such illusion when it enacted this statute, describing the "good cause" limitation as "protecting the independent counsel's ability to act independently of the President's direct control" since it permits removal only for "misconduct."

Moving on to the presumably "less important" controls that the President retains, the Court notes that no independent counsel may be appointed without a specific request from the Attorney General. As I have discussed above, the condition that renders such a request mandatory (inability to find "no reasonable grounds to believe" that further investigation is warranted) is so insubstantial that the Attorney General's discretion is severely confined. And once the referral is made, it is for the Special Division to determine the scope and duration of the investigation. And in any event, the limited power over referral is irrelevant to the question whether, *once appointed*, the independent counsel exercises executive power free from the President's control. Finally, the Court points out that the Act directs the independent counsel to abide by general Justice Department policy, except when not "possible." The exception alone shows this to be an empty promise. Even without that, however, one would be hard put to come up with many investigative or prosecutorial "policies" (other than those imposed by the Constitution or by Congress through law) that are absolute. Almost all investigative and prosecutorial decisions—including the ultimate decision whether, after a technical violation of the law has been found, prosecution is warranted—involve the balancing of innumerable legal and practical considerations. In sum, the balancing of various legal, practical and political considerations, none of which is absolute, is the very essence of prosecutorial discretion. To take this away is to remove the core of the prosecutorial function, and not merely "some" presidential control.

As I have said, however, it is ultimately irrelevant *how much* the statute reduces presidential control. The case is over when the Court acknowledges, as it must, that "[i]t is undeniable that the Act reduces the amount of control or supervision that the Attorney General and, through him, the President exercises over the investigation and prosecution of a certain class of alleged criminal activity." It effects a revolution in our constitutional jurisprudence for the Court, once it has determined that (1) purely executive functions are at issue here, and (2) those functions have been given to a person whose actions are not fully within the supervision and control of the President, nonetheless to proceed further to sit in judgment of whether "the President's need to control the exercise of [the independent counsel's] discretion is *so central* to the functioning of the Executive Branch" as to require complete control (emphasis added), whether the conferral of his powers upon someone else "*sufficiently* deprives the President of control over the independent counsel to interfere impermissibly with [his] constitutional obligation to ensure the faithful execution of the laws" (emphasis added), and whether "the Act give[s] the Executive Branch *sufficient* control over the independent counsel to ensure that the President is able to perform his constitutionally assigned duties" (emphasis added). It is not for us to determine, and we have never presumed to determine, how much of the purely executive powers of government must be within the full control of the President. The Constitution prescribes that they *all* are. . . .

The Court has, nonetheless, replaced the clear constitutional prescription that the executive power belongs to the President with a "balancing test." What are the standards to determine how the balance is to be struck, that is, how much removal of presidential power is too much? Many countries of the world get along with an Executive that is much weaker than ours—in fact, entirely dependent upon the continued support of the legislature. Once we depart from the text of the Constitution, just where short of that do we stop? The most amazing feature of the Court's opinion is that it does not even purport to give an answer. It simply *announces*, with no analysis, that the ability to control the decision whether to investigate and prosecute the President's closest advisors, and indeed the President himself, is not "so central to the functioning of the Executive Branch" as to be constitutionally required to be within the President's control. Apparently that is so because we say it is so. Evidently, the governing standard is to be what might be called the unfettered wisdom of a majority of this Court, revealed to an obedient people on a case-by-case basis. This is not only not the government of laws that the Constitution established; it is not a government of laws at all.

In my view, moreover, even as an ad hoc, standardless judgment the Court's conclusion must be wrong. Before this statute was passed, the President, in taking action disagreeable to the Congress, or an executive officer giving advice to the President or testifying before Congress concerning one of those many matters on which the two branches are from time to time at odds, could be assured that his acts and motives would be adjudged—insofar as the decision whether to conduct a criminal investigation and to prosecute is concerned—in the Executive Branch, that is, in a forum attuned to the interests and the policies of the Presidency. That was one of the natural advantages the Constitution gave to the Presidency, just as it gave Members of Congress (and their staffs) the advantage of not being prosecutable for anything said or done in their legislative capacities. See U.S. Const., Art. I, Sec. 6, cl. 1; *Gravel v. United States*, 408 U.S. 606 (1972). It is the very object of this legislation to eliminate that assurance of a sympathetic forum. Unless it can honestly be said that there are "no reasonable grounds to believe" that further investigation is warranted, further investigation must ensue; and the conduct of the investigation, and determination of whether to prosecute, will be given to a person neither selected by nor subject to the control of the President—who will in turn assemble a staff by finding out, presumably, who is willing to put aside whatever else they are doing, for an indeterminate period of time, in order to investigate and prosecute the President or a particular named individual in his administration. The prospect is frightening (as I will discuss at some greater length at the conclusion of this opinion) even outside the context of a bitter, interbranch political dispute. Perhaps the boldness of the President himself will not be affected—though I am not even sure of that. (How much easier it is for Congress, instead of accepting the political damage attendant to the commencement of impeachment proceedings against the President on trivial grounds—or, for that matter, how easy it is for one of the President's political foes outside of Congress—simply to trigger a debilitating criminal investigation of the Chief Executive under this law.) But as for the President's high-level assistants, who typically have no political base of support, it is as utterly unrealistic to think that they will not be intimidated by this prospect, and that their advice to him and their advocacy of his interests before a hostile Congress will not be affected, as it would be to think that the Members of Congress and their staffs would be unaffected by replacing the Speech or Debate Clause with a similar provision. It deeply wounds the President, by substantially reducing the President's ability to protect himself and his staff. That is the whole object of the law, of course, and I cannot imagine why the Court believes it does not succeed.

Besides weakening the Presidency by reducing the zeal of his staff, it must also be obvious that the institution of the independent counsel enfeebles him more directly in his constant confrontations with Congress, by eroding his public support. Nothing is so politically effective as the ability to charge that one's opponent and his associates are not merely wrong-headed, naive, ineffective, but, in all probability, "crooks." And nothing so effectively gives an appearance of validity to such charges as a Justice Department investigation and, even better, prosecution. The present statute provides ample means for that sort of attack. . . .

As I indicated earlier, the basic separation-of-powers principles I have discussed are what give life and content to our jurisprudence concerning the President's power to appoint and remove officers. The same result of unconstitutionality is therefore plainly indicated by our case law in these areas. . . .

Because appellant (who all parties and the Court agree is an officer of the United States) was not appointed by the President with the advice and consent of the Senate, but rather by the Special Division of the United States Court of Appeals, her appointment is constitutional only if (1) she is an "inferior" officer within the meaning of the above clause, and (2) Congress may vest her appointment in a court of law.

As to the first of these inquiries, the Court does not attempt to "decide exactly" what establishes the line between principal and "inferior" officers, but is confident that, whatever the line may be, appellant "clearly falls on the 'inferior officer' side" of it. The Court gives three reasons: *First*, she "is subject to removal by a higher Executive branch official," namely the Attorney General. *Second*, she is "empowered by the Act to perform only certain, limited duties." *Third*, her office is "limited in jurisdiction" and "limited in tenure." . . .

The first of these lends no support to the view that appellant is an inferior officer. Appellant is removable only for "good cause" or physical or mental incapacity. By contrast, most (if not all) *principal* officers in the Executive Branch may be removed by the President *at will*. I fail to see how the fact that appellant is more difficult to remove than most principal officers helps to establish that she is an inferior officer. . . .

The second reason offered by the Court—that appellant performs only certain, limited duties—may be relevant to whether she is an inferior officer, but it mischaracterizes the extent of her powers. . . .

The final set of reasons given by the Court for why the independent counsel clearly is an inferior officer emphasizes the limited nature of her jurisdiction and tenure. Taking the latter first, I find nothing unusually limited about the independent counsel's tenure. To the contrary, unlike most high-ranking Executive Branch officials, she continues to serve until she (or the Special Division) decides that her work is substantially completed. . . .

More fundamentally, however, it is not clear from the Court's opinion why the factors it discusses—even if applied correctly to the facts of this case—are determinative of the question of inferior officer status. The apparent source of these factors is a statement in *United States v. Germaine*, 99 U.S. (9 Otto) 508 (1879) (discussing *United States v. Hartwell*, 6 Wall. 385 (1868)), that "the term [officer] embraces the ideas of tenure, duration, emolument and duties." Besides the fact that this was dictum, it was dictum in a case where the distinguishing characteristics of inferior officers versus superior officers were in no way relevant, but rather only the distinguishing characteristics of an "officer of the United States" (to which the criminal statute at issue applied) as opposed to a mere *employee*. Rather than erect a theory of who is an inferior officer on the foundation of such an irrelevancy, I think it preferable to look to the text of the Constitution and the division of power that it establishes. These demonstrate, I think, that the independent counsel is not an inferior officer because she is not *subordinate* to any officer in the Executive Branch (indeed, not even to the President). Dictionaries in use at the time of the Constitutional Convention gave the word "inferiour" two meanings which it still bears today: (1) "[l]ower in place, . . . station, . . . rank of life, . . . value or excellency," and (2) "[s]ubordinate." S. Johnson, *Dictionary of the English Language* (6th ed. 1785). In a document dealing with the structure (the constitution) of a government, one would naturally expect the word to bear the latter meaning—indeed, in such a context it would be unpardonably careless to use the word *unless* a relationship of subordination was intended. If what was meant was merely "lower in station or rank," one would use instead a term such as "lesser officers." At the only other point in the Constitution at which the word "inferior" appears, it plainly connotes a relationship of subordination. Article III vests the judicial Power of the United States in "one supreme Court, and in such *inferior* Courts as the Congress may from time to time ordain and establish." U.S. Const., Art. III, Sec. 1 (emphasis added). In *Federalist* No. 81, Hamilton pauses to describe the "inferior" courts authorized by Art. III as inferior in the sense that they are "subordinate" to the Supreme Court....

That "inferior" means "subordinate" is also consistent with what little we know about the evolution of the Appointments Clause....

To be sure, it is not a *sufficient* condition for "inferior" officer status that one be subordinate to a principal officer. Even an officer who is subordinate to a department head can be a principal officer....

The independent counsel is not even subordinate to the President. The Court essentially admits as much, noting that "appellant may not be 'subordinate' to the Attorney General (and the President) insofar as she possesses a degree of independent discretion to exercise the powers delegated to her under the Act." In fact, there is no doubt about it. As noted earlier, the Act specifically grants her the "*full* power and *independent* authority to exercise *all* investigative and prosecutorial functions of the Department of Justice" and makes her removable only for "good cause," a limitation specifically intended to ensure that she be *independent* of, not *subordinate* to, the President and the Attorney General.

Because appellant is not subordinate to another officer, she is not an "inferior" officer and her appointment other than by the President with the advice and consent of the Senate is unconstitutional....

The Court could have resolved the removal power issue in this case by simply relying upon its erroneous conclusion that the independent counsel was an inferior officer, and then extending our holding that the removal of inferior officers appointed by the Executive can be restricted, to a new holding that even the removal of inferior officers appointed by the courts can be restricted. That would in my view be a considerable and unjustified extension, giving the Executive full discretion in *neither* the selection *nor* the removal of a purely executive officer. The course the Court has chosen, however, is even worse.

Since our 1935 decision in *Humphrey's Executor v. United States*—which was considered by many at the time the product of an activist, anti-New Deal court bent on reducing the power of President Franklin Roosevelt—it has been established that the line of permissible restriction upon removal of principal officers lies at the point at which the powers exercised by those officers are no longer purely executive. Thus, removal restrictions have been generally regarded as lawful for so-called "independent regulatory agencies," such as the Federal Trade Commission, the Interstate Commerce Commission, and the Consumer Products Safety Commission, which engage substantially in what has been called the "quasi-legislative activity" of rule-making, and for members of Article I courts, such as the Court of Military Appeals who engage in the "quasi-judicial" function of adjudication. It has often been observed, correctly in my view, that the line between "purely executive" functions and "quasi-legislative" or "quasi-judicial" functions is not a clear one or even a rational one.... But at least it permitted the identification of certain officers, and certain agencies, whose functions were entirely within the control of the President. Congress had to be aware of that restriction in its legislation. Today, however, *Humphrey's Executor* is swept into the dustbin of repudiated constitutional principles. "[O]ur present considered view," the Court says, "is that the determination of whether the Constitution allows Congress to impose a 'good cause'-type restriction on the President's power to remove an official cannot be made to turn on whether or not that official is classified as 'purely executive.' " What *Humphrey's Executor* (and presumably *Myers*) really means, we are now told, is not that there are any "rigid categories of those officials who may or may not be removed at will by the President," but simply that Congress cannot "interefere with the President's exercise of the 'executive power' and his constitutionally appointed duty to 'take care that the laws be faithfully executed.' " . . .

One can hardly grieve for the shoddy treatment given today to *Humphrey's Executor*, which, after all, accorded the same indignity (with much less justification) to Chief Justice TAFT's opinion 10 years earlier in *Myers v. United States,* [272 U.S. 52 (1926)]—gutting, in six quick pages devoid of textual or historical precedent for the novel principle it set forth, a carefully researched and reasoned 70-page opinion. It is in fact comforting to witness the reality that he who lives by the *ipse dixit* dies by the *ipse dixit*. But one must grieve for the Constitution. *Humphrey's Executor* at least had the decency formally to observe the constitutional principle that the President had to be the repository of *all* executive power which, as *Myers* carefully explained, necessarily means that he must be able to discharge those who do not perform executive functions according to his liking. As we noted in *Bowsher*, once an officer is appointed " 'it is only the authority that can remove him, and not the authority that appointed him, that he must fear and, in the performance of his functions, obey.' " By contrast, "our present considered view" is simply that *any* Executive officer's removal can be restricted, so long as the President remains "able to accomplish his constitutional role." There are now no lines. If the removal of a prosecutor, the virtual embodiment of the power to "take care that the laws be faithfully executed," can be restricted, what officer's removal cannot? This is an open invitation for Congress to experiment. What about a special Assistant Secretary of State, with responsibility for one very narrow area of foreign policy, who would not only have to be confirmed by the Senate but could also be removed only pursuant to certain carefully designed restrictions? Could this possibly render the President "[un]able to accomplish his constitutional role"? Or a special Assistant Secretary of Defense for Procurement? The possibilities are endless, and the Court does not understand what the separation of powers, what "[a]mbition . . . counteract[ing] ambition," *Federalist* No. 51 (Madison), is all about, if it does not expect Congress to try them. As far as I can discern from the Court's opinion, it is now open season upon the President's removal power for all executive officers, with not even the superficially principled restriction of *Humphrey's Executor* as cover. The Court essentially says to the President "Trust us. We will make sure that you are able to accomplish your constitutional role." I think the Constitution gives the President—and the people—more protection than that.

The purpose of the separation and equilibration of powers in general, and of the unitary Executive in particular, was not merely to assure effective government but to preserve individual freedom. Those who hold or have held offices covered by the Ethics in Government Act are entitled to that protection as much as the rest of us, and I conclude my discussion by considering the effect of the Act upon the fairness of the process they receive.

Only someone who has worked in the field of law enforcement can fully appreciate the vast power and the immense discretion that are placed in the hands of a prosecutor with respect to the objects of his investigation. . . .

Under our system of government, the primary check against prosecutorial abuse is a political one. The prosecutors who exercise this awesome discretion are selected and can be removed by a President, whom the people have trusted enough to elect. Moreover, when crimes are not investigated and prosecuted fairly, nonselectively with a reasonable sense of proportion, the President pays the cost in political damage to his administration. . . .

The notion that every violation of law should be prosecuted, including—indeed, *especially*—every violation by those in high places, is an attractive one, and it would be risky to argue in an election campaign that that is not an absolutely overriding value. *Fiat justitia, ruat coelum.* Let justice be done, though the heavens may fall. The reality is, however, that it is not an absolutely overriding value, and it was with the hope that we would be able to acknowledge and apply such realities that the Constitution spared us, by life tenure, the necessity of election campaigns. I cannot imagine that there are not many thoughtful men and women in Congress who realize that the benefits of this legislation are far outweighed by its harmful effect upon our system of government, and even upon the nature of justice received by those men and women who agree to serve in the Executive Branch. But it is difficult to vote not to enact, and even more difficult to vote to repeal, a statute called, appropriately enough, the Ethics in Government Act. If Congress is controlled by the party other than the one to which the President belongs, it has little incentive to repeal it; if it is controlled by the same party, it dare not. By its short-sighted action today, I fear the Court has permanently encumbered the Republic with an institution that will do it great harm.

Worse than what it has done, however, is the manner in which it has done it. A government of laws means a government of rules. Today's decision on the basic issue of fragmentation of executive power is ungoverned by rule, and hence ungoverned by law. It extends into the very heart of our most significant constitutional function the "totality of the circumstances" mode of analysis that this Court has in recent years become fond of. Taking all things into account, we conclude that the power taken away from the President here is not really *too* much. The next time executive power is assigned to someone other than the President we may conclude, taking all things into account, that it *is* too much. That opinion, like this one, will not be confined by any rule. We will describe, as we have today (though I hope more accurately) the effects of the provision in question, and will authoritatively announce: "The President's need to control the exercise of the [subject officer's] discretion *is* so central to the functioning of the Executive Branch as to require complete control." This is not analysis; it is ad hoc judgment. And it fails to explain why it is not true that—as the text of the Constitution seems to require, as the Founders seemed to expect, and as our past cases have uniformly assumed—all purely executive power must be under the control of the President.

The ad hoc approach to constitutional adjudication has real attraction, even apart from its work-saving potential. It is guaranteed to produce a result, in every case, that will make a majority of the Court happy with the law. The law is, by definition, precisely what the majority thinks, taking all things into account, it *ought* to be. I prefer to rely upon the judgment of the wise men who constructed our system, and of the people who approved it, and of two centuries of history that have shown it to be sound. Like it or not, that judgment says, quite plainly, that "[t]he executive Power shall be vested in a President of the United States."

C | *Legislative Powers in the Administrative State*

The president's role in initiating and formulating legislation as well as in overseeing and controlling its implementation has expanded enormously as a result of Congress's delegation of its powers to the executive branch and the growth of the institutional presidency. As noted earlier, the president's State of the Union address has become an occasion for the presentation of his legislative and budget recommendations to Congress. Although George Washington and John Adams personally delivered their reports to Congress, for more than a century—from Thomas Jefferson in 1801 to 1917, when Woodrow Wilson reinstated the practice—presidents sent only a written message to Congress. Although Congress is given the power of the purse (in Article I, Section 9), since the Budget and Accounting Act of 1921 the president has assumed responsibility for submitting budget estimates to Congress, which then may increase or decrease specific items in the "executive budget." More recently, the Office of Management and Budget was given the major responsibility for preparing budget estimates for the White House. Presidents may also issue executive orders and proclamations—some may be delcaraty or such as President Carter's proclamation of "Earth Day," while others are substantive such as President Reagan's ordering a "cost, risk, benefit" analysis of proposed regulations. Regulatory agencies also exercise enormous lawmaking power in rule making and issuing new regulations, subject to the Administrative Procedures Act of 1947, which requires public notice and opportunity for comment and for challenging proposed rules and regulations. In addition, Presidents Reagan and George W. Bush issued a large number of "presidential signing statements"—expressing presidential intent—when signing bills into law. (See the CONSTITUTIONAL HISTORY box in this section on Presidential Signing Statements and Legislative Powers.)

To safeguard against congressional usurpation of presidential power, the Constitutional Convention guaranteed the president a role in the passage of legislation. Article I, Section 7, requires the president's approval or disapproval of "every order, resolution, or vote to which the concurrence of the Senate and the House of Representatives may be necessary." The president may veto legislation, although not particular items in a bill, by returning a bill unsigned to the house in which it originated, along with his objections. If within ten days of receiving a bill the president neither signs nor vetoes it, the bill becomes law without his signature. But if Congress goes out of session within that period, then the president may exercise what is called a "pocket veto" by simply not returning the bill. The president's veto power over legislation is qualified, however, because it may be overridden by a two-thirds vote of both houses. Congress may also pass "concurrent resolutions," which do not require approval of the president to become law.

Broad delegations of congressional lawmaking power to the executive branch are almost invariably upheld by the Court. This is so even though the Constitution delegates the lawmaking power to Congress and despite the age-old Latin maxim—or *nondelegation doctrine*—that "delegated power may not be [re]delegated." Still, the Court's approach to reviewing the lawmaking powers of the executive branch has evolved, particularly with the growth of the administrative state in the twentieth century.

For most of the nineteenth century, Congress delegated very little and the executive branch remained small. In *Wayman v. Southard*, 23 U.S. 1 (1825), the Marshall Court initially sanctioned delegated powers as necessary "to fill in the details" and to implement the general provisions of legislation. In the late nineteenth century in response to the Industrial Revolution, though, Congress began creating independent regulatory commissions, like the Interstate Commerce Commission (ICC) in 1887 (which was abolished in 1995), and delegatingmore powers. When these delegations were challenged, the Court upheld the delegation of lawmaking power so long as Congress laid "down by legislative act an intelligible principle to which the person or body authorized to take action is directed to conform."[1] As a result, Congress delegates to agencies extensive powers under exceedingly broad standards, such as authorizing, for example, the Federal Communications Commission (FCC) to regulate the airwaves in the "public convenience, interest or necessity." In effect, Congress provides *legislative mandates* for agencies to enact regulations.

During the New Deal, when a number of new agencies were created in the 1930s, such as the Food and Drug Administration, the Court did enforce the nondelegation doctrine and imposed due process requirements on agency rulemaking. Two 1935 cases struck down major New Deal legislation aimed at easing the Depression, reasoning that it impermissibly delegated power. The "hot oil case," *Panama Refining Company v. Ryan*, 293 U.S. 388 (1935), invalidated part of the National Industrial Recovery Act of 1933 for giving the president authority to exclude from interstate commerce oil that was produced in excess of state regulations. The other was known as "the sick chickens case," *Schechter Poultry Corporation v. United States* (excerpted below). The following year the Court also struck down the Guffey Coal Act, in *Carter v. Carter Coal Co.*, 298 U.S. 238 (1936), as an impermissible delegation of power to set up a regulatory code for the coal industry.

After the "constitutional crisis" in 1937, the Court abandoned the nondelegation doctrine and has not found any other legislation to run afoul of the doctrine. The confrontation over the Court's pre-1937 rulings and the continued expansion of administrative agencies nonetheless resulted in the enactment of the Administrative Procedure Act (APA) of 1946, a uniform code for regulatory policymaking. With the APA, Congress inaugurated a new era in administrative law. A central rationalization for broad delegations of lawmaking power to the executive branch during the New Deal was administrative expertise over complex economic and social regulations. The expertise of agencies also became an important justification for judicial deference to the executive branch and Congress's broad delegation of its lawmaking power.

A second generation of new federal agencies and delegations further expanded the executive branch's regulatory powers in the 1970s with the creation of the Environmental Protection Agency (1972), the Consumer Product Safety Commission (1972), and the Occupational Safety and Health Administration (1973), among others. Congress not only gave these new and older agencies expanded responsibilities for regulating complex health-safety and environmental risks but it also provided for expanded opportunities to challenge regulations and regulatory inaction in federal courts. Congress did so because of concerns that the Republican administration of Richard Nixon would not aggressively enact health, safety, and environmental regulations. Businesses, corporations, and industry groups in turn increasingly opposed new regulations as too costly, challenging them in courts and lobbying for deregulatory reforms.

As a result, in the 1970s and 1980s federal courts became more involved in reviewing challenges to agencies' regulations and divided over the exercise of judicial review. On one hand, Judge David Bazelon championed imposing heightened due process requirements on agencies, an approach known as "strict procedures ensure correct results."[2] He contended that "the best way for courts to guard against unreasonable or erroneous administrative decisions is not for judges themselves to scrutinize the technical merits of each decision. Rather, it is to establish a decision–making process which assures a reasoned decision that can be held up to the scrutiny of the scientific community and the public." Accordingly, the judiciary had a major role in supervising the regulatory process and should ensure public participation in, and the reasoned elaboration of the basis for, agency rulemaking. On the other hand, Judge Harold Leventhal championed the so-called "hard look" approach to exercising review. Instead of imposing additional procedural requirements, he maintained that courts should engage in searching, substantive review of the technical basis for agency decisions.[3]

The Supreme Court initially embraced the "hard look" approach in *Vermont Yankee Nuclear Power Corporation v. Natural Resources Defense Council, Inc.*, 435 U.S. 519 (1978). Writing for the Court, Rehnquist repudiated the "strict procedures ensure correct results" approach as judicial "Monday morning quarterbacking" that "clearly runs the risk of 'propel[ling] the courts into the domain which Congress has set aside exclusively for the administrative agency.' " However, the "hard look" approach was not unproblematic. It was no less interventionist in sanctioning heightened judicial scrutiny of the basis for regulations and remained ill-defined as a guideline.

The ambiguity of the "hard look" approach and the inevitable problems of judges' differing views of the substantive basis for regulations were subsequently underscored in *Industrial Union Department, AFL-CIO v. American Petroleum Institute* (1980), involving a challenge to the OSHA's regulation of benzene, a carcinogen. After Democratic president Jimmy Carter won election in 1976, his administration moved to regain what it deemed ground lost in health, safety, and environmental regulation during the Nixon and Ford administrations. Like other agencies, the OSHA maintained there was no safe threshold level of carcinogenic exposure and it was impossible to calculate the number of lives that would be saved by a 1 ppm benzene standard. That standard was immediately attacked as too costly and unsupported, since the risks at such a low level of exposure were impossible to quantify. On appeal, the Court had to decide whether the OSHA had presented sufficient analysis for its regulation, but the justices split five to four and only three joined Stevens's opinion for the Court. In his view, the OSHA failed to establish a significant risk of regulating benzene below the level of 10 ppm. By contrast, Rehnquist, who cast the crucial fifth vote in a concurring opinion in *American Petroleum Institute* (excerpted below) argued that the OSHA provision should be invalidated on the basis of the nondelegation doctrine, thereby forcing Congress to establish more precise standards for agency rulemaking. The four dissenters—Justices Marshall, Brennan, White, and Blackmun—disagreed. In their view, the nondelegation doctrine was "moribund," as Marshall put in *FPC v. New England Power Co.*, 415 U.S. 345 (1974), and the majority had taken the "hard look" approach too far, imposing its own philosophy of regulating health risks for that of the agency. Just "as the Constitution does not enact Mr. Herbert Spenser's *Social Statics*," as Marshall put it, "so the responsibility to scrutinize federal administrative action does not authorize this Court to strike its own balance between the costs and benefits of occupational safety standards."

The Court's ruling in *American Petroleum Institute* generated confusion and the Court sought clarity a year later when reviewing the OSHA's cotton dust standard in *American Textile Manufacturers Institute, Inc. v. Donovan*, 452 U.S. 490 (1981). Since cotton dust is not a carcinogen, it did not fall under the OSHA's generic carcinogen policy, but the agency interpreted its legislative mandate as requiring the most protective standard feasible. Businesses challenged the standard as too costly and argued that the standard should be supported by a "cost–risk–benefit" assessment. But, the Carter administration contended that such an assessment was not required and would result in a lower standard. The controversy then escalated when in 1981 Republican president Ronald Reagan issued an executive order requiring a cost-benefit analysis for all new federal regulations, including the OSHA's cotton dust standard. On appeal, the Court held the OSH Act did not *require* but *permitted* a cost–risk–benefit assessment for the regulation. Writing for the Court, Justice Brennan emphasized that, on the one hand, judges have no technical expertise or standards to apply in such cases and, on the other hand, the executive branch has discretion in interpreting the law. In short, the principal check on the executive branch lies with Congress and presidential elections, not the courts.

The Supreme Court finally held that courts should defer to exective branch agencies' interpretation of ambiguous delegations of lawmaking power by Congress in *Chevron v. Natural Resources Defense Council*, 467 U.S. 837 (1984). In that case, the Court unanimously upheld the Reagan administration's "bubble policy" for regulating air pollution. The dispute centered on whether the EPA could abandon an earlier policy, requiring each emission source within a plant to be assessed independently, and substitute a policy giving a plant wide or "bubble" definition of polluting "sources" under the Clean Air Act.

The "bubble policy" permitted particular pollution-emitting sources to exceed air pollution control standards, so long as the emissions on a plant-wide basis were at or below overall air-quality standards. The policy was de-regulatory in that polluters would not incur the higher costs of installing expensive controls for particular pollutants. On appeal, Justice Stevens upheld the "bubble policy" and explained that courts should defer to White House directives to agencies and agencies' interpretations of their legislative mandates when those mandates are ambiguous. In his words: "if the statute is silent or ambiguous with respect to the specific issue, the question for the courts is whether the agency's answer is based on a permissible construction of the statute." Judicial deference to Congress's broad delegation of lawmaking authority and to the executive branch's interpretation of its legislative mandates was warranted, because

> judges are not experts in the field, and are not part of either political branch of the government. Courts must, in some cases, reconcile competing political interests, but not on the basis of the judges' personal policy preferences. In contrast, an agency to which Congress had delegated policymaking responsibilities may, within the limits of that delegation, properly rely upon the incumbent administration's views of wise policy to inform its judgments. While agencies are not directly accountable to the people, the Chief Executive is, and it is entirely appropriate for this political branch of the Govern-ment to make such policy choices—resolving the competing interests which Congress itself either inadvertently did not resolve, or intentionally left to be resolved by the agency charged with the administration of the statute in light of everyday realities.

The so-called *Chevron* doctrine of judicial deference has prevailed. In *Rust v. Sullivan*, 500 U.S. 173 (1991) (see Vol. 2, Ch. 5), for example, the Court upheld regulations adopted by the Reagan administration that forbid federal funding of family planning organizations that also provided abortion-related services, even though such organizations had received funding for almost two decades. There, Chief Justice Rehnquist reiterated that when statutory interpretation is ambiguous, courts should defer to the executive branch's construction, even if it reverses a prior interpretation of Congress's legislation.

The president and the executive branch also exercise significant power when interpreting and enforcing legislation under the obligation to "take Care that the Laws be faithfully executed." But controversies arise when the president and his subordinates refuse to enforce laws deemed in conflict with their legal policy goals or detrimental to the nation. While some courts have ruled that the "take care" clause poses a duty to enforce the laws, even those with which the president disagrees, the judiciary tends to defer to the executive branch in recognizing that traditional principles of prosecutorial discretion allow agencies to decide when and how to enforce laws.

A related controversy involves whether, given the obligation to faithfully execute the laws, the president may impound funds for specific programs that Congress has appropriated. Richard M. Nixon, among other presidents, claimed an inherent power to refuse to spend funds or otherwise carry out laws as authorized by Congress. The Court has not yet resolved this constitutional issue. But in *Train v. City of New York*, 420 U.S. 35 (1975), it held as a statutory matter that the president could not withhold funds provided by Congress for the enforcement of the Federal Water Pollution Control Act.

Congress nevertheless retains significant powers of overseeing its delegations to the executive branch, through its appropriation and oversight hearings in particular. When delegating broad power to executive agencies, Congress also frequently required agencies to report their decisions to Congress and authorized one or both houses to overturn, within a specified period of time, agency decisions by passing a "legislative veto." But in a far-reaching 1983 ruling, in *Immigration and Naturalization Service v. Chadha* (1983) (see excerpt below), the Court ruled that "legislative vetoes" violate the principle of separation of powers. In spite of *Chadha*, however, Congress has enacted more than 400 new legislative vetoes, requiring the executive branch to obtain for certain decisions the approval of specific congressional committees and giving those committees veto authority.[4]

The Court, however, struck down Congress's delegation to the president of the power of line-item vetoes in *Clinton v. City of New York* (1998) (excerpted below). As in *Chadha*, the Court held that the Line Item Veto Act of 1996 violates the presentment clause of Article I, Section 7, Clause 2.

NOTES

1. *J. W. Hampton, Jr. & Co. v. United States*, 276 U.S. 394 (1928).

2. *International Harvester Co. v. Ruckelshaus*, 478 F. 2d 615, 652 (D.C. Cir., 1973); and David Bazelon, "Coping with Technology through the Legal Process," 62 *Cornell Law Review* 817 (1977).

3. See Harold Leventhal, "Environmental Decisionmaking and the Role of the Courts," 122 *University of Pennsylvania Law Review* 509 (1974).

4. See Louis Fisher and Neal Devins, eds., *Political Dynamics of Constitutional Law*, 3d ed. (St. Paul, MN: West, 2001).

SELECTED BIBLIOGRAPHY

Adler, David Gray, and Genovese, Michael A., eds. *The Presidency and the Law: The Clinton Legacy*. Lawrence: University Press of Kansas, 2002.

Barber, Sotirios. *The Constitution and the Delegation of Congressional Power*. Chicago: University of Chicago Press, 1975.

Cameron, Charles. *Veto Bargaining: Presidents and the Politics of Negative Power*. New York: Cambridge University Press, 1999.

Cooper, Phillip J. *By Order of the President: The Use and Abuse of Executive Direct Action*. Lawrence: University Press of Kansas, 2002.

Craig, Barbara. *Chadha*. New York: Oxford University Press, 1988.

■ CONSTITUTIONAL HISTORY

Presidential Signing Statements and Legislative Powers

President George W. Bush opposed an amendment to an appropriations bill, sponsored by Senator John McCain (R-Az) and supported overwhelmingly in the House of Representatives, prohibiting the "cruel, inhuman, or degrading" treatment of detainees in U.S. custody. Although Bush eventually signed the bill in 2006, he issued a presidential signing statement declaring that the provision, among others, was only "advisory." He thus renewed debate over the uses of presidential signing statements and the assertion of greater presidential power in domestic and foreign affairs.

Presidential signing statements, issued when a president signs a bill into law, have served four functions. First, they explain to the public the potential impact or significance of the legislation. Second, they may direct subordinate officials in the executive branch on how to interpret and implement the law. Third, they may inform Congress and the public that the president deems a particular provision unconstitutional. However, some presidents and scholars have maintained that such bills should not be signed into law and instead returned to Congress, although four justices—Justices O'Connor, Scalia, Kennedy, and Souter—noted in a concurring opinion, in *Freytag v. C.I.R.*, 501 U.S. 868 (1991), that the president may "disregard [laws] when they are unconstitutional." Fourth, and most controversial, is the use of presidential signing

Fisher, Louis. *Presidential Spending Power.* Princeton, NJ: Princeton University Press, 1975.

Korn, Jessica. *The Power of Separation: American Constitutionalism and the Myth of the Legislative Veto.* Princeton, NJ: Princeton University Press, 1996.

May, Christopher. *Presidential Defiance of "Unconstitutional" Laws.* Westport, CT: Greenwood Press, 1998.

Murchison, Kenneth. *The Snail Darter Case: TVA versus the Endangered Species Act.* Lawrence: University Press of Kansas, 2007.

O'Brien, David M. *What Process Is Due? Courts and Science-Policy Disputes.* New York: Russell Sage Foundation, 1987.

Spitzer, Robert. *The Presidential Veto: Touchstone of the American Presidency.* Albany: State University of New York Press, 1988.

statements to add an "executive history" to the legislative history on which courts may draw when reviewing the executive branch's implementation of the law.

Prior to the 1980s administration of Ronald Reagan, the use of presidential signing statements was infrequent and limited to the first three functions. Only some sixteen times did thirteen different presidents issue them, ranging from Andrew Jackson to John Tyler, Abraham Lincoln, Andrew Johnson, Theodore Roosevelt, Woodrow Wilson, Franklin D. Roosevelt, Harry Truman, Dwight D. Eisenhower, Richard M. Nixon, Gerald Ford, and Jimmy Carter.

During the Reagan administration extensive use of presidential signing statements was made to establish an "executive history" of legislation for the use of the executive branch and the judiciary. Notably, as a young attorney then in the administration, Justice Samuel Alito, Jr., championed their use for establishing presidential intent in signing legislation and for maintaining "a unitary executive." While Presidents George H. W. Bush and Bill Clinton also issued such statements, George W. Bush made extensive use of them, even though federal courts have yet to give them much weight. In response and in opposition, the American Bar Association has sought legislation providing for judicial review of the constitutionality of the president's disregarding provisions of a bill signed into law or interpreting provisions inconsistent with the clear intent of Congress.

For further reading, see Walter Dellinger, Memorandum for Bernard N. Nussbaum, counsel to the president, "The Legal Significance of Presidential Signing Statements" (November 3, 1993), available at *www.usdoj.gov:/olc/signing.htm*; Phillip Cooper, "George W. Bush, Edgar Allan Poe, and the Use and Abuse of Presidential Signing Statements," 35 *Presidential Studies Quarterly* 525–532 (2005).

Schechter Poultry Corporation v. United States
295 U.S. 495, 55 S.CT. 837 (1935)

In 1933 Congress passed the National Industrial Recovery Act, under its power to regulate interstate commerce and as part of President Franklin D. Roosevelt's New Deal Program, to help stimulate the economy and reduce unemployment. Under the act, the National Recovery Administration was authorized to set fair codes for business competition, including standards for wages, hours, and working conditions.

The Schechter brothers operated slaughterhouses in New York City, which received live chickens from outside the state, slaughtered them, and then sold them to local stores. They were convicted in a federal district court of violating a number of standards set by the National Recovery Administration. After an appellate court affirmed, they appealed to the Supreme Court.

The Court granted the Schechters' petition for *certiorari* and ruled in their favor on two grounds. First, the Court found that the Schechters were engaged in intrastate commerce that had only an indirect effect on interstate commerce and, therefore, their business was outside the scope of Congress's regulatory power over interstate commerce. Second, in the excerpt here, Chief Justice Charles Evans Hughes found a portion of the National Industrial Recovery Act authorizing the establishment of a Live Poultry Code to be an unconstitutional delegation of power to the executive branch.

The Court's decision was unanimous, and the opinion was announced by Chief Justice Hughes. A concurring opinion was delivered by Justice Cardozo, who was joined by Justice Stone.

☐ *Chief Justice HUGHES delivers the opinion of the Court.*

The Question of the Delegation of Legislative Power.—We recently had occasion to review the pertinent decisions and the general principles which govern the determination of this question. *Panama Refining Company v. Ryan*, 293 U.S. 388 [(1935)]. The Constitution provides that "All legislative powers herein granted shall be vested in a Congress of the United States, which shall consist of a Senate and House of Representatives." Article 1, Sec. 1. And the Congress is authorized "To make all Laws which shall be necessary and proper for carrying into Execution" its general powers. Article 1, Sec. 8, par. 18. The Congress is not permitted to abdicate or to transfer to others the essential legislative functions with which it is thus vested. We have repeatedly recognized the necessity of adapting legislation to complex conditions involving a host of details with which the national Legislature cannot deal directly. We pointed out in the

Panama Refining Company Case that the Constitution has never been regarded as denying to Congress the necessary resources of flexibility and
practicality, which will enable it to perform its function in laying down
policies and establishing standards, while leaving to selected instrumentalities the making of subordinate rules within prescribed limits and the determination of facts to which the policy as declared by the Legislature is
to apply. But we said that the constant recognition of the necessity and
validity of such provisions, and the wide range of administrative authority
which has been developed by means of them, cannot be allowed to obscure the limitations of the authority to delegate, if our constitutional system is to be maintained. . . .

Accordingly, we look to the statute to see whether Congress has overstepped these limitations—whether Congress in authorizing "codes of fair
competition" has itself established the standards of legal obligation, thus performing its essential legislative function, or, by the failure to enact such standards, has attempted to transfer that function to others.

The aspect in which the question is now presented is distinct from that
which was before us in the case of the Panama Refining Company. There
the subject of the statutory prohibition was defined. National Industrial Recovery Act, Sec. 9 (c), 15 USCA Sec. 709 (c). That subject was the transportation in interstate and foreign commerce of petroleum and petroleum
products which are produced or withdrawn from storage in excess of the
amount permitted by state authority. The question was with respect to the
range of discretion given to the President in prohibiting that transportation.
As to the "codes of fair competition," under section 3 of the act, the question is more fundamental. It is whether there is any adequate definition of
the subject to which the codes are to be addressed.

What is meant by "fair competition" as the term is used in the act?
Does it refer to a category established in the law, and is the authority to
make codes limited accordingly? Or is it used as a convenient designation
for whatever set of laws the formulators of a code for a particular trade or
industry may propose and the President may approve (subject to certain
restrictions), or the President may himself prescribe, as being wise and
beneficent provisions for the government of the trade or industry in order
to accomplish the broad purposes of rehabilitation, correction, and expansion which are stated in the first section of title 1?

The act does not define "fair competition." "Unfair competition," as
known to the common law, is a limited concept. Primarily, and strictly, it relates to the palming off of one's goods as those of a rival trader. . . .

In recent years, its scope has been extended. It has been held to apply
to misappropriation as well as misrepresentation, to the selling of another's
goods as one's own—to misappropriation of what equitably belongs to a
competitor. Unfairness in competition has been predicated on acts which lie
outside the ordinary course of business and are tainted by fraud or coercion
or conduct otherwise prohibited by law. But it is evident that in its widest
range, "unfair competition," as it has been understood in the law, does not
reach the objectives of the codes which are authorized by the National Industrial Recovery Act. The codes may, indeed, cover conduct which existing
law condemns, but they are not limited to conduct of that sort. The government does not contend that the act contemplates such a limitation. It would

be opposed both to the declared purposes of the act and to its administrative construction.

The Federal Trade Commission Act (section 5 [15 USCA Sec. 45]) introduced the expression "unfair methods of competition," which were declared to be unlawful. That was an expression new in the law. Debate apparently convinced the sponsors of the legislation that the words "unfair competition," in the light of their meaning at common law, were too narrow. We have said that the substituted phrase has a broader meaning, that it does not admit of precise definition; its scope being left to judicial determination as controversies arise. . . .

What are "unfair methods of competition" are thus to be determined in particular instances, upon evidence, in the light of particular competitive conditions and of what is found to be a specific and substantial public interest. To make this possible, Congress set up a special procedure. A commission, a quasi judicial body, was created. Provision was made for formal complaint, for notice and hearing, for appropriate findings of fact supported by adequate evidence, and for judicial review to give assurance that the action of the commission is taken within its statutory authority. . . .

In providing for codes, the National Industrial Recovery Act dispenses with this administrative procedure and with any administrative procedure of an analogous character. But the difference between the code plan of the Recovery Act and the scheme of the Federal Trade Commission Act lies not only in procedure but in subject-matter. We cannot regard the "fair competition" of the codes as antithetical to the "unfair methods of competition" of the Federal Trade Commission Act. The "fair competition" of the codes has a much broader range and a new significance. The Recovery Act provides that it shall not be construed to impair the powers of the Federal Trade Commission, but, when a code is approved, its provisions are to be the "standards of fair competition" for the trade or industry concerned, and any violation of such standards in any transaction in or affecting interstate or foreign commerce is to be deemed "an unfair method of competition" within the meaning of the Federal Trade Commission Act.

For a statement of the authorized objectives and content of the "codes of fair competition," we are referred repeatedly to the "Declaration of Policy" in section 1 of title 1 of the Recovery Act (15 USCA Sec. 701). Thus the approval of a code by the President is conditioned on his finding that it "will tend to effectuate the policy of this title." The President is authorized to impose such conditions "for the protection of consumers, competitors, employees, and others, and in furtherance of the public interest, and may provide such exceptions to and exemptions from the provisions of such code, as the President in his discretion deems necessary to effectuate the policy herein declared." The "policy herein declared" is manifestly that set forth in section 1. That declaration embraces a broad range of objectives. Among them we find the elimination of "unfair competitive practices." But, even if this clause were to be taken to relate to practices which fall under the ban of existing law, either common law or statute, it is still only one of the authorized aims described in section 1. . . .

Under section 3, whatever "may tend to effectuate" these general purposes may be included in the "codes of fair competition." We think the conclusion is inescapable that the authority sought to be conferred by section 3 was not merely to deal with "unfair competitive practices" which offend against existing law, and could be the subject of judicial condemnation without further legislation, or to create administrative machinery for the application of established principles of law to particular instances of violation. Rather, the purpose is clearly disclosed to authorize new and controlling prohibitions through codes of laws which would embrace what the formulators would propose, and what the President would approve or prescribe, as wise and beneficent measures for the government of trades and industries in order to bring about their rehabilitation, correction, and development, according to the general declaration of policy in section 1. Codes of laws of this sort are styled "codes of fair competition."

We find no real controversy upon this point, and we must determine the validity of the code in question in this aspect. . . .

The question, then, turns upon the authority which section 3 of the Recovery Act vests in the President to approve or prescribe. If the codes have standing as penal statutes, this must be due to the effect of the executive action. But Congress cannot delegate legislative power to the President to exercise an unfettered discretion to make whatever laws he thinks may be needed or advisable for the rehabilitation and expansion of trade or industry. See *Panama Refining Company v. Ryan, supra,* and cases there reviewed.

Accordingly we turn to the Recovery Act to ascertain what limits have been set to the exercise of the President's discretion: First, the President, as a condition of approval, is required to find that the trade or industrial associations or groups which propose a code "impose no inequitable restrictions on admission to membership" and are "truly representative." That condition, however, relates only to the status of the initiators of the new laws and not to the permissible scope of such laws. Second, the President is required to find that the code is not "designed to promote monopolies or to eliminate or oppress small enterprises and will not operate to discriminate against them." And to this is added a proviso that the code "shall not permit monopolies or monopolistic practices." But these restrictions leave virtually untouched the field of policy envisaged by section 1, and, in that wide field of legislative possibilities, proponents of a code, refraining from monopolistic designs, may roam at will, and the President may approve or disapprove their proposals as he may see fit. That is the precise effect of the further finding that the President is to make—that the code "will tend to effectuate the policy of this title." While this is called a finding, it is really but a statement of an opinion as to the general effect upon the promotion of trade or industry of a scheme of laws. These are the only findings which Congress has made essential in order to put into operation a legislative code having the aims described in the "Declaration of Policy."

Nor is the breadth of the President's discretion left to the necessary implications of this limited requirement as to his findings. As already noted, the President in approving a code may impose his own conditions, adding to or taking from what is proposed, as "in his discretion" he thinks necessary "to effectuate the policy" declared by the act. Of course, he has no less liberty when he prescribes a code on his own motion or on complaint, and he is free to prescribe one if a code has not been approved. The act provides for the creation by the President of administrative agencies to assist him, but the action or reports of such agencies, or of his other assistants—their recommendations and findings in relation to the making of codes—have no sanction beyond the will of the President, who may accept, modify, or reject them as he pleases. Such recommendations or findings in no way limit the authority which section 3 undertakes to vest in the President with no other conditions than those there specified. And this authority relates to a host of different trades and industries, thus extending the President's discretion to all the varieties of laws which he may deem to be beneficial in dealing with the vast array of commercial and industrial activities throughout the country.

Such a sweeping delegation of legislative power finds no support in the decisions upon which the government especially relies. By the Interstate Commerce Act, Congress has itself provided a code of laws regulating the activities of the common carriers subject to the act, in order to assure the performance of their services upon just and reasonable terms, with adequate facilities and without unjust discrimination. Congress from time to time has elaborated its requirements, as needs have been disclosed. To facilitate the application of the standards prescribed by the act, Congress has provided an expert body. That administrative agency, in dealing with particular cases, is required to act upon notice and hearing, and its orders must be supported by findings of fact which in turn are sustained by evidence. . . .

To summarize and conclude upon this point: Section 3 of the Recovery Act is without precedent. It supplies no standards for any trade, industry, or activity. It does not undertake to prescribe rules of conduct to be applied to particular states of fact determined by appropriate administrative procedure. Instead of prescribing rules of conduct, it authorizes the making of codes to prescribe them. For that legislative undertaking, section 3 sets up no standards, aside from the statement of the general aims of rehabilitation, correction, and expansion described in section 1. In view of the scope of that broad declaration and of the nature of the few restrictions that are imposed, the discretion of the President in approving or prescribing codes, and thus enacting laws for the government of trade and industry throughout the country, is virtually unfettered. We think that the code-making authority thus conferred is an unconstitutional delegation of legislative power.

☐ *Justice CARDOZO, concurring.*

The delegated power of legislation which has found expression in this code is not canalized within banks that keep it from overflowing. It is unconfined and vagrant, if I may borrow my own words in an earlier opinion. *Panama Refining Co. v. Ryan.* . . .

This court has held that delegation may be unlawful, though the act to be performed is definite and single, if the necessity, time, and occasion of performance have been left in the end to the discretion of the delegate. I thought that ruling went too far. I pointed out in an opinion that there had been "no grant to the Executive of any roving commission to inquire into evils and then, upon discovering them, do anything he pleases." Choice, though within limits, had been given him "as to the occasion, but none whatever as to the means." Here, in the case before us, is an attempted delegation not confined to any single act nor to any class or group of acts identified or described by reference to a standard. Here in effect is a roving commission to inquire into evils and upon discovery correct them.

I have said that there is no standard, definite or even approximate, to which legislation must conform. Let me make my meaning more precise. If codes of fair competition are codes eliminating "unfair" methods of competition ascertained upon inquiry to prevail in one industry or another, there is no unlawful delegation of legislative functions when the President is directed to inquire into such practices and denounce them when discovered. . . .

But there is another conception of codes of fair competition, their significance and function, which leads to very different consequences, though it is one that is struggling now for recognition and acceptance. By this other conception a code is not to be restricted to the elimination of business practices that would be characterized by general acceptance as oppressive or unfair. It is to include whatever ordinances may be desirable or helpful for the well-being or prosperity of the industry affected. In that view, the function of its adoption is not merely negative, but positive; the planning of improvements as well as the extirpation of abuses. What is fair, as thus conceived, is not something to be contrasted with what is unfair or fraudulent or tricky. The extension becomes as wide as the field of industrial regulation. If that conception shall prevail, anything that Congress may do within the limits of the commerce clause for the betterment of business may be done by the President upon the recommendation of a trade association by calling it a code. This is delegation running riot. No such plenitude of power is susceptible of transfer. The statute, however, aims at nothing less, as one can learn both from its terms and from the administrative practice under it. Nothing less is aimed at by the code now submitted to our scrutiny.

The code does not confine itself to the suppression of methods of competition that would be classified as unfair according to accepted business standards or accepted norms of ethics. It sets up a comprehensive body of rules to promote the welfare of the industry, if not the welfare of the nation, without reference to standards, ethical or commercial, that could be known or predicted in advance of its adoption. . . .

☐ *I am authorized to state that Justice STONE joins in this opinion.*

Industrial Union Department, AFL-CIO v. American Petroleum Institute

448 U.S. 607, 100 S.CT. 2844 (1980)

In the Occupational Safety and Health Act, Congress delegated the power to regulate carcinogenic and toxic substances by authorizing the

Occupational Safety and Health Administration (OSHA) to set standards that "most adequately assure, to the extent feasible, on the basis of the best available evidence, that no employee will suffer impairment of health or functional capacity."

After years of study, the OSHA issued a temporary emergency standard for occupational exposure to benzene at 1 part per million (ppm). The American Petroleum Institute and a coalition of other benzene producers and users immediately challenged the standard. After the United States Court of Appeals for the Fifth Circuit struck down OSHA's standard, the Industrial Union Department of the AFL-CIO appealed to the Supreme Court.

The Court's decision was five to four, and the opinion announced by Justice Stevens commanded only three votes—those of Chief Justice Burger and Justices Stewart and Powell. Justices Powell and Rehnquist and Chief Justice Burger concurred. The dissent was by Justice Marshall, who was joined by Justices Brennan, White, and Blackmun.

The crucial fifth vote for the Court's decision was cast by Justice Rehnquist, who issued a concurring opinion (reprinted here) that invokes the nondelegation doctrine, rather than the reasons set forth by Justice Stevens, for overturning the benzene regulation.

☐ *Justice REHNQUIST, concurring.*

The statutory provision at the center of the present controversy, Sec. 6(b)(5) of the Occupational Safety and Health Act of 1970, states, in relevant part, that the Secretary of Labor

> . . . in promulgating standards dealing with toxic materials or harmful physical agents . . . shall set the standard which most adequately assures, *to the extent feasible,* on the basis of the best available evidence, that no employee will suffer material impairment of health or functional capacity even if such employee has regular exposure to the hazard dealt with by such standard for the period of his working life.

According to the Secretary, who is one of the petitioners herein, Sec. 6(b)(5) imposes upon him an absolute duty, in regulating harmful substances like benzene for which no safe level is known, to set the standard for permissible exposure at the lowest level that "can be achieved at bearable cost with available technology." While the Secretary does not attempt to refine the concept of "bearable cost," he apparently believes that a proposed standard is economically feasible so long as its impact "will not be such as to threaten the financial welfare of the affected firms or the general economy." . . .

Respondents reply, and the lower court agreed, that Sec. 6(b)(5) must be read in light of another provision in the same Act, Sec. 3(8), which defines an "occupational health and safety standard" as

> . . . a standard which requires conditions, or the adoption or use of one or more practices, means, methods, operations, or processes, reasonably necessary or appropriate to provide safe or healthful employment and places of employment.

According to respondents, Sec. 6(b)(5), as tempered by Sec. 3(8), requires the Secretary to demonstrate that any particular health standard is justifiable on the basis of a rough balancing of costs and benefits.

In considering these alternative interpretations, my colleagues manifest a good deal of uncertainty, and ultimately divide over whether the Secretary produced sufficient evidence that the proposed standard for benzene will result in any appreciable benefits at all. This uncertainty, I would suggest, is eminently justified, since I believe that this litigation presents the Court with what has to be one of the most difficult issues that could confront a decision-maker: whether the statistical possibility of future deaths should ever be disregarded in light of the economic costs of preventing those deaths. I would also suggest that the widely varying positions advanced in the briefs of the parties and in the opinions of Justice STEVENS, THE CHIEF JUS-TICE, Justice POWELL, and Justice MARSHALL demonstrate, perhaps better than any other fact, that Congress, the governmental body best suited and most obligated to make the choice confronting us in this litigation, has improperly delegated that choice to the Secretary of Labor and, derivatively, to this Court.

In his *Second Treatise of Civil Government*, published in 1690, John Locke wrote that "[t]he power of the legislative, being derived from the people by a positive voluntary grant and institution, can be no other than what that positive grant conveyed, which being only to make laws, and not to make legislators, the legislative can have no power to transfer their authority of making laws and place it in other hands." Two hundred years later, this Court expressly recognized the existence of and the necessity for limits on Congress' ability to delegate its authority to representatives of the Executive Branch: "That Congress cannot delegate legislative power to the president is a principle universally recognized as vital to the integrity and maintenance of the system of government ordained by the Constitution." *Field v. Clark*, 143 U.S. 649 [(1892)]. . . .

Viewing the legislation at issue here in light of these principles, I believe that it fails to pass muster. Read literally, the relevant portion of Sec. 6(b)(5) is completely precatory, admonishing the Secretary to adopt the most protective standard if he can, but excusing him from that duty if he cannot. In the case of a hazardous substance for which a "safe" level is either unknown or impractical, the language of Sec. 6(b)(5) gives the Secretary absolutely no indication where on the continuum of relative safety he should draw his line. Especially in light of the importance of the interests at stake, I have no doubt that the provision at issue, standing alone, would violate the doctrine against uncanalized delegations of legislative power. . . .

As formulated and enforced by this Court, the nondelegation doctrine serves three important functions. First, and most abstractly, it ensures to the extent consistent with orderly governmental administration that important choices of social policy are made by Congress, the branch of our Government most responsive to the popular will. . . . Second, the doctrine guarantees that, to the extent Congress finds it necessary to delegate authority, it provides the recipient of that authority with an "intelligible principle" to guide the exercise of the delegated discretion. . . . Third, and derivative of the second, the doctrine ensures that courts charged with reviewing the exercise of delegated legislative discretion will be able to test that exercise against ascertainable standards. . . .

I believe the legislation at issue here fails on all three counts. The decision whether the law of diminishing returns should have any place in the regulation of toxic substances is quintessentially one of legislative policy. For Congress to pass that decision on to the Secretary in the manner it did violates, in my mind, John Locke's caveat—reflected in the cases cited earlier in this opinion—that legislatures are to make laws, not legislators. Nor, as I think the prior discussion amply demonstrates, do the provisions at issue or their legislative history provide the Secretary with any guidance that might lead him to his somewhat tentative conclusion that he must eliminate exposure to benzene as far as technologically and economically possible. Finally, I would suggest that the standard of "feasibility" renders meaningful judicial review impossible. . . .

Immigration and Naturalization Service v. Chadha

462 U.S. 919, 103 S.CT. 2764 (1983)

Jagdish Rai Chadha was admitted into the United States on a non-immigrant student visa in 1966. Following the expiration of the visa in 1972, the district director of the Immigration and Naturalization Service (INS) ordered Chadha to show why he should not be deported. At a hearing in 1974, Chadha agreed that he was deportable but requested time to apply for a suspension of deportation. Upon his application, the deportation order was suspended, pending a hearing by the INS.

Under the Immigration and Naturalization Act, any suspension of deportation orders must be reported by the attorney general to Congress, which then may veto the orders under Section 244(c)2 of the INS Act. The House of Representatives subsequently passed a resolution opposing the granting of permanent residence to Chadha and five other aliens.

On the basis of the House's veto of the INS's suspension of Chadha's deportation, an immigration judge reopened deportation hear-

Jagdish Rai Chadha with his wife and one of their three daughters.
(*Terrence McCarthy/New York Times Pictures.*)

ings. Chadha unsuccessfully challenged the proceedings on the ground that Section 244(c)2 was unconstitutional. After the Board of Immigration Appeals affirmed the judge's order reinstating deportation, Chadha appealed to the Court of Appeals for the Ninth Circuit. That court held that the House's "legislative veto" overturning the INS's suspension order violated the principle of separation of powers. The Supreme Court granted a petition for *certiorari*.

The Court's decision was seven to two, and the majority's opinion was announced by Chief Justice Burger. Justice Powell delivered a concurring opinion. Justices White and Rehnquist dissented.

☐ *Chief Justice BURGER delivers the opinion of the Court.*

We granted *certiorari* ... [to consider] a challenge to the constitutionality of the provision in Sec. 244(c)(2) of the Immigration and Nationalization Act, authorizing one House of Congress, by resolution, to invalidate the decision of the Executive Branch, pursuant to authority delegated by Congress to the Attorney General of the United States, to allow a particular deportable alien to remain in the United States. . . .

We begin, of course, with the presumption that the challenged statute is valid. Its wisdom is not the concern of the courts; if a challenged action does not violate the Constitution, it must be sustained:

> Once the meaning of an enactment is discerned and its constitutionality determined, the judicial process comes to an end. We do not sit as a committee of review, nor are we vested with the power of veto. *Tennessee Valley Authority v. Hill*, 437 U.S. 153 (1978).

By the same token, the fact that a given law or procedure is efficient, convenient, and useful in facilitating functions of government, standing alone, will not save it if it is contrary to the Constitution. Convenience and efficiency are not the primary objectives—or the hallmarks—of democratic government and our inquiry is sharpened rather than blunted by the fact that Congressional veto provisions are appearing with increasing frequency in statutes which delegate authority to executive and independent agencies:

> Since 1932, when the first veto provision was enacted into law, 295 congressional veto-type procedures have been inserted in 196 different statutes as follows: from 1932 to 1939, five statutes were affected; from 1940–49, nineteen statutes; between 1950–59, thirty-four statutes; and from 1960–69, forty-nine. From the year 1970 through 1975, at least one hundred sixty-three such provisions were included in eighty-nine laws. Abourezk, The Congressional Veto: A Contemporary Response to Executive Encroachment on Legislative Prerogatives, 52 *Ind.L.Rev.* 323, 324 (1977). . . .

Justice WHITE undertakes to make a case for the proposition that the one-House veto is a useful "political invention" and we need not challenge that assertion. We can even concede this utilitarian argument although the long range political wisdom of this "invention" is arguable. But policy arguments supporting even useful "political inventions" are subject to the demands of the Constitution which defines powers and, with respect to this subject, sets out just how those powers are to be exercised.

Explicit and unambiguous provisions of the Constitution prescribe and define the respective functions of the Congress and of the Executive in the legislative process. Since the precise terms of those familiar provisions are critical to the resolution of this case, we set them out verbatim. Art. I provides:

> All legislative Powers herein granted shall be vested in a Congress of the United States, which shall consist of a Senate *and* a House of Representatives. Art. I, Sec. 1. (Emphasis added).
>
>> Every Bill which shall have passed the House of Representatives *and* the Senate, *shall*, before it becomes a Law, be presented to the President of the United States; . . . Art. I, Sec. 7, cl. 2. (Emphasis added).
>
>> *Every* Order, Resolution, or Vote to which the Concurrence of the Senate and House of Representatives may be necessary (except

on a question of Adjournment) *shall be* presented to the President
of the United States; and before the Same shall take Effect, *shall be*
approved by him, or being disapproved by him, *shall be* repassed by
two thirds of the Senate and House of Representatives, according
to the Rules and Limitations prescribed in the Case of a Bill. Art. I,
Sec. 7, cl. 3. (Emphasis added).

These provisions of Art. I are integral parts of the constitutional design for the separation of powers. We have recently noted that "[t]he principle of separation of powers was not simply an abstract generalization in
the minds of the Framers: it was woven into the documents that they
drafted in Philadelphia in the summer of 1787." *Buckley v. Valeo,* [424 U.S.
1 (1976)]. Just as we relied on the textual provision of Art. II, Sec. 2, cl. 2,
to vindicate the principle of separation of powers in *Buckley,* we find that
the purposes underlying the Presentment Clauses, Art. I, Sec. 7, cls. 2, 3,
and the bicameral requirement of Art. I, Sec. 1 and Sec. 7, cl. 2, guide our
resolution of the important question presented in this case. The very
structure of the articles delegating and separating powers under Arts. I, II,
and III exemplify the concept of separation of powers and we now turn
to Art. I. . . .

The President's role in the lawmaking process also reflects the Framers'
careful efforts to check whatever propensity a particular Congress might
have to enact oppressive, improvident, or ill-considered measures. The President's veto role in the legislative process was described later during public
debate on ratification:

It establishes a salutary check upon the legislative body, calculated
to guard the community against the effects of faction, precipitancy,
or of any impulse unfriendly to the public good which may happen
to influence a majority of that body. . . . The primary inducement
to conferring the power in question upon the Executive is to enable him to defend himself; the secondary one is to increase the
chances in favor of the community against the passing of bad
laws through haste, inadvertence, or design. The *Federalist* No. 73
(A. Hamilton). . . .

The bicameral requirement of Art. I, Secs. 1, 7 was of scarcely less
concern to the Framers than was the Presidential veto and indeed the two
concepts are interdependent. By providing that no law could take effect
without the concurrence of the prescribed majority of the Members of
both Houses, the Framers reemphasized their belief, already remarked
upon in connection with the Presentment Clauses, that legislation should
not be enacted unless it has been carefully and fully considered by the Nation's elected officials. . . .

Hamilton argued that a Congress comprised of a single House was antithetical to the very purposes of the Constitution. Were the Nation to adopt
a Constitution providing for only one legislative organ, he warned:

we shall finally accumulate, in a single body, all the most important
prerogatives of sovereignty, and thus entail upon our posterity one

of the most execrable forms of government that human infatuation ever contrived. Thus we should create in reality that very tyranny which the adversaries of the new Constitution either are, or affect to be, solicitous to avert. The *Federalist* No. 22. . . .

We see therefore that the Framers were acutely conscious that the bicameral requirement and the Presentment Clauses would serve essential constitutional functions. The President's participation in the legislative process was to protect the Executive Branch from Congress and to protect the whole people from improvident laws. The division of the Congress into two distinctive bodies assures that the legislative power would be exercised only after opportunity for full study and debate in separate settings. The President's unilateral veto power, in turn, was limited by the power of two thirds of both Houses of Congress to overrule a veto thereby precluding final arbitrary action of one person. It emerges clearly that the prescription for legislative action in Art. I, Secs. 1, 7 represents the Framers' decision that the legislative power of the Federal government be exercised in accord with a single, finely wrought and exhaustively considered, procedure.

The Constitution sought to divide the delegated powers of the new federal government into three defined categories, legislative, executive and judicial, to assure, as nearly as possible, that each Branch of government would confine itself to its assigned responsibility. The hydraulic pressure inherent within each of the separate Branches to exceed the outer limits of its power, even to accomplish desirable objectives, must be resisted.

Although not "hermetically" sealed from one another the powers delegated to the three Branches are functionally identifiable. When any Branch acts, it is presumptively exercising the power the Constitution has delegated to it. When the Executive acts, it presumptively acts in an executive or administrative capacity as defined in Art. II. And when, as here, one House of Congress purports to act, it is presumptively acting within its assigned sphere.

Beginning with this presumption, we must nevertheless establish that the challenged action under Sec. 244(c)(2) is of the kind to which the procedural requirements of Art. I, Sec. 7 apply. Not every action taken by either House is subject to the bicameralism and presentment requirements of Art. I. Whether actions taken by either House are, in law and fact, an exercise of legislative power depends not on their form but upon "whether they contain matter which is properly to be regarded as legislative in its character and effect." . . .

Examination of the action taken here by one House pursuant to Sec. 244(c)(2) reveals that it was essentially legislative in purpose and effect. In purporting to exercise power defined in Art. I, Sec. 8, cl. 4 to "establish an uniform Rule of Naturalization," the House took action that had the purpose and effect of altering the legal rights, duties and relations of persons, including the Attorney General, Executive Branch officials and Chadha, all outside the legislative branch. Section 244(c)(2) purports to authorize one House of Congress to require the Attorney General to deport an individual alien whose deportation otherwise would be cancelled under Sec. 244. The one-House veto operated in this case to overrule the Attorney General and mandate Chadha's deportation; absent the House action, Chadha would remain in the United States. Congress has *acted* and its action has altered Chadha's status.

The legislative character of the one-House veto in this case is confirmed by the character of the Congressional action it supplants. Neither the House of Representatives nor the Senate contends that, absent the veto provision in Sec. 244(c)(2), either of them, or both of them acting together, could effectively require the Attorney General to deport an alien once the Attorney General, in the exercise of legislatively delegated authority, had determined the alien should remain in the United States. Without the challenged provision in Sec. 244(c)(2), this could have been achieved, if at all, only by legislation requiring deportation. Similarly, a veto by one House of Congress under Sec. 244(c)(2) cannot be justified as an attempt at amending the standards set out in Sec. 244(a)(1), or as a repeal of Sec. 244 as applied to Chadha. Amendment and repeal of statutes, no less than enactment, must conform with Art. I.

The nature of the decision implemented by the one-House veto in this case further manifests its legislative character. After long experience with the clumsy, time-consuming private bill procedure, Congress made a deliberate choice to delegate to the Executive Branch, and specifically to the Attorney General, the authority to allow deportable aliens to remain in this country in certain specified circumstances. It is not disputed that this choice to delegate authority is precisely the kind of decision that can be implemented only in accordance with the procedures set out in Art. I. Disagreement with the Attorney General's decision on Chadha's deportation—that is, Congress' decision to deport Chadha—no less than Congress' original choice to delegate to the Attorney General the authority to make that decision, involves determinations of policy that Congress can implement in only one way; bicameral passage followed by presentment to the President. Congress must abide by its delegation of authority until that delegation is legislatively altered or revoked.

Finally, we see that when the Framers intended to authorize either House of Congress to act alone and outside of its prescribed bicameral legislative role, they narrowly and precisely defined the procedure for such action. There are but four provisions in the Constitution, explicit and unambiguous, by which one House may act alone with the unreviewable force of law, not subject to the President's veto:

(a) The House of Representatives alone was given the power to initiate impeachments. Art. I, Sec. 2, cl. 6;

(b) The Senate alone was given the power to conduct trials following impeachment on charges initiated by the House and to convict following trial. Art. I, Sec. 3, cl. 5;

(c) The Senate alone was given final unreviewable power to approve or to disapprove presidential appointments. Art. II, Sec. 2, cl. 2;

(d) The Senate alone was given unreviewable power to ratify treaties negotiated by the President. Art. II, Sec. 2, cl. 2.

Clearly, when the Draftsmen sought to confer special powers on one House, independent of the other House, or of the President, they did so in explicit, unambiguous terms. These carefully defined exceptions from presentment and bicameralism underscore the difference between the legislative functions of Congress and other unilateral but important and binding one-House acts provided for in the Constitution. These exceptions are narrow, explicit, and separately justified; none of them authorize the action challenged here. On the contrary, they provide further support for the conclusion that Congressional authority is not to be implied and for the conclusion that the veto provided for in Sec. 244(c)(2) is not authorized by the constitutional design of the powers of the Legislative Branch.

Since it is clear that the action by the House under Sec. 244(c)(2) was not within any of the express constitutional exceptions authorizing one House to act alone, and equally clear that it was an exercise of legislative power, that action was subject to the standards prescribed in Article I. The bicameral requirement, the Presentment Clauses, the President's veto, and Congress' power to override a veto were intended to erect enduring checks on each Branch and to protect the people from the improvident exercise of power by mandating certain prescribed steps. To preserve those checks, and maintain the separation of powers, the carefully defined limits on the power of each Branch must not be eroded. To accomplish what has been attempted by one House of Congress in this case requires action in conformity with the express procedures of the Constitution's prescription for legislative action: passage by a majority of both Houses and presentment to the President.

The veto authorized by Sec. 244(c)(2) doubtless has been in many respects a convenient shortcut; the "sharing" with the Executive by Congress of its authority over aliens in this manner is, on its face, an appealing compromise. In purely practical terms, it is obviously easier for action to be taken by one House without submission to the President; but it is crystal clear from the records of the Convention, contemporaneous writings and debates, that the Framers ranked other values higher than efficiency. The records of the Convention and debates in the States preceding ratification underscore the common desire to define and limit the exercise of the newly created federal powers affecting the states and the people. There is unmistakable expression of a determination that legislation by the national Congress be a step-by-step, deliberate and deliberative process.

The choices we discern as having been made in the Constitutional Convention impose burdens on governmental processes that often seem clumsy, inefficient, even unworkable, but those hard choices were consciously made by men who had lived under a form of government that permitted arbitrary governmental acts to go unchecked. There is no support in the Constitution or decisions of this Court for the proposition that the cumbersomeness and delays often encountered in complying with explicit Constitutional standards may be avoided, either by the Congress or by the President. See *Youngstown Sheet & Tube Co. v. Sawyer*, 343 U.S. 579 (1952). With all the obvious flaws of delay, untidiness, and potential for abuse, we have not yet found a better way to preserve freedom than by making the exercise of power subject to the carefully crafted restraints spelled out in the Constitution.

We hold that the Congressional veto provision in Sec. 244(c)(2) is severable from the Act and that it is unconstitutional. Accordingly, the judgment of the Court of Appeals is

Affirmed.

□ *Justice POWELL, concurring.*

The Court's decision, based on the Presentment Clauses, Art. I, Sec. 7, cls. 2 and 3, apparently will invalidate every use of the legislative veto. The breadth of this holding gives one pause. Congress has included the veto in literally hundreds of statutes, dating back to the 1930s. Congress clearly views this procedure as essential to controlling the delegation of power to administrative agencies. One reasonably may disagree with Congress' assessment of the veto's utility, but the respect due its judgment as a coordinate branch of Government cautions that our holding should be no more extensive than necessary to decide this case. In my view, the case may be decided on a narrower ground. When Congress finds that a particular person does not satisfy the statutory criteria for permanent residence in this country it has assumed a judicial function in violation of the principle of separation of powers. Accordingly, I concur only in the judgment. . . .

☐ *Justice WHITE, dissenting.*

Today the Court not only invalidates Sec. 244(c)(2) of the Immigration and Naturalization Act, but also sounds the death knell for nearly 200 other statutory provisions in which Congress has reserved a "legislative veto." For this reason, the Court's decision is of surpassing importance. And it is for this reason that the Court would have been well-advised to decide the case, if possible, on the narrower grounds of separation of powers, leaving for full consideration the constitutionality of other congressional review statutes operating on such varied matters as war powers and agency rule-making, some of which concern the independent regulatory agencies.

The prominence of the legislative veto mechanism in our contemporary political system and its importance to Congress can hardly be overstated. It has become a central means by which Congress secures the accountability of executive and independent agencies. Without the legislative veto, Congress is faced with a Hobson's choice: either to refrain from delegating the necessary authority, leaving itself with a hopeless task of writing laws with the requisite specificity to cover endless special circumstances across the entire policy landscape, or in the alternative, to abdicate its lawmaking function to the executive branch and independent agencies. To choose the former leaves major national problems unresolved; to opt for the latter risks unaccountable policymaking by those not elected to fill that role. Accordingly, over the past five decades, the legislative veto has been placed in nearly 200 statutes. The device is known in every field of governmental concern: reorganization, budgets, foreign affairs, war powers, and regulation of trade, safety, energy, the environment and the economy. . . .

[T]he legislative veto is more than "efficient, convenient, and useful." It is an important if not indispensable political invention that allows the President and Congress to resolve major constitutional and policy differences, assures the accountability of independent regulatory agencies, and preserves Congress' control over lawmaking. Perhaps there are other means of accommodation and accountability, but the increasing reliance of Congress upon the legislative veto suggests that the alternatives to which Congress must now turn are not entirely satisfactory.

The history of the legislative veto also makes clear that it has not been a sword with which Congress has struck out to aggrandize itself at the expense of the other branches—the concerns of Madison and Hamilton. Rather, the veto has been a means of defense, a reservation of ultimate authority necessary if Congress is to fulfill its designated role under Article I as the nation's lawmaker. While the President has often objected to particular legislative vetoes, generally those left in the hands of congressional committees, the Executive has more often agreed to legislative review as the price for a broad delegation of authority. To be sure, the President may have preferred unrestricted power, but that could be precisely why Congress thought it essential to retain a check on the exercise of delegated authority.

For all these reasons, the apparent sweep of the Court's decision today is regrettable. The Court's Article I analysis appears to invalidate all legislative vetoes irrespective of form or subject. Because the legislative veto is commonly found as a check upon rulemaking by administrative agencies and upon broad-based policy decisions of the Executive Branch, it is particularly unfortunate that the Court reaches its decision in a case involving the exercise of a veto over deportation decisions regarding particular individuals. Courts should always be wary of striking statutes as unconstitutional; to strike an entire class of statutes based on consideration of a somewhat atypical and more-readily indictable exemplar of the class is irresponsible. . . .

If the legislative veto were as plainly unconstitutional as the Court strives to suggest, its broad ruling today would be more comprehensible. But, the constitutionality of the legislative veto is anything but clearcut. The issue divides scholars, courts, attorneys general, and the two other branches of the National Government. If the veto devices so flagrantly disregarded the requirements of Article I as the Court today suggests, I find it incomprehensible that Congress, whose members are bound by oath to uphold the Constitution, would have placed these mechanisms in nearly 200 separate laws over a period of 50 years.

The reality of the situation is that the constitutional question posed today is one of immense difficulty over which the executive and legislative branches—as well as scholars and judges—have understandably disagreed. That disagreement stems from the silence of the Constitution on the precise question: The Constitution does not directly authorize or prohibit the legislative veto. Thus, our task should be to determine whether the legislative veto is consistent with the purposes of Art. I and the principles of Separation of Powers which are reflected in that Article and throughout the Constitution. We should not find the lack of a specific constitutional authorization for the legislative veto surprising, and I would not infer disapproval of the mechanism from its absence. From the summer of 1787 to the present the government of the United States has become an endeavor far beyond the contemplation of the Framers. Only within the last half century has the complexity and size of the Federal Government's responsibilities grown so greatly that the Congress must rely on the legislative veto as the most effective if not the only means to insure their role as the nation's lawmakers. But the wisdom of the Framers was to anticipate that the nation would grow and new problems of governance would require different solutions. Accordingly, our Federal Government was intentionally chartered with the flexibility to respond to contemporary needs without losing sight of fundamental democratic principles. This was the spirit in which Justice JACKSON penned his influential concurrence in the *Steel Seizure Case:*

The actual art of governing under our Constitution does not and cannot conform to judicial definitions of the power of any of its branches based on isolated clauses or even single Articles torn from context. While the Constitution diffuses power the better to secure liberty, it also contemplates that practice will integrate the dispersed powers into a workable government. *Youngstown Sheet & Tube Co. v. Sawyer*, 343 U.S. 579 (1952).

This is the perspective from which we should approach the novel constitutional questions presented by the legislative veto. In my view, neither Article I of the Constitution nor the doctrine of separation of powers is violated by this mechanism by which our elected representatives preserve their voice in the governance of the nation. . . .

It is long-settled that Congress may "exercise its best judgment in the selection of measures, to carry into execution the constitutional powers of the government," and "avail itself of experience, to exercise its reason, and to accommodate its legislation to circumstances." *McCulloch v. Maryland*, 4 Wheat. 316 (1819) . . .

The Court heeded this counsel in approving the modern administrative state. The Court's holding today that all legislative-type action must be enacted through the lawmaking process ignores that legislative authority is routinely delegated to the Executive branch, to the independent regulatory agencies, and to private individuals and groups. . . .

This Court's decisions sanctioning such delegations make clear that Article I does not require all action with the effect of legislation to be passed as a law.

Theoretically, agencies and officials were asked only to "fill up the details," and the rule was that "Congress cannot delegate any part of its legislative power except under a limitation of a prescribed standard." . . .

In practice, however, restrictions on the scope of the power that could be delegated diminished and all but disappeared. In only two instances did the Court find an unconstitutional delegation. *Panama Refining Co. v. Ryan*, 293 U.S. 388 (1935); *Schechter Poultry Corp. v. United States*, 295 U.S. 495 (1935).

The wisdom and the constitutionality of these broad delegations are matters that still have not been put to rest. But for present purposes, these cases establish that by virtue of congressional delegation, legislative power can be exercised by independent agencies and Executive departments without the passage of new legislation. . . .

If Congress may delegate lawmaking power to independent and executive agencies, it is most difficult to understand Article I as forbidding Congress from also reserving a check on legislative power for itself. Absent the veto, the agencies receiving delegations of legislative or quasi-legislative power may issue regulations having the force of law without bicameral approval and without the President's signature. It is thus not apparent why the reservation of a veto over the exercise of that legislative power must be subject to a more exacting test. In both cases, it is enough that the initial statutory authorizations comply with the Article I requirements. . . .

I regret that I am in disagreement with my colleagues on the fundamental questions that this case presents. But even more I regret the destructive scope of the Court's holding. It reflects a profoundly different conception of the Constitution than that held by the Courts which sanctioned the modern administrative state. Today's decision strikes down in one fell swoop provisions in more laws enacted by Congress than the Court has cumulatively invalidated in its history. . . .

Clinton v. City of New York

524 U.S. 417, 118 S.Ct. 2091 (1998)

After avoiding a ruling on the constitutionality of congressional delegation to the president of the power of line-item veto in *Raines v. Byrd*, 521 U.S. 811 (1997), by denying several senators and representatives standing to challenge the law, the Court struck down the Line Item Veto Act of 1996. The pertinent facts are discussed by Justice Stevens in his opinion for the Court.

The Court's decision was six to three and its opinion announced by Justice Stevens. Justice Kennedy filed a concurring opinion. Justice Scalia filed an opinion concurring in part and dissenting in part, which Justice O'Connor joined. Justice Breyer filed a dissenting opinion, which Justices O'Connor and Scalia joined in part.

☐ *Justice STEVENS delivered the opinion of the Court.*

The Line Item Veto Act (Act) was enacted in April 1996 and became effective on January 1, 1997. The following day, six Members of Congress who had voted against the Act brought suit in the District Court for the District of Columbia challenging its constitutionality. On April 10, 1997, the District Court entered an order holding that the Act is unconstitutional. We determined, however, that the Members of Congress did not have standing to sue because they had not "alleged a sufficiently concrete injury to have established Article III standing," *Raines v. Byrd* (1997). . . .

Less than two months after our decision in that case, the President exercised his authority to cancel one provision in the Balanced Budget Act of 1997, and two provisions in the Taxpayer Relief Act of 1997. Appellees, claiming that they had been injured by two of those cancellations, filed these cases in the District Court. That Court again held the statute invalid and we again expedited our review. We now hold that these appellees have standing to challenge the constitutionality of the Act and, reaching the merits, we agree that the cancellation procedures set forth in the Act violate the Presentment Clause, Art. I, Sec. 7, cl. 2, of the Constitution. . . .

Appellees filed two separate actions against the President and other federal officials challenging these two cancellations. The plaintiffs in the first case are the City of New York, two hospital associations, one hospital, and two unions representing health care employees. The plaintiffs in the second are a farmers' cooperative [Snake River Cooperative] consisting of about

30 potato growers in Idaho and an individual farmer who is a member and officer of the cooperative. The District Court consolidated the two cases and determined that at least one of the plaintiffs in each had standing under Article III of the Constitution. . . .

The Line Item Veto Act gives the President the power to "cancel in whole" three types of provisions that have been signed into law: "(1) any dollar amount of discretionary budget authority; (2) any item of new direct spending; or (3) any limited tax benefit." It is undisputed that the New York case involves an "item of new direct spending" and that the Snake River case involves a "limited tax benefit" as those terms are defined in the Act. It is also undisputed that each of those provisions had been signed into law pursuant to Article I, Section 7, of the Constitution before it was canceled.

The Act requires the President to adhere to precise procedures whenever he exercises his cancellation authority. In identifying items for cancellation he must consider the legislative history, the purposes, and other relevant information about the items. He must determine, with respect to each cancellation, that it will "(i) reduce the Federal budget deficit; (ii) not impair any essential Government functions; and (iii) not harm the national interest." Moreover, he must transmit a special message to Congress notifying it of each cancellation within five calendar days (excluding Sundays) after the enactment of the canceled provision. It is undisputed that the President meticulously followed these procedures in these cases.

A cancellation takes effect upon receipt by Congress of the special message from the President. If, however, a "disapproval bill" pertaining to a special message is enacted into law, the cancellations set forth in that message become "null and void." The Act sets forth a detailed expedited procedure for the consideration of a "disapproval bill," but no such bill was passed for either of the cancellations involved in these cases. A majority vote of both Houses is sufficient to enact a disapproval bill. The Act does not grant the President the authority to cancel a disapproval bill, but he does, of course, retain his constitutional authority to veto such a bill. . . .

There are important differences between the President's "return" of a bill pursuant to Article I, Section 7, and the exercise of the President's cancellation authority pursuant to the Line Item Veto Act. The constitutional return takes place before the bill becomes law; the statutory cancellation occurs after the bill becomes law. The constitutional return is of the entire bill; the statutory cancellation is of only a part. Although the Constitution expressly authorizes the President to play a role in the process of enacting statutes, it is silent on the subject of unilateral Presidential action that either repeals or amends parts of duly enacted statutes.

There are powerful reasons for construing constitutional silence on this profoundly important issue as equivalent to an express prohibition. The procedures governing the enactment of statutes set forth in the text of Article I were the product of the great debates and compromises that produced the Constitution itself. Familiar historical materials provide abundant support for the conclusion that the power to enact statutes may only "be exercised in accord with a single, finely wrought and exhaustively considered, procedure." [*INS v.*] *Chadha*, 462 U.S. [919 (1983)]. Our first President understood the text of the Presentment Clause as requiring that he either "approve all the parts of a Bill, or reject it in toto." What has emerged in these cases from the President's exercise of his statutory cancellation powers, however, are

454 | The President as Chief Executive in Domestic Affairs

truncated versions of two bills that passed both Houses of Congress. They are not the product of the "finely wrought" procedure that the Framers designed. . . .

The Government advances two related arguments to support its position that despite the unambiguous provisions of the Act, cancellations do not amend or repeal properly enacted statutes in violation of the Presentment Clause. First, relying primarily on *Field v. Clark*, 143 U.S. 649 (1892), the Government contends that the cancellations were merely exercises of discretionary authority granted to the President by the Balanced Budget Act and the Taxpayer Relief Act read in light of the previously enacted Line Item Veto Act. Second, the Government submits that the substance of the authority to cancel tax and spending items "is, in practical effect, no more and no less than the power to 'decline to spend' specified sums of money, or to 'decline to implement' specified tax measures." Neither argument is persuasive. . . .

[In *Field v. Clark*, the Court identified] three critical differences between the power to suspend the exemption from import duties and the power to cancel portions of a duly enacted statute. First, the exercise of the suspension power was contingent upon a condition that did not exist when the Tariff Act was passed: the imposition of "reciprocally unequal and unreasonable" import duties by other countries. In contrast, the exercise of the cancellation power within five days after the enactment of the Balanced Budget and Tax Reform Acts necessarily was based on the same conditions that Congress evaluated when it passed those statutes. Second, under the Tariff Act, when the President determined that the contingency had arisen, he had a duty to suspend; in contrast, while it is true that the President was required by the Act to make three determinations before he canceled a provision, those determinations did not qualify his discretion to cancel or not to cancel. Finally, whenever the President suspended an exemption under the Tariff Act, he was executing the policy that Congress had embodied in the statute. In contrast, whenever the President cancels an item of new direct spending or a limited tax benefit he is rejecting the policy judgment made by Congress and relying on his own policy judgment. Thus, the conclusion in *Field v. Clark* that the suspensions mandated by the Tariff Act were not exercises of legislative power does not undermine our opinion that cancellations pursuant to the Line Item Veto Act are the functional equivalent of partial repeals of Acts of Congress that fail to satisfy Article I, Section 7.

The Government's reliance upon other tariff and import statutes, discussed in *Field*, that contain provisions similar to the one challenged in *Field* is unavailing for the same reasons. . . .

Neither are we persuaded by the Government's contention that the President's authority to cancel new direct spending and tax benefit items is no greater than his traditional authority to decline to spend appropriated funds. . . . It is argued that the Line Item Veto Act merely confers comparable discretionary authority over the expenditure of appropriated funds. The critical difference between this statute and all of its predecessors, however, is that unlike any of them, this Act gives the President the unilateral power to change the text of duly enacted statutes. None of the Act's predecessors could even arguably have been construed to authorize such a change.

Although they are implicit in what we have already written, . . . it is appropriate to emphasize three points.

First, we express no opinion about the wisdom of the procedures authorized by the Line Item Veto Act. Many members of both major political parties who have served in the Legislative and the Executive Branches have long advocated the enactment of such procedures for the purpose of "ensuring greater fiscal accountability in Washington." . . . We do not lightly conclude that their action was unauthorized by the Constitution. We have, however, twice had full argument and briefing on the question and have concluded that our duty is clear.

Second, . . . because we conclude that the Act's cancellation provisions violate Article I, Section 7, of the Constitution, we find it unnecessary to consider the District Court's alternative holding that the Act "impermissibly disrupts the balance of powers among the three branches of government."

Third, our decision rests on the narrow ground that the procedures authorized by the Line Item Veto Act are not authorized by the Constitution. . . .

If there is to be a new procedure in which the President will play a different role in determining the final text of what may "become a law," such change must come not by legislation but through the amendment procedures set forth in Article V of the Constitution. *Cf. U.S. Term Limits, Inc. v. Thorton*, 514 U.S. 779 (1995).

The judgment of the District Court is affirmed.

It is so ordered.

☐ *Justice KENNEDY, concurring.*

I write to respond to my colleague Justice BREYER, who observes that the statute does not threaten the liberties of individual citizens, a point on which I disagree. The argument is related to his earlier suggestion that our role is lessened here because the two political branches are adjusting their own powers between themselves. To say the political branches have a somewhat free hand to reallocate their own authority would seem to require acceptance of two premises: first, that the public good demands it, and second, that liberty is not at risk. The former premise is inadmissible. The Constitution's structure requires a stability which transcends the convenience of the moment. The latter premise, too, is flawed. Liberty is always at stake when one or more of the branches seek to transgress the separation of powers.

Separation of powers was designed to implement a fundamental insight: concentration of power in the hands of a single branch is a threat to liberty. The *Federalist* states the axiom in these explicit terms: "The accumulation of all powers, legislative, executive, and judiciary, in the same hands . . . may justly be pronounced the very definition of tyranny." The *Federalist* No. 47. So convinced were the Framers that liberty of the person inheres in structure that at first they did not consider a Bill of Rights necessary. It was at Madison's insistence that the First Congress enacted the Bill of Rights. It would be a grave mistake, however, to think a Bill of Rights in Madison's scheme then or in sound constitutional theory now renders separation of powers of lesser importance. . . .

Separation of powers helps to ensure the ability of each branch to be vigorous in asserting its proper authority. In this respect the device operates on a horizontal axis to secure a proper balance of legislative, executive, and judicial authority. Separation of powers operates on a vertical axis as well, between each branch and the citizens in whose interest powers must be exercised. The citizen has a vital interest in the regularity of the exercise of governmental power. If this point was not clear before *Chadha*, it should have been so afterwards. Though *Chadha* involved the deportation of a person, while the case before us involves the expenditure of money or the grant of a tax exemption, this circumstance does not mean that the vertical operation of the separation of powers is irrelevant here. By increasing the power of the President beyond what the Framers envisioned, the statute compromises the political liberty of our citizens, liberty which the separation of powers seeks to secure. . . .

☐ *Justice BREYER, with whom Justice O'CONNOR and Justice SCALIA join as to Part III, dissenting.*

■ II

I approach the constitutional question before us with three general considerations in mind. First, the Act represents a legislative effort to provide the President with the power to give effect to some, but not to all, of the expenditure and revenue-diminishing provisions contained in a single massive appropriations bill. And this objective is constitutionally proper.

When our Nation was founded, Congress could easily have provided the President with this kind of power. In that time period, our population was less than four million, federal employees numbered fewer than 5,000, annual federal budget outlays totaled approximately $4 million, and the entire operative text of Congress's first general appropriations law read as follows:

> Be it enacted . . . that there be appropriated for the service of the present year, to be paid out of the monies which arise, either from the requisitions heretofore made upon the several states, or from the duties on import and tonnage, the following sums, viz. A sum not exceeding two hundred and sixteen thousand dollars for defraying the expenses of the civil list, under the late and present government; a sum not exceeding one hundred and thirty-seven thousand dollars for defraying the expenses of the department of war; a sum not exceeding one hundred and ninety thousand dollars for discharging the warrants issued by the late board of treasury, and remaining unsatisfied; and a sum not exceeding ninety-six thousand dollars for paying the pensions to invalids.

At that time, a Congress, wishing to give a President the power to select among appropriations, could simply have embodied each appropriation in a separate bill, each bill subject to a separate Presidential veto.

Today, however, our population is about 250 million, the Federal Government employs more than four million people, the annual federal budget is $1.5 trillion, and a typical budget appropriations bill may have a dozen titles, hundreds of sections, and spread across more than 500 pages of the Statutes at Large. Congress cannot divide such a bill into thousands, or tens of thousands, of separate appropriations bills, each one of which the President would have to sign, or to veto, separately. Thus, the question is whether the Constitution permits Congress to choose a particular novel means to achieve this same, constitutionally legitimate, end.

Second, the case in part requires us to focus upon the Constitution's generally phrased structural provisions, provisions that delegate all "legislative" power to Congress and vest all "executive" power in the President. The Court, when applying these provisions, has interpreted them generously in terms of the institutional arrangements that they permit. . . .

Third, we need not here referee a dispute among the other two branches. . . .

These three background circumstances mean that, when one measures the literal words of the Act against the Constitution's literal commands, the fact that the Act may closely resemble a different, literally unconstitutional, arrangement is beside the point. To drive exactly 65 miles per hour on an interstate highway closely resembles an act that violates the speed limit. But it does not violate that limit, for small differences matter when the question is one of literal violation of law. No more does this Act literally violate the Constitution's words.

The background circumstances also mean that we are to interpret non-literal Separation of Powers principles in light of the need for "workable government." *Youngstown Sheet and Tube Co.* [*Sawyer*, 343 U.S. 579 (1952)] (JACKSON, J., concurring). If we apply those principles in light of that objective, as this Court has applied them in the past, the Act is constitutional.

■ III

The Court believes that the Act violates the literal text of the Constitution. A simple syllogism captures its basic reasoning:

Major Premise: The Constitution sets forth an exclusive method for enacting, repealing, or amending laws.

Minor Premise: The Act authorizes the President to "repeal or amend" laws in a different way, namely by announcing a cancellation of a portion of a previously enacted law.

Conclusion: The Act is inconsistent with the Constitution.

I find this syllogism unconvincing, however, because its Minor Premise is faulty. When the President "canceled" the two appropriation measures now before us, he did not repeal any law nor did he amend any law. He simply followed the law, leaving the statutes, as they are literally written, intact. . . .

Because one cannot say that the President's exercise of the power the Act grants is, literally speaking, a "repeal" or "amendment," the fact that the Act's procedures differ from the Constitution's exclusive procedures for enacting (or repealing) legislation is beside the point. The Act itself was enacted in accordance with these procedures, and its failure to require the President to satisfy those procedures does not make the Act unconstitutional.

■ IV

Because I disagree with the Court's holding of literal violation, I must consider whether the Act nonetheless violates Separation of Powers principles—principles that arise out of the Constitution's vesting of the "executive Power" in "a President," U.S. Const., Art. II, Sec. 1, and "all legislative Powers" in "a Congress," Art. I, Sec. 1. There are three relevant Separation of Powers questions here: (1) Has Congress given the President the wrong kind of power, i.e., "non-Executive" power? (2) Has Congress given the President the power to "encroach" upon Congress' own constitutionally reserved territory? (3) Has Congress given the President too much power, violating the doctrine of "nondelegation"? These three limitations help assure "adequate control by the citizen's representatives in Congress," upon which Justice KENNEDY properly insists. And with respect to this Act, the answer to all these questions is "no."

Viewed conceptually, the power the Act conveys is the right kind of power. It is "executive." As explained above, an exercise of that power "executes" the Act. Conceptually speaking, it closely resembles the kind of delegated authority—to spend or not to spend appropriations, to change or not to change tariff rates—that Congress has frequently granted the President, any differences being differences in degree, not kind.

The fact that one could also characterize this kind of power as "legislative," say, if Congress itself (by amending the appropriations bill) prevented a provision from taking effect, is beside the point. . . .

If there is a Separation of Powers violation, then, it must rest, not upon purely conceptual grounds, but upon some important conflict between the Act and a significant Separation of Powers objective.

The Act does not undermine what this Court has often described as the principal function of the Separation of Powers, which is to maintain the tripartite structure of the Federal Government—and thereby protect individual liberty—by providing a "safeguard against the encroachment or aggrandizement of one branch at the expense of the other." *Buckley v. Valeo*, 424 U.S. 1 (1976).

[O]ne cannot say that the Act "encroaches" upon Congress' power, when Congress retained the power to insert, by simple majority, into any future appropriations bill, into any section of any such bill, or into any phrase of any section, a provision that says the Act will not apply. Congress also retained the power to "disapprove," and thereby reinstate, any of the President's cancellations. And it is Congress that drafts and enacts the appropriations statutes that are subject to the Act in the first place—and thereby defines the outer limits of the President's cancellation authority. Thus this Act is not the sort of delegation "without . . . sufficient check" that concerns Justice KENNEDY. Indeed, the President acts only in response to, and on the terms set by, the Congress.

Nor can one say that the Act's basic substantive objective is constitutionally improper, for the earliest Congresses could have, and often did, confer on the President this sort of discretionary authority over spending. And, if an individual Member of Congress, who say, favors aid to Country A but not to Country B, objects to the Act on the ground that the President may "rewrite" an appropriations law to do the opposite, one can respond, "But a majority of Congress voted that he have that power; you may vote to exempt the relevant appropriations provision from the Act; and if you command a majority, your appropriation is safe." Where the burden of overcoming legislative inertia lies is within the power of Congress to determine by rule. Where is the encroachment?

Nor can one say the Act's grant of power "aggrandizes" the Presidential office. The grant is limited to the context of the budget. It is limited to the power to spend, or not to spend, particular appropriated items, and the

power to permit, or not to permit, specific limited exemptions from generally applicable tax law from taking effect. . . .

The "nondelegation" doctrine represents an added constitutional check
upon Congress' authority to delegate power to the Executive Branch. And it
raises a more serious constitutional obstacle here. The Constitution permits
Congress to "seek assistance from another branch" of Government, the "extent and character" of that assistance to be fixed "according to common sense
and the inherent necessities of the governmental co-ordination." *J. W. Hampton, Jr. & Co. v. United States*, 276 U.S. [394 (1928)]. But there are limits on
the way in which Congress can obtain such assistance; it "cannot delegate
any part of its legislative power except under the limitation of a prescribed
standard." *United States v. Chicago, M., St. P. & P.R. Co.*, 282 U.S. 311 (1931).
Or, in Chief Justice TAFT's more familiar words, the Constitution permits
only those delegations where Congress "shall lay down by legislative act an
intelligible principle to which the person or body authorized to [act] is directed to conform." *J. W. Hampton.*

The Act before us seeks to create such a principle in three ways. The
first is procedural. The Act tells the President that, in "identifying dollar
amounts [or] . . . items . . . for cancellation" (which I take to refer to his selection of the amounts or items he will "prevent from having legal force or
effect"), he is to "consider," among other things, "the legislative history, construction, and purposes of the law which contains [those amounts or items,
and] . . . any specific sources of information referenced in such law or . . . the
best available information. . . ."

The second is purposive. The clear purpose behind the Act, confirmed
by its legislative history, is to promote "greater fiscal accountability" and to
"eliminate wasteful federal spending and . . . special tax breaks."

The third is substantive. The President must determine that, to "prevent"
the item or amount "from having legal force or effect" will "reduce the Federal budget deficit; . . . not impair any essential Government functions;
and . . . not harm the national interest."

The resulting standards are broad. But this Court has upheld standards
that are equally broad, or broader. . . .

■ V

In sum, I recognize that the Act before us is novel. In a sense, it skirts a constitutional edge. But that edge has to do with means, not ends. The means chosen
do not amount literally to the enactment, repeal, or amendment of a law. Nor,
for that matter, do they amount literally to the "line item veto" that the Act's title announces. Those means do not violate any basic Separation of Powers principle. They do not improperly shift the constitutionally foreseen balance of
power from Congress to the President. Nor, since they comply with Separation
of Powers principles, do they threaten the liberties of individual citizens. They
represent an experiment that may, or may not, help representative government
work better. The Constitution, in my view, authorizes Congress and the President to try novel methods in this way. Consequently, with respect, I dissent.

☐ *Justice SCALIA, with whom Justice O'CONNOR joins, and with whom
Justice BREYER joins as to Part III, concurring in part and dissenting in part.*

■ III

I do not believe that Executive cancellation of this item of direct spending violates the Presentment Clause.

The Presentment Clause requires, in relevant part, that "every Bill which shall have passed the House of Representatives and the Senate, shall, before it becomes a Law, be presented to the President of the United States; If he approve he shall sign it, but if not he shall return it." There is no question that enactment of the Balanced Budget Act complied with these requirements: the House and Senate passed the bill, and the President signed it into law. It was only after the requirements of the Presentment Clause had been satisfied that the President exercised his authority under the Line Item Veto Act to cancel the spending item. Thus, the Court's problem with the Act is not that it authorizes the President to veto parts of a bill and sign others into law, but

---

■ THE DEVELOPMENT OF LAW

Presidential Vetoes, 1789–2010

PRESIDENT	REGULAR VETOES	POCKET VETOES	TOTAL VETOES	OVERRIDDEN
Washington	2	0	2	0
J. Adams	0	0	0	0
Jefferson	0	0	0	0
Madison	5	2	7	0
Monroe	1	0	1	0
J. Q. Adams	0	0	0	0
Jackson	5	7	12	0
Van Buren	0	1	1	0
W. Harrison	0	0	0	0
Tyler	6	4	10	1
Polk	2	1	3	0
Taylor	0	0	0	0
Fillmore	0	0	0	0
Pierce	9	0	9	5
Buchanan	4	3	7	0
Lincoln	2	5	7	0
A. Johnson	21	8	29	15
Grant	45	49	94	4
Hayes	12	1	13	1
Garfield	0	0	0	0
Arthur	4	8	12	1

rather that it authorizes him to "cancel"—prevent from "having legal force or effect"—certain parts of duly enacted statutes.

Article I, Sec. 7 of the Constitution obviously prevents the President from cancelling a law that Congress has not authorized him to cancel. Such action cannot possibly be considered part of his execution of the law, and if it is legislative action, as the Court observes, " 'repeal of statutes, no less than enactment, must conform with Art. I.' " But that is not this case. It was certainly arguable, as an original matter, that Art. I, Sec. 7 also prevents the President from cancelling a law which itself authorizes the President to cancel it. But as the Court acknowledges, that argument has long since been made and rejected. In 1809, Congress passed a law authorizing the President to cancel trade restrictions against Great Britain and France if either revoked edicts directed at the United States. Joseph STORY regarded the conferral of that authority as entirely unremarkable in *The Orono*, 18 F. Cas. 830 (CCD Mass. 1812). The Tariff

PRESIDENT	REGULAR VETOES	POCKET VETOES	TOTAL VETOES	OVERRIDDEN
Cleveland	346	238	584	7
B. Harrison	19	25	44	1
McKinley	6	36	42	0
T. Roosevelt	42	40	82	1
Taft	30	9	39	1
Wilson	33	11	44	6
Harding	5	1	6	0
Coolidge	20	30	50	4
Hoover	21	16	37	3
F. D. Roosevelt	372	263	635	9
Truman	180	70	250	12
Eisenhower	73	108	181	2
Kennedy	12	9	21	0
L. B. Johnson	16	14	30	0
Nixon	26	17	43	7
Ford	48	18	66	12
Carter	13	18	31	2
Reagan	39	39	78	9
G. H. W. Bush	29	17	44	1
Clinton	36	0	36	2
G. W. Bush	11	1	12	4
Obama	0	1	1	0
Totals:	1,494	1,070	2,563	110

Source: U.S. Senate Historical Office, Senate Library; Congressional Research Service and www.presidency.UCSB.edu/data/vetoes.phb; as of January 3, 2010.

Act of 1890 authorized the President to "suspend, by proclamation to that effect" certain of its provisions if he determined that other countries were imposing "reciprocally unequal and unreasonable" duties. This Court upheld the constitutionality of that Act in *Field v. Clark*, reciting the history since 1798 of statutes conferring upon the President the power to "discontinue the prohibitions and restraints hereby enacted and declared," "suspend the operation of the aforesaid act," and "declare the provisions of this act to be inoperative." . . .

I turn, then, to the crux of the matter: whether Congress' authorizing the President to cancel an item of spending gives him a power that our history and traditions show must reside exclusively in the Legislative Branch. I may note, to begin with, that the Line Item Veto Act is not the first statute to authorize the President to "cancel" spending items. In *Bowsher v. Synar*, 478 U.S. 714 (1986), we addressed the constitutionality of the Balanced Budget and Emergency Deficit Control Act of 1985, which required the President, if the federal budget deficit exceeded a certain amount, to issue a "sequestration" order mandating spending reductions specified by the Comptroller General. The effect of sequestration was that "amounts sequestered . . . shall be permanently cancelled." We held that the Act was unconstitutional, not because it impermissibly gave the Executive legislative power, but because it gave the Comptroller General, an officer of the Legislative Branch over whom Congress retained removal power, "the ultimate authority to determine the budget cuts to be made," "functions . . . plainly entailing execution of the law in constitutional terms." The President's discretion under the Line Item Veto Act is certainly broader than the Comptroller General's discretion was under the 1985 Act, but it is no broader than the discretion traditionally granted the President in his execution of spending laws. . . .

Certain Presidents have claimed Executive authority to withhold appropriated funds even absent an express conferral of discretion to do so. In 1876, for example, President Grant reported to Congress that he would not spend money appropriated for certain harbor and river improvements, because "under no circumstances [would he] allow expenditures upon works not clearly national," and in his view, the appropriations were for "works of purely private or local interest, in no sense national." President Franklin D. Roosevelt impounded funds appropriated for a flood control reservoir and levee in Oklahoma. President Truman ordered the impoundment of hundreds of millions of dollars that had been appropriated for military aircraft. President Nixon, the Mahatma Ghandi of all impounders, asserted at a press conference in 1973 that his "constitutional right" to impound appropriated funds was "absolutely clear." Our decision two years later in *Train v. City of New York*, 420 U.S. 35 (1975), proved him wrong, but it implicitly confirmed that Congress may confer discretion upon the executive to withhold appropriated funds, even funds appropriated for a specific purpose. The statute at issue in *Train* authorized spending "not to exceed" specified sums for certain projects, and directed that such "sums authorized to be appropriated . . . shall be allotted" by the Administrator of the Environmental Protection Agency. Upon enactment of this statute, the President directed the Administrator to allot no more than a certain part of the amount authorized. This Court held, as a matter of statutory interpretation, that the statute did not grant the Executive discretion to withhold the funds, but required allotment of the full amount authorized.

The short of the matter is this: Had the Line Item Veto Act authorized the President to "decline to spend" any item of spending contained in the Balanced Budget Act of 1997, there is not the slightest doubt that authorization would have been constitutional. What the Line Item Veto Act does instead—authorizing the President to "cancel" an item of spending—is technically different. But the technical difference does not relate to the technicalities of the Presentment Clause, which have been fully complied with; and the doctrine of unconstitutional delegation, which is at issue here, is preeminently not a doctrine of technicalities. The title of the Line Item Veto Act, which was perhaps designed to simplify for public comprehension, or perhaps merely to comply with the terms of a campaign pledge, has succeeded in faking out the Supreme Court. The President's action it authorizes in fact is not a line-item veto and thus does not offend Art. I, Sec. 7; and insofar as the substance of that action is concerned, it is no different from what Congress has permitted the President to do since the formation of the Union. . . .

For the foregoing reasons, I respectfully dissent.

D | *Accountability and Immunities*

The president is politically accountable through the electoral process when running for reelection and in trying to win passage of his programs by Congress. Both Houses also have the power to hold hearings and investigate actions by the president and the executive branch. But the president may not be removed from office (under Article II, Section 4) except "by Impeachment for, and Conviction of, Treason, Bribery, or other High Crimes and Misdemeanors." (The Twenty-fifth Amendment, however, provides an additional procedure for removing a president who because of disability is unable to discharge the powers and duties of his office.)

Congressional investigations of actions of the executive branch may lead to confrontations, when presidents withhold information, or claim an inherent power to withhold information as a matter of "executive privilege" in the interests of preserving the confidentiality of White House communications and national security.[1] Since George Washington, presidents have asserted the power to deny Congress sensitive information, dealing with treaty negotiations, for instance, military operations, and executive branch investigations. But they have done so with greater frequency and over a broader range of matters since World War II. Most of the disputes arising between the president and Congress have thus far been resolved by negotiations. The Court, however, recognizes limits to congressional investigatory powers (see Ch. 5) and specifically that Congress "cannot inquire into matters which are within the exclusive province of one of the other branches of Government."[2]

Richard Nixon after his resignation. (*AP/Wide World Photos, Inc.*)

The Court expressly acknowledged the constitutional status of a president's claim of "executive privilege" in *United States v. Nixon* (1974) (see excerpt below). But this case involved the assertion by President Richard M. Nixon of an absolute and unreviewable claim of "executive privilege" within the context of a criminal investigation, and not a congressional hearing, by a special prosecutor assigned to investigate the administration's involvement with a break-in of the headquarters of the Democratic National Committee in the Watergate hotel and its subsequent attempts to cover up the Watergate affair.[3]

A number of other constitutional issues bearing on presidential accountability and immunity arose due to the Watergate affair. For one, questions persisted about whether the chief executive may be subject to subpoenas and injunctions and what happens if he resists. In *Mississippi v. Johnson*, 4 Wall. 162 (1875), the Court declined to issue an injunction against the president on the grounds that if he balked, it would be "without power to enforce its process." But the *Nixon* Court upheld the subpoenas against the president, and he complied with its ruling.

Another question, avoided by the Court in *Nixon*, involves whether the president may be subject to criminal indictment while in office.[4] Article I, Section 3, makes clear that on leaving office the president may be indicted and subject to criminal and civil prosecutions for actions taken while in office. After resigning, Nixon avoided further criminal prosecution because his successor, Gerald R. Ford, granted him "a full, free and absolute pardon . . . for all offenses against the United States which he . . . committed or may have committed or taken part in during" his presidency.

Although Nixon evaded criminal prosecution after leaving office, he faced several civil suits that raised the related issue of whether the president enjoys immunity from civil liability. Initially, a suit was brought by Morton Halperin, a former National Security Council employee. He sued Nixon, Henry Kissinger, and several presidential aides for maintaining wiretaps on his home telephone, even after he left government service. In *Halperin v. Kissinger*, 606 F.2d 1192 (1979), the Court of Appeals for the District of Columbia Circuit ruled that Nixon enjoyed a qualified immunity but, along with his former aides, was subject to the suit. That ruling was left undisturbed when the Supreme Court split four to four, with Justice Rehnquist not participating, when reviewing its appeal in *Kissinger v. Halperin*, 452 U.S. 713 (1981).

In two companion cases against Nixon and former senior advisers, the Court upheld absolute immunity for the president, but concluded that senior aides enjoy only qualified immunity in civil liability suits. In *Nixon v. Fitzgerald*, 457 U.S. 731 (1982), newly appointed Justice Sandra Day O'Connor cast the crucial vote in deciding that the president "is entitled to absolute immunity from damages liability predicated on his official acts." A former Pentagon employee, A. Ernest Fitzgerald, sought damages from Nixon and several White House aides after he was fired for publicly criticizing military cost overruns. The justices split five to four in sustaining Nixon's claim of absolute immunity as "a functionally mandated incident of the President's unique office, rooted in the constitutional tradition of the separation of powers and supported by our history." Yet in *Harlow v. Fitzgerald*, 457 U.S. 800 (1982), the companion case brought by Fitzgerald against several White House aides involved in his firing, the Court ruled that senior presidential advisers forfeit immunity if they know or should have known that their actions violate individuals' constitutional rights. However, the Court upheld immunity from lawsuits against members of the president's cabinet and other high federal officials for alleged constitutional violations by their subordinates. *Ashcroft v. Iqbal*, 129 S.Ct. 1937 (2009), stemmed from a suit against former attorney general John Ashcroft and others based on federal actions during the roundup and detention of men of Arab descent or identified with the Muslim faith, in the aftermath of the terrorists' attacks on September 11, 2001. On appeal the Supreme Court split five to four in holding that high government officials cannot be held responsible for actions of subordinates and are liable for only their own personal misconduct. Writing for the majority, Justice Kennedy in this case held that personal liability for alleged torture had not been established. Justices Souter and Breyer filed dissenting opinions, which Justices Stevens and Ginsburg joined.

The impeachment proceedings against Nixon posed other important constitutional questions. Under Article I, the House of Representatives has "the sole power of impeachment," which it exercises by passing, by majority vote, "articles of impeachment." The Senate is given "the sole power to try all impeachments." Basically, the House functions as a prosecutor and the Senate sits as a court in passing judgment on impeachment. Article II, section 4, further specifies that the president and other government officials may be "removed from Office on Impeachment for, and Conviction of, Treason, Bribery, or other high Crimes and Misdemeanors." Besides Nixon, impeachment proceedings have been brought against eleven federal judges—seven of whom have been convicted—one senator and three members of the executive branch, President Andrew Johnson in 1868 and the secretary of war in 1876, and President Bill Clinton in 1998–1999.

A major question in Nixon's impeachment involved the meaning of "high crimes and misdemeanors"; specifically, whether the president could be impeached for other than indictable criminal offenses. Nixon's attorneys advanced the view that impeachment requires not only "a criminal offense, but one of a very serious nature, committed in one's governmental capacity." At the other extreme, Gerald Ford, as congressman, urged in the House of Representatives during his 1970 drive to impeach Justice William O. Douglas that "an impeachable offense is whatever a majority of the House of Representatives considers it to be at a given moment in history; conviction results from whatever offense or offenses two-thirds of the other body considers to be sufficiently serious to require removal of the accused from office."[5] The staff and a majority of the House Judiciary Committee ultimately took a position midway between these two extreme views. They concluded that the violation of criminal laws was not necessary for impeachment, if the offenses were nevertheless serious. In their view, "[t]o confine impeachable conduct to indictable offenses may well be to set a standard so restrictive as not to reach conduct that might adversely affect the system of government. Some of the most grievous offenses against our constitutional form of government may not entail violations of the criminal law."[6]

In voting three articles of impeachment against President Nixon, the majority of the House Judiciary Committee adopted the latter position, charging the president with (1) obstruction of justice during the Watergate cover-up; (2) abuse of presidential power by misusing the FBI, CIA, and other governmental agencies; and (3) contempt of Congress in refusing to obey the committee's subpoenas for White House materials (see below).

The unconditional pardon granted Nixon by President Gerald Ford was controversial and elicited wide public disapproval. Article II, Section 2, gives the president the "power to grant reprieves and pardons for offenses against the United States, except in cases of impeachment." Although the constitutional convention rejected a proposal that would have limited the pardon power to cover only individuals indicted and convicted of criminal offenses, some lawyers challenged the constitutionality of Ford's pardon on the ground that Nixon had not been criminally indicted (although he was named as an unindicted co-conspirator in the Watergate cover-up). A federal district judge, in *Murphy v. Ford*, 390 F.Supp. 1372 (1975), however, upheld Ford's pardon. In doing so, the judge found support in the very broad language of the Supreme Court's opinion, in *Ex parte Garland*, 4 Wall. (71 U.S.) 333 (1867), that the president's pardoning power "extends to every offense known to the law, and may be exercised at any time after its commission, either before legal proceedings are taken, or during their pendency, or after conviction and judgment [and] cannot be fettered by legislative restrictions."

One additional constitutional question arising in the aftermath of Watergate and bearing on presidential accountability and immunities was settled in *Nixon v. Administrator of General Services*, 433 U.S. 425 (1977). Presidential papers have historically been the property of the president, but because of the circumstances of Nixon's resignation and ongoing criminal investigations of his administration, Congress passed the Presidential Recordings and Materials Preservation Act of 1974. It authorized the General Services Administration to hold and screen Nixon's presidential materials, returning purely private papers to him and making the rest available to the public. Nixon attacked the constitutionality of the act for violating separation of powers, executive privilege, and his constitutionally protected privacy rights, but the Court rejected his claims and upheld the legislation.

The issues of accountability and immunity loomed large in the presidency of William Jefferson Clinton. In *Clinton v. Jones* (1997) (excerpted below) the Court unanimously rejected President Clinton's claim of immunity while in the Oval Office from civil suits, specifically a suit filed by Paula Jones, who had sought damages for alleged sexual harassment by then-governor Clinton in 1991. That suit was subsequently dismissed and settled out of court. But almost a quarter of a century after Nixon resigned rather than face impeachment, the House of Representatives impeached Clinton. On December 11 and 12, 1998, the House Judiciary Committee approved four articles of impeachment (excerpted below). A week later, on December 17, 1998, the full House approved two of those articles. Article I impeached the president for committing perjury and giving misleading testimony to a federal grand jury investigating the Paula Jones case and his "sexual" relationship with a White House intern, Monica Lewinsky. The House also approved Article III, impeaching the president for obstructing justice in an effort to delay, conceal, and cover up evidence related to the Jones lawsuit. President Clinton, thus, became the second president to be impeached and to face a trial in the Senate; in February 1999, the Senate acquitted him. In 1868, President Andrew Johnson was impeached for firing his Secretary of War, Edwin M. Stanton, in violation of the Tenure in Office Act of 1867. That law was passed over Johnson's veto, because he deemed it an unconstitutional limitation on presidential powers, and prohibited the president from removing any official appointed by him without the consent of the Senate. Conviction in the Senate requires a two-thirds vote and Johnson was acquitted by just one vote.

Finally, in a potentially wide-ranging ruling supporting the powers of the presidency in domestic affairs, the Court limited *United States v. Nixon* (1974) in holding that confidentiality may be preserved without invoking executive privilege in *Cheney v. U.S. District Court for the District of Columbia*, 542 U.S. 367 (2004). Shortly after taking office President George W. Bush appointed Vice President Dick Cheney to head an advisory group on energy policy, the National Energy Policy Development Group (NEPDG). Subsequently, Judicial Watch and the Sierra Club filed a suit seeking copies of all records of the individuals who attended NEPDG meetings under the Federal Advisory Committee Act, which imposes disclosure requirements except for advisory groups composed completely of officers and employees of the federal government. The Judicial Watch contended that energy corporations were so active in the NEPDG's deliberations as to make them de facto members. The district court agreed and the Bush administration appealed to the Court of Appeals for the District of Columbia, asking it to vacate the decision to permit pretrial discovery of the NEPDG's records. The appellate court dismissed the appeal and the administration's claim that, instead of relying on executive privilege, confidentiality was based on the principle of separation of powers and disclosure would harm the presidency. That decision was appealed by the administration.

Writing for the Court, Justice Kennedy distinguished *United States v. Nixon*, which rejected the claim of an absolute unreviewable claim of executive privilege within a criminal proceeding, and the dispute in *Cheney* over the pretrial discovery in a civil suit for executive branch records. Justice Kennedy explained:

> The distinction *Nixon* drew between criminal and civil proceedings is not just a matter of formalism. The need for information for use in civil cases, while far from negligible, does not share the urgency

or significance of the criminal subpoena requests in *Nixon*. As *Nixon* recognized, the right to production of relevant evidence in civil proceedings does not have the same "constitutional dimensions." . . .

[In addition, the] discovery requests are directed to the Vice President and other senior Government officials who served on the NEPDG to give advice and make recommendations to the President. The Executive Branch, at its highest level, is seeking the aid of the courts to protect its constitutional prerogatives. [S]pecial considerations control when the Executive Branch's interests in maintaining the autonomy of its office and safeguarding the confidentiality of its communications are implicated. This Court has held, on more than one occasion, that "[t]he high respect that is owed to the office of the Chief Executive . . . is a matter that should inform the conduct of the entire proceeding, including the timing and scope of discovery," *Clinton* [v. *Jones*, 520 U.S. 681 (1997)], and that the Executive's "constitutional responsibilities and status [are] factors counseling judicial deference and restraint" in the conduct of litigation against it, *Nixon v. Fitzgerald*, 457 U.S. [731 (1982)]. . . .

The observation in *Nixon* that production of confidential information would not disrupt the functioning of the Executive Branch cannot be applied in a mechanistic fashion to civil litigation. In the criminal justice system, there are various constraints, albeit imperfect, to filter out insubstantial legal claims. . . . In contrast, there are no adequate checks in the civil discovery process here. . . .

Given the breadth of the discovery requests in this case [for all records] compared to the narrow subpoena orders [for specific White House tape recordings] in *United States v. Nixon*, our precedent provides no support for the proposition that the Executive Branch "shall bear the burden" of invoking executive privilege with sufficient specificity and of making particularized objections. . . .

The case was remanded for further proceedings. Dissenting Justices Ginsburg and Souter maintained the lower court which could "accommodate separation of powers concerns" by limiting discovery at the government's request. Justices Thomas and Scalia, concurring and dissenting in part, accepted Cheney's argument that the Court should bar all pretrial discovery, rather than permit the case to proceed.

NOTES

1. For an examination of the history of claims to executive privilege, see Raoul Berger, *Executive Privilege* (Cambridge, MA: Harvard University Press, 1974).

2. *Barenblatt v. United States*, 360 U.S. 109 (1959).

3. For a further discussion of some of the constitutional issues arising out of the Watergate affair, see Philip B. Kurland, *Watergate and the Constitution* (Chicago: University of Chicago Press, 1978).

4. See Raoul Berger, *Impeachment: The Constitutional Problems* (Cambridge, MA: Harvard University Press, 1973); and Raoul Berger, "The President, Congress, and the Courts—Must Impeachment Precede Indictment?" 83 *Yale Law Journal* 1111 (1974).

5. Gerald Ford, *Congressional Record*, 91st Cong., 2d sess., Apr. 15, 1970, 11912–11913.

6. Quoted and discussed in Congressional Quarterly, *1970 CQ Almanac* (Washington, DC: Congressional Quarterly, 1970), 1025.

Selected Bibliography

Baker, Peter. *Inside the Impeachment and Trial of William Jefferson Clinton*. New York: Scribner's, 2000.

Ball, Howard. *"We Have a Duty": The Supreme Court and the Watergate Tapes Litigation*. New York: Greenwood, 1990.

Berger, Raoul. *Impeachment: The Constitutional Problems*. Cambridge, MA: Harvard University Press, 1973.

————. *Executive Privilege*. Cambridge, MA: Harvard University Press, 1974.

Black, Charles. *Impeachment: A Handbook*. New Haven, CT: Yale University Press, 1998.

Fisher, Louis. *The Politics of Executive Privilege*. Durham, N.C.: Carolina Academic Press, 2004.

Gerhardt, Michael J. *The Federal Impeachment Process: A Constitutional and Historical Analysis*. Princeton, NJ: Princeton University Press, 1996.

Kurland, Philip. *Watergate and the Constitution*. Chicago: University of Chicago Press, 1978.

Posner, Richard. *An Affair of State: The Investigation, Impeachment, and Trial of President Clinton*. Cambridge, MA: Harvard University Press, 1999.

Rae, Nicol, and Campbell, Colton C. *Impeaching Clinton: Partisan Strife on Capitol Hill*. Lawrence: University Press of Kansas, 2004.

Rozell, Mark. *Executive Privilege: The Dilemma of Secrecy and Democratic Accountability*. 2d ed. Lawrence: University Press of Kansas, 2000.

Sirica, John. *To Set the Record Straight: The Break-in, the Tapes, the Conspirators, the Pardon*. New York: W. W. Norton, 1979.

Von Tassel, Emily Field, and Finkelman, Paul. *Impeachable Offenses*. Washington, DC: C. Q. Press, 1998.

United States v. Nixon

418 U.S. 683, 94 S.CT. 3090 (1974)

On the night of June 17, 1972, five men broke into the headquarters of the National Democratic Party in the Watergate complex in Washington, DC. "The plumbers," as they were called, were caught by some off-duty policemen, while planting bugging devices so they could monitor the Democratic party's campaign plans for the fall presidential election. On the next day it was learned that one of them worked for President Nixon's reelection committee.

Nixon and his associates managed to cover up involvement in the break-in and won reelection. But congressional committees continued to search for links between the break-in and the White House. At the same time, Judge John Sirica presided over the trial of the five burglars and pressed for full disclosure of White House involvement. In spring 1973, the Senate Select Committee on Presidential Activities of 1972 began its investigations. Nixon's former counsel, John Dean, became the star witness, revealing much of the president's involvement in the cover-up. A surprise witness, former White House aide Alexander Butterfield, then disclosed that Nixon had tape-recorded conversations in the Oval Office. The possibility of evidence in the tapes showing Nixon's direct involvement deepened the Watergate crisis.

The Senate committee and a special prosecutor, Archibald Cox, appointed to investigate illegal activities of the White House, immediately sought a small number of the tapes. Nixon refused to relinquish them, claiming executive privilege to withhold information that might damage national security interests.

The special prosecutor subpoenaed Nixon's attorneys to turn over the tapes. When Nixon again refused, Judge Sirica ordered their release but Nixon would still not comply. Cox appealed to the Court of Appeals for the District of Columbia Circuit, whose judges urged that a compromise be found. When none could be reached, the court ruled that Nixon had to surrender the tapes.

After the appellate court's ruling, Nixon announced that he would release summaries of the relevant conversations. But Cox found the deal unacceptable. Nixon then ordered the "Saturday Night Massacre." Chief of Staff Alexander Haig told Attorney General Elliot Richardson to fire the special prosecutor. Instead, Richardson resigned, as did the deputy attorney general. Finally, Solicitor General Robert H. Bork became the acting attorney general and fired Cox. But this unleashed a wave of public anger and within four days Nixon told Judge Sirica that nine tapes would be forthcoming.

The release of the nine tapes served only to intensify the controversy, when it was discovered that an eighteen-and-a-half-minute segment of the first conversation after the break-in had been erased. That and other revelations prodded the House of Representatives to create a committee to investigate the possibility of impeachment. And by February 1974, the House directed its Judiciary Committee to begin hearings on impeachment.

■ Constitutional History

Unraveling the Watergate Affair

June 17, 1972—Five men are arrested in the Democratic National Committee's headquarters in the Watergate Hotel in Washington, DC. One, James W. McCord, Jr., is the security director of the Committee to Re-Elect the President. Two others, E. Howard Hunt, Jr., and Gordon Liddy, who have White House and Nixon campaign ties, are linked to the burglars.

September 15—A federal grand jury indicts Hunt, Liddy, and the Watergate burglars; however, despite evidence of a wider conspiracy, the Justice Department closes its investigation.

January 8, 1973—The Watergate burglary trial begins. Five defendants plead guilty; Liddy and Hunt are convicted after trial.

March 19—In a letter to Judge John J. Sirica, McCord says that the defendants were pressured to plead guilty, that perjury was committed, and that others were involved.

April 30—The White House announces the resignation of Attorney General Richard Kleindienst and presidential aides John Ehrlichman and H. R. Haldeman, and the firing of presidential counselor John Dean.

June 25—John Dean begins testifying before the Senate Watergate Committee, revealing that the Watergate break-in was part of a White House program of political espionage and that President Nixon was part of an attempt to cover up the Watergate affair.

July 16—Alexander P. Butterfield, a former White House aide, discloses that there is a tape recorder in the Oval Office used to record presidential conversations.

July 26—After the president refuses to release the White House tapes,

---

Nixon continued to refuse to give additional tapes to the Judiciary Committee and Leon Jaworski, who had replaced Cox as special prosecutor. Then on March 1, 1974, the federal grand jury investigating Watergate indicted top White House aides. It also secretly named Nixon as an unindicted coconspirator and asked that the information against him be turned over to the House Judiciary Committee.

The Judiciary Committee subpoenaed all documents and tapes related to Watergate, but Nixon remained adamant about his right to decide what to release. Jaworski countered by asking Sirica to enforce a

the committee obtains subpoenas for several of the taped conversations.

October 20—The Saturday Night Massacre. The special Watergate prosecutor, Archibald Cox, is fired by Acting Attorney General Robert H. Bork, after Attorney General Elliot Richardson and Deputy Attorney General William Ruckelshaus refuse to dismiss Cox and resign instead.

November 5—President Nixon appoints a new special prosecutor, Leon Jaworski, who continues to request that the president turn over tapes of his conversations bearing on Watergate.

March 1, 1974—Seven former presidential aides are indicted for the Watergate cover-up and President Nixon is named as an unindicted co-conspirator.

May 9—The House Judiciary Committee begins impeachment proceedings.

July 24—The Supreme Court rules, in *United States v. Nixon*, that the president must turn over the subpoenaed White House tapes to the special prosecutor.

July 27—The House Judiciary Committee approves an article of impeachment, charging the president with obstruction of justice. Later two additional articles are approved.

August 5—The president releases transcripts of three conversations with H. R. Haldeman made six days after the break-in. They reveal that he ordered a halt to the Federal Bureau of Investigation's (FBI) probe of the Watergate break-in and cover-up to prevent discovery that his re-election campaign committee was involved.

August 8—Amid growing public outcry calling for his removal from office, President Nixon announces he will resign.

August 9—President Nixon resigns and Vice-President Gerald R. Ford is sworn in as president.

September 8—President Ford pardons former President Nixon.

---

subpoena for sixty-four tapes. When Nixon still would not yield, Jaworski appealed directly to the Supreme Court.

On May 31, 1974, the Court announced that it would grant the appeal on an expedited basis. On July 8, during oral arguments, Jaworski argued that the basic issue was who is to be the arbiter of what the Constitution says. Nixon's claim of executive privilege in withholding the tapes, he insisted, placed the president above the law. Jaworski conceded that the Constitution might provide "for such a thing as executive privilege." But what he denied was that Nixon, or any president, could claim an absolute, unreviewable privilege. If he had that power, the president, not the Court, would be the supreme interpreter of the Constitution.

After Jaworski argued for an hour, Nixon's attorney, James St. Clair, asked that the case be dismissed. He argued that there was a "fusion" between the criminal prosecution of presidential aides, on the one hand, and the impeachment proceedings against Nixon, on the other. Information used at the trial of the Watergate conspirators would be turned over to Congress for use against the president. That, he claimed, violated the principle of separation of powers. The dispute, he unsuccessfully urged, "is essentially a political dispute. It is a dispute that this Court ought not to be drawn into."

When the justices later discussed the case in private conference, all agreed that the Court had jurisdiction, that the case did not raise a political question, and that the case should be decided as soon as possible. All agreed, furthermore, that Nixon's claim of executive privilege could not withstand scrutiny. That portion of the Court's opinion dealing with the claim of executive privilege is excerpted here.

The Court's decision was unanimous; the opinion was announced by Chief Justice Burger, with Justice Rehnquist not participating.

☐ *Chief Justice BURGER delivers the opinion of the Court.*

[W]e turn to the claim that the subpoena should be quashed because it demands "confidential conversations between a President and his close advisors that it would be inconsistent with the public interest to produce." The first contention is a broad claim that the separation of powers doctrine precludes judicial review of a President's claim of privilege. The second contention is that if he does not prevail on the claim of absolute privilege, the court should hold as a matter of constitutional law that the privilege prevails over the subpoena *duces tecum*.

In the performance of assigned constitutional duties each branch of the Government must initially interpret the Constitution, and the interpretation of its powers by any branch is due great respect from the others. The President's counsel, as we have noted, reads the Constitution as providing an absolute privilege of confidentiality for all Presidential communications. Many decisions of this Court, however, have unequivocally reaffirmed the holding of *Marbury v. Madison*, [1 Cr. 137 (1803)], that "[i]t is emphatically the province and duty of the judicial department to say what the law is."

Our system of government "requires that federal courts on occasion interpret the Constitution in a manner at variance with the construction given the document by another branch." *Powell v. McCormack*, [395 U.S. 486 (1969)]. And in *Baker v. Carr*, [369 U.S. 186 (1962)], the Court stated:

> [D]eciding whether a matter has in any measure been committed
> by the Constitution to another branch of government, or whether
> the action of that branch exceeds whatever authority has been

committed, is itself a delicate exercise in constitutional interpretation, and is a responsibility of this Court as ultimate interpreter of the Constitution.

Notwithstanding the deference each branch must accord the others, the "judicial Power of the United States" vested in the federal courts by Art. III, § 1, of the Constitution can no more be shared with the Executive Branch than the Chief Executive, for example, can share with the Judiciary the veto power, or the Congress share with the Judiciary the power to override a Presidential veto. Any other conclusion would be contrary to the basic concept of separation of powers and the checks and balances that flow from the scheme of a tripartite government. We therefore reaffirm that it is the province and duty of this Court "to say what the law is" with respect to the claim of privilege presented in this case. *Marbury v. Madison.* . . .

In support of his claim of absolute privilege, the President's counsel urges two grounds, one of which is common to all governments and one of which is peculiar to our system of separation of powers. The first ground is the valid need for protection of communications between high Government officials and those who advise and assist them in the performance of their manifold duties: the importance of this confidentiality is too plain to require further discussion. Human experience teaches that those who expect public dissemination of their remarks may well temper candor with a concern for appearances and for their own interests to the detriment of the decision-making process. Whatever the nature of the privilege of confidentiality of Presidential communications in the exercise of Art. II powers, the privilege can be said to derive from the supremacy of each branch within its own assigned area of constitutional duties. Certain powers and privileges flow from the nature of enumerated powers; the protection of the confidentiality of Presidential communications has similar constitutional underpinnings.

The second ground asserted by the President's counsel in support of the claim of absolute privilege rests on the doctrine of separation of powers. Here it is argued that the independence of the Executive Branch within its own sphere, *Humphrey's Executor v. United States*, 295 U.S. 602 (1935); *Kilbourn v. Thompson*, 103 U.S. 168 (1881), insulates a President from a judicial subpoena in an ongoing criminal prosecution, and thereby protects confidential Presidential communications.

However, neither the doctrine of separation of powers, nor the need for confidentiality of high-level communications, without more, can sustain an absolute, unqualified Presidential privilege of immunity from judicial process under all circumstances. The President's need for complete candor and objectivity from advisers calls for great deference from the courts. However, when the privilege depends solely on the broad, undifferentiated claim of public interest in the confidentiality of such conversations, a confrontation with other values arises. Absent a claim of need to protect military, diplomatic, or sensitive national security secrets, we find it difficult to accept the argument that even the very important interest in confidentiality of Presidential communications is significantly diminished by production of such material for *in camera* inspection with all the protection that a district court will be obliged to provide.

The impediment that an absolute, unqualified privilege would place in the way of the primary constitutional duty of the Judicial Branch to do justice in criminal prosecutions would plainly conflict with the function of the courts under Art. III. In designing the structure of our Government and dividing and allocating the sovereign power among three co-equal branches, the Framers of the Constitution sought to provide a comprehensive system, but the separate powers were not intended to operate with absolute independence. . . .

To read the Art. II powers of the President as providing an absolute privilege as against a subpoena essential to enforcement of criminal statutes on no more than a generalized claim of the public interest in confidentiality of nonmilitary and nondiplomatic discussions would upset the constitutional balance of "a workable government" and gravely impair the role of the courts under Art. III.

Since we conclude that the legitimate needs of the judicial process may outweigh Presidential privilege, it is necessary to resolve those competing interests in a manner that preserves the essential functions of each branch. The right and indeed the duty to resolve that question does not free the Judiciary from according high respect to the representations made on behalf of the President. *United States v. Burr*, [4 Cr. (8 U.S.) 470 (1807)].

The expectation of a President to the confidentiality of his conversations and correspondence, like the claim of confidentiality of judicial deliberations, for example, has all the values to which we accord deference for the privacy of all citizens and, added to those values, is the necessity for protection of the public interest in candid, objective, and even blunt or harsh opinions in Presidential decisionmaking. A President and those who assist him must be free to explore alternatives in the process of shaping policies and making decisions and to do so in a way many would be unwilling to express except privately. These are the considerations justifying a presumptive privilege for Presidential communications. The privilege is fundamental to the operation of Government and inextricably rooted in the separation of powers under the Constitution. In *Nixon v. Sirica*, 159 U.S. App. D.C. 58 (1973), the Court of Appeals held that such Presidential communications are "presumptively privileged" and this position is accepted by both parties in the present litigation. We agree with Chief Justice MARSHALL's observation, therefore, that "[i]n no case of this kind would a court be required to proceed against the president as against an ordinary individual." *United States v. Burr*. . . .

But this presumptive privilege must be considered in light of our historic commitment to the rule of law. This is nowhere more profoundly manifest than in our view that "the twofold aim [of criminal justice] is that guilt shall not escape or innocence suffer." *Berger v. United States* [295 U.S. 78 (1935)]. We have elected to employ an adversary system of criminal justice in which the parties contest all issues before a court of law. The need to develop all relevant facts in the adversary system is both fundamental and comprehensive. The ends of criminal justice would be defeated if judgments were to be founded on a partial or speculative presentation of the facts. The very integrity of the judicial system and public confidence in the system depend on full disclosure of all the facts, within the framework of the rules of evidence. To ensure that justice is done, it is imperative to the function of courts that compulsory process be available for the production of evidence needed either by the prosecution or by the defense.

Only recently the Court restated the ancient proposition of law, albeit in the context of a grand jury inquiry rather than a trial.

> that "the public . . . has a right to every man's evidence," except for those persons protected by a constitutional, common-law, or statutory privilege. . . .

The privileges referred to by the Court are designed to protect weighty and legitimate competing interests. Thus, the Fifth Amendment to the Constitution provides that no man "shall be compelled in any criminal case to be a witness against himself." And, generally, an attorney or a priest may not be required to disclose what has been revealed in professional confidence. These and other interests are recognized in law by privileges against forced disclosure, established in the Constitution, by statute, or at common law. Whatever their origins, these exceptions to the demand for every man's evidence are not lightly created nor expansively construed, for they are in derogation of the search for truth.

In this case the President challenges a subpoena served on him as a third party requiring the production of materials for use in a criminal prosecution on the claim that he has a privilege against disclosure of confidential communications. He does not place his claim of privilege on the ground they are military or diplomatic secrets. As to these areas of Art. II duties the courts have traditionally shown the utmost deference to presidential responsibilities. No case of the Court, however, has extended this high degree of deference to a President's generalized interest in confidentiality. Nowhere in the Constitution, as we have noted earlier, is there any explicit reference to a privilege of confidentiality, yet to the extent this interest relates to the effective discharge of a President's powers, it is constitutionally based. . . .

In this case we must weigh the importance of the general privilege of confidentiality of presidential communications in performance of his responsibilities against the inroads of such a privilege on the fair administration of criminal justice. The interest in preserving confidentiality is weighty indeed and entitled to great respect. However we cannot conclude that advisers will be moved to temper the candor of their remarks by the infrequent occasions of disclosure because of the possibility that such conversations will be called for in the context of a criminal prosecution.

On the other hand, the allowance of the privilege to withhold evidence that is demonstrably relevant in a criminal trial could cut deeply into the guarantee of the process of law and gravely impair the basic function of the courts. A President's acknowledged need for confidentiality in the communications of his office is general in nature, whereas the constitutional need for production of relevant evidence in a criminal proceeding is specific and central to the fair adjudication of a particular criminal case in the administration of justice. Without access to specific facts a criminal prosecution may be totally frustrated. The President's broad interest in confidentiality of communications will not be violated by disclosure of a limited number of conversations preliminarily shown to have some bearing on the pending criminal cases.

We conclude that when the ground for asserting privilege as to subpoenaed materials sought for use in a criminal trial is based only on the generalized interest in confidentiality, it cannot prevail over the fundamental demands of due process of law in the fair administration of criminal justice. The generalized assertion of privilege must yield to the demonstrated, specific need for evidence in a pending criminal trial. We have earlier determined that the District Court did not err in authorizing the issuance of the subpoena. If a president concludes that compliance with a subpoena would be injurious to the public interest he may properly, as was done here, invoke a claim of privilege on the return of the subpoena. Upon receiving a claim of privilege from the Chief Executive, it became the further duty of the District Court to treat the subpoenaed material as presumptively privileged and to require the Special Prosecutor to demonstrate that the presidential material was "essential to the justice of the [pending criminal] case." *United States v. Burr.* Here the District Court treated the material as presumptively privileged, proceeded to find that the Special Prosecutor had made a sufficient showing to rebut the presumption and ordered an *in camera* ["in chambers"] examination of the subpoenaed material. On the basis of our examination of the record we are unable to conclude that the District Court erred in ordering the inspection. Accordingly we affirm the order of the District Court that subpoenaed materials be transmitted to that court. We now turn to the important question of the District Court's responsibilities in conducting the *in camera* examination of presidential materials or communications delivered under the compulsion of the subpoena *duces tecum.*

It is elementary that *in camera* inspection of evidence is always a procedure calling for scrupulous protection against any release or publication of material not found by the court, at that stage, probably admissible in evidence and relevant to the issues of the trial for which it is sought. That being true of an ordinary situation, it is obvious that the District Court has a very heavy responsibility to see to it that Presidential conversations, which are either not relevant or not admissible, are accorded that high degree of respect due the President of the United States. Chief Justice MARSHALL, sitting as a trial judge in the *Burr* case was extraordinarily careful to point out that

> [i]n no case of this kind would a court be required to proceed against the president as against an ordinary individual. . . .

MARSHALL's statement cannot be read to mean in any sense that a President is above the law, but relates to the singularly unique role under Art. II of a President's communications and activities related to the performance of duties under that Article. Moreover, a President's communications and activities encompass a vastly wider range of sensitive material than would be true of any "ordinary individual." It is therefore necessary in the public interest to afford Presidential confidentiality the greatest protection consistent with the fair administration of justice. The need for confidentiality even as to idle conversations with associates in which casual reference might be made concerning political leaders within the country or foreign statesmen is too obvious to call for further treatment. We have no doubt that the District Judge will at all times accord to Presidential records that high degree of deference suggested in *United States v. Burr,* and will discharge his responsibility to see to it that until released to the Special Prosecutor no *in camera* material is revealed to anyone. This burden applies with even greater force to excised material; once the decision is made to excise, the material is restored to its privileged status and should be returned under seal to its lawful custodian.

Since this matter came before the Court during the pendency of a criminal prosecution, and on representations that time is of the essence, the mandate shall issue forthwith.

Affirmed.

Articles of Impeachment against President Richard M. Nixon Recommended by the House Judiciary Committee

Resolved, That Richard M. Nixon, President of the United States, is impeached for high crimes and misdemeanors, and that the following articles of impeachment be exhibited to the Senate:

Articles of impeachment exhibited by the House of Representatives of the United States of America in the name of itself and of all of the people of the United States of America, against Richard M. Nixon, President of the United States of America, in maintenance and support of its impeachment against him for high crimes and misdemeanors.

ARTICLE I

In his conduct of the office of President of the United States, Richard M. Nixon, in violation of his constitutional oath faithfully to execute the office of President of the United States and, to the best of his ability, preserve, protect, and defend the Constitution of the United States, and in violation of his constitutional duty to take care that the laws be faithfully executed, has prevented, obstructed, and impeded the administration of justice, in that:

On June 17, 1972, and prior thereto, agents of the Committee for the Re-election of the President committed unlawful entry of the headquarters of the Democratic National Committee in Washington, District of Columbia, for the purpose of securing political intelligence. Subsequent thereto, Richard M. Nixon, using the powers of his high office, engaged, personally and through his subordinates and agents, in a course of conduct or plan designed to delay, impede, and obstruct the investigation of such unlawful entry; to cover up, conceal and protect those responsible; and to conceal the existence and scope of other unlawful covert activities.

The means used to implement this course of conduct or plan included one or more of the following:

1. Making or causing to be made false or misleading statements to lawfully authorized investigative officers and employees of the United States;

2. Withholding relevant and material evidence or information from lawfully authorized investigative officers and employees of the United States;

3. Approving, condoning, acquiescing in, and counseling witnesses with

respect to the giving of false or misleading statements to lawfully authorized investigative officers and employees of the United States and false or misleading testimony in duly instituted judicial and congressional proceedings;

4. Interfering or endeavoring to interfere with the conduct of investigations by the Department of Justice of the United States, the Federal Bureau of Investigation, the Office of Watergate Special Prosecution Force, and Congressional committees;

5. Approving, condoning, and acquiescing in, the surreptitious payment of substantial sums of money for the purpose of obtaining the silence or influencing the testimony of witnesses, potential witnesses or individuals who participated in such illegal entry and other illegal activities;

6. Endeavoring to misuse the Central Intelligence Agency, an agency of the United States;

7. Disseminating information received from officers of the Department of Justice of the United States to subjects of investigations conducted by lawfully authorized investigative officers and employees of the United States, for the purpose of aiding and assisting such subjects in their attempts to avoid criminal liability;

8. Making false or misleading public statements for the purpose of deceiving the people of the United States into believing that a thorough and complete investigation had been conducted with respect to allegations of misconduct on the part of personnel of the executive branch of the United States and personnel of the Committee for the Re-election of the President, and that there was no involvement of such personnel in such misconduct; or

9. Endeavoring to cause prospective defendants, and individuals duly tried and convicted, to expect favored treatment and consideration in return for their silence or false testimony, or rewarding individuals for their silence or false testimony.

In all of this, Richard M. Nixon has acted in a manner contrary to his trust as President and subversive of constitutional government, to the great prejudice of the cause of law and justice and to the manifest injury of the people of the United States.

Wherefore Richard M. Nixon, by such conduct, warrants impeachment and trial, and removal from office.

ARTICLE II

Using the powers of the office of president of the United States, Richard M. Nixon, in violation of his constitutional oath faithfully to execute the office of president of the United States and, to the best of his ability, preserve, protect and defend the Constitution of the United States, and in disregard of his constitutional duty to take care that the laws be faithfully executed, has repeatedly engaged in conduct violating the constitutional rights of citizens, impairing the due and proper administration of justice and the conduct of lawful inquiries, or contravening the laws governing agencies of the executive branch and the purposes of these agencies.

This conduct has included one or more of the following:

1. He has, acting personally and through his subordinates and agents, endeavored to obtain from the Internal Revenue Service, in violation of the constitutional rights of citizens, confidential information contained in in-

come tax returns for purposes not authorized by law and to cause, in violation of the constitutional rights of citizens, income tax audits or other income tax investigations to be initiated or conducted in a discriminatory manner.

2. He misused the Federal Bureau of Investigation, the Secret Service and other executive personnel in violation or disregard of the constitutional rights of citizens by directing or authorizing such agencies or personnel to conduct or continue electronic surveillance or other investigations for purposes unrelated to national security, the enforcement of laws or any other lawful function of his office; and he did direct the concealment of certain records made by the Federal Bureau of Investigation of electronic surveillance.

3. He has, acting personally and through his subordinates and agents, in violation or disregard of the constitutional rights of citizens, authorized and permitted to be maintained a secret investigative unit within the office of the president, financed in part with money derived from campaign contributions to him, which unlawfully utilized the resources of the Central Intelligence Agency, engaged in covert and unlawful activities and attempted to prejudice the constitutional right of an accused to a fair trial.

4. He has failed to take care that the laws were faithfully executed by failing to act when he knew or had reason to know that his close subordinates endeavored to impede and frustrate lawful inquiries by duly constituted executive, judicial and legislative entities concerning the unlawful entry into the headquarters of the Democratic National Committee and the cover-up thereof, and concerning other unlawful activities including those relating to the confirmation of Richard Kleindienst as attorney general of the United States, the electronic surveillance of private citizens, the break-in into the office of Dr. Lewis Fielding and the campaign financing practices of the Committee to Re-elect the President.

5. In disregard of the rule of law, he knowingly misused the executive power by interfering with agencies of the executive branch, including the Federal Bureau of Investigation, the Criminal Division and the Office of Watergate Special Prosecution Force, of the Department of Justice and the Central Intelligence Agency, in violation of his duty to take care that the laws be faithfully executed.

In all of this, Richard M. Nixon has acted in a manner contrary to his trust as president and subversive of constitutional government, to the great prejudice of the cause of law and justice and to the manifest injury of the people of the United States.

Wherefore Richard M. Nixon, by such conduct, warrants impeachment and trial and removal from office.

ARTICLE III

In his conduct of the office of president of the United States, Richard M. Nixon, contrary to his oath faithfully to execute the office of president of the United States and, to the best of his ability, preserve, protect and defend the Constitution of the United States, and in violation of his constitutional duty to take care that the laws be faithfully executed, has failed without lawful cause or excuse to produce papers and things as directed by duly authorized subpoenas issued by the Committee on the Judiciary of the House of

Representatives on April 11, 1974; May 15, 1974; May 30, 1974, and June 24, 1974, and willfully disobeyed such subpoenas.

The subpoenaed papers and things were deemed necessary by the committee in order to resolve by direct evidence fundamental, factual questions relating to presidential direction, knowledge or approval of actions demonstrated by other evidence to be substantial grounds for impeachment of the president.

In refusing to produce these papers and things Richard M. Nixon substituting his judgment as to what materials were necessary for the inquiry, interposed the powers of the presidency against the lawful subpoenas of the House of Representatives, thereby assuming to himself functions and judgments necessary to the exercise of the sole power of impeachment vested by the Constitution in the House of Representatives.

In all of this, Richard M. Nixon has acted in a manner contrary to his trust as president and subversive of constitutional government, to the great prejudice of the cause of law and justice and to the manifest injury of the people of the United States.

Wherefore, Richard M. Nixon by such conduct, warrants impeachment and trial and removal from office.

Clinton v. Jones

520 U.S. 681, 117 S.Ct. 1636 (1997)

The facts are discussed in the excerpt below. The Court's decision was unanimous and its opinion announced by Justice Stevens. Justice Breyer filed a concurring opinion.

☐ *Justice STEVENS delivered the opinion of the Court.*

This case raises a constitutional and a prudential question concerning the Office of the President of the United States. Respondent, a private citizen, seeks to recover damages from the current occupant of that office based on actions allegedly taken before his term began. The President submits that in all but the most exceptional cases the Constitution requires federal courts to defer such litigation until his term ends and that, in any event, respect for the office warrants such a stay. Despite the force of the arguments supporting the President's submissions, we conclude that they must be rejected.

Petitioner, William Jefferson Clinton, was elected to the Presidency in 1992, and re-elected in 1996. His term of office expires on January 20, 2001. In 1991 he was the Governor of the State of Arkansas. Respondent, Paula Corbin Jones, is a resident of California. In 1991 she lived in Arkansas, and was an employee of the Arkansas Industrial Development Commission.

On May 6, 1994, she commenced this action in the United States District Court for the Eastern District of Arkansas by filing a complaint naming petitioner and Danny Ferguson, a former Arkansas State Police officer, as defendants. The complaint alleges two federal claims, and two state law claims over which the federal court has jurisdiction because of the diverse citizenship of the parties. As the case comes to us, we are required to assume the truth of the detailed—but as yet untested—factual allegations in the complaint.

Those allegations principally describe events that are said to have occurred on the afternoon of May 8, 1991, during an official conference held at the Excelsior Hotel in Little Rock, Arkansas. The Governor delivered a speech at the conference; respondent—working as a state employee—staffed the registration desk. She alleges that Ferguson persuaded her to leave her desk and to visit the Governor in a business suite at the hotel, where he made "abhorrent" sexual advances that she vehemently rejected. She further claims that her superiors at work subsequently dealt with her in a hostile and rude manner, and changed her duties to punish her for rejecting those advances. Finally, she alleges that after petitioner was elected President, Ferguson defamed her by making a statement to a reporter that implied she had accepted petitioner's alleged overtures, and that various persons authorized to speak for the President publicly branded her a liar by denying that the incident had occurred. . . .

The District Judge denied the motion to dismiss on immunity grounds and ruled that discovery in the case could go forward, but ordered any trial stayed until the end of petitioner's Presidency. Although she recognized that a "thin majority" in *Nixon v. Fitzgerald* [457 U.S. 731 (1982)] had held that "the President has absolute immunity from civil damage actions arising out of the execution of official duties of office," she was not convinced that "a President has absolute immunity from civil causes of action arising prior to assuming the office." She was, however, persuaded by some of the reasoning in our opinion in *Fitzgerald* that deferring the trial if one were required would be appropriate. Relying in part on the fact that respondent had failed to bring her complaint until two days before the 3-year period of limitations expired, she concluded that the public interest in avoiding litigation that might hamper the President in conducting the duties of his office outweighed any demonstrated need for an immediate trial. . . .

Petitioner's principal submission—that "in all but the most exceptional cases," the Constitution affords the President temporary immunity from civil damages litigation arising out of events that occurred before he took office—cannot be sustained on the basis of precedent.

Only three sitting Presidents have been defendants in civil litigation involving their actions prior to taking office. Complaints against Theodore Roosevelt and Harry Truman had been dismissed before they took office; the dismissals were affirmed after their respective inaugurations. Two companion cases arising out of an automobile accident were filed against John F. Kennedy in 1960 during the Presidential campaign. After taking office, he unsuccessfully argued that his status as Commander in Chief gave him a right to a stay under the Soldiers' and Sailors' Civil Relief Act of 1940. The motion for a stay was denied by the District Court, and the matter was settled out of court. Thus, none of those cases sheds any light on the constitutional issue before us.

The principal rationale for affording certain public servants immunity from suits for money damages arising out of their official acts is inapplicable to unofficial conduct. In cases involving prosecutors, legislators, and judges we have repeatedly explained that the immunity serves the public interest in

President William Jefferson Clinton. *(Corbis/Bettman.)*

enabling such officials to perform their designated functions effectively without fear that a particular decision may give rise to personal liability. We explained in *Ferri v. Ackerman*, 444 U.S. 193 (1979): "As public servants, the prosecutor and the judge represent the interest of society as a whole. The conduct of their official duties may adversely affect a wide variety of different individuals, each of whom may be a potential source of future controversy. The societal interest in providing such public officials with the maximum ability to deal fearlessly and impartially with the public at large has long been recognized as an acceptable justification for official immunity. The point of immunity for such officials is to forestall an atmosphere of intimidation that would conflict with their resolve to perform their designated functions in a principled fashion." That rationale provided the principal basis for our holding that a former President of the United States was "entitled to absolute immunity from damages liability predicated on his official acts," *Fitzgerald*. Our central concern was to avoid rendering the President "unduly cautious in the discharge of his official duties."

This reasoning provides no support for an immunity for unofficial conduct. As we explained in *Fitzgerald*, "the sphere of protected action must be related closely to the immunity's justifying purposes." Because of the President's broad responsibilities, we recognized in that case an immunity from damages claims arising out of official acts extending to the "outer perimeter of his authority." But we have never suggested that the President, or any other official, has an immunity that extends beyond the scope of any action taken in an official capacity.

Moreover, when defining the scope of an immunity for acts clearly taken within an official capacity, we have applied a functional approach: "Frequently our decisions have held that an official's absolute immunity should extend only to acts in performance of particular functions of his office." As our opinions have made clear, immunities are grounded in "the nature of the function performed, not the identity of the actor who performed it."

Petitioner's effort to construct an immunity from suit for unofficial acts grounded purely in the identity of his office is unsupported by precedent. . . .

Petitioner's strongest argument supporting his immunity claim is based on the text and structure of the Constitution. He does not contend that the occupant of the Office of the President is "above the law," in the sense that his conduct is entirely immune from judicial scrutiny. The President argues merely for a postponement of the judicial proceedings that will determine whether he violated any law. His argument is grounded in the character of the office that was created by Article II of the Constitution, and relies on separation of powers principles that have structured our constitutional arrangement since the founding.

As a starting premise, petitioner contends that he occupies a unique office with powers and responsibilities so vast and important that the public interest demands that he devote his undivided time and attention to his public duties. He submits that—given the nature of the office—the doctrine of separation of powers places limits on the authority of the Federal Judiciary to interfere with the Executive Branch that would be transgressed by allowing this action to proceed. . . .

[But] the lines between the powers of the three branches are not always neatly defined. But in this case there is no suggestion that the Federal Judiciary is being asked to perform any function that might in some way be described as "executive." Respondent is merely asking the courts to exercise their core Article III jurisdiction to decide cases and controversies. Whatever the outcome of this case, there is no possibility that the decision will curtail the scope of the official powers of the Executive Branch. The litigation of questions that relate entirely to the unofficial conduct of the individual who happens to be the President poses no perceptible risk of misallocation of either judicial power or executive power.

Rather than arguing that the decision of the case will produce either an aggrandizement of judicial power or a narrowing of executive power, petitioner contends that—as a by-product of an otherwise traditional exercise of judicial power—burdens will be placed on the President that will hamper the performance of his official duties. We have recognized that "even when a branch does not arrogate power to itself . . . the separation-of-powers doctrine requires that a branch not impair another in the performance of its constitutional duties." As a factual matter, petitioner contends that this particular case—as well as the potential additional litigation that an affirmance of the Court of Appeals judgment might spawn—may impose an unacceptable burden on the President's time and energy, and thereby impair the effective performance of his office.

Petitioner's predictive judgment finds little support in either history or the relatively narrow compass of the issues raised in this particular case. As we have already noted, in the more-than-200-year history of the Republic, only three sitting Presidents have been subjected to suits for their private actions. If the past is any indicator, it seems unlikely that a deluge of such litigation will ever engulf the Presidency. As for the case at hand, if properly managed by the District Court, it appears to us highly unlikely to occupy any substantial amount of petitioner's time. . . .

In sum, "it is settled law that the separation-of-powers doctrine does not bar every exercise of jurisdiction over the President of the United States." *Fitzgerald*. If the Judiciary may severely burden the Executive Branch by reviewing the legality of the President's official conduct, and if it may direct appropriate process to the President himself, it must follow that the federal courts have power to determine the legality of his unofficial conduct. The burden on the President's time and energy that is a mere by-product of such review surely cannot be considered as onerous as the direct burden imposed by judicial review and the occasional invalidation of his official actions. We therefore hold that the doctrine of separation of powers does not require federal courts to stay all private actions against the President until he leaves office.

[W]e are persuaded that it was an abuse of discretion for the District Court to defer the trial until after the President leaves office. Such a lengthy and categorical stay takes no account whatever of the respondent's interest in bringing the case to trial. The complaint was filed within the statutory limitations period—albeit near the end of that period—and delaying trial would increase the danger of prejudice resulting from the loss of evidence, including the inability of witnesses to recall specific facts, or the possible death of a party. . . .

The Federal District Court has jurisdiction to decide this case. Like every other citizen who properly invokes that jurisdiction, respondent has a right to an orderly disposition of her claims. Accordingly, the judgment of the Court of Appeals is affirmed.

It is so ordered.

House of Representatives and Senate Votes on Articles of Impeachment against President William Jefferson Clinton

On December 11 and 12, 1998, the House of Representatives Judiciary Committee approved four articles of impeachment. One week later, on December 19, 1998, the full House approved two of those articles, Articles I and III, by the following votes:

Article		Democrats	Republicans	Total
I (grand jury perjury)				
	For:	5	223	**228**
	Against:	201	5	206
II (perjury in Jones case)				
	For:	5	200	205
	Against:	201	28	**229**
III (obstruction of justice)				
	For:	5	216	**221**
	Against:	200	12	212
IV (false statements to Congress)				
	For:	1	147	148
	Against:	204	81	**285**

After a trial presided over by Chief Justice Rehnquist, on February 12, 1999, the Senate voted to acquit President Clinton on both counts. The vote was:

Article		Democrats	Republicans	Total
On Perjury				
	For:	0	45	**45**
	Against:	45	10	**55**
On Obstruction of Justice				
	For:	0	50	**50**
	Against:	45	5	**50**

5

CONGRESS: MEMBERSHIP, IMMUNITIES, AND INVESTIGATORY POWERS

Article I of the Constitution provides that all legislative powers "shall be vested in a Congress of the United States." In contrast with the general powers delegated to the president, the powers given Congress are enumerated in considerable detail. Section 8 of the Article lists seventeen specific powers, including the power to regulate commerce, to coin money, to raise and support armies, and to declare war. Congress also has the residual power of passing laws "necessary and proper" to executing its authority. In addition, various constitutional amendments—notably, the Thirteenth, Fourteenth, and Fifteenth Amendments—further expand the powers of Congress.

The authority to make laws does not exhaust congressional powers, however. Congress has the implied power of investigating subjects on which it might legislate and regulate. Both houses assume a judicial function during impeachment proceedings, and the Senate has an executive role in ratifying treaties and consenting to the president's nomination of high government officials (see Ch. 4). If presidential and vice-presidential candidates fail to win a majority vote in the electoral college, the Twelfth Amendment gives both houses an electoral role in choosing the president and vice president. Finally, Article V gives Congress the power to propose constitutional amendments, subject to ratification by three-quarters of the states.

This chapter examines controversies that have arisen over the structure, membership, and immunities of Congress, as well as Congress's investigatory and contempt powers. Chapter 6 turns to the constitutional politics of the legislative, taxing, and spending powers of Congress.

A | *Membership and Immunities*

The structure of Congress is bicameral: the Senate represents the states and the House represents the people, based on each state's population. This registers a major compromise forged during the Constitutional Convention over the interests of densely and sparsely populated states in achieving representative government.

Each state is guaranteed two representatives in the Senate; hence, with the addition of new states, Alaska (1959) and Hawaii (1959), the size of the Senate has grown from 26 (two senators from each of the thirteen original states) to 100. To ensure that the Senate represents the interests of state governments, the Constitution originally provided for election of senators by state legislatures. But the Seventeenth Amendment (ratified in 1913) made direct popular vote the basis for senatorial election.

Because representation in the House turns on population, a number of controversies have arisen over its composition. The Framers initially provided for sixty-five representatives, based on an estimate of the population (or one representative for every 30,000 people in each state). They also provided for a census within three years after the first Congress, and every ten years thereafter, for determining the apportionment of representatives. Although declining to rule on the constitutional question of whether the Census clause, in Article 1, Section 2, clause 3, mandating reapportionment after each decennial census, requires an actual house-by-house count or permits adjustments based on statistical samples, the Court held that as a matter of statutory law the use of the latter is impermissible. Because of criticisms that the Census Bureau undercounts children, minorities, and the poor, in 1991 Congress authorized the bureau to study how to "achieve the most accurate population count possible." But when the bureau proposed supplementing the census count in 2000 with statistical adjustments, its plans were immediately challenged by several states and Republican members of the House of Representatives, who feared that the outcome would favor Democrats and affect congressional redistricting following the 2000 census. A bare majority, in *Department of Commerce v. U.S. House of Representatives*, 525 U.S. 316 (1999), ruled that the use of statistical samples would run afoul of the Census Act's requirement for an actual enumeration. However, in *Utah v. Evans*, 536 U.S. 452 (2002), a bare majority upheld the use of a statistical measure known as "hot-deck imputation," which estimates data on missing households in arriving at the final census count, and which Congress had approved and that had been used in four previous censuses.

In establishing the basis for representation, the Framers were forced into another compromise due to conflicting interests of Northern and Southern states. As a result, all "free persons" and indentured servants, plus "three-fifths of all other persons [slaves]," were to be counted. With the ratification of the Thirteenth Amendment in 1865, slavery was abolished and blacks were given equal weight in the apportionment of representation. The Fourteenth Amendment (1868) formally specifies that apportionment "among the several states [be] according to their respective numbers, counting the whole number of persons in each State, excluding Indians not taxed."

The basis for apportioning representatives in the House was not further specified and was left for the states and Congress to determine. State legislatures may establish "the times, places and manner of holding elections," but Congress may also "make or alter such regulations." Throughout the nineteenth century, after each census Congress passed apportionment statutes increasing the number of representatives to 435 by 1911. Congress then froze the size of the House and created a mechanism for the reapportionment of representatives after each census in 1929.

Once the size of the House was frozen, controversies emerged over the malapportionment of districts and gerrymandering—the practice of the majority party in state legislatures to redraw district lines to ensure the election of incumbents and party faithful. Beginning in 1842, Congress required the states to provide "contiguous, equal districts." But this requirement was omitted in the 1929 apportionment statute. And *Wood v. Broom*, 287 U.S. 1 (1932), held that Congress intentionally repealed the requirement for equal voting districts in each state.

The Court in the 1940s and 1950s took the position that malapportionment of districts was a "political question" for Congress to deal with. In *Colegrove v. Green*, 328 U.S. 549 (1946), for example, district lines in Illinois had not been redrawn since 1901. As a result, the voting strength of Chicago residents was significantly diluted in favor of rural districts. Such reapportionment controversies, in the words of Justice Frankfurter, constituted a "political thicket" the Court should not enter.

In *Baker v. Carr* (1962) (see excerpt in Ch. 2), however, a majority of the Warren Court held that the "political question" doctrine was no longer an obstacle to cases challenging the malapportionment of state legislative districts. Two years later, in *Wesberry v. Sanders* (1964) (excerpted in Ch. 8), Justice Black declared that the principle of equal congressional districts was constitutionally mandated. In his view, "[T]he command of Art. 1, Sec. 2, that Representatives be chosen by the People of the several States' means that as nearly as is practicable one man's vote in a congressional election is to be worth as much as another's." Still, dissenting Justices Harlan and Stewart contended that the Framers of the Constitution "would [not] have subscribed to the principle of 'one person, one vote'" and that the Court had no authority "to step into every situation where the political branch may be thought to have fallen short."

In its reapportionment rulings, the Warren Court never addressed the question of extending the principle of "one person one vote" from redistricting within a state to the allocation of congressional districts among the states. That issue was finally raised in *U.S. Department of Commerce v. Montana*, 503 U.S. 442 (1992). There, the Rehnquist Court unanimously declined to extend the principle of "one person, one vote" to representation in the House of Representatives. In an unusual move, the Court expedited an appeal of a three judge–district court ruling that the 1991 apportionment of seats in the House of Representatives violated the principle of "one person, one vote." In the lower court's words, "The goal of Article I, section 2 [which requires the representatives be apportioned 'according to their respective Numbers'] is equal representation, not relatively equal representation." Montana sued over the loss of 1 of its 2 representatives, arguing that its population of 803,000 would make it the most populous congressional district in the country; under the 1991 reapportionment scheme the average district included 570,000 people.

Since the size of the House of Representatives is not constitutionally fixed and was frozen at 435, in 1941 Congress adopted a method of reapportionment that aims at the smallest relative, rather than absolute, differences in representation. The district court, nevertheless, held that equal representation required a reduction in the state's absolute, instead of relative, difference from the theoretically ideal congressional district. Under this method of apportioning the 435 House seats, Montana would retain two seats, while Washington would forfeit one of its seats. The disparity in terms of raw numbers would be smaller, although Washington's average congressional district would be 52 percent bigger than Montana's two smaller districts. Moreover, the principle of "one person, one vote" appears impossible to enforce in this area, unless the size of the House is increased, because the Constitution mandates both that each state have at least one representative and that no congressional district cut across state lines.

When reversing the lower court's ruling in *U.S. Department of Com-*

merce v. Montana, the Court rejected both the federal government's claim that the political question doctrine applied and Montana's claim that it was unconstitutionally denied equal representation. In dismissing the argument that the case presented a nonjusticiable political question, Justice Stevens reaffirmed the holding in *Baker v. Carr* that federal courts have jurisdiction over reapportionment controversies. When turning then to the merits of the case, Stevens observed that

> [t]he constitutional guarantee of a minimum of one Representative for each State inexorably compels a significant departure from the ideal [of equal representation]. In Alaska, Vermont, and Wyoming, where the statewide districts are less populous than the ideal district, every vote is more valuable than the national average. Moreover, the need to allocate a fixed number of indivisible Representatives among 50 States of varying populations makes it virtually impossible to have the same size district in any pair of States, let alone in all 50. Accordingly, although "common sense" supports a test requiring "a good-faith effort to achieve precise mathematical equality" within each state, the constraints imposed by Article I, section 2, itself make that goal illusionary for the Nation as a whole.

Qualifications for membership in Congress are specified as well in Article I. Representatives must be at least twenty-five years old, must have been U.S. citizens for seven years, and must reside in the state from which they are elected. Besides the residency requirement, senators must be thirty years of age and must have been citizens for nine years. Members in both houses are also disqualified from simultaneously holding positions in the executive branch, although they may assume temporary diplomatic assignments.[1]

Each house is authorized to judge "the elections, returns and qualifications of its members." But questions have arisen over whether duly elected members may be denied their seats for reasons other than age, citizenship, and residency. Both houses have occasionally had additional requirements for membership. During the Civil War, for instance, the Test Oath Act of 1862 required members to pledge that they would not participate in rebellion. However, *Powell v. McCormack* (1969) (see excerpt below) held that members could not be excluded for reasons other than those specified in Article I. Subsequently, *Roudebush v. Hartke*, 405 U.S. 15 (1972), held that congressional authority over its membership did not prevent Indiana from recounting the ballots cast in a closely contested 1970 election for one of that state's U.S. senators.

In the 1990s, a grassroots movement succeeded in persuading twenty-three states to adopt term limits. Term limits was also a prominent feature of the House Republicans' "Contract with America" in the

1994 elections; however, in March 1995, the House defeated four different versions of a constitutional amendment imposing term limits. A bare majority of the Court subsequently struck down state-imposed term limits in *U.S. Term Limits, Inc. v. Thornton* (1995) (excerpted below). Justice Stevens declared unconstitutional such limits on membership in Congress and left no doubt that any term limitations on members of Congress require amending the Constitution. By contrast, Chief Justice Rehnquist and Justices O'Connor and Scalia joined Justice Thomas's dissent, maintaining that the Constitution was silent on the matter and that the states retained authority to add qualifications for their representatives in Congress beyond those specified in Article I for members' age, citizenship, and residency.

In response to the ruling in *U.S. Term Limits, Inc. v. Thornton*, a year later Missouri amended its state constitution to require placing of the words "Disregarded Voters' Instruction on Term Limits" on the ballot next to the name of an incumbent who failed to support term limits and who ran for reelection. For candidates who are not incumbents and refuse to vow to support term limits, the law required placing the label "Declined to Pledge to Support Term Limits" next to their names. Donald Gralike, a congressional candidate, challenged the constitutionality of the law. As in *U.S. Term Limits*, writing for the Court in *Cook v. Gralike*, 531 U.S. 510 (2001), Justice Stevens struck down Missouri's law for running afoul of the Elections Clause of Article 1, Section 4, by impermissibly attempting to add to the qualifications for holding congressional office beyond those specified for members' age, citizenship, and residency. Chief Justice Rehnquist and Justices Kennedy and Thomas each filed concurring opinions.

Membership in Congress carries certain privileges and immunities. Members "shall in all cases, except treason, felony and breach of the peace, be privileged from arrest during their attendance at the session of their respective houses, and in going to and returning from the same; and for any speech or debate in either house, they shall not be questioned in any other place." These privileges and immunities are rooted in the struggles between the English Parliament and the Crown that resulted in certain parliamentary privileges. They are designed to prevent harassment of representatives by the executive branch.

The speech or debate clause means that representatives may not be held legally accountable for statements made in their official capacity. *Kilbourn v. Thompson*, 103 U.S. 168 (1881), initially interpreted this protection to include "words spoken in debate" and anything "generally done in a session of the House by one of its members in relation to the business before it." However, in *Gravel v. United States* (1972) (see excerpt below) the Court drew a line between the "legislative business" of representatives and their broader "political activities." On the one hand, Senator Mike Gravel's reading of portions of the "Pentagon Papers," a classified history of America's involvement in Vietnam, into the public record during a Senate committee session was protected by the speech or debate clause. On the other hand, arrangements he made to have the papers published by a commercial publisher were deemed "not part and parcel of the legislative process."

The scope of "legislative business" covered by the speech or debate clause is broad, as demonstrated by *Eastland v. United States Servicemen's Fund*, 421 U.S. 491 (1975). There the Court upheld a Senate subcommittee's investigation, which threatened an organization's First Amendment freedoms of speech, press, and right of association, by expansively reading the speech or debate clause to be a shield against judicial scrutiny and interference with legislative work.

The Court also defers to Congress on matters "within the sphere of legitimate legislative activity," but continues to draw a sharp line between representatives' "legislative business" and "political activities." In *Hutchinson v. Proxmire* (1979) (see excerpt below) the Court decided that Senator William Proxmire was immune from libel suits for statements made on the Senate floor and read into the Congressional Record, but not for those in press releases, newsletters, and telephone calls to executive agencies.

In defining the scope of protected "legislative activities," the Court confronts particular difficulties in cases arising from criminal prosecutions of members of Congress. *United States v. Johnson*, 383 U.S. 169 (1966), unanimously found that a representative, who made a speech on the floor of the House in exchange for money, was protected against having his speeches introduced at trial for the purpose of showing his part in a conspiracy to defraud the government. This ruling forbidding the use of "legislative acts or the motivation for legislative acts" in prosecutions was narrowed in *United States v. Brewster*, 408 U.S. 501 (1972). There the Court held that newsletters mailed to constituents and speeches delivered outside of Congress could be used as evidence in prosecutions for bribery and conspiracy. Bribery and a representative's "promise to deliver a speech, a vote, or to solicit other votes is not 'speech or debate.'" Still, criminal prosecution of such activities remains difficult. For, as the Court reaffirmed in *United States v. Helstoski*, 442 U.S. 477 (1979), the speech or debate clause precludes both the use of "legislative acts" as evidence and judicial inquiry into representatives' "motivations" during criminal trials.[2]

Finally, the Court has had to grapple with whether legislative aides and others involved in the work of Congress enjoy the same immunities as elected representatives under the speech or debate clause. Recall that *Gravel* "treated as one" the senator and his aides in construing the protection afforded by the speech or debate clause. But an earlier case, *Dombrowski v. Eastland*, 387 U.S. 82 (1967), ruled that counsel for a Senate committee, although not the senator chairing the committee, could be sued for conspiring to violate the rights of a group of political activists. And despite the implications of *Gravel*, the Court maintains that legislative immunity "is less absolute, although applicable, when applied to officers or employees of a legislative body, rather than to legislators themselves." Thus in *Doe v. McMillan*, 412 U.S. 306 (1973), members of a congressional committee and their immediate staffs could not be sued for issuing a report containing libelous statements about schoolchildren in the District of Columbia whereas, other legislative personnel—including the Government Printing Office—are not likewise protected. In the Court's words, legislative personnel "who participate in distributions of actionable material beyond the reasonable bounds of the legislative task, enjoy no Speech or Debate immunity."

NOTES

1. Members of Congress often hold commissions in the Armed Forces Reserves, however. In *Schlesinger v. Reservists Committee to Stop the War*, 418 U.S. 208 (1974), the Court avoided deciding whether such commissions are incompatible with congressional membership by denying the plaintiffs standing to raise the issue.

2. In *Tenney v. Brandhove*, 341 U.S. 367 (1951), legislative immunity was extended to members of state legislatures. However, *United States v. Gillock*, 445 U.S. 360 (1980), held that the speech or debate clause did not protect state legislators from federal prosecution.

SELECTED BIBLIOGRAPHY

Balinski, Michel, and Young, H. Peyton. *Fair Representation: Meeting the Ideal of One Man, One Vote*. New Haven, CT: Yale University Press, 1982.

Bushnell, Eleanore. *Crimes, Follies, and Misfortunes: The Federal Impeachment Trials*. Champaign: University of Illinois Press, 1992.

Carey, John M., Niemi, Richard, and Powell, Lynda. *Term Limits in the State Legislatures*. Ann Arbor: University of Michigan Press, 2000.

Lee, Frances E., and Oppenheimer, Bruce I. *Sizing Up the Senate: The Unequal Consequences of Equal Representation*. Chicago: University of Chicago Press, 1999.

Volcansek, Mary. *None Called for Justice: Judicial Impeachment*. Champaign: University of Illinois Press, 1993.

Representative Adam Clayton Powell, Jr., Democrat, is shown in Washington, DC on Jan 11, 1945. *(AP Photo.)*

Powell v. McCormack

395 U.S. 486, 89 S.CT. 1944 (1969)

Adam Clayton Powell was an influential and controversial black congressman from Harlem, New York, elected initially in 1942 to Congress. In November 1966, he won reelection, amid allegations of improper use of government funds and misusing his position as chair of the House Education and Labor Committee. But in January 1967 he was denied his seat by a vote of the House of Representatives to exclude him. Powell then ran in a special election to fill his seat and again won reelection. He also filed a lawsuit against Speaker of the House John McCormack and several congressional officers, seeking an injunction ordering the House to seat him. Powell contended that the House could exclude him for no other reason than failing to meet the requirements of age, citizenship, and residency set forth in Article I. A year earlier, in *Bond v. Floyd*, 385 U.S. 116 (1966), the Supreme Court had held that the Georgia legislature violated Julian Bond's First Amendment rights by refusing to seat him due to his public opposition to the draft and the Vietnam War. Still a federal district court dismissed

Powell's complaint, ruling that it had no jurisdiction over the dispute. After a court of appeals affirmed that decision, Powell appealed to the Supreme Court. It reversed, holding that federal courts have jurisdiction over suits filed by congressmen against the sergeant at arms (who is an officer, but not an elected member of the House) and no jurisdiction over suits brought by members against the speaker (who is also an elected member of the House), that the issue presented was not a "political question," and that Powell had been unconstitutionally excluded from Congress.

The Court's decision was seven to one, with Justice Fortas not participating, and the majority's opinion was announced by Chief Justice Warren. A concurring opinion was delivered by Justice Douglas. Justice Stewart dissented.

□ *Chief Justice WARREN delivers the opinion of the Court.*

Respondents assert that the Speech or Debate Clause of the Constitution, Art. I, Sec. 6, is an absolute bar to petitioner's action. . . .

The Speech or Debate Clause, adopted by the Constitutional Convention without debate or opposition, finds its roots in the conflict between Parliament and the Crown culminating in the Glorious Revolution of 1688 and the English Bill of Rights of 1689. Drawing upon this history, we concluded in *United States v. Johnson*, [383 U.S. 169 (1966)], that the purpose of this clause was "to prevent intimidation [of legislators] by the executive and accountability before a possibly hostile judiciary." Although the clause sprang from a fear of seditious libel actions instituted by the Crown to punish unfavorable speeches made in Parliament, we have held that it would be a "narrow view" to confine the protection of the Speech or Debate Clause to words spoken in debate. Committee reports, resolutions, and the act of voting are equally covered, as are "things generally done in a session of the House by one of its members in relation to the business before it." . . .

Our cases make it clear that the legislative immunity created by the Speech or Debate Clause performs an important function in representative government. It insures that legislators are free to represent the interests of their constituents without fear that they will be later called to task in the courts for that representation. Thus, in *Tenney v. Brandhove*, [341 U.S. 367 (1951)], the Court quoted the writings of James Wilson as illuminating the reason for legislative immunity: "In order to enable and encourage a representative of the publick to discharge his publick trust with firmness and success, it is indispensably necessary, that he should enjoy the fullest liberty of speech, and that he should be protected from the resentment of every one, however powerful, to whom the exercise of that liberty may occasion offense."

Legislative immunity does not, of course, bar all judicial review of legislative acts. That issue was settled by implication as early as 1803, see *Marbury v. Madison*, 1 Cranch (5 U.S.) 137 [(1803)], and expressly in *Kilbourn v. Thompson* [103 U.S. 168 (1881)], the first of this Court's cases interpreting the reach of the Speech or Debate Clause. Challenged in *Kilbourn* was the constitutionality of a House Resolution ordering the arrest and imprisonment of a recalcitrant witness who had refused to respond to a subpoena issued by a House investigating committee. While holding that the Speech or Debate Clause barred Kilbourn's action for false imprisonment brought against several members of the House, the Court nevertheless reached the merits of Kilbourn's attack and decided that, since the House had no power to punish for contempt, Kilbourn's imprisonment pursuant to the resolution was unconstitutional. It therefore allowed Kilbourn to bring his false imprisonment action against Thompson, the House's Sergeant at Arms, who had executed the warrant for Kilbourn's arrest.

The Court first articulated in *Kilbourn* and followed in *Dombrowski v. Eastland* [387 U.S. 82 (1967)], the doctrine that, although an action against a Congressman may be barred by the Speech or Debate Clause, legislative employees who participated in the unconstitutional activity are responsible for their acts. Despite the fact that petitioners brought this suit against several House employees—the Sergeant at Arms, the Doorkeeper and the Clerk—as well as several Congressmen, respondents argue that *Kilbourn* and *Dombrowski* are distinguishable. Conceding that in *Kilbourn* the presence of the Sergeant at Arms and in *Dombrowski* the presence of a congressional subcommittee counsel as defendants in the litigation allowed judicial review of the challenged congressional action, respondents urge that both cases concerned an affirmative act performed by the employee outside the House having a direct effect upon a private citizen. Here, they continue, the relief sought relates to actions taken by House agents solely within the House. Alternatively, respondents insist that Kilbourn and Dombrowski prayed for damages while petitioner Powell asks that the Sergeant at Arms disburse funds, an assertedly greater interference with the legislative process. We reject the proffered distinctions. . . .

Freedom of legislative activity and the purposes of the Speech or Debate Clause are fully protected if legislators are relieved of the burden of defending themselves. In *Kilbourn* and *Dombrowski* we thus dismissed the action against members of Congress but did not regard the Speech or Debate Clause as a bar to reviewing the merits of the challenged congressional action since congressional employees were also sued. Similarly, though this action may be dismissed against the Congressmen petitioners are entitled to maintain their action against House employees and to judicial review of the propriety of the decision to exclude petitioner Powell. . . .

EXCLUSION OR EXPULSION.

The resolution excluding petitioner Powell was adopted by a vote in excess of two-thirds of the 434 Members of Congress—307 to 116. Article I, Sec. 5, grants the House authority to expel a member "with the Concurrence of two thirds." Respondents assert that the House may expel a member for any reason whatsoever and that, since a two-thirds vote was obtained, the procedure by which Powell was denied his seat in the 90th Congress should be regarded as an expulsion, not an exclusion. . . .

Although respondents repeatedly urge this Court not to speculate as to the reasons for Powell's exclusion, their attempt to equate exclusion with expulsion would require a similar speculation that the House would have voted to expel Powell had it been faced with that question. Powell had not been seated at the time House Resolution No. 278 was debated and passed. After

a motion to bring the Select Committee's proposed resolution to an immediate vote had been defeated, an amendment was offered which mandated
Powell's exclusion. Mr. Celler, chairman of the Select Committee, then posed
a parliamentary inquiry to determine whether a two-thirds vote was necessary to pass the resolution if so amended "in the sense that it might amount
to an expulsion." The Speaker replied that "action by a majority vote would
be in accordance with the rules." Had the amendment been regarded as an
attempt to expel Powell, a two-thirds vote would have been constitutionally
required. The Speaker ruled that the House was voting to exclude Powell,
and we will not speculate what the result might have been if Powell had
been seated and expulsion proceedings subsequently instituted. . . .

[Under] Art. I, Sec. 5, we necessarily must determine the meaning of the
phrase to "be the Judge of the Qualifications of its own Members." Petitioners argue that the records of the debates during the Constitutional Convention; available commentary from the post-Convention, pre-ratification
period; and early congressional applications of Art. 1, Sec. 5, support their
construction of the section. Respondents insist, however, that a careful examination of the pre-Convention practices of the English Parliament and
American colonial assemblies demonstrates that by 1787, a legislature's power
to judge the qualifications of its members was generally understood to encompass exclusion or expulsion on the ground that an individual's character
or past conduct rendered him unfit to serve. When the Constitution and the
debates over its adoption are thus viewed in historical perspective, argue respondents, it becomes clear that the "qualifications" expressly set forth in the
Constitution were not meant to limit the long-recognized legislative power
to exclude or expel at will, but merely to establish "standing incapacities,"
which could be altered only by a constitutional amendment. Our examination of the relevant historical materials leads us to the conclusion that petitioners are correct and that the Constitution leaves the House without
authority to *exclude* any person, duly elected by his constituents, who meets
all the requirements for membership expressly prescribed in the Constitution. . . .

Relying heavily on Charles Warren's analysis of the Convention debates,
petitioners argue that the proceedings manifest the Framers' unequivocal
intention to deny either branch of Congress the authority to add to or
otherwise vary the membership qualifications expressly set forth in the
Constitution. We do not completely agree, for the debates are subject to
other interpretations. However, we have concluded that the records of the
debates, viewed in the context of the bitter struggle for the right to freely
choose representatives which had recently concluded in England and in light
of the distinction the Framers made between the power to expel and the
power to exclude, indicate that petitioners' ultimate conclusion is correct.

The Convention opened in late May 1787. By the end of July, the delegates adopted, with a minimum of debate, age requirements for membership
in both the Senate and the House. The Convention then appointed a Committee of Detail to draft a constitution incorporating these and other resolutions adopted during the preceding months. Two days after the Committee
was appointed, George Mason of Virginia, moved that the Committee consider a clause " 'requiring certain qualifications of landed property & citizenship' " and disqualifying from membership in Congress persons who had

unsettled accounts or who were indebted to the United States. A vigorous debate ensued. Charles Pinckney and General Charles C. Pinckney both of South Carolina, moved to extend these incapacities to both the judicial and executive branches of the new government. But John Dickinson, of Delaware, opposed the inclusion of any statement of qualifications in the Constitution. He argued that it would be "impossible to make a compleat one, and a partial one would by implication tie up the hands of the Legislature from supplying the omissions." Dickinson's argument was rejected; and, after eliminating the disqualification of debtors and the limitation to "landed" property, the Convention adopted Mason's proposal to instruct the Committee of Detail to draft a property qualification. . . .

The Committee reported in early August, proposing no change in the age requirement; however, it did recommend adding citizenship and residency requirements for membership. After first debating what the precise requirements should be, on August 8, 1787, the delegates unanimously adopted the three qualifications embodied in Art. I, Sec. 2. . . .

On August 10, the Convention considered the Committee of Detail's proposal that the "Legislature of the United States shall have authority to establish such uniform qualifications of the members of each House, with regard to property, as to the said Legislature shall seem expedient." The debate on this proposal discloses much about the views of the Framers on the issue of qualifications. For example, James Madison urged its rejection, stating that the proposal would vest

> an improper & dangerous power in the Legislature. The qualifications of electors and elected were fundamental articles in a Republican Govt. and ought to be fixed by the Constitution. If the Legislature could regulate those of either, it can by degrees subvert the Constitution. A Republic may be converted into an aristocracy or oligarchy as well by limiting the number capable of being elected, as the number authorised to elect. . . . It was a power also, which might be made subservient to the views of one faction agst. another. Qualifications founded on artificial distinctions may be devised, by the stronger in order to keep out partizans of [a weaker] faction.

Significantly, Madison's argument was not aimed at the imposition of a property qualification as such, but rather at the delegation to the Congress of the discretionary power to establish any qualifications. . . .

The debates at the state conventions also demonstrate the Framers' understanding that the qualifications for members of Congress had been fixed in the Constitution. Before the New York convention, for example, Hamilton emphasized: "[T]he true principle of a republic is, that the people should choose whom they please to govern them. Representation is imperfect in proportion as the current of popular favor is checked. This great source of free government, popular election, should be perfectly pure, and the most unbounded liberty allowed." In short, both the intention of the Framers, to the extent it can be determined, and an examination of the basic principles of our democratic system persuade us that the Constitution does not vest in the Congress a discretionary power to deny membership by a majority vote. . . .

Therefore, we hold that, since Adam Clayton Powell, Jr., was duly elected by the voters of the 18th Congressional District of New York and was not ineligible to serve under any provision of the Constitution, the House was without power to exclude him from its membership. . . .

☐ *Justice DOUGLAS, concurring.*

While I join the opinion of the Court, I add a few words. As the Court says, the important constitutional question is whether the Congress has the power to deviate from or alter the qualifications for membership as a Representative contained in Art. I, Sec. 2, cl. 2, of the Constitution. Up to now the understanding has been quite clear to the effect that such authority does not exist. "Each House shall be the Judge of the Elections, Returns and Qualifications of its own Members. . . ." Contests may arise over whether an elected official meets the "qualifications" of the Constitution, in which event the House is the sole judge. But the House is not the sole judge when "qualifications" are added which are not specified in the Constitution. . . .

At the root . . . is the basic integrity of the electoral process. Today we proclaim the constitutional principle of "one man, one vote." When that principle is followed and the electors choose a person who is repulsive to the Establishment in Congress, by what constitutional authority can that group of electors be disenfranchised?

U.S. Term Limits, Inc. v. Thornton

514 U.S. 779, 115 S.Ct. 1842 (1995)

In 1992 Arkansas voters approved Amendment 73 to their state constitution and imposed term limits on three categories of elected officials. Section 1 provides that no elected official in the executive branch of the state government may serve for more than two terms. Section 2 provides that no member of the state house of representatives may serve for more than three two-year terms and no state senator may serve for more than two four-year terms. Section 3 further specified that state representatives to the U.S. House of Representatives may not be certified as candidates or be eligible for having their names placed on the ballot after having served for three or more terms. That section similarly limited candidates from running for the U.S. Senate after they served two or more terms there.

Within weeks of the adoption of Arkansas's term-limitation amendment, the League of Women Voters sought a declaratory judgment that Section 3 was an unconstitutional additional qualification under Article 1 of the U.S. Constitution. A state lower court and the Arkansas state supreme court agreed, whereupon U.S. Term Limits,

Inc., an organization advocating term limits for elected officials, appealed to the Supreme Court.

The Court's decision was five to four and the majority's opinion was announced by Justice Stevens. Justice Kennedy filed a concurring opinion. Justice Thomas filed a dissenting opinion, joined by Chief Justice Rehnquist and Justices O'Connor and Scalia.

    ☐ *Justice STEVENS delivered the opinion of the Court.*

The Constitution sets forth qualifications for membership in the Congress of the United States. Article I, Sec. 2, cl. 2, which applies to the House of Representatives, provides: "No Person shall be a Representative who shall not have attained to the Age of twenty five Years, and been seven Years a Citizen of the United States, and who shall not, when elected, be an Inhabitant of that State in which he shall be chosen." Article I, Sec. 3, cl. 3, which applies to the Senate, similarly provides: "No Person shall be a Senator who shall not have attained to the Age of thirty Years, and been nine Years a Citizen of the United States, and who shall not, when elected, be an Inhabitant of that State for which he shall be chosen."

Today's cases present a challenge to an amendment to the Arkansas State Constitution that prohibits the name of an otherwise-eligible candidate for Congress from appearing on the general election ballot if that candidate has already served three terms in the House of Representatives or two terms in the Senate. The Arkansas Supreme Court held that the amendment violates the Federal Constitution. We agree with that holding. Such a state-imposed restriction is contrary to the "fundamental principle of our representative democracy," embodied in the Constitution, that "the people should choose whom they please to govern them." *Powell v. McCormack*, 395 U.S. 486 (1969). Allowing individual States to adopt their own qualifications for congressional service would be inconsistent with the Framers' vision of a uniform National Legislature representing the people of the United States. If the qualifications set forth in the text of the Constitution are to be changed, that text must be amended. . . .

Twenty-six years ago, in *Powell v. McCormack*, we reviewed the history and text of the Qualifications Clauses in a case involving an attempted exclusion of a duly elected Member of Congress. The principal issue was whether the power granted to each House in Art. I, Sec. 5, to judge the "Qualifications of its own Members" includes the power to impose qualifications other than those set forth in the text of the Constitution. In an opinion by Chief Justice WARREN for eight Members of the Court, we held that it does not. . . .

We started our analysis in *Powell* by examining the British experience with qualifications for membership in Parliament, focusing in particular on the experience of John Wilkes. While serving as a member of Parliament, Wilkes had published an attack on a peace treaty with France. This literary endeavor earned Wilkes a conviction for seditious libel and a 22-month prison sentence. In addition, Parliament declared Wilkes ineligible for membership and ordered him expelled. Despite (or perhaps because of) these difficulties, Wilkes was reelected several times. Parliament, however, persisted in its refusal to seat him. After several years of Wilkes' efforts, the House of Commons voted to expunge the resolutions that had expelled Wilkes and had declared him ineligible, labeling those prior actions "subversive of the rights of the whole body of electors of this kingdom." After reviewing Wilkes' "long and bitter struggle for the right of the British electorate to be represented by men of their own choice," we concluded in *Powell* that "on the eve of the Constitutional Convention, English precedent stood for the proposition that 'the law of the land had regulated the qualifications of members to serve in parliament' and those qualifications were 'not occasional but fixed.'"

Against this historical background, we viewed the Convention debates as manifesting the Framers' intent that the qualifications in the Constitution be fixed and exclusive. We found particularly revealing the debate concerning a proposal made by the Committee of Detail that would have given Congress the power to add property qualifications. James Madison argued that such a power would vest "'an improper & dangerous power in the Legislature,'" by which the Legislature "'can by degrees subvert the Constitution.'" . . .

We also recognized in *Powell* that the post-Convention ratification debates confirmed that the Framers understood the qualifications in the Constitution to be fixed and unalterable by Congress. . . . Moreover, we reviewed the debates at the state conventions and found that they "also demonstrate the Framers' understanding that the qualifications for members of Congress had been fixed in the Constitution."

The exercise by Congress of its power to judge the qualifications of its Members further confirmed this understanding. We concluded that, during the first 100 years of its existence, "Congress strictly limited its power to judge the qualifications of its members to those enumerated in the Constitution."

As this elaborate summary reveals, our historical analysis in *Powell* was both detailed and persuasive. We thus conclude now, as we did in *Powell*, that history shows that, with respect to Congress, the Framers intended the Constitution to establish fixed qualifications. . . .

Our reaffirmation of *Powell*, does not necessarily resolve the specific questions presented in these cases. For petitioners argue that whatever the constitutionality of additional qualifications for membership imposed by Congress, the historical and textual materials discussed in *Powell* do not support the conclusion that the Constitution prohibits additional qualifications imposed by States. In the absence of such a constitutional prohibition, petitioners argue, the Tenth Amendment and the principle of reserved powers require that States be allowed to add such qualifications. . . .

Contrary to petitioners' assertions, the power to add qualifications is not part of the original powers of sovereignty that the Tenth Amendment reserved to the States. Petitioners' Tenth Amendment argument misconceives the nature of the right at issue because that Amendment could only "reserve" that which existed before. As Justice STORY recognized, "the states can exercise no powers whatsoever, which exclusively spring out of the existence of the national government, which the constitution does not delegate to them. . . . No state can say, that it has reserved, what it never possessed." Justice STORY's position thus echoes that of Chief Justice MARSHALL in

McCulloch v. Maryland, 17 U.S. 316 (1819). In *McCulloch*, the Court rejected the argument that the Constitution's silence on the subject of state power to tax corporations chartered by Congress implies that the States have "reserved" power to tax such federal instrumentalities. . . .

With respect to setting qualifications for service in Congress, no such right existed before the Constitution was ratified. The contrary argument overlooks the revolutionary character of the government that the Framers conceived. Prior to the adoption of the Constitution, the States had joined together under the Articles of Confederation. In that system, "the States retained most of their sovereignty, like independent nations bound together only by treaties." *Wesberry v. Sanders*, 376 U.S. 1 (1964). After the Constitutional Convention convened, the Framers were presented with, and eventually adopted a variation of, "a plan not merely to amend the Articles of Confederation but to create an entirely new National Government with a National Executive, National Judiciary, and a National Legislature." In adopting that plan, the Framers envisioned a uniform national system, rejecting the notion that the Nation was a collection of States, and instead creating a direct link between the National Government and the people of the United States. In that National Government, representatives owe primary allegiance not to the people of a State, but to the people of the Nation. . . .

Two other sections of the Constitution further support our view of the Framers' vision. First, consistent with STORY's view, the Constitution provides that the salaries of representatives should "be ascertained by Law, and paid out of the Treasury of the United States," Art. I, Sec. 6, rather than by individual States. The salary provisions reflect the view that representatives owe their allegiance to the people, and not to States. Second, the provisions governing elections reveal the Framers' understanding that powers over the election of federal officers had to be delegated to, rather than reserved by, the States. It is surely no coincidence that the context of federal elections provides one of the few areas in which the Constitution expressly requires action by the States, namely that "the Times, Places and Manner of holding Elections for Senators and Representatives, shall be prescribed in each State by the legislature thereof." This duty parallels the duty under Article II that "Each State shall appoint, in such Manner as the Legislature thereof may direct, a Number of Electors." Art. II, Sec. 1, cl. 2. These Clauses are express delegations of power to the States to act with respect to federal elections.

This conclusion is consistent with our previous recognition that, in certain limited contexts, the power to regulate the incidents of the federal system is not a reserved power of the States, but rather is delegated by the Constitution. . . .

We find further evidence of the Framers' intent in Art. 1, Sec. 5, cl. 1, which provides: "Each House shall be the Judge of the Elections, Returns and Qualifications of its own Members." That Art. I, Sec. 5 vests a federal tribunal with ultimate authority to judge a Member's qualifications is fully consistent with the understanding that those qualifications are fixed in the Federal Constitution, but not with the understanding that they can be altered by the States. If the States had the right to prescribe additional qualifications—such as property, educational, or professional qualifications—for their own representatives, state law would provide the standard for judging a Member's eligibility. As we concluded in *Murdock v. Memphis*, 87 U.S. 590

(1875), federal questions are generally answered finally by federal tribunals because rights which depend on federal law "should be the same everywhere" and "their construction should be uniform." . . . The Constitution's provision for each House to be the judge of its own qualifications thus provides further evidence that the Framers believed that the primary source of those qualifications would be federal law. . . .

Our conclusion that States lack the power to impose qualifications vindicates the same "fundamental principle of our representative democracy" that we recognized in *Powell*, namely that "the people should choose whom they please to govern them." As we noted earlier, the *Powell* Court recognized that an egalitarian ideal—that election to the National Legislature should be open to all people of merit—provided a critical foundation for the Constitutional structure. . . .

Similarly, we believe that state-imposed qualifications, as much as congressionally imposed qualifications, would undermine the second critical idea recognized in *Powell*: that an aspect of sovereignty is the right of the people to vote for whom they wish. Again, the source of the qualification is of little moment in assessing the qualification's restrictive impact.

Finally, state-imposed restrictions, unlike the congressionally imposed restrictions at issue in *Powell*, violate a third idea central to this basic principle: that the right to choose representatives belongs not to the States, but to the people. From the start, the Framers recognized that the "great and radical vice" of the Articles of Confederation was "the principle of LEGISLATION for STATES or GOVERNMENTS, in their CORPORATE or COLLECTIVE CAPACITIES, and as contradistinguished from the INDIVIDUALS of whom they consist." *The Federalist* No. 15 (Hamilton). Thus the Framers, in perhaps their most important contribution, conceived of a Federal Government directly responsible to the people, possessed of direct power over the people, and chosen directly, not by States, but by the people. The Framers implemented this ideal most clearly in the provision, extant from the beginning of the Republic, that calls for the Members of the House of Representatives to be "chosen every second Year by the People of the several States." Art. I, Sec. 2, cl. 1. Following the adoption of the 17th Amendment in 1913, this ideal was extended to elections for the Senate. The Congress of the United States, therefore, is not a confederation of nations in which separate sovereigns are represented by appointed delegates, but is instead a body composed of representatives of the people. . . .

Petitioners argue that, even if States may not add qualifications, Amendment 73 is constitutional because it is not such a qualification, and because Amendment 73 is a permissible exercise of state power to regulate the "Times, Places and Manner of Holding Elections." We reject these contentions.

Unlike Sections 1 and 2 of Amendment 73, which create absolute bars to service for long-term incumbents running for state office, Section 3 merely provides that certain Senators and Representatives shall not be certified as candidates and shall not have their names appear on the ballot. They may run as write-in candidates and, if elected, they may serve. Petitioners contend that only a legal bar to service creates an impermissible qualification, and that Amendment 73 is therefore consistent with the Constitution. . . .

The merits of term limits, or "rotation," have been the subject of debate since the formation of our Constitution, when the Framers unanimously rejected a proposal to add such limits to the Constitution. The cogent arguments on both sides of the question that were articulated during the process of ratification largely retain their force today. Over half the States have adopted measures that impose such limits on some offices either directly or indirectly, and the Nation as a whole, notably by constitutional amendment, has imposed a limit on the number of terms that the President may serve. Term limits, like any other qualification for office, unquestionably restrict the ability of voters to vote for whom they wish. On the other hand, such limits may provide for the infusion of fresh ideas and new perspectives, and may decrease the likelihood that representatives will lose touch with their constituents. It is not our province to resolve this longstanding debate.

We are, however, firmly convinced that allowing the several States to adopt term limits for congressional service would effect a fundamental change in the constitutional framework. Any such change must come not by legislation adopted either by Congress or by an individual State, but rather—as have other important changes in the electoral process—through the Amendment procedures set forth in Article V. The Framers decided that the qualifications for service in the Congress of the United States be fixed in the Constitution and be uniform throughout the Nation. That decision reflects the Framers' understanding that Members of Congress are chosen by separate constituencies, but that they become, when elected, servants of the people of the United States. They are not merely delegates appointed by separate, sovereign States; they occupy offices that are integral and essential components of a single National Government. In the absence of a properly passed constitutional amendment, allowing individual States to craft their own qualifications for Congress would thus erode the structure envisioned by the Framers, a structure that was designed, in the words of the Preamble to our Constitution, to form a "more perfect Union."

The judgment is affirmed.

☐ *Justice THOMAS, with whom THE CHIEF JUSTICE, Justice O'CONNOR, and Justice SCALIA join, dissenting.*

I dissent. Nothing in the Constitution deprives the people of each State of the power to prescribe eligibility requirements for the candidates who seek to represent them in Congress. The Constitution is simply silent on this question. And where the Constitution is silent, it raises no bar to action by the States or the people. . . .

Our system of government rests on one overriding principle: all power stems from the consent of the people. To phrase the principle in this way, however, is to be imprecise about something important to the notion of "reserved" powers. The ultimate source of the Constitution's authority is the consent of the people of each individual State, not the consent of the undifferentiated people of the Nation as a whole.

The ratification procedure erected by Article VII makes this point clear. The Constitution took effect once it had been ratified by the people gathered in convention in nine different States. But the Constitution went into effect only "between the States so ratifying the same," Art. VII; it did not bind the people of North Carolina until they had accepted it.

When they adopted the Federal Constitution, of course, the people of each State surrendered some of their authority to the United States (and hence to entities accountable to the people of other States as well as to themselves). They affirmatively deprived their States of certain powers, see, e.g., Art. I, Sec. 10, and they affirmatively conferred certain powers upon the Federal Government, see, e.g., Art. I, Sec. 8. Because the people of the several States are the only true source of power, however, the Federal Government enjoys no authority beyond what the Constitution confers: the Federal Government's powers are limited and enumerated. . . .

In each State, the remainder of the people's powers—"the powers not delegated to the United States by the Constitution, nor prohibited by it to the States," Amdt. 10—are either delegated to the state government or retained by the people. The Federal Constitution does not specify which of these two possibilities obtains; it is up to the various state constitutions to declare which powers the people of each State have delegated to their state government. As far as the Federal Constitution is concerned, then, the States can exercise all powers that the Constitution does not withhold from them. The Federal Government and the States thus face different default rules: where the Constitution is silent about the exercise of a particular power—that is, where the Constitution does not speak either expressly or by necessary implication—the Federal Government lacks that power and the States enjoy it.

These basic principles are enshrined in the Tenth Amendment, which declares that all powers neither delegated to the Federal Government nor prohibited to the States "are reserved to the States respectively, or to the people." With this careful last phrase, the Amendment avoids taking any position on the division of power between the state governments and the people of the States: it is up to the people of each State to determine which "reserved" powers their state government may exercise. But the Amendment does make clear that powers reside at the state level except where the Constitution removes them from that level. All powers that the Constitution neither delegates to the Federal Government nor prohibits to the States are controlled by the people of each State. . . .

The majority is therefore quite wrong to conclude that the people of the States cannot authorize their state governments to exercise any powers that were unknown to the States when the Federal Constitution was drafted. Indeed, the majority's position frustrates the apparent purpose of the Amendment's final phrase. The Amendment does not preempt any limitations on state power found in the state constitutions, as it might have done if it simply had said that the powers not delegated to the Federal Government are reserved to the States. But the Amendment also does not prevent the people of the States from amending their state constitutions to remove limitations that were in effect when the Federal Constitution and the Bill of Rights were ratified. . . .

The majority settles on "the Qualifications Clauses" as the constitutional provisions that Amendment 73 violates. Because I do not read those provisions to impose any unstated prohibitions on the States, it is unnecessary for me to decide whether the majority is correct to identify Arkansas' ballot-access restriction with laws fixing true term limits or otherwise prescribing "qualifications" for congressional office. . . . [T]he Qualifications Clauses are merely straightforward recitations of the minimum eligibility requirements that the Framers thought it essential for every Member of Congress to meet. They restrict state power only in that they prevent the States from abolishing all eligibility requirements for membership in Congress.

Because the text of the Qualifications Clauses does not support its position, the majority turns instead to its vision of the democratic principles that animated the Framers. But the majority's analysis goes to a question that is not before us: whether Congress has the power to prescribe qualifications for its own members. . . . [T]he democratic principles that contributed to the Framers' decision to withhold this power from Congress do not prove that the Framers also deprived the people of the States of their reserved authority to set eligibility requirements for their own representatives. . . .

To the extent that they bear on this case, the records of the Philadelphia Convention affirmatively support my unwillingness to find hidden meaning in the Qualifications Clauses, while the surviving records from the ratification debates help neither side. As for the postratification period, five States supplemented the constitutional disqualifications in their very first election laws. The historical evidence thus refutes any notion that the Qualifications Clauses were generally understood to be exclusive. Yet the majority must establish just such an understanding in order to justify its position that the Clauses impose unstated prohibitions on the States and the people. In my view, the historical evidence is simply inadequate to warrant the majority's conclusion that the Qualifications Clauses mean anything more than what they say. . . .

[T]oday's decision reads the Qualifications Clauses to impose substantial implicit prohibitions on the States and the people of the States. I would not draw such an expansive negative inference from the fact that the Constitution requires Members of Congress to be a certain age, to be inhabitants of the States that they represent, and to have been United States citizens for a specified period. Rather, I would read the Qualifications Clauses to do no more than what they say. I respectfully dissent.

Gravel v. United States

408 U.S. 606, 92 S.CT. 2614 (1972)

On the morning of June 29, 1971, the Supreme Court ruled, in *New York Times Co. v. United States*, 403 U.S. 713 (1971) (see excerpt in Vol. 1, Ch. 4), that the Nixon administration could not enjoin the publication of a stolen, top-secret history of America's involvement in the Vietnam War, known as the "Pentagon Papers." That evening, to give the "Pentagon Papers" wider circulation, Alaska's Senator Mike Gravel convened his Subcommittee on Public Buildings and Grounds. He read summaries of the papers and later entered all forty-seven volumes of the study into public record as an exhibit. In addition, he arranged to have the papers published (without profit for himself) by a private commercial publisher, the Beacon Press. Subsequently, a federal grand jury investigating the release of the "Pentagon Papers" subpoenaed Gravel's aide, Leonard Rodberg. Gravel and Rodberg moved to quash the subpoena based on the privileges afforded by the speech or debate clause. A court of appeals issued an order barring the grand jury's inquiry into Gravel's and Rodberg's motives and actions in entering the "Pentagon Papers" into public record and arranging for their publication by a private publisher. But it held that the publisher was not exempt from the grand jury's inquiry. Both Gravel and the government appealed to the Supreme Court. Gravel claimed that his arrangements to have the papers privately published were protected by the speech or debate clause, while the government maintained that they and the activities of Gravel's aide were not shielded from the grand jury's investigation.

The Court's decision was five to four, and the majority's opinion announced by Justice Blackmun was written by Justice White. Dissents were by Justices Douglas, Brennan, joined by Justice Marshall, and Stewart.

☐ *Justice BLACKMUN delivers the opinion of the Court by Justice WHITE.*

Because the claim is that a Member's aide shares the Member's constitutional privilege, we consider first whether and to what extent Senator Gravel himself is exempt from process or inquiry by a grand jury investigating the commission of a crime. Our frame of reference is Art. I, Sec. 6, cl. 1, of the Constitution. The last sentence of the Clause provides Members of Congress with two distinct privileges. Except in cases of "Treason, Felony and Breach of the Peace," the Clause shields Members from arrest while attending or traveling to and from a session of their House. History reveals, and prior cases so hold, that this part of the Clause exempts Members from arrest in civil cases only. Nor does freedom from arrest confer immunity on a Member from service of process as a defendant in civil matters . . . or as a witness in a criminal case. It is, therefore, sufficiently plain that the constitutional freedom from arrest does not exempt Members of Congress from the operation of the ordinary criminal laws, even though imprisonment may prevent or interfere with the performance of their duties as Members. Indeed, implicit in the narrow scope of the privilege of freedom from arrest is, as Jefferson noted, the judgment that legislators ought not to stand above the law they create but ought generally to be bound by it as are ordinary persons.

In recognition, no doubt, of the force of this part of Sec. 6, Senator Gravel disvows any assertion of general immunity from the criminal law. But he points out that the last portion of Sec. 6 affords Members of Congress another vital privilege—they may not be questioned in any other place for any speech or debate in either House. The claim is not that while one part of Sec. 6 generally permits prosecutions for treason, felony, and breach of the peace, another part nevertheless broadly forbids them. Rather, his insistence is that the Speech or Debate Clause at the very least protects him from criminal or civil liability and from questioning elsewhere than in the Senate, with respect to the events occurring at the subcommittee hearing at which the Pentagon Papers were introduced into the public record. To us this claim is incontrovertible. The Speech or Debate Clause was designed to assure a co-equal branch of the government wide freedom of speech, debate, and deliberation without intimidation or threats from the Executive Branch. It thus protects Members against prosecutions that directly impinge upon or threaten the legislative process. We have no doubt that Senator Gravel may not be made to answer—either in terms of questions or in terms of defending himself from prosecution—for the events that occurred at the subcommittee meeting. Our decision is made easier by the fact that the United States appears to have abandoned whatever position it took to the contrary in the lower courts.

Even so, the United States strongly urges that because the Speech or Debate Clause confers a privilege only upon "Senators and Representatives," Rodberg himself has no valid claim to constitutional immunity from grand jury inquiry. In our view, both courts below correctly rejected this position. We agree with the Court of Appeals that for the purpose of construing the privilege a Member and his aide are to be "treated as one." . . . Both courts recognized what the Senate of the United States urgently presses here: that it is literally impossible, in view of the complexities of the modern legislative process, with Congress almost constantly in session and matters of legislative concern constantly proliferating, for Members of Congress to perform their legislative tasks without the help of aides and assistants; that the day-to-day work of such aides is so critical to the Members' performance that they must be treated as the latter's alter egos; and that if they are not so recognized, the central role of the Speech or Debate Clause—to prevent intimidation of legislators by the Executive and accountability before a possibly hostile judiciary will inevitably be diminished and frustrated.

It is true that the Clause itself mentions only "Senators and Representatives," but prior cases have plainly not taken a literalistic approach in applying the privilege. The Clause also speaks only of "Speech or Debate," but the Court's consistent approach has been that to confine the protection of the Speech or Debate Clause to words spoken in debate would be an unacceptably narrow view. Committee reports, resolutions, and the act of voting are equally covered. . . . Rather than giving the clause a cramped construction, the Court has sought to implement its fundamental purpose of freeing the legislator from executive and judicial oversight that realistically threatens to control his conduct as a legislator. We have little doubt that we are neither exceeding our judicial powers nor mistakenly construing the Constitution by holding that the Speech or Debate Clause applies not only to a Member but also to his aides insofar as the conduct of the latter would be a protected legislative act if performed by the Member himself. . . .

The United States fears the abuses that history reveals have occurred when legislators are invested with the power to relieve others from the operation of otherwise valid civil and criminal laws. But these abuses, it seems to us, are for the most part obviated if the privilege applicable to the aide is viewed, as it must be, as the privilege of the Senator, and invocable only by the Senator or by the aide on the Senator's behalf, and if in all events the privilege available to the aide is confined to those services that would be immune legislative conduct if performed by the Senator himself. This view places beyond the Speech or Debate Clause a variety of services characteristically performed by aides for Members of Congress, even though within the scope of their employment. It likewise provides no protection for criminal conduct threatening the security of the person or property of others, whether performed at the direction of the Senator in preparation for or in execution of a legislative act or done without his knowledge or direction. Neither does it immunize Senator or aide from testifying at trials or grand jury proceedings involving third-party crimes where the questions do not require testimony about or impugn a legislative act. Thus our refusal to distinguish between Senator and aide in applying the Speech or Debate Clause does not mean that Rodberg is for all purposes exempt from grand jury questioning.

We are convinced also that the Court of Appeals correctly determined that Senator Gravel's alleged arrangement with Beacon Press to publish the Pentagon Papers was not protected speech or debate within the meaning of Art. I, Sec. 6, cl. 1, of the Constitution. . . . Legislative acts are not all-encompassing. The heart of the Clause is speech or debate in either House. Insofar as the Clause is construed to reach other matters, they must be an integral part of the deliberative and communicative processes by which Members participate in committee and House proceedings with respect to the consideration and passage or rejection of proposed legislation or with respect to other matters which the Constitution places within the jurisdiction of either House. As the Court of Appeals put it, the courts have extended the privilege to matters beyond pure speech or debate in either House, but "only when necessary to prevent indirect impairment of such deliberations." . . .

Here, private publication by Senator Gravel through the cooperation of Beacon Press was in no way essential to the deliberations of the Senate; nor does questioning as to private publication threaten the integrity or independence of the Senate by impermissibly exposing its deliberations to executive influence. The Senator had conducted his hearings; the record and any report that was forthcoming were available both to his committee and the Senate. Insofar as we are advised, neither Congress nor the full committee ordered or authorized the publication. We cannot but conclude that the Senator's arrangements with Beacon Press were not part and parcel of the legislative process. . . .

The Speech or Debate Clause recognizes speech, voting, and other legislative acts as exempt from liability that might otherwise attach, it does not privilege either Senator or aide to violate an otherwise valid criminal law in preparing for or implementing legislative acts. If republication of these classified papers would be a crime under an Act of Congress, it would not be entitled to immunity under the Speech or Debate Clause. It also appears that the grand jury was pursuing this very subject in the normal course of a valid investigation. The Speech or Debate Clause does not in our view extend immunity to Rodberg, as a Senator's aide, from testifying before the grand jury about the arrangement between Senator Gravel and Beacon Press or about his own participation, if any, in the alleged transaction, so long as legislative acts of the Senator are not impugned.

Similar considerations lead us to disagree with the Court of Appeals insofar as it fashioned, tentatively at least, a nonconstitutional testimonial privilege protecting Rodberg from any questioning by the grand jury concerning the matter of republication of the Pentagon Papers. This privilege, thought to be similar to that protecting executive officials from liability for libel was considered advisable "[t]o the extent that a congressman has responsibility to inform his constituents. . . ." But we cannot carry a judicially fashioned privilege so far as to immunize criminal conduct proscribed by an Act of Congress or to frustrate the grand jury's inquiry into whether publication of these classified documents violated a federal criminal statute. The so-called executive privilege has never been applied to shield executive officers from prosecution for crime, the Court of Appeals was quite sure that third parties were neither immune from liability nor from testifying about the republication matter, and we perceive no basis for conferring a testimonial privilege on Rodberg as the Court of Appeals seemed to do. . . .

Because the Speech or Debate Clause privilege applies both to Senator and aide, it appears to us that [the lower court's] order, alone, would afford ample protection for the privilege if it forbade questioning any witness, including Rodberg: (1) concerning the Senator's conduct, or the conduct of his aides, at the June 29, 1971, meeting of the subcommittee; (2) concerning the motives and purposes behind the Senator's conduct, or that of his aides, at that meeting; (3) concerning communications between the Senator and his aides during the term of their employment and related to said meeting or any other legislative act of the Senator; (4) except as it proves relevant to investigating possible third-party crime, concerning any act, in itself not criminal, performed by the Senator, or by his aides in the course of their employment, in preparation for the subcommittee hearing. We leave the final form of such an order to the Court of Appeals in the first instance, or, if that court prefers, to the District Court.

The judgment of the Court of Appeals is vacated and the cases are remanded to that court for further proceedings consistent with this opinion.

So ordered.

☐ *Justice BRENNAN, with whom Justice DOUGLAS and Justice MARSHALL join, dissenting.*

In holding that Senator Gravel's alleged arrangement with Beacon Press to publish the Pentagon Papers is not shielded from extra-senatorial inquiry by the Speech or Debate Clause, the Court adopts what for me is a far too narrow view of the legislative function. The Court seems to assume that words spoken in debate or written in congressional reports are protected by the Clause, so that if Senator Gravel had recited part of the Pentagon Papers on the Senate floor or copied them into a Senate report, those acts could not be questioned "in any other Place." Yet because he sought a wider audience, to publicize information deemed relevant to matters pending before his own committee, the Senator suddenly loses his immunity and is exposed to grand jury investigation and possible prosecution for the republication. The explanation for this anomalous result is the Court's belief that "Speech or Debate" encompasses only acts necessary to the internal deliberations of Congress concerning proposed legislation. "Here," according to the Court, "private publication by Senator Gravel through the cooperation of Beacon Press was in no way essential to the deliberations of the Senate." Therefore, "the Senator's arrangements with Beacon Press were not part and parcel of the legislative process."

Thus, the Court excludes from the sphere of protected legislative activity a function that I had supposed lay at the heart of our democratic system. I speak, of course, of the legislator's duty to inform the public about matters affecting the administration of government. That this "informing function" falls into the class of things "generally done in a session of the House by one of its members in relation to the business before it." . . .

Unlike the Court, . . . I think that the activities of Congressmen in communicating with the public are legislative acts protected by the Speech or Debate Clause. I agree with the Court that not every task performed by a legislator is privileged; intervention before Executive departments is one that is not. But the informing function carries a far more persuasive claim to the protections of the Clause. It has been recognized by this Court as something "generally done" by Congressmen, the Congress itself has established special concessions designed to lower the cost of such communication, and, most important, the function furthers several well-recognized goals of representative government. To say in the face of these facts that the informing function is not privileged merely because it is not necessary to the internal deliberations of Congress is to give the Speech or Debate Clause an artificial and narrow reading unsupported by reason. . . .

Hutchinson v. Proxmire

443 U.S. 111, 99 S.CT. 2675 (1979)

In March 1975, Senator William Proxmire initiated the "Golden Fleece of the Month" award to publicize wasteful government spending. The second award went to several government agencies for funding research on animal aggression by Dr. Ronald Hutchinson. Proxmire announced the award on a floor of the Senate in a speech (printed in part in the opinion below) and in press releases and newsletters to constituents. His legislative assistant also discussed the award and Hutchinson's study with the sponsoring agencies. Funding for the study was eventually withdrawn. And Hutchinson filed a suit in federal district court, contending that erroneous statements made by Proxmire and his aide defamed him and resulted in a loss of income. The district judge ruled that Proxmire's statements on the Senate floor and in press releases were covered by the speech or debate clause, but not those made in newsletters and television interviews. However, the court also held that

Hutchinson was a "public figure" and could collect damages only if Proxmire's statements were made with "actual malice"—with the knowing or reckless disregard of their truth or falsity. Because the judge found no evidence of actual malice, Hutchinson was not awarded damages. After an appellate court affirmed that ruling, Hutchinson appealed to the Supreme Court, which granted his petition for *certiorari*.

The Court's decision was seven to two, and the majority's opinion was announced by Chief Justice Burger. A separate opinion, in part concurring and dissenting, was delivered by Justice Stewart. Dissent was by Justice Brennan.

    ☐ *Chief Justice BURGER delivers the opinion of the Court.*

Ronald Hutchinson, a research behavioral scientist, sued respondents, William Proxmire, a United States Senator, and his legislative assistant, Morton Schwartz, for defamation arising out of Proxmire's giving what he called his "Golden Fleece" award. The "award" went to federal agencies that had sponsored Hutchinson's research. Hutchinson alleged that in making the award and publicizing it nationwide, respondents had libeled him, damaging him in his professional and academic standing, and had interfered with his contractual relations. The District Court granted summary judgment for respondents and the Court of Appeals affirmed. . . .

We reverse and remand to the Court of Appeals for further proceedings consistent with this opinion.

Respondent Proxmire is a United States Senator from Wisconsin. In March 1975, he initiated the "Golden Fleece of the Month Award" to publicize what he perceived to be the most egregious examples of wasteful governmental spending. The second such award, in April 1975, went to the National Science Foundation, the National Aeronautics and Space Administration, and the Office of Naval Research, for spending almost half a million dollars during the preceding seven years to fund Hutchinson's research. . . .

The bulk of Hutchinson's research was devoted to the study of emotional behavior. In particular, he sought an objective measure of aggression, concentrating upon the behavior patterns of certain animals, such as the clenching of jaws when they were exposed to various aggravating stressful stimuli. The National Aeronautics and Space Agency and the Navy were interested in the potential of this research for resolving problems associated with confining humans in close quarters for extended periods of time in space and undersea exploration. . . .

In the speech Proxmire described the federal grants for Hutchinson's research, concluding with the following comment:

> The funding of this nonsense makes me almost angry enough to scream and kick or even clench my jaw. It seems to me it is outrageous.
>
> Dr. Hutchinson's studies should make the taxpayers as well as his monkeys grind their teeth. In fact, the good doctor has made a fortune from his monkeys and in the process made a monkey out of the American taxpayer.

It is time for the Federal Government to get out of this "monkey business." In view of the transparent worthlessness of Hutchinson's study of jaw-grinding and biting by angry or hard-drinking monkeys, it is time we put a stop to the bite Hutchinson and the bureaucrats who fund him have been taking of the taxpayer.

In May 1975, Proxmire referred to his Golden Fleece Awards in a newsletter sent to about 100,000 people whose names were on a mailing list that included constituents in Wisconsin as well as persons in other states. The newsletter repeated the essence of the speech and the press release. Later in 1975, Proxmire appeared on a television interview program where he referred to Hutchinson's research, though he did not mention Hutchinson by name.

The Speech or Debate Clause has been directly passed on by this Court relatively few times in 190 years. . . . Literal reading of the Clause would, of course, confine its protection narrowly to a "Speech or Debate *in* either House." But the Court has given the Clause a practical rather than a strictly literal reading which would limit the protection to utterances made within the four walls of either Chamber. Thus, we have held that committee hearings are protected, even if held outside the Chambers; committee reports are also protected. . . .

Nearly a century ago, in *Kilbourn v. Thompson*, 103 U.S. 168 (1881), this Court held that the Clause extended "to things generally done *in a session* of the House by one of its members *in relation to the business before it.*" . . .

Whatever imprecision there may be in the term "legislative activities," it is clear that nothing in history or in the explicit language of the Clause suggests any intention to create an absolute privilege from liability or suit for defamatory statements made outside the Chamber. . . .

In *Gravel v. United States*, 408 U.S. 606 (1972) we recognized that the doctrine denying immunity for republication had been accepted in the United States. . . .

We reach a similar conclusion here. A speech by Proxmire in the Senate would be wholly immune and would be available to other Members of Congress and the public in the Congressional Record. But neither the newsletters nor the press release was "essential to the deliberations of the Senate" and neither was part of the deliberative process. . . .

Voting and preparing committee reports are the individual and collective expressions of opinion within the legislative process. As such, they are protected by the Speech or Debate Clause. Newsletters and press releases, by contrast, are primarily means of informing those outside the legislative forum; they represent the views and will of a single Member. It does not disparage either their value or their importance to hold that they are not entitled to the protection of the Speech or Debate Clause.

☐ *Justice BRENNAN, dissenting.*

I disagree with the Court's conclusion that Senator Proxmire's newsletters and press releases fall outside the protection of the speech or debate immunity. In my view, public criticism by legislators of unnecessary governmental expenditures, whatever its form, is a legislative act shielded by the Speech or Debate Clause.

B | Investigatory, Contempt, and Impeachment Powers

A congressional power to investigate is not expressly granted, but instead an implied power incident to lawmaking. Congress, as the Court recognized, "cannot legislate wisely or effectively in the absence of information respecting the conditions which the legislation is intended to affect or change."[1]

The power was asserted by the House in its first major investigation in 1792. Following an Indian defeat of an expedition led by Major General St. Clair, a House committee requested President George Washington to release all papers and records related to the incident. The president's cabinet considered the request and decided to turn over the materials, but also agreed that

> the Executive ought to communicate such papers as the public good would permit, and ought to refuse those, the disclosure of which would injure the public . . . [In addition, the Cabinet concluded,] that neither the committee nor House had a right to call on the Head of a Department, who and whose papers were under the President alone; but that the committee should instruct their chairman to move the House to address the President.[2]

Although the materials in the St. Clair episode were given to Congress, the basis was set for presidential claims of "executive privilege" when the president withheld documents and for confrontations between the executive branch and Congress over its investigatory power.

Congress's investigatory power is backed by the power to find in contempt individuals who disrupt its proceedings or refuse to testify before its committees and to have them arrested and imprisoned.[3] Unlike the investigative and contempt powers of the English Parliament, however, congressional exercise of these powers remains subject to judicial review. In *Anderson v. Dunn*, 6 Wheat. (19 U.S.) 204 (1821), the Marshall Court expressed concerns about the procedural safeguards afforded individuals charged with contempt, when holding that they could not be imprisoned beyond the session of the House finding them in contempt. As a result of these concerns and the irregularity of contempt proceedings, Congress passed legislation in 1857 requiring individuals summoned by either House to appear as witnesses. If they refused to appear or to answer "pertinent questions," a committee could direct the sergeant at arms to hold them until they testified. Alternatively, the committee could punish them by finding them in contempt and directing a

United States attorney to seek their indictment by a federal grand jury, and thereupon prosecute them in a federal district court.[4]

Initially, the Court took a narrow view of congressional investigatory and contempt powers in *Kilbourn v. Thompson*, 103 U.S. 168 (1881). Hallet Kilbourn refused to answer certain questions and to deliver to a House committee private papers bearing on a real estate deal. He was found in contempt and imprisoned for forty-five days. On appeal, the Court concluded that the House was overzealous in its inquiry and intruded into a matter already pending in the courts. In doing so, the Court announced three principles limiting congressional investigations: (1) they may not intrude in areas reserved for the executive branch or the courts, (2) they are limited to matters on which Congress may legitimately legislate, and (3) the House resolutions authorizing such investigations must indicate the congressional intent in legislating on the subject under investigation.

The Court later qualified *Kilbourn* and adopted a broader view of Congress's powers in a case arising from an investigation of Attorney General Harry M. Daugherty and other Department of Justice officials in connection with the Teapot Dome scandal, which involved graft and corruption in the administration of President Warren G. Harding. Mally S. Daugherty, the brother of the attorney general, refused to appear before and to bring records subpoenaed by a Senate committee. In *McGrain v. Daugherty*, 273 U.S. 135 (1927), the Court unanimously affirmed Congress's power to compel a private individual to testify. Although noting that Congress has no "general power to inquire into private matters," the Court ruled that it may investigate legitimate subjects of potential legislation, or which have a "proper legislative purpose," and require testimony pertinent to that inquiry.[5]

After affirming Congress's broad investigatory powers, the Court then confronted claims that individuals' civil liberties were being denied by congressional inquiries. This was especially so during the early Cold War years in the 1940s and 1950s, when fear of Communism was at its peak. At that time the House Un-American Activities Committee (HUAC) (finally abolished in 1974) and the Senate Permanent Investigations Subcommittee, chaired by Senator Joseph R. McCarthy, subpoenaed hundreds of individuals in and out of government to testify about alleged Communist activities of their own and their acquaintances. In response to challenges to these investigations, the Court ruled that witnesses may refuse to answer vague or irrelevant questions and that the committees' inquiries may not go beyond its authorizing resolutions.[6] In addition, the Warren Court, in 1955, reversed the convictions of individuals who had refused to testify about their alleged membership in the Communist Party on the grounds that that would violate their Fifth Amendment privilege against self-incrimination.[7]

The problem for witnesses claiming the Fifth Amendment when refusing to testify before the HUAC was that they could not "take the Fifth" selectively. If they took it for one, they took it for all questions. Those who did were then open to any form of questioning which might imply, if not prove, their support of Communist activities. As a result, many witnesses were often branded, in the words of Senator McCarthy, "Fifth Amendment Communists." They could forgo their Fifth Amendment rights by testifying in exchange for a congressional grant of immunity (which guaranteed that their testimony would not be used against them in criminal trial).[8] Still, whether they claimed the Fifth Amendment in refusing to testify or waived that right and testified, they frequently suffered damage to their reputations and lost their jobs due to the adverse publicity.

The First Amendment provides another possible defense against congressional inquiries. Claims that the HUAC abridged witnesses' freedoms of speech and association and aimed simply at punishing them for their political views, nonetheless, had little success until *Watkins v. United States* (1957) (see excerpt below). There Chief Justice Warren acknowledged the relevancy of the First Amendment, warning that "there is no congressional power to expose for the sake of exposure." But in reversing Watkins's conviction for contempt for refusing to answer certain questions, Warren ultimately rested the Court's decision on the due process clause of the Fifth Amendment.

Two years later, a First Amendment challenge to the House's investigation of the Communist Party was squarely faced and rejected. In *Barenblatt v. United States* (1959) (see excerpt below), the Court divided five to four in finding that First Amendment interests were overridden by those of Congress in ensuring society's self-preservation. This ruling provoked a sharp dissent from Justice Black in one of his most-notable opinions.

The Court remained divided five to four in finding congressional interests in investigations to outweigh First Amendment claims until Justices Frankfurter and Whittaker retired in 1962.[9] They were replaced by Democratic president John F. Kennedy's appointees, Justices Byron White and Arthur Goldberg, and the latter cast the pivotal vote in *Gibson v. Florida Legislative Investigation Committee* (1963) (see excerpt below), upholding the First Amendment in a case involving state rather than congressional investigations. Since *Gibson* the Court has continued to acknowledge First Amendment limitations on the scope of legislative investigations.[10]

The Court has not yet squarely dealt with a claim of executive privilege in withholding government documents from a congressional investigatory committee. However, in *Barenblatt* the Court noted that

Congress "cannot inquire into matters which are within the exclusive province of one of the other branches of Government." Arguably, this would include materials bearing on a treaty being negotiated, for example, or confidential White House communications, and "sensitive" investigatory files. There have been a number of clashes between Congress and the executive branch over the withholding of information from congressional committees, but thus far compromises have been achieved before litigation has reached the Court.

In *Walter L. Nixon v. United States*, 506 U.S. 224 (1993) (excerpted below), the Rehnquist Court heard a challenge to the Senate's procedure for impeachments. The Constitution gives the Senate the sole power to "try all impeachments," and throughout the nineteenth century the full Senate in effect functioned like a jury in hearing the evidence presented in impeachment trials conducted on the floor of the Senate. In 1935 the Senate adopted a new procedure, although not used until the mid-1980s, under which a committee of twelve senators conducts an impeachment hearing and then presents a report to the full Senate, which votes on each article of impeachment. Former federal judge Walter Nixon challenged the constitutionality of the Senate's committee procedure, but in his opinion for the Court Chief Justice Rehnquist held that Nixon presented a nonjusticiable political question and that the Senate's procedure was constitutional. By contrast, concurring Justices White and Blackmun found no barrier to judicial review, while also agreeing that the impeachment committee procedure did not violate the Constitution.

NOTES

1. *McGrain v. Daugherty*, 273 U.S. 135 (1927).

2. Thomas Jefferson, *The Writings of Thomas Jefferson*, Vol. 1 (Washington, DC: Memorial Edition, 1903), 303–305.

3. *Groppi v. Leslie*, 404 U.S. 496 (1972), upheld the use of contempt powers against those disrupting legislative proceedings.

4. This procedure for contempt proceedings was upheld in *In re Chapman*, 166 U.S. 661 (1897). In 1978, Congress also provided that if a witness refuses to comply with a Senate subpoena, the Senate may request a court order requiring immediate compliance, subject to its imposing the penalty of civil contempt for a witness's continued refusal to testify.

5. See also *Sinclair v. United States*, 279 U.S. 263 (1929). Note, however, that under *Eastland v. United States Servicemens' Fund* (1975) (excerpted in this chapter), the Court does not require a "predictable end result" of a "valid legislative inquiry" and that congressional investigations may lead up "blind alleys."

6. *United States v. Rumely*, 345 U.S. 41 (1953); *Deutch v. United States*, 367 U.S. 456 (1961); and *Gojack v. United States*, 384 U.S. 702 (1966).

7. See *Quinn v. United States*, 349 U.S. 155 (1955); and *Emspak v. United States*, 349 U.S. 190 (1955).

8. *Ullmann v. United States*, 350 U.S. 422 (1956), upheld the Immunity Act of 1954, permitting congressional committees to grant immunity for witnesses who waived their Fifth Amendment rights and testified. See also *Kastigar v. United States*, 406 U.S. 441 (1972).

9. See *Wilkinson v. United States*, 365 U.S. 399 (1961); and *Braden v. United States*, 365 U.S. 431 (1961).

10. See, for example, *DeGregory v. Attorney General of New Hampshire*, 383 U.S. 825 (1966). But see again the Burger Court's ruling in *Eastland v. United States Servicemens' Fund* (1975) (in this chapter) on how congressional committees are shielded by the speech or debate clause.

SELECTED BIBLIOGRAPHY

Bushnell, Eleanore. *Crimes, Follies, and Misfortunes: The Federal Impeachment Trials.* Champaign: University of Illinois Press, 1992.

Goodman, Walter. *The Committee: The Extraordinary Career of the House Committee on Un-American Activities.* New York: Farrar, Straus & Giroux, 1968.

Hamilton, James. *The Power to Probe: A Study of Congressional Investigations.* New York: Random House, 1976.

McGeary, M. Nelson. *The Development of Congressional Investigative Power.* New York: Columbia University Press, 1940.

Pritchett, C. Herman. *Congress versus the Supreme Court: 1957–1960.* Minneapolis: University of Minnesota Press, 1961.

Rehnquist, William H. *Grand Inquests: The Historic Impeachments of Justice Samuel Chase and President Andrew Johnson.* New York: Morrow, 1992.

Volcansek, Mary. *None Called for Justice: Judicial Impeachment.* Champaign: University of Illinois Press, 1993.

Watkins v. United States
354 U.S. 178, 77 S.Ct. 1173 (1957)

John Watkins was one of 129 people found in contempt of Congress for refusing to answer questions about the Communist Party and other "subversive organizations," when appearing before the House Un-American Activities Committee between 1950 and 1965. In 1954, as a labor organizer for the United Automobile Workers, he was summoned and appeared before the subcommittee. Although testifying about his activities and those of others he believed still to be members of the Communist Party, Watkins declined to answer questions about the activities of those who were no longer members. Because these questions did not bear on his activities, he could not invoke his Fifth Amendment privilege against self-incrimination when refusing to testify. Instead, Watkins contended that these questions were irrelevant and not pertinent to the committee's investigation. The House voted him in contempt and Watkins was convicted in a federal district court. After a court of appeals upheld his conviction, Watkins appealed to the Supreme Court.

The Court's decision was six to one, and the majority's opinion was announced by Chief Justice Warren, with Justices Burton and Whittaker not participating. A concurring opinion was delivered by Justice Frankfurter. Justice Clark dissented.

☐ *Chief Justice WARREN delivers the opinion of the Court.*

This is a review by *certiorari* of a conviction for "contempt of Congress." The misdemeanor is alleged to have been committed during a hearing before a congressional investigating committee. It is not the case of a truculent or contumacious witness who refuses to answer all questions or who, by boisterous or discourteous conduct, disturbs the decorum of the committee room. Petitioner was prosecuted for refusing to make certain disclosures which he asserted to be beyond the authority of the committee to demand. The controversy thus rests upon fundamental principles of the power of the Congress and the limitations upon that power. We approach the questions presented with conscious awareness of the far-reaching ramifications that can follow from a decision of this nature. . . .

We start with several basic premises on which there is general agreement. The power of the Congress to conduct investigations is inherent in the legislative process. That power is broad. It encompasses inquiries concerning the administration of existing laws as well as proposed or possibly needed statutes. It includes surveys of defects in our social, economic or political system for the purpose of enabling the Congress to remedy them. It comprehends probes into departments of the Federal Government to expose corruption, inefficiency or waste. But, broad as is this power of inquiry, it is not unlimited. There is no general authority to expose the private affairs of individuals without justification in terms of the functions of the Congress. This was freely conceded by the Solicitor General in his argument of this case. Nor is the Congress a law enforcement or trial agency. These are functions of the executive and judicial departments of government. No inquiry is an end in itself; it must be related to, and in furtherance of, a legitimate task of the Congress. Investigations conducted solely for the personal aggrandizement of the investigators or to "punish" those investigated are indefensible.

It is unquestionably the duty of all citizens to cooperate with the Congress in its efforts to obtain the facts needed for intelligent legislative action. It is their unremitting obligation to respond to subpoenas, to respect the dignity of the Congress and its committees and to testify fully with respect to matters within the province of proper investigation. This, of course, assumes that the constitutional rights of witnesses will be respected by the Congress as they are in a court of justice. The Bill of Rights is applicable to investigations as to all forms of governmental action. Witnesses cannot be compelled to give evidence against themselves. They cannot be subjected to unreasonable search and seizure. Nor can the First Amendment freedoms of speech, press, religion, or political belief and association be abridged. . . .

The history of contempt of the legislature in this country is notably different from that of England. In the early days of the United States, there lingered the direct knowledge of the evil effects of absolute power. Most of the instances of use of compulsory process by the first Congresses concerned matters affecting the qualification or integrity of their members or came about in inquiries dealing with suspected corruption or mismanagement of government officials. Unlike the English practice, from the very outset the use of contempt power by the legislature was deemed subject to judicial review. . . .

There was very little use of the power of compulsory process in early years to enable the Congress to obtain facts pertinent to the enactment of new statutes or the administration of existing laws. The first occasion for such an investigation arose in 1827 when the House of Representatives was considering a revision of the tariff laws. In the Senate, there was no use of a fact-finding investigation in aid of legislation until 1859. In the Legislative Reorganization Act, the Committee on Un-American Activities was the only standing committee of the House of Representatives that was given the power to compel disclosures. . . .

It is not surprising, from the fact that the Houses of Congress so sparingly employed the power to conduct investigations, that there have been few cases requiring judicial review of the power. The Nation was almost one hundred years old before the first case reached this Court to challenge the use of compulsory process as a legislative device, rather than in inquiries concerning the elections or privileges of Congressmen. In *Kilbourn v. Thompson*, 103 U.S. 168 [1881], decided in 1881, an investigation had been authorized by the House of Representatives to learn the circumstances surrounding the bankruptcy of Jay Cooke & Company, in which the United States had deposited funds. The committee became particularly interested in a private real estate pool that was a part of the financial structure. The Court found that the subject matter of the inquiry was "in its nature clearly judicial and therefore one in respect to which no valid legislation could be enacted." The House had thereby exceeded the limits of its own authority.

Subsequent to the decision in *Kilbourn*, until recent times, there were very few cases dealing with the investigative power. The matter came to the fore again when the Senate undertook to study the corruption in the handling of oil leases in the 1920's. In *McGrain v. Daugherty*, 273 U.S. 135 [1927], and *Sinclair v. United States*, 279 U.S. 263 [1929], the Court applied the precepts of *Kilbourn* to uphold the authority of the Congress to conduct the challenged investigations. The Court recognized the danger to effective and honest conduct of the Government if the legislature's power to probe corruption in the executive branch were unduly hampered.

In the decade following World War II, there appeared a new kind of congressional inquiry unknown in prior periods of American history. Principally this was the result of the various investigations into the threat of subversion of the United States Government, but other subjects of congressional interest also contributed to the changed scene. This new phase of legislative inquiry involved a broad-scale intrusion into the lives and affairs of private citizens. It brought before the courts novel questions of the appropriate limits of congressional inquiry. Prior cases, like *Kilbourn*, *McGrain* and *Sinclair*, had defined the scope of investigative power in terms of the inherent limitations of the sources of that power. In the more recent cases, the emphasis shifted to problems of accommodating the interest of the Government with the rights and privileges of individuals. The central theme was the application of the Bill of Rights as a restraint upon the assertion of governmental power in this form.

It was during this period that the Fifth Amendment privilege against self-incrimination was frequently invoked and recognized as a legal limit upon the authority of a committee to require that witness answer its questions. Some early doubts as to the applicability of that privilege before a legislative committee never matured. When the matter reached this Court, the Government did not challenge in any way that the Fifth Amendment protection was available to the witness, and such a challenge could not have prevailed. It confined its argument to the character of the answers sought and to the adequacy of the claim of privilege. . . .

A far more difficult task evolved from the claim by witnesses that the committees' interrogations were infringements upon the freedoms of the First Amendment. Clearly, an investigation is subject to the command that the Congress shall make no law abridging freedom of speech or press or assembly. While it is true that there is no statute to be reviewed, and that an investigation is not a law, nevertheless an investigation is part of lawmaking. It is justified solely as an adjunct to the legislative process. The First Amendment may be invoked against infringement of the protected freedoms by law or by lawmaking.

Abuses of the investigative process may imperceptibly lead to abridgement of protected freedoms. The mere summoning of a witness and compelling him to testify, against his will, about his beliefs, expressions or associations is a measure of governmental interference. And when those forced revelations concern matters that are unorthodox, unpopular, or even hateful to the general public, the reaction in the life of the witness may be disastrous. This effect is even more harsh when it is past beliefs, expressions or associations that are disclosed and judged by current standards rather than those contemporary with the matters exposed. Nor does the witness alone suffer the consequences. Those who are identified by witnesses and thereby placed in the same glare of publicity are equally subject to public stigma, scorn and obloquy. Beyond that, there is the more subtle and immeasurable effect upon those who tend to adhere to the most orthodox and uncontroversial views and associations in order to avoid a similar fate at some future time. That this impact is partly the result of nongovernmental activity by private persons cannot relieve the investigators of their responsibility for initiating the reaction.

The Court recognized the restraints of the Bill of Rights upon congressional investigations in *United States v. Rumely*, 345 U.S. 41 [(1953)]. The magnitude and complexity of the problem of applying the First Amendment to that case led the Court to construe narrowly the resolution describing the committee's authority. It was concluded that, when First Amendment rights are threatened, the delegation of power to the committee must be clearly revealed in its charter. . . .

We have no doubt that there is no congressional power to expose for the sake of exposure. The public is, of course, entitled to be informed concerning the workings of its government. That cannot be inflated into a general power to expose where the predominant result can only be an invasion of the private rights of individuals. But a solution to our problem is not to be found in testing the motives of committee members for this purpose. Such is not our function. Their motives alone would not vitiate an investigation which had been instituted by a House of Congress if that assembly's legislative purpose is being served. . . .

It would be difficult to imagine a less explicit authorizing resolution. Who can define the meaning of "un-American"? What is that single, solitary "principle of the form of government as guaranteed by our Constitution"? There is no need to dwell upon the language, however. At one time, perhaps, the resolution might have been read narrowly to confine the Committee to the subject of propaganda. The events that have transpired in the fifteen years before the interrogation of petitioner make such a construction impossible at this date. . . .

Combining the language of the resolution with the construction it has been given, it is evident that the preliminary control of the Committee exercised by the House of Representatives is slight or non-existent. No one could reasonably deduce from the charter the kind of investigation that the Committee was directed to make. As a result, we are asked to engage in a process of retroactive rationalization. Looking backward from the events that transpired, we are asked to uphold the Committee's actions unless it appears that they were clearly not authorized by the charter. As a corollary to this inverse approach, the Government urges that we must view the matter hospitably to the power of the Congress—that if there is any legislative purpose which might have been furthered by the kind of disclosure sought, the witness must be punished for withholding it. No doubt every reasonable indulgence of legality must be accorded to the actions of a coordinate branch of our Government. But such deference cannot yield to an unnecessary and unreasonable dissipation of precious constitutional freedoms.

The Government contends that the public interest at the core of the investigations of the Un-American Activities Committee is the need by the Congress to be informed of efforts to overthrow the Government by force and violence so that adequate legislative safeguards can be erected. From this core, however, the Committee can radiate outward infinitely to any topic thought to be related in some way to armed insurrection. The outer reaches of this domain are known only by the content of "un-American activities." Remoteness of subject can be aggravated by a probe for a depth of detail even farther removed from any basis of legislative action. A third dimension is added when the investigators turn their attention to the past to collect minutiae on remote topics, on the hypothesis that the past may reflect upon the present.

The consequences that flow from this situation are manifold. In the first place, a reviewing court is unable to make the kind of judgment made by the Court in *United States v. Rumely, supra.* The Committee is allowed, in essence, to define its own authority, to choose the direction and focus of its activities. In deciding what to do with the power that has been conferred upon them, members of the Committee may act pursuant to motives that seem to them to be the highest. Their decisions, nevertheless, can lead to ruthless exposure of private lives in order to gather data that is neither desired by the Congress nor useful to it. Yet it is impossible in this circumstance, with constitutional freedoms in jeopardy, to declare that the Committee has ranged beyond the area committed to it by its parent assembly because the boundaries are so nebulous.

More important and more fundamental than that, however, it insulates the House that has authorized the investigation from the witnesses who are subjected to the sanctions of compulsory process. There is a wide gulf between the responsibility for the use of investigative power and the actual exercise of that power. This is an especially vital consideration in assuring respect for constitutional liberties. Protected freedoms should not be placed in danger in the absence of a clear determination by the House or the Senate that a particular inquiry is justified by a specific legislative need.

It is, of course, not the function of this Court to prescribe rigid rules for the Congress to follow in drafting resolutions establishing investigating committees. That is a matter peculiarly within the realm of the legislature, and its decisions will be accepted by the courts up to the point where their own duty to enforce the constitutionally protected rights of individuals is affected. An excessively broad charter, like that of the House Un-American Activities Committee, places the courts in an untenable position if they are to strike a balance between the public need for a particular interrogation and the right of citizens to carry on their affairs free from unnecessary governmental interference. It is impossible in such a situation to ascertain whether any legislative purpose justifies the disclosures sought and, if so, the importance of that information to the Congress in furtherance of its legislative function. The reason no court can make this critical judgment is that the House of Representatives itself has never made it. Only the legislative assembly initiating an investigation can assay the relative necessity of specific disclosures.

Absence of the qualitative consideration of petitioner's questioning by the House of Representatives aggravates a serious problem, revealed in this case, in the relationship of congressional investigating committees and the witnesses who appear before them. Plainly these committees are restricted to the missions delegated to them, i.e., to acquire certain data to be used by the House or the Senate in coping with a problem that falls within its legislative sphere. No witness can be compelled to make disclosures on matters outside that area. This is a jurisdictional concept of pertinency drawn from the nature of a congressional committee's source of authority. It is not wholly different from nor unrelated to the element of pertinency embodied in the criminal statute under which petitioner was prosecuted. When the definition of jurisdictional pertinency is as uncertain and wavering as in the case of the Un-American Activities Committee, it becomes extremely difficult for the Committee to limit its inquiries to statutory pertinency.

Since World War II, the Congress has practically abandoned its original practice of utilizing the coercive sanction of contempt proceedings at the bar of the House. The sanction there imposed is imprisonment by the House until the recalcitrant witness agrees to testify or disclose the matters sought, provided that the incarceration does not extend beyond adjournment. The Congress has instead invoked the aid of the federal judicial system in protecting itself against contumacious conduct. It has become customary to refer these matters to the United States Attorneys for prosecution under criminal law.

The appropriate statute is found in 2 U.S.C. Sec. 192. It provides:

> Every person who having been summoned as a witness by the authority of either House of Congress to give testimony or to produce papers upon any matter under inquiry before either House, or any joint committee established by a joint or concurrent resolution of the two Houses of Congress, or any committee of either House of Congress, willfully makes default, or who, having appeared, refuses to answer any question pertinent to the question under inquiry, shall be deemed guilty of a misdemeanor, punishable by a fine of not more than $1,000 nor less than $100 and imprisonment in a common jail for not less than one month nor more than twelve months.

In fulfillment of their obligation under this statute, the courts must accord to the defendants every right which is guaranteed to defendants in all other criminal cases. Among these is the right to have available, through a sufficiently precise statute, information revealing the standard of criminality before the commission of the alleged offense. Applied to persons prosecuted under Sec. 192, this raises a special problem in that the statute defines the crime as refusal to answer "any question pertinent to the question under inquiry." Part of the standard of criminality, therefore, is the pertinency of the questions propounded to the witness.

The problem attains proportion when viewed from the standpoint of the witness who appears before a congressional committee. He must decide at the time the questions are propounded whether or not to answer. . . . An erroneous determination on his part, even if made in the utmost good faith, does not exculpate him if the court should later rule that the questions were pertinent to the question under inquiry.

It is obvious that a person compelled to make this choice is entitled to have knowledge of the subject to which the interrogation is deemed pertinent. That knowledge must be available with the same degree of explicitness and clarity that the Due Process Clause requires in the expression of any element of a criminal offense. The "vice of vagueness" must be avoided here as in all other crimes. There are several sources that can outline the "question under inquiry" in such a way that the rules against vagueness are satisfied. The authorizing resolution, the remarks of the chairman or members of the committee, or even the nature of the proceedings themselves, might sometimes make the topic clear. This case demonstrates, however, that these sources often leave the matter in grave doubt.

Fundamental fairness demands that no witness be compelled to [determine whether a question is pertinent to a legitimate legislative purpose] . . . with so little guidance. Unless the subject matter has been made to appear with undisputable clarity, it is the duty of the investigative body, upon objection of the witness on grounds of pertinency, to state for the record the subject under inquiry at that time and the manner in which the propounded questions are pertinent thereto. To be meaningful, the explanation must describe what the topic under inquiry is and the connective reasoning whereby the precise questions asked relate to it.

The statement of the Committee Chairman in this case, in response to petitioner's protest, was woefully inadequate to convey sufficient information as to the pertinency of the questions to the subject under inquiry. Petitioner was thus not accorded a fair opportunity to determine whether he was within his rights in refusing to answer, and his conviction is necessarily invalid under the Due Process Clause of the Fifth Amendment.

We are mindful of the complexities of modern government and the ample scope that must be left to the Congress as the sole constitutional depository of legislative power. Equally mindful are we of the indispensable function, in the exercise of that power, of congressional investigations. The conclusions we have reached in this case will not prevent the Congress, through its committees, from obtaining any information it needs for the proper fulfillment of its role in our scheme of government. The legislature is free to determine the kinds of data that should be collected. It is only those investigations that are conducted by use of compulsory process that give rise to a need to protect the rights of individuals against illegal encroachment. That protection can be readily achieved through procedures which prevent the separation of power from responsibility and which provide the constitutional requisites of fairness for witnesses. A measure of added care on the part of the House and the Senate in authorizing the use of compulsory process and by their committees in exercising that power would suffice. That is a small price to pay if it serves to uphold the principles of limited, constitutional government without constricting the power of the Congress to inform itself.

☐ *Justice CLARK, dissenting.*

As I see it the chief fault in the majority opinion is its mischievous curbing of the informing function of the Congress. . . .

[T]he Court reverses the judgment because: (1) The subject matter of the inquiry was not "made to appear with undisputable clarity" either through its "charter" or by the Chairman at the time of the hearing and, therefore, Watkins was deprived of a clear understanding of "the manner in which the propounded questions [were] pertinent thereto"; and (2) the present committee system of inquiry of the House, as practiced by the Un-American Activities Committee, does not provide adequate safeguards for the protection of the constitutional right of free speech. I subscribe to neither conclusion. . . .

I think the Committee here was acting entirely within its scope and that the purpose of its inquiry was set out with "undisputable clarity." In the first place, the authorizing language of the Reorganization Act must be read as a whole, not dissected. It authorized investigation into subversive activity, its extent, character, objects, and diffusion. While the language might have been more explicit than using such words as "un-American," or phrases like "principle of the form of government," still these are fairly well understood terms. We must construe them to give them meaning if we can. Our cases indicate that rather than finding fault with the use of words or phrases, we are bound to presume that the action of the legislative body in granting authority to the Committee was with a legitimate object "if [the action] is *capable* of being so construed." . . . Before we can deny the authority "it must be obvious that" the Committee has "exceeded the bounds of legislative power." *Tenney v. Brandhove*, 341 U.S. 367 [(1951)]. The fact that the Committee has often been attacked has caused close scrutiny of its acts by the House as a whole and the House has repeatedly given the Committee its approval. "Power" and "responsibility" have not been separated. But the record in this case does not stop here. It shows that at the hearings involving Watkins, the Chairman made statements explaining the functions of the Committee. And, further-more, Watkins' action at the hearing clearly reveals that he was well ac-quainted with the purpose of the hearing. It was to investigate Communist infiltration into his union. This certainly falls within the grant of authority from the Reorganization Act and the House has had ample opportunity to limit the investigative scope of the Committee if it feels that the Committee has exceeded its legitimate bounds. I do not see how any First Amendment rights were endangered here. There is nothing in the First Amendment that provides the guarantees Watkins claims. That Amendment was designed to prevent attempts by law to curtail freedom of speech. It forbids Congress from making any law "abridging the freedom of speech, or of the press." It guarantees Watkins' right to join any organization and make any speech that does not have an intent to incite to crime. . . . But Watkins was asked whether he knew named individuals and whether they were Communists. He refused to answer on the ground that his rights were being abridged. What he was actually seeking to do was to protect his former associates, not himself, from embarrassment. He had already admitted his own involvement. He sought to vindicate the rights, if any, of his associates. . . .

As already indicated, even if Watkins' associates were on the stand they could not decline to disclose their Communist connections on First Amend-ment grounds. While there may be no restraint by the Government of one's beliefs, the right of free belief has never been extended to include the with-holding of knowledge of past events or transactions. There is no general priv-ilege of silence. The First Amendment does not make speech or silence permissible to a person in such measure as he chooses. Watkins has here ex-ercised his own choice as to when he talks, what questions he answers, and when he remains silent. A witness is not given such a choice by the Amend-ment. Remote and indirect disadvantages such as "public stigma, scorn and obloquy" may be related to the First Amendment, but they are not enough to block investigation.

Barenblatt v. United States
360 U.S. 109, 79 S.CT. 1081 (1959)

The ruling in *Watkins v. United States* (1957) (see preceding excerpt) touched off a firestorm of protest in Congress. Conservative Repub-licans and southern Democrats charged that the Warren Court "[i]ntruded on Congress's right of investigation by reversing certain ci-tations for contempt of Congress" and "[e]ndangered the national security by rulings in subversive activities cases." In particular, Indiana's Senator William Jenner introduced a bill that would withdraw the Supreme Court's jurisdiction over, among other things, "any committee or subcommittee of the United States Congress or any action or proceedings against a witness charged with contempt of Congress." While the Jenner and other bills were being debated in Congress, the justices granted review of the case brought by Lloyd Barenblatt, a college professor, convicted for refusing to answer certain questions asked by a subcommittee of the House Un-American Activities Committee. Justice Harlan's opinion for a bare majority of the Court, in affirming Barenblatt's conviction, further discusses the facts of the case. Notably, on the same day this decision was announced, in *Uphaus v. Wyman*, 364 U.S. 388 (1959), the Court also ruled that a director of a summer camp could be forced to supply the names of all guests at the camp during a two-year period to the New Hampshire attorney general, who was investigating for the state legislature whether there were any "subversive persons" in the state. The rulings in *Barenblatt* and *Uphaus* helped diffuse the controversy over the Court, and Jenner's and similar Court-curbing legislation was defeated in Congress.

The Court's decision was five to four, and the majority's opinion was announced by Justice Harlan. Justice Black dissented and was joined by Chief Justice Warren and Justice Douglas, as did Justice Brennan.

☐ *Justice HARLAN delivers the opinion of the Court.*

Once more the Court is required to resolve the conflicting constitutional claims of congressional power and of an individual's right to resist its exercise. The congressional power in question concerns the internal process of Congress in moving within its legislative domain; it involves the utilization of its committees to secure "testimony needed to enable it efficiently to exercise a legislative function belonging to it under the Constitution." . . . Broad as it is, the power is not, however, without limitations. Since Congress may only investigate into those areas in which it may potentially legislate or appropriate, it cannot inquire into matters which are within the exclusive province of one of the other branches of the Government. Lacking the judicial power given to the Judiciary, it cannot inquire into matters that are exclusively the concern of the Judiciary. Neither can it supplant the Executive in what exclusively belongs to the Executive. And the Congress, in common with all branches of the Government, must exercise its powers subject to the limitations placed by the Constitution on governmental action, more particularly in the context of this case the relevant limitations of the Bill of Rights.

The congressional power of inquiry, its range and scope, and an individual's duty in relation to it, must be viewed in proper perspective. The power and the right of resistance to it are to be judged in the concrete, not on the basis of abstractions. In the present case congressional efforts to learn the extent of a nationwide, indeed worldwide, problem have brought one of its investigating committees into the field of education. Of course, broadly viewed, inquiries cannot be made into the teaching that is pursued in any of our educational institutions. When academic teaching-freedom and its corollary learning-freedom, so essential to the well-being of the Nation, are claimed, this Court will always be on the alert against intrusion by Congress into this constitutionally protected domain. But this does not mean that the Congress is precluded from interrogating a witness merely because he is a teacher. An educational institution is not a constitutional sanctuary from inquiry into matters that may otherwise be within the constitutional legislative domain merely for the reason that inquiry is made of someone within its walls. . . .

We here review petitioner's conviction . . . for contempt of Congress, arising from his refusal to answer certain questions put to him by a Sub-committee of the House Committee on Un-American Activities during the course of an inquiry concerning alleged Communist infiltration into the field of education. . . .

Pursuant to a subpoena, and accompanied by counsel, petitioner on June 28, 1954, appeared as a witness before this congressional Subcommittee. After answering a few preliminary questions and testifying that he had been a graduate student and teaching fellow at the University of Michigan from 1947 to 1950 and an instructor in psychology at Vassar College from 1950 to shortly before his appearance before the Subcommittee, petitioner objected generally to the right of the Subcommittee to inquire into his "political" and "religious" beliefs or any "other personal and private affairs" or "associational activities," upon grounds set forth in a previously prepared memorandum which he was allowed to file with the Subcommittee. Thereafter petitioner specifically declined to answer each of the following five questions:

> Are you now a member of the Communist Party? [Count One.]
> Have you ever been a member of the Communist Party? [Count Two.]
> Now, you have stated that you knew Francis Crowley. Did you know Francis Crowley as a member of the Communist Party? [Count Three.]
> Were you ever a member of the Haldane Club of the Communist Party while at the University of Michigan? [Count Four.]
> Were you a member while a student of the University of Michigan Council of Arts, Sciences, and Professions? [Count Five.]

In each instance the grounds of refusal were those set forth in the prepared statement. Petitioner expressly disclaimed reliance upon "the Fifth Amendment." . . .

Petitioner's various contentions resolve themselves into three propositions: First, the compelling of testimony by the Subcommittee was neither legislatively authorized nor constitutionally permissible because of the vagueness of Rule XI of the House of Representatives, Eighty-third Congress, the charter of authority of the parent Committee. Second, petitioner was not adequately apprised of the pertinency of the Subcommittee's questions to the subject matter of the inquiry. Third, the questions petitioner refused to answer infringed rights protected by the First Amendment.

SUBCOMMITTEE'S AUTHORITY TO COMPEL TESTIMONY.

At the outset it should be noted that Rule XI authorized this Subcommittee to compel testimony within the framework of the investigative authority conferred on the Un-American Activities Committee. Petitioner contends that *Watkins v. United States*, [354 U.S. 178 (1957)], nevertheless held the grant of this power in all circumstances ineffective because of the vagueness of Rule XI in delineating the Committee jurisdiction to which its exercise was to be appurtenant. . . .

The *Watkins* case cannot properly be read as standing for such a proposition. A principal contention in *Watkins* was that the refusals to answer were justified because the requirement of 2 U.S.C. Sec. 192, that the questions asked be "pertinent to the question under inquiry" had not been satisfied. . . . This Court reversed the conviction solely on that ground, holding that Watkins had not been adequately apprised of the subject matter of the Subcommittee's investigation or the pertinency thereto of the questions he refused to answer. In so deciding the Court drew upon Rule XI only as one of the facets in the total *mise en scène* in its search for the "question under inquiry" in that particular investigation. That the vagueness of Rule XI was not alone determinative is also shown by the Court's further statement that aside from the Rule "the remarks of the chairman or members of the committee, or even the nature of the proceedings themselves, might sometimes make the topic [under inquiry] clear." In short, while *Watkins* was critical of Rule XI, it did not involve the broad and inflexible holding petitioner now attributes to it.

Petitioner also contends, independently of *Watkins*, that the vagueness of Rule XI deprived the Subcommittee of the right to compel testimony in this investigation into Communist activity. We cannot agree with this contention which in its furthest reach would mean that the House Un-American Activities Committee under its existing authority has no right to compel testimony in any circumstances. Granting the vagueness of the Rule, we may not read it in isolation from its long history in the House of Representatives. Just as legislation is often given meaning by the gloss of legislative reports, administrative interpretation, and long usage, so the proper meaning of an authorization to a congressional committee is not to be derived alone from its abstract terms unrelated to the definite content furnished them by the course of congressional actions. The Rule comes to us with a "persuasive gloss of legislative history" which shows beyond doubt that in pursuance of its legislative concerns in the domain of "national security" the House has clothed the Un-American Activities Committee with pervasive authority to investigate Communist activities in this country. . . .

PERTINENCY CLAIM.

Undeniably a conviction for contempt under 2 U.S.C. Sec. 192 cannot stand unless the questions asked are pertinent to the subject matter of the investigation. *Watkins v. United States*. But the factors which led us to rest decision on this ground in *Watkins* were very different from those involved here.

In *Watkins* the petitioner had made specific objection to the Subcommittee's questions on the ground of pertinency; the question under inquiry had not been disclosed in any illuminating manner; and the questions asked the petitioner were not only amorphous on their face, but in some instances clearly foreign to the alleged subject matter of the investigation— "Communism in labor." . . .

In contrast, petitioner in the case before us raised no objections on the ground of pertinency at the time any of the questions were put to him. . . .

We need not, however, rest decision on petitioner's failure to object on this score, for here "pertinency" was made to appear "with undisputable clarity." First of all, it goes without saying that the scope of the Committee's authority was for the House, not a witness, to determine, subject to the ultimate reviewing responsibility of this Court. What we deal with here is whether petitioner was sufficiently apprised of "the topic under inquiry" thus authorized "and the connective reasoning whereby the precise questions asked relate[d] to it." In light of his prepared memorandum of constitutional objections there can be no doubt that this petitioner was well aware of the Subcommittee's authority and purpose to question him as it did. In addition the other sources of this information which we recognized in *Watkins* . . . leave no room for a "pertinency" objection on this record. The subject matter of the inquiry had been identified at the commencement of the investigation as Communist infiltration into the field of education. Just prior to petitioner's appearance before the Subcommittee, the scope of the day's hearings had been announced as "in the main communism in education and the experiences and background in the party by Francis X. T. Crowley. It will deal with activities in Michigan, Boston, and in some small degree, New York." Petitioner had heard the Subcommittee interrogate the witness Crowley along the same lines as he, petitioner, was evidently to be questioned, and had listened to Crowley's testimony identifying him as a former member of an alleged Communist student organization at the University of Michigan while they both were in attendance there. Further, petitioner had stood mute in the face of the Chairman's statement as to why he had been called as a witness by the Subcommittee. And, lastly, unlike *Watkins*, petitioner refused to answer questions as to his own Communist Party affiliations, whose pertinency of course was clear beyond doubt. . . .

CONSTITUTIONAL CONTENTIONS.

The precise constitutional issue confronting us is whether the Subcommittee's inquiry into petitioner's past or present membership in the Communist Party transgressed the provisions of the First Amendment, which of course reach and limit congressional investigations. . . . Undeniably, the First Amendment in some circumstances protects an individual from being compelled to disclose his associational relationships. However, the protections of the First Amendment, unlike a proper claim of the privilege against self-incrimination under the Fifth Amendment, do not afford a witness the right to resist inquiry in all circumstances. Where First Amendment rights are asserted to bar governmental interrogation resolution of the issue always involves a balancing by the courts of the competing private and public interests at stake in the particular circumstances shown. These principles were recognized in the *Watkins* case, where, in speaking of the First Amendment in relation to congressional inquiries, we said, "It is manifest that despite the adverse effects which follow upon compelled disclosure of private matters, not all such inquiries are barred. The critical element is the existence of, and the weight to be ascribed to, the interest of the Congress in demanding disclosures from an unwilling witness." . . .

That Congress has wide power to legislate in the field of Communist activity in this Country, and to conduct appropriate investigations in aid thereof, is hardly debatable. The existence of such power has never been questioned by this Court, and it is sufficient to say, without particularization, that Congress has enacted or considered in this field a wide range of legislative measures, not a few of which have stemmed from recommendations of the very Committee whose actions have been drawn in question here. In the last analysis this power rests on the right of self-preservation, "the ultimate value of any society." . . .

On these premises, this Court in its constitutional adjudications has consistently refused to view the Communist Party as an ordinary political party, and has upheld federal legislation aimed at the Communist problem which in a different context would certainly have raised constitutional issues of the gravest character. . . . To suggest that because the Communist Party may also sponsor peaceable political reforms the constitutional issues before us should now be judged as if that Party were just an ordinary political party from the standpoint of national security, is to ask this Court to blind itself to world affairs which have determined the whole course of our national policy since the close of World War II. . . . An investigation of advocacy of or preparation for overthrow certainly embraces the right to identify a witness as a member of the Communist Party, and to inquire into the various manifestations of the Party's tenets. The strict requirements of a prosecution under the Smith Act are not the measure of the permissible scope of a congressional investigation into "overthrow," for of necessity the investigatory process must proceed step by step. Nor can it fairly be concluded that this investigation was directed at controlling what is being taught at our universities rather than at overthrow. The statement of the Subcommittee Chairman at the opening of the investigation evinces no such intention, and so far as this record reveals nothing thereafter transpired which would justify our holding that the thrust of the investigation later changed. The record discloses considerable testimony concerning the foreign domination and revolutionary purposes and efforts of the Communist Party. That there was also testimony on the abstract philosophical level does not detract from the dominant theme of this investigation—Communist infiltration furthering the alleged ultimate purpose of overthrow. And certainly the conclusion would not be justified that the questioning of petitioner would have exceeded permissible bounds had he not shut off the Subcommittee at the threshold.

Nor can we accept the further contention that this investigation should not be deemed to have been in furtherance of a legislative purpose because the true objective of the Committee and of the Congress was purely "exposure." So long as Congress acts in pursuance of its constitutional power, the Judiciary lacks authority to intervene on the basis of the motives which spurred the exercise of that power. "It is, of course, true," as was said in *McCray v. United States* [195 U.S. 27 (1904)], "that if there be no authority in the judiciary to restrain a lawful exercise of power by another department of the government, where a wrong motive or purpose has impelled to the exertion of the power, that abuses of a power conferred may be temporarily effectual. The remedy for this however, lies, not in the abuse by the judicial authority of its functions, but in the people, upon whom, after all, under our institutions, reliance must be placed for the correction of abuses committed in the exercise of a lawful power." These principles of course apply as well to committee investigations into the need for legislation as to the enactments which such investigations may produce. . . .

We conclude that the balance between the individual and the governmental interests here at stake must be struck in favor of the latter, and that therefore the provisions of the First Amendment have not been offended.

We hold that petitioner's conviction for contempt of Congress discloses no infirmity, and that the judgment of the Court of Appeals must be affirmed.

Affirmed.

☐ *Justice BLACK, with whom THE CHIEF JUSTICE and Justice DOUGLAS join, dissenting.*

The First Amendment says in no equivocal language that Congress shall pass no law abridging freedom of speech, press, assembly or petition. The activities of this Committee, authorized by Congress, do precisely that, through exposure, obloquy and public scorn. See *Watkins v. United States.* The Court does not really deny this fact but relies on a combination of three reasons for permitting the infringement: (A) The notion that despite the First Amendment's command Congress can abridge speech and association if this Court decides that the governmental interest in abridging speech is greater than an individual's interest in exercising that freedom, (B) the Government's right to "preserve itself," (C) the fact that the Committee is only after Communists or suspected Communists in this investigation. . . .

To apply the Court's balancing test under such circumstances is to read the First Amendment to say "Congress shall pass no law abridging freedom of speech, press, assembly and petition, unless Congress and the Supreme Court reach the joint conclusion that on balance the interest of the Government in stifling these freedoms is greater than the interest of the people in having them exercised." This is closely akin to the notion that neither the First Amendment nor any other provision of the Bill of Rights should be enforced unless the Court believes it is *reasonable* to do so. Not only does this violate the genius of our *written* Constitution, but it runs expressly counter to the injunction to Court and Congress made by Madison when he introduced the Bill of Rights. "If they [the first ten amendments] are incorporated into the Constitution, independent tribunals of justice will consider themselves in a peculiar manner the guardians of those rights: they will be an impenetrable bulwark against *every* assumption of power in the Legislative or Executive; they will be naturally led to resist *every* encroachment upon rights expressly stipulated for in the Constitution by the declaration of rights." Unless we return to this view of our judicial function, unless we once again accept the notion that the Bill of Rights means what it says and that this Court must enforce that meaning, I am of the opinion that our great charter of liberty will be more honored in the breach than in the observance.

But even assuming what I cannot assume, that some balancing is proper in this case, I feel that the Court after stating the test ignores it completely. At most it balances the right of the Government to preserve itself, against Barenblatt's right to refrain from revealing Communist affiliations. Such a balance, however, mistakes the factors to be weighed. In the first place, it completely leaves out the real interest in Barenblatt's silence, the interest of the people as a whole in being able to join organizations, advocate causes and make political "mistakes" without later being subjected to governmental penalties for having dared to think for themselves. It is this right, the right to err politically, which keeps us strong as a Nation. For no number of laws against communism can have as much effect as the personal conviction which comes from having heard its arguments and rejected them, or from having once accepted its tenets and later recognized their worthlessness. Instead, the obloquy which results from investigations such as this not only stifles "mistakes" but prevents all but the most courageous from hazarding any views which might at some later time become disfavored. This result, whose importance cannot be overestimated, is doubly crucial when it affects the universities, on which we must largely rely for the experimentation and development of new ideas essential to our country's welfare. It is these interests of society, rather than Barenblatt's own right to silence, which I think the Court should put on the balance against the demands of the Government, if any balancing process is to be tolerated. Instead they are not mentioned, while on the other side the demands of the Government are vastly overstated and called "self preservation." . . .

Moreover, I cannot agree with the Court's notion that First Amendment freedoms must be abridged in order to "preserve" our country. That notion rests on the unarticulated premise that this Nation's security hangs upon its power to punish people because of what they think, speak or write about, or because of those with whom they associate for political purposes. The Government, in its brief, virtually admits this position when it speaks of the "communication of unlawful ideas." I challenge this premise, and deny that ideas can be proscribed under our Constitution. . . .

I would reverse this conviction.

Gibson v. Florida Legislative Investigation Committee
372 U.S. 539, 83 S.Ct. 889 (1963)

Following the watershed ruling in *Brown v. Board of Education of Topeka, Kansas*, 347 U.S. 483 (1954) (see Vol. 2, Ch. 12), the National Association for the Advancement of Colored People (NAACP) spearheaded further litigation to force Southern states to begin school desegregation. As a result, the NAACP was subject to great hostility, as state officials sought in a variety of ways to thwart its activities. In Alabama, officials endeavored to stop the NAACP's efforts by requiring it to register and produce a list of its members. The NAACP complied, except for producing its membership list on the ground that that violated its First Amendment right to freedom of association. After being found in contempt and fined $100,000 for refusing to turn over its membership lists, the NAACP appealed to the Supreme Court. In *National Association for the Advancement of Colored People v. Alabama*, 357 U.S. 449 (1958) (see Vol. 2, Ch. 5), the Court upheld the organization's claims that disclosure of its membership lists would abridge its First Amendment right of lawful association. In 1958, the Florida Supreme Court likewise ruled that the NAACP could not be compelled to release its membership lists to a state legislative committee. But it also held that the "custodian" of its records could be compelled to bring them to the hearings and to refer to them in answering questions. The next year, the Florida legislature established a Legislative Investigation Committee to investigate "subversive organizations"—such as the Communist party—and their infiltration of the NAACP. Theodore Gibson, the president of the Miami branch of the NAACP, was subpoenaed to appear and to bring the membership lists of his branch for reference to hearings of the committee. Gibson agreed to answer questions about members but refused to bring the records to the committee's hearings. He contended that that request infringed on members' freedom of association. After a state court found him in contempt and the Florida Supreme Court affirmed, Gibson appealed to the Supreme Court, and a bare majority reversed the decision of the state supreme court.

The Court's decision was five to four, and the majority's opinion was announced by Justice Goldberg. Concurring opinions were delivered by Justices Black and Douglas. Dissents were by Justices White and Harlan, who was joined by Justices Clark and Stewart.

☐ *Justice GOLDBERG delivers the opinion of the Court.*

We are here called upon once again to resolve a conflict between individual rights of free speech and association and governmental interest in conducting legislative investigations. Prior decisions illumine the contending principles.

This Court has repeatedly held that rights of association are within the ambit of the constitutional protections afforded by the First and Fourteenth Amendments. . . . The respondent Committee does not contend otherwise, nor could it, for, as was said in *N.A.A.C.P. v. Alabama*, "It is beyond debate that freedom to engage in association for the advancement of beliefs and ideas is an inseparable aspect of the 'liberty' assured by the Due Process Clause of the Fourteenth Amendment, which embraces freedom of speech." And it is equally clear that the guarantee encompasses protection of privacy of association in organizations such as that of which the petitioner is president; indeed, in both the *Bates* [*v. Little Rock*, 361 U.S. 516 (1960)] and *Alabama* cases, this Court held N.A.A.C.P. membership lists of the very type here in question to be beyond the States' power of discovery in the circumstances there presented.

The First and Fourteenth Amendment rights of free speech and free association are fundamental and highly prized, and "need breathing space to survive." *N.A.A.C.P. v. Button*, 371 U.S. 415 [1963]. "Freedoms such as these are protected not only against heavy-handed frontal attack, but also from being stifled by more subtle governmental interference." *Bates v. Little Rock*. And, as declared in *N.A.A.C.P. v. Alabama*, "It is hardly a novel perception that compelled disclosure of affiliation with groups engaged in advocacy may constitute [an] . . . effective . . . restraint on freedom of association. . . . This Court has recognized the vital relationship between freedom to associate and privacy in one's associations. . . . Inviolability of privacy in group association may in many circumstances be indispensable to preservation of freedom of association, particularly where a group espouses dissident beliefs." So it is here.

At the same time, however, this Court's prior holdings demonstrate that there can be no question that the State has power adequately to inform itself—through legislative investigation, if it so desires—in order to act and protect its legitimate and vital interests. . . .

Significantly, the parties are in substantial agreement as to the proper test to be applied to reconcile the competing claims of government and individual and to determine the propriety of the Committee's demands. As declared by the respondent Committee in its brief to this Court, "Basically, this case hinges entirely on the question of whether the evidence before the Committee [was] . . . sufficient to show probable cause or nexus between the N.A.A.C.P. Miami Branch, and Communist activities." We understand this to mean—regardless of the label applied, be it "nexus," "foundation," or whatever—that it is an essential prerequisite to the validity of an investigation which intrudes into the area of constitutionally protected rights of speech, press, association and petition that the State convincingly show a substantial relation between the information sought and a subject of overriding and compelling state interest. Absent such a relation between the N.A.A.C.P. and conduct in which the State may have a compelling regulatory concern, the Committee has not "demonstrated so cogent an interest in obtaining and making public" the membership information sought to be obtained as to "justify the substantial abridgement of associational freedom which such disclosures will effect." . . .

Applying these principles to the facts of this case, the respondent Committee contends that the prior decisions of this Court . . . compel a result here upholding the legislative right of inquiry. In *Barenblatt* [*v. United States*, 360 U.S. 109 (1959)], *Wilkinson* [*v. United States*, 365 U.S. 431 (1961)], and *Braden* [*v. United States*, 365 U.S. 431 (1961)], however, it was a refusal to answer a question or questions concerning the witness' *own* past or present membership *in the Communist Party* which supported his conviction. It is apparent that the necessary preponderating governmental interest and, in fact, the very result in those cases were founded on the holding that the Communist Party is not an ordinary or legitimate political party, as known in this country, and that, because of its particular nature, membership therein is *itself* a permissible subject of regulation and legislative scrutiny. Assuming the correctness of the premises on which those cases were decided, no further demonstration of compelling governmental interest was deemed necessary, since the direct object of the challenged questions there was discovery of membership in the Communist Party, a matter held pertinent to a proper subject then under inquiry.

Here, however, it is not alleged Communists who are the witnesses before the Committee and it is not discovery of their membership in that party which is the object of the challenged inquiries. Rather, it is the N.A.A.C.P. itself which is the subject of the investigation, and it is its local president, the petitioner, who was called before the Committee and held in contempt because he refused to divulge the contents of its membership records. There is no suggestion that the Miami branch of the N.A.A.C.P. or the national organization with which it is affiliated was, or is, itself a subversive organization. Nor is there any indication that the activities or policies of the N.A.A.C.P. were either Communist dominated or influenced. In fact, this very record indicates that the association was and is against communism and has voluntarily taken steps to keep Communists from being members. Each year since 1950, the N.A.A.C.P. has adopted resolutions barring Communists from membership in the organization. Moreover, the petitioner testified that all prospective officers of the local organization are thoroughly investigated for Communist or subversive connections and, though subversive activities constitute grounds for termination of association membership, no such expulsions from the branch occurred during the five years preceding the investigation.

Thus, unlike the situation in *Barenblatt, Wilkinson,* and *Braden, supra,* the Committee was not here seeking from the petitioner or the records of which he was custodian any information as to whether he, himself, or even other persons were members of the Communist Party, Communist front or affiliated organizations, or other allegedly subversive groups; instead, the entire thrust of the demands on the petitioner was that he disclose whether other persons were members of the N.A.A.C.P., itself a concededly legitimate and nonsubversive organization. Compelling such an organization, engaged in the exercise of First and Fourteenth Amendment rights, to disclose its membership presents, under our cases, a question wholly different from compelling the Communist Party to disclose its own membership. Moreover, even to say, as in *Barenblatt* . . . that it is permissible to inquire into the subject of Communist infiltration of educational or other organizations does not mean that it is permissible to demand or require from such other groups disclosure of their membership by inquiry into their records when such disclosure will seriously inhibit or impair the exercise of constitutional rights and has not itself been demonstrated to bear a crucial relation to a proper governmental interest or to be essential to fulfillment of a proper governmental purpose. The prior holdings that governmental interest in controlling subversion and the particular character of the Communist Party and its objectives outweigh the right of individual Communists to conceal party membership or affiliations by no means require the wholly different conclusion that other groups—concededly legitimate—automatically forfeit their rights to privacy of association simply because the general subject matter of the legislative inquiry is Communist subversion or infiltration. The fact that governmental interest was deemed compelling in *Barenblatt, Wilkinson,* and *Braden* and held to support the inquiries there made into membership in the Communist Party does not resolve the issues here, where the challenged questions go to membership in an admittedly lawful organization.

In the absence of directly determinative authority, we turn, then, to consideration of the facts now before us. Obviously, if the respondent were still seeking discovery of the entire membership list, we could readily dispose of this case on the authority of *Bates v. Little Rock*, and *N.A.A.C.P. v. Alabama, supra*; a like result would follow if it were merely attempting to do piecemeal what could not be done in a single step. Though there are indications that the respondent Committee intended to inquire broadly into the N.A.A.C.P. membership records, there is no need to base our decision today upon a prediction as to the course which the Committee might have pursued if initially unopposed by the petitioner. Instead, we rest our result on the fact that the record in this case is insufficient to show a substantial connection between the Miami branch of the N.A.A.C.P. and Communist *activities* which the respondent Committee itself concedes is an essential prerequisite to demonstrating the immediate, substantial, and subordinating state interest necessary to sustain its right of inquiry into the membership lists of the association.

Basically, the evidence relied upon by the respondent to demonstrate the necessary foundation consists of the testimony of R. J. Strickland, an investigator for the Committee and its predecessors, and Arlington Sands, a former association official.

Strickland identified by name some 14 persons whom he said either were or had been Communists or members of Communist "front" or "affiliated" organizations. His description of their connection with the association was simply that "each of them has been a member of and/or participated in the meetings and other affairs of the N.A.A.C.P. in Dade County, Florida." In addition, one of the group was identified as having made, at an unspecified time, a contribution of unspecified amount to the local organization.

We do not know from this ambiguous testimony how many of the 14 were supposed to have been N.A.A.C.P. members. For all that appears, and there is no indicated reason to entertain a contrary belief, each or all of the named persons may have attended no more than one or two wholly public meetings of the N.A.A.C.P., and such attendance, like their membership, to the extent it existed, in the association, may have been wholly peripheral and begun and ended many years prior even to commencement of the present investigation in 1956. In addition, it is not clear whether the asserted Communist affiliations and the association with the N.A.A.C.P., however slight, coincided in time. . . .

This summary of the evidence discloses the utter failure to demonstrate the existence of any substantial relationship between the N.A.A.C.P. and subversive or Communist activities. In essence, there is here merely indirect, less than unequivocal, and mostly hearsay testimony that in years past some 14 people who were asserted to be, or to have been, Communists or members of Communist front or "affiliated organizations" attended occasional meetings of the Miami branch of the N.A.A.C.P. "and/or" were members of that branch, which had a total membership of about 1,000. . . .

Of course, a legislative investigation—as any investigation—must proceed "step by step," *Barenblatt v. United States*, but step by step or in totality, an adequate foundation for inquiry must be laid before proceeding in such a manner as will substantially intrude upon and severely curtail or inhibit constitutionally protected activities or seriously interfere with similarly protected associational rights. No such foundation has been laid here. The respondent

Committee has failed to demonstrate the compelling and subordinating governmental interest essential to support direct inquiry into the membership records of the N.A.A.C.P.

Nothing we say here impairs or denies the existence of the underlying legislative right to investigate or legislate with respect to subversive activities by Communists or anyone else; our decision today deals only with the manner in which such power may be exercised and we hold simply that groups which themselves are neither engaged in subversive or other illegal or improper activities nor demonstrated to have any substantial connections with such activities are to be protected in their rights of free and private association. . . .

To permit legislative inquiry to proceed on less than an adequate foundation would be to sanction unjustified and unwarranted intrusions into the very heart of the constitutional privilege to be secure in associations in legitimate organizations engaged in the exercise of First and Fourteenth Amendment rights; to impose a lesser standard than we here do would be inconsistent with the maintenance of those essential conditions basic to the preservation of our democracy.

The judgment below must be and is reversed.

Reversed.

☐ *Justice HARLAN, with whom Justice CLARK, Justice STEWART, and Justice WHITE join, dissenting.*

This Court rests reversal on its finding that the Committee did not have sufficient justification for including the Miami Branch of the N.A.A.C.P. within the ambit of its investigation—that, in the language of our cases [*Uphaus v. Wyman*, 360 U.S. 72 (1959)], an adequate "nexus" was lacking between the N.A.A.C.P. and the subject matter of the Committee's inquiry.

The Court's reasoning is difficult to grasp. I read its opinion as basically proceeding on the premise that the governmental interest in investigating Communist infiltration into admittedly nonsubversive organizations, as distinguished from investigating organizations themselves suspected of subversive activities, is not sufficient to overcome the countervailing right to freedom of association. On this basis "nexus" is seemingly found lacking because it was never claimed that the N.A.A.C.P. Miami Branch had itself engaged in subversive activity, and because none of the Committee's evidence relating to any of the 52 alleged Communist Party members was sufficient to attribute such activity to the local branch or to show that it was dominated, influenced, or used "by Communists."

But, until today, I had never supposed that any of our decisions relating to state or federal power to investigate in the field of Communist subversion could possibly be taken as suggesting any difference in the degree of governmental investigatory interest as between Communist infiltration *of* organizations and Communist activity *by* organizations. . . .

Given the unsoundness of the basic premise underlying the Court's holding as to the absence of "nexus," this decision surely falls of its own weight. For unless "nexus" requires an investigating agency to prove in advance the very things it is trying to find out, I do not understand how it can be said that the information preliminarily developed by the Committee's investigator was not sufficient to satisfy, under any reasonable test, the requirement of "nexus." . . .

I also find it difficult to see how this case really presents any serious question as to interference with freedom of association. Given the willingness of the petitioner to testify from recollection as to individual memberships in the local branch of the N.A.A.C.P., the germaneness of the membership records to the subject matter of the Committee's investigation, and the limited purpose for which their use was sought—as an aid to refreshing the witness' recollection, involving their divulgence only to the petitioner himself . . . —this case of course bears no resemblance whatever to *N.A.A.C.P. v. Alabama*, or *Bates v. Little Rock*. In both of those cases the State had sought general divulgence of local N.A.A.C.P. membership lists without any showing of a justifying state interest. In effect what we are asked to hold here is that the petitioner had a constitutional right to give only partial or inaccurate testimony, and that indeed seems to me the true effect of the Court's holding today.

Walter L. Nixon v. United States

506 U.S. 224, 113 S.CT. 732 (1993)

Walter Nixon, a former chief judge of the federal district court for southern Mississippi, was tried and convicted by a jury of two counts of making false statements before a federal grand jury and sentenced to prison. The grand jury had investigated reports that Nixon accepted money from a friend in exchange for seeking to halt the federal prosecution of his friend's son. Subsequently, because Nixon refused to resign from his judgeship and continued to receive his judicial salary while in prison, the House of Representatives adopted three articles of impeachment; two articles charged Nixon with giving false testimony to the grand jury and the third with bringing the judiciary into disrepute. The Senate then voted to invoke its own Impeachment Rule XI, under which the presiding officer appoints a committee of Senators to "receive evidence and take testimony." That committee held four days of hearings, during which ten witnesses, including Nixon, testified. The committee subsequently presented a transcript and a report to the full Senate, which debated the articles of impeachment for three hours and allowed Nixon to make a personal appeal. Following Nixon's conviction by a vote of eighty-nine to eight in the Senate, he filed a suit claiming that the Senate's expedited impeachment procedure was unconstitutional. After a federal district and appellate court rejected his claim as nonjusticiable, Nixon appealed to the Supreme Court.

The Court's decision was unanimous, and the opinion was announced by Chief Justice Rehnquist. Concurrences were by Justices Stevens, White, and Souter.

□ *Chief Justice REHNQUIST delivers the opinion of the Court.*

In this case, we must examine Article I, Section 3, Clause 6, to determine the scope of authority conferred upon the Senate by the Framers regarding impeachment. It provides:

> The Senate shall have the sole power to try all Impeachments. When sitting for that Purpose, they shall be on Oath or Affirmation. When the President of the United States is tried, the Chief Justice shall preside: And no person shall be convicted without the Concurrence of two-thirds of the members present.

The language and structure of this Clause are revealing. The first sentence is a grant of authority to the Senate, and the word "sole" indicates that this authority is reposed in the Senate and nowhere else. . . .

Petitioner argues that the word "try" in the first sentence imposes by implication an additional requirement on the Senate in that the proceedings must be in the nature of a judicial trial. From there petitioner goes on to argue that this limitation precludes the Senate from delegating to a select committee the task of hearing the testimony of witnesses, as was done pursuant to Senate Rule XI. . . .

There are several difficulties with this position which lead us ultimately to reject it. The word "try" both in 1787 and later, has considerably broader meanings than those to which petitioner would limit it. . . .

The Framers labored over the question of where the impeachment power should lie. Significantly, in at least two considered scenarios the power was placed with the Federal Judiciary. . . . According to Alexander Hamilton, the Senate was the "most fit depositary of this important trust" because its members are representatives of the people. See *The Federalist*, No. 65. The Supreme Court was not the proper body because the Framers "doubted whether the members of that tribunal would, at all times, be endowed with so eminent a portion of fortitude as would be called for in the execution of so difficult a task" or whether the Court "would possess the degree of credit and authority" to carry out its judgment if it conflicted with the accusation brought by the Legislature—the people's representatives. . . .

There are two additional reasons why the Judiciary, and the Supreme Court in particular, were not chosen to have any role in impeachments. First, the Framers recognized that most likely there would be two sets of proceedings for individuals who commit impeachable offenses—the impeachment trail and a separate criminal trial. . . . The Framers deliberately separated the two forums to avoid raising the specter of bias and to ensure independent judgments. . . .

Second, judicial review would be inconsistent with the Framers' insistence that our system be one of checks and balances. In our constitutional system, impeachment was designed to be the only check on the Judicial Branch by the Legislature. . . .

In addition to the textual commitment argument, we are persuaded that the lack of finality and the difficulty of fashioning relief counsel against justiciability. See *Baker v. Carr.* We agree with the Court of Appeals that opening the door of judicial review to the procedures used by the Senate in trying impeachments would "expose the political life of the country to months, or perhaps years, of chaos." This lack of finality would manifest itself most dramatically if the President were impeached. The legitimacy of any successor, and hence his effectiveness, would be impaired severely, not merely while the judicial process was running its course, but during any retrial that a differently constituted Senate might conduct if its first judgment of conviction were invalidated. Equally uncertain is the question of what relief a court may give other than simply setting aside the judgment of conviction. Could it order the reinstatement of a convicted federal judge, or order Congress to create an additional judgeship if the seat had been filled in the interim?

Petitioner finally contends that a holding of nonjusticiability cannot be reconciled with our opinion in *Powell v. McCormack*, 395 U.S. 486 (1969). The relevant issue in *Powell* was whether courts could review the House of Representatives' conclusion that Powell was "unqualified" to sit as a Member because he had been accused of misappropriating public funds and abusing the process of the New York courts. We stated that the question of justiciability turned on whether the Constitution committed authority to the House to judge its members' qualifications, and if so, the extent of that commitment. Article I, Section 5 provides that "Each House shall be the Judge of the Elections, Returns and Qualifications of its own Members." In turn, Article I, Section 2 specifies three requirements for membership in the House: The candidate must be at least twenty-five years of age, a citizen of the United States for no less than seven years, and an inhabitant of the State he is chosen to represent. We held that, in light of the three requirements specified in the Constitution, the word "qualifications"—of which the House was to be the Judge—was of a precise, limited nature.

Our conclusion in *Powell* was based on the fixed meaning of "qualifications" set forth in Article I, Section 2. . . . In the case before us, there is no separate provision of the Constitution which could be defeated by allowing the Senate final authority to determine the meaning of the word "try" in the Impeachment Trial Clause. We agree with Nixon that courts possess power to review either legislative or executive action that transgresses identifiable textual limits. . . . But we conclude, after exercising that delicate responsibility, that the word "try" in the Impeachment Clause does not provide an identifiable textual limit on the authority which is committed to the Senate.

☐ *Justice SOUTER concurred in a separate opinion in which, unlike Justice WHITE, he argued that the issue was nonjusticiable, although for different reasons than given by Chief Justice REHNQUIST.*

■ CONSTITUTIONAL HISTORY

Impeachment Trials

Article I provides that the House of Representatives "shall have the sole Power of Impeachment," and that the Senate has "the sole Power to try all Impeachments," as well as requires a two-thirds vote for conviction. Article II further specifies that the president and all civil officers shall be impeached for "Treason, Bribery, or other high Crimes and Misdemeanors."

The process was designed to be difficult and infrequently employed, except for removing officials who committed "great offenses." Indeed, after the partisan-driven effort to impeach Justice Samuel Chase failed to result in conviction, Thomas Jefferson lamented that impeachment was "a mere scarecrow." Still, more than fifty judges have resigned rather than face impeachment. In addition, two judges, as well as President Richard M. Nixon in 1974, resigned in order to evade impeachment trials.

There have been only fifteen Senate trials, resulting in seven convictions. Not all of those tried had allegedly committed criminal offenses. Most had other problems. Charges of alcoholism, senility, or violations of ethical conduct have often been leveled at judges. Others were targets of opposing political forces.

NAME (YEAR)	PARTY/OFFICE	POLITICAL COMPOSITION HOUSE	SENATE	SENATE VOTE
William Blount (1799)	Democratic-Republican Senator	58 Federalists 48 Democratic-Republicans	20 Federalists 12 Democratic-Republicans	Yes 11 No 14
John Pickering (1804)	Federalist Judge	69 Republicans 36 Federalists	25 Republicans 9 Federalists	Yes 19 No 7 Convicted
Samuel Chase (1805)	Federalist Justice	102 Republicans 39 Federalists	25 Republicans 9 Federalists	Yes 19 No 15
James H. Peck (1830–1831)	Republican Judge	139 Democrats 74 Republicans	36 Democrats 6 Whigs 3 Federalists 3 Republicans	Yes 21 No 22
West H. Humphreys (1862)	Democrat Judge	105 Republicans 43 Democrats 30 Other	27 Republicans 14 Democrats 7 Other	Yes 39 No 0 Convicted

NAME (YEAR)	PARTY/OFFICE	POLITICAL COMPOSITION HOUSE	SENATE	SENATE VOTE
Andrew Johnson (1868)	Democrat President	143 Republicans 49 Democrats	42 Republicans 12 Democrats	Yes 35 No 19
William W. Belknap (1876)	Douglas Democrat Secretary of War	169 Democrats 109 Republicans 14 Other	45 Republicans 12 Democrats	Yes 37 No 19
Charles Swayne (1905)	Republican Judge	207 Republicans 178 Democrats	58 Republicans 32 Democrats	Yes 35 No 47
Robert Archbald (1913)	Republican Judge	228 Democrats 161 Republicans	51 Republicans 45 Democrats	Yes 68 No 5 Convicted
Harold Louderback (1933)	Republican Judge	220 Democrats 21 Republicans 1 Other	60 Democrats 35 Republicans 1 Other	Yes 45 No 34
Halsted Ritter (1936)	Republican Judge	319 Democrats 103 Republicans 10 Other	70 Democrats 26 Republicans	Yes 56 No 28 Convicted
Harry E. Clairborne (1986)	Democrat Judge	253 Democrats 182 Republicans	53 Republicans 47 Democrats	Yes 87 No 10 Convicted
Alcee Hastings (1989)	Democrat Judge	262 Democrats 173 Republicans	57 Democrats 43 Republicans	Yes 69 No 26 Convicted
Walter Nixon, Jr. (1989)	Democrat Judge	262 Democrats 173 Republicans	57 Democrats 43 Republicans	Yes 89 No 8 Convicted
William J. Clinton (1999)	Democrat President	229 Republicans 206 Democrats	55 Republicans 45 Democrats	Yes 45/50★ No 55/50★ (★2 counts)

Because of the difficulties of impeachment and problems with judicial discipline and removal, some scholars and politicians argue that federal judges—who under Article III, section 1 hold their offices subject to "good Behavior"—may be removed by means other than impeachment. Since Article III conditions judicial tenure upon "good Behavior," it arguably provides a broader basis for removing judges than Article II's impeachment provision.

6

CONGRESS: LEGISLATIVE, TAXING, AND SPENDING POWERS

The legislative powers of Congress, as noted in the last chapter, are expressly *enumerated*. Article 1 lists seventeen specific powers, including the power to regulate commerce, to lay and collect taxes, and to "provide for the common Defense and general welfare of the United States." In addition, in Article I, Section 8, Clause 18, Congress was given an important residual power of enacting all laws "necessary and proper" to the execution of its authority and other delegated powers.

Basically, Congress may enact four types of laws: those that (1) provide substantive or procedural rules of general application governing, for example, interstate commerce; (2) govern the collection of revenues for the national government; (3) appropriate revenues for expenditure by the government; and (4) confer benefits on or adjust claims of individuals against the government. Although extensive, this power is not unlimited. Congress may not, for example, pass *ex post facto* laws (criminal statutes that have retroactive application). Nor may it deny or infringe on guarantees of the Bill of Rights.

The detailed enumeration of Congress's legislative powers registers the Framers' aim of correcting the defects of the Articles of Confederation by creating a national government with vastly greater, although nonetheless limited, powers. As James Madison explains in *The Federalist*, No. 42, under the Articles of Confederation a central problem was that the Continental Congress could not effectively regulate commerce among the states or with foreign nations. For this reason, among seventeen areas over which legislative power is granted in Article I, the commerce clause empowers Congress "to regulate commerce with foreign nations, and among the several states, and with Indian tribes."

In specifically enumerating legislative powers, the Constitutional Convention rejected Alexander Hamilton's proposal that Congress have the "power to pass all laws which they shall judge necessary to the common defense and general welfare of the Union."[1] However, the convention agreed to add the necessary and proper clause, recognizing an *implied* power of Congress "[t]o make all Laws which shall be necessary and proper for carrying into Execution the foregoing Powers, and all other Powers vested by this Constitution in the Government of the United States, or in any Department or Officer thereof."

Besides enumerated and implied powers, Congress possesses *inherent* powers that flow from the concept of sovereignty. For example, the Constitution does not specifically confer on Congress the power to govern territories acquired by acquisition or through treaties. Yet as Chief Justice Marshall observed, "The right to govern may be the inevitable consequence of the right to acquire territory. Whichever may be the source, whence the power is derived, the possession of it is unquestioned."[2] In *United States v. Kagama*, 118 U.S. 375 (1886), the Court more emphatically acknowledged the inherent powers of Congress:

> [T]his power of Congress to organize territorial governments and make laws for their inhabitants, arises not so much from the clause in the Constitution in regard to disposing or making rules and regulations concerning the Territory and other property of the United States, as from the ownership of the country in which the Territories are, and the right of exclusive sovereignty which must exist in the National Government and can be found nowhere else.

In addition to enumerated, implied, and inherent powers, constitutional amendments are a source of expanding congressional powers. In particular, the "Reconstruction Amendments" (the Thirteenth, Fourteenth, and Fifteenth Amendments) contain provisions expanding Congress's enforcement powers; they generated major controversy over the passage of the Voting Rights Act, forbidding racial discrimination in voting, see *South Carolina v. Katzenbach* (1966) (see excerpt in Ch. 8).

While the Constitutional Convention aimed at ensuring extensive legislative powers for Congress, it also sought to preserve for the states those powers not delegated to the national government. But during the ratification period Anti-Federalists charged that Congress was given too much power, especially with "the sweeping" necessary and proper clause. As the pamphleteer Centinel cautioned in the fall of 1787, "Whatever law congress may deem necessary and proper for carrying into

■ CONSTITUTIONAL HISTORY

Formal Amendments and Methods of Amending the Constitution

Only twenty-seven of the thirty-one amendments proposed by Congress, from the over 11,500 proposed amendments introduced in Congress, have been successfully passed and ratified by the states. Two of the most recent proposals that have failed to win approval involved granting home rule and Senate representation to residents of the District of Columbia and the ill-fated Equal Rights Amendment, which would have recognized the equal rights of women.

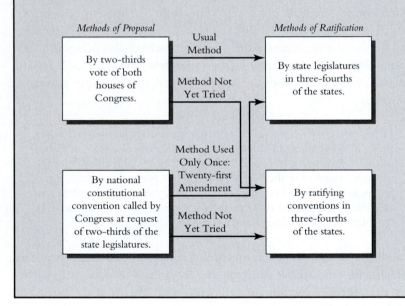

execution any of the powers vested in them, may be enacted; and by virtue of this clause, they may control and abrogate any and every of the laws of the state governments, on the allegation that they interfere with the execution of their powers."[3] Likewise, when opposing New York's ratification of the Constitution, leading Anti-Federalist Brutus warned that under the necessary and proper clause Congress "may so exercise this power as entirely to annihilate all the state governments, and reduce this country to one single government."[4]

Because of the Anti-Federalists' opposition and dire predictions, the first Congress added the Tenth Amendment. It underscores that "pow-

The Time Taken to Ratify Amendments to the Constitution

AMENDMENT NUMBER AND CONTENT		DATE	TIME TO RATIFY
1–10	The Bill of Rights	1791	1 year, 2.5 months
11	Lawsuits against states	1798	3 years, 10 months
12	Presidential elections	1804	8.5 months
13	Abolition of slavery	1865	10.5 months
14	Equal civil rights	1868	2 years, 1.5 months
15	Voting rights for freemen (black men)	1870	1 year, 1 month
16	Federal income tax	1913	3 years, 7.5 months
17	Senatorial elections	1913	1 year, 0.5 month
18	Prohibition	1919	1 year, 1.5 months
19	Women's suffrage	1920	1 year, 2.5 months
20	Terms of office	1933	11 months
21	Repeal of prohibition	1933	9.5 months
22	Limit on president's terms	1951	3 years, 11.5 months
23	Voting rights for the District of Columbia	1961	9 months
24	Abolition of poll taxes	1964	1 year, 5.5 months
25	Presidential succession	1965	1 year, 6.5 months
26	Eighteen-year-olds' suffrage	1971	4 months
27	Ban on midterm salary increases for Congress	1992	203 years

ers not delegated to the United States by the Constitution . . . are re-served to the States respectively, or to the people." However, the Tenth Amendment by no means resolved the essential tension between congressional and state powers (see Ch. 7).

Constitutional controversies continue to arise from the debate initially sparked by the Federalists and Anti-Federalists over the scope of Congress's legislative powers and competing claims of "states' rights" and federalism. In this chapter the development of Congress's expansive legislative powers is examined, and in Chapter 7 their limitations and the scope of states' regulatory powers over commerce are considered.

NOTES

1. A. Hamilton, in *Records of the Federal Convention*, Vol. 3, ed. Max Farrand (New Haven, CT: Yale University Press, 1911), 617, 627.

2. *American Insurance Co. v. Canter*, 26 U.S. (1 Pet.) 516 (1828).

3. The Centinel, in *The Complete Anti-Federalist*, Vol. 2, ed. Herbert J. Storing (Chicago: University of Chicago Press, 1981), 168–169.

4. Brutus, in *The Complete Anti-Federalist*, Vol. 2, ed. Herbert J. Storing (Chicago: University of Chicago Press, 1981), 366.

SELECTED BIBLIOGRAPHY

Devins, Neil, and Whittington, Keith, eds. *Congress and the Constitution*. Durham, NC: Duke University Press, 2005.

Frankfurter, Felix. *The Commerce Clause under Marshall, Taney and Waite*. Chapel Hill: University of North Carolina Press, 1971.

■ CONSTITUTIONAL HISTORY

A Twenty-seventh Amendment after 203 Years

In 1789 James Madison proposed twelve amendments to the Constitution, and ten known as the Bill of Rights were ratified in 1791. More than 200 years later, one of his two unratified amendments finally received the crucial vote of three-fourths of the states. Madison's proposed second amendment, which became the Twenty-seventh Amendment, provides that "[n]o law varying the compensation for the services of the Senators and Representatives shall take effect, until an election of Representatives shall have intervened."

Some congressional leaders initially disagreed about whether an amendment could take effect 203 years after its proposal. But after the archivist of the United States verified that the bills ratified in each state were the same and certified the amendment, it took effect. Subsequently, for politically symbolic reasons, Congress approved of the amendment by a vote of 99 to 0 in the Senate and 414 to 3 in the House.

Article V of the Constitution does not specify a time limit for states' ratification. Of the more than 10,000 proposed amendments, four others passed Congress and remain outstanding. One, also proposed in 1789, would base the size of the House of Representative on one representative for every 30,000 people until the House reached 100 members, then one

Gunther, Gerald, ed. *John Marshall's Defense of McCulloch v. Maryland.* Palo Alto, CA: Stanford University Press, 1969.

Kyvig, David. *Explicit and Authentic Acts: Amending the Constitution, 1776–1995.* Lawrence: University Press of Kansas, 1996.

Levinson, Sanford, ed. *Responding to Imperfection: The Theory and Practice of Constitutional Amendment.* Princeton, NJ: Princeton University Press, 1995.

Vile, John R., ed. *Proposed Amendments to the U.S. Constitution: 1787–2001.* New York: The Lawbook Exchange, 2003.

———. *Constitutional Change in the United States: A Comparative Study of the Role of Constitutional Amendments, Judicial Interpretations, and Legislative and Executive Actions.* New York: Praeger, 1994.

———. *Contemporary Questions Surrounding the Constitutional Amending Process.* New York: Praeger, 1993.

representative for every 40,000 until the House grew to 200, with Congress determining its size thereafter. An 1810 proposal would deny citizenship to anyone accepting a title or office from an "emperor, king, prince, or foreign power." In 1861 Congress passed an amendment allowing slavery to continue. And in 1924 Congress approved another allowing it to regulate child labor and overturning rulings of the Supreme Court to the contrary.

In addition, thirty-two states—two short of the necessary two-thirds—have petitioned Congress to pass a balanced budget amendment, and nineteen have asked for an amendment banning abortion. Two other amendments—the Equal Rights Amendment (Vol. 2, Ch. 12, "Constitutional History") and a proposal giving the District of Columbia representation in Congress—were defeated.

The first Congress did not set a deadline for ratification of its amendments. Nor did Congress do so until 1917 when it required ratification of the prohibition amendment within seven years. When that requirement was challenged in *Dillion v. Gloss*, 256 U.S. 368 (1921), the Court held that "ratification must be within some reasonable time after [an amendment's] proposal" and Congress's power to set a deadline was "an incident of its power to designate the mode of ratification." Subsequently, the question of whether the proposed child labor amendment could be ratified thirteen years after its proposal arose in *Coleman v. Miller*, 307 U.S. 433 (1939). In that case, the Court ruled that that was a political question for Congress, not the judiciary, to decide.

A | *The Classic View of Congress's Legislative Powers*

The scope of Congress's legislative powers, and, indeed, the power of the national government, became the focus of an enduring struggle almost immediately after ratification of the Constitution. In December 1790, Secretary of the Treasury Alexander Hamilton proposed that Congress charter a national bank. The ensuing debate over its constitutionality pitted Hamilton and the Federalists against Madison and Jefferson over not just the allocation of governmental power but fundamental principles of constitutional interpretation and politics.

Hamilton contended that a national bank was needed and would strengthen the national government by aiding in tax collection, administering public finances, and in securing loans to the government. And he persuasively argued that Congress had the broad constitutional authority to establish such a corporation:

> Now it appears to the Secretary of the Treasury, that this *general principle is inherent in the very definition of Government* and *essential* to every step of the progress to be made by that of the United States; namely—that every power vested in a Government is in its nature *sovereign*, and includes by *force* of the *term*, a right to employ all the *means* requisite, and fairly *applicable* to the attainment of the *ends* of such power; and which are not precluded by restrictions & exceptions specified in the constitution; or not immoral, or not contrary to the essential ends of political activity. . . .

> It is not denied, that there are *implied*, as well as *express* powers, and that the former are as effectually delegated as the latter. . . .

> Then it follows, that as a power of erecting a corporation may as well be *implied* as any other thing; it may as well be employed as an *instrument* or *mean* of carrying into execution any of the specified powers, as any other instrument or mean whatever. The only question must be, in this as in every other case, whether the mean to be employed, or in this instance the corporation to be erected, has a natural relation to any of the acknowledged objects or lawful ends of the government. Thus a corporation may not be erected by congress, for superintending the police of the city of Philadelphia because they are not authorized to *regulate* the *police* of that city; but one may be erected in relation to the collection of taxes, or to the trade with foreign countries, or the trade between the States, or with the Indian Tribes, because it is the province of the federal

government to regulate those objects & because it is incident to a general *sovereign* or *legislative power* to *regulate* a thing, to employ all the means which relate to its regulation to the *best & greatest advantage.* . . .

[T]he doctrine which is contended for . . . does not affirm that the National government is sovereign in all respects, but that it is sovereign to a certain extent: that is, to the extent of the objects of its specified powers.

It leaves therefore a criterion of what is constitutional, and of what is not so. This criterion is the *end* to which the measure relates as a *mean*. If the end be clearly comprehended within any of the specified powers, & if the measure have an obvious relation to that end, and is not forbidden by any particular provision of the constitution—it may be safely deemed to come within the compass of the national authority.[1]

The Senate, half of whose members had been delegates to the Constitutional Convention, unanimously endorsed Hamilton's proposal.

By contrast, in the House of Representatives, Madison maintained that creation of the bank was beyond the scope of Congress's delegated powers:

Mark the reasoning on which the validity of the bill depends. To borrow money is made the end, and the accumulation of capitals implied as the means. The accumulation of money is then the end, and the Bank implied as the means. The Bank is then the end, and a charter of incorporation . . . implied as the means.

If implications, thus remote and thus multiplied, can be linked together, a chain may be formed that will reach every object of legislation, every object within the whole compass of political economy. . . .

[T]he proposed Bank could not be called necessary to the Government; at most could be but convenient. Its uses to the Government could be supplied by keeping the taxes a little in advance; by loans from individuals; by other Banks, over which the Government would have equal command; nay greater, as it might grant or refuse to these the privilege (a free and irrevocable gift to the proposed Bank) of using their notes in the Federal Revenue.[2]

Jefferson, serving as Secretary of State, expressed similar opposition. In a memorandum to President Washington, he explained:

I consider the foundation of the Constitution as laid on this ground: That "all powers not delegated to the United States, by the Constitution, nor prohibited by it to the States, are reserved to the

States or to the people." To take a single step beyond the boundaries thus specially drawn around the powers of Congress is to take possession of a boundless field of power, no longer susceptible of any definition.

The incorporation of a bank, and the powers assumed by this bill, have not, in my opinion, been delegated to the United States by the Constitution. . . .

It has been urged that a bank will give great facility or convenience in the collection of taxes. Suppose this were true; yet the Constitution allows only the means which are *"necessary,"* not those which are merely "convenient" for effecting the enumerated powers. If such a latitude of construction be allowed to this phrase as to give any non-enumerated power, it will go to every one, for there is not one which ingenuity may not torture into a *convenience* in some instance *or other*, to *some one* of so long a list of enumerated powers. It would swallow up all the delegated powers, and reduce the whole to one power, as before observed. Therefore it was that the Constitution restrained them to the *necessary* means, that is to say, to those means without which the grant of power would be nugatory.[3]

Despite these arguments, by a vote of thirty-nine to twenty the House adopted a bill chartering the bank. On February 25, 1791, Washington signed the act incorporating, and granting a twenty-year charter to, the first Bank of the United States.

When the bank's charter expired in 1811, its renewal was defeated in Congress by just one vote. Jeffersonian-Republicans and private business and banking interests led the opposition. Notably, though, President Madison and Jefferson now supported the bank and deemed its constitutionality settled. Four years later Congress established the second Bank of the United States with another twenty-year charter. This time, economic hardships brought about by the War of 1812 and the national government's reliance on state banks for loans, rather than the constitutionality of the bank, was the overriding consideration in Congress.

Opposition to a national bank, however, remained strong in the states and eventually led to the landmark decision in *McCulloch v. Maryland* (1819) (see excerpt below). Chief Justice Marshall, an ardent Federalist, upheld the constitutionality of the bank with a broad reading of congressional powers reminiscent of Hamilton's arguments decades earlier. In his classic formulation: "Let the end be legitimate, let it be within the scope of the constitution, and all means which are appropriate, which are plainly adapted to that end, which are not prohibited, but consistent with the letter and spirit of the constitution, are constitutional."

Although Madison and Jefferson agreed with *McCulloch's* holding, they continued to bristle at the expansive interpretation of the power of Congress and the national government advanced by the Marshall Court. In Jefferson's words, "The judiciary of the United States is the subtle core of sappers and miners constantly working underground to undermine the foundations of our confederated fabric. They are construing our Constitution from a coordination of general [i.e., national] and special [i.e., state] government to a general and supreme one alone. This will lay all things at their feet."[4]

Opposition persisted and support for the bank gradually diminished by 1832, when Congress passed another bill extending the bank's charter. President Andrew Jackson vetoed the bill and again challenged the Marshall Court's interpretation of and authority over the Constitution (see "Jackson's Veto Message of 1832," excerpted in Ch. 1).

The Marshall Court nonetheless successfully established the basis for a broad interpretation of Congress's plenary power. Moreover, Marshall's analysis in *McCulloch* rests on the Constitution's structure and allocation of governmental authority, rather than primarily on its granting congressional authority to make all necessary and proper laws.[5] And that analysis was subsequently incorporated into the necessary and proper clause in justifying expansive legislation. In the *Legal Tender Cases*, 110 U.S. 421 (1884), for example, the national government's use of legal tender to repay private debts was upheld as a "necessary and proper" exercise of its power to create a national currency, based on its express authority to coin money.[6] Later, in *Katzenbach v. Morgan*, 384 U.S. 641 (1966), the Court again reaffirmed Congress's plenary power under the necessary and proper clause when upholding the Voting Rights Act of 1965, which forbids racial discrimination in voting.

Five years after *McCulloch*, Marshall further advanced his vision of national governmental power by broadly construing the commerce clause in *Gibbons v. Ogden* (1824) (see excerpt below). Congress itself did not even assert its authority over commerce among the states until the late nineteenth century. Yet *Gibbons* affirmed broad congressional authority in striking down state regulations for infringing on the power, even if unexercised, of Congress. Marshall did so by (1) defining "commerce" as all "intercourse" that (2) "affects more states than one," and holding that Congress's power over commerce is (3) complete and (4) does not stop at state boundaries.

Gibbons was immediately heralded for securing the freedom of interstate transportation. As a result, tax and other barriers erected among the states were eliminated, the basis for a national "common market" was laid, and economic growth in the country promoted. In addition, Marshall's definition of *commerce* as intercourse among the states would later serve as a basis for upholding federal regulation under

Chief Justice John Marshall. (*Portrait by Rembrandt Peale, Collection of the Supreme Court of the United States.*)

the commerce clause over an expanding range of activities, including, for example, the sale of lottery tickets,[7] "white slave trade,"[8] oil pipes running across state lines,[9] and telecommunications.[10]

Through a broad interpretation of the plenary powers of Congress in *McCulloch* and *Gibbons*, the Marshall Court advanced the interests of the national government over those of the states and buttressed its own power of judicial review.

NOTES

1. A. Hamilton, "Opinion on the Constitutionality of an Act to Establish a Bank," in *The Papers of Alexander Hamilton*, Vol. 8, ed. Harold C. Syrett (New York: Columbia University Press, 1961–1979), 97.

2. J. Madison, in *The Debates and Proceedings in the Congress of the United States*, Vol. 2 (Washington, DC: Gales and Seaton, 1834), 1944–1954.

3. T. Jefferson, "Opinion on the Constitutionality of the Bill for Establishing a National Bank," in *The Papers of Thomas Jefferson*, Vol. 19, ed. Julian Boyd (Princeton, NJ: Princeton University Press, 1974), 275.

4. Quoted and further discussed in Dumas Malone, *Jefferson: The President* (Boston: Little, Brown, 1970), 146–153.

5. See Charles Black, *Structure and Relationship in Constitutional Law* (Baton Rouge: Louisiana State University Press, 1969).

6. The Court upheld as well the Interstate Commerce Act of 1887 as a necessary and proper exercise of congressional authority, *Interstate Commerce Commission v. Brimson*, 154 U.S. 447 (1894). For other decisions relying on the necessary and proper clause, see *Lichter v. United States*, 334 U.S. 743 (1948); *Adams v. Maryland*, 347 U.S. 179 (1954); and *United States v. Oregon*, 366 U.S. 643 (1961).

7. *Champion v. Ames*, 188 U.S. 321 (1907).

8. See *Hale v. United States*, 227 U.S. 308 (1913); and *Caminetti v. United States*, 242 U.S. 470 (1917).

9. *The Pipe Line Cases*, 234 U.S. 548 (1914).

10. *Federal Radio Commission v. Nelson Brothers*, 289 U.S. 266 (1933).

SELECTED BIBLIOGRAPHY

Elkin, Stephen. *Reconstructing the Commercial Republic.* Chicago: University of Chicago Press, 2006.

Ellis, Richard E. *Aggressive Nationalism: McCulloch v. Maryland and the Foundation of Federal Authority in the Young Republic.* New York: Oxford University Press, 2007.

Frankfurter, Felix. *The Commerce Clause under Marshall, Taney and Waite.* Chapel Hill: University of North Carolina Press, 1937.

Killenbeck, Mark. *McCulloch v. Maryland: Securing A Nation.* Lawrence: University Press of Kansas, 2006.

McCulloch v. Maryland
4 WHEAT. (17 U.S.) 316 (1819)

Two years after Congress chartered the second Bank of the United States, Maryland passed a law imposing an annual tax of $15,000 on all banks operating in the state that were not chartered by the state legislature. James McCulloch, the cashier for the Maryland branch of the Bank of the United States, refused to pay the tax assessed against the bank. As a result, Maryland successfully sued McCulloch, who then appealed to the Supreme Court.

The Court's decision was unanimous, and the opinion was announced by Chief Justice Marshall.

☐ *Chief Justice MARSHALL delivers the opinion of the Court.*

In the case now to be determined, the defendant, a sovereign state, denies the obligation of a law enacted by the legislature of the Union, and the plaintiff, on his part, contests the validity of an act which has been passed by the legislature of that state. The constitution of our country, in its most interesting and vital parts, is to be considered; the conflicting powers of the government of the Union and of its members, as marked in that constitution, are to be discussed; and an opinion given, which may essentially influence the great operations of the government. No tribunal can approach such a question without a deep sense of its importance, and of the awful responsibility involved in its decision. But it must be decided peacefully, or remain a source of hostile legislation, perhaps of hostility of a still more serious nature; and if it is to be so decided, by this tribunal alone can the decision be made. On the Supreme Court of the United States has the constitution of our country devolved this important duty.

The first question made in the cause is, has Congress power to incorporate a bank?

It has been truly said that this can scarcely be considered as an open question, entirely unprejudiced by the former proceedings of the nation respecting it. The principle now contested was introduced at a very early period of our history, has been recognized by many successive legislatures, and has been acted upon by the judicial department, in cases of peculiar delicacy, as a law of undoubted obligation.

It will not be denied that a bold and daring usurpation might be resisted, after an acquiescence still longer and more complete than this. But it is conceived that a doubtful question, one on which human reason may pause, and the human judgment be suspended, in the decision of which the great principles of liberty are not concerned, but the respective powers of those who are equally the representatives of the people, are to be adjusted; if not put at rest by the practice of the government, ought to receive a considerable impression from that practice. An exposition of the constitution, deliberately established by legislative acts, on the faith of which an immense property has been advanced, ought not to be lightly disregarded.

The power now contested was exercised by the first Congress elected under the present constitution. The bill for incorporating the bank of the United States did not steal upon an unsuspecting legislature, and pass unobserved. Its principle was completely understood, and was opposed with equal zeal and ability. After being resisted, first in the fair and open field of debate, and afterwards in the executive cabinet, with as much persevering talent as any measure has ever experienced, and being supported by arguments which convinced minds as pure and as intelligent as this country can boast, it became a law. The original act was permitted to expire; but a short experience of the embarrassments to which the refusal to revive it exposed the government, convinced those who were most prejudiced against the measure of its necessity and induced the passage of the present law. It would require no ordinary share of intrepidity to assert that a measure adopted under these circumstances was a bold and plain usurpation, to which the constitution gave no countenance.

These observations belong to the cause; but they are not made under the impression that, were the question entirely new, the law would be found irreconcilable with the constitution.

In discussing this question, the counsel for the state of Maryland have deemed it of some importance, in the construction of the constitution, to consider that instrument not as emanating from the people, but as the act of sovereign and independent states. The powers of the general government, it has been said, are delegated by the states, who alone are truly sovereign; and must be exercised in subordination to the states, who alone possess supreme dominion.

It would be difficult to sustain this proposition. The convention which framed the constitution was indeed elected by the state legislatures. But the instrument, when it came from their hands, was a mere proposal, without obligation, or pretensions to it. It was reported to the then existing Congress of the United States, with a request that it might "be submitted to a convention of delegates, chosen in each state by the people thereof, under the recommendation of its legislature, for their assent and ratification." This mode of proceeding was adopted; and by the convention, by Congress, and by the state legislatures, the instrument was submitted to the people. They acted upon it in the only manner in which they can act safely, effectively, and wisely, on such a subject, by assembling in convention. It is true, they assembled in their several states—and where else should they have assembled? No political dreamer was ever wild enough to think of breaking down the lines which separate the states, and of compounding the American people into one common mass. Of consequence, when they act, they act in their states. But the measures they adopt do not, on that account, cease to be the measures of the people themselves, or become the measures of the state governments.

From these conventions the constitution derives its whole authority. The government proceeds directly from the people; is "ordained and established" in the name of the people; and is declared to be ordained, "in order to form a more perfect union, establish justice, insure domestic tranquillity, and secure the blessings of liberty to themselves and to their posterity." The assent of the states, in their sovereign capacity, is implied in calling a convention, and thus submitting that instrument to the people. But the people were at perfect liberty to accept or reject it; and their act was final. It required not the affirmance, and could not be negatived, by the state governments. The constitution, when thus adopted, was of complete obligation, and bound the state sovereignties. . . .

The government of the Union, then (whatever may be the influence of this fact on the case), is, emphatically, and truly, a government of the people. In form and in substance it emanates from them. Its powers are granted by them, and are to be exercised directly on them, and for their benefit.

This government is acknowledged by all to be one of enumerated powers. The principle, that it can exercise only the powers granted to it, would seem too apparent to have required to be enforced by all those arguments which its enlightened friends, while it was depending before the people, found it necessary to urge, that principle is now universally admitted. But the question respecting the extent of the powers actually granted, is perpetually arising, and will probably continue to arise, as long as our system shall exist.

In discussing these questions, the conflicting powers of the general and state governments must be brought into view, and the supremacy of their respective laws, when they are in opposition, must be settled.

If any one proposition could command the universal assent of mankind, we might expect it would be this—that the government of the Union, though limited in its powers, is supreme within its sphere of action. This would seem to result necessarily from its nature. It is the government of all; its powers are delegated by all; it represents all, and acts for all. Though any one state may be willing to control its operations, no state is willing to allow others to control them. The nation, on those subjects on which it can act, must necessarily bind its component parts. But this question is not left to mere reason; the people have, in express terms, decided it by saying, "this constitution, and the laws of the United States, which shall be made in pursuance thereof," "shall be the supreme law of the land," and by requiring that the members of the state legislatures, and the officers of the executive and judicial departments of the states shall take the oath of fidelity to it. . . .

Among the enumerated powers, we do not find that of establishing a bank or creating a corporation. But there is no phrase in the instrument which, like the articles of confederation, excludes incidental or implied powers; and which requires that everything granted shall be expressly and minutely described. Even the 10th amendment, which was framed for the purpose of quieting the excessive jealousies which had been excited, omits the word "expressly," and declares only that the powers "not delegated to the United States, nor prohibited to the states, are reserved to the states or to the people"; thus leaving the question, whether the particular power which may become the subject of contest has been delegated to the one government, or prohibited to the other, to depend on a fair construction of the whole instrument. The men who drew and adopted this amendment had experienced the embarrassments resulting from the insertion of this word in the articles of confederation, and probably omitted it to avoid those embarrassments. A constitution, to contain an accurate detail of all the subdivisions of which its great powers will admit, and of all the means by which they may be carried into execution, would partake of a prolixity of a legal code, and could scarcely be embraced by the human mind. It would probably never be understood by the public. Its nature, therefore, requires, that only its great outlines should be marked, its important objects designated, and the minor ingredients which compose those objects be deduced from the nature of the objects themselves. That this idea was entertained by the framers of the American constitution, is not only to be inferred from the nature of the instrument, but from the language. Why else were some of the limitations, found in the ninth section of the 1st article, introduced? It is also, in some degree warranted by their having omitted to use any restrictive term which might prevent its receiving a fair and just interpretation. In considering this question, then, we must never forget that it is a constitution we are expounding.

Although, among the enumerated powers of government, we do not find the word "bank" or "incorporation," we find the great power to lay and collect taxes; to borrow money; to regulate commerce; to declare and conduct war; and to raise and support armies and navies. The sword and the purse, all the external relations, and no inconsiderable portion of the industry of the nation, are entrusted to its government. It can never be pretended that these vast powers draw after them others of inferior importance, merely because they are inferior. Such an idea can never be advanced. But it may with great reason be contended, that a government, entrusted with such ample powers, on the due execution of which the happiness and prosperity of the nation so vitally depends, must also be entrusted with ample means for the execution. The power being given, it is the interest of the nation to facilitate its execution. It can never be their interest, as cannot be presumed to have been their intention, to clog and embarrass its execution in withholding the most appropriate means. Throughout this vast republic, from the St. Croix to the Gulf of Mexico, from the Atlantic to the Pacific, revenue is to be collected and expended, armies are to be marched and supported. The exigencies of the nation may require that the treasure raised in the north should be transported to the south, that raised in the east conveyed to the west, or that this order should be reversed. Is that construction of the constitution to be preferred which would render these operations difficult, hazardous, and expensive? Can we adopt that construction (unless the words imperiously require it) which would impute to the framers of that instrument, when granting these powers for the public good, the intention of impeding their exercise by withholding a choice of means? . . .

On what foundation does this argument rest? On this alone: The power of creating a corporation is one appertaining to sovereignty, and is not expressly conferred on Congress. This is true. But all legislative powers appertain to sovereignty. The original power of giving the law on any subject whatever, is a sovereign power; and if the government of the Union is restrained from creating a corporation, as a means for performing its functions, on the single reason that the creation of a corporation is an act of sovereignty; if the sufficiency of this reason be acknowledged, there would be some difficulty in sustaining the authority of Congress to pass other laws for the accomplishment of the same objects. . . .

But the constitution of the United States has not left the right of Congress to employ the necessary means for the execution of the powers conferred on the government to general reasoning. To its enumeration of powers is added that of making "all laws which shall be necessary and proper, for carrying into execution the foregoing powers, and all other powers vested by this constitution, in the government of the United States, or in any department thereof."

The counsel for the State of Maryland have urged various arguments, to prove that this clause, though in terms a grant of power, is not so in effect; but is really restrictive of the general right, which might otherwise be implied, of selecting means for executing the enumerated powers. . . .

[T]he argument on which most reliance is placed, is drawn from the peculiar language of this clause. Congress is not empowered by it to make all laws, which may have relation to the powers conferred on the government; but such only as may be "necessary and proper" for carrying them into execution. The word "necessary" is considered as controlling the whole sentence, and as limiting the right to pass laws for the execution of the granted powers, to such as are indispensable, and without which the power would be nugatory. That it excludes the choice of means, and leaves to Congress, in each case, that only which is most direct and simple.

Is it true that this is the sense in which the word "necessary" is always used? Does it always import an absolute physical necessity, so strong that one thing, to which another may be termed necessary, cannot exist without that other? We think it does not. If reference be had to its use, in the common affairs of the world, or in approved authors, we find that it frequently imports no more than that one thing is convenient, or useful, or essential to another.

To employ the means necessary to an end, is generally understood as employing any means calculated to produce the end, and not as being confined to those single means, without which the end would be entirely unattainable. Such is the character of human language, that no word conveys to the mind, in all situations, one single definite idea; and nothing is more common than to use words in a figurative sense. Almost all compositions contain words, which, taken in their rigorous sense, would convey a meaning different from that which is obviously intended. It is essential to just construction, that many words which import something excessive should be understood in a more mitigated sense—in that sense which common usage justifies. The word "necessary" is of this description. It has not a fixed character peculiar to itself. It admits of all degrees of comparison; and is often connected with other words, which increase or diminish the impression the mind receives of the urgency it imports. A thing may be necessary, very necessary, absolutely or indispensably necessary. To no mind would the same idea be conveyed by these several phrases. This comment on the word is well illustrated by the passage cited at the bar, from the 10th section of the 1st article of the constitution. It is, we think, impossible to compare the sentence which prohibits a state from laying "imposts or duties on imports or exports, except what may be absolutely necessary for executing its inspection laws," with that which authorizes Congress "to make all laws which shall be necessary and proper for carrying into execution" the powers of the general government, without feeling a conviction that the convention understood itself to change materially the meaning of the word "necessary," by prefixing the word "absolutely." This word, then, like others, is used in various senses; and, in its construction, the subject, the context, the intention of the person using them, are all to be taken into view.

Let this be done in the case under consideration. The subject is the execution of those great powers on which the welfare of a nation essentially depends. It must have been the intention of those who gave these powers, to insure, as far as human prudence could insure, their beneficial execution. This could not be done by confiding the choice of means to such narrow limits as not to leave it in the power of Congress to adopt any which might be appropriate, and which were conducive to the end. This provision is made in a constitution intended to endure for ages to come, and, consequently, to be adapted to the various crises of human affairs. To have prescribed the means by which government should, in all future time, execute its powers, would have been to change, entirely, the character of the instrument, and give it the properties of a legal code. It would have been an unwise attempt to provide, by immutable rules, for exigencies which, if foreseen at all, must have been seen dimly, and which can be best provided for as they occur. To have declared that the best means shall not be used, but those alone without which the power given would be nugatory, would have been to deprive the legislature of the capacity to avail itself of experience, to exercise its reason, and to accommodate its legislation to circumstances. If we apply this principle of construction to any of the powers of the government, we shall find it so pernicious in its operation that we shall be compelled to discard it. . . .

So, with respect to the whole penal code of the United States: whence arises the power to punish in cases not prescribed by the constitution? All admit that the government may, legitimately, punish any violation of its laws;

and yet, this is not among the enumerated powers of Congress. The right to enforce the observance of law, by punishing its infraction, might be denied with more plausibility because it is expressly given in some cases. Congress is empowered "to provide for the punishment of counterfeiting the securities and current coin of the United States," and "to define and punish piracies and felonies committed on the high seas, and offenses against the law of nations." The several powers of Congress may exist, in a very imperfect state, to be sure, but they may exist and be carried into execution, although no punishment should be inflicted in cases where the right to punish is not expressly given.

Take, for example, the power "to establish post-offices and post-roads." This power is executed by the single act of making the establishment. But, from this has been inferred the power and duty of carrying the mail along the post-road, from one post-office to another. And, from this implied power, has again been inferred the right to punish those who steal letters from the post-office, or rob the mail. It may be said, with some plausibility, that the right to carry the mail, and to punish those who rob it, is not indispensably necessary to the establishment of a post-office and post-road. This right is indeed essential to the beneficial exercise of the power, but not indispensably necessary to its existence. So, of the punishment of the crimes of stealing or falsifying a record or process of a court of the United States, or of perjury in such court. To punish these offenses is certainly conducive to the due administration of justice. But courts may exist, and may decide the causes brought before them, though such crimes escape punishment.

The baneful influence of this narrow construction on all the operations of the government, and the absolute impracticability of maintaining it without rendering the government incompetent to its great objects, might be illustrated by numerous examples drawn from the constitution, and from our laws. . . .

In ascertaining the sense in which the word "necessary" is used in this clause of the constitution, we may derive some aid from that with which it is associated. Congress shall have power "to make all laws which shall be necessary and proper to carry into execution" the powers of the government. If the word "necessary" was used in that strict and rigorous sense for which the counsel for the state of Maryland contend, it would be an extraordinary departure from the usual course of the human mind, as exhibited in composition, to add a word, the only possible effect of which is to qualify that strict and rigorous meaning; to present to the mind the idea of some choice of means of legislation not straightened and compressed within the narrow limits for which gentlemen contend.

But the argument which most conclusively demonstrates the error of the construction contended for by the counsel for the state of Maryland, is founded on the intention of the convention, as manifested in the whole clause. To waste time and argument in proving that without it Congress might carry its powers into execution, would be not much less idle than to hold a lighted taper to the sun. As little can it be required to prove, that in the absence of this clause, Congress would have some choice of means. That it might employ those which, in its judgment, would most advantageously effect the object to be accomplished. That any means adapted to the end, any means which tended directly to the execution of the constitutional powers of the government, were in themselves constitutional. This clause, as construed by the state of Maryland, would abridge, and almost annihilate this useful and necessary right of the legislature to select its means. That this could not be intended, is, we should think, had it not been already controverted, too apparent for controversy. We think so for the following reasons:

1st. The clause is placed among the powers of Congress, not among the limitations on those powers.

2d. Its terms purport to enlarge, not to diminish the powers vested in the government. It purports to be an additional power, not a restriction on those already granted. No reason has been, or can be assigned for thus concealing an intention to narrow the discretion of the national legislature under words which purport to enlarge it. . . .

The result of the most careful and attentive consideration bestowed upon this clause is, that if it does not enlarge, it cannot be construed to restrain the powers of Congress, or to impair the right of the legislature to exercise its best judgment in the selection of measures to carry into execution the constitutional powers of the government. If no other motive for its insertion can be suggested, a sufficient one is found in the desire to remove all doubts respecting the right to legislate on that vast mass of incidental powers which must be involved in the constitution, if that instrument be not a splendid bauble.

We admit, as all must admit, that the powers of the government are limited, and that its limits are not to be transcended. But we think the sound construction of the constitution must allow to the national legislature that discretion, with respect to the means by which the powers it confers are to be carried into execution, which will enable that body to perform the high duties assigned to it, in the manner most beneficial to the people. Let the end be legitimate, let it be within the scope of the constitution, and all means which are appropriate, which are plainly adapted to that end, which are not prohibited, but consist with the letter and spirit of the constitution, are constitutional. . . .

If a corporation may be employed indiscriminately with other means to carry into execution the powers of the government, no particular reason can be assigned for excluding the use of a bank, if required for its fiscal operations. To use one, must be within the discretion of Congress, if it be an appropriate mode of executing the powers of government. That it is a convenient, a useful, and essential instrument in the prosecution of its fiscal operations, is not now a subject of controversy. All those who have been concerned in the administration of our finances, have concurred in representing the importance and necessity; and so strongly have they been felt, that statesmen of the first class, whose previous opinions against it had been confirmed by every circumstance which can fix the human judgment, have yielded those opinions to the exigencies of the nation. Under the confederation, Congress, justifying the measure by its necessity, transcended perhaps its powers to obtain the advantage of a bank; and our own legislation attests the universal conviction of the utility of this measure. The time has passed away when it can be necessary to enter into any discussion in order to prove the importance of this instrument, as a means to effect the legitimate objects of the government.

But, were its necessity less apparent, none can deny its being an appropriate measure; and if it is, the degree of its necessity, as has been very justly observed, is to be discussed in another place. Should Congress, in the execution of its powers, adopt measures which are prohibited by the constitution; or should Congress, under the pretext of executing its powers, pass laws for the accomplishment of objects not entrusted to the government, it would become the painful duty of this tribunal, should a case requiring such a decision come before it, to say that such an act was not the law of the land. But where the law is not prohibited, and is really calculated to effect any of the objects entrusted to the government, to undertake here to inquire into the degree of its necessity, would be to pass the line which circumscribes the judicial department, and to tread on legislative ground. This court disclaims all pretensions to such a power. . . .

It being the opinion of the court that the act incorporating the bank is constitutional, and that the power of establishing a branch in the state of Maryland might be properly exercised by the bank itself, we proceed to inquire:

2. Whether the state of Maryland may, without violating the constitution, tax that branch?

That the power of taxation is one of vital importance; that it is retained by the states; that it is not abridged by the grant of a similar power to the government of the Union; that it is to be concurrently exercised by the two governments: are truths which have never been denied. But, such is the paramount character of the constitution that its capacity to withdraw any subject from the action of even this power, is admitted. The states are expressly forbidden to lay any duties on imports or exports, except what may be absolutely necessary for executing their inspection laws. If the obligation of this prohibition must be conceded—if it may restrain a state from the exercise of its taxing power on imports and exports—the same paramount character would seem to restrain, as it certainly may restrain, a state from such other exercise of this power, as is in its nature incompatible with, and repugnant to, the constitutional laws of the Union. A law, absolutely repugnant to another, as entirely repeals that other as if express terms of repeal were used.

On this ground the counsel for the bank place its claim to be exempted from the power of a state to tax its operations. There is no express provision for the case, but the claim has been sustained on a principle which so entirely pervades the constitution, is so intermixed with the materials which compose it, so interwoven with its web, so blended with its texture, as to be incapable of being separated from it without rendering it into shreds.

This great principle is, that the constitution and the laws made in pursuance thereof are supreme; that they control the constitution and laws of the respective states, and cannot be controlled by them. From this, which may be almost termed an axiom, other propositions are deduced as corollaries, on the truth or error of which, and on their application to this case, the cause has been supposed to depend. These are, 1st. that a power to create implies a power to preserve. 2d. That a power to destroy, if wielded by a different hand, is hostile to, and incompatible with these powers to create and to preserve. 3d. That where this repugnancy exists, that authority which is supreme must control, not yield to that over which it is supreme. . . .

That the power of taxing it by the states may be exercised so as to destroy it, is too obvious to be denied. But taxation is said to be an absolute power, which acknowledges no other limits than those expressly prescribed in the constitution, and like sovereign power of every other description, is trusted to the discretion of those who use it. But the very terms of this argument admit that the sovereignty of the state, in the article of taxation itself, is subordinate to, and may be controlled by the constitution of the United States. How far it has been controlled by that instrument must be a question of construction. In making this construction, no principle not declared can be admissible, which would defeat the legitimate operations of a supreme government. It is of the very essence of supremacy to remove all obstacles to its action within its own sphere, and so to modify every power vested in subordinate governments as to exempt its own operations from their own influence. This effect need not be stated in terms. It is so involved in the declaration of supremacy, so necessarily implied in it, that the expression of it could not make it more certain. We must, therefore, keep it in view while construing the constitution.

The argument on the part of the state of Maryland is, not that the states may directly resist a law of Congress, but that they may exercise their acknowledged powers upon it, and that the constitution leaves them this right in the confidence that they will not abuse it.

Before we proceed to examine this argument, and to subject it to the test of the constitution, we must be permitted to bestow a few considerations on the nature and extent of this original right of taxation, which is acknowledged to remain with the states. It is admitted that the power of taxing the people and their property is essential to the very existence of government, and may be legitimately exercised on the objects to which it is applicable, to the utmost extent to which the government may choose to carry it. The only security against the abuse of this power is found in the structure of the government itself. In imposing a tax the legislature acts upon its constituents. This is in general a sufficient security against erroneous and oppressive taxation.

The people of a state, therefore, give to their government a right of taxing themselves and their property, and as the exigencies of government cannot be limited, they prescribe no limits to the exercise of this right, resting confidently on the interest of the legislator, and on the influence of the constituents over their representative, to guard them against its abuse. But the means employed by the government of the Union have no such security, nor is the right of a state to tax them sustained by the same theory. Those means are not given by the people of a particular state, not given by the constituents of the legislature, which claim the right to tax them, but by the people of all the states. They are given by all for the benefit of all—and upon theory, should be subjected to that government only which belongs to all. . . .

We find, then, on just theory, a total failure of this original right to tax the means employed by the government of the Union, for the execution of its powers. The right never existed, and the question whether it has been surrendered, cannot arise.

But, waiving this theory for the present, let us resume the inquiry, whether this power can be exercised by the respective states, consistently with a fair construction of the constitution.

That the power to tax involves the power to destroy; that the power to destroy may defeat and render useless the power to create; that there is a plain repugnance, in conferring on one government a power to control the constitutional measures of another, which other, with respect to those very measures, is declared to be supreme over that which exerts the control, are propositions not to be denied. But all inconsistencies are to be reconciled by the magic of the word confidence. Taxation, it is said, does not necessarily and unavoidably destroy. To carry it to the excess of destruction would be an abuse, to presume which, would banish that confidence which is essential to all government.

But is this a case of confidence? Would the people of any one state trust those of another with a power to control the most insignificant operations of their state government? We know they would not. Why, then, should we suppose that the people of any one state should be willing to trust those of another with a power to control the operations of a government to which they have confided the most important and most valuable interests? In the legislature of the Union alone, are all represented. The legislature of the Union alone, therefore, can be trusted by the people with the power of controlling measures which concern all, in the confidence that it will not be abused. This, then, is not a case of confidence, and we must consider it as it really is.

If we apply the principle for which the state of Maryland contends, to the constitution generally, we shall find it capable of changing totally the character of that instrument. We shall find it capable of arresting all the measures of the government, and of prostrating it at the foot of the states. The American people have declared their constitution, and the laws made in pursuance thereof, to be supreme; but this principle would transfer the supremacy, in fact, to the states. . . .

It has also been insisted, that, as the power of taxation in the general and state governments is acknowledged to be concurrent, every argument which would sustain the right of the general government to tax banks chartered by the states, will equally sustain the right of the states to tax banks chartered by the general government.

But the two cases are not on the same reason. The people of all the states have created the general government, and have conferred upon it the general power of taxation. The people of all the states, and the states themselves, are represented in Congress, and, by their representatives, exercise this power. When they tax the chartered institutions of the states, they tax their constituents; and these taxes must be uniform. But, when a state taxes the operations of the government of the United States, it acts upon institutions created, not by their own constituents, but by people over whom they claim no control. It acts upon the measures of a government created by others as well as themselves, for the benefit of others in common with themselves. The difference is that which always exists, and always must exist, between the action of the whole on a part, and the action of a part on the whole—between the laws of a government declared to be supreme, and those of a government which, when in opposition to those laws, is not supreme.

But if the full application of this argument could be admitted, it might bring into question the right of Congress to tax the state banks, and could not prove the right of the states to tax the Bank of the United States. . . .

We are unanimously of the opinion that the law passed by the legislature of Maryland, imposing a tax on the Bank of the United States, is unconstitutional and void.

Gibbons v. Ogden
9 WHEAT. (22 U.S.) 1 (1824)

Robert Livingston and Robert Fulton were granted by the New York legislature a monopoly on the operation of steamboats in the state's waters. They in turn licensed Aaron Ogden to exclusively operate a ferry between New York City and various ports in New Jersey. Subsequently, on the basis of his license, Ogden sought in New York courts an injunction against Thomas Gibbons, who ran a competing ferry between New York City and Elizabethtown Point, New Jersey. Gibbons countered that his boats were licensed under a 1793 act of Congress for vessels "employed in the coasting trade and fisheries." But when enjoining Gibbons from operating his ferries, the New York courts upheld Ogden's claims on the grounds that the 1793 act covered only coasting vessels and Congress had not passed legislation specifically regulating steamboats. Gibbons then appealed to the Supreme Court, which held that the monopoly granted by New York interfered with Congress's power to regulate interstate commerce.

The Court's decision was unanimous, and the opinion was announced by Chief Justice Marshall. Justice Johnson concurred.

☐ *Chief Justice MARSHALL delivers the opinion of the Court.*

The appellant contends that this decree is erroneous, because the laws which purport to give the exclusive privilege it sustains, are repugnant to . . . that clause in the constitution which authorizes Congress to regulate commerce. . . .

[The Constitution] contains an enumeration of powers expressly granted by the people to their government. It has been said that these powers ought to be construed strictly. But why ought they to be so construed? Is there one sentence in the constitution which gives countenance to this rule? In the last of the enumerated powers, that which grants, expressly, the means of carrying all others into execution, Congress is authorized "to make all laws which shall be necessary and proper" for the purpose. But this limitation on the means which may be used, is not extended to the powers which are conferred; nor is there one sentence in the constitution which has been pointed out by the gentlemen of the bar, or which we have been able to discern, that prescribes this rule. We do not, therefore, think ourselves justified in adopting it. What do gentlemen mean by a strict construction? If they contend only against that enlarged construction which would extend words beyond their natural and obvious import, we might question the application of the term, but should not controvert the principle. If they contend for that narrow construction which, in support of some theory not to be found in the constitution, would deny to the government those powers which the words of the grant, as usually understood, import, and which are consistent with the general views and objects of the instrument; for that narrow construction, which would cripple the government and render it unequal to the objects for which it is declared to be instituted, and to which the powers given, as fairly understood, render it competent; then we cannot perceive the propriety of this strict construction, nor adopt it as the rule by which the constitution is to be expounded. As men, whose intentions require no concealment, generally employ the words which most directly and aptly express the ideas they intend to convey, the enlightened patriots who framed our constitution, and the people who adopted it, must be understood to have employed words in their natural sense, and to have intended what they have said. . . . We know of no rule for construing the extent of such powers, other than is given by the language of the instrument which confers them, taken in connection with the purposes for which they were conferred.

The words are: "Congress shall have power to regulate commerce with foreign nations, and among the several states, and with the Indian tribes."

The subject to be regulated is commerce; and our constitution being, as was aptly said at the bar, one of enumeration, and not of definition, to ascertain the extent of the power it becomes necessary to settle the meaning of the word. The counsel for the appellee would limit it to traffic, to buying and selling, or the interchange of commodities, and do not admit that it comprehends navigation. This would restrict a general term, applicable to many objects, to one of its significations. Commerce, undoubtedly, is traffic, but it is something more; it is intercourse. It describes the commercial intercourse between nations, and parts of nations, in all its branches, and is regulated by prescribing rules for carrying on that intercourse. The mind can scarcely conceive a system for regulating commerce between nations, which shall exclude all laws concerning navigation, which shall be silent on the admission of the vessels of the one nation into the ports of the other, and be confined to prescribing rules for the conduct of individuals, in the actual employment of buying and selling, or of barter. . . .

All America understands, and has uniformly understood, the word "commerce" to comprehend navigation. It was so understood, and must have been so understood, when the constitution was framed. The power over commerce, including navigation, was one of the primary objects for which the people of America adopted their government, and must have been contemplated in forming it. The convention must have used the word in that sense; because all have understood it in that sense, and the attempt to restrict it comes too late. . . .

The word used in the constitution, then, comprehends, and has been always understood to comprehend, navigation within its meaning; and a power to regulate navigation is as expressly granted as if that term had been added to the word "commerce."

To what commerce does this power extend? The constitution informs us, to commerce "with foreign nations, and among the several states, and with the Indian tribes."

It has, we believe, been universally admitted that these words comprehend every species of commercial intercourse between the United States and foreign nations. No sort of trade can be carried on between this country and any other, to which this power does not extend. It has been truly said, that commerce, as the word is used in the constitution, is a unit, every part of which is indicated by the term.

If this be the admitted meaning of the word, in its application to foreign nations, it must carry the same meaning throughout the sentence, and remain a unit, unless there be some plain intelligible cause which alters it.

The subject to which the power is next applied, is to commerce "among the several states." The word "among" means intermingled with. A thing which is among others, is intermingled with them. Commerce among the states cannot stop at the external boundary line of each state, but may be introduced into the interior.

It is not intended to say that these words comprehend that commerce which is completely internal, which is carried on between man and man in a state, or between different parts of the same state, and which does not extend to or affect other states. Such a power would be inconvenient, and is certainly unnecessary.

Comprehensive as the word "among" is, it may very properly be restricted to that commerce which concerns more states than one. The phrase is not one which would probably have been selected to indicate the completely interior traffic of a state, because it is not an apt phrase for that purpose; and the enumeration of the particular classes of commerce to which the power was to be extended, would not have been made had the intention been to extend the power to every description. The enumeration presupposes something not enumerated; and that something, if we regard the language or the subject of the sentence, must be the exclusively internal commerce of a state. The genius and character of the whole government seem to be, that its action is to be applied to all the external concerns of the nation, and to those internal concerns which affect the states generally; but not to those which are completely within a particular state, which do not affect other states, and with which it is not necessary to interfere, for the purpose of executing some of the general powers of the government. The completely internal commerce of a state, then, may be considered as reserved for the state itself.

But, in regulating commerce with foreign nations, the power of Congress does not stop at the jurisdictional lines of the several states. It would be a very useless power if it could not pass those lines. The commerce of the United States with foreign nations, is that of the whole United States. Every district has a right to participate in it. The deep streams which penetrate our country in every direction, pass through the interior of almost every state in the Union, and furnish the means of exercising this right. If Congress has the power to regulate it, that power must be exercised whenever the subject exists. If it exists within the states, if a foreign voyage may commence or terminate at a port within a state, then the power of Congress may be exercised within a state.

This principle is, if possible, still more clear, when applied to commerce "among the several states." They either join each other, in which case they are separated by a mathematical line, or they are remote from each other, in which case other states lie between them. What is commerce "among" them; and how is it to be conducted? Can a trading expedition between two adjoining states commence and terminate outside of each? And if the trading intercourse be between two states remote from each other, must it not commence in one, terminate in the other, and probably pass through a third? Commerce among the states must, of necessity, be commerce with the states. In the regulation of trade with the Indian tribes, the action of the law, especially when the constitution was made, was chiefly within a state. The power of Congress, then, whatever it may be, must be exercised within the territorial jurisdiction of the several states. The sense of the nation, on this subject, is unequivocally manifested by the provisions made in the laws for transporting goods, by land, between Baltimore and Providence, between New York and Philadelphia, and between Philadelphia and Baltimore.

We are now arrived at the inquiry, What is this power?

It is the power to regulate; that is, to prescribe the rule by which commerce is to be governed. This power, like all others vested in Congress, is complete in itself, may be exercised to its utmost extent, and acknowledges no limitations, other than are prescribed in the constitution. These are expressed in plain terms, and do not affect the questions which arise in this case, or which have been discussed at the bar. If, as has always been understood, the sovereignty of Congress, though limited to specified objects, is plenary as to those objects, the power over commerce with foreign nations, and among the several States, is vested in Congress as absolutely as it would be in a single government, having in its constitution the same restrictions on the exercise of the power as are found in the constitution of the United States. The wisdom and the discretion of Congress, their identity with the people, and the influence which their constituents possess at election, are, in this, as in many other instances, as that, for example, of declaring war, the sole restraints on which they have relied, to secure them from its abuse. They are the restraints on which the people must often rely solely, in all representative governments.

The power of Congress, then, comprehends navigation within the limits of every state in the Union; so far as that navigation may be, in any manner, connected with "commerce with foreign nations, or among the several states, or with the Indian tribes." It may, of consequence, pass the jurisdictional line of New York, and act upon the very waters to which the prohibition now under consideration applies.

But it has been urged with great earnestness, that although the power of Congress to regulate commerce with foreign nations, and among the several states, be co-extensive with the subject itself, and have no other limits than are prescribed in the constitution, yet the states may severally exercise the same power within their respective jurisdictions. In support of this argument, it is said that they possessed it as an inseparable attribute of sovereignty, before the formation of the constitution, and still retain it, except so far as they have surrendered it by that instrument; that this principle results from the nature of the government, and is secured by the tenth amendment; that an affirmative grant of power is not exclusive, unless in its own nature it be such that the continued exercise of it by the former possessor is inconsistent with the grant, and that this is not of that description.

The appellant, conceding these postulates, except the last, contends that full power to regulate a particular subject, implies the whole power, and leaves no residuum; that a grant of the whole is incompatible with the existence of a right in another to any part of it. . . .

The grant of the power to lay and collect taxes is, like the power to regulate commerce, made in general terms, and has never been understood to interfere with the exercise of the same power by the states; and hence has been drawn an argument which has been applied to the question under consideration. But the two grants are not, it is conceived, similar in their terms or their nature. Although many of the powers formerly exercised by the states, are transferred to the government of the Union, yet the state governments remain, and constitute a most important part of our system. The power of taxation is indispensable to their existence, and is a power which, in its own nature, is capable of residing in, and being exercised by, different authorities at the same time. . . .

Congress is authorized to lay and collect taxes, etc., to pay the debts, and provide for the common defense and general welfare of the United States. This does not interfere with the power of the states to tax for the support of their own governments; nor is the exercise of that power by the states an exercise of any portion of the power that is granted to the United States. . . . There is no analogy, then, between the power of taxation and the power of regulating commerce. . . .

The sole question is, can a state regulate commerce with foreign nations and among the states, while Congress is regulating it? . . .

[I]nspection laws are said to be regulations of commerce, and are certainly recognized in the constitution, as being passed in the exercise of a power remaining with the states.

That inspection laws may have a remote and considerable influence on commerce, will not be denied; but that a power to regulate commerce is the source from which the right to pass them is derived, cannot be admitted. The objects of inspection laws is to improve the quality of articles produced by the labor of the country; to fit them for exportation; or, it may be, for domestic use. They act upon the subject before it becomes an article of foreign commerce, or of commerce among the states, and prepared it for that purpose. They form a portion of that immense mass of legislation which embraces everything within the territory of a state not surrendered to the general government; all which can be most advantageously exercised by the states themselves. Inspection laws, quarantine laws, health laws of every description, as well as laws for regulating the internal commerce of a state, and those which respect turnpike-roads, ferries, etc., are component parts of this mass.

No direct general power over these objects is granted to Congress; and, consequently, they remain subject to state legislation. If the legislative power of the Union can reach them, it must be for national purposes; it must be where the power is expressly given for a special purpose, or is clearly incidental to some power which is expressly given. It is obvious, that the government of the Union, in the exercise of its express powers, that, for example, of regulating commerce with foreign nations and among the states, may use means that may also be employed by a state, in the exercise of its acknowledged power; that, for example, of regulating commerce within the state. If Congress license vessels to sail from one port to another, in the same state, the act is supposed to be, necessarily, incidental to the power expressly granted to Congress, and implies no claim of a direct power to regulate the purely internal commerce of a state, or to act directly on its system of police. So, if a state, in passing laws on subjects acknowledged to be within its control, and with a view to those subjects, shall adopt a measure of the same character with one which Congress may adopt, it does not derive its authority from the particular power which has been granted, but from some other, which remains with the state, and may be executed by the same means. All experience shows that the same measures, or measures scarcely distinguishable from each other, may flow from distinct powers; but this does not prove that the powers themselves are identical. Although the means used in their execution may sometimes approach each other so nearly as to be confounded, there are other situations in which they are sufficiently distinct to establish their individuality.

In our complex system, presenting the rare and difficult scheme of one general government, whose action extends over the whole, but which possesses only certain enumerated powers, and of numerous state governments, which retain and exercise all powers not delegated to the Union, contests respecting power must arise. Were it even otherwise, the measures taken by the respective governments to execute their acknowledged powers, would often be of the same description, and might, sometimes, interfere. This, however, does not prove that the one is exercising, or has a right to exercise, the powers of the other. . . .

[The Act of 1793, licensing steamboats] demonstrates the opinion of Congress, that steamboats may be enrolled and licensed, in common with vessels using sails. They are, of course, entitled to the same privileges, and can no more be restrained from navigating waters, and entering ports which are free to such vessels, than if they were wafted on their voyage by the winds, instead of being propelled by the agency of fire. The one element may be as legitimately used as the other, for every commercial purpose authorized by the laws of the Union; and the act of a state inhibiting the use of either to any vessel having a license under the act of Congress, comes, we think, in direct collision with that act. . . .

Powerful and ingenious minds, taking, as postulates, that the powers expressly granted to the government of the Union are to be contracted, by construction, into the narrowest possible compass, and that the original powers of the States are retained, if any possible construction will retain them, may, by a course of well digested, but refined and metaphysical reasoning, founded on these premises, explain away the constitution of our country, and leave it a magnificent structure indeed, to look at, but totally unfit for use. They may so entangle and perplex the understanding, as to obscure principles which were before thought quite plain, and induce doubts where, if the mind were to pursue its own course, none would be perceived. In such a case, it is peculiarly necessary to recur to safe and fundamental principles to sustain those principles, and, when sustained, to make them the tests of the arguments to be examined.

B | *From Legal Formalism to the New Deal Crisis*

Chief Justice Marshall's unitary conception of commerce and standard for determining Congress's power over commerce—whether commerce "extend[s] to or affect[s] other states"—was nationalist. Indeed, following *Gibbons* he struck down a Maryland law requiring importers to pay a license fee on the grounds that states could not tax items imported through foreign commerce so long as they remained in their "original package."[1]

Gibbons also implied, however, a distinction between Congress's power over *interstate* commerce and that of the states over *intrastate* commerce. Although holding that Congress's power over commerce "among the several states" is complete and "cannot stop at the external boundary line of each state, but may be introduced into the interior," Chief Justice Marshall also observed, "It is not intended to say that these words comprehend that commerce which is completely internal, which is carried on between man and man in a state, or between different parts of the same state, and which does not extend to or affect other states. Such a power would be inconvenient, and is certainly unnecessary." And he added, "Comprehensive as the word 'among' is, it may very properly be restricted to that commerce which concerns more states than one." Hence, "the completely internal commerce of a state," Marshall noted, "may be considered as reserved for the state itself."

From Marshall's *dicta* in *Gibbons* the Court under Chief Justice Roger Taney, who was more sympathetic to claims of states' rights, developed the interstate-intrastate distinction. In *The License Cases*, 5 How. (46 U.S.) 504 (1847), Taney suggested two separate, mutually exclusive commerce powers in noting the existence of "internal or domestic commerce, which belongs to the states, and over which congress can exercise no control." Two years later, Justice John McLean further elaborated this view: "All commercial action within the limits of a state, and which does not extend to any other state or foreign country, is exclusively under state regulation."[2]

With the introduction into constitutional law of the interstate-intrastate commerce distinction, the touchstone for determining the powers of Congress and the states became whether commerce crossed a state line. Not until after the Civil War, however, did Congress actually assert its power over commerce. And in the absence of congressional statutes the Court employed the interstate-intrastate distinction to uphold state regulations. In *Paul v. Virginia*, 8 Wall. (75 U.S.) 168 (1869), for instance, state regulation of interstate insurance companies was upheld on the grounds that "issuing a policy of insurance is not a transaction of commerce" and insurance contracts "are not articles of commerce."

By the late nineteenth century the interstate-intrastate distinction was applied in a formalistic way. This development reflected political changes in the country and in the Court. A new era in government regulation was inaugurated with the passage of the Interstate Commerce Act of 1887 and the Sherman Antitrust Act of 1890. The Interstate Commerce Act created the first regulatory commission in the United States, the ICC (which was abolished in 1995), and authorized it to investigate and regulate the operation of interstate railroads. The Sherman Antitrust Act made it illegal for interstate businesses to form trusts, combinations, or monopolies and authorized the executive branch to prosecute businesses that formed monopolies and entered into conspiracies to restrain trade and fix prices. This expansion of congressional power responded to pressures brought by the Industrial Revolution and a successful national economy. It also registered a new conception of the role of the national government in promoting freedom that had evolved since the Reconstruction era. At the same time, industries, railroad companies, and corporations, opposing regulation by the national government, contended that only states could regulate their activities; yet, states could not regulate those businesses that operated in more than one state. Coincidentally, the Court's composition also changed with the addition of justices who had been corporate lawyers and sympathized with private business interests. In 1888, Melville Fuller, a successful commercial attorney, was appointed chief justice and joined on the bench conservative Justices Stephen Field and Samuel Miller. He was then followed by others opposed to social change and embracing laissez-faire capitalism, notably, Justices David Brewer (in 1890), Edward White (in 1894), and Rufus Peckham (in 1896).[3]

Between 1887 and 1937 the Court relied on the interstate-intrastate dichotomy in upholding state regulations and striking down congressional legislation as unauthorized under the commerce clause. In doing so the Court invented some additional rules for further defining the boundaries between state and federal power. One of the most important of these was that between the activities of *production*, or *manufacturing* (over which states enjoyed virtually exclusive authority), and those of *distribution*, or *commercial transportation* (which Congress might regulate). This *production/distribution* rule enabled the Court, on the one hand, to uphold state regulation or taxation of commercial interests that sought exemption by claiming their activities were subject only to congressional regulation and, on the other hand, to strike down federal regulations and thereby limit the reach of congressional power over commerce.

For example, in *Kidd v. Pearson*, 128 U.S. 1 (1888), the Court upheld Iowa's ban on the manufacture of liquor as applied to a distillery in the state that exported its entire product to other states. In rejecting the distillery's claim that manufacturing a product sold exclusively out of state constituted interstate commerce, the Court observed, "No distinction is more popular to the common mind, or more clearly expressed in economic and political literature, than that between manufacturing and commerce. Manufacturing is transformation—the fashioning of raw materials into a change of form for use. The functions of commerce are different. The buying and selling and the transportation incident thereto constitute commerce."

United States v. E. C. Knight Company (1895) (see excerpt below) illustrates the Court's use of the production/distribution rule to defeat the congressional power under the commerce clause. In that case, over the forceful dissent of Justice Harlan, the Fuller Court ruled that the Sherman Antitrust regulation of monopolies did not apply to the country's largest sugar refining company because it viewed the company's production of sugar as a local activity distinctly separate from the industry's sugar distribution.

The Court later applied the production/distribution rule in defining the scope of congressional and state regulatory powers over mining;[4] fishing, farming, and oil production;[5] and hydroelectric power.[6] The most extreme use of the rule came in *Hammer v. Dagenhart* (1918) (see excerpt below), when a bare majority of the Court struck down the Federal Child Labor Act of 1916. A year earlier, in *Wilson v. New*, 243 U.S. 332 (1917), the justices divided five to four in upholding employment regulations for railroad workers. However, in *Hammer* the majority found that Congress impermissibly barred shipment in interstate commerce of goods produced in factories that employed children under fourteen or allowed children between the ages of fourteen and sixteen to work more than eight hours a day or more than six days a week. In his opinion for the majority, Justice Day narrowly read federal power over commerce to be limited to regulating the *means* of transportation. And he distinguished earlier cases upholding congressional regulation of lottery tickets, prostitution, and impure food[7] on the grounds that these goods are harmful per se, whereas goods produced by child labor are harmless. Justice Holmes, writing for the dissenters, rejected the majority's formalistic reasoning and blasted it for reading its own "moral conceptions" into constitutional law.

Hammer was extraordinary in challenging congressional authority and was eventually overruled in *United States v. Darby* (1941) (see excerpt below). Still, even when a majority of the Court could be mustered to uphold progressive legislation it relied on other formal rules and tests derived from the distinction between interstate and intrastate commerce. In particular, the Court rationalized federal regulation on an *"effect on commerce" rule*, that is, whether an activity within a state had an obvious effect or impact on interstate commerce so as to justify the exercise of federal power. But applying this rule required the Court to invent various tests for gauging the impact of local activities on interstate commerce.

One test used to implement the effects rule was whether local activities were in the *stream of commerce*. This was the basis for the Court's rejecting the claim of Chicago stockyard firms, made when challenging federal prosecutions for conspiring to restrain trade, that the purchase and sale of cattle in Chicago stockyards was not commerce among the states. As Justice Holmes observed in *Swift & Company v. United States*, 196 U.S. 375 (1905):

> Commerce among the states is not a technical legal conception, but a practical one, drawn from the course of business. When cattle are sent for sale from a place in one State, with the expectation that they will end their transit, after purchase, in another, and when in effect they do so, with only the interruption necessary to find a purchaser at the stock yards, and when this is a typical, constantly recurring course, the current thus existing is a current of commerce among the States, and the purchase of the cattle is a part and incident of such commerce.

The stream of commerce test was subsequently employed in sustaining federal regulation of stockyards[8] and grain and cotton exchanges.[9]

Another test centered on whether intrastate commerce was so physically *intermingled* or *intertwined* with interstate commerce as to make it impractical to distinguish federal and state regulatory powers. In *Southern Railway Co. v. United States*, 222 U.S. 20 (1911), the Court upheld federal regulations applied to a company carrying on its interstate railroad three cars not equipped with safety couplers, as required under the Safety Appliance Act, even though these cars were used solely in intrastate transportation. In Justice Van Devanter's words, "This is so, not because Congress possesses any power to regulate intrastate commerce as such, but because its power to regulate interstate commerce is plenary and consequently may be exerted to secure the safety of the persons and property transported therein and of those who are employed in such transportation, no matter what may be the source of the dangers which threaten it."

The *Shreveport doctrine* was yet another test used to justify the exercise of federal power over intrastate commerce. *The Shreveport Rate Case*, 234 U.S. 342 (1914), affirmed an order of the ICC requiring Texas intrastate rates from Dallas and Houston to be equalized with the interstate rates for travel from Shreveport, Louisiana, to Texas. This was because the interstate rates set by the ICC for transportation from Shreveport to Texas were higher than those for intrastate travel set by the Texas Railroad Commission. And as a result Shreveport was economically disadvantaged in competing for trade in Texas. In sustaining federal power here, Justice Hughes explained, "Wherever the interstate and intrastate transactions of carriers are so related that the government of the one involves the control of the other, it is Congress, and not the State, that is entitled to prescribe the final and dominant rule, for otherwise Congress would be denied the exercise of its constitutional authority and the State, and not the Nation, would be supreme within the national field."

Finally, the Court employed a distinction between *direct* and *indirect* effects on commerce. Note that in *E. C. Knight*, Chief Justice Fuller held that the government cannot forbid the merger of sugar companies under the Sherman Antitrust Act based on the possibility that "trade or commerce might be indirectly affected." But as with the other tests, the problem remained how the categories of direct and indirect effects were to be defined in practice. And the Court's rigid definition of them when striking down important pieces of President Franklin D. Roosevelt's program for economic recovery during the Depression precipitated the crisis over the New Deal.

In *Schechter Poultry Corporation v. United States*, 295 U.S. 495 (1935) (see excerpt in Ch. 4), Chief Justice Hughes struck down the National Industrial Recovery Act as an unconstitutional delegation of power. In addition, he found that the Schechter Corporation in Brooklyn, New York, was neither engaged in interstate commerce nor part of the stream of commerce. Nor did Schechter's purchase and transportation of chickens from elsewhere in New York and Pennsylvania to its slaughterhouse, where they were sold to local retailers, have a direct effect on interstate commerce. Although Hughes did not try further to define direct and indirect effects, he observed that it was "clear in principle" and "a fundamental one, essential to the maintenance of our constitutional system. Otherwise," he added, "there would be virtually no limit to the federal power and for all practical purposes we should have a completely centralized government."

One year later in *Carter v. Carter Coal Company*, 298 U.S. 238 (1936), the Court split sharply over striking down another piece of New Deal legislation, the Bituminous Coal Conservation Act, under which codes for employment practices were established for the coal industry. This time Justice Sutherland, writing for the majority, endeavored to precisely demark the difference between direct and indirect effects on commerce:

> The word "direct" implies that the activity or condition invoked or blamed shall operate proximately—not mediately, remotely, or collaterally—to produce the effect. It connotes the absence of an efficient intervening agency or condition. And the extent of the effect bears no logical relation to its character. The distinction between a direct and an indirect effect turns, not upon the magnitude of either the cause or the effect, but merely upon the manner in which the

effect has been brought about. If the production by one man of a single ton of coal intended for interstate sale and shipment . . . affects interstate commerce indirectly, the effect does not become direct by multiplying the tonnage, or increasing the number of men employed, or adding to the expense or complexities of the business, or by all combined.

In applying the distinction here, Sutherland further observed:

> Much stress is put upon the evils which come from the struggle between employers and employees over the matter of wages, working conditions, the right of collective bargaining, etc., and the resulting strikes, curtailment and irregularity of production and effect on prices; and it is insisted that interstate commerce is *greatly* affected thereby. But . . . the conclusive answer is that the evils are all local evils over which the federal government has no legislative control. The relation of employer and employee is a local relation. . . . And the controversies and evils, which it is the object of the act to regulate and minimize, are local controversies and evils affecting local work undertaken to accomplish that local result. Such effect as they may have upon commerce, however extensive it may be, is secondary and indirect. An increase in the greatness of the effect adds to its importance. It does not alter its character.

This rigid use of the direct and indirect effects test provoked a sharp dissent from Justice Cardozo who, along with Justices Brandeis and Stone, maintained that Congress's commerce power was "as broad as the need that evokes it."

The Court's striking down important New Deal legislation in *Schechter* and *Carter Coal Company* resulted in a major confrontation between it and the country. President Roosevelt, after winning a landslide reelection in 1936, was embittered by the invalidation of his programs. And he responded by proposing judicial reforms that would expand the size of the Court to fifteen. His "Court-packing plan" called for the appointment of a new member of the Court for every justice over seventy years of age. That would have enabled him to secure a majority on the Court sympathetic to his programs (see "President Roosevelt's Radio Broadcast, March 9, 1937," in Ch. 1).

Notes

1. *Brown v. Maryland*, 25 U.S. (12 Wheat.) 419 (1827).

2. *The Passenger Cases*, 7 How. 283 (1849).

3. For further discussion, see Benjamin R. Twiss, *Lawyers and the Constitution: How Laissez Faire Came to the Supreme Court* (1942); and William F. Swindler, *Court and Constitution in the 20th Century: The Old Legality, 1889–1932* (Indianapolis: Bobbs-Merrill, 1969).

4. *United Mine Workers v. Coronado Coal Company*, 259 U.S. 344 (1922).

5. *Champlin Refining Company v. Corporation Commission*, 286 U.S. 210 (1932).

6. *Utah Power and Light v. Pfost*, 286 U.S. 165 (1932).

7. See the discussion and cases cited in section A of this chapter.

8. *Stafford v. Wallace*, 258 U.S. 495 (1922).

9. *Chicago Board of Trade v. Olsen*, 262 U.S. 543 (1923); and *Allenberg Cotton Company, Inc. v. Pittman*, 419 U.S. 20 (1974).

Selected Bibliography

Corwin, Edward S. *Liberty against Government*. Baton Rouge: Louisiana State University Press, 1948.

Horowitz, Morton. *The Transformation of American Law, 1780–1860*. Cambridge, MA: Harvard University Press, 1977.

Leuchtenburg, William. *The Supreme Court Reborn: The Constitutional Revolution in the Age of Roosevelt*. New York: Oxford University Press, 1995.

McCloskey, Robert. *American Conservativism: In the Age of Enterprise 1865–1910*. Cambridge, MA: Harvard University Press, 1951.

United States v. E. C. Knight Company

156 U.S. 1, 15 S.Ct. 249 (1895)

The Sherman Antitrust Act of 1890 made it illegal for businesses to contract, combine, or conspire to create a trust or monopoly for the purpose of restraining free trade and monopolizing interstate or foreign commerce. The American Sugar Refining Company, which already controlled a majority of the sugar-refining companies in the United States, subsequently purchased stock in and arranged to control four other companies, including E. C. Knight. The American Sugar Refining Company would thereby control over 98 percent of the country's sugar-refining business. The Department of Justice sought a court order forbidding the stock sale and other ar-rangements made by E. C. Knight, the American Sugar Refining Company, and three other Philadelphia firms. It contended that the companies had conspired and entered into combinations in restraint of trade in violation of the Sherman Antitrust Act. But lower federal courts denied relief, holding that the companies were engaged in manufacturing, not interstate commerce, and hence not subject to the anti-trust regulations. The government thereupon appealed to the Supreme Court.

The Court's decision was eight to one, and the majority's opinion was announced by Chief Justice Fuller. Justice Harlan dissented.

☐ *Chief Justice FULLER delivers the opinion of the Court.*

By the purchase of the stock of the four Philadelphia refineries with shares of its own stock the American Sugar Refining Company acquired nearly complete control of the manufacture of refined sugar within the United States. The bill charged that the contracts under which these purchases were made constituted combinations in restraint of trade, and that in entering into them the defendants combined and conspired to restrain the trade and commerce in refined sugar among the several states and with foreign nations, contrary to the act of congress of July 2, 1890.

The relief sought was the cancellation of the agreements under which the stock was transferred, the redelivery of the stock to the parties respectively, and an injunction against the further performance of the agreements and further violations of the act. . . .

The fundamental question is whether, conceding that the existence of a monopoly in manufacture is established by the evidence, that monopoly can be directly suppressed under the act of congress in the mode attempted by this bill.

It cannot be denied that the power of a state to protect the lives, health, and property of its citizens, and to preserve good order and the public morals, "the power to govern men and things within the limits of its dominion," is a power originally and always belonging to the states, not surrendered by them to the general government, nor directly restrained by the constitution of the United States, and essentially exclusive. The relief of the citizens of each state from the burden of monopoly and the evils resulting from the restraint of trade among such citizens was left with the states to deal with, and this court has recognized their possession of that power even to the extent of holding that an employment or business carried on by private individuals, when it becomes a matter of such public interest and importance as to create a common charge or burden upon the citizen, in other words, when it becomes a practical monopoly, to which the citizen is compelled to resort, and by means of which a tribute can be exacted from the community,—is subject to regulation by state legislative power. On the other hand, the power of congress to regulate commerce among the several states is also exclusive. The constitution does not provide that interstate commerce shall be free, but, by the grant of this exclusive power to regulate it, it was left free, except as congress might impose restraints. Therefore it has been determined that the failure of congress to exercise this exclusive power in any case is an expression of its will that the subject shall be free from restrictions or impositions upon it by the several states, and if a law passed by a state in the exercise of its acknowledged powers comes into conflict with that will, the congress and the state cannot occupy the position of equal opposing sovereignties, because the constitution declares its supremacy, and that of the laws passed in pursuance thereof; and that which is not supreme must yield to that which is supreme. "Commerce undoubtedly is traffic," said Chief Justice MARSHALL, "but it is something more; it is intercourse. It describes the commercial intercourse between nations and parts of nations in all its branches, and is regulated by prescribing rules for carrying on that intercourse." That which belongs to commerce is within the jurisdiction of the United States, but that which does not belong to commerce is within the jurisdiction of the police power of the state. . . .

The argument is that the power to control the manufacture of refined sugar is a monopoly over a necessary of life, to the enjoyment of which by a large part of the population of the United States interstate commerce is indispensable, and that, therefore, the general government, in the exercise of the power to regulate commerce, may repress such monopoly directly, and set aside the instruments which have created it. But this argument cannot be confined to necessaries of life merely, and must include all articles of general consumption. Doubtless the power to control the manufacture of a given thing involves, in a certain sense, the control of its disposition, but this is a secondary, and not the primary, sense; and, although the exercise of that power may result in bringing the operation of commerce into play, it does not control it, and affects it only incidentally and indirectly. Commerce succeeds to manufacture, and is not a part of it. The power to regulate commerce is the power to prescribe the rule by which commerce shall be governed, and is a power independent of the power to suppress monopoly. But it may operate in repression of monopoly whenever that comes within the rules by which commerce is governed, or whenever the transaction is itself a monopoly of commerce.

It is vital that the independence of the commercial power and of the police power, and the delimitation between them, however sometimes perplexing, should always be recognized and observed, for, while the one furnishes the strongest bond of union, the other is essential to the preservation of the autonomy of the states as required by our dual form of government; and acknowledged evils, however grave and urgent they may appear to be, had better be borne, than the risk be run, in the effort to suppress them, of more serious consequences by resort to expedients of even doubtful constitutionality.

It will be perceived how far-reaching the proposition is that the power of dealing with a monopoly directly may be exercised by the general government whenever interstate or international commerce may be ultimately affected. The regulation of commerce applies to the subjects of commerce, and not to matters of internal police. Contracts to buy, sell, or exchange goods to be transported among the several states, the transportation and its instrumentalities, and articles bought, sold, or exchanged for the purposes of such transit among the states, or put in the way of transit, may be regulated; but this is because they form part of interstate trade or commerce. The fact that an article is manufactured for export to another state does not of itself make it an article of interstate commerce, and the intent of the manufacturer does not determine the time when the article or product passes from the control of the state and belongs to commerce. . . .

Contracts, combinations, or conspiracies to control domestic enterprise in manufacture, agriculture, mining, production in all its forms, or to raise or lower prices or wages, might unquestionably tend to restrain external as well as domestic trade, but the restraint would be an indirect result, however inevitable, and whatever its extent, and such result would not necessarily determine the object of the contract, combination, or conspiracy. . . .

Slight reflection will show that, if the national power extends to all contracts and combinations in manufacture, agriculture, mining, and other productive industries, whose ultimate result may affect external commerce, comparatively little of business corporations and affairs would be left for state control.

It was in the light of well-settled principles that the act of July 2, 1890, was framed. Congress did not attempt thereby to assert the power to deal with monopoly directly as such; or to limit and restrict the rights of corporations created by the states or the citizens of the states in the acquisition, control, or disposition of property; or to regulate or prescribe the price or prices at which such property or the products thereof should be sold; or to make criminal the acts of persons in the acquisition and control of property which the states of their residence or creation sanctioned or permitted. Aside from the provisions applicable where congress might exercise municipal power, what the law struck at was combinations, contracts, and conspiracies to monopolize trade and commerce among the several states or with foreign nations; but the contracts and acts of the defendants related exclusively to the acquisition of the Philadelphia refineries and the business of sugar refining in Pennsylvania, and bore no direct relation to commerce between the states or with foreign nations. The object was manifestly private gain in the manufacture of the commodity, but not through the control of interstate or foreign commerce. It is true that the bill alleged that the products of these refineries were sold and distributed among the several states, and that all the companies were engaged in trade or commerce with the several states and with foreign nations; but this was no more than to say that trade and commerce served manufacture to fulfill its function. Sugar was refined for sale, and sales were probably made at Philadelphia for consumption, and undoubtedly for resale by the first purchasers throughout Pennsylvania and other states, and refined sugar was also forwarded by the companies to other states for sale. Nevertheless it does not follow that an attempt to monopolize, or the actual monopoly of, the manufacture was an attempt, whether executory or consummated, to monopolize commerce, even though, in order to dispose of the product, the instrumentality of commerce was necessarily invoked. There was nothing in the proofs to indicate any intention to put a restraint upon trade or commerce, and the fact, as we have seen, that trade or commerce might be indirectly affected, was not enough to entitle complainants to a decree.

☐ *Justice* HARLAN, *dissenting.*

The court holds it to be vital in our system of government to recognize and give effect to both the commercial power of the nation and the police powers of the states, to the end that the Union be strengthened, and the autonomy of the states preserved. In this view I entirely concur. Undoubtedly, the preservation of the just authority of the states is an object of deep concern to every lover of his country. . . . But it is equally true that the preservation of the just authority of the general government is essential as well to the safety of the states as to the attainment of the important ends for which that government was ordained by the people of the United States; and the destruction of that authority would be fatal to the peace and well-being of the American people. . . .

It would seem to be indisputable that no combination of corporations or individuals can, of right, impose unlawful restraints upon interstate trade, whether upon transportation or upon such interstate intercourse and traffic as precede transportation, any more than it can, of right, impose unreasonable restraints upon the completely internal traffic of a state. The supposition cannot be indulged that this general proposition will be disputed. If it be true that a combination of corporations or individuals may, so far as the power of congress is concerned, subject interstate trade, in any of its stages, to unlawful restraints, the conclusion is inevitable that the constitution has failed to accomplish one primary object of the Union, which was to place commerce among the states under the control of the common government of all the people, and thereby relieve or protect it against burdens or restrictions imposed, by whatever authority, for the benefit of particular localities or special interests. . . .

The power of congress covers and protects the absolute freedom of such intercourse and trade among the states as may or must succeed manufacture and precede transportation from the place of purchase. This would seem to be conceded, for the court in the present case expressly declare that "contracts to buy, sell, or exchange goods to be transported among the several states, the transportation and its instrumentalities, and articles bought, sold, or exchanged for the purpose of such transit among the states, or put in the way of transit, may be regulated, but this is because they form part of interstate trade or commerce." Here is a direct admission—one which the settled doctrines of this court justify—that contracts to buy, and the purchasing of goods to be transported from one state to another, and transportation, with its instrumentalities, are all parts of interstate trade or commerce. Each part of such trade is then under the protection of congress. . . .

In my judgment, the citizens of the several states composing the Union are entitled of right to buy goods in the state where they are manufactured, or in any other state, without being confronted by an illegal combination whose business extends throughout the whole country, which, by the law everywhere, is an enemy to the public interests, and which prevents such buying, except at prices arbitrarily fixed by it. I insist that the free course of trade among the states cannot coexist with such combinations. When I speak of trade I mean the buying and selling of articles of every kind that are recognized articles of interstate commerce. Whatever improperly obstructs the free course of interstate intercourse and trade, as involved in the buying and selling of articles to be carried from one state to another, may be reached by congress under its authority to regulate commerce among the states. The exercise of that authority so as to make trade among the states in all recognized articles of commerce absolutely free from unreasonable or illegal restrictions imposed by combinations is justified by an express grant of power to congress, and would redound to the welfare of the whole country. I am unable to perceive that any such result would imperil the autonomy of the states, especially as that result cannot be attained through the action of any one state. . . .

To the general government has been committed the control of commercial intercourse among the states, to the end that it may be free at all times from any restraints except such as congress may impose or permit for the benefit of the whole country. The common government of all the people is the only one that can adequately deal with a matter which directly and injuriously affects the entire commerce of the country, which concerns equally all the people of the Union, and which, it must be confessed, cannot be adequately controlled by any one state. Its authority should not be so weakened by construction that it cannot reach and eradicate evils that, beyond all question, tend to defeat an object which that government is entitled, by the constitution, to accomplish. "Powerful and ingenious minds," this court has said, "taking, as postulates, that the powers expressly granted to the government of the Union are to be contracted by construction into the narrowest possible compass, and that the original powers of the states are retained, if any possible construction will retain them, may, by a course of well-digested but refined and metaphysical reasoning, founded on these premises, explain away the constitution of our country, and leave it, a magnificent structure, indeed, to look at, but totally unfit for use. They may so entangle and perplex the understanding as to obscure principles which were before thought quite plain, and induce doubts where, if the mind were to pursue its own course, none would be perceived." *Gibbons v. Ogden*, 9 Wheat. 1 [1824].

Hammer v. Dagenhart
247 U.S. 251, 38 S.Ct. 529 (1918)

The Federal Child Labor Act of 1916 forbade the shipment in interstate commerce of goods produced in factories employing children under the age of fourteen or allowing children between ages fourteen and sixteen to work more than eight hours a day, at night, or for more than six days a week. Roland Dagenhart, the father of two minor sons who worked in a cotton mill in North Carolina, sought in federal district court an injunction against W. C. Hammer, a United States attorney, from enforcing the act. The district judge granted the injunction on the ground that the legislation was unconstitutional. The government, then, appealed to the Supreme Court, which granted review and struck down the Federal Child Labor Act.

The Court's decision was five to four, and the majority's opinion was announced by Justice Day. Dissent was by Justice Holmes, who was joined by Justices McKenna, Brandeis, and Clarke.

☐ *Justice DAY delivers the opinion of the Court.*

[T]he power [to regulate commerce] is one way to control the means by which commerce is carried on, which is directly the contrary of the assumed right to forbid commerce from moving and thus destroying it as to particular commodities. But it is insisted that adjudged cases in this court establish the doctrine that the power to regulate given to Congress incidentally includes the authority to prohibit the movement of ordinary commodities and therefore that the subject is not open for discussion. The cases demonstrate the contrary. They rest upon the character of the particular subjects dealt with and the fact that the scope of governmental authority, state or national, possessed over them is such that the authority to prohibit is as to them but the exertion of the power to regulate.

The first of these cases is *Champion v. Ames*, 188 U.S. 321 [(1903)], the so-called *Lottery Case*, in which it was held that Congress might pass a law having the effect to keep the channels of commerce free from use in the transportation of tickets used in the promotion of lottery schemes. In *Hipolite Egg Co. v. United States*, 220 U. S. 45 [(1911)]. This court sustained the power of Congress to pass the Pure Food and Drug Act, which prohibited the introduction into the states by means of interstate commerce of impure foods and drugs. In *Hoke v. United States*, 227 U. S. 308 [(1913)], this court sustained the constitutionality of the so-called "White Slave Traffic Act," whereby the transportation of a woman in interstate commerce for the purpose of prostitution was forbidden. . . .

In each of these instances the use of interstate transportation was necessary to the accomplishment of harmful results. In other words, although the power over interstate transportation was to regulate, that could only be accomplished by prohibiting the use of the facilities of interstate commerce to effect the evil intended.

This element is wanting in the present case. The thing intended to be accomplished by this statute is the denial of the facilities of interstate commerce to those manufacturers in the states who employ children within the prohibited ages. The act in its effect does not regulate transportation among the states, but aims to standardize the ages at which children may be employed in mining and manufacturing within the states. The goods shipped are of themselves harmless. The act permits them to be freely shipped after thirty days from the time of their removal from the factory. When offered for shipment, and before transportation begins, the labor of their production is over, and the mere fact that they were intended for interstate commerce transportation does not make their production subject to federal control under the commerce power. . . . The making of goods and the mining of coal are not commerce, nor does the fact that these things are to be afterwards shipped, or used in interstate commerce, make their production a part thereof. . . .

Over interstate transportation, or its incidents, the regulatory power of Congress is ample, but the production of articles, intended for interstate commerce, is a matter of local regulation.

If it were otherwise, all manufacture intended for interstate shipment would be brought under federal control to the practical exclusion of the authority of the states, a result certainly not contemplated by the framers of the Constitution when they vested in Congress the authority to regulate commerce among the States. . . .

It is further contended that the authority of Congress may be exerted to control interstate commerce in the shipment of child-made goods because of the effect of the circulation of such goods in other states where the evil of this class of labor has been recognized by local legislation, and the right to thus employ child labor has been more rigorously restrained than in the state of production. In other words, that the unfair competition, thus engendered, may be controlled by closing the channels of interstate commerce to manufacturers in those states where the local laws do not meet what Congress deems to be the more just standard of other states.

There is no power vested in Congress to require the states to exercise their police power so as to prevent possible unfair competition. Many causes may co-operate to give one state, by reason of local laws or conditions, an economic advantage over others. The commerce clause was not intended to give to Congress a general authority to equalize such conditions. In some of the states laws have been passed fixing minimum wages for women, in others the local law regulates the hours of labor of women in various employments. Business done in such states may be at an economic disadvantage when compared with states which have no such regulations; surely, this fact does not give Congress the power to deny transportation in interstate commerce to those who carry on business where the hours of labor and the rate of compensation for women have not been fixed by a standard in use in other states and approved by Congress.

The grant of power to Congress over the subject of interstate commerce was to enable it to regulate such commerce, and not to give it authority to control the states in their exercise of the police power over local trade and manufacture.

The grant of authority over a purely federal matter was not intended to destroy the local power always existing and carefully reserved to the states in the Tenth Amendment to the Constitution. . . .

In interpreting the Constitution it must never be forgotten that the nation is made up of states to which are entrusted the powers of local government. And to them and to the people the powers not expressly delegated to the national government are reserved. . . . The power of the states to regulate their purely internal affairs by such laws as seem wise to the local authority is inherent and has never been surrendered to the general government. . . . To sustain this statute would not be in our judgment a recognition of the lawful exertion of congressional authority over interstate commerce, but would sanction an invasion by the federal power of the control of a matter purely local in its character, and over which no authority has been delegated to Congress in conferring the power to regulate commerce among the states. . . .

For these reasons we hold that this law exceeds the constitutional authority of Congress. It follows that the decree of the District Court must be Affirmed.

☐ *Justice HOLMES, dissenting.*

[I]f an act is within the powers specifically conferred upon Congress, it seems to me that it is not made any less constitutional because of the indirect effects that it may have, however obvious it may be that it will have those effects, and that we are not at liberty upon such grounds to hold it void.

The first step in my argument is to make plain what no one is likely to dispute—that the statute in question is within the power expressly given to Congress if considered only as to its immediate effects and that if invalid it is so only upon some collateral ground. The statute confines itself to prohibiting the carriage of certain goods in interstate or foreign commerce. Congress is given power to regulate such commerce in unqualified terms. It would not be argued today that the power to regulate does not include the power to prohibit. Regulation means the prohibition of something, and when interstate commerce is the matter to be regulated I cannot doubt that the regulation may prohibit any part of such commerce that Congress sees fit to forbid. At all events it is established by the *Lottery* Case and others that have followed it that a law is not beyond the regulative power of Congress merely because it prohibits certain transportation out and out. *Champion v. Ames*, 188 U.S. 321 [1903]. So I repeat that this statute in its immediate operation is clearly within the Congress's constitutional power.

The question then is narrowed to whether the exercise of its otherwise constitutional power by Congress can be pronounced unconstitutional because of its possible reaction upon the conduct of the States in a matter upon which I have admitted that they are free from direct control. I should have thought that that matter had been disposed of so fully as to leave no room for doubt. I should have thought that the most conspicuous decisions of this Court had made it clear that the power to regulate commerce and other constitutional powers could not be cut down or qualified by the fact that it might interfere with the carrying out of the domestic policy of any State.

The manufacture of oleomargarine is as much a matter of State regulation as the manufacture of cotton cloth. Congress levied a tax upon the compound when colored so as to resemble butter that was so great as obviously to prohibit the manufacture and sale. In a very elaborate discussion the present CHIEF JUSTICE excluded any inquiry into the purpose of an act which apart from that purpose was within the power of Congress. . . . Fifty years ago a tax on state banks, the obvious purpose and actual effect of which was to drive them, or at least their circulation, out of existence, was sustained, although the result was one that Congress had no constitutional power to require. The Court made short work of the argument as to the purpose of the Act. "The Judicial cannot prescribe to the Legislative Departments of the Government limitations upon the exercise of its acknowledged powers." *Veazie Bank v. Fenno*, 8 Wall. [75 U.S.] 533 [1869]. . . .

The notion that prohibition is any less prohibition when applied to things now thought evil I do not understand. But if there is any matter upon which civilized countries have agreed—far more unanimously than they have with regard to intoxicants and some other matters over which this country is now emotionally aroused—it is the evil of premature and excessive child labor. I should have thought that if we were to introduce our own moral conceptions where in my opinion they do not belong, this was preeminently a case for upholding the exercise of all its powers by the United States.

But I had thought that the propriety of the exercise of a power admitted to exist in some cases was for the consideration of Congress alone and that this Court always had disavowed the right to intrude its judgment upon questions of policy or morals. It is not for this Court to pronounce when prohibition is necessary to regulation if it ever may be necessary—to say that it is permissible as against strong drink but not as against the product of ruined lives.

The Act does not meddle with anything belonging to the States. They may regulate their internal affairs and their domestic commerce as they like. But when they seek to send their products across the State line they are no longer within their rights. If there were no Constitution and no Congress their power to cross the line would depend upon their neighbors. Under the Constitution such commerce belongs not to the States but to Congress to regulate. It may carry out its views of public policy whatever indirect effect they may have upon the activities of the States. Instead of being encountered by a prohibitive tariff at her boundaries the State encounters the public policy of the United States which it is for Congress to express. The public policy of the United States is shaped with a view to the benefit of the nation as a whole. . . . The national welfare as understood by Congress may require a different attitude within its sphere from that of some self-seeking State. It seems to me entirely constitutional for Congress to enforce its understanding by all the means at its command.

☐ *Justice McKENNA, Justice BRANDEIS, and Justice CLARKE concur in this opinion.*

C | *From the New Deal Crisis to the Administrative State*

A groundswell of opposition to the Court was emerging in the country by February 5, 1937, when President Roosevelt sent his "Court-packing plan" to Congress. Besides *Schechter* and *Carter Coal*, the Court had struck down provisions of the National Industrial Recovery Act in *Panama Refining Co. v. Ryan*, 293 U.S. 388 (1935); a railroad retirement program in *Railroad Retirement Board v. Alton Railroad Co.*, 295 U.S. 330 (1935); and a scheme for farm subsidies under the Agricultural Adjustment Act in *United States v. Butler*, 297 U.S. 1 (1936).[1] In addition, a New York minimum wage law for women was overturned by a five-to-four vote in *Morehead v. New York ex rel. Tipaldo*, 298 U.S. 587 (1936).[2] The only significant New Deal legislation sustained (five to four) was that dealing with eliminating the gold standard and devaluation of the dollar.[3] The constitutionality of crucial New Deal programs was thus in doubt and for the Court to still rule on, including the National Labor Relations Act (or Wagner Act), the Social Security Act, and the Public Utility Holding Company Act.

While the Senate Judiciary Committee considered FDR's proposal for expanding the Court in the spring of 1937, Senator Burton Wheeler, an opponent of the plan, at the suggestion of Justice Brandeis, asked Chief Justice Hughes if he would send a letter to the committee indicating what the justices thought about their workload and whether more justices were needed. On March 21, Hughes responded with a skillfully crafted letter implying that all the justices opposed the plan. (Hughes in fact talked only with Van Devanter and Brandeis; Cardozo and Stone later strongly disapproved of his actions and would have refused to sign the letter.) Immediately, Wheeler proclaimed that the Court was "unanimous with reference to the letter of the Chief Justice" and used the letter to mobilize opposition.

More dramatically on March 29, the Court voted five to four to uphold Washington state's minimum wage law in *West Coast Hotel Company v. Parrish*, 300 U.S. 379 (1937) (see Vol. 2, Ch. 3). Then, two weeks later in *National Labor Relations Board v. Jones & Laughlin Steel Corporation* (1937) (see excerpt below) the justices in a five-to-four decision upheld a vital part of the New Deal program, the National Labor Relations Act. Both cases signified a "switch in time that saved nine," because the Court had been split five to four when striking down progressive state and federal legislation. Justices Sutherland, McReynolds, Butler, and Van Devanter—the "Four Horsemen"—voted together as a laissez-faire protectionist bloc, while Stone and Cardozo followed Brandeis in supporting progressive economic legislation. Hughes and Roberts were the swing votes, the latter, less-tractable justice casting the pivotal vote striking down FDR's programs. But Roberts was persuaded by Hughes in December to change his mind, and when these rulings came down they dealt a death blow to FDR's Court-packing plan.

Chief Justice Hughes's opinion in *Jones & Laughlin*, upholding the National Labor Relations Board's (NLRB) jurisdiction over any person engaging in unfair labor practices "affecting commerce," reaffirmed Congress's plenary power under the commerce clause, at once returning to the themes expounded in *Gibbons* and laying the basis for the contemporary exercise of congressional power. And underscoring the Court's renewed deference to Congress on the day *Jones & Laughlin* came down, the justices approved enforcement of the Wagner Act against a trailer manufacturer and a small clothing company.[4] Almost invariably since *Jones & Laughlin*,[5] the Court has approved extending the coverage of the act over a wide range of businesses and labor relations.[6]

Congress responded to the Court's changed position and passed the Fair Labor Standards Act of 1938, one of the last major pieces of New Deal legislation. The act makes it unlawful to ship in interstate commerce goods produced in violation of employment standards set by the law for all employees "engaged in commerce or in the production of goods for commerce." The justices unanimously upheld the act in *United States v. Darby Lumber Company* (1941) (see excerpt below) and expressly overruled its earlier decision in *Hammer v. Dagenhart*.

The following year in *Wickard v. Filburn* (1942) (see excerpt below), the Court again demonstrated that it would affirm extensive congressional power and in the process discarded the direct and indirect effects rule. In this case, marketing penalties under the Agricultural Adjustment Act of 1938 were upheld against a farmer who grew only twenty-three acres of wheat for consumption on his farm alone.

These rulings typify the modern Court's approach to congressional power under the commerce clause. Congressional regulation of navigable waters and hydroelectric power,[7] for example, and extensive enforcement of the Sherman Antitrust Act were thus sanctioned.[8] With few exceptions in the aftermath of the New Deal crisis the Court legitimated a steady expansion of the reach of congressional power (see Ch. 7).

One consequence of the Court's legitimizing expansive congressional control over commerce has been to enlarge Congress's power to make federal criminal law.[9] Under the commerce clause, for instance, Congress passed the Consumer Credit Protection Act of 1968, the Omnibus Crime Control and Safe Streets Act of 1968, and the Federal Travel Act of 1970, all of which impose criminal penalties for various activities bearing some connection to interstate transportation.[10] *Perez v. United States*, 402 U.S. 146 (1971), is indicative of how deferential the Court became after its 1937 turnaround. There Justice Douglas for the majority upheld Congress's prohibition of "loan sharking"—that is, organized crime's extraction of payments for loans—under the Consumer Credit Protection Act on the grounds that congressional hearings had established a connection between local loan sharks and interstate commerce. Only dissenting Justice Stewart protested that

> the Framers of the Constitution never intended that the National Government might define as a crime and prosecute such wholly local activity through the enactment of federal criminal laws. . . . [I]t is not enough to say that some loan sharking is a national problem, for all crime is a national problem. It is not enough to say that some loan sharking has interstate characteristics, for any crime may have an interstate setting.

Another significant use of Congress's commerce power was in passing civil rights legislation. On the authority of the commerce clause, Congress enacted the Civil Rights Act of 1964, banning racial discrimination in public accommodations and, in Title VII of the act, discrimination in employment, as well as created the Equal Employment Opportunity Commission. So too, Title VIII of the Civil Rights Act of 1968 prohibits discrimination on the basis of race, color, religion, or national origin in the sale or rental of housing. When constitutional challenges were initially made to the Civil Rights Act, the Court rebuffed them in *Heart of Atlanta Motel, Inc. v. United States* (1964) (see excerpt below) and *Katzenbach v. McClung* (1964) (see excerpt below).[11] See also *South Carolina v. Katzenbach* (1966), upholding

Congress's power to enact the Voting Rights Act of 1965 (see excerpt in Ch. 8).

Congress's ever broader assertion of its power under the Commerce Clause and the Court's New Deal jurisprudence supporting the expansion of the administrative state drew increasing criticism from conservatives and advocates of "states' rights." In several sharply divided rulings, bare majorities of the Burger and Rehnquist Courts sought to resurrect the Tenth and Eleventh Amendments as a barrier to Congress's power (see Ch. 7, Section B). In addition, the Court handed down several important recent rulings on Congress's commerce power that signaled the emergence on the high bench of a majority willing to defend states' interests and to limit congressional power, at least in the area of expanding federal criminal law under the Commerce Clause.

Writing for a bare majority in *United States v. Lopez* (1995) (excerpted below), Chief Justice Rehnquist struck down the Gun-Free School Zones Act of 1990, which had made it a federal crime to possess a firearm within one thousand feet of a school. This was only the second ruling to limit Congress's power under the Commerce Clause in almost sixty years. While the chief justice's opinion was written broadly, in a concurring opinion Justice Thomas appeared to go even further by calling into question the Court's post-1937 jurisprudence in the area. Justices Stevens and Souter wrote separate dissenting opinions, while also joining, along with Justice Ginsburg, a major dissent by Justice Breyer, who sharply disagreed with both the majority's second-guessing of Congress in striking down the act and the basis for the majority's doing so.

The ruling and reasoning in *Lopez* invited further litigation attacking the constitutionality of not only Congress's power to enact federal criminal law but also legislation bearing on education, health, safety, and the environment. In *Reno v. Condon* (2000) (excerpted below), however, the Court unanimously upheld the Drivers' Privacy Protection Act, which forbids states from selling drivers' personal information, such as home address and telephone number. Over the objections of South Carolina, Chief Justice Rehnquist ruled that such information is a "thing in commerce" and thus within Congress's power to regulate. But Chief Justice Rehnquist again commanded *Lopez*'s bare majority in *United States v. Morrison* (2000) (excerpted below), striking down the Violence Against Women Act of 1994. In the majority's view Congress both failed to show that violence against women had a "substantial effect on interstate commerce" and exceeded its power under Section 5 of the Fourteenth Amendment. In the latter respect the Court reaffirmed its holding in *City of Boerne v. Flores* (1997) (excerpted below). In *City of Boerne* the Court struck down the Religious Freedom

Restoration Act of 1993 (RFRA), which Congress enacted following the ruling in *Employment Division, Department of Human Resources of Oregon v. Smith*, 492 U.S. 872 (1990) (in Vol. 2, Ch. 6) and established as a matter of federal law the pre-*Smith* test for balancing claims to religious freedom against governmental interests in generally applicable laws. In *City of Boerne*, the Court held that Congress exceeded its authority under the enforcement clause of Section 5 of the Fourteenth Amendment because Congress's power under Section 5 is solely remedial and does not authorize congressional expansion of constitutional rights beyond the scope of that recognized by the Court. *Morrison* in turn reaffirmed that limitation on congressional power.

In several recent cases, the Court also considered the scope of congressional authority and the balance between federal and state governments' powers under the Controlled Substances Act (CSA). *Gonzales v. O Centro Espirita Beneficente Uniao do Vegetal*, 546 U.S. 418 (2006), with Justice Alito not participating, unanimously held that the RFRA permitted federal courts to make exceptions on a case-by-case basis from the CSA for the importation of drugs to be used in a "sincere exercise of religion." A small religious sect challenged under the RFRA a ban on the importation of *hoasca* (pronounced "wass-ca"), used in sacramental tea originating in the Amazon rainforest, even though the CSA bans all use of the hallucinogen. Writing for the Court, Chief Justice Roberts noted that peyote, another hallucinogen, had been made an exception to the CSA for the use by Native Americans for thirty-five years and rejected the Bush administration's arguments that it had compelling governmental interests in forbidding the importation of *hoasca* based on (1) protecting the health of users, (2) preventing the diversion of the drug to recreational users, and (3) complying with the 1971 U.N. Convention on Psychotropic Substances.

In two other decisions, majorities on the Court went in different directions. On the one hand, in *Gonzales v. Raich* (2005) (excerpted below), the Court upheld congressional power and the federal prosecution of users of medicinal marijuana. Ten states had legalized the medicinal use of marijuana, but writing for the Court Justice Stevens upheld congressional power to criminalize such use. Chief Justice Rehnquist and Justices O'Connor and Thomas dissented. On the other hand, in *Gonzales v. Oregon* (2006) (excerpted below) the Court ruled that the attorney general's directive barring physician-suicide exceeded his authority under the CSA, and upheld Oregon's Death with Dignity Act, which permits doctors to prescribe certain lethal substances to assist in the painless death of competent but terminally ill individuals. Chief Justice Roberts and Justices Scalia and Thomas dissented.

Notes

1. The Court also struck down the Farm Mortgage Act and the Municipal Bankruptcy Act in, respectively, *Louisville Joint Stock Land Bank v. Radford*, 295 U.S. 555 (1935); and *Ashton v. Cameron County District*, 298 U.S. 513 (1936).

2. By five-to-four votes, however, the Court sustained New York laws on unemployment compensation and setting minimum prices for milk, in *Associated Industries v. Department of Labor*, 299 U.S. 587 (1936); and *Nebbia v. New York*, 291 U.S. 502 (1934). And in *Home Building & Loan Co. v. Blaisdell* (1934) (see Vol. 2, Ch. 3), a bare majority upheld the Minnesota Mortgage Moratorium law.

3. See *The Gold Clause Cases*, 294 U.S. 240 (1935). The Court also upheld federal legislation prohibiting the shipment in interstate commerce of convict-made goods into states that prohibited such goods. See *Whitfield v. Ohio*, 297 U.S. 431 (1936); and *Kentucky Whip and Collar Co. v. Illinois Central Railroad Co.*, 299 U.S. 334 (1937).

4. *National Labor Relations Board v. Freuhauf Trailer Co.*, 301 U.S. 49 (1937); and *National Labor Relations Board v. Friedman-Harry Marks Clothing Company*, 301 U.S. 58 (1937).

5. In *McCulloch v. Sociedad Nacional de Marineros de Honduras*, 372 U.S. 10 (1963), the Court denied the NLRB's jurisdiction over foreign seamen and, in *NLRB v. Catholic Bishop of Chicago*, 440 U.S. 490 (1979), over lay faculty in Catholic high schools.

6. See *Associated Press v. NLRB*, 301 U.S. 103 (1937); *Consolidated Edison Co. v. NLRB*, 305 U.S. 197 (1938); *Santa Cruz Fruit Packing Co. v. NLRB*, 303 U.S. 453 (1938); *NLRB v. Fainblatt*, 306 U.S. 601 (1939); *Polish Alliance v. Labor Board*, 322 U.S. 643 (1944); *Guss v. Utah Labor Board*, 353 U.S. 1 (1957); and *NLRB v. Reliance Fuel Oil Corporation*, 371 U.S. 224 (1963).

7. See *United States v. Appalachian Electric Power Co.*, 311 U.S. 377 (1940), upholding the Federal Water Power Act of 1920; *Arizona v. California*, 283 U.S. 423 (1931), upholding the Boulder Canyon Project Act of 1928; and *Tennessee Electric Power Company v. T.V.A.*, 306 U.S. 118 (1939), denying utility companies standing to challenge the constitutionality of the Tennessee Valley Authority.

8. See *United States v. South-Eastern Underwriters Association*, 322 U.S. 533 (1944), upholding application of antitrust laws to insurance companies; and *Goldfarb v. Virginia State Bar*, 421 U.S. 773 (1975), holding that a bar association's imposition of minimum fees for legal services constituted price fixing. In *Flood v. Kuhn*, 407 U.S. 258 (1972), however, the Court upheld an exemption for organized baseball from the Sherman Act, when denying a challenge to the "reserve clause," under which a club that first signs a player obtains an exclusive right to his services.

9. Prior to 1937 the Court upheld congressional power to ban interstate transportation of stolen cars, in *Brooks v. United States*, 267 U.S. 432 (1925); and to enact the Federal Kidnapping Act, in *Gooch v. United States*, 297 U.S. 124 (1936).

10. While the Court has not seriously questioned the constitutionality of such legislation, it has on occasion reversed convictions under these statutes. *United States v. Bass*, 404 U.S. 336 (1971), for example, overturned a conviction under the Omnibus Crime Control and Safe Streets Act because there was no showing that firearms were used in interstate commerce, whereas *Scarbough v. United States*, 431 U.S. 563 (1977), affirmed a conviction based on the government's showing that firearms had moved at least once in commerce.

11. In addition, in *Daniel v. Paul*, 395 U.S. 298 (1969), the Court upheld enforce-

ment of provisions of the Civil Rights against a "private club" in Arkansas, which racially discriminated in selling its "memberships" for twenty-five cents on the grounds that the club served interstate travelers and served food that had moved in interstate commerce.

SELECTED BIBLIOGRAPHY

Baker, Leonard. *Back to Back: The Duel between FDR and the Supreme Court.* New York: Macmillan, 1967.

Cortner, Richard C. *Civil Rights and Public Accommodations: The Heart of Atlanta Motel and McClung Cases.* Lawrence: University Press of Kansas, 2001.

Cushman, Barry. *Rethinking the New Deal: The Structure of a Constitutional Revolution.* New York: Oxford University Press, 1998.

Leuchtenburg, William E. *The Supreme Court Reborn: The Constitutional Revolution in the Age of Roosevelt.* New York: Oxford University Press, 1995.

Murchison, Kenneth. *The Snail Darter Case: TVA versus the Endangered Species Act.* Lawrence; University Press of Kansas, 2007.

Schoenbrod, David. *Power without Responsibility: How the Congress Abuses the People through Delegation.* New Haven, CT: Yale University Press, 1993.

National Labor Relations Board v. Jones & Laughlin Steel Corporation
301 U.S. 1, 57 S.CT. 615 (1937)

After the Court struck down the National Industrial Recovery Act in *Schechter Poultry Corporation v. United States*, 295 U.S. 495 (1935) (see excerpt in Vol. 1, Ch. 4), Congress passed the National Labor Relations Act, or so-called Wagner Act. With that act Congress again sought to protect the right of workers to organize and to encourage collective bargaining, created the new NLRB, and authorized it to prevent unfair labor practices on the rationale that they might lead to strikes that would affect the flow of commerce. An affiliate of the Amalgamated Association of Iron & Tin Workers of America charged before the NLRB that Jones & Laughlin, one of the largest steel producers in the country, discouraged employees from joining the union and fired ten employees for their union activities. Following a hearing, the NLRB ordered Jones & Laughlin to reinstate the ten employees. The corporation refused to do so, contending that the Wagner Act was unconstitutional because it governed labor relations, not commerce. The NLRB, as provided in the act, petitioned a federal court of appeals to enforce its order, but

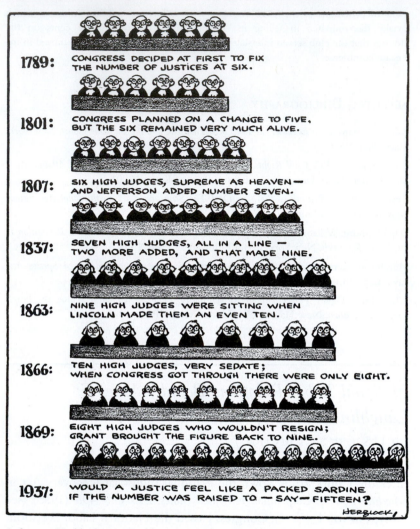

1789: CONGRESS DECIDED AT FIRST TO FIX THE NUMBER OF JUSTICES AT SIX.

1801: CONGRESS PLANNED ON A CHANGE TO FIVE, BUT THE SIX REMAINED VERY MUCH ALIVE.

1807: SIX HIGH JUDGES, SUPREME AS HEAVEN — AND JEFFERSON ADDED NUMBER SEVEN.

1837: SEVEN HIGH JUDGES, ALL IN A LINE — TWO MORE ADDED, AND THAT MADE NINE.

1863: NINE HIGH JUDGES WERE SITTING WHEN LINCOLN MADE THEM AN EVEN TEN.

1866: TEN HIGH JUDGES, VERY SEDATE; WHEN CONGRESS GOT THROUGH THERE WERE ONLY EIGHT.

1869: EIGHT HIGH JUDGES WHO WOULDN'T RESIGN; GRANT BROUGHT THE FIGURE BACK TO NINE.

1937: WOULD A JUSTICE FEEL LIKE A PACKED SARDINE IF THE NUMBER WAS RAISED TO — SAY — FIFTEEN?

HERBLOCK

A famous Herblock cartoon blasting President Franklin D. Roosevelt's 1937 "court-packing" plan. *(From* Herblock: A Cartoonist's Life, *Times Books, 1998. Courtesy of the Estate of Herbert L. Block.)*

---

that court declined, and the NLRB appealed to the Supreme Court. Although the Court had unanimously struck down the National Industrial Recovery Act two years earlier in *Schechter*, Chief Justice Hughes managed to mass a bare majority in this case for upholding Congress's power to enact the National Labor Relations Act.

The Court's decision was five to four, and the majority's opinion was announced by Chief Justice Hughes. Justice McReynolds dissented and was joined by Justices Van Devanter, Sutherland, and Butler.

☐ *Chief Justice HUGHES delivers the opinion of the Court.*

In a proceeding under the National Labor Relations Act of 1935 the National Labor Relations Board found that the respondent, Jones & Laughlin Steel Corporation, had violated the act by engaging in unfair labor practices affecting commerce. . . . The unfair labor practices charged were that the corporation was discriminating against members of the union with regard to hire and tenure of employment, and was coercing and intimidating its employees in order to interfere with their self-organization. . . .

Jones & Laughlin . . . is engaged in the business of manufacturing iron and steel in plants situated in Pittsburgh and nearby Aliquippa, Pa. It manufactures and distributes a widely diversified line of steel and pig iron, being the fourth largest producer of steel in the United States. With its subsidiaries—nineteen in number—it is a completely integrated enterprise, owning and operating ore, coal and limestone properties, lake and river transportation facilities and terminal railroads located at its manufacturing plants. It owns or controls mines in Michigan and Minnesota. It operates four ore steamships on the Great Lakes, used in the transportation of ore to its factories. It owns coal mines in Pennsylvania. It operates towboats and steam barges used in carrying coal to its factories. It owns limestone properties in various places in Pennsylvania and West Virginia. It owns the Monongahela connecting railroad which connects the plants of the Pittsburgh works and forms an interconnection with the Pennsylvania, New York Central and Baltimore & Ohio Railroad systems. It owns the Aliquippa & Southern Railroad Company, which connects the Aliquippa works with the Pittsburgh & Lake Erie, part of the New York Central system. Much of its product is shipped to its warehouses in Chicago, Detroit, Cincinnati and Memphis,—to the last two places by means of its own barges and transportation equipment. In Long Island City, New York, and in New Orleans it operates structural steel fabricating shops in connection with the warehousing of semifinished materials sent from its works. Through one of its wholly-owned subsidiaries it owns, leases, and operates stores, warehouses, and yards for the distribution of equipment and supplies for drilling and operating oil and gas mills and for pipe lines, refineries and pumping stations. It has sales offices in twenty cities in the United States and a wholly-owned subsidiary which is devoted exclusively to distributing its product in Canada. Approximately 75 per cent of its product is shipped out of Pennsylvania.

Summarizing these operations, the Labor Board concluded that the works in Pittsburgh and Aliquippa "might be likened to the heart of a self-contained, highly integrated body. They draw in the raw materials from Michigan, Minnesota, West Virginia, Pennsylvania in part through arteries and by means controlled by the respondent; they transform the materials and then pump them out to all parts of the nation through the vast mechanism which the respondent has elaborated."

To carry on the activities of the entire steel industry, 33,000 men mine ore, 44,000 men mine coal, 4,000 men quarry limestone, 16,000 men manufacture coke, 343,000 men manufacture steel, and 83,000 men transport its product. Respondent has about 10,000 employees in its Aliquippa plant, which is located in a community of about 30,000 persons.

Respondent points to evidence that the Aliquippa plant, in which the discharged men were employed, contains complete facilities for the production of finished and semifinished iron and steel products from raw materials. . . . [T]he iron ore which is procured from mines in Minnesota and Michigan and transported to respondent's plant is stored in stock piles for future use, the amount of ore in storage varying with the season but usually being enough to maintain operations from nine to ten months. . . .

Practically all the factual evidence in the case . . . supports the findings of the Board that respondent discharged these men "because of their union activity and for the purpose of discouraging membership in the union." We turn to the questions of law which respondent urges in contesting the validity and application of the act.

First. The Scope of the Act.—The act is challenged in its entirety as an attempt to regulate all industry, thus invading the reserved powers of the States over their local concerns. It is asserted that the references in the act to interstate and foreign commerce are colorable at best; that the act is not a true regulation of such commerce or of matters which directly affect it, but on the contrary has the fundamental object of placing under the compulsory supervision of the federal government all industrial labor relations within the nation.

The critical words of [the Act] prescribing the limits of the Board's authority in dealing with the labor practices, are "affecting commerce." The act specifically defines . . . 'affecting commerce' [as] in commerce, or burdening or obstructing commerce or the free flow of commerce, or having led or tending to lead to a labor dispute burdening or obstructing commerce or the free flow of commerce."

This definition is one of exclusion as well as inclusion. The grant of authority to the Board does not purport to extend to the relationship between all industrial employees and employers. Its terms do not impose collective bargaining upon all industry regardless of effects upon interstate or foreign commerce. It purports to reach only what may be deemed to burden or obstruct that commerce and, thus qualified, it must be construed as contemplating the exercise of control within constitutional bounds. It is a familiar principle that acts which directly burden or obstruct interstate or foreign commerce, or its free flow, are within the reach of the congressional power. Acts having that effect are not rendered immune because they grow out of labor disputes. . . .

It is the effect upon commerce, not the source of the injury which is the criterion. Whether or not particular action does affect commerce in such a close and intimate fashion as to be subject to federal control, and hence to lie within the authority conferred upon the Board, is left by the statute to be determined as individual cases arise. We are thus to inquire whether in the instant case the constitutional boundary has been passed.

Second. The Unfair Labor Practices in Question. . . . [I]n its present application, the statute goes no further than to safeguard the right of employees to self-organization and to select representatives of their own choosing for collective bargaining or other mutual protection without restraint or coercion by their employer.

That is a fundamental right. Employees have as clear a right to organize and select their representatives for lawful purposes as the respondent has to organize in business and select its own officers and agents. Discrimination and coercion to prevent the free exercise of the right of employees to self-organization and representation is a proper subject for condemnation by

competent legislative authority. Long ago we stated the reason for labor organizations. We said that they were organized out of the necessities of the situation; that a single employee was helpless in dealing with an employer; that
he was dependent ordinarily on his daily wage for the maintenance of himself and family; that, if the employer refused to pay him the wages that he
thought fair, he was nevertheless unable to leave the employ and resist arbitrary and unfair treatment; that union was essential to give laborers opportunity to deal on an equality with their employer. . . .

Third. *The Application of the Act to Employees Engaged in Production.*—The
Principle Involved. Respondent says that, whatever may be said of employees
engaged in interstate commerce, the industrial relations and activities in the
manufacturing department of respondent's enterprise are not subject to federal regulation. The argument rests upon the proposition that manufacturing
in itself is not commerce. . . .

The government distinguishes these cases. The various parts of respondent's enterprise are described as interdependent and as thus involving "a
great movement of iron ore, coal and limestone along well-defined paths to
the steel mills, thence through them, and thence in the form of steel products
into the consuming centers of the country—a definite and well-understood
course of business." It is urged that these activities constitute a "stream" or
"flow" of commerce, of which the Aliquippa manufacturing plant is the fo-
cal point, and that industrial strife at that point would cripple the entire
movement. . . .

We do not find it necessary to determine whether these features of defendant's business dispose of the asserted analogy to the "stream of commerce" cases. The instances in which that metaphor has been used are but
particular, and not exclusive, illustrations of the protective power which the
government invokes in support of the present act. The congressional authority to protect interstate commerce from burdens and obstructions is not limited to transactions which can be deemed to be an essential part of a "flow"
of interstate or foreign commerce. Burdens and obstructions may be due to
injurious action springing from other sources. . . . Although activities may be
intrastate in character when separately considered, if they have such a close
and substantial relation to interstate commerce that their control is essential
or appropriate to protect that commerce from burdens and obstructions,
Congress cannot be denied the power to exercise that control. *Schechter
Corporation v. United States.* Undoubtedly the scope of this power must be
considered in the light of our dual system of government and may not be
extended so as to embrace effects upon interstate commerce so indirect and
remote that to embrace them, in view of our complex society, would effectually obliterate the distinction between what is national and what is local
and create a completely centralized government. . . . The question is necessarily one of degree. . . .

That intrastate activities, by reason of close and intimate relation to
interstate commerce, may fall within federal control is demonstrated in the
case of carriers who are engaged in both interstate and intrastate transportation. There federal control has been found essential to secure the freedom of interstate traffic from interference or unjust discrimination and to
promote the efficiency of the interstate service. *The Shreveport Case (Houston,
E. & W. T. R. Co. v. United States)*, 234 U.S. 342 [1914]. . . .

The close and intimate effect which brings the subject within the reach of federal power may be due to activities in relation to productive industry although the industry when separately viewed is local. . . .

It is thus apparent that the fact that the employees here concerned were engaged in production is not determinative. The question remains as to the effect upon interstate commerce of the labor practice involved. In the *Schechter Case*, we found that the effect there was so remote as to be beyond the federal power. To find "immediacy or directness" there was to find it "almost everywhere," a result inconsistent with the maintenance of our federal system. In the *Carter Case* [*Carter v. Carter Coal Co.*, 298 U.S. 238 (1936)], the Court was of the opinion that the provisions of the statute relating to production were invalid upon several grounds,—that there was improper delegation of legislative power, and that the requirements not only went beyond any sustainable measure of protection of interstate commerce but were also inconsistent with due process. These cases are not controlling here.

Fourth. Effects of the Unfair Labor Practice in Respondent's Enterprise. Giving full weight to respondent's contention with respect to a break in the complete continuity of the "stream of commerce" by reason of respondent's manufacturing operations, the fact remains that the stoppage of those operations by industrial strife would have a most serious effect upon interstate commerce. In view of respondent's far-flung activities, it is idle to say that the effect would be indirect or remote. It is obvious that it would be immediate and might be catastrophic. We are asked to shut our eyes to the plainest facts of our national life and to deal with the question of direct and indirect effects in an intellectual vacuum. Because there may be but indirect and remote effects upon interstate commerce in connection with a host of local enterprises throughout the country, it does not follow that other industrial activities do not have such a close and intimate relation to interstate commerce as to make the presence of industrial strife a matter of the most urgent national concern. When industries organize themselves on a national scale, making their relation to interstate commerce the dominant factor in their activities, how can it be maintained that their industrial labor relations constitute a forbidden field into which Congress may not enter when it is necessary to protect interstate commerce from the paralyzing consequences of industrial war? We have often said that interstate commerce itself is a practical conception. It is equally true that interferences with that commerce must be appraised by a judgment that does not ignore actual experience.

Experience has abundantly demonstrated that the recognition of the right of employees to self-organization and to have representatives of their own choosing for the purpose of collective bargaining is often an essential condition of industrial peace. Refusal to confer and negotiate has been one of the most prolific causes of strife. This is such an outstanding fact in the history of labor disturbances that it is a proper subject of judicial notice and requires no citation of instances. . . .

The steel industry is one of the great basic industries of the United States, with ramifying activities affecting interstate commerce at every point. The Government aptly refers to the steel strike of 1919–1920 with its far-reaching consequences. The fact that there appears to have been no major disturbance in that industry in the more recent period did not dispose of the possibilities of future and like dangers to interstate commerce which Congress was entitled to foresee and to exercise its protective power to forestall. It is not necessary again to detail the facts as to respondent's enterprise. Instead of being beyond the pale, we think that it presents in a most striking way the close and intimate relation which a manufacturing industry may have to interstate commerce and we have no doubt that Congress had constitutional authority to safeguard the right of respondent's employees to self-organization and freedom in the choice of representatives for collective bargaining.

☐ *Justice McREYNOLDS, dissenting.*

Justice VAN DEVANTER, Justice SUTHERLAND, Justice BUTLER and I are unable to agree with the decisions just announced. . . .

Considering the far-reaching import of these decisions, the departure from what we understand has been consistently ruled here, and the extraordinary power confirmed to a Board of three, the obligation to present our views becomes plain.

The Court as we think departs from well-established principles followed in *Schechter Poultry Corporation v. United States*, and *Carter v. Carter Coal Co.* . . .

It puts into the hands of a Board power of control over purely local industry beyond anything heretofore deemed permissible. . . .

We are told that Congress may protect the "stream of commerce" and that one who buys raw material without the state, manufactures it therein, and ships the output to another state is in that stream. Therefore it is said he may be prevented from doing anything which may interfere with its flow.

This, too, goes beyond the constitutional limitations heretofore enforced. If a man raises cattle and regularly delivers them to a carrier for interstate shipment, may Congress prescribe the conditions under which he may employ or discharge helpers on the ranch? The products of a mine pass daily into interstate commerce; many things are brought to it from other states. Are the owners and the miners within the power of Congress in respect of the latter's tenure and discharge? May a mill owner be prohibited from closing his factory or discontinuing his business because so to do would stop the flow of products to and from his plant in interstate commerce? . . .

If the ruling of the Court just announced is adhered to, these questions suggest some of the problems certain to arise. . . .

That Congress has power by appropriate means, not prohibited by the Constitution, to prevent direct and material interference with the conduct of interstate commerce is settled doctrine. But the interference struck at must be direct and material, not some mere possibility contingent on wholly uncertain events; and there must be no impairment of rights guaranteed. A state by taxation on property may indirectly but seriously affect the cost of transportation; it may not lay a direct tax upon the receipts from interstate transportation. The first is an indirect effect, the other direct. . . .

The things inhibited by the Labor Act relate to the management of a manufacturing plant—something distinct from commerce and subject to the authority of the state. And this may not be abridged because of some vague possibility of distant interference with commerce. . . .

It seems clear to us that Congress has transcended the powers granted.

United States v. Darby Lumber Company

312 U.S. 100, 61 S.Ct. 451 (1941)

Fred Darby, the owner of a Georgia lumber business, was indicted for violating provisions of the Fair Labor Standards Act of 1938. That act prohibits in interstate commerce the shipping and producing of goods for commerce by companies whose employees are paid less than the minimum wage (set, at the time, at twenty cents per hour by the act) or who work more than forty hours a week without overtime pay, and requires companies to keep records on their employees' wages and hours. In federal district court, a judge quashed the indictment on finding the act unconstitutional because, relying on *Hammer v. Dagenhart*, 247 U.S. 251 (1918) (excerpted in section B of this chapter) and other rulings of the Supreme Court, Congress had no authority to control the conditions of production and manufacturing under the commerce clause. The Department of Justice appealed that ruling to the Supreme Court, which after granting and hearing the case reversed the lower court and overturned *Hammer v. Dagenhart*.

The Court's decision was unanimous, and the opinion was announced by Justice Stone.

☐ *Justice STONE delivers the opinion of the Court.*

The Fair Labor Standards Act set up a comprehensive legislative scheme for preventing the shipment in interstate commerce of certain products and commodities produced in the United States under labor conditions as respects wages and hours which fail to conform to standards set up by the Act. Its purpose . . . is to exclude from interstate commerce goods produced for the commerce and to prevent their production for interstate commerce, under conditions detrimental to the maintenance of the minimum standards of living necessary for health and general well-being; and to prevent the use of interstate commerce as the means of competition in the distribution of goods so produced, and as the means of spreading and perpetuating such substandard labor conditions among the workers of the several states. . . .

[We] confine our decision to the validity and construction of the statute. . . .

While manufacture is not of itself interstate commerce the shipment of manufactured goods interstate is such commerce and the prohibition of such shipment by Congress is indubitably a regulation of the commerce. The power to regulate commerce is the power "to prescribe the rule by which commerce is to be governed." *Gibbons v. Ogden.* It extends not only to those regulations which aid, foster and protect the commerce, but embraces those which prohibit it. It is conceded that the power of Congress to prohibit transportation in interstate commerce includes noxious articles, stolen articles, kidnapped persons, and articles such as intoxicating liquor or convict made goods, traffic in which is forbidden or restricted by the laws of the state of destination. . . .

But it is said that the present prohibition falls within the scope of none of these categories; that while the prohibition is nominally a regulation of the commerce its motive or purpose is regulation of wages and hours of persons engaged in manufacture, the control of which has been reserved to the states and upon which Georgia and some of the states of destination have placed no restriction; that the effect of the present statute is not to exclude the prescribed articles from interstate commerce in aid of state regulation as in *Kentucky Whip & Collar Co. v. Illinois Central R. Co.*, [299 U.S. 334 (1937)] but instead, under the guise of a regulation of interstate commerce, it undertakes to regulate wages and hours within the state contrary to the policy of the state which has elected to leave them unregulated.

The power of Congress over interstate commerce "is complete in itself, may be exercised to its utmost extent, and acknowledges no limitations, other than are prescribed by the constitution." *Gibbons v. Ogden.* That power can neither be enlarged nor diminished by the exercise or non-exercise of state power. Congress, following its own conception of public policy concerning the restrictions which may appropriately be imposed on interstate commerce, is free to exclude from the commerce articles whose use in the states for which they are destined it may conceive to be injurious to the public health, morals or welfare, even though the state has not sought to regulate their use. . . .

Such regulation is not a forbidden invasion of state power merely because either its motive or its consequence is to restrict the use of articles of commerce within the states of destination and is not prohibited unless by other Constitutional provisions. It is no objection to the assertion of the power to regulate interstate commerce that its exercise is attended by the same incidents which attend the exercise of the police power of the states. . . .

The motive and purpose of the present regulation is plainly to make effective the Congressional conception of public policy that interstate commerce should not be made the instrument of competition in the distribution of goods produced under substandard labor conditions, which competition is injurious to the commerce and to the states from and to which the commerce flows. The motive and purpose of a regulation of interstate commerce are matters for the legislative judgment upon the exercise of which the Constitution places no restriction and over which the courts are given no control. . . .

Whatever their motive and purpose, regulations of commerce which do not infringe some constitutional prohibition are within the plenary power conferred on Congress by the Commerce Clause. Subject only to that limitation, presently to be considered, we conclude that the prohibition of the shipment interstate of goods produced under the forbidden substandard labor conditions is within the constitutional authority of Congress.

In the more than a century which has elapsed since the decision of *Gibbons v. Ogden*, these principles of constitutional interpretation have been so long and repeatedly recognized by this Court as applicable to the Commerce Clause, that there would be little occasion for repeating them now were it not for the decision of this Court twenty-two years ago in *Hammer v. Dagenhart.* . . .

Hammer v. Dagenhart has not been followed. The distinction on which the decision was rested that Congressional power to prohibit interstate commerce is limited to articles which in themselves have some harmful or deleterious property—a distinction which was novel when made and un-supported by any provision of the Constitution—has long since been abandoned.

The conclusion is inescapable that *Hammer v. Dagenhart* was a departure from the principles which have prevailed in the interpretation of the commerce clause both before and since the decision and that such vitality, as a precedent, as it then had has long since been exhausted. It should be and now is overruled.

Validity of the wage and hour requirements. Section 15(a)(2) and Secs. 6 and 7 require employers to conform to the wage and hour provisions with respect to all employees engaged in the production of goods for interstate commerce. As appellee's employees are not alleged to be "engaged in interstate commerce" the validity of the prohibition turns on the question whether the employment, under other than the prescribed labor standards, of employees engaged in the production of goods for interstate commerce is so related to the commerce and so affects it as to be within the reach of the power of Congress to regulate it. . . .

[W]e think the acts alleged in the indictment are within the sweep of the statute. The obvious purpose of the Act was not only to prevent the interstate transportation of the proscribed product, but to stop the initial step toward transportation, production with the purpose of so transporting it. Congress was not unaware that most manufacturing businesses shipping their product in interstate commerce make it in their shops without reference to its ultimate destination and then after manufacture select some of it for shipment interstate and some intrastate according to the daily demands of their business, and that it would be practically impossible, without disrupting manufacturing businesses, to restrict the prohibited kind of production to the particular pieces of lumber, cloth, furniture or the like which later move in interstate rather than intrastate commerce. . . .

There remains the question whether such restriction on the production of goods for commerce is a permissible exercise of commerce power. The power of Congress over interstate commerce is not confined to the regulation of commerce among the states. It extends to those activities intrastate which so affect interstate commerce or the exercise of the power of Congress over it as to make regulation of them appropriate means to the attainment of a legitimate end, the exercise of the granted power of Congress to regulate interstate commerce. . . .

Congress, having by the present Act adopted the policy of excluding from interstate commerce all goods produced for the commerce which do not conform to the specified labor standards, it may choose the means reasonably adapted to the attainment of the permitted end, even though they involve control of intrastate activities. Such legislation has often been sustained with respect to powers, other than the commerce power granted to the national government, when the means chosen, although not themselves within the granted power, were nevertheless deemed appropriate aids to the accomplishment of some purpose within an admitted power of the national government. . . . A familiar like exercise of power is the regulation of intrastate transactions which are so commingled with or related to interstate commerce that all must be regulated if the interstate commerce is to be effectively controlled. . . .

Similarly Congress may require inspection and preventive treatment of all cattle in a disease infected area in order to prevent shipment in interstate commerce of some of the cattle without the treatment. It may prohibit the removal, at destination, of labels required by the Pure Food & Drugs Act, 21 U.S.C.A. Sec. 1 et seq., to be affixed to articles transported in interstate commerce.

We think also that Sec. 15(a)(2), now under consideration, is sustainable independently of Sec. 15(a)(1), which prohibits shipment or transportation of the proscribed goods. As we have said the evils aimed at by the Act are the spread of substandard labor conditions through the use of the facilities of interstate commerce for competition by the goods so produced with those produced under the prescribed or better labor conditions; and the consequent dislocation of the commerce itself caused by the impairment or destruction of local businesses by competition made effective through interstate commerce. The Act is thus directed at the suppression of a method or kind of competition in interstate commerce which it has in effect condemned as "unfair," as the Clayton Act has condemned other "unfair methods of competition" made effective through interstate commerce. . . .

The means adopted by Sec. 15(a) (2) for the protection of interstate commerce by the suppression of the production of the condemned goods for interstate commerce is so related to the commerce and so affects it as to be within the reach of the commerce power. . . .

Our conclusion is unaffected by the Tenth Amendment which provides: "The powers not delegated to the United States by the Constitution, nor prohibited by it to the States, are reserved to the States respectively, or to the people." The amendment states but a truism that all is retained which has not been surrendered. There is nothing in the history of its adoption to suggest that it was more than declaratory of the relationship between the national and state governments as it had been established by the Constitution before the amendment or that its purpose was other than to allay fears that the new national government might seek to exercise powers not granted, and that the states might not be able to exercise fully their reserved powers. . . .

Validity of the requirement of records of wages and hours. Sec. 15(a) (5) and Sec. 11(c). These requirements are incidental to those for the prescribed wages and hours, and hence validity of the former turns on validity of the latter. Since, as we have held, Congress may require production for interstate commerce to conform to those conditions, it may require the employer, as a means of enforcing the valid law, to keep a record showing whether he has in fact complied with it. The requirement for records even of the intrastate transaction is an appropriate means to the legitimate end.

Wickard v. Filburn

317 U.S. 111, 63 S.Ct. 82 (1941)

Under the Agricultural Adjustment Act of 1938, as amended in 1941, Secretary of Agriculture Claude Wickard was directed to set national acreage allotments for wheat to stabilize agricultural production. This required apportioning the allotments among the states and establishing quotas for individual farmers, who were subject to penalties for growing more wheat than their assigned quota. The act also provided that if more than one-third of the farmers subject to the regulations objected by referendum to the proposed national allotments, then the act would be suspended. Filburn owned a small dairy farm in Ohio and was allotted a little over eleven acres for wheat. But he planted twenty-three acres, intending to use the excess crops to feed his livestock, and harvested 239 bushels more than his allotted 222 bushels under the program. As a result, he was fined $117.11, based on a penalty of $0.49 for each bushel produced in excess of his quota. Filburn refused to pay and filed a complaint in federal district court, asking for an injunction against enforcement of the penalty and for a declaratory judgment that the legislation as applied to him violated the commerce clause and the Fifth Amendment. A three-judge court issued an injunction on the grounds that the secretary of agriculture had made misleading speeches in support of the adoption of the quotas by referendum. The government then appealed to the Supreme Court, which reversed the lower court's holding and addressed (in the excerpt here) the constitutional challenge to Congress's commerce power.

The Court's decision was unanimous, and the opinion was announced by Justice Jackson.

☐ *Justice JACKSON delivers the opinion of the Court.*

It is urged that under the Commerce Clause of the Constitution, Article I, Sec. 8, clause 3, Congress does not possess the power it has in this instance sought to exercise. The question would merit little consideration since our decision in *United States v. Darby* [(1941)], sustaining the federal power to regulate production of goods for commerce except for the fact that this Act extends federal regulation to production not intended in any part for commerce but wholly for consumption on the farm. The Act includes a definition of "market" and its derivatives so that as related to wheat in addition to its conventional meaning it also means to dispose of "by feeding (in any form) to poultry or livestock which, or the products of which, are sold, bartered, or exchanged, or to be so disposed of." Hence, marketing quotas not only embrace all that may be sold without penalty but also what may be consumed on the premises. . . .

Appellee says that this is a regulation of production and consumption of wheat. Such activities are, he urges, beyond the reach of Congressional power under the Commerce Clause, since they are local in character, and their effects upon interstate commerce are at most "indirect." In answer the Government argues that the statute regulates neither production nor consumption, but only marketing; and, in the alternative, that if the Act does go beyond the regulation of marketing it is sustainable as a "necessary and proper" implementation of the power of Congress over interstate commerce.

The Government's concern lest the Act be held to be a regulation of production or consumption rather than of marketing is attributable to a few dicta and decisions of this Court which might be understood to lay it down that activities such as "production," "manufacturing," and "mining" are strictly "local" and, except in special circumstances which are not present here, cannot be regulated under the commerce power because their effects upon interstate commerce are, as matter of law, only "indirect." Even today, when this power has been held to have great latitude, there is no decision of this Court that such activities may be regulated where no part of the product is intended for interstate commerce or intermingled with the subjects thereof. We believe that a review of the course of decision under the Commerce Clause will make plain, however, that questions of the power of Congress are not to be decided by reference to any formula which would give controlling force to nomenclature such as "production" and "indirect" and foreclose consideration of the actual effects of the activity in question upon interstate commerce.

At the beginning Chief Justice MARSHALL described the federal commerce power with a breadth never yet exceeded. *Gibbons v. Ogden* [1824]. He made emphatic the embracing and penetrating nature of this power by warning that effective restraints on its exercise must proceed from political rather than from judicial processes. . . .

For nearly a century, however, decisions of this Court under the Commerce Clause dealt rarely with questions of what Congress might do in the exercise of its granted power under the Clause and almost entirely with the permissibility of state activity which it was claimed discriminated against or burdened interstate commerce. During this period there was perhaps little occasion for the affirmative exercise of the commerce power, and the influence of the Clause on American life and law was a negative one, resulting almost wholly from its operation as a restraint upon the powers of the states. . . .

It was not until 1887 with the enactment of the Interstate Commerce Act that the interstate commerce power began to exert positive influence in American law and life. This first important federal resort to the commerce power was followed in 1890 by the Sherman Anti-Trust Act and, thereafter, mainly after 1903, by many others. These statutes ushered in new phases of adjudication, which required the Court to approach the interpretation of the Commerce Clause in the light of an actual exercise by Congress of its power thereunder.

When it first dealt with this new legislation, the Court adhered to its earlier pronouncements, and allowed but little scope to the power of Congress. *United States v. E. C. Knight Co.* [1895]. These earlier pronouncements also played an important part in several of the five cases in which this Court later held that Acts of Congress under the Commerce Clause were in excess of its power. . . .

The Court's recognition of the relevance of the economic effects in the application of the Commerce Clause exemplified by this statement has made the mechanical application of legal formulas no longer feasible. Once an economic measure of the reach of the power granted to Congress in the Commerce Clause is accepted, questions of federal power cannot be decided simply by finding the activity in question to be "production" nor can consideration of its economic effects be foreclosed by calling them "indirect." . . .

Whether the subject of the regulation in question was "production," "consumption," or "marketing" is, therefore, not material for purposes of deciding the question of federal power before us. That an activity is of local character may help in a doubtful case to determine whether Congress intended to reach it. . . .

The wheat industry has been a problem industry for some years. Largely as a result of increased foreign production and import restrictions, annual exports of wheat and flour from the United States during the ten-year period ending in 1940 averaged less than 10 per cent of total production, while during the 1920's they averaged more than 25 per cent. The decline in the export trade has left a large surplus in production which in connection with an abnormally large supply of wheat and other grains in recent years caused congestion in a number of markets; tied up railroad cars; and caused elevators in some instances to turn away grains, and railroads to institute embargoes to prevent further congestion. . . .

The maintenance by government regulation of a price for wheat undoubtedly can be accomplished as effectively by sustaining or increasing the demand as by limiting the supply. The effect of the statute before us is to restrict the amount which may be produced for market and the extent as well to which one may forestall resort to the market by producing to meet his own needs. That appellee's own contribution to the demand for wheat may be trivial by itself is not enough to remove him from the scope of federal regulation where, as here, his contribution, taken together with that of many others similarly situated, is far from trivial. . . .

One of the primary purposes of the Act in question was to increase the market price of wheat and to that end to limit the volume thereof that could affect the market. It can hardly be denied that a factor of such volume and variability as home-consumed wheat would have a substantial influence on price and market conditions. This may arise because being in marketable condition such wheat overhangs the market and if induced by rising prices tends to flow into the market and check price increases. But if we assume that it is never marketed, it supplies a need of the man who grew it which would otherwise be reflected by purchases in the open market. Home-grown wheat in this sense competes with wheat in commerce. The stimulation of commerce is a use of the regulatory function quite as definitely as prohibitions or restrictions thereon. This record leaves us in no doubt that Congress may properly have considered that wheat consumed on the farm where grown if wholly outside the scheme of regulation would have a substantial effect in defeating and obstructing its purpose to stimulate trade therein at increased prices.

It is said, however, that this Act, forcing some farmers into the market to buy what they could provide for themselves, is an unfair promotion of the markets and prices of specializing wheat growers. It is of the essence of regulation that it lays a restraining hand on the self-interest of the regulated and that advantages from the regulation commonly fall to others. The conflicts of economic interest between the regulated and those who advantage by it are wisely left under our system to resolution by the Congress under its more flexible and responsible legislative process. Such conflicts rarely lend themselves to judicial determination. And with the wisdom, workability, or fairness, of the plan of regulation we have nothing to do.

Heart of Atlanta Motel, Inc. v. United States
379 U.S. 241, 85 S.Ct. 348 (1964)

and

Katzenbach v. McClung
379 U.S. 294, 85 S.Ct. 377 (1964)

Through litigation, sit-ins, and marches, the civil rights movement sought to end racial discrimination in public schools and public accommodations. The Warren Court responded in cases such as *Peterson v. Greenville*, 373 U.S. 244 (1963), ruling that a restaurant that discriminated against blacks ran afoul of the Fourteenth Amendment's "equal protection of the law" because a city ordinance required the separation of races. However, the Court was limited by the "state action" doctrine, announced in *The Civil Rights Cases*, 109 U.S. 3 (1883) (see Vol. 2, Ch. 12), holding that the Fourteenth Amendment does not prohibit discrimination in privately owned public accommodations like hotels and restaurants unless private discrimination is "sanctioned in some way by the state" or "done under state authority." In addition, litigation was costly and had limited effectiveness.

With the Civil Rights Act of 1964, or so-called Public Accommodations Act, Congress responded by forbidding racial discrimination or segregation in hotels, motels, restaurants, and catering establishments of all kinds, as well as bars, barber shops, gasoline stations, entertainment, and other facilities on the premises of the establishments covered by the

Moreton Rolleson, Jr., owner of the Heart of Atlanta Motel, challenged the constitutionality of the Civil Rights Act of 1964, which, on the basis of Congress's power to regulate interstate commerce, prohibits racial discrimination in privately owned public accommodations. (*Corbis.*)

act—excluded were "private clubs," boarding houses with five or fewer rooms for rent, and other facilities closed to the public. In passing the act, Congress relied on its authority under the commerce clause and its enforcement power in Section 5 of the Fourteenth Amendment. When the Department of Justice sought to enforce the act, constitutional challenges were immediately raised.

In the *Heart of Atlanta Motel* case, the owners of a downtown Atlanta motel refused to rent any of their 216 rooms to blacks and unsuccessfully sought a declaratory judgment from a three-judge district court that the legislation was unconstitutional. The motel advertised in national magazines and on billboards, and about 75 percent of its guests were from out of state. The Heart of Atlanta Motel appealed the district court's injunction against its refusal to comply with the act to the Supreme Court.

In the other case, the owner of Ollie's Barbecue, a local restaurant in Birmingham, Alabama, successfully fought enforcement of the act in federal district court. In this instance, the lower court found the act's provision barring racial discrimination in any restaurant that "serves or offers to serve interstate travelers, or a substantial portion of the food which it serves . . . has moved in commerce" to apply, since about half of the food served in the restaurant had "moved" in commerce. However, the court concluded that the restaurant, which began operation in

1925, would lose substantial business if it were forced to serve blacks. Attorney General Nicholas Katzenbach appealed that decision to the Supreme Court.

Justice Tom Clark's opinion for the majority in both cases upholds the constitutionality of the Civil Rights Act solely on Congress's authority under the commerce clause, whereas Justices Douglas and Goldberg would have relied on the Fourteenth Amendment as well. Justice Black's concurring opinion raises issues about whether there are any limits on congressional power to regulate commerce.

The Court's decision was unanimous, and the opinion was announced by Justice Clark. Concurrences were by Justices Black, Douglas, and Goldberg.

☐ *Justice CLARK delivers the opinion of the Court [in* Heart of Atlanta Motel, Inc. v. United States*].*

Congress first evidenced its interest in civil rights legislation in the Civil Rights or Enforcement Act of April 9, 1866. There followed four Acts with a fifth, the Civil Rights Act of March 1, 1875, culminating the series. In 1883 this Court struck down the public accommodations sections of the 1875 Act in the *Civil Rights Cases*. No major legislation in this field had been enacted by Congress for 82 years when the Civil Rights Act of 1957 became law. It was followed by the Civil Rights Act of 1960. Three years later, on June 19, 1963, the late President Kennedy called for civil rights legislation in a message to Congress to which he attached a proposed bill. Its stated purpose was

> to promote the general welfare by eliminating discrimination based on race, color, religion, or national origin in . . . public accommodations through the exercise by Congress of the powers conferred upon it . . . to enforce the provisions of the fourteenth and fifteenth amendments, to regulate commerce among the several States, and to make laws necessary and proper to execute the powers conferred upon it by the Constitution.

Bills were introduced in each House of the Congress, embodying the President's suggestion. . . .

After extended hearings each of these bills was favorably reported to its respective house. . . . Although each bill originally incorporated extensive findings of fact these were eliminated from the bills as they were reported. . . . Our only frame of reference as to the legislative history of the Act is, therefore, the hearings, reports and debates on the respective bills in each house.

The Act as finally adopted was most comprehensive, undertaking to prevent through peaceful and voluntary settlement discrimination in voting, as well as in places of accommodation and public facilities, federally secured programs and in employment. Since Title II is the only portion under attack here, we confine our consideration to those public accommodation provisions.

TITLE II OF THE ACT.

This Title is divided into seven sections beginning with Sec. 201(a) which provides that:

> All persons shall be entitled to the full and equal enjoyment of the goods, services, facilities, privileges, advantages, and accommodations of any place of public accommodation, as defined in this section, without discrimination or segregation on the ground of race, color, religion, or national origin.

There are listed in Sec. 201(b) four classes of business establishments, each of which "serves the public" and "is a place of public accommodation" within the meaning of Sec. 201(a) "if its operations affect commerce, or if discrimination or segregation by it is supported by State action." The covered establishments are . . .

> any inn, hotel, motel, or other establishment which provides lodging to transient guests, other than an establishment located within a building which contains not more than five rooms for rent or hire and which is actually occupied by the proprietor of such establishment as his residence. . . .

Section 201(c) defines the phrase "affect commerce" as applied to the above establishments. It first declares that "any inn, hotel, motel, or other establishment which provides lodging to transient guests" affects commerce *per se*. . . .

The Civil Rights Cases, 109 U.S. 3, 3 S.CT. 18 (1883), and their Application.

In light of our ground for decision, it might be well at the outset to discuss the *Civil Rights Cases, supra,* which declared provisions of the Civil Rights Act of 1875 unconstitutional. 18 Stat. 335, 336. We think that decision inapposite, and without precedential value in determining the constitutionality of the present Act. Unlike Title II of the present legislation, the 1875 Act broadly proscribed discrimination in "inns, public conveyances on land or water, theaters, and other places of public amusement," without limiting the categories of affected businesses to those impinging upon interstate commerce. In contrast, the applicability of Title II is carefully limited to enterprises having a direct and substantial relation to the interstate flow of goods and people, except where state action is involved. Further, the fact that certain kinds of businesses may not in 1875 have been sufficiently involved in interstate commerce to warrant bringing them within the ambit of the commerce power is not necessarily dispositive of the same question today. Our populace had not reached its present mobility, nor were facilities, goods and services circulating as readily in interstate commerce as they are today. Although the principles which we apply today are those first formulated by Chief Justice MARSHALL in *Gibbons v. Ogden,* the conditions of transportation and commerce have changed dramatically, and we must apply those principles to the present state of commerce. The sheer increase in volume of interstate traffic alone would give discriminatory practices which inhibit travel a far larger impact upon the Nation's commerce than such practices had on the economy of another day. Finally, there is language in the *Civil Rights Cases* which indicates that the Court did not fully consider whether the 1875 Act could be sustained as an exercise of the commerce power. . . .

THE BASIS OF CONGRESSIONAL ACTION.

While the Act as adopted carried no congressional findings the record of its passage through each house is replete with evidence of the burdens that discrimination by race or color places upon interstate commerce. . . .

This testimony included the fact that our people have become increasingly mobile with millions of people of all races traveling from State to State; that Negroes in particular have been the subject of discrimination in transient accommodations, having to travel great distances to secure the same; that often they have been unable to obtain accommodations and have had to call upon friends to put them up overnight, and that these conditions had become so acute as to require the listing of available lodging for Negroes in a special guidebook which was itself "dramatic testimony to the difficulties" Negroes encounter in travel. . . . These exclusionary practices were found to be nationwide, the Under Secretary of Commerce testifying that there is "no question that this discrimination in the North still exists to a large degree" and in the West and Midwest as well. . . . This testimony indicated a qualitative as well as quantitative effect on interstate travel by Negroes. The former was the obvious impairment of the Negro traveler's pleasure and convenience that resulted when he continually was uncertain of finding lodging. As for the latter, there was evidence that this uncertainty stemming from racial discrimination had the effect of discouraging travel on the part of a substantial portion of the Negro community. This was the conclusion not only of the Under Secretary of Commerce but also of the Administrator of the Federal Aviation Agency who wrote the Chairman of the Senate Commerce Committee that it was his "belief that air commerce is adversely affected by the denial to a substantial segment of the traveling public of adequate and desegregated public accommodations." We shall not burden this opinion with further details since the voluminous testimony presents overwhelming evidence that discrimination by hotels and motels impedes interstate travel.

THE POWER OF CONGRESS OVER INTERSTATE TRAVEL.

The same interest in protecting interstate commerce which led Congress to deal with segregation in interstate carriers and the white-slave traffic has prompted it to extend the exercise of its power to gambling, *Lottery Case* (*Champion v. Ames*), [188 U.S. 321] (1903); to criminal enterprises, *Brooks v. United States*, [267 U.S. 432] (1925); to deceptive practices in the sale of products, *Federal Trade Comm. v. Mandel Bros., Inc.*, [359 U.S. 385] (1959); to fraudulent security transactions, *Securities & Exchange Comm. v. Ralston Purina Co.*, [346 U.S. 119] (1953); to misbranding of drugs, *Weeks v. United States*, [232 U.S. 383] (1918); to wages and hours, *United States v. Darby*, [321 U.S. 100] (1941); to members of labor unions, *National Labor Relations Board v. Jones & Laughlin Steel Corp.*, [310 U.S. 1] (1937); to crop control, *Wickard v. Filburn* (1942); to discrimination against shippers, *United States v. Baltimore & Ohio R. Co.*, [317 U.S. 111] (1948); to the protection of small business from injurious price cutting, *Moore v. Mead's Fine Bread Co.*, [333 U.S. 169] (1954);

to resale price maintenance, *Hudson Distributors, Inc. v. Eli Lilly & Co.*, [348 U.S. 115] (1964); *Schwegmann Bros. v. Calvert Distillers Corp.*, [377 U.S. 386] (1951); to professional football, *Radovich v. National Football League*, [352 U.S. 445] (1957); and to racial discrimination by owners and managers of terminal restaurants, *Boynton v. Com. of Virginia*, [362 U.S. 454] (1960).

That Congress was legislating against moral wrongs in many of these areas rendered its enactments no less valid. In framing Title II of this Act Congress was also dealing with what it considered a moral problem. But that fact does not detract from the overwhelming evidence of the disruptive effect that racial discrimination has had on commercial intercourse. It was this burden which empowered Congress to enact appropriate legislation, and, given this basis for the exercise of its power, Congress was not restricted by the fact that the particular obstruction to interstate commerce with which it was dealing was also deemed a moral and social wrong.

It is said that the operation of the motel here is of a purely local character. But, assuming this to be true, "[i]f it is interstate commerce that feels the pinch, it does not matter how local the operation which applies the squeeze." *United States v. Women's Sportswear Mfg. Ass'n*, 336 U.S. 460 (1949). . . . Thus the power of Congress to promote interstate commerce also includes the power to regulate the local incidents thereof, including local activities in both the States of origin and destination, which might have a substantial and harmful effect upon that commerce. One need only examine the evidence which we have discussed above to see that Congress may—as it has—prohibit racial discrimination by motels serving travelers, however "local" their operations may appear.

Nor does the Act deprive appellant of liberty or property under the Fifth Amendment. The commerce power invoked here by the Congress is a specific and plenary one authorized by the Constitution itself. The only questions are: (1) whether Congress had a rational basis for finding that racial discrimination by motels affected commerce, and (2) if it had such a basis, whether the means it selected to eliminate that evil are reasonable and appropriate. If they are, appellant has no "right" to select its guests as it sees fit, free from governmental regulation. . . .

We . . . conclude that the action of the Congress in the adoption of the Act as applied here to a motel which concededly serves interstate travelers is within the power granted it by the Commerce Clause of the Constitution, as interpreted by this Court for 140 years. It may be argued that Congress could have pursued other methods to eliminate the obstructions it found in interstate commerce caused by racial discrimination. But this is a matter of policy that rests entirely with the Congress not with the courts. How obstructions in commerce may be removed—what means are to be employed—is within the sound and exclusive discretion of the Congress. It is subject only to one caveat—that the means chosen by it must be reasonably adapted to the end permitted by the Constitution. We cannot say that its choice here was not so adapted. The Constitution requires no more.

☐ *Justice CLARK delivers the opinion of the Court [in* Katzenbach v. McClung*].*

Ollie's Barbecue is a family-owned restaurant in Birmingham, Alabama, specializing in barbecued meats and homemade pies, with a seating capacity

of 220 customers. It is located on a state highway 11 blocks from an interstate one and a somewhat greater distance from railroad and bus stations. The
restaurant caters to a family and white-collar trade with a take-out service
for Negroes. It employs 36 persons, two-thirds of whom are Negroes.

In the 12 months preceding the passage of the Act, the restaurant purchased locally approximately $150,000 worth of food, $69,683 or 46% of
which was meat that it bought from a local supplier who had procured it
from outside the State. The District Court expressly found that a substantial
portion of the food served in the restaurant had moved in interstate commerce. The restaurant has refused to serve Negroes in its dining accommodations since its original opening in 1927, and since July 2, 1964, it has been
operating in violation of the Act. The court below concluded that if it were
required to serve Negroes it would lose a substantial amount of business. . . .

The basic holding in *Heart of Atlanta Motel*, answers many of the contentions made by the appellees. There we outlined the overall purpose and
operational plan of Title II and found it a valid exercise of the power to regulate interstate commerce insofar as it requires hotels and motels to serve
transients without regard to their race or color. In this case we consider its
application to restaurants which serve food a substantial portion of which has
moved in commerce. . . . Sections 201(b) (2) and (c) place any "restaurant . . .
principally engaged in selling food for consumption on the premises" under
the Act "if . . . it serves or offers to serve interstate travelers or a substantial
portion of the food which it serves . . . has moved in commerce."

Ollie's Barbecue admits that it is covered by these provisions of the
Act. . . .

As we noted in *Heart of Atlanta Motel* both Houses of Congress conducted prolonged hearings on the Act. And, as we said there, while no formal
findings were made, which of course are not necessary, it is well that we
make mention of the testimony at these hearings the better to understand
the problem before Congress and determine whether the Act is a reasonable
and appropriate means toward its solution. The record is replete with testimony of the burdens placed on interstate commerce by racial discrimination
in restaurants. . . .

Moreover there was an impressive array of testimony that discrimination
in restaurants had a direct and highly restrictive effect upon interstate travel
by Negroes. This resulted, it was said, because discriminatory practices prevent Negroes from buying prepared food served on the premises while on a
trip, except in isolated and unkempt restaurants and under most unsatisfactory and often unpleasant conditions. This obviously discourages travel and
obstructs interstate commerce for one can hardly travel without eating. Likewise, it was said, that discrimination deterred professional, as well as skilled,
people from moving into areas where such practices occurred and thereby
caused industry to be reluctant to establish there. . . .

We believe that this testimony afforded ample basis for the conclusion
that established restaurants in such areas sold less interstate goods because of
the discrimination, that interstate travel was obstructed directly by it, that
business in general suffered and that many new businesses refrained from
establishing there as a result of it. Hence the District Court was in error
in concluding that there was no connection between discrimination and
the movement of interstate commerce. The court's conclusion that such a

connection is outside "common experience" flies in the face of stubborn fact. . . .

The appellees contend that Congress has arbitrarily created a conclusive presumption that all restaurants meeting the criteria set out in the Act "affect commerce." Stated another way, they object to the omission of a provision for a case-by-case determination—judicial or administrative—that racial discrimination in a particular restaurant affects commerce.

But Congress' action in framing this Act was not unprecedented. In *United States v. Darby* (1941), this Court held constitutional the Fair Labor Standards Act of 1938. . . .

Here, as there, Congress has determined for itself that refusals of service to Negroes have imposed burdens both upon the interstate flow of food and upon the movement of products generally. Of course, the mere fact that Congress has said when particular activity shall be deemed to affect commerce does not preclude further examination by this Court. But where we find that the legislators, in light of the facts and testimony before them, have a rational basis for finding a chosen regulatory scheme necessary to the protection of commerce, our investigation is at an end. The only remaining question—one answered in the affirmative by the court below—is whether the particular restaurant either serves or offers to serve interstate travelers or serves food a substantial portion of which has moved in interstate commerce. . . .

Confronted as we are with the facts laid before Congress, we must conclude that it had a rational basis for finding that racial discrimination in restaurants had a direct and adverse effect on the free flow of interstate commerce. Insofar as the sections of the Act here relevant are concerned, Secs. 201(b) (2) and (c), Congress prohibited discrimination only in those establishments having a close tie to interstate commerce, i.e., those, like the McClungs', serving food that has come from out of the State. We think in so doing that Congress acted well within its power to protect and foster commerce in extending the coverage of Title II only to those restaurants offering to serve interstate travelers or serving food, a substantial portion of which has moved in interstate commerce.

The absence of direct evidence connecting discriminatory restaurant service with the flow of interstate food, factor on which the appellees place much reliance, is not, given the evidence as to the effect of such practices on other aspects of commerce, a crucial matter.

The power of Congress in this field is broad and sweeping; where it keeps within its sphere and violates no express constitutional limitation it has been the rule of this Court, going back almost to the founding days of the Republic, not to interfere. The Civil Rights Act of 1964, as here applied, we find to be plainly appropriate in the resolution of what the Congress found to be a national commercial problem of the first magnitude. We find it in no violation of any express limitations of the Constitution and we therefore declare it valid.

The judgment is therefore reversed.

☐ *Justice BLACK, concurring.*

It requires no novel or strained interpretation of the Commerce Clause to sustain Title II as applied [here]. . . . At least since *Gibbons v. Ogden*, decided in 1824 in an opinion by Chief Justice John MARSHALL, it has been uniformly accepted that the power of Congress to regulate commerce among the States is plenary, "complete in itself, may be exercised to its utmost extent, and acknowledges no limitations, other than are prescribed in the constitution." Nor is "Commerce" as used in the Commerce Clause to be limited to a narrow, technical concept. It includes not only, as Congress has enumerated in the Act, "travel, trade, traffic, commerce, transportation, or communication," but also all other unitary transactions and activities that take place in more States than one. That some parts or segments of such unitary transactions may take place only in one State cannot, of course, take from Congress its plenary power to regulate them in the national interest. The facilities and instrumentalities used to carry on this commerce, such as railroads, truck lines, ships, rivers, and even highways are also subject to congressional regulation, so far as is necessary to keep interstate traffic upon fair and equal terms. . . .

Furthermore, it has long been held that the Necessary and Proper Clause, Art. I, Sec. 8, cl. 18, adds to the commerce power of Congress the power to regulate local instrumentalities operating within a single State if their activities burden the flow of commerce among the States. . . .

The Heart of Atlanta Motel is a large 216-room establishment strategically located in relation to Atlanta and interstate travelers. It advertises extensively by signs along interstate highways and in various advertising media. As a result of these circumstances approximately 75% of the motel guests are transient interstate travelers. It is thus an important facility for use by interstate travelers who travel on highways, since travelers in their own cars must find lodging places to make their journeys comfortably and safely. . . .

The foregoing facts are more than enough, in my judgment, to show that Congress acting within its discretion and judgment has power under the Commerce Clause and the Necessary and Proper Clause to bar racial discrimination in the Heart of Atlanta Motel.

☐ *Justice DOUGLAS, concurring.*

Though I join the Court's opinions, I am somewhat reluctant here . . . to rest solely on the Commerce Clause. My reluctance is not due to any conviction that Congress lacks power to regulate commerce in the interests of human rights. It is rather my belief that the right of people to be free of state action that discriminates against them because of race, like the "right of persons to move freely from State to State" (*Edwards v. People of the State of California*) [314 U.S. 160 (1941)], "occupies a more protected position in our constitutional system than does the movement of cattle, fruit, steel and coal across state lines." . . .

Hence I would prefer to rest on the assertion of legislative power contained in Sec. 5 of the Fourteenth Amendment which states: "The Congress shall have power to enforce, by appropriate legislation, the provisions of this article"—a power which the Court concedes was exercised at least in part in this Act.

A decision based on the Fourteenth Amendment would have a more settling effect, making unnecessary litigation over whether a particular restaurant or inn is within the commerce definitions of the Act or whether a particular customer is an interstate traveler. Under my construction, the

Act would apply to all customers in all the enumerated places of public accommodation. And that construction would put an end to all obstructionist strategies and finally close one door on a bitter chapter in American history. . . .

United States v. Lopez

514 U.S. 549, 115 S.CT. 1624 (1995)

Shortly after the enactment of the Gun-Free School Zones Act of 1990, which made it a federal crime to possess a firearm within 1,000 feet of public or private schools, Alfonso Lopez, Jr., a twelfth-grade student, was arrested for carrying a .38 caliber handgun into Edison High School in San Antonio, Texas. Lopez was initially charged with violating Texas's law against firearm possession on school premises, but those charges were dropped after federal agents charged him with violating the Gun-Free School Zones Act. Subsequently, a federal district court found Lopez guilty and sentenced him to six months imprisonment and two years probation. On appeal, Lopez's attorneys challenged his conviction on the ground the Gun-Free School Zones Act was unconstitutional because Congress exceeded its power under the Commerce Clause in enacting the legislation. The Court of Appeals for the Fifth Circuit agreed and reversed his conviction. The federal government appealed that decision.

The Court's decision was five to four and the majority's opinion was announced by Chief Justice Rehnquist. Justices Kennedy and Thomas filed concurring opinions. Justices Stevens, Souter, and Breyer filed dissenting opinions, which Justice Ginsburg joined.

□ *Chief Justice REHNQUIST delivered the opinion of the Court.*

We start with first principles. The Constitution creates a Federal Government of enumerated powers. As James Madison wrote, "the powers delegated by the proposed Constitution to the federal government are few and defined. Those which are to remain in the State governments are numerous and indefinite." *The Federalist* No. 45. . . . The Constitution delegates to Congress the power "to regulate Commerce with foreign Nations, and among the several States, and with the Indian Tribes." The Court, through Chief Justice MARSHALL, first defined the nature of Congress' commerce power in *Gibbons v. Ogden*, 9 Wheat. 1 (1824): "Commerce, undoubtedly, is traffic, but it is something more: it is intercourse. It describes the commercial intercourse between nations, and parts of nations, in all its branches, and is regulated by prescribing rules for carrying on that intercourse." The commerce power "is the power to regulate; that is, to prescribe the rule by which commerce is to be governed. This power, like all others vested in Congress, is complete in itself, may be exercised to its utmost extent, and acknowledges no limitations, other than are prescribed in the constitution." The *Gibbons* Court, however, acknowledged that limitations on the commerce power are inherent in the very language of the Commerce Clause. "It is not intended to say that these words comprehend that commerce, which is completely internal, which is carried on between man and man in a State, or between different parts of the same State, and which does not extend to or affect other States. Such a power would be inconvenient, and is certainly unnecessary." "Comprehensive as the word 'among' is, it may very properly be restricted to that commerce which concerns more States than one. . . . The enumeration presupposes something not enumerated; and that something, if we regard the language or the subject of the sentence, must be the exclusively internal commerce of a State."

For nearly a century thereafter, the Court's Commerce Clause decisions dealt but rarely with the extent of Congress' power, and almost entirely with the Commerce Clause as a limit on state legislation that discriminated against interstate commerce. Under this line of precedent, the Court held that certain categories of activity such as "production," "manufacturing," and "mining" were within the province of state governments, and thus were beyond the power of Congress under the Commerce Clause. See *Wickard v. Filburn*, 317 U.S. 111 (1942) (describing development of Commerce Clause jurisprudence).

In 1887, Congress enacted the Interstate Commerce Act, and in 1890, Congress enacted the Sherman Antitrust Act. These laws ushered in a new era of federal regulation under the commerce power. When cases involving these laws first reached this Court, we imported from our negative Commerce Clause cases the approach that Congress could not regulate activities such as "production," "manufacturing," and "mining." See, e.g., *United States v. E. C. Knight Co.*, 156 U.S. 1 (1895) ("Commerce succeeds to manufacture, and is not part of it"); *Carter v. Carter Coal Co.*, 298 U.S. 238 (1936) ("Mining brings the subject matter of commerce into existence. Commerce disposes of it."). Simultaneously, however, the Court held that, where the interstate and intrastate aspects of commerce were so mingled together that full regulation of interstate commerce required incidental regulation of intrastate commerce, the Commerce Clause authorized such regulation.

In *A. L. A. Schechter Poultry Corp. v. United States*, 295 U.S. 495 (1935), the Court struck down regulations that fixed the hours and wages of individuals employed by an intrastate business because the activity being regulated related to interstate commerce only indirectly. In doing so, the Court characterized the distinction between direct and indirect effects of intrastate transactions upon interstate commerce as "a fundamental one, essential to the maintenance of our constitutional system." . . .

Two years later, in the watershed case of *NLRB v. Jones & Laughlin Steel Corp.*, 301 U.S. 1 (1937), the Court upheld the National Labor Relations Act against a Commerce Clause challenge, and in the process, departed from the distinction between "direct" and "indirect" effects on interstate commerce. The Court held that intrastate activities that "have such a close and substantial relation to interstate commerce that their control is essential or appropriate to protect that commerce from burdens and obstructions" are within Congress' power to regulate.

In *United States v. Darby*, 312 U.S. 100 (1941), the Court upheld the Fair Labor Standards Act, stating: "The power of Congress over interstate commerce is not confined to the regulation of commerce among the states. It extends to those activities intrastate which so affect interstate commerce or the exercise of the power of Congress over it as to make regulation of them appropriate means to the attainment of a legitimate end, the exercise of the granted power of Congress to regulate interstate commerce."

In *Wickard v. Filburn*, the Court upheld the application of amendments to the Agricultural Adjustment Act of 1938 to the production and consumption of home-grown wheat. The *Wickard* Court explicitly rejected earlier distinctions between direct and indirect effects on interstate commerce, stating: "Even if appellee's activity be local and though it may not be regarded as commerce, it may still, whatever its nature, be reached by Congress if it exerts a substantial economic effect on interstate commerce, and this irrespective of whether such effect is what might at some earlier time have been defined as 'direct' or 'indirect.' " . . .

Jones & Laughlin Steel, *Darby*, and *Wickard* ushered in an era of Commerce Clause jurisprudence that greatly expanded the previously defined authority of Congress under that Clause. In part, this was a recognition of the great changes that had occurred in the way business was carried on in this country. Enterprises that had once been local or at most regional in nature had become national in scope. But the doctrinal change also reflected a view that earlier Commerce Clause cases artificially had constrained the authority of Congress to regulate interstate commerce.

But even these modern-era precedents which have expanded congressional power under the Commerce Clause confirm that this power is subject to outer limits. In *Jones & Laughlin Steel*, the Court warned that the scope of the interstate commerce power "must be considered in the light of our dual system of government and may not be extended so as to embrace effects upon interstate commerce so indirect and remote that to embrace them, in view of our complex society, would effectually obliterate the distinction between what is national and what is local and create a completely centralized government." Since that time, the Court has heeded that warning and undertaken to decide whether a rational basis existed for concluding that a regulated activity sufficiently affected interstate commerce.

Similarly, in *Maryland v. Wirtz*, 392 U.S. 183 (1968), the Court reaffirmed that "the power to regulate commerce, though broad indeed, has limits" that "the Court has ample power" to enforce. In response to the dissent's warnings that the Court was powerless to enforce the limitations on Congress' commerce powers because "all activities affecting commerce, even in the minutest degree, [*Wickard*], may be regulated and controlled by Congress," (DOUGLAS, J., dissenting), the *Wirtz* Court replied that the dissent had misread precedent as "neither here nor in *Wickard* has the Court declared that Congress may use a relatively trivial impact on commerce as an excuse for broad general regulation of state or private activities." Rather, "the Court has said only that where a general regulatory statute bears a substantial relation to commerce, the de minimis character of individual instances arising under that statute is of no consequence."

Consistent with this structure, we have identified three broad categories of activity that Congress may regulate under its commerce power. First, Congress may regulate the use of the channels of interstate commerce. Second, Congress is empowered to regulate and protect the instrumentalities of interstate commerce, or persons or things in interstate commerce, even though the threat may come only from intrastate activities. Finally, Congress' commerce authority includes the power to regulate those activities having a substantial relation to interstate commerce, those activities that substantially affect interstate commerce.

Within this final category, admittedly, our case law has not been clear whether an activity must "affect" or "substantially affect" interstate commerce in order to be within Congress' power to regulate it under the Commerce Clause. We conclude, consistent with the great weight of our case law, that the proper test requires an analysis of whether the regulated activity "substantially affects" interstate commerce.

We now turn to consider the power of Congress, in the light of this framework, to enact Section 922(q). The first two categories of authority may be quickly disposed of: Section 922(q) is not a regulation of the use of the channels of interstate commerce, nor is it an attempt to prohibit the interstate transportation of a commodity through the channels of commerce; nor can Section 922(q) be justified as a regulation by which Congress has sought to protect an instrumentality of interstate commerce or a thing in interstate commerce. Thus, if Section 922(q) is to be sustained, it must be under the third category as a regulation of an activity that substantially affects interstate commerce.

First, we have upheld a wide variety of congressional Acts regulating intrastate economic activity where we have concluded that the activity substantially affected interstate commerce. Examples include the regulation of intrastate coal mining; intrastate extortionate credit transactions, restaurants utilizing substantial interstate supplies, inns and hotels catering to interstate guests, and production and consumption of home-grown wheat. These examples are by no means exhaustive, but the pattern is clear. Where economic activity substantially affects interstate commerce, legislation regulating that activity will be sustained. . . .

Section 922(q) is a criminal statute that by its terms has nothing to do with "commerce" or any sort of economic enterprise, however broadly one might define those terms. Section 922(q) is not an essential part of a larger regulation of economic activity, in which the regulatory scheme could be undercut unless the intrastate activity were regulated. It cannot, therefore, be sustained under our cases upholding regulations of activities that arise out of or are connected with a commercial transaction, which viewed in the aggregate, substantially affects interstate commerce. . . .

The Government's essential contention, in fine, is that we may determine here that Section 922(q) is valid because possession of a firearm in a local school zone does indeed substantially affect interstate commerce. The Government argues that possession of a firearm in a school zone may result in violent crime and that violent crime can be expected to affect the functioning of the national economy in two ways. First, the costs of violent crime are substantial, and, through the mechanism of insurance, those costs are spread throughout the population. Second, violent crime reduces the willingness of individuals to travel to areas within the country that are perceived to be unsafe. The Government also argues that the presence of guns in schools poses a substantial threat to the educational process by threatening the learning environment. A handicapped educational process, in turn, will result in a less productive citizenry. That, in turn, would have an adverse effect on the Nation's economic well-being. As a result, the Government argues that Congress could rationally have concluded that Section 922(q) substantially affects interstate commerce.

We pause to consider the implications of the Government's arguments. The Government admits, under its "costs of crime" reasoning, that Congress could regulate not only all violent crime, but all activities that might lead to violent crime, regardless of how tenuously they relate to interstate commerce. . . . [I]f we were to accept the Government's arguments, we are hard-pressed to posit any activity by an individual that Congress is without power to regulate. . . .

To uphold the Government's contentions here, we would have to pile inference upon inference in a manner that would bid fair to convert congressional authority under the Commerce Clause to a general police power of the sort retained by the States. Admittedly, some of our prior cases have taken long steps down that road, giving great deference to congressional action. The broad language in these opinions has suggested the possibility of additional expansion, but we decline here to proceed any further. To do so would require us to conclude that the Constitution's enumeration of powers does not presuppose something not enumerated, and that there never will be a distinction between what is truly national and what is truly local. This we are unwilling to do.

For the foregoing reasons the judgment of the Court of Appeals is Affirmed.

☐ *Justice THOMAS, concurring.*

Although I join the majority, I write separately to observe that our case law has drifted far from the original understanding of the Commerce Clause. In a future case, we ought to temper our Commerce Clause jurisprudence in a manner that both makes sense of our more recent case law and is more faithful to the original understanding of that Clause. . . . In an appropriate case, I believe that we must further reconsider our "substantial effects" test with an eye toward constructing a standard that reflects the text and history of the Commerce Clause without totally rejecting our more recent Commerce Clause jurisprudence. . . .

At the time the original Constitution was ratified, "commerce" consisted of selling, buying, and bartering, as well as transporting for these purposes. As one would expect, the term "commerce" was used in contradistinction to productive activities such as manufacturing and agriculture. Alexander Hamilton, for example, repeatedly treated commerce, agriculture, and manufacturing as three separate endeavors. See, e.g., *The Federalist* No. 36, (referring to "agriculture, commerce, manufactures"); id., No. 21 (distinguishing commerce, arts, and industry); id., No. 12 (asserting that commerce and agriculture have shared interests).

Moreover, interjecting a modern sense of commerce into the Constitution generates significant textual and structural problems. For example, one cannot replace "commerce" with a different type of enterprise, such as manufacturing. When a manufacturer produces a car, assembly cannot take place "with a foreign nation" or "with the Indian Tribes." Parts may come from different States or other nations and hence may have been in the flow of commerce at one time, but manufacturing takes place at a discrete site. Agriculture and manufacturing involve the production of goods; commerce encompasses traffic in such articles. . . .

The Constitution not only uses the word "commerce" in a narrower sense than our case law might suggest, it also does not support the proposition that Congress has authority over all activities that "substantially affect" interstate commerce. The Commerce Clause does not state that Congress may "regulate matters that substantially affect commerce with foreign Nations, and among the several States, and with the Indian Tribes." In contrast, the Constitution itself temporarily prohibited amendments that would "affect" Congress' lack of authority to prohibit or restrict the slave trade or to enact unproportioned direct taxation. . . .

Put simply, much if not all of Art. I, Section 8 (including portions of the Commerce Clause itself) would be surplusage if Congress had been given authority over matters that substantially affect interstate commerce. An interpretation of cl. 3 that makes the rest of Section 8 superfluous simply cannot be correct. Yet this Court's Commerce Clause jurisprudence has endorsed just such an interpretation: the power we have accorded Congress has swallowed Art. I, Section 8.

Indeed, if a "substantial effects" test can be appended to the Commerce Clause, why not to every other power of the Federal Government? There is no reason for singling out the Commerce Clause for special treatment. Accordingly, Congress could regulate all matters that "substantially affect" the Army and Navy, bankruptcies, tax collection, expenditures, and so on. In that case, the clauses of Section 8 all mutually overlap, something we can assume the Founding Fathers never intended.

Our construction of the scope of congressional authority has the additional problem of coming close to turning the Tenth Amendment on its head. Our case law could be read to reserve to the United States all powers not expressly prohibited by the Constitution. Taken together, these fundamental textual problems should, at the very least, convince us that the "substantial effects" test should be reexamined. . . .

Apart from its recent vintage and its corresponding lack of any grounding in the original understanding of the Constitution, the substantial effects test suffers from the further flaw that it appears to grant Congress a police power over the Nation. When asked at oral argument if there were any limits to the Commerce Clause, the Government was at a loss for words. Likewise, the principal dissent insists that there are limits, but it cannot muster even one example. . . .

The substantial effects test suffers from this flaw, in part, because of its "aggregation principle." Under so-called "class of activities" statutes, Congress can regulate whole categories of activities that are not themselves either "interstate" or "commerce." In applying the effects test, we ask whether the class of activities as a whole substantially affects interstate commerce, not whether any specific activity within the class has such effects when considered in isolation.

The aggregation principle is clever, but has no stopping point. Suppose all would agree that gun possession within 1,000 feet of a school does not substantially affect commerce, but that possession of weapons generally (knives, brass knuckles, nunchakus, etc.) does. Under our substantial effects doctrine, even though Congress cannot single out gun possession, it can prohibit weapon possession generally. But one always can draw the circle broadly enough to cover an activity that, when taken in isolation, would not have substantial effects on commerce. Under our jurisprudence, if Congress passed an omnibus "substantially affects interstate commerce" statute, purporting to regulate every aspect of human existence, the Act apparently would be constitutional. Even though particular sections may govern only trivial activities, the statute in the aggregate regulates matters that substantially affect commerce.

This extended discussion . . . reveals that our substantial effects test is far removed from both the Constitution and from our early case law and that the Court's opinion should not be viewed as "radical" or another "wrong turn" that must be corrected in the future. . . .

☐ *Justice SOUTER, dissenting.*

In reviewing congressional legislation under the Commerce Clause, we defer to what is often a merely implicit congressional judgment that its regulation addresses a subject substantially affecting interstate commerce "if there is any rational basis for such a finding." *Hodel v. Virginia Surface Mining & Reclamation Assn., Inc.*, 452 U.S. 264 (1981). If that congressional determination is within the realm of reason, "the only remaining question for judicial inquiry is whether 'the means chosen by Congress [are] reasonably adapted to the end permitted by the Constitution.' " *Hodel*, quoting *Heart of Atlanta Motel, Inc. v. United States*, 379 U.S. 241 (1964).

The practice of deferring to rationally based legislative judgments "is a paradigm of judicial restraint." In judicial review under the Commerce Clause, it reflects our respect for the institutional competence of the Congress on a subject expressly assigned to it by the Constitution and our appreciation of the legitimacy that comes from Congress's political accountability in dealing with matters open to a wide range of possible choices.

It was not ever thus, however, as even a brief overview of Commerce Clause history during the past century reminds us. The modern respect for the competence and primacy of Congress in matters affecting commerce developed only after one of this Court's most chastening experiences, when it perforce repudiated an earlier and untenably expansive conception of judicial review in derogation of congressional commerce power. A look at history's sequence will serve to show how today's decision tugs the Court off course, leading it to suggest opportunities for further developments that would be at odds with the rule of restraint to which the Court still wisely states adherence.

Notwithstanding the Court's recognition of a broad commerce power in *Gibbons v. Ogden*, 9 Wheat. 1 (1824) (MARSHALL, C. J.), Congress saw few occasions to exercise that power prior to Reconstruction, and it was really the passage of the Interstate Commerce Act of 1887 that opened a new age of congressional reliance on the Commerce Clause for authority to exercise general police powers at the national level. Although the Court upheld a fair amount of the ensuing legislation as being within the commerce power, the period from the turn of the century to 1937 is better noted for a series of cases applying highly formalistic notions of "commerce" to invalidate federal social and economic legislation, see, e.g., *Carter v. Carter Coal Co.*, 298 U.S. 238 (1936) (striking Act prohibiting unfair labor practices in coal industry as regulation of "mining" and "production," not "commerce"); *A. L. A. Schechter Poultry Corp. v. United States*, 295 U.S. 495 (1935) (striking congressional regulation of activities affecting interstate commerce only "indirectly"); *Hammer v. Dagenhart*, 247 U.S. 251 (1918) (striking Act prohibiting shipment in interstate commerce of goods manufactured at factories using child labor because the Act regulated "manufacturing," not "commerce"); *Adair v. United States*, 208 U.S. 161 (1908) (striking protection of labor union membership as outside "commerce").

These restrictive views of commerce subject to congressional power complemented the Court's activism in limiting the enforceable scope of state economic regulation. It is most familiar history that during this same period the Court routinely invalidated state social and economic legislation under an expansive conception of Fourteenth Amendment substantive due process. See, e.g., *Lochner v. New York*, 198 U.S. 45 (1905) (striking state law establishing maximum working hours for bakers). The fulcrums of judicial review in these cases were the notions of liberty and property characteristic of laissez-faire economics, whereas the Commerce Clause cases turned on what was ostensibly a structural limit of federal power, but under each conception of judicial review the Court's character for the first third of the century showed itself in exacting judicial scrutiny of a legislature's choice of economic ends and of the legislative means selected to reach them.

It was not merely coincidental, then, that sea changes in the Court's conceptions of its authority under the Due Process and Commerce Clauses occurred virtually together, in 1937, with *West Coast Hotel Co. v. Parrish*, [300 U.S. 379], and *NLRB v. Jones & Laughlin Steel Corp.*, 301 U.S. 1. . . . In *West Coast Hotel*, the Court's rejection of a due process challenge to a state law fixing minimum wages for women and children marked the abandonment of its expansive protection of contractual freedom. Two weeks later, *Jones & Laughlin* affirmed congressional commerce power to authorize NLRB injunctions against unfair labor practices. The Court's finding that the regulated activity had a direct enough effect on commerce has since been seen as beginning the abandonment, for practical purposes, of the formalistic distinction between direct and indirect effects.

In the years following these decisions, deference to legislative policy judgments on commercial regulation became the powerful theme under both the Due Process and Commerce Clauses, and in due course that deference became articulate in the standard of rationality review. In due process litigation, the Court's statement of a rational basis test came quickly. The parallel formulation of the Commerce Clause test came later, only because complete elimination of the direct/indirect effects dichotomy and acceptance of the cumulative effects doctrine, *Wickard v. Filburn*, 317 U.S. 111 (1942), so far settled the pressing issues of congressional power over commerce as to leave the Court for years without any need to phrase a test explicitly deferring to rational legislative judgments. The moment came, however, with the challenge to congressional Commerce Clause authority to prohibit racial discrimination in places of public accommodation, when the Court simply made explicit what the earlier cases had implied: "where we find that the legislators, in light of the facts and testimony before them, have a rational basis for finding a chosen regulatory scheme necessary to the protection of commerce, our investigation is at an end." *Katzenbach v. McClung,* 379 U.S. 294 (1964), discussing *United States v. Darby;* see *Heart of Atlanta Motel, Inc. v. United States,* 379 U.S. 241 (1964). Thus, under commerce, as under due process, adoption of rational basis review expressed the recognition that the Court had no sustainable basis for subjecting economic regulation as such to judicial policy judgments, and for the past half-century the Court has no more turned back in the direction of formalistic Commerce Clause review (as in deciding whether regulation of commerce was sufficiently direct) than it has inclined toward reasserting the substantive authority of *Lochner* due process (as in the inflated protection of contractual autonomy).

There is today, however, a backward glance at both the old pitfalls, as the Court treats deference under the rationality rule as subject to gradation according to the commercial or noncommercial nature of the immediate subject of the challenged regulation. The distinction between what is patently commercial and what is not looks much like the old distinction between what directly affects commerce and what touches it only indirectly. And the act of calibrating the level of deference by drawing a line between what is patently commercial and what is less purely so will probably resemble the process of deciding how much interference with contractual freedom was fatal. Thus, it seems fair to ask whether the step taken by the Court today does anything but portend a return to the untenable jurisprudence from which the Court extricated itself almost 60 years ago. The answer is not reassuring. To be sure, the occasion for today's decision reflects the century's end, not its beginning. But if it seems anomalous that the Congress of the United States has taken to regulating school yards, the act in question is still probably no more remarkable than state regulation of bake shops 90 years ago. In any event, there is no reason to hope that the Court's qualification of rational basis review will be any more successful than the efforts at substantive economic review made by our predecessors as the century began. Taking the Court's opinion on its own terms, Justice BREYER has explained both the hopeless porosity of "commercial" character as a ground of Commerce Clause distinction in America's highly connected economy, and the inconsistency of this categorization with our rational basis precedents from the last 50 years. . . .

☐ *Justice BREYER, with whom Justice STEVENS, Justice SOUTER, and Justice GINSBURG join, dissenting.*

In my view, the statute falls well within the scope of the commerce power as this Court has understood that power over the last half-century.

In reaching this conclusion, I apply three basic principles of Commerce Clause interpretation. First, the power to "regulate Commerce . . . among the several States" encompasses the power to regulate local activities insofar as they significantly affect interstate commerce. See, e.g., *Gibbons v. Ogden,* 9 Wheat. 1 (1824) (MARSHALL, C. J.); *Wickard v. Filburn,* 317 U.S. 111 (1942). As the majority points out, the Court, in describing how much of an effect the Clause requires, sometimes has used the word "substantial" and sometimes has not. . . . I use the word "significant" because the word "substantial" implies a somewhat narrower power than recent precedent suggests. But, to speak of "substantial effect" rather than "significant effect" would make no difference in this case.

Second, in determining whether a local activity will likely have a significant effect upon interstate commerce, a court must consider, not the effect of an individual act (a single instance of gun possession), but rather the cumulative effect of all similar instances (i.e., the effect of all guns possessed in or near schools). Third, the Constitution requires us to judge the connection between a regulated activity and interstate commerce, not directly, but at one remove. Courts must give Congress a degree of leeway in determining the existence of a significant factual connection between the regulated activity and interstate commerce—both because the Constitution delegates the commerce power directly to Congress and because the determination requires an empirical judgment of a kind that a legislature is more likely than a court to make with accuracy. The traditional words "rational basis" capture this leeway. . . .

Applying these principles to the case at hand, we must ask whether Congress could have had a rational basis for finding a significant (or substantial) connection between gun-related school violence and interstate commerce. Or, to put the question in the language of the explicit finding that Congress made when it amended this law in 1994: Could Congress rationally have found that "violent crime in school zones," through its effect on the "quality of education," significantly (or substantially) affects "interstate" or "foreign commerce"? As long as one views the commerce connection, not as a "technical legal conception," but as "a practical one," *Swift & Co. v. United States*, 196 U.S. 375 (1905) (HOLMES, J.), the answer to this question must be yes. Numerous reports and studies—generated both inside and outside government—make clear that Congress could reasonably have found the empirical connection that its law, implicitly or explicitly, asserts.

For one thing, reports, hearings, and other readily available literature make clear that the problem of guns in and around schools is widespread and extremely serious. These materials report, for example, that four percent of American high school students (and six percent of inner-city high school students) carry a gun to school at least occasionally; that 12 percent of urban high school students have had guns fired at them; that 20 percent of those students have been threatened with guns; and that, in any 6-month period, several hundred thousand school children are victims of violent crimes in or near their schools. And, they report that this widespread violence in schools throughout the Nation significantly interferes with the quality of education in those schools. Based on reports such as these, Congress obviously could have thought that guns and learning are mutually exclusive. And, Congress could therefore have found a substantial educational problem—teachers unable to teach, students unable to learn—and concluded that guns near schools contribute substantially to the size and scope of that problem.

Having found that guns in schools significantly undermine the quality of education in our Nation's classrooms, Congress could also have found, given the effect of education upon interstate and foreign commerce, that gun-related violence in and around schools is a commercial, as well as a human, problem. Education, although far more than a matter of economics, has long been inextricably intertwined with the Nation's economy. When this Nation began, most workers received their education in the workplace, typically (like Benjamin Franklin) as apprentices. As late as the 1920's, many workers still received general education directly from their employers—from large corporations, such as General Electric, Ford, and Goodyear, which created schools within their firms to help both the worker and the firm. (Throughout most of the 19th century fewer than one percent of all Americans received secondary education through attending a high school.) As public school enrollment grew in the early 20th century, the need for industry to teach basic educational skills diminished. But, the direct economic link between basic education and industrial productivity remained. Scholars estimate that nearly a quarter of America's economic growth in the early years of this century is traceable directly to increased schooling. . . . Increasing global competition also has made primary and secondary education economically more important. . . .

The economic links I have just sketched seem fairly obvious. Why then is it not equally obvious, in light of those links, that a widespread, serious, and substantial physical threat to teaching and learning also substantially threatens the commerce to which that teaching and learning is inextricably tied? That is to say, guns in the hands of six percent of inner-city high school students and gun-related violence throughout a city's schools must threaten the trade and commerce that those schools support. The only question, then, is whether the latter threat is (to use the majority's terminology) "substantial." And, the evidence of (1) the extent of the gun-related violence problem, (2) the extent of the resulting negative effect on classroom learning, and (3) the extent of the consequent negative commercial effects, when taken together, indicate a threat to trade and commerce that is "substantial." At the very least, Congress could rationally have concluded that the links are "substantial."

In sum, a holding that the particular statute before us falls within the commerce power would not expand the scope of that Clause. Rather, it simply would apply pre-existing law to changing economic circumstances. See *Heart of Atlanta Motel, Inc. v. United States*, 379 U.S. 241 (1964). It would recognize that, in today's economic world, gun-related violence near the classroom makes a significant difference to our economic, as well as our social, well-being. . . .

The majority's holding—that Section 922 falls outside the scope of the Commerce Clause—creates three serious legal problems. First, the majority's holding runs contrary to modern Supreme Court cases that have upheld congressional actions despite connections to interstate or foreign commerce that are less significant than the effect of school violence. . . .

In *Katzenbach v. McClung*, 379 U.S. 294 (1964), this Court upheld, as within the commerce power, a statute prohibiting racial discrimination at local restaurants, in part because that discrimination discouraged travel by African Americans and in part because that discrimination affected purchases of food and restaurant supplies from other States. In *Daniel v. Paul*, 395 U.S. 298 (1969), this Court found an effect on commerce caused by an amusement park located several miles down a country road in the middle of Alabama—because some customers (the Court assumed), some food,

15 paddleboats, and a jukebox had come from out of State. In both of these cases, the Court understood that the specific instance of discrimination (at a local place of accommodation) was part of a general practice that, considered as a whole, caused not only the most serious human and social harm, but had nationally significant economic dimensions as well. It is difficult to distinguish the case before us, for the same critical elements are present. . . . Most importantly, like the local racial discrimination at issue in *McClung* and *Daniel*, the local instances here, taken together and considered as a whole, create a problem that causes serious human and social harm, but also has nationally significant economic dimensions. . . .

The second legal problem the Court creates comes from its apparent belief that it can reconcile its holding with earlier cases by making a critical distinction between "commercial" and noncommercial "transaction[s]." That is to say, the Court believes the Constitution would distinguish between two local activities, each of which has an identical effect upon interstate commerce, if one, but not the other, is "commercial" in nature. As a general matter, this approach fails to heed this Court's earlier warning not to turn "questions of the power of Congress" upon "formulas" that would give "controlling force to nomenclature such as 'production' and 'indirect' and foreclose consideration of the actual effects of the activity in question upon interstate commerce." *Wickard.* Moreover, the majority's test is not consistent with what the Court saw as the point of the cases that the majority now characterizes. Although the majority today attempts to categorize *Perez* [*v. United States*, 402 U.S. 146 (1971)], *McClung*, and *Wickard* as involving intrastate "economic activity," the Courts that decided each of those cases did not focus upon the economic nature of the activity regulated. Rather, they focused upon whether that activity affected interstate or foreign commerce. In fact, the *Wickard* Court expressly held that Wickard's consumption of home grown wheat, "though it may not be regarded as commerce," could nevertheless be regulated—"whatever its nature"—so long as "it exerts a substantial economic effect on interstate commerce." . . .

Regardless, if there is a principled distinction that could work both here and in future cases, Congress (even in the absence of vocational classes, industry involvement, and private management) could rationally conclude that schools fall on the commercial side of the line. In 1990, the year Congress enacted the statute before us, primary and secondary schools spent $230 billion—that is, nearly a quarter of a trillion dollars—which accounts for a significant portion of our $5.5 trillion Gross Domestic Product for that year. . . . Certainly, Congress has often analyzed school expenditure as if it were a commercial investment, closely analyzing whether schools are efficient, whether they justify the significant resources they spend, and whether they can be restructured to achieve greater returns. Why could Congress, for Commerce Clause purposes, not consider schools as roughly analogous to commercial investments from which the Nation derives the benefit of an educated work force?

The third legal problem created by the Court's holding is that it threatens legal uncertainty in an area of law that, until this case, seemed reasonably well settled. Congress has enacted many statutes (more than 100 sections of the United States Code), including criminal statutes (at least 25 sections), that use the words "affecting commerce" to define their scope. Do these, or similar, statutes regulate noncommercial activities? If so, would that alter the meaning of "affecting commerce" in a jurisdictional element? More importantly, in the absence of a jurisdictional element, are the courts nevertheless to take *Wickard* (and later similar cases) as inapplicable, and to judge the effect of a single noncommercial activity on interstate commerce without considering similar instances of the forbidden conduct? However these questions are eventually resolved, the legal uncertainty now created will restrict Congress' ability to enact criminal laws aimed at criminal behavior that, considered problem by problem rather than instance by instance, seriously threatens the economic, as well as social, well-being of Americans. . . .

Reno v. Condon

528 U.S. 141, 120 S.CT. 666 (2000)

Congress enacted the Drivers' Privacy Protection Act of 1994 to protect individuals' privacy and other interests. The law regulates the disclosure of personal information contained in the records of state motor vehicle departments. Specifically, it forbids the disclosure of personal information—name, address, telephone number, identification number, photograph, and medical information—except for certain purposes related, for instance, to driver safety and motor vehicle recalls. The law also regulates the resale of such information by private parties and imposes penalties for violations. South Carolina and some other states regularly sold such information and immediately challenged the constitutionality of the law. Charlie Condon, South Carolina's attorney general, argued that the law violated the Tenth and Eleventh Amendments and was incompatible with principles of federalism. A federal district court agreed and was affirmed by the Court of Appeals for the Fourth Circuit. Attorney General Janet Reno appealed and the Supreme Court granted review.

The appellate court's decision was reversed in a unanimous opinion for the Court delivered by Chief Justice Rhenquist.

☐ *Chief Justice REHNQUIST delivered the opinion of the Court.*

The Driver's Privacy Protection Act of 1994 (DPPA or Act) regulates the disclosure of personal information contained in the records of state motor vehicle departments (DMVs). We hold that in enacting this statute Congress did not run afoul of the federalism principles enunciated in *New York v. United States*, 505 U.S. 144 (1992), and *Printz v. United States*, 521 U.S. 898 (1997). . . .

The United States asserts that the DPPA is a proper exercise of Congress' authority to regulate interstate commerce under the Commerce

Clause. The United States bases its Commerce Clause argument on the fact that the personal, identifying information that the DPPA regulates is a "thin[g] in interstate commerce," and that the sale or release of that information in interstate commerce is therefore a proper subject of congressional regulation. *United States v. Lopez*, 514 U.S. 549 (1995). We agree with the United States' contention. The motor vehicle information which the States have historically sold is used by insurers, manufacturers, direct marketers, and others engaged in interstate commerce to contact drivers with customized solicitations. The information is also used in the stream of interstate commerce by various public and private entities for matters related to interstate motoring. Because drivers' information is, in this context, an article of commerce, its sale or release into the interstate stream of business is sufficient to support congressional regulation. We therefore need not address the Government's alternative argument that the States' individual, intrastate activities in gathering, maintaining, and distributing drivers' personal information has a sufficiently substantial impact on interstate commerce to create a constitutional base for federal legislation.

But the fact that drivers' personal information is, in the context of this case, an article in interstate commerce does not conclusively resolve the constitutionality of the DPPA. In *New York* and *Printz*, we held federal statutes invalid, not because Congress lacked legislative authority over the subject matter, but because those statutes violated the principles of federalism contained in the Tenth Amendment. . . .

We agree with South Carolina's assertion that the DPPA's provisions will require time and effort on the part of state employees, but reject the State's argument that the DPPA violates the principles laid down in either *New York* or *Printz*. We think, instead, that this case is governed by our decision in *South Carolina v. Baker*, 485 U.S. 505 (1988). In *Baker*, we upheld a statute that prohibited States from issuing unregistered bonds because the law "regulate[d] state activities," rather than "seek[ing] to control or influence the manner in which States regulate private parties." We further noted: "The NGA [National Governors Association] nonetheless contends that Section 310 has commandeered the state legislative and administrative process because many state legislatures had to amend a substantial number of statutes in order to issue bonds in registered form and because state officials had to devote substantial effort to determine how best to implement a registered bond system. Such 'commandeering' is, however, an inevitable consequence of regulating a state activity. Any federal regulation demands compliance. That a State wishing to engage in certain activity must take administrative and sometimes legislative action to comply with federal standards regulating that activity is a commonplace that presents no constitutional defect."

Like the statute at issue in *Baker*, the DPPA does not require the States in their sovereign capacity to regulate their own citizens. The DPPA regulates the States as the owners of databases. It does not require the South Carolina Legislature to enact any laws or regulations, and it does not require state officials to assist in the enforcement of federal statutes regulating private individuals. We accordingly conclude that the DPPA is consistent with the constitutional principles enunciated in *New York* and *Printz*. . . .

The judgment of the Court of Appeals is therefore Reversed.

■ In Comparative Perspective

The European Court of Justice and the European Union

The European Court of Justice (ECJ), formally known as the Court of Justice for the European Communities, was created in 1957. Along with the Council of Ministers, the European Commission, the European Parliament, and later the Court of Auditors, the ECJ was created to promote the goal of achieving economic integration in Europe. The ECJ's role is to create a uniform system of law. Originally, only six countries—Belgium, France, West Germany, Italy, Luxembourg, and the Netherlands—participated, but subsequently other countries joined in treaties creating what has evolved from the European Coal and Steel Community (ECSC) into the European Economic Community (EEC) and, as of 1995, into the European Union (EU). In 1973, Denmark, Ireland, and Britain became new members, followed by Greece in 1981, and Portugal and Spain in 1986. In 1995, Austria, Finland, and Sweden joined, bringing the total number in the European Union to fifteen. In 2004, ten more central eastern European countries joined, bringing the total to twenty-five. In 2007, Bulgaria and Romania were admitted and enlarged the EU to twenty-seven member states.

The European Court of Justice, located in Luxembourg, is independent and composed of fifteen judges, one judge recommended by each country and appointed by unanimous approval of all member states; there are also six advocates-general. The judges and advocates-general serve six-year staggered terms and vow not to consider national interests in making their decisions. All decisions are unanimous, no dissenting opinions are issued, and even the opinions announcing the decisions are not signed by their authors. ECJ judges also take an oath "to preserve the secrecy of the deliberations of the Court," as a further measure to ensure their independence and insulation from political pressures. Cases may be brought by other EU institutions, member states or "directly affected" EU citizens, or by reference from national courts for preliminary rulings on EU law that the ECJ has not yet settled. Since its inception, the ECJ's caseload has grown steadily. In 1988, a Court of First Instance was created to ease the ECJ's workload and backlog of cases. Still, in the 1990s the ECJ annually handed down around three hundred decisions and took on average two to three years to decide each case.

The ECJ has been compared to the U.S. Supreme Court in the early nineteenth century under Chief Justice John Marshall, whose rulings striking down state taxes, trade barriers, and other regulations under the Interstate Commerce Clause promoted an economic common market and solidified the Court's power of judicial review. Critics of the ECJ complain that it has become too activist, indeed, more activist than the Marshall Court, because it has turned the Treaty of Rome into a kind of constitution that gives it the power of constitutional judicial review. During the 1960s and 1970s the ECJ laid the groundwork with precedents promoting the value of European integration. By the 1980s and 1990s, the ECJ had not only established its power of judicial review but also (1) the supremacy of EU law over that of member states' legislation, (2) the competence and superiority of EU institutions over areas, such as environmental protection and human rights, that the Treaty was originally silent about, and (3) expanded the legal policy areas over which it has jurisdiction by expanding standing for private parties to sue on the basis of treaty provisions and acts of EU institutions that require implementing legislation.

In *Firma Foto-Frost v. Hauptzollamt Lübeck-Ost*, Case 314/85, 1987 ECR 4199, 53 CMLR 57 (1987), for instance, the ECJ ruled that national courts have the power to declare EU acts valid, but not invalid, within their countries. The ECJ also ruled that a national court must refuse to enforce a national law or statute that contravenes EU laws while questions concerning the compatibility of the national law and EU law are pending before the ECJ, thereby mandating a type of judicial review. (See *R. v. Secretary of State for Transport, ex parte Factortame*, A.C. 603 [1991].)

In addition, EU law based on treaties and legislation initially contained few provisions dealing with individual rights. Yet the ECJ's decisions on citizens' standing to sue when "directly affected" by EU law expanded its jurisdiction over member states' legislation and power to strike down legislation for contravening EU law. As a result, the ECJ has moved not only in the direction of promoting an economic common market, but also toward developing human rights law based on the doctrines of the "direct effect" and the supremacy of EU law. In *J. Nold, Kohlen- und Baustoffgrobhandlung v. Commission of the European Communities*, Case 4/73, 1974 ECR 491, 2 CMLR 338 (1974), the ECJ invoked an international treaty, the European Convention for the Protection of Human Rights, in addition to the constitutions of member states, as a source for its declaration of fundamental rights.

Paralleling the U.S. Supreme Court's incorporation of guarantees of the Bill of Rights into the Fourteenth Amendment and application of them to the states (see Vol. 2, Ch. 4), the ECJ has also "discovered" fundamental rights in the constitutions and treaties of member states. (See, for example, *Yvonne van Duyn v. Home Office*, Case 41/74 1974 ECR 1337 [1974]). Moreover, the ECJ has enforced human rights principles against not only the member states but also corporations and private parties. For example, in *Gabrielle Defrenne v. Société Anonyme Belge Navigation Aérienne Sabena*, Case 43/75, 1976 ECR 455 (1976), the ECJ identified a fundamental right to equal pay for equal work, citing the International Labour Organization Convention, and held that Sabena Airlines had violated that right in requiring stewardesses to retire upon their fortieth birthday.

For further reading, see Damian Chalmers, C. Hadjiemmanvil, and G. Monti, eds., *European Union Law* (New York: Cambridge University Press, 2006); Anthony Arnull, *The European Union and Its Court of Justice* (New York: Oxford University Press, 1999); Paolo Mengozzi, *European Community Law* (Boston: Kluwer Law International, 1999); Alec Stone Sweet, *Governing with Judges: Constitutional Politics in Europe* (New York: Oxford University Press, 2000); Karen J. Alter, *Establishing the Supremacy of European Law* (New York: Oxford University Press, 2001); and Gráinne de Búrca and J. H. H. Weiler, *The European Court of Justice* (New York: Oxford University Press, 2001).

City of Boerne v. Flores

521 U.S. 507, 117 S.CT. 2157 (1997)

Situated on a hill in the city of Boerne, Texas, is St. Peter Catholic Church, built in 1923 and replicating the mission style of the region's earlier history. The church seats about 230 worshipers, but in the 1990s became too small to accommodate the growing number of parishioners. Accordingly, the Archbishop of San Antonio gave permission to the parish to enlarge the building. Shortly afterward, however, the Boerne City Council passed an ordinance authorizing the city's Historic Landmark Commission to prepare a preservation plan with proposed historic landmarks and districts. Under the ordinance, the Commission must preapprove construction affecting historic landmarks or buildings in a historic district. When the Archbishop applied for a building permit so construction could proceed, city authorities, relying on the ordinance and the designation of the church as a historic landmark, denied the application. The Archbishop in turn challenged that decision in federal district court, claiming that the city violated the church's religious freedom as guaranteed by the Religious Freedom Restoration Act of 1993 (RFRA). Congress enacted that law following the Supreme Court's ruling in *Employment Division, Department of Human Resources of Oregon v. Smith*, 492 U.S. 872 (1990) (in Vol. 2, Ch. 6) and established as a matter of federal statutory law the pre-*Smith* test for balancing claims to religious freedom against governmental interests in otherwise generally applicable laws, like Boerne's zoning ordinance. And in defending the decision to deny the church a building permit, attorneys for the city countered that Congress had exceeded its enforcement powers under Section 5 of the Fourteenth Amendment in enacting the RFRA. The district court held the RFRA unconstitutional as a violation of the separation of powers. When the Court of Appeals for the Fifth Circuit reversed, the city of Boerne appealed to the Supreme Court, which granted *certiorari*.

The Court's decision was six to three and its opinion delivered by Justice Kennedy. Justices Stevens and Scalia filed concurring opinions. Justice O'Connor filed a dissenting opinion, which Justices Souter and Breyer joined in part. In a brief dissent omitted here, Justice Souter reiterated his doubts, expressed in *Church of Lukumi Babalu Aye, Inc. v. Hialeah*, 492 U.S. 872 (1990) (in Vol. 2, Ch. 6), about the precedential value of *Smith*, and indicated that the Court here should have either reconsidered the soundness of the *Smith* rule or dismissed this case as improvidently granted. In another brief dissent, Justice Breyer expressed agreement with Justice O'Connor's dissent except for her views of Congress's enforcement power under Section 5 of the Fourteenth Amendment, an issue which he would not have reached in this case.

☐ *Justice KENNEDY delivered the opinion of the Court, in which Chief Justice REHNQUIST and Justices STEVENS, THOMAS, and GINSBURG joined, and in all but Part III-A-1 of which Justice SCALIA joined.*

A decision by local zoning authorities to deny a church a building permit was challenged under the Religious Freedom Restoration Act of 1993 (RFRA). The case calls into question the authority of Congress to enact RFRA. We conclude the statute exceeds Congress' power. . . .

■ II

Congress enacted RFRA in direct response to the Court's decision in *Employment Div., Dept. of Human Resources of Ore. v. Smith*, 494 U.S. 872 (1990). There we considered a Free Exercise Clause claim brought by members of the Native American Church who were denied unemployment benefits when they lost their jobs because they had used peyote. In evaluating the claim, we declined to apply the balancing test set forth in *Sherbert v. Verner*, 374 U.S. 398 (1963), under which we would have asked whether Oregon's prohibition substantially burdened a religious practice and, if it did, whether the burden was justified by a compelling government interest. . . . The application of the *Sherbert* test, the *Smith* decision explained, would have produced an anomaly in the law, a constitutional right to ignore neutral laws of general applicability. The anomaly would have been accentuated, the Court reasoned, by the difficulty of determining whether a particular practice was central to an individual's religion. We explained, moreover, that it "is not within the judicial ken to question the centrality of particular beliefs or practices to a faith, or the validity of particular litigants' interpretations of those creeds." . . .

Four Members of the Court disagreed. They argued the law placed a substantial burden on the Native American Church members so that it could be upheld only if the law served a compelling state interest and was narrowly tailored to achieve that end. Justice O'CONNOR concluded Oregon had satisfied the test, while Justice BLACKMUN, joined by Justice BRENNAN and Justice MARSHALL, could see no compelling interest justifying the law's application to the members.

These points of constitutional interpretation were debated by Members of Congress in hearings and floor debates. Many criticized the Court's reasoning, and this disagreement resulted in the passage of RFRA. Congress announced:

(1) The framers of the Constitution, recognizing free exercise of religion as an unalienable right, secured its protection in the First Amendment to the Constitution;

(2) laws "neutral" toward religion may burden religious exercise as surely as laws intended to interfere with religious exercise;

(3) governments should not substantially burden religious exercise without compelling justification;

(4) in *Employment Division v. Smith*, 494 U.S. 872 (1990), the Supreme Court virtually eliminated the requirement that the government justify burdens on religious exercise imposed by laws neutral toward religion; and

(5) the compelling interest test as set forth in prior Federal court rulings is a workable test for striking sensible balances between religious liberty and competing prior governmental interests.

The Act's stated purposes are:

(1) to restore the compelling interest test as set forth in *Sherbert v. Verner*, 374 U.S. 398 (1963) and *Wisconsin v. Yoder*, 406 U.S. 205 (1972) and to guarantee its application in all cases where free exercise of religion is substantially burdened; and

(2) to provide a claim or defense to persons whose religious exercise is substantially burdened by government.

RFRA prohibits "government" from "substantially burdening" a person's exercise of religion even if the burden results from a rule of general applicability unless the government can demonstrate the burden "(1) is in furtherance of a compelling governmental interest; and (2) is the least restrictive means of furthering that compelling governmental interest." The Act's mandate applies to any "branch, department, agency, instrumentality, and official (or other person acting under color of law) of the United States," as well as to any "State, or . . . subdivision of a State." . . .

■ III (A)

Under our Constitution, the Federal Government is one of enumerated powers. *McCulloch v. Maryland*, 4 Wheat. 316 (1819). The judicial authority to determine the constitutionality of laws, in cases and controversies, is based on the premise that the "powers of the legislature are defined and limited; and that those limits may not be mistaken, or forgotten, the constitution is written." *Marbury v. Madison*, 1 Cranch 137 (1803).

Congress relied on its Fourteenth Amendment enforcement power in enacting the most far reaching and substantial of RFRA's provisions, those which impose its requirements on the States. . . .

The parties disagree over whether RFRA is a proper exercise of Congress' Section 5 power "to enforce" by "appropriate legislation" the constitutional guarantee that no State shall deprive any person of "life, liberty, or property, without due process of law" nor deny any person "equal protection of the laws." . . .

All must acknowledge that Section 5 is "a positive grant of legislative power" to Congress, *Katzenbach v. Morgan*, 384 U.S. 641 (1966). In *Ex parte Virginia*, 100 U.S. 339 (1880), we explained the scope of Congress' Section 5 power in the following broad terms: "Whatever legislation is appropriate, that is, adapted to carry out the objects the amendments have in view, whatever tends to enforce submission to the prohibitions they contain, and to secure to all persons the enjoyment of perfect equality of civil rights and the equal protection of the laws against State denial or invasion, if not prohibited, is brought within the domain of congressional power." Legislation which deters or remedies constitutional violations can fall within the sweep of Congress' enforcement power even if in the process it prohibits conduct which is not itself unconstitutional and intrudes into "legislative spheres of autonomy previously reserved to the States." *Fitzpatrick v. Bitzer*, 427 U.S. 445 (1976). For example, the Court upheld a suspension of literacy tests and similar voting requirements under Congress' parallel power to enforce the provisions of the Fifteenth Amendment, see U.S. Const., Amdt. 15, Sec. 2, as a measure to combat racial discrimination in voting, *South Carolina v. Katzenbach*, 383 U.S. 301 (1966), despite the facial constitutionality of the tests under *Lassiter v. Northampton County Bd. of Elections*, 360 U.S. 45 (1959). We have also concluded that other measures protecting voting rights are within Congress' power to enforce the Fourteenth and Fifteenth Amendments, despite the burdens those measures placed on the States. . . .

It is also true, however, that "as broad as the congressional enforcement power is, it is not unlimited." *Oregon v. Mitchell*, 400 U.S. 112 (1970). In assessing the breadth of Section 5's enforcement power, we begin with its text. Congress has been given the power "to enforce" the "provisions of this article." We agree with respondent, of course, that Congress can enact legislation under Section 5 enforcing the constitutional right to the free exercise of religion. The "provisions of this article," to which Section 5 refers, include the Due Process Clause of the Fourteenth Amendment. Congress' power to enforce the Free Exercise Clause follows from our holding in *Cantwell v. Connecticut*, 310 U.S. 296 (1940), that the "fundamental concept of liberty embodied in [the Fourteenth Amendment's Due Process Clause] embraces the liberties guaranteed by the First Amendment."

Congress' power under Section 5, however, extends only to "enforcing" the provisions of the Fourteenth Amendment. The Court has described this power as "remedial," *South Carolina v. Katzenbach*. The design of the Amendment and the text of Section 5 are inconsistent with the suggestion that Congress has the power to decree the substance of the Fourteenth Amendment's restrictions on the States. Legislation which alters the meaning of the Free Exercise Clause cannot be said to be enforcing the Clause. Congress does not enforce a constitutional right by changing what the right is. It has been given the power "to enforce," not the power to determine what constitutes a constitutional violation. Were it not so, what Congress would be enforcing would no longer be, in any meaningful sense, the "provisions of [the Fourteenth Amendment]."

While the line between measures that remedy or prevent unconstitutional actions and measures that make a substantive change in the governing law is not easy to discern, and Congress must have wide latitude in determining where it lies, the distinction exists and must be observed. There must be a congruence and proportionality between the injury to be prevented or remedied and the means adopted to that end. Lacking such a connection, legislation may become substantive in operation and effect. History and our case law support drawing the distinction, one apparent from the text of the Amendment.

■ 1

The Fourteenth Amendment's history confirms the remedial, rather than substantive, nature of the Enforcement Clause. The Joint Committee on Reconstruction of the 39th Congress began drafting what would become the Fourteenth Amendment in January 1866. The objections to the Committee's first draft of the Amendment, and the rejection of the draft, have a direct bearing on the central issue of defining Congress' enforcement power. In February, Republican Representative John Bingham of Ohio reported the following draft amendment to the House of Representatives on behalf of the Joint Committee: "The Congress shall have power to make all laws which shall be necessary and proper to secure to the citizens of each State all privileges and immunities of citizens in the several States, and to all persons in the several States equal protection in the rights of life, liberty, and property."

The proposal encountered immediate opposition, which continued through three days of debate. Members of Congress from across the political spectrum criticized the Amendment, and the criticisms had a common theme: The proposed Amendment gave Congress too much legislative power at the expense of the existing constitutional structure. Democrats and conservative Republicans argued that the proposed Amendment would give Congress a power to intrude into traditional areas of state responsibility, a power inconsistent with the federal design central to the Constitution. Typifying these views, Republican Representative Robert Hale of New York labeled the Amendment "an utter departure from every principle ever dreamed of by the men who framed our Constitution," and warned that under it "all State legislation, in its codes of civil and criminal jurisprudence and procedures . . . may be overridden, may be repealed or abolished, and the law of Congress established instead." . . .

As a result of these objections having been expressed from so many different quarters, the House voted to table the proposal until April. The Amendment in its early form was not again considered. Instead, the Joint Committee began drafting a new article of Amendment, which it reported to Congress on April 30, 1866.

Section 1 of the new draft Amendment imposed self-executing limits on the States. Section 5 prescribed that "the Congress shall have power to enforce, by appropriate legislation, the provisions of this article." The revised Amendment proposal did not raise the concerns expressed earlier regarding broad congressional power to prescribe uniform national laws with respect to life, liberty, and property. After revisions not relevant here, the new measure passed both Houses and was ratified in July 1868 as the Fourteenth Amendment. . . .

The design of the Fourteenth Amendment has proved significant also in maintaining the traditional separation of powers between Congress and the Judiciary. The first eight Amendments to the Constitution set forth self-executing prohibitions on governmental action, and this Court has had primary authority to interpret those prohibitions. The Bingham draft, some thought, departed from that tradition by vesting in Congress primary power to interpret and elaborate on the meaning of the new Amendment through legislation. Under it, "Congress, and not the courts, was to judge whether or not any of the privileges or immunities were not secured to citizens in the several States." While this separation of powers aspect did not occasion the widespread resistance which was caused by the proposal's threat to the federal balance, it nonetheless attracted the attention of various Members. As enacted, the Fourteenth Amendment confers substantive rights against the States which, like the provisions of the Bill of Rights, are self-executing. The power to interpret the Constitution in a case or controversy remains in the Judiciary.

■ 2

The remedial and preventive nature of Congress' enforcement power, and the limitation inherent in the power, were confirmed in our earliest cases on the Fourteenth Amendment. In the *Civil Rights Cases*, 109 U.S. 3 (1883), the Court invalidated sections of the Civil Rights Act of 1875 which prescribed criminal penalties for denying to any person "the full enjoyment of" public accommodations and conveyances, on the grounds that it exceeded Congress' power by seeking to regulate private conduct. The Enforcement Clause, the Court said, did not authorize Congress to pass "general legislation upon the rights of the citizen, but corrective legislation; that is, such as may be necessary and proper for counteracting such laws as the States may adopt or enforce, and which, by the amendment, they are prohibited from making or enforcing. . . ." Although the specific holdings of these early cases might have been superseded or modified, see, e.g., *Heart of Atlanta Motel, Inc. v. United States*, 379 U.S. 241 (1964), their treatment of Congress' Section 5 power as corrective or preventive, not definitional, has not been questioned. . . .

■ 3

Any suggestion that Congress has a substantive, non-remedial power under the Fourteenth Amendment is not supported by our case law. In *Oregon v. Mitchell*, a majority of the Court concluded Congress had exceeded its enforcement powers by enacting legislation lowering the minimum age of voters from 21 to 18 in state and local elections. The five Members of the Court who reached this conclusion explained that the legislation intruded into an area reserved by the Constitution to the States. . . .

If Congress could define its own powers by altering the Fourteenth Amendment's meaning, no longer would the Constitution be "superior paramount law, unchangeable by ordinary means." It would be "on a level with ordinary legislative acts, and, like other acts, . . . alterable when the legislature shall please to alter it." *Marbury v. Madison*. Under this approach, it is difficult to conceive of a principle that would limit congressional power. Shifting legislative majorities could change the Constitution and effectively circumvent the difficult and detailed amendment process contained in Article V.

We now turn to consider whether RFRA can be considered enforcement legislation under Section 5 of the Fourteenth Amendment.

■ III (B)

If Congress can prohibit laws with discriminatory effects in order to prevent racial discrimination in violation of the Equal Protection Clause, see *Fullilove v. Klutznick*, 448 U.S. 448 (1980), then it can do the same, respondent argues, to promote religious liberty.

While preventive rules are sometimes appropriate remedial measures, there must be a congruence between the means used and the ends to be achieved. The appropriateness of remedial measures must be considered in light of the evil presented. Strong measures appropriate to address one harm may be an unwarranted response to another, lesser one. . . .

Regardless of the state of the legislative record, RFRA cannot be considered remedial, preventive legislation, if those terms are to have any meaning. RFRA is so out of proportion to a supposed remedial or preventive object that it cannot be understood as responsive to, or designed to prevent, unconstitutional behavior. It appears, instead, to attempt a substantive change in constitutional protections. Preventive measures prohibiting certain types of laws may be appropriate when there is reason to believe that many of the laws affected by the congressional enactment have a significant likelihood of being unconstitutional. Remedial legislation under Section 5 "should be adapted to the mischief and wrong which the [Fourteenth] Amendment was intended to provide against." *Civil Rights Cases.*

RFRA is not so confined. Sweeping coverage ensures its intrusion at every level of government, displacing laws and prohibiting official actions of almost every description and regardless of subject matter. RFRA's restrictions apply to every agency and official of the Federal, State, and local Governments. RFRA has no termination date or termination mechanism. Any law is subject to challenge at any time by any individual who alleges a substantial burden on his or her free exercise of religion.

The reach and scope of RFRA distinguish it from other measures passed under Congress' enforcement power, even in the area of voting rights. In *South Carolina v. Katzenbach*, the challenged provisions were confined to those regions of the country where voting discrimination had been most flagrant and affected a discrete class of state laws, i.e., state voting laws. Furthermore, to ensure that the reach of the Voting Rights Act was limited to those cases in which constitutional violations were most likely (in order to reduce the possibility of overbreadth), the coverage under the Act would terminate "at the behest of States and political subdivisions in which the danger of substantial voting discrimination has not materialized during the preceding five years." This is not to say, of course, that Section 5 legislation requires termination dates, geographic restrictions or egregious predicates. Where, however, a congressional enactment pervasively prohibits constitutional state action in an effort to remedy or to prevent unconstitutional state action, limitations of this kind tend to ensure Congress' means are proportionate to ends legitimate under Section 5.

The stringent test RFRA demands of state laws reflects a lack of proportionality or congruence between the means adopted and the legitimate end to be achieved. If an objector can show a substantial burden on his free exercise, the State must demonstrate a compelling governmental interest and show that the law is the least restrictive means of furthering its interest. Claims that a law substantially burdens someone's exercise of religion will often be difficult to contest. Laws valid under *Smith* would fall under RFRA without regard to whether they had the object of stifling or punishing free exercise. We make these observations not to reargue the position of the majority in *Smith* but to illustrate the substantive alteration of its holding attempted by RFRA. . . .

The substantial costs RFRA exacts, both in practical terms of imposing a heavy litigation burden on the States and in terms of curtailing their traditional general regulatory power, far exceed any pattern or practice of unconstitutional conduct under the Free Exercise Clause as interpreted in *Smith*. Simply put, RFRA is not designed to identify and counteract state laws likely to be unconstitutional because of their treatment of religion. In most cases, the state laws to which RFRA applies are not ones which will have been motivated by religious bigotry. If a state law disproportionately burdened a particular class of religious observers, this circumstance might be evidence of an impermissible legislative motive. RFRA's substantial burden test, however, is not even a discriminatory effects or disparate impact test. It is a reality of the modern regulatory state that numerous state laws, such as the zoning regulations at issue here, impose a substantial burden on a large class of individuals. When the exercise of religion has been burdened in an incidental way by a law of general application, it does not follow that the persons affected have been burdened any more than other citizens, let alone burdened because of their religious beliefs. In addition, the Act imposes in every case a least restrictive means requirement—a requirement that was not used in the pre-*Smith* jurisprudence RFRA purported to codify—which also indicates that the legislation is broader than is appropriate if the goal is to prevent and remedy constitutional violations. . . .

Broad as the power of Congress is under the Enforcement Clause of the Fourteenth Amendment, RFRA contradicts vital principles necessary to maintain separation of powers and the federal balance. The judgment of the Court of Appeals sustaining the Act's constitutionality is reversed.

☐ *Justice STEVENS, concurring.*

In my opinion, the Religious Freedom Restoration Act of 1993 (RFRA) is a "law respecting an establishment of religion" that violates the First Amendment to the Constitution.

If the historic landmark on the hill in Boerne happened to be a museum or an art gallery owned by an atheist, it would not be eligible for an exemption from the city ordinances that forbid an enlargement of the structure. Because the landmark is owned by the Catholic Church, it is claimed that RFRA gives its owner a federal statutory entitlement to an exemption from a generally applicable, neutral civil law. Whether the Church would actually prevail under the statute or not, the statute has provided the Church with a legal weapon that no atheist or agnostic can obtain. This governmental preference for religion, as opposed to irreligion, is forbidden by the First Amendment. *Wallace v. Jaffree*, 472 U.S. 38 (1985).

☐ *Justice SCALIA, with whom Justice STEVENS joins, concurring in part.*

I write to respond briefly to the claim of Justice O'CONNOR's dissent (hereinafter "the dissent") that historical materials support a result contrary to the one reached in *Employment Div., Dept. of Human Resources of Ore. v. Smith*, 494 U.S. 872 (1990). The material that the dissent claims is at odds with *Smith* either has little to say about the issue or is in fact more consistent with *Smith* than with the dissent's interpretation of the Free Exercise Clause. . . .

The dissent first claims that *Smith*'s interpretation of the Free Exercise Clause departs from the understanding reflected in various statutory and constitutional protections of religion enacted by Colonies, States, and Territories in the period leading up to the ratification of the Bill of Rights. But the protections afforded by those enactments are in fact more consistent with *Smith*'s interpretation of free exercise than with the dissent's understanding of it. [T]he early "free exercise" enactments cited by the dissent protect only against action that is taken "for" or "in respect of" religion; or action taken "on account of" religion; or "discriminatory" action; or, finally (and unhelpfully for purposes of interpreting "free exercise" in the Federal Constitution), action that interferes with the "free exercise" of religion. It is eminently arguable that application of neutral, generally applicable laws of the sort the dissent refers to—such as zoning laws—would not constitute action taken "for," "in respect of," or "on account of" one's religion, or "discriminatory" action.

Assuming, however, that the affirmative protection of religion accorded by the early "free exercise" enactments sweeps as broadly as the dissent's theory would require, those enactments do not support the dissent's view, since they contain "provisos" that significantly qualify the affirmative protection they grant. According to the dissent, the "provisos" support its view because they would have been "superfluous" if "the Court was correct in *Smith* that generally applicable laws are enforceable regardless of religious conscience." I disagree. In fact, the most plausible reading of the "free exercise" enactments (if their affirmative provisions are read broadly, as the dissent's view requires) is a virtual restatement of *Smith*: Religious exercise shall be permitted so long as it does not violate general laws governing conduct. The "provisos" in the enactments negate a license to act in a manner "unfaithfull to the Lord Proprietary" (Maryland Act Concerning Religion of 1649), or "behave" in other than a "peaceable and quiet" manner (Rhode Island Charter of 1663), or "disturb the public peace" (New Hampshire Constitution), or interfere with the "peace [and] safety of the State" (New York, Maryland, and Georgia Constitutions), or "demean" oneself in other than a "peaceable and orderly manner" (Northwest Ordinance of 1787). At the time these provisos were enacted, keeping "peace" and "order" seems to have meant, precisely, obeying the laws: "Every breach of law is against the peace." Even as late as 1828, when Noah Webster published his *American Dictionary of the English Language*, he gave as one of the meanings of "peace": "8. Public tranquility; that quiet, order and security which is guaranteed by the laws; as, to keep the peace; to break the peace." This limitation upon the scope of religious exercise would have been in accord with the background political philosophy of the age (associated most prominently with John Locke), which regarded freedom as the right "to do only what was not lawfully prohibited." And while, under this interpretation, these early "free exercise" enactments support the Court's judgment in *Smith*, I see no sensible interpretation that could cause them to support what I understand to be the position of Justice O'CONNOR, or any of *Smith*'s other critics. No one in that camp, to my knowledge, contends that their favored "compelling state interest" test conforms to any possible interpretation of "breach of peace and order"—i.e., that only violence or force, or any other category of action (more limited than "violation of law") which can possibly be conveyed by the phrase "peace and order," justifies state prohibition of religiously motivated conduct.

Apart from the early "free exercise" enactments of Colonies, States, and Territories, the dissent calls attention to those bodies', and the Continental Congress's, legislative accommodation of religious practices prior to ratification of the Bill of Rights. This accommodation—which took place both before and after enactment of the state constitutional protections of religious liberty—suggests (according to the dissent) that "the drafters and ratifiers of the First Amendment . . . assumed courts would apply the Free Exercise Clause similarly." But that legislatures sometimes (though not always) found it "appropriate" to accommodate religious practices does not establish that accommodation was understood to be constitutionally mandated by the Free Exercise Clause. As we explained in *Smith*, "To say that a nondiscriminatory religious-practice exemption is permitted, or even that it is desirable, is not to say that it is constitutionally required."

The dissent's final source of claimed historical support consists of statements of certain of the Framers in the context of debates about proposed legislative enactments or debates over general principles (not in connection with the drafting of State or Federal Constitutions). Those statements are subject to the same objection as was the evidence about legislative accommodation: There is no reason to think they were meant to describe what was constitutionally required (and judicially enforceable), as opposed to what was thought to be legislatively or even morally desirable. . . .

☐ *Justice O'CONNOR, with whom Justice BREYER joins except as to a portion of Part I, dissenting.*

I dissent from the Court's disposition of this case. I agree with the Court that the issue before us is whether the Religious Freedom Restoration Act (RFRA) is a proper exercise of Congress' power to enforce Section 5 of the Fourteenth Amendment. But as a yardstick for measuring the constitutionality of RFRA, the Court uses its holding in *Employment Div., Dept. of Human Resources of Ore. v. Smith*, 494 U.S. 872 (1990), the decision that prompted Congress to enact RFRA as a means of more rigorously enforcing the Free Exercise Clause. I remain of the view that *Smith* was wrongly decided, and I would use this case to reexamine the Court's holding there. Therefore, I would direct the parties to brief the question whether *Smith* represents the correct understanding of the Free Exercise Clause and set the case for reargument. If the Court were to correct the misinterpretation of the Free Exercise Clause set forth in *Smith*, it would simultaneously put our First Amendment jurisprudence back on course and allay the legitimate concerns of a majority in Congress who believed that *Smith* improperly restricted religious liberty. We would then be in a position to review RFRA in light of a proper interpretation of the Free Exercise Clause. . . .

United States v. Morrison
529 U.S. 598, 120 S.CT. 1740 (2000)

After holding extensive hearings on gender-motivated violence and finding that such violence costs the national economy $3 billion annually, Congress enacted the Violence Against Women Act of 1994, which made violence against women a federal crime and, in Section 13981 of the U.S. Code, created as a remedy a private cause of action for victims to sue their attackers for damages. In 1994, Christy Brzonkala, a first-year student at Virginia Polytechnic Institute and State University, was allegedly raped in her dormitory room by two football players, Antonio Morrison and James Crawford. No criminal charges were filed against the latter, but subsequently Brzonkala sued them for damages under the Violence Against Women Act. A federal district court, however, concluded that the law was an unconstitutional intrusion on traditional state concerns, and the Court of Appeals for the Fourth Circuit agreed, relying on *United States v. Lopez*, 514 U.S. 549 (1995), and *City of Boerne v. Flores*, 521 U.S. 507 (1997). The U.S. government and Brzonkala appealed, and 36 states joined a brief in support of the law. The Supreme Court granted review.

The decision of the appellate court was affirmed by a five-to-four vote. Chief Justice Rehnquist delivered the opinion for the Court. Justice Thomas filed a concurring opinion. Justices Souter and Breyer filed dissenting opinions, which were joined by Justices Ginsburg and Stevens.

☐ *Chief Justice REHNQUIST delivered the opinion of the Court.*

The United States Court of Appeals for the Fourth Circuit, sitting *en banc,* struck down Section 13981 because it concluded that Congress lacked constitutional authority to enact the section's civil remedy. Believing that these cases are controlled by our decisions in *United States v. Lopez*, 514 U.S. 549 (1995), *United States v. Harris*, 106 U.S. 629 (1883), and the *Civil Rights Cases*, 109 U.S. 3 (1883), we affirm. . . .

Every law enacted by Congress must be based on one or more of its powers enumerated in the Constitution. Congress explicitly identified the sources of federal authority on which it relied in enacting Section 13981. It said that a "federal civil rights cause of action" is established "[p]ursuant to the affirmative power of Congress under section 5 of the Fourteenth Amendment to the Constitution, as well as under section 8 of Article I of the Constitution." We address Congress' authority to enact this remedy under each of these constitutional provisions in turn. . . .

As we discussed at length in *Lopez*, our interpretation of the Commerce Clause has changed as our Nation has developed. We need not repeat that detailed review of the Commerce Clause's history here; it suffices to say that, in the years since *NLRB v. Jones & Laughlin Steel Corp.*, 301 U.S. 1 (1937), Congress has had considerably greater latitude in regulating conduct and transactions under the Commerce Clause than our previous case law permitted.

As we observed in *Lopez*, modern Commerce Clause jurisprudence has "identified three broad categories of activity that Congress may regulate under its commerce power." "First, Congress may regulate the use of the channels of interstate commerce" (citing *Heart of Atlanta Motel, Inc. v. United States*, 379 U.S. 241, 256 [(1964)]; *United States v. Darby*, 312 U.S. 100 [(1941)]). "Second, Congress is empowered to regulate and protect the instrumentalities of interstate commerce, or persons or things in interstate commerce, even though the threat may come only from intrastate activities" (citing *Shreveport Rate Cases*, 234 U.S. 342 [1914]; *Southern R. Co. v. United States*, 222 U.S. 20 [(1911)]; *Perez [v. United States*, 402 U.S. 146 (1971)]). "Finally, Congress' commerce authority includes the power to regulate those activities having a substantial relation to interstate commerce, i.e., those activities that substantially affect interstate commerce" (citing *Jones & Laughlin Steel*).

Petitioners do not contend that these cases fall within either of the first two of these categories of Commerce Clause regulation. They seek to sustain Section 13981 as a regulation of activity that substantially affects interstate commerce. Given Section 13981's focus on gender-motivated violence wherever it occurs (rather than violence directed at the instrumentalities of interstate commerce, interstate markets, or things or persons in interstate commerce), we agree that this is the proper inquiry.

Since *Lopez* most recently canvassed and clarified our case law governing this third category of Commerce Clause regulation, it provides the proper framework for conducting the required analysis of Section 13981. In *Lopez*, we held that the Gun-Free School Zones Act of 1990, 18 U.S.C. Section 922(q) (1) (A), which made it a federal crime to knowingly possess a firearm in a school zone, exceeded Congress' authority under the Commerce Clause. Several significant considerations contributed to our decision.

First, . . . "Where economic activity substantially affects interstate commerce, legislation regulating that activity will be sustained." . . .

The second consideration that we found important . . . was that the statute contained "no express jurisdictional element which might limit its reach to a discrete set of firearm possessions that additionally have an explicit connection with or effect on interstate commerce." Such a jurisdictional element may establish that the enactment is in pursuance of Congress' regulation of interstate commerce.

Third, we noted that neither Section 922(q) "nor its legislative history contain[s] express congressional findings regarding the effects upon interstate commerce of gun possession in a school zone." While "Congress normally is not required to make formal findings as to the substantial burdens that an activity has on interstate commerce," the existence of such findings may "enable us to evaluate the legislative judgment that the activity in question substantially affect[s] interstate commerce, even though no such substantial effect [is] visible to the naked eye."

Finally, our decision in *Lopez* rested in part on the fact that the link between gun possession and a substantial effect on interstate commerce was attenuated. . . . We rejected these "costs of crime" and "national productivity" arguments because they would permit Congress to "regulate not only all violent crime, but all activities that might lead to violent crime, regardless of how tenuously they relate to interstate commerce."

With these principles underlying our Commerce Clause jurisprudence as reference points, the proper resolution of the present cases is clear. Gender-motivated crimes of violence are not, in any sense of the phrase, economic activity. While we need not adopt a categorical rule against aggregating the effects of any noneconomic activity in order to decide these cases, thus far in our Nation's history our cases have upheld Commerce Clause regulation of intrastate activity only where that activity is economic in nature.

Like the Gun-Free School Zones Act at issue in *Lopez*, Section 13981 contains no jurisdictional element establishing that the federal cause of action is in pursuance of Congress' power to regulate interstate commerce. Although *Lopez* makes clear that such a jurisdictional element would lend support to the argument that Section 13981 is sufficiently tied to interstate commerce, Congress elected to cast Section 13981's remedy over a wider, and more purely intrastate, body of violent crime.

In contrast with the lack of congressional findings that we faced in *Lopez*, Section 13981 is supported by numerous findings regarding the serious impact that gender-motivated violence has on victims and their families. But the existence of congressional findings is not sufficient, by itself, to sustain the constitutionality of Commerce Clause legislation. As we stated in *Lopez*, "[S]imply because Congress may conclude that a particular activity substantially affects interstate commerce does not necessarily make it so." Rather, "[w]hether particular operations affect interstate commerce sufficiently to come under the constitutional power of Congress to regulate them is ultimately a judicial rather than a legislative question, and can be settled finally only by this Court."

In these cases, Congress' findings are substantially weakened by the fact that they rely so heavily on a method of reasoning that we have already rejected as unworkable if we are to maintain the Constitution's enumeration of powers. Congress found that gender-motivated violence affects interstate commerce "by deterring potential victims from traveling interstate, from engaging in employment in interstate business, and from transacting with business, and in places involved in interstate commerce; by diminishing national productivity, increasing medical and other costs, and decreasing the supply of and the demand for interstate products." Given these findings and petitioners' arguments, the concern that we expressed in *Lopez* that Congress might use the Commerce Clause to completely obliterate the Constitution's distinction between national and local authority seems well founded. . . . If accepted, petitioners' reasoning would allow Congress to regulate any crime as long as the nationwide, aggregated impact of that crime has substantial effects on employment, production, transit, or consumption. Indeed, if Congress may regulate gender-motivated violence, it would be able to regulate murder or any other type of violence since gender-motivated violence, as a subset of all violent crime, is certain to have lesser economic impacts than the larger class of which it is a part. . . .

We accordingly reject the argument that Congress may regulate noneconomic, violent criminal conduct based solely on that conduct's aggregate effect on interstate commerce. The Constitution requires a distinction between what is truly national and what is truly local. In recognizing this fact we preserve one of the few principles that has been consistent since the Clause was adopted. The regulation and punishment of intrastate violence that is not directed at the instrumentalities, channels, or goods involved in interstate commerce has always been the province of the States.

Because we conclude that the Commerce Clause does not provide Congress with authority to enact Section 13981, we address petitioners' alternative argument that the section's civil remedy should be upheld as an exercise of Congress' remedial power under Section 5 of the Fourteenth Amendment.

The principles governing an analysis of congressional legislation under Section 5 are well settled. . . . *City of Boerne v. Flores*, 521 U.S. 507 (1997). Section 5 is "a positive grant of legislative power," *Katzenbach v. Morgan*, 384 U.S. 641 (1966), that includes authority to "prohibit conduct which is not itself unconstitutional and [to] intrud[e] into 'legislative spheres of autonomy previously reserved to the States.' " However, "[a]s broad as the congressional enforcement power is, it is not unlimited." *Oregon v. Mitchell*, 400 U.S. 112 (1970). . . .

As our cases have established, state-sponsored gender discrimination violates equal protection unless it "serves important governmental objectives and the discriminatory means employed" are "substantially related to the achievement of those objectives." *United States v. Virginia*, 518 U.S. 515 (1996). However, the language and purpose of the Fourteenth Amendment place certain limitations on the manner in which Congress may attack discriminatory conduct. These limitations are necessary to prevent the Fourteenth Amendment from obliterating the Framers' carefully crafted balance of power between the States and the National Government. Foremost among these limitations is the time-honored principle that the Fourteenth Amendment, by its very terms, prohibits only state action.

Shortly after the Fourteenth Amendment was adopted, we decided two cases interpreting the Amendment's provisions, *United States v. Harris*, 106 U.S. 629 (1883), and the *Civil Rights Cases*, 109 U.S. 3 (1883). In *Harris*, the Court considered a challenge to Section 2 of the Civil Rights Act of 1871. That section sought to punish "private persons" for "conspiring to deprive any one of the equal protection of the laws enacted by the State." We concluded that this law exceeded Congress' Section 5 power because the law was "directed exclusively against the action of private persons, without reference to the laws of the State, or their administration by her officers."

We reached a similar conclusion in the *Civil Rights Cases*. In those consolidated cases, we held that the public accommodation provisions of the Civil Rights Act of 1875, which applied to purely private conduct, were beyond the scope of the Section 5 enforcement power. . . .

Petitioners alternatively argue that, unlike the situation in the *Civil Rights Cases*, here there has been gender-based disparate treatment by state authorities, whereas in those cases there was no indication of such state action. There is abundant evidence, however, to show that the Congresses that enacted the Civil Rights Acts of 1871 and 1875 had a purpose similar to that of Congress in enacting Section 13981: There were state laws on the books bespeaking equality of treatment, but in the administration of these laws there was discrimination against newly freed slaves. . . .

But even if that distinction were valid, we do not believe it would save Section 13981's civil remedy. For the remedy is simply not "corrective in its character, adapted to counteract and redress the operation of such prohibited [s]tate laws or proceedings of [s]tate officers." *Civil Rights Cases.* Or, as we have phrased it in more recent cases, prophylactic legislation under Section 5 must have a "congruence and proportionality between the injury to be prevented or remedied and the means adopted to that end." *Florida Prepaid Postsecondary Ed. Expense Bd. v. College Savings Bank,* 527 U.S. 627 (1999); *Flores.* Section 13981 is not aimed at proscribing discrimination by officials which the Fourteenth Amendment might not itself proscribe; it is directed not at any State or state actor, but at individuals who have committed criminal acts motivated by gender bias. . . .

[Section 13981] is, therefore, unlike any of the Section 5 remedies that we have previously upheld. For example, in *Katzenbach v. Morgan,* 384 U.S. 641 (1966), Congress prohibited New York from imposing literacy tests as a prerequisite for voting because it found that such a requirement disenfranchised thousands of Puerto Rican immigrants who had been educated in the Spanish language of their home territory. That law, which we upheld, was directed at New York officials who administered the State's election law and prohibited them from using a provision of that law. In *South Carolina v. Katzenbach,* 383 U.S. 301 (1966), Congress imposed voting rights requirements on States that, Congress found, had a history of discriminating against blacks in voting. The remedy was also directed at state officials in those States. . . .

For these reasons, we conclude that Congress' power under Section 5 does not extend to the enactment of Section 13981.

☐ *Justice THOMAS, concurring.*

The majority opinion correctly applies our decision in *United States v. Lopez* and I join it in full. I write separately only to express my view that the very notion of a "substantial effects" test under the Commerce Clause is inconsistent with the original understanding of Congress' powers and with this Court's early Commerce Clause cases. By continuing to apply this rootless and malleable standard, however circumscribed, the Court has encouraged the Federal Government to persist in its view that the Commerce Clause has virtually no limits. Until this Court replaces its existing Commerce Clause jurisprudence with a standard more consistent with the original understanding, we will continue to see Congress appropriating state police powers under the guise of regulating commerce.

☐ *Justice SOUTER, with whom Justice STEVENS, Justice GINSBURG, and Justice BREYER join, dissenting.*

Congress has the power to legislate with regard to activity that, in the aggregate, has a substantial effect on interstate commerce. See *Wickard v. Filburn,* 317 U.S. 111 (1942). The fact of such a substantial effect is not an issue for the courts in the first instance, but for the Congress, whose institutional capacity for gathering evidence and taking testimony far exceeds ours. By passing legislation, Congress indicates its conclusion, whether explicitly or not, that facts support its exercise of the commerce power. The business of the courts is to review the congressional assessment, not for soundness but simply for the rationality of concluding that a jurisdictional basis exists in fact. Any explicit findings that Congress chooses to make, though not dispositive of the question of rationality, may advance judicial review by identifying factual authority on which Congress relied.

One obvious difference from *United States v. Lopez* is the mountain of data assembled by Congress here showing the effects of violence against women on interstate commerce. Passage of the Act in 1994 was preceded by four years of hearings, which included testimony from physicians and law professors; from survivors of rape and domestic violence; and from representatives of state law enforcement and private business. The record includes reports on gender bias from task forces in 21 States, and we have the benefit of specific factual findings in the eight separate Reports issued by Congress and its committees over the long course leading to enactment.

With respect to domestic violence, Congress received evidence for the following findings: "Three out of four American women will be victims of violent crimes sometime during their life." "Violence is the leading cause of injuries to women ages 15 to 44." "[A]s many as 50 percent of homeless women and children are fleeing domestic violence." "Since 1974, the assault rate against women has outstripped the rate for men by at least twice for some age groups and far more for others." "[B]attering is the single largest cause of injury to women in the United States." "An estimated 4 million American women are battered each year by their husbands or partners." "Over 1 million women in the United States seek medical assistance each year for injuries sustained [from] their husbands or other partners." "Between 2,000 and 4,000 women die every year from [domestic] abuse." "Partial estimates show that violent crime against women costs this country at least 3 billion—not million, but billion—dollars a year." "[E]stimate[s] suggest that we spend $5 to $10 billion a year on health care, criminal justice, and other social costs of domestic violence."

The evidence as to rape was similarly extensive, supporting these conclusions: "[The incidence of] rape rose four times as fast as the total national crime rate over the past 10 years." "According to one study, close to half a million girls now in high school will be raped before they graduate." "[One hundred twenty-five thousand] college women can expect to be raped during this—or any—year." "[T]hree-quarters of women never go to the movies alone after dark because of the fear of rape and nearly 50 percent do not use public transit alone after dark for the same reason." "[Forty-one] percent of judges surveyed believed that juries give sexual assault victims less credibility than other crime victims." "Less than 1 percent of all [rape] victims have collected damages." "[A]n individual who commits rape has only about 4 chances in 100 of being arrested, prosecuted, and found guilty of any offense." "Almost one-quarter of convicted rapists never go to prison and another quarter received sentences in local jails where the average sentence is 11 months." "[A]lmost 50 percent of rape victims lose their jobs or are forced to quit because of the crime's severity."

Based on the data thus partially summarized, Congress found that "crimes of violence motivated by gender have a substantial adverse effect on interstate commerce, by deterring potential victims from traveling interstate, from engaging in employment in interstate business, and from transacting with business, and in places involved, in interstate commerce[,] 'by diminishing national productivity, increasing medical and other costs, and decreasing the supply of and the demand for interstate products.' "

Congress thereby explicitly stated the predicate for the exercise of its Commerce Clause power. Is its conclusion irrational in view of the data amassed? True, the methodology of particular studies may be challenged, and some of the figures arrived at may be disputed. But the sufficiency of the evidence before Congress to provide a rational basis for the finding cannot seriously be questioned.

Indeed, the legislative record here is far more voluminous than the record compiled by Congress and found sufficient in two prior cases upholding Title II of the Civil Rights Act of 1964 against Commerce Clause challenges. In *Heart of Atlanta Motel, Inc. v. United States*, 379 U.S. 241 (1964), and *Katzenbach v. McClung*, 379 U.S. 294 (1964), the Court referred to evidence showing the consequences of racial discrimination by motels and restaurants on interstate commerce. Congress had relied on compelling anecdotal reports that individual instances of segregation costs thousands to millions of dollars.

While Congress did not, to my knowledge, calculate aggregate dollar values for the nationwide effects of racial discrimination in 1964, in 1994 it did rely on evidence of the harms caused by domestic violence and sexual assault, citing annual costs of $3 billion in 1990, and $5 to $10 billion in 1993. Equally important, though, gender-based violence in the 1990's was shown to operate in a manner similar to racial discrimination in the 1960's in reducing the mobility of employees and their production and consumption of goods shipped in interstate commerce. Like racial discrimination, "[g]ender-based violence bars its most likely targets—women—from full partic[ipation] in the national economy."

If the analogy to the Civil Rights Act of 1964 is not plain enough, one can always look back a bit further. In *Wickard*, we upheld the application of the Agricultural Adjustment Act to the planting and consumption of homegrown wheat. The effect on interstate commerce in that case followed from the possibility that wheat grown at home for personal consumption could either be drawn into the market by rising prices, or relieve its grower of any need to purchase wheat in the market. The Commerce Clause predicate was simply the effect of the production of wheat for home consumption on supply and demand in interstate commerce. Supply and demand for goods in interstate commerce will also be affected by the deaths of 2,000 to 4,000 women annually at the hands of domestic abusers, and by the reduction in the work force by the 100,000 or more rape victims who lose their jobs each year or are forced to quit. Violence against women may be found to affect interstate commerce and affect it substantially.

The Act would have passed muster at any time between *Wickard* in 1942 and *Lopez* in 1995, a period in which the law enjoyed a stable understanding that congressional power under the Commerce Clause, complemented by the authority of the Necessary and Proper Clause, Art. I. Sec. 8, cl. 18, extended to all activity that, when aggregated, has a substantial effect on interstate commerce. As already noted, this understanding was secure even against the turmoil at the passage of the Civil Rights Act of 1964, in the aftermath of which the Court not only reaffirmed the cumulative effects and rational basis features of the substantial effects test, see *Heart of Atlanta, McClung*, but declined to limit the commerce power through a formal distinction between legislation focused on "commerce" and statutes addressing "moral and social wrong[s]."

The fact that the Act does not pass muster before the Court today is therefore proof, to a degree that *Lopez* was not, that the Court's nominal adherence to the substantial effects test is merely that. Although a new jurisprudence has not emerged with any distinctness, it is clear that some congressional conclusions about obviously substantial, cumulative effects on commerce are being assigned lesser values than the once-stable doctrine would assign them. These devaluations are accomplished not by any express repudiation of the substantial effects test or its application through the aggregation of individual conduct, but by supplanting rational basis scrutiny with a new criterion of review.

Thus the elusive heart of the majority's analysis in these cases is its statement that Congress's findings of fact are "weakened" by the presence of a disfavored "method of reasoning." This seems to suggest that the "substantial effects" analysis is not a factual enquiry, for Congress in the first instance with subsequent judicial review looking only to the rationality of the congressional conclusion, but one of a rather different sort, dependent upon a uniquely judicial competence.

This new characterization of substantial effects has no support in our cases (the self-fulfilling prophecies of *Lopez* aside), least of all those the majority cites. Perhaps this explains why the majority is not content to rest on its cited precedent but claims a textual justification for moving toward its new system of congressional deference subject to selective discounts. . . .

The premise that the enumeration of powers implies that other powers are withheld is sound; the conclusion that some particular categories of subject matter are therefore presumptively beyond the reach of the commerce power is, however, a *non sequitur.* From the fact that Art. I, Sec. 8, cl. 3 grants an authority limited to regulating commerce, it follows only that Congress may claim no authority under that section to address any subject that does not affect commerce. It does not at all follow that an activity affecting commerce nonetheless falls outside the commerce power, depending on the specific character of the activity, or the authority of a State to regulate it along with Congress. My disagreement with the majority is not, however, confined to logic, for history has shown that categorical exclusions have proven as unworkable in practice as they are unsupportable in theory.

Chief Justice MARSHALL's seminal opinion in *Gibbons v. Ogden,* [9 Wheat 1 (1824)], construed the commerce power from the start with "a breadth never yet exceeded," *Wickard v. Filburn.* In particular, it is worth noting, the Court in *Wickard* did not regard its holding as exceeding the scope of Chief Justice MARSHALL's view of interstate commerce; *Wickard* applied an aggregate effects test to ostensibly domestic, noncommercial farming consistently with Chief Justice MARSHALL's indication that the commerce power may be understood by its exclusion of subjects, among others, "which do not affect other States." This plenary view of the power has either prevailed or been acknowledged by this Court at every stage of our jurisprudence. And it was this understanding, free of categorical qualifications, that prevailed in the period after 1937 through *Lopez*, as summed up by Justice HARLAN: "Of course, the mere fact that Congress has said when particular activity shall be deemed to affect commerce does not preclude further examination by this Court. But where we find that the legislators have a rational basis for finding a chosen regulatory scheme necessary to the protection of commerce, our investigation is at an end." *Maryland v. Wirtz*, 392 U.S. 183 (1968).

Justice HARLAN spoke with the benefit of hindsight, for he had seen the result of rejecting the plenary view, and today's attempt to distinguish between primary activities affecting commerce in terms of the relatively commercial or noncommercial character of the primary conduct proscribed comes with the pedigree of near-tragedy that I outlined in *United States v. Lopez* (dissenting opinion). In the half century following the modern activation of the commerce power with passage of the Interstate Commerce Act in 1887, this Court from time to time created categorical enclaves beyond congressional reach by declaring such activities as "mining," "production," "manufacturing," and union membership to be outside the definition of "commerce" and by limiting application of the effects test to "direct" rather than "indirect" commercial consequences. See, e.g., *United States v. E. C. Knight Co.*, 156 U.S. 1 (1895) (narrowly construing the Sherman Antitrust Act in light of the distinction between "commerce" and "manufacture"); *Hammer v. Dagenhart*, 247 U.S. 251 (1918) (invalidating law prohibiting interstate shipment of goods manufactured with child labor as a regulation of "manufacture"); *A. L. A. Schechter Poultry Corp. v. United States*, 295 U.S. 495 (1935) (invalidating regulation of activities that only "indirectly" affected commerce); *Carter v. Carter Coal Co.*, 298 U.S. 238 (1936) (holding that regulation of unfair labor practices in mining regulated "production," not "commerce").

Since adherence to these formalistically contrived confines of commerce power in large measure provoked the judicial crisis of 1937, one might reasonably have doubted that Members of this Court would ever again toy with a return to the days before *NLRB v. Jones & Laughlin Steel Corp.*, 301 U.S. 1 (1937), which brought the earlier and nearly disastrous experiment to an end. And yet today's decision can only be seen as a step toward recapturing the prior mistakes. . . .

Why is the majority tempted to reject the lesson so painfully learned in 1937? An answer emerges from contrasting *Wickard* with one of the predecessor cases it superseded. It was obvious in *Wickard* that growing wheat for consumption right on the farm was not "commerce" in the common vocabulary, but that did not matter constitutionally so long as the aggregated activity of domestic wheat growing affected commerce substantially. Just a few years before *Wickard*, however, it had certainly been no less obvious that "mining" practices could substantially affect commerce, even though *Carter Coal Co.* had held mining regulation beyond the national commerce power. When we try to fathom the difference between the two cases, it is clear that they did not go in different directions because the *Carter Coal* Court could not understand a causal connection that the *Wickard* Court could grasp; the difference, rather, turned on the fact that the Court in *Carter Coal* had a reason for trying to maintain its categorical, formalistic distinction, while that reason had been abandoned by the time *Wickard* was decided. The reason was laissez-faire economics, the point of which was to keep government interference to a minimum. The Court in *Carter Coal* was still trying to create a laissez-faire world out of the 20th-century economy, and formalistic commercial distinctions were thought to be useful instruments in achieving that object. The Court in *Wickard* knew it could not do any such thing and in the aftermath of the New Deal had long since stopped attempting the impossible. Without the animating economic theory, there was no point in contriving formalisms in a war with Chief Justice MARSHALL's conception of the commerce power.

If we now ask why the formalistic economic/noneconomic distinction might matter today, after its rejection in *Wickard*, the answer is not that the majority fails to see causal connections in an integrated economic world. The answer is that in the minds of the majority there is a new animating theory that makes categorical formalism seem useful again. Just as the old formalism had value in the service of an economic conception, the new one is useful in serving a conception of federalism. It is the instrument by which assertions of national power are to be limited in favor of preserving a supposedly discernible, proper sphere of state autonomy to legislate or refrain from legislating as the individual States see fit. The legitimacy of the Court's current emphasis on the noncommercial nature of regulated activity, then, does not turn on any logic serving the text of the Commerce Clause or on the realism of the majority's view of the national economy. The essential issue is rather the strength of the majority's claim to have a constitutional warrant for its current conception of a federal relationship enforceable by this Court through limits on otherwise plenary commerce power. This conception is the subject of the majority's second categorical discount applied today to the facts bearing on the substantial effects test.

The Court finds it relevant that the statute addresses conduct traditionally subject to state prohibition under domestic criminal law, a fact said to have some heightened significance when the violent conduct in question is not itself aimed directly at interstate commerce or its instrumentalities. Again, history seems to be recycling, for the theory of traditional state concern as grounding a limiting principle has been rejected previously, and more than once. . . .

The objection to reviving traditional state spheres of action as a consideration in commerce analysis, however, not only rests on the portent of incoherence, but is compounded by a further defect just as fundamental. The defect, in essence, is the majority's rejection of the Founders' considered judgment that politics, not judicial review, should mediate between state and national interests as the strength and legislative jurisdiction of the National Government inevitably increased through the expected growth of the national economy. Whereas today's majority takes a leaf from the book of the old judicial economists in saying that the Court should somehow draw the line to keep the federal relationship in a proper balance, Madison, Wilson, and MARSHALL understood the Constitution very differently.

Although Madison had emphasized the conception of a National Government of discrete powers (a conception that a number of the ratifying conventions thought was too indeterminate to protect civil liberties), Madison himself must have sensed the potential scope of some of the powers granted (such as the authority to regulate commerce), for he took care in *The Federalist* No. 46 to hedge his argument for limited power by explaining the importance of national politics in protecting the States' interests. The National Government "will partake sufficiently of the spirit [of the States], to be disinclined to invade the rights of the individual States, or the prerogatives of their governments." . . .

Politics as the moderator of the congressional employment of the commerce power was the theme many years later in *Wickard*, for after the Court acknowledged the breadth of the *Gibbons* formulation it invoked Chief Justice MARSHALL yet again in adding that "(h)e made emphatic the embracing and penetrating nature of this power by warning that effective restraints on its exercise must proceed from political rather than judicial processes." *Wickard*.

As with "conflicts of economic interest," so with supposed conflicts of sovereign political interests implicated by the Commerce Clause: the Constitution remits them to politics. The point can be put no more clearly than the Court put it the last time it repudiated the notion that some state activities categorically defied the commerce power as understood in accordance with generally accepted concepts. [In *Garcia v. San Antonio Metropolitan Transit Authority*, 469 U.S. 528 (1985), the Court] concluded that "the Framers chose to rely on a federal system in which special restraints on federal power over the States inhered principally in the workings of the National Government itself, rather than in discrete limitations on the objects of federal authority. State sovereign interests, then, are more properly protected by procedural safeguards inherent in the structure of the federal system than by judicially created limitations on federal power." . . .

All of this convinces me that today's ebb of the commerce power rests on error, and at the same time leads me to doubt that the majority's view will prove to be enduring law. There is yet one more reason for doubt. Although we sense the presence of *Carter Coal, Schechter*, and [*National League of Cities v.*] *Usery* [426 U.S. 833 (1976)], once again, the majority embraces them only at arm's-length. Where such decisions once stood for rules, today's opinion points to considerations by which substantial effects are discounted. Cases standing for the sufficiency of substantial effects are not overruled; cases overruled since 1937 are not quite revived. The Court's thinking betokens less clearly a return to the conceptual straitjackets of *Schechter* and *Carter Coal* and *Usery* than to something like the unsteady state of obscenity law between *Redrup v. New York*, 386 U.S. 767 (1967), and *Miller v. California*, 413 U.S. 15 (1973), a period in which the failure to provide a workable definition left this Court to review each case ad hoc. As our predecessors learned then, the practice of such ad hoc review cannot preserve the distinction between the judicial and the legislative, and this Court, in any event, lacks the institutional capacity to maintain such a regime for very long. This one will end when the majority realizes that the conception of the commerce power for which it entertains hopes would inevitably fail the test expressed in Justice HOLMES's statement that "[t]he first call of a theory of law is that it should fit the facts." The facts that cannot be ignored today are the facts of integrated national commerce and a political relationship between States and Nation much affected by their respective treasuries and constitutional modifications adopted by the people. The federalism of some earlier time is no more adequate to account for those facts today than the theory of laissez-faire was able to govern the national economy 70 years ago.

□ *Justice BREYER, with whom Justice STEVENS joins, and with whom Justice SOUTER and Justice GINSBURG join as to Part I-A, dissenting.*

The majority holds that the federal commerce power does not extend to such "noneconomic" activities as "noneconomic, violent criminal conduct" that significantly affects interstate commerce only if we "aggregate" the interstate "effect[s]" of individual instances. Justice SOUTER explains why history, precedent, and legal logic militate against the majority's approach. I agree and join his opinion. I add that the majority's holding illustrates the difficulty of finding a workable judicial Commerce Clause touchstone—a set of comprehensible interpretive rules that courts might use to impose some meaningful limit, but not too great a limit, upon the scope of the legislative authority that the Commerce Clause delegates to Congress.

Consider the problems. The "economic/noneconomic" distinction is not easy to apply. Does the local street corner mugger engage in "economic" activity or "noneconomic" activity when he mugs for money? See *Perez v. United States*, 402 U.S. 146 (1971) (aggregating local "loan sharking" instances); *United States v. Lopez*, 514 U.S. 549 (1995) (loan sharking is economic because it consists of "intrastate extortionate credit transactions"). Would evidence that desire for economic domination underlies many brutal crimes against women save the present statute?

The line becomes yet harder to draw given the need for exceptions. The Court itself would permit Congress to aggregate, hence regulate, "noneconomic" activity taking place at economic establishments. See *Heart of Atlanta Motel, Inc. v. United States*, 379 U.S. 241 (1964) (upholding civil rights laws forbidding discrimination at local motels); *Katzenbach v. McClung*, 379 U.S. 294 (1964) (same for restaurants); *Lopez* (recognizing congressional power to aggregate, hence forbid, noneconomically motivated discrimination at public accommodations).

More important, why should we give critical constitutional importance to the economic, or noneconomic, nature of an interstate-commerce-affecting cause? If chemical emanations through indirect environmental change cause identical, severe commercial harm outside a State, why should it matter whether local factories or home fireplaces release them? The Constitution itself refers only to Congress' power to "regulate Commerce . . . among the several States," and to make laws "necessary and proper" to implement that power. The language says nothing about either the local nature, or the economic nature, of an interstate-commerce-affecting cause. . . .

Most important, the Court's complex rules seem unlikely to help secure the very object that they seek, namely, the protection of "areas of traditional state regulation" from federal intrusion. The Court's rules, even if broadly interpreted, are underinclusive. The local pickpocket is no less a traditional subject of state regulation than is the local gender-motivated assault. Regardless, the Court reaffirms, as it should, Congress' well-established and frequently exercised power to enact laws that satisfy a commerce-related jurisdictional prerequisite—for example, that some item relevant to the federally regulated activity has at some time crossed a state line.

And in a world where most everyday products or their component parts cross interstate boundaries, Congress will frequently find it possible to redraft a statute using language that ties the regulation to the interstate movement of some relevant object, thereby regulating local criminal activity or, for that matter, family affairs. Although this possibility does not give the Federal Government the power to regulate everything, it means that any substantive limitation will apply randomly in terms of the interests the majority seeks to protect. How much would be gained, for example, were Congress to reenact the present law in the form of "An Act Forbidding Violence Against Women Perpetrated at Public Accommodations or by Those Who Have Moved in, or through the Use of Items that Have Moved in, Interstate Commerce"? Complex Commerce Clause rules creating fine distinctions that achieve only random results do little to further the important federalist interests that called them into being. That is why modern (pre-*Lopez*) case law rejected them. . . .

For these reasons, as well as those set forth by Justice SOUTER, this statute falls well within Congress's Commerce Clause authority, and I dissent from the Court's contrary conclusion. . . .

Gonzales v. Raich

545 U.S. 1, 125 S.CT. 2195 (2005)

Two seriously ill Californians, Angel McClary Raich and Diane Monson, used marijuana for medicinal purposes. Under California's Compassionate Use Act of 1996, they could legally do so; nine other states had similar laws. Raich received her marijuana free of charge from her caregivers, while Monson cultivated her own in the backyard. In 2002, deputies from the sheriff's department and federal Drug Enforcement Agency (DEA) agents arrived at Monson's home. The sheriff's deputies determined that Monson's cultivation and use of marijuana was legal under state law. But the DEA agents contended that Monson was in violation of the federal Controlled Substances Act (CSA), which designates marijuana as a Schedule I "controlled substance" and makes it unlawful to possess, manufacture, or distribute such substances. After a three-hour standoff between the county district attorney and the U.S. attorney, the DEA agents seized and destroyed Monson's cannabis plants. Subsequently, Raich and Monson filed a lawsuit and sought an injunction against the enforcement of the federal statute. A federal district court denied the motion, but on appeal the U.S. Court of Appeals for the Ninth Circuit reversed, holding that, based on rulings in *United States v. Lopez*, 514 U.S. 549 (1995), and *United States v. Morrison*, 529 U.S. 598 (2000), the application of the CSA to Raich and Monson exceeded Congress's regulatory power under the Commerce Clause, and rejected the government's argument that the "aggregation principle" upheld in *Wickard v. Filburn*, 317 U.S. 111 (1942), applied, ruling that the principle was inapplicable to the activities of Raich and Monson. The Department of Justice appealed that decision, and the Supreme Court granted review.

The appellate court's decision was reversed on a vote of six to three. Justice Stevens delivered the opinion of the Court and Justice Scalia filed a concurring opinion. Chief Justice Rehnquist and Justices O'Connor and Thomas dissented.

☐ *Justice STEVENS delivered the opinion of the Court.*

California is one of at least nine States that authorize the use of marijuana for medicinal purposes. The question presented in this case is whether the power vested in Congress by Article I, Section 8, of the Constitution "[t]o make all Laws which shall be necessary and proper for carrying into Execution" its authority to "regulate Commerce with foreign Nations, and among the several States" includes the power to prohibit the local cultivation and use of marijuana in compliance with California law. . . .

The obvious importance of the case prompted our grant of *certiorari*. The case is made difficult by respondents' strong arguments that they will suffer irreparable harm because, despite a congressional finding to the contrary, marijuana does have valid therapeutic purposes. The question before us, however, is not whether it is wise to enforce the statute in these circumstances; rather, it is whether Congress' power to regulate interstate markets for medicinal substances encompasses the portions of those markets that are supplied with drugs produced and consumed locally. Well-settled law controls our answer. The CSA is a valid exercise of federal power, even as applied to the troubling facts of this case. We accordingly vacate the judgment of the Court of Appeals.

Shortly after taking office in 1969, President Nixon declared a national "war on drugs." As the first campaign of that war, Congress set out to enact legislation that would consolidate various drug laws on the books into a comprehensive statute, provide meaningful regulation over legitimate sources of drugs to prevent diversion into illegal channels, and strengthen law enforcement tools against the traffic in illicit drugs. That effort culminated in the passage of the Comprehensive Drug Abuse Prevention and Control Act of 1970. . . .

In enacting the CSA, Congress classified marijuana as a Schedule I drug. This preliminary classification was based, in part, on the recommendation of the Assistant Secretary of HEW "that marihuana be retained within schedule I at least until the completion of certain studies now underway." Schedule I drugs are categorized as such because of their high potential for abuse, lack of any accepted medical use, and absence of any accepted safety for use in medically supervised treatment. . . .

Respondents in this case do not dispute that passage of the CSA, as part of the Comprehensive Drug Abuse Prevention and Control Act, was well within Congress' commerce power. Nor do they contend that any provision or section of the CSA amounts to an unconstitutional exercise of congressional authority. Rather, respondents' challenge is actually quite limited; they argue that the CSA's categorical prohibition of the manufacture and possession of marijuana as applied to the intrastate manufacture and possession of marijuana for medical purposes pursuant to California law exceeds Congress' authority under the Commerce Clause.

In assessing the validity of congressional regulation, none of our Commerce Clause cases can be viewed in isolation. As charted in considerable detail in *United States v. Lopez*, [514 U.S. 549 (1995)] our understanding of the reach of the Commerce Clause, as well as Congress' assertion of authority there under, has evolved over time. The Commerce Clause emerged as the Framers' response to the central problem giving rise to the Constitution itself: the absence of any federal commerce power under the Articles of Confederation. For the first century of our history, the primary use of the Clause was to preclude the kind of discriminatory state legislation that had once been permissible. Then, in response to rapid industrial development and an increasingly interdependent national economy, Congress "ushered in a new era of federal regulation under the commerce power," beginning with the enactment of the Interstate Commerce Act in 1887, and the Sherman Antitrust Act in 1890. Cases decided during that "new era," which now spans more than a century, have identified three general categories of regulation in which Congress is authorized to engage under its commerce power. First, Congress can regulate the channels of interstate commerce. *Perez v. United States*, 402 U.S. 146 (1971). Second, Congress has authority to regulate and protect the instrumentalities of interstate commerce, and persons or things in interstate commerce. Third, Congress has the power to regulate activities that substantially affect interstate commerce. *NLRB v. Jones & Laughlin Steel Corp.*, 301 U.S. 1 (1937). Only the third category is implicated in the case at hand.

Our case law firmly establishes Congress' power to regulate purely local activities that are part of an economic "class of activities" that have a substantial effect on interstate commerce. See, e.g., *Perez*; *Wickard v. Filburn*, 317 U.S. 111 (1942). As we stated in *Wickard*, "even if appellee's activity be local and though it may not be regarded as commerce, it may still, whatever its nature, be reached by Congress if it exerts a substantial economic effect on interstate commerce." We have never required Congress to legislate with scientific exactitude. When Congress decides that the " 'total incidence' " of a practice poses a threat to a national market, it may regulate the entire class. In this vein, we have reiterated that when " 'a general regulatory statute bears a substantial relation to commerce, the de minimis character of individual instances arising under that statute is of no consequence.' "

Our decision in *Wickard* is of particular relevance. In *Wickard*, we upheld the application of regulations promulgated under the Agricultural Adjustment Act of 1938, which were designed to control the volume of wheat moving in interstate and foreign commerce in order to avoid surpluses and consequent abnormally low prices. The regulations established an allotment of 11.1 acres for Filburn's 1941 wheat crop, but he sowed 23 acres, intending to use the excess by consuming it on his own farm. Filburn argued that even though we had sustained Congress' power to regulate the production of goods for commerce, that power did not authorize "federal regulation [of] production not intended in any part for commerce but wholly for consumption on the farm." Justice JACKSON's opinion for a unanimous Court rejected this submission. *Wickard* thus establishes that Congress can regulate purely intrastate activity that is not itself "commercial," in that it is not produced for sale, if it concludes that failure to regulate that class of activity would undercut the regulation of the interstate market in that commodity.

The similarities between this case and *Wickard* are striking. Like the farmer in *Wickard*, respondents are cultivating, for home consumption, a fungible commodity for which there is an established, albeit illegal, interstate market. Just as the Agricultural Adjustment Act was designed "to control the volume [of wheat] moving in interstate and foreign commerce in order to avoid surpluses . . ." and consequently control the market price, a primary purpose of the CSA is to control the supply and demand of controlled substances in both lawful and unlawful drug markets. In *Wickard*, we had no difficulty concluding that Congress had a rational basis for believing that, when viewed in the aggregate, leaving home-consumed wheat outside the regulatory scheme would have a substantial influence on price and market conditions. Here too, Congress had a rational basis for concluding that leaving home-consumed marijuana outside federal control would similarly affect price and market conditions.

More concretely, one concern prompting inclusion of wheat grown for home consumption in the 1938 Act was that rising market prices could draw such wheat into the interstate market, resulting in lower market prices. The parallel concern making it appropriate to include marijuana grown for home consumption in the CSA is the likelihood that the high demand in the interstate market will draw such marijuana into that market. While the diversion of homegrown wheat tended to frustrate the federal interest in stabilizing prices by regulating the volume of commercial transactions in the interstate market, the diversion of homegrown marijuana tends to frustrate the federal interest in eliminating commercial transactions in the interstate market in their entirety. In both cases, the regulation is squarely within Congress' commerce power because production of the commodity meant for home consumption, be it wheat or marijuana, has a substantial effect on supply and demand in the national market for that commodity.

Nonetheless, respondents suggest that *Wickard* differs from this case in three respects: (1) the Agricultural Adjustment Act, unlike the CSA, exempted small farming operations; (2) *Wickard* involved a "quintessential economic activity"—a commercial farm—whereas respondents do not sell marijuana; and (3) the *Wickard* record made it clear that the aggregate production of wheat for use on farms had a significant impact on market prices. Those differences, though factually accurate, do not diminish the precedential force of this Court's reasoning.

The fact that Wickard's own impact on the market was "trivial by itself" was not a sufficient reason for removing him from the scope of federal regulation. That the Secretary of Agriculture elected to exempt even smaller farms from regulation does not speak to his power to regulate all those whose aggregated production was significant, nor did that fact play any role in the Court's analysis. Moreover, even though Wickard was indeed a commercial farmer, the activity he was engaged in—the cultivation of wheat for home consumption—was not treated by the Court as part of his commercial farming operation. . . .

In assessing the scope of Congress' authority under the Commerce

Clause, we stress that the task before us is a modest one. We need not determine whether respondents' activities, taken in the aggregate, substantially affect interstate commerce in fact, but only whether a "rational basis" exists for so concluding. Given the enforcement difficulties that attend distinguishing between marijuana cultivated locally and marijuana grown elsewhere, and concerns about diversion into illicit channels, we have no difficulty concluding that Congress had a rational basis for believing that failure to regulate the intrastate manufacture and possession of marijuana would leave a gaping hole in the CSA. Thus, as in *Wickard*, when it enacted comprehensive legislation to regulate the interstate market in a fungible commodity, Congress was acting well within its authority to "make all Laws which shall be necessary and proper" to "regulate Commerce . . . among the several States." That the regulation ensnares some purely intrastate activity is of no moment. As we have done many times before, we refuse to excise individual components of that larger scheme.

To support their contrary submission, respondents rely heavily on two of our more recent Commerce Clause cases. In their myopic focus, they overlook the larger context of modern-era Commerce Clause jurisprudence preserved by those cases. Moreover, even in the narrow prism of respondents' creation, they read those cases far too broadly. Those two cases, of course, are *Lopez* and [*United States* v.] *Morrison*, 529 U.S. 598 [2000]. As an initial matter, the statutory challenges at issue in those cases were markedly different from the challenge respondents pursue in the case at hand. Here, respondents ask us to excise individual applications of a concededly valid statutory scheme. In contrast, in both *Lopez* and *Morrison*, the parties asserted that a particular statute or provision fell outside Congress' commerce power in its entirety. This distinction is pivotal for we have often reiterated that "[w]here the class of activities is regulated and that class is within the reach of federal power, the courts have no power 'to excise, as trivial, individual instances' of the class."

Unlike those at issue in *Lopez* and *Morrison*, the activities regulated by the CSA are quintessentially economic. "Economics" refers to "the production, distribution, and consumption of commodities." The CSA is a statute that regulates the production, distribution, and consumption of commodities for which there is an established, and lucrative, interstate market. Prohibiting the intrastate possession or manufacture of an article of commerce is a rational (and commonly utilized) means of regulating commerce in that product. Such prohibitions include specific decisions requiring that a drug be withdrawn from the market as a result of the failure to comply with regulatory requirements as well as decisions excluding Schedule I drugs entirely from the market. Because the CSA is a statute that directly regulates economic, commercial activity, our opinion in *Morrison* casts no doubt on its constitutionality.

The Court of Appeals was able to conclude otherwise only by isolating a "separate and distinct" class of activities that it held to be beyond the reach of federal power, defined as "the intrastate, noncommercial cultivation, possession and use of marijuana for personal medical purposes on the advice of a physician and in accordance with state law." The court characterized this class as "different in kind from drug trafficking." The differences between the members of a class so defined and the principal traffickers in Schedule I substances might be sufficient to justify a policy decision exempting the narrower class from the coverage of the CSA. The question, however, is whether Congress' contrary policy judgment, i.e., its decision to include this narrower "class of activities" within the larger regulatory scheme, was constitutionally deficient. We have no difficulty concluding that Congress acted rationally in determining that none of the characteristics making up the purported class, whether viewed individually or in the aggregate, compelled an exemption from the CSA; rather, the subdivided class of activities defined by the Court of Appeals was an essential part of the larger regulatory scheme.

First, the fact that marijuana is used "for personal medical purposes on the advice of a physician" cannot itself serve as a distinguishing factor. The CSA designates marijuana as contraband for any purpose. . . .

Second, limiting the activity to marijuana possession and cultivation "in accordance with state law" cannot serve to place respondents' activities beyond congressional reach. The Supremacy Clause unambiguously provides that if there is any conflict between federal and state law, federal law shall prevail. It is beyond peradventure that federal power over commerce is " 'superior to that of the States to provide for the welfare or necessities of their inhabitants,' ". . . .

So, from the "separate and distinct" class of activities identified by the Court of Appeals (and adopted by the dissenters), we are left with "the intrastate, noncommercial cultivation, possession and use of marijuana." Thus the case for the exemption comes down to the claim that a locally cultivated product that is used domestically rather than sold on the open market is not subject to federal regulation. Given the findings in the CSA and the undisputed magnitude of the commercial market for marijuana, our decisions in *Wickard v. Filburn* and the later cases endorsing its reasoning foreclose that claim. . . .

☐ *Justice SCALIA, concurring in the judgment.*

Since *Perez v. United States*, 402 U.S. 146 (1971), our cases have mechanically recited that the Commerce Clause permits congressional regulation of three categories: (1) the channels of interstate commerce; (2) the instrumentalities of interstate commerce, and persons or things in interstate commerce; and (3) activities that "substantially affect" interstate commerce. The first two categories are self-evident, since they are the ingredients of interstate commerce itself. The third category, however, is different in kind, and its recitation without explanation is misleading and incomplete.

It is misleading because, unlike the channels, instrumentalities, and agents of interstate commerce, activities that substantially affect interstate commerce are not themselves part of interstate commerce, and thus the power to regulate them cannot come from the Commerce Clause alone. Rather, as this Court has acknowledged, Congress's regulatory authority over intrastate activities that are not themselves part of interstate commerce (including activities that have a substantial effect on interstate commerce) derives from the Necessary and Proper Clause. And the category of "activities that substantially affect interstate commerce" is incomplete because the authority to enact laws necessary and proper for the regulation of interstate commerce is not limited to laws governing intrastate activities that substantially affect interstate commerce. Where necessary to make a regulation of interstate commerce effective, Congress may regulate even those intrastate activities that do not themselves substantially affect interstate commerce.

Our cases show that the regulation of intrastate activities may be necessary to and proper for the regulation of interstate commerce in two general circumstances. Most directly, the commerce power permits Congress not only to devise rules for the governance of commerce between States but also to facilitate interstate commerce by eliminating potential obstructions, and to restrict it by eliminating potential stimulants. See *NLRB v. Jones & Laughlin Steel Corp.*, 301 U.S. 1 (1937). That is why the Court has repeatedly sustained congressional legislation on the ground that the regulated activities had a substantial effect on interstate commerce. *Lopez* and *Morrison* recognized the expansive scope of Congress's authority in this regard: "[T]he pattern is clear. Where economic activity substantially affects interstate commerce, legislation regulating that activity will be sustained."

This principle is not without limitation. In *Lopez* and *Morrison*, the Court—conscious of the potential of the "substantially affects" test to "'obliterate the distinction between what is national and what is local,'"— rejected the argument that Congress may regulate noneconomic activity based solely on the effect that it may have on interstate commerce through a remote chain of inferences. Thus, although Congress's authority to regulate intrastate activity that substantially affects interstate commerce is broad, it does not permit the Court to "pile inference upon inference" in order to establish that noneconomic activity has a substantial effect on interstate commerce. As we implicitly acknowledged in *Lopez*, however, Congress's authority to enact laws necessary and proper for the regulation of interstate commerce is not limited to laws directed against economic activities that have a substantial effect on interstate commerce. Though the conduct in *Lopez* was not economic, the Court nevertheless recognized that it could be regulated as "an essential part of a larger regulation of economic activity, in which the regulatory scheme could be undercut unless the intrastate activity were regulated." This statement referred to those cases permitting the regulation of intrastate activities "which in a substantial way interfere with or obstruct the exercise of the granted power."

Although this power "to make . . . regulation effective" commonly overlaps with the authority to regulate economic activities that substantially affect interstate commerce, and may in some cases have been confused with that authority, the two are distinct. The regulation of an intrastate activity may be essential to a comprehensive regulation of interstate commerce even though the intrastate activity does not itself "substantially affect" interstate commerce. Moreover, as the passage from *Lopez* quoted above suggests, Congress may regulate even noneconomic local activity if that regulation is a necessary part of a more general regulation of interstate commerce. The relevant question is simply whether the means chosen are "reasonably adapted" to the attainment of a legitimate end under the commerce power. . . .

As the Court said in the *Shreveport Rate Cases*, [234 U.S. 342 (1914)], the Necessary and Proper Clause does not give "Congress . . . the authority to regulate the internal commerce of a State, as such," but it does allow Congress "to take all measures necessary or appropriate to" the effective regulation of the interstate market, "although intrastate transactions . . . may thereby be controlled."

Today's principal dissent objects that, by permitting Congress to regulate activities necessary to effective interstate regulation, the Court reduces *Lopez* and *Morrison* to "little more than a drafting guide." (O'CONNOR, J.). I think that criticism unjustified. Unlike the power to regulate activities that have a substantial effect on interstate commerce, the power to enact laws enabling effective regulation of interstate commerce can only be exercised in conjunction with congressional regulation of an interstate market, and it extends only to those measures necessary to make the interstate regulation effective. As *Lopez* itself states, and the Court affirms today, Congress may regulate noneconomic intrastate activities only where the failure to do so "could . . . undercut" its regulation of interstate commerce. This is not a power that threatens to obliterate the line between "what is truly national and what is truly local." . . .

Lopez and *Morrison* affirm that Congress may not regulate certain "purely local" activity within the States based solely on the attenuated effect that such activity may have in the interstate market. But those decisions do not declare noneconomic intrastate activities to be categorically beyond the reach of the Federal Government. . . .

The application of these principles to the case before us is straightforward. In the CSA, Congress has undertaken to extinguish the interstate market in Schedule I controlled substances, including marijuana. The Commerce Clause unquestionably permits this. The power to regulate interstate commerce "extends not only to those regulations which aid, foster and protect the commerce, but embraces those which prohibit it." To effectuate its objective, Congress has prohibited almost all intrastate activities related to Schedule I substances—both economic activities (manufacture, distribution, possession with the intent to distribute) and noneconomic activities (simple possession). That simple possession is a noneconomic activity is immaterial to whether it can be prohibited as a necessary part of a larger regulation. Rather, Congress's authority to enact all of these prohibitions of intrastate controlled-substance activities depends only upon whether they are appropriate means of achieving the legitimate end of eradicating Schedule I substances from interstate commerce.

By this measure, I think the regulation must be sustained. . . .

☐ *Justice O'CONNOR, with whom THE CHIEF JUSTICE and Justice THOMAS join as to all but Part III, dissenting.*

We enforce the "outer limits" of Congress' Commerce Clause authority not for their own sake, but to protect historic spheres of state sovereignty from excessive federal encroachment and thereby to maintain the distribution of power fundamental to our federalist system of government. One of federalism's chief virtues, of course, is that it promotes innovation by allowing for the possibility that "a single courageous State may, if its citizens choose, serve as a laboratory; and try novel social and economic experiments without risk to the rest of the country." *New State Ice Co. v. Liebmann*, 285 U.S. 262 (1932) (BRANDEIS, J., dissenting).

This case exemplifies the role of States as laboratories. The States' core police powers have always included authority to define criminal law and to protect the health, safety, and welfare of their citizens. Exercising those powers, California (by ballot initiative and then by legislative codification) has come to its own conclusion about the difficult and sensitive question of whether marijuana should be available to relieve severe pain and suffering. Today the Court sanctions an application of the federal Controlled Substances Act that extinguishes that experiment, without any proof that the personal cultivation, possession, and use of marijuana for medicinal purposes, if economic activity in the first place, has a substantial effect on interstate commerce and is therefore an appropriate subject of federal regulation. In so doing, the Court announces a rule that gives Congress a perverse incentive to legislate broadly pursuant to the Commerce Clause—nestling questionable assertions of its authority into comprehensive regulatory schemes— rather than with precision. That rule and the result it produces in this case are irreconcilable with our decisions in *Lopez* and *United States v. Morrison*, 529 U.S. 598 (2000). Accordingly I dissent. . . .

☐ *Justice THOMAS, dissenting.*

As I explained at length in *United States v. Lopez*, 514 U.S. 549 (1995), the Commerce Clause empowers Congress to regulate the buying and selling of goods and services trafficked across state lines. The Clause's text, structure, and history all indicate that, at the time of the founding, the term " 'commerce' consisted of selling, buying, and bartering, as well as transporting for these purposes." Commerce, or trade, stood in contrast to productive activities like manufacturing and agriculture. Throughout founding-era dictionaries, Madison's notes from the Constitutional Convention, *The Federalist Papers*, and the ratification debates, the term "commerce" is consistently used to mean trade or exchange—not all economic or gainful activity that has some attenuated connection to trade or exchange. The term "commerce" commonly meant trade or exchange (and shipping for these purposes) not simply to those involved in the drafting and ratification processes, but also to the general public.

Even the majority does not argue that respondents' conduct is itself "Commerce among the several States." Monson and Raich neither buy nor sell the marijuana that they consume. They cultivate their cannabis entirely in the State of California—it never crosses state lines, much less as part of a commercial transaction. Certainly no evidence from the founding suggests that "commerce" included the mere possession of a good or some purely personal activity that did not involve trade or exchange for value. In the early days of the Republic, it would have been unthinkable that Congress could prohibit the local cultivation, possession, and consumption of marijuana.

On this traditional understanding of "commerce," the Controlled Substances Act (CSA) regulates a great deal of marijuana trafficking that is interstate and commercial in character. The CSA does not, however, criminalize only the interstate buying and selling of marijuana. Instead, it bans the entire market—intrastate or interstate, noncommercial or commercial—for marijuana. Respondents are correct that the CSA exceeds Congress' commerce power as applied to their conduct, which is purely intrastate and noncommercial. . . .

The majority prevents States like California from devising drug policies that they have concluded provide much-needed respite to the seriously ill. It does so without any serious inquiry into the necessity for federal regulation or the propriety of "displac[ing] state regulation in areas of traditional state concern." Our federalist system, properly understood, allows California and a growing number of other States to decide for themselves how to safeguard the health and welfare of their citizens. I would affirm the judgment of the Court of Appeals. I respectfully dissent.

Gonzales v. Oregon

546 U.S. 243, 126 S.Ct. 904 (2006)

In 1994, Oregon voters approved a ballot initiative and enacted the Death with Dignity Act, permitting doctors to legally prescribe certain lethal substances to assist in the death of competent terminally-ill individuals. However, in 2001 former U.S. Attorney General John Ashcroft took the position that physician-assisted suicide violates the Controlled Substances Act (CSA) of 1970, because assisting in suicide is not a "legitimate medical purpose" that justifies the dispensing of any controlled substance. He issued what became known as the "Ashcroft Directive," under which doctors distributing controlled substances to assist suicide could have their registration under the act revoked and criminally prosecuted for violating federal law. In 2002, a doctor, a pharmacist, a group of terminally-ill patients, and Oregon challenged the directive in federal district court. That court ruled that the directive was invalid and enjoined its enforcement. Subsequently, a divided three-judge panel of the U.S. Court of Appeals for the Ninth Circuit agreed. The court emphasized the issue of "states' rights," observing that: "The principle that state governments bear the primary responsibility for evaluating physician assisted suicide follows from our concept of federalism, which requires that state lawmakers, not the federal government are the primary regulators of professional [medical] conduct." The Department of Justice appealed that decision and the Supreme Court granted review.

The appellate court's decision was affirmed by a six to three vote. Justice Kennedy delivered the opinion of the Court. Justice Scalia, joined by Chief Justice Roberts, and Justice Thomas filed dissenting opinions.

☐ *Justice KENNEDY delivered the opinion of the Court.*

The question before us is whether the Controlled Substances Act allows the United States Attorney General to prohibit doctors from prescribing regulated drugs for use in physician–assisted suicide, notwithstanding a state law permitting the procedure. As the Court has observed, "Americans are engaged in an earnest and profound debate about the morality, legality, and practicality of physician–assisted suicide." *Washington v. Glucksberg*, 521 U. S. 702 (1997). The dispute before us is in part a product of this political and moral debate, but its resolution requires an inquiry familiar to the courts: interpreting a federal statute to determine whether Executive action is authorized by, or otherwise consistent with, the enactment. . . .

We turn first to the text and structure of the CSA. Enacted in 1970 with the main objectives of combating drug abuse and controlling the legitimate and illegitimate traffic in controlled substances, the CSA creates a comprehensive, closed regulatory regime criminalizing the unauthorized manufacture, distribution, dispensing, and possession of substances classified in any of the Act's five schedules. *Gonzales v. Raich*, 545 U. S. 1 (2005). The Act places substances in one of five schedules based on their potential for abuse or dependence, their accepted medical use, and their accepted safety for use under medical supervision. Schedule I contains the most severe restrictions on access and use, and Schedule V the least. Congress classified a host of substances when it enacted the CSA, but the statute permits the Attorney General to add, remove, or reschedule substances. He may do so, however, only after making particular findings, and on scientific and medical matters he is required to accept the findings of the Secretary of Health and Human Services (Secretary).

The present dispute involves controlled substances listed in Schedule II, substances generally available only pursuant to a written, nonrefillable prescription by a physician. A 1971 regulation promulgated by the Attorney General requires that every prescription for a controlled substance "be issued for a legitimate medical purpose by an individual practitioner acting in the usual course of his professional practice.". . .

Executive actors often must interpret the enactments Congress has charged them with enforcing and implementing. The parties before us are in sharp disagreement both as to the degree of deference we must accord the Interpretive Rule's substantive conclusions and whether the Rule is authorized by the statutory text at all. Although balancing the necessary respect for an agency's knowledge, expertise, and constitutional office with the courts' role as interpreter of laws can be a delicate matter, familiar principles guide us. An administrative rule may receive substantial deference if it interprets the issuing agency's own ambiguous regulation. *Auer v. Robbins*, 519 U. S. 452 (1997). An interpretation of an ambiguous statute may also receive substantial deference. *Chevron U. S. A. Inc. v. Natural Resources Defense Council, Inc.*, 467 U. S. 837 (1984). Deference in accordance with *Chevron*, however, is warranted only "when it appears that Congress delegated authority to the agency generally to make rules carrying the force of law, and that the agency interpretation claiming deference was promulgated in the exercise of that authority." *United States v. Mead Corp.*, 533 U. S. 218 (2001). Otherwise, the interpretation is "entitled to respect" only to the extent it has the "power to persuade." *Skidmore v. Swift & Co.*, 323 U. S. 134 (1944).

In our view *Auer* and the standard of deference it accords to an agency are inapplicable here. *Auer* involved a disputed interpretation of the Fair Labor Standards Act of 1938 as applied to a class of law enforcement officers.

Under regulations promulgated by the Secretary of Labor, an exemption from overtime pay depended, in part, on whether the employees met the "salary basis" test. In this Court the Secretary of Labor filed an *amicus* brief explaining why, in his view, the regulations gave exempt status to the officers. We gave weight to that interpretation, holding that because the applicable test was "a creature of the Secretary's own regulations, his interpretation of it is, under our jurisprudence, controlling unless plainly erroneous or inconsistent with the regulation."

In *Auer*, the underlying regulations gave specificity to a statutory scheme the Secretary was charged with enforcing and reflected the considerable experience and expertise the Department of Labor had acquired over time with respect to the complexities of the Fair Labor Standards Act. Here, on the other hand, the underlying regulation does little more than restate the terms of the statute itself. The language the Interpretive Rule addresses comes from Congress, not the Attorney General, and the near-equivalence of the statute and regulation belies the Government's argument for *Auer* deference. . . .

Just as the Interpretive Rule receives no deference under *Auer*, neither does it receive deference under *Chevron*. If a statute is ambiguous, judicial review of administrative rulemaking often demands *Chevron* deference; and the rule is judged accordingly. All would agree, we should think, that the statutory phrase "legitimate medical purpose" is a generality, susceptible to more precise definition and open to varying constructions, and thus ambiguous in the relevant sense. *Chevron* deference, however, is not accorded merely because the statute is ambiguous and an administrative official is involved. To begin with, the rule must be promulgated pursuant to authority Congress has delegated to the official.

The Attorney General has rulemaking power to fulfill his duties under the CSA. The specific respects in which he is authorized to make rules, however, instruct us that he is not authorized to make a rule declaring illegitimate a medical standard for care and treatment of patients that is specifically authorized under state law.

The starting point for this inquiry is, of course, the language of the delegation provision itself. In many cases authority is clear because the statute gives an agency broad power to enforce all provisions of the statute. The CSA does not grant the Attorney General this broad authority to promulgate rules.

The CSA gives the Attorney General limited powers, to be exercised in specific ways. His rulemaking authority under the CSA is described in two provisions: (1) "The Attorney General is authorized to promulgate rules and regulations and to charge reasonable fees relating to the registration and control of the manufacture, distribution, and dispensing of controlled substances and to listed chemicals," and (2) "The Attorney General may promulgate and enforce any rules, regulations, and procedures which he may deem necessary and appropriate for the efficient execution of his functions under this subchapter." As is evident from these sections, Congress did not delegate to the Attorney General authority to carry out or effect all provisions of the CSA. Rather, he can promulgate rules relating only to "registration" and "control" [of drugs] and "for the efficient execution of his functions" under the statute. . . .

The structure of the CSA, then, conveys unwillingness to cede medical judgments to an Executive official who lacks medical expertise....

In deciding whether the CSA can be read as prohibiting physician-assisted suicide, we look to the statute's text and design. The statute and our case law amply support the conclusion that Congress regulates medical practice insofar as it bars doctors from using their prescription-writing powers as a means to engage in illicit drug dealing and trafficking as conventionally understood. Beyond this, however, the statute manifests no intent to regulate the practice of medicine generally. The silence is understandable given the structure and limitations of federalism, which allow the States " 'great latitude under their police powers to legislate as to the protection of the lives, limbs, health, comfort, and quiet of all persons.' " *Medtronic, Inc. v. Lohr,* 518 U. S. 470 (1996)....

In the face of the CSA's silence on the practice of medicine generally and its recognition of state regulation of the medical profession it is difficult to defend the Attorney General's declaration that the statute impliedly criminalizes physician-assisted suicide....

☐ *Justice SCALIA, with whom Chief Justice ROBERTS and Justice THOMAS join, dissenting.*

Contrary to the Court's analysis, this case involves not one but three independently sufficient grounds for reversing the Ninth Circuit's judgment. First, the Attorney General's interpretation of "legitimate medical purpose" is clearly valid, given the substantial deference we must accord it under *Auer v. Robbins* and his two remaining conclusions follow naturally from this interpretation. Second, even if this interpretation of the regulation is entitled to lesser deference or no deference at all, it is by far the most natural interpretation of the Regulation—whose validity is not challenged here. Third, even if that interpretation of the Regulation were incorrect, the Attorney General's independent interpretation of the statutory phrase "public interest" and his implicit interpretation of the statutory phrase "public health and safety" are entitled to deference under *Chevron U. S. A. Inc. v. Natural Resources Defense Council, Inc.,* and they are valid under *Chevron.* For these reasons, I respectfully dissent....

☐ *Justice THOMAS, dissenting.*

When Angel Raich and Diane Monson challenged the application of the Controlled Substances Act (CSA) to their purely intrastate possession of marijuana for medical use as authorized under California law, a majority of this Court determined that the CSA effectively invalidated California's law because "the CSA is a comprehensive regulatory regime specifically designed to regulate which controlled substances can be utilized for medicinal purposes, and in what manner." *Gonzales v. Raich* (2005). The majority employed unambiguous language, concluding that the "manner" in which controlled substances can be utilized "for medicinal purposes" is one of the "core activities regulated by the CSA." And, it described the CSA as creating a comprehensive framework for regulating the production, distribution, and possession of . . . 'controlled substances,' " including those substances that " 'have a useful and legitimate medical purpose,' " in order to "foster the beneficial use of those medications" and "to prevent their misuse."

Today the majority beats a hasty retreat from these conclusions. . . . The majority does so based on its conclusion that the CSA is only concerned with the regulation of "medical practice insofar as it bars doctors from using their prescription-writing powers as a means to engage in illicit drug dealing and trafficking as conventionally understood." In other words, in stark contrast to *Raich*'s broad conclusions about the scope of the CSA as it pertains to the medicinal use of controlled substances, today this Court concludes that the CSA is merely concerned with fighting " 'drug abuse' " and only insofar as that abuse leads to "addiction or abnormal effects on the nervous system."

The majority's newfound understanding of the CSA as a statute of limited reach is all the more puzzling because it rests upon constitutional principles that the majority of the Court rejected in *Raich*. Notwithstanding the States' " 'traditional police powers to define the criminal law and to protect the health, safety, and welfare of their citizens,' " the *Raich* majority concluded that the CSA applied to the intrastate possession of marijuana for medicinal purposes authorized by California law because "Congress could have rationally" concluded that such an application was necessary to the regulation of the "larger interstate marijuana market." Here, by contrast, the majority's restrictive interpretation of the CSA is based in no small part on "the structure and limitations of federalism, which allow the States "great latitude under their police powers to legislate as to the protection of the lives, limbs, health, comfort, and quiet of all persons." According to the majority, these "background principles of our federal system . . . belie the notion that Congress would use . . . an obscure grant of authority to regulate areas traditionally supervised by the States' police power." . . .

I agree with limiting the applications of the CSA in a manner consistent with the principles of federalism and our constitutional structure. *Raich* (THOMAS, J., dissenting). But that is now water over the dam. The relevance of such considerations was at its zenith in *Raich*, when we considered whether the CSA could be applied to the intrastate possession of a controlled substance consistent with the limited federal powers enumerated by the Constitution. Such considerations have little, if any, relevance where, as here, we are merely presented with a question of statutory interpretation, and not the extent of constitutionally permissible federal power. . . . Accordingly, I respectfully dissent.

D | *Taxing and Spending Powers*

Congress has broad (but not unlimited) powers to tax and spend under Sections 8 and 9 of Article 1. The first clause of Section 8 provides that "[t]he Congress shall have power to lay and collect Taxes, Duties, Imposts and Excises, to pay the debts and provide for the common defense and general welfare of the United States." Since *McCulloch v. Maryland* (1819) (excerpted in Section A of this chapter), congressional power to tax has been construed to be plenary and to reach virtually "every subject."[1] Article 1, Section 9, though, limits Congress's power in providing that "[n]o capitation, or other direct tax shall be laid, unless in proportion to the census or enumeration herein before directed to be taken." This prohibition of "direct" taxation was interpreted as barring only capitation and land taxes in *Hylton v. United States*, 3 U.S. (3 Dall.) 171 (1796), which upheld a federal tax on carriages.

A major controversy, however, erupted over Congress's levying federal income taxes. Congress resorted to taxing incomes to raise revenues during the Civil War and the Court initially rebuffed the argument that income taxes were unconstitutional direct taxes in *Springer v. United States*, 102 U.S. 586 (1881). Charles Pollock, a major stockholder in the Farmers' Loan and Trust Company, challenged the constitutionality of congressional legislation in 1894 that imposed a tax of 2 percent on income in excess of $4,000. He sought to enjoin his bank from paying the tax on the grounds that it amounted to direct taxation and a denial of property rights under the due process clause.

Federal income tax was a piece of progressive legislation and attacked by Pollock's attorney, Joseph H. Choate, as "communistic in its purposes and tendencies, and is defended here upon principles as communistic, socialistic—what should I call them—populistic as ever have been addressed to any political assembly in the world."[2] Justice Howell E. Jackson was ill with tuberculosis and absent from the bench when the Fuller Court heard *Pollock v. Farmer's Loan and Trust Co.*, 157 U.S. 428 (1895). Six of the eight justices who heard the case accepted Choate's argument that an income tax levied on land violated Article I, Section 9. But the eight justices were equally divided over whether income from personal property was a direct tax.

Because of the importance of the controversy, Choate asked that the Court rehear the case. And six weeks later, in *Pollock v. Farmer's Loan and Trust Co.*, 158 U.S. 601 (1895), a bare majority struck down as unconstitutional the entire system of federal income tax. Giving vent to the Court's defense of property rights and laissez-faire capitalism (see Vol. 2, Ch. 3), Chief Justice Fuller announced, "Taxes on real estate being indisputably direct taxes, taxes on the rents or income of real estate are equally direct taxes. . . . [And] taxes on personal property, or on the income from personal property, are likewise direct taxes."

The four dissenters in *Pollock* protested the majority's turning its back on a century of precedents upholding Congress's plenary power in an attempt to block the forces of change brought by the current of progressive politics. In Justice John Harlan's words,

> The practical effect of the decision today is to give certain kinds of property a position of favoritism and advantage inconsistent with

the fundamental principles of our social organization, and to invest them with power and influence that may be perilous to that portion of the American people upon whom rests the larger part of the burden of the government, and who ought not to be subjected to the dominion of aggregated wealth any more than the property of the country should be at the mercy of the lawless.

As a result of *Pollock* and the Court's defense of interests in private property under the guise of a "liberty of contract" (see Vol. 2, Ch. 3) between 1887 and 1937, the Court was criticized by progressives for becoming the instrument of the rich and of corporate America. A movement to overturn the Court's ruling finally led to the passage and ratification in 1913 of the Sixteenth Amendment, which provides that "Congress shall have power to lay and collect taxes on incomes, from whatever source derived, without apportionment among the several States, and without regard to any census or enumeration."

The Court's defense of laissez-faire capitalism and stand against progressive legislation ultimately concluded with the "constitutional crisis" of 1937 and the Court's reversal of its interpretation of Congress's power under the commerce clause and abandonment of the doctrine of a "liberty of contract" (see section C, in this chapter, and Vol. 2, Ch. 3). In the 1920s and 1930s, though, the Court carried its defense of laissez-faire capitalism over to its construction of Congress's taxing power and thereby sharply limited that power. This was so in spite of the fact that since 1789 Congress had passed protective tariffs and laws taxing activities for purposes other than primarily raising revenues. In *J. W. Hampton, Jr., & Co. v. United States*, 276 U.S. 294 (1928), the Court affirmed the constitutionality of such uses of taxation, observing that "the existence of other motives in the selection of the subjects of taxes can not invalidate Congressional action." Indeed, in *McCray v. United States*, 194 U.S. 27 (1904), a congressional tax on oleomargarine that was colored to look like butter was upheld with the Court disclaiming any power to scrutinize "the motives or purposes of Congress when enacting legislation."[3]

In the Court's confrontation with progressive legislation and the New Deal, Congress's power to tax for purposes other than raising revenues was nevertheless sharply limited. In response to the Court's striking down the Child Labor Act of 1916 in *Hammer v. Dagenhart* (1918) (excerpted in Section B of this chapter), Congress passed the Federal Child Labor Tax Act of 1919, imposing a 10 percent tax on the annual profits of businesses using child labor in violation of the law's standards for employing child labor. When this law was attacked in *Bailey v. Drexel Furniture Co.*, 259 U.S. 20 (1922), the Taft Court struck it down for imposing a regulatory penalty on the use of child labor instead of being a tax per se.[4]

Along with the Court's "switch in time that saved nine" in *National Labor Relations Board v. Jones & Laughlin Steel Corporation* (1937) (excerpted in Section C of this chapter) and *West Coast Hotel v. Parrish*, 300 U.S. 379 (1937) (see Vol. 2, Ch. 3), a bare majority of the Court affirmed a major piece of New Deal legislation, the Social Security Act of 1935, in *Steward Machine Co. v. Davis* (1937) (see excerpt below). Notice that as in *NLRB* and *West Coast Hotel*, the Four Horsemen —Justices Butler, McReynolds, Sutherland, and Van Devanter— dissented from the revolution in constitutional politics that these rulings signified.

The Court, though, persisted for a time in imposing its notion of "dual federalism," which it initially developed as a limitation on congressional power over commerce (see Vol. 1, Ch. 7). In *United States v. Kahriger*, 345 U.S. 22 (1953), the doctrine of "dual federalism" remained infused in the Court's interpretation of the use of Congress's taxing power to regulate certain activities. *Kahriger* sustained Congress's power to tax the earnings of gamblers and to require them to register, but was eventually overturned as an infringement of an individual's Fifth Amendment privilege against self-incrimination in *Marchetti v. United States*, 390 U.S. 39 (1968).

Since the constitutional revolution forged in 1937, the Court has generally upheld Congress's broad powers to tax and spend when rejecting arguments, like those advanced by the four dissenters in *Steward Machine Co.*, that the Tenth Amendment's reserved powers for the states limit Congress. In *Brown v. Public Agencies Opposed to Social Security Entrapment*, 477 U.S. 41 (1986), for example, the Burger Court unanimously upheld Congress's amending the Social Security Act to deny the right of states to withdraw participating state and local employees from the social security system.

Since 1937 the Court has also consistently affirmed Congress's broad power to spend for the purpose of promoting the general welfare. *Buckley v. Valeo*, 424 U.S. 1 (1976) (see Vol. 1, Ch. 8), for instance, upheld the major provisions of the Federal Election Campaign Act of 1976 and when doing so turned aside the argument that public financing of presidential elections was contrary to the "general welfare." The general welfare clause, observed the Court, is "a general grant of power, the scope of which is quite expansive [and] for Congress to decide which expenditures will promote the general welfare."

South Dakota v. Dole (1987) (see excerpt below), sustained Congress's authorizing the secretary of transportation to withhold federal highway funds from states that failed to enact laws setting the minimum drinking age at twenty-one. Notably, dis-senting Justices Brennan and O'Connor contended that Congress's spending power was limited by the Twenty-first Amendment, which repealed the Eighteenth Amendment's prohibition on the manufacturing and sale of liquor and reserved the power of regulating liquor to the states.

Finally, it bears noting that the taxing power is a concurrent power, exercised by Congress and the states. Article I, Section 10, though, prohibits the states from laying "any Imposts or Duties on Imports or Exports, except what may be absolutely necessary for executing its inspection Laws." The major limitation on states' powers of taxation is, nonetheless, Congress's power over interstate commerce. Basically, states may not adopt taxes that discriminate against interstate commerce or that have "the practical effect" of unduly favoring states and localities. In *Davis v. Michigan Department of Treasury*, 489 U.S. 803 (1989), for example, the Rehnquist Court, with only Justice Stevens dissenting, ruled that states may not tax federal pensions if they exempt from taxation the pensions of retired state and local employees. In *Wardair Canada, Inc. v. Florida Department of Revenue*, 477 U.S. 1 (1986), Justice Brennan summarized the tests used by the Court in determining the constitutionality of a state tax affecting interests in interstate commerce: "When a state tax is challenged as violative of the dormant interstate Commerce Clause, we have asked four questions: is the tax applied to an activity with a substantial nexus with the taxing State; is the tax fairly apportioned; does the tax discriminate against interstate commerce; is the tax fairly related to the services provided by the State."

NOTES

1. *License Tax Cases*, 5 Wall. 462 (1867). See also *Brushaber v. Union Pacific Railroad*, 240 U.S. 1 (1916).

2. Quoted in Alpheus T. Mason and William Beany, *The Supreme Court in a Free Society* (Englewood Cliffs, NJ: Prentice-Hall, 1959), 131.

3. See also *Head Money Cases*, 112 U.S. 580 (1884); *United States v. Doremus*, 249 U.S. 86 (1919); and *Sunshine Anthracite Coal Co. v. Adkins*, 310 U.S. 381 (1940).

4. See also *United States v. Constantine*, 296 U.S. 287 (1935).

Steward Machine Co. v. Davis
301 U.S. 548, 57 S.Ct. 883 (1937)

As part of the New Deal, Congress passed the Social Security Act of 1935, requiring employers of eight or more employees to pay a federal excise tax on a percentage of their employees' wages. Under the program, the funds were collected as general revenue and deposited in the United States Treasury. Employers who contributed to state unemployment funds could credit such payments against the federal tax, but state unemployment compensation funds had to meet federal standards and to be deposited with the U.S. Treasury.

Steward Machine Company paid $46.14 to the federal government under the law, but then promptly sued Harwell Davis, an Internal Revenue Service official, for a refund on the grounds that the Social Security Act was unconstitutional. A federal district court dismissed the complaint. After that decision was upheld by a court of appeals, Steward Machine Company appealed to the Supreme Court, which affirmed the ruling of the appellate court.

The Court's decision was five to four, and the majority's opinion was announced by Justice Cardozo. Justices McReynolds, Sutherland, who was joined by Justice Van Devanter, and Butler filed dissents.

☐ *Justice CARDOZO delivers the opinion of the Court.*

The validity of the tax imposed by the Social Security Act (42 U.S.C.A. Secs. 301-1305) on employers of eight or more is here to be determined. . . .

The assault on the statute proceeds on an extended front. Its assailants take the ground that the tax is not an excise; that it is not uniform throughout the United States as excises are required to be; that its exceptions are so many and arbitrary as to violate the Fifth Amendment; that its purpose was not revenue, but an unlawful invasion of the reserved powers of the states; and that the states in submitting to it have yielded to coercion and have abandoned governmental functions which they are not permitted to surrender.

The objections will be considered seriatim with such further explanation as may be necessary to make their meaning clear.

First: The tax, which is described in the statute as an excise, is laid with uniformity throughout the United States as a duty, an impost, or an excise upon the relation of employment. . . .

The subject-matter of taxation open to the power of the Congress is as comprehensive as that open to the power of the states, though the method of apportionment may at times be different. "The Congress shall have Power to lay and collect Taxes, Duties, Imposts and Excises." Article 1, Sec. 8. If the tax is a direct one, it shall be apportioned according to the census or enumeration. If it is a duty, impost, or excise, it shall be uniform throughout the United States. Together, these classes include every form of tax appropriate to sovereignty. . . . Whether the tax is to be classified as an "excise" is in truth not of critical importance. If not that, it is an "impost." A capitation or other "direct" tax it certainly is not. "Although there have been, from time to time, intimations that there might be some tax which was not a direct tax, nor included under the words 'duties, imposts, and excises,' such a tax, for more than 100 years of national existence, has as yet remained undiscovered, notwithstanding the stress of particular circumstances has invited thorough investigation into sources of revenue." There is no departure from that thought in later cases, but rather a new emphasis of it. . . .

The tax being an excise, its imposition must conform to the canon of uniformity. There has been no departure from this requirement. According to the settled doctrine, the uniformity exacted is geographical, not intrinsic. . . .

Second: The excise is not invalid under the provisions of the Fifth Amendment by force of its exemptions.

The statute does not apply, as we have seen, to employers of less than eight. It does not apply to agricultural labor, or domestic service in a private home or to some other classes of less importance. Petitioner contends that the effect of these restrictions is an arbitrary discrimination vitiating the tax.

The Fifth Amendment unlike the Fourteenth has no equal protection clause. . . .

The classifications and exemptions directed by the statute now in controversy have support in considerations of policy and practical convenience that cannot be condemned as arbitrary. . . .

Third: The excise is not void as involving the coercion of the states in contravention of the Tenth Amendment or of restrictions implicit in our federal form of government.

The proceeds of the excise when collected are paid into the Treasury at Washington, and thereafter are subject to appropriation like public moneys generally. No presumption can be indulged that they will be misapplied or wasted. Even if they were collected in the hope or expectation that some other and collateral good would be furthered as an incident, that without more would not make the act invalid. This indeed is hardly questioned. The case for the petitioner is built on the contention that here an ulterior aim is wrought into the very structure of the act, and what is even more important that the aim is not only ulterior, but essentially unlawful. In particular, the 90 per cent credit is relied upon as supporting that conclusion. But before the statute succumbs to an assault upon these lines, two propositions must be made out by the assailant. There must be a showing in the first place that separated from the credit the revenue provisions are incapable of standing by themselves. There must be a showing in the second place that the tax and the credit in combination are weapons of coercion, destroying or impairing the autonomy of the states. The truth of each proposition being essential to the success of the assault, we pass for convenience to a consideration of the second, without pausing to inquire whether there has been a demonstration of the first.

To draw the line intelligently between duress and inducement, there is need to remind ourselves of facts as to the problem of unemployment that are now matters of common knowledge. . . . The relevant statistics are gathered in the brief of counsel for the government. Of the many available figures a few only will be mentioned. During the years 1929 to 1936, when the country was passing through a cyclical depression, the number of the unemployed mounted to unprecedented heights. Often the average was more than 10 million; at times a peak was attained of 16 million or more. Disaster to the breadwinner meant disaster to dependents. Accordingly the roll of the unemployed, itself formidable enough, was only a partial roll of the destitute or needy. The fact developed quickly that the states were unable to give the requisite relief. The problem had become national in area and dimensions. There was need of help from the nation if the people were not to starve. It is too late today for the argument to be heard with tolerance that in a crisis so extreme the use of the moneys of the nation to relieve the unemployed and their dependents is a use for any purpose narrower than the promotion of the general welfare. . . .

The Social Security Act is an attempt to find a method by which all these public agencies may work together to a common end. Every dollar of the new taxes will continue in all likelihood to be used and needed by the nation as long as states are unwilling, whether through timidity or for other motives, to do what can be done at home. At least the inference is permissible that Congress so believed, though retaining undiminished freedom to spend the money as it pleased. On the other hand, fulfillment of the home duty will be lightened and encouraged by crediting the taxpayer upon his account with the Treasury of the nation to the extent that his contributions under the laws of the locality have simplified or diminished the problem of relief . . .

Who then is coerced through the operation of this statute? Not the taxpayer. He pays in fulfillment of the mandate of the local legislature. Not the state. Even now she does not offer a suggestion that in passing the unemployment law she was affected by duress. For all that appears, she is satisfied with her choice, and would be sorely disappointed if it were now to be annulled. The difficulty with the petitioner's contention is that it confuses motive with coercion. "Every tax is in some measure regulatory. To some extent it interposes an economic impediment to the activity taxed as compared with others not taxed." *Sonzinsky v. United States* [300 U.S. 506 (1937)]. In like manner every rebate from a tax when conditioned upon conduct is in some measure a temptation. But to hold that motive or temptation is equivalent to coercion is to plunge the law in endless difficulties. . . .

In ruling as we do, we leave many questions open. We do not say that a tax is valid, when imposed by act of Congress, if it is laid upon the condition that a state may escape its operation through the adoption of a statute unrelated in subject-matter to activities fairly within the scope of national policy and power. No such question is before us. . . .

The judgment is affirmed.

☐ *Justice McREYNOLDS, dissenting.*

That portion of the Social Security legislation here under consideration, I think, exceeds the power granted to Congress. It unduly interferes with the orderly government of the state by her own people and otherwise offends the Federal Constitution. . . .

Forever, so far as we can see, the states are expected to function under federal direction concerning an internal matter. By the sanction of this adventure, the door is open for progressive inauguration of others of like kind under which it can hardly be expected that the states will retain genuine independence of action. And without independent states a Federal Union as contemplated by the Constitution becomes impossible. . . .

☐ *Justice SUTHERLAND, with whom Justice VAN DEVANTER joins, dissenting.*

[T]he question with which I have difficulty is whether the administrative provisions of the act invade the governmental administrative powers of the several states reserved by the Tenth Amendment. A state may enter into contracts; but a state cannot, by contract or statute, surrender the execution, or a share in the execution, of any of its governmental powers either to a sister state or to the federal government, any more than the federal government can surrender the control of any of its governmental powers to a foreign nation. The power to tax is vital and fundamental, and, in the highest degree, governmental in character. Without it, the state could not exist. Fundamental also, and no less important, is the governmental power to expend the moneys realized from taxation, and exclusively to administer the laws in respect of the character of the tax and the methods of laying and collecting it and expending the proceeds. . . .

The precise question, therefore, which we are required to answer by an application of these principles is whether the congressional act contemplates a surrender by the state to the federal government, in whole or in part, of any state governmental power to administer its own unemployment law or the state pay roll-tax funds which it has collected for the purposes of that law. An affirmative answer to this question, I think, must be made.

I do not, of course, doubt the power of the state to select and utilize a depository for the safe-keeping of its funds; but it is quite another thing to agree with the selected depository that the funds shall be withdrawn for certain stipulated purposes, and for no other. Nor do I doubt the authority of the federal government and a state government to co-operate to a common end, provided each of them is authorized to reach it. But such co-operation must be effectuated by an exercise of the powers which they severally possess, and not by an exercise, through invasion or surrender, by one of them of the governmental power of the other. . . .

For the foregoing reasons, I think the judgment below should be reversed.

South Dakota v. Dole

483 U.S. 203, 107 S.Ct. 2793 (1987)

In response to widespread concern over the numbers of minors involved in automobile accidents while under the influence of alcohol and at the insistence of the administration of President Ronald Reagan, Congress amended the Surface Transportation Assistance Act in 1984 to encourage states to raise the minimum drinking age to twenty-one. The secretary of transportation was authorized to withhold part of a state's federal highway funds for 1987 and 1988 if, by October 1986, the state did not raise its minimum drinking age.

In South Dakota individuals nineteen years old or older could purchase beer with a 3.2 percent alcohol content, and the state refused to change its law because the state legislature deemed Congress's action an intrusion on the powers of the states under the Tenth and Twenty-first

Amendments. As a result, the state was expected to lose $4 million in federal highway funds in 1987 and double that in 1988. The state, therefore, sued Elizabeth Dole, the secretary of transportation. The suit was dismissed by a federal district court and the state appealed the affirmance of that decision by a federal appellate court to the Supreme Court. Although considered a strong supporter of the powers of the states, Chief Justice William Rehnquist delivered the Court's opinion upholding Congress's spending power, whereas dissenting Justices William Brennan and Sandra Day O'Connor agreed that Congress here had run afoul of the Twenty-first Amendment.

The Court's decision was seven to two, and the majority's opinion was announced by Chief Justice Rehnquist. Justices Brennan and O'Connor dissented.

☐ *Chief Justice REHNQUIST delivers the opinion of the Court.*

Here, Congress has acted indirectly under its spending power to encourage uniformity in the States' drinking ages. As we explain below, we find this legislative effort within constitutional bounds even if Congress may not regulate drinking ages directly.

The Constitution empowers Congress to "lay and collect Taxes, Duties, Imposts, and Excises, to pay the Debts and provide for the common Defence and general Welfare of the United States." Art. I, Sec. 8, cl. 1. Incident to this power, Congress may attach conditions on the receipt of federal funds, and has repeatedly employed the power "to further broad policy objectives by conditioning receipt of federal moneys upon compliance by the recipient with federal statutory and administrative directives." *Fullilove v. Klutznick*, 448 U.S. 448 [1980]. The breadth of this power was made clear in *United States v. Butler*, 297 U.S. 1 (1936), where the Court, resolving a longstanding debate over the scope of the Spending Clause, determined that "the power of Congress to authorize expenditure of public moneys for public purposes is not limited by the direct grants of legislative power found in the Constitution." Thus, objectives not thought to be within Article I's "enumerated legislative fields," may nevertheless be attained through the use of the spending power and the conditional grant of federal funds.

The spending power is of course not unlimited, but is instead subject to several general restrictions articulated in our cases. The first of these limitations is derived from the language of the Constitution itself: the exercise of the spending power must be in pursuit of "the general welfare." Second, we have required that if Congress desires to condition the States' receipt of federal funds, it "must do so unambiguously, . . . enabl[ing] the States to exercise their choice knowingly, cognizant of the consequences of their participation." Third, our cases have suggested (without significant elaboration) that conditions on federal grants might be illegitimate if they are unrelated "to the federal interest in particular national projects or programs." Finally, we have noted that other constitutional provisions may provide an independent bar to the conditional grant of federal funds. . . .

South Dakota does not seriously claim that Sec. 158 is inconsistent with any of the first three restrictions mentioned above. We can readily conclude that the provision is designed to serve the general welfare, especially in light of the fact that "the concept of welfare or the opposite is shaped by Congress. . . ." *Helvering v. Davis* [301 U.S. 619 (1937)]. Congress found that the differing drinking ages in the States created particular incentives for young persons to combine their desire to drink with their ability to drive, and that this interstate problem required a national solution. The means it chose to address this dangerous situation were reasonably calculated to advance the general welfare. . . .

The remaining question about the validity of Sec. 158—and the basic point of disagreement between the parties—is whether the Twenty-first Amendment constitutes an "independent constitutional bar" to the conditional grant of federal funds. Petitioner, relying on its view that the Twenty-first Amendment prohibits *direct* regulation of drinking ages by Congress, asserts that "Congress may not use the spending power to regulate that which it is prohibited from regulating directly under the Twenty-first Amendment." But our cases show that this "independent constitutional bar" limitation on the spending power is not of the kind petitioner suggests. *United States v. Butler* [297 U.S. 1 (1936)], for example, established that the constitutional limitations on Congress when exer-cising its spending power are less exacting than those on its authority to regulate directly.

We have also held that a perceived Tenth Amendment limitation on congressional regulation of state affairs did not concomitantly limit the range of conditions legitimately placed on federal grants.

Our decisions have recognized that in some circumstances the financial inducement offered by Congress might be so coercive as to pass the point at which "pressure turns into compulsion." *Steward Machine Co. v. Davis* [301 U.S. 548 (1937)]. Here, however, Congress has directed only that a State desiring to establish a minimum drinking age lower than 21 lose a relatively small percentage of certain federal highway funds. Petitioner contends that the coercive nature of the program is evident from the degree of success it has achieved. We cannot conclude however, that a conditional grant of federal money of this sort is unconstitutional simply by reason of its success in achieving the congressional objective. . . .

Accordingly, the judgment of the Court of Appeals is
Affirmed.

☐ *Justice BRENNAN, dissenting.*

I agree with Justice O'CONNOR that regulation of the minimum age of purchasers of liquor falls squarely within the ambit of those powers reserved to the State by the Twenty-first Amendment. Since States possess this constitutional power, Congress can not condition a federal grant in a manner that abridges this right. The Amendment, itself, strikes the proper balance between federal and state authority. I therefore dissent.

☐ *Justice O'CONNOR, dissenting.*

The Court today upholds the National Minimum Drinking Age Amendment, 23 U.S.C. Sec. 158 (1982 ed., Supp. III), as a valid exercise of the Spending Power conferred by Article I, Sec. 8. But Sec. 158 is not a condition on spending reasonably related to the expenditure of federal funds and cannot be justified on that ground. Rather, it is an attempt to regulate the sale of liquor, an attempt that lies outside Congress' power to regulate commerce because it falls within the ambit of Sec. 2 of the Twenty-first Amendment. . . .

When Congress appropriates money to build a highway, it is entitled to insist that the highway be a safe one. But it is not entitled to insist as a condition of the use of highway funds that the State impose or change regulations in other areas of the State's social and economic life because of an attenuated or tangential relationship to highway use or safety. Indeed, if the rule were otherwise, the Congress could effectively regulate almost any area of a State's social, political, or economic life on the theory that use of the interstate transportation system is somehow enhanced. . . .

If the Spending Power is to be limited only by Congress' notion of the general welfare, the reality, given the vast financial resources of the Federal Government, is that the Spending Clause gives "power to the Congress to tear down the barriers, to invade the states' jurisdiction, and to become a parliament of the whole people, subject to no restrictions save such as are self-imposed." *United States v. Butler.* This, of course, as *Butler* held, was not the Framers' plan and it is not the meaning of the Spending Clause.

Our later cases are consistent with the notion that, under the Spending Power, the Congress may only condition grants in ways that can fairly be said to be related to the expenditure of federal funds. For example, in *Fullilove v. Klutznick*, 448 U.S. 448 (1980), the Court upheld a condition on federal grants that 10% of the money be "set aside" for contracts with minority business enterprises. But the Court found that the condition could be justified as a valid regulation under the Commerce Power and Sec. 5 of the Fourteenth Amendment. . . .

As discussed above, a condition that a State will raise its drinking age to 21 cannot fairly be said to be reasonably related to the expenditure of funds for highway construction. The only possible connection, highway safety, has nothing to do with how the funds Congress has appropriated are expended. Rather than a condition determining how federal highway money shall be expended, it is a regulation determining who shall be able to drink liquor. As such it is not justified by the Spending Power.

7

THE STATES AND AMERICAN FEDERALISM

Federalism is a distinctive feature and integral part of American constitutional politics and the administration of public affairs. Yet, in denoting the separation of state and national powers, federalism conceals complex and ambiguous connections. This is because there occurred a fundamental conceptual change in the understanding of federalism during the founding period. The Constitutional Convention rejected the eighteenth-century notion of federalism as a confederation or league of equal and independent sovereign states. But there still remained wide-ranging disagreement over the exact relationship of the national government to the states. In creating a new form of federalism, the Constitution thus laid the basis for ongoing debates and political struggles over the roles and responsibilities of national and state governments in providing social services. In addition, as Ronald L. Watts underscores: " 'Federalism' is basically not a descriptive but a normative term and refers to the advocacy of multi-tiered government combining elements of shared-rule and regional self-rule."[1] (For further discussion see the IN COMPARATIVE PERSPECTIVE box in this section).

During the founding period, the meaning of federalism was less clear and more controversial than today. The terms of constitutional politics were fluid and ambiguous. States were spoken of as sovereign, free, and independent, yet coordinate, coequal, and coextensive with the national government. As one delegate opposing Maryland's ratification of the Constitution, Luther Martin, complained, "the language of the States being *sovereign* and *independent* was once familiar and understood" but now "strange and obscure."[2]

Referring to the states as both independent and coordinate projected the appealing imagery of a union of two gravitational centers of authority: nation and state. This "compound government of the United States," James Madison explained, "is without a model, and to be explained by itself, not by similitude or analogies."³ Still, it seems fair to say the meaning of federalism was not fully grasped by its supporters or opponents; without any such model, each side was continuing to proffer its own definition during a process of political give and take.

Supporters of the Constitution shrewdly co-opted the label "Federalist" and worked an irreversible change in the meaning of *federalism*. In the eighteenth century, *federalism* denoted a "confederal system," a league of formally equal and independent sovereign states, much like the European Union today. And the Constitutional Convention in 1787 was called for the purpose of remedying the defects of (con)federalism in the nation's first constitution. The Articles of Confederation specified (in Article II) that "[e]ach State retains its sovereignty, freedom and independence, and every power, jurisdiction and right, which is not by this confederation expressly delegated to the United States, in Congress assembled."

What had been associated with federalism—namely, states' sovereignty—was denied during the Constitutional Convention. Even before the convention, Madison among others sought a middle ground between the existing (con)federation of states and their complete consolidation into a single republic. Yet states' sovereignty was even excluded from this middle ground. "[A] due supremacy of national authority," along with room for "the local authorities wherever they can be subordinately useful," is what Madison wanted. In any event, a national veto "*in all cases whatsoever* on the legislative acts of the States [was] the least possible encroachment on the State jurisdictions."⁴

During the convention, compromises forced acceptance of a "mixed form" of government, combining national and federal elements. As Madison analyzed the proposed constitution in *The Federalist*, No. 39, "In its foundation it is federal, not national; in the sources from which the ordinary powers of the government are drawn, it is partly federal and partly national; in the operation of these powers, it is national, not federal; in the extent of them, again, it is federal, not national; and, finally in the authoritative mode of introducing amendments, it is neither wholly federal nor wholly national." This account implicitly denies the sovereignty, although not the existence or status, of the states. Nor could it have been otherwise. By definition *sovereignty* is indivisible and absolute. Supporters and opponents of the second constitution agreed it was "a solecism in politics for two co-ordinate sovereignties to exist together."[5]

The drafters and defenders of the Constitution did not claim sovereignty for the proposed federal government, any more than did most of those in opposition, the Anti-Federalists, claim absolute sovereignty for the states. Sovereignty was considered to reside in the nation, in the people of the several states.

The method of ratifying the Constitution called for by the convention (in Article VII) is revealing in this regard. Under the Articles of Confederation, amendments were to be ratified by *all* state legislatures. Instead of having the Constitution submitted to state legislatures, however, the convention recommended that Congress send the document to the states for ratification by special conventions of the people, and that at least *nine* states give their approval. Congress and the thirteen states agreed, thereby amending the Articles of Confederation and affirming the principle of popular sovereignty.

Ratification by special state conventions was politically strategic. It also signified that the Constitution was not a mere treaty "among the Governments and Independent States," but the expression of "the supreme authority of the people themselves."[6] This was in keeping with the widely held view, expressed in the Declaration of Independence, that "the good people of these colonies" acted, in some respects, as one people. And popular, not state, sovereignty is boldly proclaimed in the opening line of the Constitution's Preamble, "We the People . . . form a more Perfect Union."

The significance of such explicit repudiation of states' sovereignty was not lost on some Anti-Federalists. During Virginia's ratifying convention, Patrick Henry thundered, "what right had they to say, *We, the People?* . . . [W]ho authorized them to speak the language of, *We, the People*, instead of *We, the States?* States are the characteristics, and the soul of a confederation. If the States are not the agents of this compact, it must be one great consolidated National Government of the people of all the States."[7] But Henry's position was on the losing side of history. The pretense of state sovereignty had undermined the Articles of Confederation and discredited the traditional understanding of federalism. The Constitution remedied that defect, Federalists and most Anti-Federalists agreed, much as Abraham Lincoln later claimed the existence of the states depended on a union older than the states themselves.[8]

Most Anti-Federalists were as committed to the union as to the states. Far from inflexible in their understanding of federalism, they reluctantly accepted a constitution that by earlier standards hardly embodied principles of federalism. They considered themselves the "true" Federalists in defending the states because states, smaller in size and more accountable to the people, were deemed essential to preserving individual liberty.

The Federal Farmer, an Anti-Federalist pamphleteer, referred to those insisting on "distinct republics" connected under a "federal head" as "pretended federalists." Traditional federalism could not "answer the purposes of government," any more than complete consolidation would prove practical. Like other "true federalists" and those "honest federalists" among the Constitution's supporters, he embraced a "partial consolidation" of the states "united under an efficient federal head."[9]

The deep division between the Federalists and Anti-Federalists was over republicanism and preservation of individual liberty. The debate no longer revolved around "whether the proposed union deprived states of the full sovereignty befitting members of a federal system, but whether the proposed union threatened to deprive them of their independence."[10] Differences turned on questions of degree: how far and in what form the federal government's power would extend. Federal power was limited, but "limitations were not to be imposed by considerations of state sovereignty."[11] Such considerations were ruled out by the way in which *federalism* was redefined as a separation of governmental power within a union of states sharing in a larger national political structure and process.

The meaning of America's new federalism was by no means settled with ratification of the Constitution or the Bill of Rights in 1791. That and other important questions of constitutional politics remained unresolved. As John Mercer anticipated toward the end of the Constitutional Convention, "It is a great mistake to suppose that the paper we are to propose will govern the United States. It is the men whom it will bring into the government and interest in maintaining it that is to govern them. The paper will only mark out the mode and the form. Men are the substance and must do the business."[12] The "true and safe construction" of the Constitution, Madison likewise allowed, would emerge with the "uniform sanction of successive legislative bodies; through a period of years and under the varied ascendency of parties."[13]

The idea of states' sovereignty continued to inspire imaginations. Differences within the Court provoked the first crisis over federalism in 1793. In *Chisholm v. Georgia*, 2 Dall. 419 (1793), Justice James Wilson, a former delegate to the Constitutional Convention and Pennsylvania's ratifying convention, held that citizens of one state could sue another state in federal courts. "As to the purposes of the union," he emphatically stated, "Georgia is not a sovereign state." That provoked an angry dissent from Justice James Iredell, a Southerner who had attended North Carolina's ratifying convention. His dissent invited the adoption of the Eleventh Amendment, overturning *Chisholm* and guaranteeing sovereign immunity for states from lawsuits brought by citizens of other states.

Five years later, a major reassertion of state sovereignty came from none other than James Madison and Thomas Jefferson, during their heated confrontation with the Federalists. In 1798, they issued the Virginia and Kentucky Resolutions (see Ch. 1) in response to the Alien and Sedition Acts, which aimed at silencing Jeffersonian-Republicans. Besides contending the acts ran afoul of the First Amendment, Madison and Jefferson claimed the states had the power to judge the constitutionality of federal law. Jefferson went so far as to assert that states could nullify federal laws they deemed unconstitutional. The "sovereign and independent" states, in his words, "have the unquestionable right to judge . . . and, that a nullification [by] those sovereignties, of all unauthorized acts done under color of that instrument is the rightful remedy."[14]

The Virginia and Kentucky Resolutions were extreme in both claiming state nullification of federal laws and returning to the older view of federalism. That view of federalism, to be sure, periodically resurfaced in various parts of the country. But Madison's and Jefferson's invocation of states' sovereignty failed to command support among the states. Moreover, it neither accurately reflected their understanding of the Constitution nor accorded with their practices once each became president. The language of the Virginia and Kentucky Resolutions was that of protest marshaled in a moment of personal and political confrontation.[15]

Although no longer prevailing, the doctrine of states' sovereignty survived into the 1800s. Its revival came in the South, where it gradually evolved along with the political career of South Carolina's John C. Calhoun. Elected to Congress in 1810 as a fierce nationalist, Calhoun emerged in the 1820s as an advocate of states' sovereignty and an apologist for slavery. In futile efforts to preserve the South's way of life, he advanced the ideas of state nullification of federal law and of a "concurrent majority," by which either the North or South could veto the will of the national majority as registered in congressional legislation. Calhoun's theory of state sovereignty survived his death in 1850 as a rationale for the Confederacy.

It took three decades for these ideas to culminate in the Civil War. In 1832, no state followed South Carolina in nullifying a federal tariff based on then Vice President Calhoun's theory of state sovereignty. President Andrew Jackson rebuffed the state's action as inconsistent with the union, and the state backed down. No state, again, joined South Carolina's 1851 call to secede in protest of the Compromise of 1850, which admitted California into the Union as a "free state."

Southern states continued to look for accommodation and vindication of their interests in the Supreme Court under Chief Justice Roger B. Taney. He did not disappoint them. But his decision in *Dred Scott v. Sandford*, 60 U.S. 393 (1857) (see Vol. 2, Ch. 12), spelled disaster for the Court and the country. Taney sustained the power of southern states by striking down Congress's Missouri Compromise, excluding slavery from the territories. As far as the Constitution and the federal government were concerned, he proclaimed, blacks possessed "no rights." His decision triggered resistance in northern states, which in turn underscored for Southerners that their interests could not be preserved within the union. Immediately following Lincoln's inauguration in 1861, ten slaveholding states sided with South Carolina in forming the Confederate States of America.

The Civil War was as much over constitutional principle as economics, slavery, and differences in northern and southern ways of life. Secessionists frankly denied what earlier Anti-Federalists, even if reluctantly, conceded; namely, state sovereignty has no place within the framework of the Constitution. Alas, the nation's sovereignty had to be redeemed on the battlefield.

Defenders of states' sovereignty were defeated but not laid to rest by the war. During the Reconstruction period, the Supreme Court sought to accommodate both by developing a non sequitur, the doctrine of "dual federalism." "The Constitution," as the Supreme Court observed in *Texas v. White*, 7 Wall. (74 U.S.) 700 (1869), "look[ed] to an indestructable Union composed of indestructable States." Justice Samuel Miller pushed further in *The Slaughterhouse Cases*, 16 Wall. 36 (1873) (see Vol. 2, Ch. 3), advancing the idea of dual citizenship in sharply limiting the Fourteenth Amendment's application to the states. In *The Civil Rights Cases*, 109 U.S. 3 (1883) (see Vol. 2, Ch. 12), the last major piece of Reconstruction legislation, the Civil Rights Act of 1875, was overturned. The Supreme Court then effectively returned control of race relations to the states by upholding the doctrine of separate but equal in *Plessy v. Ferguson*, 163 U.S. 537 (1896) (see Vol. 2, Ch. 12), which upheld an 1890 Louisiana law requiring "equal but separate accommodations for the white and colored races" in all state passenger railway cars.

When the doctrine of separate but equal was held inapplicable to public schools in *Brown v. Board of Education*, 347 U.S. 483 (1954) (see Vol. 2, Ch. 12), the Warren Court's landmark school desegregation decision provoked massive resistance, violent protests, and widespread noncompliance. Controversy over states' sovereignty was rekindled, and the discredited idea of state nullification, or interposition, revived. But in *Bush v. Orleans School Board*, 364 U.S. 500 (1960), in response to states' resistance to desegregation, the Court underscored that "[t]he conclusion is clear that [state] interposition is not a *constitutional* doctrine."

While the vices and virtues of the national political process for safeguarding the interests of the states continue to be debated,[16] it bears pointing out that the Constitution recognizes few "attributes of state sovereignty" and even fewer present insurmountable barriers to the exercise of federal power. Article I guarantees the people of each state representation in the House and the representation of the states in the Senate. Article IV provides that no new state shall be created from territory in an existing state or group of states without the states' consent. Article V guarantees equal state representation in the Senate. The Tenth Amendment suggests other attributes, such as the power to tax and legislate, but only to the extent that they are not superseded or preempted by Congress. And the Eleventh Amendment protects states from being sued in federal courts by citizens of other states or foreign countries.

That the Constitution omits any affirmative mention of states' sovereignty does not appear fatal for its defenders, because the Constitution limits federal powers to those specifically enumerated and does so against the background of existing state governments. In other words, the enumeration of federal powers presupposed the states, whose powers are not conferred by the Constitution. Still, the absence of any constitutional affirmation of states' sovereignty carries great weight in light of the disassociation of federalism from states' sovereignty, and indeed the rejection of the latter, during the adoption and ratification of the Constitution.

In addition, the Constitution expressly grants plenary powers to the federal government and sharply limits states' powers. The states are prohibited, in Article I, from conducting independent foreign and monetary policies, imposing export duties, impairing the obligations of contract, granting titles of nobility, and passing bills of attainder or *ex post facto* laws. Under Article III, they have no sovereign immunity from suits by other states or the United States.[17] Article IV further constrains them in several ways, including limiting their powers to determine state citizenship and to control their geographical boundaries. Most notably, Article IV puts into the hands of the federal government, not the states, the responsibility for guaranteeing that each state has a "Republican Form of Government." Finally, the supremacy clause in Article VI not only declares the supremacy of federal over state laws but forces state courts in certain cases to apply federal law. Support for states' sovereignty thus cannot be constitutionally grounded in geographical territory or in terms of exclusive authority over its people, due to the co-existence and supremacy of the federal government.

In creating a new form of federalism, the Constitution presumed the existence, not the sovereignty, of the states. Indisputably, the states have a crucial role and responsibility in the administration of social services. Congress and the federal government depend heavily on them in sharing the burdens of governing. Individuals find continued protection for civil liberties and civil rights in the states and state constitutional law. As Justice Louis Brandeis pointed out, dissenting in *New State Ice Co. v. Liebmann*, 285 U.S. 262 (1932): "It is one of the happy incidents of the federal system that a single courageous state may, if its citizens choose, serve as a laboratory; and try novel social and economic experiments without risk to the rest of the country."

This chapter examines the constitutional politics of federalism and continuing controversies over the powers of the states and intergovernmental relations. Issues involving state powers to regulate commerce and other subjects not preempted by Congress are taken up (see also Vol. 1, Ch. 6). Then the focus is on the contemporary debate within the Court over the Tenth Amendment, which recognizes the "reserved" powers of the states. Finally, judicial federalism, the independence and interrelation of federal and state courts, as well as changes in the role of state supreme courts in interpreting federal and state constitutions are discussed.

NOTES

1. Ronald Watts, *Comparing Federal Systems*, 2d ed. (Montreal: McGill-Queen's University Press, 1999), 6. See also David M. O'Brien, "Federalism as a Metaphor in the Constitutional Politics of Public Administration," 49 *Public Administration Review* 411 (1989).

2. Quoted in James Madison, *Notes of Debates in the Federal Convention of 1787* (Athens: Ohio University Press, 1966), 217.

3. Quoted and further discussed in Rufas S. Davis, *The Federal Principle* (Berkeley: University of California Press, 1978), 118.

4. James Madison to George Washington, April 16, 1787, reprinted in Philip Kurland and Ralph Lerner, eds., *The Founders' Constitution*, Vol. 1 (Chicago: University of Chicago Press, 1987), 250.

5. Quoted and discussed in Herbert J. Storing, *What the Anti-Federalists Were For* (Chicago: University of Chicago Press, 1981), 12.

6. James Madison, in *The Records of the Federal Convention of 1787*, Vol. 1, ed. Max Farrand (New Haven, CT: Yale University Press, 1974), 122–123.

7. Patrick Henry, in *The Complete Anti-Federalist*, Vol. 5, ed. Herbert J. Storing (Chicago: University of Chicago Press, 1981), 211.

8. See Abraham Lincoln, "Message to Congress, Special Session," July 4, 1861, in *A*

Compilation of the Messages and Papers of the Presidents, 20 vols., ed. J. D. Richardson (New York: Bureau of National Literature, 1917).

9. Federal Farmer, in *The Founders' Constitution*, Vol. 1, ed. Kurland and Lerner, 258–259, 273.

10. Kurland and Lerner, *The Founders' Constitution*, Vol. 1, ed. Kurland and Lerner, 243.

11. William Murphy, *The Triumph of Nationalism* (Chicago: Quadrangle, 1967), 410.

12. Quoted in Madison, *Notes of Debates in the Federal Convention of 1787*, 455–456.

13. Quoted and further discussed in Robert Morgan, *James Madison on the Constitution and the Bill of Rights* (Westport, CT: Greenwood, 1988), 196.

14. See "Virginia Resolutions of 1798," and "Kentucky Resolutions of 1798 and 1799," in *The Debates in the Several State Conventions on the Adoption of the Federal Constitution*, Vol. 4, ed. Jonathan Elliot (New York: Burt Franklin Reprints, 1974), Ch. 1, 528–529, 540–544.

15. See Dumas Malone, *Jefferson and the Ordeal of Liberty* (Boston: Little, Brown, 1962), 395.

16. See and compare Jesse Choper, *Judicial Review and the National Political Process* (Chicago: University of Chicago Press, 1980) with Martin H. Redish, *The Constitution as Political Structure* (New York: Oxford University Press, 1995).

17. See *Monaco v. Mississippi*, 292 U.S. 313 (1934).

SELECTED BIBLIOGRAPHY

Beer, Samuel. *To Make a Nation: The Rediscovery of American Federalism*. Cambridge, MA: Harvard University Press, 1993.

Berger, Raoul. *Federalism: The Founders' Design*. Norman: University of Oklahoma Press, 1987.

Chemerinsky, Erwin. *Enhancing Government: Federalism for the 21st Century*. Palo Alto, CA: Stanford University Press, 2008.

Elkins, Stanley, and Mckitrick, Eric. *The Age of Federalism*. New York: Oxford University Press, 1993.

Greve, Michael S. *Real Federalism: Why It Matters, How It Could Happen*. Washington, DC: American Enterprise Institute, 1999.

Kincaid, John, and G.A. Tarr, eds., *Constitutional Origins, Structure, and Change in Federal Countries*. Montreal: McGill-Queens University Press, 2005.

Marbach, Joseph, Katz, Ellis, and Smith, Troy, eds. *Federalism in America: An Encyclopedia*. Westport, CT: Greenwood Press, 2006.

Nicolaidis, Kalypso, and Howse, Robert, eds. *The Federal Vision: Legitimacy and Levels of Governance in the United States and the European Union*. New York: Oxford University Press, 2002.

Noonan, John. *Narrowing the Nation's Power: The Supreme Court Sides with the States*. Berkeley: University of California Press, 2002.

Redish, Martin H. *The Constitution as Political Structure*. New York: Oxford University Press, 1995.

Waltenberg, Eric, and Swinford, Bill. *Litigating Federalism: The States before the Supreme Court*. Westport, CT: Greenwood Press, 1999.

Watts, Ronald L. *Comparing Federal Systems*. 2d ed. Montreal: McGill-Queen's University Press, 1999.

■ IN COMPARATIVE PERSPECTIVE

Federalism, Federations, and Confederations

In revising the Articles of Confederation in 1787, the Constitutional Convention rejected the premise of that document and the prevailing European theory of sovereign state by recognizing instead that sovereignty resides in the people and that units of government—national, state, and local—exercise only delegated powers. Most other contemporary federal systems have borrowed from the American model of federalism because of its success in promoting political unification and integration, while also allowing for power sharing in intergovernmental relations and for setting limits on governmental authority.

The three other principal models for contemporary federalism are the Canadian, German, and Swiss systems. Canada combines a federal system with a parliamentary form of government that has authority to legislate on all matters pertaining to "peace, order, and good government." The system was established in 1867, in part to prevent the conflicts similar to those between the states that led to the American Civil War. In each of the ten provinces, the lieutenant governor is appointed by the prime minister and must approve any provincial law before it goes into effect. The legislative powers of the provinces are thus checked and limited. However, the provinces retain residual powers, and unlike the U.S. Supreme Court, the Canadian judiciary has generally encouraged decentralization in recognition of its multicultural society. As a consequence, Canadian provinces exercise greater power and the national government is weaker than in the United States. In addition, the special status claimed by French-speaking Quebec has led to intergovernmental relations that alternate between periods of centralization and decentralization.

The Federal Republic of Germany, whose Basic Laws of 1949 became the constitution with the reunification of East and West Germany in 1990, is often referred to as an example of cooperative federalism. Its sixteen states, or länder, exercise a great deal of power, far more than states do in the United States. The central government has a president and a bicameral parliament composed of an upper house, the Federal Council, and a lower house, the National Assembly, as well as an independent judiciary. The central government has exclusive authority over foreign affairs, money, immigration, and telecommunications. But the länder retain residual powers over all other matters and have concurrent powers over civil and criminal law, health, and the public welfare. Moreover, national legislation does not become law unless approved by a majority of the

Federal Council, whose members are selected by legislatures in the länder, not by popular elections.

Switzerland established a confederation on the basis of regional governments (cantons). The cantons reflect the ethnic and linguistic differences of their German-, French-, and Italian-speaking populations. All three languages are officially recognized by the central government. But of the twenty-two cantons, eighteen are unilingual, three are bilingual, and one is trilingual. They exercise most lawmaking powers and are represented in the National Council, a bicameral legislature, and the Council of States. In 2000, a new federal constitution was adopted that further entrenches the triparite division of powers at the levels of the federal government, the cantons, and the municipalities.

Among the countries with federal systems are these:

Argentine Republic	Malaysia
Commonwealth of Australia	United Mexican States
Federal Republic of Austria	Islamic Republic of Pakistan
Federative Republic of Brazil	Russian Federation
Canada	Swiss Confederation
Federal Islamic Republic of	United Arab Emirates
Comoros	United States of America
Federal Republic of Germany	Republic of Venezuela
Republic of India	

In addition, a number of other countries have federal relations or decentralized arrangements within a unitary government. Those countries include Belgium, South Africa, and the United Kingdom of Great Britain and Northern Ireland.

Finally, with the emergence of permanent multinational communities and the dissolution of the former Soviet Union, there is a kind of revival in the formation of confederations and confederal arrangements of sovereign states, largely due to the forces of international economic competition and the goal of promoting economic common markets through the elimination of trade barriers. The European Union is a prime example, but there are others, such as the Association of the South East Asian Nations (ASEAN).

For further reading see Kalypso Nicolaidis and Robert Howse, eds., *The Federal Vision: Legitimacy and Levels of Government in the United States and the European Union* (New York: Oxford University Press, 2002); John Kincaid and G. Alan Tarr, eds., *A Global Dialogue on Federalism* (Montreal: McGill-Queen's University Press, 2005); and Ann L. Griffiths, ed., *Handbook of Federal Countries 2005* (Montreal; McGill-Queen's University Press, 2005).

A | States' Power over Commerce and Regulation

Congress's ineffective regulation of commerce, as Madison explained in the *Federalist*, No. 42, was a central problem with the Articles of Confederation. For that reason, Article I of the Constitution specifically empowers Congress "to regulate commerce with foreign nations, and among the several states, and with Indian tribes (as examined in Chapter 6)."

Congress remained reluctant to assert its authority over commerce until the late nineteenth century. But in *Gibbons v. Ogden*, 9 Wheat. 1 (1824) (see Vol. 1, Ch. 6). Chief Justice John Marshall set forth an enduring principle of constitutional law. He held that Congress's power is plenary and does not stop at state lines, while defining *commerce* as all "intercourse" that "affects more states than one." His standard for determining the scope of congressional power was nationalist and immediately heralded for securing the freedom of interstate transportation. As a result, tax and other barriers erected among the states were eliminated, the basis for a national "common market" was laid, and economic growth in the country was promoted.

In *Gibbons*, though, Marshall also implied a distinction between Congress's power over *interstate* commerce and that of the states over *intrastate* commerce. "[T]he completely internal commerce of a State," he noted, "may be considered as reserved for the State itself." Under Marshall's successor, Chief Justice Taney, the Court proved much more sympathetic to state power over commerce. In *Mayor of City of New York v. Miln*, 36 U.S. (11 Pet.) 102 (1837), for example, the Taney Court upheld a New York law aimed at discouraging the immigration of indigents. The law required shipmasters entering New York's port from another state or country to report on their passengers and, if demanded by the mayor, to pay bonds for foreign passengers who later went on welfare rolls. When holding that the law was an exercise of state police powers, akin to inspection laws and "not a regulation of commerce," Justice Philip Barbour explained, "We think it as competent and as necessary for a State to provide precautionary measures against the moral pestilence of paupers, vagabonds, and possibly convicts, as it is to guard against the physical pestilence which may arise from unsound and infectious articles imported, or from a ship, the crew of which may be laboring under an infectious disease." But dissenting Justice Joseph Story, who was a leading intellectual influence as a Harvard law school professor and Chief Justice Marshall's closest ally on the Court, countered that the law was an unconstitutional restraint on interstate commerce and fell "directly within the principles established in the case of *Gibbons v. Ogden.*"

The Taney Court's interpretation in *Miln* was extreme and is no longer controlling. In *Edwards v. California*, 314 U.S. 160 (1941), the Court unanimously struck down California's law making it a misdemeanor to knowingly bring an indigent into the state. A majority agreed that California's law was "an unconstitutional barrier to interstate commerce," while four other justices deemed the law to violate a fundamental right to interstate travel. The Court further repudiated *Miln* in *Shapiro v. Thompson*, 394 U.S. 618 (1969), when holding that states may not impose one-year residency requirements as a condition for receiving public assistance.

Of far more lasting significance than *Miln* is *Cooley v. The Board of Wardens of the Port of Philadelphia* (1852) (see excerpt below), in which the Taney Court held that in some areas the regulation of commerce is a shared power of national and state governments. And for the first time the Court grappled with the issue of what standard should be employed in drawing the line differentiating the areas of permissible state regulation from those exclusively subject to Congress's power under the commerce clause.

The commerce clause is not, of course, self-interpreting. And there have been four rival interpretive theories of the relationship between the national government and the states in regulating commerce. In *Gibbons*, Marshall rejected Ogden's argument that there is a *concurrent power* over commerce, akin to the taxing power that both national and state governments may exercise. On this theory, no area of commerce would be exclusively reserved for Congress. Under the supremacy clause of Article VI, federal regulation would displace that of the states, but states could regulate in the absence of federal regulation. Marshall, though, rejected this theory and the analogy drawn between the powers to tax and to regulate commerce.

Justice William Johnson's concurring opinion in *Gibbons* advanced what has been called the *dormant power* theory. On this interpretation, the commerce clause would bar state regulation of commerce regardless of whether Congress had exercised its powers over commerce. Marshall took no position on this theory in *Gibbons*, but a majority embraced it in *The Passenger Cases*, 7 How. 283 (1849), holding that state taxing power is limited over interstate commerce by the "affirmative grants of power to the general government."[1] However, writing for the Court in *Cooley*, Justice Benjamin Curtis rejected this theory.

Curtis also rejected a third interpretation, that of *mutual exclusiveness*. In *Gibbons*, Marshall appeared to accept this view when rejecting

Chief Justice Roger B. Taney. A photograph (the subject's name is misspelled on the mat but is the correct pronunciation) taken in the 1850s. (*National Portrait Gallery, Smithsonian Institution.*)

the concurrent powers theory and noting that states could regulate internal commerce with inspection and health laws, for example, as well as "everything within the territory of a State, not surrendered to [the] general government."

In *Cooley*, Curtis proposed a fourth theory, that of *selective exclusiveness*. According to this theory, Congress's power is complete and exclusive in some areas, while in others the states are free to regulate commerce. As to the standard for distinguishing the subjects of national versus state regulation, Curtis proposed, "Whatever subjects of this power are in their nature national, or admit only of one uniform system, or plan of regulation, may justly be said to be of such a nature as to require exclusive legislation by Congress."

As a result of the Court's writing the theory of selective exclusiveness into the constitutional law of the commerce clause, it inevitably had to define the categories subject to state regulation and those exclusively reserved for Congress. Central to the Court's subsequent interpretation and line drawing has been whether or not states regulate commerce in the absence of federal legislation.

In those areas where Congress has not yet legislated—the so-called *dormant commerce clause*—the Court applies the standard set down in *Cooley.* State regulation is valid if the activity is basically local and the Court determines there is no need for a uniform national standard. In *Bob-Lo Excursion Co. v. Michigan,* 333 U.S. 28 (1948), for example, Michigan's civil rights act was upheld as applied against an amusement park running an excursion steamer to an island on the Canadian side of the Detroit river. Bob-Lo Excursion Company refused to transport blacks and contended that the state law was inapplicable because it was engaged in foreign commerce and hence subject only to congressional legislation. The Court rejected that claim, observing, "It is difficult to imagine what national interest or policy, whether of securing uniformity in regulating commerce, affecting relations with foreign nations or otherwise, could reasonably be found to be adversely affected by applying Michigan's statute to those facts or to outweigh her interest in doing so."

When determining whether an activity subject to state regulation is "essentially local," the Court considers the burden placed on interstate commerce by a state regulation. *South Carolina Highway Department v. Barnwell Brothers,* 303 U.S. 177 (1938), upheld a state law forbidding on state highways trucks and trailers wider than ninety inches and weighing more than 20,000 pounds, despite its being stricter than the laws of surrounding states. However, *Southern Pacific Co. v. Arizona* (1945) (see excerpt below), overturned a regulation of the length of trains as an undue burden on interstate commerce, touching a subject requiring a national standard. See also *Bibb v. Navajo Freight Lines, Inc.* (1959) (see excerpt below).

A related controversy involves whether state regulation aims to discriminate against businesses in other states so as to erect commercial or other barriers. In such controversies, the Court must decide whether a state regulation is too burdensome and what kinds and levels of burdens are acceptable. *Maine v. Taylor* (1986) (see excerpt below) is instructive on the Court's analysis of this kind of controversy.

In a significant ruling that could increase the number of dormant commerce clause cases coming to the Court, *Wyoming v. Oklahoma,* 502 U.S. 437 (1992) (further discussed in Ch. 2), extended standing to states to challenge the constitutionality of other states' regulations under the commerce clause on the grounds that those regulations diminished the state's tax revenues.

When Congress has enacted legislation regulating interstate commerce, challenges to state regulation require the Court to decide

■ CONSTITUTIONAL HISTORY

The Court's Rulings on Federal Preemption of State Laws in Historical Perspective

The Court in a series of recent rulings has sharply limited the federal government's regulatory powers by limiting Congress's power to enact legislation under the Interstate Commerce Clause and Section 5 of the Fourteenth Amendment (as discussed in Vol. 1, Ch. 6), as well as under the Tenth and Eleventh Amendments (as discussed in the next section). However, the Court continues to uphold federal preemption of state laws. The tables below put the Court's record into historical perspective.

RULINGS ON STATUTORY FEDERAL PREEMPTION, 1921–2009

COURT	NUMBER	UPHELD PREEMPTION (%)	STATE OR LOCAL LAWS NOT PREEMPTED (%)
Taft Court (1921–1930)	2	1 (50)	1 (50)
Hughes Court (1930–1941)	6	3 (50)	3 (50)
Stone Court (1941–1946)	6	4 (66)	2 (33)
Vinson Court (1946–1953)	4	3 (75)	1 (25)
Warren Court (1953–1969)	33	18 (55)	15 (45)
Burger Court (1969–1986)	77	36 (46)	41 (53)
Rehnquist Court (1986–2005)	106	57 (54)	49 (45)
Roberts Court (2005–)	9	5 (55)	4 (44)
Total	243	127 (52)	116 (47)

RULINGS ON PREEMPTION IN THE ABSENCE OF A CONGRESSIONAL STATUTE, DORMANT COMMERCE CLAUSE CASES, 1921–2009

COURT	NUMBER	UPHELD PREEMPTION (%)	STATE OR LOCAL LAWS NOT PREEMPTED (%)
Taft Court (1921–1930)	2	1 (50)	1 (50)
Hughes Court (1930–1941)	1		1 (100)
Stone Court (1941–1946)	3	3 (100)	
Vinson Court (1946–1953)			
Warren Court (1953–1969)	4	1 (25)	3 (75)
Burger Court (1969–1986)	20	8 (40)	12 (60)
Rehnquist Court (1986–2005)	33	20 (60)	13 (40)
Roberts Court (2005–)	2	1 (50)	1(50)
Total	65	34 (52)	31 (48)

Source: David M. O'Brien, "The Rehnquist Court and Federal Preemption: In Search of a Theory," *23 Publius: The Journal of Federalism* 15 (1993), and as updated by the author in consultation and with appreciation for the database constructed by Michael Greve and Kim Hendrickson of the American Enterprise Institute, and as updated by the author through the Court's October 2009–2010 term.

whether Congress has completely occupied the field and whether states may still enact nonconflicting legislation. Since *McCulloch v. Maryland*, 4 Wheat. 316 (1819) (excerpted in Ch. 6), the Court has maintained that federal legislation preempts conflicting state regulation under the supremacy clause of Article VI.[2]

Cooley's holding that some subjects are inherently local far from solved the problem of determining which subjects are "national" and which are exclusively "local." In the early nineteenth century, the Court attempted to resolve this problem in several ways. In *Brown v. Maryland*, 25 U.S. 419 (1827), the Marshall Court ruled that states could not tax items of interstate commerce as long as they remained in their "original package."[3] And in *Wilson v. Black Bird Creek Marsh Co.*, 27 U.S. 245 (1829), the Marshall Court suggested that the purpose of legislation may be important, when ruling that a state's authorization for a dam on a stream deep enough to be used by boats in interstate commerce did not violate the commerce clause.

Rather than attempting to define activities that are inherently local or determine the purpose of state legislation, the Court now generally employs the *doctrine of federal preemption*—that Congress has preempted state regulation in an area by its own legislation. Sometimes a federal statute expressly preempts state regulation. In *Shaw v. Delta Air Lines*, 463 U.S. 85 (1983), the Court held that the federal Employment Retirement Income Security Act (ERISA) preempted "all State laws insofar as they . . . relate to any employee benefit plan." In other circumstances, though, Congress may not explicitly state that it is preempting state regulation, and the Court must analyze the costs and benefits of state regulation under the federal preemption doctrine. The doctrine has been applied in a large number of areas. In *Pennsylvania v. Nelson* (1956) (see excerpt below), Chief Justice Warren outlined the basic considerations in applying the doctrine. Other important rulings limiting state regulatory powers are *Missouri v. Holland*, 252 U.S. 416 (1920) (excerpted in Vol. 1, Ch. 3); *Steward Machine Co. v. Davis*, 301 U.S. 548 (1937) (excerpted in Vol. 1, Ch. 6); and *South Dakota v. Dole*, 483 U.S. 203 (1987) (excerpted in Vol. 1, Ch. 6).

Notes

1. See also *The License Cases*, 5 How. 504 (1847).

2. See also *Havenstein v. Lynham*, 100 U.S. 483 (1880).

3. See also *Leisy v. Hardin*, 135 U.S. 100 (1890). *Brown v. Maryland*, however, was limited in *Michigan Tire Co. v. Wages*, 423 U.S. 276 (1976).

Selected Bibliography

Corwin, Edward S. *The Commerce Clause versus States Rights.* Princeton, NJ: Princeton University Press, 1936.

Frankfurter, Felix. *The Commerce Clause.* Introduction by Wallace Mendelson. Chicago: Quadrangle, 1964.

Goodman, Frank, ed. *The Supreme Court's Federalism: Real or Imagined?* Thousand Oaks, CA: Sage, 2001.

Zimmerman, Joseph F. *Congressional Preemption; Regulatory Federalism.* Albany: State University of New York, 2005.

Cooley v. The Board of Wardens of the Port of Philadelphia
12 How. (53 U.S.) 229 (1851)

In 1803, Pennsylvania passed a law requiring, with certain exceptions, ships entering or leaving Philadelphia's harbor to employ a pilot from the city to navigate and provided that shipowners who failed to comply were required to pay one-half of the pilotage fees into a pilot's pension fund. When two of Aaron Cooley's ships did not use local pilots, the Board of Wardens of the Port of Philadelphia sued in a court of common pleas, which found in their favor. The Pennsylvania Supreme Court affirmed, and Cooley appealed to the Supreme Court, arguing that the law was an unconstitutional tax on commerce and not a pilot regulation, since Congress had passed in 1789 a law permitting the states to regulate pilots.

The Court's decision was seven to two, and the opinion was announced by Justice Curtis. A separate opinion, concurring in the decision but dissenting from the Court's reasoning, was delivered by Justice Daniel. Justices Wayne and McLean dissented.

☐ *Justice CURTIS delivers the opinion of the court.*

That the power to regulate commerce includes the regulation of navigation, we consider settled. And when we look to the nature of the service performed by pilots, to the relations which that service and its compensations bear to navigation between the several States, and between the ports of the United States, and foreign countries, we are brought to the conclusion, that the regulation of the qualifications of pilots, of the modes and times of offering and rendering their services, of the responsibilities which shall rest upon them, of the powers they shall possess, of the compensation they may demand, and of the penalties by which their rights and duties may be enforced, do constitute regulations of navigation, and consequently of commerce, within the just meaning of this clause of the Constitution. . . .

It becomes necessary, therefore, to consider whether this law of Pennsylvania, being a regulation of commerce, is valid.

The Act of Congress of the 7th of August, 1789, sec. 4, is as follows:

> That all pilots in the bays, inlets, rivers, harbors, and ports of the United States, shall continue to be regulated in conformity with the existing laws of the States, respectively, wherein such pilots may be, or with such laws as the States may respectively hereafter enact for the purpose, until further legislative provision shall be made by Congress.

If the law of Pennsylvania, now in question, had been in existence at the date of this Act of Congress, we might hold it to have been adopted by Congress, and thus made a law of the United States, and so valid. Because this Act does, in effect, give the force of an Act of Congress, to the then existing state laws on this subject, so long as they should continue unrepealed by the State which enacted them.

But the law on which these actions are founded was not enacted till 1803. What effect, then, can be attributed to so much of the Act of 1789 as declares that pilots shall continue to be regulated in conformity "with such laws as the States may respectively hereafter enact for the purpose, until further legislative provision shall be made by Congress?"

If the States were divested of the power to legislate on this subject by the grant of the commercial power to Congress, it is plain this Act could not confer upon them power thus to legislate. If the Constitution excluded the States from making any law regulating commerce, certainly Congress cannot regrant, or in any manner reconvey to the States that power. And yet this Act of 1789 gives its sanction only to laws enacted by the States. This necessarily implies a constitutional power to legislate; for only a rule created by the sovereign power of a state acting in its legislative capacity, can be deemed a law, enacted by a state; and if the State has so limited its sovereign power that it no longer extends to a particular subject, manifestly it cannot, in any proper sense, be said to enact laws thereon. Entertaining these views we are brought directly and unavoidably to the consideration of the question, whether the grant of the commercial power to Congress, did per se deprive the States of all power to regulate pilots. This question has never been decided by this court, nor, in our judgment, has any case depending upon all the considerations which must govern this one, come before this court. The grant of commercial power to Congress does not contain any terms which expressly exclude the States from exercising an authority over its subject matter. If they are excluded it must be because the nature of the power, thus granted to Congress, requires that a similar authority should not exist in the States. If it were conceded on the one side, that the nature of this power, like that to legislate for the District of Columbia, is absolutely and totally repugnant to the existence of similar power in the States, probably no one would deny that the grant of the power to Congress, as effectually and perfectly excludes the States from all future legislation on the subject, as if express words had been used to exclude them. And on the other hand, if it were admitted that the existence of this power in Congress, like the power of taxation, is compatible with the existence of a similar power in the States, then it would be in conformity with the contemporary exposition of the Constitution (*Federalist*, No. 32), and with the judicial construction, given from time to time by this court, after the most deliberate consideration, to hold that the mere grant of such a power to Congress, did not imply a prohibition on the States to exercise the same power; that it is not the mere existence of such a power, but its exercise by Congress, which may be in-compatible with the exercise of the same power by the States, and that the States may legislate in the absence of congressional regulations. . . .

The diversities of opinion, therefore, which have existed on this subject, have arisen from the different views taken of the nature of this power. But when the nature of a power like this is spoken of, when it is said that the nature of the power requires that it should be exercised exclusively by Congress, it must be intended to refer to the subjects of that power, and to say they are of such a nature as to require exclusive legislation by Congress. Now, the power to regulate commerce, embraces a vast field, containing not only many, but exceedingly various subjects, quite unlike in their nature; some imperatively demanding a single uniform rule, operating equally on the commerce of the United States in every port; and some like the subject now in question, as imperatively demanding that diversity, which alone can meet the local necessities of navigation.

Either absolutely to affirm, or deny, that the nature of this power requires exclusive legislation by Congress, is to lose sight of the nature of the subjects of this power, and to assert concerning all of them, what is really applicable but to a part. Whatever subjects of this power are in their nature national, or admit only of one uniform system, or plan of regulation, may justly be said to be of such a nature as to require exclusive legislation by Congress. That this cannot be affirmed of laws for the regulation of pilots and pilotage is plain. The Act of 1789 contains a clear and authoritative declaration by the first Congress, that the nature of this subject is such, that until Congress should find it necessary to exert its power, it should be left to the legislation of the States; that it is local and not national; that it is likely to be the best provided for, not by one system, or plan of regulations, but by as many as the legislative discretion of the several States should deem applicable to the local peculiarities of the ports within their limits.

Viewed in this light, so much of this Act of 1789 as declares that pilots shall continue to be regulated "by such laws as the States may respectively hereafter enact for that purpose," instead of being held to be inoperative, as an attempt to confer on the States a power to legislate, of which the Constitution had deprived them, is allowed an appropriate and important signification. It manifests the understanding of Congress, at the outset of the government, that the nature of this subject is not such as to require its exclusive legislation. The practice of the States, and of the national government, has been in conformity with this declaration, from the origin of the national government to this time; and the nature of the subject, when examined, is such as to leave no doubt of the superior fitness and propriety, not to say the absolute necessity, of different systems of regulation, drawn from local knowledge and experience, and conformed to local wants. How, then, can we say, that by the mere grant of power to regulate commerce, the States are deprived of all the power to legislate on this subject, because from the nature of the power the legislation of Congress must be exclusive. This would be to affirm that the nature of the power is, in any case, something different from the nature of the subject to which, in such case, the power extends, and that the nature of the power necessarily demands, in all cases, exclusive legislation by Congress, while the nature of one of the subjects of that power, not only does not require such exclusive legislation, but may be best provided for by many different systems enacted by the States, in conformity with the circumstances of the ports within their limits. In construing an instrument designed for the formation of a government, and in determining the extent of one of its important grants of power to legislate, we can make no such distinction between the nature of the power and the nature of the subject on which that power was intended practically to operate, nor consider the grant more extensive by affirming of the power, what is not true of its subject now in question.

It is the opinion of a majority of the court that the mere grant to Congress of the power to regulate commerce, did not deprive the States of power to regulate pilots, and that although Congress has legislated on this subject, its legislation manifests an intention, with a single exception, not to regulate this subject, but to leave its regulation to the several States. To these precise questions, which are all we are called on to decide, this opinion must be understood to be confined. It does not extend to the question what other subjects, under the commercial power, are within the exclusive control of Congress, or may be regulated by the States in the absence of all congressional legislation; nor to the general question how far any regulation of a subject by Congress may be deemed to operate as an exclusion of all legislation by the States upon the same subject. We decide the precise questions before us, upon what we deem sound principles, applicable to this particular subject in the state in which the legislation of Congress has left it. We go no farther. . . .

We are of opinion that this state law was enacted by virtue of a power, residing in the State to legislate; that it is not in conflict with any law of Congress; that it does not interfere with any system which Congress has established by making regulations, or by intentionally leaving individuals to their own unrestricted action; that this law is therefore valid, and the judgement of the Supreme Court of Pennsylvania in each case must be affirmed.

☐ *Justice McLEAN, dissenting.*

It is with regret that I feel myself obliged to dissent from the opinion of a majority of my brethren in this case.

As expressing my views on the question involved, I will copy a few sentences from the opinion of Chief Justice MARSHALL in the opinion in *Gibbons v. Ogden*. "It has been said," says that illustrious judge, "that the Act of August 7th, 1789, acknowledges a concurrent power in the States to regulate the conduct of pilots, and hence is inferred an admission of their concurrent right with Congress to regulate commerce with foreign nations and amongst the States. But this inference is not, we think, justified by the fact." . . .

"The Act unquestionably manifests an intention to leave this subject entirely to the States, until Congress should think proper to interpose; but the very enactment of such a law indicates an opinion that it was necessary; that the existing system would not be applicable to the new state of things, unless expressly applied to it by Congress. But this section is confined to pilots within the bays, inlets, rivers, harbors, and ports of the United States, which are, of course, in whole or in part, also within the limits of some particular state. The acknowledged power of a state to regulate its police, its domestic trade, and to govern its own citizens, may enable it to legislate on this subject, to a considerable extent; and the adoption of its system by Congress, and the application of it to the whole subject of commerce, does not seem to the court to imply a right in the States so to apply it of their own authority. But the adoption of the state system being temporary, being only 'until further legislative provision shall be made by Congress,' shows conclusively, an opinion that Congress could control the whole subject, and might adopt the system of the States or provide one of its own."

Why did Congress pass the Act of 1789, adopting the pilot laws of the respective States? Laws they unquestionably were, having been enacted by the States before the adoption of the Constitution. But were they laws under the Constitution? If they had been so considered by Congress, they would not have been adopted by a special Act. There is believed to be no instance in the legislation of Congress, where a state law has been adopted, which, before its adoption, applied to federal powers. To suppose such a case, would be an imputation of ignorance as to federal powers, least of all chargeable against the men who formed the Constitution and who best understood it.

Congress adopted the pilot laws of the States, because it was well understood, they could have had no force, as regulations of foreign commerce or of commerce among the States, if not so adopted. By their adoption they were made Acts of Congress, and ever since they have been so considered and enforced.

Each State regulates the commerce within its limits; which is not within the range of federal powers. So far, and no farther could effect have been given to the pilot laws of the States, under the Constitution. But those laws were only adopted "until further legislative provisions shall be made by Congress."

This shows that Congress claimed the whole commercial power on this subject, by adopting the pilot laws of the States, making them Acts of Congress; and also by declaring that the adoption was only until some further legislative provision could be made by Congress.

☐ *Justice DANIEL, concurring in the judgment and dissenting from the Court's reasoning.*

I agree with the majority in their decision, that the judgments of the Supreme Court of Pennsylvania in these cases should be affirmed, though I cannot go with them in the process or argument by which their conclusion has been reached. . . . The power delegated to Congress by the Constitution relates properly to the terms on which commercial engagements may be prosecuted; the character of the articles which they may embrace; the permission or terms according to which they may be introduced; and do not necessarily nor even naturally extend to the means of precaution and safety adopted within the waters or limits of the States by the authority of the latter for the preservation of vessels and cargoes, and the lives of navigators or passengers. These last subjects are essentially local—they must depend upon local necessities which call them into existence, must differ according to the degrees of that necessity. It is admitted, on all hands, that they cannot be uniform or even general, but must vary so as to meet the purposes to be accomplished. . . . The true question here is, whether the power to enact pilot laws is appropriate and necessary, or rather most appropriate and necessary to the State or the federal governments. It being conceded that this power has been exercised by the States from their very dawn of existence; that it can be practically and beneficially applied by the local authorities only; it being conceded, as it must be, that the power to pass pilot laws, as such, has not been in any express terms delegated to Congress, and does not necessarily conflict with the right to establish commercial regulations, I am forced to conclude that this is an original and inherent power in the States, and not one to be merely tolerated, or held subject to the sanction of the federal government.

Southern Pacific Co. v. Arizona

325 U.S. 761, 65 S.Ct. 1515 (1945)

In 1940, Arizona's state attorney general sued the Southern Pacific Company for operating two interstate trains in violation of the state's Train Limit Law of 1912, prohibiting the operation of trains with more than fourteen passenger or seventy freight cars. Attorneys for the company attacked the constitutionality of the law on grounds that it violated the commerce clause and the due process clause of the Fourteenth Amendment. The trial court found in favor of the Southern Pacific Company but the Supreme Court of Arizona reversed. Southern Pacific then appealed to the Supreme Court.

The Court's decision was seven to two, and the majority's opinion was announced by Chief Justice Stone. Justice Rutledge concurred, and Justices Black and Douglas dissented.

☐ *Chief Justice STONE delivers the opinion of the Court.*

Although the commerce clause conferred on the national government power to regulate commerce, its possession of the power does not exclude all state power of regulation. . . . [I]t has been recognized that, in the absence of conflicting legislation by Congress, there is a residuum of power in the state to make laws governing matters of local concern which nevertheless in some measure affect interstate commerce or even, to some extent, regulate it. . . . Thus the states may regulate matters which, because of their number and diversity, may never be adequately dealt with by Congress. . . . When the regulation of matters of local concern is local in character and effect, and its impact on the national commerce does not seriously interfere with its operation, and the consequent incentive to deal with them nationally is slight, such regulation has been generally held to be within state authority.

But ever since *Gibbons v. Ogden*, the states have not been deemed to have authority to impede substantially the free flow of commerce from state to state, or to regulate those phases of the national commerce which, because of the need of national uniformity, demand that their regulation, if any, be prescribed by a single authority. Whether or not this long recognized distribution of power between the national and the state governments is predicated upon the implications of the commerce clause itself, or upon the presumed intention of Congress, where Congress has not spoken, the result is the same.

In the application of these principles some enactments may be found to be plainly within and others plainly without state power. But between these extremes lies the infinite variety of cases in which regulation of local matters may also operate as a regulation of commerce, in which reconciliation of the conflicting claims of state and national power is to be attained only by some appraisal and accommodation of the competing demands of the state and national interests involved. . . .

For a hundred years it has been accepted constitutional doctrine that the commerce clause, without the aid of Congressional legislation, thus affords some protection from state legislation inimical to the national commerce, and that in such cases, where Congress has not acted, this Court, and not the state legislature, is under the commerce clause the final arbiter of the competing demands of state and national interests. . . .

Congress has undoubted power to redefine the distribution of power over interstate commerce. It may either permit the states to regulate the commerce in a manner which would otherwise not be permissible, or exclude state regulation even of matters of peculiarly local concern which nevertheless affect interstate commerce. . . .

But in general Congress has left it to the courts to formulate the rules thus interpreting the commerce clause in its application, doubtless because it has appreciated the destructive consequences to the commerce of the nation if their protection were withdrawn and has been aware that in their application state laws will not be invalidated without the support of relevant factual material which will "afford a sure basis" for an informed judgment. Meanwhile, Congress has accommodated its legislation, as have the states, to these rules as an established feature of our constitutional system. There has thus been left to the states wide scope for the regulation of matters of local state concern, even though it in some measure affects the commerce, provided it does not materially restrict the free flow of commerce across state lines, or interfere with it in matters with respect to which uniformity of regulation is of predominant national concern.

Hence the matters for ultimate determination here are the nature and extent of the burden which the state regulation of interstate trains, adopted as a safety measure, imposes on interstate commerce, and whether the relative weights of the state and national interests involved are such as to make inapplicable the rule, generally observed, that the free flow of interstate commerce and its freedom from local restraints in matters requiring uniformity of regulation are interests safeguarded by the commerce clause from state interference. . . .

The findings show that the operation of long trains, that is trains of more than fourteen passenger and more than seventy freight cars, is standard practice over the main lines of the railroads of the United States, and that, if the length of trains is to be regulated at all, national uniformity in the regulation adopted, such as only Congress can prescribe, is practically indispensable to the operation of an efficient and economical national railway system. On many railroads passenger trains of more than fourteen cars and freight trains of more than seventy cars are operated, and on some systems freight trains are run ranging from one hundred and twenty-five to one hundred and sixty cars in length. . . .

In Arizona, approximately 93% of the freight traffic and 95% of the passenger traffic is interstate. Because of the Train Limit Law appellant is required to haul over 30% more trains in Arizona than would otherwise have been necessary. The record shows a definite relationship between operating costs and the length of trains, the increase in length resulting in a reduction of operating costs per car. The additional cost of operation of trains complying with the Train Limit Law in Arizona amounts for the two railroads traversing that state to about $1,000,000 a year. The reduction in train lengths also impedes efficient operation. More locomotives and more manpower are required; the necessary conversion and reconversion of train lengths at terminals and the delay caused by breaking up and remaking long trains upon entering and leaving the state in order to comply with the law, delays the traffic and diminishes its volume moved in a given time, especially when traffic is heavy. . . .

The unchallenged findings leave no doubt that the Arizona Train Limit Law imposes a serious burden on the interstate commerce conducted by appellant. It materially impedes the movement of appellant's interstate trains through that state and interposes a substantial obstruction to the national policy proclaimed by Congress, to promote adequate, economical and efficient railway transportation service. Enforcement of the law in Arizona, while train lengths remain unregulated or are regulated by varying standards in other states, must inevitably result in an impairment of uniformity of efficient railroad operation because the railroads are subjected to regulation which is not uniform in its application. . . .

We think, as the trial court found, that the Arizona Train Limit Law, viewed as a safety measure, affords at most slight and dubious advantage, if any, over unregulated train lengths. . . .

Here we conclude that the state does go too far. Its regulation of train lengths, admittedly obstructive to interstate train operation, and having a seriously adverse effect on transportation efficiency and economy, passes beyond what is plainly essential for safety since it does not appear that it will lessen rather than increase the danger of accident. Its attempted regulation of the operation of interstate trains cannot establish nation-wide control such as is essential to the maintenance of an efficient transportation system, which Congress alone can prescribe. The state interest cannot be preserved at the expense of the national interest by an enactment which regulates interstate train lengths without securing such control, which is a matter of national concern. To this the interest of the state here asserted is subordinate. . . .

 ☐ *Justice BLACK, dissenting.*

[W]hether it is in the interest of society for the length of trains to be governmentally regulated is a matter of public policy. Someone must fix that policy—either the Congress, or the state, or the courts. A century and a half of constitutional history and government admonishes this Court to leave that choice to the elected legislative representatives of the people themselves, where it properly belongs both on democratic principles and the requirements of efficient government.

 ☐ *Justice DOUGLAS, dissenting.*

My view has been that the courts should intervene only where the state legislation discriminated against interstate commerce or was out of harmony with laws which Congress had enacted. It seems to me particularly appropriate that that course be followed here. For Congress has given the Interstate Commerce Commission broad powers of regulation over interstate carriers. The Commission is the national agency which has been entrusted with the task of promoting a safe, adequate, efficient, and economical transportation service. It is the expert on this subject. It is in a position to police the field. And if its powers prove inadequate for the task, Congress, which has paramount authority in this field, can implement them. . . .

Whether the question arises under the Commerce Clause or the Fourteenth Amendment, I think the legislation is entitled to a presumption of validity. If a State passed a law prohibiting the hauling of more than one freight car at a time, we would have a situation comparable in effect to a state law requiring all railroads within its borders to operate on narrow gauge tracks. The question is one of degree and calls for a close appraisal of the facts. I am not persuaded that the evidence adduced by the railroads overcomes the presumption of validity to which this train limit law is entitled.

Bibb v. Navajo Freight Lines, Inc.
359 U.S. 520, 79 S.CT. 962 (1959)

Attorneys for Navajo Freight Lines, Inc., a New Mexico corporation, sought an injunction in federal district court against the enforcement of an Illinois law requiring all trucks and trailers to have special mudguards, unlike those required in other states. A federal district court found this an undue burden on interstate commerce. Joseph Bibb, the director of Illinois's Department of Public Safety, appealed to the Supreme Court.

The Court's decision was unanimous, and the opinion was announced by Justice Douglas. Justice Harlan concurred and was joined by Justice Stewart.

☐ *Justice DOUGLAS delivers the opinion of the Court.*

We are asked in this case to hold that an Illinois statute requiring the use of a certain type of rear fender mudguard on trucks and trailers operated on the highways of that State conflicts with the Commerce Clause of the Constitution. . . .

The power of the State to regulate the use of its highways is broad and pervasive. We have recognized the peculiarly local nature of this subject of safety, and have upheld state statutes applicable alike to interstate and intrastate commerce, despite the fact that they may have an impact on interstate commerce. The regulation of highways "is akin to quarantine measures, game laws, and like local regulations of rivers, harbors, piers, and docks, with respect to which the state has exceptional scope for the exercise of its regulatory power, and which, Congress not acting, have been sustained even though they materially interfere with interstate commerce." *Southern Pacific Co. v. State of Arizona.* . . .

These safety measures carry a strong presumption of validity when challenged in court. If there are alternative ways of solving a problem, we do not sit to determine which of them is best suited to achieve a valid state objective. Policy decisions are for the state legislature, absent federal entry into the field. Unless we can conclude on the whole record that "the total effect of the law as a safety measure in reducing accidents and casualties is so slight or problematical as not to outweigh the national interest in keeping interstate commerce free from interferences which seriously impede it" (*Southern Pacific Co. v. State of Arizona*), we must uphold the statute.

The District Court found that "since it is impossible for a carrier operating in interstate commerce to determine which of its equipment will be used in a particular area, or on a particular day, or days, carriers operating into or through Illinois . . . will be required to equip all their trailers in accordance with the requirements of the Illinois Splash Guard statute." With two possible exceptions the mudflaps required in those States which have mudguard regulations would not meet the standards required by the Illinois statute. The cost of installing the contour mudguards is $30 or more per vehicle. The District Court found that the initial cost of installing those mudguards on all the trucks owned by the appellees ranged from $4,500 to $45,840. There was also evidence in the record to indicate that the cost of maintenance and replacement of these guards is substantial.

Illinois introduced evidence seeking to establish that contour mudguards had a decided safety factor in that they prevented the throwing of debris into the faces of drivers of passing cars and into the windshields of a following vehicle. But the District Court in its opinion stated that it was "conclusively shown that the contour mud flap possesses no advantages over the conventional or straight mud flap previously required in Illinois and presently required in most of the states" and that "there is rather convincing testimony that use of the contour flap creates hazards previously unknown to those using the highways."

These findings on cost and on safety are not the end of our problem. . . . State control of the width and weight of motor trucks and trailers sustained in *South Carolina State Highway Dept. v. Barnwell Bros.*, [303 U.S. 177 (1935)], involved nice questions of judgment concerning the need of those regulations so far as the issue of safety was concerned. That case also presented the problem whether interstate motor carriers, who were required to replace all equipment or keep out of the State, suffered an unconstitutional restraint on interstate commerce. The matter of safety was said to be one essentially for the legislative judgment; and the burden of redesigning or replacing equipment was said to be a proper price to exact from interstate and intrastate motor carriers alike. . . .

Cost taken into consideration with other factors might be relevant in some cases to the issue of burden on commerce. But it has assumed no such proportions here. If we had here only a question whether the cost of adjusting an interstate operation to these new local safety regulations prescribed by Illinois unduly burdened interstate commerce, we would have to sustain the law under the authority of the *Sproles* [*v. Binford*, 286 U.S. 347 (1937)], *Barnwell*, and *Maurer* [*v. Hamilton*, 309 U.S. 598 (1940)], cases. The same result would obtain if we had to resolve the much discussed issues of safety presented in this case.

This case presents a different issue. The equipment in the *Sproles, Barnwell,* and *Maurer* cases could pass muster in any State, so far as the records in those cases reveal. We were not faced there with the question whether one State could prescribe standards for interstate carriers that would conflict with the standards of another State, making it necessary, say, for an interstate carrier to shift its cargo to differently designed vehicles once another state line was reached. We had a related problem in *Southern Pacific Co. v. State of Arizona,* where the Court invalidated a statute of Arizona prescribing a maximum length of 70 cars for freight trains moving through that State. . . .

An order of the Arkansas Commerce Commission, already mentioned, requires that trailers operating in that State be equipped with straight or conventional mudflaps. Vehicles equipped to meet the standards of the Illinois statute would not comply with Arkansas standards, and vice versa. Thus if a trailer is to be operated in both States, mudguards would have to be interchanged, causing a significant delay in an operation where prompt movement may be of the essence. It was found that from two to four hours of labor are required to install or remove a contour mudguard. Moreover, the contour guard is attached to the trailer by welding and if the trailer is conveying a cargo of explosives (e.g., for the United States Government) it would be exceedingly dangerous to attempt to weld on a contour mudguard without unloading the trailer. . . .

This in summary is the rather massive showing of burden on interstate commerce which appellees made at the hearing. . . .

This is one of those cases—few in number—where local safety measures that are nondiscriminatory place an unconstitutional burden on interstate commerce. . . . The conflict between the Arkansas regulation and the Illinois regulation also suggests that this regulation of mudguards is not one of those matters "admitting of diversity of treatment, according to the special requirements of local conditions," to use the words of Chief Justice HUGHES in *Sproles v. Binford*. A State which insists on a design out of line with the requirements of almost all the other States may sometimes place a great burden of delay and inconvenience on those interstate motor carriers entering or crossing its territory. Such a new safety device—out of line with the requirements of the other States—may be so compelling that the innovating State need not be the one to give way. But the present showing—balanced against the clear burden on commerce—is far too inconclusive to make this mudguard meet that test.

We deal not with absolutes but with questions of degree. The state legislatures plainly have great leeway in providing safety regulations for all vehicles—interstate as well as local. Our decisions so hold. Yet the heavy burden which the Illinois mudguard law places on the interstate movement of trucks and trailers seems to us to pass the permissible limits even for safety regulations.
Affirmed.

Maine v. Taylor

477 U.S. 131, 106 S.CT. 2440 (1986)

Justice Harry Blackmun discusses the facts of this case, challenging Maine's law prohibiting the importation of live baitfish, in his opinion for the Court.

The Court's decision was eight to one, and the majority's opinion was announced by Justice Blackmun. Justice Stevens dissented.

☐ *Justice BLACKMUN delivers the opinion of the Court.*

Appellee Robert J. Taylor operates a bait business in Maine. Despite a Maine statute prohibiting the importation of live baitfish, he arranged to have 158,000 live golden shiners delivered to him from outside the State. The shipment was intercepted, and a federal grand jury in the District of Maine indicted Taylor for violating and conspiring to violate the Lacey Act Amendments of 1981. Section 3(a)(2)(A) of those Amendments makes it a federal crime "to import, export, transport, sell, receive, acquire, or purchase in interstate or foreign commerce . . . any fish or wildlife taken, possessed, transported, or sold in violation of any law or regulation of any State or in violation of any foreign law."

Taylor moved to dismiss the indictment on the ground that Maine's import ban unconstitutionally burdens interstate commerce and therefore may not form the basis for a federal prosecution under the Lacey Act. . . . Maine intervened to defend the validity of its statute, arguing that the ban legitimately protects the State's fisheries from parasites and non-native species that might be included in shipments of live baitfish. The District Court found the statute constitutional and denied the motion to dismiss. The Court of Appeals for the First Circuit reversed, agreeing with Taylor that the underlying state statute impermissibly restricts interstate trade. . . . Maine appealed. . . .

Maine's statute restricts interstate trade in the most direct manner possible, blocking all inward shipments of live baitfish at the State's border. Still, as both the District Court and the Court of Appeals recognized, this fact alone does not render the law unconstitutional. The limitation imposed by the Commerce Clause on state regulatory power "is by no means absolute," and "the States retain authority under their general police powers to regulate matters of 'legitimate local concern,' even though interstate commerce may be affected." . . .

In determining whether a State has overstepped its role in regulating interstate commerce, this Court has distinguished between state statutes that burden interstate transactions only incidentally, and those that affirmatively discriminate against such transactions. While statutes in the first group violate the Commerce Clause only if the burdens they impose on interstate trade are "clearly excessive in relation to the putative local benefits" statutes in the second group are subject to more demanding scrutiny. The Court explained in *Hughes v. Oklahoma*, 441 U.S. 322 (1979), that once a state law is shown to discriminate against interstate commerce "either on its face or in practical effect," the burden falls on the State to demonstrate both that the statute "serves a legitimate local purpose," and that this purpose could not be served as well by available nondiscriminatory means. . . .

The District Court and the Court of Appeals both reasoned correctly that, since Maine's import ban discriminates on its face against interstate trade, it should be subject to the strict requirements of *Hughes v. Oklahoma*, notwithstanding Maine's argument that those requirements were waived by the Lacey Act Amendments of 1981. It is well established that Congress may authorize the States to engage in regulation that the Commerce Clause would otherwise forbid. But because of the important role the Commerce Clause plays in protecting the free flow of interstate trade, this Court has exempted state statutes from the implied limitations of the Clause only when the congressional direction to do so has been "unmistakably clear." . . .

Maine's ban on the importation of live baitfish thus is constitutional only if it satisfies the requirements ordinarily applied under *Hughes v. Oklahoma* to local regulation that discriminates against interstate trade: the statute must serve a legitimate local purpose, and the purpose must be one that cannot be served as well by available nondiscriminatory means.

The District Court found after an evidentiary hearing that both parts of the *Hughes* test were satisfied, but the Court of Appeals disagreed. We conclude that the Court of Appeals erred in setting aside the findings of the District Court. . . .

Nor do we think that much doubt is cast on the legitimacy of Maine's purposes by what the Court of Appeals took to be signs of protectionist intent. Shielding in-state industries from out-of-state competition is almost never a legitimate local purpose, and state laws that amount to "simple economic protectionism" consequently have been subject to a "virtually *per se* rule of invalidity." . . .

The Commerce Clause significantly limits the ability of States and localities to regulate or otherwise burden the flow of interstate commerce, but it does not elevate free trade above all other values. As long as a State does not needlessly obstruct interstate trade or attempt to "place itself in a position of economic isolation," *Baldwin v. G.A.F. Seelig, Inc.*, 294 U.S. 511 (1935), it retains broad regulatory authority to protect the health and safety of its citizens and the integrity of its natural resources. The evidence in this case amply supports the District Court's findings that Maine's ban on the importation of live baitfish serves legitimate local purposes that could not adequately be served by available nondiscriminatory alternatives. This is not a case of arbitrary discrimination against interstate commerce; the record suggests that Maine has legitimate reasons, "apart from their origin, to treat [out-of-state baitfish] differently," *Philadelphia v. New Jersey*, 437 U.S. [617 (1978)]. The judgment of the Court of Appeals setting aside appellee's conviction is therefore reversed.

☐ *Justice STEVENS, dissenting.*

There is something fishy about this case. Maine is the only State in the Union that blatantly discriminates against out-of-state baitfish by flatly prohibiting their importation. Although golden shiners are already present and thriving in Maine (and, perhaps not coincidentally, the subject of a flourishing domestic industry), Maine excludes golden shiners grown and harvested (and, perhaps not coincidentally sold) in other States. This kind of stark discrimination against out-of-state articles of commerce requires rigorous justification by the discriminating State. . . .

This is not to derogate the State's interest in ecological purity. But the invocation of environmental protection or public health has never been thought to confer some kind of special dispensation from the general principle of nondiscrimination in interstate commerce. . . .

If Maine wishes to rely on its interest in ecological preservation, it must show that interest, and the infeasibility of other alternatives, with far greater specificity. Otherwise, it must further that asserted interest in a manner far less offensive to the notions of comity and cooperation that underlie the Commerce Clause. . . .

Pennsylvania v. Nelson

350 U.S. 497, 76 S.Ct. 477 (1956)

Steve Nelson, a member of the Communist Party, was convicted in a state trial court of violating Pennsylvania's Sedition Act, making the advocacy of the overthrow of the government a crime. He was sentenced to twenty years of imprisonment, fined $10,000, and assigned the costs of his prosecution in the sum of $13,000. On appeal, the Pennsylvania State Supreme Court overturned Nelson's conviction after concluding that the state law was superseded by federal legislation, the Smith Act of 1940. The Commonwealth of Pennsylvania appealed that ruling to the Supreme Court of the United States.

The Court's decision was six to three, and the majority's opinion was announced by Chief Justice Warren. Justice Reed dissented and was joined by Justices Burton and Minton.

☐ *Chief Justice WARREN delivers the opinion of the Court.*

It should be said at the outset that the decision in this case does not affect the right of States to enforce their sedition laws at times when the Federal Government has not occupied the field and is not protecting the entire country from seditious conduct. The distinction between the two situations was clearly recognized by the court below. Nor does it limit the jurisdiction of the States where the Constitution and Congress have specifically given them concurrent jurisdiction, as was done under the Eighteenth Amendment and the Volstead Act. . . . Neither does it limit the right of the State to protect itself at any time against sabotage or attempted violence of all kinds.

Nor does it prevent the State from prosecuting where the same act constitutes both a federal offense and a state offense under the police power. . . .

Where, as in the instant case, Congress has not stated specifically whether a federal statute has occupied a field in which the States are otherwise free to legislate, different criteria have furnished touchstones for decision. Thus,

> [t]his Court, in considering the validity of state laws in the light of . . . federal laws touching the same subject, has made use of the following expressions: conflicting; contrary to; occupying the field; repugnance; difference; irreconcilability; inconsistency; violation; curtailment; and interference. But none of these expressions provides an infallible constitutional test or an exclusive constitutional yardstick. In the final analysis, there can be no one crystal clear distinctly marked formula. *Hines v. Davidowitz*, 312 U.S. 52 [1941].

In this case, we think that each of several tests of supersession is met.

First, "[t]he scheme of federal regulation [is] so pervasive as to make reasonable the inference that Congress left no room for the States to supplement it." *Rice v. Santa Fe Elevator Corp.* [331 U.S. 218 (1947)]. The Congress determined in 1940 that it was necessary for it to re-enter the field of antisubversive legislation, which had been abandoned by it in 1921. In that year, it enacted the Smith Act which proscribes advocacy of the overthrow of any government—federal, state or local—by force and violence and organization of and knowing membership in a group which so advocates. Conspiracy to commit any of these acts is punishable under the general criminal conspiracy provisions in 18 U.S.C. Sec. 371, 18 U.S. C.A. Sec. 371. The Internal Security Act of 1950 is aimed more directly at Communist organizations. It distinguishes between "Communist-action organizations" and "Communist-front organizations," requiring such organizations to register and to file annual reports with the Attorney General giving complete details as to their officers and funds. Members of Communist-action organizations who have not been registered by their organization must register as individuals. Failure to register in accordance with the requirements of Sections 786–787 is punishable by a fine of not more than $10,000 for an offending organization and by a fine of not more than $10,000 or imprisonment for not more than five years or both for an individual offender—each day of failure to register constituting a separate offense. And the Act imposes certain sanctions upon both "action" and "front" organizations and their members. The Communist Control Act of 1954 declares "that the Communist Party of the United States, although purportedly a political party, is in fact an instrumentality of a conspiracy to overthrow the Government of the United States" and that "its role as the agency of a hostile foreign power renders its existence a clear present and continuing danger to the security of the United States." It also contains a legislative finding that the Communist Party is a " 'communist-action' organization" within the meaning of the Internal Security Act of 1950 and provides that "knowing" members of the Communist Party are "subject to all the provisions and penalties" of that Act. It furthermore sets up a new classification of "Communist-infiltrated organizations" and provides for the imposition of sanctions against them.

We examine these Acts only to determine the congressional plan. Looking to all of them in the aggregate, the conclusion is inescapable that Congress has intended to occupy the field of sedition. Taken as a whole, they evince a congressional plan which makes it reasonable to determine that no room has been left for the States to supplement it. Therefore, a state sedition statute is superseded regardless of whether it purports to supplement the federal law. . . .

Second, the federal statutes "touch a field in which the federal interest is so dominant that the federal system [must] be assumed to preclude enforcement of state laws on the same subject." *Rice v. Santa Fe Elevator Corp.* Congress has devised an all-embracing program for resistance to the various forms of totalitarian aggression. Our external defenses have been strengthened, and a plan to protect against internal subversion has been made by it. It has appropriated vast sums, not only for our own protection, but also to strengthen freedom throughout the world. It has charged the Federal Bureau of Investigation and the Central Intelligence Agency with responsibility for intelligence concerning Communist seditious activities against our Government, and has denominated such activities as part of a world conspiracy. It accordingly proscribed sedition against all government in the nation—national, state and local. Congress declared that these steps were taken "to provide for the common defense, to preserve the sovereignty of the United States as an independent nation, and to guarantee to each State a republican form of government. . . ." Congress having thus treated seditious conduct as a matter of vital national concern, it is in no sense a local enforcement problem. . . .

Third, enforcement of state sedition acts presents a serious danger of conflict with the administration of the federal program. Since 1939, in order to avoid a hampering of uniform enforcement of its program by sporadic local prosecutions, the Federal Government has urged local authorities not to intervene in such matters, but to turn over to the federal authorities immediately and unevaluated all information concerning subversive activities. . . .

In his brief, the Solicitor General states that forty-two States plus Alaska and Hawaii have statutes which in some form prohibit advocacy of the violent overthrow of established government. These statutes are entitled anti-sedition statutes, criminal anarchy laws, criminal syndicalist laws, etc. Although all of them are primarily directed against the overthrow of the United States Government, they are in no sense uniform. And our attention has not been called to any case where the prosecution has been successfully directed against an attempt to destroy state or local government. Some of these Acts are studiously drawn and purport to protect fundamental rights by appropriate definitions, standards of proof and orderly procedures in keeping with the avowed congressional purpose "to protect freedom from those who would destroy it, without infringing upon the freedom of all our people." Others are vague and are almost wholly without such safeguards. Some even purport to punish mere membership in subversive organizations which the federal statutes do not punish where federal registration requirements have been fulfilled.

When we were confronted with a like situation in the field of labor-management relations, Justice JACKSON wrote:

> A multiplicity of tribunals and a diversity of procedures are quite as apt to produce incompatible or conflicting adjudications as are different rules of substantive law.

Should the States be permitted to exercise a concurrent jurisdiction in this area, federal enforcement would encounter not only the difficulties mentioned by Justice JACKSON, but the added conflict engendered by different criteria of substantive offenses.

Since we find that Congress has occupied the field to the exclusion of

---

■ THE DEVELOPMENT OF LAW

Other Rulings on State Regulation of Commerce in the Absence of Federal Legislation

CASE	RULING
Dean Milk Company v. City of Madison, 340 U.S. 349 (1956)	Invalidated an ordinance prohibiting the sale of milk in the city of Madison, Wisconsin, unless it was bottled at an approved plant, for erecting an economic barrier against the sale of milk produced in Illinois.
Head v. New Mexico Board of Examiners, 374 U.S. 424 and (1963)	Upheld a state law forbidding the advertising of the price of eyeglasses and rejected the claim of an out-of-state optometrist that the law burdened interstate commerce.
Colorado Anti-Discrimination Commission, v. Continental Airlines, 372 U.S. 714 (1963)	Upheld a state antidiscrimination law as applied to Continental Airlines, an interstate carrier, as posing no undue burden.
Great Atlantic & Pacific Tea Co. v. Cottrell, 424 U.S. 366 (1976)	Held that Mississippi may not bar sales of milk produced in Louisiana that met its health standards simply because Louisiana refused to sign a reciprocity agreement.
Hunt v. Washington State Apple Advertising Commission, 432 U.S. 333 (1977)	Struck down North Carolina's labeling requirements for apples as an undue burden on and discrimination against Washington state apple growers.
City of Philadelphia v. New Jersey, 437 U.S. 617 (1978)	Struck down New Jersey's ban on the disposal of out-of-state garbage as an undue burden on interstate commerce.

parallel state legislation, that the dominant interest of the Federal Government precludes state intervention, and that administration of state Acts would conflict with the operation of the federal plan, we are convinced that the decision of the Supreme Court of Pennsylvania is unassailable. . . .

The judgment of the Supreme Court of Pennsylvania is affirmed.

CASE	RULING
Exxon Corporation v. Governor of Maryland, 437 U.S. 117 (1978)	Upheld a state prohibition against producers and refiners of petroleum products from operating service stations in the state.
Hughes v. Oklahoma, 441 U.S. 322 (1979)	Struck down a law forbidding the shipping of minnows for out-of-state sales.
Raymond Motor Transportation v. Rice and Kassell v. Consolidated Freightways Corporation, 450 U.S. 662 (1981)	Invalidated Wisconsin's and Iowa's bans on the operation on state highways of sixty-five-foot double trucks as burdens on interstate commerce.
Minnesota v. Clover Leaf Creamery Co., 449 U.S. 459 (1981)	Upheld a conservation law "banning the retail sale of milk in plastic nonreturnable, nonrefillable containers, but permitting such sale in other nonre-

turnable, nonrefillable containers, such as paperboard milk cartons" as an "incidental burden imposed on commerce."

New England Power Co. v. New Hampshire, 455 U.S. 331 (1982)	Held that states may not forbid companies from selling power to other states even though produced by utilities in the state.
Sporhase v. Nebraska, 458 U.S. 941 (1982)	Upheld a Nebraska law requiring permits for the shipment and sale of ground water insofar as permits were

issued on findings that the shipment and sale were (1) reasonable, (2) not contrary to the conservation of water, and (3) not detrimental to the public welfare, but held that the state could not require a reciprocity agreement with the state to which the water was shipped and sold.

Hartigan v. General Electric Company and Don't Waste Washington Legal Defense Foundation v. Washington, 461 U.S. 913 (1983)	Let stand lower court rulings that states may not ban out-of-state nuclear waste from being transported and stored within their borders.

(continues)

■ THE DEVELOPMENT OF LAW
Other Rulings on State Regulation of Commerce in the
Absence of Federal Legislation (continued)

CASE	RULING
White v. Massachusetts Council, 460 U.S. 204 (1983)	Upheld a restriction on public works contracts to companies agreeing to use Boston workers in at least half of their jobs.
South-Central Timber Development, Inc. v. Wunnicke, 467 U.S. 82 (1984)	Congress authorized Alaska to require that timber cut on federal land in the state be processed within the state prior to export, but failed to similarly

regulate timber on state land. Alaska's requirement that timber cut on state land be processed within the state, nevertheless, has an undue burden on interstate commerce in affecting out-of-state processing markets.

Brown-Forman Distillers Corp. v. New York Liquor Authority, 476 U.S. 573 (1986)	Held that states may not force an out-of-state merchant to seek regulatory approval in one state before conducting business in another.
Goldberg v. Sweet, 488 U.S. 980 (1988)	A 5 percent state tax on all telephone calls, including interstate calls, does not violate the commerce clause.
Cotton Petroleum v. New Mexico, 490 U.S. 163 (1989)	States are not specifically preempted by Congress from taxing oil and gas taken from Indian reservations.
Healy v. Beer Institute, Inc., 491 U.S. 324 (1989)	Struck down as an undue burden on commerce Connecticut's statute requiring out-of-state shippers of beer to

affirm that their prices for products sold in state are not higher than the prices of those products sold out of state.

Trinova Corporation v. Michigan Department of Treasury, 498 U.S. 358 (1991)	Upheld Michigan's "single business tax," a value-added tax (VAT), levied against a multistate business. With Justice Souter not participating, Justice

Kennedy held for the majority that Michigan's tax did not discriminate against out-of-state business or run afoul of either the commerce clause or the due process clause. State taxes, when challenged by multistate businesses for violating the commerce clause, are permissible, observed Justice

Kennedy, so long as they meet a four-pronged text: "the tax is applied to an activity with a substantial nexus with the taxing State, is fairly apportioned, does not discriminate against interstate commerce, and is fairly related to the services provided by the State." *Complete Auto Transit, Inc. v. Brady*, 430 U.S 274 (1977).

CASE	RULING
Wyoming v. Oklahoma, 502 U.S. 437 (1992)	To promote local jobs and to increase tax revenues, Oklahoma in 1986 enacted a law requiring its public utilities

to purchase a certain percentage of Oklahoma-mined coal. As a result, its public utilities purchased less Wyoming-mined coal, and Wyoming lost revenues that it would have received from severance taxes on coal that would have otherwise been sold to Oklahoma's public utilities. Writing for the Court, Justice White struck down Oklahoma's statute as violating the commerce clause, which "prohibits economic protectionism—that is, regulatory measures designed to benefit in-state economic interests by burdening out-of-state competitors." In a dissenting opinion, Justice Scalia, joined by Chief Justice Rehnquist and Justice Thomas, argued that Wyoming did not have standing to bring the suit and objected to the majority's finding that the state's loss of revenue was within the "zone of interests" covered by the commerce clause.

Chemical Waste Management v. Hunt, 504 U.S. 334 (1992)	States may not impose a fee on hazardous waste generated in another state and dumped at a commercial facility

in its jurisdiction, while not imposing the same fee on waste generated and dumped within its borders. The Alabama State Supreme Court held that although the fee posed a burden on interstate commerce, the fee was permissible because it aimed at protecting health and safety and not economic protectionism for in-state businesses. But by an eight-to-one vote the Court reversed on the basis of its prior ruling in *Philadelphia v. New Jersey*, 437 U.S. 617 (1978), that state prohibitions of solid waste imported from other states amount to economic protectionism in violation of the commerce clause.

Fort Gratiot Sanitary Landfill v. Michigan Department of Natural Resources, 504 U.S. 353 (1992)	Held that a county's refusal, authorized by state law, to allow the disposal within the county of any solid waste generated outside the county unconstitu-

tionally discriminates against interstate commerce. A federal appellate court had upheld the law on the grounds that the county's policy treated both out-of-county and out-of-state solid waste equally. But by a seven-to-two vote the Court struck down Michigan's waste import restrictions as protectionist and discriminatory in violation of the interstate commerce clause. Chief Justice Rehnquist and Justice Blackmun dissented.

(continues)

■ THE DEVELOPMENT OF LAW
Other Rulings on State Regulation of Commerce in the Absence of Federal Legislation (continued)

CASE	RULING
Quill Corporation v. North Dakota, 504 U.S. 298 (1992)	Quill Corporation challenged a state law that required companies located in other states to collect a state sales

tax on mail order sales as a violation of the due process clause and Congress's power to regulate interstate commerce. Writing for the majority, Justice Stevens overturned in part a ruling in *National Bellas Hess v. Department of Revenue of Illinois*, 386 U.S. 753 (1967), that had upheld a due process challenge to such state sales taxes. Although now reversing that holding, Stevens reaffirmed *National Bellas Hess*'s ruling that such taxes pose an undue burden on interstate commerce in the absence of congressional legislation. He underscored, however, that Congress could authorize states to levy such taxes. The sole dissenter, Justice White, argued that even in the absence of congressional legislation, states should have the power to collect such taxes and *National Bellas Hess* should be given "the complete burial it justly deserves."

Kraft General Foods v. Iowa Dept. of Revenue, 505 U.S. 71 (1992)	Struck down Iowa's provision disallowing tax credits for business taxes paid to foreign countries. Writing for the Court, Justice Stevens held that that

provision discriminates against foreign commerce in violation of the commerce clause.

Itel Containers International Corporation v. Huddleston, 507 U.S. 60 (1993)	Writing for the Court, Justice Kennedy upheld a state tax on international transport containers and rejected a commerce clause challenge upon concluding

that Congress had not intended to preempt such taxation in approving an international Container Convention.

Northwest Airlines, Inc. v. County of Kent, Michigan, 510 U.S. 355 (1994)	Rejected a dormant commerce-clause challenge to an airport fee scheme that discriminated between commercial airlines and general aviation by assessing higher fees on the former.
Oregon Waste Systems, Inc. v. Department of Environmental Quality of the State of Oregon, 511 U.S. 93 (1994)	Struck down Oregon's surcharge on the disposal of out-of-state solid waste in its landfills as discriminatory economic protectionism in violation of the dormant commerce clause.

CASE	RULING
C&A Carbone, Inc. v. Town of Clarkstown, New York, 511 U.S. 383 (1994)	Struck down an ordinance requiring all nonhazardous solid waste within the town to be deposited at a local transfer station. Writing for the majority, Jus-

tice Kennedy held that the ordinance deprived out-of-state businesses of access to the local market and thereby unconstitutionally discriminated in favor of local businesses.

Associated Industries of Missouri v. Lohman, 511 U.S. 641 (1994)	Writing for the Court, Justice Thomas invalidated a statewide "additional use tax" on goods purchased outside of the state for impermissibly discriminating against interstate commerce.

West Lynn Creamery, Inc. v. Healy, 512 U.S. 186 (1994)	Struck down a Massachusetts pricing order on all milk sold within the state and subsidy for in-state dairy farmers

as economically discriminatory and a violation of the commerce clause. Justice Stevens wrote for the majority, and Chief Justice Rehnquist, joined by Justice Thomas, dissented.

Barclays Bank PLC v. Franchise Tax Board of California and Colgate-Palmolive Co. v. Franchise Tax Board of California, 512 U.S. 1201 (1994)	Writing for the Court's majority, Justice Ginsburg upheld a controversial state policy of taxing multinational corporations based on their worldwide income, rather than on their earnings within the state, over objections that

the policy discriminates against foreign and interstate commerce. The majority reaffirmed that state tax policies may run afoul of the commerce clause if the tax (1) applies to an activity lacking a "substantial nexus to the taxing state"; (2) is not fairly apportioned; (3) discriminates against interstate commerce; or (4) is not fairly related to the services provided by a state. In addition, in cases involving the taxation of foreign commerce the Court examines (5) whether there is an "enhanced risk of multiple taxation," and (6) whether a state's tax interferes with the federal government's capacity to "speak with one voice when regulating commercial relations with foreign governments." Justice Ginsburg found California's "worldwide combined reporting" method of taxation to survive all but the third criterion. However, the justice concluded that Barclays had failed to show that the state's method of taxation in fact operated to impose an inordinate burden on multinational corporations. Justice O'Connor, joined by Justice Thomas, dissented.

(continues)

■ The Development of Law
*Other Rulings on State Regulation of Commerce in the
Absence of Federal Legislation (continued)*

CASE	RULING
Oklahoma Tax Commission v. Jefferson Lines, Inc., 514 U.S. 175 (1995)	Writing for the majority, Justice Souter upheld a state sales tax on bus tickets for interstate travel sold within the state over the objection that the tax

imposed an undue burden on interstate commerce and was inconsistent with the Commerce Clause. Justices Breyer and O'Connor dissented.

| *Fulton Corporation v. Faulkner*, 516 U.S. 325 (1996) | Writing for the Court, Justice Souter struck down North Carolina's tax on state residents who own stock in |

companies that do no business within the state, while exempting residents who own stock in companies doing business within the state, as a violation of the dormant commerce clause.

| *General Motors Corporation v. Tracy, Tax Commissioner of Ohio*, 519 U.S. 278 (1997) | Ohio imposes general sales and use taxes on natural gas purchases from all sellers, whether in-state or out-of-state, including state regulated utili- |

ties but not independent producers and marketers. In an appeal of a challenge to the constitutionality of that distinction, Justice Souter held that Ohio's differential tax treatment of natural gas sales does not violate the dormant commerce clause.

| *Camps Newfound/Owatonna, Inc. v. Town of Harrison*, 520 U.S. 564 (1997) | Writing for a bare majority, Justice tStevens struck down Maine's statute governing tax exemptions for chari- table institutions that gave more lim- |

ited benefits to institutions serving primarily nonresidents as a violation of the dormant commerce clause. Chief Justice Rehnquist and Justices Scalia, Thomas, and Ginsburg dissented.

| *Pharmaceutical Research and Manufacturers of America v. Walsh*, 538 U.S. 644 (2003) | Held that Maine's Act to Establish Fairer Pricing for Prescription Drugs does not violate the dormant com- merce clause. Due to increasing |

Medicaid costs for prescription drugs, Congress authorized requiring drug companies to pay rebates to states for their Medicaid purchases. Under Maine's program, the state negotiates rebates with drug companies. If a company does not enter into an agreement, then doctors are required to obtain the state's approval for reimbursement for prescription drugs under Medicaid. Writing for the Court, Justice Stevens held that Maine's law, aimed at promoting discount drugs, did not discriminate against out-of-state drug manufacturers in violation of the commerce clause.

CASE	RULING
American Insurance Association v. Garamendi, 539 U.S. 396 (2003)	Invalidated California's 1999 Holocaust Victim Insurance Relief Act, which required all insurance companies in the state

that sold individual policies in Europe between 1920 and 1945 to disclose the names of policyholders and beneficiaries, in order to assist Holocaust survivors in collecting benefits. Writing for the Court, Justice Souter held that the law infringed on the president's foreign policy-making powers, and in particular the German Foundation Agreement, under which the United States and Germany established a fund and a procedure for compensating insurance companies' victims during the Nazi era. Justice Souter also rejected California's assertion that Congress had authorized in the McCarran-Ferguson Act, rather than preempting under its interstate commerce power, state laws of the sort at issue. Justices Ginsburg, Stevens, Scalia, and Thomas dissented.

Granholm v. Heald, 544 U.S. 460 (2005)	A bare majority struck down Michigan and New York laws that forbid wineries located out

of state from shipping wine directly to consumers. The ruling will have wide-ranging consequences for alcohol sales on the Internet and affect laws in eighteen other states. Writing for the Court, Justice Kennedy noted that there was a "patchwork of laws," with some states banning all direct shipments, others only out-of-state shipments, and some requiring reciprocity. That amounted to "an ongoing, low-level trade war" that discriminated against interstate commerce. Such discrimination, Justice Kennedy ruled, was "neither authorized nor permitted by the Twenty-first Amendment," which gives states the authority to regulate the importation of liquor. Justice Kennedy emphasized that the Twenty-first Amendment "should not be subordinated to the dormant Commerce Clause," and that "in all but the narrowest circumstances, state laws violate the Commerce Clause if they mandate differential treatment of in-state and out-of-state economic interests that benefits the former and burdens the later." Justices Stevens and Thomas issued dissenting opinions, which Chief Justice Rehnquist and Justice O'Connor joined.

(continues)

■ THE DEVELOPMENT OF LAW
Other Rulings on State Regulation of Commerce in the
Absence of Federal Legislation (continued)

CASE	RULING
American Trucking Associations, Inc. v. Michigan Public Service Commission,545 U.S. 429 (2005)	Writing for the Court, Justice Breyer ruled that the dormant Commerce Clause does not preclude Michigan from imposing a $100 annual fee on trucks engaged in intrastate commer-

cial hauling, and does not discriminate against interstate commerce.

United Haulers Association v. Onedia-Herkimer Solid Waste Management Authority, 550 U.S. 330	Writing for the Court, Chief Justice tice Roberts held that the dormant commerce clause is not violated when state and local governments impose

■ THE DEVELOPMENT OF LAW

Other Rulings on State Regulatory Powers in Alleged Conflict with Federal Legislation

CASE	RULING
Allen-Bradley Local v. Wisconsin Employment Relations Board, 315 U.S. 740 (1942)	Federal legislation did not preempt states from punishing offensive con- duct related to "traditionally local matters as public safety and order and the use of streets and highways."
Hill v. Florida, 325 U.S. 528 (1945)	State law requiring licenses for labor union agents conflicted with the Na- tional Labor Relations Act.
International Union v. O'Brien, 339 U.S. 454 (1950)	State laws interfering with the right to strike are preempted by federal legisla- tion.
Garner v. Teamsters Union, 346 U.S. 485 (1953)	State forbidden from barring peaceful picketing.

additional fees on private haulers of solid waste, so long as they do not discriminate between in and out public disposal authorities. Justice Alito, joined by Justices Stevens and Kennedy, dissented.

CASE	RULING
Department of Revenue of Kentucky v. Davis, 128 S.Ct. 1801 (2008)	The Court upheld Kentucky's law exempting interest on bonds issued by the state from taxation, while permitting the taxing of interest on out-of-

state bonds. Writing for the Court, Justice Souter held that while the dormant commerce clause bars "economic protectionism" (regulations that benefit in-state economic interests by burdening out-of-state competitors), in this case, the state's interests in financing its own civic responsibilities and state autonomy outweighed the claim of economic protectionism. Justice Stevens and Thomas filed concurring opinions, while Justices Kennedy and Alito dissented, and Chief Justice Roberts and Justice Scalia filed separate opinions concurring in part.

CASE	RULING
Weber v. Anheuser-Busch, 348 U.S. 468 (1955), and *Teamsters Union v. Oliver*, 358 U.S. 283 (1957)	State antitrust laws preempted as applied to enjoying labor strikes and collective bargaining agreements.
Farmers Educational & Cooperative Union v. WDAY, 360 U.S. 525 (1958)	The Federal Communications Act, requiring broadcasters to carry some political speeches without censoring them, occupied the field and thus im-

munized broadcasters from liability under state libel laws.

Huron Portland Cement Co. v. Detroit, 362 U.S. 440 (1960)	Upheld the conviction of a ship operating in interstate commerce and whose boiler met federal standards, for

violating Detroit's smoke-abatement ordinance.

City of Burbank v. Lockheed Air Terminal, 411 U.S. 624 (1973)	Struck down local noise abatement ordinance as being preempted by federal airline regulations.

(continues)

- ### THE DEVELOPMENT OF LAW
Other Rulings on State Regulatory Powers in Alleged
Conflict with Federal Legislation (continued)

CASE	RULING
Jackson Transit Authority v. Amalgamated Transit Union, 457 U.S. 15 (1982)	Held that the urban Mass Transportation Act of 1964 did not preempt states from their traditional control over labor relations involving local governments and unions.
Pacific Gas & Electric Co. v. State Energy Commission, 461 U.S. 190 (1983)	Held the Atomic Energy Act does not preempt states from some regulation of nuclear power plants; states may forbid the building of plants until the

federal government has approved of the methods of nuclear waste disposal.

Silkwood v. Kerr-McGee Corporation, 464 U.S. 283 (1984)	Held that state laws for awarding punitive damages for injuries resulting from escaped plutonium at a nuclear

power plant are not preempted; held that state safety, but not economic, regulations are preempted.

Metropolitan Life Insurance Co. v. Ward, 470 U.S. 869 (1985)	Upheld state regulation of insurance contracts as not constituting interstate commerce.
Nantahala Power & Light Co. v. Thornburg, 476 U.S. 953 (1986)	States may not differ from the Federal Energy Regulatory Commission's standards in setting intrastate retail rates.
Mississippi Power & Light Co. v. Mississippi ex rel. Moore, 487 U.S. 354 (1988)	Federal Energy Regulatory Commission preempted state rate-making authority.
Felder v. Casey, 487 U.S. 131 (1988)	Section 1983 of the United States Code, providing for federal civil rights suits, preempts Wisconsin's notice-of-

claim statute (which had barred lawsuits against any state governmental agency or officer unless a written notice of the injury suffered was submitted within 120 days of the injury).

California v. Federal Energy Regulatory Commission, 495 U.S. 490 (1990)	Held that California's regulations setting standards for minimum stream lows on a river, in which federally li-

censed hydroelectric power plant was located, were preempted by the Federal Power Act.

CASE	RULING

Perpich v. Department of Defense, **496 U.S. 334 (1990)**   The Court held that, over the objections of a state governor, the federal government may order state National Guard troops to take part in peacetime training abroad, and reaffirmed federal preemption based on the recognition of "the supremacy of the federal government in the area of military affairs."

Gregory v. Ashcroft, **501 U.S. 452 (1991)**   Upheld Missouri's law requiring mandatory retirement of state judges at the age of seventy over objections that the law violated the Fourteenth Amendment equal protection clause and the federal Age Discrimination in Employment Act.

Wisconsin Public Intervenor v. Mortier, **501 U.S. 597 (1991)**   The Court held that local and state uses governments may regulate pesticide because such regulations were not preempted by the Federal, Fungicide, Insecticide, and Rodenticide Act of 1972.

Dennis v. Higgins, **498 U.S. 439 (1991)**   The Court held that government officials could be held liable under Section 1983 of the U.S. Code when they are found to have violated the commerce clause. Writing for the majority, Justice White construed the commerce clause to confer "rights, privileges, or immunities" within the meaning of Section 1983. Justice Kennedy, joined by Chief Justice Rehnquist, dissented from the Court's expansive reading of the commerce clause, pointing out that the majority's ruling would increase "the burden that a state or local government will face in defending its economic regulation and taxation."

Ingersoll-Rand v. McClendon, **498 U.S. 133 (1991)**   The Court unanimously held that employees who claim they were fired so their employers would not have to pay pension benefits may not bring suits in state courts for punitive damages. Writing for the Court, Justice O'Connor held that the Employee Retirement Income Security Act of 1974 preempts such action in state courts by barring such firing and providing for reinstatement of employees and payment of lost wages and benefits.

(continues)

■ THE DEVELOPMENT OF LAW
Other Rulings on State Regulatory Powers in Alleged
Conflict with Federal Legislation (continued)

CASE	RULING
County of Yakima v. Confederated Tribes and Bands of the Yakima Indian Nation, 502 U.S. 251 (1992)	Held that the Indiana General Allotment Act of 1887 permits states and localities to impose *ad valorem* taxes on land owned by Native Americans but does not allow excise taxes on the sale of Indian lands.
Gade v. National Solid Wastes Management Association, 505 U.S. 88 (1992)	The Court affirmed a federal appellate court decision that struck Illinois's licensing and training requirements for workers in hazardous waste sites on

the grounds that the Occupational Safety and Health Act (OSHA) preempted states from adopting standards stricter than mandated by OSHA, even though the state asserted its requirements were adopted for environment, and not occupational, reasons. Justices Souter, Blackmun, Stevens, and Thomas dissented.

Morales v. Trans World Airlines, 504 U.S. 374 (1992)	Held that states may not ban deceptive advertising by airplane companies. A federal appellate court held that state

regulations of how airlines advertise their fares were preempted by the Federal Aviation Act, which gives the federal government sole regulatory authority over airline "rates, routes, or services." With Justice Souter not participating, a bare majority affirmed the lower court's decision that states were preempted by federal law from regulating airlines' advertising.

Arkansas v. Oklahoma and Environmental Protection Agency v. Oklahoma, 503 U.S. 91 (1992)	Upheld the Environmental Protection Agency's (EPA) action permitting discharges from a new disposal site in Arkansas, located thirty-eight miles

above the Oklahoma state line, over the objections that the discharges would violate Oklahoma's environmental standards, and ruled that the EPA's regulatory decisions under the Clean Water Act preempt state common law and the federal common law of nuisance.

Cipollone v. Liggett Group, Inc., 505 U.S. 504 (1992)	Held that the Federal Cigarette Labeling and Advertising Act of 1965, as amended by the Public Health Ciga-

rette Smoking Act of 1969, preempts some lawsuits but not those based on breach of warranty, intentionally fraudulent misrepresentation, and concealment of health risks as well as conspiracy to misrepresent the health consequences of smoking. Justice Scalia and Thomas, dissenting in part, would have held that all suits were preempted.

CASE	RULING
The District of Columbia v. The Greater Washington Board of Trade, 506 U.S. 125 (1992)	Held that the Employee Retirement Income Security Act (ERISA) does not preempt a District of Columbia statute requiring employers who provide

health-insurance coverage to continue to provide coverage to employees who are receiving workers' compensation.

CSX Transportation v. Easterbrook, 507 U.S. 658 (1993)	Held that the Federal Railroad Safety Act of 1970 preempts a wrongful-death suit against a railroad for the

death of a truck driver who collided with a train, allegedly due to inadequate warnings at crossing and the train's excessive speed.

Northwest Airlines, Inc. v. County of Kent, Michigan, 510 U.S. 355 (1994)	Rebuffed a challenge to an airport system of collecting fees based on charging commercial airlines 100 percent of their square footage allocation costs,

but only 20 percent of the same costs incurred by general aviation. Writing for the majority, Justice Ginsburg held that that system did not violate the Anti-Head Tax Act or burden interstate commerce. Justice Thomas dissented.

Livades v. Bradshaw, 512 U.S. 107 (1994)	Writing for the Court, Justice Souter held that a collective-bargaining agreement was preempted under provisions of the National Labor Relations Act.

Doctor's Associates, Inc. v. Casarotto, 517 U.S. 681 (1996)	Writing for the Court, Justice Ginsburg struck down a Montana law governing arbitration agreements as pre-

empted by the Federal Arbitration Act. Justice Thomas dissented.

United States v. Locke, 529 U.S. 89 (2000)	The Court unanimously struck down Washington's navigational regulations as preempted by the Oil Pollution Act

of 1990. Following the oil spill of the Exxon Valdez in 1989, Washington enacted regulations that were more extensive and stringent than those set forth in federal statutes and international treaties.

(continues)

■ The Development of Law
Other Rulings on State Regulatory Powers in Alleged
Conflict with Federal Legislation (continued)

CASE	RULING
Crosby v. National Foreign Trade Council, 530 U.S. 363 (2000)	The Court unanimously invalidated Massachusetts's 1996 law restricting public agencies from contracting with

companies that also conduct business with Burma (Myanmar). Writing for the Court, Justice Souter held that federal laws imposing conditional sanctions on Burma preempted the state law and the state law ran contrary to Congress's authorization for the president to set national policy toward Burma.

Egelhoff v. Egelhoff, 532 U.S. 141 (2001)	Writing for the Court, Justice Thomas invalidated a Washington statute, providing that the designation of a spouse

as the beneficiary of a nonprobate asset is automatically revoked upon divorce, as preempted by the Employee Retirement Income Security Act of 1974 (ERISA). Justices Breyer and Stevens dissented.

Lorillard Tobacco v. Reilly, 533 U.S. 901 (2001)	Invalidated Massachusetts's restrictions on the advertising of tobacco products as preempted by the Federal Cigarette Labeling and Advertising Act.

Kentucky Association of Health Plans, Inc. v. Miller, 538 U.S. 329 (2003)	Writing for a unanimous Court, Justice Scalia held that the Employment Retirement Income Security Act (ERISA) does not preempt Ken-

tucky's Any Willing Provider (AWP) laws because they are regulations of the insurance industry. Health Management Organizations (HMOs) had exclusive networks with health-care providers and sought to have the state's AWP laws invalidated on the ground they were preempted by ERISA's regulation of employee benefit plans. But the Court held that Kentucky's laws regulated insurance programs and thus HMOs in the state could not restrict access to particular health-care providers.

Beneficial National Bank v. Anderson, 539 U.S. 1 (2003)	Held that the National Bank Act provides the exclusive basis for usury claims against national banks and preempts state usury laws.

CASE	RULING

Hillside Dairy, Inc. v. Lyons, 539 U.S. 59 (2003)   Held that California's milk pricing regulations, which favored in-state farmers, were not exempt from Congress's interstate commerce power and the Federal Agriculture and Reform Act of 1996.

Aetna Health Inc. v. Davila, 542 U.S. 200 (2004)   Held that the Employee Retirement Income Security Act of 1974 (ERISA) preempts the Texas Health Care Liability Act and bars suits against health maintenance organizations (HMOs) for their refusal to provide certain services in state courts, rather than federal courts where the potential liability of HMOs is more limited.

Bates v. Dow Agrosciences, 544 U.S. 4331 (2005)   Writing for the Court, Justice Stevens held that the Federal Insecticide, Fungicide and Rodenticide Act (FIFRA) does not preempt state laws and tort relief lawsuits in state courts against manufacturers for negligently designed and manufactured products. Because the FIFRA does not provide for suits in federal courts, the ruling was significant since a contrary ruling would have denied consumers any opportunity to sue manufacturers. However, Justice Stevens also emphasized that not all state lawsuits under federal statutes are permitted. Preemption of each federal statute must be determined in light of its own statutory language, legislative history, and the history of litigation over a regulated product.

Mid-Con Freight Systems, Inc. v. Michigan Public Service Commission, 545 U.S. 440 (2005)   Federal law requires interstate truckers to obtain a federal permit and by 1991 some thirty-nine states also demanded such proof. Because of differences in the states, Congress created a Single State Registration System (SSRS), which allows companies to file one set of state and federal registration forms, and prohibits states from imposing additional registration fees. Michigan imposed an annual $100 fee for state licensed trucks and its law was challenged. Writing for the Court, Justice Breyer held that the federal law did not preempt Michigan's law because the federal statute only applies to the SSRS registration and does not preclude additional state regulations.

(continues)

■ THE DEVELOPMENT OF LAW
*Other Rulings on State Regulatory Powers in Alleged
Conflict with Federal Legislation (continued)*

CASE	RULING
Rowe v. New Hampshire TransportationAssociation, 128 S.Ct. 989 (2008)	Writing for the Court, Justice Breyer held that provisions of the Federal Aviation Administration Authorization Act (FAAAA) preempted Maine's law re-

quiring tobacco shippers to verify that the buyer was of legal age and prohibiting unlicensed tobacco shippers from out of state. Several other states have similar laws aimed at cutting down on the delivery of cigarettes bought over the Internet.

Preston v. Ferrer, 128 S.Ct. 978 (2008)	Writing for the Court, Justice Ginsburg held that the Federal Arbitration Act preempts a state law that would refer a

dispute to an administrative agency. Justice Thomas dissented.

Riegel v. Medtronic, Inc., 128 S.Ct. 999 (2008)	Writing for the Court, Chief Justice Roberts held that the Medical Device Amendments preemption clause over-

rides state common-law claims against producers of medical devices that were approved by the Food and Drug Administration. Justice Ginsburg dissented.

Chamber of Commerce of the United States of America v. Brown 128 S.Ct. 2408 (2008)	The majority held that the National Labor Relations, Act as amended by the Taft-Hartley Act of 1947 preempted a California law that prohibited employers who receive state grants of

more than $10,000 per year from using the money "to assist, promote, or deter union organizing." Writing for the Court, Justice Stevens held that federal law demonstrated a "congressional intent to encourage free debate on issues dividing labor and management." Justices Ginsburg and Breyer dissented.

CASE	RULING
Altria Group, Inc. v. Good, 129 S.Ct. 538 (2008)	Writing for a bare majority, Justice Stevens held that the Federal Cigarette Labeling and Advertising Act, which

prohibits states from placing "smoking and health" requirements on cigarette advertisements, does not preempt suits against tobacco manufacturers for deceptive advertising. The Altria Group was sued under Maine's Unfair Trade Practices Act for fraudulently advertising that their "light" cigarettes delivered less tar and nicotine than regular brands. Justice Stevens emphasized that such suits are "predicated on the duty not to deceive" and thus are separate from the federal government's regulation of warnings on cigarette packs. Chief Justice Roberts and Justices Scalia and Alito joined Justice Thomas's dissent.

Wyeth v. Levine, 129 S.Ct. 1187 (2009)	Writing for the Court, Justice Stevens held that the Food, Drug, and Cosmetic Act's (FDCA) labeling requirements for

drugs do not preempt state court tort claims against drug manufactures for failure to fully warn about potential harms of the usage of a drug. Chief Justice Roberts and Justices Scalia and Alito dissented.

Cuomo v. Clearing House Association, 129 S.Ct. 2710 (2009)	Writing for the Court, Justice Scalia held that under the 1864 National Bank Act, "visitorial" powers preempt a state attorney from issuing executive subpoenas

in order to enforce state free-lending laws against national banks, though not the state's power of law enforcement. Justice Thomas issued a separate opinion, in part concurring and dissenting, which was joined by Chief Justice Roberts and Justices Kennedy and Alito.

B | *The Tenth and Eleventh Amendments and the States*

In response to the Anti-Federalists' concerns about safeguarding individual liberty, the first Congress adopted the Bill of Rights, including the Tenth Amendment, which provides that "[t]he powers not delegated to the United States by the Constitution, nor prohibited by it to the States, are reserved to the States respectively, or to the people." The amendment long stood, as the Court put it in *United States v. Darby Lumber Company*, 312 U.S. 100 (1941) (excerpted in Ch. 6), as a truism, without independent force in constraining federal powers. It reaffirms the Constitution's structure and limitations of federal powers to those specifically granted. Indeed, during the First Congress's debate over the amendment, Elbridge Gerry, who had been a delegate from Massachusetts to the Constitutional Convention, proposed inserting the word *expressly* so the amendment would read, "the powers not *expressly* delegated by the Constitution, nor prohibited to the States, are reserved to the States respectively, or to the people." Rejection of his proposal and the addition of the last clause—reserving powers "to the people"—underscores that the federal government's powers are delegated and plenary; any others belong to the people of the states.

Chief Justice William Rehnquist championed the idea of states' sovereignty. In *National League of Cities v. Usery*, 426 U.S. 833 (1976), he persuaded four other justices to hold that the exercise of congressional power over commerce threatened "the separate and independent existence" of the states as "sovereign political entit[ies]." On that basis, he struck down three 1974 amendments to the Fair Labor Standards Act extending minimum-wage and maximum-hours standards to all state, county, and municipal employees.

National League of Cities v. Usery bitterly divided the Court, however. Just a year before, with only Rehnquist dissenting, the Court upheld federal restrictions on salary increases for state employees.[1] Indeed, not since striking down much of the early New Deal legislation and the constitutional crisis of 1937 had the Court sought to limit Congress's power in this area. And Rehnquist was forced to overturn *Maryland v. Wirtz*, 392 U.S. 183 (1968), upholding similar labor standards for state employees in hospitals, institutions, and schools. In that earlier ruling, Justice John Harlan saw no point in denying congressional power over state employees when it indisputably covered all private-sector employees. Rehnquist conceded that federal regulation of state em-

Chief justice nominee John Roberts (front, right) carrying the coffin of Chief Justice Rehnquist into the Supreme Court on September 6, 2005. *(Kevin Wolf/Associated Press.)*

ployees was "within the scope of the Commerce Clause." But he asserted that "there are attributes of sovereignty attaching to every state government that may not be impaired by Congress, not because Congress lacks an affirmative grant of legislative authority to reach the matter, but because the Constitution prohibits it from exercising the authority in that manner."

Rehnquist supported his decision with a textualist and structural reading of the Tenth Amendment. As interpreted by Rehnquist, the amendment is an "affirmative limitation" on Congress "akin to" others in the Bill of Rights, "running in favor of the States *as States.*" Congress may not regulate the "States *qua* States" or deny their "freedom to structure integral operations in areas of traditional governmental functions." Thus despite conceding Congress's power to regulate the working conditions of state employees and finding no express prohibitions to its doing so, Rehnquist held that extending federal labor standards to state employees was "not within the authority granted Congress." In delivering his opinion in *National League of Cities v. Usery*, Rehnquist wrote,

It is one thing to recognize the authority of Congress to enact laws regulating individual businesses necessarily subject to the dual sovereignty of the government of the Nation and of the State in which they reside. It is quite another to uphold a similar exercise of congressional authority directed not to private citizens, but to the States as States. We have repeatedly recognized that there are attributes of sovereignty attaching to every state government which may not be impaired by Congress, not because Congress may lack an affirmative grant of legislative authority to reach the matter, but because the Constitution prohibits it from exercising the authority in that manner. . . .

One undoubted attribute of state sovereignty is the State's power to determine the wages which shall be paid to those whom they employ in order to carry out their governmental functions, what hours those persons will work, and what compensation will be provided where these employees may be called upon to work overtime.

Among the four dissenters in *National League of Cities*, Justice William J. Brennan, Jr., protested that the Constitution neither guarantees state sovereignty nor requires or permits its judicial enforcement and reiterated that "restraints on [Congress's commerce power] must proceed from political rather than judicial processes."

It bears emphasizing, though, that Rehnquist's interpretation of the Tenth Amendment was modest in limiting congressional powers only under the commerce clause. Within a week of *National League of Cities*, he held the Fourteenth Amendment empowers Congress to prohibit state and local employers, no less than those in the private sector, from practicing racial discrimination in violation of the Civil Rights Act of 1964.[2] Moreover, he relied on *South Carolina v. Katzenbach*, 383 U.S. 301 (1966) (excerpted in Ch. 8), a decision clearly denying states' sovereignty in upholding the 1965 Voting Rights Act, which authorizes federal examiners to determine voter qualifications and approve state voting laws. Nor does the Tenth Amendment stand as an obstacle to Congress's taxing and spending powers. In *South Dakota v. Dole*, 483 U.S. 203 (1987) (excerpted in Ch. 6), Rehnquist upheld the withholding of federal highway funds from states refusing to adopt a minimum drinking age of twenty-one.

National League of Cities nonetheless renewed debate over federalism. Besides raising states' sovereignty to the level of constitutional law, Rehnquist left unexplained both how "traditional" or "essential" state activities were to be determined and why the Court, not Congress, should define and defend them. Subsequent decisions reformulated Rehnquist's ruling into a three-pronged test for curbing Congress's commerce power based on showing that legislation (1) regulated "States as States," (2) addressed "matters that are indisputably 'attributes of state sovereignty,' " and (3) would force "States' compliance" in ways that "directly impair their ability 'to structure integral operations in areas of traditional function.' "[3] But on this test, a majority of the Court refused to further limit Congress's control over state and local employees.[4]

Finally, Justice Harry Blackmun, who cast the crucial fifth vote in *National League of Cities*, changed his mind about the wisdom of judicial line-drawing in defense of interests of the states as states. In *Garcia v. San Antonio Metropolitan Transit Authority* (1985) (see excerpt below), he joined the four justices who had dissented in *National League of Cities* and expressly overturned that ruling. *Garcia's* majority reaffirmed that federalism is a political structure in which states' interests are represented, for better or worse, in the national political process. And that is precisely what *Garcia's* dissenters deny in maintaining that the national political process inadequately safeguards states' "sphere of sovereignty," and that the Court stands as a last defense for states' sovereignty.

State powers have been eroded, *Garcia's* dissenters point out, due to several factors: "the recent expansion of the commerce power," the "unprecedented growth of federal regulatory activity," the Seventeenth Amendment's substitution of popular election of senators for that of selection by state legislatures as originally provided, and "the expanded influence of national interest groups" in Congress and the national political process. In addition to other developments, the Fourteenth Amendment greatly expanded congressional power, the Sixteenth Amendment gave Congress the power to levy a federal income tax, the Court has expansively read Congress's taxing and spending powers since the New Deal, and (see Vol. 2, Ch. 4) the Court nationalized the Bill of Rights, making those guarantees limit the powers of the states no less than the federal government.

As the Court's composition changed in the late 1980s and early 1990s, support for defending the states' interests appeared to grow among the justices. One of the most important initial rulings in which the Rehnquist Court defended states' interests involved two Missouri state judges who attacked the constitutionality of the state's age-seventy mandatory retirement for judges and other public officials. They contended that Missouri's retirement law violated the Fourteenth Amendment equal protection clause and the federal Age Discrimination in Employment Act (ADEA) of 1967. But attorneys for the state defended the retirement law on federalist grounds. Writing for the Court in *Gregory v. Ashcroft*, 501 U.S. 452 (1991), Justice O'Connor upheld Missouri's mandatory retirement law as applied to state judges upon recognizing the "dual sovereignty" of the national and state governments. In her words,

As every schoolchild learns, our Constitution establishes a system of dual sovereignty between the States and the Federal Government. This Court also has recognized this fundamental principle [in *Texas v. White*, 7 Wall. 700, 725 (1869), and *Lane County v. Oregon*, 7 Wall. 71, 76 (1869)]. . . . The Constitution created a Federal Government of limited powers. "The powers not delegated to the United States by the Constitution, nor prohibited by it to the States, are reserved to the States respectively, or to the people." U.S. Const., Amdt. 10. The States thus retain substantial sovereign authority under our constitutional system. . . .

Upon that constitutional analysis, Justice O'Connor reasoned that when important principles of federalism are at stake, Congress must make a "plain statement" that it "intends to preempt the historic powers of the States." "This plain statement rule," according to O'Connor, "is nothing more than an acknowledgment that the States retain substantial sovereign powers under our constitutional scheme, powers with which Congress does not readily interfere." O'Connor also noted with regard to Congress's powers under Section 5 of the Fourteenth Amendment and the Court's application of the Fourteenth Amendment equal protection clause that prior cases had upheld state regulations—pertaining to the denial of public employment to aliens (see Vol. 2, Ch. 12)—upon a "political function" exception-theory. On that basis, the Court had held that States may exclude individuals from positions "intimately related to the process of democratic self-government." "These cases," O'Connor claimed, also "stand in recognition of the authority of the people of the States to determine the qualifications of their most important government officials. . . ."

Conceding that the Court was "constrained in our ability to consider the limits that the state-federal balance places in Congress's powers under the Commerce Clause," O'Connor nonetheless emphasized that "the plain statement rule" would permit the Court to strike down the application of a federal regulation to the states, and uphold state regulations, unless Congress expressly stated that it intended to preempt the states. As O'Connor put it, "[I]nasmuch as this Court in *Garcia* has left primarily to the political process the protection of the States against intrusive exercises of Congress's Commerce Clause powers, we must be absolutely certain that Congress intended such an exercise."

In a separate opinion, in part concurring and dissenting, and in which Justice Stevens joined, Justice White took strong exception to the majority's analysis and its broad application of the "plain statement rule" in determining whether Congress has preempted state laws and regulations. As Justice White explained:

The majority's plain statement rule is not only unprecedented, it directly contravenes our decisions in *Garcia v. San Antonio Metropolitan*

Transit Authority, 469 U.S. 528 (1985), and *South Carolina v. Baker*, 485 U.S. 505 (1988). In those cases we made it clear "that States must find their protection from congressional regulation through the national political process, not through judicially defined spheres of unregulable state activity." We also rejected as "unsound in principle and unworkable in practice" any test for state immunity that requires a judicial determination of which state activities are "traditional," "integral," or "necessary." The majority disregards those decisions in its attempt to carve out areas of state activity that will receive special protection from federal legislation.

The majority's approach is also unsound because it will serve only to confuse the law. First, the majority fails to explain the scope of its rule. Is the rule limited to federal regulation of the qualifications of state officials? Or does it apply more broadly to the regulation of any "state governmental functions"? Second, the majority does not explain its requirement that Congress's intent to regulate a particular state activity be "plain to anyone reading [the federal statute]." Does that mean that it is now improper to look to the purpose or history of a federal statute in determining the scope of the statute's limitations on state activities? If so, the majority's rule is completely inconsistent with our preemption jurisprudence. See, e.g., *Hillsborough County v. Automated Medical Laboratories, Inc.*, 471 U.S. 707 (1985) (preemption will be found where there is a "clear and manifest purpose" to displace state law). The vagueness of the majority's rule undoubtedly will lead States to assert that various federal statutes no longer apply to a wide variety of State activities if Congress has not expressly referred to those activities in the statute. Congress, in turn, will be forced to draft long and detailed lists of which particular state functions it meant to regulate.

My disagreement with the majority does not end with its unwarranted announcement of the plain statement rule. Even more disturbing is its treatment of Congress's power under Section 5 of the Fourteenth Amendment. Section 5 provides that "[t]he Congress shall have power to enforce, by appropriate legislation, the provisions of this article." Despite that sweeping constitutional delegation of authority to Congress, the majority holds that its plain statement rule will apply with full force to legislation enacted to enforce the Fourteenth Amendment. . . .

The Rehnquist Court's renewed deference to the states in *Gregory v. Ashcroft* and *Coleman v. Thompson*, 501 U.S. 722 (1991), prompted speculation that the Court might overrule *Garcia*. Yet, when the Court was asked to reconsider *Garcia* in *New York v. United States*, 505 U.S. 144 (1992) (excerpted below), it declined to do so. Writing for the majority in *New York v. United States*, Justice O'Connor nonetheless strongly defended "state sovereignty" when striking down one section of Congress's 1985 statute requiring states that fail to comply with their obligation to provide sites for radioactive waste by 1996 to take title of and assume liability for all undisposed waste. Notably, though, O'Connor rests the decision not on *Garcia* and the Tenth Amendment, but instead on Congress's exceeding its power under the commerce clause. Finally, without invoking the Tenth Amendment, a bare majority of the Court held that Congress exceeded its power and intruded on states' powers when enacting the Gun-Free School Zones Act of 1990, in *United States v. Lopez*, 514 U.S. 549 (1995) (excerpted in Vol. 1, Ch. 6). However, the Tenth Amendment as a limitation on congressional power was reemphasized by Justice Scalia in his opinion for a bare majority in *Printz v. United States* and *Mack v. United States* (excerpted below). There, the Court struck down a key provision of the Brady Handgun Violence Prevention Act of 1993, requiring state and local law enforcement officials to conduct background checks on gun purchasers.

In addition, a bare majority of the Rehnquist Court resurrected the Eleventh Amendment as a limitation on congressional power under Article I. In *Seminole Tribe of Florida v. Florida* (1996) (excerpted below) Chief Justice Rehnquist ruled that Congress, in the Indian Gaming Regulatory Act of 1988, impermissibly gave Indian tribes standing to sue states in federal courts in order to force them to negotiate compacts for the tribes to run casinos and other gambling activities on reservations. In that and subsequent cases, Justices Stevens, Souter, Ginsburg, and Breyer dissented.

In a series of five to four rulings, the Court extended its ruling in *Seminole Tribe* (see in this section the box THE DEVELOPMENT OF LAW: Other Recent Rulings on the Eleventh Amendment). Notably, in *Alden v. Maine* (1999) (excerpted below) a bare majority held that the "structure and history" of the Constitution not only shields states from suits filed in federal courts but also makes them immune from lawsuits in state courts that seek to enforce federal rights against them. Here, Maine's probation officers sought to force the state to pay for overtime work, as provided by amendments to the Fair Labor Standards Act of 1938.

However, *Nevada Department of Human Resources v. Hibbs*, 538 U.S. 721 (2003) (excerpted below), affirmed congressional power to abrogate states' immunity in authorizing private lawsuits against states for violations of the Family and Medical Leave Act of 1993. Congress, reasoned Chief Justice Rehnquist, had the power to do so under Section 5 of the Fourteenth Amendment in order to enforce the amendment's bar against gender discrimination. The ruling reaffirmed that Congress may abrogate states' Eleventh Amendment immunity if it bases legislation on its remedial power under Section 5 of the Fourteenth Amendment to enforce the constitutional guarantee of the equal protection of the law; gender discrimination, unlike age discrimination, is impermissible under the Fourteenth Amendment (see Vol. 2, Ch. 12). In addition, a bare majority, in *Tennessee v. Lane*, 541 U.S. 428 (2004), held that Congress may abrogate state immunity in Title 2 of the Americans with Disabilities Act (ADA) of 1990 but limited its holding to suits to force states to provide access for the disabled to courthouses, and did not address access to other public facilities. Writing for the Court, Justice Stevens found Congress had established a nationwide problem of discrimination against the disabled and their exercise of a fundamental right to judicial proceedings. On that basis he distinguished *Board of Trustees of University of Alabama v. Garrett*, 531 U.S. 356 (2001), in which for a bare majority Chief Justice Rehnquist held that Congress lacked the authority to abrogate state immunity from lawsuits filed under Title 1 of the ADA, which forbids discrimination against the disabled in state employment. (For a further discussion see THE DEVELOPMENT OF LAW box in this chapter.)

NOTES

1. See *Fry v. United States*, 421 U.S. 524 (1975).

2. *Fitzpatrick v. Bitzer*, 427 U.S. 445 (1976).

3. *Hodel v. Virginia Surface Mining*, 452 U.S. 264, 287–288 (1981). In a footnote, the majority added a fourth requirement and important qualification: "Demonstrating that these three requirements are met does not, however, guarantee that a Tenth Amendment challenge to congressional commerce power action will succeed. There are situations in which the nature of the federal interest advanced may be such that it justifies state submission."

4. See *Hodel v. Virginia Surface Mining*, 452 U.S. 264 (1981); *FERC v. Mississippi*, 456 U.S. 742 (1982); *United Transportation Union v. Long Island Railroad Company*, 455 U.S. 678 (1982); and *EEOC v. Wyoming*, 460 U.S. 222 (1983).

SELECTED BIBLIOGRAPHY

Beer, Samuel H. *To Make a Nation: The Rediscovery of American Federalism*. Cambridge, MA: Belknap Press, 1993.

Berger, Raoul. *Federalism: The Founders' Design*. Norman: University of Oklahoma Press, 1987.

Greve, Michael S. *Real Federalism: Why It Matters, How It Could Happen*. Washington, DC: American Enterprise Institute, 1999.

Lofgren, Charles A. *Government from Reflection and Choice*. New York: Oxford University Press, 1986.

Mason, Alpheus Thomas. *The States Rights Debate*. Englewood Cliffs, NJ: Prentice-Hall, 1964.

McAffee, Thomas; Bybee, Jay and Bryant, Christopher. *Powers Reserved for the People and the States: A History of the Ninth and Tenth Amendments*. Westport, CT: Praeger, 2006.

McDonald, Forrest. *States' Rights and the Union: Imperium in Imperio, 1776–1876.* Lawrence: University Press of Kansas, 2000.

Noonan, John T., Jr. *Narrowing the Nation's Power: The Supreme Court Sides with the States.* Berkeley: University of California Press, 2002.

Storing, Herbert. *The Complete Anti-Federalist,* 7 Vols. Chicago: University of Chicago Press, 1981.

■ INSIDE THE COURT

Rethinking Federalism in Garcia v. San Antonio Metropolitan Transit Authority

In *National League of Cities v. Usery,* 426 U.S. 833 (1976), a bare majority for the first time since the 1937 New Deal crisis resurrected the Tenth Amendment as an affirmative limitation on Congress, when striking down an amendment to the Fair Labor Standards Act of 1938. The justices were bitterly divided over whether there was a principle for the Court to enforce in order to protect "traditional state functions," or whether they should defer to the political process to define the boundaries of federalism. Justice Harry Blackmun cast the pivotal vote and expressed his concerns in a concurrence.

Almost a decade later, in *Garcia v. San Antonio Metropolitan Transit Authority (SAMTA)* (excerpted in this chapter), the SAMTA contended that it did not have to pay Joe Garcia and other employees federal overtime wages because it was exempt from such federal mandates under *National League of Cities.* After hearing oral arguments on March 19, 1984, the justices discussed their votes in private conference on March 21, with Chief Justice Burger leading the discussion:

BURGER: This case presents a constitutional policy choice. Private mass transit has faded out and large cities have gone public. Yet, water and transit systems are basically local. This is like water in that respect and is here to stay. The federal government can attach conditions. I don't think that [*United Transportation Union v.*] *Long Island* [455 U.S. 678 (1982), in which a majority of the Court held that the federal Railway Labor Act preempted state laws governing a state-owned railroad] controls this case. Pass until draft circulates, but inclined to affirm.

BRENNAN: The issue presented is whether a publicly owned and operated mass transit system is a "traditional state function" for the purposes of the Tenth Amendment. In my view, it is not.

Over 80 percent of the publicly owned mass transit systems became public after 1966, when the Fair Labor Standards Act was amended to apply to publicly owned mass transit. As in *Long Island Railroad*, these states acquired their mass transit operations knowing that the operations would be subject to federal regulation. Reverse.

WHITE: Agree with Brennan.

MARSHALL: Agree with Brennan.

BLACKMUN: This is a tough case for me after my concurrence in *National League*. Municipal mass transit reeks of localism, like police, fire, and so forth. A good opinion can be written either way. I come down on the side that this is local, and vote to affirm.

POWELL: A principled decision could be written either way. Agree with Harry. But, we are talking here of driving people to and from their work—a service that is essential to provide in cities like Richmond. Vote to affirm.

REHNQUIST: Agree with Harry and Lewis. Affirm.

STEVENS: Let the democratic process work. Otherwise, the Court would basically be engaging in substantive due process; it has no standards to enforce here. Municipalities have political power and it is not for the Court to protect them from Congress. Reverse.

O'CONNOR: The third *National League* test—traditional state functions—is the point. History does not freeze traditional public service—the issue is whether Congress goes too far. Affirm.

With Justice Blackmun at the center, though inclined to adhere to *National League of Cities*, the justices appeared equally divided and, thus, after conference Chief Justice Burger assigned him to write the opinion for the Court. But when working on the draft, Justice Blackmun changed his mind about what is and how to determine a "traditional state function." As a result, he produced a draft questioning *National League of Cities*. In the first draft that circulated on June 11, 1986, he explained:

A review of the operation of the "traditional governmental function" standard in this and other cases now persuades us that the attempt to draw the boundaries of state regulatory immunity in terms of "traditional governmental functions" is both unworkable and inconsistent with the principles of federalism on which *National League of Cities* rests.

(continues)

- INSIDE THE COURT
Rethinking Federalism in Garcia v. San Antonio
Metropolitan Transit Authority *(continued)*

However, he stopped short of overruling *National League of Cities* and in-stead reaffirmed "the fundamental premise of *National League of Cities* that Congress's authority under the Commerce Clause must accommo-date the special rule of the States in the federal system. We hold, however, that the necessary accommodation between federal power and state au-tonomy is realized when Congress places no burden on the States that it has not placed on private parties as well."

Along with his draft opinion, in a memorandum to the conference, Blackmun further explained the course he had taken:

> You will recall that the conference vote in these cases was 5–4 to affirm, with my own vote shaky on the affirming side. I as-sume that it is because of this that the Chief Justice assigned the cases to me, on his frequently stated reference to the "least per-suaded."
>
> I have spent a lot of time on these cases. I have finally decided to come down on the side of reversal. I have been able to find no principled way in which to affirm. It seems to me that our customary reliance on the "historical" and the "traditional" is misplaced and that something more fundamental is required to eliminate the widespread confusion in the area. The enclosed draft of a proposed opinion reflects my views.
>
> I realize that this means (1) that the cases should be reassigned and (2) that some of you may feel the cases should go over for reargument. Perhaps this can be discussed at conference.

Chief Justice Burger was angry over Blackmun's writing an opinion that reached a result contrary to the conference vote. Moreover, the Court was two weeks from ending the term and he therefore did not fa-vor reassigning the opinion for the Court. Instead, Chief Justice Burger immediately moved to carry the case over for reargument the next term. Justices O'Connor, Powell, and Rehnquist immediately agreed. By con-trast, Justice Stevens strongly objected to hearing rearguments. Justices Brennan, Blackmun, and Marshall agreed with him. Although agreeing to join the Blackmun draft, Justice White was ambivalent about hearing rearguments, but at conference he voted to carry the case over. Justices Powell and O'Connor also pressed for asking counsel to address the ques-tion of "whether or not the principles of the Tenth Amendment as set forth in *National League of Cities v. Usery*, 426 U.S. 833 (1976), should be reconsidered." They aimed to force Blackmun's hand and to make him take a stand on that issue, which his original draft had evaded. For his part, Blackmun promptly shot back, warning: "I venture to say . . . that if the question is to be presented, *National League of Cities* just might end up being overruled. In the opinion I prepared this Term, and as to which some took umbrage, it was not overruled."

The justices heard rearguments on the first Monday in October 1984. Afterward, on October 3, they discussed the case at conference:

BURGER: 79 percent of mass transit is now public. Congress may want federal control, but Congress must assert its conditions. Affirm.

BRENNAN: I was ready to join Harry's opinion last term, and stand ready to do so. If there is sentiment for expressly overruling *National League of Cities*, I would join that. In fact, that may be required by Harry's analysis. Reverse.

WHITE: Reverse and overrule *National League.*

MARSHALL: Still with Harry and would overrule *National League.*

BLACKMUN: It was a disappointing oral argument from all concerned. The traditional government function test does not work. Reverse.

POWELL: Agree with the traditional governmental function test as whether it is essentially a matter of local or national concern. A balancing test is required. I don't think that the federal interest here is that great. Affirm.

REHNQUIST: Affirm.

STEVENS: There is no doubt what Congress meant here. Any balancing here is for Congress to do, as Brennan says. This is a classic case where it is wrong for the judiciary to intervene. Reverse.

O'CONNOR: This is a watershed case. . . . The Framers encouraged a system of dual sovereignty, state and federal sovereignty. The pay of state employees is for the states to determine. The Court has a role in protecting the states. Affirm.

The conference discussion only served to solidify Justice Blackmun's decision to remain aligned with the four dissenters in *National League of Cities* and to revise his draft opinion from the previous term and overrule *National League of Cities* in *Garcia.*

Sources: Justice William J. Brennan, Jr., Papers, and Justice Harry A. Blackmun Papers, Box 412, Manuscripts Division, Library of Congress; and Del Dickson, ed., *The Supreme Court in Conference (1940–1985)* (New York: Oxford University Press, 2001).

Garcia v. San Antonio Metropolitan Transit Authority

469 U.S. 528, 105 S.Ct. 1005 (1985)

In 1974, Congress amended the Fair Labor Standards Act (FLSA) to apply to virtually all state and local government employees and to require state and local governments to comply with minimum-wage and overtime standards. The San Antonio Metropolitan Transit Authority (SAMTA) sought in federal district court a declaratory judgment exempting it from FLSA's provisions on the grounds that the amendment to the law violated the Tenth Amendment. The court entered a summary judgment, without hearing oral arguments, for the transit authority. Joe Garcia, a transit authority employee, appealed that decision to the Supreme Court.

The Court's decision was five to four, and the majority's opinion was announced by Justice Blackmun. Dissents were by Justices Powell, O'Connor, and Rehnquist and joined by Chief Justice Burger.

☐ *Justice BLACKMUN delivers the opinion of the Court.*

We revisit in these cases an issue raised in *National League of Cities v. Usery*, 426 U.S. 833 (1976). In that litigation, this Court, by a sharply divided vote, ruled that the Commerce Clause does not empower Congress to enforce the minimum-wage and overtime provisions of the Fair Labor Standards Act (FLSA) against the States "in areas of traditional governmental functions." Although *National League of Cities* supplied some examples of "traditional governmental functions," it did not offer a general explanation of how a "traditional" function is to be distinguished from a "nontraditional" one. Since then, federal and state courts have struggled with the task, thus imposed, of identifying a traditional function for purposes of state immunity under the Commerce Clause.

In the present cases, a Federal District Court concluded that municipal ownership and operation of a mass-transit system is a traditional governmental function and thus, under *National League of Cities*, is exempt from the obligations imposed by the FLSA. Faced with the identical question, three Federal Courts of Appeals and one state appellate court have reached the opposite conclusion.

Our examination of this "function" standard applied in these and other cases over the last eight years now persuades us that the attempt to draw the boundaries of state regulatory immunity in terms of "traditional governmental function" is not only unworkable but is inconsistent with established principles of federalism and, indeed, with those very federalism principles on which *National League of Cities* purported to rest. That case, accordingly, is overruled....

Appellees have not argued that SAMTA [San Antonio Metropolitan Transit Authority] is immune from regulation under the FLSA on the ground that it is a local transit system engaged in intrastate commercial activity. In a practical sense, SAMTA's operations might well be characterized as "local." Nonetheless, it long has been settled that Congress' authority under the Commerce Clause extends to intrastate economic activities that affect interstate commerce. See, e.g., *Hodel v. Virginia Surface Mining & Recl. Assn.*, 452 U.S. 264 (1981); *Heart of Atlanta Motel, Inc. v. United States*, 379 U.S. 241 (1964); *Wickard v. Filburn*, 317 U.S. 111 (1942); *United States v. Darby*, 312 U.S. 100 (1941). Were SAMTA a privately owned and operated enterprise, it could not credibly argue that Congress exceeded the bounds of its Commerce Clause powers in prescribing minimum wages and overtime rates for SAMTA's employees. Any constitutional exemption from the requirements of the FLSA therefore must rest on SAMTA's status as a governmental entity rather than on the "local" nature of its operations.

The prerequisites for governmental immunity under *National League of Cities* were summarized by this Court in *Hodel*. . . . Under that summary, four conditions must be satisfied before a state activity may be deemed immune from a particular federal regulation under the Commerce Clause. First, it is said that the federal statute at issue must regulate "the 'States as States.' " Second, the statute must "address matters that are indisputably 'attribute[s] of state sovereignty.' " Third, state compliance with the federal obligation must "directly impair [the States'] ability 'to structure integral operations in areas of traditional governmental functions.' " Finally, the relation of state and federal interests must not be such that "the nature of the federal interest . . . justifies state submission." . . .

The controversy in the present cases has focused on the third *Hodel* requirement—that the challenged federal statute trench on "traditional governmental functions." The District Court voiced a common concern: "Despite the abundance of adjectives, identifying which particular state functions are immune remains difficult." Just how troublesome the task has been is revealed by the results reached in other federal cases. Thus, [lower] courts have held that regulating ambulance services, . . . licensing automobile drivers, . . . operating a municipal airport, . . . performing solid waste disposal, . . . and operating a highway authority, . . . are functions *protected* under *National League of Cities*. At the same time, courts have held that issuance of industrial development bonds, . . . regulation of intrastate natural gas sales, . . . regulation of traffic on public roads, . . . regulation of air transportation, . . . operation of a telephone system, . . . leasing and sale of natural gas, . . . operation of a mental health facility, . . . and provision of in-house domestic services for the aged and handicapped, . . . are *not* entitled to immunity. We find it difficult, if not impossible, to identify an organizing principle that places each of the cases in the first group on one side of a line and each of the cases in the second group on the other side. The constitutional distinction between licensing drivers and regulating traffic, for example, or between operating a highway authority and operating a mental health facility, is elusive at best.

Thus far, this Court itself has made little headway in defining the scope of the governmental functions deemed protected under *National League of Cities*. In that case the Court set forth examples of protected and unprotected functions, . . . but provided no explanation of how those examples were identified. The only other case in which the Court has had occasion to address the problem is [*Transportation Union v.*] *Long Island* [455 U.S. 678 (1982)]. We there observed: "The determination of whether a federal law impairs a state's authority with respect to 'areas of traditional [state] functions' may at times be a difficult one." The accuracy of that statement is demonstrated by this Court's own difficulties in *Long Island* in developing a workable standard for "traditional governmental functions." We relied in large part there on "the *historical reality* that the operation of railroads is not among the functions *traditionally* performed by state and local governments," but we simultaneously disavowed "a static historical view of state functions generally immune from federal regulation" (first emphasis added; second emphasis in original). We held that the inquiry into a particular function's "traditional" nature was merely a means of determining whether the federal statute at issue unduly handicaps "basic state prerogatives" but we did not offer an explanation of what makes one state function a "basic prerogative" and another function not basic. Finally, having disclaimed a rigid reliance on the historical pedigree of state involvement in a particular area, we nonetheless found it appropriate to emphasize the extended historical record of *federal* involvement in the field of rail transportation. . . .

Many constitutional standards involve "undoubte[d] . . . gray areas," *Fry v. United States*, 421 U.S. 542 (1975) (dissenting opinion), and, despite the difficulties that this Court and other courts have encountered so far, it normally might be fair to venture the assumption that case-by-case development would lead to a workable standard for determining whether a particular governmental function should be immune from federal regulation under the Commerce Clause. A further cautionary note is sounded, however, by the Court's experience in the related field of state immunity from federal taxation. In *South Carolina v. United States* [199 U.S. 437] (1905), the Court held for the first time that the state tax immunity recognized in *Collector v. Day* [11 Wall. 113] (1871), extended only to the "ordinary" and "strictly governmental" instrumentalities of state governments and not to instrumentalities "used by the State in the carrying on of an ordinary private business." While the Court applied the distinction outlined in *South Carolina* for the following 40 years, at no time during that period did the Court develop a consistent formulation of the kinds of governmental functions that were entitled to immunity. The Court identified the protected functions at various times as "essential," "usual," "traditional," or "strictly governmental." While "these differences in phraseology . . . must not be too literally contradistinguished" . . . they reflect an inability to specify precisely what aspects of a governmental function made it necessary to the "unimpaired existence" of the States. Indeed, the Court ultimately chose "not, by an attempt to formulate any general test, [to] risk embarrassing the decision of cases [concerning] activities of a different kind which may arise in the future." . . .

If these tax immunity cases had any common thread, it was in the attempt to distinguish between "governmental" and "proprietary" functions. To say that the distinction between "governmental" and "proprietary" proved to be stable, however, would be something of an overstatement. . . . It was this uncertainty and instability that led the Court in *New York v. United States* [326 U.S. 572] (1946), unanimously to conclude that the distinction between "governmental" and "proprietary" functions was "untenable" and must be abandoned. . . .

The distinction the Court discarded as unworkable in the field of tax immunity has proved no more fruitful in the field of regulatory immunity under the Commerce Clause. Neither do any of the alternative standards that might be employed to distinguish between protected and unprotected governmental functions appear manageable. We rejected the possibility of making immunity turn on a purely historical standard of "tradition" in *Long Island*, and properly so. The most obvious defect of a historical approach to state immunity is that it prevents a court from accommodating changes in the historical functions of States, changes that have resulted in a number of once-private functions like education being assumed by the States and their subdivisions. At the same time, the only apparent virtue of a rigorous historical standard, namely, its promise of a reasonably objective measure for state immunity, is illusory. Reliance on history as an organizing principle results in linedrawing of the most arbitrary sort; the genesis of state governmental functions stretches over a historical continuum from before the Revolution to the present, and courts would have to decide by fiat precisely how longstanding a pattern of state involvement had to be for federal regulatory authority to be defeated.

A nonhistorical standard for selecting immune governmental functions is likely to be just as unworkable as is a historical standard. The goal of identifying "uniquely" governmental functions, for example, has been rejected by the Court in the field of governmental tort liability in part because the notion of a "uniquely" governmental function is unmanageable. Another possibility would be to confine immunity to "necessary" governmental services, that is, services that would be provided inadequately or not at all unless the government provided them. . . . The set of services that fits into this category, however, may well be negligible. The fact that an unregulated market produces less of some service than a State deems desirable does not mean that the State itself must provide the service; in most if not all cases, the State can "contract out" by hiring private firms to provide the service or simply by providing subsidies to existing suppliers. It also is open to question how well equipped courts are.

We believe, however, that there is a more fundamental problem at work here, a problem that explains why the Court was never able to provide a basis for the governmental/proprietary distinction in the intergovernmental tax immunity cases and why an attempt to draw similar distinctions with respect to federal regulatory authority under *National League of Cities* is unlikely to succeed regardless of how the distinctions are phrased. The problem is that neither the governmental proprietary distinction nor any other that purports to separate out important governmental functions can be faithful to the role of federalism in a democratic society. The essence of our federal system is that within the realm of authority left open to them under the Constitution, the States must be equally free to engage in any activity that their citizens choose for the common weal, no matter how unorthodox or unnecessary anyone else—including the judiciary—deems state involvement to be. Any rule of state immunity that looks to the "traditional," "integral," or "necessary" nature of governmental functions inevitably invites an unelected federal judiciary to make decisions about which state policies it favors and which ones it dislikes. "The science of government . . . is the science of experiment," *Anderson v. Dunn* [19 U.S. 204] (1821), and the States cannot serve as laboratories for social and economic experiment, see *New State Ice Co. v. Liebmann*, 285 U.S. 262 (1932) (BRANDEIS, J., dissenting), if they must pay an added price when they meet the changing needs of their citizenry by taking up functions that an earlier day and a different society left in private hands. . . .

We therefore now reject, as unsound in principle and unworkable in practice, a rule of state immunity from federal regulation that turns on a judicial appraisal of whether a particular governmental function is "integral" or "traditional." Any such rule leads to inconsistent results at the same time that it disserves principles of democratic self-governance, and it breeds inconsistency precisely because it is divorced from those principles. If there are to be limits on the Federal Government's power to interfere with state functions— as undoubtedly there are—we must look elsewhere to find them. We accordingly return to the underlying issue that confronted this Court in *National League of Cities*—the manner in which the Constitution insulates States from the reach of Congress' power under the Commerce Clause.

The central theme of *National League of Cities* was that the States occupy a special position in our constitutional system and that the scope of Congress' authority under the Commerce Clause must reflect that position. Of course, the Commerce Clause by its specific language does not provide any special limitation on Congress' actions with respect to the States. . . . It is equally true, however, that the text of the Constitution provides the beginning rather than the final answer to every inquiry into questions of federalism, for "[b]ehind the words of the constitutional provisions are postulates which limit and control." *Monaco v. Mississippi*, 292 U.S. 313 (1934). *National League of Cities* reflected the general conviction that the Constitution precludes "the National Government [from] devour[ing] the essentials of state sovereignty." *Maryland v. Wirtz*, 392 U.S. [183 (1968)] (dissenting opinion).

In order to be faithful to the underlying federal premises of the Constitution, courts must look for the "postulates which limit and control."

What has proved problematic is not the perception that the Constitution's federal structure imposes limitations on the Commerce Clause, but rather the nature and content of those limitations. One approach to defining the limits on Congress' authority to regulate the States under the Commerce Clause is to identify certain underlying elements of political sovereignty that are deemed essential to the States' "separate and independent existence." *Lane County v. Oregon* [7 Wall. 71] (1869). This approach obviously underlay the Court's use of the "traditional governmental function" concept in *National League of Cities*. It also has led to the separate requirement that the challenged federal statute "address matters that are indisputably 'attribute[s] of state sovereignty.' " *Hodel*. In *National League of Cities* itself, for example, the Court concluded that decisions by a State concerning the wages and hours of its employees are an "undoubted attribute of state sovereignty." . . . The opinion did not explain what aspects of such decisions made them such an "undoubted attribute," and the Court since then has remarked on the uncertain scope of the concept. See *EEOC v. Wyoming*, [460 U.S. 266 (1983)]. The point of the inquiry, however, has remained to single out particular features of a State's internal governance that are deemed to be intrinsic parts of state sovereignty.

We doubt that courts ultimately can identify principled constitutional limitations on the scope of Congress' Commerce Clause powers over the States merely by relying on *a priori* definitions of state sovereignty. In part, this is because of the elusiveness of objective criteria for "fundamental" elements of state sovereignty, a problem we have witnessed in the search for "traditional governmental functions." There is, however, a more fundamental reason: the sovereignty of the States is limited by the Constitution itself. A variety of sovereign powers, for example, are withdrawn from the States by Article I, Section 10, Section 8 of the same Article works an equally sharp contraction of state sovereignty by authorizing Congress to exercise a wide range of legislative powers and (in conjunction with the Supremacy Clause of Article VI) to displace contrary state legislation. By providing for final review of questions of federal law in this Court, Article III curtails the sovereign power of the States' judiciaries to make authoritative determinations of law. See *Martin v. Hunter's Lessee*, 1 Wheat. 304 (1816). Finally, the developed application, through the Fourteenth Amendment, of the greater part of the Bill of Rights to the States limits the sovereign authority that States otherwise would possess to legislate with respect to their citizens and to conduct their own affairs.

The States unquestionably do "retai[n] a significant measure of sovereign authority." They do so, however, only to the extent that the Constitution has not divested them of their original powers and transferred those powers to the Federal Government. In the words of James Madison to the Members of the First Congress: "Interference with the power of the States was no constitutional criterion of the power of Congress. If the power was not given, Congress could not exercise it; if given, they might exercise it, although it should interfere with the laws, or even the Constitution of the States." . . .

As a result, to say that the Constitution assumes the continued role of the States is to say little about the nature of that role. Only recently, this Court recognized that the purpose of the constitutional immunity recognized in *National League of Cities* is not to preserve "a sacred province of state autonomy." *EEOC v. Wyoming*. With rare exceptions, like the guarantee, in Article IV, Sec. 3, of state territorial integrity, the Constitution does not carve out express elements of state sovereignty that Congress may not employ its delegated powers to displace. James Wilson reminded the Pennsylvania ratifying convention in 1787: "It is true, indeed, sir, although it presupposes the existence of state governments, yet this Constitution does not suppose them to be the sole power to be respected." 2 *Debates in the Several State Conventions on the Adoption of the Federal Constitution* 439 (J. Elliot 2d ed. 1876). The power of the Federal Government is a "power to be respected" as well, and the fact that the States remain sovereign as to all powers not vested in Congress or denied them by the Constitution offers no guidance about where the frontier between state and federal power lies. In short, we have no license to employ freestanding conceptions of state sovereignty when measuring congressional authority under the Commerce Clause.

When we look for the States' "residuary and inviolable sovereignty," *The Federalist* No. 39 (J. Madison), in the shape of the constitutional scheme rather than in predetermined notions of sovereign power, a different measure of state sovereignty emerges. Apart from the limitation on federal authority inherent in the delegated nature of Congress' Article I powers, the principal means chosen by the Framers to ensure the role of the States in the federal system lies in the structure of the Federal Government itself. It is no novelty to observe that the composition of the Federal Government was designed in large part to protect the States from over-reaching by Congress. The Framers thus gave the States a role in the selection both of the Executive and the Legislative Branches of the Federal Government. The States were vested with indirect influence over the House of Representatives and the Presidency by their control of electoral qualifications and their role in presidential elections. U.S. Const., Art. I, Sec. 2, and Art. II, Sec. 1. They were given more direct influence in the Senate, where each State received equal representation and each Senator was to be selected by the legislature of his State. Art. I, Sec. 3. The significance attached to the States' equal representation in the Senate is underscored by the prohibition of any constitutional amendment divesting a State of equal representation without the State's consent. Art. V. . . .

In short, the Framers chose to rely on a federal system in which special restraints on federal power over the States inhered principally in the workings of the National Government itself, rather than in discrete limitations on the objects of federal authority. State sovereign interests, then, are more properly protected by procedural safeguards inherent in the structure of the federal system than by judicially created limitations on federal power.

The effectiveness of the federal political process in preserving the States' interests is apparent even today in the course of federal legislation. On the one hand, the States have been able to direct a substantial proportion of federal revenues into their own treasuries in the form of general and program-specific grants in aid. The federal role in assisting state and local governments is a longstanding one; Congress provided federal land grants to finance state governments from the beginning of the Republic, and direct cash grants were awarded as early as 1887 under the Hatch Act. In the past quarter-century alone, federal grants to States and localities have grown from $7 billion to $96 billion. As a result, federal grants now account for about one-fifth of state and local government expenditures. The States have obtained federal funding for such services as police and fire protection, education, public health and hospitals, parks and recreation, and sanitation. Moreover, at the same time that the States have exercised their influence to obtain federal support, they have been able to exempt themselves from a wide variety of obligations imposed by Congress under the Commerce Clause. For example, the Federal Power Act, the National Labor Relations Act, the Labor-Management Reporting and Disclosure Act, the Occupational Safety and Health Act, the Employee Retirement Insurance Security Act, and the Sherman Act all contain express or implied exemptions for States and their subdivisions. The fact that some federal statutes such as the FLSA extend general obligations to the States cannot obscure the extent to which the political position of the States in the federal system has served to minimize the burdens that the States bear under the Commerce Clause. . . .

[A]gainst this background, we are convinced that the fundamental limitation that the constitutional scheme imposes on the Commerce Clause to protect the "States as States" is one of process rather than one of result. Any substantive restraint on the exercise of Commerce Clause powers must find its justification in the procedural nature of this basic limitation, and it must be tailored to compensate for possible failings in the national political process rather than to dictate a "sacred province of state autonomy." . . .

Insofar as the present cases are concerned, then, we need go no further than to state that we perceive nothing in the overtime and minimum-wage requirements of the FLSA, as applied to SAMTA, that is destructive of state sovereignty or violative of any constitutional provision. SAMTA faces nothing more than the same minimum-wage and overtime obligations that hundreds of thousands of other employers, public as well as private, have to meet.

This analysis makes clear that Congress' action in affording SAMTA employees the protections of the wage and hour provisions of the FLSA contravened no affirmative limit on Congress' power under the Commerce Clause. The judgment of the District Court therefore must be reversed. . . .

☐ *Justice POWELL, with whom THE CHIEF JUSTICE, Justice REHNQUIST and Justice O'CONNOR join, dissenting.*

The Court today, in its 5–4 decision, overrules *National League of Cities v. Usery* (1976), a case in which we held that Congress lacked authority to impose the requirements of the Fair Labor Standards Act on state and local governments. Because I believe this decision substantially alters the federal system embodied in the Constitution, I dissent.

There are, of course, numerous examples over the history of this Court in which prior decisions have been reconsidered and overruled. There have been few cases, however, in which the principle of *stare decisis* and the rationale of recent decisions were ignored as abruptly as we now witness. The reasoning of the Court in *National League of Cities*, and the principle applied there, have been reiterated consistently over the past eight years. Since its decision in 1976, *National League of Cities* has been cited and quoted in opinions joined by every member of the present Court. . . .

Whatever effect the Court's decision may have in weakening the application of *stare decisis*, it is likely to be less important than what the Court has done to the Constitution itself. A unique feature of the United States is the *federal* system of government guaranteed by the Constitution and implicit in the very name of our country. Despite some genuflecting in Court's opinion to the concept of federalism, today's decision effectively reduces the Tenth Amendment to meaningless rhetoric when Congress acts pursuant to the Commerce Clause. . . .

Much of the Court's opinion is devoted to arguing that it is difficult to define *a priori* "traditional governmental functions." *National League of Cities* neither engaged in, nor required, such a task. The Court discusses and condemns as standards "traditional governmental function[s]," "purely historical" functions, " 'uniquely' governmental functions," and " 'necessary' governmental services." But nowhere does it mention that *National League of Cities* adopted a familiar type of balancing test for determining whether Commerce Clause enactments transgress constitutional limitations imposed by the federal nature of our system of government. This omission is noteworthy, since the author of today's opinion joined *National League of Cities* and concurred separately to point out that the Court's opinion in that case "adopt[s] a balancing approach [that] does not outlaw federal power in areas . . . where the federal interest is demonstrably greater and where state . . . compliance with imposed federal standards would be essential." (BLACKMUN, J., concurring). . . .

In overruling *National League of Cities*, the Court incorrectly characterizes the mode of analysis established therein and developed in subsequent cases.

Moreover, the statute at issue in this case, the FLSA, is the identical statute that was at issue in *National League of Cities*. Although Justice BLACKMUN's concurrence noted that he was "not untroubled by certain possible implications of the Court's opinion" in *National League of Cities*, it also stated that "the result with respect to the statute under challenge here [the FLSA] is *necessarily correct*" (emphasis added). His opinion for the Court today does not discuss the statute, nor identify any changed circumstances that warrant the conclusion today that *National League of Cities* is *necessarily wrong*.

Today's opinion does not explain how the States' role in the electoral process guarantees that particular exercises of the Commerce Clause power will not infringe on residual State sovereignty. Members of Congress are elected from the various States, but once in office they are members of the federal government. . . .

The Court apparently thinks that the State's success at obtaining federal funds for various projects and exemptions from the obligations of some federal statutes is indicative of the "effectiveness of the federal political process in preserving the States' interests." But such political success is not relevant to the question whether the political *processes* are the proper means of enforcing constitutional limitations. The fact that Congress generally does not transgress constitutional limits on its power to reach State activities does not make judicial review any less necessary to rectify the cases in which it does do so. The States' role in our system of government is a matter of constitutional law, not of legislative grace. "The powers not delegated to the United States by the Constitution, nor prohibited by it to the States, are reserved to the States, respectively, or to the people." U.S. Const., Amend. 10.

More troubling than the logical infirmities in the Court's reasoning is the result of its holding, i.e., that federal political officials, invoking the Commerce Clause, are the sole judges of the limits of their own power. This result is inconsistent with the fundamental principles of our constitutional system. At least since *Marbury v. Madison* it has been the settled province of the federal judiciary "to say what the law is" with respect to the constitutionality of acts of Congress. In rejecting the role of the judiciary in protecting the States from federal overreaching, the Court's opinion offers no explanation for ignoring the teaching of the most famous case in our history.

In our federal system, the States have a major role that cannot be preempted by the national government. As contemporaneous writings and the debates at the ratifying conventions make clear, the States' ratification of the Constitution was predicated on this understanding of federalism. Indeed, the Tenth Amendment was adopted specifically to ensure that the important role promised the States by the proponents of the Constitution was realized. . . .

[T]he harm to the States that results from federal overreaching under the Commerce Clause is not simply a matter of dollars and cents. Nor is it a matter of the wisdom or folly of certain policy choices. Rather, by usurping functions traditionally performed by the States, federal overreaching under the Commerce Clause undermines the constitutionally mandated balance of power between the States and the federal government, a balance designed to protect our fundamental liberties.

The emasculation of the powers of the States that can result from the Court's decision is predicated on the Commerce Clause as a power "delegated to the United States" by the Constitution. The relevant language states: "Congress shall have power . . . to regulate commerce with foreign nations and among the several states and with the Indian tribes." Art. I, Sec. 8. Section eight identifies a score of powers, listing the authority to lay taxes, borrow money on the credit of the United States, pay its debts, and provide for the common defense and the general welfare *before* its brief reference to "Commerce." It is clear from the debates leading up to the adoption of the Constitution that the commerce to be regulated was that which the states themselves lacked the practical capability to regulate. Indeed, the language of the clause itself focuses on activities that only a national government could regulate: commerce with foreign nations and Indian tribes and "*among*" the several states.

To be sure, this Court has construed the Commerce Clause to accommodate unanticipated changes over the past two centuries. As these changes have occurred, the Court has had to decide whether the federal government has exceeded its authority by regulating activities beyond the capability of a single state to regulate or beyond legitimate federal interests that outweighed the authority and interests of the States. In so doing, however, the Court properly has been mindful of the essential role of the States in our federal system.

The opinion for the Court in *National League of Cities* was faithful to history in its understanding of federalism. The Court observed that "our federal system of government imposes definite limits upon the authority of Congress to regulate the activities of States as States by means of the commerce power." The Tenth Amendment was invoked to prevent Congress from exercising its "power in a fashion that impairs the States' integrity or their ability to function effectively in a federal system." . . .

This Court has recognized repeatedly that state sovereignty is a fundamental component of our system of government. More than a century ago, in *Lane County v. Oregon* (1868), the Court stated that the Constitution recognized "the necessary existence of the States, and, within their proper spheres, the independent authority of the States." . . .

In contrast, the Court today propounds a view of federalism that pays only lip service to the role of the States. Although it says that the States "unquestionably do 'retai[n]' a significant measure of sovereign authority,' " it fails to recognize the broad, yet specific areas of sovereignty that the Framers intended the States to retain. Indeed, the Court barely acknowledges that the Tenth Amendment exists. That Amendment states explicitly that "[t]he powers not delegated to the United States . . . are reserved to the States." U.S. Const., Amend. 10. The Court recasts this language to say that the States retain their sovereign powers "only to the extent that the Constitution has not divested them of their original powers and transferred those powers to the Federal Government." This rephrasing is not a distinction without a difference; rather, it reflects the Court's unprecedented view that Congress is free under the Commerce Clause to assume a State's traditional sovereign power, and to do so without judicial review of its action. Indeed, the Court's view of federalism appears to relegate the States to precisely the trivial role that opponents of the Constitution feared they would occupy.

In *National League of Cities*, we spoke of fire prevention, police protection, sanitation, and public health as "typical of [the services] performed by state and local governments in discharging their dual functions of administering the public law and furnishing public services." Not only are these activities remote from any normal concept of interstate commerce, they are also activities that epitomize the concerns of local, democratic self-government. In emphasizing the need to protect traditional governmental functions, we identified the kinds of activities engaged in by state and local governments that affect the everyday lives of citizens. These are services that people are in a position to understand and evaluate, and in a democracy, have the right to oversee. We recognized that "it is functions such as these which governments are created to provide . . ." and that the states and local governments are better able than the national government to perform them.

The Court maintains that the standard approved in *National League of Cities* "disserves principles of democratic self-government." In reaching this conclusion, the Court looks myopically only to persons elected to positions in the federal government. It disregards entirely the far more effective role of democratic self-government at the state and local levels. One must compare realistically the operation of the state and local governments with that of the federal government. Federal legislation is drafted primarily by the staffs of the congressional committees. In view of the hundreds of bills introduced at each session of Congress and the complexity of many of them, it is virtually impossible for even the most conscientious legislators to be truly familiar with many of the statutes enacted. Federal departments and agencies customarily are authorized to write regulations. Often these are more important than the text of the statutes. As is true of the original legislation, these are drafted largely by staff personnel. The administration and enforcement of federal laws and regulations necessarily are largely in the hands of staff and civil service employees. These employees may have little or no knowledge of the States and localities that will be affected by the statutes and regulations for which they are responsible. In any case, they hardly are as accessible and responsive as those who occupy analogous positions in State and local governments. . . .

The question presented in this case is whether the extension of the FLSA to the wages and hours of employees of a city-owned transit system unconstitutionally impinges on fundamental state sovereignty. The Court's sweeping holding does far more than simply answer this question in the negative. In overruling *National League of Cities*, today's opinion apparently authorizes federal control, under the auspices of the Commerce Clause, over the terms and conditions of employment of all state and local employees. Thus, for purposes of federal regulation, the Court rejects the distinction between public and private employers that had been drawn carefully in *National League of Cities*. The Court's action reflects a serious misunderstanding, if not an outright rejection, of the history of our country and the intention of the Framers of the Constitution. . . .

☐ *Justice O'CONNOR, with whom Justice POWELL and Justice REHNQUIST join, dissenting.*

. . .

In my view, federalism cannot be reduced to the weak "essence" distilled by the majority today. There is more to federalism than the nature of the constraints that can be imposed on the States in "the realm of authority left open to them by the Constitution." The central issue of federalism, of course, is whether any realm *is* left open to the States by the Constitution— whether any area remains in which a State may act free of federal interference. . . . The true "essence" of federalism is that the States *as States* have legitimate interests which the National Government is bound to respect even though its laws are supreme. *Younger v. Harris*, 401 U.S. 37 (1971). If federalism so conceived and so carefully cultivated by the Framers of our Constitution is to remain meaningful, this Court cannot abdicate its constitutional responsibility to oversee the Federal Government's compliance with its duty to respect the legitimate interests of the States.

Due to the emergence of an integrated and industrialized national economy, this Court has been required to examine and review a breathtaking expansion of the powers of Congress. In doing so the Court correctly perceived that the Framers of our Constitution intended Congress to have sufficient power to address national problems. But the Framers were not single-minded. The Constitution is animated by an array of intentions. . . . Just as surely as the Framers envisioned a National Government capable of solving national problems, they also envisioned a republic whose vitality was assured by the diffusion of power not only among the branches of the Federal Government, but also between the Federal Government and the States. . . .

We would do well to recall the constitutional basis for federalism and the development of the commerce power which has come to displace it. The text of the Constitution does not define the precise scope of state authority other than to specify, in the Tenth Amendment, that the powers not delegated to the United States by the Constitution are reserved to the States. In the view of the Framers, however, this did not leave state authority weak or defenseless; the powers delegated to the United States, after all, were "few and defined." *The Federalist* No. 45. The Framers' comments indicate that the sphere of state activity was to be a significant one, as Justice POWELL's opinion clearly demonstrates. The States were to retain authority over those local concerns of greatest relevance and importance to the people. . . .

The problems of federalism in an integrated national economy are capable of more responsible resolution than holding that the States as States retain no status apart from that which Congress chooses to let them retain. The proper resolution, I suggest, lies in weighing state autonomy as a factor in the balance when interpreting the means by which Congress can exercise its authority on the States as States. It is insufficient, in assessing the validity of congressional regulation of a State pursuant to the commerce power, to ask only whether the same regulation would be valid if enforced against a private party. . . . As far as the Constitution is concerned, a State should not be equated with any private litigant. . . . Instead, the autonomy of a State is an essential component of federalism. If state autonomy is ignored in assessing the means by which Congress regulates matters affecting commerce, then federalism becomes irrelevant simply because the set of activities remaining beyond the reach of such a commerce power "may well be negligible."

It has been difficult for this Court to craft bright lines defining the scope of the state autonomy protected by *National League of Cities*. Such difficulty is to be expected whenever constitutional concerns as important as federalism and the effectiveness of the commerce power come into conflict. Regardless of the difficulty, it is and will remain the duty of this Court to reconcile these concerns in the final instance. That the Court shuns the task today by appealing to the "essence of federalism" can provide scant comfort to those who believe our federal system requires something more than a unitary, centralized

Tenth Amendment Rulings in Historical Perspective

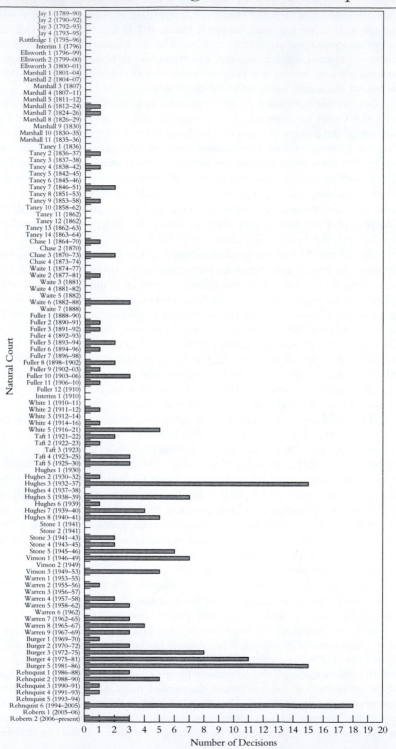

Source: William Grayson Lambert's Honors Thesis at the University of Virginia (2009).
"Natural Courts" are periods in which the Court's composition did not change.

government. I would not shirk the duty acknowledged by *National League of Cities* and its progeny, and I share Justice REHNQUIST's belief that this Court will in time again assume its constitutional responsibility.

I respectfully dissent.

New York v. United States

505 U.S. 144, 112 S.CT. 2408 (1992)

In the late 1970s, federal policy makers began confronting the prospect that the country would soon run out of disposal sites for low-level radioactive waste. Federal authorities began targeting three states—Nevada, South Carolina, and Washington—as possible disposal sites but encountered widespread criticism from those and other states. Finally, based largely on recommendations made by the National Governors' Association, Congress enacted the Low-Level Radioactive Waste Policy Act of 1980, which established a federal policy of holding each state "responsible for providing for the availability of capacity either within or outside the State for the disposal of low-level radioactive waste generated within its borders," upon finding that such waste could be disposed of "most safely and efficiently . . . on a regional basis." The act authorized the states to enter into regional compacts that, after ratification by Congress, would have authority in 1986 to restrict the use of disposal facilities to waste generated by states within each region.

By 1985, however, only three regional compacts had been formed, all around the three targeted states. As a result, the following year the authorities for three regional compacts would have the authority to exclude the disposal of radioactive waste generated in states not belonging to one of the compacts, and thirty-one states would thus be left with no ensured site for the disposal of their radioactive wastes. Congress therefore amended its earlier legislation with the Low-Level Radioactive Waste Policy Amendments Act of 1985.

The 1985 act, which was also based on proposals submitted by the National Governors' Association, achieved a kind of political compromise between the targeted and untargeted states. The targeted states agreed to continue, for seven years, to dispose of radioactive waste generated in other states, while the nontargeted states agreed to provide disposal sites for their own waste by 1992. The law also provided three kinds of incentives for states to comply with their obligation to dispose of waste generated within their own borders by 1992: (1) Monetary incentives: States or compacts disposing of all radioactive waste generated within their borders by January 1, 1993, might receive special funding from surcharges collected by the targeted states and held in escrow by the Department of Energy. (2) Access incentives: States or compacts that failed to meet specified deadlines for disposing of their waste would be charged double surcharges and be denied access to disposal sites in targeted states thereafter, and those states failing to operate disposal facilities by January 1, 1992, could be charged triple surcharges. (3) A "take-title provision": States or compacts that failed to provide disposal sites for all wastes generated within the state or compact by January 1, 1996, would be obligated to take title of all undisposed waste and assume liability for all damages incurred by the waste's generator, which could not dispose of it because of the state's or compact's failure to provide a disposal site.

New York, which generates a large share of the nation's low-level radioactive waste, complied with the 1985 law's requirements for siting and financing of disposal facilities by selecting five potential disposal sites. But residents in two of the counties selected as disposal sites filed suit and were later joined by New York State authorities. They argued that the 1985 amendments were unconstitutional and intruded on states' rights as guaranteed by the Tenth Amendment. The Court of Appeals for the Second Circuit, however, rejected that argument and New York appealed to the Supreme Court.

The Court's decision was six to three; the majority's opinion was announced by Justice O'Connor. Justices White and Stevens delivered separate opinions, in part concurring and in part dissenting, in which Justice Blackmun joined.

☐ *Justice O'CONNOR delivers the opinion of the Court.*

[T]he Tenth Amendment "states but a truism that all is retained which has not been surrendered." *United States v. Darby*, 312 U.S. 100 (1941). . . . This has been the Court's consistent understanding: "The States unquestionably do retain a significant measure of sovereign authority . . . to the extent that the Constitution has not divested them of their original powers and transferred those powers to the Federal Government." *Garcia v. San Antonio Metropolitan Transit Authority.* [469 U.S. 528 (1985)].

Congress exercises its conferred powers subject to the limitations contained in the Constitution. Thus, for example, under the Commerce Clause Congress may regulate publishers engaged in interstate commerce, but Congress is constrained in the exercise of that power by the First Amendment. The Tenth Amendment likewise restrains the power of Congress, but this limit is not derived from the text of the Tenth Amendment itself, which, as we have discussed, is essentially a tautology. Instead, the Tenth Amendment confirms that the power of the Federal Government is subject to limits that may, in a given instance, reserve power to the States. The Tenth Amendment thus directs us to determine, as in this case, whether an incident of state sovereignty is protected by a limitation on an Article I power. . . .

[The federal] framework has been sufficiently flexible over the past two centuries to allow for enormous changes in the nature of government. The Federal Government undertakes activities today that would have been unimaginable to the Framers in two senses; first, because the Framers would not have conceived that any government would conduct such activities; and second, because the Framers would not have believed that the Federal Government, rather than the States, would assume such responsibilities. Yet the powers conferred upon the Federal Government by the Constitution were phrased in language broad enough to allow for the expansion of the Federal Government's role. Among the provisions of the Constitution that have been particularly important in this regard, three concern us here.

First, the Constitution allocates to Congress the power "to regulate Commerce . . . among the several States." Art. I, Sec. 8, cl. 3. . . . Second, the Constitution authorizes Congress "to pay the Debts and provide for the . . . general Welfare of the United States." Art. I, Sec. 8, cl. 1. . . . The Court's broad construction of Congress' power under the Commerce and Spending Clauses has of course been guided, as it has with respect to Congress' power generally, by the Constitution's Necessary and Proper Clause, which authorizes Congress "to make all Laws which shall be necessary and proper for carrying into Execution the foregoing Powers." U.S. Const., Art. I., Sec. 8, cl. 18.

Finally, The Constitution provides that "the Laws of the United States . . . shall be the supreme Law of the Land . . . anything in the Constitution or Laws of any State to the Contrary notwithstanding." U.S. Const., Art. VI, cl. 2. . . .

The actual scope of the Federal Government's authority with respect to the States has changed over the years, therefore, but the constitutional structure underlying and limiting that authority has not. In the end, just as a cup may be half empty or half full, it makes no difference whether one views the question at issue in this case as one of ascertaining the limits of the power delegated to the Federal Government under the affirmative provisions of the Constitution or one of discerning the core of sovereignty retained by the States under the Tenth Amendment. Either way, we must determine whether any of the three challenged provisions of the Low-Level Radioactive Waste Policy Amendments Act of 1985 oversteps the boundary between federal and state authority. . . .

Most of our recent cases interpreting the Tenth Amendment have concerned the authority of Congress to subject state governments to generally applicable laws. The Court's jurisprudence in this area has traveled an unsteady path. See *Maryland v. Wirtz*, 392 U.S. 183 (1968) (state schools and hospitals are subject to Fair Labor Standards Act); *Garcia v. San Antonio Metropolitan Transit Authority*, 469 U.S. 528 (1985) (overruling *National League of Cities*) (state employers are once again subject to Fair Labor Standards Act). This case presents no occasion to apply or revisit the holdings of any of these cases, as this is not a case in which Congress has subjected a State to the same legislation applicable to private parties. Cf. *FERC v. Mississippi*, 456 U.S. 742 (1982).

This case instead concerns the circumstances under which Congress may use the States as implements of regulation; that is, whether Congress may direct or otherwise motivate the States to regulate in a particular field or a particular way. Our cases have established a few principles that guide our resolution of the issue.

As an initial matter, Congress may not simply "commandeer the legislative processes of the States by directly compelling them to enact and enforce a federal regulatory program." *Hodel v. Virginia Surface Mining & Reclamation Assn., Inc.*, 452 U.S. 264 (1981). . . .

While Congress has substantial powers to govern the Nation directly, including in areas of intimate concern to the States, the Constitution has never been understood to confer upon Congress the ability to require the States to govern according to Congress' instructions. . . .

This is not to say Congress lacks the ability to encourage a State to regulate in a particular way, or that Congress may not hold out incentives to the States as a method of influencing a State's policy choices. Our cases have identified a variety of methods, short of outright coercion, by which Congress may urge a State to adopt a legislative program consistent with federal interests. Two of these methods are of particular relevance here.

First, under Congress' spending power, "Congress may attach conditions on the receipt of federal funds." *South Dakota v. Dole*, 483 U.S. [203 (1987)]. . . .

Second, where Congress has the authority to regulate private activity under the Commerce Clause, we have recognized Congress' power to offer States the choice of regulating that activity according to federal standards or having state law preempted by federal regulation. . . .

By contrast, where the Federal Government compels States to regulate, the accountability of both state and federal officials is diminished. If the citizens of New York, for example, do not consider that making provision for the disposal of radioactive waste is in their best interest, they may elect state officials who share their view. That view can always be preempted under the Supremacy Clause if it is contrary to the national view, but in such a case it is the Federal Government that makes the decision in full view of the public, and it will be federal officials that suffer the consequences if the decision turns out to be detrimental or unpopular. But where the Federal Government directs the States to regulate, it may be state officials who will bear the brunt of public disapproval, while the federal officials who devised the regulatory program may remain insulated from the electoral ramifications of their decision. Accountability is thus diminished when, due to federal coercion, elected state officials cannot regulate in accordance with the views of the local electorate in matters not preempted by federal regulation.

With these principles in mind, we turn to the three challenged provisions of the Low-Level Radioactive Waste Policy Amendments Act of 1985.

The first set of incentives works in three steps. First, Congress has authorized States with disposal sites to impose a surcharge on radioactive waste received from other States. Second, the Secretary of Energy collects a portion of this surcharge and places the money in an escrow account. Third, States achieving a series of milestones receive portions of this fund.

The first of these steps is an unexceptionable exercise of Congress' power to authorize the States to burden interstate commerce. . . .

The second step, the Secretary's collection of a percentage of the surcharge, is no more than a federal tax on interstate commerce, which petitioners do not claim to be an invalid exercise of either Congress' commerce or taxing power.

The third step is a conditional exercise of Congress' authority under the

Spending Clause: Congress has placed conditions—the achievement of the milestones—on the receipt of federal funds. . . .

This third so-called "incentive" offers States, as an alternative to regulating pursuant to Congress' direction, the option of taking title to and possession of the low level radioactive waste generated within their borders and becoming liable for all damages waste generators suffer as a result of the States' failure to do so promptly. In this provision, Congress has crossed the line distinguishing encouragement from coercion. . . .

The take title provision offers state governments a "choice" of either accepting ownership of waste or regulating according to the instructions of Congress. . . . Because an instruction to state governments to take title to waste, standing alone, would be beyond the authority of Congress, and because a direct order to regulate, standing alone, would also be beyond the authority of Congress, it follows that Congress lacks the power to offer the States a choice between the two. Unlike the first two sets of incentives, the take title incentive does not represent the conditional exercise of any congressional power enumerated in the Constitution. In this provision, Congress has not held out the threat of exercising its spending power or its commerce power; it has instead held out the threat, should the States not regulate according to one federal instruction, of simply forcing the States to submit to another federal instruction. A choice between two unconstitutionally coercive regulatory techniques is no choice at all. Either way, "the Act commandeers the legislative processes of the States by directly compelling them to enact and enforce a federal regulatory program," *Hodel v. Virginia Surface Mining & Reclamation Assn., Inc.*, an outcome that has never been understood to lie within the authority conferred upon Congress by the Constitution. . . .

The take title provision appears to be unique. No other federal statute has been cited which offers a state government no option other than that of implementing legislation enacted by Congress. Whether one views the take title provision as lying outside Congress' enumerated powers, or as infringing upon the core of state sovereignty reserved by the Tenth Amendment, the provision is inconsistent with the federal structure of our Government established by the Constitution. . . .

The Constitution permits both the Federal Government and the States to enact legislation regarding the disposal of low level radioactive waste. The Constitution enables the Federal Government to preempt state regulation contrary to federal interests, and it permits the Federal Government to hold out incentives to the States as a means of encouraging them to adopt suggested regulatory schemes. It does not, however, authorize Congress simply to direct the States to provide for the disposal of the radioactive waste generated within their borders. While there may be many constitutional methods of achieving regional self-sufficiency in radioactive waste disposal, the method Congress has chosen is not one of them. The judgment of the Court of Appeals is accordingly

Affirmed in part and reversed in part.

☐ *Justice WHITE, with whom Justices BLACKMUN and STEVENS join, concurring and dissenting in part.*

My disagreement with the Court's analysis begins at the basic descriptive level of how the legislation at issue in this case came to be enacted. . . .

To read the Court's version of events, one would think that Congress was the sole proponent of a solution to the Nation's low-level radioactive waste problem. Not so. The Low-Level Radioactive Waste Policy Act of 1980 (1980 Act), and its amendatory Act of 1985, resulted from the efforts of state leaders to achieve a state-based set of remedies to the waste problem. They sought not federal preemption or intervention, but rather congressional sanction of interstate compromises they had reached. . . .

In my view, New York's actions subsequent to enactment of the 1980 and 1985 Acts fairly indicate its approval of the interstate agreement process embodied in those laws within the meaning of Art. I, Sec. 10, cl. 3, of the Constitution, which provides that "no State shall, without the Consent of Congress, . . . enter into any Agreement or Compact with another State." First, the States—including New York—worked through their Governors to petition Congress for the 1980 and 1985 Acts. As I have attempted to demonstrate, these statutes are best understood as the products of collective state action, rather than as impositions placed on States by the Federal Government. Second, New York acted in compliance with the requisites of both statutes in key respects, thus signifying its assent to the agreement achieved among the States as codified in these laws. . . .

The Court announces that it has no occasion to revisit such decisions as *Gregory v. Ashcroft*, [501 U.S. 452] (1991); *South Carolina v. Baker*, 485 U.S. 505 (1988); *Garcia v. San Antonio Metropolitan Transit Authority*, 469 U.S. 528 (1985); *EEOC v. Wyoming*, 460 U.S. 226 (1983); and *National League of Cities v. Usery*, 426 U.S. 833 (1976), because "this is not a case in which Congress has subjected a State to the same legislation applicable to private parties." Although this statement sends the welcome signal that the Court does not intend to cut a wide swath through our recent Tenth Amendment precedents, it nevertheless is unpersuasive. I have several difficulties with the Court's analysis in this respect: it builds its rule around an insupportable and illogical distinction in the types of alleged incursions on state sovereignty; it derives its rule from cases that do not support its analysis; it fails to apply the appropriate tests from the cases on which it purports to base its rule; and it omits any discussion of the most recent and pertinent test for determining the take title provision's constitutionality.

The Court's distinction between a federal statute's regulation of States and private parties for general purposes, as opposed to a regulation solely on the activities of States, is unsupported by our recent Tenth Amendment cases. In no case has the Court rested its holding on such a distinction. Moreover, the Court makes no effort to explain why this purported distinction should affect the analysis of Congress' power under general principles of federalism and the Tenth Amendment. The distinction, facilely thrown out, is not based on any defensible theory. Certainly one would be hard-pressed to read the spirited exchanges between the Court and dissenting Justices in *National League of Cities*, and in *Garcia v. San Antonio Metropolitan Transit Authority*, as having been based on the distinction now drawn by the Court. An incursion on state sovereignty hardly seems more constitutionally acceptable if the federal statute that "commands" specific action also applies to private parties. The alleged diminution in state authority over its own affairs is not any less because the federal mandate restricts the activities of private parties. . . .

Printz v. United States and *Mack v. United States*
521 U.S. 898, 117 S.Ct. 2365 (1997)

In 1993, after seven years of debate Congress enacted the Brady Hand-gun Violence Prevention Act as an amendment to the Gun Control Act of 1968. The law was named after James S. Brady, who was disabled in the 1981 assassination attempt on President Ronald Reagan. Among other provisions, the law required state and local law enforcement offi-cials to conduct background checks on prospective handgun pur-chasers. That provision was challenged by two chief law enforcement officers, Jay Printz of Ravalli County, Montana, and Richard Mack of Graham County, Arizona. They argued that the federal provision was unconstitutional because Congress has no authority to require state and local officials to carry out federal laws. Besides claiming that the law was an unfunded federal mandate, they claimed that the law was burdensome and diverted resources and time from their investigative responsibilities. A federal district court agreed but the Court of Appeals for the Ninth Circuit reversed and Printz and Mack, supported by the National Rifle Association, appealed.

The Court's decision was five to four and its opinion delivered by Justice Scalia. Justices O'Connor and Thomas filed concurring opin-ions. Justice Stevens filed a dissenting opinion, which was joined by Justices Souter, Ginsburg, and Breyer. Justices Souter and Breyer also filed separate dissenting opinions.

☐ *Justice SCALIA delivered the opinion of the Court.*

The question presented in these cases is whether certain interim provi-sions of the Brady Handgun Violence Prevention Act, commanding state and local law enforcement officers to conduct background checks on prospective handgun purchasers and to perform certain related tasks, violate the Consti-tution. . . .

[T]he Brady Act purports to direct state law enforcement officers to participate, albeit only temporarily, in the administration of a federally en-acted regulatory scheme. Regulated firearms dealers are required to forward Brady Forms not to a federal officer or employee, but to the CLEOs [chief law enforcement officers], whose obligation to accept those forms is implicit in the duty imposed upon them to make "reasonable efforts" within five days to determine whether the sales reflected in the forms are lawful. While the CLEOs are subjected to no federal requirement that they prevent the sales determined to be unlawful (it is perhaps assumed that their state-law duties will require prevention or apprehension), they are empowered to grant, in effect, waivers of the federally prescribed 5-day waiting period for handgun purchases by notifying the gun dealers that they have no reason to believe the transactions would be illegal.

The petitioners here object to being pressed into federal service, and contend that congressional action compelling state officers to execute federal laws is unconstitutional.

Because there is no constitutional text speaking to this precise question, the answer to the CLEOs' challenge must be sought in historical understanding and practice, in the structure of the Constitution, and in the jurisprudence of this Court. We treat those three sources in that order. . . .

The Government observes that statutes enacted by the first Congresses required state courts to record applications for citizenship, to transmit abstracts of citizenship applications and other naturalization records to the Secretary of State, and to register aliens seeking naturalization and issue certificates of registry. It may well be, however, that these requirements applied only in States that authorized their courts to conduct naturalization proceedings. Other statutes of that era apparently or at least arguably required state courts to perform functions unrelated to naturalization, such as resolving controversies between a captain and the crew of his ship concerning the seaworthiness of the vessel, hearing the claims of slave owners who had apprehended fugitive slaves and issuing certificates authorizing the slave's forced removal to the State from which he had fled, taking proof of the claims of Canadian refugees who had assisted the United States during the Revolutionary War, and ordering the deportation of alien enemies in times of war.

These early laws establish, at most, that the Constitution was originally understood to permit imposition of an obligation on state judges to enforce federal prescriptions, insofar as those prescriptions related to matters appropriate for the judicial power. That assumption was perhaps implicit in one of the provisions of the Constitution, and was explicit in another. In accord with the so-called Madisonian Compromise, Article III, Sec. 1, established only a Supreme Court, and made the creation of lower federal courts optional with the Congress—even though it was obvious that the Supreme Court alone could not hear all federal cases throughout the United States. And the Supremacy Clause, Art. VI, cl. 2, announced that "the Laws of the United States . . . shall be the supreme Law of the Land; and the Judges in every State shall be bound thereby." It is understandable why courts should have been viewed distinctively in this regard; unlike legislatures and executives, they applied the law of other sovereigns all the time. The principle underlying so-called "transitory" causes of action was that laws which operated elsewhere created obligations in justice that courts of the forum state would enforce. The Constitution itself, in the Full Faith and Credit Clause, Art. IV, Sec. 1, generally required such enforcement with respect to obligations arising in other States.

For these reasons, we do not think the early statutes imposing obligations on state courts imply a power of Congress to impress the state executive into its service. Indeed, it can be argued that the numerousness of these statutes, contrasted with the utter lack of statutes imposing obligations on the States' executive (notwithstanding the attractiveness of that course to

Congress), suggests an assumed absence of such power. The only early federal law the Government has brought to our attention that imposed duties on state executive officers is the Extradition Act of 1793, which required the "executive authority" of a State to cause the arrest and delivery of a fugitive from justice upon the request of the executive authority of the State from which the fugitive had fled. That was in direct implementation, however, of the Extradition Clause of the Constitution itself; see Art. IV, Sec. 2.

Not only do the enactments of the early Congresses, as far as we are aware, contain no evidence of an assumption that the Federal Government may command the States' executive power in the absence of a particularized constitutional authorization, they contain some indication of precisely the opposite assumption. On September 23, 1789—the day before its proposal of the Bill of Rights—the First Congress enacted a law aimed at obtaining state assistance of the most rudimentary and necessary sort for the enforcement of the new Government's laws: the holding of federal prisoners in state jails at federal expense. Significantly, the law issued not a command to the States' executive, but a recommendation to their legislatures. . . . Moreover, when Georgia refused to comply with the request, Congress' only reaction was a law authorizing the marshal in any State that failed to comply with the Recommendation of September 23, 1789, to rent a temporary jail until provision for a permanent one could be made.

In addition to early legislation, the Government also appeals to other sources we have usually regarded as indicative of the original understanding of the Constitution. It points to portions of *The Federalist* which reply to criticisms that Congress's power to tax will produce two sets of revenue officers—for example, "Brutus's" assertion in his letter to the New York Journal of December 13, 1787, that the Constitution "opens a door to the appointment of a swarm of revenue and excise officers to prey upon the honest and industrious part of the community, eat up their substance, and riot on the spoils of the country." "Publius" responded that Congress will probably "make use of the State officers and State regulations, for collecting" federal taxes, *The Federalist* No. 36 (A. Hamilton), and predicted that "the eventual collection [of internal revenue] under the immediate authority of the Union, will generally be made by the officers, and according to the rules, appointed by the several States," No. 45 (J. Madison). The Government also invokes *The Federalist's* more general observations that the Constitution would "enable the [national] government to employ the ordinary magistracy of each [State] in the execution of its laws," No. 27 (A. Hamilton), and that it was "extremely probable that in other instances, particularly in the organization of the judicial power, the officers of the States will be clothed in the correspondent authority of the Union," No. 45 (J. Madison). But none of these statements necessarily implies—what is the critical point here—that Congress could impose these responsibilities without the consent of the States. They appear to rest on the natural assumption that the States would consent to allowing their officials to assist the Federal Government. . . .

Justice SOUTER contends that his interpretation of *Federalist* No. 27 is "supported by No. 44," written by Madison, wherefore he claims that "Madison and Hamilton" together stand opposed to our view. In fact, *Federalist* No. 44 quite clearly contradicts Justice SOUTER's reading. In that

Number, Madison justifies the requirement that state officials take an oath to support the Federal Constitution on the ground that they "will have an essential agency in giving effect to the federal Constitution." If the dissent's reading of *Federalist* No. 27 were correct (and if Madison agreed with it), one would surely have expected that "essential agency" of state executive officers (if described further) to be described as their responsibility to execute the laws enacted under the Constitution. Instead, however, *Federalist* No. 44 continues with the following description: "The election of the President and Senate will depend, in all cases, on the legislatures of the several States. And the election of the House of Representatives will equally depend on the same authority in the first instance; and will, probably, forever be conducted by the officers and according to the laws of the States." It is most implausible that the person who labored for that example of state executive officers' assisting the Federal Government believed, but neglected to mention, that they had a responsibility to execute federal laws. If it was indeed Hamilton's view that the Federal Government could direct the officers of the States, that view has no clear support in Madison's writings, or as far as we are aware, in text, history, or early commentary elsewhere.

To complete the historical record, we must note that there is not only an absence of executive-commandeering statutes in the early Congresses, but there is an absence of them in our later history as well, at least until very recent years. The Government points to the Act of August 3, 1882, which enlisted state officials "to take charge of the local affairs of immigration in the ports within such State, and to provide for the support and relief of such immigrants therein landing as may fall into distress or need of public aid"; to inspect arriving immigrants and exclude any person found to be a "convict, lunatic, idiot," or indigent; and to send convicts back to their country of origin "without compensation." The statute did not, however, mandate those duties, but merely empowered the Secretary of the Treasury "to enter into contracts with such State . . . officers as may be designated for that purpose by the governor of any State." . . .

The constitutional practice we have examined above tends to negate the existence of the congressional power asserted here, but is not conclusive. We turn next to consideration of the structure of the Constitution, to see if we can discern among its "essential postulates," *Principality of Monaco v. Mississippi*, 292 U.S. 313 (1934), a principle that controls the present cases.

It is incontestible that the Constitution established a system of "dual sovereignty." *Gregory v. Ashcroft*, 501 U.S. 452 (1991). Although the States surrendered many of their powers to the new Federal Government, they retained "a residuary and inviolable sovereignty," *The Federalist* No. 39 (J. Madison). This is reflected throughout the Constitution's text, including (to mention only a few examples) the prohibition on any involuntary reduction or combination of a State's territory, Art. IV, Sec. 3; the Judicial Power Clause, Art. III, Sec. 2, and the Privileges and Immunities Clause, Art. IV, Sec. 2, which speak of the "Citizens" of the States; the amendment provision, Article V, which requires the votes of three-fourths of the States to amend the Constitution; and the Guarantee Clause, Art. IV, Sec. 4, which "presupposes the continued existence of the states and . . . those means and instrumentalities which are the creation of their sovereign and reserved rights," *Helvering v. Gerhardt*, 304 U.S. 405 (1938). Residual state sovereignty was also implicit, of course, in the Constitution's conferral upon Congress of not all governmental powers, but only discrete, enumerated ones, Art. I, Sec. 8, which implication was rendered express by the Tenth Amendment's assertion that "the powers not delegated to the United States by the Constitution, nor prohibited by it to the States, are reserved to the States respectively, or to the people."

The Framers' experience under the Articles of Confederation had persuaded them that using the States as the instruments of federal governance was both ineffectual and provocative of federal-state conflict. Preservation of the States as independent political entities being the price of union, and "the practicality of making laws, with coercive sanctions, for the States as political bodies" having been, in Madison's words, "exploded on all hands" of the Federal Convention of 1787, the Framers rejected the concept of a central government that would act upon and through the States, and instead designed a system in which the state and federal governments would exercise concurrent authority over the people—who were, in Hamilton's words, "the only proper objects of government," *The Federalist* No. 15. We have set forth the historical record in more detail elsewhere, see *New York v. United States*, and need not repeat it here. It suffices to repeat the conclusion: "The Framers explicitly chose a Constitution that confers upon Congress the power to regulate individuals, not States." The great innovation of this design was that "our citizens would have two political capacities, one state and one federal, each protected from incursion by the other"—"a legal system unprecedented in form and design, establishing two orders of government, each with its own direct relationship, its own privity, its own set of mutual rights and obligations to the people who sustain it and are governed by it." *U.S. Term Limits, Inc. v. Thornton*, 514 U.S. 779 (1995) (KENNEDY, J., concurring). The Constitution thus contemplates that a State's government will represent and remain accountable to its own citizens. See *New York; United States v. Lopez*, 514 U.S. 549 (1995) (KENNEDY, J., concurring). As Madison expressed it: "The local or municipal authorities form distinct and independent portions of the supremacy, no more subject, within their respective spheres, to the general authority than the general authority is subject to them, within its own sphere." *The Federalist* No. 39. . . .

When we were at last confronted squarely with a federal statute that unambiguously required the States to enact or administer a federal regulatory program, our decision should have come as no surprise. At issue in *New York v. United States*, 505 U.S. 144 (1992), were the so-called "take title" provisions of the Low-Level Radioactive Waste Policy Amendments Act of 1985, which required States either to enact legislation providing for the disposal of radioactive waste generated within their borders, or to take title to, and possession of the waste—effectively requiring the States either to legislate pursuant to Congress's directions, or to implement an administrative solution. We concluded that Congress could constitutionally require the States to do neither. "The Federal Government," we held, "may not compel the States to enact or administer a federal regulatory program." . . .

Finally, the Government puts forward a cluster of arguments that can be grouped under the heading: "The Brady Act serves very important purposes, is most efficiently administered by CLEOs during the interim period, and places a minimal and only temporary burden upon state officers." There is considerable disagreement over the extent of the burden, but we need not pause over that detail. Assuming all the mentioned factors were true, they might be relevant if we were evaluating whether the incidental application to the States of a federal law of general applicability excessively interfered with the functioning of state governments. But where, as here, it is the whole object of the law to direct the functioning of the state executive, and hence to compromise the structural framework of dual sovereignty, such a "balancing" analysis is inappropriate. It is the very principle of separate state sovereignty that such a law offends, and no comparative assessment of the various interests can overcome that fundamental defect. . . .

What we have said makes it clear enough that the central obligation imposed upon CLEOs by the interim provisions of the Brady Act—the obligation to "make a reasonable effort to ascertain within 5 business days whether receipt or possession [of a handgun] would be in violation of the law, including research in whatever State and local recordkeeping systems are available and in a national system designated by the Attorney General"—is unconstitutional. Extinguished with it, of course, is the duty implicit in the background-check requirement that the CLEO accept notice of the contents of, and a copy of, the completed Brady Form, which the firearms dealer is required to provide to him. . . .

We held in *New York* that Congress cannot compel the States to enact or enforce a federal regulatory program. Today we hold that Congress cannot circumvent that prohibition by conscripting the State's officers directly. The Federal Government may neither issue directives requiring the States to address particular problems, nor command the States' officers, or those of their political subdivisions, to administer or enforce a federal regulatory program. It matters not whether policymaking is involved, and no case-by-case weighing of the burdens or benefits is necessary; such commands are fundamentally incompatible with our constitutional system of dual sovereignty. Accordingly, the judgment of the Court of Appeals for the Ninth Circuit is reversed.

☐ *Justice O'CONNOR, concurring.*

Our precedent and our Nation's historical practices support the Court's holding today. The Brady Act violates the Tenth Amendment to the extent it forces States and local law enforcement officers to perform background checks on prospective handgun owners and to accept Brady Forms from firearms dealers. Our holding, of course, does not spell the end of the objectives of the Brady Act. States and chief law enforcement officers may voluntarily continue to participate in the federal program. Moreover, the directives to the States are merely interim provisions scheduled to terminate November 30, 1998. Congress is also free to amend the interim program to provide for its continuance on a contractual basis with the States if it wishes, as it does with a number of other federal programs. . . .

☐ *Justice STEVENS, with whom Justice SOUTER, Justice GINSBURG, and Justice BREYER join, dissenting.*

When Congress exercises the powers delegated to it by the Constitution, it may impose affirmative obligations on executive and judicial officers of state and local governments as well as ordinary citizens. This conclusion is firmly supported by the text of the Constitution, the early history of the Nation, decisions of this Court, and a correct understanding of the basic structure of the Federal Government.

These cases do not implicate the more difficult questions associated with congressional coercion of state legislatures addressed in *New York v. United States*, 505 U.S. 144 (1992). Nor need we consider the wisdom of relying on local officials rather than federal agents to carry out aspects of a federal program, or even the question whether such officials may be required to perform a federal function on a permanent basis. The question is whether Congress, acting on behalf of the people of the entire Nation, may require local law enforcement officers to perform certain duties during the interim needed for the development of a federal gun control program. It is remarkably similar to the question, heavily debated by the Framers of the Constitution, whether the Congress could require state agents to collect federal taxes. Or the question whether Congress could impress state judges into federal service to entertain and decide cases that they would prefer to ignore.

Indeed, since the ultimate issue is one of power, we must consider its implications in times of national emergency. Matters such as the enlistment of air raid wardens, the administration of a military draft, the mass inoculation of children to forestall an epidemic, or perhaps the threat of an international terrorist, may require a national response before federal personnel can be made available to respond. If the Constitution empowers Congress and the President to make an appropriate response, is there anything in the Tenth Amendment, "in historical understanding and practice, in the structure of the Constitution, [or] in the jurisprudence of this Court" that forbids the enlistment of state officers to make that response effective? More narrowly, what basis is there in any of those sources for concluding that it is the Members of this Court, rather than the elected representatives of the people, who should determine whether the Constitution contains the unwritten rule that the Court announces today?

Perhaps today's majority would suggest that no such emergency is presented by the facts of these cases. But such a suggestion is itself an expression of a policy judgment. And Congress' view of the matter is quite different from that implied by the Court today. . . .

The text of the Constitution provides a sufficient basis for a correct disposition of this case.

Article I, Sec. 8, grants the Congress the power to regulate commerce among the States. Putting alongside the revisionist views expressed by Justice THOMAS in his concurring opinion in *United States v. Lopez*, 514 U.S. 549 (1995), there can be no question that that provision adequately supports the regulation of commerce in handguns effected by the Brady Act. Moreover, the additional grant of authority in that section of the Constitution "to make all Laws which shall be necessary and proper for carrying into Execution the foregoing Powers" is surely adequate to support the temporary enlistment of local police officers in the process of identifying persons who should not be entrusted with the possession of handguns. In short, the affirmative delegation of power in Article I provides ample authority for the congressional enactment.

Unlike the First Amendment, which prohibits the enactment of a category of laws that would otherwise be authorized by Article I, the Tenth Amendment imposes no restriction on the exercise of delegated powers. Using language that plainly refers only to powers that are "not" delegated to Congress, it provides: "The powers not delegated to the United States by the Constitution, nor prohibited by it to the States, are reserved to the States respectively, or to the people." U.S. Const., Amdt. 10. The Amendment confirms the principle that the powers of the Federal Government are limited to those affirmatively granted by the Constitution, but it does not purport to limit the scope or the effectiveness of the exercise of powers that are delegated to Congress. Thus, the Amendment provides no support for a rule that immunizes local officials from obligations that might be imposed on ordinary citizens. Indeed, it would be more reasonable to infer that federal law may impose greater duties on state officials than on private citizens because another provision of the Constitution requires that "all executive and judicial Officers, both of the United States and of the several States, shall be bound by Oath or Affirmation, to support this Constitution." U.S. Const., Art. VI, cl. 3.

There is not a clause, sentence, or paragraph in the entire text of the Constitution of the United States that supports the proposition that a local police officer can ignore a command contained in a statute enacted by Congress pursuant to an express delegation of power enumerated in Article I.

Under the Articles of Confederation the National Government had the power to issue commands to the several sovereign states, but it had no authority to govern individuals directly. Thus, it raised an army and financed its operations by issuing requisitions to the constituent members of the Confederacy, rather than by creating federal agencies to draft soldiers or to impose taxes.

That method of governing proved to be unacceptable, not because it demeaned the sovereign character of the several States, but rather because it was cumbersome and inefficient. Indeed, a confederation that allows each of its members to determine the ways and means of complying with an overriding requisition is obviously more deferential to state sovereignty concerns than a national government that uses its own agents to impose its will directly on the citizenry. The basic change in the character of the government that the Framers conceived was designed to enhance the power of the national government, not to provide some new, unmentioned immunity for state officers. Because indirect control over individual citizens ("the only proper objects of government") was ineffective under the Articles of Confederation, Alexander Hamilton explained that "we must extend the authority of the Union to the persons of the citizens." *The Federalist* No. 15.

Indeed, the historical materials strongly suggest that the Founders intended to enhance the capacity of the federal government by empowering it—as a part of the new authority to make demands directly on individual citizens—to act through local officials. Hamilton made clear that the new Constitution, "by extending the authority of the federal head to the individual citizens of the several States, will enable the government to employ the ordinary magistracy of each, in the execution of its laws." *The Federalist* No. 27. Hamilton's meaning was unambiguous; the federal government was to have the power to demand that local officials implement national policy programs. As he went on to explain: "It is easy to perceive that this will tend to destroy, in the common apprehension, all distinction between the sources from which [the state and federal governments] might proceed; and will give the federal government the same advantage for securing a due obedience to its authority which is enjoyed by the government of each State."

More specifically, during the debates concerning the ratification of the Constitution, it was assumed that state agents would act as tax collectors for the federal government. Opponents of the Constitution had repeatedly expressed fears that the new federal government's ability to impose taxes directly on the citizenry would result in an overbearing presence of federal tax collectors in the States. Federalists rejoined that this problem would not arise because, as Hamilton explained, "the United States . . . will make use of the State officers and State regulations for collecting" certain taxes. No. 36. Similarly, Madison made clear that the new central government's power to raise taxes directly from the citizenry would "not be resorted to, except for supplemental purposes of revenue . . . and that the eventual collection, under the immediate authority of the Union, will generally be made by the officers . . . appointed by the several States." No. 45. . . .

We are far truer to the historical record by applying a functional approach in assessing the role played by these early state officials. The use of state judges and their clerks to perform executive functions was, in historical context, hardly unusual. And, of course, judges today continue to perform a variety of functions that may more properly be described as executive. The majority's insistence that this evidence of federal enlistment of state officials to serve executive functions is irrelevant simply because the assistance of "judges" was at issue rests on empty formalistic reasoning of the highest order. . . .

The Court concludes its review of the historical materials with a reference to the fact that our decision in *INS v. Chadha,* 462 U.S. 919 (1983), invalidated a large number of statutes enacted in the 1970's, implying that recent enactments by Congress that are similar to the Brady Act are not entitled to any presumption of validity. But in *Chadha,* unlike this case, our decision rested on the Constitution's express bicameralism and presentment requirements, not on judicial inferences drawn from a silent text and a historical record that surely favors the congressional understanding. Indeed, the majority's opinion consists almost entirely of arguments against the substantial evidence weighing in opposition to its view; the Court's ruling is strikingly lacking in affirmative support. Absent even a modicum of textual foundation for its judicially crafted constitutional rule, there should be a presumption that if the Framers had actually intended such a rule, at least one of them would have mentioned it.

The Court's "structural" arguments are not sufficient to rebut that presumption. The fact that the Framers intended to preserve the sovereignty of the several States simply does not speak to the question whether individual state employees may be required to perform federal obligations, such as registering young adults for the draft, creating state emergency response commissions designed to manage the release of hazardous substances, collecting and reporting data on underground storage tanks that may pose an environmental hazard, and reporting traffic fatalities, and missing children to a federal agency.

As we explained in *Garcia v. San Antonio Metropolitan Transit Authority,* 469 U.S. 528 (1985): "The principal means chosen by the Framers to ensure the role of the States in the federal system lies in the structure of the Federal Government itself. It is no novelty to observe that the composition of the Federal Government was designed in large part to protect the States from overreaching by Congress." Given the fact that the Members of Congress are elected by the people of the several States, with each State receiving an equivalent number of Senators in order to ensure that even the smallest

States have a powerful voice in the legislature, it is quite unrealistic to assume that they will ignore the sovereignty concerns of their constituents. It is far more reasonable to presume that their decisions to impose modest burdens on state officials from time to time reflect a considered judgment that the people in each of the States will benefit therefrom. . . .

Accordingly, I respectfully dissent.

☐ *Justice SOUTER, dissenting.*

In deciding these cases, which I have found closer than I had anticipated, it is *The Federalist* that finally determines my position. I believe that the most straightforward reading of No. 27 is authority for the Government's position here, and that this reading is both supported by No. 44 and consistent with Nos. 36 and 45.

Hamilton in No. 27 first notes that because the new Constitution would authorize the National Government to bind individuals directly through national law, it could "employ the ordinary magistracy of each [State] in the execution of its laws." Were he to stop here, he would not necessarily be speaking of anything beyond the possibility of cooperative arrangements by agreement. But he then addresses the combined effect of the proposed Supremacy Clause, and state officers' oath requirement, U.S. Const., Art. VI, cl. 3, and he states that "the Legislatures, Courts and Magistrates of the respective members will be incorporated into the operations of the national government, as far as its just and constitutional authority extends; and will be rendered auxiliary to the enforcement of its laws." *The Federalist* No. 27. The natural reading of this language is not merely that the officers of the various branches of state governments may be employed in the performance of national functions; Hamilton says that the state governmental machinery "will be incorporated" into the Nation's operation, and because the "auxiliary" status of the state officials will occur because they are "bound by the sanctity of an oath," I take him to mean that their auxiliary functions will be the products of their obligations thus undertaken to support federal law, not of their own, or the States', unfettered choices. Madison in No. 44 supports this reading in his commentary on the oath requirement. He asks why state magistrates should have to swear to support the National Constitution, when national officials will not be required to oblige themselves to support the state counterparts. His answer is that national officials "will have no agency in carrying the State Constitutions into effect. The members and officers of the State Governments, on the contrary, will have an essential agency in giving effect to the Federal Constitution." *The Federalist* No. 44 (J. Madison). He then describes the state legislative "agency" as action necessary for selecting the President, see U.S. Const., Art. II, Sec. 1, and the choice of Senators, see U.S. Const., Art. I, Sec. 3 (repealed by Amendment XVII). The Supremacy Clause itself, of course, expressly refers to the state judges' obligations under federal law, and other numbers of *The Federalist* give examples of state executive "agency" in the enforcement of national revenue laws. . . .

In the light of all these passages, I cannot persuade myself that the statements from No. 27 speak of anything less than the authority of the National Government, when exercising an otherwise legitimate power (the commerce power, say), to require state "auxiliaries" to take appropriate action. To be sure, it does not follow that any conceivable requirement may be imposed on any state official. I continue to agree, for example, that Congress may not require a state legislature to enact a regulatory scheme and that *New York v. United States*, 505 U.S. 144 (1992) was rightly decided (even though I now believe its *dicta* went too far toward immunizing state administration as well as state enactment of such a scheme from congressional mandate); after all, the essence of legislative power, within the limits of legislative jurisdiction, is a discretion not subject to command. But insofar as national law would require nothing from a state officer inconsistent with the power proper to his branch of tripartite state government (say, by obligating a state judge to exercise law enforcement powers), I suppose that the reach of federal law as Hamilton described it would not be exceeded, cf. *Garcia v. San Antonio Metropolitan Transit Authority*, 469 U.S. 528 (1965) (without precisely delineating the outer limits of Congress's Commerce Clause power, finding that the statute at issue was not "destructive of state sovereignty"). . . .

Seminole Tribe of Florida v. Florida
517 U.S. 44, 116 S.Ct. 1114 (1996)

In 1988, Congress enacted the Indian Gaming Regulatory Act, authorizing Indian tribes to conduct gaming activities in conformance with compacts agreed to by the tribe and the state in which the gaming activities are located. The act also imposed on the states a duty to negotiate compacts in "good faith" with Indian tribes and authorized tribes to bring suits in federal courts against a state that failed to negotiate a gaming compact. Subsequently, after negotiations between Florida and the Seminole Tribe broke down in 1991, the tribe sued the state in federal court. Attorneys for Florida, however, moved to have the suit dismissed on the grounds that the act violated the Eleventh Amendment and that the suit violated the state's sovereign immunity from suits in federal court. The federal district court dismissed that motion and the state's attorneys appealed to the Court of Appeals for the Eleventh Circuit, which reversed the lower court upon concluding that the Eleventh Amendment bars Congress from abrogating a state's Eleventh Amendment immunity from suits in federal courts. The Seminole Tribe appealed that decision to the Supreme Court, which granted review.

The Court's decision was five to four. Chief Justice Rehnquist announced the opinion for the majority, and Justices Stevens and Souter filed dissenting opinions. Justices Ginsburg and Breyer joined the latter justice's dissent.

☐ *Chief Justice REHNQUIST delivered the opinion of the Court.*

The Indian Gaming Regulatory Act provides that an Indian tribe may conduct certain gaming activities only in conformance with a valid compact between the tribe and the State in which the gaming activities are located.

The Act, passed by Congress under the Indian Commerce Clause, U.S. Const., Art. I, sec. 10, cl. 3, imposes upon the States a duty to negotiate in good faith with an Indian tribe toward the formation of a compact, and authorizes a tribe to bring suit in federal court against a State in order to compel performance of that duty. We hold that notwithstanding Congress' clear intent to abrogate the States' sovereign immunity, the Indian Commerce Clause does not grant Congress that power, and therefore [provisions of the act] cannot grant jurisdiction over a State that does not consent to be sued. We further hold that the doctrine of *Ex parte Young*, 209 U.S. 123 (1908), may not be used to enforce [the act's provisions] against a state official. . . .

The Eleventh Amendment provides: "The Judicial power of the United States shall not be construed to extend to any suit in law or equity, commenced or prosecuted against one of the United States by Citizens of another State, or by Citizens or Subjects of any Foreign State." Although the text of the Amendment would appear to restrict only the Article III diversity jurisdiction of the federal courts, "we have understood the Eleventh Amendment to stand not so much for what it says, but for the presupposition . . . which it confirms." *Blatchford v. Native Village of Noatak*, 501 U.S. 775 (1991). That presupposition, first observed over a century ago in *Hans v. Louisiana*, 134 U.S. 1 (1890), has two parts: first, that each State is a sovereign entity in our federal system; and second, that " 'it is inherent in the nature of sovereignty not to be amenable to the suit of an individual without its consent.' " . . .

[O]ur inquiry into whether Congress has the power to abrogate unilaterally the States' immunity from suit is narrowly focused on one question: Was the Act in question passed pursuant to a constitutional provision granting Congress the power to abrogate? Previously, in conducting that inquiry, we have found authority to abrogate under only two provisions of the Constitution. In *Fitzpatrick [v. Bitzer*, 427 U.S. 445 (1976)], we recognized that the Fourteenth Amendment, by expanding federal power at the expense of state autonomy, had fundamentally altered the balance of state and federal power struck by the Constitution. We noted that Section 1 of the Fourteenth Amendment contained prohibitions expressly directed at the States and that Section 5 of the Amendment expressly provided that "The Congress shall have the power to enforce, by appropriate legislation, the provisions of this article." We held that through the Fourteenth Amendment, federal power extended to intrude upon the province of the Eleventh Amendment and therefore that Section 5 of the Fourteenth Amendment allowed Congress to abrogate the immunity from suit guaranteed by that Amendment.

In only one other case has congressional abrogation of the States' Eleventh Amendment immunity been upheld. In *Pennsylvania v. Union Gas Co.*, 491 U.S. 1 (1989), a plurality of the Court found that the Interstate Commerce Clause granted Congress the power to abrogate state sovereign immunity, stating that the power to regulate interstate commerce would be "incomplete without the authority to render States liable in damages." Justice WHITE added the fifth vote necessary to the result in that case, but wrote separately in order to express that he "[did] not agree with much of [the plurality's] reasoning." . . .

Both parties make their arguments from the plurality decision in *Union Gas*, and we, too, begin there. We think it clear that Justice BRENNAN's opinion finds Congress' power to abrogate under the Interstate Commerce Clause from the States' cession of their sovereignty when they gave Congress plenary power to regulate interstate commerce. Respondents' focus elsewhere is misplaced. While the plurality decision states that Congress' power under the Interstate Commerce Clause would be incomplete without the power to abrogate, that statement is made solely in order to emphasize the broad scope of Congress' authority over interstate commerce. Moreover, respondents' rationale would mean that where Congress has less authority, and the States have more, Congress' means for exercising that power must be greater. We read the plurality opinion to provide just the opposite. Indeed, it was in those circumstances where Congress exercised complete authority that Justice BRENNAN thought the power to abrogate most necessary.

Following the rationale of the *Union Gas* plurality, our inquiry is limited to determining whether the Indian Commerce Clause, like the Interstate Commerce Clause, is a grant of authority to the Federal Government at the expense of the States. The answer to that question is obvious. If anything, the Indian Commerce Clause accomplishes a greater transfer of power from the States to the Federal Government than does the Interstate Commerce Clause. This is clear enough from the fact that the States still exercise some authority over interstate trade but have been divested of virtually all authority over Indian commerce and Indian tribes. Under the rationale of *Union Gas*, if the States' partial cession of authority over a particular area includes cession of the immunity from suit, then their virtually total cession of authority over a different area must also include cession of the immunity from suit. We agree with the petitioner that the plurality opinion in *Union Gas* allows no principled distinction in favor of the States to be drawn between the Indian Commerce Clause and the Interstate Commerce Clause.

Never before the decision in *Union Gas* had we suggested that the bounds of Article III could be expanded by Congress operating pursuant to any constitutional provision other than the Fourteenth Amendment. Indeed, it had seemed fundamental that Congress could not expand the jurisdiction of the federal courts beyond the bounds of Article III. The plurality's citation of prior decisions for support was based upon what we believe to be a misreading of precedent. The plurality claimed support for its decision from a case holding the unremarkable, and completely unrelated, proposition that the States may waive their sovereign immunity, and cited as precedent propositions that had been merely assumed for the sake of argument in earlier cases.

Reconsidering the decision in *Union Gas*, we conclude that none of the policies underlying *stare decisis* require our continuing adherence to its holding. The decision has, since its issuance, been of questionable precedential value, largely because a majority of the Court expressly disagreed with the rationale of the plurality. The case involved the interpretation of the Constitution and therefore may be altered only by constitutional amendment or revision by this Court. Finally, both the result in *Union Gas* and the plurality's rationale depart from our established understanding of the Eleventh Amendment and undermine the accepted function of Article III. We feel bound to conclude that *Union Gas* was wrongly decided and that it should be, and now is, overruled. . . .

In overruling *Union Gas* today, we reconfirm that the background principle of state sovereign immunity embodied in the Eleventh Amendment is not so ephemeral as to dissipate when the subject of the suit is an area, like the regulation of Indian commerce, that is under the exclusive control of the Federal Government. Even when the Constitution vests in Congress complete law-making authority over a particular area, the Eleventh Amendment prevents congressional authorization of suits by private parties against unconsenting States. The Eleventh Amendment restricts the judicial power under Article III, and Article I cannot be used to circumvent the constitutional limitations placed upon federal jurisdiction. Petitioner's suit against the State of Florida must be dismissed for a lack of jurisdiction. . . .

☐ *Justice SOUTER, with whom Justice GINSBURG and Justice BREYER join, dissenting.*

I part company from the Court because I am convinced that its decision is fundamentally mistaken, and for that reason I respectfully dissent.

It is useful to separate three questions: (1) whether the States enjoyed sovereign immunity if sued in their own courts in the period prior to ratification of the National Constitution; (2) if so, whether after ratification the States were entitled to claim some such immunity when sued in a federal court exercising jurisdiction either because the suit was between a State and a non-state litigant who was not its citizen, or because the issue in the case raised a federal question; and (3) whether any state sovereign immunity recognized in federal court may be abrogated by Congress.

The answer to the first question is not clear, although some of the Framers assumed that States did enjoy immunity in their own courts. The second question was not debated at the time of ratification, except as to citizen-state diversity jurisdiction; there was no unanimity, but in due course the Court in *Chisholm v. Georgia* [2 Dall. 419 (1793)] answered that a state defendant enjoyed no such immunity. As to federal question jurisdiction, state sovereign immunity seems not to have been debated prior to ratification, the silence probably showing a general understanding at the time that the States would have no immunity in such cases.

The adoption of the Eleventh Amendment soon changed the result in *Chisholm*, not by mentioning sovereign immunity, but by eliminating citizen-state diversity jurisdiction over cases with state defendants. I will explain why the Eleventh Amendment did not affect federal question jurisdiction, a notion that needs to be understood for the light it casts on the soundness of *Hans*'s holding that States did enjoy sovereign immunity in federal question suits. The *Hans* Court erroneously assumed that a State could plead sovereign immunity against a noncitizen suing under federal question jurisdiction, and for that reason held that a State must enjoy the same protection in a suit by one of its citizens. The error of *Hans*'s reasoning is underscored by its clear inconsistency with the Founders' hostility to the implicit reception of common-law doctrine as federal law, and with the Founders' conception of sovereign power as divided between the States and the National Government for the sake of very practical objectives.

The Court's answer today to the third question is likewise at odds with the Founders' view that common law, when it was received into the new American legal systems, was always subject to legislative amendment. In ignoring the reasons for this pervasive understanding at the time of the ratification, and in holding that a nontextual common-law rule limits a clear grant of congressional power under Article I, the Court follows a course that has brought it to grief before in our history, and promises to do so again.

Beyond this third question that elicits today's holding, there is one further issue. To reach the Court's result, it must not only hold the *Hans* doctrine to be outside the reach of Congress, but must also displace the doctrine of *Ex parte Young*, 209 U. S. 123 (1908), that an officer of the government may be ordered prospectively to follow federal law, in cases in which the government may not itself be sued directly. None of its reasons for displacing *Young's* jurisdictional doctrine withstand scrutiny.

The doctrine of sovereign immunity comprises two distinct rules, which are not always separately recognized. The one rule holds that the King or the Crown, as the font of law, is not bound by the law's provisions; the other provides that the King or Crown, as the font of justice, is not subject to suit in its own courts. The one rule limits the reach of substantive law; the other, the jurisdiction of the courts. We are concerned here only with the latter rule, which took its common-law form in the high middle ages. . . .

Whatever the scope of sovereign immunity might have been in the Colonies, however, or during the period of Confederation, the proposal to establish a National Government under the Constitution drafted in 1787 presented a prospect unknown to the common law prior to the American experience: the States would become parts of a system in which sovereignty over even domestic matters would be divided or parcelled out between the States and the Nation, the latter to be invested with its own judicial power and the right to prevail against the States whenever their respective substantive laws might be in conflict. With this prospect in mind, the 1787 Constitution might have addressed state sovereign immunity by eliminating whatever sovereign immunity the States previously had, as to any matter subject to federal law or jurisdiction; by recognizing an analogue to the old immunity in the new context of federal jurisdiction, but subject to abrogation as to any matter within that jurisdiction; or by enshrining a doctrine of inviolable state sovereign immunity in the text, thereby giving it constitutional protection in the new federal jurisdiction.

The 1787 draft in fact said nothing on the subject, and it was this very silence that occasioned some, though apparently not widespread, dispute among the Framers and others over whether ratification of the Constitution would preclude a State sued in federal court from asserting sovereign immunity as it could have done on any matter of nonfederal law litigated in its own courts. . . .

The argument among the Framers and their friends about sovereign immunity in federal citizen-state diversity cases, in any event, was short lived and ended when this Court, in *Chisholm v. Georgia*, chose between the constitutional alternatives of abrogation and recognition of the immunity enjoyed at common law. The 4-to-1 majority adopted the reasonable (although not compelled) interpretation that the first of the two Citizen-State Diversity Clauses abrogated for purposes of federal jurisdiction any immunity the States might have enjoyed in their own courts, and Georgia was accordingly held subject to the judicial power in a common-law assumpsit action by a South Carolina citizen suing to collect a debt. . . .

The Eleventh Amendment, of course, repudiated *Chisholm* and clearly divested federal courts of some jurisdiction as to cases against state parties: "The Judicial power of the United States shall not be construed to extend to any suit in law or equity, commenced or prosecuted against one of the United States by Citizens of another State, or by Citizens or Subjects of any Foreign State." There are two plausible readings of this provision's text. Under the first, it simply repeals the Citizen-State Diversity Clauses of Article III for all cases in which the State appears as a defendant. Under the second, it strips the federal courts of jurisdiction in any case in which a state defendant is sued by a citizen not its own, even if jurisdiction might otherwise rest on the existence of a federal question in the suit. Neither reading of the Amendment, of course, furnishes authority for the Court's view in today's case, but we need to choose between the competing readings for the light that will be shed on the *Hans* doctrine and the legitimacy of inflating that doctrine to the point of constitutional immutability as the Court has chosen to do.

The history and structure of the Eleventh Amendment convincingly show that it reaches only to suits subject to federal jurisdiction exclusively under the Citizen-State Diversity Clauses. In precisely tracking the language in Article III providing for citizen-state diversity jurisdiction, the text of the Amendment does, after all, suggest to common sense that only the Diversity Clauses are being addressed. . . . If the Framers of the Eleventh Amendment had meant it to immunize States from federal question suits like those that might be brought to enforce the Treaty of Paris, they would surely have drafted the Amendment differently.

It should accordingly come as no surprise that the weightiest commentary following the amendment's adoption described it simply as constricting the scope of the Citizen-State Diversity Clauses. In *Cohens v. Virginia*, 6 Wheat. 264 (1821), for instance, Chief Justice MARSHALL, writing for the Court, emphasized that the amendment had no effect on federal courts' jurisdiction grounded on the "arising under" provision of Article III and concluded that "a case arising under the constitution or laws of the United States, is cognizable in the Courts of the Union, whoever may be the parties to that case." The point of the Eleventh Amendment, according to *Cohens*, was to bar jurisdiction in suits at common law by Revolutionary War debt creditors, not "to strip the government of the means of protecting, by the instrumentality of its Courts, the constitution and laws from active violation."

In sum, reading the Eleventh Amendment solely as a limit on citizen-state diversity jurisdiction has the virtue of coherence with this Court's practice, with the views of John MARSHALL, with the history of the Amendment's drafting, and with its allusive language. Today's majority does not appear to disagree, at least insofar as the constitutional text is concerned; the Court concedes, after all, that "the text of the Amendment would appear to restrict only the Article III diversity jurisdiction of the federal courts." . . .

Hans was indeed a leap in the direction of today's holding, even though it does not take the Court all the way. The parties in *Hans* raised, and the Court in that case answered, only what I have called the second question, that is, whether the Constitution, without more, permits a State to plead sovereign immunity to bar the exercise of federal question jurisdiction. Although the Court invoked a principle of sovereign immunity to cure what it took to be the Eleventh Amendment's anomaly of barring only those state suits brought by noncitizen plaintiffs, the *Hans* Court had no occasion to consider whether Congress could abrogate that background immunity by statute. Indeed (except in the special circumstance of Congress's power to enforce the Civil War Amendments), this question never came before our Court until *Union Gas*, and any intimations of an answer in prior cases were mere *dicta*. In *Union Gas* the Court held that the immunity recognized in *Hans* had no constitutional status and was subject to congressional abrogation. Today the Court overrules *Union Gas* and holds just the opposite. In deciding how to choose between these two positions, the place to begin is with *Hans*'s holding that a principle of sovereign immunity derived from the common law insulates a state from federal question jurisdiction at the suit of its own citizen. A critical examination of that case will show that it was wrongly decided, as virtually every recent commentator has concluded. It follows that the Court's further step today of constitutionalizing *Hans*'s rule against abrogation by Congress compounds and immensely magnifies the century-old mistake of *Hans* itself and takes its place with other historic examples of textually untethered elevations of judicially derived rules to the status of inviolable constitutional law. . . .

Three critical errors in *Hans* weigh against constitutionalizing its holding as the majority does today. The first we have already seen: the *Hans* Court misread the Eleventh Amendment. It also misunderstood the conditions under which common-law doctrines were received or rejected at the time of the Founding, and it fundamentally mistook the very nature of sovereignty in the young Republic that was supposed to entail a State's immunity to federal question jurisdiction in a federal court. . . .

While the States had limited their reception of English common law to principles appropriate to American conditions, the 1787 draft Constitution contained no provision for adopting the common law at all. This omission stood in sharp contrast to the state constitutions then extant, virtually all of which contained explicit provisions dealing with common-law reception. Since the experience in the States set the stage for thinking at the national level, this failure to address the notion of common-law reception could not have been inadvertent. Instead, the Framers chose to recognize only particular common-law concepts, such as the writ of *habeas corpus*, U. S. Const., Art. I, Sec. 9, cl. 2, and the distinction between law and equity, U. S. Const., Amdt. VII, by specific reference in the constitutional text. This approach reflected widespread agreement that ratification would not itself entail a general reception of the common law of England.

The Framers also recognized that the diverse development of the common law in the several states made a general federal reception impossible. "The common law was not the same in any two of the Colonies," Madison observed; "in some the modifications were materially and extensively different." . . .

Given the refusal to entertain any wholesale reception of common law, given the failure of the new Constitution to make any provision for adoption of common law as such, and given the protests already quoted that no general reception had occurred, the *Hans* Court and the Court today cannot reasonably argue that something like the old immunity doctrine somehow slipped in as a tacit but enforceable background principle. The evidence is even more specific, however, that there was no pervasive understanding that sovereign immunity had limited federal question jurisdiction. . . .

As a matter of political theory, this federal arrangement of dual delegated sovereign powers truly was a more revolutionary turn than the late war had been. Before the new federal scheme appeared, 18th-century political theorists had assumed that "there must reside somewhere in every political unit a single, undivided, final power, higher in legal authority than any other power, subject to no law, a law unto itself." The American development of divided sovereign powers, which "shattered . . . the categories of government that had dominated Western thinking for centuries," was made possible only by a recognition that the ultimate sovereignty rests in the people themselves. The people possessing this plenary bundle of specific powers were free to parcel them out to different governments and different branches of the same government as they saw fit. . . .

Given this metamorphosis of the idea of sovereignty in the years leading up to 1789, the question whether the old immunity doctrine might have been received as something suitable for the new world of federal question jurisdiction is a crucial one. The answer is that sovereign immunity as it would have been known to the Framers before ratification thereafter became inapplicable as a matter of logic in a federal suit raising a federal question. The old doctrine, after all, barred the involuntary subjection of a sovereign to the system of justice and law of which it was itself the font, since to do otherwise would have struck the common-law mind from the Middle Ages onward as both impractical and absurd. But the ratification demonstrated that state governments were subject to a superior regime of law in a judicial system established, not by the State, but by the people through a specific delegation of their sovereign power to a National Government that was paramount within its delegated sphere. When individuals sued States to enforce federal rights, the Government that corresponded to the "sovereign" in the traditional common-law sense was not the State but the National Government, and any state immunity from the jurisdiction of the Nation's courts would have required a grant from the true sovereign, the people, in their Constitution, or from the Congress that the Constitution had empowered. . . .

State immunity to federal question jurisdiction would, moreover, have run up against the common understanding of the practical necessity for the new federal relationship. According to Madison, the "multiplicity," "mutability," and "injustice" of then-extant state laws were prime factors requiring the formation of a new government. These factors, Madison wrote to Jefferson, "contributed more to that uneasiness which produced the Convention, and prepared the Public mind for a general reform, than those which accrued to our national character and interest from the inadequacy of the Confederation to its immediate objects." These concerns ultimately found concrete expression in a number of specific limitations on state power, including provisions barring the States from enacting bills of attainder or ex post facto laws, coining money or emitting bills of credit, denying the privileges and immunities of out-of-staters, or impairing the obligation of contracts. But the proposed Constitution also dealt with the old problems affirmatively by granting the powers to Congress enumerated in Article I, Section 8, and by providing through the Supremacy Clause that Congress could preempt State action in areas of concurrent state and federal authority.

Given the Framers' general concern with curbing abuses by state governments, it would be amazing if the scheme of delegated powers embodied in the Constitution had left the National Government powerless to render the States judicially accountable for violations of federal rights. And of course the Framers did not understand the scheme to leave the government powerless. . . .

History confirms the wisdom of Madison's abhorrence of constitution-alizing common-law rules to place them beyond the reach of congressional amendment. The Framers feared judicial power over substantive policy and the ossification of law that would result from transforming common law into constitutional law, and their fears have been borne out every time the Court has ignored Madison's counsel on subjects that we generally group under economic and social policy. It is, in fact, remarkable that as we near the end of this century the Court should choose to open a new constitutional chapter in confining legislative judgments on these matters by resort to tex-tually unwarranted common-law rules, for it was just this practice in the century's early decades that brought this Court to the nadir of competence that we identify with *Lochner v. New York*, 198 U.S. 45 (1905).

It was the defining characteristic of the *Lochner* era, and its charac-teristic vice, that the Court treated the common-law background (in those days, common-law property rights and contractual autonomy) as paramount, while regarding congressional legislation to abrogate the common law on these economic matters as constitutionally suspect. See, e.g., *Adkins v. Chil-dren's Hospital of D.C.*, 261 U. S. 525 (1923) (finding abrogation of common-law freedom to contract for any wage an unconstitutional "compulsory exaction"). And yet the superseding lesson that seemed clear after *West Coast Hotel Co. v. Parrish*, 300 U. S. 379 (1937), that action within the legislative power is not subject to greater scrutiny merely because it trenches upon the case law's ordering of economic and social relationships, seems to have been lost on the Court.

The majority today, indeed, seems to be going *Lochner* one better. When the Court has previously constrained the express Article I powers by resort to common-law or background principles, it has done so at least in an ostensible effort to give content to some other written provision of the Constitution, like the Due Process Clause, the very object of which is to limit the exercise of governmental power. . . . Today, however, the Court is not struggling to fulfill a responsibility to reconcile two arguably conflicting and Delphic constitutional provisions, nor is it struggling with any Delphic text at all. For even the Court concedes that the Constitution's grant to Congress of plenary power over re-lations with Indian tribes at the expense of any state claim to the contrary is unmistakably clear, and this case does not even arguably implicate a textual trump to the grant of federal question jurisdiction. . . .

In *Ex parte Young*, this Court held that a federal court has jurisdiction in a suit against a state officer to enjoin official actions violating federal law, even though the State itself may be immune. Under *Young*, "a federal court, consistent with the Eleventh Amendment, may enjoin state officials to con-form their future conduct to the requirements of federal law." . . .

Absent the application of *Ex parte Young*, I would, of course, follow *Union Gas* in recognizing congressional power under Article I to abrogate *Hans* immunity. Since the reasons for this position, *supra*, tend to unsettle *Hans* as well as support *Union Gas*, I should add a word about my reasons for continuing to accept *Hans's* holding as a matter of *stare decisis*.

The *Hans* doctrine was erroneous, but it has not previously proven to be unworkable or to conflict with later doctrine or to suffer from the effects of facts developed since its decision (apart from those indicating its original er-rors). I would therefore treat *Hans* as it has always been treated in fact until to-day, as a doctrine of federal common law. For, as so understood, it has formed one of the strands of the federal relationship for over a century now, and the stability of that relationship is itself a value that *stare decisis* aims to respect.

In being ready to hold that the relationship may still be altered, not by the Court but by Congress, I would tread the course laid out elsewhere in our cases. The Court has repeatedly stated its assumption that insofar as the relative positions of States and Nation may be affected consistently with the Tenth Amendment, they would not be modified without deliberately expressed intent. See *Gregory v. Ashcroft*, 501 U.S. [452 (1991)]. The plain statement rule, which "assures that the legislature has in fact faced, and intended to bring into issue, the critical matters involved in the judicial decision," is particularly appropriate in light of our primary reliance on "the effectiveness of the federal political process in preserving the States' interests." *Garcia v. San Antonio Metropolitan Authority*, 469 U. S. 528 (1985). Hence, we have required such a plain statement when Congress preempts the historic powers of the States, *Rice v. Santa Fe Elevator Corp.*, 331 U. S. 218 (1947), imposes a condition on the grant of federal moneys, *South Dakota v. Dole*, 483 U.S. 203 (1987), or seeks to regulate a State's ability to determine the qualifications of its own officials.

When judging legislation passed under unmistakable Article I powers, no further restriction could be required. Nor does the Court explain why more could be demanded. In the past, we have assumed that a plain statement requirement is sufficient to protect the States from undue federal encroachments upon their traditional immunity from suit. It is hard to contend that this rule has set the bar too low, for (except in *Union Gas*) we have never found the requirement to be met outside the context of laws passed under Section 5 of the Fourteenth Amendment. The exception I would recognize today proves the rule, moreover, because the federal abrogation of state immunity comes as part of a regulatory scheme which is itself designed to invest the States with regulatory powers that Congress need not extend to them. This fact suggests to me that the political safeguards of federalism are working, that a plain statement rule is an adequate check on congressional overreaching, and that today's abandonment of that approach is wholly unwarranted. . . .

Alden v. Maine

527 U.S. 706, 119 S.CT. 2240 (1999)

The pertinent facts are discussed by Justice Kennedy in his opinion for the Court, affirming the decision of the Maine Supreme Judicial Court. The Court's decision was five to four. Justice Souter filed a dissenting opinion, which was joined by Justices Stevens, Ginsburg, and Breyer.

☐ *Justice KENNEDY delivered the opinion of the Court.*

In 1992, petitioners, a group of probation officers, filed suit against their employer, the State of Maine, in the United States District Court for the

District of Maine. The officers alleged the State had violated the overtime provisions of the Fair Labor Standards Act of 1938 (FLSA), and sought compensation and liquidated damages. While the suit was pending, this Court decided *Seminole Tribe of Fla. v. Florida*, 517 U.S. 44 (1996), which made it clear that Congress lacks power under Article I to abrogate the States' sovereign immunity from suits commenced or prosecuted in the federal courts. Upon consideration of *Seminole Tribe*, the District Court dismissed petitioners' action, and the Court of Appeals affirmed. Petitioners then filed the same action in state court. The state trial court dismissed the suit on the basis of sovereign immunity, and the Maine Supreme Judicial Court affirmed. . . .

We hold that the powers delegated to Congress under Article I of the United States Constitution do not include the power to subject nonconsenting States to private suits for damages in state courts. We decide as well that the State of Maine has not consented to suits for overtime pay and liquidated damages under the FLSA. On these premises we affirm the judgment sustaining dismissal of the suit.

The Eleventh Amendment makes explicit reference to the States' immunity from suits "commenced or prosecuted against one of the United States by Citizens of another State, or by Citizens or Subjects of any Foreign State." We have, as a result, sometimes referred to the States' immunity from suit as "Eleventh Amendment immunity." The phrase is convenient shorthand but something of a misnomer, for the sovereign immunity of the States neither derives from nor is limited by the terms of the Eleventh Amendment. Rather, as the Constitution's structure, and its history, and the authoritative interpretations by this Court make clear, the States' immunity from suit is a fundamental aspect of the sovereignty which the States enjoyed before the ratification of the Constitution, and which they retain today (either literally or by virtue of their admission into the Union upon an equal footing with the other States) except as altered by the plan of the Convention or certain constitutional Amendments.

Although the Constitution establishes a National Government with broad, often plenary authority over matters within its recognized competence, the founding document "specifically recognizes the States as sovereign entities." *Seminole Tribe of Fla*. Various textual provisions of the Constitution assume the States' continued existence and active participation in the fundamental processes of governance. See *Printz v. United States*, 521 U.S. 898 (1997) (citing Art. III, Sec. 2; Art. IV, Secs. 2–4; Art. V). The limited and enumerated powers granted to the Legislative, Executive, and Judicial Branches of the National Government, moreover, underscore the vital role reserved to the States by the constitutional design. Any doubt regarding the constitutional role of the States as sovereign entities is removed by the Tenth Amendment, which, like the other provisions of the Bill of Rights, was enacted to allay lingering concerns about the extent of the national power. The Amendment confirms the promise implicit in the original document: "The powers not delegated to the United States by the Constitution, nor prohibited by it to the States, are reserved to the States respectively, or to the people."

The federal system established by our Constitution preserves the sovereign status of the States in two ways. First, it reserves to them a substantial portion of the Nation's primary sovereignty, together with the dignity and essential attributes inhering in that status. . . .

Second, even as to matters within the competence of the National Government, the constitutional design secures the founding generation's rejection of "the concept of a central government that would act upon and through the States" in favor of "a system in which the State and Federal Governments would exercise concurrent authority over the people—who were, in Hamilton's words, "the only proper objects of government." *Printz*. In this the founders achieved a deliberate departure from the Articles of Confederation: Experience under the Articles had "exploded on all hands" the "practicality of making laws, with coercive sanctions, for the States as political bodies." . . .

The generation that designed and adopted our federal system considered immunity from private suits central to sovereign dignity. When the Constitution was ratified, it was well established in English law that the Crown could not be sued without consent in its own courts. See *Chisholm v. Georgia*, 2 Dall. 419 (1793) (IREDELL, J., dissenting). . . .

[The Court's decision in *Chisholm v. Georgia* met with widespread opposition and resulted in the adoption and ratification of the Eleventh Amendment, guaranteeing states' sovereign immunity against lawsuits by citizens of other states.] Each House spent but a single day discussing the Amendment, and the vote in each House was close to unanimous. All attempts to weaken the Amendment were defeated. . . .

It might be argued that the *Chisholm* decision was a correct interpretation of the constitutional design and that the Eleventh Amendment represented a deviation from the original understanding. This, however, seems unsupportable. First, despite the opinion of Justice IREDELL, the majority failed to address either the practice or the understanding that prevailed in the States at the time the Constitution was adopted. Second, even a casual reading of the opinions suggests the majority suspected the decision would be unpopular and surprising. . . .

The text and history of the Eleventh Amendment also suggest that Congress acted not to change but to restore the original constitutional design. Although earlier drafts of the Amendment had been phrased as express limits on the judicial power granted in Article III, the adopted text addressed the proper interpretation of that provision of the original Constitution, see U.S. Const., Amdt. 11 ("The Judicial Power of the United States shall not be construed to extend to any suit in law or equity, commenced or prosecuted against one of the United States"). By its terms, then, the Eleventh Amendment did not redefine the federal judicial power but instead overruled the Court. . . .

The Court has been consistent in interpreting the adoption of the Eleventh Amendment as conclusive evidence "that the decision in *Chisholm* was contrary to the well-understood meaning of the Constitution," *Seminole Tribe*, and that the views expressed by Hamilton, Madison, and Marshall during the ratification debates, and by Justice IREDELL in his dissenting opinion in *Chisholm*, reflect the original understanding of the Constitution. In accordance with this understanding, we have recognized a "presumption that no anomalous and unheard-of proceedings or suits were intended to be raised up by the Constitution—anomalous and unheard of when the constitution was adopted." As a consequence, we have looked to "history and experience, and the established order of things," rather than "[a]dhering to the mere letter" of the Eleventh Amendment in determining the scope of the States' constitutional immunity from suit. . . .

[Prior] holdings reflect a settled doctrinal understanding, consistent with the views of the leading advocates of the Constitution's ratification, that sovereign immunity derives not from the Eleventh Amendment but from the structure of the original Constitution itself. The Eleventh Amendment confirmed rather than established sovereign immunity as a constitutional principle; it follows that the scope of the States' immunity from suit is demarcated not by the text of the Amendment alone but by fundamental postulates implicit in the constitutional design. . . .

In this case we must determine whether Congress has the power, under Article I, to subject nonconsenting States to private suits in their own courts. As the foregoing discussion makes clear, the fact that the Eleventh Amendment by its terms limits only "[t]he Judicial power of the United States" does not resolve the question. To rest on the words of the Amendment alone would be to engage in the type of ahistorical literalism we have rejected in interpreting the scope of the States' sovereign immunity since the discredited decision in *Chisholm*.

While the constitutional principle of sovereign immunity does pose a bar to federal jurisdiction over suits against nonconsenting States, this is not the only structural basis of sovereign immunity implicit in the constitutional design. Rather, "[t]here is also the postulate that States of the Union, still possessing attributes of sovereignty, shall be immune from suits, without their consent, save where there has been a surrender of this immunity in the plan of the convention." This separate and distinct structural principle is not directly related to the scope of the judicial power established by Article III, but inheres in the system of federalism established by the Constitution. In exercising its Article I powers Congress may subject the States to private suits in their own courts only if there is "compelling evidence" that the States were required to surrender this power to Congress pursuant to the constitutional design.

Petitioners contend the text of the Constitution and our recent sovereign immunity decisions establish that the States were required to relinquish this portion of their sovereignty. [But, we disagree.] The Constitution, by delegating to Congress the power to establish the supreme law of the land when acting within its enumerated powers, does not foreclose a State from asserting immunity to claims arising under federal law merely because that law derives not from the State itself but from the national power. A contrary view could not be reconciled with . . . *Employees of Dept. of Public Health and Welfare of Mo. v. Department of Public Health and Welfare of Mo.*, 411 U.S. 279 (1973), which recognized that the FLSA was binding upon Missouri but nevertheless upheld the State's immunity to a private suit to recover under that Act; or with numerous other decisions to the same effect. We reject any contention that substantive federal law by its own force necessarily overrides the sovereign immunity of the States. When a State asserts its immunity to suit, the question is not the primacy of federal law but the implementation of the law in a manner consistent with the constitutional sovereignty of the States. . . .

Whether Congress has authority under Article I to abrogate a State's immunity from suit in its own courts is, then, a question of first impression. In determining whether there is "compelling evidence" that this derogation of the States' sovereignty is "inherent in the constitutional compact," we continue our discussion of history, practice, precedent, and the structure of the Constitution.

We look first to evidence of the original understanding of the Constitution. Petitioners contend that because the ratification debates and the events surrounding the adoption of the Eleventh Amendment focused on the States' immunity from suit in federal courts, the historical record gives no instruction as to the founding generation's intent to preserve the States' immunity from suit in their own courts.

We believe, however, that the founders' silence is best explained by the simple fact that no one, not even the Constitution's most ardent opponents, suggested the document might strip the States of the immunity. In light of the overriding concern regarding the States' war-time debts, together with the well known creativity, foresight, and vivid imagination of the Constitution's opponents, the silence is most instructive. It suggests the sovereign's right to assert immunity from suit in its own courts was a principle so well established that no one conceived it would be altered by the new Constitution. . . .

[W]hile the Eleventh Amendment by its terms addresses only "the Judicial power of the United States," nothing in *Chisholm*, the catalyst for the Amendment, suggested the States were not immune from suits in their own courts. . . .

In light of the language of the Constitution and the historical context, it is quite apparent why neither the ratification debates nor the language of the Eleventh Amendment addressed the States' immunity from suit in their own courts. The concerns voiced at the ratifying conventions, the furor raised by *Chisholm*, and the speed and unanimity with which the Amendment was adopted, moreover, underscore the jealous care with which the founding generation sought to preserve the sovereign immunity of the States. . . .

A general federal power to authorize private suits for money damages would place unwarranted strain on the States' ability to govern in accordance with the will of their citizens. Today, as at the time of the founding, the allocation of scarce resources among competing needs and interests lies at the heart of the political process. While the judgment creditor of the State may have a legitimate claim for compensation, other important needs and worthwhile ends compete for access to the public fisc. Since all cannot be satisfied in full, it is inevitable that difficult decisions involving the most sensitive and political of judgments must be made. If the principle of representative government is to be preserved to the States, the balance between competing interests must be reached after deliberation by the political process established by the citizens of the State, not by judicial decree mandated by the Federal Government and invoked by the private citizen.

By "split[ting] the atom of sovereignty," the founders established "two orders of government, each with its own direct relationship, its own privity, its own set of mutual rights and obligations to the people who sustain it and are governed by it." *Saenz v. Roe*, 526 U.S. 489 (1999). When the Federal Government asserts authority over a State's most fundamental political processes, it strikes at the heart of the political accountability so essential to our liberty and republican form of government.

The asserted authority would blur not only the distinct responsibilities of the State and National Governments but also the separate duties of the judicial and political branches of the state governments, displacing "state decisions that 'go to the heart of representative government.' " *Gregory v.*

Ashcroft, 501 U.S. 452 (1991). A State is entitled to order the processes of its own governance, assigning to the political branches, rather than the courts, the responsibility for directing the payment of debts. If Congress could displace a State's allocation of governmental power and responsibility, the judicial branch of the State, whose legitimacy derives from fidelity to the law, would be compelled to assume a role not only foreign to its experience but beyond its competence as defined by the very constitution from which its existence derives. . . .

In light of history, practice, precedent, and the structure of the Constitution, we hold that the States retain immunity from private suit in their own courts, an immunity beyond the congressional power to abrogate by Article I legislation.

The constitutional privilege of a State to assert its sovereign immunity in its own courts does not confer upon the State a concomitant right to disregard the Constitution or valid federal law. The States and their officers are bound by obligations imposed by the Constitution and by federal statutes that comport with the constitutional design. We are unwilling to assume the States will refuse to honor the Constitution or obey the binding laws of the United States.

Sovereign immunity, moreover, does not bar all judicial review of state compliance with the Constitution and valid federal law. Rather, certain limits are implicit in the constitutional principle of state sovereign immunity.

The first of these limits is that sovereign immunity bars suits only in the absence of consent. Many States, on their own initiative, have enacted statutes consenting to a wide variety of suits. The rigors of sovereign immunity are thus "mitigated by a sense of justice which has continually expanded by consent the suability of the sovereign." *Great Northern Life Ins. Co.* [*v. Read,* 322 U.S. 47 (1944)]. Nor, subject to constitutional limitations, does the Federal Government lack the authority or means to seek the States' voluntary consent to private suits. Cf. *South Dakota v. Dole,* 483 U.S. 203 (1987).

We have held also that in adopting the Fourteenth Amendment, the people required the States to surrender a portion of the sovereignty that had been preserved to them by the original Constitution, so that Congress may authorize private suits against nonconsenting States pursuant to its Section 5 enforcement power. By imposing explicit limits on the powers of the States and granting Congress the power to enforce them, the Amendment "fundamentally altered the balance of state and federal power struck by the Constitution." *Seminole Tribe.* When Congress enacts appropriate legislation to enforce this Amendment, see *City of Boerne v. Flores,* 521 U.S. 507 (1997), federal interests are paramount, and Congress may assert an authority over the States which would be otherwise unauthorized by the Constitution.

The second important limit to the principle of sovereign immunity is that it bars suits against States but not lesser entities. The immunity does not extend to suits prosecuted against a municipal corporation or other governmental entity which is not an arm of the State. Nor does sovereign immunity bar all suits against state officers. Some suits against state officers are barred by the rule that sovereign immunity is not limited to suits which name the State as a party if the suits are, in fact, against the State. The rule, however, does not bar certain actions against state officers for injunctive or declaratory relief. Compare *Ex parte Young,* 209 U.S. 123 (1908), and *In re Ayers, supra,* with *Seminole Tribe, supra,* and *Edelman v. Jordan,* 415 U.S. 651

(1974). Even a suit for money damages may be prosecuted against a state officer in his individual capacity for unconstitutional or wrongful conduct fairly attributable to the officer himself, so long as the relief is sought not from the state treasury but from the officer personally. . . .

[Finally, t]he State of Maine has not questioned Congress' power to prescribe substantive rules of federal law to which it must comply. Despite an initial good-faith disagreement about the requirements of the FLSA, it is conceded by all that the State has altered its conduct so that its compliance with federal law cannot now be questioned. The Solicitor General of the United States has appeared before this Court, however, and asserted that the federal interest in compensating the States' employees for alleged past violations of federal law is so compelling that the sovereign State of Maine must be stripped of its immunity and subjected to suit in its own courts by its own employees. Yet, despite specific statutory authorization, the United States apparently found the same interests insufficient to justify sending even a single attorney to Maine to prosecute this litigation. The difference between a suit by the United States on behalf of the employees and a suit by the employees implicates a rule that the National Government must itself deem the case of sufficient importance to take action against the State; and history, precedent, and the structure of the Constitution make clear that, under the plan of the Convention, the States have consented to suits of the first kind but not of the second. The judgment of the Supreme Judicial Court of Maine is Affirmed.

☐ *Justice SOUTER, with whom Justice STEVENS, Justice GINSBURG, and Justice BREYER join, dissenting.*

In *Seminole Tribe of Fla. v. Florida*, 517 U.S. 44 (1996), a majority of this Court invoked the Eleventh Amendment to declare that the federal judicial power under Article III of the Constitution does not reach a private action against a State, even on a federal question. In the Court's conception, however, the Eleventh Amendment was understood as having been enhanced by a "background principle" of state sovereign immunity (understood as immunity to suit) that operated beyond its limited codification in the Amendment, dealing solely with federal citizen-state diversity jurisdiction. To the *Seminole Tribe* dissenters, of whom I was one, the Court's enhancement of the Amendment was at odds with constitutional history and at war with the conception of divided sovereignty that is the essence of American federalism.

Today's issue arises naturally in the aftermath of the decision in *Seminole Tribe*. . . . In thus complementing its earlier decision, the Court of course confronts the fact that the state forum renders the Eleventh Amendment beside the point, and it has responded by discerning a simpler and more straightforward theory of state sovereign immunity than it found in *Seminole Tribe*: a State's sovereign immunity from all individual suits is a "fundamental aspect" of state sovereignty "confirm[ed]" by the Tenth Amendment. As a consequence, *Seminole Tribe*'s contorted reliance on the Eleventh Amendment and its background was presumably unnecessary; the Tenth would have done the work with an economy that the majority in *Seminole Tribe* would have welcomed. Indeed, if the Court's current reasoning is correct, the Eleventh Amendment itself was unnecessary. Whatever Article III may originally have said about the federal judicial power, the embarrassment to the State of Georgia occasioned by attempts in federal court to enforce the State's war debt could easily have been avoided if only the Court that decided *Chisholm v. Georgia*, 2 Dall. 419 (1793), had understood a State's inherent, Tenth Amendment right to be free of any judicial power, whether the court be state or federal, and whether the cause of action arise under state or federal law.

The sequence of the Court's positions prompts a suspicion of error, and skepticism is confirmed by scrutiny of the Court's efforts to justify its holding. There is no evidence that the Tenth Amendment constitutionalized a concept of sovereign immunity as inherent in the notion of statehood, and no evidence that any concept of inherent sovereign immunity was understood historically to apply when the sovereign sued was not the font of the law. Nor does the Court fare any better with its subsidiary lines of reasoning, that the state–court action is barred by the scheme of American federalism, a result supposedly confirmed by a history largely devoid of precursors to the action considered here. The Court's federalism ignores the accepted authority of Congress to bind States under the FLSA and to provide for enforcement of federal rights in state court. The Court's history simply disparages the capacity of the Constitution to order relationships in a Republic that has changed since the founding.

On each point the Court has raised it is mistaken, and I respectfully dissent from its judgment.

Nevada Department of Human Resources v. Hibbs
538 U.S. 721, 123 S.CT. 1972 (2003)

The Family and Medical Leave Act of 1993 (FMLA) entitles eligible employees to take up to twelve weeks of unpaid leave annually for attending to illnesses within the immediate family. The FMLA also creates a private right of action to seek damages against an employer for violating provisions of the law. William Hibbs worked for the Nevada Department of Human Resources and in 1997 sought leave under the FMLA in order to care for his ailing wife. His request was granted but after twelve weeks on leave the agency notified him that he must return to work. When Hibbs failed to do so, his employment was terminated. Subsequently, Hibbs sued Nevada in federal district court for violations of the FMLA. The district court held that Hibbs was barred from filing the FMLA claim against the state on the basis of the Eleventh Amendment. However, on appeal the Court of Appeals for the Ninth Circuit reversed that decision and ruled that states' sovereign immunity under the Eleventh Amendment was overridden by Congress's power under Section 5 of the Fourteenth Amendment to enact laws aimed at enforcing the equal protection of the law and address the persistence of gender discrimination. The state appealed that decision and the Supreme Court granted *certiorari*.

The Supreme Court affirmed by a vote of six to three. Chief Justice Rehnquist delivered the opinion for the Court. Justices Souter and Stevens each filed concurring opinions. Justices Scalia and Kennedy filed dissenting opinions; Justice Thomas joined the dissent.

☐ *Chief Justice REHNQUIST delivered the opinion of the Court.*

The Family and Medical Leave Act of 1993 (FMLA or Act) entitles eligible employees to take up to 12 work weeks of unpaid leave annually for any of several reasons, including the onset of a "serious health condition" in an employee's spouse, child, or parent. The Act creates a private right of action to seek both equitable relief and money damages "against any employer (including a public agency) in any Federal or State court of competent jurisdiction," Section 2617 (a) (2), should that employer "interfere with, restrain, or deny the exercise of" FMLA rights. We hold that employees of the State of Nevada may recover money damages in the event of the State's failure to comply with the family-care provision of the Act. . . .

For over a century now, we have made clear that the Constitution does not provide for federal jurisdiction over suits against nonconsenting States. *Board of Trustees of Univ. of Ala. v. Garrett*, 531 U.S. 356 (2001); *Kimel v. Florida Bd. of Regents*, 528 U.S. 62 (2000); *College Savings Bank v. Florida Prepaid Postsecondary Ed. Expense Bd.*, 527 U. S. 666 (1999); *Seminole Tribe of Fla. v. Florida*, 517 U.S. 44, 54 (1996); *Hans v. Louisiana*, 134 U.S. 1 (1890).

Congress may, however, abrogate such immunity in federal court if it makes its intention to abrogate unmistakably clear in the language of the statute and acts pursuant to a valid exercise of its power under Section 5 of the Fourteenth Amendment. The clarity of Congress' intent here is not fairly debatable. The Act enables employees to seek damages "against any employer (including a public agency) in any Federal or State court of competent jurisdiction," and Congress has defined "public agency" to include both "the government of a State or political subdivision thereof" and "any agency of . . . a State, or a political subdivision of a State." We held in *Kimel* that, by using identical language in the Age Discrimination in Employment Act of 1967 (ADEA), Congress satisfied the clear statement rule of *Dellmuth* [*v, Muth*, 491 U.S. 223 (1989)]. This case turns, then, on whether Congress acted within its constitutional authority when it sought to abrogate the States' immunity for purposes of the FMLA's family-leave provision.

In enacting the FMLA, Congress relied on two of the powers vested in it by the Constitution: its Article I commerce power and its power under Section 5 of the Fourteenth Amendment to enforce that Amendment's guarantees. Congress may not abrogate the States' sovereign immunity pursuant to its Article I power over commerce. *Seminole Tribe*. Congress may, however, abrogate States' sovereign immunity through a valid exercise of its Section 5 power, for "the Eleventh Amendment, and the principle of state sovereignty which it embodies, are necessarily limited by the enforcement provisions of Section 5 of the Fourteenth Amendment." *Fitzpatrick v. Bitzer*, 427 U.S. 445 (1976). See also *Garrett; Kimel*.

Two provisions of the Fourteenth Amendment are relevant here: Section 5 grants Congress the power "to enforce" the substantive guarantees of Section 1—among them, equal protection of the laws—by enacting "appropriate legislation." Congress may, in the exercise of its Section 5 power, do more than simply proscribe conduct that we have held unconstitutional. "Congress' power to enforce the Amendment includes the authority both to remedy and to deter violation of rights guaranteed thereunder by prohibiting a somewhat broader swath of conduct, including that which is not itself forbidden by the Amendment's text." *Garrett; City of Boerne v. Flores*, 521 U.S. 507 (1997); *Katzenbach v. Morgan*, 384 U.S. 641 (1966). In other words, Congress may enact so-called prophylactic legislation that proscribes facially constitutional conduct, in order to prevent and deter unconstitutional conduct.

City of Boerne also confirmed, however, that it falls to this Court, not Congress, to define the substance of constitutional guarantees. "The ultimate interpretation and determination of the Fourteenth Amendment's substantive meaning remains the province of the Judicial Branch." *Kimel.* Section 5 legislation reaching beyond the scope of Section 1's actual guarantees must be an appropriate remedy for identified constitutional violations, not "an attempt to substantively redefine the States' legal obligations." We distinguish appropriate prophylactic legislation from "substantive redefinition of the Fourteenth Amendment right at issue" by applying the test set forth in *City of Boerne*: Valid Section 5 legislation must exhibit "congruence and proportionality between the injury to be prevented or remedied and the means adopted to that end."

The FMLA aims to protect the right to be free from gender-based discrimination in the workplace. We have held that statutory classifications that distinguish between males and females are subject to heightened scrutiny. See, e.g., *Craig v. Boren*, 429 U.S. 190 (1976). For a gender-based classification to withstand such scrutiny, it must "serv[e] important governmental objectives," and "the discriminatory means employed [must be] substantially related to the achievement of those objectives." *United States v. Virginia*, 518 U.S. 515 (1996). The State's justification for such a classification "must not rely on overbroad generalizations about the different talents, capacities, or preferences of males and females." We now inquire whether Congress had evidence of a pattern of constitutional violations on the part of the States in this area.

The history of the many state laws limiting women's employment opportunities is chronicled in—and, until relatively recently, was sanctioned by—this Court's own opinions. For example, in *Bradwell v. State*, 16 Wall. 130 (1873) (Illinois), and *Goesaert v. Cleary*, 335 U.S. 464 (1948) (Michigan), the Court upheld state laws prohibiting women from practicing law and tending bar, respectively. State laws frequently subjected women to distinctive restrictions, terms, conditions, and benefits for those jobs they could take. In *Muller v. Oregon*, 208 U.S. 412 (1908), for example, this Court approved a state law limiting the hours that women could work for wages, and observed that 19 States had such laws at the time. Such laws were based on the related beliefs that (1) woman is, and should remain, "the center of home and family life," *Hoyt v. Florida*, 368 U.S. 57 (1961), and (2) "a proper discharge of [a woman's] maternal functions—having in view not merely her own health, but the well-being of the race—justif[ies] legislation to protect her from the greed as well as the passion of man," *Muller*. Until our decision in *Reed v. Reed*, 404 U.S. 71 (1971), "it remained the prevailing doctrine that government, both federal and state, could withhold from women opportunities accorded men so long as any 'basis in reason'"—such as the above beliefs—"could be conceived for the discrimination." *Virginia*.

Congress responded to this history of discrimination by abrogating States' sovereign immunity in Title VII of the Civil Rights Act of 1964, and we sustained this abrogation in *Fitzpatrick*. But state gender discrimination did not cease. "[I]t can hardly be doubted that . . . women still face pervasive, although at times more subtle, discrimination . . . in the job market." *Frontiero v. Richardson*, 411 U.S. 677 (1973). According to evidence that was before Congress when it enacted the FMLA, States continue to rely on invalid gender stereotypes in the employment context, specifically in the administration of leave benefits. Reliance on such stereotypes cannot justify the States' gender discrimination in this area. *Virginia*. The long and extensive history of sex discrimination prompted us to hold that measures that differentiate on the basis of gender warrant heightened scrutiny; here, as in *Fitzpatrick*, the persistence of such unconstitutional discrimination by the States justifies Congress' passage of prophylactic Section 5 legislation.

As the FMLA's legislative record reflects, a 1990 Bureau of Labor Statistics (BLS) survey stated that 37 percent of surveyed private-sector employees were covered by maternity leave policies, while only 18 percent were covered by paternity leave policies. The corresponding numbers from a similar BLS survey the previous year were 33 percent and 16 percent, respectively. While these data show an increase in the percentage of employees eligible for such leave, they also show a widening of the gender gap during the same period. Thus, stereotype-based beliefs about the allocation of family duties remained firmly rooted, and employers' reliance on them in establishing discriminatory leave policies remained widespread.

Congress also heard testimony that "[p]arental leave for fathers . . . is rare. Even . . . [w]here child-care leave policies do exist, men, both in the public and private sectors, receive notoriously discriminatory treatment in their requests for such leave." (Washington Council of Lawyers). Many States offered women extended "maternity" leave that far exceeded the typical 4- to 8-week period of physical disability due to pregnancy and childbirth, but very few States granted men a parallel benefit: Fifteen States provided women up to one year of extended maternity leave, while only four provided men with the same. This and other differential leave policies were not attributable to any differential physical needs of men and women, but rather to the pervasive sex-role stereotype that caring for family members is women's work.

Finally, Congress had evidence that, even where state laws and policies were not facially discriminatory, they were applied in discriminatory ways. . . .

In sum, the States' record of unconstitutional participation in, and fostering of, gender-based discrimination in the administration of leave benefits is weighty enough to justify the enactment of prophylactic Section 5 legislation.

We reached the opposite conclusion in *Garrett* and *Kimel*. In those cases, the Section 5 legislation under review responded to a purported tendency of state officials to make age- or disability-based distinctions. Under our equal protection case law, discrimination on the basis of such characteristics is not judged under a heightened review standard, and passes muster if there is "a rational basis for doing so at a class-based level, even if it 'is probably not true' that those reasons are valid in the majority of cases." *Kimel*. Thus, in order to impugn the constitutionality of state discrimination against the disabled or the elderly, Congress must identify, not just the existence of age- or disability-based state decisions, but "a widespread pattern" of irrational reliance on such criteria. We found no such showing with respect to the ADEA and Title I of the Americans with Disabilities Act of 1990 (ADA). *Kimel.*

Here, however, Congress directed its attention to state gender discrimination, which triggers a heightened level of scrutiny. Because the standard for demonstrating the constitutionality of a gender-based classification is more difficult to meet than our rational-basis test—it must "serv[e] important governmental objectives" and be "substantially related to the achievement of those objectives," *Virginia,*—it was easier for Congress to show a pattern of state constitutional violations. Congress was similarly successful in *South Carolina v. Katzenbach*, 383 U.S. 301 (1966), where we upheld the Voting Rights Act of 1965: Because racial classifications are presumptively invalid, most of the States' acts of race discrimination violated the Fourteenth Amendment. . . .

Unlike the statutes at issue in *City of Boerne, Kimel,* and *Garrett,* which applied broadly to every aspect of state employers' operations, the FMLA is narrowly targeted at the fault line between work and family—precisely where sex-based overgeneralization has been and remains strongest—and effects only one aspect of the employment relationship. . . .

The judgment of the Court of Appeals is therefore Affirmed.

☐ *Justice KENNEDY, with whom Justice SCALIA Justice THOMAS join, dissenting.*

The specific question is whether Congress may impose on the States this entitlement program of its own design, with mandated minimums for leave time, and then enforce it by permitting private suits for money damages against the States. This in turn must be answered by asking whether subjecting States and their treasuries to monetary liability at the insistence of private litigants is a congruent and proportional response to a demonstrated pattern of unconstitutional conduct by the States. If we apply the teaching of these and related cases, the family leave provision of the Act, Section 2612 (a) (1) (C), in my respectful view, is invalid to the extent it allows for private suits against the unconsenting States.

Congress does not have authority to define the substantive content of the Equal Protection Clause; it may only shape the remedies warranted by the violations of that guarantee. *City of Boerne.* This requirement has special force in the context of the Eleventh Amendment, which protects a State's fiscal integrity from federal intrusion by vesting the States with immunity from private actions for damages pursuant to federal laws. The Commerce Clause likely would permit the National Government to enact an entitlement program such as this one; but when Congress couples the entitlement with the authorization to sue the States for monetary damages, it blurs the line of accountability the State has to its own citizens. These basic concerns underlie cases such as *Garrett* and *Kimel.* . . .

The Court is unable to show that States have engaged in a pattern of unlawful conduct which warrants the remedy of opening state treasuries to private suits. The inability to adduce evidence of alleged discrimination, coupled with the inescapable fact that the federal scheme is not a remedy but a benefit program, demonstrate the lack of the requisite link between any problem Congress has identified and the program it mandated.

In examining whether Congress was addressing a demonstrated "pattern of unconstitutional employment discrimination by the States," the Court gives superficial treatment to the requirement that we "identify with some precision the scope of the constitutional right at issue." *Garrett.* The Court suggests the issue is "the right to be free from gender-based discrimination in the workplace," and then it embarks on a survey of our precedents speaking to "[t]he history of the many state laws limiting women's employment opportunities." All would agree that women historically have been subjected to conditions in which their employment opportunities are more limited than those available to men. As the Court acknowledges, however, Congress responded to this problem by abrogating States' sovereign immunity in Title VII of the Civil Rights Act of 1964. The provision now before us has a different aim than Title VII. It seeks to ensure that eligible employees, irrespective of gender, can take a minimum amount of leave time to care for an ill relative.

The relevant question, as the Court seems to acknowledge, is whether, notwithstanding the passage of Title VII and similar state legislation, the States continued to engage in widespread discrimination on the basis of gender in the provision of family leave benefits. If such a pattern were shown, the Eleventh Amendment would not bar Congress from devising a congruent and proportional remedy. The evidence to substantiate this charge must be far more specific, however, than a simple recitation of a general history of employment discrimination against women. When the federal statute seeks to abrogate state sovereign immunity, the Court should be more careful to insist on adherence to the analytic requirements set forth in its own precedents. Persisting overall effects of gender-based discrimination at the workplace must not be ignored; but simply noting the problem is not a substitute for evidence which identifies some real discrimination the family leave rules are designed to prevent. . . .

The paucity of evidence to support the case the Court tries to make demonstrates that Congress was not responding with a congruent and proportional remedy to a perceived course of unconstitutional conduct. Instead, it enacted a substantive entitlement program of its own. If Congress had been concerned about different treatment of men and women with respect to family leave, a congruent remedy would have sought to ensure the benefits of any leave program enacted by a State are available to men and women on an equal basis. Instead, the Act imposes, across the board, a requirement that States grant a minimum of 12 weeks of leave per year. This requirement may represent Congress' considered judgment as to the optimal balance between the family obligations of workers and the interests of employers, and the States may decide to follow these guidelines in designing their own family leave benefits. It does not follow, however, that if the States choose to enact a different benefit scheme, they should be deemed to engage in unconstitutional conduct and forced to open their treasuries to private suits for damages. . . .

■ The Development of Law

Other Recent Rulings on the Eleventh Amendment

CASE	VOTE	RULING
Florida Prepaid Postsecondary Education Expense Board v. College Savings Bank, 527 U.S. 627 (1999)	5:4	Writing for the Court, Chief Justice Rehnquist held that Congress exceeded its powers in abrogating states' sovereign immunity in enacting

the Patent and Plant Variety Protection Remedy Clarification Act. Relying on *Seminole Tribe of Florida v. Florida,* 517 U.S. 44 (1996), Chief Justice Rehnquist also ruled that Congress exceeded its power under the Commerce Clause of Article I and its enforcement power under Section 5 of the Fourteenth Amendment, as interpreted in *City of Boerne v. Flores,* 521 U.S. 507 (1997) (excerpted in Vol. 1, Ch. 6). Justices Stevens, Souter, Ginsburg, and Breyer dissented.

CASE	VOTE	RULING
Kimel v. Florida Board of Regents, 527 U.S. 62 (2000)	5:4	Writing for the Court, Justice O'Connor held that Congress exceeded its powers in abrogating states' sov-

ereign immunity under the Eleventh Amendment in extending the Age Discrimination in Employment Act to state employees and ruled that state employees may not bring suits in federal courts to enforce provisions of the law. Justices Stevens, Souter, Ginsburg, and Breyer dissented.

CASE	VOTE	RULING
Board of Trustees of the University of Alabama v. Garrett, 531 U.S. 356 (2001)	5:4	The Court held that state emloyees may not sue their state employers under the Americans with Disabilities Act of 1990 (ADA), which

prohibits employers from "discriminat[ing] against a qualified individual with a disability" in employment. Writing for the Court, Chief Justice Rehnquist reaffirmed that Congress may abrogate states' Eleventh Amendment immunity when it both unequivocally intends to do so and acts pursuant to its constitutional authority. *Kimel v. Florida Bd. of Regents,* 528 U.S. 62 (2000). While Congress may not base abrogation of state immunity upon its Article I power to regulate interstate commerce, it may do so under Section 5 of the Fourteenth

(continues)

■ THE DEVELOPMENT OF LAW
Other Recent Rulings on the Eleventh Amendment (continued)

CASE	VOTE	RULING

Amendment, which authorizes Congress to enforce the Fourteenth Amendment's protection by enacting "appropriate legislation." *City of Boerne v. Flores*, 521 U.S. 507 (1997). The Court has held, however, that disability, like age, is not a protected suspect or quasi-suspect classification under the Fourteenth Amendment. *City of Cleburne, Texas v. Cleburne Living Center*, 473 U.S. 432 (1985) (discussed in Vol. 2, Ch. 12). Thus, Congress exceeded its enforcement and remedial powers under the Fourteenth Amendment and unconstitutionally abrogated states' sovereign immunity under the Eleventh Amendment.

| *Kansas v. Colorado,* 533 U.S. 1 (2001) | 6:3 | Writing for the Court, Justice Stevens rejected the contention that the Eleventh Amendment |

bars a state from recovering monetary damages from another state in a suit on original jurisdiction; Kansas sued Colorado over the diversion of water from the Arkansas River and sought a damage award. Justice O'Connor filed an opinion in part concurring and dissenting, which Justices Scalia and Thomas joined.

| *Lapides v. Board of Regents of The University System of Georgia*, 534 U.S. 1052 (2002) | 8:0 | Writing for a unanimous Court, Justice Breyer held that a state's removal of a lawsuit filed against it from a state court to a federal court constitutes a waiver |

of the state's Eleventh Amendment immunity.

| *Verizon Maryland v. Public Service Commission of Maryland*, 535 U.S. 467 (2002) | 8:0 | With Justice O'Connor not participating, the Court held unanimously that states are not immune from suits brought over implementation of the Telecommunications Act of 1996. |

| *Federal Maritime Commission v. South Carolina State Ports Authority*, 535 U.S. 743 (2002) | 5:4 | Writing for the Court, Justice Thomas held that states' sovereign immunity bars the Federal Maritime Commission (FMC) from adjudicating a private |

party's complaint against a nonconsenting state in an administrative law proceeding. Justice Thomas reasoned that dual sovereignty is a defining feature of the nation and an integral component of states' sovereignty is their immunity from private suits. Although the Eleventh Amendment provides that the "judicial Power of the United States" does not "extend to any suit, in law or equity," brought by citizens of one state against another state, that provision does not define states' sovereign immunity but instead is only one particular exemplification of that immunity. Since administrative adjudications were virtually unheard of in the eighteenth and nineteenth centuries, so there was little evidence of the framers' intent. Accordingly, Justice Thomas reasoned that based on the presumption that the Constitution was not intended to permit any proceedings against states that were "anomalous and unheard of when the Constitution was adopted," *Hans v. Louisiana*, 134 U.S. 1 (1890), the Court should give great weight to the fact that the states were not subject to private suits in administrative adjudications at the time of the founding. In holding that *Hans's* presumption of immunity applies, Justice Thomas observed that administrative law judges and trial judges play similar roles and administrative and judicial proceedings share similar features. In addition, he concluded that it would be strange if Congress were prohibited from exercising its Article I powers to abrogate state sovereign immunity in Article III judicial proceedings, but permitted to use its powers to create court-like administrative tribunals to which state sovereign immunity did not apply. Justices Stevens and Breyer issued dissenting options and were joined by Justices Souter and Ginsburg.

CASE	VOTE	RULING
Nevada Department of Human Resources v. Hibbs, 538 U.S. 721 (2003)	6:3	Writing for the Court, Chief Justice Rehnquist held that Congress had the power to abrogate states' sovereign immu-

nity in authorizing private lawsuits against states for violations of the Family and Medical Leave Act of 1993. Congress, reasoned the chief justice, passed the act, and had the power to do so under Section 5 of the Fourteenth Amendment, in enforcing the amendment's prohibition against gender discrimination. Justices Scalia, Kennedy, and Thomas dissented.

Frew v. Hawkins, 540 U.S. 431 (2004)	9:0	Writing for the Court, Justice Kennedy held that states are not immune under the Eleventh

Amendment from complying with their obligations under a consent degree enforcing federal law, even for monetary damages for retrospective relief for failure to enforce federal laws. Linda Frew sued Texas for failing to provide medical care for her children under the federal Early and Periodic Screening, Diagnostic, and Treatment (EPSDT) program. State offi-

(continues)

■ The Development of Law
Other Recent Rulings on the Eleventh Amendment (continued)

CASE	VOTE	RULING

cials did not raise an Eleventh Amendment claim or object to the suit in federal court. But after the court approved a consent degree they claimed that it was unenforceable under the Eleventh Amendment. Justice Kennedy ruled that the Eleventh Amendment does not bare enforcement of a consent degree pertaining to states' providing EPSDT services and, although generally not for damages for retrospective relief for a state's failure to comply with federal law, here the damages were enforceable as part of a federal court order that enforced states' compliance with federal law.

Tennessee v. Lane,   5:4   Writing for the Court, Justice
541 U.S. 509 (2004)   Stevens held that Congress has
                                       the power under Section 5 of
the Fourteenth Amendment to authorize lawsuits against states to force their compliance with Title 2 of the Americans with Disabilities Act (ADA) of 1990 and rejected the claim that such suits are barred by the Eleventh Amendment. But, the holding was narrow and limited to suits against states to force them to provide access for the disabled to courthouses. The ruling did not address access to other public "services, programs, or activities" where fundamental rights are not at issue. Justice Stevens justified the exercise of Congress's remedial power on finding that "Congress learned that many individuals, in many states across the country, were being excluded from courthouses and court proceedings by reason of their disabilities." On that basis he distinguished the five-to-four decision, in *Board of Trustees of University of Alabama v. Garrett*, 531 U.S. 356 (2001), in which Chief Justice Rehnquist held that Title I of the ADA, barring discrimination against people with disabilities in state employment, did not abrogate states' Eleventh Amendment immunity. Writing for the dissenters—Justices Scalia, Kennedy, and Thomas—in *Lane*, Chief Justice Rehnquist maintained that Congress lacked the authority to abrogate state immunity from suits to enforce the ADA under all of its provisions, and dismissed evidence of a congressional finding of discrimination against the disabled as merely "anecdotal" and insufficient to establish systematic discrimination. Justice O'Connor cast the pivotal vote in *Garrett* and *Lane*.

CASE	VOTE	RULING

United States v. Georgia, 546 U.S. 151 (2006) — 9:0 — Writing for the Court, Justice Scalia held that Title II of the Americans with Disabilities Act (ADA) of 1990 created a private cause of action to sue state officials for monetary damages for violating constitutional rights and that Section 5 of the Fourteenth Amendment, which gives Congress the power to enact legislation to enforce the amendment, includes the power to abrogate Eleventh Amendment state immunity. The case, involving a paraplegic prison inmate claiming that prison officials violated his Eight Amendment rights, was remanded for reconsideration of whether the state had violated the inmate's rights.

Central Virginia Community College v. Katz, 546 U.S. 356 (2006) — 5:4 — Writing for the majority, Justice Stevens held that states are not immune from bankruptcy proceedings and, like other creditors, are bound to a bankruptcy court's orders. After reviewing the history of the bankruptcy clause in Article I, Section 8, Justice Stevens concluded that the Constitution created a national uniform bankruptcy system. Justice Thomas filed a dissent, which was joined by Chief Justice Roberts and Justices Scalia and Kennedy.

Northern Insurance Co. v. Chatham County, Georgia, 547 U.S. 189 (2006) — 9:0 — Writing for the Court, Justice Thomas held that the Eleventh Amendment does not bar admiralty suits against counties and that counties do not qualify as an "arm of the state" in such cases.

C | *Judicial Federalism*

Judicial power is divided and decentralized in the United States. Alongside the federal judiciary, each state has its own independent judicial system. Article III, Section 2 (see Ch. 2) gives the Supreme Court jurisdiction over cases "arising under the Constitution" and controversies between states and citizens of different states. The supremacy clause of Article VI, of course, necessitates that the Court has authority to review decisions of state supreme courts when in conflict with federal law. In addition, the Judiciary Act of 1789 in Section 5 extended federal appellate jurisdiction to the final judgments and decrees "in the highest court of law or equity of a State in which a decision in the suit could be had" in three areas: where a state draws into question the validity of federal law; where a state statute was challenged as "repugnant to the constitution, treaties or laws of the United States" but upheld; and where state courts construing federal law decide against the title, right, privilege, or exemption claimed.

The Court's review of state supreme court decisions has been a source of long-standing controversy in constitutional politics. In *Fairfax's Devisee v. Hunter's Lessee*, 7 Cr. (11 U.S.) 603 (1813), for example, Virginia refused to honor a ruling of the Marshall Court reversing a decision of that state's supreme court on the rights of British subjects under the Jay Treaty. Virginia maintained that despite being bound by the Constitution, its interpretations of federal law (not those of federal courts) were controlling. Three years later, Justice Joseph Story reasserted federal judicial power to review state court decisions in *Martin v. Hunter's Lessee* (1816) (see excerpt below), when rebuffing Virginia's contention by pointing out that the Constitution was established not by the states but the "people of the United States."[1]

Periodically, state courts, legislatures, and government officials have balked at enforcing federal law and asserted the power of state nullification. In one of the Court's first encounters with such a controversy, arising from the Pennsylvania legislature's refusal to comply with a lower federal court decision, in *United States v. Peters*, 5 Cr. 115 (1809), Chief Justice Marshall dismissed out of hand the state's position: "If the legislatures of the several States may, at will, annul the judgments of the courts of the United States, and destroy the rights acquired under those judgments, the constitution itself becomes a solemn mockery; and the nation is deprived of the means of enforcing its laws by the instrumentality of its own tribunals."

Prior to the Civil War, a number of northern states refused to comply with the Fugitive Slave Act of 1850 requiring the return of escaped slaves. In *Ableman v. Booth*, 21 How. (62 U.S.) 506 (1859), arising from the Wisconsin state supreme court's declaration that the fugitive slave law was unconstitutional, the Taney Court resoundingly reasserted federal supremacy. Although a strong defender of state power, Chief Justice Taney declared that "no power is more clearly conferred by the Constitution and laws of the United States, than the power of this court to decide, ultimately and finally, all cases arising under such Constitution and laws."

State nullification or interposition was revived by southern states in opposition to the Warren Court's 1954 landmark ruling on school desegregation. The Alabama legislature, for example, declared,

> WHEREAS the states, being the parties to the constitutional compact, it follows of necessity that there can be no tribunal above their authority to decide, in the last resort, whether the compact made by them be violated; and consequently, they must decide themselves, in the last resort, such questions as may be of sufficient magnitude to require their interposition. . . .

> The decisions and orders of the Supreme Court of the United States relating to the separation of races in the public schools are, as a matter of right, null, void, and of no effect; and . . . as a matter of right, this State is not bound to abide thereby.

The Court, however, once again rejected that contention in the controversy over the opposition of Little Rock, Arkansas, to school desegregation in *Cooper v. Aaron* (1958) (see excerpt below).

State courts may exercise concurrent jurisdiction with federal courts, unless Congress has conferred exclusive jurisdiction on the federal judiciary. Article VI also provides that "the judges in every state shall be bound [by the Supremacy Clause], anything in the Constitution or laws of any state to the contrary notwithstanding."[2]

Although neither federal nor state courts may issue injunctions enjoining each others' proceedings,[3] federal courts may enjoin state officials from enforcing unconstitutional state laws. The injunctive power was first asserted in *Osborn v. Bank of the United States*, 9 Wheat. 738 (1824), though the Marshall Court held that state officials could be enjoined only after a court had declared a state law invalid. *Ex parte Young*, 209 U.S. 123 (1908) further expanded federal injunctive powers, when holding that a state attorney general could be enjoined from enforcing a statute while the statute's validity is being determined in a federal court. In response to that ruling, in 1910 Congress enacted legislation forbidding federal judges sitting alone from enjoining the enforcement of state laws and requiring that such injunctions be issued by a panel or three-judge court.

The injunctive power of federal courts was greatly expanded in *Dombrowski v. Pfister* 380 U.S. 82 (1967). There the Warren Court held that where a state law is vague and susceptible to unconstitutional application, federal courts may enjoin its enforcement until a state court has issued a declaratory judgment narrowing its construction. Subsequent rulings, however, have substantially limited *Dombrowski*.[4] The leading case is *Younger v. Harris* (1971) (see excerpt below).[5]

Another important instrument for federal supervision of state courts is the use of *habeas corpus* review of the constitutionality for holding a person in prison and the law and procedure under which he was convicted and sentenced. The Court requires that defendants exhaust state remedies before seeking *habeas corpus* review in federal district courts.[6] As a result of the Warren Court's extension of the guarantees of the Bill of Rights to the states (see Vol. 2, Ch. 4), the number of applications for *habeas corpus* review escalated in the 1970s and 1980s. In response, the Court moved to cut back sharply on the availability of federal *habeas corpus* review.[7] *Stone v. Powell* (1976) (excerpted below) is a leading illustrative case.

The Rehnquist Court went much further in cutting back on the opportunities for inmates in state prisons to pursue *habeas corpus* appeals in federal courts. In the process the Court overturned *Fay v. Noia*, 372 U.S. 391 (1963), which had held that federal courts could consider the petitions of prison inmates who had failed properly to appeal their cases in state courts, so long as they had not "deliberately bypassed" the appellate system in state courts. Writing for the Court in *Coleman v. Thompson*, 501 U.S. 722 (1991), however, Justice O'Connor took exactly the opposite view in laying down a new rule under which almost any failure by a prison convict to satisfy a state's appellate procedures will result in his or her forfeiting the right to file a *habeas corpus* petition in federal courts. Justice O'Connor observed that

> [t]his is a case about federalism. It concerns the respect that federal courts owe the States and the States' procedural rules when reviewing the claims of state prisoners in federal *habeas corpus*. . . .

> This Court will not review a question of federal law decided by a state court if the decision of that court rests on a state law ground that is independent of the federal question and adequate to support the judgment. . . .

> In the *habeas* context, the application of the independent and adequate state ground doctrine is grounded in concerns of comity and

federalism. Without the rule, a federal district court would be able to do in *habeas* what this Court could not do on direct review; *habeas* would offer state prisoners whose custody was supported by independent and adequate state grounds an end run around the limits of this Court's jurisdiction and a means to undermine the States' interest in enforcing its laws. . . .

In *Michigan v. Long*, 463 U.S. 1032 (1983) . . . [the Court ruled that] a state court that wishes to look to federal law for guidance or as an alternative holding while still relying on an independent and adequate state ground can avoid the presumption by stating "clearly and expressly that [its decision] is . . . based on bona fide separate, adequate, and independent grounds." . . . *Long* [involved the direct review of a state supreme court decision. By contrast] the problem of ambiguous state court decisions in the application of the independent and adequate state ground doctrine in a federal *habeas* case [was first addressed] in *Harris v. Reed*, 489 U.S. 255 (1989). . . . In *Harris* [the Court] applied in federal *habeas* the presumption this Court adopted in *Long* for direct review cases. . . . After *Harris*, federal courts on *habeas corpus* review of state prisoner claims, like this Court on direct review of state court judgments, will presume that there is no independent and adequate state ground for a state court decision when the decision "fairly appears to rest primarily on federal law, or to be interwoven with the federal law, and when the adequacy and independence of any possible state law ground is not clear from the face of the opinion." . . .

In all cases in which a state prisoner has defaulted his federal claims in state court pursuant to an independent and adequate state procedural rule, federal *habeas* review of the claims is barred unless the prisoner can demonstrate cause for the default and actual prejudice as a result of the alleged violation of federal law, or demonstrate that failure to consider the claims will result in a fundamental miscarriage of justice. . . .

In addition, the Court redrew the lines of judicial federalism in other ways that further reduce federal courts' supervisory role over both the enforcement of federal legislation and decisions of state courts. Writing for the Court in *Sue Suter v. Artist M.*, 503 U.S. 347 (1992), Chief Justice Rehnquist held that abused and neglected children do not have an implied right to sue in federal court to enforce provisions of the Adoption Assistance and Child Welfare Act of 1980. That act requires, as a condition of receiving federal funding for children's foster care and adoption services, that states "make reasonable efforts" to prevent child abuse and neglect. Rehnquist construed the statute to "not unambiguously confer an enforceable right" on the children and held that it was up to federal agencies, not private citizens or federal courts, to ensure states' compliance with the statute.

Still, a bare majority stopped short of substantially cutting back on federal courts' *habeas corpus* review of claims of *Miranda* and Fifth Amendment violations in *Withrow v. Williams*, 507 U.S. 680 (1993). In that case Michigan prosecutors had asked the Court to extend the reasoning in *Stone v. Powell*, 428 U.S. 465 (1976) (see excerpt below), to requests for federal *habeas corpus* review of state prisoners' claim of *Miranda* violations. Note that the bare majority in *Withrow* declined to extend *Stone v. Powell* on the ground that *Stone* dealt with *habeas* review of cases involving violations of the exclusionary rule—a rule that the Court deems not to be "a personal constitutional right," but only a prudential rule aimed at deterring illegal searches and seizures. By contrast, in his opinion for the Court Justice Souter held that *Miranda* protects "a fundamental trial right" that justifies federal *habeas* review.

However, another bare majority affirmed a more rigorous standard for federal courts setting aside convictions of state prisoners who claim violations of their *Miranda* rights. Chief Justice Rehnquist ruled that when exercising *habeas* review federal courts may set aside convictions only if the errors made at trial in not honoring *Miranda* have a "substantial and injurious effect or influence in determining the jury's verdict." In doing so, the chief justice rejected the less-stringent standard of whether the error was "harmless beyond a reasonable doubt." As a result, prisoners must show that they suffered "actual prejudice" due to a state trial court's errors. Here, in *Brecht v. Abrahamson*, 507 U.S. 619 (1993), Justices White, Souter, Blackmun, and O'Connor dissented.

Finally, in a splintered ruling the Court stopped just short of jettisoning much of *Ex parte Young*, 209 U.S. 123 (1908). Although the Eleventh Amendment's provision for the states' immunity generally bars suits against states in federal courts, *Ex parte Young* held that state officials may be sued and enjoined from enforcing state laws that are said to be unconstitutional, even though those laws have not yet been ruled invalid. At issue in *Idaho v. Coeur d'Alene Tribe*, 521 U.S. 261 (1997), was whether the state could be sued in federal court in a dispute over ownership of a lake bed, part of which is on an Indian reservation. A bare majority—including Chief Justice Rehnquist and Justices Kennedy, O'Connor, Scalia, and Thomas—held that the suit bore too directly and intrusively on Idaho's "sovereign interest in its lands and waters."

NOTES

1. See also *Cohens v. Virginia*, 6 Wheat. 264 (1821).

2. *Prigg v. Pennsylvania*, 16 Pet. 539 (1942), held that states could not be forced to enforce federal penal statutes, but that ruling was subsequently abandoned.

3. Congress limited the powers of the federal courts in 1793 and with a number of later statutes. The Court denied the power of states to enjoin the proceedings of

lower federal courts as essential to the independence of the two judicial systems. See *McKim v. Voorhies*, 7 Cr. 279 (1812); and *United States ex rel. Riggs v. Johnson County*, 6 Wall. 166 (1868).

4. See *Steffel v. Thompson*, 415 U.S. 452 (1974); *Kugler v. Helfant*, 421 U.S. 117 (1975); *Rizzo v. Goode*, 423 U.S. 362 (1976); *Justice v. Vail*, 430 U.S. 327 (1977); and *Middlesex County Ethics Committee v. Garden State Bar Association*, 457 U.S. 423 (1982).

5. *Huffman v. Purse, Ltd.*, 420 U.S. 592 (1975), extended *Younger* to civil proceedings.

6. See, for example, *Pitchess v. Davis*, 421 U.S. 482 (1975).

7. See also *Francis v. Henderson*, 425 U.S. 536 (1976); *Estelle v. Williams*, 425 U.S. 501 (1976); *Holmberg v. Parratt*, 431 U.S. 969 (1977); and *Rose v. Lundy*, 455 U.S. 509 (1982).

SELECTED BIBLIOGRAPHY

Latzer, Barry. *State Constitutions and Criminal Law.* Westport, CT: Greenwood, 1991.

Lopeman, Charles. *The Activist Advocate: Policy Making in State Supreme Courts.* New York: Praeger, 1999.

Solimine, Michael, and Walker, James. *Respecting State Courts.* Westport, CT: Greenwood, 1999.

Stumpf, Harry, and Culver, John. *The Politics of State Courts.* White Plains, NY: Longman, 1992.

Tarr, G. Allan, and Porter, Mary C. *State Supreme Courts in State and Nation.* New Haven, CT: Yale University Press, 1988.

Martin v. Hunter's Lessee

1 WHEAT. (14 U.S.) 304, 14 S.CT. 97 (1816)

Denny Martin sought to recover a body of land in Virginia he inherited from Lord Fairfax and contended that his rights were secured under the Treaty of Peace with Great Britian in 1783. Virginia's highest appellate court had denied his and other British citizens' land rights, but the Supreme Court reversed that decision in *Fairfax's Devisee v. Hunter's Lessee*, 7 Cr. (11 U.S.) 603 (1813). However, on remand of that case the Virginia court refused to abide by the Supreme Court's ruling and held unconstitutional the portion of Section 25 of the Judiciary Act of 1789 which extended federal jurisdiction over decisions of state supreme courts. Martin once again appealed to the Supreme Court.

The Court's decision was unanimous, and the opinion was announced by Justice Story. Justice Johnson concurred.

☐ *Justice STORY delivers the opinion of the Court.*

The third article of the constitution is that which must principally attract our attention. The first section declares, "the judicial power of the United States shall be vested in one Supreme Court, and in such other [*sic*] inferior courts as the Congress may, from time to time, ordain and establish." The second section declares, that "the judicial power shall extend to all cases in law or equity, arising under this constitution, the laws of the United States, and the treaties made, or which shall be made, under their authority; to all cases affecting ambassadors, other public ministers and consuls; to all cases of admiralty and maritime jurisdiction; to controversies to which the United States shall be a party; to controversies between two or more states; between a state and citizens of another state; between citizens of different states; between citizens of the same state, claiming lands under the grants of different states; and between a state or the citizens thereof, and foreign states, citizens, or subjects." It then proceeds to declare, that "in all cases affecting ambassadors, other public ministers and consuls, and those in which a state shall be a party, the Supreme Court shall have original jurisdiction. In all the other cases before mentioned the Supreme Court shall have appellate jurisdiction, both as to law and fact, with such exceptions, and under such regulations, as the Congress shall make." . . .

Let this article be carefully weighed and considered. The language of the article throughout is manifestly designed to be mandatory upon the legislature. Its obligatory force is so imperative that Congress could not, without a violation of its duty, have refused to carry it into operation. The judicial power of the United States shall be vested (not may be vested) in one supreme court, and in such inferior courts as Congress may, from time to time, ordain and establish. . . .

The judicial power must, therefore, be vested in some court, by Congress; and to suppose that it was not an obligation binding on them, but might, at their pleasure, be omitted or declined, is to suppose that, under the sanction of the constitution they might defeat the constitution itself; a construction which would lead to such a result cannot be sound. . . .

If, then, it is the duty of Congress to vest the judicial power of the United States, it is a duty to vest the whole judicial power. The language, if imperative as to one part, is imperative as to all. If it were otherwise, this anomaly would exist, that Congress might successively refuse to vest the jurisdiction in any one class of cases enumerated in the constitution, and thereby defeat the jurisdiction as to all; for the constitution has not singled out any class on which Congress are bound to act in preference to others. . . .

This leads us to the consideration of the great question as to the nature and extent of the appellate jurisdiction of the United States. We have already seen that appellate jurisdiction is given by the constitution to the Supreme Court in all cases, where it has not original jurisdiction; subject, however, to such exceptions and regulations as Congress may prescribe. It is, therefore, capable of embracing every case enumerated in the constitution, which is not exclusively to be decided by way of original jurisdiction. . . .

[B]y the terms of the constitution, the . . . appellate power is not limited by the terms of the third article to any particular courts. The words are, "the judicial power (which includes appellate power) shall extend to all cases," etc., and "in all other cases before mentioned the Supreme Court shall have appellate jurisdiction." It is the case, then, and not the court, that gives the jurisdiction. If the judicial power extends to the case, it will be in vain to search in the letter of the constitution for any qualification as to the tribunal where it depends. . . .

If the constitution meant to limit the appellate jurisdiction to cases pending in the courts of the United States, it would necessarily follow that the jurisdiction of these courts would, in all the cases enumerated in the constitution, be exclusive of state tribunals. How otherwise could the jurisdiction extend to all cases arising under the constitution, laws and treaties of the United States, or to all cases of admiralty and maritime jurisdiction? If some of these cases might be entertained by state tribunals, and no appellate jurisdiction as to them should exist, then the appellate power would not extend to all, but to some, cases. If state tribunals might exercise concurrent jurisdiction over all or some of the other classes of cases in the constitution without control, then the appellate jurisdiction of the United States might, as to such cases, have no real existence, contrary to the manifest intent of the constitution. Under such circumstances, to give effect to the judicial power, it must be construed to be exclusive; and this not only when the casus faederis should arise directly, but when it should arise, incidentally, in cases pending in state courts. This construction would abridge the jurisdiction of such courts far more than has been ever contemplated in any act of Congress. . . .

[I]t is plain that the framers of the constitution did contemplate that cases within the judicial cognizance of the United States not only might but would arise in the state courts, in the exercise of their ordinary jurisdiction. With this view the sixth article declares, that "this constitution, and the laws of the United States which shall be made in pursuance thereof, and all treaties made, or which shall be made, under the authority of the United States, shall be the supreme law of the land and the judges in every state shall be bound thereby, anything in the constitution or laws of any state to the contrary notwithstanding." It is obvious that this obligation is imperative upon the state judges in their official, and not merely in their private, capacities. From the very nature of their judicial duties they would be called upon to pronounce the law applicable to the case in judgment. They were not to decide merely according to the laws or constitution of the state, but according to the constitution, laws and treaties of the United States—"the supreme law of the land." . . .

It must, therefore, be conceded that the constitution not only contemplated, but meant to provide for cases within the scope of the judicial power of the United States, which might yet depend before state tribunals. It was foreseen that in the exercise of their ordinary jurisdiction, state courts would incidentally take cognizance of cases arising under the constitution, the laws and treaties of the United States. Yet to all these cases the judicial power, by the very terms of the constitution, is to extend. It cannot extend by original jurisdiction if that was already rightfully and exclusively attached in the state courts, which (as has been already shown) may occur; it must, therefore, extend by appellate jurisdiction, or not at all. It would seem to follow that the appellate power of the United States must, in such cases, extend to state tribunals; and if in such cases, there is no reason why it should not equally attach upon all others within the purview of the constitution.

It has been argued that such an appellate jurisdiction over state courts is inconsistent with the genius of our governments, and the spirit of the constitution. That the latter was never designed to act upon state sovereignties, but only upon the people, and that if the power exists, it will materially impair the sovereignty of the states, and the independence of their courts. We cannot yield to the force of this reasoning; it assumes principles which we cannot admit, and draws conclusions to which we do not yield our assent.

It is a mistake that the constitution was not designed to operate upon states, in their corporate capacities. It is crowded with provisions which restrain or annul the sovereignty of the states in some of the highest branches of their prerogatives. The tenth section of the first article contains a long list of disabilities and prohibitions imposed upon the states. Surely, when such essential portions of state sovereignty are taken away, or prohibited to be exercised, it cannot be correctly asserted that the constitution does not act upon the states. The language of the constitution is also imperative upon the states as to the performance of many duties. It is imperative upon the state legislatures to make laws prescribing the time, places, and manner of holding elections for senators and representatives, and for electors of President and Vice-President. And in these, as well as some other cases, Congress have a right to revise, amend, or supersede the laws which may be passed by state legislatures. When, therefore, the states are stripped of some of the highest attributes of sovereignty, and the same are given to the United States; when the legislatures of the states are, in some respects, under the control of Congress, and in every case are, under the constitution, bound by the paramount authority of the United States; it is certainly difficult to support the argument that the appellate power over the decisions of state courts is contrary to the genius of our institutions. The courts of the United States can, without question, revise the proceedings of the executive and legislative authorities of the states, and if they are found to be contrary to the constitution, may declare them to be of no legal validity. Surely the exercise of the same right over judicial tribunals is not a higher or more dangerous act of sovereign power.

Nor can such a right be deemed to impair the independence of state judges. It is assuming the very ground in controversy to assert that they possess an absolute independence of the United States. In respect to the powers granted to the United States, they are not independent; they are expressly bound to obedience by the letter of the constitution; and if they should unintentionally transcend their authority, or misconstrue the constitution, there is no more reason for giving their judgments an absolute and irresistible force than for giving it to the acts of the other co-ordinate departments of state sovereignty. . . .

There is an additional consideration, which is entitled to great weight. The constitution of the United States was designed for the common and equal benefit of all the people of the United States. The judicial power was granted for the same benign and salutary purposes. It was not to be exercised exclusively for the benefit of parties who might be plaintiffs, and would elect the national forum, but also for the protection of defendants who might be entitled to try their rights, or assert their privileges, before the same forum. Yet, if the construction contended for be correct, it will follow, that as the plaintiff may always elect the state court, the defendant, may be deprived of all the security which the constitution intended in aid of his rights. Such a state of things can in no respect be considered as giving equal rights. . . .

On the whole, the court are of opinion that the appellate power of the United States does extend to cases pending in the state courts; and that the

25th section of the judiciary act, which authorizes the exercise of this jurisdiction in the specified cases, by a writ of error, is supported by the letter
and spirit of the constitution. We find no clause in that instrument which
limits this power; and we dare not interpose a limitation where the people
have not been disposed to create one.

Cooper v. Aaron

358 U.S. 1, 78 S.Ct. 1401 (1958)

In 1958, Governor Orval Faubus encouraged southern segregationists
to oppose the Supreme Court's ruling on school desegregation, and violence erupted in Little Rock, Arkansas. The federal National Guard
had to be called out to maintain order. The school board in Little Rock
pleaded with the Supreme Court to postpone its mandate for the desegregation of public schools. The Court granted the petition and expedited proceedings, hearing oral arguments three days after the
petition was filed.

After the justices unanimously voted to deny the school board's request for a delay in desegregating its public schools, Justice Brennan
prepared a draft of the opinion that would announce the Court's decision. But in an unusual move all nine justices gathered in their private
conference room and reworked portions of the opinion. The Court
also took the unusual step of noting in the opinion that three justices—Brennan, Harlan, and Whittaker—were not on the Court when
the landmark ruling in *Brown v. Board of Education of Topeka, Kansas*
(1954) (see Vol. 2, Ch. 12) was handed down but that they would have
joined the unanimous decision if they had been. All nine justices then
signed the Court's opinion to emphasize their unanimity and because
Justice Frankfurter insisted on adding a concurring opinion. This departure from the typical practice of having one justice sign the opinion
was strongly opposed by Douglas and angered Brennan and Chief Justice Warren. But all agreed to depart in this way so that Frankfurter's
concurring opinion "would not be accepted as any dilution or interpretation of the views expressed in the Court's joint opinion." Frankfurter insisted on publishing a concurring opinion because many of his
former students at Harvard Law School were leading members of the
southern bar and because the ex-justice (and former governor of South
Carolina) James Byrnes had published an attack on *Brown* and an article
written by one of Frankfurter's favorite former law clerks, Alexander
Bickel. As a clerk, Bickel had prepared a lengthy research report on seg-

regated schools when the Court first considered *Brown*. Later, when back at Harvard, Bickel revised and published it in the *Harvard Law Review*. Given Byrnes's attack, Frankfurter personally felt the need to lecture southern lawyers on the legitimacy of the Court's ruling in *Brown*.

☐ *THE CHIEF JUSTICE, Justice BLACK, Justice FRANKFURTER, Justice DOUGLAS, Justice BURTON, Justice CLARK, Justice HARLAN, Justice BRENNAN, and Justice WHITTAKER deliver the opinion of the Court.*

As this case reaches us it raises questions of the highest importance to the maintenance of our federal system of government. It necessarily involves a claim by the Governor and Legislature of a State that there is no duty on state officials to obey federal court orders resting on this Court's considered interpretation of the United States Constitution. Specifically it involves actions by the Governor and Legislature of Arkansas upon the premise that they are not bound by our holding in *Brown v. Board of Education* [1954]. That holding was that the Fourteenth Amendment forbids States to use their governmental powers to bar children on racial grounds from attending schools where there is state participation through any arrangement, management, funds or property. We are urged to uphold a suspension of the Little Rock School Board's plan to do away with segregated public schools in Little Rock until state laws and efforts to upset and nullify our holding in *Brown v. Board of Education* have been further challenged and tested in the courts. We reject these contentions. . . .

In affirming the judgment of the Court of Appeals which reversed the District Court we have accepted without reservation the position of the School Board, the Superintendent of Schools, and their counsel that they displayed entire good faith in the conduct of these proceedings and in dealing with the unfortunate and distressing sequence of events which has been outlined. We likewise have accepted the findings of the District Court as to the conditions at Central High School during the 1957–1958 school year, and also the findings that the educational progress of all the students, white and colored, of that school has suffered and will continue to suffer if the conditions which prevailed last year are permitted to continue.

The significance of these findings, however, is to be considered in light of the fact, indisputably revealed by the record before us, that the conditions they depict are directly traceable to the actions of legislators and executive officials of the State of Arkansas, taken in their official capacities, which reflect their own determination to resist this Court's decision in the *Brown* case and which have brought about violent resistance to that decision in Arkansas. In its petition for certiorari filed in this Court, the School Board itself describes the situation in this language: "The legislative, executive, and judicial departments of the state government opposed the desegregation of Little Rock schools by enacting laws, calling out troops, making statements villifying federal law and federal courts, and failing to utilize state law enforcement agencies and judicial processes to maintain public peace."

One may well sympathize with the position of the Board in the face of the frustrating conditions which have confronted it, but, regardless of the Board's good faith, the actions of the other state agencies responsible for those conditions compel us to reject the Board's legal position. Had Central High School been under the direct management of the State itself, it could hardly be suggested that those immediately in charge of the school should be heard to assert their own good faith as a legal excuse for delay in implementing the constitutional rights of these respondents, when vindication of those rights was rendered difficult or impossible by the actions of other state officials. The situation here is in no different posture because the members of the School Board and the Superintendent of Schools are local officials; from the point of view of the Fourteenth Amendment, they stand in this litigation as the agents of the State. . . .

The controlling legal principles are plain. The command of the Fourteenth Amendment is that no "State" shall deny to any person within its jurisdiction the equal protection of the laws. "A State acts by its legislative, its executive, or its judicial authorities. It can act in no other way. The constitutional provision, therefore, must mean that no agency of the State, or of the officers or agents by whom its powers are exerted, shall deny to any person within its jurisdiction the equal protection of the laws. Whoever, by virtue of public position under a State government . . . denies or takes away the equal protection of the laws, violates the constitutional inhibition; and as he acts in the name and for the State, and is clothed with the State's power, his act is that of the State. This must be so, or the constitutional prohibition has no meaning." *Ex parte Virginia*, 100 U.S. 339 [1880]. Thus the prohibitions of the Fourteenth Amendment extend to all action of the State denying equal protection of the laws; whatever the agency of the State taking the action, or whatever the guise in which it is taken. In short, the constitutional rights of children not to be discriminated against in school admission on grounds of race or color declared by this Court in the *Brown* case can neither be nullified openly and directly by state legislators or state executive or judicial officers, nor nullified indirectly by them through evasive schemes for segregation whether attempted "ingeniously or ingenuously." *Smith v. Texas*, 311 U.S. 128 [1940]. . . .

What has been said, in the light of the facts developed, is enough to dispose of the case. However, we should answer the premise of the actions of the Governor and Legislature that they are not bound by our holding in the *Brown* case. It is necessary only to recall some basic constitutional propositions which are settled doctrine.

Article VI of the Constitution makes the Constitution the "supreme Law of the Land." In 1803, Chief Justice MARSHALL, speaking for a unanimous Court, referring to the Constitution as "the fundamental and paramount law of the nation," declared in the notable case of *Marbury v. Madison* that "It is emphatically the province and duty of the judicial department to say what the law is." This decision declared the basic principle that the federal judiciary is supreme in the exposition of the law of the Constitution, and that principle has ever since been respected by this Court and the Country as a permanent and indispensable feature of our constitutional system. It follows that the interpretation of the Fourteenth Amendment enunciated by this Court in the *Brown* case is the supreme law of the land, and Art. VI of the Constitution makes it of binding effect on the States "any Thing in the Constitution or Laws of any State to the Contrary notwithstanding." Every state legislator and executive and judicial officer is solemnly committed by oath taken pursuant to Art. VI, Sec. 3 "to support this Constitution." . . .

No state legislator or executive or judicial officer can war against the Constitution without violating his undertaking to support it. Chief Justice MARSHALL spoke for a unanimous Court in saying that: "If the legislatures of the several states may, at will, annul the judgments of the courts of the United States, and destroy the rights acquired under those judgments, the constitution itself becomes a solemn mockery. . . ." *United States v. Peters*, 5 Cranch 115 [(1809)].

It is, of course, quite true that the responsibility for public education is primarily the concern of the States, but it is equally true that such responsibilities, like all other state activity, must be exercised consistently with federal constitutional requirements as they apply to state action. The Constitution created a government dedicated to equal justice under law. The Fourteenth Amendment embodied and emphasized that ideal. State support of segregated schools through any arrangement, management, funds, or property cannot be squared with the Amendment's command that no State shall deny to any person within its jurisdiction the equal protection of the laws. The right of a student not to be segregated on racial grounds in schools so maintained is indeed so fundamental and pervasive that it is embraced in the concept of due process of law. *Bolling v. Sharpe*, 347 U.S. 497 [1954]. The basic decision in *Brown* was unanimously reached by this Court only after the case had been briefed and twice argued and the issues had been given the most serious consideration. Since the first *Brown* opinion three new Justices have come to the Court. They are at one with the Justices still on the Court who participated in that basic decision as to its correctness, and that decision is now unanimously reaffirmed. The principles announced in that decision and the obedience of the States to them, according to the command of the Constitution, are indispensable for the protection of the freedoms guaranteed by our fundamental charter for all of us. Our constitutional ideal of equal justice under law is thus made a living truth.

☐ *Justice FRANKFURTER, concurring.*

While unreservedly participating with my brethren in our joint opinion, I deem it appropriate also to deal individually with the great issue here at stake. . . .

We are now asked to hold that the illegal, forcible interference by the State of Arkansas with the continuance of what the Constitution commands, and the consequences in disorder that it entrained, should be recognized as justification for undoing what the Board of Education had formulated, what the District Court in 1955 had directed to be carried out, and what was in process of obedience. No explanation that may be offered in support of such a request can obscure the inescapable meaning that law should bow to force. To yield to such a claim would be to enthrone official lawlessness and lawlessness if not checked is the precursor of anarchy. . . .

The duty to abstain from resistance to "the supreme Law of the Land," U.S. Const., Art. VI, Sec. 2, as declared by the organ of our Government for ascertaining it, does not require immediate approval of it nor does it deny the right of dissent. Criticism need not be stilled. Active obstruction or defiance is barred. Our kind of society cannot endure if the controlling authority of the Law as derived from the Constitution is not to be the tribunal specially charged with the duty of ascertaining and declaring what is "the supreme Law of the Land."

Younger v. Harris

401 U.S. 37, 91 S.Ct. 746 (1971)

John Harris, Jr., was indicted in state court for violating California's Criminal Syndicalism Act, which forbade the advocacy of criminal syndicalism or teaching of the "necessity or propriety of committing any crime, sabotage, violence or any unlawful method of terrorism as a means of accomplishing" economic and political change. While his prosecution was pending in state court, he promptly filed a complaint in federal district court, asking that it enjoin Evelle Younger, the district attorney of Los Angeles County, from prosecuting him on the grounds that the law unconstitutionally denied him the freedom of speech and press under the First and Fourteenth Amendments. A three-judge federal court held in a declaratory judgment that California's law was void for vagueness and overbreadth in violation of the First and Fourteenth Amendments and, accordingly, issued an injunction restraining Younger from prosecuting Harris in state court. Younger then appealed to the Supreme Court, which reversed the lower federal court's declaratory judgment and injunction.

The Court's decision was eight to one; the majority's opinion was announced by Justice Black. Justices Brennan and Stewart concurred and were joined by Justices White, Marshall, and Harlan. Justice Douglas delivered a dissenting opinion.

☐ *Justice BLACK delivers the opinion of the Court.*

Since the beginning of this country's history Congress has, subject to few exceptions, manifested a desire to permit state courts to try state cases free from interference by federal courts. In 1793 an Act unconditionally provided: "[N]or shall a writ of injunction be granted to stay proceedings in any court of a state. . . ." A comparison of the 1793 Act with 28 U.S.C. Sec. 2283, its present-day successor, graphically illustrates how few and minor have been the exceptions granted from the flat, prohibitory language of the old Act. During all this lapse of years from 1793 to 1970 the statutory exceptions to the 1793 congressional enactment have been only three: (1) "except as expressly authorized by Act of Congress"; (2) "where necessary in aid of its jurisdiction"; and (3) "to protect or effectuate its judgments." In addition, a judicial exception to the long-standing policy evidenced by the statute has been made where a person about to be prosecuted in a state court can show that he will, if the proceeding in the state court is not enjoined, suffer irreparable damages. See *Ex parte Young*, 209 U.S. 123 (1908).

The precise reasons for this long-standing public policy against federal court interference with state court proceedings have never been specifically identified but the primary sources of the policy are plain. One is the basic doctrine of equity jurisprudence that courts of equity should not act, and particularly should not act to restrain a criminal prosecution, when the moving party has an adequate remedy at law and will not suffer irreparable injury if denied equitable relief. The doctrine may originally have grown out of circumstances peculiar to the English judicial system and not applicable in this country, but its fundamental purpose of restraining equity jurisdiction within narrow limits is equally important under our Constitution, in order to prevent erosion of the role of the jury and avoid a duplication of legal proceedings and legal sanctions where a single suit would be adequate to protect the rights asserted. This underlying reason for restraining courts of equity from interfering with criminal prosecutions is reinforced by an even more vital consideration, the notion of "comity," that is, a proper respect for state functions, a recognition of the fact that the entire country is made up of a Union of separate state governments, and a continuance of the belief that the National Government will fare best if the States and their institutions are left free to perform their separate functions in their separate ways. This, perhaps for lack of a better and clearer way to describe it, is referred to by many as "Our Federalism," and one familiar with the profound debates that ushered our Federal Constitution into existence is bound to respect those who remain loyal to the ideals and dreams of "Our Federalism." The concept does not mean blind deference to "States' Rights" any more than it means centralization of control over every important issue in our National Government and its courts. The Framers rejected both these courses. What the concept does represent is a system in which there is sensitivity to the legitimate interests of both State and National Governments, and in which the National Government, anxious though it may be to vindicate and protect federal rights and federal interests, always endeavors to do so in ways that will not unduly interfere with the legitimate activities of the States. It should never be forgotten that this slogan, "Our Federalism," born in the early struggling days of our Union of States, occupies a highly important place in our Nation's history and its future.

This brief discussion should be enough to suggest some of the reasons why it has been perfectly natural for our cases to repeat time and time again that the normal thing to do when federal courts are asked to enjoin pending proceedings in state courts is not to issue such injunctions....

In [earlier] cases the Court stressed the importance of showing irreparable injury, the traditional prerequisite to obtaining an injunction. In addition, however, the Court also made clear that in view of the fundamental policy against federal interference with state criminal prosecutions, even irreparable injury is insufficient unless it is "both great and immediate." Certain types of injury, in particular, the cost, anxiety, and inconvenience of having to defend against a single criminal prosecution, could not by themselves be considered "irreparable" in the special legal sense of that term. Instead, the threat to the plaintiff's federally protected rights must be one that cannot be eliminated by his defense against a single criminal prosecution....

[I]n *Douglas* [*v. City of Jeannette*, 319 U.S. 157 (1943)], we made clear, after reaffirming this rule, that:

> It does not appear from the record that petitioners have been threatened with any injury other than that incidental to every criminal proceeding brought lawfully and in good faith....

This is where the law stood when the Court decided *Dombrowski v. Pfister*, 380 U.S. 479 (1965), and held that an injunction against the enforcement of certain state criminal statutes could properly issue under the circumstances presented in that case. In *Dombrowski*, unlike many of the earlier cases denying injunctions, the complaint made substantial allegations that:

> the threats to enforce the statutes against appellants are not made with any expectation of securing valid convictions, but rather are part of a plan to employ arrests, seizures, and threats of prosecution under color of the statutes to harass appellants and discourage them and their supporters from asserting and attempting to vindicate the constitutional rights of Negro citizens of Louisiana. . . .

[T]he Court in *Dombrowski* went on to say:

> But the allegations in this complaint depict a situation in which defense of the State's criminal prosecution will not assure adequate vindication of constitutional rights. They suggest that a substantial loss of or impairment of freedoms of expression will occur if appellants must await the state court's disposition and ultimate review in this Court of any adverse determination. These allegations, if true, clearly show irreparable injury. . . .

And the Court made clear that even under these circumstances the District Court issuing the injunction would have continuing power to lift it at any time and remit the plaintiffs to the state courts if circumstances warranted. . . .

It is against the background of these principles that we must judge the propriety of an injunction under the circumstances of the present case. Here a proceeding was already pending in the state court, affording Harris an opportunity to raise his constitutional claims. There is no suggestion that this single prosecution against Harris is brought in bad faith or is only one of a series of repeated prosecutions to which he will be subjected. In other words, the injury that Harris faces is solely "that incidental to every criminal proceeding brought lawfully and in good faith," *Douglas*, and therefore under the settled doctrine we have already described he is not entitled to equitable relief "even if such statutes are unconstitutional." . . .

It is undoubtedly true, as the Court stated in *Dombrowski*, that "[a] criminal prosecution under a statute regulating expression usually involves imponderables and contingencies that themselves may inhibit the full exercise of First Amendment freedoms." But this sort of "chilling effect," as the Court called it, should not by itself justify federal intervention. In the first place, the chilling effect cannot be satisfactorily eliminated by federal injunctive relief. . . .

Moreover, the existence of a "chilling effect," even in the area of First Amendment rights, has never been considered a sufficient basis, in and of itself, for prohibiting state action. Where a statute does not directly abridge free speech, but—while regulating a subject within the State's power—tends to have the incidental effect of inhibiting First Amendment rights, it is well settled that the statute can be upheld if the effect on speech is minor in relation to the need for control of the conduct and the lack of alternative means for doing so. . . .

Beyond all this is another, more basic consideration. Procedures for testing the constitutionality of a statute "on its face" in the manner apparently contemplated by *Dombrowski*, and for then enjoining all action to enforce the statute until the State can obtain court approval for a modified version, are fundamentally at odds with the function of the federal courts in our constitutional plan. The power and duty of the judiciary to declare laws unconstitutional is in the final analysis derived from its responsibility for resolving concrete disputes brought before the courts for decision; a statute apparently governing a dispute cannot be applied by judges, consistently with their obligations under the Supremacy Clause, when such an application of the statute would conflict with the Constitution. *Marbury v. Madison* (1803). But this vital responsibility, broad as it is, does not amount to an unlimited power to survey the statute books and pass judgment on laws before the courts are called upon to enforce them. . . .

For these reasons, fundamental not only to our federal system but also to the basic functions of the Judicial Branch of the National Government under our Constitution, we hold that the *Dombrowski* decision should not be regarded as having upset the settled doctrines that have always confined very narrowly the availability of injunctive relief against state criminal prosecutions.

☐ *Justice DOUGLAS, dissenting.*

Dombrowski represents an exception to the general rule that federal courts should not interfere with state criminal prosecutions. The exception does not arise merely because prosecutions are threatened to which the First Amendment will be the proffered defense. *Dombrowski* governs statutes which are a blunderbuss by themselves or when used *en masse*—those that have an "overbroad" sweep. "If the rule were otherwise, the contours of regulation would have to be hammered out case by case—and tested only by those hardy enough to risk criminal prosecution to determine the proper scope of regulation." It was in the context of overbroad state statutes that we spoke of the "chilling effect upon the exercise of First Amendment rights" caused by state prosecutions. . . .

The special circumstances when federal intervention in a state criminal proceeding is permissible are not restricted to bad faith on the part of state officials or the threat of multiple prosecutions. They also exist where for any reason the state statute being enforced is unconstitutional on its face.

Stone v. Powell

428 U.S. 465, 96 S.CT. 3037 (1976)

Lloyd Powell was convicted of murder in state court, in part on the basis of his testimony concerning a revolver found in his possession when he was arrested for violating an ordinance prohibiting vagrancy. The trial judge rejected his claim that the testimony should have been excluded because the ordinance was unconstitutional and that, therefore, the arrest was invalid. A state appellate court agreed, and Powell then applied for *habeas corpus* relief in federal district court. The federal district court concluded that the arresting officer had probable cause to arrest Powell. And even if the vagrancy ordinance were unconstitutional, the deterrent purpose of the Fourth Amendment's exclusionary rule did not require the suppression at trial of statements Powell made to the arresting officer at the time of his arrest. The Court of Appeals for the Ninth Circuit then reversed. And California's prison warden, W. T. Stone, appealed to the Supreme Court.

The Court's decision was six to three, and the majority's opinion was announced by Justice Powell. Chief Justice Burger delivered a concurring opinion. Dissents were by Justice White and Justice Brennan, who was joined by Justice Marshall.

☐ *Justice POWELL delivers the opinion of the Court.*

The question presented is whether a federal court should consider, in ruling on a petition for *habeas corpus* relief filed by a state prisoner, a claim that evidence obtained by an unconstitutional search or seizure was introduced at his trial, when he has previously been afforded an opportunity for full and fair litigation of his claim in the state courts. The issue is of considerable importance to the administration of criminal justice. . . .

Respondents allege violations of Fourth Amendment rights guaranteed them through the Fourteenth Amendment. The question is whether state prisoners—who have been afforded the opportunity for full and fair consideration of their reliance upon the exclusionary rule with respect to seized evidence by the state courts at trial and on direct review—may invoke their claim again on federal *habeas corpus* review. The answer is to be found by weighing the utility of the exclusionary rule against the costs of extending it to collateral review of Fourth Amendment claims.

The costs of applying the exclusionary rule even at trial and on direct review are well known: the focus of the trial, and the attention of the participants therein, is diverted from the ultimate question of guilt or innocence that should be the central concern in a criminal proceeding. Moreover, the physical evidence sought to be excluded is typically reliable and often the most probative information bearing on the guilt or innocence of the defendant. . . . Application of the rule thus deflects the truthfinding process and often frees the guilty. The disparity in particular cases between the error committed by the police officer and the windfall afforded a guilty defendant by application of the rule is contrary to the idea of proportionality that is essential to the concept of justice. Thus, although the rule is thought to deter unlawful police activity in part through the nurturing of respect for Fourth Amendment values, if applied indiscriminately it may well have the opposite effect of generating disrespect for the law and administration of justice. These long-recognized costs of the rule persist when a criminal conviction is sought to be overturned on collateral review on the ground that a search-and-seizure claim was erroneously rejected by two or more tiers of state courts.

Evidence obtained by police officers in violation of the Fourth Amendment is excluded at trial in the hope that the frequency of future violations will decrease. Despite the absence of supportive empirical evidence, we have assumed that the immediate effect of exclusion will be to discourage law enforcement officials from violating the Fourth Amendment by removing the incentive to disregard it. More importantly, over the long term, this demonstration that our society attaches serious consequences to violation of constitutional rights is thought to encourage those who formulate law enforcement policies, and the officers who implement them, to incorporate Fourth Amendment ideals into their value system.

We adhere to the view that these considerations support the implementation of the exclusionary rule at trial and its enforcement on direct appeal of state court convictions. But the additional contribution, if any, of the consideration of search-and-seizure claims of state prisoners on collateral review is small in relation to the costs. To be sure, each case in which such claim is considered may add marginally to an awareness of the values protected by the Fourth Amendment. There is no reason to believe, however, that the overall educative effect of the exclusionary rule would be appreciably diminished if search-and-seizure claims could not be raised in federal *habeas corpus* review of state convictions. Nor is there reason to assume that any specific disincentive already created by the risk of exclusion of evidence at trial or the reversal of convictions on direct review would be enhanced if there were the further risk that a conviction obtained in state court and affirmed on direct review might be overturned in collateral proceedings often occurring years after the incarceration of the defendant. The view that the deterrence of Fourth Amendment violations would be furthered rests on the dubious assumption that law enforcement authorities would fear that federal *habeas* review might reveal flaws in a search or seizure that went undetected at trial and on appeal. Even if one rationally could assume that some additional incremental deterrent effect would be presented in isolated cases, the resulting advance of the legitimate goal of furthering Fourth Amendment rights would be outweighed by the acknowledged costs to other values vital to a rational system of criminal justice.

In sum, we conclude that where the State has provided an opportunity for full and fair litigation of a Fourth Amendment claim, a state prisoner may not be granted federal *habeas corpus* relief on the ground that evidence obtained in an unconstitutional search or seizure was introduced at his trial. In this context the contribution of the exclusionary rule, if any, to the effectuation of the Fourth Amendment is minimal, and the substantial societal costs of application of the rule persist with special force.

Accordingly, the judgments of the Courts of Appeals are
Reversed.

☐ *Justice BRENNAN, with whom Justice MARSHALL joins, dissenting.*

The Court adheres to the holding of *Mapp* [*v. Ohio*, 367 U.S. 643 (1961)] that the Constitution "require[d] exclusion" of the evidence admitted at respondents' trials. However, the Court holds that the Constitution "does not require" that respondents be accorded *habeas* relief if they were accorded "an opportunity for full and fair litigation of [their] Fourth Amendment claim[s]" in state courts. Yet once the Constitution was interpreted by *Mapp* to require exclusion of certain evidence at trial, the Constitution became irrelevant to the manner in which that constitutional right was to be enforced in the federal courts; *that* inquiry is only a matter of respecting Congress' allocation of federal judicial power between this Court's appellate jurisdiction and a federal district court's *habeas* jurisdiction. Indeed, by conceding that today's "decision does not mean that the federal [district] court lacks jurisdiction over [respondents'] claim[s]" the Court admits that respondents have sufficiently alleged that they are "in custody in violation of the Constitution" within the meaning of Sec. 2254 and that there is no "constitutional" rationale for today's holding. Rather, the constitutional "interest balancing" approach to this case is untenable, and I can only view the constitutional garb in which the Court dresses its result as a disguise for rejection of the longstanding principle that there are no "second class" constitutional rights for purposes of federal *habeas* jurisdiction; it is nothing less than an attempt to provide a veneer of respectability for an obvious usurpation of Congress' Art. III power to delineate the jurisdiction of the federal courts.

[T]he real ground of today's decision—a ground that is particularly troubling in light of its portent for *habeas* jurisdiction generally—is the Court's novel reinterpretation of the *habeas* statutes; this would read the statutes as requiring the District Courts routinely to deny *habeas* relief to prisoners "in custody in violation of the Constitution or laws of the United States" as a matter of judicial "discretion"—a "discretion" judicially manufactured today contrary to the express statutory language—because such claims are "different in kind" from other constitutional violations in that they "do not 'impugn the integrity of the fact-finding process'" and because application of such constitutional strictures "often frees the guilty." Much in the Court's opinion suggests that a construction of the *habeas* statutes to deny relief for non-"guilt-related" constitutional violations, based on this Court's vague notions of comity and federalism is the actual premise for today's decision, and although the Court attempts to bury its underlying premises in footnotes, those premises mark this case as a harbinger of future eviscerations of the *habeas* statutes that plainly does violence to congressional power to frame the statutory contours of *habeas* jurisdiction. . . .

To the extent the Court is actually premising its holding on an interpretation of 28 U.S.C. Sec. 2243 or Sec. 2254, it is overruling the heretofore settled principle that federal *habeas* relief is available to redress *any* denial of asserted constitutional rights, whether or not denial of the right affected the truth or fairness of the fact-finding process. . . .

Without even paying the slightest deference to principles of *stare decisis* or acknowledging Congress' failure for two decades to alter the *habeas* statutes in light of our interpretation of congressional intent to render all federal constitutional contentions cognizable on *habeas*, the Court today rewrites Congress' jurisdictional statutes as heretofore construed and bars access to federal courts by state prisoners with constitutional claims distasteful to a majority of my Brethren. . . .

I would address the Court's concerns for effective utilization of scarce judicial resources, finality principles, federal-state friction, and notions of "federalism" only long enough to note that such concerns carry no more force with respect to non-"guilt-related" constitutional claims than they do with respect to claims that affect the accuracy of the fact-finding process. Congressional conferral of federal *habeas* jurisdiction for the purpose of entertaining petitions from state prisoners necessarily manifested a conclusion that such concerns could not be controlling, and any argument for discriminating among constitutional rights must therefore depend on the nature of the constitutional right involved. . . .

[U]nlike the Court I consider that the exclusionary rule is a constitutional ingredient of the Fourth Amendment, any modification of that rule should at least be accomplished with some modicum of logic and justification not provided today. . . .

The Court does not disturb the holding of *Mapp v. Ohio* that, as a matter of federal constitutional law, illegally obtained evidence must be excluded from the trial of a criminal defendant whose rights were transgressed during the search that resulted in acquisition of the evidence. In light of that constitutional rule it is a matter for Congress, not this Court, to prescribe what federal courts are to review state prisoners' claims of constitutional error committed by state courts. Until this decision, our cases have never departed from the construction of the *habeas* statutes as embodying a congressional intent that, however substantive constitutional rights are delineated or expanded, those rights may be asserted as a procedural matter under federal *habeas* jurisdiction. Employing the transparent tactic that today's is a decision construing the Constitution, the Court usurps the authority—vested by the Constitution in the Congress—to reassign federal judicial responsibility for reviewing state prisoners' claims of failure of state courts to redress violations of their Fourth Amendment rights. Our jurisdiction is eminently unsuited for that task, and as a practical matter the only result of today's holding will be that denials by the state courts of claims by state prisoners of violations of their Fourth Amendment rights will go unreviewed by a federal tribunal. I fear that the same treatment ultimately will be accorded state prisoners' claims of violations of other constitutional rights; thus the potential ramifications of this case for federal *habeas* jurisdiction generally are ominous. The Court, no longer content just to restrict forthrightly the constitutional rights of the citizenry, has embarked on a campaign to water down even such constitutional rights as it purports to acknowledge by the device of foreclosing resort to the federal *habeas* remedy for their redress.

I would affirm the judgments of the Courts of Appeals.

D | *State Courts and State Constitutional Law*

State courts handle the overwhelming volume of all litigation—well over 90 percent of all filings. Over 300,000 civil and 50,000 criminal cases are annually filed in federal courts. By comparison, state courts annually face over 26 million filings. The type of litigation in state courts also tends to diverge from that in federal courts. Apart from criminal cases, the largest portion of state supreme court litigation involves economic issues—whether relating to state regulation of public utilities, zoning, and small businesses or labor relations and workmen's compensation, natural resources, energy, and the environment. Litigation varies from state to state as well, depending on factors such as population size, urbanization, and socioeconomic conditions.[1]

The Supreme Court's nationalization of guarantees of the Bill of Rights (see Vol. 2, Ch. 4) profoundly altered constitutional politics and the federal–state court relationships. With the increasing prominence of the federal judiciary, the role of state courts and state constitutional law tended to be overshadowed, but that is no longer the case.

The important role of state courts in interpreting their own state constitutions is underscored by the fact the Supreme Court intrudes on state court policy making in only a very narrow class of litigation—the class of cases in which state courts deal with questions of federal legislation and federal constitutional law. Federal questions rarely emerge from the grist of state courts, emphasized Justice Brennan, a former New Jersey state supreme court judge: "If cases were grains of sand, federal question cases would be hard to find on the beach. The final and vital decisions of most controversies upon which depend life, liberty, and property are made by the state courts."[2] If a case does not raise a substantial federal question or is decided on *independent state grounds*—a state constitution or bill of rights—then the Court declines review and respects the principle of comity between federal and state judiciaries.

Federal–state court relations have always been uneasy, but they have evolved rather dramatically in the last thirty years with the changes in the composition and direction of the Supreme Court. In the 1950s and 1960s, when state supreme courts tended to be much more conservative than the Warren Court, relations were often especially acrimonious. The Conference of State Chief Justices in 1958 went so far as to pass a resolution condemning the Warren Court for its erosion of federalism and its tendency "to adopt the role of policymaker without proper judicial restraint."[3] By contrast, from the mid-1970s to the present the Court's policy-making moved in a more conservative direction, while some state supreme courts became far more protective of individual rights. Although not outright reversing some of the most controversial and landmark Warren Court rulings, the Burger, Rehnquist, and Roberts Courts refused further extensions and achieved retrenchment in a number of areas. More liberal state supreme courts accordingly refused to follow the rulings of the Court when interpreting individual rights under state constitutional law. "Why should we always be the tail being wagged by the Federal dog?" asked New Hampshire State Supreme Court Justice Charles Douglas and other state judges. "Liberal state courts have taken the doctrines of federalism and states' rights, heretofore associated with [conservatives] like George Wallace,"

California's Justice Stanley Mosk explained, "and adapted them to give citizens more rights under their state constitutions rather than to oppress them."[4]

The resurgence in state constitutional law protecting individual rights has renewed controversy within the Supreme Court over its power to patrol the decisions of state supreme courts, particularly in the area of individual rights. The shift in state constitutional law in the view of Brennan was a sign of "the strength of our federal system."[5] Oregon State Supreme Court Justice Hans Linde, a leading influence on the development of state constitutional law, agreed. He argued that state courts should turn to their state constitutions first because they are "first in time and first in logic:"

> It was not unheard of in 1776, long before the drafting of the Federal Constitution, for the revolutionaries of that day to declare in their charters of their new states that [individuals enjoyed certain fundamental rights and liberties]. . . .
>
> Far from being the model for the states, the Federal Bill of Rights was added to the Constitution to meet demands for the same guarantees against the new central government that people had secured against their own local officials. Moreover, the states that adopted new constitutions during the following decades took their bills of rights from the preexisting state constitutions rather than from the federal amendments. . . .
>
> The Federal Bill of Rights did not supersede those of the states. It was not interposed between the citizen and his state. When the Fifth Amendment was invoked against the City of Baltimore in 1833, John Marshall replied that its adoption "could never have occurred to any human being, as a mode of doing that which might be effected by the state itself." Only the Civil War made it clear that it might sometimes be necessary to use federal law as a mode of doing that which a state could but did not effect for itself—the protection of some of its citizens against those in control of its government.
>
> It is the Fourteenth Amendment that has bound the states to observe the guarantees of the Federal Bill of Rights. . . .
>
> We tend to forget how recently the application of the Federal Bill of Rights to the states developed. Throughout the nineteenth century and the first quarter of the twentieth, state courts decided questions on constitutional rights under their own state constitutions. In 1925, it was only a hypothesis that the states were bound by the First Amendment. That was really settled only after 1937. Fifth Amendment guarantees against compulsory self-incrimination and double jeopardy did not bind the states until 1964 and 1969, respectively. I shall not go through the catalogue; most of the decisions binding the states to observe the procedures of the Fourth,

Fifth, and Sixth amendments date from the same period. Of course, the states had all these guarantees in their own laws long before the Federal Bill of Rights was applied to the states. State courts had been administering these laws, sometimes generously, more often not, for a century or more without awaiting an interpretation of the United States Supreme Court.

Historically, the states' commitment to individual rights came first. Restraints on the federal government were patterned upon the states' declarations of rights. . . .

Just as rights under state constitutions were first in time, they also are first in the logic of constitutional law. For lawyers, the point is quickly made. Whenever a person asserts a particular right, and a state court recognizes and protects that right under state law, then the state is not depriving the person of whatever federal claim he or she might otherwise assert. There is no federal question.[6]

In contrast to what Justice Brennan maintained, and others who share his views, the more conservative members of the Court have sought to bring state courts into line by reversing decisions vindicating broader constitutional rights than they approved. *Michigan v. Long* (1983) (excerpted below) is illustrative of the Court's concern. There Justice O'Connor for the majority ruled that state supreme courts must clearly indicate that their rulings rest on *adequate and independent state grounds*; otherwise the Court will feel free to reverse those rulings with which it disagrees. *People v. P. J. Video, Inc.* (1986) (excerpted below) illustrates how state supreme courts may nevertheless refuse to back down from their interpretation of guarantees for individual rights, even after their prior decisions have been reversed by the Supreme Court. For another state supreme court ruling declining to follow the Supreme Court, see, for example, *Commonwealth of Kentucky v. Wasson* (1992) (in Vol. 1, Ch. 2).

NOTES

1. See for example, Henry Glick and Kenneth Vines, *State Court Systems* (Englewood Cliffs, NJ: Prentice-Hall, 1973).

2. William J. Brennan, "Address," 31 *Pennsylvania Bar Association Quarterly* 394 (1960).

3. "Report of the Committee on Federal-State Relationships as Affected by Judicial Decisions," reprinted in *Cong. Record*, 73rd Cong., 2d sess., Appendix, A7784 (Aug. 25, 1958).

4. Quoted in David M. O'Brien, *Storm Center: The Supreme Court in American Politics*, 9th ed. (New York: W. W. Norton, 2011).

5. See William J. Brennan, Jr., "State Constitutions and the Protection of Individual Rights," 90 *Harvard Law Review* 489 (1977).

6. Hans Linde, "First Things First: Rediscovering the States' Bill of Rights," 9 *University of Baltimore Law Review* 379 (1980).

SELECTED BIBLIOGRAPHY

Brennan, William J., Jr. "Guardians of Our Liberties—State Courts No Less Than Federal." In *Judges on Judging: Views from the Bench*. 3d ed. Edited by David M. O'Brien. Washington, DC: C.Q. Press, 2009.

Friesen, Jennifer. *State Constitutional Law.* New York: Bender, 1995, and updates.

Langer, Laura. *Judicial Review in State Supreme Courts: A Comparative Study*. Albany: State University of New York Press, 2002.

Latzer, Barry. *State Constitutions and Criminal Justice*. New York: Greenwood Press, 1991.

Lopeman, Charles. *The Activist Advocate: Policy Making in State Supreme Courts*. New York: Praeger, 1999.

Porter, Mary, and Tarr, Allan, eds. *State Supreme Courts: Policymakers in the Federal System*. Westport, CT: Greenwood Press, 1982.

Stumpf, Harry, and Culver, John. *The Politics of State Courts.* New York: Longman, 1992.

Solimine, Michael, and Walker, James. *Respecting State Courts*. Westport, CT: Greenwood Press, 1999.

Tarr, G. Alan. *Understanding State Constitutions*. Princeton, NJ: Princeton University Press, 1998.

Michigan v. Long

463 U.S. 1036, 103 S.CT. 3469 (1983)

David Long was convicted of possession of marijuana, and he appealed. A state appellate court affirmed his conviction, but the Michigan Supreme Court reversed on the grounds that police had made an illegal search in violation of "the Fourth Amendment to the United States Constitution *and* Art. 1, Sec. 11 of the Michigan Constitution" (emphasis added). The state attorney general appealed that ruling to the Supreme Court.

The Court's decision was six to three, and the majority's opinion was announced by Justice O'Connor. Concurrence was by Justice Blackmun. Dissents were by Justices Brennan, whom Justice Marshall joined, and Stevens.

☐ *Justice O'CONNOR delivers the opinion of the Court.*

In *Terry v. Ohio*, 392 U.S. 1 (1968), we upheld the validity of a protective search for weapons in the absence of probable cause to arrest because it is unreasonable to deny a police officer the right "to neutralize the threat of physical harm," when he possesses an articulable suspicion that an individual is armed and dangerous. We did not, however, expressly address whether such a protective search for weapons could extend to an area beyond the person in the absence of probable cause to arrest. In the present case, respondent David Long was convicted for possession of marihuana found by police in the passenger compartment and trunk of the automobile that he was driving. The police searched the passenger compartment because they had reason to believe that the vehicle contained weapons potentially dangerous to the officers. We hold that the protective search of the passenger compartment was reasonable under the principles articulated in *Terry* and other decisions of this Court. We also examine Long's argument that the decision below rests upon an adequate and independent state ground, and we decide in favor of our jurisdiction. . . .

Before reaching the merits, we must consider Long's argument that we are without jurisdiction to decide this case because the decision below rests on an adequate and independent state ground. The court below referred twice to the State Constitution in its opinion, but otherwise relied exclusively on federal law. Long argues that the Michigan courts have provided greater protection from searches and seizures under the State Constitution than is afforded under the Fourth Amendment, and the references to the State Constitution therefore establish an adequate and independent ground for the decision below.

Although we have announced a number of principles in order to help us determine whether various forms of references to state law constitute adequate and independent state grounds, we openly admit that we have thus far not developed a satisfying and consistent approach for resolving this vexing issue. In some instances, we have taken the strict view that if the ground of decision was at all unclear, we would dismiss the case. . . . In other instances, we have vacated or continued a case in order to obtain clarification about the nature of a state-court decision. . . . In more recent cases, we have ourselves examined state law to determine whether state courts have used federal law to guide their application of state law or to provide the actual basis for the decision that was reached. . . .

This ad hoc method of dealing with cases that involve possible adequate and independent state grounds is antithetical to the doctrinal consistency that is required when sensitive issues of federal-state relations are involved. Moreover, none of the various methods of disposition that we have employed thus far recommends itself as the preferred method that we should apply to the exclusion of others, and we therefore determine that it is appropriate to reexamine our treatment of this jurisdictional issue in order to achieve the consistency that is necessary.

The process of examining state law is unsatisfactory because it requires us to interpret state laws with which we are generally unfamiliar, and which often, as in this case, have not been discussed at length by the parties. Vacation and continuance for clarification have also been unsatisfactory both because of the delay and decrease in efficiency of judicial administration and, more important, because these methods of disposition place significant burdens on state courts to demonstrate the presence or absence of our jurisdiction. . . . Finally, outright dismissal of cases is clearly not a panacea because it cannot be doubted that there is an important need for uniformity in federal law, and that this need goes unsatisfied when we fail to review an opinion that rests primarily upon federal grounds and where the *independence* of an alleged state ground is not apparent from the four corners of the opinion. We have long recognized that dismissal is inappropriate "where there is strong indication . . . that the federal constitution as judicially construed controlled the decision below." . . .

Respect for the independence of state courts, as well as avoidance of rendering advisory opinions, have been the cornerstones of this Court's refusal to decide cases where there is an adequate and independent state ground. It is precisely because of this respect for state courts, and this desire to avoid advisory opinions, that we do not wish to continue to decide issues of state law that go beyond the opinion that we review, or to require state courts to reconsider cases to clarify the grounds of their decisions. Accordingly, when, as in this case, a state court decision fairly appears to rest primarily on federal law, or to be interwoven with the federal law, and when the adequacy and independence of any possible state law ground is not clear from the face of the opinion, we will accept as the most reasonable explanation that the state court decided the case the way it did because it believed that federal law required it to do so. If a state court chooses merely to rely on federal precedents as it would on the precedents of all other jurisdictions, then it need only make clear by a plain statement in its judgment or opinion that the federal cases are being used only for the purpose of guidance, and do not themselves compel the result that the court has reached. In this way, both justice and judicial administration will be greatly improved. If the state court decision indicates clearly and expressly that it is alternatively based on bona fide separate, adequate, and independent grounds, we, of course, will not undertake to review the decision.

This approach obviates in most instances the need to examine state law in order to decide the nature of the state court decision, and will at the same time avoid the danger of our rendering advisory opinions. It also avoids the unsatisfactory and intrusive practice of requiring state courts to clarify their decisions to the satisfaction of this Court. We believe that such an approach will provide state judges with a clearer opportunity to develop state jurisprudence unimpeded by federal interference, and yet will preserve the integrity of federal law. . . .

The principle that we will not review judgments of state courts that rest on adequate and independent state grounds is based, in part, on "the limitations of our own jurisdiction." The jurisdictional concern is that we not "render an advisory opinion, and if the same judgment would be rendered by the state court after we corrected its views of federal laws, our review could amount to nothing more than an advisory opinion." Our requirement of a "plain statement" that a decision rests upon adequate and independent state grounds does not in any way authorize the rendering of advisory opinions. Rather, in determining, as we must, whether we have jurisdiction to review a case that is alleged to rest on adequate and independent state grounds . . . we merely assume that there are no such grounds when it is not clear from the opinion itself that the state court relied upon an adequate and independent state ground and when it fairly appears that the state court rested its decision primarily on federal law.

Our review of the decision below under this framework leaves us unconvinced that it rests upon an independent state ground. Apart from its two citations to the State Constitution, the court below relied *exclusively* on its understanding of *Terry* and other federal cases. Not a single state case was cited to support the state court's holding that the search of the passenger compartment was unconstitutional. Indeed, the court declared that the search in this case was unconstitutional because "[t]he Court of Appeals erroneously applied the principles of *Terry v. Ohio* to the search of the interior of the vehicle in this case." The references to the State Constitution in no way indicate that the decision below rested on grounds in any way *independent* from the state court's interpretation of federal law. Even if we accept that the Michigan Constitution has been interpreted to provide independent protection for certain rights also secured under the Fourth Amendment, it fairly appears in this case that the Michigan Supreme Court rested its decision primarily on federal law.

Rather than dismissing the case, or requiring that the state court reconsider its decision on our behalf solely because of a mere possibility that an adequate and independent ground supports the judgment, we find that we have jurisdiction in the absence of a plain statement that the decision below rested on an adequate and independent state ground. It appears to us that the state court "felt compelled by what it understood to be federal constitutional considerations to construe . . . its own law in the manner it did." . . .

The court below held, and respondent Long contends, that Deputy Howell's entry into the vehicle cannot be justified under the principles set forth in *Terry* because "*Terry* authorized only a limited pat-down search of a *person* suspected of criminal activity" rather than a search of an area. Although *Terry* did involve the protective frisk of a person, we believe that the police action in this case is justified by the principles that we have already established in *Terry* and other cases. . . .

The judgment of the Michigan Supreme Court is reversed, and the case is remanded for further proceedings not inconsistent with this opinion.

It is so ordered.

☐ *Justice STEVENS, dissenting.*

The jurisprudential questions presented in this case are far more important than the question whether the Michigan police officer's search of respondent's car violated the Fourth Amendment. The case raises profoundly significant questions concerning the relationship between two sovereigns— the State of Michigan and the United States of America.

The Supreme Court of the State of Michigan expressly held "that the deputies' search of the vehicle was proscribed by the Fourth Amendment to the United States Constitution and *Art. 1, Sec. 11 of the Michigan Constitution*" (emphasis added). The state law ground is clearly adequate to support the judgment, but the question whether it is independent of the Michigan Supreme Court's understanding of federal law is more difficult. Four possible ways of resolving that question present themselves: (1) asking the Michigan Supreme Court directly, (2) attempting to infer from all possible sources of state law what the Michigan Supreme Court meant, (3) presuming that adequate state grounds are independent unless it clearly appears otherwise, or (4) presuming that adequate state grounds are *not* independent unless it clearly appears otherwise. This Court has, on different occasions, employed each of the first three approaches; never until today has it even hinted at the fourth. In order to "achieve the consistency that is necessary," the Court to-day undertakes a reexamination of all the possibilities. It rejects the first approach as inefficient and unduly burdensome for state courts, and rejects the second approach as an inappropriate expenditure of our resources. Although I find both of those decisions defensible in themselves, I cannot accept the Court's decision to choose the fourth approach over the third—to presume that adequate state grounds are intended to be dependent on federal law unless the record plainly shows otherwise. I must therefore dissent. . . .

I believe that in reviewing the decisions of state courts, the primary role of this Court is to make sure that persons who seek to *vindicate* federal rights have been fairly heard. That belief resonates with statements in many of our prior cases. . . .

Until recently we had virtually no interest in cases of this type. Thirty years ago, this Court reviewed only one. *Nevada v. Stacher*, 358 U.S. 907 (1953). Indeed, that appears to have been the only case during the entire 1953 Term in which a State even sought review of a decision by its own judiciary. Fifteen years ago, we did not review any such cases, although the total number of requests had mounted to three. Some time during the past decade, perhaps about the time of the 5-to-4 decision in *Zacchini v. Scripps-Howard Broadcasting Co.*, 433 U.S. 562 (1977), our priorities shifted. The result is a docket swollen with requests by States to reverse judgments that their courts have rendered in favor of their citizens. I am confident that a future Court will recognize the error of this allocation of resources. When that day comes, I think it likely that the Court will also reconsider the propriety of today's expansion of our jurisdiction.

The Court offers only one reason for asserting authority over cases such as the one presented today: "an important need for uniformity in federal law [that] goes unsatisfied when we fail to review an opinion that rests primarily upon federal grounds and where the independence of an alleged state ground is not apparent from the four corners of the opinion." Of course, the supposed need to "review an opinion" clashes directly with our oft-repeated reminder that "our power is to correct wrong judgments, not to revise opinions." The clash is not merely one of form: the "need for uniformity in federal law" is truly an ungovernable engine. That same need is no less present when it is perfectly clear that a state ground is both independent and adequate. . . .

I respectfully dissent.

People v. P. J. Video, Inc.

68 N.Y. 2d 296, 501 N.E. 2d 556 (N.Y., 1986)

In *New York v. P. J. Video, Inc.*, 475 U.S. 868 (1986), the Supreme Court reversed a ruling of the New York Court of Appeals (the state's highest appellate court), which had held that a state court judge erred when issuing a search warrant for the seizure of allegedly obscene videocassette films. The New York court ruled that for the seizure of books and films, which are subject to First Amendment protection, a "higher" standard of probable cause applies than the usual "fair probability" that evidence of crime will be found on a police search. The Supreme Court reversed and remanded the case back to the New York court for further proceedings not inconsistent with its rejection of a "higher" standard of probable cause for search warrants for allegedly obscene materials. But the New York Court of Appeals responded with the opinion delivered by Judge Simons.

☐ *Judge SIMONS.*

In our earlier decision in this case we held that the issuing magistrate erred in approving a warrant authorizing the seizure of video cassette films as evidence that defendants were promoting obscenity. . . .

On *certiorari* review, the Supreme Court judged probable cause by applying the totality of the circumstances/fair probability test of *Illinois v. Gates* [462 U.S. 213 (1983)]. The *Gates* rule originally was adopted to test the reliability of anonymous informants' tips. It overruled the established two-pronged *Aguilar-Spinelli* test (*Aguilar v. Texas*, 378 U.S. 108 [(1964)]; *Spinelli v. United States*, 393 U.S. 410 [(1969)]) which required a court to review both the basis of the informant's knowledge and the reliability of his information, to permit a magistrate to now decide whether, given all the circumstances set forth in the police affidavit, there is a *fair probability* that contraband or evidence of a crime will be found in a particular place. In this case, the Supreme Court extended the reach of this "totality of the circumstances/fair probability" standard and applied it, for the first time, to an obscenity case to permit the magistrate to focus generally on the explicit nature of pornographic material without specifically considering the other statutory elements of the crime (*see, New York v. P. J. Video*). Having done so, it remanded the case to us for our further consideration.

State courts are bound by the decisions of the Supreme Court when reviewing Federal statutes or applying the Federal Constitution. Under established principles of federalism, however, the States also have sovereign powers. When their courts interpret State statutes or the State Constitution the decisions of these courts are conclusive if not violative of Federal law. Although State courts may not circumscribe rights guaranteed by the Federal Constitution, they may interpret their own law to supplement or expand them. . . . Thus, notwithstanding that the evidence before the magistrate was sufficient to establish probable cause under the Federal Constitution, we have the power on remand to interpret article I, Sec. 12 of the New York Constitution as requiring more. We turn then to the question whether we should measure probable cause in this case by different standards under the State Constitution.

Courts and commentators have identified many considerations and concerns upon which a State court may rely when determining that its Constitution accords greater protection to individual liberties and rights than the protection guaranteed by the Federal Constitution. . . .

One basis for relying on the State Constitution arises from an interpretive review of its provisions. If the language of the State Constitution differs from that of its Federal counterpart, then the court may conclude that there is a basis for a different interpretation of it. Such an analysis considers whether the textual language of the State Constitution specifically recognizes rights not enumerated in the Federal Constitution; whether language in the State Constitution is sufficiently unique to support a broader interpretation of the individual right under State law; whether the history of the adoption of the text reveals an intention to make the State provision co-extensive with, or broader than, the parallel Federal provision; and whether the very structure and purpose of the State Constitution serves to expressly affirm certain rights rather than merely restrain the sovereign power of the State. To contrast, noninterpretive review proceeds from a judicial perception of sound policy, justice and fundamental fairness. . . . A noninterpretive analysis attempts to discover, for example, any preexisting State statutory or common law defining the scope of the individual right in question; the history and traditions of the State in its protection of the individual right; any identification of the right in the State Constitution as being one of peculiar State or local concern; and any distinctive attitudes of the State citizenry toward the definition, scope or protection of the individual right.

Our determination rests on noninterpretive grounds. We rely principally on established Federal and State law because we believe the arguments supporting that body of law are more persuasive than the arguments supporting application of the *Gates* rule in this obscenity case, and are consistent with the admonition of an earlier Supreme Court that constitutional provisions for the security of persons and property are to be liberally construed (*see, Boyd v. United States*, 116 U.S. 616 [(1886)]). Our decision, however, is also based on principles of federalism and on New York's long tradition of interpreting our State Constitution to protect individual rights. In this case, we consider two fundamental rights, the right of free expression and the right of citizens to be free from unlawful governmental intrusions.

In the past we have frequently applied the State Constitution, in both civil and criminal matters, to define a broader scope of protection than that accorded by the Federal Constitution in cases concerning individual rights and liberties. Our conduct in the area of Fourth Amendment rights has been somewhat more restrained because the history of Section 12 supports the presumption that the provision "against unlawful searches and seizures contained in NY Constitution, Article I, Section 12 conforms with that found in the 4th Amendment, and that this identity of language supports a policy of uniformity between State and Federal courts." . . . Based on this, we have sought to fashion search and seizure rules that promote consistency in the interpretations we have given these parallel clauses. The interest of Federal-State uniformity, however, is simply one consideration to be balanced against other considerations that may argue for a different State rule. When weighed against the ability to protect fundamental constitutional rights, the practical need for uniformity can seldom be a decisive factor. Thus, notwithstanding an interest in conforming our State Constitution's restrictions on searches and seizures to those of the Federal Constitution where desirable, this court has adopted independent standards under the State Constitution when doing so best promotes "predictability and precision in judicial review of search and seizure cases and the protection of the individual rights of our citizens." . . .

In addition, we have sought to provide and maintain "bright line" rules to guide the decisions of law enforcement and judicial personnel who must understand and implement our decisions in their day-to-day operations in the field. To this end, we have rejected the reasoning behind the so-called good-faith exception to the warrant requirement recently articulated by the Supreme Court, refusing, on State constitutional grounds, to apply it. Similarly, although asked to do so, we have not reached out to adopt the *Gates* "totality of the circumstances" test in warrant cases, and we have declined to extend it to review warrantless arrests predicated on hearsay information. . . .

These decisions reflect a concern that the Fourth Amendment rules governing police conduct have been muddied, and judicial supervision of the warrant process diluted, thus heightening the danger that our citizens' rights against unreasonable police intrusions might be violated. We see the Supreme Court's present ruling as a similar dilution of the requirements of judicial supervision in the warrant process and as a departure from prior law on the subject. As we read the court's decision, it condones a probable cause determination by a magistrate based only upon the strength of the showing of probable cause as it relates to one of several necessary elements of the crime involved. While the "totality of the circumstances/fair probability" formulation may satisfy some as an acceptable analytical framework when used to evaluate whether an informant's tip should be credited as *one* element bearing on probable cause, the argument for its validity breaks down where, as here, the standard is applied in a different, nonhearsay, probable cause context. . . .

Several years ago we summarized our past decisions on the subject, restating a rigorous, fact-specific standard of review imposed upon the magistrate determining probable cause. . . . It imposed a specific, nondelegable burden on the magistrate which required that he, not the police, determine probable cause, and it required that his determination be objectively verifiable. . . . This is the standard that should be applied to protect the rights of New York citizens.

Our decision to rely on Article I, Section 12, rather than on the Supreme Court's Fourth Amendment pronouncement in this case, is motivated also by concerns of federalism and separation of powers. The States exist as sovereign entities independent of the national Government and the Tenth Amendment reserves to them and the people "[t]he powers not delegated to the United States by the Constitution, nor prohibited by it to the States" (U.S. Const. 10th Amend.). . . . One of the powers reserved to the States is the power to define what conduct shall be criminal within its borders. . . . Given that our Legislature, consonant with Federal constitutional mandates has determined that an offensive, explicit depiction of sexual conduct, standing alone, is not obscene, neither an issuing magistrate nor a reviewing court can legitimately override that legislative intent and find probable cause that the crime of obscenity has been committed based solely on a showing that sexually oriented material is explicit and offensive. The Supreme Court's decision in this case has, in effect, stated that certain elements of our statutory definition of a crime are not significant. We are not free to similarly ignore or recast the legislative mandate. . . .

The legal reasoning supporting our views, our understanding of principles of federalism, and this State's legal and cultural traditions all lead us to conclude that we should depart from the Federal rule stated in this case. We hold, therefore, that this warrant application did not demonstrate the probable cause required under the provisions of Article I, Sec. 12 of the State

Constitution and accordingly, on reargument following remand from the United States Supreme Court, we affirm the order of the County Court.

Commonwealth of Kentucky v. Wasson

842 S.W. 2D 487 (1992) (reprise)

In this case, the Kentucky Supreme Court rejected the analysis in *Bowers v. Hardwick*, 478 U.S. 186 (1986) and struck down its state ban on homosexual sodomy. Pertinent portions of the opinion appear in Volume 1, Chapter 2. See also THE DEVELOPMENT OF LAW: Other Recent State Supreme Court Decisions Declining to Follow the U.S. Supreme Court's Rulings in Volume 1, Chapter 2, and Volume 2, Chapter 2.

■ THE DEVELOPMENT OF LAW

Other Recent State Supreme Court Decisions Declining to Follow the U.S. Supreme Court's Rulings

(reprise; see Volume 1, Chapter 2.)

8

Representative Government, Voting Rights, and Electoral Politics

Fair and representative government is the bedrock for the constitutional politics of free government. It is the basis for political struggles over governmental accountability, federalism, majority rule versus minority rights, and much else. The idea was not new to the Framers, but the Constitution provided a foundation for an unprecedented experiment in representative government and for later expansion of the franchise.

John Locke, the English philosopher, championed "fair and *equal*" representation in his *Second Treatise of Government* (1689), when attacking the rotten boroughs of the British system of representing towns and counties:

[Section] 157. Things of this World are in so constant a Flux, that nothing remains long in the same State. . . . But things not always changing equally, and private interest often keeping up Customs and Priviledges, when the reasons of them are ceased, it often comes to pass, that in Governments, where part of the Legislative consists of *Representatives* chosen by the People, that in tract of time this *Representation* becomes very *unequal* and disproportionate to the reasons it was at first establish'd upon. To what gross absurdities the following of Custom, when Reason has left it, may lead, we may be satisfied when we see the bare Name of a Town, of which there remains not so much as the ruines, where scarce so much Housing as a Sheep-

■ CONSTITUTIONAL HISTORY

Thomas Paine on the Right to Vote and Representative Government

The revolutionary pamphleteer, Thomas Paine, in his *Dissertation on the First Principles of Government* (1795), linked the right to vote with representative government in a natural rights argument:

> The true and only true basis of representative government is equally of rights. Every man has a right to one vote, and no more in the choice of representatives. The rich have no more right to exclude the poor from the right of voting, or of electing and being elected, than the poor have to exclude the rich; and wherever it is attempted, or proposed, on either side, it is a question of force and not of right. Who is he that would exclude another? That other has a right to exclude him. . . .

> Personal rights, of which the right of voting for representatives is one, are a species of property of the most sacred kind: and he that would employ his pecuniary property, or presume upon the influence it gives him, to dispossess or rob another of his property as he would use fire-arms, and merits to have it taken from him.

> Inequality of rights is credited by a combination in one part of the community to exclude another part from its rights. Whenever it be made an article of a constitution, or a law, that the right of voting, or of electing and being elected, shall appertain exclusively to persons possessing that quantity to exclude those who do not possess the same quantity. It is investing themselves with powers as a self-created part of society, to the exclusion of the rest. . . .

> To take away this right is to reduce a man to slavery, for slavery consists in being subject to the will of another, and he that has not a vote in the election of representatives is in this case. The proposal therefore to disfranchise any class of men is as criminal as the proposal to take away property.

coat; or more inhabitants than a Shepherd is to be found, sends *as many Representatives* to the Assembly of Lawmakers, as a whole County numerous in People, and powerful in riches. This Stranger stands amazed at, and every one must confess needs a remedy. . . .

[W]henever the People shall chuse their *Representatives upon* just and undeniable *equal measures* suitable to the original Frame of the Government, it cannot be doubted to be the will and act of the Society, whoever permitted, or caused them so to do.[1]

Denial of representation to the colonies gave rise to the slogan "No taxation without representation." On October 14, 1774, the Continental Congress proclaimed,

> [T]he foundation of English liberty, of all free government, is a right in the people to participate in their legislative council: and as the English colonists are not represented, and from their local and other circumstances, cannot properly be represented in the British parliament, they are entitled to a free and exclusive power of legislation in their several provincial legislatures, where their right of representation can alone be preserved, in all cases of taxation and internal policy, subject only to the negative of their sovereign, in such manner as has been heretofore used and accustomed.[2]

Two years later, the failure of King George III to respond to colonial demands for fair and equal representation was cited as one of the justifications for revolution in the Declaration of Independence: "He has dissolved Representative Houses repeatedly, for opposing with manly firmness his invasions in the rights of the people. He has refused for a long time, after such dissolutions, to cause others to be elected, whereby the Legislative Powers, incapable of Annihilation, have returned to the People at large for their exercise."

Following the Declaration of Independence and the Revolutionary War, novel institutions of representative government emerged in the states and in the eventual formulation of the national government. But that was only the beginning. The history of the constitutional politics of the franchise and representative government is one of long-fought struggles to expand voting rights and to make the electoral process more democratic.

NOTES

1. John Locke, *Two Treatises of Government*, ed. Peter Laslett (New York: Mentor, 1960), 418–419.

2. "Declaration and Resolves of the First Continental Congress, 1774," reprinted in *The Roots of the Bill of Rights*, Vol. 1, ed. Bernard Schwartz (New York: Chelsea House, 1980), 217.

SELECTED BIBLIOGRAPHY

Goldwin, Robert, and Schambra, William, eds. *How Democratic Is the Constitution?* Washington, DC: American Enterprise Institute, 1980.

Kurland, Philip B., and Lerner, Ralph, eds. *The Founders' Constitution*, Vol. 1. Chicago: University of Chicago Press, 1987.

Kromkowski, Charles. *Recreating the American Republic: Rules of Apportionment, Constitutional Change, and American Political Development, 1700–1870*. Cambridge, MA: Cambridge University Press, 2002.

McDonald, Forrest. *Novus Ordo Seclorum: The Intellectual Origins of the Constitution*. Lawrence: University of Kansas Press, 1985.

White, Morton. *The Philosophy of the American Revolution*. New York: Oxford University Press, 1978.

A | *Representative Government and the Franchise*

The Framers agreed that representative government was the only alternative to both the tyranny of being ruled and that of direct democracy; both were deemed politically unacceptable. Still, there was disagreement as to who was to be represented as well as to how to achieve representation.

Anti-Federalists, such as the Federal Farmer, argued that "a full and equal representation is that in which the interests, feelings, opinions, and views of the people are collected, in such a manner as they would be were all the people assembled."[1] Anti-Federalists tended to reside in rural and agricultural areas and wanted assurance of representation of their people. They distrusted the Federalists, those in urban areas along the Atlantic seaboard and associated with commercial and banking interests. As Republicus, the pen name of a Kentucky Anti-Federalist, put it, "the constitution should provide for a fair and equal representation. That is that every member of the union have a freedom of suffrage and that every equal number of people have an equal number of representatives."[2]

By contrast, Federalists tended to take a dim view of those who, in Alexander Hamilton's words, wanted "an actual representation of all classes of the people by persons of each class." The Federalists favored representation by a natural aristocracy—"gentlemen of fortune and ability," as Hamilton put it during the Constitutional Convention.[3] So, too, John Adams feared that representation might be carried so far as "to confound and destroy all distinctions, and prostrate all ranks to one common level."[4]

To allay the fears of both supporters and opponents of the Constitution, in *The Federalist*, Nos. 10 and 63, James Madison made the ingenious argument that representative government in a large, "extended republic" would prevent the spread of two kinds of political "diseases": the corruption of representatives who play on their popularity to exploit voters and to dominate the people, and the election of representatives bent on venting popular passions and prejudices by denying individual rights.

[T]he greater number of citizens and extent of territory which may be brought within the compass of republican, than of democratic government; and it is this circumstance principally which renders factious combinations less to be dreaded in the former, than in the latter. The smaller the society, the fewer probably will be the distinct parties and interests composing it; the fewer the distinct parties and interests, the more frequently will a majority be found of the same party; and the smaller the number of individuals composing a majority, and the smaller the compass within which they are placed, the more easily will they concert and execute their plans of oppression. Extend the sphere, and you take in a greater variety of parties and interests; you make it less probable that a majority of the whole will have a common motive to invade the rights of other citizens; or if such a common motive exists, it will be more difficult for all who feel it to discover their own strength, and to act in unison with each other. . . .

The influence of factious leaders may kindle a flame within their particular States, but will be unable to spread a general conflagration through the other States: a religious sect, may degenerate into a political faction in a part of the Confederacy; but the variety of sects dispersed over the entire face of it, must secure the national Councils against any danger from that source. . . .

In the extent and proper structure of the Union, therefore, we behold a Republican remedy for the diseases most incident to Republican Government. And accordingly to the degree of pleasure and pride, we feel in being Republicans, ought to be our zeal in cherishing the spirit and supporting the character of Federalists.

In granting the franchise, however, the states followed the British-colonial model. Voting rights were generally limited to "freeholders" (white males who owned land and were at least twenty-one years old) and some states imposed religious qualifications as well. Under the Articles of Confederation, each state was free to determine the qualifications of voters. The Constitution did not change that. At the Constitutional Convention, Gouverneur Morris had proposed that the federal franchise be limited to freeholders. But Benjamin Franklin, among others, took issue with that, observing that "[i]t is of great consequence that we should not depress the virtue & public spirit of our common people; of which they displayed a great deal during the war."[5] In spite of the revolutionary rhetoric, there thus remained great inequalities. Thomas Jefferson, for instance, lamented that Virginia's constitution of 1776 limited voting rights only to the minority of that state's freeholders and disenfranchised the majority of those "who pay and fight."[6]

The Constitution, along with subsequent amendments, deals with voting rights more than any other subject. Remarkably, though, the universe and qualification of voters are not affirmatively defined. Instead, the Constitution and amendments have made the franchise more inclusive by progressively eliminating barriers for exercising voting rights and excluding blacks, women, poor, and the young from the electorate. Representation and voting rights are addressed in two sections of Article 1. Section 2, providing that electors of members of the House of Representatives "have the qualification requisite for electors of the most numerous branch of the state legislature," was a compromise designed to ensure a popular basis for the House without creating a national electorate independent of state electorates. The times, places, and manner clause of Section 4 gives Congress the power to require that representatives be elected from districts, rather than on a statewide basis. As discussed in Chapter 3, the Seventeenth Amendment (ratified in 1913) provides for the popular election of senators. Five other amendments greatly expanded the franchise and made the electoral process more democratic: the Fourteenth, Fifteenth, Nineteenth, Twenty-fourth, and Twenty-sixth Amendments.

The Framers, however, wholly failed to foresee the rise of political parties. Yet, after more than a decade of Federalist domination of the presidency and Congress, the fourth presidential election in 1800 brought into office Thomas Jefferson and the Jeffersonian-Republicans. Ever since, state and federal elections have been a contest between candidates of opposing political parties. And one consequence of the emergence of political parties was the expansion of the franchise and electorate. Notably, during Andrew Jackson's presidency (1829–1837) the property qualification was eliminated or replaced with a taxpayer qualification. Still, the electorate remained principally that of white males over twenty-one years old.

The struggle for further extension of suffrage grew from an 1848 convention of women in Seneca Falls, New York. There, Elizabeth Stanton pushed for the convention's adoption of a resolution "that it is the duty of the women of this country to secure to themselves their sacred right to the elective franchise." Stanton was supported by Frederick Douglass, the great black orator and abolitionist. Douglass tied equal rights for women with the abolition of slavery. And from this early beginning of the women's movement through the Civil War, suffrage for women and suffrage for blacks were linked.

Following the Civil War, two Reconstruction amendments held out the possibility of voting rights for women and blacks. Ratified in 1868, the Fourteenth Amendment's first section guaranteed "the privileges and immunities of citizens of the United States" against abridgement by the states. Section 2 provides that any state denying participation in state or federal elections to "any of the male inhabitants of such State, being twenty-one years of age, and citizens of the United States . . . except for participating in rebellion, or other crime" shall have the number of its representatives and delegates to the Electoral College proportionately reduced.

The narrow victory of General Ulysses S. Grant in the 1868 presidential election then convinced the Republican party that to maintain its control of Congress it needed black votes. And so it proposed the Fifteenth Amendment (ratified in 1870), specifically guaranteeing black voting rights by forbidding the abridgement of any citizen's right to vote "on account of race, color, or previous condition of servitude."

Despite continued disenfranchisement, some women held out hope that they might win the right to vote in federal election by claiming it was a guarantee of the Fourteenth Amendment's privileges and immunities clause. This was Susan B. Anthony's defense when prosecuted for casting a ballot in a federal election in 1872, but it was rejected by a lower federal court. The Court then dashed the hopes of another woman seeking to vote in a Missouri election. *Minor v. Happersett*, 21 Wall, (88 U.S.) 162 (1875), held that "the Constitution of the United States does not confer the right of suffrage upon anyone." Two more cases the following year rejected the argument that the Fifteenth Amendment affirmatively grants voting rights.[7]

Women had somewhat greater success in winning the right to vote in the states. In 1870, Wyoming's territorial legislature extended the right to them. Still, by 1913 only nine states allowed women to vote. In 1912, however, the Progressive Party of Theodore Roosevelt supported woman's suffrage. Political pressure continued to mount during World War I as larger numbers of women entered the work force and contributed to the war effort. In 1918, President Woodrow Wilson endorsed women's suffrage, and the next year Congress submitted a constitutional amendment to the states. The Nineteenth Amendment was ratified in 1920.

Although blacks were guaranteed the right to vote by the Fourteenth and Fifteenth Amendments, and were elected to office in the South during Reconstruction, barriers of various sorts soon emerged. Poll taxes, literacy tests, and other obstacles (discussed in section C of this chapter) effectively disenfranchised blacks by the turn of the twentieth century. *Breedlove v. Suttles*, 302 U.S. 277 (1937), held that poll taxes did not violate the Fourteenth and Fifteenth Amendments. That ruling sparked a campaign in the 1940s and 1950s to get the states and Congress to abolish poll taxes. The campaign had considerable success in the states; by 1960 only Alabama, Arkansas, Mississippi, Texas, and Virginia retained poll taxes. Congress finally banned poll taxes in federal elections with the Twenty-fourth Amendment (ratified in 1964).

When Virginia's powerful Harry Byrd political machine sought to evade the law by requiring voters to either pay a poll tax or file a certificate of residency at least six months before an election, it was rebuffed in *Harman v. Forssenius*, 380 U.S. 578 (1965). The Warren Court went even further in *Harper v. Virginia State Board of Elections*, 383 U.S. 663 (1966), ruling that while the Twenty-fourth Amendment barred poll taxes in *federal* elections, the Fourteenth Amendment equal protection clause forbade poll taxes in *state* elections, and thereby overturned *Breedlove*.

Among the goals of the civil rights movement in the 1950s and 1960s was the elimination of all barriers to black voting rights. Martin Luther King, Jr., launched voter-registration drives in the South, where there was widespread resistance and often violence. Congress had passed civil rights acts in 1957 and 1960, but they proved ineffective in placing the burden of eliminating voter discrimination on federal district court judges.

Finally, on the authority of Section 2 of the Fifteenth Amendment, which gives Congress the power to enforce "by appropriate legislation" the amendment's prohibition against racial discrimination in voting, Congress passed the Voting Rights Act of 1965. It outlaws any "voting qualification or prerequisite to voting" that denies the right to vote on account of race or color. Specifically banned are literacy tests,[8] tests for educational achievement and understanding,[9] proofs of "good moral character," and vouchers for the qualifications of registered voters. Such tests were banned in any state or subdivision where less than 50 percent of the persons of voting age were registered on November 1, 1964, or voted in that November's election. Moreover, while the above voting restrictions were suspended, the act provides that states and localities must receive the approval of the district court of the District of Columbia or the U.S. attorney general prior to implementing any changes in election laws. In addition, the law authorizes the U.S. Civil Service Commission to appoint federal voting-examiners to register voters where the attorney general deemed that was necessary to the enforcement of the Fifteenth Amendment.

The Voting Rights Act of 1965 remains controversial. The Court, though, affirmed its constitutionality in *South Carolina v. Katzenbach* (1966) (excerpted below).[10] In 1970 the act, which had a five-year limitation, was extended and amended to ban all literacy tests and modified the factors triggering the attorney general's preclearance of changes in states' voting laws. The law was again extended in 1975 for seven more years.

When amending the Voting Rights Act in 1970, Congress also enacted a provision forbidding in any local, state, and federal election the denial of the right to vote "on account of age if such citizen is eighteen years or older." Although opposing the lowering of the voting age at a time when there was widespread opposition among college students to the Vietnam War, President Nixon signed the act into law but directed Attorney General John Mitchell to challenge its constitutionality. In *Oregon v. Mitchell*, 400 U.S. 112 (1970), the Court was sharply split over Congress's power to extend the franchise in *state* as well as in national elections. Four justices thought Congress had the power; four justices disagreed. Justice Hugo Black cast the deciding vote, holding that Congress could lower the voting age in national but not in state and local elections. Congress immediately responded to that decision, and within six months the states ratified the Twenty-sixth Amendment (1971).

Despite some resistance from within the Reagan administration, the law was further extended in 1982 for twenty-five years. The principal controversy revolved around the standards for determining whether states or localities had discriminatory voting practices. In *City of Mobile v. Bolden*, 446 U.S. 55 (1980), the Burger Court upheld Mobile's system of electing a three-member city commission with at-large elections. At-large elections may work to the disadvantage of blacks and other minorities, and in Mobile, although 40 percent of the city was black, no black had ever been elected to the commission.[11] Civil rights organizations contended that Congress should ban election systems that "result" in discrimination. But opponents countered that a "results test" would eventually lead to proportional elections. In the end, the Voting Rights Act of 1982 provides that in cases challenging electoral discrimination, judges should look at "the totality of circumstances," the process and results of an election.

The renewed and revised Voting Rights Act in turn sparked a new round of litigation that finally reached the Supreme Court in the early 1990s. Congress amended the act in 1982 so as to reverse the Court's ruling in *City of Mobile v. Bolden*, 446 U.S. 55 (1980), which had construed the act to require proof of a "discriminatory intent" for establishing a violation of the Voting Rights Act. Instead of a "discriminatory intent" test, Congress wrote into law a "results test" under which minority voters simply must show that they had less opportunity than other residents in a district to elect representatives and public officials. In addition, the 1982 amendments substituted "representatives" for "legislators" in the act. And that invited the question of whether "representatives" includes elected state judges and provided a basis for challenging state judicial election systems.

In 1988 a group of black voters challenged Georgia's judicial-election system, pointing out that only 5 of that state's 135 trial judges were black. A three-judge federal district court ruled against Georgia, and on that basis the Department of Justice declared that the state's judicial election system was discriminatory in diluting the strength of black voters by requiring candidates to attain a majority, rather than a mere plurality, vote and by requiring them to run for specific judgeships in multijudge districts. In a separate lawsuit, black and Hispanic citizens challenged the at-large system for electing district judges in a number of Texas's metropolitan counties; at-large elections tend to work against electing minority candidates. They pointed out, for example, that in Harris County, Texas's largest district, blacks counted for 18 percent of the voting age population, while only 3 of the 59 judges (or 5 percent) were black. Although a federal district court held that the Texas judicial election system was subject to the Voting Rights Act, the Court of Appeals for the Fifth Circuit held that judicial elections are not covered because judges "do not represent the people, they serve the people," and the Voting Rights Act only guarantees minorities an equal opportunity to elect "representatives of their choice." Likewise, in the Georgia case, the state contended that Section 5 did not apply to judicial elections, and even if it did, it should not apply here because while Georgia had created new judgeships since 1964, its electoral system was not new. But, in contrast to the Fifth Circuit, a federal district court rejected those arguments.

The Court thus confronted two separate questions: (1) Do provisions of the Voting Rights Act apply to judicial elections? (2) If the act applies, what methods of electing state judges run afoul of the act? Without hearing oral arguments on the first, threshold, question, the Court unanimously said "yes" and rejected the argument that judicial elections are exempt from provisions of the Voting Rights Act. It did so in a simple one-sentence order that "summarily affirmed" the ruling of the district court, in *Georgia State Board of Elections v. Brooks*, 498 U.S. 916 (1990).

By summarily affirming the lower court in the Georgia cases, however, the Court provided no guidance for the Justice Department or lower courts when reviewing challenges to various state judicial election systems. Accordingly, the Court also granted review of several other cases involving attacks on various methods of electing state judges.

Three cases that involved Louisiana's judicial elections were granted as well. Two, *Chisom v. Roemer*, 501 U.S. 380 (1991), and *United States v. Roemer*, 501 U.S. 380 (1991), challenged Louisiana's method of electing justices to its seven-member state supreme court. Five of those justices are elected from single-member districts, while two are elected in at-large elections in a sixth voting district. Black voters in the sixth district argued that the at-large elections diluted their voting strength. They also contended that if the at-large district were divided along parish lines and split into two districts, a majority of the black voters in one of those new districts would have a chance to elect a black justice; no black has been elected to the Louisiana state supreme court in this century.

By a vote of six to three in *Chisom*, the Court held that Section 2 of the Voting Rights Act applies to judicial elections. Writing for the majority, Justice Stevens reasoned that if Congress had intended to exclude judicial elections from the coverage of the Voting Rights Act, it would have explicitly said so. The Court's holding in *Wells v. Edwards*, 409 U.S. 1095 (1973), that the "one-person, one-vote" rule was inapplicable to judicial elections, Stevens observed, does not mean that judicial elections are entirely immune from vote dilution claims. *Wells*, he pointed out, rejected a constitutional claim and, therefore, had no relevance to a correct interpretation of the Voting Rights Act, which was enacted to provide additional protection for voting rights not adequately protected by the Constitution itself.

The Voting Rights Act, without major controversy except from Southern states objecting to the continuation of the requirement for DoJ preapproval of changes in their voting laws, was again renewed in 2006.

NOTES

1. Letters of the Federal Farmer, in *The Complete Anti-Federalist*, Vol. 2, ed. Herbert J. Storing (Chicago: University of Chicago Press, 1980), 287–288.

2. Republicus, in *The Complete Anti-Federalist*, Vol. 5, ed. Herbert J. Storing (Chicago: University of Chicago Press, 1980), 167.

3. Alexander Hamilton, in *The Records of the Federal Convention of 1787*, Vol. 2, ed. Max Farrand (New Haven, CT: Yale University Press, 1937), 298–299.

4. John Adams to James Sullivan, May 26, 1776, in *The Founders' Constitution*, Vol. 1, ed. Philip Kurland and Ralph Lerner (Chicago: University of Chicago Press, 1987), 394–395.

5. Benjamin Franklin, *The Records of the Federal Convention of 1787*, Vol. 2, ed. Max Farrand (New Haven, CT: Yale University Press, 1974), 204.

6. Thomas Jefferson, *Notes on the State of Virginia* (Chapel Hill: University of North Carolina Press, 1954), 118–119.

7. See *United States v. Reese*, 92 U.S. 214 (1876); and *United States v. Cruikshank*, 92 U.S. 542 (1876). The Court, however, reconsidered these rulings with respect to black, although not female, voting rights in *Ex Parte Yarbrough*, 110 U.S. 651 (1884).

8. The Court upheld literacy tests in *Guinn v. United States*, 23 U.S. 347 (1915); and *Lassiter v. Northhampton County Board of Elections*, 360 U.S. 45 (1959).

9. The Court upheld tests for whether potential voters understood their state and federal constitution in *Williams v. Mississippi*, 170 U.S. 213 (1898).

10. See also *Allen v. State Board of Elections*, 393 U.S. 544 (1969); *Perkins v. Matthews*, 400 U.S. 379 (1971); *Georgia v. United States*, 411 U.S. 526 (1973); *City of Rome v. United States*, 446 U.S. 156 (1980); and the discussion in section B of this chapter.

11. The Court struck down at-large elections where it found invidious discrimination. See *Rogers v. Herman Lodge*, 458 U.S. 613 (1982). But held that there was no voter discrimination in *City of Lockhart v. United States*, 460 U.S. 125 (1983). See also *Thornburg v. Gingles*, 478 U.S. 30 (1986).

SELECTED BIBLIOGRAPHY

Ball, Howard, Krane, Dale, and Lauth, Thomas P. *Compromised Compliance: Implementation of the 1965 Voting Rights Act*. Westport, CT: Greenwood Press, 1982.

Goldman, Robert. *Reconstruction and Black Suffrage: Losing the Vote in Reese and Cruikshank*. Lawrence: University of Kansas Press, 2001.

Guinier, Lani. *The Tyranny of the Majority: Fundamental Fairness and Representative Democracy*. New York: Free Press, 1994.

Hamilton, Charles. *The Bench and the Ballot: Southern Federal Judges and Black Voters*. New York: Oxford University Press, 1973.

Hasen, Richard L. *The Supreme Court and Election Law: Judging Equality from Baker v. Carr to Bush v. Gore*, New York: New York University Press, 2003.

Keyssar, Alexander. *The Right to Vote: The Contested History of Democracy in the United States*. New York: Basic Books, 2000.

Landsberg, Brian. *Free to Vote at Last: The Alabama Origins of the 1965 Voting Rights Act*. Lawrence: University Press of Kansas, 2007.

Moore, Wayne. *Constitutional Rights and the Powers of the People*. Princeton, NJ: Princeton University Press, 1996.

Thernstrom, Abigail. *Whose Votes Count? Affirmative Action and Minority Voting Rights*. Cambridge, MA: Harvard University Press, 1987.

South Carolina v. Katzenbach

383 U.S. 301, 86 S.CT. 803 (1966)

Shortly after the passage of the Voting Rights Act of 1965, South Carolina filed suit in the Supreme Court, under its original jurisdiction, seeking a declaration of the unconstitutionality of several sections of the law and an order refraining Nicholas Katzenbach, the attorney general, from enforcing its provisions. South Carolina contended that the act violated the Tenth Amendment and the principle of equal treatment of the states. Katzenbach defended the law as appropriate legislation pursuant to the enforcement of the Fifteenth Amendment.

The Court's decision was unanimous; and the opinion was announced by Chief Justice Warren. Justice Black concurred.

□ *Chief Justice WARREN delivers the opinion of the Court.*

The Voting Rights Act was designed by Congress to banish the blight of racial discrimination in voting, which has infected the electoral process in parts of our country for nearly a century. The Act creates stringent new remedies for voting discrimination where it persists on a pervasive scale, and in addition the statute strengthens existing remedies for pockets of voting discrimination elsewhere in the country. Congress assumed the power to prescribe these remedies from Sec. 2 of the Fifteenth Amendment, which authorizes the National Legislature to effectuate by "appropriate" measures the constitutional prohibition against racial discrimination in voting. We hold that the sections of the Act which are properly before us are an appropriate means for carrying out Congress' constitutional responsibilities and are consonant with all other provisions of the Constitution. We therefore deny South Carolina's request that enforcement of these sections of the Act be enjoined.

The constitutional propriety of the Voting Rights Act of 1965 must be judged with reference to the historical experience which it reflects. Before enacting the measure, Congress explored with great care the problem of racial discrimination in voting. . . .

Two points emerge vividly from the voluminous legislative history of the Act contained in the committee hearings and floor debates. First: Congress felt itself confronted by an insidious and pervasive evil which had been perpetuated in certain parts of our country through unremitting and ingenious defiance of the Constitution. Second: Congress concluded that the unsuccessful remedies which it had prescribed in the past would have to be replaced by sterner and more elaborate measures in order to satisfy the clear commands of the Fifteenth Amendment. . . .

The Fifteenth Amendment to the Constitution was ratified in 1870. Promptly thereafter Congress passed the Enforcement Act of 1870, which made it a crime for public officers and private persons to obstruct exercise of the right to vote. The statute was amended in the following year to provide for detailed federal supervision of the electoral process, from registration to the certification of returns. As the years passed and fervor for racial equality waned, enforcement of the laws became spotty and ineffective, and most of their provisions were repealed in 1894. The remnants have had little significance in the recently renewed battle against voting discrimination.

Meanwhile, beginning in 1890, the States of Alabama, Georgia, Louisiana, Mississippi, North Carolina, South Carolina, and Virginia enacted tests still in use which were specifically designed to prevent Negroes from voting. Typically, they made the ability to read and write a registration qualification and also required completion of a registration form. These laws were based on the fact that as of 1890 in each of the named States, more than two-thirds of the adult Negroes were illiterate while less than one-quarter of the adult whites were unable to read or write. At the same time, alternate tests were prescribed in all of the named States to assure that white illiterates would not be deprived of the franchise. These included grandfather clauses, property qualifications, "good character" tests, and the requirement that registrants "understand" or "interpret" certain matters.

The course of subsequent Fifteenth Amendment litigation in this Court demonstrates the variety and persistence of these and similar institutions designed to deprive Negroes of the right to vote. Grandfather clauses were invalidated in *Guinn v. United States*, 238 U.S. 347 [1915]; and *Myers v. Anderson*, 238 U.S. 368 [1915]. Procedural hurdles were struck down in *Lane v. Wilson*, 307 U.S. 268 [1939]. The white primary was outlawed in *Smith v. Allwright*, 321 U.S. 649 [1944]; and *Terry v. Adams*, 345 U.S. 461 [1953]. Improper challenges were nullified in *United States v. Thomas*, 362 U.S. 58 [1960]. Racial gerrymandering was forbidden by *Gomillion v. Lightfoot*, 364 U.S. 339 [1960]. Finally, discriminatory application of voting tests was condemned in *Schnell v. Davis*, 336 U.S. 933 [1949]; *Alabama v. United States*, 371 U.S. 37 [1962]; and *Louisiana v. United States*, 380 U.S. 145 [1965].

According to the evidence in recent Justice Department voting suits, the latter stratagem is now the principal method used to bar Negroes from the polls. . . .

In recent years, Congress has repeatedly tried to cope with the problem by facilitating case-by-case litigation against voting discrimination. The Civil Rights Act of 1957 authorized the Attorney General to seek injunctions against public and private interference with the right to vote on racial grounds. Perfecting amendments in the Civil Rights Act of 1960 permitted the joinder of States as parties defendant, gave the Attorney General access to local voting records, and authorized courts to register voters in areas of systematic discrimination. Title I of the Civil Rights Act of 1964 expedited the hearing of voting cases before three-judge courts and outlawed some of the tactics used to disqualify Negroes from voting in federal elections.

Despite the earnest efforts of the Justice Department and of many federal judges, these new laws have done little to cure the problem of voting discrimination. According to estimates by the Attorney General during hearings on the Act, registration of voting-age Negroes in Alabama rose only from 14.2% to 19.4% between 1958 and 1964; in Louisiana it barely inched ahead from 31.7% to 31.8% between 1956 and 1965; and in Mississippi it increased only from 4.4% to 6.4% between 1954 and 1964. In each instance, registration of voting-age whites ran roughly 50 percentage points or more ahead of Negro registration. . . .

The Voting Rights Act of 1965 reflects Congress' firm intention to rid the country of racial discrimination in voting. The heart of the Act is a complex scheme of stringent remedies aimed at areas where voting discrimination has been most flagrant. Section 4 (a)–(d) lays down a formula defining the States and political subdivisions to which these new remedies apply. The first of the remedies, contained in Sec. 4 (a), is the suspension of literacy tests and similar voting qualifications for a period of five years from the last occurrence of substantial voting discrimination. Section 5 prescribes a second remedy, the suspension of all new voting regulations pending review by federal authorities to determine whether their use would perpetuate voting discrimination. The third remedy, covered in Secs. 6(b), 7, 9, and 13(a), is the assignment of federal examiners on certification by the Attorney General to list qualified applicants who are thereafter entitled to vote in all elections.

Other provisions of the Act prescribe subsidiary cures for persistent voting discrimination. Section 8 authorizes the appointment of federal poll-watchers in places to which federal examiners have already been assigned.

Section 10(d) excuses those made eligible to vote in sections of the country covered by Sec. 4 (b) of the Act from paying accumulated past poll taxes for state and local elections. Section 12(e) provides for balloting by persons denied access to the polls in areas where federal examiners have been appointed.

The remaining remedial portions of the Act are aimed at voting discrimination in any area of the country where it may occur. Section 2 broadly prohibits the use of voting rules to abridge exercise of the franchise on racial grounds. Sections 3, 6(a), and 13(b) strengthen existing procedures for attacking voting discrimination by means of litigation. Section 4(e) excuses citizens educated in American schools conducted in a foreign language from passing English-language literacy tests. Section 10(a)–(c) facilitates constitutional litigation challenging the imposition of all poll taxes for state and local elections. Sections 11 and 12(a)–(d) authorize civil and criminal sanctions against interference with the exercise of rights guaranteed by the Act. . . .

These provisions of the Voting Rights Act of 1965 are challenged on the fundamental ground that they exceed the powers of Congress and encroach on an area reserved to the States by the Constitution. South Carolina and certain of the *amici curiae* also attack specific sections of the Act for more particular reasons. They argue that the coverage formula prescribed in Sec. 4(a)–(d) violates the principle of the equality of States, denies due process by employing an invalid presumption and by barring judicial review of administrative findings, constitutes a forbidden bill of attainder, and impairs the separation of powers by adjudicating guilt through legislation. They claim that the review of new voting rules required in Sec. 5 infringes Article III by directing the District Court to issue advisory opinions. They contend that the assignment of federal examiners authorized in Sec. 6(b) abridges due process by precluding judicial review of administrative findings and impairs the separation of powers by giving the Attorney General judicial functions; also that the challenge procedure prescribed in Sec. 9 denies due process on account of its speed. Finally, South Carolina and certain of the *amici curiae* maintain that Secs. 4(a) and 5, buttressed by Sec. 14(b) of the Act, abridge due process by limiting litigation to a distant forum.

Some of these contentions may be dismissed at the outset. The word "person" in the context of the Due Process Clause of the Fifth Amendment cannot, by any reasonable mode of interpretation, be expanded to encompass the States of the Union, and to our knowledge this has never been done by any court. . . . Likewise, courts have consistently regarded the Bill of Attainder Clause of Article I and the principle of the separation of powers only as protections for individual persons and private groups, those who are peculiarly vulnerable to non-judicial determinations of guilt. Nor does a State have standing as the parent of its citizens to invoke these constitutional provisions against the Federal Government, the ultimate *parens patriae* of every American citizen. The objections to the Act which are raised under these provisions may therefore be considered only as additional aspects of the basic question presented by the case: Has Congress exercised its powers under the Fifteenth Amendment in an appropriate manner with relation to the States?

The ground rules for resolving this question are clear. The language and purpose of the Fifteenth Amendment, the prior decisions construing its several provisions, and the general doctrines of constitutional interpretation, all point to one fundamental principle. As against the reserved powers of the States, Congress may use any rational means to effectuate the constitutional prohibition of racial discrimination in voting. . . .

The basic test to be applied in a case involving Sec. 2 of the Fifteenth Amendment is the same as in all cases concerning the express powers of Congress with relation to the reserved powers of the States. Chief Justice MARSHALL laid down the classic formulation, 50 years before the Fifteenth Amendment was ratified:

> Let the end be legitimate, let it be within the scope of the constitution, and all means which are appropriate, which are plainly adapted to that end, which are not prohibited, but consist with the letter and spirit of the constitution, are constitutional. *McCulloch v. Maryland*, 4 Wheat. 316 [1819]. . . .

We therefore reject South Carolina's argument that Congress may appropriately do no more than to forbid violations of the Fifteenth Amendment in general terms—that the task of fashioning specific remedies or of applying them to particular localities must necessarily be left entirely to the courts. Congress is not circumscribed by any such artificial rules under Sec. 2 of the Fifteenth Amendment. In the oft-repeated words of Chief Justice MARSHALL, referring to another specific legislative authorization in the Constitution, "This power, like all others vested in Congress, is complete in itself, may be exercised to its utmost extent, and acknowledges no limitations, other than are prescribed in the constitution." *Gibbons v. Ogden*, 9 Wheat. 1 [1824]. . . .

After enduring nearly a century of widespread resistance to the Fifteenth Amendment, Congress has marshalled an array of potent weapons against the evil, with authority in the Attorney General to employ them effectively. Many of the areas directly affected by this development have indicated their willingness to abide by any restraints legitimately imposed upon them. We here hold that the portions of the Voting Rights Act properly before us are a valid means for carrying out the commands of the Fifteenth Amendment. Hopefully, millions of non-white Americans will now be able to participate for the first time on an equal basis in the government under which they live. We may finally look forward to the day when truly "[t]he right of citizens of the United States to vote shall not be denied or abridged by the United States or by any State on account of race, color, or previous condition of servitude."

The bill of complaint is dismissed.

Bill dismissed.

☐ *Justice BLACK, concurring in part.*

Though . . . I agree with most of the Court's conclusions, I dissent from its holding that every part of Sec. 5 of the Act is constitutional. Section 4(a), to which Sec. 5 is linked, suspends for five years all literacy tests and similar devices in those States coming within the formula of Sec. 4(b). Section 5 goes on to provide that a State covered by Sec. 4(b) can in no way amend its constitution or laws relating to voting without first trying to persuade the Attorney General of the United States or the Federal District Court for the District of Columbia that the new proposed laws do not have the purpose and will not have the effect of denying the right to vote to citizens on account of their race or color. I think this section is unconstitutional on at least two grounds. . . .

[I]t is hard for me to believe that a justiciable controversy can arise in the constitutional sense from a desire by the United States Government or some of its officials to determine in advance what legislative provisions a State may enact or what constitutional amendments it may adopt. If this dispute between the Federal Government and the States amounts to a case or controversy it is a far cry from the traditional constitutional notion of a case or controversy as a dispute over the meaning of enforceable laws or the manner in which they are applied. And if by this section Congress has created a case or controversy, and I do not believe it has, then it seems to me that the most appropriate judicial forum for settling these important questions is this Court acting under its original Art. III, Sec. 2, jurisdiction to try cases in which a State is a party. At least a trial in this Court would treat the States with the dignity to which they should be entitled as constituent members of our Federal Union. . . .

My second and more basic objection to Sec. 5 is that Congress has here exercised its power under Sec. 2 of the Fifteenth Amendment through the adoption of means that conflict with the most basic principles of the Constitution. . . . Section 5, by providing that some of the States cannot pass state laws or adopt state constitutional amendments without first being compelled to beg federal authorities to approve their policies, so distorts our constitutional structure of government as to render any distinction drawn in the Constitution between state and federal power almost meaningless. One of the most basic premises upon which our structure of government was founded was that the Federal Government was to have certain specific and limited powers and no others, and all other power was to be reserved either "to the States respectively, or to the people." Certainly if all the provisions of our Constitution which limit the power of the Federal Government and reserve other power to the States are to mean anything, they mean at least that the States have power to pass laws and amend their constitutions without first sending their officials hundreds of miles away to beg federal authorities to approve them. Moreover, it seems to me that Sec. 5 which gives federal officials power to veto state laws they do not like is in direct conflict with the clear command of our Constitution that "The United States shall guarantee to every State in this Union a Republican Form of Government." I cannot help but believe that the inevitable effect of any such law which forces any one of the States to entreat federal authorities in faraway places for approval of local laws before they can become effective is to create the impression that the State or States treated in this way are little more than conquered provinces. And if one law concerning voting can make the States plead for this approval by a distant federal court or the United States Attorney General, other laws on different subjects can force the States to seek the advance approval not only of the Attorney General but of the President himself or any other chosen members of his staff. It is inconceivable to me that such a radical degradation of state power was intended in any of the provisions of our Constitution or its Amendments. Of course I do not mean to cast any doubt whatever upon the indisputable power of the Federal Government to invalidate a state law once enacted and operative on the ground that it intrudes into the area of supreme federal power. But the Federal Government has heretofore always been content to exercise this power to protect federal supremacy by authorizing its agents to bring lawsuits against state officials once an operative state law has created an actual case and controversy. A federal law which assumes the power to compel the States to submit in advance any proposed legislation they have for approval by federal agents approaches dangerously near to wiping the States out as useful and effective

---

■ THE DEVELOPMENT OF LAW

Other Rulings Interpreting the Voting Rights Act

CASE	VOTE	RULING
Gaston County v. United States, 395 U.S. 285 (1969)	7:1	Because of past racial discrimination in the electoral system, the Court held that "impartial"

administration of literacy tests would serve only to "perpetuate these [past] inequities in a different form."

Perkins v. Matthews, 400 U.S. 379 (1971)	7:2	Localities covered by the Voting Rights Act may not annex territory or move polling places without prior federal approval.

City of Richmond, Virginia v. United States, 422 U.S. 358 (1975)	6:3	Upheld the annexation of twenty-three square miles of the the county of Richmond that resulted in a black population

of 42 percent rather than 52 percent prior to annexation; no violation of the Voting Rights Act.

Beer v. United States, 425 130 (1976)	5:3	The Voting Rights Act does U.S. not require redrawing district lines to give black voters proportional

tional representation; the act only bars dilution of the black vote and any "retrogression in the position of racial minorities with respect to their effective exercise of the electoral franchise."

units in the government of our country. I cannot agree to any constitutional interpretation that leads inevitably to such a result. . . .

In this and other prior Acts Congress has quite properly vested the Attorney General with extremely broad power to protect voting rights of citizens against discrimination on account of race or color. Section 5 viewed in this context is of very minor importance and in my judgment is likely to serve more as an irritant to the States than as an aid to the enforcement of the Act. I would hold Sec. 5 invalid for the reasons stated above with full confidence that the Attorney General has ample power to give vigorous, expeditious and effective protection to the voting rights of all citizens.

CASE	VOTE	RULING
United Jewish Organizations v. Carey, 430 (1976)	8:0	Held that the Fourteenth and Fifteenth Amendments and the Civil Rights Act were not violated by a reapportionment plan that diluted the votes of Hasidic Jews by splitting their community into two assembly districts to secure several predominantly nonwhite voting districts.
United States v. Board of Commissioners of Sheffield, Alabama, 435 U.S. 110 (1978)	6:3	Held that the Voting Rights Act requirement for preclearance by the Department of Justice of changes in election laws applies to all elections; here, to the municipal election of city councilmen.
City of Mobile, Alabama v. Bolden, 446 U.S. 55 (1980)	6:3	At-large elections did not violate black voting rights.
City of Rome v. United States, 446 U.S. 156 (1980)	7:2	Annexation violated the Voting Rights Act.
Rogers v. Lodge, 458 U.S. 613 (1982)	6:3	Held that "intent" is necessary to show that changes in election law result in invidious voting dilution.
City of Lockhart v. United States, 460 U.S. 125 (1983)	6:3	City's election plan subject to preclearance.

(continues)

■ THE DEVELOPMENT OF LAW
Other Rulings Interpreting the Voting Rights Act (continued)

CASE	VOTE	RULING
Thornburg v. Gingles, 478 U.S. 30 (1986)	6:3	Held that (1) the use of multi-member districts does not impede minority voters to elect representatives, unless a block of majority voters usually defeats minority candidates; (2) minority voters who challenge the use of multimember districts must demonstrate impermissible vote dilution; and (3) concluded that in the last six elections there was proportionate representation of blacks.
Chisom v. Roemer, 501 U.S. 380 (1991)	6:3	Held that the Voting Rights Act, as amended, applies to state judicial elections. Chief Justice Rehnquist and Justices Kennedy and Scalia dissented.
Houston Lawyers' Association v. Texas Attorney General, 501 U.S. 449 (1991)	6:3	The Court held that Section 2 of the Voting Rights Act applied to Texas's elections of state trial court judges. Justice Stevens wrote for the majority and Justice Scalia for the dissenters.
Presley v. Etowah County Commission, 502 U.S. 491 (1992)	6:3	The Court gave local governments greater freedom to change their political structure without obtaining prior approval from the Department of Justice under Section 5 of the Voting Rights Act. After the election of a black commissioner, the white majority county commission changed its system of allocating money, from one in which each commissioner had full authority over funds allocated to his or her district to a common fund under the control of the voting majority on the commission. Justice Kennedy held that the county did not have to obtain prior approval because the change did not involve "voting changes" covered by the act. The Voting Rights Act, according to Justice Kennedy, covers only four kinds of "voting changes": (1) in the manner of voting, such as switching from single-district to at-large elections; (2) in candidacy qualifications; (3) in voter registration; and (4) affecting the creation or abolition of an elected office. Each of these kinds of changes relates directly to the electoral process, whereas Justice Kennedy deemed changes in the internal operations of an elected body to have no direct relation to voting. Justices Stevens, Blackmun, and White dissented.

CASE	VOTE	RULING

Growe, Secretary of State of Minnesota v. Emison, 507 U.S. 25 (1993) — 9:0 — Unanimously reversing a district court decision that imposed a reapportionment plan creating a minority-dominated state senate district in Minnesota's legislature, the Court held that federal courts must defer to state courts when parallel lawsuits challenging redistricting plans are pending.

Voinovich v. Quilter, 507 U.S. 149 (1993) — 9:0 — Unanimously reversing a lower court ruling that struck down the creation of black-majority voting districts, the Court held that states are free to design reapportionment plans that include majority-minority districts so long as the end result does not violate the Voting Rights Act by "diminishing or abridging the voting strength of the protected class." Here, Ohio Democrats challenged a Republican-sponsored plan that Democrats claimed packed minorities into voting districts that already had elected black state legislators, while diluting blacks' voting strength in other predominantly white districts. Writing for the Court, Justice O'Connor observed that "the practice challenged here, the creation of majority-minority districts, does not invariably minimize or maximize minority voting strength. Instead, it can have either effect or neither. On the one hand, creating majority-black districts necessarily leaves few black voters and therefore diminishes black-voter influence in predominantly white districts. On the other hand, the creation of majority-black districts can enhance the influence of black voters. Placing black voters in a district in which they constitute a sizeable and therefore 'safe' majority ensures that they are able to elect their candidate of choice. Which effect the practice has, if any at all, depends entirely on the facts and circumstances of each case."

Morse v. Republican Party of Virginia, 517 U.S. 116 (1996) — 5:4 — A bare majority of the Court ruled that provisions of the Voting Rights Act extend to changes made in political parties' requirements for primary elections. Virginia delegated its authority over primary elections to the major political parties in the state. The Court held that the party's nominating convention effectively constituted a state primary election and thus was subject to the provisions of the Voting Rights Act. The four dissenters—Chief Justice Rehnquist and Justices Kennedy, Scalia, and Thomas—countered that the act did not extend to parties' nominating conventions, because political parties are not "state actors."

(continues)

■ THE DEVELOPMENT OF LAW
Other Rulings Interpreting the Voting Rights Act (continued)

CASE	VOTE	RULING
Young v. Fordice, 520 U.S. 273 (1997)	9:0	Held that Mississippi was required under Section 5 of the Voting Rights Act to obtain

the Department of Justice's preclearance approval before implementing the federal Motor Voter law of 1995 in a way that would make it the only state with separate registration procedures for federal and state elections. Writing for the Court, Justice Breyer observed that the dual registration system "contains numerous examples of new, significantly different administrative practices" that posed "a potential for discriminatory impact" on minority voters.

| *Reno v. Bossier Parish School Board*, 520 U.S. 1206 (1997) | 7:2 | Writing for the majority, Justice O'Connor rejected the Department of Justice's decade- |

old policy of denying preclearance under Section 5 of the Voting Rights Act to changes in electoral redistricting in the nine southern states not only when they would weaken the position of minority voters but also when redistricting plans would not improve those voters' position as much as theoretically possible. Under the policy of the Department of Justice, preclearance under Section 5 was denied if redistricting plans failed to satisfy the standard of Section 2 of the act, which applies nationwide and does not require proof that minority voters would be in a worse position but rather that they would not be in as strong a position to elect minorities as possible. However, Justice O'Connor held that policy to make it more difficult for the nine southern states to obtain preclearance under Section 5 than Congress had intended.

| *Abrams v. Johnson*, 521 U.S. 74 (1997) | 5:4 | In *Miller v. Johnson*, 512 U.S. 622 (1995), the Court invalidated Georgia's congressional redis- |

tricting plan, which created three majority-black districts out of the state's eleven districts, because race was the predominant factor in the redistricting plan. On remand, the federal district court deferred to the legislature to draw a new plan, but it could not reach agreement. The district court thus drew its own plan, containing only one majority-black district. The 1996 generalelections were held under that plan, but voters and the Department of Justice challenged the plan on the ground that it did not adequately take into account the interests of the state's black population. Writing for a bare majority as in *Miller v. Johnson*, Justice Kennedy upheld the lower court's redistricting plan and held that the court had abused neither its remedial powers nor its discretion in deciding that it could not draw two majority-black districts without engaging in racial gerrymandering. In holding that the redistricting did not violate either Section 2 or Section 5 of the Voting Rights Act and did not violate the constitutional guarantee of "one person, one vote" under Article 1, Section 2, Justice Kennedy reaffirmed that race "must not be a predominant factor in drawing the district lines." As in *Miller v. Johnson*, Justices Breyer, Ginsburg, Souter, and Stevens dissented.

CASE	VOTE	RULING
Lopez v. Monterey County, 525 U.S. 266 (1999)	8:1	Writing for the Court, Justice O'Connor held that a county covered by Section 5 of the

Voting Rights Act of 1965, which requires designated states and subdivisions to obtain Department of Justice approval for any proposed changes in election laws, in a state (California) not covered by Section 5, must still receive federal preclearance for voting changes. Justice Thomas dissented.

Reno v. Bossier Parish School Board, 528 U.S. 320 (2000)	5:4	Writing for the majority, Justice tice Scalia ruled that Section 5 of the Voting Rights Act does

not prohibit Department of Justice preclearance of a redistricting plan adopted with an ostensibly discriminatory but nonretrogressive purpose. The Department of Justice had objected to a plan to give all twelve voting districts white majorities, even though about 20 percent of the population was black. The department contended that it could deny preclearance approval because the plan would dilute black voting strength. But Justice Scalia rejected that interpretation of the Voting Rights Act in holding that preclearance could be denied only if a redistricting plan would put blacks in a worse position or to prevent "backsliding." That narrower interpretation was deemed by the Court's majority to be justified given "the substantial federalism costs that the preclearance procedure already exacts" from state and local governments. Justices Stevens, Souter, Ginsburg, and Breyer dissented.

Georgia v. Ashcroft, 539 U.S. 461 (2003)	5:4	Held that under Section 5 of the Voting Rights Act, legislative and congressional dis-

tricts may be redrawn in ways that shrink black voting majorities in order to create more Democratic-leaning districts. Georgia's redistricting reduced black majorities in three districts to just over 50 percent, down from 62 to 55 percent, in order to increase the likelihood that Democrats would be elected. A federal district court held that this action violated the Voting Rights Act, but the Supreme Court reversed, holding that in assessing the racial regressive effect all factors may be considered, including a minority group's voting participation in a coalitional district. Justices Stevens, Souter, Ginsburg, and Breyer dissented.

(continues)

■ The Development of Law
Other Rulings Interpreting the Voting Rights Act (continued)

CASE	VOTE	RULING
Northwest Austin Municipal Utility District No. 1 v. Holder, 129 S.Ct. 2504 (2009)	8:1	Although declining to declare unconstitutional the 2006 extension of Section 5 of the Voting Rights Act

of 1965, which requires Department of Justice preclearance of changes in election procedures in southern states and some counties in Alaska, California, Florida, Michigan, and elsewhere that once discriminated against minority voters, the Court held that a Texas utility district (which does not register voters) could apply for a "bailout," under Section 4 of the law, from the required Section 5 preclearance review if they could demonstrate that they had not recently engaged in voter discrimination; this holding also invited further constitutional challenges to law. Writing for the Court, Chief Justice Roberts observed: "more than forty years ago, this Court concluded that 'exceptional conditions' prevailing in certain parts of the country justified extraordinary legislation otherwise unfamiliar to our federal system. In part due to the success of that legislation, we are now a very different Nation. Whether conditions continue to justify such legislation is a difficult constitutional question we do not answer today." When extending the Voting Rights Act in 2006, Congress relied on evidence of voter discrimination that was decades old and offered no evidence of the persistence of such discrimination. Dissenting, Justice Clarence Thomas would have struck down Section 5 as unconstitutional.

B | *Voting Rights and the Reapportionment Revolution*

Despite disenfranchisement of large segments of the population in the nineteenth century, Congress and the states by and large adhered to the principle of representation based on equal population. In the Northwest Ordinance of 1787, for example, Congress provided that representation in territorial legislatures was to be based on population. As discussed in Chapter 5, from 1842 to 1929 Congress required that members of the House of Representatives be elected from "contiguous, equal districts." Between 1790 and 1889, no state was admitted into the union that did not guarantee representation in its state legislature based on population.

But in the late nineteenth and early twentieth centuries, with the influx of immigrants and the emergence of large urban areas due to the Industrial Revolution, many states bowed to political pressures and refused to reapportion state legislative districts. As a result, votes in rural areas greatly outweighed those in urban areas. As discussed in Chapter 2, Justice Frankfurter insisted in *Colegrove v. Green*, 328 U.S. 549 (1946), that reapportionment was a "political question" for Congress and state legislatures, not the Court, to decide. In that case, Illinois had not redrawn its electoral district lines since 1901 and the voting inequalities were as great as nine to one in some districts. But Illinois was by no means unique in failing to reapportion its legislative houses. In 1910, 41.9 million people lived in urban areas, while 49.9 lived in rural areas. Fifty years later, in 1960, 125.2 million lived in urban areas, whereas only 54 million lived in rural areas.

In 1960, the Warren Court confronted the related issue of racial malapportionment. In *Gomillion v. Lightfoot* (1960) (excerpted below), the Court rebuffed an attempt by Tuskegee, Alabama, to redraw its electoral lines so as to exclude virtually all black voters from within the city's limits.

Finally, in *Baker v. Carr*, 369 U.S. 186 (1962) (excerpted in Volume 1, Chapter 2), the Court responded to the malapportionment controversy, holding that reapportionment was no longer a nonjusticiable controversy. Years later, after leaving the bench, Chief Justice Earl Warren explained in a television interview that *Baker* was more important than the Court's landmark school desegregation ruling:

> [I]n my mind the most important case we have had in all those years was the case of *Baker v. Carr*, which is what we might call the parent case of the one man, one vote doctrine, which guarantees to every American citizen participating in government an equal value of his vote to that of any other vote that is cast in the particular election. And the reason I say that is not because it decided any particular issue at the time but the courts had vacillated on that question for a great many years and there were decisions that ended up three, three, three, without a majority of the vote in any of them. And which were, the net result of which were to stratify the situation in states where the legislature was grossly malapportioned, and some places it remained that way for sixty or seventy years and there was no way that the people of the state could get a constitutional amendment on which to vote, because the people who were [in] the malapportioned legislatures wouldn't submit that kind of an amendment to them, and there was no way under their state

government for the people to initiate such a measure. . . . [W]e held in *Baker v. Carr* that it was a judicial question, and that the courts, therefore, had jurisdiction. . . . And I believe that if we had had the decision shortly after the Fourteenth Amendment was adopted, that most of these problems that are confronting us today, particularly the racial problems, would have been solved by the political process where they should have been decided, rather than through the courts acting only under the bare bones of the Constitution. And if Blacks and everybody else could vote, the people who were in the majority in these various states had an opportunity to elect their people instead of having some district with large votes that were just about like the old so-called rotten boroughs over in England.[1]

While *Baker* announced the coming of the "reapportionment revolution" by inviting litigation challenging malapportioned legislatures, it did not address head-on the merits of the reapportionment controversy. Not until the following year did Justice Douglas announce the principle of "one person, one vote." When striking down Georgia's county-unit system of primary elections for state offices for diluting the votes of urbanites in *Gray v. Sanders*, 372 U.S. 368 (1963), Douglas declared that "[t]he conception of political equality from the Declaration of Independence, to Lincoln's Gettysburg address, to the Fifteenth, Seventeenth, and Nineteenth Amendments can mean only one thing—one person, one vote."

The next year, the Warren Court handed down seventeen reapportionment rulings. In the two leading cases, the Court advanced the principle of one person, one vote as the "essence of self-government" when extending it to malapportioned congressional districts, in *Wesberry v. Sanders* (1964) (excerpted below), and to state legislative districts in *Reynolds v. Sims* (1964) (excerpted below).

The Court's 1964 reapportionment rulings far from settled the controversy or put an end to litigation. The Court's rulings affected the apportionment of forty-eight states and there were already challenges to forty-one states' apportionment in the lower federal courts.

The Court also further extended the principle of one person, one vote to most elections for local offices, although not all.[2] In *Hadley v. Junior College District of Metropolitan Kansas City, Missouri*, 397 U.S. 50 (1970), Justice Black underscored the Court's determination to apply the principle of one person, one vote to virtually every local election:

We . . . hold today that as a general rule, whenever a state or local government decides to select persons by popular election or perform governmental functions, the equal protection clause of the Fourteenth Amendment requires that each qualified voter must be given an equal opportunity to participate in that election, and when members of an elected body are chosen from separate districts, each district must be established on a basis which will insure, as far as practicable, that equal numbers of voters can vote for proportionally equal numbers of officials.

Note, however, that the Court unanimously refused to apply the principle of "one person, one vote" to the apportionment of the House of Representatives, in *U.S. Department of Commerce v. Montana*, 503 U.S. 442 (1992) (see Vol. 1, Ch. 5). In a related controversy growing out of the 1990 census, the Court held that the federal government did not have to adjust census figures that undercounted blacks, Hispanics, and other minorities in some metropolitan areas and along the country's borders. New York City challenged the census figures, which are used in congressional redistricting and in calculating federal funding for the states, as a violation of minority voting rights. Although acknowledging that blacks were undercounted by 4.8 percent, Hispanics by 5.2 percent, Native Americans by 5 percent, and Asian-Pacific Islanders by 3.1 percent, the secretary of the Department of Commerce, who oversees the Census Bureau, decided that it was too costly to adjust the headcount to make it more accurate. Subsequently, Wisconsin and Oklahoma joined the suit on the side of the Commerce Department, in order to preserve their federal funding under the 1990 census. Without dissent, the Supreme Court held that Congress, which delegated its authority to the commerce secretary, has virtually unlimited discretion in deciding how to conduct the decennial census. Writing for the Court in *Wisconsin v. City of New York*, 517 U.S. 1 (1996), Chief Justice Rehnquist observed that the Census Bureau had "made an extraordinary effort to conduct an accurate enumeration, and was successful in counting 98.4 percent of the population."

The Court also continued to confront controversies arising from the use of multimember districts. These districts have been attacked, and sometimes adopted, for aiming to dilute the vote of minorities by expanding the size of a district. The Court held that multimember districts are not unconstitutional per se.[3] *Whitcomb v. Chavis*, 403 U.S. 124 (1971), upheld the use of multimember districts, despite considerable evidence that the votes of black and poor residents were diluted. Although the Court has expressed a preference for single-member districts in court-drawn plans,[4] *City of Mobile v. Bolden*, 446 U.S. 55 (1980), reaffirmed that vote dilution in multimember districts is unconstitutional only if there is evidence of an "intent" to discriminate. But as already noted, Congress responded to that ruling in the Voting Rights Act of 1982 by rejecting an "intent" standard and substituting a "totality of circumstances" standard for determining whether an electoral system is discriminatory. In *Rogers v. Herman Lodge*, 458 U.S. 613 (1982), the Burger Court ordered the establishment of single-member districts as a remedy for invidious discrimination in the at-large electoral system in Burke County, Georgia.[5]

The Court continues as well to confront litigation challenging the disparity in the weight of votes in electoral systems. Notably, the Court has continued to grapple with the line-drawing problem created by the Warren Court's holding that mathematical exactitude is not necessary to ensure the principle of one person, one vote, but rather "honest and good faith effort[s] to construct districts . . . as nearly of equal population as is practicable."

As further indicated in the box THE DEVELOPMENT OF LAW: Judicial Standards in Reapportionment Cases, the Court has consis-

---

■ The Development of Law

Rulings Extending the Principle of One Person, One Vote to Local Governments

CASE	VOTE	RULING
Avery v. Midland County, Texas, 390 U.S. 474 (1968)	6:3	Held that district lines for county commissioners were disproportiontionate and diluted local votes.
Kramer v. Union Free School District, 395 U.S. 621 (1969)	6:3	Held that New York a statute limiting voting in school district elections to
homeowners violated the Fourteenth Amendment.		
Hadley v. Junior College District of Metropolitan Kansas City, 397 U.S. 50 (1970)	6:3	Found that the selection of junior college trustees was based on disproportionate voting and held
that virtually all state and local elections must abide by the principle of one person, one vote.		
Board of Estimate of City of New York v. United States, 489 U.S. 688 (1989)	9:0	Applied principle of "one person, one vote" to New York Board of Estimate.

The Warren Court made sweeping changes in constitutional law and politics. But with the exception of the Court's 1954 landmark ruling on school desegregation, a solid majority on the Warren Court did not emerge until after the appointments of Justices Byron White and Arthur Goldberg in 1962. Seated, left to right, are Justices Tom C. Clark and Hugo L. Black, Chief Justice Earl Warren, and Justices William O. Douglas and John Harlan. Standing, left to right, are Justices Byron R. White, William J. Brennan, Jr., Potter Stewart, and Arthur J. Goldberg. (*Photo by Harris & Ewing, Collection of the Supreme Court of the United States.*)

tently allowed greater variations in the population ranges for state legislative districts than for congressional districts. At the same time, the Court also rather consistently approved a narrowing of the acceptable population ranges for both state legislative and congressional districts. Notably, *Gaffney v. Cummings*, 412 U.S. 735 (1973), upheld a population range of plus-or-minus 7.8 percent in Connecticut's state legislative districts and observed that states may undertake "not to minimize or eliminate the political strength of any group or party, but to recognize it and, through districting, provide a rough sort of proportional representation." In *Gaffney*, the Court also held that the burden of proof shifts to the plaintiffs who are claiming malapportionment. A decade later, in *Karcher v. Daggett*, 462 U.S. 725 (1983), a bare majority rejected New Jersey's plan for congressional districting with a total population variation of 0.69 percent. Writing for the Court and a plurality in *Karcher*, Justice Brennan held that the "as nearly as practicable" standard for apportioning congressional districts is inconsistent with the adoption of fixed numerical standards for justifying population variations,

- The Development of Law

Judicial Standards in Reapportionment Cases

STATE LEGISLATIVE DISTRICTS	CONGRESS
Swann v. Adams, 385 U.S. 440 (1967). Rejected population variations of 30 percent in Florida state senate and 40 percent in house districts.	*Duddleston v. Grills*, 385 U.S. 155 (1967). Rejected Indiana's congressional districting plan with 12.8 percent maximum deviation among district populations.
Kilgarlin v. Hill, 386 U.S. 120 (1967). Held that states must justify deviations in population of plus 14.8 percent and minus 11.6 percent.	*Kirkpatrick v. Priesler*, 394 U.S. 542 (1969). Rejected Missouri's congressional population deviations of plus-or-minus 3 percent. *Wells v. Rockefeller*, 394 U.S. 542 (1969). Rejected redistricting with population range of approximately 6 percent each way and defended as regional communities of interest.
Mahan v. Howell, 410 U.S. 315 (1973). Approved Virginia's 16.4 percent maximum population variance range, as justified by consistent patterns of following local subdivision lines.	*White v. Weiser* 412 U.S. 783 (1973). Rejected Texas's population range among congressional districts of plus 2.43 percent to minus 1.7 percent and suggested the adoption of an alternative plan with no significant population deviations.
White v. Regester, 412 U.S. 755 (1973). Upheld redistricting with population variations in the range of 10 percent, plus or minus, unless plaintiffs show discrimination.	*Karcher v. Daggett*, 462 U.S. 725 (1983). Rejected New Jersey's congressional districting with a total variation in population of 0.69 percent.
Gaffney v. Cummings, 412 U.S. 735 (1973). Upheld Connecticut's population range of plus-or-minus 7.8 percent for state legislative districts and ruled that the burden of proving malapportionment shifts to the plaintiff.	

The original gerrymander in 1812, with head, wings, and claws by Gilbert Stuart. (*The Granger Collection, New York.*)

and that the acceptability of the justification for population variations turns on the circumstances of each case.

In *Karcher v. Daggett*, a majority—a majority consisting of concurring Justice Stevens and the four dissenters (Chief Justice Burger and Justices Powell, Rehnquist, and White)—indicated that political gerrymandering may be a greater threat to fair representation than population variations in voting districts. *Gerrymandering* is a term describing efforts to draw district lines to preserve partisan power. It originated in Massachusetts in 1812, where the state legislature produced a salamander-shaped district, named after the governor, Elbridge Gerry. Since then it has been commonplace in the politics of congressional and state legislative districting.

Gerrymandering is principally used either to safeguard incumbents' seats or, more recently, to create districts in urban areas that will ensure the election of an ethnic or racial minority. The Warren Court repeatedly rejected opportunities to supervise this practice, except in cases like *Gomillion* involving gerrymandering aimed at disenfrachising minorities. In *United Jewish Organizations v. Carey*, 430 U.S. 144 (1977), the Burger Court likewise dismissed the claims of Hasidic Jews, who challenged the constitutionality of New York's redistricting plan that divided their community to establish two predominantly nonwhite voting districts—one Puerto Rican and the other Hispanic. The Hasidic Jews' votes were not diluted, but it was more difficult to elect a Hasidic Jew to the New York Assembly. The Court held that there was no way to distinguish one minority from another and that there was no principle to apply except for that of "one person, one vote." Besides that, the Court emphasized judicial deference to the political process in the area of redistricting.

However, in *Davis v. Bandemer*, 478 U.S. 106 (1986), the Court held that political gerrymandering was a justiciable controversy. But a majority could not agree on a standard for adjudicating such disputes. Almost two decades later the Court revisited the issue in *Vieth v. Jubelirer* (2004) (excerpted below). There, a plurality—Chief Justice Rehnquist and Justices O'Connor, Scalia, and Thomas—would have overruled *Davis v. Bandemer* and held that political gerrymandering controversies are nonjusticiable. Justice Kennedy, who cast the pivotal vote, would not go along with that and maintained that an enforceable standard might still emerge. The four dissenters—Justices Stevens, Souter, Ginsburg, and Breyer—countered that the Court could formulate standards for adjudicating political gerrymandering disputes, but they could not agree on a standard.

In a major and divisive ruling with broad political ramifications in *Shaw v. Reno*, 509 U.S. 630 (1993) (excerpted below), the Court held that the Fourteenth Amendment forbids racial gerrymandering unless the government demonstrates a "compelling reason" for creating black or Hispanic congressional districts. Following the 1990 census, twenty-six new so-called minority-majority districts were created in order to ensure black and Hispanic representation in Congress. Yet, Justice O'Connor's opinion for the Court applied the most rigorous standard of review, or "strict scrutiny" test (for a further discussion see the Rehnquist Court's rulings on affirmative action in Vol. 2, Ch. 12), and inspired each of the four dissenters to file separate dissenting opinions.

The bare majority on the Rehnquist Court that decided *Shaw v. Reno* held together in a series of other decisions interpreting the Voting Rights Act (see THE DEVELOPMENT OF LAW: Other Post–*Shaw v. Reno* Rulings on Racial Gerrymandering in this section), so as to strike down the creation of most minority-majority voting districts. The Court did finally uphold the racial redistricting of North Carolina's twelfth congressional district, which a bare majority had struck down in *Shaw v. Reno*, in *Hunt v. Cromartie* (2001) (excerpted below), as a result of Justice O'Connor's joining the four dissenters from the previous *Shaw v. Reno* line of rulings. However, in another five-to-four decision with Justice O'Connor rejoining the four conservatives and writing the opinion for the Court, *Georgia v. Ashcroft* (2003) (excerpted below) held that redistricting that shrinks black voting majorities in order to create more Democratic-leaning or coalitional districts may be permissible and not retrogressive in violation of the Voting Rights Act.

Finally, in a highly controversial case involving the Texas Republicans' mid-decennial redistricting and gerrymandering of congressional districts, the Court was sharply fragmented. Traditionally, redistricting has taken place after each census and partisan gerrymandering remains controversial. The Republican-dominated legislature redrew district lines in order to disadvantage Democrats, increase the size of the Republican majority in the House of Representatives, and preserve the seat of an incumbent—Representative Henry Bonilla—who was losing support among the Latino majority in his district. In *League of United Latin American Citizens v. Perry*, 548 U.S. 399 (2006), Justice Kennedy held for a plurality that such partisan redistricting is permissible. Chief Justice Roberts and Justices Stevens, Scalia, Souter, and Breyer each issued separate opinions in part concurring and in part dissenting.

NOTES

1. "A Conversation with Earl Warren," WGBH-TV (Boston) Education Foundation (1972), transcript pp. 15–16.

2. The Court approved a system for electing the board of directors of a water district that limited the electorate to landowners and weighted their votes in *Salyer Land Company v. Tulare Water Storage District*, 410 U.S. 719 (1973). See also *Gordon v. Lance*, 403 U.S. 1 (1971); *Holt Civic Club v. City of Tuscaloosa*, 439 U.S. 60 (1978); and *Ball v. James*, 451 U.S. 355 (1981).

3. See *Fortson v. Dorsey*, 379 U.S. 433 (1965); and *Burns v. Richardson*, 384 U.S. 73 (1966).

4. See *Connor v. Johnson*, 402 U.S. 690 (1971); *Chapman v. Meier*, 420 U.S. 1 (1975); and *East Carrol Parish School Board v. Marshall*, 424 U.S. 636 (1976).

5. But see *Thornburg v. Gingles*, 478 U.S. 30 (1986), in the table in section A of this chapter.

SELECTED BIBLIOGRAPHY

Baker, Gordon. *The Reapportionment Revolution*. New York: Random House, 1966.

Bybee, Keith. *Mistaken Identity: The Supreme Court and the Politics of Minority Representation*. Princeton, NJ: Princeton University Press, 1998.

Canon, David T. *Race, Redistricting, and Representation*. Chicago: University of Chicago Press, 1999.

Davidson, Chandler, and Grofman, Bernard, eds. *Quiet Revolution in the South*. Princeton, NJ: Princeton University Press, 1994.

Grofman, Bernard, ed. *Race and Redistricting in the 1990s*. New York: Agathon Press, 1999.

Guinier, Lani. *The Tyranny of the Majority: Fundamental Fairness and Representative Democracy*. New York: Free Press, 1994.

Kousser, J. Morgan. *Colorblind Justice: Minority Voting Rights and the Undoing of the Second Reconstruction*. Chapel Hill: University of North Carolina Press, 1999.

Lubin, David. *The Paradox of Representation: Minority Interests in Congress*. Princeton, NJ: Princeton University Press, 1997.

Monmonier, Mark S. *Bushmanders and Bullwinkles: How Politicians Manipulate Electronic Maps*. Chicago: University of Chicago Press, 2001.

Skerry, Peter. *Counting on the Census? Race, Group Identity, and the Evasion of Politics*. Washington, DC: Brookings Institution Press, 2001.

Thernstrom, Abigail. *Voting Rights—And Wrongs: The Elusive Quest for Racially Fair Elections*. Washington, DC: American Enterprise Institute, 2009.

Valelly, Richard. *The Voting Rights Act*. Washington, DC: C. Q. Press, 2005.

Yarbrough, Tinsley E. *Race and Redistricting: The Shaw-Cromartie Cases*. Lawrence: University Press of Kansas, 2003.

Gomillion v. Lightfoot

364 U.S. 339, 81 S.Ct. 125 (1960)

Charles Gomillion and several other black voters sued Phil Lightfoot, the mayor of Tuskegee, Alabama, for denying their voting rights as guaranteed under the Fifteenth Amendment. In 1957, Alabama's legislature redrew the boundaries of Tuskegee's electoral district from a square shape to that of a figure with twenty-eight sides. The redistricting placed virtually all black voters outside the city limits and in a district that had no whites. (See map, following, which the Court included in an appendix to its opinion.) A federal district court dismissed the suit, and a court of appeals affirmed that ruling. Gomillion then appealed to the Supreme Court, which granted review.

The Court's decision was unanimous, and the opinion was announced by Justice Frankfurter.

☐ *Justice FRANKFURTER delivers the opinion of the Court.*

The complaint amply alleges a claim of racial discrimination. Against this claim the respondents have never suggested, either in their brief or in oral argument, any countervailing municipal function which Act 140 is designed to serve. The respondents invoke generalities expressing the State's unrestricted power—unlimited, that is, by the United States Constitution—to establish, destroy, or reorganize by contraction or expansion its politi-

TUSKEGEE, ALABAMA, BEFORE AND AFTER ACT 140

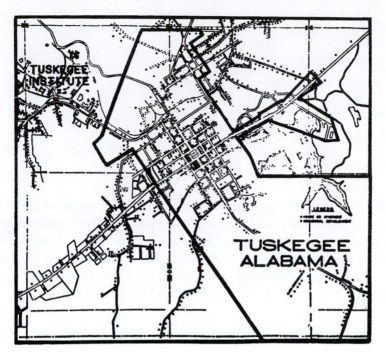

The entire area of the square comprised the city prior to Act 140. The irregular black-bordered figure within the square represents the postenactment city.

---

cal subdivisions, to wit, cities, counties, and other local units. We freely recognize the breadth and importance of this aspect of the State's political power. . . .

In no case involving unequal weight in voting distribution that has come before the Court did the decision sanction a differentiation on racial lines whereby approval was given to unequivocal withdrawal of the vote solely from colored citizens. Apart from all else, these considerations lift this controversy out of the so-called "political" arena and into the conventional sphere of constitutional litigation. . . .

When a State exercises power wholly within the domain of state interest, it is insulated from federal judicial review. But such insulation is not carried over when state power is used as an instrument for circumventing a federally protected right. This principle has had many applications. It has long been recognized in cases which have prohibited a State from exploiting a power acknowledged to be absolute in an isolated context to justify the imposition of an "unconstitutional condition." What the Court has said in those cases is equally applicable here, viz., that "Acts generally lawful may become unlawful when done to accomplish an unlawful end, *United States v. Reading Co.*, 226 U.S. 324 [1913], and a constitutional power cannot be used by way of condition to attain an unconstitutional result." *Western Union*

Telegraph Co. v. Foster, 247 U.S. 105 [(1918)]. The petitioners are entitled to prove their allegations at trial.

For these reasons, the principal conclusions of the District Court and the Court of Appeals are clearly erroneous and the decision below must be reversed.

Reversed.

Baker v. Carr

369 U.S. 186, 82 S.Ct. 691 (1962) (reprise)

This watershed case inaugurated the "reapportionment revolution," in holding that federal courts had jurisdiction and reapportionment controversies were justiciable, and not "political questions" to be decided by the other branches of government. Although *Baker* did not address the merits of the reapportionment dispute, it is no less important to this chapter. Pertinent parts of this case are reprinted in Volume 1, Chapter 2.

Wesberry v. Sanders

376 U.S. 1, 84 S.Ct. 526 (1964)

James Wesberry, Jr., and several other registered voters filed a suit in federal district court, asking it to declare unconstitutional Georgia's statute prescribing congressional districts. The 1931 statute created ten districts. But according to the 1960 census, the Fifth Congressional District had a population of 823,680, while the average population of the ten districts was 394,312, less than half of the Fifth District's population. Moreover, the Ninth District had a population of only 272,154, less than one-third as many as the Fifth District. Wesberry contended that because there was only one congressman for each district, the Fifth District's congressman had to represent from two to three times as many people as other congressmen. A three-judge federal district court, however, dismissed the suit. Wesberry then appealed to the Supreme Court.

The Court's decision was six to three, and the majority's opinion was announced by Justice Black. A separate opinion, in part concurring and dissenting, was delivered by Justice Clark. Justice Harlan dissented and was joined in part by Justice Stewart.

☐ *Justice BLACK delivers the opinion of the Court.*

We agree with the District Court that the 1931 Georgia apportionment grossly discriminates against voters in the Fifth Congressional District. A single Congressman represents from two to three times as many Fifth District voters as are represented by each of the Congressmen from the other Georgia congressional districts. The apportionment statute thus contracts the value of some votes and expands that of others. If the Federal Constitution intends that when qualified voters elect members of Congress each vote be given as much weight as any other vote, then this statute cannot stand.

We hold that, construed in its historical context, the command of Art. I, Sec. 2, that Representatives be chosen "by the People of the several States" means that as nearly as is practicable one man's vote in a congressional election is to be worth as much as another's. This rule is followed automatically, of course, when Representatives are chosen as a group on a statewide basis, as was a widespread practice in the first 50 years of our Nation's history. It would be extraordinary to suggest that in such statewide elections the votes of inhabitants of some parts of a State, for example, Georgia's thinly populated Ninth District, could be weighted at two or three times the value of the votes of people living in more populous parts of the State, for example, the Fifth District around Atlanta. Cf. *Gray v. Sanders*, 372 U.S. 368 [1963]. We do not believe that the Framers of the Constitution intended to permit the same vote-diluting discrimination to be accomplished through the device of districts containing widely varied numbers of inhabitants. To say that a vote is worth more in one district than in another would not only run counter to our fundamental ideas of democratic government, it would cast aside the principle of a House of Representatives elected "by the People," a principle tenaciously fought for and established at the Constitutional Convention. The history of the Constitution, particularly that part of it relating to the adoption of Art. I, Sec. 2, reveals that those who framed the Constitution meant that, no matter what the mechanics of an election, whether statewide or by districts, it was population which was to be the basis of the House of Representatives.

During the Revolutionary War the rebelling colonies were loosely allied in the Continental Congress, a body with authority to do little more than pass resolutions and issue requests for men and supplies. Before the war ended the Congress had proposed and secured the ratification by the States of a somewhat closer association under the Articles of Confederation. Though the Articles established a central government for the United States, as the former colonies were even then called, the States retained most of their sovereignty, like independent nations bound together only by treaties. There were no separate judicial or executive branches: only a Congress consisting of a single house. Like the members of an ancient Greek league, each State, without regard to size or population, was given only one vote in that house. It soon became clear that the Confederation was without adequate power to collect needed revenues or to enforce the rules its Congress adopted. Farsighted men felt that a closer union was necessary if the States were to be saved from foreign and domestic dangers.

The result was the Constitutional Convention of 1787, called for "the sole and express purpose of revising the Articles of Confederation. . . ." When the Convention met in May, this modest purpose was soon abandoned for the greater challenge of creating a new and closer form of government than was possible under the Confederation. Soon after the Convention assembled, Edmund Randolph of Virginia presented a plan not merely to amend the Articles of Confederation but to create an entirely new National Government with a National Executive, National Judiciary, and a National Legislature of two Houses, one house to be elected by "the people," the second house to be elected by the first.

The question of how the legislature should be constituted precipitated the most bitter controversy of the Convention. One principle was uppermost in the minds of many delegates: that, no matter where he lived, each voter should have a voice equal to that of every other in electing members of Congress. In support of this principle, George Mason of Virginia

> argued strongly for an election of the larger branch by the people. It was to be the grand depository of the democratic principle of the Govt.

James Madison agreed, saying "If the power is not immediately derived from the people, in proportion to their numbers, we may make a paper confederacy, but that will be all." . . .

Some delegates opposed election by the people. The sharpest objection arose out of the fear on the part of small States like Delaware that if population were to be the only basis of representation the populous States like Virginia would elect a large enough number of representatives to wield overwhelming power in the National Government. Arguing that the Convention had no authority to depart from the plan of the Articles of Confederation which gave each State an equal vote in the National Congress, William Paterson of New Jersey said, "If the sovereignty of the States is to be maintained, the Representatives must be drawn immediately from the States, not from the people: and we have no power to vary the idea of equal sovereignty." To this end he proposed a single legislative chamber in which each State, as in the Confederation, was to have an equal vote. A number of delegates supported this plan.

The delegates who wanted every man's vote to count alike were sharp in their criticism of giving each State, regardless of population, the same voice in the National Legislature. Madison entreated the Convention "to renounce a principle wch. was confessedly unjust," and Rufus King of Massachusetts "was prepared for every event, rather than sit down under a Govt. founded in a vicious principle of representation and which must be as short-lived as it would be unjust."

The dispute came near ending the Convention without a Constitution. Both sides seemed for a time to be hopelessly obstinate. Some delegations threatened to withdraw from the Convention if they did not get their way. Seeing the controversy growing sharper and emotions rising, the wise and highly respected Benjamin Franklin arose and pleaded with the delegates on both sides to "part with some of their demands, in order that they may join in some accommodating proposition." At last those who supported representation of the people in both houses and those who supported it in neither were brought together, some expressing the fear that if they did not reconcile their differences, "some foreign sword will probably do the work for us." The deadlock was finally broken when a majority of the States agreed to what has been called the Great Compromise, based on a proposal which had been repeatedly advanced by Roger Sherman and other delegates from Connecticut. It provided on the one hand that each State, including little Delaware and Rhode Island, was to have two Senators. As a further guarantee that these Senators would be considered state emissaries, they were to be elected by the state legislatures, Art. I, Sec. 3, and it was specially provided in Article V that no State should ever be deprived of its equal representation in the Senate. The other side of the compromise was that, as provided in Art. I, Sec. 2, members of the House of Representatives should be chosen "by the People of the several States" and should be "apportioned among the several States . . . according to their respective Numbers." While those who wanted both houses to represent the people had yielded on the Senate, they had not yielded on the House of Representatives. William Samuel Johnson of Connecticut had summed it up well: "in *one* branch the *people*, ought to be represented; in the *other*, the *States*."

The debates at the Convention make at least one fact abundantly clear: that when the delegates agreed that the House should represent "people" they intended that in allocating Congressmen the number assigned to each State should be determined solely by the number of the State's inhabitants. . . .

It would defeat the principle solemnly embodied in the Great Compromise—equal representation in the House for equal numbers of people—for us to hold that, within the States, legislatures may draw the lines of congressional districts in such a way as to give some voters a greater voice in choosing a Congressman than others. The House of Representatives, the Convention agreed, was to represent the people as individuals, and on a basis of complete equality for each voter. The delegates were quite aware of what Madison called the "vicious representation" in Great Britain whereby "rotten boroughs" with few inhabitants were represented in Parliament on or almost on a par with cities of greater population. Wilson urged that people must be represented as individuals, so that America would escape the evils of the English system under which one man could send two members to Parliament to represent the borough of Old Sarum while London's million people sent but four. The delegates referred to rotten borough apportionments in some of the state legislatures as the kind of objectionable governmental action that the Constitution should not tolerate in the election of congressional representatives. . . .

It is in the light of such history that we must construe Art. I, Sec. 2, of the Constitution, which, carrying out the ideas of Madison and those of like views, provides that Representatives shall be chosen "by the People of the several States" and shall be "apportioned among the several States . . . according to their respective Numbers." It is not surprising that our Court has held that this Article gives persons qualified to vote a constitutional right to vote and to have their votes counted. *United States v. Mosley*, 238 U.S. 383, [1915]. *Ex parte Yarbrough*, 110 U.S. 651 [1884]. Not only can this right to vote not be denied outright, it cannot, consistently with Article I, be destroyed by alteration of ballots, see *United States v. Classic*, 313 U.S. 299 [1941], or diluted by stuffing of the ballot box, see *United States v. Saylor*, 322 U.S. 385 [1944]. No right is more precious in a free country than that of having a voice in the election of those who make the laws under which, as good citizens, we must live. Other rights, even the most basic, are illusory if the right to vote is undermined. Our Constitution leaves no room for classification of people in a way that unnecessarily abridges this right. In urging the people to adopt the Constitution, Madison said in No. 57 of *The Federalist*:

> Who are to be the electors of the Federal Representatives? Not the rich more than the poor; not the learned more than the ignorant; not the haughty heirs of distinguished names, more than the humble sons of obscure and unpropitious fortune. The electors are to be the great body of the people of the United States. . . .

Readers surely could have fairly taken this to mean, "one person, one vote." Cf. *Gray v. Sanders.* . . .

While it may not be possible to draw congressional districts with mathematical precision, that is no excuse for ignoring our Constitution's plain objective of making equal representation for equal numbers of people the fundamental goal for the House of Representatives. That is the high standard of justice and common sense which the Founders set for us.

Reversed and remanded.

☐ *Justice HARLAN, dissenting.*

I had not expected to witness the day when the Supreme Court of the United States would render a decision which casts grave doubt on the constitutionality of the composition of the House of Representatives. It is not an exaggeration to say that such is the effect of today's decision. The Court's holding that the Constitution requires States to select Representatives either by elections at large or by elections in districts composed "as nearly as is practicable" of equal population places in jeopardy the seats of almost all the members of the present House of Representatives. . . .

Although the Court finds necessity for its artificial construction of Article I in the undoubted importance of the right to vote, that right is not involved in this case. All of the appellants do vote. The Court's talk about "debasement" and "dilution" of the vote is a model of circular reasoning, in which the premises of the argument feed on the conclusion. Moreover, by focusing exclusively on numbers in disregard of the area and shape of a congressional district as well as party affiliations within the district, the Court deals in abstractions which will be recognized even by the politically unsophisticated to have little relevance to the realities of political life.

In any event, the very sentence of Art. I, Sec. 2, on which the Court exclusively relies confers the right to vote for Representatives only on those whom *the State* has found qualified to vote for members of "the most numerous Branch of the State Legislature." So far as Article I is concerned, it is within the State's power to confer that right only on persons of wealth or of a particular sex or, if the State chose, living in specified areas of the State. Were Georgia to find the residents of the Fifth District unqualified to vote for Representatives to the State House of Representatives, they could not vote for Representatives to Congress, according to the express words of Art. I, Sec. 2. Other provisions of the Constitution would, of course, be relevant, *but, so far as Art. I, Sec. 2, is concerned*, the disqualification would be within Georgia's power. How can it be, then, that this very same sentence prevents Georgia from apportioning its Representatives as it chooses? The truth is that it does not.

The Court purports to find support for its position in the third paragraph of Art. I, Sec. 2, which provides for the apportionment of Representatives among the States. The appearance of support in that section derives from the Court's confusion of two issues: direct election of Representatives within the States and the apportionment of Representatives among the States. Those issues are distinct, and were separately treated in the Constitution. The fallacy of the Court's reasoning in this regard is illustrated by its slide, obscured by intervening discussion from the intention of the delegates at the Philadelphia Convention "that in allocating Congressmen the number assigned to each State should be determined solely by the number of the State's inhabitants," to a "principle solemnly embodied in the Great Compromise—equal representation in the House for equal numbers of people." The delegates did have the former intention and made clear provision for it., Although many, perhaps most, of them also believed generally—but assuredly not in the precise, formalistic way of the majority of the Court— that within the States representation should be based on population, they did not surreptitiously slip their belief into the Constitution in the phrase "by the People," to be discovered 175 years later like a Shakespearian anagram.

Far from supporting the Court, the apportionment of Representatives among the States shows how blindly the Court has marched to its decision. Representatives were to be apportioned among the States on the basis of free population plus three-fifths of the slave population. Since no slave voted, the inclusion of three-fifths of their number in the basis of apportionment gave the favored States representation far in excess of their voting population. If, then, slaves were intended to be without representation, Article I did exactly what the Court now says it prohibited: it "weighted" the vote of voters in the slave States. Alternatively, it might have been thought that Representatives elected by free men of a State would speak also for the slaves. But since the slaves added to the representation only of their own State, Representatives from the slave States could have been thought to speak only for the slaves of their own States, indicating both that the Convention believed it possible for a Representative elected by one group to speak for another nonvoting group and that Representatives were in large degree still thought of as speaking for the whole population *of a State*.

There is a further basis for demonstrating the hollowness of the Court's assertion that Article I requires "one man's vote in a congressional election . . . to be worth as much as another's." Nothing that the Court does today will disturb the fact that although in 1960 the population of an average congressional district was 410,481, the States of Alaska, Nevada, and Wyoming each have a Representative in Congress, although their respective populations are 226,167, 285,278, and 330,066. In entire disregard of population, Art. I, Sec. 2, guarantees each of these States and every other State "at Least one Representative." It is whimsical to assert in the face of this guarantee that an absolute principle of "equal representation in the House for equal numbers of people" is "solemnly embodied" in Article I. All that there is is a provision which bases representation in the House, generally but not entirely, on the population of the States. The provision for representation of *each State* in the House of Representatives is not a mere exception to the principle framed by the majority; it shows that no such principle is to be found.

Finally in this array of hurdles to its decision which the Court surmounts only by knocking them down is Sec. 4 of Art. I which states simply:

> The Times, Places and *Manner* of holding Elections for Senators and Representatives, shall be prescribed in each State by the Legislature thereof; but the Congress may at any time by Law make or alter such Regulations, except as to the Places of chusing Senators. (Emphasis added.)

The delegates were well aware of the problem of "rotten boroughs," as material cited by the Court and hereafter makes plain. It cannot be supposed that delegates to the Convention would have labored to establish a principle of equal representation only to bury it, one would have thought beyond discovery, in Sec. 2, and omit all mention of it from Sec. 4, which deals explicitly with the conduct of elections. Section 4 states without qualification that the state legislatures shall prescribe regulations for the conduct of elections for Representatives and, equally without qualification, that Congress may make or alter such regulations. There is nothing to indicate any limitation whatsoever on this grant of plenary initial and supervisory power. The Court's holding is, of course, derogatory not only of the power of the state legislatures but also of the power of Congress, both theoretically and as they have actually exercised their power. It freezes upon both, for no reason other than that it seems wise to the majority of the present Court, a particular political theory for the selection of Representatives. . . .

The upshot of all this is that the language of Art. I, Secs. 2 and 4, the surrounding text, and the relevant history are all in strong and consistent direct contradiction of the Court's holding. The constitutional scheme vests in the States plenary power to regulate the conduct of elections for Representatives, and, in order to protect the Federal Government, provides for congressional supervision of the States' exercise of their power. Within this scheme, the appellants do not have the right which they assert, in the absence of provision for equal districts by the Georgia Legislature or the Congress. The constitutional right which the Court creates is manufactured out of whole cloth. . . .

Believing that the complaint fails to disclose a constitutional claim, I would affirm the judgment below dismissing the complaint.

☐ *Justice STEWART disagreed with Justice HARLAN on the justiciability of the controversy, but otherwise joined his opinion.*

Reynolds v. Sims

377 U.S. 533, 84 S.Ct. 1362 (1964)

M. O. Sims and several other voters sued state and party officials in federal district court, alleging that Alabama's legislature was malapportioned and denied them an equal voting right. Although the state's constitution provided for a reapportionment every ten years, none had been undertaken since 1901. As a result, about one-fourth of the state's population could elect a majority of the state senators and representatives. The ratios of people to legislators varied by as much as fourteen to one in senate districts and up to sixteen to one in the lower house. The district court judge agreed that Sims's rights under the Fourteenth Amendment equal protection clause were violated and ordered the state to undertake reapportionment plans. Alabama's legislature came up with two plans but neither was based strictly on population. And the district court declared them unconstitutional. At that, B. A. Reynolds and several other state officials appealed to the Supreme Court.

The Court's decision was eight to one, and the majority's opinion was announced by Chief Justice Warren. Justices Clark and Stewart concurred; Justice Harlan dissented.

☐ *Chief Justice WARREN delivers the opinion of the Court.*

A predominant consideration in determining whether a State's legislative apportionment scheme constitutes an invidious discrimination violative of rights asserted under the Equal Protection Clause is that the rights allegedly impaired are individual and personal in nature. As stated by the Court in *United States v. Bathgate*, 246 U.S. 220 [1918], "[t]he right to vote is personal. . . ." While the result of a court decision in a state legislative apportionment controversy may be to require the restructuring of the geographical distribution of seats in a state legislature, the judicial focus must be concentrated upon ascertaining whether there has been any discrimination against certain of the State's citizens which constitutes an impermissible impairment of their constitutionally protected right to vote. Like *Skinner v. Oklahoma*, 316 U.S. 535 [1942], such a case "touches a sensitive and important area of human rights," and "involves one of the basic civil rights of man," presenting questions of alleged "invidious discriminations . . . against groups or types of individuals in violation of the constitutional guaranty of just and equal laws." Undoubtedly, the right of suffrage is a fundamental matter in a free and democratic society. Especially since the right to exercise the franchise in a free and unimpaired manner is preservative of other basic civil and political rights, any alleged infringement of the right of citizens to vote must be carefully and meticulously scrutinized. . . .

Legislators represent people, not trees or acres. Legislators are elected by voters, not farms or cities or economic interests. As long as ours is a representative form of government, and our legislatures are those instruments of government elected directly by and directly representative of the people, the right to elect legislators in a free and unimpaired fashion is a bedrock of our political system. It could hardly be gainsaid that a constitutional claim had been asserted by an allegation that certain otherwise qualified voters had been entirely prohibited from voting for members of their state legislature. And, if a State should provide that the votes of citizens in one part of the State should be given two times, or five times, or 10 times the weight of votes of citizens in another part of the State, it could hardly be contended that the right to vote of those residing in the disfavored areas had not been effectively diluted. It would appear extraordinary to suggest that a State could be constitutionally permitted to enact a law providing that certain of the State's voters could vote two, five, or 10 times for their legislative representatives, while voters living elsewhere could vote only once. And it is inconceivable that a state law to the effect that, in counting votes for legislators, the votes of citizens in one part of the State would be multiplied by two, five, or 10, while the votes of persons in another area would be counted only at face value, could be constitutionally sustainable. Of course, the effect of state legislative districting schemes which give the same number of representatives to unequal numbers of constituents is identical. . . .

Logically, in a society ostensibly grounded on representative government, it would seem reasonable that a majority of the people of a State could elect a majority of that State's legislators. To conclude differently, and to sanction minority control of state legislative bodies, would appear to deny majority rights in a way that far surpasses any possible denial of minority rights that might otherwise be thought to result. Since legislatures are responsible for enacting laws by which all citizens are to be governed, they should be bodies which are collectively responsive to the popular will. And the concept of equal protection has been traditionally viewed as requiring the uniform treatment of persons standing in the same relation to the governmental action questioned or challenged. With respect to the allocation of legislative representation, all voters, as citizens of a State, stand in the same relation regardless of where they live. Any suggested criteria for the differentiation of citizens are insufficient to justify any discrimination, as to the weight of their votes, unless relevant to the permissible purposes of legislative apportionment. Since the achieving of fair and effective representation for all citizens is concededly the basic aim of legislative apportionment, we conclude that the Equal Protection Clause guarantees the opportunity for equal participation by all voters in the election of state legislators. Diluting the weight of votes because of place of residence impairs basic constitutional rights under the Fourteenth Amendment. . . .

We are told that the matter of apportioning representation in a state legislature is a complex and many-faceted one. We are advised that States can rationally consider factors other than population in apportioning legislative representation. We are admonished not to restrict the power of the States to impose differing views as to political philosophy on their citizens. We are cautioned about the dangers of entering into political thickets and mathematical quagmires. Our answer is this: a denial of constitutionally protected rights demands judicial protection; our oath and our office require no less of us. . . . To the extent that a citizen's right to vote is debased, he is that much less a citizen. The fact that an individual lives here or there is not a legitimate reason for overweighting or diluting the efficacy of his vote. The complexions of societies and civilizations change, often with amazing rapidity. A nation once primarily rural in character becomes predominantly urban. Representation schemes once fair and equitable become archaic and outdated. But the basic principle of representative government remains, and must remain, unchanged—the weight of a citizen's vote cannot be made to depend on where he lives. . . .

We hold that, as a basic constitutional standard, the Equal Protection

Clause requires that the seats in both houses of a bicameral state legislature must be apportioned on a population basis. Simply stated, an individual's right to vote for state legislators is unconstitutionally impaired when its weight is in a substantial fashion diluted when compared with votes of citizens living in other parts of the State. . . .

Much has been written since our decision in *Baker v. Carr* about the applicability of the so-called federal analogy to state legislative apportionment arrangements. After considering the matter, the court below concluded that no conceivable analogy could be drawn between the federal scheme and the apportionment of seats in the Alabama Legislature under the proposed constitutional amendment. We agree with the District Court, and find the federal analogy inapposite and irrelevant to state legislative districting schemes. Attempted reliance on the federal analogy appears often to be little more than an after-the-fact rationalization offered in defense of maladjusted state apportionment arrangements. The original constitutions of 36 of our States provided that representation in both houses of the state legislatures would be based completely, or predominantly, on population. And the Founding Fathers clearly had no intention of establishing a pattern or model for the apportionment of seats in state legislatures when the system of representation in the Federal Congress was adopted. Demonstrative of this is the fact that the Northwest Ordinance, adopted in the same year, 1787, as the Federal Constitution, provided for the apportionment of seats in territorial legislatures solely on the basis of population.

The system of representation in the two Houses of the Federal Congress is one ingrained in our Constitution, as part of the law of the land. It is one conceived out of compromise and concession indispensable to the establishment of our federal republic. Arising from unique historical circumstances, it is based on the consideration that in establishing our type of federalism a group of formerly independent States bound themselves together under one national government. Admittedly, the original 13 States surrendered some of their sovereignty in agreeing to join together "to form a more perfect Union." But at the heart of our constitutional system remains the concept of separate and distinct governmental entities which have delegated some, but not all, of their formerly held powers to the single national government. . . .

Political subdivisions of States—counties, cities, or whatever—never were and never have been considered as sovereign entities. Rather, they have been traditionally regarded as subordinate governmental instrumentalities created by the State to assist in the carrying out of state governmental functions. . . . The relationship of the States to the Federal Government could hardly be less analogous. . . .

Since we find the so-called federal analogy inapposite to a consideration of the constitutional validity of state legislative apportionment schemes, we necessarily hold that the Equal Protection Clause requires both houses of a state legislature to be apportioned on a population basis. The right of a citizen to equal representation and to have his vote weighted equally with those of all other citizens in the election of members of one house of a bicameral state legislature would amount to little if States could effectively submerge the equal-population principle in the apportionment of seats in the other house. . . .

By holding that as a federal constitutional requisite both houses of a state legislature must be apportioned on a population basis, we mean that the Equal Protection Clause requires that a State make an honest and good faith effort to construct districts, in both houses of its legislature, as nearly of equal population as is practicable. We realize that it is a practical impossibility to arrange legislative districts so that each one has an identical number of residents, or citizens, or voters. Mathematical exactness or precision is hardly a workable constitutional requirement.

In *Wesberry v. Sanders*, the Court stated that congressional representation must be based on population as nearly as is practicable. In implementing the basic constitutional principle of representative government as enunciated by the Court in *Wesberry*—equality of population among districts—some distinctions may well be made between congressional and state legislative representation. Since, almost invariably, there is a significantly larger number of seats in state legislative bodies to be distributed within a State than congressional seats, it may be feasible to use political subdivision lines to a greater extent in establishing state legislative districts than in congressional districting while still affording adequate representation to all parts of the State. To do so would be constitutionally valid, so long as the resulting apportionment was one based substantially on population and the equal-population principle was not diluted in any significant way. . . .

So long as the divergences from a strict population standard are based on legitimate considerations incident to the effectuation of a rational state policy, some deviations from the equal-population principle are constitutionally permissible with respect to the apportionment of seats in either or both of the two houses of a bicameral state legislature. But neither history alone, nor economic or other sorts of group interests, are permissible factors in attempting to justify disparities from population-based representation. Citizens, not history or economic interests, cast votes. Considerations of area alone provide an insufficient justification for deviations from the equal-population principle. Again, people, not land or trees or pastures, vote. Modern developments and improvements in transportation and communications make rather hollow, in the mid-1960's, most claims that deviations from population-based representation can validly be based solely on geographical considerations. Arguments for allowing such deviations in order to insure effective representation for sparsely settled areas and to prevent legislative districts from becoming so large that the availability of access of citizens to their representatives is impaired are today, for the most part, unconvincing.

A consideration that appears to be of more substance in justifying some deviations from population-based representation in state legislatures is that of insuring some voice to political subdivisions, as political subdivisions. Several factors make more than insubstantial claims that a State can rationally consider according political subdivisions some independent representation in at least one body of the state legislature, as long as the basic standard of equality of population among districts is maintained. Local governmental entities are frequently charged with various responsibilities incident to the operation of state government. In many States much of the legislature's activity involves the enactment of so-called local legislation, directed only to the concerns of particular political subdivisions. And a State may legitimately desire to construct districts along political subdivision lines to deter the possibilities of gerrymandering. However, permitting deviations from population-based representation does not mean that each local governmental unit or political subdivision can be given separate representation, regardless of population. Carried too far, a scheme of giving at least one seat in one house to each political subdivision (for example, to each county) could easily result, in many States, in a total subversion of the equal-population principle in that legislative body. This would be especially true in a State where the number of counties is large and many of them are sparsely populated, and the number of seats in the legislative body being apportioned does not significantly exceed the number of counties. Such a result, we conclude, would be constitutionally impermissible. And careful judicial scrutiny must of course be given, in evaluating state apportionment schemes, to the character as well as the degree of deviations from a strict population basis. But if, even as a result of a clearly rational state policy of according some legislative representation to political subdivisions, population is submerged as the controlling consideration in the apportionment of seats in the particular legislative body, then the right of all of the State's citizens to cast an effective and adequately weighted vote would be unconstitutionally impaired. . . .

Affirmed and remanded.

☐ *Justice HARLAN, dissenting.*

In my judgment, today's decisions are refuted by the language of the Amendment which they construe and by the inference fairly to be drawn from subsequently enacted Amendments. They are unequivocally refuted by history and by consistent theory and practice from the time of the adoption of the Fourteenth Amendment until today.

The Court's elaboration of its new "constitutional" doctrine indicates how far—and how unwisely—it has strayed from the appropriate bounds of its authority. The consequence of today's decision is that in all but the handful of States which may already satisfy the new requirements the local District Court or, it may be, the state courts, are given blanket authority and the constitutional duty to supervise apportionment of the State Legislatures. It is difficult to imagine a more intolerable and inappropriate interference by the judiciary with the independent legislatures of the States. . . .

Although the Court—necessarily, as I believe—provides only generalities in elaboration of its main thesis, its opinion nevertheless fully demonstrates how far removed these problems are from fields of judicial competence. Recognizing that "indiscriminate districting" is an invitation to "partisan gerrymandering," the Court nevertheless excludes virtually every basis for the formation of electoral districts other than "indiscriminate districting." In one or another of today's opinions, the Court declares it unconstitutional for a State to give effective consideration to any of the following in establishing legislative districts:

(1) history;
(2) "economic or other sorts of group interests";
(3) area;
(4) geographical considerations;
(5) a desire "to insure effective representation for sparsely settled areas";
(6) "availability of access of citizens to their representatives";
(7) theories of bicameralism (except those approved by the Court);

(8) occupation;

(9) "an attempt to balance urban and rural power";

(10) the preference of a majority of voters in the State.

So far as presently appears, the *only* factor which a State may consider, apart from numbers, is political subdivisions. But even "a clearly rational state policy" recognizing this factor is unconstitutional if "population is submerged as the controlling consideration. . . ."

I know of no principle of logic or practical or theoretical politics, still less any constitutional principle, which establishes all or any of these exclusions. Certain it is that the Court's opinion does not establish them. So far as the Court says anything at all on this score, it says only that "legislators represent people, not trees or acres"; that "citizens, not history or economic interests, cast votes," that "people, not land or trees or pastures, vote." All this may be conceded. But it is surely equally obvious, and, in the context of elections, more meaningful to note that people are not ciphers and that legislators can represent their electors only by speaking for their interests— economic, social, political—many of which do reflect the place where the electors live. The Court does not establish, or indeed even attempt to make a case for the proposition that conflicting interests within a State can only be adjusted by disregarding them when voters are grouped for purposes of representation. . . .

These decisions also cut deeply into the fabric of our federalism. What must follow from them may eventually appear to be the product of state legislatures. Nevertheless, no thinking person can fail to recognize that the aftermath of these cases, however desirable it may be thought in itself, will have been achieved at the cost of a radical alteration in the relationship between the States and the Federal Government, more particularly the Federal Judiciary. Only one who has an overbearing impatience with the federal system and its political processes will believe that that cost was not too high or was inevitable.

Finally, these decisions give support to a current mistaken view of the Constitution and the constitutional function of this Court. This view, in a nutshell, is that every major social ill in this country can find its cure in some constitutional "principle," and that this Court should "take the lead" in promoting reform when other branches of government fail to act. The Constitution is not a panacea for every blot upon the public welfare, nor should this Court, ordained as a judicial body, be thought of as a general haven for reform movements. The Constitution is an instrument of government, fundamental to which is the premise that in a diffusion of governmental authority lies the greatest promise that this Nation will realize liberty for all its citizens. This Court, limited in function in accordance with that premise, does not serve its high purpose when it exceeds its authority, even to satisfy justified impatience with the slow workings of the political process. For when, in the name of constitutional interpretation, the Court *adds* something to the Constitution that was deliberately excluded from it, the Court in reality substitutes its view of what should be so for the amending process. . . .

Vieth v. Jubelirer

541 U.S. 267, 124 S.CT. 1769 (2004)

After the 2000 census Pennsylvania lost two seats in the House of Representatives, and the Republican-controlled legislature redrew the congressional district lines in ways that disadvantaged Democratic candidates. Three Democrats—Richard Vieth, Norman Jean Vieth, and Susan Furey—challenged the constitutionality of that political gerrymander as a violation of the principle of one person, one vote. The Supreme Court held, in *Davis v. Bandemer*, 478 U.S. 109 (1986), that political gerrymandering controversies are justiciable but provided no standard for adjudicating such disputes. Accordingly, the three-judge district court dismissed Vieth's claim. And an appeal was made to the Supreme Court.

The lower court was affirmed by a vote of five to four. Justice Scalia delivered the opinion for the Court, which was joined by Chief Justice Rehnquist and Justices O'Connor and Thomas. They would have overruled *Davis v. Bandemer* and ruled that political gerrymandering controversies are nonjusticiable. In a concurring opinion, however, Justice Kennedy agreed with the result but declined to overrule *Davis* and held out the possibility of developing a standard for adjudicating the constitutionality of political gerrymanders. Dissenting opinions were filed by Justice Souter, which Justice Ginsburg joined; and Justices Stevens and Breyer.

□ *Justice SCALIA announced the judgment of the Court and delivered an opinion, in which THE CHIEF JUSTICE, Justice O'CONNOR, and Justice THOMAS join.*

In *Davis v. Bandemer* (1986), this Court held that political gerrymandering claims are justiciable, but could not agree upon a standard to adjudicate them. The present appeal presents the questions whether our decision in *Bandemer* was in error, and, if not, what the standard should be. . . .

Political gerrymanders are not new to the American scene. One scholar traces them back to the Colony of Pennsylvania at the beginning of the 18th century, where several counties conspired to minimize the political power of the city of Philadelphia by refusing to allow it to merge or expand into surrounding jurisdictions, and denying it additional representatives. The political gerrymander remained alive and well (though not yet known by that name) at the time of the framing.

It is significant that the Framers provided a remedy for such practices in the Constitution. Article 1, Sec. 4, while leaving in state legislatures the initial power to draw districts for federal elections, permitted Congress to "make or alter" those districts if it wished. . . .

The power bestowed on Congress to regulate elections, and in particular to restrain the practice of political gerrymandering, has not lain dormant. In the Apportionment Act of 1842, Congress provided that Representatives must be elected from single-member districts "composed of contiguous territory." Congress again imposed these requirements in the Apportionment Act of 1862, and in 1872 further required that districts "contai[n] as nearly as practicable an equal number of inhabitants." In the Apportionment Act of 1901, Congress imposed a compactness requirement. The requirements of contiguity, compactness, and equality of population were repeated in the 1911 apportionment legislation, but were not thereafter continued. Today, only the single-member-district-requirement remains. Recent history, however, attests to Congress's awareness of the sort of districting practices appellants protest, and of its power under Article I, Sec. 4, to control them. Since 1980, no fewer than five bills have been introduced to regulate gerrymandering in congressional districting.

Eighteen years ago, we held that the Equal Protection Clause grants judges the power—and duty—to control political gerrymandering, see *Davis v. Bandemer* (1986). It is to consideration of this precedent that we now turn.

As Chief Justice MARSHALL proclaimed two centuries ago, "[i]t is emphatically the province and duty of the judicial department to say what the law is." *Marbury v. Madison*, 1 Cranch 137, 177 (1803). Sometimes, however, the law is that the judicial department has no business entertaining the claim of unlawfulness—because the question is entrusted to one of the political branches or involves no judicially enforceable rights. See, e.g., *Nixon v. United States*, 506 U.S. 224 (1993) (challenge to procedures used in Senate impeachment proceedings). . . .

"The judicial Power" created by Article III, Sec. 1, of the Constitution is not whatever judges choose to do, or even whatever Congress chooses to assign them, see *Lujan v. Defenders of Wildlife*, 504 U.S. 555 (1992). It is the power to act in the manner traditional for English and American courts. One of the most obvious limitations imposed by that requirement is that judicial action must be governed by standard, by rule. Laws promulgated by the Legislative Branch can be inconsistent, illogical, and ad hoc; law pronounced by the courts must be principled, rational, and based upon reasoned distinctions.

Over the dissent of three Justices, the Court held in *Davis v. Bandemer* that, since it was "not persuaded that there are no judicially discernible and manageable standards by which political gerrymander cases are to be decided" such cases were justiciable. The clumsy shifting of the burden of proof for the premise (the Court was "not persuaded" that standards do not exist, rather than "persuaded" that they do) was necessitated by the uncomfortable fact that the six-Justice majority could not discern what the judicially discernable standards might be. . . . The lower courts have lived with that assurance of a standard (or more precisely, lack of assurance that there is no standard), coupled with that inability to specify a standard, for the past 18 years. In that time, they have considered numerous political gerrymandering claims; this Court has never revisited the unanswered question of what standard governs. . . .

Eighteen years of judicial effort with virtually nothing to show for it justify us in revisiting the question whether the standard promised by *Bandemer* exists. As the following discussion reveals, no judicially discernible and manageable standards for adjudicating political gerrymandering claims have emerged. Lacking them, we must conclude that political gerrymandering claims are nonjusticiable and that *Bandemer* was wrongly decided.

We begin our review of possible standards with that proposed by Justice WHITE's plurality opinion in *Bandemer* because, as the narrowest ground for our decision in that case, it has been the standard employed by the lower courts. The plurality concluded that a political gerrymandering claim could succeed only where plaintiffs showed "both intentional discrimination against an identifiable political group and an actual discriminatory effect on that group." As to the intent element, the plurality acknowledged that "[a]s long as redistricting is done by a legislature, it should not be very difficult to prove that the likely political consequences of the reapportionment were intended." However, the effects prong was significantly harder to satisfy. Relief could not be based merely upon the fact that a group of persons banded together for political purposes had failed to achieve representation commensurate with its numbers, or that the apportionment scheme made its winning of elections more difficult. Rather, it would have to be shown that, taking into account a variety of historic factors and projected election results, the group had been "denied its chance to effectively influence the political process" as a whole, which could be achieved even without electing a candidate. It would not be enough to establish, for example, that Democrats had been "placed in a district with a supermajority of other Democratic voters" or that the district "departs from pre-existing political boundaries." Rather, in a challenge to an individual district the inquiry would focus "on the opportunity of members of the group to participate in party deliberations in the slating and nomination of candidates, their opportunity to register and vote, and hence their chance to directly influence the election returns and to secure the attention of the winning candidate." A statewide challenge, by contrast, would involve an analysis of "the voters' direct or indirect influence on the elections of the state legislature as a whole." With what has proved to be a gross understatement, the plurality acknowledged this was "of necessity a difficult inquiry." . . .

Because this standard was misguided when proposed, has not been improved in subsequent application, and is not even defended before us today by the appellants, we decline to affirm it as a constitutional requirement. . . .

Our one-person, one-vote cases, see *Reynolds v. Sims*, 377 U.S. 533 (1964); *Wesberry v. Sanders*, 376 U.S. 1 (1964), have no bearing upon this question, neither in principle nor in practicality. Not in principle, because to say that each individual must have an equal say in the selection of representatives, and hence that a majority of individuals must have a majority say, is not at all to say that each discernable group, whether farmers or urban dwellers or political parties, must have representation equivalent to its numbers. And not in practicality, because the easily administrable standard of population equality adopted by *Wesberry* and *Reynolds* enables judges to decide whether a violation has occurred (and to remedy it) essentially on the basis of three readily determined factors—where the plaintiff lives, how many voters are in his district, and how many voters are in other districts; whereas requiring judges to decide whether a districting system will produce a statewide majority for a majority party casts them forth upon a sea of imponderables, and asks them to make determinations that not even election experts can agree upon. . . .

We turn next to consideration of the standards proposed by today's dissenters. . . .

Justice STEVENS would . . . require courts to consider political gerrymandering challenges at the individual–district level. Much of his dissent is addressed to the incompatibility of severe partisan gerrymanders with democratic principles. We do not disagree with that judgment, any more than we disagree with the judgment that it would be unconstitutional for the Senate to employ, in impeachment proceedings, procedures that are incompatible with its obligation to "try" impeachments. See *Nixon v. United States* (1993). The issue we have discussed is not whether severe partisan gerrymanders violate the Constitution, but whether it is for the courts to say when a violation has occurred, and to design a remedy. On that point, Justice STEVENS's dissent is less helpful, saying, essentially, that if we can do it in the racial gerrymandering context we can do it here. . . .

Justice SOUTER recognizes that there is no existing workable standard for adjudicating such claims. He proposes a "fresh start," a newly constructed standard loosely based in form on our Title VII cases, and complete with a five-step prima facie test sewn together from parts of, among other things, our Voting Rights Act jurisprudence, law review articles, and apportionment cases. Even if these self-styled "clues" to unconstitutionality could be manageably applied, which we doubt, there is no reason to think they would detect the constitutional crime which Justice SOUTER is investigating—an "extremity of unfairness" in partisan competition.

Under Justice SOUTER's proposed standard, in order to challenge a particular district, a plaintiff must show (1) that he is a member of a "cohesive political group"; (2) "that the district of his residence . . . paid little or no heed" to traditional districting principles; (3) that there were "specific correlations between the district's deviations from traditional districting principles and the distribution of the population of his group"; (4) that a hypothetical district exists which includes the plaintiff's residence, remedies the packing or cracking of the plaintiff's group, and deviates less from traditional districting principles; and (5) that "the defendants acted intentionally to manipulate the shape of the district in order to pack or crack his group." When those showings have been made, the burden would shift to the defendants to justify the district "by reference to objectives other than naked partisan advantage."

While this five-part test seems eminently scientific, upon analysis one finds that each of the last four steps requires a quantifying judgment that is unguided and ill suited to the development of judicial standards: How much disregard of traditional districting principles? How many correlations between deviations and distribution? How much remedying of packing or cracking by the hypothetical district? How many legislators must have had the intent to pack and crack—and how efficacious must that intent have been (must it have been, for example, a sine qua non cause of the districting, or a predominant cause)? . . . What is a lower court to do when, as will often be the case, the district adheres to some traditional criteria but not others? Justice SOUTER's only response to this question is to evade it: "It is not necessary now to say exactly how a district court would balance a good showing on one of these indices against a poor showing on another, for that sort of detail is best worked out case by case." But the devil lurks precisely in such detail. The central problem is determining when political gerrymandering has gone too far. It does not solve that problem to break down the original unanswerable question (How much political motivation and effect is too much?) into four more discrete but equally unanswerable questions.

Justice SOUTER's proposal is doomed to failure for a more basic reason: No test—yea, not even a five-part test—can possibly be successful unless one knows what he is testing for. Justice SOUTER . . . vaguely describes the harm he is concerned with as vote dilution, a term which usually implies some actual effect on the weight of a vote. But no element of his test looks to the effect of the gerrymander on the electoral success, the electoral opportunity, or even the political influence, of the plaintiff group. We do not know the precise constitutional deprivation his test is designed to identify and prevent. . . .

We agree with much of Justice BREYER's dissenting opinion, which convincingly demonstrates that "political considerations will likely play an important, and proper, role in the drawing of district boundaries." This places Justice BREYER, like the other dissenters, in the difficult position of drawing the line between good politics and bad politics. Unlike them, he would tackle this problem at the statewide level.

The criterion Justice BREYER proposes is nothing more precise than "the unjustified use of political factors to entrench a minority in power." While he invokes in passing the Equal Protection Clause, it should be clear to any reader that what constitutes unjustified entrenchment depends on his own theory of "effective government." While one must agree with Justice BREYER's incredibly abstract starting point that our Constitution sought to create a "basically democratic" form of government, that is a long and impassable distance away from the conclusion that the judiciary may assess whether a group (somehow defined) has achieved a level of political power (somehow defined) commensurate with that to which they would be entitled absent unjustified political machinations (whatever that means).

Justice BREYER provides no real guidance for the journey. Despite his promise to do so, he never tells us what he is testing for, beyond the unhelpful "unjustified entrenchment." . . .

Justice KENNEDY recognizes that we have "demonstrat[ed] the shortcomings of the other standards that have been considered to date." He acknowledges, moreover, that we "lack . . . comprehensive and neutral principles for drawing electoral boundaries," and that there is an "absence of rules to limit and confine judicial intervention." From these premises, one might think that Justice KENNEDY would reach the conclusion that political gerrymandering claims are nonjusticiable. Instead, however, he concludes that courts should continue to adjudicate such claims because a standard may one day be discovered. . . .

Justice KENNEDY asserts that to declare nonjusticiability would be incautious. Our rush to such a holding after a mere 18 years of fruitless litigation "contrasts starkly" he says, "with the more patient approach" that this Court has taken in the past. We think not. . . .

We conclude that neither Article I, Sec. 2, nor the Equal Protection Clause, nor (what appellants only fleetingly invoke) Article I, Sec. 4, provides a judicially enforceable limit on the political considerations that the States and Congress may take into account when districting.

Considerations of *stare decisis* do not compel us to allow *Bandemer* to stand. . . . Eighteen years of essentially pointless litigation have persuaded us that *Bandemer* is incapable of principled application. We would therefore overrule that case, and decline to adjudicate these political gerrymandering claims. The judgment of the District Court is affirmed.

☐ *Justice KENNEDY, concurring in the judgment.*

I would not foreclose all possibility of judicial relief if some limited and precise rationale were found to correct an established violation of the Constitution in some redistricting cases. . . .

The object of districting is to establish "fair and effective representation for all citizens." *Reynolds v. Sims*, 377 U.S. 533 (1964). At first it might seem that courts could determine, by the exercise of their own judgment, whether political classifications are related to this object or instead burden representational rights. The lack, however, of any agreed upon model of fair and effective representation makes this analysis difficult to pursue. . . .

It is not in our tradition to foreclose the judicial process from the attempt to define standards and remedies where it is alleged that a constitutional right is burdened or denied. Nor is it alien to the Judiciary to draw or approve election district lines. Courts, after all, already do so in many instances. A determination by the Court to deny all hopes of intervention could erode confidence in the courts as much as would a premature decision to intervene.

Our willingness to enter the political thicket of the apportionment process with respect to one-person, one-vote claims makes it particularly difficult to justify a categorical refusal to entertain claims against this other type of gerrymandering. The plurality's conclusion that absent an "easily administrable standard," the appellants' claim must be nonjusticiable contrasts starkly with the more patient approach of *Baker v. Carr* (1962), not to mention the controlling precedent on the question of justiciability of *Davis v. Bandemer*, the case the plurality would overrule. . . .

Even putting *Baker* to the side—and so assuming that the existence of a workable standard for measuring a gerrymander's burden on representational rights distinguishes one-person, one-vote claims from partisan gerrymandering claims for justiciability purposes—I would still reject the plurality's conclusions as to nonjusticiability. Relying on the distinction between a claim having or not having a workable standard of that sort involves a difficult proof: proof of a categorical negative. That is, the different treatment of claims otherwise so alike hinges entirely on proof that no standard could exist. This is a difficult proposition to establish, for proving a negative is a challenge in any context.

That no such standard has emerged in this case should not be taken to prove that none will emerge in the future. Where important rights are involved, the impossibility of full analytical satisfaction is reason to err on the side of caution. Allegations of unconstitutional bias in apportionment are most serious claims, for we have long believed that "the right to vote" is one of "those political processes ordinarily to be relied upon to protect minorities." . . .

If suitable standards with which to measure the burden a gerrymander imposes on representational rights did emerge, hindsight would show that the Court prematurely abandoned the field. That is a risk the Court should not take. . . .

☐ *Justice STEVENS, dissenting.*

The central question presented by this case is whether political gerrymandering claims are justiciable. Although our reasons for coming to this conclusion differ, five Members of the Court are convinced that the plurality's answer to that question is erroneous. Moreover, as is apparent from our separate writings today, we share the view that, even if these appellants are not entitled to prevail, it would be contrary to precedent and profoundly unwise to foreclose all judicial review of similar claims that might be advanced in the future. That we presently have somewhat differing views—concerning both the precedential value of some of our recent cases and the standard that should be applied in future cases—should not obscure the fact that the areas of agreement set forth in the separate opinions are of far greater significance.

The concept of equal justice under law requires the State to govern impartially. See *Romer v. Evans*, 517 U.S. 620 (1996). . . . In my view, when partisanship is the legislature's sole motivation—when any pretense of neutrality is forsaken unabashedly and all traditional districting criteria are subverted for partisan advantage—the governing body cannot be said to have acted impartially.

Although we reaffirm the central holding of the Court in *Davis v. Bandemer*, we have not reached agreement on the standard that should govern partisan gerrymandering claims. I would decide this case on a narrow ground. . . .

State action that discriminates against a political minority for the sole and unadorned purpose of maximizing the power of the majority plainly violates the decisionmaker's duty to remain impartial. Gerrymanders necessarily rest on legislators' predictions that "members of certain identifiable groups . . . will vote in the same way." *Mobile v. Bolden*, 446 U.S. 55 (1980). "In the line-drawing process, racial, religious, ethnic, and economic gerrymanders are all species of political gerrymanders." Thus, the critical issue in both racial and political gerrymandering cases is the same: whether a single non-neutral criterion controlled the districting process to such an extent that the Constitution was offended. This Court has treated that precise question as justiciable in *Gomillion* [*v. Lightfoot*, 364 U.S. 339 (1960)] and in the *Shaw* [*v. Reno*, 509 U.S. 630 (1993)] line of cases, and today's plurality has supplied no persuasive reason for distinguishing the justiciability of partisan gerrymanders. Those cases confirm and reinforce the holding that partisan gerrymandering claims are justiciable. . . .

[W]hile political considerations may properly influence the decisions of our elected officials, when such decisions disadvantage members of a minority group—whether the minority is defined by its members' race, religion, or political affiliation—they must rest on a neutral predicate. Thus, the Equal Protection Clause implements a duty to govern impartially that requires, at the very least, that every decision by the sovereign serve some nonpartisan public purpose.

In evaluating a claim that a governmental decision violates the Equal Protection Clause, we have long required a showing of discriminatory purpose. See *Washington v. Davis*, 426 U.S. 229 (1976). That requirement applies with full force to districting decisions. The line that divides a racial or ethnic minority unevenly between school districts can be entirely legitimate if chosen on the basis of neutral factors—county lines, for example, or a natural boundary such as a river or major thoroughfare. But if the district lines were chosen for the purpose of limiting the number of minority students in the school, or the number of families holding unpopular religious or political views, that invidious purpose surely would invalidate the district. . . .

In sum, in evaluating a challenge to a specific district, I would apply the standard set forth in the *Shaw* cases and ask whether the legislature allowed partisan considerations to dominate and control the lines drawn, forsaking all neutral principles. Under my analysis, if no neutral criterion can be identified to justify the lines drawn, and if the only possible explanation for a district's bizarre shape is a naked desire to increase partisan strength, then no rational basis exists to save the district from an equal protection challenge. Such a narrow test would cover only a few meritorious claims, but it would preclude extreme abuses . . . and it would perhaps shorten the time period in which the pernicious effects of such a gerrymander are felt. This test would mitigate the current trend under which partisan considerations are becoming the be-all and end-all in apportioning representatives. . . .

☐ *Justice SOUTER, with whom Justice GINSBURG joins, dissenting.*

The notion of fairness assumed to be denied . . . has been described as "each political group in a State [having] the same chance to elect representatives of its choice as any other political group," and as a "right to 'fair and effective representation.' " It is undeniable that political sophisticates understand such fairness and how to go about destroying it, although it cannot possibly be described with the hard edge of one person, one vote. The difficulty has been to translate these notions of fairness into workable criteria, as distinct from mere opportunities for reviewing courts to make episodic judgments that things have gone too far, the sources of difficulty being in the facts that some intent to gain political advantage is inescapable whenever political bodies devise a district plan, and some effect results from the intent. Thus, the issue is one of how much is too much, and we can be no more exact in stating a verbal test for too much partisanship than we can be in defining too much race consciousness when some is inevitable and legitimate. Instead of coming up with a verbal formula for too much, then, the Court's job must be to identify clues, as objective as we can make them, indicating that partisan competition has reached an extremity of unfairness. . . .

Since this Court has created the problem no one else has been able to solve, it is up to us to make a fresh start. . . . I would therefore preserve *Davis's* holding that political gerrymandering is a justiciable issue, but otherwise start anew. I would adopt a political gerrymandering test analogous to the summary judgment standard crafted in *McDonnell Douglas Corp. v. Green*, 411 U.S. 792 (1973), calling for a plaintiff to satisfy elements of a prima facie cause of action, at which point the State would have the opportunity not only to rebut the evidence supporting the plaintiff's case, but to offer an affirmative justification for the districting choices, even assuming the proof of the plaintiff's allegations. My own judgment is that we would have better luck at devising a workable prima facie case if we concentrated as much as possible on suspect characteristics of individual districts instead of statewide patterns. It is not that a statewide view of districting is somehow less important; the usual point of gerrymandering, after all, is to control the greatest number of seats overall. But, as will be seen, we would be able to call more readily on some existing law when we defined what is suspect at the district level, and for now I would conceive of a statewide challenge as itself a function of claims that individual districts are illegitimately drawn. Finally, in the same interest of threshold simplicity, I would stick to problems of single-member districts; if we could not devise a workable scheme for dealing with claims about these, we would have to forget the complications posed by multi-member districts.

For a claim based on a specific single-member district, I would require the plaintiff to make out a prima facie case with five elements. First, the resident plaintiff would identify a cohesive political group to which he belonged, which would normally be a major party, as in this case and in *Davis*. There is no reason in principle, however, to rule out a claimant from a minor political party (which might, if it showed strength, become the target of vigorous hostility from one or both major parties in a State) or from a different but politically coherent group whose members engaged in bloc voting, as a large labor union might do.

Second, a plaintiff would need to show that the district of his residence, see *United States v. Hays*, 515 U.S. 737 (1995) (requiring residence in a challenged district for standing), paid little or no heed to those traditional districting principles whose disregard can be shown straightforwardly: contiguity, compactness, respect for political subdivisions, and conformity with geographic features like rivers and mountains. Because such considerations are already relevant to justifying small deviations from absolute population equality, and because compactness in particular is relevant to demonstrating possible majority-minority districts under the Voting Rights Act of 1965, there is no doubt that a test relying on these standards would fall within judicial competence. . . .

Third, the plaintiff would need to establish specific correlations between the district's deviations from traditional districting principles and the distribution of the population of his group. For example, one of the districts to which appellants object most strongly in this case is District 6, which they say "looms like a dragon descending on Philadelphia from the west, splitting up towns and communities throughout Montgomery and Berks Counties." To make their claim stick, they would need to point to specific protuberances on the draconian shape that reach out to include Democrats, or fissures in it that squirm away from Republicans. They would need to show that when towns and communities were split, Democrats tended to fall on one side and Republicans on the other.

Fourth, a plaintiff would need to present the court with a hypothetical district including his residence, one in which the proportion of the plaintiff's group was lower (in a packing claim) or higher (in a cracking one) and which at the same time deviated less from traditional districting principles than the actual district. This hypothetical district would allow the plaintiff to claim credibly that the deviations from traditional districting principles were not only correlated with, but also caused by, the packing or cracking of his group. Drawing the hypothetical district would, of course, necessarily involve redrawing at least one contiguous district, and a plaintiff would have to show that this could be done subject to traditional districting principles without packing or cracking his group (or another) worse than in the district being challenged.

Fifth, and finally, the plaintiff would have to show that the defendants acted intentionally to manipulate the shape of the district in order to pack or crack his group. See *Washington v. Davis*, 426 U.S. 229 (1976). In substantiating claims of political gerrymandering under a plan devised by a single major party, proving intent should not be hard, once the third and fourth (correlation and cause) elements are established. . . .

A plaintiff who got this far would have shown that his State intentionally acted to dilute his vote, having ignored reasonable alternatives consistent with traditional districting principles. I would then shift the burden to the defendants to justify their decision by reference to objectives other than naked partisan advantage. . . . The State might, for example, posit the need to avoid racial vote dilution. . . . This is not, however, the time or place for a comprehensive list of legitimate objectives a State might present. The point here is simply that the Constitution should not petrify traditional districting objectives as exclusive, and it is enough to say that the State would be required to explain itself, to demonstrate that whatever reasons it gave were more than a mere pretext for an old-fashioned gerrymander.

As for a statewide claim, I would not attempt an ambitious definition without the benefit of experience with individual district claims, and for now I would limit consideration of a statewide claim to one built upon a number of district-specific ones. Each successful district-specific challenge would necessarily entail redrawing at least one contiguous district, and the more the successful claims, the more surrounding districts to be redefined. At a certain point, the ripples would reach the state boundary, and it would no longer make any sense for a district court to consider the problems piecemeal. . . .

☐ *Justice BREYER, dissenting.*

I start with a fundamental principle. "We the People," who "ordain[ed] and establish[ed]" the American Constitution, sought to create and to protect a workable form of government that is in its " 'principles, structure, and whole mass,' " basically democratic. In a modern Nation of close to 300 million people, the workable democracy that the Constitution foresees must mean more than a guaranteed opportunity to elect legislators representing equally populous electoral districts. . . .

Why do I refer to these elementary constitutional principles? Because I believe they can help courts identify at least one abuse at issue in this case. To understand how that is so, one should begin by asking why single-member electoral districts are the norm, why the Constitution does not insist that the membership of legislatures better reflect different political views held by different groups of voters. History, of course, is part of the answer, but it does not tell the entire story. The answer also lies in the fact that a single-member-district system helps to assure certain democratic objectives better than many "more representative" (i.e., proportional) electoral systems. Of course, single-member districts mean that only parties with candidates who finish "first past the post" will elect legislators. That fact means in turn that a party with a bare majority of votes or even a plurality of votes will often obtain a large legislative majority, perhaps freezing out smaller parties. But single-member districts thereby diminish the need for coalition governments. And that fact makes it easier for voters to identify which party is responsible for government decisionmaking (and which rascals to throw out), while simultaneously providing greater legislative stability.

If single-member districts are the norm, however, then political considerations will likely play an important, and proper, role in the drawing of district boundaries. In part, that is because politicians, unlike nonpartisan observers, normally understand how "the location and shape of districts" determine "the political complexion of the area." It is precisely because politicians are best able to predict the effects of boundary changes that the districts they design usually make some political sense.

More important for present purposes, the role of political considerations reflects a surprising mathematical fact. Given a fairly large state population with a fairly large congressional delegation, districts assigned so as to be perfectly random in respect to politics would translate a small shift in political sentiment, say a shift from 51% Republican to 49% Republican, into a seismic shift in the makeup of the legislative delegation, say from 100% Republican to 100% Democrat. Any such exaggeration of tiny electoral changes—virtually wiping out legislative representation of the minority party—would itself seem highly undemocratic.

Given the resulting need for single-member districts with nonrandom boundaries, it is not surprising that "traditional" districting principles have rarely, if ever, been politically neutral. Rather, because, in recent political memory, Democrats have often been concentrated in cities while Republicans have often been concentrated in suburbs and sometimes rural areas, geographically drawn boundaries have tended to "pac[k]" the former.

This is to say that traditional or historically-based boundaries are not, and should not be, "politics free." Rather, those boundaries represent a series of compromises of principle—among the virtues of, for example, close representation of voter views, ease of identifying "government" and "opposition" parties, and stability in government. They also represent an uneasy truce, sanctioned by tradition, among different parties seeking political advantage.

As I have said, reference back to these underlying considerations helps to explain why the legislature's use of political boundary drawing considerations ordinarily does not violate the Constitution's Equal Protection Clause. The reason lies not simply in the difficulty of identifying abuse or finding an appropriate judicial remedy. The reason is more fundamental: Ordinarily, there simply is no abuse. The use of purely political boundary-drawing factors, even where harmful to the members of one party, will often nonetheless find justification in other desirable democratic ends, such as maintaining relatively stable legislatures in which a minority party retains significant representation.

At the same time, these considerations can help identify at least one circumstance where use of purely political boundary-drawing factors can amount to a serious, and remediable, abuse, namely the unjustified use of political factors to entrench a minority in power. By entrenchment I mean a situation in which a party that enjoys only minority support among the populace has nonetheless contrived to take, and hold, legislative power. By unjustified entrenchment I mean that the minority's hold on power is purely the result of partisan manipulation and not other factors. These "other" factors that could lead to "justified" (albeit temporary) minority entrenchment include sheer happenstance, the existence of more than two major parties, the unique constitutional requirements of certain representational bodies such as the Senate, or reliance on traditional (geographic, communities of interest, etc.) districting criteria. . . .

Courts need not intervene often to prevent the kind of abuse I have described, because those harmed constitute a political majority, and a majority normally can work its political will. Where a State has improperly gerrymandered legislative or congressional districts to the majority's disadvantage, the majority should be able to elect officials in statewide races—particularly the Governor—who may help to undo the harm that districting has caused the majority's party, in the next round of districting if not sooner. And where a State has improperly gerrymandered congressional districts, Congress retains the power to revise the State's districting determinations.

Moreover, voters in some States, perhaps tiring of the political boundary-drawing rivalry, have found a procedural solution, confiding the task to a commission that is limited in the extent to which it may base districts on partisan concerns. . . .

But we cannot always count on a severely gerrymandered legislature itself to find and implement a remedy. The party that controls the process has no incentive to change it. . . . When it is necessary, a court should prove capable of finding an appropriate remedy. Courts have developed districting remedies in other cases. . . . The bottom line is that courts should be able to identify the presence of one important gerrymandering evil, the unjustified entrenching in power of a political party that the voters have rejected. They should be able to separate the unjustified abuse of partisan boundary-drawing considerations to achieve that end from their more ordinary and justified use. And they should be able to design a remedy for extreme cases. . . .

Shaw v. Reno

509 U.S. 630, 113 S.Ct. 2816 (1993)

After the 1990 census, North Carolina became eligible for a twelfth congressional seat. But in order to comply with Section 5 of the Voting Rights Act of 1965, which requires a covered jurisdiction to obtain federal authorization for changes in its election practices and procedures, North Carolina submitted to the Department of Justice a congressional reapportionment plan with one majority-black district. The Bush administration's Department of Justice, however, objected to the state's initial plan because a second congressional district could have

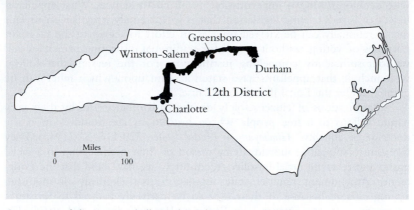

Congressional district 12, challenged in *Shaw v. Reno* (1993).

been created to give blacks greater voting strength in the state's south-central and southeastern region. North Carolina's general assembly thus revised its plan to include a second majority-black district in the north-central region. That new district stretched approximately 160 miles along Interstate 85 and for much of its length was no wider than the I-85 corridor. The constitutionality of that district was in turn attacked by several white voters, including a Duke University law school professor. A three-judge district court dismissed the complaint on the ground that under *United Jewish Organizations of Williamsburgh, Inc. v. Carey*, 430 U.S. 144 (1977), favoring minority voters was not discriminatory in the constitutional sense and that the plan did not proportionally under-represent white voters statewide. That decision was appealed to the Supreme Court, which granted *certiorari*.

The Court's decision was five to four, with the majority's opinion announced by Justice O'Connor and dissents by Justices White, Blackmun, Stevens, and Souter.

☐ *Justice O'CONNOR delivers the opinion of the Court.*

An understanding of the nature of appellants' claim is critical to our resolution of the case. In their complaint, appellants did not claim that the General Assembly's reapportionment plan unconstitutionally "diluted" white voting strength. They did not even claim to be white. Rather, appellants' complaint alleged that the deliberate segregation of voters into separate districts on the basis of race violated their constitutional right to participate in a "color-blind" electoral process.

Despite their invocation of the ideal of a "color-blind" Constitution, see *Plessy v. Ferguson*, 163 U.S. 537 (1896) (HARLAN, J., dissenting), appellants appear to concede that race-conscious redistricting is not always unconstitutional. That concession is wise: This Court never has held that race-conscious state decisionmaking is impermissible in all circumstances. What appellants object to is redistricting legislation that is so extremely irregular on its face that it rationally can be viewed only as an effort to segregate the races for purposes of voting, without regard for traditional districting principles and without sufficiently compelling justification. For the reasons that follow, we conclude that appellants have stated a claim upon which relief can be granted under the Equal Protection Clause. . . .

Classifications of citizens solely on the basis of race "are by their very nature odious to a free people whose institutions are founded upon the doctrine of equality." *Hirabayashi v. United States*, 320 U.S. 81 (1943). They threaten to stigmatize individuals by reason of their membership in a racial group and to incite racial hostility. Accordingly, we have held that the Fourteenth Amendment requires state legislation that expressly distinguishes among citizens because of their race to be narrowly tailored to further a compelling governmental interest. See, e.g., *Wygant v. Jackson Bd. of Ed.*, 476 U.S. 267 (1986).

These principles apply not only to legislation that contains explicit racial distinctions, but also to those "rare" statutes that, although race-neutral, are, on their face, "unexplainable on grounds other than race." *Arlington Heights v. Metropolitan Housing Development Corp.*, 429 U.S. 252 (1977). . . .

The Court applied the same reasoning to the "uncouth twenty-eight-sided" municipal boundary line at issue in *Gomillion* [*v. Lightfoot*, 364 U.S. 339 (1960)]. Although the statute that redrew the city limits of Tuskegee was race-neutral on its face, plaintiffs alleged that its effect was impermissibly to remove from the city virtually all black voters and no white voters. . . .

The Court extended the reasoning of *Gomillion* to congressional districting in *Wright v. Rockefeller*, 376 U.S. 52 (1964). At issue in *Wright* were four districts contained in a New York apportionment statute. The plaintiffs alleged that the statute excluded nonwhites from one district and concentrated them in the other three. Every member of the Court assumed that the plaintiffs' allegation that the statute "segregated eligible voters by race and place of origin" stated a constitutional claim. The Justices disagreed only as to whether the plaintiffs had carried their burden of proof at trial. The dissenters thought the unusual shape of the district lines could "be explained only in racial terms." The majority, however, accepted the District Court's finding that the plaintiffs had failed to establish that the districts were in fact drawn on racial lines. Although the boundary lines were somewhat irregular, the majority reasoned, they were not so bizarre as to permit of no other conclusion. Indeed, because most of the nonwhite voters lived together in one area, it would have been difficult to construct voting districts without concentrations of nonwhite voters.

Wright illustrates the difficulty of determining from the face of a single-member districting plan that it purposefully distinguishes between voters on the basis of race. A reapportionment statute typically does not classify persons at all; it classifies tracts of land, or addresses. Moreover, redistricting differs from other kinds of state decisionmaking in that the legislature always is aware of race when it draws district lines, just as it is aware of age, economic status, religious and political persuasion, and a variety of other demographic factors. That sort of race consciousness does not lead inevitably to impermissible race discrimination. As *Wright* demonstrates, when members of a racial group live together in one community, a reapportionment plan that concentrates members of the group in one district and excludes them from others may reflect wholly legitimate purposes. The district lines may be drawn, for example, to provide for compact districts of contiguous territory, or to maintain the integrity of political subdivisions.

The difficulty of proof, of course, does not mean that a racial gerrymander, once established, should receive less scrutiny under the Equal Protection Clause than other state legislation classifying citizens by race. Moreover, it seems clear to us that proof sometimes will not be difficult at all. In some exceptional cases, a reapportionment plan may be so highly irregular that, on its face, it rationally cannot be understood as anything other than an effort to "segregate . . . voters" on the basis of race. *Gomillion*, in which a tortured municipal boundary line was drawn to exclude black voters, was such a case. So, too, would be a case in which a State concentrated a dispersed minority population in a single district by disregarding traditional districting principles such as compactness, contiguity, and respect for political subdivisions. We emphasize that these criteria are important not because they are constitutionally required—they are not—but because they are objective factors that may serve to defeat a claim that a district has been gerrymandered on racial lines. . . .

Put differently, we believe that reapportionment is one area in which appearances do matter. A reapportionment plan that includes in one district individuals who belong to the same race, but who are otherwise widely separated by geographical and political boundaries, and who may have little in common with one another but the color of their skin, bears an uncomfortable resemblance to political apartheid. It reinforces the perception that members of the same racial group—regardless of their age, education, economic status, or the community in which they live—think alike, share the same political interests, and will prefer the same candidates at the polls. We have rejected such perceptions elsewhere as impermissible racial stereotypes. . . .

For these reasons, we conclude that a plaintiff challenging a reapportionment statute under the Equal Protection Clause may state a claim by alleging that the legislation, though race-neutral on its face, rationally cannot be understood as anything other than an effort to separate voters into different districts on the basis of race, and the separation lacks sufficient justification. It is unnecessary for us to decide whether or how a reapportionment plan that, on its face, can be explained in nonracial terms successfully could be challenged. Thus, we express no view as to whether "the intentional creation of majority-minority districts, without more" always gives rise to an equal protection claim. We hold only that, on the facts of this case, plaintiffs have stated a claim sufficient to defeat the state appellees' motion to dismiss. . . . It is [also] for these reasons that race-based districting by our state legislatures demands close judicial scrutiny. . . .

☐ *Justice WHITE, with whom Justices BLACKMUN and STEVENS join, dissenting.*

The facts of this case mirror those presented in *United Jewish Organizations of Williamsburgh, Inc. v. Carey*, 430 U.S. 144 (1977), where the Court rejected a claim that creation of a majority-minority district violated the Constitution, either as a per se matter or in light of the circumstances leading to the creation of such a district. Of particular relevance, five of the Justices reasoned that members of the white majority could not plausibly argue that their influence over the political process had been unfairly cancelled, or that such had been the State's intent. Accordingly, they held that plaintiffs were not entitled to relief under the Constitution's Equal Protection Clause. On the same reasoning, I would affirm the district court's dismissal of appellants' claim in this instance.

The Court today chooses not to overrule, but rather to sidestep, *United Jewish Organizations of Williamsburgh*. It does so by glossing over the striking similarities, focusing on surface differences, most notably the (admittedly unusual) shape of the newly created district, and imagining an entirely new cause of action. Because the holding is limited to such anomalous circumstances, it perhaps will not substantially hamper a State's legitimate efforts to redistrict in favor of racial minorities. Nonetheless, the notion that North Carolina's plan, under which whites remain a voting majority in a disproportionate number of congressional districts, and pursuant to which the State has sent its first black representatives since Reconstruction to the United States Congress, might have violated appellants' constitutional rights is both a fiction and a departure from settled equal protection principles. Seeing no good reason to engage in either, I dissent. . . .

□ *Justice STEVENS, dissenting.*

For the reasons stated by Justice WHITE, the decision of the District Court should be affirmed. I add these comments to emphasize that the two critical facts in this case are undisputed: first, the shape of District 12 is so bizarre that it must have been drawn for the purpose of either advantaging or disadvantaging a cognizable group of voters; and, second, regardless of that shape, it was drawn for the purpose of facilitating the election of a second black representative from North Carolina.

These unarguable facts, which the Court devotes most of its opinion to proving, give rise to three constitutional questions: Does the Constitution impose a requirement of contiguity or compactness on how the States may draw their electoral districts? Does the Equal Protection Clause prevent a State from drawing district boundaries for the purpose of facilitating the election of a member of an identifiable group of voters? And, finally, if the answer to the second question is generally "No," should it be different when the favored group is defined by race? Since I have already written at length about these questions, my negative answer to each can be briefly explained.

The first question is easy. There is no independent constitutional requirement of compactness or contiguity, and the Court's opinion (despite its many references to the shape of District 12) does not suggest otherwise. . . .

As for the second question, I believe that the Equal Protection Clause is violated when the Court creates the kind of uncouth district boundaries seen in *Karcher v. Daggett*, 462 U.S. 725 (1983), *Gomillion v. Lightfoot*, 364 U.S. 339 (1960), and this case, for the sole purpose of making it more difficult for members of a minority group to win an election. The duty to govern impartially is abused when a group with power over the electoral process defines electoral boundaries solely to enhance its own political strength at the expense of any weaker group. That duty, however, is not violated when the majority acts to facilitate the election of a member of a group that lacks such power because it remains underrepresented in the state legislature—whether that group is defined by political affiliation, by common economic interests, or by religious, ethnic, or racial characteristics. The difference between constitutional and unconstitutional gerrymanders has nothing to do with whether they are based on assumptions about the groups they affect, but whether their purpose is to enhance the power of the group in control of the districting process at the expense of any minority group, and thereby to strengthen the unequal distribution of electoral power. . . .

Finally, we must ask whether otherwise permissible redistricting to benefit an underrepresented minority group becomes impermissible when the minority group is defined by its race. The Court today answers this question in the affirmative, and its answer is wrong. If it is permissible to draw boundaries to provide adequate representation for rural voters, for union members, for Hasidic Jews, for Polish Americans, or for Republicans, it necessarily follows that it is permissible to do the same thing for members of the very minority group whose history in the United States gave birth to the Equal Protection Clause. A contrary conclusion could only be described as perverse.

☐ *Justice SOUTER, dissenting.*

Until today, the Court has analyzed equal protection claims involving race in electoral districting differently from equal protection claims involving other forms of governmental conduct, and before turning to the different regimes of analysis it will be useful to set out the relevant respects in which such districting differs from the characteristic circumstances in which a State might otherwise consciously consider race. Unlike other contexts in which we have addressed the State's conscious use of race, see, e.g., *Richmond v. J. A. Croson Co.*, 488 U.S. 469 (1989) [city contracting]; *Wygant v. Jackson Bd. of Ed.*, 476 U.S. 267 (1986) [teacher layoffs], electoral districting calls for decisions that nearly always require some consideration of race for legitimate reasons where there is a racially mixed population. As long as members of racial groups have the commonality of interest implicit in our ability to talk about concepts like "minority voting strength," and "dilution of minority votes," *Thornburg v. Gingles*, 478 U.S. 30 (1986), and as long as racial bloc voting takes place, legislators will have to take race into account in order to avoid dilution of minority voting strength in the districting plans they adopt. One need look no further than the Voting Rights Act to understand that this may be required, and we have held that race may constitutionally be taken into account in order to comply with that Act. *United Jewish Organizations of Williamsburgh, Inc. v. Carey*, 430 U.S. 144 (1977).

A second distinction between districting and most other governmental decisions in which race has figured is that those other decisions using racial criteria characteristically occur in circumstances in which the use of race to the advantage of one person is necessarily at the obvious expense of a member of a different race. Thus, for example, awarding government contracts on a racial basis excludes certain firms from competition on racial grounds. See *Richmond v. J. A. Croson Co., supra.* . . . In districting, by contrast, the mere placement of an individual in one district instead of another denies no one a right or benefit provided to others. All citizens may register, vote, and be represented. . . .

A consequence of this categorical approach is the absence of any need for further searching "scrutiny" once it has been shown that a given district-ing decision has a purpose and effect falling within one of those categories. If a cognizable harm like dilution or the abridgment of the right to partici-pate in the electoral process is shown, the districting plan violates the Four-teenth Amendment. If not, it does not. Under this approach, in the absence of an allegation of such cognizable harm, there is no need for further scrutiny because a gerrymandering claim cannot be proven without the ele-ment of harm. . . .

The Court offers no adequate justification for treating the narrow cate-gory of bizarrely shaped district claims differently from other districting claims. The only justification I can imagine would be the preservation of "sound districting principles," such as compactness and contiguity. But as Jus-tice WHITE points out, and as the Court acknowledges, we have held that such principles are not constitutionally required, with the consequence that their absence cannot justify the distinct constitutional regime put in place by the Court today. . . .

I respectfully dissent.

Hunt v. Cromartie

532 U.S. 234, 121 S.CT. 1452 (2001)

For the fourth time, the Court reviewed a challenge to the "racial districting" of North Carolina's congressional District 12, one of two districts initially drawn in 1992 that contained a majority of African American voters. Subsequently, as a result of further litigation, the dis-trict was again redrawn in 1997 and 1998, and again challenged. The district as drawn in 1992, 1997, and 1998 is shown below.

In *Shaw v. Reno*, 509 U.S. 630 (1993) (*Shaw I*) (excerpted in this chapter), the Court held that the legislature had drawn the former

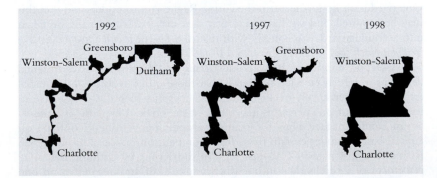

Congressional district 12 as drawn and redrawn in 1992, 1997, and 1998.

district's boundaries for race-based reasons in violation of the Equal Protection Clause, observing that a violation may exist where the legislature's boundary drawing, though "race neutral on its face," nonetheless can be understood only as an effort to "separate voters into different districts on the basis of race," and where the "separation lacks sufficient justification."

In *Shaw v. Hunt,* 517 U.S. 899 (1996) (*Shaw II*), the Court reversed a three-judge district court's holding that the 1992 district did not violate the Constitution. The Court deemed the district's "unconventional" snakelike shape, its predominantly African American racial makeup, and its history to demonstrate a deliberate effort to create an impermissible "majority-black" district.

The Court, then, considered a challenge to a new district as redrawn in 1997, in *Hunt v. Cromartie,* 526 U.S. 541 (1999) (*Hunt I*). A three-judge district court found the legislature again to have used criteria that were "facially race driven," in violation of the Equal Protection Clause. It based this conclusion upon "uncontroverted material facts" showing that the boundaries created an unusually shaped district; split counties and cities; and placed almost all heavily Democratic-registered, predominantly African American voting precincts inside the district, while locating some heavily Democratic-registered, predominantly white precincts outside the district. This latter circumstance, the court concluded, showed that the legislature was trying to maximize the new district's African American voting strength, not the district's Democratic voting strength. That decision, however, was reversed by the Supreme Court in *Hunt I* on finding that neither the evidence by itself nor this evidence coupled with the data on Democratic registration was sufficient to show the unconstitutional race-based objective that plaintiffs claimed.

On remand, the parties undertook additional discovery, the district was redrawn in 1998, and the three-judge district court again held that the legislature had unconstitutionally drawn the district's boundaries. The court found that the legislature had tried to cure the previous district's constitutional defects while also drawing a plan to maintain the existing partisan balance in the State's congressional delegation. It noted that to achieve the latter goal, the legislature "drew the new plan (1) to avoid placing two incumbents in the same district and (2) to preserve the partisan core of the existing districts." But the court also found the legislature to have used criteria that were "facially race driven" without any compelling justification for doing so. The court based its conclusion in part on the district's snakelike shape, the way in which it split cities and towns, and its heavily African American (47%) voting population. The court also concluded that the legislature drew the boundaries in order "to collect precincts with high racial identification rather than political identification." The state appealed that decision and the Supreme Court granted review.

The district court's decision was reversed. The Court's decision was five to four and its opinion delivered by Justice Breyer. Justice Thomas filed a dissenting opinion, which Chief Justice Rehnquist and Justices Scalia and Kennedy joined.

☐ *Justice BREYER delivered the opinion of the Court.*

The issue in this case is evidentiary. We must determine whether there is adequate support for the District Court's key findings, particularly the ultimate finding that the legislature's motive was predominantly racial, not political. In making this determination, we are aware that, under *Shaw I* and later cases, the burden of proof on the plaintiffs (who attack the district) is a "demanding one." *Miller v. Johnson*, 515 U.S. 900 (1995) (O'CONNOR, J., concurring). The Court has specified that those who claim that a legislature has improperly used race as a criterion, in order, for example, to create a majority-minority district, must show at a minimum that the "legislature subordinated traditional race-neutral districting principles . . . to racial considerations." Race must not simply have been "a motivation for the drawing of a majority minority district," *Bush v. Vera*, 517 U.S. 952 (1996) (O'CONNOR, J., principal opinion), but "the 'predominant factor' motivating the legislature's districting decision," *Cromartie [I]*.

The Court also has made clear that the underlying districting decision is one that ordinarily falls within a legislature's sphere of competence. Hence, the legislature "must have discretion to exercise the political judgment necessary to balance competing interests," and courts must "exercise extraordinary caution in adjudicating claims that a State has drawn district lines on the basis of race." Caution is especially appropriate in this case, where the State has articulated a legitimate political explanation for its districting decision, and the voting population is one in which race and political affiliation are highly correlated. . . .

The critical District Court determination—the matter for which we remanded this litigation—consists of the finding that race rather than politics predominantly explains District 12's 1997 boundaries. That determination rests upon three findings (the district's shape, its splitting of towns and counties, and its high African-American voting population) that we previously found insufficient to support summary judgment. Given the undisputed evidence that racial identification is highly correlated with political affiliation in North Carolina, these facts in and of themselves cannot, as a matter of law, support the District Court's judgment. The District Court rested, however, upon five new subsidiary findings to conclude that District 12's lines are the product of no "mer[e] correlat[ion]," but are instead a result of the predominance of race in the legislature's line-drawing process.

In considering each subsidiary finding, we have given weight to the fact that the District Court was familiar with this litigation, heard the testimony of each witness, and considered all the evidence with care. Nonetheless, we cannot accept the District Court's findings as adequate for reasons which we shall spell out in detail and which we can summarize as follows:

First, the primary evidence upon which the District Court relied for its "race, not politics," conclusion is evidence of voting registration, not voting behavior; and that is precisely the kind of evidence that we said was inadequate the last time this case was before us. Second, the additional evidence to which appellees' expert, Dr. Weber, pointed, and the statements made by Senator Cooper and Gerry Cohen, simply do not provide significant additional support for the District Court's conclusion. Third, the District Court, while not accepting the contrary conclusion of appellants' expert, Dr. Peterson, did not (and as far as the record reveals, could not) reject much of the significant supporting factual information he provided. Fourth, in any event, appellees themselves have provided us with charts summarizing evidence of voting behavior and those charts tend to refute the court's "race, not politics," conclusion.

The District Court primarily based its "race, not politics," conclusion upon its finding that "the legislators excluded many heavily-Democratic precincts from District 12, even when those precincts immediately border the Twelfth and would have established a far more compact district." This finding, however—insofar as it differs from the remaining four—rests solely upon evidence that the legislature excluded heavily white precincts with high Democratic Party registration, while including heavily African-American precincts with equivalent, or lower, Democratic Party registration. Indeed, the District Court cites at length figures showing that the legislature included "several precincts with racial compositions of 40 to 100 percent African-American," while excluding certain adjacent precincts "with less than 35 percent African-American population" but which contain between 54% and 76% registered Democrats.

As we said before, the problem with this evidence is that it focuses upon party registration, not upon voting behavior. And we previously found the same evidence inadequate because registration figures do not accurately predict preference at the polls. In part this is because white voters registered as Democrats "cross-over" to vote for a Republican candidate more often than do African-Americans, who register and vote Democratic between 95% and 97% of the time. A legislature trying to secure a safe Democratic seat is interested in Democratic voting behavior. Hence, a legislature may, by placing reliable Democratic precincts within a district without regard to race, end up with a district containing more heavily African-American precincts, but the reasons would be political rather than racial.

Insofar as the District Court relied upon voting registration data, particularly data that were previously before us, it tells us nothing new; and the data do not help answer the question posed when we previously remanded this litigation. . . .

The District Court also relied on two pieces of "direct" evidence of discriminatory intent. The court found that a legislative redistricting leader, Senator Roy Cooper, when testifying before a legislative committee in 1997, had said that the 1997 plan satisfies a "need for 'racial and partisan' balance." The court concluded that the words "racial balance" referred to a 10-to-2 Caucasian/African-American balance in the State's 12-member congressional delegation. Hence, Senator Cooper had admitted that the legislature had drawn the plan with race in mind. . . . We agree that one can read the statement about "racial . . . balance" as the District Court read it—to refer to the current congressional delegation's racial balance. But even as so read, the phrase shows that the legislature considered race, along with other partisan and geographic considerations; and as so read it says little or nothing about whether race played a predominant role comparatively speaking.

The second piece of "direct" evidence relied upon by the District Court is a February 10, 1997, e-mail sent from Gerry Cohen, a legislative staff member responsible for drafting districting plans, to Senator Cooper and Senator Leslie Winner. Cohen wrote: "I have moved Greensboro Black community into the 12th, and now need to take [about] 60,000 out of the 12th. I await your direction on this."

The reference to race—i.e., "Black community"—is obvious. But the e-mail does not discuss the point of the reference. It does not discuss why Greensboro's African-American voters were placed in the 12th District; it does not discuss the political consequences of failing to do so; it is addressed only to two members of the legislature; and it suggests that the legislature paid less attention to race in respect to the 12th District than in respect to the 1st District, where the e-mail provides a far more extensive, detailed discussion of racial percentages. It is less persuasive than the kinds of direct evidence we have found significant in other redistricting cases. Nonetheless, the e-mail offers some support for the District Court's conclusion. . . .

We concede the record contains a modicum of evidence offering support for the District Court's conclusion. That evidence includes the Cohen e-mail, Senator Cooper's reference to "racial balance," and to a minor degree, some aspects of Dr. Weber's testimony. The evidence taken together, however, does not show that racial considerations predominated in the drawing of District 12's boundaries. That is because race in this case correlates closely with political behavior. The basic question is whether the legislature drew District 12's boundaries because of race rather than because of political behavior (coupled with traditional, nonracial districting considerations). It is not, as the dissent contends, whether a legislature may defend its districting decisions based on a "stereotype" about African-American voting behavior. And given the fact that the party attacking the legislature's decision bears the burden of proving that racial considerations are "dominant and controlling," given the "demanding" nature of that burden of proof, and given the sensitivity, the "extraordinary caution," that district courts must show to avoid treading upon legislative prerogatives, the attacking party has not successfully shown that race, rather than politics, predominantly accounts for the result. The record leaves us with the "definite and firm conviction" that the District Court erred in finding to the contrary. And we do not believe that providing appellees a further opportunity to make their "precinct swapping" arguments in the District Court could change this result.

We can put the matter more generally as follows: In a case such as this one where majority-minority districts (or the approximate equivalent) are at issue and where racial identification correlates highly with political affiliation, the party attacking the legislatively drawn boundaries must show at the least that the legislature could have achieved its legitimate political objectives in alternative ways that are comparably consistent with traditional districting principles. That party must also show that those districting alternatives would have brought about significantly greater racial balance. Appellees failed to make any such showing here. We conclude that the District Court's contrary findings are clearly erroneous.

The judgment of the District Court is Reversed.

☐ *Justice THOMAS, with whom THE CHIEF JUSTICE, Justice SCALIA, and Justice KENNEDY join, dissenting.*

The District Court's conclusion that race was the predominant factor motivating the North Carolina Legislature is a factual finding. See *Hunt v. Cromartie*, 526 U.S. 541 (1999); *Shaw v. Hunt*, 517 U.S. 899 (1996); *Miller v. Johnson*, 515 U.S. 900 (1995). Accordingly, we should not overturn the District Court's determination unless it is clearly erroneous. . . .

Reviewing for clear error, I cannot say that the District Court's view of the evidence was impermissible. First, the court relied on objective measures of compactness, which show that District 12 is the most geographically scattered district in North Carolina, to support its conclusion that the district's design was not dictated by traditional districting concerns. Although this evidence was available when we held that summary judgment was inappropriate, we certainly did not hold that it was irrelevant in determining whether racial gerrymandering occurred. On the contrary, we determined that there was a triable issue of fact. Moreover, although we acknowledged "that a district's unusual shape can give rise to an inference of political motivation," we "doubt[ed] that a bizarre shape equally supports a political inference and a racial one." *Hunt.* As we explained, "[s]ome districts . . . are 'so highly irregular that [they] rationally cannot be understood as anything other than an effort to segregat[e] voters' on the basis of race."

Second, the court relied on the expert opinion of Dr. Weber, who interpreted statistical data to conclude that there were Democratic precincts with low black populations excluded from District 12, which would have created a more compact district had they been included. And contrary to the Court's assertion, Dr. Weber did not merely examine the registration data in reaching his conclusions. Dr. Weber explained that he refocused his analysis on performance. He did so in response to our concerns, when we reversed the District Court's summary judgment finding, that voter registration might not be the best measure of the Democratic nature of a precinct. This fact was not lost on the District Court, which specifically referred to those pages of the record covering Dr. Weber's analysis of performance.

Third, the court credited Dr. Weber's testimony that the districting decisions could not be explained by political motives. In the first instance, I, like the Court, might well have concluded that District 12 was not significantly "safer" than several other districts in North Carolina merely because its Democratic reliability exceeded the optimum by only 3 percent. And I might have concluded that it would make political sense for incumbents to adopt a "the more reliable the better" policy in districting. However, I certainly cannot say that the court's inference from the facts was impermissible.

Fourth, the court discredited the testimony of the State's witness, Dr. Peterson. Again, like the Court, if I were a district court judge, I might have found that Dr. Weber's insistence that one could not ignore the core was unpersuasive. However, even if the core could be ignored, it seems to me that Dr. Weber's testimony—that Dr. Peterson had failed to analyze all of the segments and thus that his analysis was incomplete—reasonably could have supported the court's conclusion.

Finally, the court found that other evidence demonstrated that race was foremost on the legislative agenda: an e-mail from the drafter of the 1992 and 1997 plans to senators in charge of legislative redistricting, the computer capability to draw the district by race, and statements made by Senator Cooper that the legislature was going to be able to avoid *Shaw*'s majority-minority trigger by ending just short of the majority. The e-mail, in combination with the indirect evidence, is evidence ample enough to support the District Court's finding for purposes of clear error review. The drafter of the redistricting plans reported in the bluntest of terms: "I have moved Greensboro Black community into the 12th [District], and now need to take . . . 60,000 out of the 12th [District]." Certainly the District Court was entitled to believe that the drafter was targeting voters and shifting district boundaries purely on the basis of race. The Court tries to belittle the import of this evidence by noting that the e-mail does not discuss why blacks were being targeted. However, the District Court was assigned the task of determining

---

■ THE DEVELOPMENT OF LAW

Other Post–Shaw v. Reno *Rulings on Racial Gerrymandering*

CASE	VOTE	RULING
Johnson v. De Grandy, 512 U.S. 997 (1994)	7:2	Writing for the majority, Justice Souter overturned a court-ordered redistricting

plan for Florida's House of Representatives. The plan would have increased the number of Hispanic majority districts from nine to eleven out of a total of twenty districts. Although observing that such minority-majority districts are permissible under the Voting Rights Act and sometimes necessary in order to increase minorities' representation, Justice Souter held that the act does not require creating the greatest possible number of minority-majority districts. Once a minority group has achieved representation in "rough proportion to its population," said Souter, the Voting Rights Act requires nothing more. Notably, though, Justice Souter avoided ruling on such related issues as how to measure the size of minority groups, whether as part of the overall population, the voting-age population, or the number of citizens eligible to vote. Specifying a "magic parameter," claimed the justice, was not necessary here. Justices Scalia and Thomas dissented.

whether, not why, race predominated. As I see it, this inquiry is sufficient to answer the constitutional question because racial gerrymandering offends the Constitution whether the motivation is malicious or benign. It is not a defense that the legislature merely may have drawn the district based on the stereotype that blacks are reliable Democratic voters. And regardless of whether the e-mail tended to show that the legislature was operating under an even stronger racial motivation when it was drawing District 1 than when it was drawing District 12, I am convinced that the District Court permissibly could have accorded great weight to this e-mail as direct evidence of a racial motive. . . .

The only question that this Court should decide is whether the District Court's finding of racial predominance was clearly erroneous. In light of the direct evidence of racial motive and the inferences that may be drawn from the circumstantial evidence, I am satisfied that the District Court's finding was permissible, even if not compelled by the record.

CASE	VOTE	RULING
Holder v. Hall, 512 U.S. 874 (1994)	5:4	The decision, reversing an appellate court's decision ordering the change from a

single-member county commission to a five-member commission with districts drawn so that at least one black commissioner could be elected, splintered the Court's bare majority three ways in different opinions. Black voters had challenged the permissibility of the single-member commission under Section 2 of the Voting Rights Act, in Bleckley, Georgia, where 20 percent of the population is black but where a black commissioner had never been elected to office. With only Chief Justice Rehnquist and Justice O'Connor joining his opinion for the Court, Justice Kennedy rejected the claim that the Voting Rights Act permits challenges to the size of a governmental body or organization. He did so upon concluding that it was impossible to determine what size or structure would be best. The result reached by these three justices was joined by concurring Justices Scalia and Thomas, though for different reasons and in order to form a bare majority. They agreed with the result, but they would have held that the Voting Rights Act does not govern race-conscious districting in the first place. Justice Thomas also expressly rejected over two decades of the Court's jurisprudence in the area of voting rights and the idea that minority-vote dilution is central to interpreting the Voting Rights Act. The four dissenters—Justices Blackmun, Ginsburg, Souter, and Stevens—countered that it was "clear" from the history of Bleckley County that the single-member commission had the effect of diluting the voting power of blacks.

(continues)

■ The Development of Law
*Other Post–*Shaw v. Reno *Rulings on Racial Gerrymandering (continued)*

CASE	VOTE	RULING
Miller v. Johnson, 512 U.S. 622 (1995)	5:4	After the 1990 census, it was determined that Georgia's population, 27 percent of

whom are black, merited an additional eleventh congressional district. Subsequently, Georgia's general assembly redrew district lines so as to create two minority-majority districts and another in which blacks comprised more than 35 percent of the votingage population. The Bush administration's Department of Justice, however, rejected the plan and pushed an alternative "Max-Black plan" that created three minority-majority districts. The assembly accordingly redrew the districts, but the constitutionality of that redistricting was challenged as impermissible racial gerrymandering under the Fourteenth Amendment. Writing for the Court, Justice Kennedy held that the bizarreness of the redrawn district was not problematic, but the preoccupation with the racial composition of the districts triggered strict scrutiny, and constituted impermissible redistricting, under the Fourteenth Amendment. Justices Stevens, Souter, Ginsburg, and Breyer dissented.

CASE	VOTE	RULING
Bush v. Vera, 517 U.S. 952 (1996)	5:4	Following the 1990 census, Texas was entitled to three additional congressional seats.

Using a computer program called "REDAPPL," which permitted the manipulation of district lines on a block-by-block level according to racial and other socioeconomic data, the Texas legislature created two districts that were predominantly Hispanic and one that was predominantly African American. The constitutionality of those districts was subsequently challenged. Writing for the Court, Justice O'Connor held that the redistricting based on the use of REDAPPL was constitutionally impermissible. But Justice O'Connor did not rule out the use of race as one factor in redistricting and in a separate concurring opinion emphasized that compliance with Section 2 of the Voting Rights Act may in some circumstances require the creation of minority-majority districts. Dissenting Justice Stevens, joined by Justices Souter, Ginsburg, and Breyer, countered that based on the facts of the case it was not clear that race was the predominant factor in redrawing the district line and emphasized that under the plan 97 percent of the incumbents were reelected.

CASE	VOTE	RULING

Shaw v. Hunt, (Shaw II) 517 U.S. 899 5:4 (1996)   5:4   Following the ruling in *Shaw v. Reno (Shaw I)* (1993) (excerpted in this chapter), the Court held that the redistricting of North Carolina's congressional districts and creation of a second minority-majority district was permissible and narrowly tailored to the state's compelling interests in complying with Sections 2 and 5 of the Voting Rights Act. Writing for the Court, Chief Justice Rehnquist ruled that compliance with Sections 2 and 5 of the Voting Rights Act does not justify race-conscious redistricting and reaffirmed that race-dominated redistricting does not survive strict scrutiny and runs afoul of the Fourteenth Amendment. Dissenting Justice Stevens, joined by Justices Souter, Ginsburg, and Breyer, countered that race was not the predominant factor in the redistricting.

Lawyer v. Department of Justice, 521 U.S. 567 (1997)   5:4   Writing for a bare majority, Justice Souter rejected a challenge to the configuration of a Florida legislative district under the Fourteenth Amendment's equal protection clause and the contention that a federal district court should have found a proposed districting plan unconstitutional before approving a mediated redistricting settlement. Following the 1990 census the state legislature adopted a reapportionment plan, but the Department of Justice declined to give it preclearance approval under the Voting Rights Act on the grounds that it failed to create a minority-majority in the Tampa district. When the state legislature failed to redraw the district because it was out of session, the Supreme Court of Florida revised the redistricting plan to address the Justice Department's objection. That plan called for an irregularly shaped district with a voting-age population 45.8 percent black and 9.4 percent Hispanic, comprising portions of four counties. In 1994, six residents of that proposed district challenged its constitutionality in federal district court. A three-judge district court was convened and permitted intervention in the suit by the state legislature, the governor, and a group of black and Hispanic voters. Shortly after the Court decided *Miller v. Johnson*, 512 U.S. 622 (1995), all the parties agreed to the appointment of a mediator for the dispute. Subsequently, in 1995 a settlement agreement was signed by all the parties except the appellant. The agreement proposed revising the Tampa district by decreasing its length by 58 percent, reducing the black voting-age population from 45.8 to 36.2 percent, and including portions of three counties instead of four.

(continues)

■ THE DEVELOPMENT OF LAW
*Other Post–*Shaw v. Reno *Rulings on Racial
Gerrymandering (continued)*

CASE	VOTE	RULING

The appellant, however, maintained that the district court was required to hold the original plan unconstitutional before adopting the revised plan. The district court disagreed and in March 1996 approved the settlement, concluding that the constitutional objection to the proposed district was not established. In its view, the district's shape and composition was "demonstrably benign and satisfactorily tidy, especially given the prevailing geography." Dissenting from the majority's affirmance of that decision, Justice Scalia, joined by Justices O'Connor, Kennedy, and Thomas, countered that the lower court's decision represented "an unprecedented intrusion upon state sovereignty."

Meadows v. Moon, **521 U.S. 1113 (1997)** — 9:0 — Without comment, the Court Court affirmed a federal district court's ruling invalidating Virginia's only majority-black congressional district as an unconstitutional racial gerry-mander. The challenged district ran from Richmond to the Tidewater area in irregular ways that made for a 64 percent black voting population.

Georgia v. Ashcroft, **539 U.S. 461 (2003)** — 5:4 — The Court held that under Section 5 of the Voting Rights Act, legislative and congressional districts may be redrawn in ways that shrink black voting majorities in order to create more Democratic-leaning districts. Georgia's redistricting reduced black majorities in three districts to just over 50 percent, down from 62 to 55 percent. Writing for the Court, Justice O'Connor held that in assessing the racial regressive effect all factors may be considered, including a minority group's voting participation in a coalitional district. Dissenting Justices Stevens, Souter, Ginsburg, and Breyer accused the majority of gutting the act's prohibition against redistricting that is regressive for minority voting rights.

CASE	VOTE	RULING
Bartlett v. Strickland, 129 S.C. 1231 (2009)	5:4	Writing for a plurality, Justice Kennedy held that Section 2 of the Voting Rights

Act does not require states to redraw voting district lines to allow racial minorities to vote in a district where a minority group comprises 50 percent of the population. In spite of North Carolina's constitutional "whole county" provision, prohibiting the general assembly from dividing counties when redrawing legislative districts, in 1991 the legislature redrew House District 18 to include portions of four counties, including Pender County, which at the time was a geographically compact majority-minority voting district. However, when that district was to be redrawn in 2003, the African American population had fallen below 50 percent, and instead of redrawing Pender County whole, the legislature split the district and crossed over portions of other districts. As a result, District 18 African American voting age population was 39.36 percent, whereas if Pender County's district had remained whole it would have had an African American voting age population of 35.33 percent. The rationale was that splitting Pender County gave African American voters the potential to elect a minority group's candidate, while leaving Pender County whole would have violated Section 2 of the Voting Rights Act. In Justice Kennedy's words, "There is an underlying principle of fundamental importance: We must be most cautious before interpreting a statute to require courts to make inquiries based on racial classifications and race-based predictions," though adding that "Racial discrimination and racially polarized voting are not ancient history. . . . Much remains to be done to ensure that citizens of all races have equal opportunity to share and participate in our democratic processes and traditions." By contrast, concurring Justice Thomas, joined by Justice Scalia, contended that the Voting Rights Act does not authorize any claim by minority voters that their influence is diluted in redistricting, no matter the size of the minority. Justices Stevens, Souter, Ginsburg, and Breyer dissented.

C | *Campaigns and Elections*

Since the 1960s, the Supreme Court has increasingly assumed a supervisory role in overseeing the electoral process. This is only partially due to the reapportionment revolution and the Court's duty to ensure compliance with the Voting Rights Act. In addition, the Court has applied the Fourteenth Amendment equal protection clause to bar invidious forms of discrimination in the electoral process and interpreted the First Amendment guarantee for freedom of association to protect some aspects of political parties, campaigns, and elections.

Notably, in an extraordinary ruling in *Bush v. Gore* (2000) (excerpted below) the Court reversed the Florida state supreme court's decision ordering manual recounts of statewide votes in the 2000 presidential election. Seven members of the Court deemed the state supreme court's recount order to be standardless and thus in violation of the Fourteenth Amendment equal protection clause. But a bare majority of the Court held that there was no remedy available, thereby securing the election of President George W. Bush.

Besides striking down poll taxes and literacy tests,[1] the Court has limited the power of states to control access to elections through residency requirements for voters. The Voting Rights Act of 1970 limited residency requirements to a thirty-day registration period for presidential elections. While the Court in *Dunn v. Blumstein*, 405 U.S. 330 (1972), indicated that that period of time appeared "ample" for state elections as well, fifty-day registration periods were subsequently upheld.[2] The Court also ruled that states may not bar military personnel, or others in a federal enclave, from voting in state elections.[3] States may deny convicted felons the right to vote, but *O'Brien v. Kinner*, 414 U.S. 524 (1974), held that persons in jail awaiting trial must be provided with absentee ballots or an alternative means of voting.

Under the Fourteenth Amendment equal protection clause, the Court strictly scrutinizes electoral systems for discriminating against minorities and the poor by imposing special burdens on their running for office and voting. In *Newberry v. United States*, 256 U.S. 232 (1921), however, the Court took the view that primaries were "in no real sense part of the manner of holding [an] election." Consequently, some southern states sought to discriminate against blacks at this stage of the electoral process. But *Nixon v. Herndon*, 273 U.S. 536 (1927), invalidated Texas's prohibition on blacks voting in primary elections as a denial of the Fourteenth Amendment equal protection clause. *Nixon v. Condon*, 286 U.S. 73 (1932), then struck down another attempt by Texas to disenfranchise blacks by authorizing political parties to specify the qualifications of voters in primary elections. Following that ruling and in the absence of state legislation, the Texas Democratic Party voted to deny the participation of blacks in its primary elections. The Court upheld this practice in *Grovey v. Townsend*, 295 U.S. 45 (1935), on *Newberry's* theory that primaries are exempt from the constitutional restraints that bind official state action. Six years later, though, the Hughes Court ruled that primaries are "an integral part" of the political process, when sustaining the convictions of several Louisiana officials who tampered with primary ballots in a congressional election. Finally, in *Smith v. Allwright*, 321 U.S. 649 (1944), *Newberry* and *Grovey* were abandoned. There the Court held that primaries and political parties, which are in various ways subject to state regulation, are integral to the operation of state and local governments and as such constitute "an agent of the state" subject to the proscriptions of the Fourteenth and Fifteenth Amendments. *Terry v. Adams*, 345 U.S. 461 (1953), extended this ruling to unofficial primaries in Texas run by the Jaybird Party, a Democratic county organization that excluded blacks. In the Court's words, the "Jaybird primary has become an integral part, indeed the only effective part, of the elective process that determines who shall rule and govern in the county." As such, the Jaybird Party primary was invalid under the Fifteenth Amendment.

The Court has also stood against other attempts by states to keep third-party candidates off the ballot. *Williams v. Rhodes*, 393 U.S. 23 (1968), for example, invalidated an Ohio law requiring third parties (although not established political parties) to file petitions with more than 400,000 signatures of registered voters to have a candidate's name placed on the ballot. In several other cases the Court struck down similar state requirements for the submission of petitions and early filing deadlines as a precondition for a candidate's being placed on the ballot.[4] *Communist Party of Indiana v. Whitcomb*, 414 U.S. 441 (1974), overturned a law requiring loyalty oaths of candidates of minority parties as an infringement of the First Amendment right of free speech and association. A series of other rulings invalidated state laws imposing exorbitant filing fees for getting on the ballot.[5]

The Court has dealt as well with a number of controversies arising from political parties' organization, conventions, and campaigns. After a couple of contradictory rulings on the seating of delegates at party conventions, *Cousins v. Wigoda*, 419 U.S. 477 (1975), held that the national party convention has the power to decide the credentials of convention delegates and how delegates from state political parties will be seated at a national convention. There the Court affirmed political parties' freedom to determine the composition of their conventions as protected by First Amendment right of association. *Democratic Party v. LaFollette*, 450 U.S. 107 (1981), further ruled that states could not mandate that state delegates to a national political convention cast their votes for the winner of the state's presidential primary. However, *Marchioro v. Chaney*, 442 U.S. 191 (1979), allowed that states could demand that state political parties have at least two persons from each county in the state.

Controversies over campaign finance have increasingly come to the Court since Congress passed the Federal Election Campaign Act of 1971. That law limits the amount of money individuals and groups may contribute to candidates and political parties, imposes spending limits and reporting requirements, and created an eight-member commission to oversee the law's implementation. The Court was badly split in *Buckley v. Valeo* (1976) (see excerpt below), when upholding limitations on political contributions but overturning restrictions on campaign spending. In *Brown v. Socialist Workers 74 Campaign Committee*, 459 U.S. 87 (1982), requirements for the disclosure of lists of contributors as applied to the Socialist Workers Party were deemed to violate the First Amendment right of freedom of association. Subsequently, *Federal Election Commission v. National Conservative Political Action Committee (NCPAC)* (1985) (excerpted below) invalidated the law's restrictions on campaign expenditures by political action committees. In both *Buckley* and *NCPAC*, the Court balanced the First Amendment right of association against Congress's interest in eliminating corruption in campaigns and electoral politics. The Court also struck down as a violation of the First Amendment the limitations on independent campaign expenditures by political parties as set forth in the Federal Election Campaign Act (FECA). Under FECA, political parties may not spend more than $20,000, or two cents times the voting age population of a state, in Senate races; limits on expenditures in races for the House of Representatives are about $30,000. In *Colorado Republican Federal Campaign Committee v. Federal Election Commission*, 518 U.S. 515 (1996), the Court held that the limits on expenditures in Senate races were unconstitutional but it did not address the constitutionality of spending limits on congressional elections or the larger issue of the FECA's limitations on political parties' campaign expenditures made in conjunction with a candidate's campaign committee. In *Federal Election Commission v. Colorado Republican Federal Campaign Committee*, 533 U.S. 431 (2001), a bare majority upheld that restriction on political parties' expenditures. The Court also upheld a 1907 restriction on corporations from directly contributing to candidates for federal office in rejecting a challenge to that law by a nonprofit advocacy corporation, the North Carolina Right to Life, Inc., in *Federal Election Commission v. Beaumont*, 539 U.S. 146 (2003).

In *McConnell v. Federal Election Commission* (2003) (excerpted below) a bare majority not only reaffirmed but extended *Buckley v. Valeo* in upholding most of the provisions of the Bipartisan Campaign Reform Act (BCRA) of 2002. The BCRA bans the spending of "soft money" (unregulated money) and "issue advocacy" (communications by corporations and unions) that target a specific audience and mention a candidate by name, without mentioning the election, within thirty days of a primary and 60 days of a general election. Under the campaign finance reforms, individuals' campaign contributions are limited to $4,000 per candidate in an election cycle, and PACs are limited to spending $10,000 per election cycle (primary and general elections). So-called 527 groups, named for a section of the Internal Revenue Service code, may still spend, as they notably did in the 2004 presidential election, unlimited money on election activities, so long as they do not do so thirty days before a primary or in the last sixty days before a general election, and they still use "hard money" to pay for ads closer to election days. Although upholding most of the restrictions of the BCRA, the Court struck down a provision that would have banned all campaign contributions by individuals under the age of eighteen.

However, a bare majority of the Roberts Court held, in *Federal Election Commission v. Wisconsin Right to Life, Inc.* (2007) (excerpted below), that Section 203 of the Bipartisan Campaign Reform Act (BCRA), known as the "McCain-Feingold law" after its sponsors, which made it a crime for corporations and unions to use general funds for "electioneering communications" that refer to a candidate within thirty days of federal primary elections and sixty days of a general election, was unconstitutional "as applied" to the campaign ads by the Wisconsin Right to Life, Inc. and other organizations. Writing for a plurality, Chief Justice Roberts, though, declined to overturn the bare majority's upholding of the provision in *McConnell v. Federal Election Commission*, (2003) (excerpted below). Concurring Justices Scalia, Kennedy, and Thomas agreed, but would have expressly overruled *McConnell*. By contrast, dissenting Justice Souter, joined by Justices Stevens, Ginsburg, and Breyer, sharply disagreed and countered that the majority had effectively overturned *McConnell*. Subsequently in *Davis v. Federal Election Commission* 128 S.Ct. 2759 (2008), the Court invalidated Section 319, the so-called Millionaires' Amendment to the Bipartisan Campaign Reform Act of 2002 (BCRA), for violating the First and Fifth Amendments. The Millionaires' Amendment provided equalizing advantages to a candidate relying primarily on contributed funds in campaigns against a self-financed candidate. House of Representatives candidate Jack Davis challenged the law in federal district court in anticipation that his personal expenditures would exceed the statutory limitation in an upcoming election. Davis claimed that the provision violated his First and Fifth Amendment rights through its disclosure requirements and contribution limitations. Under the law, a candidate for the House who spent more than $350,000 of his or her own money triggered additional reporting requirements; the law also permitted the candidate's opponents to solicit three times the normal limit of $2,300 per contributor and granted greater spending by the opponent's party on behalf of the candidate. Writing for the majority, Justice Alito held that the provisions forced self-financed candidates "to choose between the right to engage in unfettered political speech and subjection to discriminatory fund raising levels," and that "the resulting drag on First Amendment right" was unconstitutional. Justices Stevens and Ginsburg issued separate opinions, in part concurring and dissenting, which Justices Souter and Breyer joined. The decision invites further challenges to state laws, such as Arizona's, North Carolina's, and Maine's, that penalize private funding of elections and promote public funding of campaigns. Finally, a bare majority of the Roberts Court overturned two prior rulings, including portions of *McConnell*, in a major holding that the First Amendment protects corporations' direct expenditures for candidates for federal office, in *Citizens United v. Federal Election Commission* (2010) (excerpted below).

Other issues affecting campaigns and elections have been dealt with under the First Amendment's safeguards for freedom of speech and press. *CBS, Inc. v. Federal Communications Commission*, 453 U.S. 367 (1981), for instance, affirmed an FCC order that CBS, Inc., sell airtime for advertisements for candidates running in the 1980 presidential election.[6] For other rulings, see THE DEVELOPMENT OF LAW box in this section.

Under the First Amendment commercial speech doctrine (see Vol. 2, Ch. 5), the Court has struck down state laws restricting the political expenditures and advertising of corporations. *First National Bank of Boston v. Bellotti*, 435 U.S. 765 (1978), overturned Massachusetts's law forbidding corporations from publicizing their views on an income-tax referendum and making campaign contributions. *Consolidated Edison Company of New York v. Public Service Commission of the State of New York*, 447 U.S. 530 (1980), and *Pacific Gas & Electric v. Public Utilities Commission of California*, 475 U.S. 1 (1986), held that states may not force public utility companies to include in their newsletters and billing statements the materials of third parties addressing controversial issues of public policy with which the companies disagree.

In recent years, there has also been a growing concern not only about limiting campaign contributions and expenditures but also about imposing limits on what candidates may say in elections for judicial office. In *Republican Party of Minnesota v. White* (2002) (excerpted below), however, a bare majority struck down, as a violation of the First Amendment, a state prohibition on candidates for judicial office announcing their views on controversial legal and political issues.

In a highly controversial ruling in *Elrod v. Burns*, 427 U.S. 347 (1976), the justices, voting five to three, with Justice Stevens not participating, struck down the practice of patronage dismissals as an unconstitutional restriction on city employees' First Amendment freedoms. The controversy and struggle within the Court over the permissibility of political patronage continued in *Branti v. Finkel*, 445 U.S. 507 (1980). There the justices, six to three, with Stewart, Powell, and Rehnquist dissenting, ruled that the First Amendment protects district attorneys from being discharged for expressing their political views. But after Justice Stewart retired in 1981 and was replaced by Justice O'Connor, the Court held five to four (with Brennan, Blackmun, Marshall, and Stevens now dissenting), in *Connick v. Myers*, 461 U.S. 138 (1983), that the firing of state attorneys general for political reasons does not violate the First Amendment. But in *Rutan v. Republican Party of Illinois* (1990) (excerpted below), Justice Brennan pulled together a bare majority for sharply limiting political patronage in the hiring, promoting, and transferring of most public employees.

The First Amendment protections recognized in *Elrod, Branti,* and *Rutan* were in turn extended to independent contractors with the government in *Board of County Commissioners, Wabaunsee County, Kansas v. Umbehr*, 518 U.S. 668 (1996), and *O'Hare Truck Service, Inc. v. City of Northlake*, 518 U.S. 712 (1996). Keen Umbehr, a trash hauler for the county and an outspoken critic of the county board, had his contract terminated (so that it would not be automatically renewed) and contended that the county's retaliation for his criticisms violated the First Amendment. The Court agreed, holding that the First Amendment protects independent contractors from termination of their government contracts in retaliation for the exercise of their free speech. However, reaffirming rulings in *Connick v. Myers*, 461 U.S. 128 (1983), and *Pickering v. Board of Education of Township High School District*, 391 U.S. 563 (1968), Justice O'Connor in her opinion for the Court emphasized that

> Umbehr must show that the termination of his contract was motivated by his speech on a matter of public concern, an initial showing that requires him to prove more than the mere fact that he criticized the Board members before they terminated him. If he can make that showing, the Board will have a valid defense if it can show, by a preponderance of the evidence, that, in light of their knowledge, perceptions and policies at the time of the termination,

the Board members would have terminated the contract regardless of his speech. The Board will also prevail if it can persuade the District Court that the County's legitimate interests as contractor, deferentially viewed, outweigh the free speech interests at stake. And, if Umbehr prevails, evidence that the Board members discovered facts after termination that would have led to a later termination anyway, and evidence of mitigation of his loss by means of his subsequent contracts with the cities, would be relevant in assessing what remedy is appropriate.

In *O'Hare Truck Service, Inc.*, the protections accorded in *Elrod*, *Branti*, and *Rutan* to government employees were extended by the Court to independent contractors or regular providers of service to the government. Here, the owner of O'Hare Truck Service, Inc., refused to contribute to the mayor's reelection campaign and instead supported his opponent. After the mayor's reelection, the owner's contract was terminated and he sued. Writing for the Court, Justice Breyer held that independent contractors, no less than public employees, may not be discharged for refusing to support a political party or its candidates. As in *Rutan*, Justice Scalia dissented in *Umbehr* and *O'Hare Truck Service*; both of his dissents were joined by Justice Thomas.

Most recently, in *Garcetti v. Ceballos*, 547 U.S. 410 (2006), the Roberts Court split five to four in holding that government employees do not receive First Amendment free speech protection against a supervisor's alleged retaliation for their on-the-job speech criticizing office policy and practices. Writing for the majority, however, Justice Kennedy noted that employees still have First Amendment protection as citizens to voice their views publicly in, for example, letters to the editor or in op-ed articles in newspapers. Justices Souter, Stevens, Ginsburg, and Breyer dissented.

Finally, in *McCormick v. United States*, 500 U.S. 257 (1991), the Court revisited the issue of how and on what basis the line between bribery and campaign contributions should be drawn. At issue in *McCormick* was whether federal prosecutors may use, and on what evidentiary basis, federal extortion laws to prosecute and punish state-elected officials who allegedly extort bribery money but who claim they were merely soliciting campaign contributions. A former West Virginia state legislator, Robert McCormick, appealed his conviction for violating federal law by soliciting money a week before a state primary election from a group of foreign doctors, who repeatedly failed to qualify for medical licenses and who sought special legislation enabling them to practice in the state. McCormick received five cash contributions, totaling $5,250, in violation of state laws limiting campaign contributions to $50. In addition, he failed to report the money on both campaign disclosure forms and his state and federal income tax returns. Both federal prosecutors and McCormick's attorney agreed that campaign contributions do not constitute extortion without evidence of out-and-out vote selling. But McCormick's attorney argued that the logic and evidence used to convict him would potentially render every lawmaker who solicits campaign contributions a federal felon.

By a six-to-three vote overturning McCormick's conviction, the Rehnquist Court made it harder for federal prosecutors to prosecute politicians for extortion in soliciting campaign contributions. Writing for the majority, Justice Byron White held that prosecutors must show that a campaign contributor gave money to a politician in exchange for an "explicit promise" of help. "Money," as Justice White put it, "is constantly being solicited on behalf of candidates, who run on platforms and who claim support on the basis of their views and what they intend to do or have done." Regardless of "[w]hatever ethical considerations and appearances may indicate," he ruled that it would be "unrealistic" to hold that legislators commit extortion when they do something for constituents who have donated money to their campaigns in response to their solicitations. "To hold otherwise," White concluded, "would open to prosecution not only conduct that has long been thought to be well within the law but also conduct that in a very real sense is unavoidable so long as election campaigns are financed by private contributions or expenditures, as they have been from the beginning of the nation."

NOTES

1. In addition, the Court struck down so-called grandfather clauses, which exempted persons from literacy tests if their ancestors were entitled to vote at some specified time. See *Guinn v. United States*, 238 U.S. 347 (1915); and *Lane v. Wilson*, 307 U.S. 268 (1939).

2. *Marston v. Lewis*, 410 U.S. 679 (1973); and *Burns v. Fortson*, 410 U.S. 686 (1973).

3. See *Carrington v. Rash*, 380 U.S. 89 (1965); and *Evans v. Cornman*, 398 U.S. 419 (1970).

4. See *Moore v. Ogilvie*, 394 U.S. 814 (1969), overturning Illinois's requirement that for candidates to get on the ballot, they must file petitions signed by 25,000 registered voters, and the Court's earlier ruling in *MacDougall v. Green*, 335 U.S. 281 (1948). *Anderson v. Celebrezze*, 460 U.S. 780 (1983), struck down Ohio's early filing deadline for candidates not belonging to a major political party.

5. See *Bullock v. Carter*, 405 U.S. 134 (1972), striking down a Texas law requiring a filing fee of up to $8,900; and *Lubin v. Parish*, 415 U.S. 709 (1974), finding that California's filing fees (of $701.50) for candidates was not unreasonable but, because there were no alternative ways of getting on the ballot, the requirement was discriminatory. See also *Illinois State Board of Elections v. Socialist Workers Party*, 440 U.S. 173 (1979).

6. But see also *CBS v. Democratic National Committee*, 412 U.S. 94 (1973), approving CBS's policy of refusing paid editorial advertisements (see Vol. 2, Ch. 5).

SELECTED BIBLIOGRAPHY

Banks, Christopher, ed. *Superintending Democracy: The Courts and the Political Process.* Akron, OH: University of Akron Press, 2001.

————, Cohen, David B., and Green, John, eds. *The Final Arbiter: The Consequences of Bush v. Gore for Law and Politics.* Albany: State University of New York Press, 2005.

Dershowitz, Alan M. *Supreme Injustice: How the High Court Hijacked Election 2000.* New York: Oxford University Press, 2001.

Gais, Thomas. *Improper Influence: Campaign Finance Law, Political Interest Groups, and the Problem of Equality.* Ann Arbor: University of Michigan Press, 1996.

Gillman, Howard. *The Votes that Counted: How the Court Decided the 2000 Presidential Election.* Chicago: University of Chicago Press, 2001.

Morris, Roy, Jr. *Fraud of the Century: Rutherford B. Hayes, Samuel Tilden, and the Stolen Election of 1876.* New York: Simon & Schuster, 2003.

Pinaire, Brian. *The Constitution of Electoral Speech Law: The Supreme Court and Freedom of Expression in Campaigns and Elections.* Palo Alto, CA: Stanford University Press, 2008.

Posner, Richard. *Breaking the Deadlock: The 2000 Election, the Constitution, and the Courts.* Princeton, NJ: Princeton University Press, 2001.

Ryden, David. *Representation in Crisis: The Constitution, Interest Groups, and Political Parties.* Albany: SUNY Press, 1996.

————. *The U.S. Supreme Court and the Electoral Process.* Washington, DC: Georgetown University Press, 2000.

Smith, Bradley. *Unfree Speech: The Folly of Campaign Finance Reform.* Princeton, NJ: Princeton University Press, 2001.

Urofsky, Melvin, *Money and Free Speech: Campaign Finance Reform and the Courts,* Lawrence: University of Kansas Press, 2005.

Washington Post Staff. *Deadlock: The Inside Story of America's Closest Election.* New York: Public Affairs Press, 2001.

Bush v. Gore

531 U.S. 98, 121 S.CT. 525 (2000)

On the night of the presidential election, November 7, 2000, the Democratic candidate, Vice President Albert Gore, won the national popular vote but was locked in a bitter fight with the Republican candidate, Texas Governor George W. Bush, for Florida's twenty-five electoral votes, which would have put either over 270 votes, the portion of the 528 votes of the Electoral College required to win. Based on projections, CNN and other news services initially declared Gore and then Bush the winner, but ultimately concluded the election was too close to call. The next day the Florida Division of Elections reported that

Bush had received 2,909,135 votes and Gore 2,907,351 votes, a margin of 1,784 for Bush. Because the margin was less than one-half of one percent of the votes cast, an automatic machine recount was conducted, as required under Florida law. The result diminished Bush's lead to 327 votes and Gore then sought manual recounts in three counties—Volusia, Broward, and Miami-Dade—as allowed under Florida's law for *protesting* election results. Palm Beach County subsequently announced that it would manually recount all votes and Bush filed suit in federal district court to bar that recounting. In the meantime, a dispute arose over the deadline for canvassing boards to submit their returns to the Florida secretary of state for certification. The secretary's decision declining to waive a November 14 deadline for certification was challenged in state courts, and the Florida supreme court ruled that the manual recounts should be included in the final vote and extended the certification deadline to November 26. Attorneys for Bush appealed that decision to the U.S. Supreme Court, arguing that the state supreme court had rewritten state election law. Before the Supreme Court heard oral arguments in that case, the secretary of state certified Bush as the winner of the election by 537 votes and Gore filed suit, as provided under Florida law, *contesting* the election.

On Friday, December 1, oral arguments in *Bush v. Palm Beach County Canvassing Board,* 531 U. S. 70 (2000), (*Bush I*), were heard, and for the first time an audio recording of the arguments was made available for public broadcasting immediately after the arguments. The following Monday, December 4, the Court unanimously vacated and remanded the Florida Supreme Court's decision extending the certification date. The Court also directed the state supreme court to clarify the basis for its decision—specifically, whether its ruling violated the due process clause; Section 5 of the Electoral Count Act of 1887, which provides a "safe harbor" for electoral votes receiving certification by December 12; and Article II of the U.S. Constitution, which provides that "[e]ach state shall appoint, in such Manner as the Legislature thereof may direct" the electors for president and vice president.

On December 7, the Florida Supreme Court heard oral arguments in Gore's contest of the vote certification and the following day, voting four to three, ordered an immediate manual recount of all votes in the state where no vote for president was machine recorded. That decision was in turn immediately appealed by Bush attorneys to the U.S. Supreme Court which granted a stay of the statewide vote recount and also granted review and set the date for oral arguments the following Monday, December 11, in *Bush v. Gore.* In addition to arguing that the vote recount ran afoul of Article II and Section 5 of the Electoral Count Act, attorneys for Bush contended that the manual recount was

standardless and, thus, violated the Fourteenth Amendment equal protection clause. By contrast, Gore's lawyers claimed that every vote should
be counted. The following night at 10 P.M., December 12, the Court
handed down its decision reversing the state supreme court upon finding
that a standardless manual recount violated the equal protection clause
but that a remedy—a remedy providing for a recount of votes based on
clear standards—was impossible given the December 12 deadline.

The decision of the Court was delivered in a *per curiam* opinion. By
a vote of seven to two, with Justices Stevens and Ginsburg dissenting,
the state supreme court's decision was held to run afoul of the equal
protection clause. By a vote of five to four, the Court held that there
was no remedy available. Chief Justice Rehnquist, joined by Justices
Scalia and Thomas, filed a concurring opinion. Justices Stevens, Souter,
Ginsburg, and Breyer each filed dissenting opinions.

PER CURIAM

The petition presents the following questions: whether the Florida Supreme
Court established new standards for resolving Presidential election contests,
thereby violating Art. II, Sec. 1, cl. 2, of the United States Constitution and
failing to comply with [Section 5 of the Electoral Count Act of 1887] and
whether the use of standardless manual recounts violates the Equal Protection and Due Process Clauses. With respect to the equal protection question,
we find a violation of the Equal Protection Clause. . . .

This case has shown that punch card balloting machines can produce an
unfortunate number of ballots which are not punched in a clean, complete
way by the voter. After the current counting, it is likely legislative bodies
nationwide will examine ways to improve the mechanisms and machinery
for voting.

The individual citizen has no federal constitutional right to vote for
electors for the President of the United States unless and until the state legislature chooses a statewide election as the means to implement its power to
appoint members of the Electoral College. . . . The State, of course, after
granting the franchise in the special context of Article II, can take back the
power to appoint electors.

The right to vote is protected in more than the initial allocation of the
franchise. Equal protection applies as well to the manner of its exercise. Having once granted the right to vote on equal terms, the State may not, by later
arbitrary and disparate treatment, value one person's vote over that of another. It must be remembered that "the right of suffrage can be denied by a
debasement or dilution of the weight of a citizen's vote just as effectively as
by wholly prohibiting the free exercise of the franchise." *Reynolds v. Sims*, 377
U.S. 533 (1964).

The question before us . . . is whether the recount procedures the
Florida Supreme Court has adopted are consistent with its obligation to
avoid arbitrary and disparate treatment of the members of its electorate.

Much of the controversy seems to revolve around ballot cards designed
to be perforated by a stylus but which, either through error or deliberate

omission, have not been perforated with sufficient precision for a machine to count them. In some cases a piece of the card—a chad—is hanging, say by two corners. In other cases there is no separation at all, just an indentation.

For purposes of resolving the equal protection challenge, it is not necessary to decide whether the Florida Supreme Court had the authority under the legislative scheme for resolving election disputes to define what a legal vote is and to mandate a manual recount implementing that definition. The recount mechanisms implemented in response to the decisions of the Florida Supreme Court do not satisfy the minimum requirement for non-arbitrary treatment of voters necessary to secure the fundamental right. Florida's basic command for the count of legally cast votes is to consider the "intent of the voter." This is unobjectionable as an abstract proposition and a starting principle. The problem inheres in the absence of specific standards to ensure its equal application. The formulation of uniform rules to determine intent based on these recurring circumstances is practicable and, we conclude, necessary. . . .

The want of those rules here has led to unequal evaluation of ballots in various respects. As seems to have been acknowledged at oral argument, the standards for accepting or rejecting contested ballots might vary not only from county to county but indeed within a single county from one recount team to another. . . .

The State Supreme Court ratified this uneven treatment. It mandated that the recount totals from two counties, Miami-Dade and Palm Beach, be included in the certified total. The court also appeared to hold *sub silentio* that the recount totals from Broward County, which were not completed until after the original November 14 certification by the Secretary of State, were to be considered part of the new certified vote totals even though the county certification was not contested by Vice President Gore. Yet each of the counties used varying standards to determine what was a legal vote. Broward County used a more forgiving standard than Palm Beach County, and uncovered almost three times as many new votes, a result markedly disproportionate to the difference in population between the counties.

In addition, the recounts in these three counties were not limited to so-called undervotes but extended to all of the ballots. The distinction has real consequences. A manual recount of all ballots identifies not only those ballots which show no vote but also those which contain more than one, the so-called overvotes. Neither category will be counted by the machine. This is not a trivial concern. At oral argument, respondents estimated there are as many as 110,000 overvotes statewide. As a result, the citizen whose ballot was not read by a machine because he failed to vote for a candidate in a way readable by a machine may still have his vote counted in a manual recount; on the other hand, the citizen who marks two candidates in a way discernable by the machine will not have the same opportunity to have his vote count, even if a manual examination of the ballot would reveal the requisite indicia of intent. Furthermore, the citizen who marks two candidates, only one of which is discernable by the machine, will have his vote counted even though it should have been read as an invalid ballot. The State Supreme Court's inclusion of vote counts based on these variant standards exemplifies concerns with the remedial processes that were under way.

That brings the analysis to yet a further equal protection problem. The votes certified by the court included a partial total from one county, Miami-Dade. The Florida Supreme Court's decision thus gives no assurance that the recounts included in a final certification must be complete. Indeed, it is respondent's submission that it would be consistent with the rules of the recount procedures to include whatever partial counts are done by the time of final certification, and we interpret the Florida Supreme Court's decision to permit this. This accommodation no doubt results from the truncated contest period established by the Florida Supreme Court in *Bush I*, at respondents' own urging. The press of time does not diminish the constitutional concern. A desire for speed is not a general excuse for ignoring equal protection guarantees.

In addition to these difficulties the actual process by which the votes were to be counted under the Florida Supreme Court's decision raises further concerns. That order did not specify who would recount the ballots. The county canvassing boards were forced to pull together ad hoc teams comprised of judges from various Circuits who had no previous training in handling and interpreting ballots. Furthermore, while others were permitted to observe, they were prohibited from objecting during the recount.

The recount process, in its features here described, is inconsistent with the minimum procedures necessary to protect the fundamental right of each voter in the special instance of a statewide recount under the authority of a single state judicial officer. Our consideration is limited to the present circumstances, for the problem of equal protection in election processes generally presents many complexities. . . .

Upon due consideration of the difficulties identified to this point, it is obvious that the recount cannot be conducted in compliance with the requirements of equal protection and due process without substantial additional work. It would require not only the adoption (after opportunity for argument) of adequate statewide standards for determining what is a legal vote, and practicable procedures to implement them, but also orderly judicial review of any disputed matters that might arise. . . .

The Supreme Court of Florida has said that the legislature intended the State's electors to "participat[e] fully in the federal electoral process," as provided in [Section 5 of the Electoral Count Act]. That statute, in turn, requires that any controversy or contest that is designed to lead to a conclusive selection of electors be completed by December 12. That date is upon us, and there is no recount procedure in place under the State Supreme Court's order that comports with minimal constitutional standards. Because it is evident that any recount seeking to meet the December 12 date will be unconstitutional for the reasons we have discussed, we reverse the judgment of the Supreme Court of Florida ordering a recount to proceed.

Seven Justices of the Court agree that there are constitutional problems with the recount ordered by the Florida Supreme Court that demand a remedy. See SOUTER, J., dissenting; BREYER, J., dissenting. The only disagreement is as to the remedy. Because the Florida Supreme Court has said that the Florida Legislature intended to obtain the safe-harbor benefits of [Section 5] Justice BREYER's proposed remedy—remanding to the Florida Supreme Court for its ordering of a constitutionally proper contest until December 18—contemplates action in violation of the Florida election code, and hence could not be part of an "appropriate" order authorized by [Florida law].

The judgment of the Supreme Court of Florida is reversed, and the case is remanded for further proceedings not inconsistent with this opinion.

☐ *Chief Justice REHNQUIST, with whom Justice SCALIA and Justice THOMAS join, concurring.*

We deal here not with an ordinary election, but with an election for the President of the United States. . . . In most cases, comity and respect for federalism compel us to defer to the decisions of state courts on issues of state law. . . . But there are a few exceptional cases in which the Constitution imposes a duty or confers a power on a particular branch of a State's government. This is one of them. Article II, Sec. 1, cl. 2, provides that "[e]ach State shall appoint, in such Manner as the Legislature thereof may direct," electors for President and Vice President. Thus, the text of the election law itself, and not just its interpretation by the courts of the States, takes on independent significance. . . .

If we are to respect the legislature's Article II powers, therefore, we must ensure that postelection state–court actions do not frustrate the legislative desire to attain the "safe harbor" provided by [Section 5 of the Electoral Count Act].

In Florida, the legislature has chosen to hold statewide elections to appoint the State's 25 electors. Importantly, the legislature has delegated the authority to run the elections and to oversee election disputes to the Secretary of State, and to state circuit courts. Isolated sections of the code may well admit of more than one interpretation, but the general coherence of the legislative scheme may not be altered by judicial interpretation so as to wholly change the statutorily provided apportionment of responsibility among these various bodies. . . .

[I]n a Presidential election the clearly expressed intent of the legislature must prevail. And there is no basis for reading the Florida statutes as requiring the counting of improperly marked ballots, as an examination of the Florida Supreme Court's textual analysis shows. We will not parse that analysis here, except to note that the principal provision of the election code on which it relied was . . . entirely irrelevant. The State's Attorney General (who was supporting the Gore challenge) confirmed in oral argument here that never before the present election had a manual recount been conducted on the basis of the contention that "undervotes" should have been examined to determine voter intent. For the court to step away from this established practice, prescribed by the Secretary of State, the state official charged by the legislature with "responsibility to '[o]btain and maintain uniformity in the application, operation, and interpretation of the election laws,' " was to depart from the legislative scheme.

The scope and nature of the remedy ordered by the Florida Supreme Court jeopardizes the "legislative wish" to take advantage of the safe harbor provided by [Section 5]. December 12, 2000, is the last date for a final determination of the Florida electors that will satisfy [Section] 5. Yet in the late afternoon of December 8th—four days before this deadline—the Supreme Court of Florida ordered recounts of tens of thousands of so-called "undervotes" spread through 64 of the State's 67 counties. This was done in a search for elusive—perhaps delusive—certainty as to the exact count of 6 million votes. But no one claims that these ballots have not previously been tabulated; they were initially read by voting machines at the time of the election, and thereafter reread by virtue of Florida's automatic recount provision. No one claims there was any fraud in the election. The Supreme Court of Florida ordered this additional recount under the provision of the election code giving the circuit judge the authority to provide relief that is "appropriate under such circumstances." . . .

Given all these factors, and in light of the legislative intent identified by the Florida Supreme Court to bring Florida within the "safe harbor" provision of [Section] 5, the remedy prescribed by the Supreme Court of Florida cannot be deemed an "appropriate" one as of December 8. It significantly departed from the statutory framework in place on November 7, and authorized open-ended further proceedings which could not be completed by December 12, thereby preventing a final determination by that date.

For these reasons, in addition to those given in the *per curiam*, we would reverse.

□ *Justice STEVENS, with whom Justice GINSBURG and Justice BREYER join, dissenting.*

The federal questions that ultimately emerged in this case are not substantial. Article II provides that "[e]ach State shall appoint, in such Manner as the Legislature thereof may direct, a Number of Electors." It does not create state legislatures out of whole cloth, but rather takes them as they come—as creatures born of, and constrained by, their state constitutions. Lest there be any doubt, we stated over 100 years ago in *McPherson v. Blacker*, 146 U.S. 1 (1892), that "[w]hat is forbidden or required to be done by a State" in the Article II context "is forbidden or required of the legislative power under state constitutions as they exist." In the same vein, we also observed that "[t]he [State's] legislative power is the supreme authority except as limited by the constitution of the State." The legislative power in Florida is subject to judicial review pursuant to Article V of the Florida Constitution, and nothing in Article II of the Federal Constitution frees the state legislature from the constraints in the state constitution that created it. . . .

It hardly needs stating that Congress, pursuant to [Section] 5 did not impose any affirmative duties upon the States that their governmental branches could "violate." Rather, [Section] 5 provides a safe harbor for States to select electors in contested elections "by judicial or other methods" established by laws prior to the election day. Section 5, like Article II, assumes the involvement of the state judiciary in interpreting state election laws and resolving election disputes under those laws. Neither [Section] 5 nor Article II grants federal judges any special authority to substitute their views for those of the state judiciary on matters of state law.

Nor are petitioners correct in asserting that the failure of the Florida Supreme Court to specify in detail the precise manner in which the "intent of the voter" is to be determined rises to the level of a constitutional violation. We found such a violation when individual votes within the same State were weighted unequally, see *Reynolds v. Sims*, 377 U.S. 533 (1964), but we have never before called into question the substantive standard by which a State determines that a vote has been legally cast. And there is no reason to think that the guidance provided to the factfinders, specifically the various canvassing boards, by the "intent of the voter" standard is any less sufficient—or will lead to results any less uniform—than, for example, the "beyond a reasonable doubt" standard employed every day by ordinary citizens in courtrooms across this country.

[T]he majority effectively orders the disenfranchisement of an unknown number of voters whose ballots reveal their intent—and are therefore legal votes under state law—but were for some reason rejected by ballot-counting machines. . . .

What must underlie petitioners' entire federal assault on the Florida election procedures is an unstated lack of confidence in the impartiality and capacity of the state judges who would make the critical decisions if the vote count were to proceed. Otherwise, their position is wholly without merit. The endorsement of that position by the majority of this Court can only lend credence to the most cynical appraisal of the work of judges throughout the land. It is confidence in the men and women who administer the judicial system that is the true backbone of the rule of law. Time will one day heal the wound to that confidence that will be inflicted by today's decision. One thing, however, is certain. Although we may never know with complete certainty the identity of the winner of this year's Presidential election, the identity of the loser is perfectly clear. It is the Nation's confidence in the judge as an impartial guardian of the rule of law.

I respectfully dissent.

☐ *Justice SOUTER, with whom Justice BREYER joins and with whom Justice STEVENS and Justice GINSBURG join with regard to all but Part C, dissenting.*

The Court should not have reviewed either *Bush v. Palm Beach County Canvassing Bd.*, or this case, and should not have stopped Florida's attempt to recount all undervote ballots by issuing a stay of the Florida Supreme Court's orders during the period of this review. If this Court had allowed the State to follow the course indicated by the opinions of its own Supreme Court, it is entirely possible that there would ultimately have been no issue requiring our review, and political tension could have worked itself out in the Congress following the procedure provided in [Section 15 of the Electoral Count Act]. The case being before us, however, its resolution by the majority is another erroneous decision. . . .

The [Section] 5 issue is not serious. . . . Conclusiveness requires selection under a legal scheme in place before the election, with results determined at least six days before the date set for casting electoral votes. But no State is required to conform to [Section] 5 if it cannot do that (for whatever reason); the sanction for failing to satisfy the conditions of [Section] 5 is simply loss of what has been called its "safe harbor." And even that determination is to be made, if made anywhere, in the Congress.

The second matter here goes to the State Supreme Court's interpretation of certain terms in the state statute governing election "contests." . . . The issue is whether the judgment of the state supreme court has displaced the state legislature's provisions for election contests: is the law as declared by the court different from the provisions made by the legislature, to which the national Constitution commits responsibility for determining how each State's Presidential electors are chosen? . . .

The starting point for evaluating the claim that the Florida Supreme Court's interpretation effectively re-wrote [Florida law] must be the language of the provision on which Gore relies to show his right to raise this contest: that the previously certified result in Bush's favor was produced by "rejection of a number of legal votes sufficient to change or place in doubt the result of the election." None of the state court's interpretations is unreasonable to the point of displacing the legislative enactment quoted. . . .

In sum, the interpretations by the Florida court raise no substantial questions under Article II. . . .

▪ C

It is only on the third issue before us that there is a meritorious argument for relief, as this Court's *Per Curiam* opinion recognizes. . . . Petitioners have raised an equal protection claim (or, alternatively, a due process claim, see generally *Logan v. Zimmerman Brush Co.*, 455 U.S. 422 (1982)), in the charge that unjustifiably disparate standards are applied in different electoral jurisdictions to otherwise identical facts. . . .

In deciding what to do about this, we should take account of the fact that electoral votes are due to be cast in six days. I would therefore remand the case to the courts of Florida with instructions to establish uniform standards for evaluating the several types of ballots that have prompted differing treatments, to be applied within and among counties when passing on such identical ballots in any further recounting (or successive recounting) that the courts might order.

Unlike the majority, I see no warrant for this Court to assume that Florida could not possibly comply with this requirement before the date set for the meeting of electors, December 18. . . .

I respectfully dissent.

◻ *Justice GINSBURG, with whom Justice STEVENS joins, and with whom Justice SOUTER and Justice BREYER join as to Part I, dissenting.*

▪ I

The extraordinary setting of this case has obscured the ordinary principle that dictates its proper resolution: Federal courts defer to state high courts' interpretations of their state's own law. This principle reflects the core of federalism, on which all agree. THE CHIEF JUSTICE's solicitude for the Florida Legislature comes at the expense of the more fundamental solicitude we owe to the legislature's sovereign. Were the other members of this Court as mindful as they generally are of our system of dual sovereignty, they would affirm the judgment of the Florida Supreme Court.

▪ II

I agree with Justice STEVENS that petitioners have not presented a substantial equal protection claim. Ideally, perfection would be the appropriate standard for judging the recount. But we live in an imperfect world, one in which thousands of votes have not been counted. I cannot agree that the recount adopted by the Florida court, flawed as it may be, would yield a result any less fair or precise than the certification that preceded that recount.

Even if there were an equal protection violation, I would agree with Justice STEVENS, Justice SOUTER, and Justice BREYER that the Court's concern about "the December 12 deadline" is misplaced. . . . More fundamentally, the Court's reluctance to let the recount go forward—despite its suggestion that "[t]he search for intent can be confined by specific rules designed to ensure uniform treatment"—ultimately turns on its own judgment about the practical realities of implementing a recount, not the judgment of those much closer to the process. . . .

The Court assumes that time will not permit "orderly judicial review of any disputed matters that might arise." But no one has doubted the good faith and diligence with which Florida election officials, attorneys for all sides of this controversy, and the courts of law have performed their duties. Notably, the Florida Supreme Court has produced two substantial opinions within 29 hours of oral argument. In sum, the Court's conclusion that a constitutionally adequate recount is impractical is a prophecy the Court's own judgment will not allow to be tested. Such an untested prophecy should not decide the Presidency of the United States.

I dissent.

☐ *Justice BREYER, with whom Justice STEVENS and Justice GINSBURG join except as to Part I A (1), and with whom Justice SOUTER joins as to Part I, dissenting.*

■ I A (1)

The majority raises three Equal Protection problems with the Florida Supreme Court's recount order: first, the failure to include overvotes in the manual recount; second, the fact that all ballots, rather than simply the undervotes, were recounted in some, but not all, counties; and third, the absence of a uniform, specific standard to guide the recounts. As far as the first issue is concerned, petitioners presented no evidence, to this Court or to any Florida court, that a manual recount of overvotes would identify additional legal votes. The same is true of the second, and, in addition, the majority's reasoning would seem to invalidate any state provision for a manual recount of individual counties in a statewide election.

The majority's third concern does implicate principles of fundamental fairness. The majority concludes that the Equal Protection Clause requires that a manual recount be governed not only by the uniform general standard of the "clear intent of the voter," but also by uniform subsidiary standards (for example, a uniform determination whether indented, but not perforated, "undervotes" should count). . . . I agree that, in these very special circumstances, basic principles of fairness may well have counseled the adoption of a uniform standard to address the problem. In light of the majority's disposition, I need not decide whether, or the extent to which, as a remedial matter, the Constitution would place limits upon the content of the uniform standard.

■ (2)

Nonetheless, there is no justification for the majority's remedy, which is simply to reverse the lower court and halt the recount entirely. An appropriate remedy would be, instead, to remand this case with instructions that, even at this late date, would permit the Florida Supreme Court to require recounting all undercounted votes in Florida, including those from Broward, Volusia, Palm Beach, and Miami-Dade Counties, whether or not previously recounted prior to the end of the protest period, and to do so in accordance with a single-uniform substandard. . . .

By halting the manual recount, and thus ensuring that the uncounted legal votes will not be counted under any standard, this Court crafts a remedy out of proportion to the asserted harm. And that remedy harms the very fairness interests the Court is attempting to protect. . . .

■ II

The decision by both the Constitution's Framers and the 1886 Congress to minimize this Court's role in resolving close federal presidential elections is as wise as it is clear. However awkward or difficult it may be for Congress to resolve difficult electoral disputes, Congress, being a political body, expresses the people's will far more accurately than does an unelected Court. And the people's will is what elections are about.

Moreover, Congress was fully aware of the danger that would arise should it ask judges, unarmed with appropriate legal standards, to resolve a hotly contested Presidential election contest. Just after the 1876 Presidential election, Florida, South Carolina, and Louisiana each sent two slates of electors to Washington. Without these States, Tilden, the Democrat, had 184 electoral votes, one short of the number required to win the Presidency. With those States, Hayes, his Republican opponent, would have had 185. In order to choose between the two slates of electors, Congress decided to appoint an electoral commission composed of five Senators, five Representatives, and five Supreme Court Justices. Initially the Commission was to be evenly divided between Republicans and Democrats, with Justice DAVID DAVIS, an Independent, to possess the decisive vote. However, when at the last minute the Illinois Legislature elected Justice DAVIS to the United States Senate, the final position on the Commission was filled by Supreme Court Justice JOSEPH P. BRADLEY. The Commission divided along partisan lines, and the responsibility to cast the deciding vote fell to Justice BRADLEY. He decided to accept the votes by the Republican electors, and thereby awarded the Presidency to Hayes.

Justice BRADLEY immediately became the subject of vociferous attacks. BRADLEY was accused of accepting bribes, of being captured by railroad interests, and of an eleventh-hour change in position after a night in which his house "was surrounded by the carriages" of Republican partisans and railroad officials.

For present purposes, the relevance of this history lies in the fact that the participation in the work of the electoral commission by five Justices, including Justice BRADLEY, did not lend that process legitimacy. Nor did it assure the public that the process had worked fairly, guided by the law. Rather, it simply embroiled Members of the Court in partisan conflict, thereby undermining respect for the judicial process. And the Congress that later enacted the Electoral Count Act knew it.

This history may help to explain why I think it not only legally wrong, but also most unfortunate, for the Court simply to have terminated the Florida recount. . . . [A]bove all, in this highly politicized matter, the appearance of a split decision runs the risk of undermining the public's confidence in the Court itself. That confidence is a public treasure. . . . It is a vitally necessary ingredient of any successful effort to protect basic liberty and, indeed, the rule of law itself. We run no risk of returning to the days when a President (responding to this Court's efforts to protect the Cherokee Indians) might have said, "JOHN MARSHALL has made his decision; now let him enforce it!" But we do risk a self-inflicted wound—a wound that may harm not just the Court, but the Nation. . . .

I respectfully dissent.

Buckley v. Valeo

424 U.S. 1, 96 S.Ct. 612 (1976)

In 1971, Congress enacted the Federal Election Campaign Act to safeguard against corruption in federal elections. The act, as amended in 1974, among other things provided that

1. Political contributions by individuals and groups were limited to $1,000 each and by political committees to $5,000 for any single candidate in an election, with an annual limit of $25,000 on any individual contributor.
2. Independent spending by an individual or group "relative to a clearly identified candidate" was limited to $1,000 per election.
3. Personal contributions by both the candidate and relatives toward a campaign were limited according to the office being sought.
4. Overall expenditures by a candidate in an election were limited according to the office being sought.
5. Political committees were required to keep records on contributions and expenditures and to publicly disclose the identity of contributors and the reason for expenditures above a certain amount.
6. An eight-member commission was created to oversee enforcement of the law.
7. The Internal Revenue Code was amended to provide for public financing of primary and general elections with major party candidates receiving "full" funding and "minor" or "new" party candidates receiving a reduced proportion of funding on a dollar-matching basis.

Republican Senator James Buckley and former Democratic senator and presidential candidate Eugene McCarthy, among others, sued Francis Valeo, the secretary of the Senate, the clerk of the House of Representatives, and others. Buckley contended that various provisions of the law were unconstitutional and in violation of the appointments clause of Article II, Section 2, Clause 2, and the First and Fifth Amendments. The Court of Appeals for the District of Columbia Circuit, however, rejected most of Buckley's arguments, and he appealed to the Supreme Court.

The Court's decision on the various provisions challenged was extraordinarily fragmented and its opinion announced *per curiam*, with Justice Stevens not participating and *five* justices dissenting in part. Separate opinions, concurring in part and dissenting in part, were delivered by Chief Justice Burger and Justices White, Marshall, Rehnquist, and Blackmun.

PER CURIAM

These appeals present constitutional challenges to the key provisions of the Federal Election Campaign Act of 1971 as amended in 1974. . . .

The Act, summarized in broad terms, contains the following provisions: (a) individual political contributions are limited to $1,000 to any single candidate per election, with an overall annual limitation of $25,000 by any contributor; independent expenditures by individuals and groups "relative to a clearly identified candidate" are limited to $1,000 a year; campaign spending by candidates for various federal offices and spending for national conventions by political parties are subject to prescribed limits; (b) contributions and expenditures above certain threshold levels must be reported and publicly disclosed; (c) a system for public funding of Presidential campaign activities is established by Subtitle H of the Internal Revenue Code; and (d) a Federal Election Commission is established to administer and enforce the Act. . . .

In this Court, appellants argue that the Court of Appeals failed to give this legislation the critical scrutiny demanded under accepted First Amendment and equal protection principles. In appellants' view, limiting the use of money for political purposes constitutes a restriction on communication violative of the First Amendment, since virtually all meaningful political communications in the modern setting involve the expenditure of money. Further, they argue that the reporting and disclosure provisions of the Act unconstitutionally impinge on their right to freedom of association. Appellants also view the federal subsidy provisions of Subtitle H as violative of the General Welfare Clause, and as inconsistent with the First and Fifth Amendments. Finally, appellants renew their attack on the Commission's composition and powers. . . .

I. CONTRIBUTION AND EXPENDITURE LIMITATIONS

The intricate statutory scheme adopted by Congress to regulate federal election campaigns includes restrictions on political contributions and expenditures that apply broadly to all phases of and all participants in the election process. The major contribution and expenditure limitations in the Act prohibit individuals from contributing more than $25,000 in a single year or more than $1,000 to any single candidate for an election campaign and from spending more than $1,000 a year "relative to a clearly identified candidate." Other provisions restrict a candidate's use of personal and family resources in his campaign and limit the overall amount that can be spent by a candidate in campaigning for federal office. . . .

A. General Principles The Act's contribution and expenditure limitations operate in an area of the most fundamental First Amendment activities. Discussion of public issues and debate on the qualifications of candidates are integral to the operation of the system of government established by our Constitution. . . .

In upholding the constitutional validity of the Act's contribution and expenditure provisions on the ground that those provisions should be viewed as regulating conduct not speech, the Court of Appeals relied upon *United States v. O'Brien*, 391 U.S. 367 (1968). The *O'Brien* case involved a defendant's claim that the First Amendment prohibited his prosecution for burning his draft card because his act was "symbolic speech" engaged in as a " 'demonstration against the war and against the draft.' " . . .

We cannot share the view that the present Act's contribution and expenditure limitations are comparable to the restrictions on conduct upheld in *O'Brien*. The expenditure of money simply cannot be equated with such conduct as destruction of a draft card. Some forms of communication made possible by the giving and spending of money involve speech alone, some involve conduct primarily, and some involve a combination of the two. Yet this Court has never suggested that the dependence of a communication on the expenditure of money operates itself to introduce a nonspeech element or to reduce the exacting scrutiny required by the First Amendment. . . .

Even if the categorization of the expenditure of money as conduct were accepted, the limitations challenged here would not meet the *O'Brien* test because the governmental interests advanced in support of the Act involve "suppressing communication." The interests served by the Act include restricting the voices of people and interest groups who have money to spend and reducing the overall scope of federal election campaigns. Although the Act does not focus on the ideas expressed by persons or groups subjected to its regulations, it is aimed in part at equalizing the relative ability of all voters to affect electoral outcomes by placing a ceiling on expenditures for political expression by citizens and groups. Unlike *O'Brien*, where the Selective Service System's administrative interest in the preservation of draft cards was wholly unrelated to their use as a means of communication, it is beyond dispute that the interest in regulating the alleged "conduct" of giving or spending money "arises in some measure because the communication allegedly integral to the conduct is itself thought to be harmful." . . .

Nor can the Act's contribution and expenditure limitations be sustained, as some of the parties suggest, by reference to the constitutional principles reflected in such decisions as *Cox v. Louisiana* [379 U.S. 536 (1965)], *Adderley v. Florida*, 385 U.S. 39 (1966), and *Kovacs v. Cooper*, 336 U.S. 77 (1949). Those cases stand for the proposition that the government may adopt reasonable time, place, and manner regulations, which do not discriminate between speakers or ideas, in order to further an important governmental interest unrelated to the restriction of communication. In contrast to *O'Brien*, where the method of expression was held to be subject to prohibition, *Cox*, *Adderley*, and *Kovacs* involved place or manner restrictions on legitimate modes of expression—picketing, parading, demonstrating, and using a soundtruck. The critical difference between this case and those time, place and manner cases is that the present Act's contribution and expenditure limitations impose direct quantity restrictions on political communication and association by persons, groups, candidates and political parties in addition to any reasonable time, place, and manner regulations otherwise imposed.

A restriction on the amount of money a person or group can spend on political communication during a campaign necessarily reduces the quantity of expression by restricting the number of issues discussed, the depth of their exploration, and the size of the audience reached. This is because virtually every means of communicating ideas in today's mass society requires the expenditure of money. The distribution of the humblest handbill or leaflet entails printing, paper, and circulation costs. Speeches and rallies generally necessitate hiring a hall and publicizing the event. The electorate's increasing dependence on television, radio, and other mass media for news and information has made these expensive modes of communication indispensible instruments of effective political speech.

The expenditure limitations contained in the Act represent substantial rather than merely theoretical restraints on the quantity and diversity of political speech. The $1,000 ceiling on spending "relative to a clearly identified candidate," 18 U.S.C. Sec. 608(e)(1), would appear to exclude all citizens and groups except candidates, political parties and the institutional press from any significant use of the most effective modes of communication. Although the Act's limitations on expenditures by campaign organizations and political parties provide substantially greater room for discussion and debate, they would have required restrictions in the scope of a number of past congressional and Presidential campaigns and would operate to constrain campaigning by candidates who raise sums in excess of the spending ceiling.

By contrast with a limitation upon expenditures for political expression, a limitation upon the amount that any one person or group may contribute to a candidate or political committee entails only a marginal restriction upon the contributor's ability to engage in free communication. A contribution serves as a general expression of support for the candidate and his views, but does not communicate the underlying basis for the support. The quantity of communication by the contributor does not increase perceptibly with the size of his contribution, since the expression rests solely on the undifferentiated, symbolic act of contributing. At most, the size of the contribution provides a very rough index of the intensity of the contributor's support for the candidate. A limitation on the amount of money a person may give to a candidate or campaign organization thus involves little direct restraint on his political communication, for it permits the symbolic expression of support evidenced by a contribution but does not in any way infringe the contributor's freedom to discuss candidates and issues. While contributions may result in political expression if spent by a candidate or an association to present views to the voters, the transformation of contributions into political debate involves speech by someone other than the contributor.

Given the important role of contributions in financing political campaigns, contribution restrictions could have a severe impact on political dialogue if the limitations prevented candidates and political committees from amassing the resources necessary for effective advocacy. There is no indication, however, that the contribution limitations imposed by the Act would have any dramatic adverse effect on the funding of campaigns and political associations. The overall effect of the Act's contribution ceilings is merely to require candidates and political committees to raise funds from a greater number of persons and to compel people who would otherwise contribute amounts greater than the statutory limits to expend such funds on direct political expression, rather than to reduce the total amount of money potentially available to promote political expression. . . .

In sum, although the Act's contribution and expenditure limitations both implicate fundamental First Amendment interests, its expenditure ceilings impose significantly more severe restrictions on protected freedoms of political expression and association than do its limitations on financial contributions.

Section 608(b) provides, with certain limited exceptions, that "no person shall make contributions to any candidate with respect to any election for Federal office which, in the aggregate, exceeds $1,000." . . .

[T]he primary First Amendment problem raised by the Act's contribution limitations is their restriction of one aspect of the contributor's freedom of political association. The Court's decisions involving associational freedoms establish that the right of association is a "basic constitutional freedom" that is "closely allied to freedom of speech and a right which, like free speech, lies at the foundation of a free society." In view of the fundamental nature of the right to associate, governmental "action which may have the effect of curtailing the freedom to associate is subject to the closest scrutiny." *NAACP v. Alabama* [377 U.S. 288 (1968)]. Yet, it is clear that "[n]either the right to associate nor the right to participate in political activities is absolute." Even a " 'significant interference' with protected rights of political association" may be sustained if the State demonstrates a sufficiently important interest and employs means closely drawn to avoid unnecessary abridgement of associational freedoms. . . .

It is unnecessary to look beyond the Act's primary purpose—to limit the actuality and appearance of corruption resulting from large individual financial contributions—in order to find a constitutionally sufficient justification for the $1,000 contribution limitation. Under a system of private financing of elections, a candidate lacking immense personal or family wealth must depend on financial contributions from others to provide the resources necessary to conduct a successful campaign. The increasing importance of the communications media and sophisticated mass mailing and polling operations to effective campaigning make the raising of large sums of money an ever more essential ingredient of an effective candidacy. To the extent that large contributions are given to secure political *quid pro quos* from current and potential office holders, the integrity of our system of representative democracy is undermined. . . .

Of almost equal concern as the danger of actual *quid pro quo* arrangements is the impact of the appearance of corruption stemming from public awareness of the opportunities for abuse inherent in a regime of large individual financial contributions. . . . Congress could legitimately conclude that the avoidance of the appearance of improper influence "is also critical . . . if confidence in the system of representative Government is not to be eroded. . . ."

Appellants contend that the contribution limitations must be invalidated because bribery laws and narrowly drawn disclosure requirements constituted a less restrictive means of dealing with "proven and suspected *quid pro quo* arrangements." But laws making criminal the giving and taking of bribes deal with only the most blatant and specific attempts of those with money to influence governmental action. And while disclosure requirements serve the many salutary purposes discussed elsewhere in the opinion, Congress was surely entitled to conclude that disclosure was only a partial measure, and that contribution ceilings were a necessary legislative concomitant to deal with the reality or appearance of corruption inherent in a system permitting unlimited financial contributions, even when the identities of the contributors and the amounts of their contributions are fully disclosed. . . .

We find that, under the rigorous standard of review established by our prior decisions, the weighty interests served by restricting the size of financial contributions to political candidates are sufficient to justify the limited effect upon First Amendment freedoms caused by the $1,000 contribution ceiling. . . .

Apart from these First Amendment concerns, appellants argue that the contribution limitations work such an invidious discrimination between incumbents and challengers that the statutory provisions must be declared unconstitutional on their face. . . .

[But t]here is no . . . evidence to support the claim that the contribution limitations in themselves discriminate against major-party challengers to incumbents. Challengers can and often do defeat incumbents in federal elections. Major-party challengers in federal elections are usually men and women who are well known and influential in their community or State. Often such challengers are themselves incumbents in important local, state, or federal offices. Statistics in the record indicate that major-party challengers as well as incumbents are capable of raising large sums for campaigning. Indeed, a small but nonetheless significant number of challengers have in recent elections outspent their incumbent rivals. And, to the extent that incumbents generally are more likely than challengers to attract very large contributions, the Act's $1,000 ceiling has the practical effect of benefiting challengers as a class. Contrary to the broad generalization drawn by the appellants, the practical impact of the contribution ceilings in any given election will clearly depend upon the amounts in excess of the ceilings that, for various reasons, the candidates in that election would otherwise have received and the utility of these additional amounts to the candidates. . . .

In view of these considerations, we conclude that the impact of the Act's $1,000 contribution limitation on major-party challengers and on minor-party candidates does not render the provision unconstitutional on its face. . . .

Section 608(b)(2) of Title 18 permits certain committees, designated as "political committees," to contribute up to $5,000 to any candidate with respect to any election for federal office. In order to qualify for the higher contribution ceiling, a group must have been registered with the Commission as a political committee under 2 U.S.C. Sec. 433 for not less than 6 months, have received contributions from more than 50 persons and, except for state political party organizations, have contributed to five or more candidates for federal office. Appellants argue that these qualifications unconstitutionally discriminate against ad hoc organizations in favor of established interest groups and impermissibly burden free association. The argument is without merit. Rather than undermining freedom of association, the basic provision enhances the opportunity of bona fide groups to participate in the election process, and the registration, contribution, and candidate conditions serve the permissible purpose of preventing individuals from evading the applicable contribution limitations by labeling themselves committees. . . .

C. *Expenditure Limitations* The Act's expenditure ceilings impose direct and substantial restraints on the quantity of political speech. The most drastic of the limitations restricts individuals and groups, including political parties that fail to place a candidate on the ballot, to an expenditure of $1,000 "relative to a clearly identified candidate during a calendar year." Sec. 608(e)(1). Other expenditure ceilings limit spending by candidates, Sec. 608(a), their campaigns, Sec. 608(c), and political parties in connection with election campaigns, Sec. 608(f). It is clear that a primary effect of these expenditure limitations is to restrict the quantity of campaign speech by individuals, groups, and candidates. The restrictions, while neutral as to the ideas expressed, limit political expression "at the core of our electoral process and of the First Amendment freedoms." . . .

1. The $1,000 Limitation on Expenditures "Relative to a Clearly Identified Candidate"

Section 608(e)(1) provides that "[n]o person may make any expenditure . . . relative to a clearly identified candidate during a calendar year which, when added to all other expenditures made by such person during the year advocating the election or defeat of such candidate, exceeds $1,000." The plain effect of Sec. 608(e)(1) is to prohibit all individuals, who are neither candidates nor owners of institutional press facilities, and all groups, except political parties and campaign organizations, from voicing their views "relative to a clearly identified candidate" through means that entail aggregate expenditures of more than $1,000 during a calendar year. The provision, for example, would make it a federal criminal offense for a person or association to place a single one-quarter page advertisement "relative to a clearly identified candidate" in a major metropolitan newspaper. . . .

We turn then to the basic First Amendment question—whether Sec. 608(c)(1), even as thus narrowly and explicitly construed, impermissibly burdens the constitutional right of free expression. . . .

The discussion, *supra*, explains why the Act's expenditure limitations impose far greater restraints on the freedom of speech and association than do its contribution limitations. . . .

We find that the governmental interest in preventing corruption and the appearance of corruption is inadequate to justify Sec. 608(e)(1)'s ceiling on independent expenditures. First . . . Sec. 608(e)(1) prevents only some large expenditures. So long as persons and groups eschew expenditures that in express terms advocate the election or defeat of a clearly identified candidates they are free to spend as much as they want to promote the candidate and their views. The exacting interpretation of the statutory language necessary to avoid unconstitutional vagueness thus undermines the limitation's effectiveness as a loophole-closing provision by facilitating circumvention by those seeking to exert improper influence upon a candidate or office-holder. . . .

Second . . . parties defending Sec. 608(e)(1) contend that it is necessary to prevent would-be contributors from avoiding the contribution limitations by the simple expedient of paying directly for media advertisements or for other portions of the candidate's campaign activities. They argue that expenditures controlled by or coordinated with the candidate and his campaign might well have virtually the same value to the candidate as a contribution and would pose similar dangers of abuse. Yet such controlled or coordinated expenditures are treated as contributions rather than expenditures under the Act. Section 608(b)'s contribution ceilings rather than Sec. 608(e)(1)'s independent expenditure limitation prevent attempts to circumvent the Act through prearranged or coordinated expenditures amounting to disguised contributions. By contrast Sec. 608(e)(1) limits expenditures for express advocacy of candidates made totally independently of the candidate and his campaign. Unlike contributions, such independent expenditures may well provide little assistance to the candidate's campaign and indeed may prove counter-productive. The absence of prearrangement and coordination of an expenditure with the candidate or his agent not only undermines the value of the expenditure to the candidate, but also alleviates the danger that expenditures will be given as a *quid pro quo* for improper commitments from the candidate. Rather than preventing circumvention of the contribution limitations, Sec. 608(e)(1) severely restricts all independent advocacy despite its substantially diminished potential for abuse. . . .

It is argued, however, that the ancillary governmental interest in equalizing the relative ability of individuals and groups to influence the outcome of elections serves to justify the limitation on express advocacy of the election or defeat of candidates imposed by Sec. 608(e)(1)'s expenditure ceiling. But the concept that government may restrict the speech of some elements of our society in order to enhance the relative voice of others is wholly foreign to the First Amendment, which was designed "to secure 'the widest possible dissemination of information from diverse and antagonistic sources,'" and "'to assure unfettered interchange of ideas for the bringing about of political and social changes desired by the people.'" *New York Times Co. v. Sullivan* [376 U.S. 254 (1964)]. The First Amendment's protection against governmental abridgement of free expression cannot properly be made to depend on a person's financial ability to engage in public discussion. . . .

For the reasons stated, we conclude that Sec. 608(e)(1)'s independent expenditure limitation is unconstitutional under the First Amendment.

2. Limitation on Expenditures by Candidates from Personal or Family Resources

The Act also sets limits on expenditures by a candidate "from his personal funds, or the personal funds of his immediate family, in connection with his campaigns during any calendar year." . . .

The ceiling on personal expenditures by candidates on their own behalf, like the limitations on independent expenditures contained in Sec. 608(e)(1), imposes a substantial restraint on the ability of persons to engage in protected First Amendment expression. The candidate, no less than any other person, has a First Amendment right to engage in the discussion of public issues and vigorously and tirelessly to advocate his own election and the election of other candidates.... Section 608(a)'s ceiling on personal expenditures by a candidate in furtherance of his own candidacy thus clearly and directly interferes with constitutionally protected freedoms....

3. Limitations on Campaign Expenditures

Section 608(c) of the Act places limitations on overall campaign expenditures by candidates seeking nomination for election and election to federal office. Presidential candidates may spend $10,000,000 in seeking nomination for office and an additional $20,000,000 in the general election campaign. Sec. 608(c)(1)(A), (B). The ceiling on Senate campaigns is pegged to the size of the voting age population of the State with minimum dollar amounts applicable to campaigns in States with small populations....

No governmental interest that has been suggested is sufficient to justify the restriction on the quantity of political expression imposed by Sec. 608(c)'s campaign expenditure limitations. The major evil associated with rapidly increasing campaign expenditures is the danger of candidate dependence on large contributions. The interest in alleviating the corrupting influence of large contributions is served by the Act's contribution limitations and disclosure provisions rather than by Sec. 608(c)'s campaign expenditure ceilings. The Court of Appeals's assertion that the expenditure restrictions are necessary to reduce the incentive to circumvent direct contribution limits is not persuasive. There is no indication that the substantial criminal penalties for violating the contribution ceilings combined with the political repercussion of such violations will be insufficient to police the contribution provisions. Extensive reporting, auditing, and disclosure requirements applicable to both contributions and expenditures by political campaigns are designed to facilitate the detection of illegal contributions....

The interest in equalizing the financial resources of candidates competing for federal office is no more convincing a justification for restricting the scope of federal election campaigns. Given the limitation on the size of outside contributions, the financial resources available to a candidate's campaign, like the number of volunteers recruited, will normally vary with the size and intensity of the candidate's support....

In any event, the mere growth in the cost of federal election campaigns in and itself provides no basis for government restrictions on the quantity of campaign spending and the resulting limitation on the scope of federal campaigns. The First Amendment denies government the power to determine that spending to promote one's political views is wasteful, excessive, or unwise. In the free society ordained by our Constitution it is not to government, but the people—individually as citizens and candidates and collectively as associations and political committees—who must retain control over the quantity and range of debate on public issues in a political campaign.

For these reasons we hold that Sec. 608(c) is constitutionally invalid.

In sum, the provisions of the Act that impose a $1,000 limitation on contributions to a single candidate, Sec. 608(b)(2), a $5,000 limitation on contributions by political committee to a single candidate, Sec. 608(b)(2), and a $25,000 limitation of total contributions by an individual during any calendar year, Sec. 608(b)(3), are constitutionally valid. These limitations along with the disclosure provisions, constitute the Act's primary weapons against the reality or appearance of improper influence stemming from the dependence of candidates on large campaign contributions. The contribution ceilings thus serve the basic governmental interest in safeguarding the integrity of the electoral process without directly impinging upon the rights of individual citizens and candidates to engage in political debate and discussion. By contrast, the First Amendment requires the invalidation of the Act's independent expenditure ceiling, Sec. 608(e)(1), its limitation on a candidate's expenditures from his own personal funds, Sec. 608(a), and ceilings on overall campaign expenditures, Sec. 608(c). These provisions place substantial and direct restrictions on the ability of candidates, citizens, and associations to engage in protected political expression, restrictions that the First Amendment cannot tolerate. . . .

CONCLUSION

In summary, we sustain the individual contribution limits, the disclosure and reporting provisions, and the public financing scheme. We conclude, however, that the limitations on campaign expenditures, on independent expenditures by individuals and groups, and on expenditures by a candidate from his personal funds are constitutionally infirm.

☐ *Chief Justice BURGER, concurring in part and dissenting in part.*

I dissent from those parts of the Court's holding sustaining the Act's provisions (a) for disclosure of small contributions, (b) for limitations on contributions, and (c) for public financing of Presidential campaigns. In my view, the Act's disclosure scheme is impermissibly broad and violative of the First Amendment as it relates to reporting $10 and $100 contributions. . . .

For me contributions and expenditures are two sides of the same First Amendment coin. . . .

The Court's attempt to distinguish the communication inherent in political *contributions* from the speech aspects of political *expenditures* simply will not wash. We do little but engage in word games unless we recognize that people—candidates and contributors—spend money on political activity because they wish to communicate ideas, and their constitutional interest in doing so is precisely the same whether they or someone else utter the words. . . .

☐ *Justice WHITE, concurring in part and dissenting in part.*

I dissent . . . from the Court's view that the expenditure limitations of 18 U.S.C. Sec. 608(c) and (e) violate the First Amendment. . . .

The congressional judgment, which I would also accept, was that . . . steps must be taken to counter the corrosive effects of money in federal election campaigns. One of these steps is Sec. 608(e), which, aside from those funds that are given to the candidate or spent at his request or with his approval or cooperation limits what a contributor may independently spend in support or denigration of one running for federal office. Congress was plainly of the view that these expenditures also have corruptive potential; but the Court strikes down the provision, strangely enough claiming more insight as to what may improperly influence candidates than is possessed by the majority of Congress that passed this Bill and the President who signed it. . . .

I would take the word of those who know—that limiting independent expenditures is essential to prevent transparent and widespread evasion of the contribution limits. . . .

[T]he argument that money is speech and that limiting the flow of money to the speaker violates the First Amendment proves entirely too much. Compulsory bargaining and the right to strike, both provided for or protected by federal law, inevitably have increased the labor costs of those who publish newspapers, which are in turn an important factor in the recent disappearance of many daily papers. . . . But it has not been suggested, nor could it be successfully, that these laws, and many others, are invalid because they siphon off or prevent the accumulation of large sums that would otherwise be available for communicative activities. . . .

☐ *Justice BLACKMUN, concurring in part and dissenting in part.*

I am not persuaded that the Court makes, or indeed is able to make, a principled constitutional distinction between the contribution limitations, on the one hand, and the expenditure limitations on the other, that are involved here. I therefore do not join [all] of the Court's opinion . . . [and] dissent [in part].

Federal Election Commission v. National Conservative Political Action Committee (NCPAC) and Democratic Party of the United States v. National Conservative Political Action Committee (NCPAC)
470 U.S. 480, 105 S.CT. 1459 (1985)

The Court's ruling in *Buckley v. Valeo* did not put an end to the controversies surrounding the Federal Election Campaign Act. Under the act, if a presidential candidate accepts public financing for his or her election campaign, independent political action committees (PACs) may not spend more than $1,000 to support the election of their presidential candidate. In 1975, the National Conservative Political Action Committee (NCPAC) was formed to help promote the election of political conservatives. When the Federal Election Commission, which monitors campaign contributions for federal elections, and the Democratic Party of the United States charged that NCPAC was violating the provisions of the Federal Election Campaign Act, NCPAC countered that the law violated its First Amendment rights of freedom of speech and association. A federal district court agreed that the restrictions on PACs' campaign contributions ran afoul of the First Amendment. The Federal Election Commission and the Democratic Party of the United States appealed that decision to the Supreme Court. Justice William H. Rehnquist further discusses the pertinent facts in his opinion announcing the decision of the Court.

The Court's decision was five to four; the majority's opinion was announced by Justice Rehnquist. A separate opinion, in part concurring and dissenting, was delivered by Justice Stevens. Dissents were by Justices White and Marshall, joined by Justice Brennan.

☐ *Justice REHNQUIST delivers the opinion of the Court.*

The Presidential Election Campaign Fund Act (Fund Act), 26 U.S.C. Sec. 9001 *et seq.*, offers the Presidential candidates of major political parties the option of receiving public financing for their general election campaigns. If a Presidential candidate elects public financing, Sec. 9012(f) makes it a criminal offense for independent "political committees," such as appellees National Conservative Political Action Committee (NCPAC) and Fund For A Conservative Majority (FCM), to expend more than $1,000 to further that candidate's election. A three-judge District Court for the Eastern District of Pennsylvania, in companion lawsuits brought respectively by the Federal Election Commission (FEC) and by the Democratic Party of the United States and the Democratic National Committee (DNC), held Sec. 9012(f) unconstitutional on its face because it violated the First Amendment to the United States Constitution. . . . [We now affirm the lower court's ruling.]

NCPAC is a nonprofit, nonmembership corporation formed under the District of Columbia Nonprofit Corporation Act in August 1975 and registered with the FEC as a political committee. Its primary purpose is to attempt to influence directly or indirectly the election or defeat of candidates for federal, state, and local offices by making contributions and by making its own expenditures. It is governed by a three-member board of directors which is elected annually by the existing board. The board's chairman and the other two members make all decisions concerning which candidates to support or oppose, the strategy and methods to employ, and the amounts of money to spend. Its contributors have no role in these decisions. It raises money by general and specific direct mail solicitations. It does not maintain separate accounts for the receipts from its general and specific solicitations, nor is it required by law to do so. . . .

Both NCPAC and FCM are self-described ideological organizations with a conservative political philosophy. They solicited funds in support of President Reagan's 1980 campaign, and they spent money on such means as radio and television advertisements to encourage voters to elect him President. On the record before us, these expenditures were "independent" in that they were not made at the request of or in coordination with the official Reagan election campaign committee or any of its agents. . . .

In this case we consider provisions of the Fund Act that make it a criminal offense for political committees such as NCPAC and FCM to make independent expenditures in support of a candidate who has elected to accept public financing. . . .

There is no question that NCPAC and FCM are political committees and that President Reagan was a qualified candidate, and it seems plain enough that the PACs' expenditures fall within the term "qualified campaign expense." The PACs have argued in this Court, though apparently not below, that Sec. 9012(f) was not intended to cover truly independent expenditures such as theirs, but only coordinated expenditures. But "expenditures in co-operation, consultation, or concert, with, or at the request or suggestion of, a candidate, his authorized political committees, or their agents," are considered "contributions" under the FECA and as such are already subject to FECA's $1,000 and $5,000 limitations in Secs. 441a(a)(1), (2). Also, as noted above, one of the requirements for public funding is the candidate's agreement not to accept such contributions. Under the PAC's construction, Sec. 9012(f) would be wholly superfluous, and we find no support for that construction in the legislative history. We conclude that the PACs' independent expenditures at issue in this case are squarely prohibited by Sec. 9012(f), and we proceed to consider whether that prohibition violates the First Amendment.

There can be no doubt that the expenditures at issue in this case produce speech at the core of the First Amendment. . . .

The PACs in this case, of course, are not lone pamphleteers or street corner orators in the Tom Paine mold; they spend substantial amounts of money in order to communicate their political ideas through sophisticated media advertisements. . . . But for purposes of presenting political views in connection with a nationwide Presidential election, allowing the presentation of views while forbidding the expenditure of more than $1,000 to present them is much like allowing a speaker in a public hall to express his views while denying him the use of an amplifying system. . . .

We also reject the notion that the PACs' form of organization or method of solicitation diminishes their entitlement to First Amendment protection. The First Amendment freedom of association is squarely implicated in this case. NCPAC and FCM are mechanisms by which large numbers of individuals of modest means can join together in organizations which serve to "amplif[y] the voice of their adherents." *Buckley v. Valeo.* . . .

Having concluded that the PAC expenditures are entitled to full First Amendment protection, we now look to see if there is a sufficiently strong governmental interest served by Sec. 9012(f)'s restriction on them and whether the section is narrowly tailored to the evil that may legitimately be regulated. . . .

Corruption is a subversion of the political process. Elected officials are influenced to act contrary to their obligations of office by the prospect of financial gain to themselves or infusions of money into their campaigns. The hallmark of corruption is the financial *quid pro quo*: dollars for political favors. But here the conduct proscribed is not contributions to the candidate, but independent expenditures in support of the candidate. The amounts given to the PACs are overwhelmingly small contributions, well under the $1,000 limit on contributions upheld in *Buckley*; and the contributions are by definition not coordinated with the campaign of the candidate. The Court concluded in *Buckley* that there was a fundamental constitutional difference between money spent to advertise one's views independently of the candidate's campaign and money contributed to the candidate to be spent on his campaign. . . .

We think the same conclusion must follow here. It is contended that, because the PACs may by the breadth of their organizations spend larger amounts than the individuals in *Buckley*, the potential for corruption is greater. But precisely what the "corruption" may consist of we are never told with assurance. The fact that candidates and elected officials may alter or reaffirm their own positions on issues in response to political messages paid for by the PACs can hardly be called corruption, for one of the essential features of democracy is the presentation to the electorate of varying points of view.

☐ *Justice STEVENS concurred in part and dissented in part on a question of standing to sue.*

☐ *Justice WHITE, with whom Justice BRENNAN and Justice MARSHALL join, dissenting.*

Section 9012(f) of the Internal Revenue Code limits to $1000 the annual independent expenditures a PAC can make to further the election of a candidate receiving public funds. Because these expenditures "produce speech at the core of the First Amendment," the majority concludes that they can only be regulated in order to avoid real or apparent corruption. Perceiving no such danger, since the money does not go directly to political candidates or their committees, it strikes down Sec. 9012(f).

My disagreements with this analysis, which continues this Court's dismemberment of congressional efforts to regulate campaign financing, are many. First, I continue to believe that *Buckley v. Valeo* (1976), was wrongly decided. Congressional regulation of the amassing and spending of money in political campaigns without doubt involves First Amendment concerns, but restrictions such as the one at issue here are supported by governmental interests—including, but not limited to, the need to avoid real or apparent corruption—sufficiently compelling to withstand scrutiny. Second, even were *Buckley* correct, I consider today's holding a mistaken application of that precedent. The provision challenged here more closely resembles the contribution limitations that were upheld in *Buckley*, and later cases, than the limitations on uncoordinated individual expenditures that were struck down. Finally, even if *Buckley* requires that in general PACs be allowed to make independent expenditures, I do not think that that proposition applies to Sec. 9012(f). As part of an integrated and complex system of public funding for presidential campaigns, Sec. 9012(f) is supported by governmental interests that were absent in *Buckley*, which was premised on a system of private campaign financing. . . .

In short, as I said in *Buckley*, I cannot accept the cynic's "money talks" as a proposition of constitutional law. Today's holding also rests on a second aspect of the *Buckley* holding with which I disagree, *viz.*, its distinction between "independent" and "coordinated" expenditures. The Court was willing to accept that expenditures undertaken in consultation with a candidate or his committee should be viewed as contributions. But it rejected Congress' judgment that independent expenditures were matters of equal concern, concluding that they did not pose the danger of real or apparent corruption that supported limits on contributions. . . . The distinction is not tenable. "Independent" PAC expenditures function as contributions. Indeed, a significant portion of them no doubt would be direct contributions to campaigns had the FECA not limited such contributions to $5,000. . . .

☐ *Justice MARSHALL, dissenting.*

Although I joined the portion of the *Buckley per curiam* that distinguished contributions from independent expenditures for First Amendment purposes, I now believe that the distinction has no constitutional significance. . . .

I disagree that the limitations on contributions and expenditures have significantly different impacts on First Amendment freedoms. First, the underlying rights at issue—freedom of speech and freedom of association—are both core First Amendment rights. Second, in both cases the regulation is of the same form: It concerns the amount of money that can be spent for political activity. Thus, I do not see how one interest can be deemed more compelling than the other. . . .

McConnell v. Federal Election Commission
540 U.S. 93, 124 S.Ct. 619 (2003)

In 2002, Congress enacted and President George W. Bush signed into law the Bipartisan Campaign Reform Act (BCRA), popularly known "the McCain-Feingold law" after its sponsors, Arizona Republican senator John McCain and Wisconsin Democratic senator Russ Feingold. The most comprehensive reform of campaign finance in over a quarter of a century, it addressed developments since *Buckley v. Valeo*, 424 U.S. 1 (1976) (excerpted above), particularly the increased use of "soft money"—unregulated money under the Federal Election Campaign Act (FECA) of 1971—and the proliferation of "issue ads" or "attack ads." Proponents of the law contended that soft money had a corrupting influence on the political process. In the 2000 election, nearly half of the money spent—$498 million or 42 percent—by political parties was soft money—money spent in unlimited amounts for get-out-the-vote drives and attack ads. Moreover, 60 percent of that money came from only 800 individuals and organizations. Opponents countered that the restrictions violated the First Amendment guarantees for free speech and association.

Title I of the BCRA restricts the spending of soft money by political parties, officeholders, and candidates; and Title II prohibits corporations and unions from using their general funds for "issue ads" and other "electioneering communications" aimed at influencing the outcome of federal elections. Titles III, IV, and V contain additional restrictions requiring broadcasters to sell time to qualified candidates forty-five days prior to a primary and sixty days before the general election; and so-called millionaire provisions that specify staggered contribution limits if an opponent spends a triggering amount of personal funds. Title IV forbade individuals "17 years old or younger" from making campaign contributions, and Title V imposed a requirement on broadcasters to keep publicly available records of politically related broadcast requests.

The constitutionality of the BCRA was immediately challenged by Kentucky Republican senator Mitch McConnell and a wide range of interest groups, including the AFL-CIO, the American Civil Liberties Union, the National Rifle Association, and the National Right to Life Committee. A three-judge panel heard the challenges to the law and issued a 1,698-page decision upholding most of the BCRA but striking down restrictions on soft money. Subsequently, twelve appeals by different individuals and groups were made to the Supreme Court and consolidated. The Court granted the case on an expedited basis and heard four hours of oral arguments in September 2003.

In December 2003, the Supreme Court handed down almost 300 pages of opinions, affirming and reversing in part the lower court. The justices divided five to four, eight to one, and voted unanimously on part of one opinion. For the first time in history four justices issued three opinions for the Court. Justices Stevens and O'Connor issued the opinion for the Court upholding the BCRA's restrictions on soft money and issue ads. Chief Justice Rehnquist issued an opinion for the Court denying the petitioners standing to challenge the "millionaire provisions" and striking down the ban on campaign contributions by individuals younger than eighteen. Justice Breyer issued an opinion for the Court upholding the requirements for broadcasters to maintain publicly available records on politically related broadcast requests. Justice Stevens filed a dissent from Chief Justice Rehnquist's opinion holding that the challenge to the "millionaire provisions" was nonjusticiable. Chief Justice Rehnquist also filed a dissenting opinion. Justices Kennedy, Scalia, and Thomas each filed opinions in part dissenting and concurring. The lineup of the justices is shown on page 945.

JUSTICES IN THE MAJORITY

HOLDING	VOTE	REHNQUIST	STEVENS	O'CONNOR	SCALIA	KENNEDY	SOUTER	THOMAS	GINSBURG	BREYER
Upheld ban on soft money	5:4		X	X			X		X	X
Upheld restrictions on issue ads by corporations and unions	5:4		X	X			X		X	X
Struck down ban on contributions by individuals under 18	9:0	X	X	X	X	X	X	X	X	X
Upheld requirement that certain ads authorized by a candidate or committee clearly identify them	8:1	X	X	X	X	X	X		X	X
Upheld record-keeping requirement for broadcasters	5:4		X	X			X		X	X

□ *Justice STEVENS and Justice O'CONNOR delivered the opinion of the
Court with respect to BCRA Titles I and II, [which Justices SOUTER,
GINSBURG, and BREYER joined].*

In this opinion we discuss Titles I and II of BCRA. The opinion of the
Court delivered by THE CHIEF JUSTICE discusses Titles III and IV, and
the opinion of the Court delivered by Justice BREYER discusses Title V. . . .

BCRA is the most recent federal enactment designed "to purge national politics of what was conceived to be the pernicious influence of 'big
money' campaign contributions." [The] 1907 [Tillman Act] completely
banned corporate contributions of "money . . . in connection with" any
federal election. In 1925 Congress extended the prohibition of "contributions" "to include 'anything of value,' and made acceptance of a corporate
contribution as well as the giving of such a contribution a crime." *Federal
Election Comm'n v. National Right to Work Comm.*, 459 U.S. 197 (1982). . . .
During and shortly after World War II, Congress reacted to the "enormous
financial outlays" made by some unions in connection with national elections. Congress first restricted union contributions in the Hatch Act, and
it later prohibited "union contributions in connection with federal elections . . . altogether." . . .

In early 1972 Congress continued its steady improvement of the national election laws by enacting FECA. . . . As the 1972 presidential elections made clear, however, FECA's passage did not deter unseemly
fundraising and campaign practices. Evidence of those practices persuaded
Congress to enact the Federal Election Campaign Act Amendments of
1974. The 1974 amendments closed the loophole that had allowed candidates to use an unlimited number of political committees for fundraising
purposes and thereby to circumvent the limits on individual committees'
receipts and disbursements. They also limited individual political contributions to any single candidate to $1,000 per election, with an overall annual
limitation of $25,000 by any contributor; imposed ceilings on spending by
candidates and political parties for national conventions; required reporting
and public disclosure of contributions and expenditures exceeding certain
limits; and established the Federal Election Commission (FEC) to administer and enforce the legislation. . . .

This Court . . . concluded that each set of limitations raised serious—
though different—concerns under the First Amendment. *Buckley v. Valeo*
(1976). We treated the limitations on candidate and individual expenditures
as direct restraints on speech, but we observed that the contribution limitations, in contrast, imposed only "a marginal restriction upon the contributor's ability to engage in free communication." "[W]e determined that
limiting contributions served an interest in protecting "the integrity of our
system of representative democracy." In the end, the Act's primary purpose—
"to limit the actuality and appearance of corruption resulting from large individual financial contributions"—provided "a constitutionally sufficient
justification for the $1,000 contribution limitation."

We prefaced our analysis of the $1,000 limitation on expenditures by
observing that it broadly encompassed every expenditure " 'relative to a
clearly identified candidate.' " . . . We concluded . . . that as so narrowed, the
provision would not provide effective protection against the dangers of *quid*

pro quo arrangements, because persons and groups could eschew expenditures that expressly advocated the election or defeat of a clearly identified candidate while remaining "free to spend as much as they want to promote the candidate and his views." . . . We therefore held that Congress' interest in preventing real or apparent corruption was inadequate to justify the heavy burdens on the freedoms of expression and association that the expenditure limits imposed. . . .

As a preface to our discussion of the specific provisions of BCRA, we comment briefly on the increased importance of "soft money" [and] the proliferation of "issue ads." . . .

SOFT MONEY

Under FECA, "contributions" must be made with funds that are subject to the Act's disclosure requirements and source and amount limitations. Such funds are known as "federal" or "hard" money. FECA defines the term "contribution," however, to include only the gift or advance of anything of value "made by any person for the purpose of influencing any election for Federal office." Donations made solely for the purpose of influencing state or local elections are therefore unaffected by FECA's requirements and prohibitions. As a result, prior to the enactment of BCRA, federal law permitted corporations and unions, as well as individuals who had already made the maximum permissible contributions to federal candidates, to contribute "nonfederal money"—also known as "soft money"—to political parties for activities intended to influence state or local elections.

Shortly after *Buckley* was decided, questions arose concerning the treatment of contributions intended to influence both federal and state elections. Although a literal reading of FECA's definition of "contribution" would have required such activities to be funded with hard money, the FEC ruled that political parties could fund mixed-purpose activities—including get-out-the-vote drives and generic party advertising—in part with soft money. In 1995 the FEC concluded that the parties could also use soft money to defray the costs of "legislative advocacy media advertisements," even if the ads mentioned the name of a federal candidate, so long as they did not expressly advocate the candidate's election or defeat.

As the permissible uses of soft money expanded, the amount of soft money raised and spent by the national political parties increased exponentially. Of the two major parties' total spending, soft money accounted for 5% ($21.6 million) in 1984, 11% ($45 million) in 1988, 16% ($80 million) in 1992, 30% ($272 million) in 1996, and 42% ($498 million) in 2000. . . .

ISSUE ADVERTISING

In *Buckley* we construed FECA's disclosure and reporting requirements, as well as its expenditure limitations, "to reach only funds used for communications that expressly advocate the election or defeat of a clearly identifiable candidate." As a result of that strict reading of the statute, the use or omission of "magic words" such as "Elect John Smith" or "Vote Against Jane Doe" marked a bright statutory line separating "express advocacy" from "issue advocacy." Express advocacy was subject to FECA's limitations and could be financed only using hard money. The political parties, in other words, could not use soft money to sponsor ads that used any magic words, and corporations and unions could not fund such ads out of their general treasuries. So-called issue ads, on the other hand, not only could be financed with soft money, but could be aired without disclosing the identity of, or any other information about, their sponsors.

While the distinction between "issue" and express advocacy seemed neat in theory, the two categories of advertisements proved functionally identical in important respects. Both were used to advocate the election or defeat of clearly identified federal candidates, even though the so-called issue ads eschewed the use of magic words. Little difference existed, for example, between an ad that urged viewers to "vote against Jane Doe" and one that condemned Jane Doe's record on a particular issue before exhorting viewers to "call Jane Doe and tell her what you think." . . .

BCRA's central provisions are designed to address Congress' concerns about the increasing use of soft money and issue advertising to influence federal elections. . . . Title I is Congress' effort to plug the soft-money loophole. The cornerstone of Title I is new FECA Sec. 323(a), which prohibits national party committees and their agents from soliciting, receiving, directing, or spending any soft money. In short, Sec. 323(a) takes national parties out of the soft-money business.

The remaining provisions of new FECA Sec. 323 largely reinforce the restrictions in Sec. 323(a). New FECA Sec. 323(b) [for example] prevents the wholesale shift of soft-money influence from national to state party committees by prohibiting state and local party committees from using such funds for activities that affect federal elections. These "Federal election activit[ies]," defined in new FECA Sec. 301 (20)(A), are almost identical to the mixed-purpose activities that have long been regulated under the FEC's pre-BCRA allocation regime. . . .

In *Buckley* and subsequent cases, we have subjected restrictions on campaign expenditures to closer scrutiny than limits on campaign contributions. See, e.g., *Federal Election Comm'n v. Beaumont*, [539 U.S. 146] (2003); see also *Nixon v. Shrink Missouri Government PAC*, 528 U.S. 377 (2000). In these cases we have recognized that contribution limits, unlike limits on expenditures, "entai[l] only a marginal restriction upon the contributor's ability to engage in free communication." . . .

Because the electoral process is the very "means through which a free society democratically translates political speech into concrete governmental action," *Shrink Missouri*, contribution limits, like other measures aimed at protecting the integrity of the process, tangibly benefit public participation in political debate. For that reason, [the] less rigorous standard of review we have applied to contribution limits (*Buckley*'s "closely drawn" scrutiny) shows proper deference to Congress' ability to weigh competing constitutional interests in an area in which it enjoys particular expertise. . . .

Like the contribution limits we upheld in *Buckley*, Sec. 323's restrictions have only a marginal impact on the ability of contributors, candidates, officeholders, and parties to engage in effective political speech. Complex as its provisions may be, Sec. 323, in the main, does little more than regulate the ability of wealthy individuals, corporations, and unions to contribute large sums of money to influence federal elections, federal candidates, and federal officeholders. . . .

☐ *New FECA Sec. 323(a)'s Restrictions on National Party Committees*

The core of Title I is new FECA Sec. 323(a), which provides that "national committee[s] of a political party . . . may not solicit, receive, or direct to another person a contribution, donation, or transfer of funds or any other thing of value, or spend any funds, that are not subject to the limitations, prohibitions, and reporting requirements of this Act."

The main goal of Sec. 323(a) is modest. In large part, it simply effects a return to the scheme that was approved in *Buckley* and that was subverted by the creation of the FEC's allocation regime, which permitted the political parties to fund federal electioneering efforts with a combination of hard and soft money. Under that allocation regime, national parties were able to use vast amounts of soft money in their efforts to elect federal candidates. Consequently, as long as they directed the money to the political parties, donors could contribute large amounts of soft money for use in activities designed to influence federal elections. New Sec. 323(a) is designed to put a stop to that practice.

1. GOVERNMENTAL INTERESTS UNDERLYING HEW FECA SEC. 323(a)

The Government defends Sec. 323(*a*)'s ban on national parties' involvement with soft money as necessary to prevent the actual and apparent corruption of federal candidates and officeholders. Our cases have made clear that the prevention of corruption or its appearance constitutes a sufficiently important interest to justify political contribution limits. We have not limited that interest to the elimination of cash-for-votes exchanges. . . .

The question for present purposes is whether large soft-money contributions to national party committees have a corrupting influence or give rise to the appearance of corruption. Both common sense and the ample record in these cases confirm Congress' belief that they do. . . .

The evidence in the record shows that candidates and donors alike have in fact exploited the soft-money loophole, the former to increase their prospects of election and the latter to create debt on the part of officeholders, with the national parties serving as willing intermediaries. Thus, despite FECA's hard-money limits on direct contributions to candidates, federal officeholders have commonly asked donors to make soft-money donations to national and state committees "solely in order to assist federal campaigns," including the officeholder's own. . . .

Despite this evidence and the close ties that candidates and officeholders have with their parties, Justice KENNEDY would limit Congress' regulatory interest only to the prevention of the actual or apparent *quid pro quo* corruption "inherent in" contributions made directly to, contributions made at the express behest of, and expenditures made in coordination with, a federal officeholder or candidate. . . . This crabbed view of corruption, and particularly of the appearance of corruption, ignores precedent, common sense, and the realities of political fundraising exposed by the record in this litigation. . . .

2. NEW FECA SEC. 323(a)'S RESTRICTION ON SPENDING

AND RECEIVING SOFT MONEY

Plaintiffs and THE CHIEF JUSTICE contend that Sec. 323(a) is impermissibly overbroad because it subjects all funds raised and spent by national parties to FECA's hard-money source and amount limits, including, for example, funds spent on purely state and local elections in which no federal office is at stake. Such activities, THE CHIEF JUSTICE asserts, pose "little or no potential to corrupt . . . federal candidates or officeholders." This observation is beside the point. . . .

Access to federal officeholders is the most valuable favor the national party committees are able to give in exchange for large donations. The fact that officeholders comply by donating their valuable time indicates either that officeholders place substantial value on the soft-money contribution themselves, without regard to their end use, or that national committees are able to exert considerable control over federal officeholders. . . .

3. NEW FECA SEC. 323(a)'S RESTRICTION ON SOLICITING OR DIRECTING SOFT MONEY

Plaintiffs also contend that Sec. 323(a)'s prohibition on national parties' soliciting or directing soft-money contributions is substantially overbroad. The reach of the solicitation prohibition, however, is limited. It bars only solicitations of soft money by national party committees and by party officers in their official capacities. The committees remain free to solicit hard money on their own behalf, as well as to solicit hard money on behalf of state committees and state and local candidates. They also can contribute hard money to state committees and to candidates. In accordance with FEC regulations, furthermore, officers of national parties are free to solicit soft money in their individual capacities, or, if they are also officials of state parties, in that capacity. . . .

4. NEW FECA SEC. 323(a)'S APPLICATION TO MINOR PARTIES

The McConnell and political party plaintiffs contend that Sec. 323(a) is substantially overbroad and must be stricken on its face because it impermissibly infringes the speech and associational rights of minor parties such as the Libertarian National Committee, which, owing to their slim prospects for electoral success and the fact that they receive few large soft-money contributions from corporate sources, pose no threat of corruption comparable to that posed by the RNC and DNC. In *Buckley*, we rejected a similar argument concerning limits on contributions to minor-party candidates, noting that "any attempt to exclude minor parties and independents en masse from the Act's contribution limitations overlooks the fact that minor-party candidates may win elective office or have a substantial impact on the outcome of an election." We have thus recognized that the relevance of the interest in avoiding actual or apparent corruption is not a function of the number of legislators a given party manages to elect. It applies as much to a minor party that manages to elect only one of its members to federal office as it does to a major party whose members make up a majority of Congress. It is therefore reasonable to require that all parties and all candidates follow the same set of rules designed to protect the integrity of the electoral process. . . .

5. NEW FECA SEC. 323(a)'S ASSOCIATIONAL BURDENS

Finally, plaintiffs assert that Sec. 323(a) is unconstitutional because it impermissibly interferes with the ability of national committees to associate with state and local committees. By way of example, plaintiffs point to the Republican Victory Plans, whereby the RNC acts in concert with the state and local committees of a given State to plan and implement joint, full-ticket fundraising and electioneering programs. The political parties assert that Sec. 323(a) outlaws any participation in Victory Plans by RNC officers, including merely sitting down at a table and engaging in collective decision-making about how soft money will be solicited, received, and spent.

We are not persuaded by this argument because it hinges on an unnaturally broad reading of the terms "spend," "receive," "direct," and "solicit." Nothing on the face of Sec. 323(a) prohibits national party officers, whether acting in their official or individual capacities, from sitting down with state and local party committees or candidates to plan and advise how to raise and spend soft money. As long as the national party officer does not personally spend, receive, direct, or solicit soft money, Sec. 323(a) permits a wide range of joint planning and electioneering activity.

NEW FECA SEC. 323(b)'S RESTRICTIONS ON STATE AND LOCAL PARTY COMMITTEES

Section 323(b) is designed to foreclose wholesale evasion of Sec. 323(a)'s anticorruption measures by sharply curbing state committees' ability to use large soft-money contributions to influence federal elections. The core of Sec. 323(b) is a straightforward contribution regulation: It prevents donors from contributing nonfederal funds to state and local party committees to help finance "Federal election activity." The term "Federal election activity" encompasses four distinct categories of electioneering: (1) voter registration activity during the 120 days preceding a regularly scheduled federal election; (2) voter identification, get-out-the-vote (GOTV), and generic campaign activity that is "conducted in connection with an election in which a candidate for Federal office appears on the ballot"; (3) any "public communication" that "refers to a clearly identified candidate for Federal office" and "promotes," "supports," "attacks," or "opposes" a candidate for that office; and (4) the services provided by a state committee employee who dedicates more than 25% of his or her time to "activities in connection with a Federal election." The Act explicitly excludes several categories of activity from this definition: public communications that refer solely to nonfederal candidates; contributions to nonfederal candidates; state and local political conventions; and the cost of grassroots campaign materials like bumper stickers that refer only to state candidates. All activities that fall within the statutory definition must be funded with hard money.

Section 323(b)(2), the so-called Levin Amendment, carves out an exception to this general rule. A refinement on the pre-BCRA regime that permitted parties to pay for certain activities with a mix of federal and nonfederal funds, the Levin Amendment allows state and local party committees to pay for certain types of federal election activity with an allocated ratio of hard money and "Levin funds"—that is, funds raised within an annual limit of $10,000 per person. Except for the $10,000 cap and certain related restrictions to prevent circumvention of that limit, Sec. 323(b)(2) leaves regulation of such contributions to the States.

We begin by noting that, in addressing the problem of soft-money contributions to state committees, Congress both drew a conclusion and made a prediction. Its conclusion, based on the evidence before it, was that the corrupting influence of soft money does not insinuate itself into the political process solely through national party committees. Rather, state committees function as an alternate avenue for precisely the same corrupting forces. . . . Section 323(b) thus promotes an important governmental interest by confronting the corrupting influence that soft-money donations to political parties already have.

Congress also made a prediction. Having been taught the hard lesson of circumvention by the entire history of campaign finance regulation, Congress knew that soft-money donors would react to Sec. 323(a) by scrambling to find another way to purchase influence. It was "neither novel nor implausible" for Congress to conclude that political parties would react to Sec. 323(a) by directing soft-money contributors to the state committees, and that federal candidates would be just as indebted to these contributors as they had been to those who had formerly contributed to the national parties. . . .

We accordingly conclude that Sec. 323(b), on its face, is closely drawn to match the important governmental interests of preventing corruption and the appearance of corruption.

NEW FECA SEC. 323(D)'S RESTRICTIONS ON PARTIES' SOLICITATIONS FOR, AND DONATIONS TO, TAX–EXEMPT ORGANIZATIONS

Section 323(d) prohibits national, state, and local party committees, and their agents or subsidiaries, from "solicit[ing] any funds for, or mak[ing] or direct[ing] any donations" to, any organization established under Sec. 501(c) of the Internal Revenue Code that makes expenditures in connection with an election for federal office, and any political organizations established under Sec. 527 "other than a political committee, a State, district, or local committee of a political party, or the authorized campaign committee of a candidate for State or local office." The District Court struck down the provision on its face. We reverse and uphold Sec. 323(d), narrowly construing the section's ban on donations to apply only to the donation of funds not raised in compliance with FECA. . . .

Title II of BCRA, entitled "Noncandidate Campaign Expenditures," is divided into two subtitles: "Electioneering Communications" and "Independent and Coordinated Expenditures."

BCRA SEC. 201'S DEFINITION OF "ELECTIONEERING COMMUNICATION"

The first section of Title II, Sec. 201, comprehensively amends FECA Sec. 304, which requires political committees to file detailed periodic financial reports with the FEC. The amendment coins a new term, "electioneering communication," to replace the narrowing construction of FECA's disclosure provisions adopted by this Court in *Buckley*. As discussed further below, that construction limited the coverage of FECA's disclosure requirement to communications expressly advocating the election or defeat of particular candidates. By contrast, the term "electioneering communication" is not so limited, but is defined to encompass any "broadcast, cable, or satellite communication" that "(I) refers to a clearly identified candidate for Federal office; (II) is made within (aa) 60 days before a general, special, or run-off election for the office sought by the candidate; or (bb) 30 days before a primary or preference election, or a convention or caucus of a political party that has authority to nominate a candidate, for the office sought by the candidate; and (III) in the case of a communication which refers to a candidate other than President or Vice President, is targeted to the relevant electorate." . . .

In addition to setting forth this definition, BCRA's amendments to FECA Sec. 304 specify significant disclosure requirements for persons who fund electioneering communications. BCRA's use of this new term is not, however, limited to the disclosure context: A later section of the Act (BCRA Sec. 203) restricts corporations' and labor unions' funding of electioneering communications. Plaintiffs challenge the constitutionality of the new term as it applies in both the disclosure and the expenditure contexts.

The major premise of plaintiffs' challenge to BCRA's use of the term "electioneering communication" is that *Buckley* drew a constitutionally mandated line between express advocacy and so-called issue advocacy, and that speakers possess an inviolable First Amendment right to engage in the latter category of speech. . . .

That position misapprehends our prior decisions, for the express advocacy restriction was an endpoint of statutory interpretation, not a first principle of constitutional law. . . . [A] plain reading of *Buckley* makes clear that the express advocacy limitation, in both the expenditure and the disclosure contexts, was the product of statutory interpretation rather than a constitutional command. In narrowly reading the FECA provisions in *Buckley* to avoid problems of vagueness and overbreadth, we nowhere suggested that a statute that was neither vague nor overbroad would be required to toe the same express advocacy line.

In short, the concept of express advocacy and the concomitant class of magic words were born of an effort to avoid constitutional infirmities. . . . Nor are we persuaded, independent of our precedents, that the First Amendment erects a rigid barrier between express advocacy and so-called issue advocacy. That notion cannot be squared with our longstanding recognition that the presence or absence of magic words cannot meaningfully distinguish electioneering speech from a true issue ad. Indeed, the unmistakable lesson from the record in this litigation is that *Buckley*'s magic-words requirement is functionally meaningless. Not only can advertisers easily evade the line by eschewing the use of magic words, but they would seldom choose to use such words even if permitted. And although the resulting advertisements do not urge the viewer to vote for or against a candidate in so many words, they are no less clearly intended to influence the election. *Buckley*'s express advocacy line, in short, has not aided the legislative effort to combat real or apparent corruption, and Congress enacted BCRA to correct the flaws it found in the existing system. . . .

BCRA SEC. 203'S PROHIBITION OF CORPORATE AND LABOR
DISBURSEMENTS FOR ELECTIONEERING COMMUNICATIONS

Since our decision in *Buckley*, Congress' power to prohibit corporations and unions from using funds in their treasuries to finance advertisements expressly advocating the election or defeat of candidates in federal elections has been firmly embedded in our law. The ability to form and administer separate segregated funds authorized by FECA Sec. 316 has provided corporations and unions with a constitutionally sufficient opportunity to engage in express advocacy. That has been this Court's unanimous view, and it is not challenged in this litigation.

Section 203 of BCRA amends FECA Sec. 316(b)(2) to extend this rule, which previously applied only to express advocacy, to all "electioneering communications" covered by the definition of that term in amended FECA Sec. 304(f)(3). Thus, under BCRA, corporations and unions may not use their general treasury funds to finance electioneering communications, but they remain free to organize and administer segregated funds, or PACs, for that purpose. Because corporations can still fund electioneering communications with PAC money, it is "simply wrong" to view the provision as a "complete ban" on expression rather than a regulation. . . .

We are under no illusion that BCRA will be the last congressional statement on the matter. Money, like water, will always find an outlet. What problems will arise, and how Congress will respond, are concerns for another day. In the main we uphold BCRA's two principal, complementary features: the control of soft money and the regulation of electioneering communications. Accordingly, we affirm in part and reverse in part the District Court's judgment with respect to Titles I and II.

□ *Chief Justice REHNQUIST delivered the opinion of the Court with respect to BCRA Titles III and IV.*

This opinion addresses issues involving miscellaneous Title III and IV provisions of the Bipartisan Campaign Reform Act of 2002 (BCRA). For the reasons discussed below, we affirm the judgment of the District Court with respect to these provisions.

BCRA Sec. 305 amends the federal Communications Act of 1934, which requires that, 45 days before a primary or 60 days before a general election, broadcast stations must sell a qualified candidate the "lowest unit charge of the station for the same class and amount of time for the same period." . . .

The McConnell plaintiffs challenge Sec. 305. They argue that Senator McConnell's testimony that he plans to run advertisements critical of his opponents in the future and that he had run them in the past is sufficient to establish standing. We think not.

Article III of the Constitution limits the "judicial power" to the resolution of "cases" and "controversies." One element of the "bedrock" case-or-controversy requirement is that plaintiffs must establish that they have standing to sue. On many occasions, we have reiterated the three requirements that constitute the " 'irreducible constitutional minimum' " of standing. First, a plaintiff must demonstrate an "injury in fact," which is "concrete," "distinct and palpable," and "actual or imminent." Second, a plaintiff must establish "a causal connection between the injury and the conduct complained of—the injury has to be 'fairly trace[able] to the challenged action of the defendant, and not . . . th[e] result [of] some third party not before the court.' " *Lujan v. Defenders of Wildlife*, 504 U.S. 555 (1992). Third, a plaintiff must show the " 'substantial likelihood' that the requested relief will remedy the alleged injury in fact."

Because Senator McConnell's current term does not expire until 2009, the earliest day he could be affected by Sec. 305 is 45 days before the Republican primary election in 2008. This alleged injury in fact is too remote temporally to satisfy Article III standing. [Chief Justice REHNQUIST proceeds to deny standing to other plaintiffs' challenges to contribution limits and to the "millionaire provisions," before addressing the challenge to restrictions on campaign contributions by individuals under the age of 18.] . . .

BCRA Sec. 318 prohibits individuals "17 years old or younger" from making contributions to candidates and contributions or donations to political parties. The McConnell and Echols plaintiffs . . . argue that Sec. 318 violates the First Amendment rights of minors. We agree.

Minors enjoy the protection of the First Amendment. See, e.g., *Tinker v. Des Moines Independent Community School Dist.*, 393 U. S. 503 (1969). Limitations on the amount that an individual may contribute to a candidate or political committee impinge on the protected freedoms of expression and association. When the Government burdens the right to contribute, we apply heightened scrutiny. We ask whether the statute is "closely drawn" to avoid unnecessary abridgment of First Amendment freedoms. The Government asserts that the provision protects against corruption by conduit; that is, donations by parents through their minor children to circumvent contribution limits applicable to the parents. But the Government offers scant evidence of this form of evasion. . . .

For the foregoing reasons, we affirm the District Court's judgment finding the plaintiffs' challenges to BCRA Secs. 305, 307, and the millionaire provisions nonjusticiable, striking down as unconstitutional BCRA Sec. 318, and upholding BCRA Sec. 311.

☐ *[Justice BREYER delivered the opinion of the Court with respect to BCRA Title V and upheld the constitutionality of Sec. 504, amending the Communications Act of 1934, and requiring broadcasters to keep publicly available records of politically related broadcasting requests. He found no evidence that the requirements impose onerous administrative burdens, lack any offsetting justification, and consequently violate the First Amendment. In addition, he noted that the Court should defer the FEC's interpretation of the requirements.]*

☐ *Justice STEVENS, dissenting with respect to Sec. 305 [and which Justices GINSBURG and BREYER join].*

THE CHIEF JUSTICE, writing for the Court, concludes that the McConnell plaintiffs lack standing to challenge Sec. 305 of BCRA because Senator McConnell cannot be affected by the provision until "45 days before the Republican primary election in 2008." I am not persuaded that Article III's case-or-controversy requirement imposes such a strict temporal limit on our jurisdiction. By asserting that he has run attack ads in the past, that he plans to run such ads in his next campaign, and that Sec. 305 will adversely affect his campaign strategy, McConnell has identified a "concrete," " 'distinct,' " and " 'actual' " injury. That the injury is distant in time does not make it illusory. . . .

Like BCRA's other disclosure requirements, Sec. 305 evenhandedly regulates speech based on its electioneering content. In sum, I would uphold Sec. 305.

☐ *Chief Justice REHNQUIST, dissenting with respect to BCRA*
Titles I and V [and which Justices SCALIA and KENNEDY join].

The Court fails to recognize that the national political parties are exemplars of political speech at all levels of government, in addition to effective fundraisers for federal candidates and officeholders. . . . Indeed, some national political parties exist primarily for the purpose of expressing ideas and generating debate.

When political parties engage in pure political speech that has little or no potential to corrupt their federal candidates and officeholders, the government cannot constitutionally burden their speech any more than it could burden the speech of individuals engaging in these same activities. . . .

☐ *Justice THOMAS, concurring with respect to BCRA Titles III and IV, except for BCRA Secs. 311 and 318, concurring in the result with respect to BCRA Sec. 318, concurring in the judgment in part and dissenting in part with respect to BCRA Title II, and dissenting with respect to BCRA Titles I, V, and Sec. 311 (and which Justice SCALIA joins in part].*

With breathtaking scope, the Bipartisan Campaign Reform Act of 2002 (BCRA), directly targets and constricts core political speech, the "primary object of First Amendment protection." *Nixon v. Shrink Missouri Government PAC*, 528 U.S. 377 (2000) (THOMAS, J., dissenting). . . .

The very "purpose of the First Amendment [is] to preserve an uninhibited marketplace of ideas in which truth will ultimately prevail." *Red Lion Broadcasting Co. v. FCC*, 395 U.S. 367 (1969). Yet today the fundamental principle that "the best test of truth is the power of the thought to get itself accepted in the competition of the market," *Abrams v. United States*, 250 U.S. 616 (1919) (HOLMES, J., dissenting), is cast aside in the purported service of preventing "corruption," or the mere "appearance of corruption." *Buckley v. Valeo*. . . .

☐ *Justice KENNEDY, concurring in the judgment in part and dissenting in part with respect to BCRA Titles I and II, [which Chief Justice REHNQUIST joined and Justices SCALIA and THOMAS joined in part].*

Until today's consolidated cases, the Court has accepted but two principles to use in determining the validity of campaign finance restrictions. First is the anticorruption rationale. The principal concern, of course, is the agreement for a *quid pro quo* between officeholders (or candidates) and those who would seek to influence them. The Court has said the interest in preventing corruption allows limitations on receipt of the *quid* by a candidate or officeholder, regardless of who gives it or of the intent of the donor or officeholder. Second, the Court has analyzed laws that classify on the basis of the speaker's corporate or union identity under the corporate speech rationale.

The Court has said that the willing adoption of the entity form by corpora-tions and unions justifies regulating them differently: Their ability to give candidates *quids* may be subject not only to limits but also to outright bans; their electoral speech may likewise be curtailed. . . .

Buckley made clear, by its express language and its context, that the cor-ruption interest only justifies regulating candidates' and officeholders' receipt of what we can call the "*quids*" in the *quid pro quo* formulation. The Court rested its decision on the principle that campaign finance regulation that re-stricts speech without requiring proof of particular corrupt action with-stands constitutional challenge only if it regulates conduct posing a demonstrable *quid pro quo* danger. . . .

The Court . . . in effect interprets the anticorruption rationale to al-low regulation not just of "actual or apparent *quid pro quo* arrangements," but of any conduct that wins goodwill from or influences a Member of Congress. . . . The very aim of *Buckley's* standard, however, was to define un-due influence by reference to the presence of *quid pro quo* involving the of-ficeholder. The Court, in contrast, concludes that access, without more, proves influence is undue. Access, in the Court's view, has the same legal ramifications as actual or apparent corruption of officeholders. This new def-inition of corruption sweeps away all protections for speech that lie in its path. . . .

Today's decision breaks faith with our tradition of robust and unfettered debate. . . .

☐*Justice SCALIA, concurring with respect to BCRA Titles III and IV, dis-senting with respect to BCRA Titles I and V, and concurring in the judgment in part and dissenting in part with respect to BCRA Title II.*

This is a sad day for the freedom of speech. Who could have imagined that the same Court which, within the past four years, has sternly disapproved of restrictions upon such inconsequential forms of expression as virtual child pornography, *Ashcroft v. Free Speech Coalition*, 535 U.S. 234 (2002), tobacco ad-vertising, *Lorillard Tobacco Co. v. Reilly*, 533 U.S. 525 (2001), dissemination of illegally intercepted communications, *Bartnicki v. Vopper*, 532 U.S. 514 (2001), and sexually explicit cable programming, *United States v. Playboy Entertainment Group, Inc.*, 529 U.S. 803 (2000), would smile with favor upon a law that cuts to the heart of what the First Amendment is meant to protect: the right to criticize the government. For that is what the most offensive provisions of this legislation are all about. We are governed by Congress, and this legislation prohibits the criticism of Members of Congress by those entities most capa-ble of giving such criticism loud voice: national political parties and cor-porations, both of the commercial and the not-for-profit sort. It forbids pre-election criticism of incumbents by corporations, even not-for-profit corporations, by use of their general funds; and forbids national-party use of "soft" money to fund "issue ads" that incumbents find so offensive. . . .

Beyond that, however, the present legislation targets for prohibition cer-tain categories of campaign speech that are particularly harmful to in-cumbents. Is it accidental, do you think, that incumbents raise about three times as much "hard money"—the sort of funding generally not restricted by this legislation—as do their challengers? . . .

I wish to address three fallacious propositions that might be thought to justify some or all of the provisions of this legislation—only the last of which is explicitly embraced by the principal opinion for the Court, but all of which underlie, I think, its approach to these cases.

MONEY IS NOT SPEECH

It was said by congressional proponents of this legislation that since this legislation regulates nothing but the expenditure of money for speech, as opposed to speech itself, the burden it imposes is not subject to full First Amendment scrutiny; the government may regulate the raising and spending of campaign funds just as it regulates other forms of conduct, such as burning draft cards, see *United States v. O'Brien*, 391 U.S. 367 (1968), or camping out on the National Mall, see *Clark v. Community for Creative Non-Violence*, 468 U.S. 288 (1984).

Our traditional view was correct, and today's cavalier attitude toward regulating the financing of speech (the "exacting scrutiny" test of *Buckley* is not uttered in any majority opinion, and is not observed in the ones from which I dissent) frustrates the fundamental purpose of the First Amendment.

In any economy operated on even the most rudimentary principles of division of labor, effective public communication requires the speaker to make use of the services of others. An author may write a novel, but he will seldom publish and distribute it himself. . . . Division of labor requires a means of mediating exchange, and in a commercial society, that means is supplied by money. The publisher pays the author for the right to sell his book; it pays its staff who print and assemble the book; it demands payments from booksellers who bring the book to market. . . . The right to speak would be largely ineffective if it did not include the right to engage in financial transactions that are the incidents of its exercise.

[W]here the government singles out money used to fund speech as its legislative object, it is acting against speech as such, no less than if it had targeted the paper on which a book was printed or the trucks that deliver it to the bookstore. . . .

We have kept faith with the Founders' tradition by prohibiting the selective taxation of the press. *Minneapolis Star & Tribune Co. v. Minnesota Comm'r of Revenue*, 460 U.S. 575 (1983) (ink and paper tax). And we have done so whether the tax was the product of illicit motive or not. These press-taxation cases belie the claim that regulation of money used to fund speech is not regulation of speech itself. . . .

It should be obvious, then, that a law limiting the amount a person can spend to broadcast his political views is a direct restriction on speech. . . .

POOLING MONEY IS NOT SPEECH

Another proposition which could explain at least some of the results of today's opinion is that the First Amendment right to spend money for speech does not include the right to combine with others in spending money for speech. . . . The freedom to associate with others for the dissemination of ideas—not just by singing or speaking in unison, but by pooling financial resources for expressive purposes—is part of the freedom of speech. . . .

If it were otherwise, Congress would be empowered to enact legislation requiring newspapers to be sole proprietorships, banning their use of partnership or corporate form. That sort of restriction would be an obvious violation of the First Amendment, and it is incomprehensible why the conclusion should change when what is at issue is the pooling of funds for the most important (and most perennially threatened) category of speech: electoral speech. . . .

SPEECH BY CORPORATIONS CAN BE ABRIDGED

The last proposition that might explain at least some of today's casual abridgment of free-speech rights is this: that the particular form of association known as a corporation does not enjoy full First Amendment protection. Of course the text of the First Amendment does not limit its application in this fashion. . . . In *First Nat. Bank of Boston v. Bellotti*, 435 U.S. 765 (1978), we held unconstitutional a state prohibition of corporate speech designed to influence the vote on referendum proposals.

The Court changed course in *Austin v. Michigan Chamber of Commerce*, 494 U.S. 652 (1990), upholding a state prohibition of an independent corporate expenditure in support of a candidate for state office. I dissented in that case, and remain of the view that it was error. In the modern world, giving the government power to exclude corporations from the political debate enables it effectively to muffle the voices that best represent the most significant segments of the economy and the most passionately held social and political views. People who associate—who pool their financial resources—for purposes of economic enterprise overwhelmingly do so in the corporate form; and with increasing frequency, incorporation is chosen by those who associate to defend and promote particular ideas—such as the American Civil Liberties Union and the National Rifle Association, parties to these cases. . . .

Federal Election Commission v. Wisconsin Right to Life, Inc.

127 S.Ct. 2652 (2007)

Following the fragmented ruling upholding major provisions of the Bipartisan Campaign Reform Act (BCRA) in *McConnell v. Federal Election Commission*, 540 U.S. 93 (2003) (excerpted above), the Wisconsin Right to Life, Inc. ran television ads (which would have been permissible in newspapers and on the Internet) that allegedly ran afoul of Section 203 of the BCRA, which forbids "electioneering communications" or "issue ads" that name candidates within thirty days of federal primary elections and sixty days prior to a general election. A three-judge district court held that the provisions of Section 203 were unconstitutional "as applied" to the ads, as further discussed by Chief

Justice Roberts in his opinion for the Court. The lower court held that the ads were genuine issue ads, not express advocacy or its "functional equivalent" under *McConnell*.

The lower court's decision was affirmed by a five-to-four vote. Chief Justice Roberts delivered the opinion for the Court but declined to overrule the bare majority's upholding of Section 203 in *McConnell*. By contrast, concurring Justices Scalia, Kennedy, and Thomas would have overruled *McConnell* and BCRA's limitation on union and corporate electioneering ads. Justice Souter filed a dissenting opinion, joined by Justices Stevens, Breyer, and Ginsburg.

☐ *Chief Justice ROBERTS announced the judgment of the Court and delivered the opinion of the Court with respect to Parts I and II, and an opinion with respect to Parts III and IV, in which Justice ALITO joins.*

Section 203 of the Bipartisan Campaign Reform Act of 2002 (BCRA) makes it a federal crime for any corporation to broadcast, shortly before an election, any communication that names a federal candidate for elected office and is targeted to the electorate. In *McConnell v. Federal Election Comm'n*, 540 U.S. 93 (2003), this Court considered whether Sec. 203 was facially overbroad under the First Amendment because it captured within its reach not only campaign speech, or "express advocacy," but also speech about public issues more generally, or "issue advocacy," that mentions a candidate for federal office. The Court concluded that there was no overbreadth concern to the extent the speech in question was the "functional equivalent" of express campaign speech. On the other hand, the Court "assume[d]" that the interests it had found to "justify the regulation of campaign speech might not apply to the regulation of genuine issue ads." The Court nonetheless determined that Sec. 203 was not facially overbroad. Even assuming Sec. 203 "inhibit[ed] some constitutionally protected corporate and union speech," the Court concluded that those challenging the law on its face had failed to carry their "heavy burden" of establishing that all enforcement of the law should therefore be prohibited.

Last Term, we reversed a lower court ruling, arising in the same litigation before us now, that our decision in *McConnell* left "no room" for as-applied challenges to Sec. 203. We held on the contrary that "[i]n upholding Sec. 203 against a facial challenge, we did not purport to resolve future as-applied challenges." *Wisconsin Right to Life, Inc. v. Federal Election Comm'n*, 546 U.S. 410 (2006).

We now confront such an as-applied challenge. Resolving it requires us first to determine whether the speech at issue is the "functional equivalent" of speech expressly advocating the election or defeat of a candidate for federal office, or instead a "genuine issue a[d]." We have long recognized that the distinction between campaign advocacy and issue advocacy "may often dissolve in practical application. Candidates, especially incumbents, are intimately tied to public issues involving legislative proposals and governmental actions." *Buckley v. Valeo*, 424 U. S. 1 (1976). Our development of the law in this area requires us, however, to draw such a line, because we have recognized that the interests held to justify the regulation of campaign speech and its "functional equivalent" "might not apply" to the regulation of issue advocacy.

In drawing that line, the First Amendment requires us to err on the side of protecting political speech rather than suppressing it. We conclude that the speech at issue in this as-applied challenge is not the "functional equivalent" of express campaign speech. We further conclude that the interests held to justify restricting corporate campaign speech or its functional equivalent do not justify restricting issue advocacy, and accordingly we hold that BCRA Sec. 203 is unconstitutional as applied to the advertisements at issue in these cases.

■ I

BCRA significantly cut back on corporations' ability to engage in political speech. BCRA Sec. 203, at issue in these cases, makes it a crime for any labor union or incorporated entity—whether the United Steelworkers, the American Civil Liberties Union, or General Motors—to use its general treasury funds to pay for any "electioneering communication." BCRA's definition of "electioneering communication" is clear and expansive. It encompasses any broadcast, cable, or satellite communication that refers to a candidate for federal office and that is aired within 30 days of a federal primary election or 60 days of a federal general election in the jurisdiction in which that candidate is running for office.

Appellee Wisconsin Right to Life, Inc. (WRTL), is a nonprofit, nonstock, ideological advocacy corporation recognized by the Internal Revenue Service as tax exempt under Sec 501(c)(4) of the Internal Revenue Code. On July 26, 2004, as part of what it calls a "grassroots lobbying campaign," WRTL began broadcasting a radio advertisement entitled "Wedding." The transcript of "Wedding" reads as follows:

> PASTOR: And who gives this woman to be married to this man?
> BRIDE'S FATHER: Well, as father of the bride, I certainly could. But instead, I'd like to share a few tips on how to properly install drywall. Now you put the drywall up . . .
> VOICE-OVER: Sometimes it's just not fair to delay an important decision.
> But in Washington it's happening. A group of Senators is using the filibuster delay tactic to block federal judicial nominees from a simple "yes" or "no" vote. So qualified candidates don't get a chance to serve. It's politics at work, causing gridlock and backing up some of our courts to a state of emergency.
> Contact Senators Feingold and Kohl and tell them to oppose the filibuster.
> Visit: BeFair.org
> Paid for by Wisconsin Right to Life (befair.org), which is responsible for the content of this advertising and not authorized by any candidate or candidate's committee.

On the same day, WRTL aired a similar radio ad entitled "Loan." It had also invested treasury funds in producing a television ad entitled "Waiting," which is similar in substance and format to "Wedding" and "Loan."

WRTL planned on running "Wedding," "Waiting," and "Loan" throughout August 2004 and financing the ads with funds from its general treasury. It recognized, however, that as of August 15, 30 days prior to the Wisconsin primary, the ads would be illegal "electioneering communication[s]" under BCRA Sec. 203.

Believing that it nonetheless possessed a First Amendment right to broadcast these ads, WRTL filed suit against the Federal Election Commission (FEC) on July 28, 2004, seeking declaratory and injunctive relief before a three-judge District Court. WRTL alleged that BCRA's prohibition on the use of corporate treasury funds for "electioneering communication[s]" as defined in the Act is unconstitutional as applied to "Wedding," "Loan," and "Waiting," as well as any materially similar ads it might seek to run in the future.

Just before the BCRA blackout period was to begin, the District Court denied a preliminary injunction, concluding that "the reasoning of the *McConnell* Court leaves no room for the kind of 'as applied' challenge WRTL propounds before us." In response to this ruling, WRTL did not run its ads during the blackout period. The District Court subsequently dismissed WRTL's complaint. On appeal, we vacated the District Court's judgment, holding that *McConnell* "did not purport to resolve future as-applied challenges" to BCRA Sec. 203, and remanded "for the District Court to consider the merits of WRTL's as-applied challenge in the first instance."

On remand, after allowing four Members of Congress to intervene as defendants, the three-judge District Court granted summary judgment for WRTL, holding BCRA Sec. 203 unconstitutional as applied to the three advertisements WRTL planned to run during the 2004 blackout period. . . .

■ III

WRTL rightly concedes that its ads are prohibited by BCRA Sec. 203. Each ad clearly identifies Senator Feingold, who was running (unopposed) in the Wisconsin Democratic primary on September 14, 2004, and each ad would have been "targeted to the relevant electorate," during the BCRA blackout period. WRTL further concedes that its ads do not fit under any of BCRA's exceptions to the term "electioneering communication." The only question, then, is whether it is consistent with the First Amendment for BCRA Sec. 203 to prohibit WRTL from running these three ads. . . .

When the *McConnell* Court considered the possible facial overbreadth of Sec. 203, it looked to the studies in the record analyzing ads broadcast during the blackout periods, and those studies had classified the ads in terms of intent and effect. The Court's assessment was accordingly phrased in the same terms, which the Court regarded as sufficient to conclude, on the record before it, that the plaintiffs had not "carried their heavy burden of proving" that Sec. 203 was facially overbroad and could not be enforced in any circumstances. The Court did not explain that it was adopting a particular test for determining what constituted the "functional equivalent" of express advocacy. . . .

More importantly, this Court in *Buckley* had already rejected an intent-and-effect test for distinguishing between discussions of issues and candidates. After noting the difficulty of distinguishing between discussion of issues on the one hand and advocacy of election or defeat of candidates on the other, the *Buckley* Court explained that analyzing the question in terms "'of intent and of effect'" would afford "'no security for free discussion.'" It therefore rejected such an approach, and *McConnell* did not purport to overrule *Buckley* on this point—or even address what *Buckley* had to say on the subject.

For the reasons regarded as sufficient in *Buckley*, we decline to adopt a test for as-applied challenges turning on the speaker's intent to affect an election. The test to distinguish constitutionally protected political speech from speech that BCRA may proscribe should provide a safe harbor for those who wish to exercise First Amendment rights. The test should also "reflec[t] our 'profound national commitment to the principle that debate on public issues should be uninhibited, robust, and wide-open.' " *Buckley* (quoting *New York Times Co. v. Sullivan*, 376 U.S. 254 (1964)). A test turning on the intent of the speaker does not remotely fit the bill.

Far from serving the values the First Amendment is meant to protect, an intent-based test would chill core political speech by opening the door to a trial on every ad within the terms of Sec. 203, on the theory that the speaker actually intended to affect an election, no matter how compelling the indications that the ad concerned a pending legislative or policy issue. . . .

Buckley also explains the flaws of a test based on the actual effect speech will have on an election or on a particular segment of the target audience. Such a test " 'puts the speaker . . . wholly at the mercy of the varied understanding of his hearers.' " It would also typically lead to a burdensome, expert-driven inquiry, with an indeterminate result. Litigation on such a standard may or may not accurately predict electoral effects, but it will unquestionably chill a substantial amount of political speech. . . .

In light of these considerations, a court should find that an ad is the functional equivalent of express advocacy only if the ad is susceptible of no reasonable interpretation other than as an appeal to vote for or against a specific candidate. Under this test, WRTL's three ads are plainly not the functional equivalent of express advocacy. First, their content is consistent with that of a genuine issue ad: The ads focus on a legislative issue, take a position on the issue, exhort the public to adopt that position, and urge the public to contact public officials with respect to the matter. Second, their content lacks indicia of express advocacy: The ads do not mention an election, candidacy, political party, or challenger; and they do not take a position on a candidate's character, qualifications, or fitness for office. . . .

■ IV

BCRA Sec. 203 can be constitutionally applied to WRTL's ads only if it is narrowly tailored to further a compelling interest. This Court has never recognized a compelling interest in regulating ads, like WRTL's, that are neither express advocacy nor its functional equivalent. The District Court below considered interests that might justify regulating WRTL's ads here, and found none sufficiently compelling. We reach the same conclusion. . . .

McConnell held that express advocacy of a candidate or his opponent by a corporation shortly before an election may be prohibited, along with the functional equivalent of such express advocacy. We have no occasion to revisit that determination today. But when it comes to defining what speech qualifies as the functional equivalent of express advocacy subject to such a ban—the issue we do have to decide—we give the benefit of the doubt to speech, not censorship. The First Amendment's command that "Congress shall make no law . . . abridging the freedom of speech" demands at least that.

☐ *Justice SCALIA, with whom Justice KENNEDY and Justice THOMAS join, concurring in part and concurring in the judgment.*

A Moroccan cartoonist once defended his criticism of the Moroccan monarch (*lese majesté* being a serious crime in Morocco) as follows: " 'I'm not a revolutionary, I'm just defending freedom of speech. . . . I never said we had to change the king—no, no, no, no! But I said that some things the king is doing, I do not like. Is that a crime?' " Well, in the United States (making due allowance for the fact that we have elected representatives instead of a king) it is a crime, at least if the speaker is a union or a corporation (including not-for-profit public-interest corporations) and if the representative is identified by name within a certain period before a primary or congressional election in which he is running. That is the import of Sec. 203 of the Bi-partisan Campaign Reform Act of 2002 (BCRA), the constitutionality of which we upheld three Terms ago in *Mc-Connell v. Federal Election Comm'n* (2003). As an element essential to that determination of constitutionality, our opinion left open the possibility that a corporation or union could establish that, in the particular circumstances of its case, the ban was unconstitutional because it was (to pursue the analogy) only the king's policies and not his tenure in office that was criticized. Today's cases present the question of what sort of showing is necessary for that purpose. For the reasons I set forth below, it is my view that no test for such a showing can both (1) comport with the requirement of clarity that unchilled freedom of political speech demands, and (2) be compatible with the facial validity of Sec. 203 (as pronounced in *McConnell*). . . .

There is wondrous irony to be found in both the genesis and the consequences of BCRA. In the fact that the institutions it was designed to muzzle—unions and nearly all manner of corporations—for all the "corrosive and distorting effects" of their "immense aggregations of wealth," were utterly impotent to prevent the passage of this legislation that forbids them to criticize candidates (including incumbents). In the fact that the effect of BCRA has been to concentrate more political power in the hands of the country's wealthiest individuals and their so-called 527 organizations, unregulated by Sec. 203. (In the 2004 election cycle, a mere 24 individuals contributed an astounding total of $142 million to 527s). And in the fact that while these wealthy individuals dominate political discourse, it is this small, grass-roots organization of Wisconsin Right to Life that is muzzled.

I would overrule that part of the Court's decision in *McConnell* upholding Sec. 203(a) of BCRA. Accordingly, I join Parts I and II of today's principal opinion and otherwise concur only in the judgment.

☐ *Justice ALITO, concurring.*

I join the principal opinion because I conclude (a) that Sec. 203 of the Bipartisan Campaign Reform Act of 2002, as applied, cannot constitutionally ban any advertisement that may reasonably be interpreted as anything other than an appeal to vote for or against a candidate, (b) that the ads at issue here may reasonably be interpreted as something other than such an appeal, and (c) that because Sec. 203 is unconstitutional as applied to the advertisements before us, it is unnecessary to go further and decide whether Sec. 203 is unconstitutional on its face. If it turns out that the implementation of the as-applied standard set out in the principal opinion impermissibly chills political speech, we will presumably be asked in a future case to reconsider the holding that Sec. 203 is facially constitutional.

☐ *Justice SOUTER, with whom Justice STEVENS, Justice GINSBURG, and Justice BREYER join, dissenting.*

The significance and effect of today's judgment, from which I respectfully dissent, turn on three things: the demand for campaign money in huge amounts from large contributors, whose power has produced a cynical electorate; the congressional recognition of the ensuing threat to democratic integrity as reflected in a century of legislation restricting the electoral leverage of concentrations of money in corporate and union treasuries; and *McConnell v. Federal Election Comm'n* (2003), declaring the facial validity of the most recent Act of Congress in that tradition, a decision that is effectively, and unjustifiably, overruled today.

The indispensable ingredient of a political candidacy is money for advertising. In the 2004 campaign, more than half of the combined expenditures by the two principal presidential candidates (excluding fundraising) went for media time and space. And in the 2005–2006 election cycle, the expenditure of more than $2 billion on television shattered the previous record, even without a presidential contest. The portent is for still greater spending. By the end of March 2007, almost a year before the first primary and more than 18 months before the general election, presidential candidates had already raised over $150 million.

The indispensability of these huge sums has two significant consequences for American Government that are particularly on point here. The enormous demands, first, assign power to deep pockets. Candidates occasionally boast about the number of contributors they have, but the headlines speaking in dollars reflect political reality. . . .

Devoting concentrations of money in self-interested hands to the support of political campaigning therefore threatens the capacity of this democracy to represent its constituents and the confidence of its citizens in their capacity to govern themselves. These are the elements summed up in the notion of political integrity, giving it a value second to none in a free society.

If the threat to this value flowing from concentrations of money in politics has reached an unprecedented enormity, it has been gathering force for generations. Before the turn of the last century, as now, it was obvious that the purchase of influence and the cynicism of voters threaten the integrity and stability of democratic government, each derived from the responsiveness of its law to the interests of citizens and their confidence in that focus. The danger has traditionally seemed at its apex when no reasonable limits constrain the campaign activities of organizations whose "unique legal and economic characteristics" are tailored to "facilitat[e] the amassing of large treasuries," *Austin v. Michigan Chamber of Commerce*, 494 U.S. 652 (1990). Corporations were the earliest subjects of concern; the same characteristics that have made them engines of the Nation's extraordinary prosperity have given them the financial muscle to gain "advantage in the political marketplace" when they turn from core corporate activity to electioneering, *Federal Election Comm'n v. Massachusetts Citizens for Life, Inc.*, 479 U.S. 238 (1986), and in "Congress' judgment" the same concern extends to labor unions as to corporations, *Federal Election Comm'n v. National Right to Work Comm.*, 459 U.S. 197 (1982). . . .

In *McConnell* . . . [w]e understood that Congress had a compelling interest in limiting this sort of electioneering by corporations and unions, for Sec. 203 exemplified a tradition of "repeatedly sustained legislation aimed at 'the corrosive and distorting effects of immense aggregations of wealth that are accumulated with the help of the corporate form and that have little or no correlation to the public's support for the corporation's political ideas.' " Nor did we see any plausible claim of substantial overbreadth from incidentally prohibiting ads genuinely focused on issues rather than elections, given the limitation of "electioneering communication" by time, geographical coverage, and clear reference to candidate. "Far from establishing that BCRA's application to pure issue ads is substantial, either in an absolute sense or relative to its application to election-related advertising, the record strongly supports the contrary conclusion." Finally, we underscored the reasonableness of the Sec. 203 line by emphasizing that it defined a category of limited, but not prohibited, corporate and union speech: "Because corporations can still fund electioneering communications with PAC money, it is 'simply wrong' to view [Sec. 203] as a 'complete ban' on expression rather than a regulation." Thus "corporations and unions may finance genuine issue ads [in the runup period] by simply avoiding any specific reference to federal candidates, or in doubtful cases by paying for the ad from a segregated [PAC] fund." . . .

WRTL's planned airing of the ads had no apparent relation to any Senate filibuster vote but was keyed to the timing of the senatorial election. WRTL began broadcasting the ads on July 26, 2004, four days after the Senate recessed for the summer, and although the filibuster controversy raged on through 2005, WRTL did not resume running the ads after the election. During the campaign period that the ads did cover, Senator Feingold's support of the filibusters was a prominent issue. His position was well known, and his Republican opponents, who vocally opposed the filibusters, made the issue a major talking point in their campaigns against him.

In sum, any Wisconsin voter who paid attention would have known that Democratic Senator Feingold supported filibusters against Republican presidential judicial nominees, that the propriety of the filibusters was a major issue in the senatorial campaign, and that WRTL along with the Senator's Republican challengers opposed his reelection because of his position on filibusters. Any alert voters who heard or saw WRTL's ads would have understood that WRTL was telling them that the Senator's position on the filibusters should be grounds to vote against him.

Given these facts, it is beyond all reasonable debate that the ads are constitutionally subject to regulation under *McConnell*. There, we noted that BCRA was meant to remedy the problem of "[s]o-called issue ads" being used "to advocate the election or defeat of clearly identified federal candidates." We then gave a paradigmatic example of these electioneering ads subject to regulation, saying that "[l]ittle difference existed . . . between an ad that urged viewers to 'vote against Jane Doe' and one that condemned Jane Doe's record on a particular issue before exhorting viewers to 'call Jane Doe and tell her what you think.'" . . .

McConnell's holding that Sec. 203 is facially constitutional is overruled. By what steps does the principal opinion reach this unacknowledged result less than four years after *McConnell* was decided?

First, it lays down a new test to identify a severely limited class of ads that may constitutionally be regulated as electioneering communications, a test that is flatly contrary to *McConnell.* An ad is the equivalent of express advocacy and subject to regulation, the opinion says, only if it is "susceptible of no reasonable interpretation other than as an appeal to vote for or against a specific candidate." Since the Feingold ads could, in isolation, be read as at least including calls to communicate views on filibusters to the two Senators, those ads cannot be treated as the functional equivalent of express advocacy to elect or defeat anyone, and therefore may not constitutionally be regulated at all. . . .

The principal opinion, in other words, simply inverts what we said in *McConnell.* While we left open the possibility of a "genuine" or "pure" issue ad that might not be open to regulation under Sec. 203, we meant that an issue ad without campaign advocacy could escape the restriction. . . .

Second, the principal opinion seems to defend this inversion of *McConnell* as a necessary alternative to an unadministrable subjective test for the equivalence of express (and regulable) electioneering advocacy. The principal opinion acknowledges, of course, that in *McConnell* we said that "[t]he justifications for the regulation of express advocacy apply equally to ads aired during [the period shortly before an election] if the ads are intended to influence the voters' decisions and have that effect." But THE CHIEF JUSTICE says that statement in *McConnell* cannot be accepted at face value because we could not, consistent with precedent, have focused our First Amendment enquiry on whether "the speaker actually intended to affect an election." THE CHIEF JUSTICE suggests it is more likely that the *McConnell* opinion inadvertently borrowed the language of "intended . . . effect[s]" from academic studies in the record of viewers' perceptions of the ads' purposes.

If THE CHIEF JUSTICE were correct that *McConnell* made the constitutional application of Sec. 203 contingent on whether a corporation's "motives were pure," or its issue advocacy "subjective[ly] sincer[e]," then I, too, might be inclined to reconsider *McConnell's* language. But *McConnell* did not do that. It did not purport to draw constitutional lines based on the subjective motivations of corporations (or their principals) sponsoring political ads, but merely described our test for equivalence to express advocacy as resting on the ads' "electioneering purpose," which will be objectively apparent from those ads' content and context (as these cases and the examples cited in *McConnell* readily show). We therefore held that Sec. 203 was not substantially overbroad because "the vast majority of ads clearly had such a purpose," and consequently could be regulated consistent with the First Amendment. . . .

Third, it may be that the principal opinion rejects *McConnell* on the erroneous assumption that Sec. 203 flatly bans independent electioneering communications by a corporation. THE CHIEF JUSTICE argues that corporations must receive "the benefit of any doubt," whenever we undertake the task of "separating . . . political speech protected under the First Amendment from that which may be banned." But this is a fundamental misconception of the task at hand: we have already held that it is " 'simply wrong' to view [Sec. 203] as a 'complete ban' on expression," because PAC financing provides corporations "with a constitutionally sufficient opportunity to engage in express advocacy." *McConnell*. Thus, a successful as-applied challenger to Sec. 203 should necessarily show, at the least, that it could not constitutionally be subjected to the administrative rules that govern a PAC's formation and operation. . . .

Finally, the suggestion that Sec. 203 is a ban on political speech is belied by MCFL's safe harbor for nonprofit advocacy corporations: under that rule, WRTL would have been free to attack Senator Feingold by name at any time with ads funded from its corporate treasury, if it had not also chosen to serve as a funnel for hundreds of thousands of dollars from other corporations. Thus, what is called a "ban" on speech is a limit on the financing of electioneering broadcasts by entities that refuse to take advantage of the PAC structure but insist on acting as conduits from the campaign war chests of business corporations.

In sum, *McConnell* does not graft a subjective standard onto campaign regulation, the context of campaign advertising cannot sensibly be ignored, and Sec. 203 is not a ban on speech. What cannot be gainsaid, in any event, is that in treating these subjects as it does, the operative opinion produces the result of overruling *McConnell's* holding on Sec. 203. . . .

The price of *McConnell's* demise as authority on Sec. 203 seems to me to be a high one. The Court (and, I think, the country) loses when important precedent is overruled without good reason, and there is no justification for departing from our usual rule of *stare decisis* here. The same combination of alternatives that was available to corporations affected by *McConnell* in 2003 is available today: WRTL could have run a newspaper ad, could have paid for the broadcast ads through its PAC, could have established itself as an MCFL organization free of corporate money, and could have said "call your Senators" instead of naming Senator Feingold in its ads broadcasted just before the election. Nothing in the related law surrounding Sec. 203 has changed in any way, let alone in any way that undermines *McConnell's* rationale. . . .

I cannot tell what the future will force upon us, but I respectfully dissent from this judgment today.

Citizens United v. Federal Election Commission

130 S.CT. 876 (2010)

Citizens United, a nonprofit corporation, released a film entitled *Hillary: The Movie*. The ninety-minute documentary was about then senator Hillary Clinton, who was a candidate in the Democratic Party's 2008 presidential primary elections. The film mentioned Senator Clinton by name and featured interviews with political commentators and other persons, most of them quite critical of Senator Clinton. The film was released in theaters and on DVD, but Citizens United wanted to increase distribution by making it available through video-on-demand. Video-on-demand allows digital cable subscribers to select programming from various menus, including movies, television shows, sports, news, and music. In December 2007, a cable company offered, for a payment of $1.2 million, to make Hillary available on a video-on-demand channel called "Elections '08."

Before and after the Bipartisan Campaign Reform Act of 2002 (BCRA), federal law prohibited corporations and unions from using general funds to make direct contributions to candidates or independent expenditures that expressly advocate the election or defeat of a candidate, through any form of media, in connection with certain federal elections. The Federal Election Commission's (FEC) regulations further defined an electioneering communication as a communication that is "publicly distributed." Corporations and unions were barred from using their general funds for express advocacy or electioneering communications. They may establish, however, a "separate segregated fund" (known as a political action committee, or PAC) for these purposes. Citizens United wanted to make Hillary available through video-on-demand within 30 days of the 2008 primary elections. It feared, however, that both the film and the ads would be covered by Section 441b's ban on corporate-funded independent expenditures, thus subjecting the corporation to civil and criminal penalties under Section 437g. In December 2007, Citizens United sought declaratory and injunctive relief against the FEC. It argued that (1) Section 441b was unconstitutional as applied to Hillary; and (2) BCRA's disclaimer and disclosure requirements, BCRA Sections 201 and 311, were unconstitutional as applied to Hillary and to the three ads for the movie.

A federal district court denied Citizens United's motion for a preliminary injunction, and then granted the FEC's motion for summary judgment. The Court held that Section 441b was facially constitutional under *McConnell v. Federal Election Commission*, 540 U.S. 93 (2003) (excerpted in Vol. 1, Ch. 8) and that Section 441b was constitutional as applied to Hillary because it was "susceptible of no other interpretation than to inform the electorate that Senator Clinton is unfit for office, that the United States would be a dangerous place in a President Hillary Clinton world, and that viewers should vote against her." The Court also rejected Citizens United's challenge to BCRA's disclaimer and disclosure requirements.

The district court's decision was reversed in part and affirmed in part. Justice Kennedy delivered the opinion for the Court. Chief Justice Roberts and Justice Scalia filed concurring opinions. Justice Stevens and Thomas each filed opinions concurring and dissenting in part. Justices Ginsburg, Breyer, and Sotomayor joined Justice Stevens's opinion.

☐ *Justice KENNEDY delivered the opinion of the Court.*

Limits on electioneering communications were upheld in *McConnell v. Federal Election Comm'n*, 540 U.S. 93 (2003). The holding of *McConnell* rested to a large extent on an earlier case, *Austin v. Michigan Chamber of Commerce*, 494 U. S. 652 (1990). *Austin* had held that political speech may be banned based on the speaker's corporate identity.

In this case we are asked to reconsider *Austin* and, in effect, *McConnell*. It has been noted that "*Austin* was a significant departure from ancient First Amendment principles," *Federal Election Comm'n v. Wisconsin Right to Life, Inc.*, 551 U. S. 449 (2007) (*WRTL*) (SCALIA, J., concurring). We agree with that conclusion and hold that *stare decisis* does not compel the continued acceptance of *Austin*. The Government may regulate corporate political speech through disclaimer and disclosure requirements, but it may not suppress that speech altogether. . . .

As the District Court found, there is no reasonable interpretation of *Hillary* other than as an appeal to vote against Senator Clinton. Under the standard stated in *McConnell* and further elaborated in *WRTL*, the film qualifies as the functional equivalent of express advocacy. . . .

When the statute now at issue came before the Court in *McConnell*, both the majority and the dissenting opinions considered the question of its facial validity. The holding and validity of *Austin* were essential to the reasoning of the *McConnell* majority opinion, which upheld BCRA's extension of Sec. 441b. *McConnell* permitted federal felony punishment for speech by all corporations, including nonprofit ones, that speak on prohibited subjects shortly before federal elections. . . .

The First Amendment provides that "Congress shall make no law . . . abridging the freedom of speech." . . .

The law before us is an outright ban, backed by criminal sanctions. Section 441b makes it a felony for all corporations—including nonprofit advocacy corporations—either to expressly advocate the election or defeat of candidates or to broadcast electioneering communications within 30 days of a primary election and 60 days of a general election. Thus, the following acts would all be felonies under Sec. 441b: The Sierra Club runs an ad, within the crucial phase of 60 days before the general election, that exhorts the public to disapprove of a Congressman who favors logging in national forests; the National Rifle Association publishes a book urging the public to vote for the challenger because the incumbent U.S. Senator supports a handgun ban; and the American Civil Liberties Union creates a Web site telling the public to vote for a Presidential candidate in light of that candidate's defense of free speech. These prohibitions are classic examples of censorship.

Section 441b is a ban on corporate speech notwithstanding the fact that a PAC created by a corporation can still speak. A PAC is a separate association from the corporation. So the PAC exemption from Sec. 441b's expenditure ban does not allow corporations to speak. Even if a PAC could somehow allow a corporation to speak—and it does not—the option to form PACs does not alleviate the First Amendment problems with Sec. 441b.

Section 441b's prohibition on corporate independent expenditures is thus a ban on speech. As a "restriction on the amount of money a person or group can spend on political communication during a campaign," that statute "necessarily reduces the quantity of expression by restricting the number of issues discussed, the depth of their exploration, and the size of the audience reached." *Buckley v. Valeo*, 424 U. S. 1 (1976) *(per curiam)*. Were the Court to uphold these restrictions, the Government could repress speech by silencing certain voices at any of the various points in the speech process. . . .

Speech is an essential mechanism of democracy, for it is the means to hold officials accountable to the people. The right of citizens to inquire, to hear, to speak, and to use information to reach consensus is a precondition to enlightened self-government and a necessary means to protect it.

For these reasons, political speech must prevail against laws that would suppress it, whether by design or inadvertence. Laws that burden political speech are "subject to strict scrutiny," which requires the Government to prove that the restriction "furthers a compelling interest and is narrowly tailored to achieve that interest." . . .

We find no basis for the proposition that, in the context of political speech, the Government may impose restrictions on certain disfavored speakers. Both history and logic lead us to this conclusion.

At least since the latter part of the 19th century, the laws of some States and of the United States imposed a ban on corporate direct contributions to candidates. Yet not until 1947 did Congress first prohibit independent expenditures by corporations and labor unions in Sec. 304 of the Labor Management Relations Act 1947.

For almost three decades thereafter, the Court did not reach the question whether restrictions on corporate and union expenditures are constitutional.

In *Buckley*, the Court addressed various challenges to the Federal Election Campaign Act of 1971 (FECA) as amended in 1974. These amendments created 18 U.S.C. Sec. 608(e), an independent expenditure ban separate from Sec. 610 that applied to individuals as well as corporations and labor unions.

Before addressing the constitutionality of Sec. 608(e)'s independent expenditure ban, *Buckley* first upheld Sec. 608(b), FECA's limits on direct contributions to candidates. The *Buckley* Court recognized a "sufficiently important" governmental interest in "the prevention of corruption and the appearance of corruption." This followed from the Court's concern that large contributions could be given "to secure a political *quid pro quo.*" . . .

Buckley did not consider Sec. 610's separate ban on corporate and union independent expenditures. . . .

Less than two years after *Buckley*, *Bellotti* reaffirmed the First Amendment principle that the Government cannot restrict political speech based on the speaker's corporate identity. *Bellotti* could not have been clearer when it struck down a state-law prohibition on corporate independent expenditures related to referenda issues. . . .

Bellotti did not address the constitutionality of the State's ban on corporate independent expenditures to support candidates. In our view, however, that restriction would have been unconstitutional under *Bellotti's* central principle: that the First Amendment does not allow political speech restrictions based on a speaker's corporate identity.

Thus the law stood until *Austin*. *Austin* "uph[eld] a direct restriction on the independent expenditure of funds for political speech for the first time in [this Court's] history." (KENNEDY, J., dissenting). There, the Michigan Chamber of Commerce sought to use general treasury funds to run a newspaper ad supporting a specific candidate. Michigan law, however, prohibited corporate independent expenditures that supported or opposed any candidate for state office. A violation of the law was punishable as a felony. The Court sustained the speech prohibition.

To bypass *Buckley* and *Bellotti*, the *Austin* Court identified a new governmental interest in limiting political speech: an antidistortion interest. *Austin* found a compelling governmental interest in preventing "the corrosive and distorting effects of immense aggregations of wealth that are accumulated with the help of the corporate form and that have little or no correlation to the public's support for the corporation's political ideas."

The Court is thus confronted with conflicting lines of precedent: a pre-*Austin* line that forbids restrictions on political speech based on the speaker's corporate identity and a post-*Austin* line that permits them. No case before *Austin* had held that Congress could prohibit independent expenditures for political speech based on the speaker's corporate identity. Before *Austin* Congress had enacted legislation for this purpose, and the Government urged the same proposition before this Court.

In its defense of the corporate-speech restrictions in Sec. 441b, the Government notes the antidistortion rationale on which *Austin* and its progeny rest in part, yet it all but abandons reliance upon it. It argues instead that two other compelling interests support *Austin's* holding that corporate expenditure restrictions are constitutional: an anticorruption interest. We consider the three points in turn.

As for *Austin's* antidistortion rationale, the Government does little to defend it. And with good reason, for the rationale cannot support Sec. 441b.

If the First Amendment has any force, it prohibits Congress from fining or jailing citizens, or associations of citizens, for simply engaging in political speech. If the antidistortion rationale were to be accepted, however, it would permit Government to ban political speech simply because the speaker is an association that has taken on the corporate form. . . .

The Court reaffirmed these conclusions when it invalidated the BCRA [Bipartisan Campaign Reform Act] provision that increased the cap on contributions to one candidate if the opponent made certain expenditures from personal funds. The rule that political speech cannot be limited based on a speaker's wealth is a necessary consequence of the premise that the First Amendment generally prohibits the suppression of political speech based on the speaker's identity. . . .

There is simply no support for the view that the First Amendment, as originally understood, would permit the suppression of political speech by media corporations. The Framers may not have anticipated modern business and media corporations. Yet television networks and major newspapers owned by media corporations have become the most important means of mass communication in modern times. The First Amendment was certainly not understood to condone the suppression of political speech in society's most salient media. . . .

The purpose and effect of this law is to prevent corporations, including small and nonprofit corporations, from presenting both facts and opinions to the public. This makes *Austin's* antidistortion rationale all the more an aberration. . . .

Even if Sec. 441b's expenditure ban were constitutional, wealthy corporations could still lobby elected officials, although smaller corporations may not have the resources to do so. And wealthy individuals and unincorporated associations can spend unlimited amounts on independent expenditures. . . .

What we have said also shows the invalidity of other arguments made by the Government. For the most part relinquishing the antidistortion rationale, the Government falls back on the argument that corporate political speech can be banned in order to prevent corruption or its appearance. In *Buckley*, the Court found this interest "sufficiently important" to allow limits on contributions but did not extend that reasoning to expenditure limits. When *Buckley* examined an expenditure ban, it found "that the governmental interest in preventing corruption and the appearance of corruption [was] inadequate to justify [the ban] on independent expenditures." . . .

When *Buckley* identified a sufficiently important governmental interest in preventing corruption or the appearance of corruption, that interest was limited to *quid pro quo* corruption. The fact that speakers may have influence over or access to elected officials does not mean that these officials are corrupt. . . .

The Government contends further that corporate independent expenditures can be limited because of its interest in protecting dissenting shareholders from being compelled to fund corporate political speech. This asserted interest, like *Austin's* antidistortion rationale, would allow the Government to ban the political speech even of media corporations. . . .

Those reasons are sufficient to reject this shareholder-protection interest; and, moreover, the statute is both underinclusive and overinclusive. As to the first, if Congress had been seeking to protect dissenting shareholders, it would not have banned corporate speech in only certain media within 30 or 60 days before an election. A dissenting shareholder's interests would be implicated by speech in any media at any time. As to the second, the statute is overinclusive because it covers all corporations, including nonprofit corporations and for-profit corporations with only single shareholders. As to other corporations, the remedy is not to restrict speech but to consider and explore other regulatory mechanisms. The regulatory mechanism here, based on speech, contravenes the First Amendment. . . .

Rapid changes in technology—and the creative dynamic inherent in the concept of free expression—counsel against upholding a law that restricts political speech in certain media or by certain speakers. Today, 30-second television ads may be the most effective way to convey a political message. Soon, however, it may be that Internet sources, such as blogs and social networking Web sites, will provide citizens with significant information about political candidates and issues. Yet, Sec. 441b would seem to ban a blog post expressly advocating the election or defeat of a candidate if that blog were created with corporate funds. The First Amendment does not permit Congress to make these categorical distinctions based on the corporate identity of the speaker and the content of the political speech. . . .

Austin is overruled, so it provides no basis for allowing the Government to limit corporate independent expenditures. . . .

Given our conclusion we are further required to overrule the part of

McConnell that upheld BCRA Sec. 203's extension of Sec. 441b's restrictions on corporate independent expenditures. The *McConnell* Court relied on the antidistortion interest recognized in *Austin* to uphold a greater restriction on speech than the restriction upheld in *Austin*, and we have found this interest unconvincing and insufficient. This part of *McConnell* is now overruled.

Citizens United next challenges BCRA's disclaimer and disclosure provisions as applied to *Hillary* and the three advertisements for the movie. Under BCRA Sec. 311, televised electioneering communications funded by anyone other than a candidate must include a disclaimer that " 'is responsible for the content of this advertising.' " The required statement must be made in a "clearly spoken manner," and displayed on the screen in a "clearly readable manner" for at least four seconds. It must state that the communication "is not authorized by any candidate or candidate's committee"; it must also display the name and address (or Web site address) of the person or group that funded the advertisement. . . .

Disclaimer and disclosure requirements may burden the ability to speak, but they "impose no ceiling on campaign-related activities," *Buckley*. The Court has subjected these requirements to "exacting scrutiny," which requires a "substantial relation" between the disclosure requirement and a "sufficiently important" governmental interest. . . .

The judgment of the District Court is reversed with respect to the constitutionality of 2 U. S. C. Sec. 441b's restrictions on corporate independent expenditures. The judgment is affirmed with respect to BCRA's disclaimer and disclosure requirements. The case is remanded for further proceedings consistent with this opinion.

☐ *Justice SCALIA, with whom Justice ALITO joins, and with whom Justice THOMAS joins in part, concurring.*

I write separately to address Justice STEVENS' discussion of "Original Understandings." This section of the dissent purports to show that today's decision is not supported by the original understanding of the First Amendment. The dissent attempts this demonstration, however, in splendid isolation from the text of the First Amendment. It never shows why "the freedom of speech" that was the right of Englishmen did not include the freedom to speak in association with other individuals, including association in the corporate form. To be sure, in 1791 (as now) corporations could pursue only the objectives set forth in their charters; but the dissent provides no evidence that their speech in the pursuit of those objectives could be censored.

Instead of taking this straightforward approach to determining the Amendment's meaning, the dissent embarks on a detailed exploration of the Framers' views about the "role of corporations in society." The Framers didn't like corporations, the dissent concludes, and therefore it follows (as night the day) that corporations had no rights of free speech. Of course the Framers' personal affection or disaffection for corporations is relevant only insofar as it can be thought to be reflected in the understood meaning of the text they enacted—not, as the dissent suggests, as a freestanding substitute for that text. But the dissent's distortion of proper analysis is even worse than that. Though faced with a constitutional text that makes no distinction between types of speakers, the dissent feels no necessity to provide even an isolated statement from the founding era to the effect that corporations are not covered, but places the burden on petitioners to bring forward statements showing that they are ("there is not a scintilla of evidence to support the notion that anyone believed [the First Amendment] would preclude regulatory distinctions based on the corporate form."

Despite the corporation-hating quotations the dissent has dredged up, it is far from clear that by the end of the 18th century corporations were despised. If so, how came there to be so many of them? The dissent's statement that there were few business corporations during the eighteenth century— "only a few hundred during all of the 18th century"—is misleading. There were approximately 335 charters issued to business corporations in the United States by the end of the 18th century. This was a "considerable extension of corporate enterprise in the field of business," and represented "unprecedented growth." Moreover, what seems like a small number by today's standards surely does not indicate the relative importance of corporations when the Nation was considerably smaller. . . .

The lack of a textual exception for speech by corporations cannot be explained on the ground that such organizations did not exist or did not speak. To the contrary, colleges, towns and cities, religious institutions, and guilds had long been organized as corporations at common law and under the King's charter, and as I have discussed, the practice of incorporation only expanded in the United States. Both corporations and voluntary associations actively petitioned the Government and expressed their views in newspapers and pamphlets. . . .

But to return to, and summarize, my principal point, which is the conformity of today's opinion with the original meaning of the First Amendment. The Amendment is written in terms of "speech," not speakers. Its text offers no foothold for excluding any category of speaker, from single individuals to partnerships of individuals, to unincorporated associations of individuals, to incorporated associations of individuals—and the dissent offers no evidence about the original meaning of the text to support any such exclusion. We are therefore simply left with the question whether the speech at issue in this case is "speech" covered by the First Amendment. No one says otherwise. A documentary film critical of a potential Presidential candidate is core political speech, and its nature as such does not change simply because it was funded by a corporation. Nor does the character of that funding produce any reduction whatever in the "inherent worth of the speech" and "its capacity for informing the public," *First Nat. Bank of Boston v. Bellotti*. Indeed, to exclude or impede corporate speech is to muzzle the principal agents of the modern free economy. We should celebrate rather than condemn the addition of this speech to the public debate.

☐ *Chief Justice ROBERTS, with whom Justice ALITO joins, concurring.*

The Government urges us in this case to uphold a direct prohibition on political speech. It asks us to embrace a theory of the First Amendment that would allow censorship not only of television and radio broadcasts, but of pamphlets, posters, the Internet, and virtually any other medium that corporations and unions might find useful in expressing their views on matters of public concern. Its theory, if accepted, would empower the Government to prohibit newspapers from running editorials or opinion pieces supporting or opposing candidates for office, so long as the newspapers were owned by corporations—as the major ones are. First Amendment rights could be confined to individuals, subverting the vibrant public discourse that is at the foundation of our democracy.

The Court properly rejects that theory, and I join its opinion in full. The First Amendment protects more than just the individual on a soapbox and the lonely pamphleteer. . . .

□ *Justice THOMAS, concurring in part and dissenting in part.*

Political speech is entitled to robust protection under the First Amendment. Section 203 of the Bipartisan Campaign Reform Act of 2002 (BCRA) has never been reconcilable with that protection. By striking down Sec. 203, the Court takes an important first step toward restoring full constitutional protection to speech that is "indispensable to the effective and intelligent use of the processes of popular government." *McConnell v. Federal Election Comm'n,* (THOMAS, J., concurring in part, and dissenting in part). I dissent from Part IV of the Court's opinion, however, because the Court's constitutional analysis does not go far enough. The disclosure, disclaimer, and reporting requirements in BCRA Secs. 201 and 311 are also unconstitutional.

Congress may not abridge the "right to anonymous speech" based on the "'simple interest in providing voters with additional relevant information,'" In continuing to hold otherwise, the Court misapprehends the import of "recent events" that some *amici* describe "in which donors to certain causes were blacklisted, threatened, or otherwise targeted for retaliation." The Court properly recognizes these events as "cause for concern," but fails to acknowledge their constitutional significance. In my view, *amici's* submissions show why the Court's insistence on upholding Secs. 201 and 311 will ultimately prove as misguided (and ill fated) as was its prior approval of Sec. 203. . . .

□ *Justice STEVENS, with whom Justice GINSBURG, Justice BREYER, and Justice SOTOMAYOR join, concurring in part and dissenting in part.*

The basic premise underlying the Court's ruling is its iteration, and constant reiteration, of the proposition that the First Amendment bars regulatory distinctions based on a speaker's identity, including its "identity" as a corporation. While that glittering generality has rhetorical appeal, it is not a correct statement of the law. Nor does it tell us when a corporation may engage in electioneering that some of its shareholders oppose. It does not even resolve the specific question whether Citizens United may be required to finance some of its messages with the money in its PAC. The conceit that corporations must be treated identically to natural persons in the political sphere is not only inaccurate but also inadequate to justify the Court's disposition of this case.

In the context of election to public office, the distinction between corporate and human speakers is significant. Although they make enormous contributions to our society, corporations are not actually members of it. They cannot vote or run for office. Because they may be managed and controlled by nonresidents, their interests may conflict in fundamental respects with the interests of eligible voters. The financial resources, legal structure, and instrumental orientation of corporations raise legitimate concerns about their role in the electoral process. Our lawmakers have a compelling constitutional basis, if not also a democratic duty, to take measures designed to guard against the potentially deleterious effects of corporate spending in local and national races.

The majority's approach to corporate electioneering marks a dramatic break from our past. Congress has placed special limitations on campaign spending by corporations ever since the passage of the Tillman Act in 1907. We have unanimously concluded that this "reflects a permissible assessment of the dangers posed by those entities to the electoral process," *FEC v. National Right to Work Comm.*, 459 U.S. 197 (1982) (*NRWC*), and have accepted the "legislative judgment that the special characteristics of the corporate structure require particularly careful regulation." The Court today rejects a century of history when it treats the distinction between corporate and individual campaign spending as an invidious novelty born of *Austin v. Michigan Chamber of Commerce*, 494 U.S. 652 (1990). Relying largely on individual dissenting opinions, the majority blazes through our precedents, overruling or disavowing a body of case law including *FEC v. Wisconsin Right to Life, Inc.*, 551 U.S. 449 (2007) (*WRTL*), *McConnell v. FEC*, 540 U.S. 93 (2003), *FEC v. Beaumont*, 539 U.S. 146 (2003), *FEC v. Massachusetts Citizens for Life, Inc.*, 479 U.S. 238 (1986) (*MCFL*), *NRWC*, and *California Medical Assn. v. FEC*, 453 U.S. 182 (1981). . . .

Although I concur in the Court's decision to sustain BCRA's disclosure provisions and join Part IV of its opinion, I emphatically dissent from its principal holding. . . .

The ruling rests on several premises. First, the Court claims that *Austin* and *McConnell* have "banned" corporate speech. Second, it claims that the First Amendment precludes regulatory distinctions based on speaker identity, including the speaker's identity as a corporation. Third, it claims that *Austin* and *McConnell* were radical outliers in our First Amendment tradition and our campaign finance jurisprudence. Each of these claims is wrong.

Pervading the Court's analysis is the ominous image of a "categorical ba[n]" on corporate speech. Indeed, the majority invokes the specter of a "ban" on nearly every page of its opinion. This characterization is highly misleading, and needs to be corrected. . . .

Our cases have repeatedly pointed out that, "[c]ontrary to the [majority's] critical assumptions," the statutes upheld in *Austin* and *McConnell* do "not impose an absolute ban on all forms of corporate political spending." For starters, both statutes provide exemptions for PACs, separate segregated funds established by a corporation for political purposes. "The ability to form and administer separate segregated funds," we observed in *McConnell*, "has provided corporations and unions with a constitutionally sufficient opportunity to engage in express advocacy. That has been this Court's unanimous view."

Under BCRA, any corporation's "stockholders and their families and its executive or administrative personnel and their families" can pool their resources to finance electioneering communications. A significant and growing number of corporations avail themselves of this option; during the most recent election cycle, corporate and union PACs raised nearly a billion dollars. . . .

At the time Citizens United brought this lawsuit, the only types of speech that could be regulated under Sec. 203 were: (1) broadcast, cable, or satellite communications; (2) capable of reaching at least 50,000 persons in the relevant electorate; (3) made within 30 days of a primary or 60 days of a general federal election; (4) by a labor union or a non–MCFL, nonmedia corporation; (5) paid for with general treasury funds; and (6) "susceptible of no reasonable interpretation other than as an appeal to vote for or against a specific candidate." The category of communications meeting all of these criteria is not trivial, but the notion that corporate political speech has been "suppress[ed] . . . altogether," that corporations have been "exclu[ded] . . . from the general public dialogue," or that a work of fiction such as *Mr. Smith Goes to Washington* might be covered, is nonsense. Even the plaintiffs in *McConnell*, who had every incentive to depict BCRA as negatively as possible, declined to argue that Sec. 203's prohibition on certain uses of general treasury funds amounts to a complete ban.

In many ways, then, Sec. 203 functions as a source restriction or a time, place, and manner restriction. . . .

The second pillar of the Court's opinion is its assertion that "the Government cannot restrict political speech based on the speaker's . . . identity." The case on which it relies for this proposition is *First Nat. Bank of Boston v. Bellotti*, 435 U. S. 765 (1978). As I shall explain, the holding in that case was far narrower than the Court implies.

"Our jurisprudence over the past 216 years has rejected an absolutist interpretation" of the First Amendment. *WRTL*. The First Amendment provides that "Congress shall make no law . . . abridging the freedom of speech, or of the press." Apart perhaps from measures designed to protect the press, that text might seem to permit no distinctions of any kind. Yet in a variety of contexts, we have held that speech can be regulated differentially on account of the speaker's identity, when identity is understood in categorical or institutional terms. The Government routinely places special restrictions on the speech rights of students, prisoners, members of the Armed Forces, foreigners, and its own employees. When such restrictions are justified by a legitimate governmental interest, they do not necessarily raise constitutional problems. In contrast to the blanket rule that the majority espouses, our cases recognize that the Government's interests may be more or less compelling with respect to different classes of speakers.

In short, the Court dramatically overstates its critique of identity-based distinctions, without ever explaining why corporate identity demands the same treatment as individual identity. Only the most wooden approach to the First Amendment could justify the unprecedented line it seeks to draw.

A third fulcrum of the Court's opinion is the idea that *Austin* and *McConnell* are radical outliers, "aberration[s]," in our First Amendment tradition. The Court has it exactly backwards. It is today's holding that is the radical departure from what had been settled First Amendment law. To see why, it is useful to take a long view.

Let us start from the beginning. The Court invokes "ancient First Amendment principles," and original understandings, to defend today's ruling, yet it makes only a perfunctory attempt to ground its analysis in the principles or understandings of those who drafted and ratified the Amendment. Perhaps this is because there is not a scintilla of evidence to support the notion that anyone believed it would preclude regulatory distinctions based on the corporate form. To the extent that the Framers' views are discernible and relevant to the disposition of this case, they would appear to cut strongly against the majority's position. . . .

Although Justice SCALIA makes a perfectly sensible argument that an individual's right to speak entails a right to speak with others for a common cause, he does not explain why those two rights must be precisely identical, or why that principle applies to electioneering by corporations that serve no "common cause." Nothing in his account dislodges my basic point that members of the founding generation held a cautious view of corporate power and a narrow view of corporate rights (not that they "despised" corporations), and that they conceptualized speech in individualistic terms. If no prominent Framer bothered to articulate that corporate speech would have lesser status than individual speech, that may well be because the contrary proposition—if not also the very notion of "corporate speech"—was inconceivable. . . .

Today's decision is backwards in many senses. It elevates the majority's agenda over the litigants' submissions, facial attacks over as-applied claims, broad constitutional theories over narrow statutory grounds, individual dissenting opinions over precedential holdings, assertion over tradition, absolutism over empiricism, rhetoric over reality. Our colleagues have arrived at the conclusion that *Austin* must be overruled and that Sec. 203 is facially unconstitutional only after mischaracterizing both the reach and rationale of those authorities, and after bypassing or ignoring rules of judicial restraint used to cabin the Court's lawmaking power. Their conclusion that the societal interest in avoiding corruption and the appearance of corruption does not provide an adequate justification for regulating corporate expenditures on candidate elections relies on an incorrect description of that interest, along with a failure to acknowledge the relevance of established facts and the considered judgments of state and federal legislatures over many decades.

In a democratic society, the longstanding consensus on the need to limit corporate campaign spending should outweigh the wooden application of judge-made rules. The majority's rejection of this principle "elevate[s] corporations to a level of deference which has not been seen at least since the days when substantive due process was regularly used to invalidate regulatory legislation thought to unfairly impinge upon established economic interests." *Bellotti* (WHITE, J., dissenting). At bottom, the Court's opinion is thus a rejection of the common sense of the American people, who have recognized a need to prevent corporations from undermining self-government since the founding, and who have fought against the distinctive corrupting potential of corporate electioneering since the days of Theodore Roosevelt. It is a strange time to repudiate that common sense. While American democracy is imperfect, few outside the majority of this Court would have thought its flaws included a dearth of corporate money in politics.

■ THE DEVELOPMENT OF LAW

Other Rulings on Campaign Finance

CASE	VOTE	RULING
Citizens Against Rent Control / Coalition for Fair Housing v. Berkeley, California, 454 U.S. 290 (1981)	8:1	Declared unconstitutional a California ordinance imposing a $250 ceiling on each contributor to organizations supporting or opposing issues

placed on referendums, as an infringement of the First Amendment right of association.

Brown v. Hartlage, 456 U.S. 45 (1982)	9:0	Overturned as an infringement of the First Amendment the application of Kentucky's

Corrupt Practices Act as applied to a candidate for the office of county commissioner who pledged to lower commissioners' salaries if elected.

Federal Election Commission v. Massachusetts Citizens for Life, Inc., 479 U.S. 238 (1986)	5:4	Held a section of the Federal Election Campaign Act, banning corporate expenditures for endorsing particular candidates

for public office, to violate the First Amendment freedom of expression.

Meyer v. Grant, 486 U.S. 414 (1988)	9:0	Held unconstitutional a ban on paying circulators of petitions for signatures of registered

voters supporting the placement of a referendum on the ballot.

Austin v. Michigan Chamber of Commerce, 494 U.S. 652 (1990)	6:3	Held that States may ban corporations, even nonprofit corporations, from making independent

financial expenditures in support or opposition of political candidates.

CASE	VOTE	RULING

Colorado Republican Federal Campaign Committee v. Federal Election Commission, 518 U.S. 694 (1996) — **7:2** — Held that the party expenditure provision of Federal Election Campaign Act of 1976 did not preclude the Republican party from making independent campaign expenditures and that applying the provisions to political parties would violate the First Amendment. Writing for the Court, Justice Breyer concluded that there was no evidence that "a limitation on political parties' independent expenditures [was] necessary to combat a substantial danger of corruption of the electoral system." Justices Stevens and Ginsburg dissented.

Nixon v. Shrink Missouri Government PAC, 528 U.S. 377 (2000) — **6:3** — Reaffirming the basic holding in *Buckley v. Valeo*, 424 U.S. 1 (1976), which sustained a $1,000 cap on donations to federal candidates over First Amendment objections, the Court upheld Missouri's $1,075 limit on campaign contributions to candidates for state office. Writing for the Court, Justice Souter ruled that the prevention of corruption and the appearance of corruption was a constitutionally sufficient justification for such campaign contribution limits. Justices Kennedy, Scalia, and Thomas dissented, contending that the majority had abandoned "the rigors of our traditional First Amendment structure."

Federal Election Commission v. Colorado Republican Campaign Committee, 533 U.S. 431 (2001) — **5:4** — Writing for the Court, Justice Souter upheld the Federal Election Campaign Act's Limitations on political parties' campaign expenditures made in conjunction with a candidate's campaign committee. Justice Thomas dissented and was joined by Chief Justice Rehnquist and Justices Scalia and Kennedy.

Federal Election Commission v. Beaumont, 539 U. S. 146 (2003) — **7:2** — Upheld a 1907 restriction on corporations, including nonprofit advocacy corporations, from directly contributing to or making expenditures for candidates for federal office. Justices Scalia and Thomas dissented.

(continues)

Republican Party of Minnesota v. White

536 U. S. 765, 122 S.CT. 2528 (2002)

The Minnesota Supreme Court adopted a canon of judicial conduct prohibiting candidates for judicial office from announcing their views on disputed legal and political issues. While running for the position of associate justice on that court, Gregory Wersal filed a lawsuit seeking a declaration that this "announce clause" violates the First Amendment. A federal district court disagreed and the Court of the Appeals for the Eighth Circuit affirmed, whereupon the Republican Party appealed.

The appellate court's decision was reversed by a five-to-four vote and an opinion for the Court was delivered by Justice Scalia. Justices Stevens and Ginsburg filed dissenting opinions, which Justices Souter and Breyer joined.

□ *Justice SCALIA delivered the opinion of the Court.*

The question presented in this case is whether the First Amendment permits the Minnesota Supreme Court to prohibit candidates for judicial election in that State from announcing their views on disputed legal and political issues. . . .

Before considering the constitutionality of the announce clause, we must be clear about its meaning. Its text says that a candidate for judicial office shall not "announce his or her views on disputed legal or political issues."

We know that "announc[ing] . . . views" on an issue covers much more than promising to decide an issue a particular way. The prohibition extends to the candidate's mere statement of his current position, even if he does not bind himself to maintain that position after election. All the parties agree this is the case, because the Minnesota Code contains a so-called pledges or promises clause, which separately prohibits judicial candidates from making "pledges or promises of conduct in office other than the faithful and impartial performance of the duties of the office"—a prohibition that is not challenged here and on which we express no view.

There are, however, some limitations that the Minnesota Supreme Court has placed upon the scope of the announce clause that are not (to put it politely) immediately apparent from its text. . . . The Judicial Board issued an opinion stating that judicial candidates may criticize past decisions. . . . The Eighth Circuit relied on the Judicial Board's opinion in upholding the announce clause, and the Minnesota Supreme Court recently embraced the Eighth Circuit's interpretation.

There are yet further limitations upon the apparent plain meaning of the announce clause: In light of the constitutional concerns, the District Court construed the clause to reach only disputed issues that are likely to come before the candidate if he is elected judge. . . .

It seems to us, however, that—like the text of the announce clause itself—these limitations upon the text of the announce clause are not all that they appear to be. First, respondents acknowledged at oral argument that statements critical of past judicial decisions are not permissible if the candidate also states that he is against *stare decisis*. Thus, candidates must choose between stating their views critical of past decisions and stating their views in opposition to *stare decisis*. . . .

[I]t is clear that the announce clause prohibits a judicial candidate from stating his views on any specific nonfanciful legal question within the province of the court for which he is running, except in the context of discussing past decisions—and in the latter context as well, if he expresses the view that he is not bound by *stare decisis*. . . .

We think it plain that the announce clause is not narrowly tailored to serve impartiality (or the appearance of impartiality). . . . Indeed, the clause is barely tailored to serve that interest at all, inasmuch as it does not restrict speech for or against particular parties, but rather speech for or against particular issues. . . .

It is perhaps possible to use the term "impartiality" in the judicial context (though this is certainly not a common usage) to mean lack of preconception in favor of or against a particular legal view. This sort of impartiality would be concerned, not with guaranteeing litigants equal application of the law, but rather with guaranteeing them an equal chance to persuade the court on the legal points in their case. Impartiality in this sense may well be an interest served by the announce clause, but it is not a compelling state interest, as strict scrutiny requires. A judge's lack of predisposition regarding the relevant legal issues in a case has never been thought a necessary component of equal justice, and with good reason. For one thing, it is virtually impossible to find a judge who does not have preconceptions about the law. . . .

A third possible meaning of "impartiality" (again not a common one) might be described as openmindedness. This quality in a judge demands, not that he have no preconceptions on legal issues, but that he be willing to consider views that oppose his preconceptions, and remain open to persuasion, when the issues arise in a pending case. This sort of impartiality seeks to guarantee each litigant, not an equal chance to win the legal points in the case, but at least some chance of doing so. . . .

Respondents argue that the announce clause serves the interest in openmindedness, or at least in the appearance of openmindedness, because it relieves a judge from pressure to rule a certain way in order to maintain consistency with statements the judge has previously made. The problem is, however, that statements in election campaigns are such an infinitesimal portion of the public commitments to legal positions that judges (or judges-to-be) undertake, that this object of the prohibition is implausible. Before they arrive on the bench (whether by election or otherwise) judges have often committed themselves on legal issues that they must later rule upon. . . .

The short of the matter is this: In Minnesota, a candidate for judicial office may not say "I think it is constitutional for the legislature to prohibit same-sex marriages." He may say the very same thing, however, up until the very day before he declares himself a candidate, and may say it repeatedly (until litigation is pending) after he is elected. As a means of pursuing the objective of open-mindedness that respondents now articulate, the announce clause is so woefully underinclusive as to render belief in that purpose a challenge to the credulous. . . .

There is an obvious tension between the article of Minnesota's popularly approved Constitution which provides that judges shall be elected, and the Minnesota Supreme Court's announce clause which places most subjects of interest to the voters off limits. The disparity is perhaps unsurprising, since the ABA, which originated the announce clause, has long been an opponent of judicial elections. That opposition may be well taken (it certainly had the support of the Founders of the Federal Government), but the First Amendment does not permit it to achieve its goal by leaving the principle of elections in place while preventing candidates from discussing what the elections are about.

The Minnesota Supreme Court's canon of judicial conduct prohibiting candidates for judicial election from announcing their views on disputed legal and political issues violates the First Amendment. Accordingly, we reverse the grant of summary judgment to respondents and remand the case for proceedings consistent with this opinion. It is so ordered.

□ *Justice GINSBURG, with whom Justice STEVENS, Justice SOUTER, and Justice BREYER join, dissenting.*

Whether state or federal, elected or appointed, judges perform a function fundamentally different from that of the people's elected representatives. Legislative and executive officials act on behalf of the voters who placed them in office; "judge[s] represen[t] the Law." *Chisom v. Roemer*, 501 U.S. 380 (1991) (SCALIA, J., dissenting). Unlike their counterparts in the political branches, judges are expected to refrain from catering to particular constituencies or committing themselves on controversial issues in advance of adversarial presentation. Their mission is to decide "individual cases and controversies" on individual records, *Plaut v. Spendthrift Farm, Inc.*, 514 U.S. 211 (1995) (STEVENS, J., dissenting), neutrally applying legal principles, and, when necessary, "stand[ing] up to what is generally supreme in a democracy: the popular will," SCALIA, The Rule of Law as a Law of Rules, 56 *U. Chi. L. Rev.* 1175 (1989). . . .

The speech restriction must fail, in the Court's view, because an electoral process is at stake; if Minnesota opts to elect its judges, the Court asserts, the State may not rein in what candidates may say.

I do not agree with this unilocular, "an election is an election," approach. Instead, I would differentiate elections for political offices, in which the First Amendment holds full sway, from elections designed to select those whose office it is to administer justice without respect to persons. Minnesota's choice to elect its judges, I am persuaded, does not preclude the State from installing an election process geared to the judicial office.

Legislative and executive officials serve in representative capacities. . . . Judges, however, are not political actors. They do not sit as representatives of particular persons, communities, or parties; they serve no faction or constituency. "[I]t is the business of judges to be indifferent to popularity." *Chisom*. They must strive to do what is legally right, all the more so when the result is not the one "the home crowd" wants. Even when they develop common law or give concrete meaning to constitutional text, judges act only in the context of individual cases, the outcome of which cannot depend on the will of the public.

Thus, the rationale underlying unconstrained speech in elections for political office—that representative government depends on the public's ability to choose agents who will act at its behest—does not carry over to campaigns for the bench. . . .

In view of the magisterial role judges must fill in a system of justice, a role that removes them from the partisan fray, States may limit judicial campaign speech by measures impermissible in elections for political office. . . .

Accordingly, I would affirm the judgment of the Court of Appeals for the Eighth Circuit.

☐ *Justice STEVENS, with whom Justice SOUTER, Justice GINSBURG, and Justice BREYER join, dissenting.*

I add these comments to emphasize the force of her arguments and to explain why I find the Court's reasoning even more troubling than its holding. . . . By obscuring the fundamental distinction between campaigns for the judiciary and the political branches, and by failing to recognize the difference between statements made in articles or opinions and those made on the campaign trail, the Court defies any sensible notion of the judicial office and the importance of impartiality in that context.

The Court's disposition rests on two seriously flawed premises—an inaccurate appraisal of the importance of judicial independence and impartiality, and an assumption that judicial candidates should have the same freedom "'to express themselves on matters of current public importance'" as do all other elected officials. Elected judges, no less than appointed judges, occupy an office of trust that is fundamentally different from that occupied by policymaking officials. Although the fact that they must stand for election makes their job more difficult than that of the tenured judge, that fact does not lessen their duty to respect essential attributes of the judicial office that have been embedded in Anglo-American law for centuries. . . .

The disposition of this case on the flawed premise that the criteria for the election to judicial office should mirror the rules applicable to political elections is profoundly misguided. I therefore respectfully dissent.

Rutan v. Republican Party of Illinois
497 U.S. 62, 110 S.Ct. 2729 (1990)

In 1980, Illinois's Republican Governor James Thompson issued an executive order freezing all hiring of state employees and placing virtually all of the state's 62,000 civil service positions under the jurisdiction of his personnel office. Cynthia Rutan and several other public employees who had never supported the Republican party were subsequently denied promotions. Rutan contended that her promotion was denied simply for partisan reasons and that that violated her First Amendment rights to freedom of speech and association. In his opinion announcing the decision of the Court, Justice Brennan further discusses the facts in this case.

The Court's decision was five to four; and the majority's opinion was announced by Justice Brennan. Justice Stevens delivered a concurring opinion. Justice Scalia, joined by Chief Justice Rehnquist and Justices Kennedy and O'Connor, dissented.

☐ *Justice BRENNAN delivers the opinion of the Court.*

To the victor belong only those spoils that may be constitutionally obtained. *Elrod v. Burns*, 427 U.S. 347 (1976), and *Branti v. Finkel*, 445 U.S. 507

(1980), decided that the First Amendment forbids government officials to discharge or threaten to discharge public employees solely for not being supporters of the political party in power, unless party affiliation is an appropriate requirement for the position involved. Today we are asked to decide the constitutionality of several related political patronage practices—whether promotion, transfer, recall, and hiring decisions involving low-level public employees may be constitutionally based on party affiliation and support. We hold that they may not. . . .

In *Elrod*, we decided that a newly elected Democratic sheriff could not constitutionally engage in the patronage practice of replacing certain office staff with members of his own party "when the existing employees lack or fail to obtain requisite support from, or fail to affiliate with, that party." . . .

Four years later, in *Branti*, we decided that the First Amendment prohibited a newly appointed public defender, who was a Democrat, from discharging assistant public defenders because they did not have the support of the Democratic Party. . . .

Respondents urge us to view *Elrod* and *Branti* as inapplicable because the patronage dismissals at issue in those cases are different in kind from failure to promote, failure to transfer, and failure to recall after layoff. Respondents initially contend that the employee petitioners' First Amendment rights have not been infringed because they have no entitlement to promotion, transfer, or rehire. We rejected just such an argument in *Elrod*. . . .

Respondents next argue that the employment decisions at issue here do not violate the First Amendment because the decisions are not punitive, do not in any way adversely affect the terms of employment, and therefore do not chill the exercise of protected belief and association by public employees. This is not credible. Employees who find themselves in dead-end positions due to their political backgrounds *are* adversely affected. They will feel a significant obligation to support political positions held by their superiors, and to refrain from acting on the political views they actually hold, in order to progress up the career ladder. Employees denied transfers to workplaces reasonably close to their homes until they join and work for the Republican Party will feel a daily pressure from their long commutes to do so. And employees who have been laid off may well feel compelled to engage in whatever political activity is necessary to regain regular paychecks and positions corresponding to their skill and experience.

The same First Amendment concerns that underlay our decisions in *Elrod*, and *Branti*, are implicated here. Employees who do not compromise their beliefs stand to lose the considerable increases in pay and job satisfaction attendant to promotions, the hours and maintenance expenses that are consumed by long daily commutes, and even their jobs if they are not rehired after a "temporary" layoff. These are significant penalties and are imposed for the exercise of rights guaranteed by the First Amendment. Unless these patronage practices are narrowly tailored to further vital government interests, we must conclude that they impermissibly encroach on First Amendment freedoms. . . .

We hold that the rule of *Elrod* and *Branti* extends to promotion, transfer, recall, and hiring decisions based on party affiliation and support and that all of the petitioners and cross-respondents have stated claims upon which relief may be granted. We affirm the Seventh Circuit insofar as it remanded Ru-

tan's, Taylor's, Standefer's, and O'Brien's claims. However, we reverse the Circuit Court's decision to uphold the dismissal of Moore's claim. All five claims are remanded for proceedings consistent with this opinion.
It is so ordered.

☐ *Justice SCALIA, with whom THE CHIEF JUSTICE and Justice KENNEDY join, and with whom Justice O'CONNOR joins as to Parts II and III, dissenting.*

Today the Court establishes the constitutional principle that party membership is not a permissible factor in the dispensation of government jobs, except those jobs for the performance of which party affiliation is an "appropriate requirement." It is hard to say precisely (or even generally) what that exception means, but if there is any category of jobs for whose performance party affiliation is not an appropriate requirement, it is the job of being a judge, where partisanship is not only unneeded but positively undesirable. It is, however, rare that a federal administration of one party will appoint a judge from another party. And it has always been rare. See *Marbury v. Madison*, 1 Cranch 137 (1803). Thus, the new principle that the Court today announces will be enforced by a corps of judges (the Members of this Court included) who overwhelmingly owe their office to its violation. Something must be wrong here, and I suggest it is the Court.

The merit principle for government employment is probably the most favored in modern America, having been widely adopted by civil-service legislation at both the state and federal levels. But there is another point of view, described in characteristically Jacksonian fashion by an eminent practitioner of the patronage system, George Washington Plunkitt of Tammany Hall:

> I ain't up on sillygisms, but I can give you some arguments that nobody can answer.
> First, this great and glorious country was built up by political parties; second, parties can't hold together if their workers don't get offices when they win; third, if the parties go to pieces, the government they built up must go to pieces, too; fourth, then there'll be hell to pay. W. Riordon, *Plunkitt of Tammany Hall* 13 (1963).

It may well be that the Good Government Leagues of America were right, and that Plunkitt, James Michael Curley and their ilk were wrong; but that is not entirely certain. As the merit principle has been extended and its effects increasingly felt; as the Boss Tweeds, the Tammany Halls, the Pendergast Machines, the Byrd Machines and the Daley Machines have faded into history; we find that political leaders at all levels increasingly complain of the helplessness of elected government, unprotected by "party discipline," before the demands of small and cohesive interest-groups.

The choice between patronage and the merit principle—or, to be more realistic about it, the choice between the desirable mix of merit and patronage principles in widely varying federal, state, and local political contexts—is not so clear that I would be prepared, as an original matter, to chisel a single, inflexible prescription into the Constitution. Fourteen years ago, in *Elrod v. Burns* (1976), the Court did that. *Elrod* was limited however, as was the later decision of *Branti v. Finkel* (1980), to patronage firings, leaving it to state and federal legislatures to determine when and where political affiliation could be taken into account in hirings and promotions. Today the Court makes its constitutional civil-service reform absolute, extending to all decisions regarding government employment. Because the First Amendment has never been thought to require this disposition, which may well have disastrous consequences for our political system, I dissent.

■ I

The restrictions that the Constitution places upon the government in its capacity as lawmaker, *i.e.*, as the regulator of private conduct, are not the same as the restrictions that it places upon the government in its capacity as employer. We have recognized this in many contexts, with respect to many different constitutional guarantees. Private citizens perhaps cannot be prevented from wearing long hair, but policemen can. *Kelley v. Johnson*, 425 U.S. 238 (1976). Private citizens cannot have their property searched without probable cause, but in many circumstances government employees can. *O'Connor v. Ortega*, 480 U.S. 709 (1987). Private citizens cannot be punished for refusing to provide the government information that may incriminate them, but government employees can be dismissed when the incriminating information that they refuse to provide relates to the performance of their job. *Gardner v. Broderick*, 392 U.S. 273 (1968). With regard to freedom of speech in particular: Private citizens cannot be punished for speech of merely private concern, but government employees can be fired for that reason. *Connick v. Myers*, 461 U.S. 138, (1983). Private citizens cannot be punished for partisan political activity, but federal and state employees can be dismissed and otherwise punished for that reason. *Public Workers v. Mitchell*, 330 U.S. 75 (1947); *CSC v. Letter Carriers*, 413 U.S. 548 (1973); *Broadrick v. Oklahoma*, 413 U.S. 601 (1973).

Once it is acknowledged that the Constitution's prohibition against laws "abridging the freedom of speech" does not apply to laws enacted in the government's capacity as employer the same way it does to laws enacted in the government's capacity as regulator of private conduct, it may sometimes be difficult to assess what employment practices are permissible and what are not. That seems to me not a difficult question, however, in the present context. The provisions of the Bill of Rights were designed to restrain transient majorities from impairing long-recognized personal liberties. They did not create by implication novel individual rights overturning accepted political norms. Thus, when a practice not expressly prohibited by the text of the Bill of Rights bears the endorsement of a long tradition of open, widespread, and unchallenged use that dates back to the beginning of the Republic, we have no proper basis for striking it down. Such a venerable and accepted tradition is not to be laid on the examining table and scrutinized for its conformity to some abstract principle of First-Amendment adjudication devised by this Court. To the contrary, such traditions are themselves the stuff out of which the Court's principles are to be formed. They are, in these uncertain areas, the very points of reference by which the legitimacy or illegitimacy of *other* practices are to be figured out. When it appears that the latest "rule," or "three-part test," or "balancing test" devised by the Court has placed us on a collision course with such a landmark practice, it is the former that must be recalculated by us, and not the latter that must be abandoned by our citizens. I know of no other way to formulate a constitutional jurisprudence that reflects, as it should, the principles adhered to, over time, by the American people, rather than those favored by the personal (and necessarily shifting) philosophical dispositions of a majority of this Court. . . .

■ II

Even accepting the Court's own mode of analysis, however, and engaging in "balancing," a tradition that ought to be part of the scales, *Elrod, Branti,* and today's extension of them seem to me wrong.

The Court limits patronage on the ground that the individual's interest in uncoerced belief and expression outweighs the systemic interests invoked to justify the practice. The opinion indicates that the government may prevail only if it proves that the practice is "narrowly tailored to further vital government interests."

That strict-scrutiny standard finds no support in our cases. Although our decisions establish that government employees do not lose all constitutional rights, we have consistently applied a lower level of scrutiny when "the governmental function operating . . . [is] not the power to regulate or license, as lawmaker, an entire trade or profession, or to control an entire branch of private business, but, rather, as proprietor, to manage [its] internal operatio[ns]. . . ." *Cafeteria & Restaurant Workers v. McElroy,* 367 U.S. 886 (1961). When dealing with its own employees, the government may not act in a manner that is "patently arbitrary or discriminatory," but its regulations are valid if they bear a "rational connection" to the governmental end sought to be served, *Kelley v. Johnson.* . . .

Because the restriction on speech is more attenuated when the government conditions employment than when it imposes criminal penalties, and because "government offices could not function if every employment decision became a constitutional matter," *Connick v. Myers,* we have held that government employment decisions taken on the basis of an employee's speech do not "abridg[e] the freedom of speech," merely because they fail the narrow-tailoring and compelling-interest tests applicable to direct regulation of speech. We have not subjected such decisions to strict scrutiny, but have accorded "a wide degree of deference to the employer's judgment" that an employee's speech will interfere with close working relationships.

When the government takes adverse action against an employee on the basis of his political affiliation (an interest whose constitutional protection is derived from the interest in speech), the same analysis applies. . . .

The whole point of my dissent is that the desirability of patronage is a policy question to be decided by the people's representatives; I do not mean, therefore, to endorse that system. But in order to demonstrate that a legislature could reasonably determine that its benefits outweigh its "coercive" effects, I must describe those benefits as the proponents of patronage see them: As Justice POWELL discussed at length in his *Elrod* dissent, patronage stabilizes political parties and prevents excessive political fragmentation—both of which are results in which States have a strong governmental interest. Party strength requires the efforts of the rank-and-file, especially in "the dull periods between elections," to perform such tasks as organizing precincts, registering new voters, and providing constituent services. Even the most enthusiastic supporter of a party's program will shrink before such drudgery, and it is folly to think that ideological conviction alone will motivate sufficient numbers to keep the party going through the off-years. . . .

The Court simply refuses to acknowledge the link between patronage and party discipline, and between that and party success . . .

It is self-evident that eliminating patronage will significantly undermine party discipline; and that as party discipline wanes, so will the strength of the two-party system. But, says the Court, "[p]olitical parties have already survived the substantial decline in patronage employment practices in this century." This is almost verbatim what was said in *Elrod*. Fourteen years later it seems much less convincing. Indeed, now that we have witnessed, in 18 of the last 22 years, an Executive Branch of the Federal Government under the control of one party while the Congress is entirely or (for two years) partially within the control of the other party; now that we have undergone the most recent federal election, in which 98% of the incumbents, of whatever party, were returned to office; and now that we have seen elected officials changing their political affiliation with unprecedented readiness, the statement that "political parties have already survived" has a positively whistling-in-the-graveyard character to it. Parties have assuredly survived—but as what? As the forges upon which many of the essential compromises of American political life are hammered out? Or merely as convenient vehicles for the conducting of national presidential elections?

The patronage system does not, of course, merely foster political parties in general; it fosters the two-party system in particular. When getting a job, as opposed to effectuating a particular substantive policy, is an available incentive for party-workers, those attracted by that incentive are likely to work for the party that has the best chance of displacing the "ins," rather than for some splinter group that has a more attractive political philosophy but little hope of success. Not only is a two-party system more likely to emerge, but the differences between those parties are more likely to be moderated, as each has a relatively greater interest in appealing to a majority of the electorate and a relatively lesser interest in furthering philosophies or programs that are far from the mainstream. The stabilizing effects of such a system are obvious. . . .

Equally apparent is the relatively destabilizing nature of a system in which candidates cannot rely upon patronage-based party loyalty for their campaign support, but must attract workers and raise funds by appealing to various interest-groups. There is little doubt that our decisions in *Elrod* and *Branti*, by contributing to the decline of party strength, have also contributed to the growth of interest-group politics in the last decade. Our decision to-day will greatly accelerate the trend. It is not only campaigns that are affected, of course, but the subsequent behavior of politicians once they are in power. The replacement of a system firmly based in party discipline with one in which each office-holder comes to his own accommodation with competing interest groups produces "a dispersion of political influence that may inhibit a political party from enacting its programs into law."

Patronage, moreover, has been a powerful means of achieving the social and political integration of excluded groups. By supporting and ultimately dominating a particular party "machine," racial and ethnic minorities have—on the basis of their politics rather than their race or ethnicity—acquired the patronage awards the machine had power to confer. No one disputes the historical accuracy of this observation, and there is no reason to think that patronage can no longer serve that function. The abolition of patronage, however, prevents groups that have only recently obtained political power, especially blacks, from following this path to economic and social advancement. . . .

While the patronage system has the benefits argued for above, it also has undoubted disadvantages. It facilitates financial corruption, such as salary kickbacks and partisan political activity on government-paid time. It reduces the efficiency of government, because it creates incentives to hire more and less-qualified workers and because highly qualified workers are reluctant to accept jobs that may only last until the next election. And, of course, it applies some greater or lesser inducement for individuals to join and work for the party in power. . . .

Even were I not convinced that *Elrod* and *Branti* were wrongly decided, I would hold that they should not be extended beyond their facts, *viz.*, actual discharge of employees for their political affiliation. Those cases invalidated patronage firing in order to prevent the "restraint it places on freedoms of belief and association." The loss of one's current livelihood is an appreciably greater constraint than such other disappointments as the failure to obtain a promotion or selection for an uncongenial transfer. Even if the "coercive" effect of the former has been always to outweigh the benefits of party-based employment decisions, the "coercive" effect of the latter should not be. We have drawn a line between firing and other employment decisions in other contexts, see *Wygant v. Jackson Bd. of Education*, 476 U.S. 267 (1986) and should do so here as well. . . . If *Elrod* and *Branti* are not to be reconsidered in light of their demonstrably unsatisfactory consequences, I would go no further than to allow a cause of action when the employee has lost his position, that is, his formal title and salary. That narrow ground alone is enough to resolve the constitutional claims in the present case. . . .

The Court's opinion, of course, not only declines to confine *Elrod* and *Branti* to dismissals in the narrow sense I have proposed, but, unlike the Seventh Circuit, even extends those opinions beyond "constructive" dismissals— indeed, even beyond adverse treatment of current employees—to all hiring decisions. In the long run there may be cause to rejoice in that extension. When the courts are flooded with litigation under that most unmanageable of standards (*Branti*) brought by that most persistent and tenacious of suitors (the disappointed office-seeker) we may be moved to reconsider our intrusion into this entire field.

In the meantime, I dissent.

McIntyre v. Ohio Elections Organization

514 U.S. 334, 115 S.Ct. 1511 (1995)

In 1988, Mrs. Margaret McIntyre distributed leaflets outside of a public meeting at a middle school in Westerville, Ohio. At the meeting the school superintendent discussed an upcoming referendum on a proposed school tax levy, which Mrs. McIntyre's leaflets opposed. Some of the leaflets identified her as the author, but others purported to express the views of "Concerned Parents and Tax Payers." The levy was subsequently defeated in two elections but finally passed in a third. Five months after that election, a school official filed a complaint with the Ohio Elections Organization, charging Mrs. McIntyre with violating Section 3599.09(A) of the Ohio state code proscribing the distribution of anonymous campaign literature. Mrs. McIntyre was fined $100 and appealed to a court of common pleas, which found the restriction unconstitutional. However, a state appellate court reversed and the Ohio Supreme Court agreed, upholding the state's law. In the process of the litigation, Mrs. McIntyre died but her husband, as executor of her estate, appealed to the U.S. Supreme Court which granted review.

The Court's decision was seven to two and announced by Justice Stevens. Justices Ginsburg and Thomas filed separate concurrences. Justice Scalia filed a dissenting opinion, which was joined by Chief Justice Rehnquist.

☐ *Justice STEVENS delivered the opinion of the Court.*

"Anonymous pamphlets, leaflets, brochures and even books have played an important role in the progress of mankind." *Talley v. California*, 362 U.S. 60 (1960). Great works of literature have frequently been produced by authors writing under assumed names. Despite readers' curiosity and the public's interest in identifying the creator of a work of art, an author generally is free to decide whether or not to disclose her true identity. The decision in favor of anonymity may be motivated by fear of economic or official retaliation, by concern about social ostracism, or merely by a desire to preserve as much of one's privacy as possible. Whatever the motivation may be, at least in the field of literary endeavor, the interest in having anonymous works enter the marketplace of ideas unquestionably outweighs any public interest in requiring disclosure as a condition of entry. Accordingly, an author's decision to remain anonymous, like other decisions concerning omissions or additions to the content of a publication, is an aspect of the freedom of speech protected by the First Amendment.

The freedom to publish anonymously extends beyond the literary realm. In *Talley*, the Court held that the First Amendment protects the distribution of unsigned handbills urging readers to boycott certain Los Angeles merchants who were allegedly engaging in discriminatory employment practices. Writing for the Court, Justice BLACK noted that "persecuted groups and sects from time to time throughout history have been able to criticize oppressive practices and laws either anonymously or not at all." Justice BLACK recalled England's abusive press licensing laws and seditious libel prosecutions, and he reminded us that even the arguments favoring the ratification of the Constitution advanced in *The Federalist Papers* were published under fictitious names. On occasion, quite apart from any threat of persecution, an advocate may believe her ideas will be more persuasive if her readers are unaware of her identity. Anonymity thereby provides a way for a writer who may be personally unpopular to ensure that readers will not prejudge her message simply because they do not like its proponent. . . .

[A]s we have explained on many prior occasions, the category of speech regulated by the Ohio statute occupies the core of the protection afforded by the First Amendment: "Discussion of public issues and debate on the qualifications of candidates are integral to the operation of the system of government established by our Constitution. The First Amendment affords the broadest protection to such political expression in order 'to assure [the] unfettered interchange of ideas for the bringing about of political and social changes desired by the people.' " *Roth v. United States*, 354 U.S. 476 (1957). . . .

Nevertheless, the State argues that even under the strictest standard of review, the disclosure requirement in Section 3599.09(A) is justified by two important and legitimate state interests. Ohio judges its interest in preventing fraudulent and libelous statements and its interest in providing the electorate with relevant information to be sufficiently compelling to justify the anonymous speech ban. These two interests necessarily overlap to some extent, but it is useful to discuss them separately.

Insofar as the interest in informing the electorate means nothing more than the provision of additional information that may either buttress or undermine the argument in a document, we think the identity of the speaker is no different from other components of the document's content that the author is free to include or exclude. We have already held that the State may not compel a newspaper that prints editorials critical of a particular candidate to provide space for a reply by the candidate. *Miami Herald Publishing Co. v. Tornillo*, 418 U.S. 241 (1974). The simple interest in providing voters with additional relevant information does not justify a state requirement that a writer make statements or disclosures she would otherwise omit. . . .

The state interest in preventing fraud and libel stands on a different footing. We agree with Ohio's submission that this interest carries special weight during election campaigns when false statements, if credited, may have serious adverse consequences for the public at large. Ohio does not, however, rely solely on Section 3599.09(A) to protect that interest. Its Election Code includes detailed and specific prohibitions against making or disseminating false statements during political campaigns. These regulations apply both to candidate elections and to issue-driven ballot measures. Thus, Ohio's prohibition of anonymous leaflets plainly is not its principal weapon against fraud. Rather, it serves as an aid to enforcement of the specific prohibitions and as a deterrent to the making of false statements by unscrupulous prevaricators. Although these ancillary benefits are assuredly legitimate, we are not persuaded that they justify Section 3599.09(A)'s extremely broad prohibition. . . .

Under our Constitution, anonymous pamphleteering is not a pernicious, fraudulent practice, but an honorable tradition of advocacy and of dissent. Anonymity is a shield from the tyranny of the majority. See generally J. S. Mill, *On Liberty*. It thus exemplifies the purpose behind the Bill of Rights, and of the First Amendment in particular: to protect unpopular individuals from retaliation—and their ideas from suppression—at the hand of an intolerant society. The right to remain anonymous may be abused when it shields fraudulent conduct. But political speech by its nature will sometimes have unpalatable consequences, and, in general, our society accords greater weight to the value of free speech than to the dangers of its misuse. Ohio has not shown that its interest in preventing the misuse of anonymous election-related speech justifies a prohibition of all uses of that speech. The State may, and does, punish fraud directly. But it cannot seek to punish fraud indirectly by indiscriminately outlawing a category of speech, based on its content, with no necessary relationship to the danger sought to be prevented. One would be hard pressed to think of a better example of the pitfalls of Ohio's blunderbuss approach than the facts of the case before us.

The judgment of the Ohio Supreme Court is reversed.

□ *Justice THOMAS, concurring in the judgment.*

I agree with the majority's conclusion that Ohio's election law is inconsistent with the First Amendment. I would apply, however, a different methodology to this case. Instead of asking whether "an honorable tradition" of anonymous speech has existed throughout American history, or what the "value" of anonymous speech might be, we should determine whether the phrase "freedom of speech, or of the press," as originally understood, protected anonymous political leafletting. I believe that it did. . . . [A lengthy review of the use anonymous publications, like *The Federalist Papers*, during the period of the Constitution's ratification follows and is omitted here.]

The ratification of the Constitution was not the only issue discussed via anonymous writings in the press. James Madison and Alexander Hamilton, for example, resorted to pseudonyms in the famous "Helvidius" and "Pacificus" debates over President Washington's declaration of neutrality in the war between the British and French. Anonymous writings continued in such Republican papers as the *Aurora* and Federalists organs such as the *Gazette of the United States* at least until the election of Thomas Jefferson.

This evidence leads me to agree with the majority's result, but not its reasoning. The majority fails to seek the original understanding of the First Amendment, and instead attempts to answer the question in this case by resorting to three approaches. First, the majority recalls the historical practice of anonymous writing from Shakespeare's works to *The Federalist Papers* to Mark Twain. Second, it finds that anonymous speech has an expressive value both to the speaker and to society that outweighs public interest in disclosure. Third, it finds that Section 3599.09(A) cannot survive strict scrutiny because it is a "content-based" restriction on speech.

I cannot join the majority's analysis because it deviates from our settled approach to interpreting the Constitution and because it superimposes its modern theories concerning expression upon the constitutional text. Whether "great works of literature"—by Voltaire or George Eliot have been published anonymously should be irrelevant to our analysis, because it sheds no light on what the phrases "free speech" or "free press" meant to the people who drafted and ratified the First Amendment. . . .

□ *Justice SCALIA, with whom THE CHIEF JUSTICE joins, dissenting.*

The question posed by the present case is not the easiest sort to answer for those who adhere to the Court's (and the society's) traditional view that the Constitution bears its original meaning and is unchanging. That technique is simple of application when government conduct that is claimed to violate the Bill of Rights or the Fourteenth Amendment is shown, upon investigation, to have been engaged in without objection at the very time the Bill of Rights or the Fourteenth Amendment was adopted. There is no doubt, for example, that laws against libel and obscenity do not violate "the freedom of speech" to which the First Amendment refers; they existed and were universally approved in 1791. Application of the principle of an unchanging Constitution is also simple enough at the other extreme, where the government conduct at issue was not engaged in at the time of adoption, and there is ample evidence that the reason it was not engaged in is that it was thought to violate the right embodied in the constitutional guarantee. . . .

The present case lies between those two extremes. Anonymous electioneering was not prohibited by law in 1791 or in 1868. In fact, it was widely practiced at the earlier date, an understandable legacy of the revolutionary era in which political dissent could produce governmental reprisal. I need not dwell upon the evidence of that, since it is described at length in today's concurrence.

But to prove that anonymous electioneering was used frequently is not to establish that it is a constitutional right. Quite obviously, not every restriction upon expression that did not exist in 1791 or in 1868 is *ipso facto* unconstitutional, or else modern election laws such as those involved in *Burson v. Freeman*, 504 U.S. 191 (1992), and *Buckley v. Valeo*, 424 U.S. 1 (1976), would be prohibited, as would (to mention only a few other categories) modern antinoise regulation of the sort involved in *Kovacs v. Cooper*, 336 U.S. 77 (1949), and *Ward v. Rock Against Racism*, 491 U.S. 781 (1989), and modern parade-permitting regulation of the sort involved in *Cox v. New Hampshire*, 312 U.S. 569 (1941).

Evidence that anonymous electioneering was regarded as a constitutional right is sparse, and as far as I am aware evidence that it was generally regarded as such is nonexistent. The concurrence points to "freedom of the press" objections that were made against the refusal of some Federalist newspapers to publish unsigned essays opposing the proposed constitution (on the ground that they might be the work of foreign agents). But of course if every partisan cry of "freedom of the press" were accepted as valid, our Constitution would be unrecognizable; and if one were to generalize from these particular cries, the First Amendment would be not only a protection for newspapers but a restriction upon them. . . .

The concurrence recounts other pre- and post-Revolution examples of defense of anonymity in the name of "freedom of the press," but not a single one involves the context of restrictions imposed in connection with a free, democratic election, which is all that is at issue here. . . .

Thus, the sum total of the historical evidence marshalled by the concurrence for the principle of constitutional entitlement to anonymous electioneering is partisan claims in the debate on ratification (which was almost like an election) that a viewpoint-based restriction on anonymity by newspaper editors violates freedom of speech. This absence of historical testimony concerning the point before us is hardly remarkable. The issue of a governmental prohibition upon anonymous electioneering in particular (as opposed to a government prohibition upon anonymous publication in general) simply never arose. Indeed, there probably never arose even the abstract question of whether electoral openness and regularity was worth such a governmental restriction upon the normal right to anonymous speech. The idea of close government regulation of the electoral process is a more modern phenomenon, arriving in this country in the late 1800's.

What we have, then, is the most difficult case for determining the meaning of the Constitution. No accepted existence of governmental restrictions of the sort at issue here demonstrates their constitutionality, but neither can their nonexistence clearly be attributed to constitutional objections. In such a case, constitutional adjudication necessarily involves not just history but judgment: judgment as to whether the government action under challenge is consonant with the concept of the protected freedom (in this case, the freedom of speech and of the press) that existed when the constitutional protection was accorded. In the present case, *absent other indication*, I would be inclined to agree with the concurrence that a society which used anonymous political debate so regularly would not regard as constitutional even moderate restrictions made to improve the election process.

But there *is* other indication, of the most weighty sort: the widespread and longstanding traditions of our people. Principles of liberty fundamental enough to have been embodied within constitutional guarantees are not readily erased from the Nation's consciousness. A governmental practice that has become general throughout the United States, and particularly one that has the validation of long, accepted usage, bears a strong presumption of constitutionality. And that is what we have before us here. Section 3599.09(A) was enacted by the General Assembly of the State of Ohio almost 80 years ago. Even at the time of its adoption, there was nothing unique or extraordinary about it. The earliest statute of this sort was adopted by Massachusetts in 1890, little more than 20 years after the Fourteenth Amendment was ratified. No less than 24 States had similar laws by the end of World War I, and today every State of the Union except California has one, as does the District of Columbia, and as does the Federal Government where advertising relating to candidates for federal office is concerned. Such a universal and long established American legislative practice must be given precedence, I think, over historical and academic speculation regarding a restriction that assuredly does not go to the heart of free speech. . . .

It can be said that we ignored a tradition as old, and almost as widespread, in *Texas v. Johnson*, 491 U.S. 397 (1989), where we held unconstitutional a state law prohibiting descreation of the United States flag. But those cases merely stand for the proposition that post-adoption cannot alter the core meaning of a constitutional guarantee. As we said in *Johnson*, "if there is a bedrock principle underlying the First Amendment, it is that the government may not prohibit the expression of an idea simply because society finds the idea itself offensive or disagreeable." . . .

The foregoing analysis suffices to decide this case for me. Where the meaning of a constitutional text (such as "the freedom of speech") is unclear, the widespread and long-accepted practices of the American people are the best indication of what fundamental beliefs it was intended to enshrine. Even if I were to close my eyes to practice, however, and were to be guided exclusively by deductive analysis from our case law, I would reach the same result. . . . I respectfully dissent.

■ The Development of Law

Other Rulings on Campaigns and Elections

CASE	VOTE	RULING
Williams v. Rhodes, 393 U.S. 23 (1968)	8:1	Struck down an Ohio law precluding the Socialist Labor party from being placed on the ballot.
Gordon v. Lance, 403 U.S. 1 (1971)	9:0	Upheld West Virginia law allowing 60 percent of voters in a referendum to approve tax increases.
Jenneas v. Fortson, 403 U.S. 431 (1971)	9:0	Upheld Georgia's requirement that any political organization other than those receiving 20 percent or more in the last gubernatorial election must file a

nominating petition with not less than 15 percent of eligible voters signing it within 180 days of filing deadline for candidates in primaries.

Roudebush v. Hartke, 405 U.S. 15 (1972)	5:2	Constitutional provision that each house will judge elections does not prohibit Indi-

ana from conducting a re-count of 1970 election ballots.

Rosario v. Rockefeller, 410 U.S. 752 (1973)	5:4	State does not violate First Amendment right of freedom of association by requir-

ing that voters in primary elections enroll in the party at least thirty days before the last general election.

Kusper v. Pontikes, 414 U.S. 51 (1973)	7:2	States impermissibly abridge First Amendment by forbidding citizens to vote in the

primary of one party if they have voted in that of another party in the preceding twenty-three months.

Storer v. Brown and Frommhagen v. Brown, 415 U.S. 724 (1974)	6:3	States may require that independent candidates disassociate themselves from an es-

tablished party at least one year before the primary election of the year in which they plan to run for office.

CASE	VOTE	RULING

American Party of Texas v. White, U.S. 767 (1974) — **8:1** — A state's compelling interest in protecting the integrity of the nominating process may require new and minority parties to secure a certain number of voter signatures on petitions, excluding those who voted in a party primary in the same year, to place candidate's name on the ballot.

Anderson v. United States, 417 U.S. 211 (1974) — **7:2** — State and local officials may be prosecuted under federal law for tampering with ballots in local election because voters have an unimpeded right to vote in congressional and senatorial primaries held at the same time.

Hill v. Stone, 421 U.S. 709 (1974) — **5:3** — Struck down section of Texas election code limiting to property owners the right to vote in city bond issues; held that only age, residence, and citizenship distinctions may be made.

Richardson v. Ramirez, 418 U.S. 24 (1974) — **6:3** — Held that state may disenfranchise convicted felons who have completed their prison sentences.

Town of Lockport v. Citizens for Community Action, 430 U.S. 259 (1977) — **9:0** — Upheld a New York law requiring that new county charters go into effect only if approved by concurrent majorities of voters living within cities in the county and voters living outside of the cities.

Hunter v. Underwood, 471 U.S. 222 (1985) — **9:0** — Held that Alabama constitution disenfranchising people convicted of crimes of moral turpitude violated the Fouteenth Amendment's equal protection clause.

Tashjian v. Republican Party of Connecticut, 479 U.S. 208 (1986) — **5:4** — Connecticut's primary statute, barring unaffiliated voters from participating in elections, violated political party's First Amendment right of association.

(continues)

■ THE DEVELOPMENT OF LAW
Other Rulings on Campaigns and Elections (continued)

CASE	VOTE	RULING
Eu v. San Francisco County Democratic Central Committee, 489 U.S. 214 (1989)	8:0	Struck down an ordinance forbidding primary endorsement of political parties and restrictions on the organization and composition of official governing bodies of state political parties.
Renne v. Geary, 501 U.S. 312 (1991)	6:3	The Court held that a challenge to a state law banning political parties from endorsing candidates in nonpartisan elections for judgeships and local government positions was nonjusticiable. Justices Blackmun, Marshall, and White dissented.
Burson v. Freeman, 504 U.S. 191 (1992)	4:3	With Justice Thomas not participating, the Court upheld a Tennessee law forbidding the display and distribution of campaign materials, along with the solicitation of votes, near polling places on election day, while permitting other forms of speech there. Justices O'Connor, Souter, and Stevens dissented.
Norman v. Reed, 502 U.S. 279 (1992)	8:1	Struck down an ordinance requiring new political parties to gather 50,000 signatures on nominating petitions to place their candidates on ballots for local offices, whereas for other statewide offices only 25,000 signatures were required. With only Justice Scalia dissenting, the Court reaffirmed citizens' First and Fourteenth Amendments right to form political parties and deemed the ordinance to lack a "compelling state interest."
Burdick v. Takuski, 505 U.S. 1202 (1992)	6:3	Upheld Hawaii's law prohibiting write-in votes in state elections as imposing reasonable burdens on citizen's First and Fourteenth Amendment rights. Justices Blackmun, Kennedy, and Stevens dissented.
McIntyre v. Ohio Elections Commission, 514 U.S. 334 (1995)	7:2	Writing for the majority, Justice Stevens struck down Ohio's law against the distribution of anonymous campaign literature, and by implication similar laws in forty-eight other states, as a violation of the First Amendment. Justice Scalia and Chief Justice Rehnquist dissented.

CASE	VOTE	RULING

Timmons v. Twin Cities Area New Party, 520 U.S. 351 (1997) — 6:3 — Rejected a First Amendment challenge to Minnesota's law barring the listing on ballots of candidates supported by one of the major parties, Republican or Democrat, as well as a third party. The New Party argued that the ban on such a "fusion" in listing candidates relegated third parties to the margins and violated their First Amendment rights of freedom of speech and association. But only dissenting Justices Stevens, Souter, and O'Connor agreed.

Foster v. Love, 522 U.S. 67 (1997) — 9:0 — Struck down Louisiana's 1975 "open primary" law, under which elections are held in October and if a candidate for a congressional seat receives a majority vote, the candidate "is elected" and not subject to run on the federal election day of the Tuesday after the first Monday in November, which was established in 1872. Writing for the Court, Justice Souter held that the law infringed on Congress's "power to override state regulations" by establishing uniform rules for federal elections.

Arkansas Educational Television Commission v. Forbes, 523 U.S. 666 (1998) — 6:3 — Writing for the Court, Justice Kennedy held that a public television station may exclude "marginal" candidates from its televised debates of major candidates for political office. In refusing to extend the concept of a "public forum" to such debates, he held that the decision to exclude Steve Forbes, an independent candidate, was under the circumstances a reasonable, viewpoint-neutral exercise of journalistic discretion consistent with the First Amendment. Dissenting Justice Stevens, joined by Justices Ginsburg and Souter, countered that the majority failed to hold public television stations to a higher standard, requiring them to have "preestablished, objective criteria" for determining access to televised debates.

Buckley v. American Constitutional Law Foundation, 525 U.S. 182 (1999) — 6:3 — Writing for the majority, Justice Ginsburg invalidated Colorado's restrictions on its initiative-petition process that had required petition proponents and circulators to (1) be registered voters, (2) wear identification badges when gathering signatures, and (3) disclose the names of all paid circulators, for infringing on the First Amendment's guarantee for freedom of speech. Chief Justice Rehnquist and Justices O'Connor and Breyer dissented.

(continues)

■ THE DEVELOPMENT OF LAW
Other Rulings on Campaigns and Elections (continued)

CASE	VOTE	RULING
California Democratic Party v. Jones, 530 U. S 567 (2000)	7:2	Writing for the Court, Justice Scalia struck down California's "blanket primary," under

which all persons eligible (even those not affiliated with a party) may vote for any candidate, regardless of the candidate's political affiliation, and voters may pick and choose among different parties' candidates for various offices. Washington and Alaska had similar primaries, whereas twenty other states have "open primaries," allowing voters to decide on election day which party primary they want to participate in. Here, the "blanket primary" was held to violate political parties' First Amendment freedom of association. Justices Stevens and Ginsburg dissented.

Rice v. Cayetanno, 528 U.S. 495 (2000)	7:2	The Court held that the denial of a citizen's right to vote for trustees of the Office of

Hawaiian Affairs (OHA) violates the Fifteenth Amendment. The OHA administers programs for two subclasses of Hawaiians: "Hawaiians" and "native Hawaiians," both of which trace their ancestry back to 1778. Rice, a Hawaiian citizen who lacked ancestry to be designated a "Hawaiian," applied to vote in OHA trustee elections but was denied. Writing for the Court, Justice Kennedy ruled that the ancestry requirements were a proxy for race and as such forbidden by the Fifteenth Amendment. Justices Stevens and Ginsburg dissented.

Cook v. Gralike, 531 U.S. 510 (2001)	9:0	In response to the ruling in *U.S. Term Limits, Inc. v. Thornton*, 514 U.S. 779 (1995) (ex-

cerpted in Vol. 1, Ch. 5), Missouri amended its state constitution to require placing of the words "Disregarded Voters' Instruction on Term Limits" on the ballot next to the name of an incumbent who failed to support term limits and who runs for reelection. For candidates who are not incumbents and refuse to vow to support term limits, the law required placing the label "Declined to Pledge to Support Term Limits" next to their names. Writing for the Court, Justice Stevens struck down Missouri's law for running afoul of Elections Clause of Article 1, Section 4, by impermissibly attempting to add to the qualifications for holding congressional office beyond those specified for members' age, citizenship, and residency.

CASE	VOTE	RULING

Clingman v. Beaver, 544 U.S. 581 (2005)   **6:3**   Justice Thomas upheld Oklahoma's semiclosed primary law, under which political parties may permit only their registered voters and independents to vote in a primary. The Libertarian Party had wanted to open its primary to voters of other parties and challenged the law for infringing on the freedom of association. Justice Thomas, though, ruled that the restriction imposed only minor burdens and advanced the state's interest in preserving parties as viable interest groups.

Randall v. Sorrell, 548 U.S. 230 (2006)   **6:3**   In a plurality opinion Justice Breyer, joined by Chief Justice Roberts and Justice Alito, struck down Vermont's 1997 law imposing restrictions on campaign spending and contributions, which ranged from $200 per election cycle for state house candidates to $400 for statewide candidates. Justice Breyer held that the $200 limitation was "way, way, way lower" than the $1,000 federal campaign contribution limit upheld in *Buckley v. Valeo,* 424 U.S. 1 (1976), but the restriction was disproportionate to the state's interest in preventing the appearance of corruption in elections. In separate concurring opinions, Justices Alito, Thomas (joined by Justice Scalia), and Kennedy took the position that all contribution restrictions violate the First Amendment. Justices Souter and Stevens, joined by Justice Ginsburg, dissented.

New York State Board of Elections v. Lopez Torres, 128 S.Ct. 791 (2008)   **9:0**   Writing for the Court, Justice Scalia upheld New York's process for selecting its supreme court justices through party conventions. Under the state law, each political party selects one candidate to run in the general election. That law was challenged as a violation of the First Amendment freedom of association for discriminating against challengers to party-selected candidates. But the Court held that political parties have First Amendment protection to determine their own selection process and rejected the claims of candidates who do not have party leadership support.

(continues)

■ THE DEVELOPMENT OF LAW
Other Rulings on Campaigns and Elections (continued)

CASE	VOTE	RULING
Washington State Grange v. Washington State Republican, Party, 128 S.Ct. 1194 (2008)	7:2	Writing for the Court, Justice Thomas upheld Washington state's law requiring candidates for elective office to be identified on the ballot by their

self-designated "party preference." The majority held that the requirement did not unduly burden political parties' freedom of association under the First Amendment. Justices Scalia and Kennedy dissented.

| *Crawford v. Marion County Election Board*, 128 S.Ct. 1610 (2008) | 6:3 | Writing for a plurality and delivering the opinion, Justice Stevens rejected a Fourteenth Amendment and |

Voting Rights Act challenge to a state law requiring voters to produce a photo identification before casting a ballot in an election. Petitioners had argued that the Law had a discriminatory effect on the poor, the elderly, and the disabled. Justice Scalia, joined by Justices Thomas and Alito, filed a concurring opinion. Justices Souter and Breyer filed separate dissenting opinions; Justice Ginsburg joined the former's dissent.

| *Ysuria v. Pocatello Education Association*, 129 S.Ct. 1093 (2009) | 6:3 | Writing for the Court, Chief Justice Roberts held that states may order local governments to forbid payroll |

deductions for unions' political activities and rejected the union's claim that that violated the First Amendment. In his words: "The First Amendment prohibits government from 'abridging the freedom of speech'; it does not confer an affirmative right to use government payroll mechanisms for the purpose of obtaining funds for expression."

| *Caperton v. A. T. Massey Coal Co., Inc.* 129 S.Ct. 2252 (2009) | 5:4 | By a five-to-four vote, the Court held that it is unconstitutional for a state supreme court justice to sit on a case |

involving the financial interests of a major donor to the justice's election campaign. Writing for the majority, Justice Kennedy held that West Virginia Supreme Court Chief Justice Brent Benjamin should have recused himself from a case that overturned a $50-million verdict against a company headed by a man who contributed $3 million to the justice's election. The failure to do so ran afoul of the Due Process Clause that incorporates the common-law rule requiring recusal when a judge has "a direct, personal, substantial, pecuniary interest" in a case and, according to the Court's precedents, recusal is required where "the probability of actual bias on the part of the judge or decisionmaker is too high to be constitutionally tolerable." In Justice Kennedy's words: "Not every campaign contribution by a litigant or attorney creates a probability of bias that requires a judge's recusal, but this is an exceptional case." By contrast, dissenting Chief Justice Roberts, joined by Justices Scalia, Thomas, and Alito, countered that the ruling "requires state and federal judges simultaneously to act as political scientists (why did candidate X win the election?), economists (was the financial support disproportionate?), and psychologists (is there likely to be a debt of gratitude?)."

CASE	VOTE	RULING
Doe v. Reed, 130 S.Ct 2811 (2010)	8:1	Writing for the Court, Chief Justice Roberts held that the First Amendment does not

necessarily bar the required disclosure of the names of those who sign petitions for state referendums. In 2009, a new state law expanded the rights of same-sex partners and some Washington citizens decided to file a referendum to repeal the law. The Washington Public Records Act required the public release of those who signed the petition. Signatories of the referendum petition, afraid of reprisal, sought to enjoin the release of their identities and contended that the release violated the First Amendment. A federal disrict court held that the First Amendment granted a right to anonymity, but the Court of Appeals for the Ninth Circuit reversed, holding that there was no absolute right to anonymity under the First Amendment. Although the Court agreed with the appellate court that there was no absolute right to anonymity, Chief Justice Roberts ruled that there might be in this case since disclosure might lead to harassment of signatories and therefore the First Amendment might grant protection; thus, the case was remanded for consideration on narrower First Amendment analysis. Justice Thomas dissented.

9

ECONOMIC RIGHTS AND AMERICAN CAPITALISM

Private property is not mentioned in the Constitution even though its protection was one of the central purposes of the Constitution. Sections 8 and 10 of Article I and Section 1 of Article IV govern various matters related to private property—taxes, duties, imposts, excises, commerce, bankruptcies, bills of credit, debts, the impairment of contracts, and the rights of authors and inventors. Yet private property did not receive specific protection until the ratification in 1791 of the Fifth Amendment. The due process and takings clauses of that amendment provide that "No person shall . . . be deprived of life, liberty, or property without due process of law; nor shall private property be taken for public use without just compensation."

Liberty and property were, nevertheless, closely tied together in the minds of the Framers of the Constitution. Property conditioned suffrage and was closely linked with representation (see Vol. 1, Chs. 5 and 8). When defending the Constitution in *The Federalist*, Alexander Hamilton sought to show that it would provide security "to liberty and to property." Noah Webster, a prominent New York publisher, even more bluntly claimed "that *property* is the basis of *power*" when differentiating America from England and Europe, where property was concentrated in the hands of a few:

> [I]n America, and here alone, we have gone at once to the *foundation of liberty*, and raised the people to their true dignity. Let the lands be possessed by the people in fee-simple, let the fountain be kept pure, and the streams will be pure of course. Our jealousy of *trial by jury, the liberty of the press, &c.*, is totally groundless. Such rights are inseparably connected with the *power* and *dignity* of the

people, which rest on their *property*. They cannot be abridged. All *other* [free] nations have wrested *property* and *freedom* from *barons* and *tyrants; we* begin our empire with full possession of property and all its attending rights.[1]

The Framers took to heart the teaching of the English philosopher John Locke, in his *Second Treatise of Government*, that property is a natural right—a right preceding the establishment of government—and its preservation one of the chief ends of government. On Locke's labor theory of value, property was but an extension of liberty. "The *labour* that was mine, removing [objects] out of that common state [of nature] they were in, hath *fixed* my *Property* in them," argued Locke. "Thus the Grass my Horse has bit; the Turfs my Servant has cut; and the Ore I have digg'd in any place where I have a right to them in common with others, become my *Property*."[2] No less influential than Locke on the Framers was Sir William Blackstone, who also maintained in his *Commentaries on the Laws of England* that property was an "absolute right, inherent in every Englishman."[3]

Given this background and understanding of the fundamental nature of property, it is perhaps not surprising that the Supreme Court emerged within a generation of the ratification of the Constitution as a defender of property rights and economic liberty. Through an expansive interpretation of the contract clause in the early nineteenth century, and the creation of a "liberty of contract" in the latter part of that century, the Court laid the basis in constitutional law for the growth of American capitalism.

NOTES

1. Noah Webster, "An Examination into the Leading Principles of the Federal Constitution" (Oct. 10, 1787), in *The Founders' Constitution*, Vol. 1, ed. Philip Kurland and Ralph Lerner (Chicago: University of Chicago Press, 1987), 596–597.

2. John Locke, "Second Treatise of Government" (1689), in *Two Treatises of Government*, ed. Peter Laslett (New York: Mentor Books, 1960), 330.

3. Sir William Blackstone, *Commentaries on the Laws of England* (1765–1769) (Chicago: University of Chicago Press, 1979).

SELECTED BIBLIOGRAPHY

Barber, Sotirios. *Welfare and the Constitution*. Princeton, NJ: Princeton University Press, 2004.

Ely, James W. *The Guardian of Every Other Right: A Constitutional History of Property Rights*. New York: Oxford University Press, 1992.

Goldwin, Robert A., and Schambra, William A., eds. *How Capitalistic Is the Constitution?* Washington, DC: American Enterprise Institute, 1982.

Levy, Leonard. "Property as a Human Right." 5 *Constitutional Commentary* 169 (1988).

Paul, Ellen F., and Dickman, Howard. *Liberty, Property, and the Future of Constitutional Development.* Albany: State University of New York Press, 1990.

Pennock, J. Roland, and Chapman, John, eds. *Property.* New York: New York University Press, 1980.

A | *The Contract Clause and Vested Interests in Property*

Article I, Section 10, forbids the states from "impairing the Obligation of Contracts." That provision was ostensibly aimed at preventing the states from reneging on private contracts (such as loans made by banks) and passing laws favoring debtors, as was done in the 1780s in the aftermath of the Revolutionary War. As such, the guarantee presumably covered only private contracts. But in a series of rulings, the Marshall Court (1801–1836) broadly interpreted the contract clause to apply to public contracts (that is, contracts between a governmental agency and private individuals) and to safeguard vested interests in private property.

The famous "*Yazoo* case," *Fletcher v. Peck* (1810) (excerpted below), was the first important ruling of the Marshall Court in which the contract clause was turned into a guarantee for public contracts, in addition to a limitation on states' powers over private contracts. Notice that besides broadly construing the contract clause, Chief Justice Marshall notes that Georgia's law revoking its earlier land grants contravened "general principles, which are common to our free institutions, or by the particular provisions of the constitution of the United States." Chief Justice Marshall pushed his theory further two years later in *New Jersey v. Wilson*, 7 Cr. 164 (11 U.S.) (1812). New Jersey had made Indian lands tax-exempt, but when the land was sold to a non-Indian the state sought to tax the new owner. However, the Marshall Court ruled that the original contract with the Indians was still valid and the state could not tax the land. In one of the few cases involving private contracts, *Sturges v. Crowninshield*, 4 Wheat. (17 U.S.) 122 (1819), Chief Justice Marshall struck down a New York bankruptcy law as applied to a contract made before the law was passed. However, he found himself in the minority in *Ogden v. Sanders*, 12 Wheat. (25 U.S.) 213 (1827), when the Court upheld another bankruptcy law that had been enacted before a contested contract was made.

Next to *Fletcher v. Peck*, the second-most important Marshall Court ruling on the contract clause is *Trustees of Dartmouth College v. Woodward* (1819) (see excerpt below). Again, the clause was expansively read to protect the vested interests in a corporate charter granted by the English Crown in 1769, prior to the Revolutionary War.

The Marshall Court's interpretation of the contract clause was controversial and was viewed as a severe limitation on states' regulatory powers. Yet it remained the dominant feature in the early development of constitutional law and the vehicle by which the power of judicial review was asserted and established. Indeed, the contract clause was used in almost 40 percent of the cases challenging state legislation before 1889 and that the Court and lower federal courts used it to strike down some seventy-five state laws.[1]

The Court under Chief Justice Roger Taney (1836–1864) maintained respect for proprietary interests but was more deferential to the powers of states. In its leading ruling on the contract clause, *Charles River Bridge Co. v. Warren Bridge Co.* (1837) (see excerpt below), notice that Chief Justice Taney emphasizes that "[w]hile the rights of private property are sacredly guarded, we must not forget that the community also have rights, and that the happiness and well-being of every citizen depends on their faithful preservation." Taney thus established the principle that public contracts were to be strictly construed on the recognition that states have an important role in promoting the general welfare and technological advances in the public interest.

Despite the expansive interpretation given the contract clause in the early and mid-nineteenth century, its protection for proprietary interests did not override state police powers or the power of eminent domain (the government's taking of private property for public use without just compensation) (see section C, in this chapter). Nor did it foreclose the possibility of state regulations aimed at promoting public morals, health, safety, and welfare. In *Stone v. Mississippi*, 101 U.S. 814 (1880), for instance, the Court unanimously upheld state police power over John Stone's claim of vested property rights. Stone had been granted by the Mississippi legislature a twenty-five-year franchise to sell lottery tickets, but two years later the state adopted a new constitution prohibiting the sale of lottery tickets. When Stone sought to evade prosecution for selling lottery tickets, the Court rejected his invocation of the contract clause, just as it did when state prohibition laws were attacked for infringing on contracts for the sale of beer,[2] and when employment contracts were superseded by workmen's compensation laws.[3] As Justice Mahlon Pitney, in *Atlantic Coastline Railroad Co. v. City of Goldsboro*, 232 U.S. 548 (1914), explained for a unanimous Court, when affirming that states may delegate to cities the power to regulate health, safety, and welfare:

> [I]t is settled that neither the "contract" clause nor the "due process" clause has the effect of overriding the power of the state to establish all regulations that are reasonably necessary to secure the health, safety, good order, comfort, or general welfare of the community; that this power can neither be abdicated nor bargained away, and is inalienable even by express grant; and that all contract and property rights are held subject to its fair exercise.

Justice Pitney expressed the modern view of the contract clause. *Home Building & Loan Association v. Blaisdell* (1934) (see excerpt below) illustrates how far the Court in the twentieth century moved away from its

---

■ CONSTITUTIONAL HISTORY

John Locke on the Ends of Political Society and Government

123. If Man in the State of Nature be so free, as has been said; If he be absolute Lord of his own Person and Possessions, equal to the greatest, and subject to no Body, why will he part with his Freedom? Why will he give up this Empire, and subject himself to the Dominion and Controul of any other Power? To which 'tis obvious to Answer, that though in the state of Nature he hath such a right, yet the Enjoyment of it is very uncertain, and constantly exposed to the Invasion of others. For all being Kings as much as he, every Man his Equal, and the greater part no strict Observers of Equity and Justice, the enjoyment of the property he has in this state is very unsafe, very unsecure. This makes him willing to quit a Condition, which however free, is full of fears and continual dangers: And 'tis not without reason, that he seeks out, and is willing to joyn in Society with others who are already united, or have a mind to unite for the mutual *Preservation* of their Lives, Liberties and Estates, which I call by the general Name, *Property*.

124. The great and *chief end*, therefore, of Mens uniting into Commonwealths, and putting themselves under Government, *is the Preservation of their Property*. To which in the state of Nature there are many things wanting.

earlier application of the contract clause. There a bare majority of the Hughes Court upheld Minnesota's law, passed during the Great Depression, preventing the repossession of mortgaged property. The principle of judicial deference to legislative regulation of private contracts asserted in *Blaisdell* was reaffirmed in *City of El Paso v. Simmons* (1965) (see excerpt below). However, *United States Trust Co. of New York v. State of New Jersey* (1977) (see excerpt below) indicates that the Court gives heightened scrutiny and greater weight to claims under the contract clause in controversies involving a state's impairment of its own contracts.

Why did the Court's reliance on and enforcement of the contract clause decline in the late nineteenth and twentieth centuries? There are a number of reasons. For one thing, the Industrial Revolution brought

---

First, There wants an *establish'd*, settled, known *Law*, received and allowed by common consent to be the Standard of Right and Wrong, and the common measure to decide all Controversies between them. For though the Law of Nature be plain and intelligible to all rational Creatures; yet Men being biassed by their Interest, as well as ignorant for want of study of it, are not apt to allow of it as a Law binding to them in the application of it to their particular Cases.

125. *Secondly*, In the State of Nature there wants a *known and indifferent Judge*, with Authority to determine all differences according to the established Law. For every one in that state being both Judge and Executioner of the Law of Nature, Men being partial to themselves, Passion and Revenge is very apt to carry them too far, and with too much heat, in their own Cases; as well as negligence, and unconcernedness, to make them too remiss, in other Mens.

126. *Thirdly*, In the state of Nature there often wants *Power* to back and support the Sentence when right, and to *give* it due *Execution*. They who by any Injustice offended, will seldom fail, where they are able, by force to make good their Injustice: such resistance many times makes the punishment dan-gerous, and frequently destructive, to those who attempt it.

Source: John Locke, "Second Treatise of Government," in *Two Treatises of Government*, ed. Peter Laslett (New York: Mentor Books, 1960), ch. 5.

a growth in the number of corporations and economic problems that could not be accommodated even with a broad reading of the contract clause. Second, the Court developed its contract clause jurisprudence in the absence of congressional legislation. But in the late nineteenth century Congress responded to the social and economic pressures that accompanied industrialization and urbanization. Finally, as discussed below, the Court invented and enforced a "liberty of contract" under the Fourteenth Amendment's due process clause in defense of vested property rights against progressive economic legislation.

NOTES

1. Benjamin Wright, *The Contract Clause of the Constitution* (Cambridge, MA: Harvard University Press, 1938), 95.

2. See *Boston Beer Co. v. Massachusetts*, 97 U.S. 25 (1878).

3. *New York Central Railroad Co. v. White*, 243 U.S. 188 (1917).

SELECTED BIBLIOGRAPHY

Ackerman, Bruce. *Private Property and the Constitution*. New Haven, CT: Yale University Press, 1977.

Kutler, Stanley I. *Privilege and Creative Destruction: The Charles River Bridge Case*. 2d ed. Baltimore, MD: Johns Hopkins University Press, 1990.

Magrath, C. Peter. *Yazoo: The Case of Fletcher v. Peck*, New York: W. W. Norton & Company, 1967.

Stites, Francis. *Private Interest and Public Gain: The Dartmouth College Case*. Amherst: University of Massachusetts, 1972.

Wright, Benjamin. *The Contract Clause of the Constitution*. Cambridge, MA: Harvard University Press, 1938.

Fletcher v. Peck

6 CR. (10 U.S.) 87 (1810)

Robert Fletcher sued John Peck for the breach of a covenant on land that Peck had sold him. The land was part of a larger land grant in 1795 of the Georgia legislature to four land-holding companies, which had bribed several members of the legislature to win passage of the land grant. The next year, however, the state enacted legislation declaring the 1795 law and all rights and claims to it null and void. Peck had acquired the land in 1800 and sold it three years later to Fletcher, at which time he claimed that all past sales of the land had been lawful. Fletcher, though, contended that because the original sale of the land had been declared invalid by the Georgia legislature, Peck could not legally sell the land and was guilty of breach of contract. A federal circuit court found in favor of Peck, and Fletcher appealed directly to the Supreme Court.

The Court's decision was six to one, and the opinion was announced by Chief Justice Marshall. A separate opinion was delivered by Justice Johnson.

☐ *Chief Justice MARSHALL delivers the opinion of the Court.*

The suit was instituted on several covenants contained in a deed made by John Peck, the defendant in error, conveying to Robert Fletcher, the plaintiff in error, certain lands which were part of a large purchase made by James Gunn and others, in the year 1795, from the state of Georgia, the contract for which was made in the form of a bill passed by the legislature of that state. . . .

Titles which, according to every legal test, are perfect, are acquired with that confidence which is inspired by the opinion that the purchaser is safe. If there be any concealed defect, arising from the conduct of those who had held the property long before he acquired it, of which he had no notice, that concealed defect cannot be set up against him. He has paid his money for a title good at law, he is innocent, whatever may be the guilt of others, and equity will not subject him to the penalties attached to that guilt. All titles would be insecure, and the intercourse between man and man would be very seriously obstructed, if this principle be overturned. . . .

If the legislature felt itself absolved from those rules of property which are common to all the citizens of the United States, and from those principles of equity which are acknowledged in all our courts, its act is to be supported by its power alone, and the same power may devest any other individual of his lands, if it shall be the will of the legislature so to exert it.

It is not intended to speak with disrespect of the legislature of Georgia, or of its acts. Far from it. The question is a general question and is treated as one. For although such powerful objections to a legislative grant, as are alleged against this, may not again exist, yet the principle, on which alone this rescinding act is to be supported, may be applied to every case to which it shall be the will of any legislature to apply it. The principle is this: that a legislature may, by its own act, devest the vested estate of any man whatever, for reasons which shall, by itself, be deemed sufficient. . . .

Is the power of the legislature competent to the annihilation of such title, and to a resumption of the property thus held?

The principle asserted is, that one legislature is competent to repeal any act which a former legislature was competent to pass; and that one legislature cannot abridge the powers of a succeeding legislature.

The correctness of this principle, so far as respects general legislation, can never be controverted. But, if an act be done under a law, a succeeding legislature cannot undo it. The past cannot be recalled by the most absolute power. Conveyances have been made; those conveyances have vested legal estates, and, if those estates may be seized by the sovereign authority, still, that they originally vested is a fact, and cannot cease to be a fact.

When, then, a law is in its nature a contract, when absolute rights have vested under that contract; a repeal of the law cannot devest those rights; and the act of annulling them, if legitimate, is rendered so by a power applicable to the case of every individual in the community. . . .

It is the peculiar province of the legislature to prescribe general rules for the government of society; the application of those rules to individuals in society would seem to be the duty of other departments. How far the power of giving the law may involve every other power, in cases where the constitution is silent, never has been, and perhaps never can be, definitely stated.

The validity of this rescinding act, then, might well be doubted, were Georgia a single sovereign power. But Georgia cannot be viewed as a single, unconnected, sovereign power, on whose legislature no other restrictions are imposed than may be found in its own constitution. She is a part of a large empire; she is a member of the American Union; and that Union has a constitution the supremacy of which all acknowledge, and which imposes limits to the legislatures of the several states, which none claim a right to pass. The constitution of the United States declares that no state shall pass any bill of attainder, ex post facto law or law impairing the obligation of contracts.

Does the case now under consideration come within this prohibitory section of the constitution?

In considering this very interesting question, we immediately ask ourselves what is a contract? Is a grant a contract?

A contract is a compact between two or more parties, and is either executory or executed. An executory contract is one in which a party binds himself to do, or not to do, a particular thing; such was the law under which the conveyance was made by the governor. A contract executed is one in which the object of contract is performed; and this, says Blackstone, differs in nothing from a grant. The contract between Georgia and the purchasers was executed by the grant. A contract executed, as well as one which is executory, contains obligations binding on the parties. A grant, in its own nature, amounts to an extinguishment of the right of the grantor, and implies a contract not to re-assert that right. A party is, therefore, always estopped by his own grant.

Since, then, in fact, a grant is a contract executed, the obligation of which still continues, and since the constitution uses the general term contract, without distinguishing between those which are executory and those which are executed, it must be construed to comprehend the latter as well as the former. A law annulling conveyances between individuals, and declaring that the grantors should stand seized of their former estates, notwithstanding those grants, would be as repugnant to the constitution as a law discharging the vendors of property from the obligation of executing their contracts by conveyances. It would be strange if a contract to convey was secured by the constitution, while an absolute conveyance remained unprotected.

If, under a fair construction of the constitution, grants are comprehended under the term contracts, is a grant from the state excluded from the operation of the provision? Is the clause to be considered as inhibiting the state from impairing the obligation of contracts between two individuals, but as excluding from that inhibition contracts made with itself?

The words themselves contain no such distinction. They are general, and are applicable to contracts of every description. . . .

It is, then, the unanimous opinion of the court, that, in this case, the estate having passed into the hands of a purchaser for a valuable consideration, without notice, the state of Georgia was restrained, either by general principles, which are common to our free institutions, or by the particular provisions of the constitution of the United States, from passing a law whereby the estate of the plaintiff in the premises so purchased could be constitutionally and legally impaired and rendered null and void. . . .

☐ *Justice JOHNSON delivering a separate opinion.*

In this case I entertain . . . an opinion different from that which has been delivered by the court. . . .

[My] opinion . . . is not founded on the provision in the constitution of the United States, relative to laws impairing the obligation of contracts. It is much to be regretted that words of less equivocal signification had not been adopted in that article of the constitution. There is reason to believe, from the letters of Publius, which are well known to be entitled to the highest respect, that the object of the convention was to afford a general protection to individual rights against the acts of the state legislatures. Whether the words, "acts impairing the obligation of contracts," can be construed to have the same force as must have been given to the words "obligation and effect of contracts," is the difficulty in my mind.

There can be no solid objection to adopting the technical definition of the word "contract," given by Blackstone. The etymology, the classical signification, and the civil law idea of the word, will all support it. But the difficulty arises on the word "obligation," which certainly imports an existing moral or physical necessity. Now, a grant or conveyance by no means necessarily implies the continuance of an obligation beyond the moment of executing it. . . .

I enter with great hesitation upon this question, because it involves a subject of the greatest delicacy and much difficulty. The states and the United States are continually legislating on the subject of contracts, prescribing the mode of authentication, the time within which suits shall be prosecuted for them, in many cases affecting existing contracts by the laws which they pass, and declaring them to cease or lose their effect for want of compliance, in the parties, with such statutory provisions. All these acts appear to be within the most correct limits of legislative powers, and most beneficially exercised, and certainly could not have been intended to be affected by this constitutional provision; yet where to draw the line, or how to define or limit the words, "obligation of contracts," will be found a subject of extreme difficulty.

To give it the general effect of a restriction of the state powers in favor of private rights, is certainly going very far beyond the obvious and necessary import of the words, and would operate to restrict the states in the exercise of that right which every community must exercise, of possessing itself of the property of the individual, when necessary for public uses; a right which a magnanimous and just government will never exercise without amply indemnifying the individual, and which perhaps amounts to nothing more than a power to oblige him to sell and convey, when the public necessities require it.

Trustees of Dartmouth College v. Woodward
4 WHEAT. (17 U.S.) 518 (1819)

Dartmouth College was incorporated in 1769 under a charter granted by the English Crown, which authorized a twelve-member board of trustees to govern the college and to appoint their successors. The New Hampshire legislature, however, amended the charter in 1816 with legislation increasing the size of the board of trustees to twenty-one, establishing a board of overseers, and authorizing the governor to appoint new trustees and members of the board of overseers. The incumbent trustees refused to recognize the legislation as binding and sued William Woodward, the college's treasurer, to recover corporate property that was temporarily entrusted to him under the legislation. A trial court failed to resolve the question of the constitutionality of the legislation, but it was upheld by a state superior court. The trustees of Dartmouth College then appealed to the Supreme Court. As was the practice through most of the nineteenth century, they hired a member of the Supreme Court's bar, Daniel Webster, to argue their case. As was also the practice, attorneys for both sides were given unlimited time to present their arguments. Webster was one of the greatest orators and rather dramatically concluded his argument before the bench, observing,

> Sir, you may destroy this little institution. It is weak. It is in your hands! I know it is one of the lesser lights in the literary horizon of the country. You may put it out. But if you do so, you must carry through your work. You must extinguish, one after another, all those great lights of science which, for more than a century, have thrown their radiance over our land.
>
> It is, Sir, as I have said, a small college and yet, there are those who love it. . . .
>
> Sir, I care not how others may feel, but, for myself, when I see my Alma Mater surrounded, like Caesar in the senate-house, by those who are reiterating stab on stab, I would not, for this right hand, have her turn to me, and say *et tu quoque, mi fili!*

The Court's decision was six to one; the opinion was announced by Chief Justice Marshall. Justices Washington and Story concurred, and Justice Duvall dissented.

☐ *Chief Justice MARSHALL delivers the opinion of the Court.*

It can require no argument to prove that the circumstances of this case constitute a contract. An application is made to the crown for a charter to incorporate a religious and literary institution. In the application, it is stated that large contributions have been made for the object, which will be conferred on the corporation as soon as it shall be created. The charter is granted, and on its faith the property is conveyed. Surely in this transaction every ingredient of a complete and legitimate contract is to be found.

The points for consideration are:

1. Is this contract protected by the constitution of the United States?

2. Is it impaired by the acts under which the defendant holds?

1. On the first point it . . . becomes, then, the duty of the court most seriously to examine this charter, and to ascertain its true character. . . .

From [a] review of the charter, it appears that Dartmouth College is an eleemosynary institution, incorporated for the purpose of perpetuating the application of the bounty of the donors, to the specified objects of that bounty; that its trustees or governors were originally named by the founder, and invested with the power of perpetuating themselves; that they are not public officers, nor is it a civil institution, participating in the administration of government; but a charity school, or a seminary of education, incorporated for the preservation of its property, and the perpetual application of that property to the objects of its creation.

Yet a question remains to be considered, of more real difficulty, on which more doubt has been entertained than on all that have been discussed. The founders of the college, at least those whose contributions were in money, have parted with the property bestowed upon it, and their representatives have no interest in that property. The donors of land are equally without interest, so long as the corporation shall exist. Could they be found, they are unaffected by any alteration in its constitution, and probably regardless of its form, or even of its existence. The students are fluctuating, and no individual among our youth has a vested interest in the institution, which can be asserted in a court of justice. Neither the founders of the college nor the youth for whose benefit it was founded, complain of the alteration made in its charter, or think themselves injured by it. The trustees alone complain, and the trustees have no beneficial interest to be protected. Can this be such a contract as the constitution intended to withdraw from the power of state legislation? Contracts, the parties to which have a vested beneficial interest, and those only, it has been said, are the objects about which the constitution is solicitous, and to which its protection is extended.

The court has bestowed on this argument the most deliberate consideration, and the result will be stated. Dr. Wheelock, acting for himself, and for those who, at his solicitation, had made contributions to his school, applied for this charter, as the instrument which should enable him, and them, to perpetuate their beneficent intention. It was granted. An artificial, immortal being, was created by the crown, capable of receiving and distributing forever, according to the will of the donors, the donations which should be made to it. On this being, the contributions which had been collected were immediately bestowed. These gifts were made, not, indeed, to make a profit for the donors, or their posterity, but for something in their opinion of inestimable value; for something which they deemed a full equivalent for the money with which it was purchased. The consideration for which they stipulated, is the perpetual application of the fund to its object, in the mode prescribed by themselves. Their descendants may take no interest in the preservation of this consideration. But in this respect their descendants are not their representatives. They are represented by the corporation. The corporation is the assignee of their rights, stands in their place, and distributes their bounty, as they would themselves have distributed it, had they been immortal. So with respect to the students who are to derive learning from this source. The corporation is a trustee for them also. Their potential rights, which, taken distributively, are imperceptible, amount collectively to a most important interest. These are, in the aggregate, to be exercised, asserted and protected, by the corporation. They were as completely out of the donors, at the instant of their being vested in the corporation, and as incapable of being asserted by the students, as at present. . . .

This is plainly a contract to which the donors, the trustees, and the crown (to whose rights and obligations New Hampshire succeeds), were the original parties. It is a contract made on a valuable consideration. It is a contract for the security and disposition of property. It is a contract, on the faith of which real and personal estate has been conveyed to the corporation. It is then a contract within the letter of the constitution, and within its spirit also, unless the fact that the property is invested by the donors in trustees for the promotion of religion and education, for the benefit of persons who are perpetually changing, though the objects remain the same, shall create a particular exception, taking this case out of the prohibition contained in the constitution.

It is more than possible that the preservation of rights of this description was not particularly in the view of the framers of the constitution when the clause under consideration was introduced into that instrument. It is probable that interferences of more frequent recurrence, to which the temptation was stronger, and of which the mischief was more extensive, constituted the great motive for imposing this restriction on the state legislatures. But although a particular and a rare case may not, in itself, be of sufficient magnitude to induce a rule, yet it must be governed by the rule, when established unless some plain and strong reason for excluding it can be given. It is not enough to say that this particular case was not in the mind of the convention when the article was framed, nor of the American people when it was adopted. It is necessary to go farther, and to say that, had this particular case been suggested, the language would have been so varied, as to exclude it, or it would have been made a special exception. The case being within the words of the rule, must be within its operation likewise, unless there be something in the literal construction so obviously absurd, or mischievous, or repugnant to the general spirit of the instrument, as to justify those who expound the constitution in making it an exception.

On what safe and intelligible ground can this exception stand? There is no exception in the constitution, no sentiment delivered by its contemporaneous expounders, which would justify us in making it. In the absence of all authority of this kind, is there, in the nature and reason of the case itself, that which would sustain a construction of the constitution, not warranted by its words? Are contracts of this description of a character to excite so little interest that we must exclude them from the provisions of the constitution, as being unworthy of the attention of those who framed the instrument? Or does public policy so imperiously demand their remaining exposed to legislative alteration, as to compel us, or rather permit us to say that these words, which were introduced to give stability to contracts, and which in their plain import comprehend this contract, must yet be so construed as to exclude it?

Almost all eleemosynary corporations, those which are created for the promotion of religion, of charity, or of education, are of the same character. The law of this case is the law of all. . . .

The opinion of the court, after mature deliberation, is, that this is a contract, the obligation of which cannot be impaired without violating the constitution of the United States. This opinion appears to us to be equally supported by reason, and by the former decisions of this court.

2. We next proceed to the inquiry whether its obligation has been impaired by those acts of the legislature of New Hampshire to which the special verdict refers.

From the review of this charter, which has been taken, it appears that the whole power of governing the college, of appointing and removing tutors, of fixing their salaries, of directing the course of study to be pursued by the students, and of filling up vacancies created in their own body, was vested in the trustees. On the part of the crown it was expressly stipulated that this corporation, thus constituted, should continue forever; and that the number of trustees should forever consist of twelve, and no more. By this contract the crown was bound, and could have made no violent alteration in its essential terms, without impairing its obligation. . . .

It has been already stated that the act "to amend the charter, and enlarge and improve the corporation of Dartmouth College," increases the number of trustees to twenty-one, gives the appointment of the additional members to the executive of the state, and creates a board of overseers, to consist of twenty-five persons, of whom twenty-one are also appointed by the executive of New Hampshire, who have power to inspect and control the most important acts of the trustees. . . .

The whole power of governing the college is transferred from trustees appointed according to the will of the founder, expressed in the charter, to the executive of New Hampshire. The management and application of the funds of this eleemosynary institution, which are placed by the donors in the hands of trustees named in the charter, and empowered to perpetuate themselves, are placed by this act under the control of the government of the state. The will of the state is substituted for the will of the donors in every essential operation of the college. This is not an immaterial change. The founders of the college contracted, not merely for the perpetual application of the funds which they gave, to the objects for which those funds were given; they contracted also to secure that application by the constitution of the corporation. They contracted for a system which should, as far as human foresight can provide, retain forever the government of the literary institution they had formed, in the hands of persons approved by themselves. This system is totally changed. The charter of 1769 exists no longer. It is reorganized; and reorganized in such a manner as to convert a literary institution, moulded according to the will of its founders, and placed under the control of private literary men, into a machine entirely subservient to the will of government. This may be for the advantage of this college in particular, and may be for the advantage of literature in general, but it is not according to the will of the donors, and is subversive of that contract, on the faith of which their property was given. . . .

It results from this opinion, that the acts of the legislature of New Hampshire, which are stated in the special verdict found in this cause, are repugnant to the constitution of the United States; and that the judgment on this special verdict ought to have been for the plaintiffs. The judgment of the State Court must therefore be reversed.

Charles River Bridge Co. v. Warren Bridge Co.

11 PET. (36 U.S.) 420 (1837)

In 1785, the Massachusetts legislature incorporated the Charles River Bridge Company and authorized it to build a toll bridge over the Charles River. The company was obligated to pay Harvard College £200 annually as compensation in lieu of its right to operate a ferry that had been granted the college in 1650. In 1792, the charter was extended for another seventy years. But in 1832 the legislature incorporated the Warren Bridge Company and authorized it to build a bridge for free public use just 275 yards away from the Charles River Bridge. That prompted the owners of the Charles River Bridge Company to seek an injunction against the construction of the Warren Bridge. The Massachusetts Supreme Judicial Court dismissed the complaint and Charles River Bridge Company appealed to the Supreme Court.

The Court's decision was five to two, and the majority's opinion was announced by Chief Justice Taney. Justice McLean concurred. Dissent was by Justice Story, who was joined by Justice Thompson.

☐ *Chief Justice TANEY delivers the opinion of the Court.*

[On] what ground can the plaintiffs in error contend that the ferry rights of the college have been transferred to the proprietors of the bridge? If they have been thus transferred, it must be by some mode of transfer known to the law, and the evidence relied on to prove it can be pointed out in the record. How was it transferred? It is not suggested that there ever was in point of fact, a deed of conveyance executed by the college to the bridge company. Is there any evidence in the record from which such a conveyance may, upon legal principle, be presumed? The testimony before the court, so far from laying the foundation for such a presumption, repels it in the most positive terms. The petition to the Legislature in 1785, on which the charter was granted, does not suggest an assignment, nor any agreement or consent on the part of the college; and the petitioners do not appear to have regarded the wishes of that institution, as by any means necessary to insure their success. They place their application entirely on considerations of public interest and public convenience, and the superior advantages of a communication across Charles River by a bridge instead of a ferry. The Legislature, in granting the charter, show, by the language of the law, that they acted on the principles assumed by the petitioners. The preamble recites that the bridge "will be of great public utility;" and that is the only reason they assign for passing the law which incorporates this company. The validity of the charter is not made to depend on the consent of the college, nor of any assignment or surrender on their part; and the Legislature deal with the subject, as if it were one exclusively within their own power, and as if the ferry right were not to be transferred to the bridge company, but to be extinguished; and they appear to have acted on the principle that the State, by virtue of its sovereign powers and eminent domain, had a right to take away the franchise of the ferry; because in their judgment, the public interest and convenience would be better promoted by a bridge in the same place; and upon that principle they proceed to make a pecuniary compensation to the college for the franchise thus taken away. . . .

It does not, by any means, follow that because the legislative power in Massachusetts, in 1650, may have granted to a justly favored seminary of learning, the exclusive right of ferry between Boston and Charlestown, they would, in 1785, give the same extensive privilege to another corporation, who were about to erect a bridge in the same place. The fact that such a right was granted to the college cannot, by any sound rule of construction, be used to extend the privileges of the bridge company beyond what the words of the charter naturally and legally import. Increased population longer experienced in legislation, the different character of the corporations which owned the ferry from that which owned the bridge, might well have induced a change in the policy of the State in this respect; and as the franchise of the ferry and that of the bridge are different in their nature. . . .

[T]here is no rule of legal interpretation which would authorize the court to associate these grants together, and to infer that any privilege was intended to be given to the bridge company, merely because it had been conferred on the ferry. The charter to the bridge is a written instrument which must speak for itself, and be interpreted by its own terms.

This brings us to the Act of the Legislature of Massachusetts of 1785, by which the plaintiffs were incorporated by the name of "The Proprietors of the Charles River Bridge;" and it is here, and in the law of 1792, prolonging their charter, that we must look for the extent and nature of the franchise conferred upon the plaintiffs. . . .

"This, like many other cases, is a bargain between a company of adventurers and the public, the terms of which are expressed in the statute; and the rule of construction in all such cases, is now fully established to be this—that any ambiguity in the terms of the contract, must operate against the adventurers, and in favor of the public, and the plaintiffs can claim nothing that is not clearly given them by the act." And the doctrine thus laid down is abundantly sustained by the authorities referred to, in this decision. . . .

[T]he object and end of all government is to promote the happiness and prosperity of the community by which it is established, and it can never be assumed that the government intended to diminish its power of accomplishing the end for which it was created. And in a country like ours, free, active and enterprising, continually advancing in numbers and wealth; new channels of communication are daily found necessary, both for travel and trade, and are essential to the comfort, convenience, and prosperity of the people. A State ought never to be presumed to surrender this power, because, like the taxing power, the whole community have an interest in preserving it undiminished. And when a corporation alleges that a State has surrendered for seventy years its power of improvement and public accommodation, in a great and important line of travel, along which a vast number of its citizens must daily pass; the community have a right to insist, in the language of this court above quoted, "that its abandonment ought not to be presumed, in a case in which the deliberate purpose of the State to abandon it does not appear." The continued existence of a government would be of no great value, if by implications and presumptions, it was disarmed of the powers necessary to accomplish the ends of its creation, and the functions it was designed to perform, transferred to the hands of privileged corporations. The rule of construction announced by the court was not confined to the taxing power, nor is it so limited in the opinion delivered. On the contrary, it was distinctly placed on the ground that the interests of the community were concerned in preserving, undiminished, the power then in question; and whenever any power of the State is said to be surrendered or diminished, whether it be the taxing power or any other affecting the public interest, the same principle applies, and the rule of construction must be the same. No one will question that the interests of the great body of the people of the State, would, in this instance, be affected by the surrender of this great line of travel to a single corporation, with the right to exact toll, and exclude competition for seventy years. While the rights of private property are sacredly guarded, we must not forget that the community also have rights, and that the happiness and well being of every citizen depends on their faithful preservation.

Adopting the rule of construction above stated as the settled one, we proceed to apply it to the charter of 1785, to the proprietors of the Charles River Bridge. This act of incorporation is in the usual form, and the privileges such as are commonly given to corporations of that kind. It confers on them the ordinary faculties of a corporation, for the purpose of building the bridge; and establishes certain rates of toll, which the company are authorized to take. This is the whole grant. There is no exclusive privilege given to them over the waters of Charles River, above or below their bridge. No right to erect another bridge themselves, nor to prevent other persons from erecting one. No engagement from the State that another shall not be erected, and no undertaking not to sanction competition, nor to make improvements that may diminish the amount of its income. Upon all these subjects the charter is silent, and nothing is said in it about a line of travel, so much insisted on in the argument, in which they are to have exclusive privileges. No words are used from which an intention to grant any of these rights can be inferred. If the plaintiff is entitled to them, it must be implied simply from the nature of the grant, and cannot be inferred from the words by which the grant is made.

The relative position of the Warren Bridge has already been described. It does not interrupt the passage over the Charles River Bridge, nor make the way to it or from it less convenient. None of the faculties or franchises granted to that corporation have been revoked by the Legislature; and its right to take the tolls granted by the charter remains unaltered. In short, all the franchises and rights of property enumerated in the charter, and there mentioned to have been granted to it, remain unimpaired. But its income is destroyed by the Warren Bridge; which, being free, draws off the passengers and property which would have gone over it, and renders their franchise of no value. This is the gist of the complaint. For it is not pretended that the erection of the Warren Bridge would have done them any injury, or in any degree affected their right of property, if it had not diminished the amount of their tolls. In order, then, to entitle themselves to relief, it is necessary to show that the Legislature contracted not to do the act of which they complain; and that they impaired, or in other words violated, that contract, by the erection of the Warren Bridge.

The inquiry then is, does the charter contain such a contract on the part of the State? Is there any such stipulation to be found in that instrument? It must be admitted on all hands, that there is none—no words that even relate to another bridge, or to the diminution of their tolls, or to the line of travel. If a contract on that subject can be gathered from the charter, it must be by implication, and cannot be found in the words used. Can such an agreement be implied? The rule of construction before stated is an answer to the question. In charters of this description, no rights are taken from the public or given to the corporation, beyond those which the words of the charter, by their natural and proper construction, purport to convey. There are no words which import such a contract as the plaintiffs in error contend for, and none can be implied. . . .

Indeed, the practice and usage of almost every State in the Union, old enough to have commenced the work of internal improvement, is opposed to the doctrine contended for on the part of the plaintiffs in error. Turnpike roads have been made in succession, on the same line of travel; the latter ones interfering materially with the profits of the first. These corporations have, in some instances, been utterly ruined by the introduction of newer and better modes of transportation and traveling. In some cases railroads have rendered the turnpike roads on the same line of travel so entirely useless, that the franchise of the turnpike corporation is not worth preserving. Yet in none of these cases have the corporations supposed that their privileges were invaded, or any contract violated on the part of the State. . . .

If this court should establish the principles now contended for, what is to become of the numerous railroads established on the same line of travel with turnpike companies; and which have rendered the franchises of the turnpike corporations of no value? Let it once be understood that such charters carry with them these implied contracts, and give this unknown and undefined property in a line of traveling, and you will soon find the old turnpike corporations awakening from their sleep, and calling upon this court to put down the improvements which have taken their place. The millions of property which have been invested in railroads and canals, upon lines of travel which had been before occupied by turnpike corporations, will be put in jeopardy. We shall be thrown back to the improvements of the last century, and obliged to stand still until the claims of the old turnpike corporations shall be satisfied, and they shall consent to permit these States to avail themselves of the lights of modern science, and to partake of the benefit of those improvements which are now adding to the wealth and prosperity, and the convenience and comfort, of every other part of the civilized world. . . .

The judgment of the Supreme Judicial Court of the Commonwealth of Massachusetts, dismissing the plaintiffs' bill, must, therefore, be affirmed with costs.

☐ *Justice McLEAN concurred in a separate opinion, expressing his view that the case should be dismissed for lack of jurisdiction.*

☐ *Justice STORY, dissenting.*

I admit that where the terms of a grant are to impose burdens upon the public, or to create a restraint injurious to the public interest, there is sound reason for interpreting the terms, if ambiguous, in favor of the public. But at the same time, I insist that there is not the slightest reason for saying, even in such a case, that the grant is not to be construed favorably to the grantee, so as to secure him in the enjoyment of what is actually granted. . . .

This charter is not . . . any restriction upon the legislative power, unless it be true that because the Legislature cannot grant again what it has already granted, the legislative power is restricted. If so, then every grant of the public land is a restriction upon that power; a doctrine that has never yet been established, nor (as far as I know) ever contended for. Every grant of a franchise is, so far as that grant extends, necessarily exclusive; and cannot be resumed, or interfered with. All the learned judges in the State court admitted that the franchise of Charles River Bridge, whatever it be, could not be resumed or interfered with. The Legislature could not recall its grant or destroy it. It is a contract, whose obligation cannot be constitutionally impaired. In this respect, it does not differ from a grant of lands. In each case, the particular land, or the particular franchise, is withdrawn from the legislative operation. . . .

Then, again, how is it established that this is a grant in derogation of the rights and interests of the people? No individual citizen has any right to build a bridge over navigable waters; and consequently he is deprived of no right, when a grant is made to any other persons for that purpose. Whether it promotes or injures the particular interest of an individual citizen, constitutes no ground for judicial or legislative interference, beyond what his own rights justify. When, then, it is said that such a grant is in derogation of the rights and interests of the people, we must understand that reference is had to the rights and interests common to the whole people, as such (such as the right of navigation), or belonging to them as a political body; or, in other words, the rights and interests of the State. Now, I cannot understand how any grant of a franchise is a derogation from the rights of the people of the State, any more than a grant of public land. The right, in each case, is gone to the extent of the thing granted, and so far may be said to derogate from, that is to say, to lessen the rights of the people, or of the State. But that is not the sense in which the argument is pressed; for, by derogation, is here meant an injurious or mischievous detraction from the sovereign rights of the State. On the other hand, there can be no derogation from the rights of the people, as such, except it applies to rights common there before; which the building of a bridge over navigable waters certainly is not. If it had been said that the grant of this bridge was in derogation of the common right of navigating the Charles River, by reason of its obstructing, pro tanto, a free and open passage, the ground would have been intelligible. So, if it had been an exclusive grant of the navigation of that stream. But, if at the same time, equivalent public rights of a different nature, but of greater public accommodation and use, had been obtained; it could hardly have been said, in a correct sense, that there was any derogation from the rights of the people, or the rights of the State. It would be a mere exchange of one public right for another. . . .

No sound lawyer will, I presume, assert that the grant of a right to erect a bridge over a navigable stream, is a grant of a common right. Before such grant, had all the citizens of the State a right to erect bridges over navigable streams? Certainly they had not; and, therefore, the grant was no restriction of any common right. It was neither a monopoly, nor, in a legal sense, had it any tendency to a monopoly. It took from no citizen what he possessed before, and had no tendency to take it from him. It took, indeed, from the Legislature the power of granting the same identical privilege or franchise to any other persons. But this made it no more a monopoly than the grant of the public stock or funds of a State for a valuable consideration. Even in cases of monopolies, strictly so called, if the nature of the grant be such that it is for the public good, as in cases of patents for inventions, the rule has always been to give them a favorable construction in support of the patent. . . .

I have thus endeavored to answer, and I think I have successfully answered all the arguments (which indeed run into each other) adduced to justify a strict construction of the present charter. I go farther, and maintain not only that it is not a case for strict construction, but that the charter upon its very face, by its terms, and for its professed objects, demands from the court, upon undeniable principles of law, a favorable construction for the grantees. In the first place, the Legislature has declared that the erecting of the bridge will be of great public utility; and this exposition of its own motives for the grant requires the court to give a liberal interpretation, in order to promote, and not to destroy an enterprise of great public utility. In the next place, the grant is a contract for a valuable consideration, and a full and adequate consideration. The proprietors are to lay out a large sum of money (and in those times it was a very large outlay of capital) in erecting a bridge; they are to keep it in repair during the whole period of forty years; they are to surrender it in good repair at the end of that period to the State, as its own property; they are to pay, during the whole period, an annuity of two hundred pounds to Harvard College; and they are to incur other heavy expenses and burdens, for the public accommodation. In return for all these charges, they are entitled to no more than the receipt of the tolls during the forty years, for their reimbursement of capital, interest and expenses. With all this they are to take upon themselves the chances of success; and if the enterprise fails, the loss is exclusively their own. Nor let any man imagine that there was not, at the time when this charter was granted, much solid ground for doubting success. In order to entertain a just view of this subject, we must go back to that period of general bankruptcy, and distress and difficulty. The Constitution of the United States was not only not then in existence, but it was not then even dreamed of. The union of the States was crumbling into ruins, under the old confederation. Agriculture, manufactures and commerce were at their lowest ebb. There was infinite danger to all the States from local interests and jealousies, and from the apparent impossibility of a much longer adherence to that shadow of a government the Continental Congress. And even four years afterwards, when every evil had been greatly aggravated, and civil war was added to other calamities, the Constitution of the United States was all but shipwrecked in passing through the State conventions. It was adopted by very slender majorities. These are historical facts which required no coloring to give them effect, and admitted of no concealment to seduce men into schemes of future aggrandizement. I would even now put it to the common sense of every man, whether, if the Constitution of the United States had not been adopted, the charter would have been worth a forty years' purchase of the tolls. . . .

Now, I put it to the common sense of every man, whether if at the moment of granting the charter the Legislature had said to the proprietors— you shall build the bridge; you shall bear the burdens; you shall be bound by the charges; and your sole re-imbursement shall be from the tolls of forty years: and yet we will not even guaranty you any certainty of receiving any tolls. On the contrary, we reserve to ourselves the full power and authority to erect other bridges, toll or free bridges, according to our own free will and pleasure, contiguous to yours, and having the same termini with yours; and if you are successful we may thus supplant you, divide, destroy your profits, and annihilate your tolls, without annihilating your burdens: if, I say, such had been the language of the Legislature, is there a man living of ordinary discretion or prudence, who would have accepted such a charter upon such terms? I fearlessly answer no. . . .

Yet, this is the very form and pressure of the present case. It is not an imaginary and extravagant case. Warren Bridge has been erected, under such a supposed reserved authority, in the immediate neighborhood of Charles River Bridge; and with the same termini, to accommodate the same line of travel. For a half dozen years it was to be a toll bridge for the benefit of the proprietors, to reimburse them for their expenditures. At the end of that period, the bridge is to become the property of the State, and free of toll, unless the Legislature should hereafter impose one. In point of fact, it has since become, and now is, under the sanction of the act of incorporation, and other subsequent acts, a free bridge without the payment of any tolls for all persons. So that, in truth, here now is a free bridge, owned by and erected under the authority of the Commonwealth, which necessarily takes away all the tolls from Charles River Bridge, while its prolonged charter has twenty years to run. And yet the act of the Legislature establishing Warren Bridge is said to be no violation of the franchise granted to the Charles River Bridge. . . .

To sum up, then, the whole argument on this head, I maintain that, upon the principles of common reason and legal interpretation, the present grant carries with it a necessary implication that the Legislature shall do no act to destroy or essentially to impair the franchise: that (as one of the learned judges of the State court expressed it) there is an implied agreement that the State will not grant another bridge between Boston and Charlestown, so near as to draw away the custom from the old one: and (as another learned judge expressed it) that there is an implied agreement of the State to grant the undisturbed use of the bridge and its tolls, so far as respects any acts of its own, or of any persons acting under its authority. In other words, the State, impliedly, contracts not to resume its grant, or to do any act to the prejudice or destruction of its grant.

Home Building & Loan Association v. Blaisdell

290 U.S. 398, 54 S.Ct. 231 (1934)

In response to the social pressures arising from the economic depression in the early 1930s, Minnesota's legislature passed the Minnesota Moratorium Act of 1934. The law authorized state courts to postpone the payments of homeowners and farmers on mortgages to prevent their foreclosures. Under the act, John Blaisdell sought an extension of time on the payment of his mortgage to Home Building & Loan Association. But a trial court granted a motion to dismiss Blaisdell's petition. The Minnesota Supreme Court reversed and the trial court subsequently granted Blaisdell an extension of time on his mortgage payments. Home Building & Loan Association appealed, contending that Minnesota's moratorium law violated state and federal protections for private contracts and the taking of property without the due process of law.

The Court's decision was five to four; the majority's opinion was announced by Chief Justice Hughes. Justice Sutherland dissented and was joined by Justices Van Devanter, McReynolds, and Butler.

☐ *Chief Justice HUGHES delivers the opinion of the Court.*

In determining whether the provision for this temporary and conditional relief exceeds the power of the state by reason of the clause in the Federal Constitution prohibiting impairment of the obligations of contracts, we must consider the relation of emergency to constitutional power, the historical setting of the contract clause, the development of the jurisprudence of this Court in the construction of that clause, and the principles of construction which we may consider to be established.

Emergency does not create power. Emergency does not increase granted power or remove or diminish the restrictions imposed upon power granted or reserved. The Constitution was adopted in a period of grave emergency. Its grants of power to the federal government and its limitations of the power of the States were determined in the light of emergency, and they are not altered by emergency. What power was thus granted and what limitations were thus imposed are questions which have always been, and always will be, the subject of close examination under our constitutional system.

While emergency does not create power, emergency may furnish the occasion for the exercise of power. . . . The constitutional question presented in the light of an emergency is whether the power possessed embraces the particular exercise of it in response to particular conditions. . . .

In the construction of the contract clause, the debates in the Constitutional Convention are of little aid. But the reasons which led to the adoption of that clause, and of the other prohibitions of section 10 of article 1, are not left in doubt, and have frequently been described with eloquent emphasis. The widespread distress following the revolutionary period and the plight

A "Hooverville," named after President Herbert Hoover, in New York City during the Great Depression. Hoover was president from 1929 to 1933, when he lost the presidential election to Democrat Franklin D. Roosevelt. The economic collapse that began in Hoover's first year as president led to the Great Depression. (*Corbis/Bettmann.*)

of debtors had called forth in the States an ignoble array of legislative schemes for the defeat of creditors and the invasion of contractual obligations. Legislative interferences had been so numerous and extreme that the confidence essential to prosperous trade had been undermined and the utter destruction of credit was threatened. "The sober people of America" were convinced that some "thorough reform" was needed which would "inspire a general prudence and industry, and give a regular course to the business of society." *The Federalist*, No. 44. It was necessary to interpose the restraining power of a central authority in order to secure the foundations even of "private faith." The occasion and general purpose of the contract clause are summed up in the terse statement of Chief Justice MARSHALL in *Ogden v. Saunders*, 12 Wheat. 213 [1827]. "The power of changing the relative situation of debtor and creditor, of interfering with contracts, a power which comes home to every man, touches the interest of all, and controls the conduct of every individual in those things which he supposes to be proper for his own exclusive management, had been used to such an excess by the state legislatures, as to break in upon the ordinary intercourse of society, and destroy all confidence between man and man. This mischief had become so great, so alarming, as not only to impair commercial intercourse, and threaten the existence of credit, but to sap the morals of the people, and destroy the sanctity of private faith. To guard against the continuance of the evil, was an object of deep interest with all the truly wise, as well as the virtuous, of this great community, and was one of the important benefits expected from a reform of the government." . . .

The obligation of a contract is the law which binds the parties to perform their agreement. This Court has said that "the laws which subsist at the time and place of the making of a contract, and where it is to be performed, enter into and form a part of it, as if they were expressly referred to or incorporated in its terms." This principle embraces alike those which affect its validity, construction, discharge, and enforcement. . . .

Not only is the constitutional provision qualified by the measure of control which the state retains over remedial processes, but the state also continues to possess authority to safeguard the vital interests of its people. It does not matter that legislation appropriate to that end "has the result of modifying or abrogating contracts already in effect." Not only are existing laws read into contracts in order to fix obligations as between the parties, but the reservation of essential attributes of sovereign power is also read into contracts as a postulate of the legal order. The policy of protecting contracts against impairment presupposes the maintenance of a government by virtue of which contractual relations are worth while,—a government which retains adequate authority to secure the peace and good order of society. This principle of harmonizing the constitutional prohibition with the necessary residuum of state power has had progressive recognition in the decisions of this Court. . . .

The question is not whether the legislative action affects contracts incidentally, or directly or indirectly, but whether the legislation is addressed to a legitimate end and the measures taken are reasonable and appropriate to that end. . . .

Undoubtedly, whatever is reserved of state power must be consistent with the fair intent of the constitutional limitation of that power. The reserved power cannot be construed so as to destroy the limitation, nor is the limitation to be construed to destroy the reserved power in its essential aspects. They must be construed in harmony with each other. This principle precludes a construction which would permit the state to adopt as its policy the repudiation of debts or the destruction of contracts or the denial of means to enforce them. But it does not follow that conditions may not arise in which a temporary restraint of enforcement may be consistent with the spirit and purpose of the constitutional provision and thus be found to be within the range of the reserved power of the state to protect the vital interests of the community. It cannot be maintained that the constitutional prohibition should be so construed as to prevent limited and temporary interpositions with respect to the enforcement of contracts if made necessary by a great public calamity such as fire, flood, or earthquake. . . .

Where, in earlier days, it was thought that only the concerns of individuals or of classes were involved, and that those of the state itself were touched only remotely, it has later been found that the fundamental interests of the state are directly affected; and that the question is no longer merely that of one party to a contract as against another, but of the use of reasonable means to safeguard the economic structure upon which the good of all depends.

It is no answer to say that this public need was not apprehended a century ago, or to insist that what the provision of the Constitution meant to the vision of that day it must mean to the vision of our time. If by the statement that what the Constitution meant at the time of its adoption it means today, it is intended to say that the great clauses of the Constitution must be confined to the interpretation which the framers, with the conditions and outlook of their time, would have placed upon them, the statement carries its own refutation. It was to guard against such a narrow conception that Chief Justice MARSHALL uttered the memorable warning: "We must never forget, that it is *a constitution* we are expounding" (*McCulloch v. Maryland*, 4 Wheat. 316 [1819] "a constitution intended to endure for ages to come, and, consequently, to be adapted to the various *crises* of human affairs." . . . When we are dealing with the words of the Constitution, said this Court in *Missouri v. Holland*, 252 U.S. 416 [1920], "we must realize that they have called into life a being the development of which could not have been foreseen completely by the most gifted of its begetters. . . . The case before us must be considered in the light of our whole experience and not merely in that of what was said a hundred years ago."

Nor is it helpful to attempt to draw a fine distinction between the intended meaning of the words of the Constitution and their intended application. When we consider the contract clause and the decisions which have expounded it in harmony with the essential reserved power of the states to protect the security of their peoples, we find no warrant for the conclusion that the clause has been warped by these decisions from its proper significance or that the founders of our government would have interpreted the clause differently had they had occasion to assume that responsibility in the conditions of the later day. The vast body of law which has been developed was unknown to the fathers, but it is believed to have preserved the essential content and the spirit of the Constitution. With a growing recognition of public needs and the relation of individual right to public security, the court has sought to prevent the perversion of the clause through its use as an instrument to throttle the capacity of the states to protect their fundamental interests. This development is a growth from the seeds which the fathers planted. It is a development forecast by the prophetic words of Justice JOHNSON in *Ogden v. Saunders*, already quoted. And the germs of the later decisions are found in the early cases of the *Charles River Bridge* [11 Pet. 420 (1837)] and the *West River Bridge* [*Co. v. Dix*, 6 How. (47 U.S.) 506 (1848)], which upheld the public right against strong insistence upon the contract clause. The principle of this development is, as we have seen, that the reservation of the reasonable exercise of the protective power of the state is read into all contracts, and there is no greater reason for refusing to apply this principle to Minnesota mortgages. . . .

Applying the criteria established by our decisions, we conclude:

1. An emergency existed in Minnesota which furnished a proper occasion for the exercise of the reserved power of the state to protect the vital interests of the community. The declarations of the existence of this emergency by the Legislature and by the Supreme Court of Minnesota cannot be regarded as a subterfuge or as lacking in adequate basis. . . .

2. The legislation was addressed to a legitimate end; that is, the legislation was not for the mere advantage of particular individuals but for the protection of a basic interest of society.

3. In view of the nature of the contracts in question—mortgages of unquestionable validity—the relief afforded and justified by the emergency, in order not to contravene the constitutional provision, could only be of a character appropriate to that emergency, and could be granted only upon reasonable conditions.

4. The conditions upon which the period of redemption is extended do not appear to be unreasonable. . . .

5. The legislation is temporary in operation. It is limited to the exigency which called it forth. While the postponement of the period of redemption from the foreclosure sale is to May 1, 1935, that period may be reduced by the order of the court under the statute, in case of a change in circumstances, and the operation of the statute itself could not validly outlast the emergency or be so extended as virtually to destroy the contracts.

We are of the opinion that the Minnesota statute as here applied does not violate the contract clause of the Federal Constitution. Whether the legislation is wise or unwise as a matter of policy is a question with which we are not concerned.

☐ *Justice SUTHERLAND dissenting, joined by Justices VAN DEVANTER, McREYNOLDS, and BUTLER.*

Few questions of greater moment than that just decided have been submitted for judicial inquiry during this generation. He simply closes his eyes to the necessary implications of the decision who fails to see in it the potentiality of future gradual but ever-advancing encroachments upon the sanctity of private and public contracts. . . .

A provision of the Constitution, it is hardly necessary to say, does not admit of two distinctly opposite interpretations. It does not mean one thing at one time and an entirely different thing at another time. If the contract impairment clause, when framed and adopted, meant that the terms of a contract for the payment of money could not be altered *in invitum* by a state statute enacted for the relief of hardly pressed debtors to the end and with the effect of postponing payment or enforcement during and because of an economic or financial emergency, it is but to state the obvious to say that it means the same now. . . .

[W]e are here dealing, not with a power granted by the Federal Constitution, but with the state police power, which exists in its own right. Hence the question is, not whether an emergency furnishes the occasion for the exercise of that state power, but whether an emergency furnishes an occasion for the relaxation of the restrictions upon the power imposed by the contract impairment clause; and the difficulty is that the contract impairment clause forbids state action under any circumstances, if it have the effect of impairing the obligation of contracts. That clause restricts every state power in the particular specified, no matter what may be the occasion. It does not contemplate that an emergency shall furnish an occasion for softening the restriction or making it any the less a restriction upon state action in that contingency than it is under strictly normal conditions.

The Minnesota statute either impairs the obligation of contracts or it does not. If it does not, the occasion to which it relates becomes immaterial, since then the passage of the statute is the exercise of a normal, unrestricted, state power and requires no special occasion to render it effective. If it does, the emergency no more furnishes a proper occasion for its exercise than if the emergency were nonexistent. And so, while, in form, the suggested distinction seems to put us forward in a straight line, in reality it simply carries us back in a circle, like bewildered travelers lost in a wood, to the point where we parted company with the view of the state court.

If what has now been said is sound, as I think it is, we come to what really is the vital question in the case: Does the Minnesota statute constitute an impairment of the obligation of the contract now under review? . . .

It is quite true . . . that "the reservation of essential attributes of sovereign power is also read into contracts"; and that the Legislature cannot "bargain away the public health or the public morals." General statutes to put an end to lotteries, the sale or manufacture of intoxicating liquors, the maintenance of nuisances, to protect the public safety, etc., although they have the indirect effect of absolutely destroying private contracts previously made in contemplation of a continuance of the state of affairs then in existence but subsequently prohibited, have been uniformly upheld as not violating the contract impairment clause. The distinction between legislation of that character and the Minnesota statute, however, is readily observable. . . .

[T]he statute denies appellant for a period of two years the ownership and possession of the property—an asset which, in any event, is of substantial character, and which possibly may turn out to be of great value. The statute, therefore, is not merely a modification of the remedy; it effects a material and injurious change in the obligation.

City of El Paso v. Simmons
379 U.S. 497, 85 S.Ct. 577 (1965)

Since 1876, Texas had offered land for sale to raise funds for public schools and to settle the state. Under its law, land could be bought with a down payment of one-fortieth of the purchase price and the annual payment of 3 percent interest. If a purchaser missed an interest payment, the land was forfeited to the state unless the purchaser paid the interest before a third party obtained title to the land. Under this program, Greenberry Simmons bought some forfeited land which he in turn forfeited to the state in 1947. Two days and five years later, however, Simmons offered to pay the interest and applied to have his land reinstated. The state denied his request, citing a 1941 amendment to its law barring the reinstatement of forfeited land after five years from the date of forfeiture. Texas then sold the land to the City of El Paso in 1955. And Simmons sued in federal district court for the return of the land title, claiming that Texas's 1941 amendment to its law violated the contract clause of the Constitution. A district court judge decided for the city but a federal appellate court reversed. The City of El Paso then appealed to the Supreme Court.

The Court's decision was eight to one, with the majority's opinion announced by Justice White. Justice Black dissented.

☐ *Justice WHITE delivers the opinion of the Court.*

The City seeks to bring this case within the long line of cases recognizing a distinction between contract obligation and remedy and permitting a modification of the remedy as long as there is no substantial impairment of the value of the obligation.

We do not pause to consider further whether the Court of Appeals correctly ascertained the Texas law at the time these contracts were made, or to chart again the dividing line under federal law between "remedy" and "obligation," or to determine the extent to which this line is controlled by state court decisions, decisions often rendered in contexts not involving Contract Clause considerations. For it is not every modification of a contractual promise that impairs the obligation of contract under federal law, any more than it is every alteration of existing remedies that violates the Contract Clause. . . .

The decisions "put it beyond question that the prohibition is not an absolute one and is not to be read with literal exactness like a mathematical formula," as Chief Justice HUGHES said in *Home Building & Loan Assn. v. Blaisdell*, 290 U.S. 398 [1934], The *Blaisdell* opinion, which amounted to a comprehensive restatement of the principles underlying the application of the Contract Clause, makes it quite clear that "[n]ot only is the constitutional provision qualified by the measure of control which the state retains over remedial processes, but the state also continues to possess authority to safeguard the vital interests of its people. It does not matter that legislation appropriate to that end 'has the result of modifying or abrogating contracts already in effect.'" . . .

Of course, the power of a State to modify or affect the obligation of contract is not without limit. . . . But we think the objects of the Texas statute make abundantly clear that it impairs no protected right under the Contract Clause. . . .

The circumstances behind the 1941 amendment are well described in the Reports of the Commissioner of the General Land Office. The general purpose of the legislation enacted in 1941 was to restore confidence in the stability and integrity of land titles and to enable the State to protect and administer its property in a businesslike manner. . . .

The State's policy of quick resale of forfeited lands did not prove entirely successful; forfeiting purchasers who repurchased the lands again defaulted and other purchasers bought without any intention of complying with their contracts unless mineral wealth was discovered. The market for land contracted during the depression. These developments hardly to be expected or foreseen, operated to confer considerable advantages on the purchaser and his successors and a costly and difficult burden on the State. . . .

Laws which restrict a party to those gains reasonably to be expected from the contract are not subject to attack under the Contract Clause, notwithstanding that they technically alter an obligation of a contract. The five-year limitation allows defaulting purchasers with a bona fide interest in their lands a reasonable time to reinstate. It does not and need not allow defaulting purchasers with a speculative interest in the discovery of minerals to remain in endless default while retaining a cloud on title. . . .

The measure taken to induce defaulting purchasers to comply with their contracts, requiring payment of interest in arrears within five years, was a mild one indeed, hardly burdensome to the purchaser who wanted to adhere to his contract of purchase, but nonetheless an important one to the State's interest. The Contract Clause does not forbid such a measure.

The judgment is reversed.

☐ *Justice BLACK, dissenting.*

I have previously had a number of occasions to dissent from judgments of this Court balancing away the First Amendment's unequivocally guaranteed rights of free speech, press, assembly and petition. In this case I am compelled to dissent from the Court's balancing away the plain guarantee of Art. 1. Sec. 10, that

> No State shall . . . pass any . . . Law impairing the Obligation of Contracts . . . ,

a balancing which results in the State of Texas' taking a man's private property for public use without compensation in violation of the equally plain guarantee of the Fifth Amendment, made applicable to the States by the Fourteenth, that

> . . . private property [shall not] be taken for public use, without just compensation.

The respondent, Simmons, is the loser and the treasury of the State of Texas the ultimate beneficiary of the Court's action. . . .

United States Trust Co. of New York v. State of New Jersey
431 U.S. 1, 97 S.Ct. 1505 (1977)

In 1962, New York and New Jersey made an interstate compact limiting the Port Authority's ability to subsidize mass transit through bonds. But during the 1974 energy crisis, the New York and New Jersey legislatures repealed the covenant. The United States Trust Company of New York, a trustee and bondholder of the Port Authority, contended that repealing the covenant violated the contract clause and filed a lawsuit which a state court dismissed. The New Jersey Supreme Court affirmed and United States Trust Company of New York appealed to the Supreme Court.

The Court's decision was four to three, with Justices Powell and Stewart not participating and with the majority's opinion announced by Justice Blackmun. Chief Justice Burger concurred. Justice Brennan, joined by Justices White and Marshall, dissented.

☐ *Justice BLACKMUN delivers the opinion of the Court.*

This case presents a challenge to a New Jersey statute as violative of the Contract Clause of the United States Constitution. That statute, together with a concurrent, and parallel New York statute repealed a statutory covenant made by the two States in 1962 that had limited the ability of The Port Authority of New York and New Jersey to subsidize rail passenger transportation from revenues and reserves. . . .

The trial court concluded that repeal of the 1962 covenant was a valid exercise of New Jersey's police power because repeal served important public interests in mass transportation, energy conservation, and environmental protection. Yet the Contract Clause limits otherwise legitimate exercises of state legislative authority, and the existence of an important public interest is not always sufficient to overcome that limitation. . . .

Of course, to say that the financial restrictions of the 1962 covenant were valid when adopted does not finally resolve this case. The Contract Clause is not an absolute bar to subsequent modification of a State's own financial obligations. As with laws impairing the obligations of private contracts, an impairment may be constitutional if it is reasonable and necessary to serve an important public purpose. In applying this standard, however, complete deference to a legislative assessment of reasonableness and necessity is not appropriate because the State's self-interest is at stake. A governmental entity can always find a use for extra money, especially when taxes do not have to be raised. If a State could reduce its financial obligations whenever it wanted to spend the money for what it regarded as an important public purpose, the Contract Clause would provide no protection at all. . . .

Mass transportation, energy conservation, and environmental protection are goals that are important and of legitimate public concern. Appellees contend that these goals are so important that any harm to bondholders from repeal of the 1962 covenant is greatly outweighed by the public benefit. We do not accept this invitation to engage in a utilitarian comparison of public benefit and private loss. Contrary to Justice BLACK's fear expressed in sole dissent in *El Paso v. Simmons* [379 U.S. 497 (1965)], the Court has not "balanced away" the limitation on state action imposed by the Contract Clause. Thus a State cannot refuse to meet its legitimate financial obligations simply because it would prefer to spend the money to promote the public good rather than the private welfare of its creditors. We can only sustain the repeal of the 1962 covenant if that impairment was both reasonable and necessary to serve the admittedly important purposes claimed by the State.

The more specific justification offered for the repeal of the 1962 covenant was the States' plan for encouraging users of private automobiles to shift to public transportation. The States intended to discourage private automobile use by raising bridge and tunnel tolls and to use the extra revenue from those tolls to subsidize improved commuter railroad service. Appellees contend that repeal of the 1962 covenant was necessary to implement this plan because the new mass transit facilities could not possibly be self-supporting and the covenant's "permitted deficits" level had already been exceeded. We reject this justification because the repeal was neither necessary to achievement of the plan nor reasonable in light of the circumstances.

The determination of necessity can be considered on two levels. First, it cannot be said that total repeal of the covenant was essential; a less drastic modification would have permitted the contemplated plan without entirely removing the covenant's limitations on the use of Port Authority revenues and reserves to subsidize commuter railroads. Second, without modifying the covenant at all, the States could have adopted alternative means of achieving their twin goals of discouraging automobile use and improving mass transit. . . .

We also cannot conclude that repeal of the covenant was reasonable in light of the surrounding circumstances. In this regard a comparison with *El Paso v. Simmons, supra,* again is instructive. There a 19th century statute had effects that were unforeseen and unintended by the legislature when originally adopted. As a result speculators were placed in a position to obtain windfall benefits. The Court held that adoption of a statute of limitation was a reasonable means to "restrict a party to those gains reasonably to be expected from the contract" when it was adopted. . . .

By contrast, in the instant case the need for mass transportation in the New York metropolitan area was not a new development, and the likelihood that publicly owned commuter railroads would produce substantial deficits was well known. As early as 1922, over a half century ago, there were pressures to involve the Port Authority in mass transit. It was with full knowledge of these concerns that the 1962 covenant was adopted. . . .

During the 12-year period between adoption of the covenant and its repeal, public perception of the importance of mass transit undoubtedly grew because of increased general concern with environmental protection and energy conservation. But these concerns were not unknown in 1962, and the subsequent changes were of degree and not of kind. We cannot say that these changes caused the covenant to have a substantially different impact in 1974 than when it was adopted in 1962. And we cannot conclude that the repeal was reasonable in the light of changed circumstances.

We therefore hold that the Contract Clause of the United States Constitution prohibits the retroactive repeal of the 1962 covenant. The judgment of the Supreme Court of New Jersey is reversed.

It is so ordered.

☐ *Justice BRENNAN, with whom Justice WHITE and Justice MARSHALL join, dissenting.*

Decisions of this Court for at least a century have construed the Contract Clause largely to be powerless in binding a State to contracts limiting the authority of successor legislatures to enact laws in furtherance of the health, safety, and similar collective interests of the polity. In short, those decisions established the principle that lawful exercises of a State's police powers stand paramount to private rights held under contract. Today's decision, in invalidating the New Jersey Legislature's 1974 repeal of its predecessor's 1962 covenant, rejects this previous understanding and remolds the Contract Clause into a potent instrument for overseeing important policy determinations of the state legislature. At the same time, by creating a constitutional safe haven for property rights embodied in a contract, the decision substantially distorts modern constitutional jurisprudence governing regulation of private economic interests. . . .

One of the fundamental premises of our popular democracy is that each generation of representatives can and will remain responsive to the needs and desires of those whom they represent. Crucial to this end is the assurance that new legislators will not automatically be bound by the policies and undertakings of earlier days. In accordance with this philosophy, the Framers of our Constitution conceived of the Contract Clause primarily as protection for economic transactions entered into by purely private parties, rather than obligations involving the State itself. The Framers fully recognized that nothing would so jeopardize the legitimacy of a system of government that relies upon the ebbs and flows of politics to "clean out the rascals" than the possibility that those same rascals might perpetuate their policies simply by locking them into binding contracts.

Following an early opinion of the Court, however, that took the first step of applying the Contract Clause to public undertakings, *Fletcher v. Peck*, 6 Cranch 87 (1810), later decisions attempted to define the reach of the Clause consistently with the demands of our governing processes. The central principle developed by these decisions, beginning at least a century ago, has been that Contract Clause challenges such as that raised by appellant are to be resolved by according unusual deference to the lawmaking authority of state and local governments. . . .

This theme of judicial self-restraint and its underlying premise that a State always retains the sovereign authority to legislate in behalf of its people was commonly expressed by the doctrine that the Contract Clause will not even recognize efforts of a State to enter into contracts limiting the authority of succeeding legislators to enact laws in behalf of the health, safety, and similar collective interests of the polity—in short, that that State's police power is inalienable by contract. . . .

I would not want to be read as suggesting that the States should blithely proceed down the path of repudiating their obligations, financial or otherwise. Their credibility in the credit market obviously is highly dependent on exercising their vast lawmaking powers with self-restraint and discipline, and I, for one, have little doubt that few, if any, jurisdictions would choose to use their authority "so foolish[ly] as to kill a goose that lays golden eggs for them," *Erie R. Co. v. Public Util. Comm'rs.*, [254 U.S. 394 (1921)]. But in the final analysis, there is no reason to doubt that appellant's financial welfare is being adequately policed by the political processes and the bond marketplace itself. The role to be played by the Constitution is at most a limited one. For this Court should have learned long ago that the Constitution—be it through the Contract or Due Process Clause—can actively intrude into such economic and policy matters only if my Brethren are prepared to bear enormous institutional and social costs. Because I consider the potential dangers of such judicial interference to be intolerable, I dissent.

B | *The Development and Demise of a "Liberty of Contract"*

Ratification of the Fourteenth Amendment in 1868 provided the Supreme Court with a new basis for protecting economic rights. The amendment overturned the Taney Court's ruling in *Dred Scott v. Sandford*, 60 U.S. 393 (1857) (see Vol. 2, Chapter 12), that blacks were not citizens of the United States. Section 1 of the amendment aimed at ensuring that states would not deny blacks their citizenship by providing that "[n]o State shall make or enforce any law which shall abridge the privileges or immunities of citizens of the United States; nor shall any State deprive any person of life, liberty, or property, without due process of law; nor deny to any person within its jurisdiction the equal protection of the laws." The drafters of the amendment in the Thirty-ninth Congress thought that the privileges or immunities clause was the most important guarantee, because it expressly prohibited states from denying the privileges and immunities of being a citizen of the United States. Its importance is underscored by its almost literal repetition of the privileges and immunities clause of Article IV, Section 2, which provides that "[t]he Citizens of each State shall be entitled to all Privileges and Immunities of Citizens in the several States."

What counted among the privileges and immunities, however, was far from certain. In *Dred Scott*, Chief Justice Taney construed Article IV to protect only the privileges and immunities of citizens of states who were also citizens of the United States and who were temporarily in a state other than their own. The Fourteenth Amendment overturned this interpretation by extending citizenship to blacks, but offered no further clarification.

An obvious, although narrow, view is that the privileges or immunities clause simply forbids states from discriminating against citizens of other states.[1] Yet during the House and Senate debates on the amendment's adoption a frequently cited opinion was that of Justice Bushrod Washington. While sitting on a circuit court, he had interpreted the privileges or immunities clause in *Corfield v. Coryell*, 6 Fed. Cases 3230 (1825), upholding a New Jersey statute prohibiting nonresidents from gathering oysters in the state. Gathering oysters was not among the privileges and immunities of citizenship, but Washington added that citizens were guaranteed those rights "which are, in their nature, fundamental; which belong of right, to the citizens of all free governments." He listed (notably without mentioning the Bill of Rights) a rather wide-ranging set of fundamental rights; among others, he included the right to possess property, to travel from one state to another, to be protected by the government, to be exempt from higher taxes than paid by other citizens, and the right to bring suits in courts of law.

Whatever potential the Fourteenth Amendment's privileges or immunities clause had was soon dashed in *Butchers' Benevolent Association v. Cresent City Livestock Landing & Slaughterhouse Co.* (1873) (see excerpt below). When upholding a Louisiana law that created a monopoly on the operation of slaughterhouses, Justice Samuel Miller construed citizenship in the states and the United States to be distinct and separate and the Fourteenth Amendment to apply only to national citizenship. The independent butchers who opposed the legislative creation of a monopoly thus could not claim protection under the Fourteenth Amendment.

Four dissenters in *The Slaughterhouse Cases* disagreed. Justice Stephen Field rejected the majority's notion of dual citizenship, while Justice Joseph Bradley contended that the butchers had a right to practice their profession under the due process clauses of the Fifth and Fourteenth Amendments. Bradley was the only one to accept the interpretation of the amendment advanced by the butchers' attorney, John Campbell, a former member of the Court who resigned when his state seceded from the Union.

Campbell had argued that the Fourteenth Amendment had a grander purpose than just guaranteeing the rights of former slaves. Its due process clause guaranteed individual freedom, free enterprise, and laissez-faire individualism. His argument was an invitation for the Court to interpret the due process clause as something more than a mere procedural guarantee. Although Campbell failed to carry the day, his argument proved prophetic of what would come.

Due process was generally understood to mean "the law of the land," but the law of the land and due process were on the brink of transformation. The due process clauses of the Fifth and Fourteenth Amendments were rooted in the English common law, running back to the Magna Carta of 1215. The Magna Carta granted that "[n]o freeman shall be arrested, or imprisoned, or disseized, or outlawed, or exiled, or in any way molested; nor will [the Crown] proceed against him, unless by lawful judgment of his peers or by the law of the land." That guarantee was reaffirmed and reformed in the Petition of Right in 1628, which specified that freemen could "be imprisoned or detained only by the law of the land, or by due process of law, and not by the King's special command without any charge." Later, colonial charters and state constitutions incorporated this provision as well.

The Court's first opportunity to interpret the Fifth Amendment's due process clause had come in 1856. *Murray's Lessee v. Hoboken Land & Improvement Company*, 18 How. (59 U.S.) 272 (1856), upheld a congressional statute authorizing the Treasury Department to issue administrative warrants (without prior judicial approval) for the property of revenue collectors found to be indebted to the United States. The Taney Court rejected the claim that this amounted to the taking of property without due process because it found no conflict between this procedure and any guarantee of the Bill of Rights or settled common-law practices.

The following year in *Dred Scott*, Chief Justice Taney relied in part on the Fifth Amendment's due process clause when upholding slave-owners' proprietary interests in slaves. Taney thereby suggested that the due process of law included substantive rights as well as procedural guarantees. Moreover, state courts were beginning to acknowledge protection for property rights and economic liberties as a matter of due process of law. In *Wynehamer v. New York*, 13 N.Y. 378 (1856), New York's highest court struck down a law prohibiting the possession of liquor as a denial of due process of law.[2]

Campbell's due process argument and Justice Bradley's dissent in *The Slaughterhouse Cases* were thus early manifestations of the legal movement toward extending greater protection to economic liberties under constitutional guarantees other than that of the contract clause. In 1870, the Legal Tender Act of 1862 was invalidated, partially on the grounds that it deprived creditors of property without the due process of law, in *Hepburn v. Griswold*, 8 Wall. 608 (1870). Five years later, in *Loan Association v. Topeka*, 20 Wall. (87 U.S.) 655 (1875), a Kansas tax designed to help local industries was overturned, in Justice Miller's words, as an "unauthorized invasion of [the] private right [of property which grows] . . . out of the essential nature of free government."

By 1877, the Court under Chief Justice Morrison Waite (1874–1888) was prepared to acknowledge the due process clause's *substantive* protection for economic liberty. Although upholding Illinois's law regulating grain elevators as "clothed with the public interest" in *Munn v. Illinois* (1877) (see excerpt below), Waite conceded that economic legislation might constitute the taking of property without due process of law. And while he cautioned that "[f]or protection against abuses by legislatures, the people must resort to the polls, not to the courts," *Munn* signaled that the Court might be persuaded to supervise legislation regulating economic activities. In any event, the Court faced a growing stream of litigation attacking legislation on due process grounds. In *Davidson v. New Orleans*, 96 U.S. 97 (1878), Justice Miller was thus moved to complain that

Cartoon depicting the Supreme Court's backlog of cases in 1883 due to the growing amount of litigation challenging government regulations. (*Puck Magazine/Library of Congress.*)

the docket of this court is crowded with cases in which we are asked to hold that State courts and State legislatures have deprived their own citizens of life, liberty, or property without due process of law. There is here abundant evidence that there exists some strange misconception of the scope of this provision as found in the Fourteenth Amendment. In fact, it would seem, from the character of many of the cases before us, and the arguments made in them, that the clause under consideration is looked upon as means of bringing to the test of the decision of this court the abstract opinions of every unsuccessful litigant in a State court of justice of the decision against him, and of the merits of the legislation on which such a decision may be founded.

"The great tides and currents which engulf the rest of men," as Justice Benjamin Cardozo observed, "do not turn aside in their course, and pass the judges by."[3] The country's economic expansion in the late nineteenth century was reinforced by the intellectual currents of Conservative Social Darwinism—the philosophy of the survival of the fittest as applied to social and economic relations and perpetuating the myth of rugged individualism and laissez-faire capitalism.

The Court was gradually infused with this philosophy of laissez-faire capitalism, as its composition changed between 1877 and 1890 with the elevation of corporate lawyers to the ranks of justices.[4] And its assumption of the guardianship of economic liberty manifested itself in various ways. Notably, in an otherwise uninteresting tax case, *Santa Clara County v. Southern Pacific Railroad Company*, 118 U.S. 398 (1886), corporations were proclaimed to be "legal persons" entitled to full protection of the Fourteenth Amendment. Chief Justice Waite evidently thought this was so self-evident that he did not bother to emphasize it in his opinion, and the reporter of the Court's decisions decided on his own initiative that it merited special note in the headnotes accompanying the Court's opinion. The significance of that ruling, of course, was not lost on lawyers for railroads, corporations, and other businesses attacking government regulations.

Ten years after *Santa Clara County*, the Court explicitly held that the Fourteenth Amendment's due process clause protects a substantive, but unenumerated, "liberty of contract." *Allgeyer v. Louisiana*, 165 U.S. 578 (1897), invalidated a Louisiana law restricting the issuance of insurance policies and imposing a $1,000 fine on anyone having an illegal policy. Allgeyer & Company had a maritime insurance policy with a New York insurance firm in violation of Louisiana's law and appealed a ruling of that state's supreme court upholding the law and a fine on Allgeyer. When striking down the law, Justice Rufus Peckham boldly announced the doctrine of a liberty of contract:

> The "liberty" mentioned in [the Fourteenth] Amendment means not only the right of the citizen to be free from the mere physical restraint of his person, as by incarceration, but the term is deemed to embrace the right of the citizen to be free in the enjoyment of all his faculties; to be free to use them in all lawful ways; to live and work where he will; to earn his livelihood by any lawful calling; to pursue any livelihood or avocation, and for that purpose to enter into all contracts which may be proper, necessary and essential to his carrying out to a successful conclusion the purposes above mentioned.

Allgeyer ushered in what became known as the *Lochner* era of substantive due process economic protectionism, after one of the most notorious rulings on the liberty of contract, *Lochner v. New York* (1905) (see excerpt below). There, speaking for a bare majority, Justice Peckham struck down New York's labor law limiting the number of hours bakers could work as an interference with their liberty of contract. And in one of his most famous dissenting opinions, Justice Oliver Wendell Holmes sharply criticized his brethren for reading their own conservative economic philosophy into the Constitution. Under the guise of a liberty of contract and its substantive due process analysis, Holmes charged, the Court had become a superlegislature in overseeing economic regulations.

Justice Holmes's dissent brought the insights of "American legal realism" to bear on the majority's ruling in *Lochner* and embodies the principal liberal and progressive criticism of the *Lochner* era: the majority in *Lochner* was making rather than interpreting the law, and through its creation and enforcement of an unenumerated "liberty of contract" imposed its own conservative economic philosophy on the country. But, note that the other dissenting opinion filed in *Lochner* by Justice Harlan, and joined by Justices White and Day, represents a rival interpretation of the ruling in and the era associated with *Lochner*. Justice Harlan considered the liberty of contract a vital constitutional guarantee, rooted in the Reconstruction Amendments and the antislavery movement's emphasis on self-ownership. That liberty, though, as Harlan reminded his colleagues, remained subject to legislation aimed at promoting public health, safety, and general welfare. The majority in *Lochner*, on Harlan's view, mistakenly construed New York's law as a protectionist measure for bakery workers, rather than as a legitimate piece of health and safety legislation promoting the general welfare. That is why Justice Harlan marshalled empirical studies showing that working long hours in bakeries may indeed be injurious to workers' health. In other words, the majority in *Lochner* failed to see how New York's law promoted the general welfare and got carried away with its stand against protectionist legislation favoring one occupation or group over another.[5]

Lochner and the era that it represents, in sum, invites two rival interpretations. On the Holmesian view, *Lochner* represents the Court's purblind imposition of a laissez-faire economic philosophy against the growing forces of economic progressives. Alternatively, the *Lochner* era was a time of great class conflict and political struggles during which the Court tried to draw (not always successfully) a principled distinction between, on the one hand, legitimate economic legislation promoting health, safety, and the general welfare; and, on the other hand, economic legislation that was invalid because it was deemed to advance the special interests of particular groups or classes.

For four decades (from 1897 to 1937) the philosophy of laissez-faire capitalism and defensive stand against special interests' protective economic legislation held sway with a majority of the Court under Chief Justices Waite, Melville Fuller (1888–1910), Edward White (1910–1921), William Howard Taft (1921–1930), and Charles Evans Hughes (1930–1941). Never before or since were economic regulations more severely scrutinized. Close to 200 state and federal laws were overturned during the *Lochner* era.

The Court did not strike down all legislation, however, as Justice Harlan's dissent in *Lochner* emphasized. Where legislation sought to enforce health, safety, or moral standards with little or no impact on economic liberty, the Court deferred to the states and Congress. In *Mugler v. Kansas*, 123 U.S. 623 (1887), for instance, when sustaining a state prohibition law, Justice John Harlan explained that

> [t]here is no justification for holding that the State, under the guise merely of police regulation, is here aiming to deprive the citizen of his constitutional rights; for we cannot shut out of view the fact, within the knowledge of all, that the public health, the public morals, and the public safety, may be endangered by the general use of intoxicating drinks; nor the fact, established by statistics accessible to everyone, that the idleness, disorder, pauperism, and crime existing in the country are, in some degree at least, traceable to this evil.

But Harlan also cautioned that not every law enacted for the promotion of public welfare would survive or

> be accepted as a legitimate exertion of the police powers of the State. There are, of necessity, limits beyond which legislation cannot rightfully go. . . . The courts are not bound by mere forms, nor are they to be misled by mere pretenses. They are at liberty—indeed, are under a solemn duty—to look at the substance of things, whenever they enter upon the inquiry whether the legislature has transcended the limits of its authority. If, therefore, a statute purporting to have been enacted to protect the public health, the public morals, or the public safety, has no real or substantial relation to those objects, or is a palpable invasion of rights secured by the fundamental law, it is the duty of the courts to so adjudge, and thereby give affect to the Constitution.

On this reasoning, the Court also upheld federal laws prohibiting the sale of liquor[6] and state laws banning sales and advertisements for cigarettes,[7] as well as zoning and land-use laws.[8]

The extent to which the Court was predisposed to defer to states when regulations had no direct economic impact is underscored in two further rulings during the *Lochner* era. In *Jacobson v. Massachusetts*, 197 U.S. 11 (1905), the Court refused to question the basis for a state law requiring smallpox vaccinations. In Justice Harlan's words:

> We must assume that when the statute in question was passed, the legislature of Massachusetts was not unaware of . . . opposing theories [of the effectiveness of vaccinations], and was compelled, of necessity, to choose between them. It was not compelled to commit a matter involving the public health and safety to the final decision of a court or jury. It is no part of the function of a court or a jury to determine which one of two modes was likely to be the most

effective for the protection of the public against disease. That was for the legislative department to determine in the light of all the information it had or could obtain.

Nor was the Court inclined to scrutinize the basis for Virginia's law, passed in response to the eugenics movement, requiring the sterilization of those who were mentally defective or afflicted with epilepsy. It affirmed the compulsory sterilization of Carrie Buck, a seventeen-year-old, "feebleminded" female in a state mental institution, whose mother had also been an inmate and who had already given birth to a mentally defective child. Justice Holmes's opinion for the Court revealed not only his deference to legislatures but his acceptance of the tooth and claw of Social Darwinism. In *Buck v. Bell*, 274 U.S. 200 (1927) (excerpted in Vol. 2, Ch. 11), he observed that

> [w]e have seen more than once that the public welfare may call upon the best citizens for their lives. It would be strange if it could not call upon those who already sap the strength of the State for these lesser sacrifices, often not felt to be such by those concerned, in order to prevent our being swamped with incompetence. It is better for all the world, if instead of waiting to execute degenerate offspring for crime, or to let them starve for the imbecility, society can prevent those who are manifestly unfit from continuing their kind. The principle that sustains compulsory vaccination is broad enough to cover cutting the Fallopian tubes. . . . Three generations of imbeciles are enough.

When legislation aimed at promoting health, safety, or welfare *and* directly affected economic activities, the Court did not automatically strike it down. But the Court had to be convinced of the reasonableness of the regulations. In *Holden v. Hardy*, 169 U.S. 366 (1898), with only Justices Peckham and David Brewer dissenting, the Court upheld Utah's law limiting the number of hours in a day miners could work in mines and smelters to eight.

In *Muller v. Oregon*, (1908) (excerpted below), the Court unanimously approved a state law limiting the workday for women in industries to ten hours per day. There the Court was persuaded by what became known as "the Brandeis brief." When defending Oregon's law, the progressive and highly regarded labor lawyer, Louis Brandeis, filed an extraordinary brief, containing only two pages of legal argument and more than a hundred pages of statistics and social science studies showing how long hours of labor endangered the health of women and thus the reasonableness of the state's law.[9] (Notably, after Brandeis was named to the Court in 1916, he never cited social science materials when writing an opinion for the Court upholding state legislation.

Instead, he only cited these materials when writing dissenting opinions, criticizing the majority for overturning state laws and showing the reasonableness of the legislation.)

Although upholding state regulations in cases like *Muller* and *Bunting v. Oregon*, 243 U.S. 426 (1917), sustaining a labor law limiting workdays to ten hours a day for men and women, the Court's prevailing practice was nevertheless to strike down economic regulations. The problem for the Court and the country was that while the development of the doctrine of a liberty of contract may have been in response, in Holmes's classic phrase, "to the felt necessities of the time," it ran against the political currents of the early twentieth century. Reform Social Darwinism had replaced Conservative Social Darwinism in teaching that humans not only adapt to the environment but may change it as well.[10] Under pressure from reformers, labor unions, and the progressive movement, legislatures were passing new laws in response to the plight of workers in sweatshops, child labor, and generally dismal working conditions as depicted in novels by Upton Sinclair. The justices were no longer in tune with the times. The Court and the country were on a collision course in constitutional politics.

In *Adair v. United States*, 208 U.S. 161 (1908), for example, the Court, with only Justices Holmes and Joseph McKenna dissenting, struck down a section of a congressional labor-relations law banning yellow-dog contracts—contracts signed by workers promising they would not join labor unions—and forbidding the firing of employees who belonged to unions. When approving of Adair's firing of O. B. Coppage from the Louisville & Nashville Railroad Company because he was a union member, Justice Harlan disabused any thought of abandoning the liberty of contract:

> While ... the right of liberty and property guaranteed by the Constitution against deprivation without due process of law is subject to such reasonable restraints as the common good or the general welfare may require, it is not within the functions of government—at least, in the absence of contract between the parties—to compel any person, in the course of his business and against his will, to accept or retain the personal services of another, or to compel any person, against his will, to perform personal services for another. The right of a person to sell his labor upon such terms as he deems proper is, in its essence, the same as the right of the purchaser of labor to prescribe the conditions upon which he will accept such labor from the person offering to sell it. So the right of the employee to quit the service of the employer, for whatever reason, is the same as the right of the employer, for whatever reason, to dispense with the services of such employee. It was the legal right of the defendant Adair,—however unwise such a course might have been,—to

discharge Coppage because of his being a member of a labor organization, as it was the legal right of Coppage, if he saw fit to do so,—however unwise such a course on his part might have been,—to quit the service in which he was engaged, because the defendant employed some persons who were not members of a labor organization. In all such particulars the employer and the employee have equality of right, and any legislation that disturbs that equality is an arbitrary interference with the liberty of contract which no government can legally justify in a free land.

In *Coppage v. Kansas*, 236 U.S. 1 (1915), with Justices Holmes, Rufus Day, and Charles Evans Hughes dissenting, the Court struck down a state law outlawing yellow-dog contracts. The Kansas state supreme court had upheld the law and the conviction of T. B. Coppage for firing a switchman for the St. Louis & San Francisco Railway Company because the employee refused to give up his union membership. In another vintage expression of the doctrine of a liberty of contract, Justice Mahlon Pitney explained that

it is said by the Kansas supreme court to be a matter of common knowledge that "employees, as a rule, are not financially able to be as independent in making contracts for the sale of their labor as are employers in making a contract of purchase thereof." No doubt; wherever the right of private property exists, there must and will be inequalities of fortune; and thus it naturally happens that parties negotiating about a contract are not equally unhampered by circumstances. This applies to all contracts, and not merely to that between employer and employee. Indeed, a little reflection will show that wherever the right of private property and the right of a free contract coexist, each party when contracting is inevitably more or less influenced by the question whether he has much property, or little, or none; for the contract is made to the very end that each may gain something that he needs or desires more urgently than that which he proposes to give in exchange. And, since it is self-evident that, unless all things are held in common, some persons must have more property than others, it is from the nature of things impossible to uphold freedom of contract and the right of private property without at the same time recognizing as legitimate those inequalities of fortune that are the necessary result of the exercise of those rights. But the 14th Amendment, in declaring that a state shall not "deprive any person of life, liberty, or property without due process of law," gives to each of these an equal sanction; it recognizes "liberty" and "property" as coexistent human rights, and debars the states from any unwarranted interference with either.

And since a state may not strike them down directly, it is clear that it may not do so indirectly, as by declaring in effect that the public good requires the removal of those inequalities that are but the normal and inevitable result of their exercise. . . . The police power is broad, and not easily defined, but it cannot be given the wide scope that is here asserted for it, without in effect nullifying the constitutional guaranty.

In the 1920s the Court's defense of the liberty of contract reached the high-water mark and the controversy was exacerbated by the Great Depression. In *Adkins v. Children's Hospital*, 261 U.S. 525 (1923), a bare majority struck down the District of Columbia's minimum wage law for women and again made clear that *Lochner* was still alive. The minimum wage law, according to Justice George Sutherland, was "simply and exclusively a price-fixing law." "Women," he added, "are legally as capable of contracting for themselves as men." In dissent, Chief Justice Taft maintained that *Muller*, not *Lochner*, should control the decision and questioned whether *Lochner* had not been "overruled *sub silentio*," that is, overruled without expressly saying so. But *Wolf Packing Co. v. Court of Industrial Relations*, 262 U.S. 522 (1923), with none other than Taft delivering the Court's opinion, underscored that economic liberty was a "preferred freedom," when striking down Kansas's law creating an industrial-relations court to handle labor-management disputes. And there remained a die-hard majority on the Court into the 1930s for defending the vestiges of laissez-faire capitalism. In *Morehead v. Tipaldo*, 298 U.S. 587 (1936), the four remaining justices from *Adkins's* majority—Sutherland, Pierce Butler, Willis Van Devanter, and James McReynolds—were thus joined by Owen Roberts in overturning New York's minimum wage law.

The controversy over the Court finally erupted into the most serious crisis in constitutional politics since *Dred Scott*. During President Franklin D. Roosevelt's first term, the Court invalidated most of his early New Deal programs thereby thwarting his plans for the country's recovery from the Great Depression. After FDR's landslide reelection in 1936, he boldly proposed judicial reforms that would allow him to expand the size of the Court to fifteen by appointing a new member for every justice over seventy years of age. Then in the spring of 1937 when the Senate Judiciary Committee was debating his Court-packing plan, the Court abruptly upheld major pieces of the New Deal legislation. The Court had become badly split five to four in striking down progressive New Deal legislation. Sutherland, McReynolds, Butler, and Van Devanter—the "Four Horsemen"—voted as a bloc against economic legislation for violating economic liberty, while Stone and Cardozo followed Brandeis in supporting progressive legislation. Hughes and Roberts were the swing votes, although the latter, more conservative justice, had cast the crucial fifth vote to strike down FDR's programs. Roberts, however, was persuaded by Hughes to change his mind. In March he abandoned the Four Horsemen in *West Coast Hotel Co. v. Parrish* (1937) (see excerpt below) to uphold Washington State's minimum wage law. Two weeks later, in *National Labor Relations Board v. Jones & Laughlin Steel Corporation*, 301 U.S. 1 (1937) (see Ch. 6), Roberts again switched sides to affirm a major piece of New Deal legislation, the National Labor Relations Act.

The Court's "switch in time that saved nine" was widely speculated to have been due to FDR's Court-packing plan. But even though the rulings did not come down until the spring, Roberts had switched his vote at conference in December 1936, two months before FDR announced his plan. The reversal of the Court's position nonetheless contributed to the Senate Judiciary Committee's rejection of FDR's proposal in May. Then Van Devanter—one of the president's staunchest opponents—told the president that he would resign at the end of the next term. FDR had the first of eight appointments in the next six years to infuse his own political philosophy into the Court.

The Court's about-face in 1937 ended a constitutional crisis and an era. With the Court's abandonment of the liberty of contract and turning its back on substantive due process came a virtual abdication of judicial supervision of economic regulations. *Lincoln Federal Labor Union v. Northwestern Iron & Metal Co.*, 335 U.S. 525 (1949), for example, expressly repudiated *Adair* and *Coppage*. As FDR's first appointee to the Court, Justice Hugo Black, in *Ferguson v. Skrupa*, 372 U.S. 726 (1963), exclaimed, "[I]t is up to legislatures, not courts, to decide on the wisdom and utility of legislation."[11] The Burger Court, when upholding a state law requiring employees to be compensated when on jury duty by their employers, in *Dean v. Gadsden Times Publishing Corporation*, 412 U.S. 543 (1973), underscored that "[i]f our recent cases mean anything, they leave debatable issues as respects business, economic, and social affairs to legislative decision. We could strike down this law only if we returned to the philosophy of *Lochner, Coppage*, and *Adkins* cases."

Since the 1937 revolution in constitutional politics, the Court has evolved a proverbial double standard: it gives economic regulation only minimal scrutiny, requiring only that it have some rational basis, while giving that affecting civil liberties heightened scrutiny, often upholding legislation only if the government's interest in regulation is compelling. And since 1937 the Court has assumed a special role in overseeing voting rights and access to the political process (see Ch. 8); the freedom of speech, press, and association (see Vol. 2, Ch. 15); and invidious forms of racial and nonracial discrimination (see Vol. 2, Ch. 12).

It appears highly unlikely that the Court will once again heighten its scrutiny of economic legislation under the due process clause, let alone return to the days of the liberty of contract. Justice William Rehnquist, for example, in *United States Railroad Retirement Board v. Fritz*, 449 U.S. 166 (1980), rebuffed a due process attack on legislation eliminating railroad retirees' social security and retirement benefits with the observation that "[t]he plain language [of the statute] marks the beginning and end of our inquiry."

Finally, it bears noting that although the Court turned its back on the doctrine of a liberty of contract in 1937, it did not abandon reading substantive guarantees into the due process clause of the Fourteenth Amendment, as further discussed in Volume 2, Chapters 4 and 10.

Notes

1. For further discussion, see Charles Fairman, "Does the Fourteenth Amendment Incorporate the Bill of Rights?" 2 *Stanford Law Review* 5 (1949); and William Crosskey, "Charles Fairman, 'Legislative History,' and the Constitutional Limitations on State Authority," 22 *University of Chicago Law Review* 1 (1954).

2. See Edward Corwin, *Liberty against Government: The Rise, Flowering and Decline of a Famous Judicial Concept* (Baton Rouge: Louisiana State University Press, 1948).

3. Benjamin Cardozo, *The Nature of the Judicial Process* (New Haven, CT: Yale University Press, 1921), 168.

4. For further discussion, see Benjamin Twiss, *Lawyers and the Constitution: How Laissez Faire Came to the Supreme Court* (Princeton, NJ: Princeton University Press, 1942); Robert McCloskey, *American Conservatism in the Age of Enterprise* (Cambridge, MA: Harvard University Press, 1951); and James Willard Hurst, *Law and the Conditions of Freedom in the Nineteenth-Century United States* (Madison: University of Wisconsin Press, 1956).

5. For further discussion, see Howard Gillman, *The Constitution Besieged: The Rise and Demise of Lochner Era Police Powers Jurisprudence* (Durham, NC: Duke University Press, 1993).

6. *Hamilton v. Kentucky Distilleries and Warehouse Co.*, 251 U.S. 146 (1919).

7. See *Austin v. Tennessee*, 179 U.S. 343 (1900); and *Packer Corporation v. Utah*, 285 U.S. 105 (1932).

8. A leading case is *Euclid v. Ambler Realty Co.*, 272 U.S. 365 (1926). See also *Welch v. Swasey*, 214 U.S. 91 (1909); *Cusack v. Chicago*, 242 U.S. 526 (1917); and *Berman v. Parker*, 348 U.S. 26 (1954).

9. Other rulings upholding labor laws for women include *Cotting v. Godard*, 183 U.S. 79 (1901); *German Alliance Insurance Co. v. Lewis*, 233 U.S. 389 (1914); and *Townsend v. Yeomans*, 301 U.S. 441 (1937).

10. For further discussion, see Morton White, *Social Thought in America: The Revolt against Formalism* (New York: Viking Press, 1949).

11. See also *Williamson v. Lee Optical of Oklahoma*, 348 U.S. 483 (1955); and *Olsen v. Nebraska*, 313 U.S. 236 (1952).

SELECTED BIBLIOGRAPHY

Brigham, John. *Property and the Politics of Entitlement.* Philadelphia: Temple University Press, 1990.

Freyer, Tony. *Producers versus Capitalists: Constitutional Conflict in Antebellum America.* Charlottesville: University Press of Virginia, 1994.

Gillman, Howard. *The Constitution Besieged: The Rise and Demise of Lochner Era Police Powers Jurisprudence.* Durham, NC: Duke University Press, 1993.

Kens, Paul. *Judicial Power and Reform Politics: The Anatomy of Lochner v. New York.* Lawrence: University Press of Kansas, 1990.

Labbé, Ronald, and Lurie, Jonathan. *The Slaughterhouse Cases.* Lawrence: University Press of Kansas, 2003.

Leuchtenburg, William E. *The Supreme Court Reborn: The Constitutional Revolution in the Age of Roosevelt.* New York: Oxford University Press, 1995.

Miller, Arthur S. *The Supreme Court and American Capitalism.* New York: Free Press, 1968.

Paul, Arnold. *Conservative Crisis and the Rule of Law: Attitudes of Bench and Bar, 1887–1895.* Ithaca, NY: Cornell University Press, 1960.

Twiss, Benjamin. *Lawyers and the Constitution: How Laissez Faire Came to the Supreme Court.* Princeton, NJ: Princeton University Press, 1942.

Butchers' Benevolent Association v. Crescent City Livestock Landing & Slaughterhouse Co. (The Slaughterhouse Cases)

16 WALL. (83 U.S.) 36 (1873)

In 1869 due to the pollution and the spread of cholera, the Louisiana legislature passed a law aimed at cleaning up the Mississippi River by prohibiting all slaughtering of livestock in the City of New Orleans and surrounding parishes except at one slaughterhouse, which was given an exclusive franchise for twenty-five years. The Butchers' Benevolent Association, a group of independent slaughterers, challenged the constitutionality of the legislation on the grounds that it violated the Thirteenth and Fourteenth Amendments by depriving them of their livelihood. A state court and the Louisiana State Supreme Court upheld the law, and the Butchers' Benevolent Association appealed to the Supreme Court.

The Court's decision was five to four, with the majority's opinion announced by Justice Miller. Justices Field, Bradley, and Swayne dissented, joined by Chief Justice Chase.

☐ *Justice MILLER delivers the opinion of the Court.*

The plaintiffs . . . allege that the statute is a violation of the Constitution of the United States in these several particulars:

That it creates an involuntary servitude forbidden by the 13th article of amendment;

That it abridges the privileges and immunities of citizens of the United States;

That it denies to the plaintiffs the equal protection of the laws; and,

That it deprives them of their property without due process of law; contrary to the provisions of the 1st section of the 14th article of amendment.

This court is thus called upon for the first time to give construction to these articles. . . .

The most cursory glance at these articles discloses a unity of purpose, when taken in connection with the history of the times, which cannot fail to have an important bearing on any question of doubt concerning their true meaning. . . .

[N]o one can fail to be impressed with the one pervading purpose found in [the 13th, 14th and 15th Amendments], lying at the foundation of each, and without which none of them would have been even suggested; we mean the freedom of the slave race, the security and firm establishment of that freedom, and the protection of the newly made freemen and citizens from the oppressions of those who had formerly exercised unlimited dominion over him. It is true that only the 15th Amendment, in terms, mentions the negro by speaking of his color and his slavery. But it is just as true that each of the other articles was addressed to the grievances of that race, and designed to remedy them as the fifteenth.

We do not say that no one else but the negro can share in this protection. Both the language and spirit of these articles are to have their fair and just weight in any question of construction. Undoubtedly, while negro slavery alone was in the mind of the Congress which proposed the 13th article, it forbids any other kind of slavery, now or hereafter. . . .

The next observation is more important in view of the arguments of counsel in the present case. It is that the distinction between citizenship of the United States and citizenship of a state is clearly recognized and established. Not only may a man be a citizen of the United States without being a citizen of a state, but an important element is necessary to convert the former into the latter. He must reside within the state to make him a citizen of it, but it is only necessary that he should be born or naturalized in the United States to be a citizen of the Union.

It is quite clear, then, that there is a citizenship of the United States and a citizenship of a state, which are distinct from each other and which depend upon different characteristics or circumstances in the individual.

We think this distinction and its explicit recognition in this Amendment of great weight in this argument, because the next paragraph of this same section, which is the one mainly relied on by the plaintiffs in error, speaks only of privileges and immunities of citizens of the United States, and does not speak of those of citizens of the several states. The argument, however, in favor of the plaintiffs, rests wholly on the assumption that the citizenship is the same and the privileges and immunities guaranteed by the clause are the same.

The language is: "No state shall make or enforce any law which shall abridge the privileges or immunities of citizens of the United States." It is a little remarkable, if this clause was intended as a protection to the citizen of a state against the legislative power of his own state, that the words "citizen of the state" should be left out when it is so carefully used, and used in contradistinction to "citizens of the United States" in the very sentence which precedes it. It is too clear for argument that the change in phraseology was adopted understandingly and with a purpose.

Of the privileges and immunities of the citizens of the United States, and of the privileges and immunities of the citizen of the state, and what they respectively are, we will presently consider; but we wish to state here that it is only the former which are placed by this clause under the protection of the Federal Constitution, and that the latter, whatever they may be, are not intended to have any additional protection by this paragraph of the Amendment.

If, then, there is a difference between the privileges and immunities belonging to a citizen of the United States as such, and those belonging to the citizen of the state as such, the latter must rest for their security and protection where they have heretofore rested; for they are not embraced by this paragraph of the Amendment. . . .

In the Constitution of the United States, which superseded the Articles of Confederation, the corresponding provision is found in section two of the 4th article, in the following words: The citizens of each state shall be entitled to all the privileges and immunities of citizens of the several states.

There can be but little question that the purpose of both these provisions is the same, and that the privileges and immunities intended are the same in each. In the Articles of the Confederation we have some of these specifically mentioned, and enough perhaps to give some general idea of the class of civil rights meant by the phrase. . . .

The constitutional provision there alluded to did not create those rights, which it called privileges and immunities of citizens of the states. It threw around them in that clause no security for the citizen of the state in which they were claimed or exercised. Nor did it profess to control the power of the state governments over the rights of its own citizens.

Its sole purpose was to declare to the several states, that whatever those rights, as you grant or establish them to your own citizens, or as you limit or qualify, or impose restrictions on their exercise, the same, neither more nor less, shall be the measure of the rights of citizens of other states within your jurisdiction. . . .

The argument has not been much pressed in these cases that the defendant's charter deprives the plaintiffs of their property without due process of law, or that it denies to them the equal protection of the law. The first of these paragraphs has been in the Constitution since the adoption of the 5th Amendment, as a restraint upon the Federal power. It is also to be found in some form of expression in the constitutions of nearly all the states, as a restraint upon the power of the states. This law, then, has practically been the same as it now is during the existence of the government, except so far as the present Amendment may place the restraining power over the states in this matter in the hands of the Federal government.

We are not without judicial interpretation, therefore, both state and national, of the meaning of this clause. And it is sufficient to say that under no construction of that provision that we have ever seen, or any that we deem admissible, can the restraint imposed by the state of Louisiana upon the exercise of their trade by the butchers of New Orleans be held to be a deprivation of property within the meaning of that provision.

"Nor shall any state deny to any person within its jurisdiction the equal protection of the laws."

In the light of the history of these amendments, and the pervading purpose of them, which we have already discussed, it is not difficult to give a meaning to this clause. The existence of laws in the states where the newly emancipated negroes resided, which discriminated with gross injustice and hardship against them as a class, was the evil to be remedied by this clause, and by it such laws are forbidden.

☐ *Justice FIELD, dissenting.*

The question presented is . . . nothing less than the question whether the recent Amendments to the Federal Constitution protect the citizens of the United States against the deprivation of their common rights by state legislation. In my judgment the 14th Amendment does afford such protection, and was so intended by the Congress which framed and the states which adopted it.

The counsel for the plaintiffs in error have contended, with great force, that the act in question is also inhibited by the 13th Amendment.

That Amendment prohibits slavery and involuntary servitude, except as a punishment for crime, but I have not supposed it was susceptible of a construction which would cover the enactment in question. I have been so accustomed to regard it as intended to meet that form of slavery which had previously prevailed in this country, and to which the recent Civil War owed its existence, that I was not prepared, nor am I yet, to give to it the extent and force ascribed by counsel. Still it is evident that the language of the Amendment is not used in a restrictive sense. It is not confined to African slavery alone. It is general and universal in its application. Slavery of white men as well as of black men is prohibited, and not merely slavery in the strict sense of the term, but involuntary servitude in every form. . . .

The first clause of the fourteenth amendment . . . recognizes in express terms, if it does not create, citizens of the United States, and it makes the citizenship dependent upon the place of the birth, or the fact of their adoption, and not upon the Constitution or laws of any state or the condition of their ancestry. A citizen of a state is now only a citizen of the United States residing in that state. The fundamental rights, privileges, and immunities which belong to him as a free man and a free citizen, now belong to him as a citizen of the United States, and are not dependent upon his citizenship of any state. . . .

The Amendment does not attempt to confer any new privileges or immunities upon citizens or to enumerate or define those already existing. It assumes that there are such privileges and immunities which belong of right to citizens as such, and ordains that they shall not be abridged by state legislation. If this inhibition has no reference to privileges and immunities of this character, but only refers, as held by the majority of the court in their opinion, to such privileges and immunities as were before its adoption specially designated in the Constitution or necessarily implied as belonging to citizens of the United States, it was a vain and idle enactment, which accomplished nothing, and most unnecessarily excited Congress and the people on its passage. With privileges and immunities thus designated no state could ever have interfered by its laws, and no new constitutional provision was required to inhibit such interference. The supremacy of the Constitution and the laws of the United States always controlled any state legislation of that character. But if the Amendment refers to the natural and inalienable rights which belong to all citizens, the inhibition has a profound significance and consequence.

What, then, are the privileges and immunities which are secured against abridgement by state legislation? . . .

The privileges and immunities designated are those which of right belong to the citizens of all free governments. Clearly among these must be placed the right to pursue a lawful employment in a lawful manner, without other restraint than such as equally affects all persons. . . .

This equality of right, with exemption from all disparaging and partial enactments, in the lawful pursuits of life, throughout the whole country, is the distinguishing privilege of citizens of the United States. To them, everywhere, all pursuits, all professions, all avocations are open without other restrictions than such as are imposed equally upon all others of the same age, sex and condition. The state may prescribe such regulations for every pursuit and calling of life as will promote the public health, secure the good order and advance the general prosperity of society, but when once prescribed, the pursuit or calling must be free to be followed by every citizen who is within the conditions designated, and will conform to the regulations. This is the fundamental idea upon which our institutions rest, and unless adhered to in the legislation of the country our government will be a Republic only in name. The 14th Amendment, in my judgment, makes it essential to the validity of the legislation of every state that this equality of right should be respected. . . .

I am authorized by Chief Justice CHASE, Justice SWAYNE and Justice BRADLEY, to state that they concur with me in this dissenting opinion.

☐ *Justice BRADLEY, dissenting.*

In my view, a law which prohibits a large class of citizens from adopting a lawful employment, or from following a lawful employment previously adopted, does deprive them of liberty as well as property, without due process of law. Their right of choice is a portion of their liberty; their occupation is their property. Such a law also deprives those citizens of the equal protection of the laws, contrary to the last clause of the section. . . .

It is futile to argue that none but persons of the African race are intended to be benefited by this Amendment. That may have been the primary cause of the Amendment, but its language is general, embracing all citizens, and I think it was purposely so expressed.

Munn v. Illinois

4 OTTO (94 U.S.) 113, 24 L.ED. 77 (1877)

In 1871 in response to the Granger movement—a movement to pro-mote the interests of independent farmers in midwest states—and pres-sures to stop the exploitation of farmers by grain-elevator operators, Illinois's legislature enacted a law requiring operating licenses and set-ting the maximum rates that grain warehouses and elevators could charge for the storage of grain. Ira Munn was found in violation of the law and attacked its constitutionality as a violation of the commerce clause and the due process clause of the Fourteenth Amendment. The Illinois State Supreme Court, however, upheld Munn's conviction and Munn appealed to the Supreme Court.

The Court's decision was seven to two, with the majority's opinion announced by Chief Justice Waite. Justices Field and Strong dissented.

☐ *Chief Justice WAITE delivers the opinion of the Court.*

Every statute is presumed to be constitutional. The courts ought not to declare one to be unconstitutional, unless it is clearly so. If there is doubt, the expressed will of the Legislature should be sustained.

The Constitution contains no definition of the word "deprive," as used in the 14th Amendment. To determine its signification, therefore, it is neces-sary to ascertain the effect which usage has given it, when employed in the same or a like connection.

While this provision of the Amendment is new in the Constitution of the United States as a limitation upon the powers of the States, it is old as a principle of civilized government. It is found in Magna Charta, and, in sub-stance if not in form, in nearly or quite all the constitutions that have been from time to time adopted by the several States of the Union. By the 5th Amendment, it was introduced into the Constitution of the United States as a limitation upon the powers of the National Government, and by the 14th, as a guaranty against any encroachment upon an acknowledged right of citizenship by the Legislatures of the States. . . .

This Act was passed at a time when Magna Charta had been recognized as the fundamental law of England for hundreds of years.

This great charter embodied the principle that no person shall be de-prived of life, liberty or property, but by the judgment of his peers or the law of the land, which is an equivalent for the modern phrase, "due process of law." . . .

[I]t is apparent that, down to the time of the adoption of the 14th Amendment, it was not supposed that statutes regulating the use, or even the price of the use, of private property necessarily deprived an owner of his property without due process of law. Under some circumstances they may, but not under all. The Amendment does not change the law in this particular; it simply prevents the States from doing that which will operate as such a deprivation.

This brings us to inquire as to the principles upon which this power of regulation rests, in order that we may determine what is within and what without its operative effect. Looking, then, to the common law, from whence came the right which the Constitution protects, we find that when private property is "affected with a public interest, it ceases to be *juris privati* only." This was said by Lord Chief Justice Hale more than two hundred years ago, in his treatise *De Portibus Maris*, and has been accepted without objection as an essential element in the law of property ever since. Property does become clothed with a public interest when used in a manner to make it of public consequence, and affect the community at large. When, therefore, one devotes his property to a use in which the public has an interest, he, in effect, grants to the public an interest in that use, and must submit to be controlled by the public for the common good, to the extent of the interest he has thus created. He may withdraw his grant by discontinuing the use; but, so long as he maintains the use, he must submit to the control. . . .

It remains only to ascertain whether the warehouses of these plaintiffs in error, and the business which is carried on there, come within the operation of this principle. . . .

[I]t is difficult to see why, if the common carrier, or the miller, or the ferryman, or the innkeeper, or the wharfinger, or the baker, or the cartman, or the hackney-coachman, pursues a public employment and exercises "a sort of public office," these plaintiffs in error do not. They stand, to use again the language of their counsel, in the very "gateway of commerce," and take toll from all who pass. Their business most certainly "tends to a common charge, and is become a thing of public interest and use." Every bushel of grain for its passage "pays a toll, which is a common charge," and, therefore, according to Lord Hale, every such warehouseman "ought to be under public regulation, viz.: that he . . . take but reasonable toll." Certainly, if any business can be clothed "with a public interest, and cease to be *juris privati* only," this has been. It may not be made so by the operation of the Constitution of Illinois or this statute, but it is by the facts. . . .

We know that this is a power which may be abused; but that is no argument against its existence. For protection against abuses by Legislatures the people must resort to the polls; not to the courts. . . .

We come now to consider the effect upon this statute of the power of Congress to regulate commerce. . . . The warehouses of these plaintiffs in error are situated and their business carried on exclusively within the limits of the State of Illinois. They are used as instruments by those engaged in State as well as those engaged in interstate commerce, but they are no more necessarily a part of commerce itself than the dray or the cart by which, but for them, grain would be transferred from one railroad station to another. Incidentally they may become connected with interstate commerce, but not necessarily so. Their regulation is a thing of domestic concern and, certainly, until Congress acts in reference to their interstate relations, the State may exercise all the powers of government over them, even though in so doing it may indirectly operate upon commerce outside its immediate jurisdiction. We do not say that a case may not arise in which it will be found that a State, under the form of regulating its own affairs, has encroached upon the exclusive domain of Congress in respect to interstate commerce, but we do say that, upon the facts as they are represented to us in this record, that has not been done. . . .

The judgment is affirmed.

☐ *Justice FIELD, dissenting.*

I am compelled to dissent from the decision of the court in this case, and from the reasons upon which that decision is founded. The principle upon which the opinion of the majority proceeds is, in my judgment, subversive of the rights of private property, heretofore believed to be protected by constitutional guaranties against legislative interference, and is in conflict with the authorities cited in its support. . . .

There is nothing in the character of the business of the defendants as warehousemen which called for the interference complained of in this case. Their buildings are not nuisances; their occupation of receiving and storing grain infringes upon no rights of others, disturbs no neighborhood, infects not the air, and in no respect prevents others from using and enjoying their property as to them may seem best. The legislation in question is nothing less than a bold assertion of absolute power by the State to control, at its discretion, the property and business of the citizen, and fix the compensation he shall receive. . . .

The business of a warehouseman was, at common law, a private business, and is so in its nature. It has no special privileges connected with it, nor did the law ever extend to it any greater protection than it extended to all other private business. No reason can be assigned to justify legislation interfering with the legitimate profits of that business, that would not equally justify an intermeddling with the business of every man in the community, so soon, at least, as his business became generally useful.

I am of opinion that the judgment of the Supreme Court of Illinois should be reversed.

Lochner v. New York

198 U.S. 45, 25 S.Ct. 539 (1905)

Joseph Lochner was found guilty and fined $50 for violating an 1897 New York law prohibiting employers from having their employees work more than sixty hours a week in a bakery. Lochner's conviction was affirmed by two state courts and he applied for a writ of error from the Supreme Court.

The Court's decision was five to four; the majority's opinion was announced by Justice Peckham. Dissents were by Justices Holmes and Harlan, who was joined by Justices White and Day.

☐ *Justice PECKHAM delivers the opinion of the Court.*

The mandate of the statute, that "no employee shall be required or permitted to work," is the substantial equivalent of an enactment that "no employee shall contract or agree to work," more than ten hours per day; and, as there is no provision for special emergencies, the statute is mandatory in all cases. It is not an act merely fixing the number of hours which shall constitute a legal day's work, but an absolute prohibition upon the employer permitting, under any circumstances, more than ten hours' work to be done in his establishment. The employee may desire to earn the extra money which would arise from his working more than the prescribed time, but this statute forbids the employer from permitting the employee to earn it.

The statute necessarily interferes with the right of contract between the employer and employees, concerning the number of hours in which the latter may labor in the bakery of the employer. The general right to make a contract in relation to his business is part of the liberty of the individual protected by the 14th Amendment of the Federal Constitution. *Allgeyer v. Louisiana*, 165 U.S. 578 [1897]. Under that provision no state can deprive any person of life, liberty, or property without due process of law. The right to purchase or to sell labor is part of the liberty protected by this amendment, unless there are circumstances which exclude the right. There are, however, certain powers, existing in the sovereignty of each state in the Union, somewhat vaguely termed police powers, the exact description and limitation of which have not been attempted by the courts. Those powers, broadly stated, and without, at present, any attempt at a more specific limitation, relate to the safety, health, morals, and general welfare of the public. Both property and liberty are held on such reasonable conditions as may be imposed by the governing power of the state in the exercise of those powers, and with such conditions the 14th Amendment was not designed to interfere. . . .

The state, therefore, has power to prevent the individual from making certain kinds of contracts, and in regard to them the Federal Constitution offers no protection. If the contract be one which the state, in the legitimate exercise of its police power, has the right to prohibit, it is not prevented from prohibiting it by the 14th Amendment. Contracts in violation of a statute, either of the Federal or state government, or a contract to let one's property for immoral purposes, or to do any other unlawful act, could obtain no protection from the Federal Constitution, as coming under the liberty of person or of free contract. Therefore, when the state, by its legislature, in the assumed exercise of its police powers, has passed an act which seriously limits the right to labor or the right of contract in regard to their means of livelihood between persons who are *sui juris* (both employer and employee), it becomes of great importance to determine which shall prevail,—the right of the individual to labor for such time as he may choose, or the right of the state to prevent the individual from laboring, or from entering into any contract to labor, beyond a certain time prescribed by the state.

This court has recognized the existence and upheld the exercise of the police powers of the states in many cases which might fairly be considered as border ones, and it has, in the course of its determination of questions regarding the asserted invalidity of such statutes, on the ground of their violation of the rights secured by the Federal Constitution, been guided by rules of a very liberal nature, the application of which has resulted, in numerous instances, in upholding the validity of state statutes thus assailed. . . .

It must, of course, be conceded that there is a limit to the valid exercise of the police power by the state. . . . Otherwise the 14th Amendment would have no efficacy and the legislatures of the states would have unbounded power, and it would be enough to say that any piece of legislation was enacted to conserve the morals, the health, or the safety of the people; such legislation would be valid, no matter how absolutely without foundation the claim might be. The claim of the police power would be a mere pretext,— become another and delusive name for the supreme sovereignty of the state to be exercised free from constitutional restraint. . . . In every case that comes before this court, therefore, where legislation of this character is concerned, and where the protection of the Federal Constitution is sought, the question necessarily arises: Is this a fair, reasonable, and appropriate exercise of the police power of the state, or is it an unreasonable, unnecessary, and arbitrary interference with the right of the individual to his personal liberty, or to enter into those contracts in relation to labor which may seem to him appropriate or necessary for the support of himself and his family? Of course the liberty of contract relating to labor includes both parties to it. The one has as much right to purchase as the other to sell labor.

This is not a question of substituting the judgment of the court for that of the legislature. If the act be within the power of the state it is valid, although the judgment of the court might be totally opposed to the enactment of such a law. . . .

The question whether this act is valid as a labor law, pure and simple, may be dismissed in a few words. There is no reasonable ground for interfering with the liberty of person or the right of free contract, by determining the hours of labor, in the occupation of a baker. There is no contention that bakers as a class are not equal in intelligence and capacity to men in other trades or manual occupations, or that they are not able to assert their rights and care for themselves without the protecting arm of the state, interfering with their independence of judgment and of action. They are in no sense wards of the state. Viewed in the light of a purely labor law, with no reference whatever to the question of health, we think that a law like the one before us involves neither the safety, the morals, nor the welfare, of the public, and that the interest of the public is not in the slightest degree affected by such an act. The law must be upheld, if at all, as a law pertaining to the health of the individual engaged in the occupation of a baker. It does not affect any other portion of the public than those who are engaged in that occupation. Clean and wholesome bread does not depend upon whether the baker works but ten hours per day or only sixty hours a week. The limitation of the hours of labor does not come within the police power on that ground.

It is a question of which of two powers or rights shall prevail,—the power of the state to legislate or the right of the individual to liberty of person and freedom of contract. The mere assertion that the subject relates, though but in a remote degree, to the public health, does not necessarily render the enactment valid. The act must have a more direct relation, as a means to an end, and the end itself must be appropriate and legitimate, before an act can be held to be valid which interferes with the general right of an individual to be free in his person and in his power to contract in relation to his own labor. . . .

We think that there can be no fair doubt that the trade of a baker, in and of itself, is not an unhealthy one to that degree which would authorize the legislature to interfere with the right to labor, and with the right of free contract on the part of the individual, either as employer or employee. In looking through statistics regarding all trades and occupations, it may be true that the trade of a baker does not appear to be as healthy as some other trades, and is also vastly more healthy than still others. To the common understanding the trade of a baker has never been regarded as an unhealthy one. . . .

It seems to us that the real object and purpose were simply to regulate the hours of labor between the master and his employees (all being men, *sui juris*), in a private business, not dangerous in any degree to morals, or in any real and substantial degree to the health of the employees. Under such circumstances the freedom of master and employee to contract with each other in relation to their employment, and in defining the same, cannot be prohibited or interfered with, without violating the Federal Constitution.

☐ *Justice HOLMES, dissenting.*

This case is decided upon an economic theory which a large part of the country does not entertain. If it were a question whether I agreed with that theory, I should desire to study it further and long before making up my mind. But I do not conceive that to be my duty, because I strongly believe that my agreement or disagreement has nothing to do with the right of a majority to embody their opinions in law. It is settled by various decisions of this court that state constitutions and state laws may regulate life in many ways which we as legislators might think as injudicious, or if you like as tyrannical, as this, and which equally with this, interfere with the liberty to contract. Sunday laws and usury laws are ancient examples. A more modern one is the prohibition of lotteries. The liberty of the citizen to do as he likes so long as he does not interfere with the liberty of others to do the same, which has been a shibboleth for some well-known writers, is interfered with by school laws, by the Postoffice, by every state or municipal institution which takes his money for purposes thought desirable, whether he likes it or not. The 14th Amendment does not enact Mr. Herbert Spencer's *Social Statics*. The other day we sustained the Massachusetts vaccination law. *Jacobson v. Massachusetts*, 197 U.S. 11 [1905]. United States and state statutes and decisions cutting down the liberty to contract by way of combination are familiar to this court. *Northern Securities Co. v. United States*, 193 U.S. 197 [1904]. Two years ago we upheld the prohibition of sales of stock on margins, or for future delivery, in the Constitution of California. *Otis v. Parker*, 187 U.S. 606 [1903]. The decision sustaining an eight-hour law for miners is still recent. *Holden v. Hardy* [169 U.S. 366 (1898)]. Some of these laws embody convictions or prejudices which judges are likely to share. Some may not. But a

Constitution is not intended to embody a particular economic theory, whether of paternalism and the organic relation of the citizen to the state or of *laissez faire*. It is made for people of fundamentally differing views, and the accident of our finding certain opinions natural and familiar, or novel, and even shocking, ought not to conclude our judgment upon the question whether statutes embodying them conflict with the Constitution of the United States.

General propositions do not decide concrete cases. The decision will depend on a judgment or intuition more subtle than any articulate major premise. But I think that the proposition just stated, if it is accepted, will carry us far toward the end. Every opinion tends to become a law. I think that the word "liberty," in the 14th Amendment, is perverted when it is held to prevent the natural outcome of a dominant opinion, unless it can be said that a rational and fair man necessarily would admit that the statute proposed would infringe fundamental principles as they have been understood by the traditions of our people and our law. It does not need research to show that no such sweeping condemnation can be passed upon the statute before us. A reasonable man might think it a proper measure on the score of health. Men whom I certainly could not pronounce unreasonable would uphold it as a first installment of a general regulation of the hours of work. Whether in the latter aspect it would be open to the charge of inequality I think it unnecessary to discuss.

☐ *Justice HARLAN, with whom Justices WHITE and DAY join, dissenting.*

[Granting] that there is a liberty of contract which cannot be violated even under the sanction of direct legislative enactment, but assuming, as according to settled law we may assume, that such liberty of contract is subject to such regulations as the State may reasonably prescribe for the common good and the well-being of society, what are the conditions under which the judiciary may declare such regulations to be in excess of legislative authority and void? Upon this point there is no room for dispute; for, the rule is universal that a legislative enactment, Federal or state, is never to be disregarded or held invalid unless it be, beyond question, plainly and palpably in excess of legislative power. . . .

Let these principles be applied to the present case. By the statute in question it is provided that, "No employee shall be required or permitted to work in a biscuit, bread or cake bakery or confectionery establishment more than sixty hours in any one week, or more than ten hours in any one day, unless for the purpose of making a shorter work day on the last day of the week; nor more hours in any one week than will make an average of ten hours per day for the number of days during such week in which such employee shall work."

It is plain that this statute was enacted in order to protect the physical well-being of those who work in bakery and confectionery establishments. It may be that the statute had its origin, in part, in the belief that employers and employees in such establishments were not upon an equal footing, and that the necessities of the latter often compelled them to submit to such exactions as unduly taxed their strength. Be this as it may, the statute must be taken as expressing the belief of the people of New York that, as a general rule, and in the case of the average man, labor in excess of sixty hours during a week in such establishments may endanger the health of those who thus labor. Whether or not this be wise legislation it is not the province of the court to inquire. Under our systems of government the courts are not concerned with the wisdom or policy of legislation. So that in determining the question of power to interfere with liberty of contract, the court may inquire whether the means devised by the State are germane to an end which may be lawfully accomplished and have a real or substantial relation to the protection of health, as involved in the daily work of the persons, male and female, engaged in bakery and confectionery establishments. But when this inquiry is entered upon I find it impossible, in view of common experience, to say that there is here no real or substantial relation between the means employed by the State and the end sought to be accomplished by its legislation. Nor can I say that the statute has no appropriate or direct connection with that protection to health which each State owes to her citizens, or that it is not promotive of the health of the employees in question, or that the regulation prescribed by the State is utterly unreasonable and extravagant or wholly arbitrary. Still less can I say that the statute is, beyond question, a plain, palpable invasion of rights secured by the fundamental law. Therefore I submit that this court will transcend its functions if it assumes to annul the statute of New York. It must be remembered that this statute does not apply to all kinds of business. It applies only to work in bakery and confectionery establishments, in which, as all know, the air constantly breathed by workmen is not as pure and healthful as that to be found in some other establishments or out of doors.

Professor Hirt in his treatise on the *Diseases of the Workers* has said: "The labor of the bakers is among the hardest and most laborious imaginable, because it has to be performed under conditions injurious to the health of those engaged in it. . . ." Another writer says: "The constant inhaling of flour dust causes inflammation of the lungs and of the bronchial tubes. The eyes also suffer through this dust, which is responsible for the many cases of running eyes among the bakers. The long hours of toil to which all bakers are subjected produce rheumatism, cramps and swollen legs. The intense heat in the workshops induces the workers to resort to cooling drinks, which together with their habit of exposing the greater part of their bodies to the change in the atmosphere, is another source of a number of diseases of various organs. Nearly all bakers are pale-faced and of more delicate health than the workers of other crafts, which is chiefly due to their hard work and their irregular and unnatural mode of living whereby the power of resistance against disease is greatly diminished. The average age of a baker is below that of other workmen; they seldom live over their fiftieth year, most of them dying between the ages of forty and fifty. During periods of epidemic diseases the bakers are generally the first to succumb to the disease, and the number swept away during such periods far exceeds the number of other crafts in comparison to the men employed in the respective industries. . . ."

We judicially know that the question of the number of hours during which a workman should continuously labor has been, for a long period, and is yet, a subject of serious consideration among civilized peoples, and by those having special knowledge of the laws of health. Suppose the statute prohibited labor in bakery and confectionery establishments in excess of eighteen hours each day. No one, I take it, could dispute the power of the State to enact such a statute. But the statute before us does not embrace extreme or exceptional cases. It may be said to occupy a middle ground in respect of the hours of labor. What is the true ground for the State to take between legitimate protection, by legislation, of the public health and liberty of contract is not a question easily solved, nor one in respect of which there is or can be absolute certainty. There are very few, if any, questions in political economy about which entire certainty may be predicated. . . .

We also judicially know that the number of hours that should constitute a day's labor in particular occupations involving the physical strength and safety of workmen has been the subject of enactments by Congress and by nearly all of the States. Many, if not most, of those enactments fix eight hours as the proper basis of a day's labor. . . .

If such reasons exist that ought to be the end of this case, for the State is not amenable to the judiciary, in respect of its legislative enactments, unless such enactments are plainly, palpably, beyond all question, inconsistent with the Constitution of the United States. We are not to presume that the State of New York has acted in bad faith. Nor can we assume that its legislature acted without due deliberation, or that it did not determine this question upon the fullest attainable information, and for the common good. We cannot say that the State has acted without reason nor ought we to proceed upon the theory that its action is a mere sham. Our duty, I submit, is to sustain the statute as not being in conflict with the Federal Constitution, for the reason—and such is an all-sufficient reason—it is not shown to be plainly and palpably inconsistent with that instrument. . . .

The judgment in my opinion should be affirmed.

Muller v. Oregon

208 U.S. 412, 28 S.CT. 324 (1908)

At the dawn of the twentieth century, the Progressive Movement, led by organizations such as the National Consumers' League (NCL), promoted legislation setting maximum working hours and minimum wages. After *Lochner v. New York* (1905), however, many such state laws appeared in jeopardy. When the owner of a laundry, Curt Muller, challenged the constitutionality of his conviction for violating Oregon's law limiting the number of hours women could work to ten hours per day, the NCL decided to make a "test case" out of the suit and recruited the well-known Progressive reformer and advocate Louis D. Brandeis to argue the case on appeal. In light of *Lochner*, his strategy was try to persuade the Court of the reasonableness of and factual basis for Oregon's law. Accordingly, he had the NCL gather extensive social, economic, and public health information on the effect of women's working long hours. Nearly thirty reports from other countries and states were compiled and quoted in the 113-page brief submitted to the Court. It later became known as the "Brandeis brief" because it contained only two pages of legal arguments, with the rest being data and expert opinion supporting the position that "long hours of labor are dangerous for women primarily because of their special physical organization."

The Court's decision was unanimous in affirming the state supreme court's ruling upholding Oregon's law. Justice Brewer delivered the opinion of the Court.

☐ *Justice BREWER delivered the opinion of the court.*

It is the law of Oregon that women, whether married or single, have equal contractual and personal rights with men. [P]utting to one side the elective franchise, in the matter of personal and contractual rights they stand on the same plane as the other sex. Their rights in these respects can no more be infringed than the equal rights of their brothers. We held in *Lochner v. New York*, 198 U.S. 45 [1905], that a law providing that no laborer shall be required or permitted to work in a bakery more than sixty hours in a week or ten hours in a day was not as to men a legitimate exercise of the police power of the State, but an unreasonable, unnecessary and arbitrary interference with the right and liberty of the individual to contract in relation to his labor, and as such was in conflict with, and void under, the Federal Constitution. That decision is invoked by plaintiff in error as decisive of the question before us. But this assumes that the difference between the sexes does not justify a different rule respecting a restriction of the hours of labor.

It may not be amiss, in the present case, before examining the constitutional question, to notice the course of legislation as well as expressions of opinion from other than judicial sources. In the brief filed by Mr. Louis D. Brandeis, for the defendant in error, is a very copious collection of all these matters, an epitome of which is found in the margin.

In foreign legislation Mr. Brandeis calls attention to these statutes: Great Britain: Factories Act of 1844; Factory and Workshop Act of 1901. France, 1848; Act Nov. 2, 1892, and March 30, 1900. Switzerland, Canton of Glarus, 1848; Federal Law 1877. Austria, 1855; Acts 1897. Holland, 1889; art. 5, Sec. 1. Italy, June 19, 1902, art. 7. Germany, Laws 1891.

Then follow extracts from over ninety reports of committees, bureaus of statistics, commissioners of hygiene, inspectors of factories, both in this country and in Europe, to the effect that long hours of labor are dangerous for women, primarily because of their special physical organization. The matter is discussed in these reports in different aspects, but all agree as to the danger. It would of course take too much space to give these reports in detail. Following them are extracts from similar reports discussing the general benefits of short hours from an economic aspect of the question. In many of these reports individual instances are given tending to support the general conclusion. Perhaps the general scope and character of all these reports may be summed up in what an inspector for Hanover says: "The reasons for the reduction of the working day to ten hours—(a) the physical organization of women, (b) her maternal functions, (c) the rearing and education of the children, (d) the maintenance of the home—are all so important and so far reaching that the need for such reduction need hardly be discussed." . . .

The legislation and opinions referred to in the margin may not be, technically speaking, authorities, and in them is little or no discussion of the constitutional question presented to us for determination, yet they are significant of a widespread belief that woman's physical structure, and the functions she performs in consequence thereof, justify special legislation restricting or qualifying the conditions under which she should be permitted to toil. Constitutional questions, it is true, are not settled by even a consensus of present public opinion, for it is the peculiar value of a written constitution that it places in unchanging form limitations upon legislative action, and thus gives a permanence and stability to popular government which otherwise would be lacking. At the same time, when a question of fact is debated and debatable, and the extent to which a special constitutional limitation goes is affected by the truth in respect to that fact, a widespread and long continued belief concerning it is worthy of consideration. We take judicial cognizance of all matters of general knowledge.

It is undoubtedly true, as more than once declared by this court, that the general right to contract in relation to one's business is part of the liberty of the individual, protected by the Fourteenth Amendment to the Federal Constitution; yet it is equally well settled that this liberty is not absolute and extending to all contracts, and that a State may, without conflicting with the provisions of the Fourteenth Amendment, restrict in many respects the individual's power of contract. Without stopping to discuss at length the extent to which a State may act in this respect, we refer to the following cases in which the question has been considered: *Allgeyer v. Louisiana*, 165 U.S. 578 [1897]; *Lochner v. New York*.

That woman's physical structure and the performance of maternal functions place her at a disadvantage in the struggle for subsistence is obvious. This is especially true when the burdens of motherhood are upon her. Even when they are not, by abundant testimony of the medical fraternity continuance for a long time on her feet at work, repeating this from day to day, tends to injurious effects upon the body, and as healthy mothers are essential to vigorous offspring, the physical well-being of woman becomes an object of public interest and care in order to preserve the strength and vigor of the race.

Still again, history discloses the fact that woman has always been dependent upon man. . . . As minors, though not to the same extent, she has been looked upon in the courts as needing especial care that her rights may be preserved. Education was long denied her, and while now the doors of the school room are opened and her opportunities for acquiring knowledge are great, yet even with that and the consequent increase of capacity for business affairs it is still true that in the struggle for subsistence she is not an equal competitor with her brother. Though limitations upon personal and contractual rights may be removed by legislation, there is that in her disposition and habits of life which will operate against a full assertion of those rights. She will still be where some legislation to protect her seems necessary to secure a real equality of right. Doubtless there are individual exceptions, and there are many respects in which she has an advantage over him; but looking at it from the viewpoint of the effort to maintain an independent position in life, she is not upon an equality. Differentiated by these matters from the other sex, she is properly placed in a class by herself, and legislation designed for her protection may be sustained, even when like legislation is not necessary for men and could not be sustained. It is impossible to close one's eyes to the fact that she still looks to her brother and depends upon him. . . . Many words cannot make this plainer. The two sexes differ in structure of body, in the functions to be performed by each, in the amount of physical strength, in the capacity for long-continued labor, particularly when done standing, the influence of vigorous health upon the future well-being of the race, the self-reliance which enables one to assert full rights, and in the capacity to maintain the struggle for subsistence. This difference justifies a difference in legislation and upholds that which is designed to compensate for some of the burdens which rest upon her. . . .

For these reasons, and without questioning in any respect the decision in *Lochner v. New York*, we are of the opinion that it cannot be adjudged that the act in question is in conflict with the Federal Constitution, so far as it respects the work of a female in a laundry, and the judgment of the Supreme Court of Oregon is

Affirmed.

West Coast Hotel Co. v. Parrish

300 U.S. 379, 57 S.Ct. 578 (1937)

An employee of the West Coast Hotel Company, Elsie Parrish, sued to recover the difference between her wage and the minimum wage of $14.50 per forty-eight-hour week as set by the Industrial Welfare Committee of Washington State. In 1913, Washington's legislature passed legislation to protect the health and welfare of women and minors by setting a minimum wage. But the trial court denied Parrish's claim. When the Washington Supreme Court reversed, attorneys for West Coast Hotel Company appealed to the Supreme Court, arguing that the law ran afoul of the Fourteenth Amendment's due process clause.

The Court's decision was five to four, with the majority's opinion announced by Chief Justice Hughes. Justice Sutherland dissented and was joined by Justices Van Devanter, McReynolds, and Butler.

☐ *Chief Justice* HUGHES *delivers the opinion of the Court.*

This case presents the question of the constitutional validity of the minimum wage law of the state of Washington. . . .

The appellant conducts a hotel. The appellee Elsie Parrish was employed as a chambermaid and (with her husband) brought this suit to recover the difference between the wages paid her and the minimum wage fixed pursuant to the state law. The minimum wage was $14.50 per week of 48 hours. The appellant challenged the act as repugnant to the due process clause of the Fourteenth Amendment of the Constitution of the United States. The Supreme Court of the state, reversing the trial court, sustained the statute and directed judgment for the plaintiffs. *Parrish v. West Coast Hotel Co.*, 185 Wash. 581, 55 P.(2d) 1083 [1936]. The case is here on appeal.

The appellant relies upon the decision of this Court in *Adkins v. Children's Hospital*, 261 U.S. 525 [1923], which held invalid the District of Columbia Minimum Wage Act (40 Stat. 960) which was attacked under the due process clause of the Fifth Amendment. . . .

The recent case of *Morehead v. New York ex rel. Tipaldo*, 298 U.S. 587 [1936], came here on *certiorari* to the New York court which had held the New York minimum wage act for women to be invalid. A minority of this Court thought that the New York statute was distinguishable in a material feature from that involved in the *Adkins* Case and that for that and other reasons the New York statute should be sustained. But the Court of Appeals of New York had said that it found no material difference between the two statutes and this Court held that the "meaning of the statute" as fixed by the decision of the state court "must be accepted here as if the meaning had been specifically expressed in the enactment." That view led to the affirmance by this Court of the judgment in the *Morehead Case*, as the Court considered that the only question before it was whether the *Adkins Case* was distinguishable and that reconsideration of that decision had not been sought. . . .

We think that the question which was not deemed to be open in the *Morehead Case* is open and is necessarily presented here. . . .

The principle which must control our decision is not in doubt. The constitutional provision invoked is the due process clause of the Fourteenth Amendment governing the states, as the due process clause invoked in the *Adkins Case* governed Congress. In each case the violation alleged by those attacking minimum wage regulation for women is deprivation of freedom of contract. What is this freedom? The Constitution does not speak of freedom of contract. It speaks of liberty and prohibits the deprivation of liberty without due process of law. In prohibiting that deprivation, the Constitution does not recognize an absolute and uncontrollable liberty. Liberty in each of its phases has its history and connotation. But the liberty safe-guarded is liberty in a social organization which requires the protection of law against the evils which menace the health, safety, morals, and welfare of the people. Liberty under the Constitution is thus necessarily subject to the restraints of due process, and regulation which is reasonable in relation to its subject and is adopted in the interests of the community is due process.

This essential limitation of liberty in general governs freedom of contract in particular. More than twenty-five years ago we set forth the applicable principle in these words, after referring to the cases where the liberty guaranteed by the Fourteenth Amendment had been broadly described. . . .

This power under the Constitution to restrict freedom of contract has had many illustrations. That it may be exercised in the public interest with respect to contracts between employer and employee is undeniable. Thus statutes have been sustained limiting employment in underground mines and smelters to eight hours a day; in requiring redemption in cash of store orders or other evidences of indebtedness issued in the payment of wages; in forbidding the payment of seamen's wages in advance; in making it unlawful to contract to pay miners employed at quantity rates upon the basis of screened coal instead of the weight of the coal as originally produced in the mine; in prohibiting contracts limiting liability for injuries to employees; in limiting hours of work of employees in manufacturing establishments; and in maintaining workmen's compensation laws. In dealing with the relation of employer and employed, the Legislature has necessarily a wide field of discretion in order that there may be suitable protection of health and safety, and that peace and good order may be promoted through regulations designed to insure wholesome conditions of work and freedom from oppression. . . .

This array of precedents and the principles they applied were thought by the dissenting Justices in the *Adkins Case* to demand that the minimum wage statute be sustained. The validity of the distinction made by the Court between a minimum wage and a maximum of hours in limiting liberty of contract was especially challenged. That challenge persists and is without any satisfactory answer. . . .

We think that the views thus expressed are sound and that the decision in the *Adkins Case* was a departure from the true application of the principles governing the regulation by the state of the relation of employer and employed. . . .

There is an additional and compelling consideration which recent economic experience has brought into a strong light. The exploitation of a class of workers who are in an unequal position with respect to bargaining power and are thus relatively defenseless against the denial of a living wage is not only detrimental to their health and well being, but casts a direct burden for their support upon the community. What these workers lose in wages the taxpayers are called upon to pay. The bare cost of living must be met. We may take judicial notice of the unparalleled demands for relief which arose during the recent period of depression and still continue to an alarming extent despite the degree of economic recovery which has been achieved. It is unnecessary to cite official statistics to establish what is of common knowledge through the length and breadth of the land. While in the instant case no factual brief has been presented, there is no reason to doubt that the state of Washington has encountered the same social problem that is present elsewhere. The community is not bound to provide what is in effect a subsidy for unconscionable employers. The community may direct its law-making power to correct the abuse which springs from their selfish disregard of the public interest. . . .

Our conclusion is that the case of *Adkins v. Children's Hospital, supra*, should be, and it is, overruled. The judgment of the Supreme Court of the state of Washington is affirmed.

Affirmed.

☐ *Justice SUTHERLAND*

Justice VAN DEVANTER, Justice McREYNOLDS, Justice BUTLER, and I think the judgment of the court below should be reversed.

It is urged that the question involved should now receive fresh consideration, among other reasons, because of "the economic conditions which have supervened"; but the meaning of the Constitution does not change with the ebb and flow of economic events. We frequently are told in more general words that the Constitution must be construed in the light of the present. If by that it is meant that the Constitution is made up of living words that apply to every new condition which they include, the statement is quite true. But to say, if that be intended, that the words of the Constitution mean today what they did not mean when written—that is, that they do not apply to a situation now to which they would have applied then—is to rob that instrument of the essential element which continues it in force as the people have made it until they, and not their official agents, have made it otherwise. . . .

The judicial function is that of interpretation; it does not include the power of amendment under the guise of interpretation. To miss the point of difference between the two is to miss all that the phrase "supreme law of the land" stands for and to convert what was intended as inescapable and enduring mandates into mere moral reflections.

If the Constitution, intelligently and reasonably construed in the light of these principles, stands in the way of desirable legislation, the blame must rest upon that instrument, and not upon the court for enforcing it according to its terms. The remedy in that situation—and the only true remedy—is to amend the Constitution. . . .

In the *Adkins Case* we . . . said that while there was no such thing as absolute freedom of contract, but that it was subject to a great variety of restraints, nevertheless, freedom of contract was the general rule and restraint the exception; and that the power to abridge that freedom could only be justified by the existence of exceptional circumstances. This statement of the rule has been many times affirmed; and we do not understand that it is questioned by the present decision.

C | The "Takings Clause" and Just Compensation

A final source for the Court's protection of proprietary interests is the Fifth Amendment's provision that "private property [shall not] be taken for public use, without just compensation." It is also one area of constitutional law in which the Rehnquist Court moved toward giving somewhat greater protection for property rights: see *Nollan v. California Coastal Commission*, 483 U.S. 825 (1987) and THE DEVELOPMENT OF LAW box in this section.

The takings clause broadly guarantees government the power of eminent domain—the power to take private property for public purposes—subject to the just compensation of the owners. But what is a "public purpose"? What constitutes the "taking" of property? And what amounts to "just" compensation?

The requirement that government put private property to public use has been rather loosely interpreted. The only limitations appear to be that government may not take property for the sole purpose of making money for itself or for a private enterprise. However, government may take property and then resell it to private companies for such purposes as urban renewal, the development of industrial parks, or shopping centers, and for use by (even privately owned) public utilities. In *Hawaii Housing Authority v. Midkiff*, 467 U.S. 229 (1984) (excerpted below), for example, the Burger Court approved a state land reform act. As a vestige of Hawaiian feudalism, 96 percent of the state was owned by seventy-two landowners or state and federal governments. In 1967, Hawaii's legislature authorized the use of the power of eminent domain to condemn residential lots and to sell and transfer ownership to existing tenants on the land. The Court unanimously rejected the contention that this program constituted a taking of private property for private, not public, purposes.

General benefit to the public, not public ownership, is what matters, and the Court tends to be highly deferential to legislatures as to what benefits the public. "Subject to specific constitutional limitations," as the Court observed in *Berman v. Parker*, 348 U.S. 26 (1954), "when the legislature has spoken, the public interest has been declared in terms wellnigh conclusive."

Private property does not have to be physically taken by the government for an individual to win compensation. However, *Loretto v. Teleprompter Manhattan CATV*, 458 U.S. 419 (1982), held that permanent physical occupation of property by the government is per se taking and *First English Evangelical Lutheran Church v. County of Los Angeles*, 482 U.S. 304 (1987), ruled that temporary land-use laws may constitute a taking of private property, so-called *regulatory takings* (see THE DEVELOPMENT OF LAW box in this section).

In the classic case of *United States v. Causby*, 328 U.S. 258 (1946), the Court upheld a demand for compensation by a farmer whose land was adjacent to a military airport. The noise of airplane flights over the farm rendered it virtually worthless and the Court upheld the farmer's claim that the government was using his farmland as an extension of its runway and had to pay for it.

Not everyone next to an airport or highway, however, may demand compensation because of the accompanying noise or, for that matter, inconvenience of government regulations. Instead, for property to be "taken" in a constitutional sense, an owner must show a nearly total loss of the use of the property. In *Pennsylvania Coal Co. v. Mahon*, 260 U.S. 393 (1922), Justice Holmes formulated a practical rule, when holding that "property may be regulated to a certain extent, [but] if regulation goes too far it will be recognized as a taking." There is no "brightline rule," but rather, the burden is placed on the property owner of showing a virtually complete loss of the use of his or her property to win compensation.

In another important ruling in *Penn Central Transportation Co. v. New York*, 438 U.S. 104 (1978), the Burger Court affirmed a historic preservation law prohibiting the owners of Grand Central Terminal in New York City from building a high-rise office tower above.

Finally, the Court largely avoided controversies over whether a property owner has received just compensation. In general, just compensation means what, in the absence of the government's acquisition of the property, a willing buyer would pay, or the fair market value. As the Court observed in *Backus v. Fort Street Union Depot Co.*, 169 U.S. 557 (1898): "All that is essential is that in some appropriate way, before some properly constituted tribunal, inquiry shall be made as to the amount of compensation, and when this has been provided there is that due process of law which is required by the Federal Constitution."

The Rehnquist Court signaled renewed interest in, and invited litigation over, regulatory takings–clause jurisprudence in its 1987 rulings in *Nollan v. California Coastal Commission*, 483 U.S. 825 (1987), and *First English Evangelical Lutheran Church v. County of Los Angeles*, 482 U.S. 304 (1987), as well as revisited challenges to land-use regulations in several other cases.[1] In *Nollan*, Justice Scalia commanded a bare majority for holding that the just compensation clause was violated by California's regulations requiring homeowners of beachfront property to agree to a public easement across their property as a condition of receiving a building permit. However, a majority of the Court was unwilling to further extend *Nollan's* analysis. In a leading regulatory "takings clause" case after *Nollan*, *Lucas v. South Carolina Coastal Council* (1992) (excerpted below), the owner of beachfront property appealed a decision of the South Carolina Supreme Court that upheld a regulation barring the rebuilding of houses on the shoreline. Writing for the majority in *Lucas*, Justice Scalia held, on the one hand, that property owners who suffer total economic loss of the value of their land may have a takings-clause claim. Historically, the Court recognized takings claims only when the government actually took physical possession of a property, as in an eminent domain proceeding. But, in *Nollan* and *Lucas*, the Court recognized regulatory takings requiring the government to pay compensation when its regulations diminish the value of private property. In *Lucas*, Scalia held that it is not enough for the government to defend its environmental, land-use, and zoning regulations as in the "public interest." Governments must also defend their regulations as necessary to avoid a public harm or the "harmful or noxious use" of private property; thus a property owner might be denied a permit to run a landfill operation because it would result in flooding of nearby land. Because the state courts failed to identify the public nuisances that would justify the building restrictions in this case, the court remanded *Lucas* for further consideration.

Justice Scalia's opinion, on the other hand, limited its takings-clause analysis to apply only when property owners are totally deprived of the economic value of their land. As he put it, "When the owner of real property has been called upon to sacrifice *all* economically beneficial uses in the name of the common good, that is, to leave his property economically idle, he has suffered a taking." That, however, significantly limited the Court's holding because, as dissenting Justice Stevens observed, "A land-owner whose property is diminished in value 95 percent recovers nothing, while an owner whose property is diminished 100 percent recovers the land's full value." Since most environmental and land-use regulations do not deprive property owners of all economic use or value of their property, Justice Scalia's analysis in *Lucas* is severely limited.

Finally, in a major ruling with wide-ranging ramifications for urban planners and homeowners, by a five-to-four vote the Court upheld the use of the government's power of eminent domain to condemn and take, with just compensation, private property for the purpose of advancing the economic development of the community. Writing for the Court in *Kelo v. City of New London* (excerpted below), Justice Stevens held that "public use" was not limited to the use of public domain to build a road or a bridge; or to redistribute land ownership, as in *Hawaii Housing Authority v. Midkiff*; but includes "promoting economic development," even if the property was taken and sold for development by private developers. Justice Stevens emphasized that courts should be deferential to the decisions of state and local authorities. Justice Kennedy cast the pivotal fifth vote and filed a concurring opinion, underscoring that courts should still exercise review in such cases in order to ensure that governments do not use their power of eminent domain to simply reward or advance the interests of businesses and powerful private interests. Justice O'Connor filed a dissenting opinion which was joined by Chief Justice Rehnquist, and Justices Scalia and Thomas dissented. For further discussion see the INSIDE THE COURT and THE DEVELOPMENT OF LAW boxes in this section. See also the Court's rulings on substantive due process and punitive damages awards in Vol. 2, Ch. 4 and *BMW of North America v. Gore* (excerpted there).

■ INSIDE THE COURT

Hawaii Housing Authority v. Midkiff (1984) and Kelo v. City of New London, Connecticut (2005)

A major controversy erupted over the Court's ruling in *Kelo v. City of New London, Connecticut* (2005) (excerpted in this chapter), holding that private property may be taken by the government, with just compensation, in order to promote economic development, even if the property is then turned over for development by private businesses. Some states and local governments responded with constitutional amendments and ordinances prohibiting such takings whereas other cities moved to condemn property in order to promote economic revitalization. Yet, *Hawaii Housing Authority v. Midkiff* (1984) (excerpted in this chapter) upheld a state land reform that transferred ownership of law from feudal owners to tenants. While *Kelo* was widely criticized, *Midkiff* was praised for promoting equality and the redistribution of the wealth, even though both upheld the government's taking of private property for "public use" and selling it to private developers and owners.

Ironically, Justice O'Connor delivered the opinion for the Court in *Midkiff*, but issued a stinging dissent in *Kelo*. Moreover, Justice O'Connor circulated a draft opinion in *Midkiff* that swept very broadly in justifying the government's taking of property for public use for virtually any social purpose. In response, Justice Lewis F. Powell suggested some modifying language to narrow the opinion. On May 18, 1984, Justice Powell sent the following memo to Justice O'Connor:[1]

> Dear Sandra:
>
> This refers to our brief conversation yesterday. I should have been in touch with you sooner. My suggested changes, set forth below, do not affect your basic analysis. I have been concerned by the sweep of language that can be read as saying that any "social" purpose may justify the taking of private property. The language to this effect is primarily on page 14.
>
> I suggest the following as a substitute for the next to the last sentence in the paragraph on p. 14 that carries over from p. 13:
>
>> As the unique way titles were held in Hawaii skewed the land market, exercise of the power of eminent domain was justified. The Act advances its purposes without the state taking actual possession of the land. In such cases,

The paragraph that begins on p. 14 also can be read broadly to the effect that "social problems" may be addressed by taking private property pursuant to "social legislation". I suggest revisions of some of the language of this paragraph, beginning with the second sentence, along the following lines:

> Judicial deference is required here because, in our system of government, legislatures are better able to assess what public purposes should be advanced by an exercise of the taking power. State legislatures are as capable as Congress of making such determinations within their respective spheres of authority. See *Berman v. Parker*, 348 U.S. [26 (1954)], at 32. Thus, if there are substantial reasons for an exercise of the taking power, courts must . . .

The first full sentence on page 13 states that "redistribution offered simply to reduce the economic and social evils . . . is a rational exercise of the power of eminent domain." Again, I am troubled by the emphasis without limits on "economic and social evils". In this case we are concerned only with a very specific and unique evil. I would suggest omission of the phrase "reduce the economic evils", replacing it with "correct deficiencies in the market".

This *is* a unique case, and I think we may regret language that could encourage Congress and state legislatures to justify taking private property for any perceived social evil.

I am not sending this letter to the Conference, in the hope that changes along these lines will be acceptable to you. If not, I probably will write briefly.

I do appreciate your willingness to consider these.

Sincerely,

[LFP]

Justice Powell's suggested changes were incorporated by Justice O'Connor, though her opinion still swept broadly on the government's power of eminent domain. See and compare her opinion (for a unanimous Court, with Justice Marshall not participating) in *Midkiff*, along with her dissenting opinion (joined by Chief Justice Rehnquist and Justices Scalia and Thomas) in *Kelo*, and consider how to define "public use," for what purposes, and whether courts or state and local governments should determine the justification for the government's taking of private property.

1. Source: Justice Lewis F. Powell, Jr., Papers, Washington & Lee University School of Law, Lexington, Virginia.

Note

1. See also *Yee v. The City of Escondido, California*, 503 U.S. 519 (1992), holding that a rent-control ordinance did not amount to a takings per se. Writing for the Court, Justice O'Connor distinguished two kinds of takings-clause cases: (1) those in which the government has actually physically taken private property for public use and (2) those challenging regulations of the use of private property. The former generally requires compensation of the owners and "courts to apply a clear rule," whereas the latter requires courts to assess the purposes and economic effects of the regulations. And O'Connor reaffirmed that "[s]tates have broad power to regulate housing conditions in general and the landlord-tenant relationship in particular." The Court also rejected a takings-clause challenge in *General Motors v. Romein*, 503 U.S. 181 (1992).

Selected Bibliography

Ely, James W. *The Guardian of Every Other Right: A Constitutional History of Property Rights*. 3d ed. New York: Oxford University Press, 2008.

Epstein, Richard. *Supreme Neglect: How to Revive Constitutional Protection for Private Property*. New York: Oxford University Press, 2008.

Fischel, William. *Regulatory Takings: Law, Economics, and Politics*. Cambridge, MA: Harvard University Press, 1995.

Levy, Leonard. *A License to Steal: Forfeiture of Property*. Chapel Hill: University of North Carolina Press, 1996.

Siegan, Bernard. *Property and Freedom: The Constitution, The Courts, and Land-Use Regulation*. New Brunswick, NJ: Transaction Books, 1998.

Wolf, Michael Allan. *The Zoning of America: Euclid v. Ambler*. Lawrence: University Press of Kansas, 2008.

Hawaii Housing Authority v. Midkiff
467 U.S. 229, 104 S.Ct. 2321 (1984)

The Hawaiian islands were originally settled by Polynesian immigrants from the western Pacific. These settlers developed an economy around a feudal land-tenure system in which one island high chief controlled the land and assigned it for development to subchiefs. Beginning in the early 1800s, Hawaiian leaders and American settlers attempted to divide the lands of the kingdom among the crown, the chiefs, and the common people. These efforts proved largely unsuccessful, however. Finally, in the mid-1960s the Hawaii legislature held hearings and discovered that while the state and federal governments owned almost 49 percent of the state's land, another 47 percent was owned by 72 landholders. The legislature concluded that such concentrated land ownership was responsible for skewing the state's land prices and injuring the public tranquillity and welfare. Accordingly, the legislature enacted legislation to compel the large landowners to break up their estates. The Land Reform Act of 1967 created a mechanism for condemning residential tracts and for transferring ownership of condemned land to lessees. Under the act's condemnation scheme, tenants living on single-family lots within development tracts at least five acres in size were entitled to ask the Hawaii Housing Authority (HHA) to condemn the property on which they lived. When 25 eligible tenants, or tenants on half of the lots in the tract, whichever was less, filed appropriate applications, the act authorized the HHA to hold a public hearing to determine whether the acquisition of the land would "effectuate the public purposes" of the law. If the HHA found that these purposes would be served, it was authorized to acquire the land, at prices set either by a condemnation trial or by negotiations with the landowners.

After HHA held a public hearing on the proposed acquisition of appellees' lands and found that such acquisition would effectuate the act's public purposes, it directed appellees to negotiate with certain lessees concerning the sale of the designated properties. When these negotiations failed, HHA ordered appellees to submit to compulsory arbitration as provided by the act. Rather than comply with this order, appellees filed suit in federal district court, asking that the act be declared unconstitutional. That court held the act to be constitutional under the Public Use Clause of the Fifth Amendment. But the Court of Appeals for the Ninth Circuit reversed, holding that the law violated the Fifth Amendment. The Hawaiian Housing Authority appealed and the Supreme Court granted review and reversed the appellate court.

The Court's decision, with Justice Marshall not participating, was unanimous and delivered by Justice O'Connor.

□ *Justice O'CONNOR delivered the opinion of the Court.*

The Fifth Amendment of the United States Constitution provides, in pertinent part, that "private property [shall not] be taken for public use, without just compensation." These cases present the question whether the Public Use Clause of that Amendment, made applicable to the States through the Fourteenth Amendment, prohibits the State of Hawaii from taking, with just compensation, title in real property from lessors and transferring it to lessees in order to reduce the concentration of ownership of fees simple in the State. We conclude that it does not. . . .

The starting point for our analysis of the Act's constitutionality is the Court's decision in *Berman v. Parker*, 348 U.S. 26 (1954). In *Berman*, the Court held constitutional the District of Columbia Redevelopment Act of 1945. That Act provided both for the comprehensive use of the eminent domain power to redevelop slum areas and for the possible sale or lease of the con-

demned lands to private interests. In discussing whether the takings authorized by that Act were for a "public use," the Court stated:

> We deal, in other words, with what traditionally has been known as
> the police power. An attempt to define its reach or trace its outer lim-
> its is fruitless, for each case must turn on its own facts. The definition
> is essentially the product of legislative determinations addressed to
> the purposes of government, purposes neither abstractly nor histori-
> cally capable of complete definition. Subject to specific constitutional
> limitations, when the legislature has spoken, the public interest has
> been declared in terms well-nigh conclusive. In such cases the legisla-
> ture, not the judiciary, is the main guardian of the public needs to be
> served by social legislation, whether it be Congress legislating con-
> cerning the District of Columbia . . . or the States legislating con-
> cerning local affairs. . . . This principle admits of no exception merely
> because the power of eminent domain is involved. . . .

The Court explicitly recognized the breadth of the principle it was announcing, noting:

> Once the object is within the authority of Congress, the right to re-
> alize it through the exercise of eminent domain is clear. For the power
> of eminent domain is merely the means to the end. . . . Once the ob-
> ject is within the authority of Congress, the means by which it will be
> attained is also for Congress to determine. Here one of the means
> chosen is the use of private enterprise for redevelopment of the area.
> Appellants argue that this makes the project a taking from one
> businessman for the benefit of another businessman. But the means of
> executing the project are for Congress and Congress alone to deter-
> mine, once the public purpose has been established.

The "public use" requirement is thus coterminous with the scope of a
sovereign's police powers. There is, of course, a role for courts to play in reviewing a legislature's judgment of what constitutes a public use, even when
the eminent domain power is equated with the police power. But the Court
in *Berman* made clear that it is "an extremely narrow" one. The Court in
Berman cited with approval the Court's decision in *Old Dominion Co. v.
United States*, 269 U.S. 55 (1925), which held that deference to the legislature's "public use" determination is required "until it is shown to involve an
impossibility." . . . To be sure, the Court's cases have repeatedly stated that
"one person's property may not be taken for the benefit of another private
person without a justifying public purpose, even though compensation be
paid." *Thompson v. Consolidated Gas Corp.*, 300 U.S. 55 (1937). Thus, in *Missouri Pacific R. Co. v. Nebraska*, 164 U.S. 403 (1896), where the "order in question was not, and was not claimed to be, . . . a taking of private property for
a public use under the right of eminent domain," the Court invalidated a
compensated taking of property for lack of a justifying public purpose. But
where the exercise of the eminent domain power is rationally related to a
conceivable public purpose, the Court has never held a compensated taking
to be proscribed by the Public Use Clause. On this basis, we have no trouble
concluding that the Hawaii Act is constitutional. The people of Hawaii have
attempted, much as the settlers of the original 13 Colonies did, to reduce the

perceived social and economic evils of a land oligopoly traceable to their monarchs. The land oligopoly has, according to the Hawaii Legislature, created artificial deterrents to the normal functioning of the State's residential land market and forced thousands of individual homeowners to lease, rather than buy, the land underneath their homes. Regulating oligopoly and the evils associated with it is a classic exercise of a State's police powers. We cannot disapprove of Hawaii's exercise of this power. . . .

The State of Hawaii has never denied that the Constitution forbids even a compensated taking of property when executed for no reason other than to confer a private benefit on a particular private party. A purely private taking could not withstand the scrutiny of the public use requirement; it would serve no legitimate purpose of government and would thus be void. But no purely private taking is involved in these cases. The Hawaii Legislature enacted its Land Reform Act not to benefit a particular class of identifiable individuals but to attack certain perceived evils of concentrated property ownership in Hawaii—a legitimate public purpose. Use of the condemnation power to achieve this purpose is not irrational. Since we assume for purposes of these appeals that the weighty demand of just compensation has been met, the requirements of the Fifth and Fourteenth Amendments have been satisfied. Accordingly, we reverse the judgment of the Court of Appeals, and remand these cases for further proceedings in conformity with this opinion.

Lucas v. South Carolina Coastal Council

505 U.S. 1003, 112 S.Ct. 2886 (1992)

In 1986, petitioner David H. Lucas paid $975,000 for two residential lots on the Isle of Palms in Charleston County, South Carolina, on which he intended to build single-family homes. In 1988, however, the South Carolina Legislature enacted the Beachfront Management Act, which had the effect of barring Lucas from building on the land. A state trial court found that this prohibition rendered Lucas's parcels "valueless," for which he was entitled to just compensation. On appeal, the state supreme court reversed and Lucas appealed to the U.S. Supreme Court.

The state supreme court's decision was reversed by a vote of six to three. Justice Scalia delivered the opinion for the Court. Justice Kennedy filed a concurring opinion. Justices Blackmun and Stevens filed separate dissenting opinions, and Justice Souter filed a statement indicating that the case should have been dismissed as improvidently granted.

☐ *Justice SCALIA delivered the opinion of the Court.*

Prior to Justice HOLMES's exposition in *Pennsylvania Coal Co. v. Mahon*, 260 U.S. 393 (1922), it was generally thought that the Takings Clause reached only a "direct appropriation" of property, *Legal Tender Cases*, 79 U.S. (12 Wall.) 457 (1871), or the functional equivalent of a "practical ouster of [the owner's] possession," *Transportation Co. v. Chicago*, 99 U.S. 635 (1879). Justice HOLMES recognized in *Mahon*, however, that if the protection against physical appropriations of private property was to be meaningfully enforced, the government's power to redefine the range of interests included in the ownership of property was necessarily constrained by constitutional limits. If, instead, the uses of private property were subject to unbridled, uncompensated qualification under the police power, "the natural tendency of human nature [would be] to extend the qualification more and more until at last private property disappeared." These considerations gave birth in that case to the oft-cited maxim that, "while property may be regulated to a certain extent, if regulation goes too far it will be recognized as a taking."

Nevertheless, our decision in *Mahon* offered little insight into when, and under what circumstances, a given regulation would be seen as going "too far" for purposes of the Fifth Amendment. In 70-odd years of succeeding "regulatory takings" jurisprudence, we have generally eschewed any " 'set formula' " for determining how far is too far, preferring to "engage in . . . essentially ad hoc, factual inquiries." *Penn Central Transportation Co. v. New York City*, 438 U.S. 104 (1978). We have, however, described at least two discrete categories of regulatory action as compensable without case-specific inquiry into the public interest advanced in support of the restraint. The first encompasses regulations that compel the property owner to suffer a physical "invasion" of his property. In general (at least with regard to permanent invasions), no matter how minute the intrusion, and no matter how weighty the public purpose behind it, we have required compensation. For example, in *Loretto v. Teleprompter Manhattan CATV Corp.*, 458 U.S. 419 (1982), we determined that New York's law requiring landlords to allow television cable companies to emplace cable facilities in their apartment buildings constituted a taking, even though the facilities occupied at most only 1½ cubic feet of the landlord's property.

The second situation in which we have found categorical treatment appropriate is where regulation denies all economically beneficial or productive use of land. As we have said on numerous occasions, the Fifth Amendment is violated when land-use regulation "does not substantially advance legitimate state interests or denies an owner economically viable use of his land."

We have never set forth the justification for this rule. Perhaps it is simply, as Justice BRENNAN suggested, that total deprivation of beneficial use is, from the landowner's point of view, the equivalent of a physical appropriation. See *San Diego Gas & Electric Co. v. San Diego*, 450 U.S. [627] (1981). . . . We think . . . that there are good reasons for our frequently expressed belief that when the owner of real property has been called upon to sacrifice all economically beneficial uses in the name of the common good, that is, to leave his property economically idle, he has suffered a taking.

The trial court found Lucas's two beachfront lots to have been rendered valueless by respondent's enforcement of the coastal-zone construction ban. Under Lucas's theory of the case, which rested upon our "no economically viable use" statements, that finding entitled him to compensation. . . . The South Carolina Supreme Court, however, thought otherwise. In its view, the Beachfront Management Act was no ordinary enactment, but involved an exercise of South Carolina's "police powers" to mitigate the harm to the public interest that petitioner's use of his land might occasion. . . . In the court's view, these concessions brought petitioner's challenge within a long line of this Court's cases sustaining against Due Process and Takings Clause challenges the State's use of its "police powers" to enjoin a property owner from activities akin to public nuisances. See *Mugler v. Kansas*, 123 U.S. 623 (1887) (law prohibiting manufacture of alcoholic beverages).

For a number of reasons, however, we think the South Carolina Supreme Court was too quick to conclude that that principle decides the present case. The "harmful or noxious uses" principle was the Court's early attempt to describe in theoretical terms why government may, consistent with the Takings Clause, affect property values by regulation without incurring an obligation to compensate—a reality we nowadays acknowledge explicitly with respect to the full scope of the State's police power. . . . "Harmful or noxious use" analysis was, in other words, simply the progenitor of our more contemporary statements that "land-use regulation does not effect a taking if it 'substantially advances legitimate state interests'. . . ."

The transition from our early focus on control of "noxious" uses to our contemporary understanding of the broad realm within which government may regulate without compensation was an easy one, since the distinction between "harm-preventing" and "benefit-conferring" regulation is often in the eye of the beholder. It is quite possible, for example, to describe in either fashion the ecological, economic, and esthetic concerns that inspired the South Carolina Legislature in the present case. One could say that imposing a servitude on Lucas's land is necessary in order to prevent his use of it from "harming" South Carolina's ecological resources; or, instead, in order to achieve the "benefits" of an ecological preserve. Whether one or the other of the competing characterizations will come to one's lips in a particular case depends primarily upon one's evaluation of the worth of competing uses of real estate. A given restraint will be seen as mitigating "harm" to the adjacent parcels or securing a "benefit" for them, depending upon the observer's evaluation of the relative importance of the use that the restraint favors. Whether Lucas's construction of single-family residences on his parcels should be described as bringing "harm" to South Carolina's adjacent ecological resources thus depends principally upon whether the describer believes that the State's use interest in nurturing those resources is so important that any competing adjacent use must yield.

When it is understood that "prevention of harmful use" was merely our early formulation of the police power justification necessary to sustain (without compensation) any regulatory diminution in value; and that the distinction between regulation that "prevents harmful use" and that which "confers benefits" is difficult, if not impossible, to discern on an objective, value-free basis; it becomes self-evident that noxious-use logic cannot serve as a touchstone to distinguish regulatory "takings"—which require compensation—from regulatory deprivations that do not require compensation. . . .

Where the State seeks to sustain regulation that deprives land of all economically beneficial use, we think it may resist compensation only if the logically antecedent inquiry into the nature of the owner's estate shows that the proscribed use interests were not part of his title to begin with. This accords, we think, with our "takings" jurisprudence, which has traditionally been guided by the understandings of our citizens regarding the content of, and the State's power over, the "bundle of rights" that they acquire when they obtain title to property. It seems to us that the property owner necessarily expects the uses of his property to be restricted, from time to time, by various measures newly enacted by the State in legitimate exercise of its police

powers; "as long recognized, some values are enjoyed under an implied limitation and must yield to the police power." *Pennsylvania Coal Co. v. Mahon.*
And in the case of personal property, by reason of the State's traditionally
high degree of control over commercial dealings, he ought to be aware of
the possibility that new regulation might even render his property economically worthless (at least if the property's only economically productive use is
sale or manufacture for sale). In the case of land, however, we think the notion pressed by the Council that title is somehow held subject to the "implied limitation" that the State may subsequently eliminate all economically
valuable use is inconsistent with the historical compact recorded in the Takings Clause that has become part of our constitutional culture.

Where "permanent physical occupation" of land is concerned, we have refused to allow the government to decree it anew (without compensation), no
matter how weighty the asserted "public interests" involved, *Loretto v. Teleprompter
Manhattan CATV Corp.*—though we assuredly would permit the government
to assert a permanent easement that was a pre-existing limitation upon the
landowner's title. We believe similar treatment must be accorded confiscatory
regulations, i.e., regulations that prohibit all economically beneficial use of land:
Any limitation so severe cannot be newly legislated or decreed (without compensation), but must inhere in the title itself, in the restrictions that background
principles of the State's law of property and nuisance already place upon land
ownership. A law or decree with such an effect must, in other words, do no
more than duplicate the result that could have been achieved in the courts—by
adjacent landowners (or other uniquely affected persons) under the State's law
of private nuisance, or by the State under its complementary power to abate
nuisances that affect the public generally, or otherwise.

On this analysis, the owner of a lakebed, for example, would not be entitled to compensation when he is denied the requisite permit to engage in a
landfilling operation that would have the effect of flooding others' land. . . .
Such regulatory action may well have the effect of eliminating the land's
only economically productive use, but it does not proscribe a productive use
that was previously permissible under relevant property and nuisance principles. The use of these properties for what are now expressly prohibited purposes was always unlawful, and (subject to other constitutional limitations) it
was open to the State at any point to make the implication of those background principles of nuisance and property law explicit. In light of our
traditional resort to "existing rules or understandings that stem from an independent source such as state law" to define the range of interests that qualify
for protection as "property" under the Fifth and Fourteenth Amendments,
this recognition that the Takings Clause does not require compensation
when an owner is barred from putting land to a use that is proscribed by
those "existing rules or understandings" is surely unexceptional. When, however, a regulation that declares "off-limits" all economically productive or
beneficial uses of land goes beyond what the relevant background principles
would dictate, compensation must be paid to sustain it.

The "total taking" inquiry we require today will ordinarily entail (as the
application of state nuisance law ordinarily entails) analysis of, among other
things, the degree of harm to public lands and resources, or adjacent private
property, posed by the claimant's proposed activities, the social value of the
claimant's activities and their suitability to the locality in question, and the relative ease with which the alleged harm can be avoided through measures

taken by the claimant and the government (or adjacent private landowners) alike. The fact that a particular use has long been engaged in by similarly situated owners ordinarily imports a lack of any common-law prohibition (though changed circumstances or new knowledge may make what was previously permissible no longer so). So also does the fact that other landowners, similarly situated, are permitted to continue the use denied to the claimant.

It seems unlikely that common-law principles would have prevented the erection of any habitable or productive improvements on petitioner's land; they rarely support prohibition of the "essential use" of land. The question, however, is one of state law to be dealt with on remand. We emphasize that to win its case South Carolina must do more than proffer the legislature's declaration that the uses Lucas desires are inconsistent with the public interest, or the conclusory assertion that they violate a common-law maxim. . . . As we have said, a "State, by *ipse dixit*, may not transform private property into public property without compensation. . . ." *Webb's Fabulous Pharmacies, Inc. v. Beckwith*, 449 U.S. 155 (1980). Instead, as it would be required to do if it sought to restrain Lucas in a common-law action for public nuisance, South Carolina must identify background principles of nuisance and property law that prohibit the uses he now intends in the circumstances in which the property is presently found. Only on this showing can the State fairly claim that, in proscribing all such beneficial uses, the Beachfront Management Act is taking nothing.

The judgment is reversed, and the case is remanded for proceedings not inconsistent with this opinion.

☐ *Justice BLACKMUN, dissenting.*

Today the Court launches a missile to kill a mouse.

The State of South Carolina prohibited petitioner Lucas from building a permanent structure on his property from 1988 to 1990. Relying on an unreviewed (and implausible) state trial court finding that this restriction left Lucas' property valueless, this Court granted review to determine whether compensation must be paid in cases where the State prohibits all economic use of real estate. According to the Court, such an occasion never has arisen in any of our prior cases, and the Court imagines that it will arise "relatively rarely" or only in "extraordinary circumstances." Almost certainly it did not happen in this case.

Nonetheless, the Court presses on to decide the issue, and as it does, it ignores its jurisdictional limits, remakes its traditional rules of review, and creates simultaneously a new categorical rule and an exception (neither of which is rooted in our prior case law, common law, or common sense). I protest not only the Court's decision, but each step taken to reach it. More fundamentally, I question the Court's wisdom in issuing sweeping new rules to decide such a narrow case. [T]he Court could have reached the result it wanted without inflicting this damage upon our Takings Clause juris-prudence. . . .

☐ *Justice STEVENS, dissenting.*

In addition to lacking support in past decisions, the Court's new rule is wholly arbitrary. A landowner whose property is diminished in value 95% recovers nothing, while an owner whose property is diminished 100% recovers the land's full value. The case at hand illustrates this arbitrariness well. The Beachfront Management Act not only prohibited the building of new dwellings in certain areas, it also prohibited the rebuilding of houses that were "destroyed beyond repair by natural causes or by fire." Thus, if the homes adjacent to Lucas' lot were destroyed by a hurricane one day after the Act took effect, the owners would not be able to rebuild, nor would they be assured recovery. Under the Court's categorical approach, Lucas (who has lost the opportunity to build) recovers, while his neighbors (who have lost both the opportunity to build and their homes) do not recover. The arbitrariness of such a rule is palpable.

Moreover, because of the elastic nature of property rights, the Court's new rule will also prove unsound in practice. In response to the rule, courts may define "property" broadly and only rarely find regulations to effect total takings. This is the approach the Court itself adopts in its revisionist reading of venerable precedents. We are told that—notwithstanding the Court's findings to the contrary in each case—the brewery in *Mugler*—could be put to "other uses" and that, therefore, those cases did not involve total regulatory takings. . . .

Finally, the Court's justification for its new categorical rule is remarkably thin. The Court mentions in passing three arguments in support of its rule; none is convincing. First, the Court suggests that "total deprivation of feasible use is, from the landowner's point of view, the equivalent of a physical appropriation." This argument proves too much. From the "landowner's point of view," a regulation that diminishes a lot's value by 50% is as well "the equivalent" of the condemnation of half of the lot. Yet, it is well established that a 50% diminution in value does not by itself constitute a taking. Thus, the landowner's perception of the regulation cannot justify the Court's new rule.

Second, the Court emphasizes that because total takings are "relatively rare" its new rule will not adversely affect the government's ability to "go on." This argument proves too little. Certainly it is true that defining a small class of regulations that are per se takings will not greatly hinder important governmental functions—but this is true of any small class of regulations. The Court's suggestion only begs the question of why regulations of this particular class should always be found to effect takings. . . .

In short, the Court's new rule is unsupported by prior decisions, arbitrary and unsound in practice, and theoretically unjustified. In my opinion, a categorical rule as important as the one established by the Court today should be supported by more history or more reason than has yet been provided. . . .

Kelo v. City of New London, Connecticut
545 U.S. 469, 125 S.Ct. 2655 (2005)

The city of New London is at the junction of the Thames River and the Long Island Sound in southeastern Connecticut. Decades of economic decline led the state in 1990 to designate the city a "distressed municipality." In 1996, the federal government closed the Naval Undersea Warfare Center, which had been located in the Fort Trumbull area of the city and had employed over 1,500 people. In 1998, the city's unemployment rate was nearly double that of the state, and its population of just under 24,000 residents was at its lowest since 1920. These conditions prompted state and local officials to target New London, and particularly its Fort Trumbull area, for economic revitalization. The New London Development Corporation (NLDC), a private nonprofit entity, was authorized to assist the city in planning economic development. In January 1998, Connecticut approved a $5.35 million bond issue to support the NLDC's planning activities and a $10 million bond issue for the creation of a Fort Trumbull State Park. In February, the pharmaceutical company Pfizer announced that it would build a $300 million research facility in the Fort Trumbull area, and the NLDC hoped that that would draw new business to the area. The Fort Trumbull area is on a peninsula that juts into the Thames River and includes approximately 115 privately owned properties, as well as the thirty-two acres of land formerly occupied by the naval facility. The NLDC's development plan called for the creation of a waterfront conference hotel at the center of a "small urban village," including restaurants and stores, as well as a pedestrian "riverwalk" that would continue down the coast, along with a new U.S. Coast Guard Museum, a renovated marina, and research and development office space. The NLDC's development plan aimed to capitalize on the arrival of the Pfizer facility and the new commerce it would attract. In addition to creating jobs and generating tax revenue, the plan sought to create recreational opportunities on the waterfront and in the park. The city council approved the plan in January 2000 and designated the NLDC its development agent. The city council also authorized the NLDC to purchase property or to acquire property by exercising eminent domain in the city's name. The NLDC successfully negotiated the purchase of most of the real estate in the ninety-acre area, but its negotiations with some homeowners failed and the NLDC initiated the condemnation proceedings against them.

Susette Kelo lived in the Fort Trumbull area and had made extensive improvements to her well-maintained house, which overlooks the Thames River. In December 2000, Kelo and a few other homeowners of condemned property sued New London, claiming that the taking of their properties, even with just compensation, violated the "public use" restriction in the Fifth Amendment, because their properties would not be used for a public purpose, like building a road, but instead sold to private parties for development—development that the city claimed would economically benefit the community. A trial court granted a restraining order prohibiting New London's taking of some of the properties, but on appeal the state supreme court ruled that the city could take all of the properties. Kelo appealed that decision and the Supreme Court granted review.

The state supreme court's decision was affirmed by a five-to-four vote. Justice Stevens delivered the opinion of the Court. Justice Kennedy filed a concurring opinion. Justice O'Connor, joined by Chief Justice Rehnquist and Justices Scalia and Thomas, dissented. Justice Thomas also filed a dissenting opinion.

☐ *Justice STEVENS delivered the opinion of the Court.*

We granted *certiorari* to determine whether a city's decision to take property for the purpose of economic development satisfies the "public use" requirement of the Fifth Amendment. Two polar propositions are perfectly clear. On the one hand, it has long been accepted that the sovereign may not take the property of A for the sole purpose of transferring it to another private party B, even though A is paid just compensation. On the other hand, it is equally clear that a State may transfer property from one private party to another if future "use by the public" is the purpose of the taking; the condemnation of land for a railroad with common-carrier duties is a familiar example. Neither of these propositions, however, determines the disposition of this case.

As for the first proposition, the City would no doubt be forbidden from taking petitioners' land for the purpose of conferring a private benefit on a particular private party. See [*Hawaii Housing Authority v.*] *Midkiff*, 467 U.S. [229 (1984)] ("A purely private taking could not withstand the scrutiny of the public use requirement; it would serve no legitimate purpose of government and would thus be void"). Nor would the City be allowed to take property under the mere pretext of a public purpose, when its actual purpose was to bestow a private benefit. The takings before us, however, would be executed pursuant to a "carefully considered" development plan. The trial judge and all the members of the Supreme Court of Connecticut agreed that there was no evidence of an illegitimate purpose in this case. Therefore, as was true of the statute challenged in *Midkiff*, the City's development plan was not adopted "to benefit a particular class of identifiable individuals."

On the other hand, this is not a case in which the City is planning to open the condemned land—at least not in its entirety—to use by the general public. Nor will the private lessees of the land in any sense be required to operate like common carriers, making their services available to all comers. But although such a projected use would be sufficient to satisfy the public use requirement, this "Court long ago rejected any literal requirement that condemned property be put into use for the general public." Indeed, while many state courts in the mid-19th century endorsed "use by the public" as the proper definition of public use, that narrow view steadily eroded over time. Not only was the "use by the public" test difficult to administer (e.g., what proportion of the public need have access to the property? at what price?), but it proved to be impractical given the diverse and always evolving needs of society. Accordingly, when this Court began applying the Fifth Amendment to the States at the close of the 19th century, it embraced the broader and more natural interpretation of public use as "public purpose." Thus, in a case upholding a mining company's use of an aerial bucket line to transport ore over property it did not own, Justice HOLMES' opinion for the Court stressed "the inadequacy of use by the general public as a universal test." *Strickley v. Highland Boy Gold Mining Co.*, 200 U.S. 527 (1906). We have repeatedly and consistently rejected that narrow test ever since.

The disposition of this case therefore turns on the question whether the City's development plan serves a "public purpose." Without exception, our cases have defined that concept broadly, reflecting our longstanding policy of deference to legislative judgments in this field.

In *Berman v. Parker*, 348 U.S. 26 (1954), this Court upheld a redevelopment plan targeting a blighted area of Washington, DC, in which most of the housing for the area's 5,000 inhabitants was beyond repair. Under the plan, the area would be condemned and part of it utilized for the construction of streets, schools, and other public facilities. The remainder of the land would be leased or sold to private parties for the purpose of redevelopment, including the construction of low-cost housing.

The owner of a department store located in the area challenged the condemnation, pointing out that his store was not itself blighted and arguing that the creation of a "better balanced, more attractive community" was not a valid public use. Writing for a unanimous Court, Justice DOUGLAS refused to evaluate this claim in isolation, deferring instead to the legislative and agency judgment that the area "must be planned as a whole" for the plan to be successful. The Court explained that "community redevelopment programs need not, by force of the Constitution, be on a piecemeal basis—lot by lot, building by building." The public use underlying the taking was unequivocally affirmed: "We do not sit to determine whether a particular housing project is or is not desirable. The concept of the public welfare is broad and inclusive. . . . The values it represents are spiritual as well as physical, aesthetic as well as monetary. It is within the power of the legislature to determine that the community should be beautiful as well as healthy, spacious as well as clean, well-balanced as well as carefully patrolled. In the present case, the Congress and its authorized agencies have made determinations that take into account a wide variety of values. It is not for us to reappraise them. If those who govern the District of Columbia decide that the Nation's Capital should be beautiful as well as sanitary, there is nothing in the Fifth Amendment that stands in the way."

In *Hawaii Housing Authority v. Midkiff*, the Court considered a Hawaii statute whereby fee title was taken from lessors and transferred to lessees (for just compensation) in order to reduce the concentration of land ownership. We unanimously upheld the statute and rejected the Ninth Circuit's view that it was "a naked attempt on the part of the state of Hawaii to take the property of A and transfer it to B solely for B's private use and benefit." Reaffirming *Berman's* deferential approach to legislative judgments in this field, we concluded that the State's purpose of eliminating the "social and economic evils of a land oligopoly" qualified as a valid public use. Our opinion also rejected the contention that the mere fact that the State immediately transferred the properties to private individuals upon condemnation somehow diminished the public character of the taking. . . .

Those who govern the City were not confronted with the need to remove blight in the Fort Trumbull area, but their determination that the area was sufficiently distressed to justify a program of economic rejuvenation is entitled to our deference. The City has carefully formulated an economic development plan that it believes will provide appreciable benefits to the community, including—but by no means limited to—new jobs and increased tax revenue. As with other exercises in urban planning and development, the City is endeavoring to coordinate a variety of commercial, residential, and recreational uses of land, with the hope that they will form a whole greater than the sum of its parts. To effectuate this plan, the City has invoked a state statute that specifically authorizes the use of eminent domain to promote economic development. . . . Because that plan unquestionably serves a public purpose, the takings challenged here satisfy the public use requirement of the Fifth Amendment.

To avoid this result, petitioners urge us to adopt a new bright-line rule that economic development does not qualify as a public use. Putting aside the unpersuasive suggestion that the City's plan will provide only purely economic benefits, neither precedent nor logic supports petitioners' proposal. Promoting economic development is a traditional and long accepted function of government. There is, moreover, no principled way of distinguishing economic development from the other public purposes that we have recognized. . . .

Petitioners contend that using eminent domain for economic development impermissibly blurs the boundary between public and private takings. Again, our cases foreclose this objection. Quite simply, the government's pursuit of a public purpose will often benefit individual private parties. For example, in *Midkiff*, the forced transfer of property conferred a direct and significant benefit on those lessees who were previously unable to purchase their homes. . . .

It is further argued that without a bright-line rule nothing would stop a city from transferring citizen A's property to citizen B for the sole reason that citizen B will put the property to a more productive use and thus pay more taxes. Such a one-to-one transfer of property, executed outside the confines of an integrated development plan, is not presented in this case. While such an unusual exercise of government power would certainly raise a suspicion that a private purpose was afoot, the hypothetical cases posited by petitioners can be confronted if and when they arise. They do not warrant the crafting of an artificial restriction on the concept of public use.

Alternatively, petitioners maintain that for takings of this kind we should require a "reasonable certainty" that the expected public benefits will actually accrue. Such a rule, however, would represent an even greater departure from our precedent. "When the legislature's purpose is legitimate and its means are not irrational, our cases make clear that empirical debates over the wisdom of takings—no less than debates over the wisdom of other kinds of socioeconomic legislation—are not to be carried out in the federal courts." *Midkiff* . . .

Just as we decline to second-guess the City's considered judgments about the efficacy of its development plan, we also decline to second-guess the City's determinations as to what lands it needs to acquire in order to effectuate the project. "It is not for the courts to oversee the choice of the boundary line nor to sit in review on the size of a particular project area. Once the question of the public purpose has been decided, the amount and character of land to be taken for the project and the need for a particular tract to complete the integrated plan rests in the discretion of the legislative branch."

In affirming the City's authority to take petitioners' properties, we do not minimize the hardship that condemnations may entail, notwithstanding the payment of just compensation. We emphasize that nothing in our opinion precludes any State from placing further restrictions on its exercise of the takings power. Indeed, many States already impose "public use" requirements that are stricter than the federal baseline. Some of these requirements have been established as a matter of state constitutional law, while others are expressed in state eminent domain statutes that carefully limit the grounds upon which takings may be exercised. . . .

The judgment of the Supreme Court of Connecticut is affirmed.

☐ *Justice KENNEDY, concurring.*

I join the opinion for the Court and add these further observations. This Court has declared that a taking should be upheld as consistent with the Public Use Clause, U.S. Const., Amdt. 5., as long as it is "rationally related to a conceivable public purpose." *Hawaii Housing Authority v. Midkiff;* see also *Berman v. Parker*, 348 U.S. 26 (1954). This deferential standard of review echoes the rational-basis test used to review economic regulation under the Due Process and Equal Protection Clauses. The determination that a rational-basis standard of review is appropriate does not, however, alter the fact that transfers intended to confer benefits on particular, favored private entities, and with only incidental or pretextual public benefits, are forbidden by the Public Use Clause.

A court applying rational-basis review under the Public Use Clause should strike down a taking that, by a clear showing, is intended to favor a particular private party, with only incidental or pretextual public benefits, just as a court applying rational-basis review under the Equal Protection Clause must strike down a government classification that is clearly intended to injure a particular class of private parties, with only incidental or pretextual public justifications. See *Cleburne v. Cleburne Living Center, Inc.*, 473 U.S. 432 (1985). As the trial court in this case was correct to observe, "Where the purpose [of a taking] is economic development and that development is to be carried out by private parties or private parties will be benefited, the court must decide if the stated public purpose—economic advantage to a city sorely in need of it—is only incidental to the benefits that will be confined on private parties of a development plan." . . .

☐ *Justice O'CONNOR, with whom THE CHIEF JUSTICE, Justice SCALIA, and Justice THOMAS join, dissenting.*

Over two centuries ago, just after the Bill of Rights was ratified, Justice CHASE wrote: "An act of the Legislature (for I cannot call it a law) contrary to the great first principles of the social compact, cannot be considered a rightful exercise of legislative authority. . . . A few instances will suffice to explain what I mean. . . . [A] law that takes property from A. and gives it to B: It is against all reason and justice, for a people to entrust a Legislature with such powers; and, therefore, it cannot be presumed that they have done it." *Calder v. Bull*, 3 Dall. 386 (1798). Today the Court abandons this long-held, basic limitation on government power. Under the banner of economic development, all private property is now vulnerable to being taken and transferred to another private owner, so long as it might be upgraded—i.e., given to an owner who will use it in a way that the legislature deems more beneficial to the public—in the process. To reason, as the Court does, that the incidental public benefits resulting from the subsequent ordinary use of private property render economic development takings "for public use" is to wash out any distinction between private and public use of property—and thereby effectively to delete the words "for public use" from the Takings Clause of the Fifth Amendment. Accordingly I respectfully dissent. . . .

[W]e have read the Fifth Amendment's language to impose two distinct conditions on the exercise of eminent domain: "the taking must be for a 'public use' and 'just compensation' must be paid to the owner." *Brown v. Legal Foundation of Wash.*, 538 U.S. 216 (2003). These two limitations serve to protect "the security of Property," which Alexander Hamilton described to the Philadelphia Convention as one of the "great obj[ects] of Gov[ernment]." Together they ensure stable property ownership by providing safeguards against excessive, unpredictable, or unfair use of the government's eminent domain power—particularly against those owners who, for whatever reasons, may be unable to protect themselves in the political process against the majority's will.

While the Takings Clause presupposes that government can take private property without the owner's consent, the just compensation requirement spreads the cost of condemnations and thus "prevents the public from loading upon one individual more than his just share of the burdens of government." *Monongahela Nav. Co. v. United States*, 148 U.S. 312 (1893). The public use requirement, in turn, imposes a more basic limitation, circumscribing the very scope of the eminent domain power: Government may compel an individual to forfeit her property for the public's use, but not for the benefit of another private person. This requirement promotes fairness as well as security.

Where is the line between "public" and "private" property use? We give considerable deference to legislatures' determinations about what governmental activities will advantage the public. But were the political branches the sole arbiters of the public-private distinction, the Public Use Clause would amount to little more than hortatory fluff. An external, judicial check on how the public use requirement is interpreted, however limited, is necessary if this constraint on government power is to retain any meaning.

Our cases have generally identified three categories of takings that comply with the public use requirement, though it is in the nature of things that the boundaries between these categories are not always firm. Two are relatively straightforward and uncontroversial. First, the sovereign may transfer private property to public ownership—such as for a road, a hospital, or a military base. Second, the sovereign may transfer private property to private parties, often common carriers, who make the property available for the public's use—such as with a railroad, a public utility, or a stadium. But "public ownership" and "use-by-the-public" are sometimes too constricting and impractical ways to define the scope of the Public Use Clause. Thus we have allowed that, in certain circumstances and to meet certain exigencies, takings that serve a public purpose also satisfy the Constitution even if the property is destined for subsequent private use.

This case returns us for the first time in over 20 years to the hard question of when a purportedly "public purpose" taking meets the public use requirement. It presents an issue of first impression: Are economic development takings constitutional? I would hold that they are not. We are guided by two precedents about the taking of real property by eminent domain. In *Berman*, we upheld takings within a blighted neighborhood of Washington, DC. The neighborhood had so deteriorated that, for example, 64.3% of its dwellings were beyond repair. . . .

In *Midkiff*, we upheld a land condemnation scheme in Hawaii whereby title in real property was taken from lessors and transferred to lessees. At that time, the State and Federal Governments owned nearly 49% of the State's land, and another 47% was in the hands of only 72 private landowners. Concentration of land ownership was so dramatic that on the State's most urbanized island, Oahu, 22 landowners owned 72.5% of the fee simple titles. The Hawaii Legislature had concluded that the oligopoly in land ownership was "skewing the State's residential fee simple market, inflating land prices, and injuring the public tranquility and welfare," and therefore enacted a condemnation scheme for redistributing title.

In those decisions, we emphasized the importance of deferring to legislative judgments about public purpose. Because courts are ill-equipped to evaluate the efficacy of proposed legislative initiatives, we rejected as unworkable the idea of courts' " 'deciding on what is and is not a governmental function and . . . invalidating legislation on the basis of their view on that question at the moment of decision, a practice which has proved impracticable in other fields.' " Likewise, we recognized our inability to evaluate whether, in a given case, eminent domain is a necessary means by which to pursue the legislature's ends.

Yet for all the emphasis on deference, *Berman* and *Midkiff* hewed to a bedrock principle without which our public use jurisprudence would collapse: "A purely private taking could not withstand the scrutiny of the public use requirement; it would serve no legitimate purpose of government and would thus be void." *Midkiff*. To protect that principle, those decisions reserved "a role for courts to play in reviewing a legislature's judgment of what constitutes a public use . . . [though] the Court in *Berman* made clear that it is 'an extremely narrow' one."

The Court's holdings in *Berman* and *Midkiff* were true to the principle underlying the Public Use Clause. In both those cases, the extraordinary, precondemnation use of the targeted property inflicted affirmative harm on society—in *Berman* through blight resulting from extreme poverty and in *Midkiff* through oligopoly resulting from extreme wealth. And in both cases, the relevant legislative body had found that eliminating the existing property use was necessary to remedy the harm. Thus a public purpose was realized when the harmful use was eliminated. Because each taking directly achieved a public benefit, it did not matter that the property was turned over to private use. Here, in contrast, New London does not claim that Susette Kelo's . . . well-maintained [home is] the source of any social harm. Indeed, it could not so claim without adopting the absurd argument that any single-family home that might be razed to make way for an apartment building, or any church that might be replaced with a retail store, or any small business that might be more lucrative if it were instead part of a national franchise, is inherently harmful to society and thus within the government's power to condemn.

In moving away from our decisions sanctioning the condemnation of harmful property use, the Court today significantly expands the meaning of public use. It holds that the sovereign may take private property currently put to ordinary private use, and give it over for new, ordinary private use, so long as the new use is predicted to generate some secondary benefit for the public—such as increased tax revenue, more jobs, maybe even aesthetic pleasure. But nearly any lawful use of real private property can be said to generate some incidental benefit to the public. Thus, if predicted (or even guaranteed) positive side-effects are enough to render transfer from one private party to another constitutional, then the words "for public use" do not realistically exclude any takings, and thus do not exert any constraint on the eminent domain power. . . .

It was possible after *Berman* and *Midkiff* to imagine unconstitutional transfers from A to B. Those decisions endorsed government intervention when private property use had veered to such an extreme that the public was suffering as a consequence. Today nearly all real property is susceptible to condemnation on the Court's theory. Any property may now be taken for the benefit of another private party, but the fallout from this decision will not be random. The beneficiaries are likely to be those citizens with disproportionate influence and power in the political process, including large corporations and development firms. As for the victims, the government now has license to transfer property from those with fewer resources to those with more. . . .

□ *Justice THOMAS, dissenting.*

Long ago, William Blackstone wrote that "the law of the land . . . postpone[s] even public necessity to the sacred and inviolable rights of private property." *Commentaries on the Laws of England* (1765). The Framers embodied that principle in the Constitution, allowing the government to take property not for "public necessity," but instead for "public use." Amdt. 5. Defying this understanding, the Court replaces the Public Use Clause with a " '[P]ublic [P]urpose' " Clause, a restriction that is satisfied, the Court instructs, so long as the purpose is "legitimate" and the means "not irrational." This deferential shift in phraseology enables the Court to hold, against all common sense, that a costly urban-renewal project whose stated purpose is a vague promise of new jobs and increased tax revenue, but which is also suspiciously agreeable to the Pfizer Corporation, is for a "public use."

I cannot agree. If such "economic development" takings are for a "public use," any taking is, and the Court has erased the Public Use Clause from our Constitution, as Justice O'CONNOR powerfully argues in dissent. I do not believe that this Court can eliminate liberties expressly enumerated in the Constitution and therefore join her dissenting opinion. Regrettably, however, the Court's error runs deeper than this. Today's decision is simply the latest in a string of our cases construing the Public Use Clause to be a virtual nullity, without the slightest nod to its original meaning. In my view, the Public Use Clause, originally understood, is a meaningful limit on the government's eminent domain power. Our cases have strayed from the Clause's original meaning, and I would reconsider them. . . .

The consequences of today's decision are not difficult to predict, and promise to be harmful. So-called "urban renewal" programs provide some compensation for the properties they take, but no compensation is possible for the subjective value of these lands to the individuals displaced and the indignity inflicted by uprooting them from their homes. Allowing the government to take property solely for public purposes is bad enough, but extending the concept of public purpose to encompass any economically beneficial goal guarantees that these losses will fall disproportionately on poor communities. Those communities are not only systematically less likely to put their lands to the highest and best social use, but are also the least politically powerful. If ever there were justification for intrusive judicial review of constitutional provisions that protect "discrete and insular minorities," *United States v. Carolene Products Co.*, 304 U.S. 144 (1938), surely that principle would apply with great force to the powerless groups and individuals the Public Use Clause protects. The deferential standard this Court has adopted for the Public Use Clause is therefore deeply perverse. It encourages "those citizens with disproportionate influence and power in the political process, including large corporations and development firms" to victimize the weak.

Those incentives have made the legacy of this Court's "public purpose" test an unhappy one. In the 1950's, no doubt emboldened in part by the expansive understanding of "public use" this Court adopted in *Berman*, cities "rushed to draw plans" for downtown development. "Of all the families displaced by urban renewal from 1949 through 1963, 63 percent of those whose race was known were nonwhite, and of these families, 56 percent of nonwhites and 38 percent of whites had incomes low enough to qualify for public housing, which, however, was seldom available to them." Public works projects in the 1950's and 1960's destroyed predominantly minority communities in St. Paul, Minnesota, and Baltimore, Maryland. In 1981, urban planners in Detroit, Michigan, uprooted the largely "lower-income and elderly" Poletown neighborhood for the benefit of the General Motors Corporation. Urban renewal projects have long been associated with the displacement of blacks; "[i]n cities across the country, urban renewal came to be known as 'Negro removal.' " Over 97 percent of the individuals forcibly removed from their homes by the "slum-clearance" project upheld by this Court in *Berman* were black. Regrettably, the predictable consequence of the Court's decision will be to exacerbate these effects. . . .

■ THE DEVELOPMENT OF LAW
Other Important Rulings on the Takings Clause

CASE	VOTE	RULING
Agins v. City of Tiburon, 447 U.S. 255 (1980)	9:0	Relying on *Village of Euclid v. Ambler Realty Co.*, 272 U.S. 365 (1926), the Court approved a San

San Francisco zoning ordinance requiring the construction of single-family homes on a minimum of one-acre lots, over the objections of owners of five acres of undeveloped land of great value because of its view of San Francisco Bay. The owners had contended the zoning restriction amounted to a taking of their property.

Loretto v. Teleprompter Man-hattan CATV Corporation, 458 U.S. 419 (1982)	6:3	Affirmed a takings-clause challenge of a New York law prohibiting landlords from interfering with cable companies' installation

of cables and boxes in their buildings and specifying that property owners may not demand compensation in excess of a limit set by a state commission. When so holding, the Court observed that "Teleprompter's cable installation on appellant's building constitutes a taking under the traditional test. The installation involved a direct physical attachment of plates, boxes, wires, bolts, and screws to the building, completely occupying space immediately above and upon the roof and along the building's exterior wall."

Nollan v. California Coastal Commission, 483 U.S. 825 (1987)	5:4	Writing for a bare majority, Justice Scalia held that the just compensation clause was violated by California's regulations requi-

ring beachfront property owners to agree to a public easement across their property as a condition of receiving a building permit.

Keystone Bituminous Coal Association v. DeBene-dictis, 480 U.S. 470 (1987)	5:4	Rejected the claims of a coal company attacking the constitutionality of a Pennsylvania law limiting the mining of more than 50

percent of the coal beneath government and commercial buildings, private residences, and cemeteries to ensure surface support.

First English Evangelical Lutheran Church v. County of Los Angeles, 482 U.S. 304 (1987)	6:3	Held that the just compensation clause was violated by an ordinance, passed after a major flood, that prohibited the construction

and reconstruction of buildingson certain land affected by the flood. Writing for the majority, Chief Justice Rehnquist held that the ordinance constituted a taking of property, for which the city owed the owner just compensation. Justices Stevens, O'Connor, and Blackmun dissented.

CASE	VOTE	RULING
Pennell v. City of San Jose, 485 U.S. 1 (1988)	6:2	Rejected an attack by landlords lords on a city rent control ordinance limiting rent increases to

18 percent and allowing tenants to demand a hearing as to whether a rent increase was "reasonable under the circumstances"—circumstances that included the tenant's hardship.

| *Dolan v. City of Tigard,* 512 U.S. 374 (1994) | 5:4 | Writing for a bare majority, Chief Justice Rehnquist held that when government sets downland-use |

restrictions affecting private property it must show a "rough proportionality" between the restrictions and the harm to be prevented. Notably, the chief justice reaffirmed that the government may simply ban all development in flood plains, for instance, and that "no precise mathematical calculation" was required to justify land-use restrictions. As a result of *Dolan,* state and local governments must satisfy a two-pronged test: first, they must show that their restrictions serve a "legitimate public purpose" and, second, when imposing their restrictions they must undertake "some sort of individualized determination" establishing a "rough proportionality" between the restrictions and the harms to be averted.

| *Bennis v. Michigan,* 516 U.S. 442 (1996) | 5:4 | Writing for the majority, Chief Justice Rehnquist rejected the claim that the government vio- |

lates due process and the Fifth Amendment's takings clause when it undertakes the forfeiture of an innocent person's property, which was used in an illegal activity. Justices Breyer, Kennedy, Souter, and Stevens dissented.

| *Phillips v. Washington Legal Foundation,* 524 U.S. 156 (1998) | 5:4 | In the 1980s, Texas and 48 other states established Interest on Lawyers Trust Account (IOLTA) pro- |

grams. Under them, certain funds from clients received by attorneys are held in federally authorized "Negotiable Order of Withdrawal" accounts. The interest income of these accounts is paid to the state and used to finance legal services for low-income people. In a narrow ruling for a bare majority, Chief Justice

(continues)

■ THE DEVELOPMENT OF LAW
Other Important Rulings on the Takings Clause (continued)

Rehnquist held that the interest income does constitute "property" under the Fifth Amendment, but declined to rule on whether IOLTA programs constitute a "takings" and whether "just compensation" is required, because those issues had not been addressed by the lower courts.

CASE	VOTE	RULING
Tahoe-Sierra Preservation Council, Inc. v. Tahoe Regional Planning Agency, 535 U.S. 302 (2002)	6:3	Upheld a three-year building moratorium on construction surrounding Lake Tahoe, in order for regional governments to develop natural resources preserva-

tion and development plans, over the claim that the temporary moratorium constituted a "categorical" takings under the Fifth Amendment and deprived developers of the economically viable use of their land. Chief Justice Rehnquist and Justices Scalia and Thomas dissented.

CASE	VOTE	RULING
Lingle v. Chevron, 544 U.S. 528 (2005)	9:0	Writing for a unanimous Court, Justice O'Connor upheld Hawaii's law capping the rent paid

by gasoline dealers and ruled that it was not an unconstitutional takings. The appellate court had applied a test, suggested in *Agins v. City of*

Tiburon, 447 U.S. 255 (1980), that "[t]he application of a general zoning law to particular property effects a takings if the ordinance does not substantially advance state interests." But Justice O'Connor ruled that the "substantially advance state interests" test was *dictum* and inappropriate for determining when a takings of private property occurs. Instead, as other precedents established, in particular *Penn Central Transportation Co. v. New York*, 438 U.S. 104 (1978), a multi-factored and more deferential test should apply because taxes and fees, like that at issue here, are not per se takings.

CASE	VOTE	RULING
Stop the Beach Renourishment v. Florida, 130 S.Ct. 2592 (2010)	8:1	Writing for the Court, Justice Scalia affirmed the state supreme court's ruling rejecting the claim that beach restoration of

submerged land constituted takings under the Fifth Amendment, reaffirming the previous ruling in *Lucas v. South Carolina Coastal Council*, 505 U.S. 1003 (1992). Florida's Shore Preservation Act established procedures to restore eroded shorelines damaged by hurricanes and was challenged by beachfront property owners as a takings without just compensation, because it extended the beach line for public use. The state supreme court held that the law fixing shoreline boundaries did not unconstitutionally deprive upland owners of their property rights without just compensation. Justice Thomas dissented.

RESEARCHING LEGAL MATERIALS

The Internet offers numerous resources for legal research. Conducting legal research on the Internet is similar to researching printed legal documents in libraries. Indeed, most of those legal documents, such as court decisions, may be found on the Internet. Conducting legal research on the Internet, thus, may be more efficient and convenient for those with access to it. But, however legal research is conducted, the researcher must have an understanding of legal sources as well as a research strategy.

I. Conducting Legal Research:

A. LEGAL SOURCES:

Generally, legal research aims to discover *primary* and *secondary* legal authorities to support a legal argument or position (i.e., thesis statement).

1. PRIMARY AUTHORITIES:

Primary authorities are the most persuasive sources because they represent most accurately what the law "is." Examples of primary authorities include federal and state constitutions, statutes, case opinions (written by judges deciding specific cases or controversies), and administrative regulations.

The decisions of the Supreme Court are officially published in the *United States Reports.* In addition, two companies print editions of the Court's decisions. There is the *Lawyers' Edition,* published by the Lawyers' Cooperative, and *The Supreme Court Reporter,* published by West Publishing Company. The decisions of federal courts of appeals are usually found in West's *Federal Reporter* (or *Federal Reporter,* 2d, 3d, or 4th series, respectively). Federal district court decisions may be found in West's *Federal Supplement* series. Most states publish some of the rulings of their courts and West publishes a series of regional reporters that reprint the decisions and opinions of the highest courts in the states. These sources may be found on the Internet (as discussed below) through university and law school Internet servers, or through commercial servers such as *Lexis-Nexis* and *Westlaw.*

Note that primary legal authorities differ in their weight or authoritativeness. The decisions and opinions of the Supreme Court, for instance, are more authoritative than those of lower federal courts. Likewise, the Court's decision usually carries more weight than a concurring or dissenting opinion.

2. SECONDARY AUTHORITIES:

Secondary authorities provide "secondary" perspectives on the law or, more precisely, on how the law may or should be interpreted. Examples of secondary authorities include law review articles (written by law students or scholars), legal treatises and annotations, legal encyclopedias, books, and academic journals (in law, legal history, jurisprudence, and social sciences, like *Judicature* and *The Journal of Supreme Court History*), as well as legal newspapers (such as *Legal Times* and *The National Law Journal*).

B. DEVELOPING A RESEARCH STRATEGY:

While it is impossible to outline a research strategy that would work best for everyone, there are some general considerations in developing one. First, legal research usually involves gaining a broad understanding of the context of a case or controversy, and then moving to the narrower, specific issues presented, as well as to the competing arguments and justifications for resolving those issues one way or the other. In other words, initially consider the historical, philosophical, and political bases for, as well as the subsequent development of, a legal doctrine, such as federalism or free speech, before turning to the specific case or controversy to be addressed. If you know very little about the subject, it is wise to consult secondary authorities *first* about what the law is and how and why it has developed. Second, once you have an understanding of the general legal issues and law involved, then examine the most relevant *primary authorities*, described above. The most critical step in conducting legal research is to read (or re-read) the pertinent provision(s) of the Constitution, statute, or administrative regulation, and then consider *what the Supreme Court has said* about those provisions and the issue presented, carefully analyzing the relevant or governing judicial opinions. Remember that the aim of legal research is to advance a position, a thesis, by persuasively justifying it with an analysis of and arguments drawn from the primary and secondary authorities discussed above.

II. Legal Materials and Law-Related Sources on the Web:

Legal materials, documents, judicial opinions, and other law-related sources on the Web are available through a number of legal search engines. One of the most useful is *Findlaw* at **www.findlaw.com**. Another useful site to government links is *Firstgov*'s at **www.firstgov.org**. The Supreme Court of the United States maintains a site at **www.supremecourt.gov**, containing transcripts of oral arguments and opinions in recent cases. Also useful for researching decisions, areas of law, and votes is the Supreme Court Database at **www.supremecourtdatabase.org**.

These and other law-related resources are linked and available at the web site that W. W. Norton maintains for the casebook and the annual *Supreme Court Watch* at **www.wwnorton.com/scww/**.

THE HOW, WHY, AND WHAT TO BRIEFING AND CITING COURT CASES

A. HOW TO BRIEF A CASE:

There is no one "best way" to read and analyze cases. However, an understanding of the decision and opinions may best be acquired by following a prescribed pattern or outline that points up the essential issues of each case. It is suggested that students read the case in its entirety at least once before "briefing" the case along the lines suggested below.

1. TITLE AND CITATION: (*Marbury v. Madison*, 1 Cranch (5 U.S.) 137 (1803).)

2. FACTS OF THE CASE: A brief statement of the circumstances that brought about this case or controversy, identifying the parties and the holding of lower courts.

(Outgoing President Adams commissioned Marbury to serve as a district judge, but the commission went undelivered by his secretary of state, John Marshall. When President Jefferson came into office, he directed his secretary of state, James Madison, not to deliver Marbury's commission. Marbury filed an affidavit requiring Madison to show cause why a writ of mandamus should not be issued directing him to deliver the commission. Section 13 of the Judiciary Act of 1789, Marbury argued, empowered the Court to issue writs of mandamus.)

3. LEGAL QUESTION(S) PRESENTED: The question presented is revealed by the statement of facts, which should indicate the nature of the conflict of interests the Court must resolve. The legal question presented is often concisely stated by the Court at the outset of an opinion or the sections in an opinion dealing with specific questions presented. You should answer each question presented "yes" or "no."

(1. Has Marbury a right to his commission? Yes.

2. If a right has been violated do the laws afford a remedy? Yes.

3. Is the Court the legal body to afford such a remedy? No.

4. Does the Court have the power to declare a law unconstitutional? Yes.)

4. HOLDING: A statement of the Court's ruling and whether it affirmed or reversed the lower court's decision.

(Section 13 of the Judiciary Act of 1789 is unconstitutional.)

5. Opinion for the Court: The opinion refers to the legal reasoning which the Court offers as a justification for its holding. The Court's reasoning should be outlined point by point.

(1-A. Completion of the appointment establishes that Marbury has a legal right to his commission. 2-A. Authorities (Blackstone) show that where there is a legal right there exists a legal remedy. 2-B. Madison violated Marbury's right, and thus a remedy is due Marbury. 3-A. The Court cannot provide the remedy requested, however, since that would require an exercise of its original jurisdiction in violation of Article III of the Constitution. 3-B. Congress cannot alter the Court's original jurisdiction or expand its powers specified there. Section 13 appears to have enlarged the Court's power by giving it the power to issue writs of mandamus in original and appellate cases. 4-A. The Court has the power to declare a law unconstitutional because (1) of the Supremacy Clause of Article VI and (2) Congress may not enlarge the Court's original jurisdiction under Article III. 4-B. It is the duty of the Court "to say what the law is" because (1) judges take an oath to uphold the Constitution and (2) "the Constitution specifies that a law repugnant to the Constitution is void, and courts as well as other departments are bound by it." (3) Since the Court's power extends to all cases and controversies under the Constitution, the Court must declare Section 13 unconstitutional.)

6. Separate Opinions: Both concurring opinions (opinions that agree with the Court's holding but disagree with some or all of its reasoning) and dissenting opinions (opinions that disagree with the Court's result and reasoning) should be noted and their major points emphasized.

(There were no separate opinions filed in this case.)

7. Comments and Evaluation: A statement of the case's legal, history, and political importance, as well as criticisms of the justices' opinions and reasoning.

(1. Chief Justice Marshall should have disqualified himself from participating in the case. 2. The case did not need to be decided; it could have been remanded to a district court, since the Court had no jurisdiction. 3. Marshall's reading of Section 13 is open to criticism. 4. The case is the watershed ruling in which the Court asserted and rationalized the power of judicial review. 5. However, the Court's reasoning is not unassailable—Article III does not expressly provide for judicial review and other officials take an oath to uphold the Constitution as well; *Eakin v. Raub* on triparite or "departmental theory" of constitutional interpretation. 6. *Marbury v. Madison*, however, does not assert "judicial supremacy" as some Court-watchers and justices subsequently claimed.)

B. WHY BRIEF CASES?

Briefing cases has immediate and long-term benefits: the student will have read the case thoroughly and carefully and will have a permanent condensed record of the case. The exercise itself forces the student to come to terms with his or her understanding of the case, prepares the student for lectures and discussion, and will prove an invaluable aid in studying for the midterm and final examination.

C. CASE CITATION: Why, What, Where, and How

1. WHY FOLLOW LEGAL CITATION FORM?

a. Legal writing requires frequent citation of authority and evaluation of that authority depends on proper citation form.

b. In this context, citations in the text greatly aid the reader, eliminating the necessity of moving back and forth between text and footnotes.

2. WHAT TO CITE (in order of their decreasing legal weight):

a. Opinions (majority) for the Supreme Court.

b. Supreme Court plurality, concurring or dissenting opinions.

c. Circuit Court opinions.

d. District Court opinions.

e. Other sources: (1) state court opinions if the issue is one of state law; (2) law review articles *only* if there is no Supreme Court opinion or if the issue involves, for example, economic analysis.

f. Do not cite a lower court opinion or a non-majority opinion as binding precedent; they are persuasive authority only.

3. WHERE DOES THE CITATION APPEAR?

a. As appositives: In *Brown v. Board of Education*, 347 U.S. 483 (1954), the Court struck down racial segregation of public schools.

b. In citation sentences: Racial segregation of public schools violates the equal protection clause. *Brown v. Board of Education*, 347 U.S. 483 (1954).

4. HOW TO CITE CASES PROPERLY:

a. An opinion for the Supreme Court: *Katzenback v. Morgan*, 384 U.S. 641 (1966), or *Katzenbach v. Morgan*, 384 U.S. 641 (1966) (Brennan, J.).

b. A specific page in the Court's opinion: *Katzenbach v. Morgan*, 384 U.S. 641, 644 (1966).

c. Concurring and dissenting opinions:
Sherbert v. Verner, 374 U.S. 398, 477 (1963) (Stewart, J., con. op.).
Sherbert v. Verner, 374 U.S. 398, 495 (1963) (Harlan and White, J.J., dis. op.).

d. Circuit Court cases: *Yeager v. Estelle*, 489 F.2d 276 (5th Cir., 1973).

e. District Court cases: *Dodd v. Smith*, 389 F. Supp. 154 (D. Mass., 1975).

f. Explanatory phrases and case history: *Jackson v. Metropolitan Edison Co.*, 348 F. Supp. 954 (M.D., Pa., 1972), *aff'd.*, 483 F. 2d 754 (3d Cir., 1974), *rev'd.*, 419 U.S. 345 (1974).

g. Later references to a case previously cited in full:

(1) Use *Id.* (legal version of *Ibid.*) when the later citation immediately follows the full citation: *Id., at 427.*

(2) Use abbreviated case names, if desired, where other case citations intervene: *Jackson,* at 420 (specific page), or *Jackson, supra.* (full opinion).

5. Additional References:

See Albert Melone, *Researching Constitutional Law* (New York: Scott, Foresman/Little, Brown, 1990), or the "Blue Book," *A Uniform System of Citation* (Cambridge, MA: Harvard Law Review Association, 1999).

MEMBERS OF THE
SUPREME COURT
OF THE UNITED STATES

CHIEF JUSTICES

	APPOINTING PRESIDENT	DATES OF SERVICE
Jay, John	Washington	1789–1795
Rutledge, John	Washington	1795–1795
Ellsworth, Oliver	Washington	1796–1800
Marshall, John	Adams, J.	1801–1835
Taney, Roger Brooke	Jackson	1836–1864
Chase, Salmon Portland	Lincoln	1864–1873
Waite, Morrison Remick	Grant	1874–1888
Fuller, Melville Weston	Cleveland	1888–1910
White, Edward Douglass	Taft	1910–1921
Taft, William Howard	Harding	1921–1930
Hughes, Charles Evans	Hoover	1930–1941
Stone, Harlan Fiske	Roosevelt, F.	1941–1946
Vinson, Frederick Moore	Truman	1946–1953
Warren, Earl	Eisenhower	1953–1969
Burger, Warren Earl	Nixon	1969–1986
Rehnquist, William Hubbs	Reagan	1986–2005
Roberts, Jr., John G.	Bush, G. W.	2005–

ASSOCIATE JUSTICES

	APPOINTING PRESIDENT	DATES OF SERVICE
Rutledge, John	Washington	1790–1791
Cushing, William	Washington	1790–1810
Wilson, James	Washington	1789–1798
Blair, John	Washington	1790–1796
Iredell, James	Washington	1790–1799
Johnson, Thomas	Washington	1792–1793
Paterson, William	Washington	1793–1806
Chase, Samuel	Washington	1796–1811

	APPOINTING PRESIDENT	DATES OF SERVICE
Washington, Bushrod	Adams, J.	1799–1829
Moore, Alfred	Adams, J.	1800–1804
Johnson, William	Jefferson	1804–1834
Livingston, Henry Brockholst	Jefferson	1807–1823
Todd, Thomas	Jefferson	1807–1826
Duvall, Gabriel	Madison	1811–1835
Story, Joseph	Madison	1812–1845
Thompson, Smith	Monroe	1823–1843
Trimble, Robert	Adams, J. Q.	1826–1828
McLean, John	Jackson	1830–1861
Baldwin, Henry	Jackson	1830–1844
Wayne, James Moore	Jackson	1835–1867
Barbour, Philip Pendleton	Jackson	1836–1841
Catron, John	Van Buren	1837–1865
McKinley, John	Van Buren	1838–1852
Daniel, Peter Vivian	Van Buren	1842–1860
Nelson, Samuel	Tyler	1845–1872
Woodbury Levi	Polk	1845–1851
Grier, Robert Cooper	Polk	1846–1870
Curtis, Benjamin Robbins	Fillmore	1851–1857
Campbell, John Archibald	Pierce	1853–1861
Clifford, Nathan	Buchanan	1858–1881
Swayne, Noah Haynes	Lincoln	1862–1881
Miller, Samuel Freeman	Lincoln	1862–1890
Davis, David	Lincoln	1862–1877
Field, Stephen Johnson	Lincoln	1863–1897
Strong, William	Grant	1870–1880
Bradley, Joseph P.	Grant	1870–1892
Hunt, Ward	Grant	1873–1882
Harlan, John Marshall	Hayes	1877–1911
Woods, William Burnham	Hayes	1881–1887
Matthews, Stanley	Garfield	1881–1889
Gray, Horace	Arthur	1882–1902
Blatchford, Samuel	Arthur	1882–1893
Lamar, Lucius Quintus C.	Cleveland	1888–1893
Brewer, David Josiah	Harrison	1890–1910
Brown, Henry Billings	Harrison	1891–1906
Shiras, George, Jr.	Harrison	1892–1903
Jackson, Howell Edmunds	Harrison	1893–1895
White, Edward Douglass	Cleveland	1894–1910
Peckham Rufus Wheeler	Cleveland	1896–1909
McKenna, Joseph	McKinley	1898–1925
Holmes, Oliver Wendell	Roosevelt, T.	1902–1932

ASSOCIATE JUSTICES *(continued)*

	APPOINTING PRESIDENT	DATES OF SERVICE
Day, William Rufus	Roosevelt, T.	1903–1922
Moody, William Henry	Roosevelt, T.	1906–1910
Lurton, Horace Harmon	Taft	1910–1914
Hughes, Charles Evans	Taft	1910–1916
Van Devanter, Willis	Taft	1911–1937
Lamar, Joseph Rucker	Taft	1911–1916
Pitney, Mahlon	Taft	1912–1922
McReynolds, James Clark	Wilson	1914–1941
Brandeis, Louis Dembitz	Wilson	1916–1939
Clarke, John Hessin	Wilson	1916–1922
Sutherland, George	Harding	1921–1938
Butler, Pierce	Harding	1923–1939
Sanford, Edward Terry	Harding	1923–1930
Stone, Harlan Fiske	Coolidge	1925–1941
Roberts, Owen Josephus	Hoover	1930–1945
Cardozo, Benjamin Nathan	Hoover	1932–1938
Black, Hugo Lafayette	Roosevelt, F.	1937–1971
Reed, Stanley Forman	Roosevelt, F.	1938–1957
Frankfurter, Felix	Roosevelt, F.	1939–1962
Douglas, William Orville	Roosevelt, F.	1939–1975
Murphy, Frank	Roosevelt, F.	1940–1949
Byrnes, James Francis	Roosevelt, F.	1941–1942
Jackson, Robert Houghwout	Roosevelt, F.	1941–1954
Rutledge, Wiley Blount	Roosevelt, F.	1943–1949
Burton, Harold Hitz	Truman	1945–1958
Clark, Thomas Campbell	Truman	1949–1967
Minton, Sherman	Truman	1949–1956
Harlan, John Marshall	Eisenhower	1955–1971
Brennan, William Joseph, Jr.	Eisenhower	1956–1990
Whittaker, Charles Evans	Eisenhower	1957–1962
Stewart, Potter	Eisenhower	1958–1981
White, Byron Raymond	Kennedy	1962–1993
Goldberg, Arthur Joseph	Kennedy	1962–1965
Fortas, Abe	Johnson, L.	1965–1969
Marshall, Thurgood	Johnson, L.	1967–1991
Blackmun, Harry A.	Nixon	1970–1994
Powell, Lewis Franklin, Jr.	Nixon	1972–1987
Rehnquist, William Hubbs	Nixon	1972–1986
Stevens, John Paul	Ford	1975–2010
O'Connor, Sandra Day	Reagan	1981–2006
Scalia, Antonin	Reagan	1986–

	APPOINTING PRESIDENT	DATES OF SERVICE
Kennedy, Anthony	Reagan	1988–
Souter, David Hackett	Bush, G. H. W.	1990–2009
Thomas, Clarence	Bush, G. H. W.	1991–
Ginsburg, Ruth Bader	Clinton	1993–
Breyer, Stephen G.	Clinton	1994–
Alito, Jr., Samuel A.	Bush, G. W.	2006–
Sotomayor, Sonia	Obama	2009–
Kagan, Elena	Obama	2010–

Biographies of Current Justices

Chief Justice John G. Roberts, Jr., was born in Buffalo, New York, on January 27, 1955. After attending a Catholic boarding school in Indiana, he earned his B.A. from Harvard University and his J.D. from Harvard Law School, where he served as managing editor of the *Harvard Law Review.* Upon graduating he served as a law clerk for U.S. Court of Appeals for the Second Circuit Judge Henry Friendly and, subsequently, for then Associate Justice William H. Rehnquist. From 1981 to 1982 he worked in the administration of President Ronald Reagan as a special assistant to the attorney general and as an associate counsel to the White House Council from 1982 to 1986. Roberts then went into private legal practice in Washington, DC, but left to serve as deputy solicitor general in the administration of President George H. W. Bush from 1989 to 1993. In 1992 President Bush nominated him to serve on the U.S. Court of Appeals for the District of Columbia Circuit, but no Senate vote on his confirmation was taken and he returned to private legal practice. During his time in government and private practice Roberts argued thirty-nine cases, and won twenty-five, before the Supreme Court. In 2001, President George W. Bush renominated him to the Court of Appeals for the District of Columbia Circuit, but his nomination failed to make it out of the Democratic-controlled Senate Judiciary Committee. He was, again, renominated in 2003 and confirmed for a seat on the appellate bench. In 2005, following the announced retirement of Justice Sandra Day O'Connor, President Bush nominated him to fill her seat on the Supreme Court, but following the death of Chief Justice William H. Rehnquist, Justice Roberts was nominated for the chief justiceship. He received the Senate's confirmation as the seventeenth chief justice and 109th justice by a vote of 78 to 22. See *Confirmation Hearing on the Nomination of John G. Roberts, Jr. to be Chief Justice of the United States: Hearing Before the Senate Committee on the Judiciary*, 109th Cong. (2005). Among his extrajudicial writings is "Oral Advocacy and the Re-emergence of a Supreme Court Bar," 30 *Journal of Supreme Court History* 68 (2005). Since becoming chief justice, Roberts has appeared on ABC's *Nightline* and has given a number of interviews; see, e.g., Jeffrey Rosen, "Roberts' Rules," *The Atlantic Monthly* (Jan./Feb., 2007). See also Laura Krugman Ray, "The Style of a Skeptic: The Opinions of Chief Justice Roberts," 83 *Indiana Law Journal* 997 (2008).

Justice Samuel Anthony Alito, Jr., was born in Trenton, New Jersey, on April 1, 1950. After graduating with an A.B. from Princeton University in 1972, he earned his J.D. from Yale Law School in 1975. He subsequently clerked for U.S. Court of Appeals for the Third Circuit Judge Leonard Garth, and then worked as an assistant U.S. attorney and during the administration of President Ronald Reagan as an assistant to the solicitor general (from 1981 to 1985) and as a deputy assistant attorney general (from 1985 to 1987). During the administration of President George H. W. Bush, he served as a U.S. attorney, before President Bush nominated him to and he was confirmed for a seat on the U.S. Court of Appeals for the Third Circuit in 1990. In 2005 he was nominated by President George W. Bush to fill the seat of retiring Justice Sandra Day O'Connor. He was confirmed by the Senate as the 110th justice in January 2006 by a vote of 58 to 42.

Justice Stephen G. Breyer was born in San Francisco, California, on August 15, 1938. After graduating from Stanford University, he earned a second B.A. as a Marshall Scholar at Oxford University and then received his law degree from Harvard Law School. After clerking for a year with liberal Justice Arthur J. Goldberg, Breyer went into private practice for a few years. In 1970, he went back to Harvard Law School, where he taught administrative law and regulation. During the Watergate investigation of the Nixon administration's illegal activities, he served as an assistant special prosecutor before returning to teaching at Harvard until 1979, when he became chief counsel for the Senate Judiciary Committee. In 1980, Democratic president Jimmy Carter appointed him to the Court of Appeals for the First Circuit, where he served until President Clinton appointed him to the Supreme Court in 1994. See U.S. Congress, Senate, Committee on the Judiciary, *Hearings before the Committee on the Judiciary, U.S. Senate, One Hundred Third Congress, 2nd Session, on the Nomination of Judge Stephen G. Breyer to the Supreme Court of the United States, July 12, 13, 14, and 15, 1994* (Washington, DC: Government Printing Office, 1995). Among Justice Breyer's many publications are "Our Democratic Constitution," 77 *New York University Law Review* 245 (2002); "Judicial Review," 78 *Texas Law Review* 761 (2000); and *Active Liberty: Interpreting Our Democratic Constitution* (New York: Knopf, 2005). For a discussion of Justice Breyer's judicial philosophy, see and compare Paul Gewirtz, "The Pragmatic Passion of Stephen Breyer," 115 *Yale Law Journal* 1675 (2006); Cass Sunstein, "Justice Breyer's Democratic Pragmatism," 115 *Yale Law Journal* 1719 (2006); Robert Bork, "Enforcing a 'Mood,' " *New Criterion* 63 (Feb., 2006); Richard Posner, "Justice Breyer Throws Down the Gauntlet," 115 *Yale Law Journal* 1699 (2006); and Linda Greenhouse, "The Breyer Project: "Why Couldn't You Work This Thing Out?" 4 *Charleston Law Review* 37 (2009).

Justice Ruth Bader Ginsburg was born on March 15, 1933, in Brooklyn, New York. After graduating from Cornell University, she attended Harvard Law School but transferred and graduated from Columbia University School of Law. Unable to find a law firm in New York that would hire a female attorney,

Ginsburg served for several years as a research associate at Columbia Law School and then joined Rutgers University School of Law, where she rose to the rank of full professor before becoming the first female professor at Columbia Law School. Besides teaching, Ginsburg served as the director of the American Civil Liberties Union's Women's Rights Project and argued six (won five) important gender-based discrimination cases before the Supreme Court. In 1980 she was appointed to the Court of Appeals for the District of Columbia Circuit, and in 1993 she was appointed to the Supreme Court by President Bill Clinton. Justice Ginsburg is the second woman to sit on the high court and the first Jewish justice to sit there since the retirement of Justice Arthur J. Goldberg in 1965. See U.S. Congress, Senate, Committee on the Judiciary, *Hearings before the Committee on the Judiciary, U.S. Senate, One Hundred Third Congress, 1st Session, on the Nomination of Judge Ruth Bader Ginsburg, to Be Associate Justice of the Supreme Court, July 20, 21, 22, and 23, 1993* (Washington, DC: Government Printing Office, 1994), and Amy Leigh Campbell, "Raising the Bar: Ruth Bader Ginsburg and the ACLU Women's Rights Project," 11 *Texas Journal of Women and the Law* 157 (2002). Among Justice Ginsburg's extrajudicial publications are "Speaking in a Judicial Voice" 67 *New York University Law Review* 1185 (1992); "The Progression of Women in the Law," 28 *Valparaiso University Law Review* 1161 (1994); "Some Thoughts on Autonomy and Equality in Relation to *Roe v. Wade*," 63 *North Carolina Law Review* 375 (1985); "Remarks on Writing Separately," 65 *Washington Law Review* 133 (1990); and "Constitutional Adjudication in the United States as a Means of Advancing the Equal Stature of Men and Women under the Law," 83 *Georgetown Law Review* 263 (1997).

Justice Elena Kagan was born on the Lower East Side of Manhattan, New York, in 1960. She received her B.A. from Princeton (1981), an M. Phil. from Oxford University (1983), and her J.D. from Harvard Law School (1986). Subsequently, she clerked for Justice Thurgood Marshall, practiced law for three years, and then taught at the University of Chicago Law School before serving (1995–1999) in the Clinton administration. Afterward, she taught at Harvard Law School and became dean before President Barack Obama appointed her solicitor general in 2009. Her few prejudicial publications focused primarily on the First Amendment, administrative law, and tributes to former teachers. At age fifty, Kagan became the 112th justice, the fourth woman and eighth Jewish justice to serve on the Court.

Justice Anthony M. Kennedy was born on July 23, 1936, in Sacramento, California, where he grew up in a Roman Catholic family and lived most of his life, prior to his appointment to the Supreme Court by President Ronald Reagan in 1988. After studying at the London School of Economics and Stanford University, where he received his B.A., Kennedy attended Harvard Law School and then went into private practice in Sacramento. In 1965, he began a part-time career teaching constitutional law at the McGeorge School of Law of the University of the Pacific. Based on his activities in the Republican Party in California, then Governor Reagan recommended

Kennedy for an opening on the Court of Appeals for the Ninth Circuit, to which he was appointed by President Gerald R. Ford in 1974. Following the defeat of President Reagan's nomination in 1987 of Judge Robert H. Bork to fill the seat of Justice Lewis F. Powell, Jr., and the withdrawal of Judge Douglas H. Ginsburg from nomination for that seat, Kennedy, a more moderate conservative than either Judge Bork or Judge Ginsburg, was nominated and confirmed as an associate justice. See U.S. Congress, Senate, Committee on the Judiciary, *Hearings before the Committee on the Judiciary, U.S. Senate, One Hundredth Congress, 1st Session, on the Nomination of Anthony M. Kennedy to Be Associate Justice of the Supreme Court of the United States, December 14, 15, and 16, 1987* (Washington, DC: Government Printing Office, 1989). See also Justice Kennedy, "The Voice of Thurgood Marshall," 44 *Stanford Law Review* 1221 (1992). For discussions of Justice Kennedy's judicial philosophy, see Frank Colucci, *Justice Kennedy's Jurisprudence: The Full and Necessary Meaning of Liberty* (Lawrence: University Press of Kansas, 2009); Christopher E. Smith, "Supreme Court Surprise: Justice Anthony Kennedy's Move toward Moderation," 45 *Oklahoma Law Review* 459 (1992); Jeffrey Toobin, "How Anthony Kennedy's Passion for Foreign Law Could Change the Supreme Court," *The New Yorker* (Sept. 5, 2005); and Helen Knowles, *The Tie Goes to Freedom: Justice Anthony M. Kennedy on Liberty* (Lanham, MD: Rowman & Littlefield, 2009).

Justice Antonin Scalia was born in Trenton, New Jersey, on March 11, 1936. The son of an Italian immigrant professor, he became the first Roman Catholic to sit on the Court since the appointment of liberal Justice William J. Brennan, Jr., in 1956. After graduating from Georgetown University, he spent a year studying in Switzerland and then pursued his law degree at Harvard Law School. After working for several years in a leading Cleveland law firm, in 1967 he began teaching at the University of Virginia School of Law. From 1971 to 1977 he served in the administrations of Richard M. Nixon and Gerald R. Ford, after which he spent a year at the American Enterprise Institute, where he wrote articles attacking affirmative action and advocating deregulation. He then moved to the University of Chicago School of Law, where he helped found the Federalist Society, a conservative association of law students, lawyers, and judges. In 1982, President Ronald Reagan appointed him to the Court of Appeals for the District of Columbia Circuit, where he served until his nomination to fill the seat of Associate Justice William H. Rehnquist in 1986. See U.S. Congress, Senate, Committee on the Judiciary, *Hearings before the Committee on the Judiciary, U.S. Senate, Ninety-ninth Congress, 2d Session, on the Nomination of Judge Antonin Scalia, to Be Associate Justice of the Supreme Court of the United States, August 5 and 6, 1986* (Washington, DC: Government Printing Office, 1987). Among Justice Scalia's many off-the-bench publications are "The Dissenting Opinion," *1994 Journal of Supreme Court History* 33 (1994); "Originalism: The Lesser Evil," 57 *University of Cincinnati Law Review* 849 (1989); "The Rule of Law as a Law of Rules," 56 *University of Chicago Law Review* 1175 (1989); "Assorted Canards of Contemporary Legal Analysis," 40 *Case Western Reserve*

Law Review 581 (1990); *A Matter of Interpretation* (Princeton, NJ: Princeton University Press, 1997); and, with Bryan Garner, *Making Your Case: The Art of Persuading Judges* (St. Paul, MN: West, 2008). For discussions of his judicial philosophy, see Richard Brisbin, Jr., *Justice Antonin Scalia and the Conservative Revival* (Baltimore, MD: Johns Hopkins University Press, 1997); Christopher E. Smith, *Justice Antonin Scalia and the Supreme Court's Conservative Moment* (Westport, CT: Praeger, 1993); Kevin Ring, *Scalia Dissents: Writings of the Supreme Court's Wittiest, Most Outspoken Justice* (Washington, DC: Regnery, 2004); Ralph Rossum, *Antonin Scalia's Jurisprudence: Text and Tradition* (Lawrence: University Press of Kansas, 2005); James Staab, *The Political Thought of Justice Antonin Scalia* (Lanham: Rowman & Littlefield, 2006); and Joan Biskupic, *American Original: The Life and Constitution of Supreme Court Justice Antonin Scalia* (New York: Farrar, Straus and Giroux, 2009).

Justice Sonia Sotomayor, a daughter of immigrants from Puerto Rico, grew up in the Bronx, New York. After graduating from Princeton University and from Yale Law School, where she was an editor of the *Yale Law Journal*, she spent five years as a prosecutor in Manhattan, and then worked in private corporate legal practice. In 1992, Republican President George H. W. Bush appointed her to a federal district court, and Democratic President Bill Clinton elevated her to the U.S. Court of Appeals for the Second Circuit in 1998. In 2009, Democratic President Barack Obama nominated her, at age 55, to the Supreme Court, and Justice Sotomayor was confirmed by a vote of 68 to 31 as the 111th justice, first Latina, and third woman to sit on the Court. Among her off-the-bench publications as an appellate judge is "A Latina Judge's Voice," 13 *Berkley La Raza Law Journal* 87 (2002).

Justice Clarence Thomas was born in Pin Point, Georgia, on June 23, 1948. Raised as a Catholic, Thomas completed his undergraduate degree at Holy Cross College and then attended Yale Law School. After graduating in 1974, Thomas joined the staff of the attorney general of Missouri, John Danforth, a young Republican who became his political mentor. When Danforth was elected to the Senate, Thomas went into private practice for two years but subsequently rejoined Senator Danforth's staff as a legislative assistant and became active in the movement of conservative blacks opposed to welfare, busing, and affirmative action. Thomas's involvement in the conservative movement within the Republican Party brought him to the attention of the administration of President Ronald Reagan. In 1981, he was appointed assistant secretary for civil rights in the Department of Education. Within a year, Reagan promoted him to the position of director of the Equal Employment Opportunity Commission (EEOC). In 1990, he was named to the Court of Appeals for the District of Columbia Circuit, and the following year President George Bush named him to replace retiring Justice Thurgood Marshall. See U.S. Congress, Senate, Committee on the Judiciary, *Hearings before the Committee on the Judiciary, U.S. Senate, 1st Session, on the Nomination of Judge Clarence Thomas to Be Associate Justice of the Supreme Court of the United States*

(Washington, DC: Government Printing Office, 1993). See also Justice Thomas's article, "Freedom: A Responsibility, Not a Right," 21 *Ohio Northern University Law Review* 5 (1994); and his publications prior to his appointment to the Supreme Court, such as "Toward a 'Plain Reading' of the Constitution—The Declaration of Independence in Constitutional Interpretation," 30 *Howard Law Journal* 983 (1987); and "The Higher Law Background of the Privileges or Immunities Clause of the Fourteenth Amendment," 12 *Harvard Journal of Law & Public Policy* 63 (1989); "Judging," 45 *Kansas Law Review* 1 (1996). For a discussion of Justice Thomas's judicial philosophy, see Scott D. Gerber, *First Principles: The Jurisprudence of Clarence Thomas* (New York: New York University Press, 1999); Christopher E. Smith and Joyce Baugh, *The Real Clarence Thomas: Confirmation Veracity Meets Performance* (New York: Peter Lang, 2000); Ken Foskett, *Judging Thomas: The Life and Times of Clarence Thomas* (New York: William Morrow, 2004); Andrew P. Thomas, *Clarence Thomas: A Biography* (San Francisco: Encounter Books, 2001); and Kevin Merida and Michael Fletcher, *Supreme Discomfort: The Divided Soul of Clarence Thomas* (New York: Doubleday, 2007). See, generally, Clarence Thomas, *My Grandfather's Son: A Memoir* (New York: Harper, 2007).

GLOSSARY

Abatement. A reduction or the suspension, in whole or part, of a continuing charge or activity.

Actual malice. See malice.

Advisory opinion. An opinion or interpretation of law that does not have binding effect. The Court does not give advisory opinions, for example, on hypothetical disputes; it decides only actual cases or controversies.

Affirm. In an appellate court, to reach a decision that agrees with the result reached in a case by the lower court.

Affirmative action programs. Programs required by federal or state laws designed to remedy discriminatory practices by hiring minority-group persons and/or women.

A fortiori. With stronger reason; a term denoting that because a fact exists, therefore another, included in it though less probable or unusual, must also exist.

Ambulatory retroactivity. The changeable or alterable retroapplication of a constitutional decision, so that the decision applies only to prospective or pending cases.

Amicus curiae. A friend of the court, a person not a party to litigation, who volunteers or is invited by the court to give his views on a case.

Appeal. To take a case to a higher court for review. Generally, a party losing in a trial court may appeal once to an appellate court as a matter of right. If the party loses in the appellate court, appeal to a higher court is within the discretion of the higher court. Most appeals to the Supreme Court are within its discretion to deny or grant a hearing.

Appellant. The party that appeals a lower-court decision to a higher court.

Appellee. One who has an interest in upholding the decision of a lower court and is compelled to respond when the case is appealed to a higher court by the appellant.

Bill of Attainder. A legislative act that inflicts punishment on a named individual or members of a group without a judicial trial.

Brief. A document prepared by counsel to serve as the basis for an argument in court, setting out the facts and legal arguments in support of his case.

Case. A general term for an action, cause, suit, or controversy, at law or equity; a question contested before a court.

Case law. The law as defined by previously decided cases, distinct from statutes and other sources of law.

Certification, writ of. A method of taking a case from appellate court to the Supreme Court in which the lower court asks that some question or interpretation of law be certified, clarified, and made more certain.

Certiorari, **writ of.** A writ issued from the Supreme Court, at its discretion and at the request of a petitioner, to order a lower court to send the record of a case to the Court for its review.

Civil law. The body of law dealing with the private rights of individuals, as distinguished from criminal law.

Class action. A lawsuit brought by one person or group on behalf of all persons similarly situated.

Comity. Courtesy, respect; referring to the deference federal courts pay to state court decisions that are based on state law.

Common law. The collection of principles and rules, particularly from unwritten English law, that derive their authority from long-standing usage and custom or from courts recognizing and enforcing those customs.

Compelling state interest. A test used to uphold state action against First Amendment and equal protection challenges because of the serious need for government action.

Concurring opinion. An opinion by a justice that agrees with the result reached by the Court in a case but disagrees with the Court's rationale or reasoning for its decision.

Contempt (civil and criminal). Civil contempt is the failure to do something for the benefit of another party after being ordered to do so by a court. Criminal contempt occurs when a person exhibits disrespect for a court or obstructs the administration of justice.

Contract. An agreement between two or more persons that creates an obligation to do or not do a particular thing.

Controversies. *See* Justiciable controversy.

Criminal law. The body of law that deals with the enforcement of laws and the punishment of persons who, by breaking laws, commit crimes against the state.

Declaratory judgment. A court pronouncement declaring a legal right or interpretation but not ordering a special action.

De facto. In fact, in reality.

Defendant. In a civil action, the party denying or defending itself against charges brought by a plaintiff. In a criminal action, the person indicted for the commission of an offense.

De jure. As a result of law, as a result of official action.

Delegation of powers. The transfer of authority by one branch of government to another branch or administrative agency.

Dicta. *See Obiter dictim.*

Discretionary jurisdiction. Jurisdiction that a court may accept or reject in particular cases. The Supreme Court has discretionary jurisdiction in over 90 percent of the cases that come to it.

Dismissal. An order disposing of a case without a hearing or trial.

Dissenting opinion. An opinion by a justice that disagrees with the result reached by the Court in a case.

Docket. All cases filed in a court.

Due process. Fair and regular procedure. The Fifth and Fourteenth Amendments guarantee persons that they will not be deprived of life, liberty, or property by the government until fair and usual procedures have been followed. (see also "substantive due process")

Enfranchisement. The act of making free (as from slavery); giving a franchise or freedom; conferring the privilege of voting on a class of people.

Enemy belligerent/combatant. Citizens who associate with an enemy government or organization in order to perform hostile acts.

Equal protection of the law. The guarantee that no person or class of persons shall be denied the same protection of the law in their lives, liberty, and property.

Error, writ of. A writ issued from an appeals court to a lower court requiring that it send the record of a case so that it may review it for error.

Exclusionary rule. This rule commands that evidence obtained in violation of the rights guaranteed by the Fourth and Fifth Amendments must be excluded at trial.

Executive agreement. A treaty-like agreement with another country made by the president.

Executive privilege. Exemption from the disclosure requirements for ordinary citizens because of the executive's need for confidentiality in discharging highly important governmental functions.

Ex parte. From, or on, only one side. Application to a court for some ruling or action on behalf of only one party.

Ex post facto. After the fact; by an act or fact occurring after some previous act or fact.

Federalism. The interrelationships among the states and the relationship between the states and the national government.

Federal preemption. The federal government's exclusive power over certain matters such as interstate commerce and sedition to the exclusion of state jurisdiction and law.

Full faith and credit clause. Article IV, Section I, of the Constitution provides that states must recognize the judicial decisions and laws of other states.

Gerrymander. The process of dividing a state or other division into legal divisions in order to accomplish an ulterior purpose, such as reelecting an incumbent.

Grand jury. A jury of twelve to twenty-three persons that hears in private evidence for serving an indictment.

Habeas corpus. Literally, "you have the body"; a writ issued to inquire whether a person is lawfully imprisoned or detained. The writ demands that the persons holding the prisoner justify his detention or release him.

Immunity. A grant of exemption from prosecution in return for evidence by testimony.

In camera. "In chambers," referring to court hearings in private without spectators.

Indictment. A formal charge of offenses based on evidence presented by a prosecutor from a grand jury.

In forma pauperis. In the manner of a pauper, without liability for the costs of filing cases before a court.

Information. A written set of charges, similar to an indictment, filed by a prosecutor but without a grand jury's consideration of evidence.

Inherent powers. Powers originating from the structure of government or sovereignty that go beyond those expressly granted or which could be construed to have been implied from those expressly granted.

Injunction. A court order prohibiting a person from performing a particular act.

In re. In the affair of, concerning; often used in judicial proceedings where there is no adversary but where the matter (such as a bankrupt's estate) requires judicial action.

Intestate. Without making a will.

Judgment. The official decision of a court.

Judicial review. The power to review and strike down any legislation or other government action that is inconsistent with federal or state constitutions. The Supreme Court reviews government action only under the Constitution of the United States and federal laws.

Jurisdiction. The power of a court to hear a case or controversy, which exists when the proper parties are present and when the point to be decided is among the issues authorized to be handled by a particular court.

Justiciable controversy. A controversy in which a claim of right is asserted against another who has an interest in contesting it. Courts will consider only justiciable controversies, as distinguished from hypothetical disputes.

Malice. The intentional doing of a wrongful act. In libel, "actual malice" is the knowing or reckless disregard of the falsity of a statement.

Majority opinion. An opinion in a case that is subscribed to by a majority of the justices who participated in the decision.

Mandamus, writ of. "We command"; an order issued from a superior court directing a lower court or other government authority to perform a particular act.

Mandatory jurisdiction. Jurisdiction that a court must accept. The Supreme Court must decide cases coming under its appellate jurisdiction, though it may avoid giving them plenary consideration.

Moot. Unsettled, undecided. A moot question is also one that is no longer material, or that has already been resolved, and has become hypothetical.

Motion. A written or oral application to a court or judge to obtain a rule or order.

Natural rights. Rights based on the nature of man and independent of those rights secured by positive laws.

Negligence. The failure to do something that a reasonable person would do.

Obiter dictum. A statement by a judge or justices expressing an opinion and included with, but not essential to, an opinion resolving a case before the court. Dicta are not necessarily binding in later cases.

Opinion for the court. The opinion announcing the decision of a court.

Original jurisdiction. The jurisdiction of a court of first instance, or trial court. The Supreme Court has original jurisdiction under Article III of the Constitution.

Per curiam. "By the court"; an unsigned opinion of the court.

Petitioner. One who files a petition with a court seeking action or relief, including the plaintiff or appellant. When a writ of certiorari is granted by the Supreme Court, the party seeking review is called the petitioner, and the party responding is called the respondent.

Petit jury. A trial jury, traditionally a common law jury of twelve persons, but since 1970 the Supreme Court has permitted states to use juries composed of less than twelve persons.

Plea bargaining. The process in which the accused and the prosecutor in a criminal case agree to a mutually acceptable disposition of a case without a trial.

Plenary consideration. Full consideration. When the Supreme Court grants a case review, it may give it full consideration, permitting the parties to submit briefs on the merits of the case and to present oral arguments, before the Court reaches its decision.

Plurality opinion. An opinion announcing the decision of the Court, but which has the support of less than a majority of the Court.

Political question. Questions that courts refuse to decide because they are deemed to be essentially political in nature, or because their determination would involve an intrusion on the powers of the executive or legislature, or because courts could not provide a judicial remedy.

Probable cause. Reasonable cause, having more evidence for, rather than against, when establishing the basis for obtaining a search warrant, for example.

Procedural due process. The safeguards to a person's liberty and property, such as a right to counsel and the right to confrontation.

Rational basis test. A test used by appellate courts to uphold legislation if there is evidence of a rational basis for the law's enactment.

Reasonable and probable cause. The grounds for suspecting a person of a crime and placing him in custody, and which would persuade a reasonable person that they are true.

Reapportionment. A realignment or change in electoral districts due to changes in population.

Remand. To send back. After a decision in a case, the case is often sent back by a higher court to the court from which it came for further action in light of its decision.

Republic. A commonwealth; a form of government open to all.

Respondent. The party that is compelled to answer the claims or questions posed in a court by a petitioner.

Reverse. In an appellate court, to reach a decision that disagrees with the result reached in a case by a lower court.

Ripeness. When a case is ready for adjudication and decision; the issues presented must not be hypothetical, and the parties must have exhausted other avenues of appeal.

Search warrant. An order issued by a judge or magistrate directing a law enforcement official to search and seize evidence of the commission of a crime, contraband, the fruits of crime, or things otherwise unlawfully possessed.

Separation of powers. The division of the powers of the national government according to the three branches of government: the legislative, which is empowered to make laws; the executive, which is required to carry out the laws; and the judicial, which has the power to interpret and adjudicate disputes under the law.

Seriatim. Separately, individually, one by one. The Court's practice was once to have each justice give his opinion on a case separately.

Sovereign immunity. The doctrine that precludes a litigant from suing a sovereign without its consent to the suit.

Sovereignty. Supreme political authority; the absolute and uncontrollable power by which an independent nation-state is governed.

Standing. Having the appropriate characteristics to bring or participate in a case; in particular, having a personal interest and stake in the outcome.

Stare decisis. "Let the decision stand." The principle of adherence to settled cases, the doctrine that principles of law established in earlier cases should be accepted as authoritative in similar subsequent cases.

State action. Actions undertaken by a state government and those done "under the color of state law"; that is, those actions required or sanctioned by a state.

Statute. A written law enacted by a legislature.

Stream of commerce. Refers to local goods that for a brief period of time are in interstate commerce.

Subpoena. An order to present oneself before a grand jury, court, or legislative hearing.

Subpoena duces tecum. An order to produce specified documents or papers.

Substantive due process. The interpretation of the Fourteenth Amendment due process clause to extend protection to substantive rights and liberties, and not simply to guarantee procedural safeguards. The process of selectively incorporating guarantees of the Bill of Rights into the Fourteenth Amendment and applying them to the states involved substantive due process analysis, as did the Court's creation and enforcement of the "liberty of contract" and the "right of privacy."

Summary decision. A decision in a case that does not give it full consideration; when the Court decides a case without having the parties submit briefs on the merits of the case or present oral arguments before the Court.

Tort. An injury or wrong to the person or property of another.

Transactional immunity. Immunity granted a person in exchange for evidence or testimony, which protects that person from prosecution, regardless of independent evidence against him; *see* Use immunity.

Treaties. A compact made between two or more independent nations; treaties are made in the United States by the president with the advice and consent of the Senate.

Use immunity. Immunity granted a person in exchange for evidence or testimony but that only protects that person from prosecution based on the use of his own testimony.

Vacate. To make void, annul, or rescind the decision of a lower court.

War power. The power of the national government to wage war; Congress has the power to declare war, while the president, as commander in chief, has authority over the conduct of war.

Writ. An order commanding someone to perform or not perform acts specified in the order.

GENERAL INDEX

Page numbers with an *n* refer to notes.

INDEX OF CASES

Cases and page numbers in **boldface** refer to case excerpts. Page numbers with an *n* refer to notes.

MEMBERS OF THE SUPREME COURT OF THE UNITED STATES AND THEIR DATES OF SERVICE (through November 2010)

1. John Jay: 1789–1795*
2. James Wilson: 1789–1798
3. John Blair, Jr.: 1790–1796
4. James Iredell: 1790–1799
5. William Cushing: 1790–1810
6. Thomas Johnson: 1792–1793
7. William Paterson: 1793–1806
8. John Rutledge: 1795*
9. Oliver Ellsworth: 1796–1800*
10. Samuel Chase: 1796–1811
11. Bushrod Washington: 1799–1829
12. Alfred Moore: 1800–1804
13. John Marshall: 1801–1835*
14. William Johnson: 1804–1834
15. H. Brockholst Livingston: 1807–1823
16. Thomas Todd: 1807–1826
17. Gabriel Duvall: 1811–1835
18. Joseph Story: 1812–1845
19. Smith Thompson: 1823–1843
20. Robert Trimble: 1826–1828
21. Henry Baldwin: 1830–1844
22. John McLean: 1830–1861
23. James M. Wayne: 1835–1867
24. Philip P. Barbour: 1836–1841
25. Roger Brooke Taney: 1836–1864*
26. John Catron: 1837–1865
27. John McKinley: 1838–1852
28. Peter V. Daniel: 1842–1860
29. Levi Woodbury: 1845–1851
30. Samuel Nelson: 1845–1872
31. Robert C. Grier: 1846–1870
32. Benjamin R. Curtis: 1851–1857
33. John A. Campbell: 1853–1861
34. Nathan Clifford: 1858–1881
35. David Davis: 1862–1877
36. Noah H. Swayne: 1862–1881
37. Samuel F. Miller: 1862–1890
38. Stephen J. Field: 1863–1897
39. Salmon Portland Chase: 1864–1873*
40. William Strong: 1870–1880
41. Joseph P. Bradley: 1870–1892
42. Ward Hunt: 1873–1882
43. Morrison R. Waite: 1874–1888*
44. John Marshall Harlan: 1877–1911
45. William B. Woods: 1881–1887
46. Stanley Matthews: 1881–1889
47. Samuel Blatchford: 1882–1893
48. Horace Gray: 1882–1902
49. Lucius Q. C. Lamar: 1888–1893
50. Melville Weston Fuller: 1888–1910*
51. David J. Brewer: 1890–1910
52. Henry B. Brown: 1891–1906
53. George Shiras, Jr.: 1892–1903
54. Howell E. Jackson: 1893–1895
55. Rufus W. Peckham: 1896–1909
56. Joseph McKenna: 1898–1925
57. Oliver Wendell Holmes, Jr.: 1902–1932
58. William R. Day: 1903–1922
59. William H. Moody: 1906–1910
60. Horace H. Lurton: 1910–1914
61. Edward Douglass White: 1910–1921*
62. Joseph Rucker Lamar: 1911–1916
63. Willis Van Devanter: 1911–1937
64. Mahlon Pitney: 1912–1922
65. James Clark McReynolds: 1914–1941
66. John H. Clarke: 1916–1922
67. Louis D. Brandeis: 1916–1939
68. William Howard Taft: 1921–1930*
69. George Sutherland: 1922–1938
70. Edward T. Sanford: 1923–1930
71. Pierce Butler: 1923–1939
72. Charles Evans Hughes: 1930–1941*
73. Owen J. Roberts: 1930–1945
74. Benjamin Nathan Cardozo: 1932–1938
75. Hugo Black: 1937–1971
76. Stanley F. Reed: 1938–1957
77. Felix Frankfurter: 1939–1962
78. William O. Douglas: 1939–1975
79. Frank W. Murphy: 1940–1949
80. James F. Byrnes: 1941–1942
81. Harlan Fiske Stone: 1941–1946*
82. Robert H. Jackson: 1941–1954
83. Wiley B. Rutledge: 1943–1949
84. Harold H. Burton: 1945–1958
85. Fred M. Vinson: 1946–1953*
86. Sherman Minton: 1949–1956
87. Tom C. Clark: 1949–1967
88. Earl Warren: 1953–1969*
89. John Marshall Harlan II: 1955–1971
90. William J. Brennan, Jr.: 1956–1990
91. Charles E. Whittaker: 1957–1962
92. Potter Stewart: 1958–1981
93. Arthur J. Goldberg: 1962–1965
94. Byron R. White: 1962–1993
95. Abe Fortas: 1965–1969
96. Thurgood Marshall: 1967–1991
97. Warren E. Burger: 1969–1986*
98. Harry A. Blackmun: 1970–1994
99. Lewis F. Powell, Jr.: 1972–1987
100. William H. Rehnquist: 1972–2005*
101. John Paul Stevens: 1975–2010
102. Sandra Day O'Connor: 1981–2006
103. Antonin Scalia: 1986–
104. Anthony M. Kennedy: 1988–
105. David H. Souter: 1990–2009
106. Clarence Thomas: 1991–
107. Ruth Bader Ginsburg: 1993–
108. Stephen G. Breyer: 1994–
109. John G. Roberts, Jr.: 2005–*
110. Samuel A. Alito, Jr.: 2006–
111. Sonia Sotomayer: 2009–
112. Elena Kagan: 2010–

*Served as Chief Justice